CHAMBERS

OFFICIAL SCRABBLE®

W4 O1 R1 D2 S1

CHAMBERS

OFFICIAL SCRABBLE®

WORDS

4th EDITION

Managing Editor
Catherine Schwarz

CHAMBERS
An imprint of Chambers Harrap Publishers Ltd
7 Hopetoun Crescent
Edinburgh EH7 4AY

This edition first published by Chambers 1999
First published by Chambers 1988; second edition published 1990; third edition published 1994

Reprinted 1999, 2000

A CIP catalogue record for this book is available from the British Library.

ISBN 0-550-14190-1 Hardback

Publishing Manager
Elaine Higgleton

Designed and typeset by Chambers Harrap Publishers Ltd
Printed and bound in Great Britain by Clays Ltd, St Ives plc

Preface to fourth edition

Official Scrabble® Words (OSW) is established as the definitive work on Scrabble, indispensable whether solving those family arguments or dealing with word challenges in Scrabble clubs and tournaments all around the world. This fourth edition is published following on from publication of a new edition of *The Chambers Dictionary* in 1998.

Despite company changes, a close relationship, dating back to Spear's decision to use *The Chambers Dictionary* at the 1980 National Scrabble Championships, still exists between Spear's Games (now part of Mattel Inc) and Chambers (now part of Chambers Harrap Publishers Ltd). I know that Scrabble players throughout the English-speaking world are most appreciative of the rich fund of useful Scrabble words contained in *The Chambers Dictionary*, which is complementary to OSW and should be consulted when you want to check the meaning of a word.

With the many changes in the 1998 edition of the Dictionary, a complete review of all the words in it was required for OSW. Once again, the Main Committee, many of whom have been involved in producing all four editions of OSW, deserve thanks, along with Catherine Schwarz and her colleagues at Chambers for their painstaking work. Special mention is also due to the Initial Adjudicating Committee, both in the UK and in Australia, for their dedication in highlighting areas of change.

I, and I'm sure many others, have derived huge satisfaction from playing Scrabble over many years now. This new edition of OSW and the many new words it contains are going to make Scrabble even more enjoyable and entertaining.

Philip Nelkon
Manager–Scrabble Clubs
Spear's Games

Main Committee

Darryl Francis, *London Scrabble League*
Ian Gucklhorn, *London Scrabble League*
Terry Kirk, *London Scrabble League*
Allan Simmons, *Onwords Scrabble Magazine*
Jim Warmington, *Australian Scrabble Players Association*

Initial adjudicating committee

UK

David Acton, *Middlesex League*
Amy Byrne, *Edinburgh Scrabble Club*
Andrew Cook, *Oxford City Scrabble Club*
Andrew Fisher, *UK-Scrabble*
Helen R Gipson, *East Berks Scrabble Club*
Helen Grayson, *Aireborough Scrabble Club*
Mary Grylls, *Melton Scrabble Club*
Barry Grossman, *London Scrabble League*
Sheila Hockey, *London Scrabble League*
Terry Hollington, *Southampton Scrabble Club*
Josef Kollar, *Hythe Scrabble Club*
Donald Macleod, *Edinburgh Scrabble Club*
Roger Phillips
Evan Simpson, *Middlesex League*
Roy Upton, *Derby Scrabble Club*
Wilma Warwick, *Leith Scrabble Club*

Australia

Roger Blom, *Camberwell Scrabble Club*
Ruth Fewings, *Bendigo Scrabble Club*
Alistair Kane, *Dandenong Scrabble Club*
Sue Kyatt, *Knox Scrabble Club*
Joan Rosenthal, *Balmain BUGS Scrabble Club*
Margaret Warmington, *Balwyn Scrabble Club*

The publishers wish to acknowledge with thanks the computing help of Peter Schwarz in the compilation and revision of this edition of *Official Scrabble® Words*, and the support of Philip Nelkon of Spear's Games.

Introduction

This fourth edition of *Official Scrabble® Words* is based on *The Chambers Dictionary* (1998), the latest in a long line of Chambers dictionaries. All words listed in that dictionary are permitted in Scrabble except:

those only spelt with an initial capital letter;
abbreviations and symbols;
prefixes and suffixes;
those requiring apostrophes and hyphens.

Official Scrabble® Words (OSW) lists, and is the official authority for, all allowable words of up to 9 letters long and their inflections (plurals etc). For longer words, *The Chambers Dictionary* is the authority. A number of words listed in *The Chambers Dictionary*, and hence in OSW, may be offensive to some people, or may not conform to 'political correctness'. These words are however part of the English language, which the Dictionary naturally reflects. We therefore have not followed the American Scrabble movement in disallowing such words for Scrabble.

Every relevant entry in *The Chambers Dictionary* has been thoroughly examined and considered for inclusion in OSW. Derivative forms have been carefully considered too, and appropriate inflections - plurals, verb forms, and comparatives and superlatives - have been included. Many new words have been added to the Dictionary, and there have been other changes: some words have changed or augmented their labels (both part-of-speech and classification), some have changed their hyphenation or capitalization status, others have moved on from being abbreviations - all resulting in hundreds of new entries in this edition of OSW. Inevitably such changes, along with other Dictionary judgements, have resulted in a small number of deletions from the previous edition of OSW.

In the compilation of this edition of OSW, a small number of errors were found in *The Chambers Dictionary*. Those confirmed by the publisher have not been perpetuated in OSW.

Allowable words

This edition of *Official Scrabble® Words* is the final authority on allowed Scrabble words where the uninflected form of the word is up to 9 letters long. It is based on the 1998 edition of *The Chambers Dictionary.* All words listed in that dictionary are permitted in Scrabble except for those in the categories mentioned above.

It should be noted that the entries that are labelled 'symbol' (for example FF, LM) are now, as well as abbreviations, barred from Scrabble use.

One particular entry in OSW worthy of special mention is PH. Since in the Dictionary the capitalized letter is not the initial letter, and since PH is not deemed to be an abbreviation or a symbol, it has been included here, along with its plural PHS.

The approaches that have been taken to various groups of words in this edition of OSW are explained below.

Accents

Accents are not shown in this edition of *Official Scrabble® Words.* As there are no accented letters in the English-language Scrabble sets, it was felt unnecessary to retain accents in OSW. Where *The Chambers Dictionary* shows a word with an accent, the accent has been ignored in OSW.

Adverbs

Adverbs have been included in *Official Scrabble® Words* if they are included in *The Chambers Dictionary.* No attempt has been made to include adverbial forms which are not explicitly shown in the Dictionary.

Comparatives and Superlatives

This edition of *Official Scrabble® Words* sees the inclusion of more comparative and superlative forms than were in the previous edition. We have considered the possible comparative and superlative forms of all adjectives in OSW, and we have based our final selection on a range of criteria. These have included commonness or familiarity of the adjective, number of syllables, meaning, and whether the adjective is dialect, obsolete or foreign. We also took into account the euphony of the -ER and -EST forms, current usage, data from language corpora, including the British National Corpus®, and listings in other

other dictionaries. We cannot say that we have applied a mechanical formula in deciding which comparatives and superlatives to include. We have allowed the -IER and the -IEST forms of most one- and two-syllable adjectives ending in -Y, and some of three syllables, but not all. We have not excluded the comparative and superlative forms of all adjectives of three syllables or more - some have been included. We have not excluded the comparative and superlative forms of all adjectives ending in certain specific groups of letters, such as -ATE, -ENT, and -ID. Again, some have been included.

Definitions

This edition of *Official Scrabble® Words* contains a separate appendix listing the 2- and 3-letter words, with basic definitions, intended as aids in memorizing these important Scrabble words. For fuller treatment of these words, and to know the meaning of any other word in OSW, *The Chambers Dictionary* should be consulted.

Foreign Words

Foreign words appearing in *The Chambers Dictionary* have been included in *Official Scrabble® Words*. Where a specific plural form appears in the Dictionary, we have included only that form. Where no plural is shown in the Dictionary, we have used our judgement, and the appropriate plural form has been included. In some instances, this will be a foreign plural; in others, it will be an English plural (usually the addition of an -S). Occasionally, both types of plural will be included. Do be aware that not all plural forms in OSW are explicitly shown in *The Chambers Dictionary*. For example, as no plural form is shown in the Dictionary for STERNUM, we have included both of the plural forms STERNA and STERNUMS.

Interjections

Interjections are not treated as nouns, but as parts of speech which do not permit plurals. In *Official Scrabble® Words*, an interjection has no inflected forms, unless explicitly indicated in *The Chambers Dictionary*. A plural is only allowed if an interjection is also shown to be a noun; and verb forms are only allowed if an interjection is also shown to be a verb.

Some examples:

> AW, QUOTHA and UM are interjections only, so no inflected forms are allowed;
> EH is an interjection and a verb, so the inflected verb forms EHS, EHED and EHING are allowed;

OOH is an interjection, verb and noun, so the verb forms OOHS, OOHED and OOHING are allowed;
OOHS is also the plural form of the noun.

If *The Chambers Dictionary* quite clearly lists a plural form of an interjection (for example, as at LO and OHO),then that is allowable.

Letters and letter sounds

Names of letters and letter sounds appearing in *The Chambers Dictionary* are included in *Official Scrabble® Words*, as there is nothing in the rules of Scrabble to bar the use of such words. Accordingly, OSW lists familiar letter names (for example, AITCH, MU, NU, and XI) as well as unfamiliar ones (for example, DIGAMMA, SAMPI, VAU and WYNN). Their plural forms are also included.

Obsolete Words

Obsolete words are included in *Official Scrabble® Words*, along with many of their relevant inflected forms (such as plurals and verb inflections). We have included plurals of obsolete nouns, and we have included verb inflections of obsolete verbs. We have not included comparative and superlative forms of obsolete adjectives, or derivatives of obsolete words, unless these are explicitly shown in *The Chambers Dictionary.* (For example, BROACH and BROACHER are both allowable words, and BROCH is in the Dictonary as an obsolete spelling of BROACH - so BROACH, BROACHER and BROCH are all allowable, but we have not included BROCHER.)

Words marked in *The Chambers Dictionary* as being from the works of Shakespeare, Spenser and Milton have been treated in the same way as obsolete words.

Order of Words

All the words in *Official Scrabble® Words* are listed in strict alphabetical sequence, regardless of length. It is important to bear this in mind, particularly when checking the validity of plurals.

For example:

the plural of FAD is not listed immediately after FAD but is shown at its correct alphabetical place between FADOS and FADY;
to determine whether FAB has a plural or not it is neccesary to check between the entries FABRICS and FABULAR. It is not listed there, so FABS is not allowed.

Plurals

With few exceptions, we have included in *Official Scrabble® Words* the plurals of all nouns. Plural forms have been shown for all nouns ending in -ISM, -ITY and -NESS; while these plurals may be little used in regular English, all are available for use if needed in the English language. We have also included the plural forms of chemicals, chemical elements, minerals, man-made materials, natural minerals, fibres, drugs, gases, rocks, oils, vitamins, enzymes, diseases, illnesses and the like.

The plurals of many foreign words are included. For many words there are now two plural forms - an English plural and a foreign plural (for example, STERNUMS and STERNA). However, some words that previously only had an -S plural now only have a foreign plural. Where the compilers have found no evidence for these -S forms, only the foreign plurals are now included. For example, the plural of ANCILE is now only ANCILIA, although previously it was only ANCILES.

Word Lengths

Official Scrabble® Words users may well want to understand what criteria have been employed in considering word lengths. In compliling OSW we began by listing all the valid but uninflected words of length up to (and including) 9 letters. We then allowed the relevant inflections of these (namely plurals, verb forms, and comparatives and superlatives), resulting in words up to 13 letters long. (It is possible for a 9-letter verb to double a final consonant before adding -ING, giving 13 letters in all!)

Here are some examples:

> the 9-letter noun CACODEMON gives rise to the 10-letter plural CACODEMONS;
> the 9-letter noun CACOPHONY gives rise to the 10-letter plural CACOPHONIES;
> the 9-letter noun CANTHARIS gives rise to the 11-letter plural CANTHARIDES;
> the 9-letter verb CALCULATE gives rise to these verb inflections: CACULATED, CALCULATES and CACULATING, having 10 or 11 letters;
> the 8-letter verb CARBURET gives rise to these verb inflections: CARBURETS, CARBURETTED and CARBURETTING, having 9, 11 or 12 letters

If any inflected form of a 9-letter word is also a singular noun in its own right, then a plural form of that noun is also included.

For example:

> the 9-letter verb CATERWAUL gives rise to these verb inflections: CATERWAULS, CATERWAULED and CATERWAULING; but since CATERWAULING is also shown in *The Chambers Dictionary* as a noun, the plural form of CATERWAULINGS has been included here;
> the 8-letter verb CROSSCUT gives rise to these verb inflections: CROSSCUTS and CROSSCUTTING; but since CROSSCUTTING is also shown in the Dictionary as a noun, the plural form CROSSCUTTINGS has been included here.

There are a few instances of 9-letter adjectives which add an -S to become 10-letter nouns. For example, CANONICAL thus becomes CANONICALS, which is included. For convenience in adjudication, other similar cases are treated likewise: for example, the adverbs EARTHWARD and EARTHWARDS are both included.

There are instances of singular nouns having more than 9 letters, but with plurals of 9 letters or less. The singulars have not been included here, but the plurals have. For example, the singular AUDITORIUM has 10 letters, so hasn't been included, but its plural AUDITORIA has 9 letters, so is included.

Official Scrabble® Words will not answer every possible query regarding the validity of words. Remember that for words longer than 9 letters, and their inflected forms, you will have to turn to *The Chambers Dictionary.* For example, AUDITORIUM, mentioned above, is perfectly valid for use in Scrabble; it's just that it isn't included here. There are plenty of other 10-15 letter words that could be played legitimately in Scrabble, and are in *The Chambers Dictionary.*

A

AA
AARDVARK
AARDVARKS
AARDWOLF
AARDWOLVES
AAS
AASVOGEL
AASVOGELS
ABA
ABAC
ABACA
ABACAS
ABACI
ABACK
ABACS
ABACTINAL
ABACTOR
ABACTORS
ABACUS
ABACUSES
ABAFT
ABALONE
ABALONES
ABAMPERE
ABAMPERES
ABAND
ABANDED
ABANDING
ABANDON
ABANDONED
ABANDONEE
ABANDONEES
ABANDONING
ABANDONS
ABANDS
ABAS
ABASE
ABASED
ABASEMENT
ABASEMENTS
ABASES
ABASH
ABASHED
ABASHEDLY
ABASHES
ABASHING
ABASHLESS
ABASHMENT
ABASHMENTS
ABASING
ABASK
ABATABLE
ABATE
ABATED
ABATEMENT
ABATEMENTS
ABATES
ABATING
ABATIS
ABATOR
ABATORS
ABATTIS
ABATTOIR
ABATTOIRS
ABATTU
ABATURE
ABATURES
ABAXIAL
ABAYA
ABAYAS
ABB
ABBA
ABBACIES
ABBACY
ABBAS
ABBATIAL
ABBE
ABBES
ABBESS
ABBESSES
ABBEY
ABBEYS
ABBOT
ABBOTS
ABBOTSHIP
ABBOTSHIPS
ABBS
ABCEE
ABCEES
ABDABS
ABDICABLE
ABDICANT
ABDICATE
ABDICATED
ABDICATES
ABDICATING
ABDICATOR
ABDICATORS
ABDOMEN
ABDOMENS
ABDOMINA
ABDOMINAL
ABDUCE
ABDUCED
ABDUCENT
ABDUCES
ABDUCING
ABDUCT
ABDUCTED
ABDUCTEE
ABDUCTEES
ABDUCTING
ABDUCTION
ABDUCTIONS
ABDUCTOR
ABDUCTORS
ABDUCTS
ABEAM
ABEAR
ABEARING
ABEARS
ABED
ABEIGH
ABELE
ABELES
ABELIA
ABELIAS
ABERRANCE
ABERRANCES
ABERRANCIES
ABERRANCY
ABERRANT
ABERRATE
ABERRATED
ABERRATES
ABERRATING
ABESSIVE
ABESSIVES
ABET
ABETMENT
ABETMENTS
ABETS
ABETTAL
ABETTALS
ABETTED
ABETTER
ABETTERS
ABETTING
ABETTOR
ABETTORS
ABEYANCE
ABEYANCES
ABEYANCIES
ABEYANCY
ABEYANT
ABHOR
ABHORRED
ABHORRENT
ABHORRER
ABHORRERS
ABHORRING
ABHORRINGS
ABHORS
ABID
ABIDANCE
ABIDANCES
ABIDDEN
ABIDE
ABIDED
ABIDES
ABIDING
ABIDINGLY
ABIDINGS
ABIES
ABIGAIL
ABIGAILS
ABILITIES
ABILITY
ABIOSES
ABIOSIS
ABIOTIC
ABJECT
ABJECTED
ABJECTING
ABJECTION
ABJECTIONS
ABJECTLY
ABJECTS
ABJOINT
ABJOINTED
ABJOINTING
ABJOINTS
ABJURE
ABJURED
ABJURER
ABJURERS
ABJURES
ABJURING
ABLATE
ABLATED
ABLATES
ABLATING
ABLATION
ABLATIONS
ABLATIVAL
ABLATIVE
ABLATIVES
ABLATOR
ABLATORS
ABLAUT
ABLAUTS
ABLAZE
ABLE
ABLED
ABLEISM
ABLEISMS
ABLEIST
ABLER
ABLES
ABLEST
ABLET
ABLETS
ABLING
ABLINS
ABLOOM
ABLOW
ABLUSH
ABLUTION
ABLUTIONS
ABLY
ABNEGATE
ABNEGATED
ABNEGATES
ABNEGATING
ABNEGATOR
ABNEGATORS
ABNORMAL
ABNORMALS
ABNORMITIES
ABNORMITY
ABNORMOUS
ABOARD
ABODE
ABODED
ABODEMENT
ABODEMENTS
ABODES
ABODING
ABOIDEAU
ABOIDEAUS
ABOIL
ABOITEAU
ABOITEAUS
ABOLISH
ABOLISHED
ABOLISHES
ABOLISHING
ABOLITION
ABOLITIONS
ABOLLA
ABOLLAE
ABOLLAS
ABOMASA
ABOMASAL
ABOMASI
ABOMASUM
ABOMASUS
ABOMASUSES
ABOMINATE
ABOMINATED

The Chambers Dictionary is the authority for many longer words; see *OSW* Introduction, page xii

ABOMINATES
ABOMINATING
ABONDANCE
ABONDANCES
ABORAL
ABORD
ABORDED
ABORDING
ABORDS
ABORE
ABORIGEN
ABORIGENS
ABORIGIN
ABORIGINE
ABORIGINES
ABORIGINS
ABORNE
ABORNING
ABORT
ABORTED
ABORTEE
ABORTEES
ABORTING
ABORTION
ABORTIONS
ABORTIVE
ABORTS
ABORTUARIES
ABORTUARY
ABOUGHT
ABOULIA
ABOULIAS
ABOUND
ABOUNDED
ABOUNDING
ABOUNDS
ABOUT
ABOUTS
ABOVE
ABRADANT
ABRADANTS
ABRADE
ABRADED
ABRADES
ABRADING
ABRAID
ABRAIDED
ABRAIDING
ABRAIDS
ABRAM
ABRASION
ABRASIONS
ABRASIVE
ABRASIVES
ABRAXAS
ABRAXASES
ABRAY
ABRAYED
ABRAYING
ABRAYS
ABRAZO
ABRAZOS
ABREACT
ABREACTED
ABREACTING
ABREACTS
ABREAST
ABREGE
ABREGES
ABRICOCK
ABRICOCKS
ABRIDGE
ABRIDGED
ABRIDGER
ABRIDGERS
ABRIDGES
ABRIDGING
ABRIM
ABRIN
ABRINS
ABROACH
ABROAD
ABROADS
ABROGATE
ABROGATED
ABROGATES
ABROGATING
ABROGATOR
ABROGATORS
ABROOKE
ABROOKED
ABROOKES
ABROOKING
ABRUPT
ABRUPTER
ABRUPTEST
ABRUPTION
ABRUPTIONS
ABRUPTLY
ABRUPTS
ABSCESS
ABSCESSED
ABSCESSES
ABSCIND
ABSCINDED
ABSCINDING
ABSCINDS
ABSCISE
ABSCISED
ABSCISES
ABSCISIN
ABSCISING
ABSCISINS
ABSCISS
ABSCISSA
ABSCISSAE
ABSCISSAS
ABSCISSE
ABSCISSES
ABSCISSIN
ABSCISSINS
ABSCOND
ABSCONDED
ABSCONDER
ABSCONDERS
ABSCONDING
ABSCONDS
ABSEIL
ABSEILED
ABSEILING
ABSEILINGS
ABSEILS
ABSENCE
ABSENCES
ABSENT
ABSENTED
ABSENTEE
ABSENTEES
ABSENTING
ABSENTLY
ABSENTS
ABSEY
ABSEYS
ABSINTH
ABSINTHE
ABSINTHES
ABSINTHS
ABSIT
ABSITS
ABSOLUTE
ABSOLUTER
ABSOLUTES
ABSOLUTEST
ABSOLVE
ABSOLVED
ABSOLVER
ABSOLVERS
ABSOLVES
ABSOLVING
ABSONANT
ABSORB
ABSORBATE
ABSORBATES
ABSORBED
ABSORBENT
ABSORBENTS
ABSORBER
ABSORBERS
ABSORBING
ABSORBS
ABSTAIN
ABSTAINED
ABSTAINER
ABSTAINERS
ABSTAINING
ABSTAINS
ABSTERGE
ABSTERGED
ABSTERGES
ABSTERGING
ABSTINENT
ABSTRACT
ABSTRACTED
ABSTRACTER
ABSTRACTERS
ABSTRACTEST
ABSTRACTING
ABSTRACTS
ABSTRICT
ABSTRICTED
ABSTRICTING
ABSTRICTS
ABSTRUSE
ABSTRUSER
ABSTRUSEST
ABSURD
ABSURDER
ABSURDEST
ABSURDISM
ABSURDISMS
ABSURDIST
ABSURDISTS
ABSURDITIES
ABSURDITY
ABSURDLY
ABTHANE
ABTHANES
ABULIA
ABULIAS
ABUNA
ABUNAS
ABUNDANCE
ABUNDANCES
ABUNDANCIES
ABUNDANCY
ABUNDANT
ABUNE
ABURST
ABUSAGE
ABUSAGES
ABUSE
ABUSED
ABUSER
ABUSERS
ABUSES
ABUSING
ABUSION
ABUSIONS
ABUSIVE
ABUSIVELY
ABUT
ABUTILON
ABUTILONS
ABUTMENT
ABUTMENTS
ABUTS
ABUTTAL
ABUTTALS
ABUTTED
ABUTTER
ABUTTERS
ABUTTING
ABUZZ
ABVOLT
ABVOLTS
ABY
ABYE
ABYEING
ABYES
ABYING
ABYSM
ABYSMAL
ABYSMALLY
ABYSMS
ABYSS
ABYSSAL
ABYSSES
ACACIA
ACACIAS
ACADEME
ACADEMES
ACADEMIA
ACADEMIAS
ACADEMIC
ACADEMICS
ACADEMIES
ACADEMISM
ACADEMISMS
ACADEMIST
ACADEMISTS
ACADEMY
ACAJOU
ACAJOUS
ACALEPH
ACALEPHAN
ACALEPHANS
ACALEPHE
ACALEPHES
ACALEPHS
ACANTH
ACANTHA
ACANTHAS
ACANTHIN
ACANTHINE
ACANTHINS
ACANTHOID
ACANTHOUS
ACANTHS
ACANTHUS
ACANTHUSES
ACAPNIA
ACAPNIAS
ACARI
ACARIAN
ACARIASES
ACARIASIS
ACARICIDE
ACARICIDES
ACARID
ACARIDAN
ACARIDANS
ACARIDEAN
ACARIDEANS
ACARIDIAN
ACARIDIANS
ACARIDS
ACARINE
ACAROID
ACAROLOGIES
ACAROLOGY
ACARPOUS
ACARUS
ACATER
ACATERS
ACATES
ACATOUR
ACATOURS
ACAUDAL
ACAUDATE
ACAULINE

ACAULOSE
ACCABLE
ACCEDE
ACCEDED
ACCEDENCE
ACCEDENCES
ACCEDER
ACCEDERS
ACCEDES
ACCEDING
ACCEND
ACCENDED
ACCENDING
ACCENDS
ACCENSION
ACCENSIONS
ACCENT
ACCENTED
ACCENTING
ACCENTOR
ACCENTORS
ACCENTS
ACCENTUAL
ACCEPT
ACCEPTANT
ACCEPTANTS
ACCEPTED
ACCEPTER
ACCEPTERS
ACCEPTING
ACCEPTIVE
ACCEPTOR
ACCEPTORS
ACCEPTS
ACCESS
ACCESSARIES
ACCESSARY
ACCESSED
ACCESSES
ACCESSING
ACCESSION
ACCESSIONED
ACCESSIONING
ACCESSIONS
ACCESSORIES
ACCESSORY
ACCIDENCE
ACCIDENCES
ACCIDENT
ACCIDENTS
ACCIDIE
ACCIDIES
ACCINGE
ACCINGED
ACCINGES
ACCINGING
ACCIPITER
ACCIPITERS
ACCITE
ACCITED
ACCITES
ACCITING
ACCLAIM
ACCLAIMED
ACCLAIMING
ACCLAIMS
ACCLIMATE
ACCLIMATED
ACCLIMATES
ACCLIMATING
ACCLIVITIES
ACCLIVITY
ACCLIVOUS
ACCLOY
ACCLOYED
ACCLOYING
ACCLOYS
ACCOAST
ACCOASTED
ACCOASTING
ACCOASTS
ACCOIED
ACCOIL
ACCOILS
ACCOLADE
ACCOLADES
ACCOMPANIED
ACCOMPANIES
ACCOMPANY
ACCOMPANYING
ACCOMPT
ACCOMPTED
ACCOMPTING
ACCOMPTS
ACCORAGE
ACCORAGED
ACCORAGES
ACCORAGING
ACCORD
ACCORDANT
ACCORDED
ACCORDER
ACCORDERS
ACCORDING
ACCORDION
ACCORDIONS
ACCORDS
ACCOST
ACCOSTED
ACCOSTING
ACCOSTS
ACCOUNT
ACCOUNTED
ACCOUNTING
ACCOUNTINGS
ACCOUNTS
ACCOURAGE
ACCOURAGED
ACCOURAGES
ACCOURAGING
ACCOURT
ACCOURTED
ACCOURTING
ACCOURTS
ACCOUTER
ACCOUTERED
ACCOUTERING
ACCOUTERS
ACCOUTRE
ACCOUTRED
ACCOUTRES
ACCOUTRING
ACCOY
ACCOYED
ACCOYING
ACCOYLD
ACCOYS
ACCREDIT
ACCREDITED
ACCREDITING
ACCREDITS
ACCRETE
ACCRETED
ACCRETES
ACCRETING
ACCRETION
ACCRETIONS
ACCRETIVE
ACCREW
ACCREWED
ACCREWING
ACCREWS
ACCRUAL
ACCRUALS
ACCRUE
ACCRUED
ACCRUES
ACCRUING
ACCUMBENT
ACCURACIES
ACCURACY
ACCURATE
ACCURSE
ACCURSED
ACCURSES
ACCURSING
ACCURST
ACCUSABLE
ACCUSAL
ACCUSALS
ACCUSE
ACCUSED
ACCUSER
ACCUSERS
ACCUSES
ACCUSING
ACCUSTOM
ACCUSTOMED
ACCUSTOMING
ACCUSTOMS
ACE
ACED
ACEDIA
ACEDIAS
ACELLULAR
ACER
ACERATE
ACERB
ACERBATE
ACERBATED
ACERBATES
ACERBATING
ACERBER
ACERBEST
ACERBIC
ACERBITIES
ACERBITY
ACEROSE
ACEROUS
ACERS
ACERVATE
ACES
ACESCENCE
ACESCENCES
ACESCENCIES
ACESCENCY
ACESCENT
ACETABULA
ACETAL
ACETALS
ACETAMIDE
ACETAMIDES
ACETATE
ACETATES
ACETIC
ACETIFIED
ACETIFIES
ACETIFY
ACETIFYING
ACETONE
ACETONES
ACETOSE
ACETOUS
ACETYL
ACETYLENE
ACETYLENES
ACETYLS
ACH
ACHAENIA
ACHAENIUM
ACHAENIUMS
ACHAGE
ACHAGES
ACHARNE
ACHARYA
ACHARYAS
ACHATES
ACHE
ACHED
ACHENE
ACHENES
ACHENIA
ACHENIAL
ACHENIUM
ACHENIUMS
ACHES
ACHIER
ACHIEST
ACHIEVE
ACHIEVED
ACHIEVER
ACHIEVERS
ACHIEVES
ACHIEVING
ACHILLEA
ACHILLEAS
ACHIMENES
ACHING
ACHINGLY
ACHINGS
ACHKAN
ACHKANS
ACHROMAT
ACHROMATS
ACHY
ACICULAR
ACICULATE
ACID
ACIDER
ACIDEST
ACIDFREAK
ACIDFREAKS
ACIDIC
ACIDIER
ACIDIEST
ACIDIFIED
ACIDIFIER
ACIDIFIERS
ACIDIFIES
ACIDIFY
ACIDIFYING
ACIDITIES
ACIDITY
ACIDLY
ACIDNESS
ACIDNESSES
ACIDOSES
ACIDOSIS
ACIDS
ACIDULATE
ACIDULATED
ACIDULATES
ACIDULATING
ACIDULENT
ACIDULOUS
ACIDY
ACIERAGE
ACIERAGES
ACIERATE
ACIERATED
ACIERATES
ACIERATING
ACIFORM
ACING
ACINI
ACINIFORM
ACINOSE
ACINOUS
ACINUS
ACKEE
ACKEES
ACKERS
ACKNEW
ACKNOW
ACKNOWING
ACKNOWN
ACKNOWNE
ACKNOWS
ACLINIC
ACME

ACMES
ACMITE
ACMITES
ACNE
ACNES
ACOCK
ACOEMETI
ACOLD
ACOLUTHIC
ACOLYTE
ACOLYTES
ACOLYTH
ACOLYTHS
ACONITE
ACONITES
ACONITIC
ACONITINE
ACONITINES
ACONITUM
ACONITUMS
ACORN
ACORNED
ACORNS
ACOSMISM
ACOSMISMS
ACOSMIST
ACOSMISTS
ACOUCHI
ACOUCHIES
ACOUCHIS
ACOUCHY
ACOUSTIC
ACOUSTICS
ACQUAINT
ACQUAINTED
ACQUAINTING
ACQUAINTS
ACQUEST
ACQUESTS
ACQUIESCE
ACQUIESCED
ACQUIESCES
ACQUIESCING
ACQUIGHT
ACQUIGHTING
ACQUIGHTS
ACQUIRAL
ACQUIRALS
ACQUIRE
ACQUIRED
ACQUIRES
ACQUIRING
ACQUIST
ACQUISTS
ACQUIT
ACQUITE
ACQUITES
ACQUITING
ACQUITS
ACQUITTAL
ACQUITTALS
ACQUITTED
ACQUITTING
ACRASIA
ACRASIAS
ACRATIC
ACRAWL
ACRE
ACREAGE
ACREAGES
ACRED
ACRES
ACRID
ACRIDER
ACRIDEST
ACRIDIN
ACRIDINE
ACRIDINES
ACRIDINS
ACRIDITIES
ACRIDITY
ACRIMONIES
ACRIMONY
ACROBAT
ACROBATIC
ACROBATICS
ACROBATS
ACROGEN
ACROGENIC
ACROGENS
ACROLEIN
ACROLEINS
ACROLITH
ACROLITHS
ACROMIA
ACROMIAL
ACROMION
ACRONICAL
ACRONYCAL
ACRONYM
ACRONYMIC
ACRONYMS
ACROPETAL
ACROPHONIES
ACROPHONY
ACROPOLIS
ACROPOLISES
ACROSOME
ACROSOMES
ACROSPIRE
ACROSPIRES
ACROSS
ACROSTIC
ACROSTICS
ACROTER
ACROTERIA
ACROTERS
ACROTISM
ACROTISMS
ACRYLIC
ACRYLICS
ACT
ACTA
ACTABLE
ACTED
ACTIN
ACTINAL
ACTINALLY
ACTING
ACTINGS
ACTINIA
ACTINIAE
ACTINIAN
ACTINIANS
ACTINIAS
ACTINIC
ACTINIDE
ACTINIDES
ACTINISM
ACTINISMS
ACTINIUM
ACTINIUMS
ACTINOID
ACTINOIDS
ACTINON
ACTINONS
ACTINS
ACTION
ACTIONED
ACTIONER
ACTIONERS
ACTIONING
ACTIONIST
ACTIONISTS
ACTIONS
ACTIVATE
ACTIVATED
ACTIVATES
ACTIVATING
ACTIVATOR
ACTIVATORS
ACTIVE
ACTIVELY
ACTIVISM
ACTIVISMS
ACTIVIST
ACTIVISTS
ACTIVITIES
ACTIVITY
ACTON
ACTONS
ACTOR
ACTORS
ACTRESS
ACTRESSES
ACTS
ACTUAL
ACTUALISE
ACTUALISED
ACTUALISES
ACTUALISING
ACTUALIST
ACTUALISTS
ACTUALITE
ACTUALITES
ACTUALITIES
ACTUALITY
ACTUALIZE
ACTUALIZED
ACTUALIZES
ACTUALIZING
ACTUALLY
ACTUARIAL
ACTUARIES
ACTUARY
ACTUATE
ACTUATED
ACTUATES
ACTUATING
ACTUATION
ACTUATIONS
ACTUATOR
ACTUATORS
ACTURE
ACTURES
ACUITIES
ACUITY
ACULEATE
ACULEATED
ACULEI
ACULEUS
ACUMEN
ACUMENS
ACUMINATE
ACUMINATED
ACUMINATES
ACUMINATING
ACUMINOUS
ACUPOINT
ACUPOINTS
ACUSHLA
ACUSHLAS
ACUTE
ACUTELY
ACUTENESS
ACUTENESSES
ACUTER
ACUTES
ACUTEST
ACYCLIC
ACYCLOVIR
ACYCLOVIRS
ACYL
ACYLS
AD
ADAGE
ADAGES
ADAGIO
ADAGIOS
ADAMANT
ADAMANTLY
ADAMANTS
ADAPT
ADAPTABLE
ADAPTED
ADAPTER
ADAPTERS
ADAPTING
ADAPTION
ADAPTIONS
ADAPTIVE
ADAPTOR
ADAPTORS
ADAPTS
ADAW
ADAWED
ADAWING
ADAWS
ADAXIAL
ADAYS
ADD
ADDAX
ADDAXES
ADDEBTED
ADDED
ADDEEM
ADDEEMED
ADDEEMING
ADDEEMS
ADDEND
ADDENDA
ADDENDS
ADDENDUM
ADDER
ADDERS
ADDERWORT
ADDERWORTS
ADDICT
ADDICTED
ADDICTING
ADDICTION
ADDICTIONS
ADDICTIVE
ADDICTS
ADDING
ADDIO
ADDIOS
ADDITION
ADDITIONS
ADDITIVE
ADDITIVES
ADDLE
ADDLED
ADDLEMENT
ADDLEMENTS
ADDLES
ADDLING
ADDOOM
ADDOOMED
ADDOOMING
ADDOOMS
ADDORSED
ADDRESS
ADDRESSED
ADDRESSEE
ADDRESSEES
ADDRESSER
ADDRESSERS
ADDRESSES
ADDRESSING
ADDRESSOR
ADDRESSORS
ADDREST
ADDS
ADDUCE
ADDUCED
ADDUCENT
ADDUCER
ADDUCERS
ADDUCES

ADDUCIBLE
ADDUCING
ADDUCT
ADDUCTED
ADDUCTING
ADDUCTION
ADDUCTIONS
ADDUCTIVE
ADDUCTOR
ADDUCTORS
ADDUCTS
ADEEM
ADEEMED
ADEEMING
ADEEMS
ADEMPTION
ADEMPTIONS
ADENINE
ADENINES
ADENITIS
ADENITISES
ADENOID
ADENOIDAL
ADENOIDS
ADENOMA
ADENOMAS
ADENOMATA
ADENOSINE
ADENOSINES
ADEPT
ADEPTER
ADEPTEST
ADEPTLY
ADEPTNESS
ADEPTNESSES
ADEPTS
ADEQUACIES
ADEQUACY
ADEQUATE
ADERMIN
ADERMINS
ADESPOTA
ADESSIVE
ADESSIVES
ADHARMA
ADHARMAS
ADHERE
ADHERED
ADHERENCE
ADHERENCES
ADHERENT
ADHERENTS
ADHERER
ADHERERS
ADHERES
ADHERING
ADHESION
ADHESIONS
ADHESIVE
ADHESIVES
ADHIBIT
ADHIBITED
ADHIBITING
ADHIBITS
ADIABATIC
ADIAPHORA
ADIEU
ADIEUS
ADIEUX
ADIOS
ADIPOCERE
ADIPOCERES
ADIPOSE
ADIPOSITIES
ADIPOSITY
ADIT
ADITS
ADJACENCIES
ADJACENCY
ADJACENT
ADJECTIVE
ADJECTIVES
ADJOIN
ADJOINED
ADJOINING
ADJOINS
ADJOINT
ADJOINTS
ADJOURN
ADJOURNED
ADJOURNING
ADJOURNS
ADJUDGE
ADJUDGED
ADJUDGES
ADJUDGING
ADJUNCT
ADJUNCTLY
ADJUNCTS
ADJURE
ADJURED
ADJURES
ADJURING
ADJUST
ADJUSTED
ADJUSTER
ADJUSTERS
ADJUSTING
ADJUSTOR
ADJUSTORS
ADJUSTS
ADJUTAGE
ADJUTAGES
ADJUTANCIES
ADJUTANCY
ADJUTANT
ADJUTANTS
ADJUVANCIES
ADJUVANCY
ADJUVANT
ADJUVANTS
ADLAND
ADLANDS
ADMAN
ADMASS
ADMASSES
ADMEASURE
ADMEASURED
ADMEASURES
ADMEASURING
ADMEN
ADMIN
ADMINICLE
ADMINICLES
ADMINS
ADMIRABLE
ADMIRABLY
ADMIRAL
ADMIRALS
ADMIRANCE
ADMIRANCES
ADMIRE
ADMIRED
ADMIRER
ADMIRERS
ADMIRES
ADMIRING
ADMISSION
ADMISSIONS
ADMISSIVE
ADMIT
ADMITS
ADMITTED
ADMITTING
ADMIX
ADMIXED
ADMIXES
ADMIXING
ADMIXTURE
ADMIXTURES
ADMONISH
ADMONISHED
ADMONISHES
ADMONISHING
ADMONITOR
ADMONITORS
ADNASCENT
ADNATE
ADNATION
ADNATIONS
ADNOMINAL
ADNOUN
ADNOUNS
ADO
ADOBE
ADOBES
ADONISE
ADONISED
ADONISES
ADONISING
ADONIZE
ADONIZED
ADONIZES
ADONIZING
ADOORS
ADOPT
ADOPTED
ADOPTEE
ADOPTEES
ADOPTER
ADOPTERS
ADOPTING
ADOPTION
ADOPTIONS
ADOPTIOUS
ADOPTIVE
ADOPTS
ADORABLE
ADORABLY
ADORATION
ADORATIONS
ADORE
ADORED
ADORER
ADORERS
ADORES
ADORING
ADORINGLY
ADORN
ADORNED
ADORNING
ADORNMENT
ADORNMENTS
ADORNS
ADOS
ADOWN
ADPRESS
ADPRESSED
ADPRESSES
ADPRESSING
ADRAD
ADREAD
ADREADED
ADREADING
ADREADS
ADRED
ADRENAL
ADRENALIN
ADRENALINS
ADRENALS
ADRIFT
ADROIT
ADROITER
ADROITEST
ADROITLY
ADRY
ADS
ADSCRIPT
ADSCRIPTS
ADSORB
ADSORBATE
ADSORBATES
ADSORBED
ADSORBENT
ADSORBENTS
ADSORBING
ADSORBS
ADSUM
ADULARIA
ADULARIAS
ADULATE
ADULATED
ADULATES
ADULATING
ADULATION
ADULATIONS
ADULATOR
ADULATORS
ADULATORY
ADULT
ADULTERER
ADULTERERS
ADULTERIES
ADULTERY
ADULTHOOD
ADULTHOODS
ADULTS
ADUMBRATE
ADUMBRATED
ADUMBRATES
ADUMBRATING
ADUNC
ADUNCATE
ADUNCATED
ADUNCITIES
ADUNCITY
ADUNCOUS
ADUST
ADUSTED
ADUSTING
ADUSTS
ADVANCE
ADVANCED
ADVANCES
ADVANCING
ADVANTAGE
ADVANTAGED
ADVANTAGES
ADVANTAGING
ADVECTION
ADVECTIONS
ADVENE
ADVENED
ADVENES
ADVENING
ADVENT
ADVENTIVE
ADVENTIVES
ADVENTS
ADVENTURE
ADVENTURED
ADVENTURES
ADVENTURING
ADVERB
ADVERBIAL
ADVERBS
ADVERSARIES
ADVERSARY
ADVERSE
ADVERSELY
ADVERSER
ADVERSEST
ADVERSITIES
ADVERSITY
ADVERT
ADVERTED
ADVERTENT
ADVERTING
ADVERTISE
ADVERTISED

ADVERTISES
ADVERTISING
ADVERTISINGS
ADVERTIZE
ADVERTIZED
ADVERTIZES
ADVERTIZING
ADVERTS
ADVEW
ADVEWED
ADVEWING
ADVEWS
ADVICE
ADVICEFUL
ADVICES
ADVISABLE
ADVISABLY
ADVISE
ADVISED
ADVISEDLY
ADVISER
ADVISERS
ADVISES
ADVISING
ADVISINGS
ADVISOR
ADVISORS
ADVISORY
ADVOCAAT
ADVOCAATS
ADVOCACIES
ADVOCACY
ADVOCATE
ADVOCATED
ADVOCATES
ADVOCATING
ADVOCATOR
ADVOCATORS
ADVOUTRER
ADVOUTRERS
ADVOUTRIES
ADVOUTRY
ADVOWSON
ADVOWSONS
ADWARD
ADWARDED
ADWARDING
ADWARDS
ADYNAMIA
ADYNAMIAS
ADYNAMIC
ADYTA
ADYTUM
ADZ
ADZE
ADZES
AE
AECIA
AECIDIA
AECIDIUM
AECIUM
AEDES
AEDILE
AEDILES
AEFALD
AEFAULD
AEGIRINE
AEGIRINES
AEGIRITE
AEGIRITES
AEGIS
AEGISES
AEGLOGUE
AEGLOGUES
AEGROTAT
AEGROTATS
AEMULE
AEMULED
AEMULES
AEMULING
AENEOUS
AEOLIAN
AEOLIPILE
AEOLIPILES
AEOLIPYLE
AEOLIPYLES
AEON
AEONIAN
AEONS
AERATE
AERATED
AERATES
AERATING
AERATION
AERATIONS
AERATOR
AERATORS
AERIAL
AERIALIST
AERIALISTS
AERIALITIES
AERIALITY
AERIALLY
AERIALS
AERIE
AERIER
AERIES
AERIEST
AERIFORM
AERO
AEROBE
AEROBES
AEROBIC
AEROBICS
AEROBIONT
AEROBIONTS
AEROBOMB
AEROBOMBS
AEROBUS
AEROBUSES
AEROBUSSES
AERODART
AERODARTS
AERODROME
AERODROMES
AERODYNE
AERODYNES
AEROFOIL
AEROFOILS
AEROGRAM
AEROGRAMS
AEROGRAPH
AEROGRAPHS
AEROLITE
AEROLITES
AEROLITH
AEROLITHS
AEROLITIC
AEROLOGIES
AEROLOGY
AEROMANCIES
AEROMANCY
AEROMETER
AEROMETERS
AEROMETRIES
AEROMETRY
AEROMOTOR
AEROMOTORS
AERONAUT
AERONAUTS
AERONOMIES
AERONOMY
AEROPHOBE
AEROPHOBES
AEROPHONE
AEROPHONES
AEROPHYTE
AEROPHYTES
AEROPLANE
AEROPLANES
AEROS
AEROSHELL
AEROSHELLS
AEROSOL
AEROSOLS
AEROSPACE
AEROSPACES
AEROSTAT
AEROSTATS
AEROTAXES
AEROTAXIS
AEROTONE
AEROTONES
AEROTRAIN
AEROTRAINS
AERY
AESC
AESCES
AESCULIN
AESCULINS
AESIR
AESTHESES
AESTHESIA
AESTHESIAS
AESTHESIS
AESTHETE
AESTHETES
AESTHETIC
AESTHETICS
AESTIVAL
AESTIVATE
AESTIVATED
AESTIVATES
AESTIVATING
AETHER
AETHERS
AETIOLOGIES
AETIOLOGY
AFALD
AFAR
AFARA
AFARAS
AFAWLD
AFEAR
AFEARD
AFEARED
AFEARING
AFEARS
AFFABLE
AFFABLY
AFFAIR
AFFAIRE
AFFAIRES
AFFAIRS
AFFEAR
AFFEARD
AFFEARE
AFFEARED
AFFEARES
AFFEARING
AFFEARS
AFFECT
AFFECTED
AFFECTER
AFFECTERS
AFFECTING
AFFECTION
AFFECTIONED
AFFECTIONING
AFFECTIONS
AFFECTIVE
AFFECTS
AFFEER
AFFEERED
AFFEERING
AFFEERS
AFFERENT
AFFIANCE
AFFIANCED
AFFIANCES
AFFIANCING
AFFICHE
AFFICHES
AFFIDAVIT
AFFIDAVITS
AFFIED
AFFIES
AFFILIATE
AFFILIATED
AFFILIATES
AFFILIATING
AFFINE
AFFINED
AFFINES
AFFINITIES
AFFINITY
AFFIRM
AFFIRMANT
AFFIRMANTS
AFFIRMED
AFFIRMER
AFFIRMERS
AFFIRMING
AFFIRMS
AFFIX
AFFIXED
AFFIXES
AFFIXING
AFFLATED
AFFLATION
AFFLATIONS
AFFLATUS
AFFLATUSES
AFFLICT
AFFLICTED
AFFLICTING
AFFLICTINGS
AFFLICTS
AFFLUENCE
AFFLUENCES
AFFLUENT
AFFLUENTS
AFFLUENZA
AFFLUENZAS
AFFLUX
AFFLUXES
AFFLUXION
AFFLUXIONS
AFFOORD
AFFOORDED
AFFOORDING
AFFOORDS
AFFORCE
AFFORCED
AFFORCES
AFFORCING
AFFORD
AFFORDED
AFFORDING
AFFORDS
AFFOREST
AFFORESTED
AFFORESTING
AFFORESTS
AFFRAP
AFFRAPPED
AFFRAPPING
AFFRAPS
AFFRAY
AFFRAYED
AFFRAYING
AFFRAYS
AFFRENDED
AFFRET
AFFRETS
AFFRICATE
AFFRICATES
AFFRIGHT
AFFRIGHTED
AFFRIGHTING

AFFRIGHTS
AFFRONT
AFFRONTE
AFFRONTED
AFFRONTEE
AFFRONTING
AFFRONTINGS
AFFRONTS
AFFUSION
AFFUSIONS
AFFY
AFFYDE
AFFYING
AFGHAN
AFGHANS
AFIELD
AFIRE
AFLAJ
AFLAME
AFLATOXIN
AFLATOXINS
AFLOAT
AFLUTTER
AFOOT
AFORE
AFOREHAND
AFORESAID
AFORETIME
AFOUL
AFRAID
AFREET
AFREETS
AFRESH
AFRIT
AFRITS
AFRO
AFRONT
AFROS
AFT
AFTER
AFTERCARE
AFTERCARES
AFTERDECK
AFTERDECKS
AFTEREYE
AFTEREYED
AFTEREYEING
AFTEREYES
AFTEREYING
AFTERGAME
AFTERGAMES
AFTERGLOW
AFTERGLOWS
AFTERHEAT
AFTERHEATS
AFTERINGS
AFTERMATH
AFTERMATHS
AFTERMOST
AFTERNOON
AFTERNOONS
AFTERS
AFTERTIME
AFTERTIMES
AFTERWARD
AFTERWARDS
AFTERWORD
AFTERWORDS
AFTMOST
AGA
AGACANT
AGACANTE
AGACERIE
AGACERIES
AGAIN
AGAINST
AGALACTIA
AGALACTIAS
AGALLOCH
AGALLOCHS
AGAMI
AGAMIC
AGAMID
AGAMIDS
AGAMIS
AGAMOID
AGAMOIDS
AGAMOUS
AGAPAE
AGAPE
AGAR
AGARIC
AGARICS
AGARS
AGAS
AGAST
AGATE
AGATES
AGATEWARE
AGATEWARES
AGAVE
AGAVES
AGAZE
AGAZED
AGE
AGED
AGEDNESS
AGEDNESSES
AGEE
AGEING
AGEINGS
AGEISM
AGEISMS
AGEIST
AGEISTS
AGELAST
AGELASTIC
AGELASTS
AGELESS
AGELONG
AGEN
AGENCIES
AGENCY
AGENDA
AGENDAS
AGENE
AGENES
AGENT
AGENTED
AGENTIAL
AGENTING
AGENTIVE
AGENTIVES
AGENTS
AGERATUM
AGERATUMS
AGES
AGGER
AGGERS
AGGRACE
AGGRACED
AGGRACES
AGGRACING
AGGRADE
AGGRADED
AGGRADES
AGGRADING
AGGRATE
AGGRATED
AGGRATES
AGGRATING
AGGRAVATE
AGGRAVATED
AGGRAVATES
AGGRAVATING
AGGREGATE
AGGREGATED
AGGREGATES
AGGREGATING
AGGRESS
AGGRESSED
AGGRESSES
AGGRESSING
AGGRESSOR
AGGRESSORS
AGGRI
AGGRIEVE
AGGRIEVED
AGGRIEVES
AGGRIEVING
AGGRO
AGGROS
AGGRY
AGHA
AGHAS
AGHAST
AGILA
AGILAS
AGILE
AGILELY
AGILER
AGILEST
AGILITIES
AGILITY
AGIN
AGING
AGINGS
AGINNER
AGINNERS
AGIO
AGIOS
AGIOTAGE
AGIOTAGES
AGIST
AGISTED
AGISTER
AGISTERS
AGISTING
AGISTMENT
AGISTMENTS
AGISTOR
AGISTORS
AGISTS
AGITATE
AGITATED
AGITATES
AGITATING
AGITATION
AGITATIONS
AGITATIVE
AGITATO
AGITATOR
AGITATORS
AGITPROP
AGITPROPS
AGLEAM
AGLEE
AGLET
AGLETS
AGLEY
AGLIMMER
AGLITTER
AGLOW
AGMA
AGMAS
AGNAIL
AGNAILS
AGNAME
AGNAMED
AGNAMES
AGNATE
AGNATES
AGNATIC
AGNATICAL
AGNATION
AGNATIONS
AGNISE
AGNISED
AGNISES
AGNISING
AGNIZE
AGNIZED
AGNIZES
AGNIZING
AGNOMEN
AGNOMENS
AGNOMINA
AGNOMINAL
AGNOSIA
AGNOSIAS
AGNOSTIC
AGNOSTICS
AGO
AGOG
AGOGE
AGOGES
AGOGIC
AGOGICS
AGOING
AGON
AGONE
AGONIC
AGONIES
AGONISE
AGONISED
AGONISES
AGONISING
AGONIST
AGONISTES
AGONISTIC
AGONISTICS
AGONISTS
AGONIZE
AGONIZED
AGONIZES
AGONIZING
AGONS
AGONY
AGOOD
AGORA
AGORAS
AGOROT
AGOUTA
AGOUTAS
AGOUTI
AGOUTIES
AGOUTIS
AGOUTY
AGRAFFE
AGRAFFES
AGRAPHA
AGRAPHIA
AGRAPHIAS
AGRAPHIC
AGRAPHON
AGRARIAN
AGRASTE
AGRAVIC
AGREE
AGREEABLE
AGREEABLY
AGREED
AGREEING
AGREEMENT
AGREEMENTS
AGREES
AGREGE
AGREGES
AGREMENS
AGREMENT
AGREMENTS
AGRESTAL
AGRESTIAL
AGRESTIC
AGRIMONIES
AGRIMONY
AGRIN
AGRIOLOGIES
AGRIOLOGY
AGRISE

AGRISED
AGRISES
AGRISING
AGRIZE
AGRIZED
AGRIZES
AGRIZING
AGROLOGIES
AGROLOGY
AGRONOMIC
AGRONOMICS
AGRONOMIES
AGRONOMY
AGROUND
AGRYZE
AGRYZED
AGRYZES
AGRYZING
AGUACATE
AGUACATES
AGUE
AGUED
AGUES
AGUISE
AGUISED
AGUISES
AGUISH
AGUISHLY
AGUISING
AGUIZE
AGUIZED
AGUIZES
AGUIZING
AGUTI
AGUTIS
AH
AHA
AHEAD
AHEAP
AHED
AHEIGHT
AHEM
AHENT
AHIGH
AHIMSA
AHIMSAS
AHIND
AHING
AHINT
AHOLD
AHORSE
AHOY
AHS
AHULL
AHUNGERED
AHUNGRY
AI
AIA
AIAS
AIBLINS
AID
AIDANCE
AIDANCES
AIDANT
AIDE
AIDED
AIDER
AIDERS
AIDES
AIDFUL
AIDING
AIDLESS
AIDOI
AIDOS
AIDS
AIERIES
AIERY
AIGLET
AIGLETS
AIGRETTE
AIGRETTES
AIGUILLE
AIGUILLES
AIKIDO
AIKIDOS
AIKONA
AIL
AILANTHUS
AILANTHUSES
AILANTO
AILANTOS
AILED
AILERON
AILERONS
AILETTE
AILETTES
AILING
AILMENT
AILMENTS
AILS
AIM
AIMED
AIMING
AIMLESS
AIMLESSLY
AIMS
AIN
AINE
AINEE
AIOLI
AIOLIS
AIR
AIRBASE
AIRBASES
AIRBORNE
AIRBURST
AIRBURSTS
AIRBUSSES
AIRCRAFT
AIRDRAWN
AIRDROME
AIRDROMES
AIRED
AIRER
AIRERS
AIRFIELD
AIRFIELDS
AIRFLOW
AIRFLOWS
AIRFOIL
AIRFOILS
AIRFRAME
AIRFRAMES
AIRGAP
AIRGAPS
AIRGLOW
AIRGLOWS
AIRGRAPH
AIRGRAPHS
AIRHEAD
AIRHEADS
AIRHOLE
AIRHOLES
AIRIER
AIRIEST
AIRILY
AIRINESS
AIRINESSES
AIRING
AIRINGS
AIRLESS
AIRLIFT
AIRLIFTED
AIRLIFTING
AIRLIFTS
AIRLINE
AIRLINER
AIRLINERS
AIRLINES
AIRLOCK
AIRLOCKS
AIRMAIL
AIRMAILED
AIRMAILING
AIRMAILS
AIRMAN
AIRMEN
AIRN
AIRNED
AIRNING
AIRNS
AIRPLANE
AIRPLANES
AIRPORT
AIRPORTS
AIRS
AIRSCREW
AIRSCREWS
AIRSHAFT
AIRSHAFTS
AIRSHIP
AIRSHIPS
AIRSICK
AIRSIDE
AIRSIDES
AIRSPACE
AIRSPACES
AIRSPEED
AIRSPEEDS
AIRSTOP
AIRSTOPS
AIRSTREAM
AIRSTREAMS
AIRSTRIP
AIRSTRIPS
AIRT
AIRTED
AIRTIGHT
AIRTIME
AIRTIMES
AIRTING
AIRTS
AIRWARD
AIRWARDS
AIRWAVE
AIRWAVES
AIRWAY
AIRWAYS
AIRWOMAN
AIRWOMEN
AIRWORTHY
AIRY
AIS
AISLE
AISLED
AISLES
AISLING
AISLINGS
AIT
AITCH
AITCHBONE
AITCHBONES
AITCHES
AITS
AITU
AITUS
AIZLE
AIZLES
AJAR
AJEE
AJOWAN
AJOWANS
AJUTAGE
AJUTAGES
AJWAN
AJWANS
AKARYOTE
AKARYOTES
AKE
AKED
AKEDAH
AKEDAHS
AKEE
AKEES
AKENE
AKENES
AKES
AKIMBO
AKIN
AKINESES
AKINESIA
AKINESIAS
AKINESIS
AKING
AKKAS
AKOLUTHOS
AKOLUTHOSES
AKVAVIT
AKVAVITS
ALA
ALAAP
ALAAPS
ALABAMINE
ALABAMINES
ALABASTER
ALABASTERS
ALACK
ALACRITIES
ALACRITY
ALAE
ALAIMENT
ALAIMENTS
ALALAGMOI
ALALAGMOS
ALALIA
ALALIAS
ALAMEDA
ALAMEDAS
ALAMODE
ALAMODES
ALAMORT
ALAND
ALANG
ALANGS
ALANINE
ALANINES
ALANNAH
ALANNAHS
ALAP
ALAPA
ALAPAS
ALAPS
ALAR
ALARM
ALARMED
ALARMEDLY
ALARMING
ALARMISM
ALARMISMS
ALARMIST
ALARMISTS
ALARMS
ALARUM
ALARUMED
ALARUMING
ALARUMS
ALARY
ALAS
ALASTRIM
ALASTRIMS
ALATE
ALATED
ALAY
ALAYED
ALAYING
ALAYS
ALB
ALBACORE
ALBACORES
ALBARELLI

ALBARELLO
ALBARELLOS
ALBATA
ALBATAS
ALBATROSS
ALBATROSSES
ALBE
ALBEDO
ALBEDOS
ALBEE
ALBEIT
ALBERGHI
ALBERGO
ALBERT
ALBERTITE
ALBERTITES
ALBERTS
ALBESCENT
ALBESPINE
ALBESPINES
ALBESPYNE
ALBESPYNES
ALBICORE
ALBICORES
ALBINESS
ALBINESSES
ALBINIC
ALBINISM
ALBINISMS
ALBINO
ALBINOISM
ALBINOISMS
ALBINOS
ALBINOTIC
ALBITE
ALBITES
ALBITIC
ALBITISE
ALBITISED
ALBITISES
ALBITISING
ALBITIZE
ALBITIZED
ALBITIZES
ALBITIZING
ALBRICIAS
ALBS
ALBUGO
ALBUGOS
ALBUM
ALBUMEN
ALBUMENS
ALBUMIN
ALBUMINS
ALBUMS
ALBURNOUS
ALBURNUM
ALBURNUMS
ALCAHEST
ALCAHESTS
ALCAIDE
ALCAIDES
ALCALDE
ALCALDES
ALCARRAZA
ALCARRAZAS
ALCATRAS
ALCATRASES
ALCAYDE
ALCAYDES
ALCAZAR
ALCAZARS
ALCHEMIC
ALCHEMIES
ALCHEMISE
ALCHEMISED
ALCHEMISES
ALCHEMISING
ALCHEMIST
ALCHEMISTS
ALCHEMIZE
ALCHEMIZED
ALCHEMIZES
ALCHEMIZING
ALCHEMY
ALCHERA
ALCHERAS
ALCHYMIES
ALCHYMY
ALCOHOL
ALCOHOLIC
ALCOHOLICS
ALCOHOLS
ALCOPOP
ALCOPOPS
ALCORZA
ALCORZAS
ALCOVE
ALCOVES
ALDEA
ALDEAS
ALDEHYDE
ALDEHYDES
ALDER
ALDERMAN
ALDERMEN
ALDERN
ALDERS
ALDOSE
ALDOSES
ALDRIN
ALDRINS
ALE
ALEATORIC
ALEATORIES
ALEATORY
ALEBENCH
ALEBENCHES
ALECOST
ALECOSTS
ALECTRYON
ALECTRYONS
ALEE
ALEFT
ALEGAR
ALEGARS
ALEGGE
ALEGGED
ALEGGES
ALEGGING
ALEMBIC
ALEMBICS
ALEMBROTH
ALEMBROTHS
ALENGTH
ALEPH
ALEPHS
ALEPINE
ALEPINES
ALERCE
ALERCES
ALERION
ALERIONS
ALERT
ALERTED
ALERTER
ALERTEST
ALERTING
ALERTLY
ALERTNESS
ALERTNESSES
ALERTS
ALES
ALETHIC
ALEURON
ALEURONE
ALEURONES
ALEURONS
ALEVIN
ALEVINS
ALEW
ALEWASHED
ALEWIFE
ALEWIVES
ALEWS
ALEXIA
ALEXIAS
ALEXIC
ALEXIN
ALEXINS
ALEYE
ALEYED
ALEYES
ALEYING
ALFA
ALFALFA
ALFALFAS
ALFAQUI
ALFAQUIS
ALFAS
ALFERECES
ALFEREZ
ALFORJA
ALFORJAS
ALFRESCO
ALGA
ALGAE
ALGAL
ALGAROBA
ALGAROBAS
ALGARROBA
ALGARROBAS
ALGARROBO
ALGARROBOS
ALGATE
ALGATES
ALGEBRA
ALGEBRAIC
ALGEBRAS
ALGERINE
ALGERINES
ALGESES
ALGESIA
ALGESIAS
ALGESIS
ALGICIDE
ALGICIDES
ALGID
ALGIDITIES
ALGIDITY
ALGIN
ALGINATE
ALGINATES
ALGINIC
ALGINS
ALGOID
ALGOLOGIES
ALGOLOGY
ALGORISM
ALGORISMS
ALGORITHM
ALGORITHMS
ALGUACIL
ALGUACILS
ALGUAZIL
ALGUAZILS
ALGUM
ALGUMS
ALIAS
ALIASES
ALIASING
ALIASINGS
ALIBI
ALIBIS
ALICANT
ALICANTS
ALICYCLIC
ALIDAD
ALIDADE
ALIDADES
ALIDADS
ALIEN
ALIENABLE
ALIENAGE
ALIENAGES
ALIENATE
ALIENATED
ALIENATES
ALIENATING
ALIENATOR
ALIENATORS
ALIENED
ALIENEE
ALIENEES
ALIENING
ALIENISM
ALIENISMS
ALIENIST
ALIENISTS
ALIENOR
ALIENORS
ALIENS
ALIFORM
ALIGARTA
ALIGARTAS
ALIGHT
ALIGHTED
ALIGHTING
ALIGHTS
ALIGN
ALIGNED
ALIGNING
ALIGNMENT
ALIGNMENTS
ALIGNS
ALIKE
ALIMENT
ALIMENTAL
ALIMENTED
ALIMENTING
ALIMENTS
ALIMONIES
ALIMONY
ALINE
ALINED
ALINEMENT
ALINEMENTS
ALINES
ALINING
ALIPED
ALIPEDS
ALIPHATIC
ALIQUANT
ALIQUOT
ALISMA
ALISMAS
ALIT
ALITERACIES
ALITERACY
ALITERATE
ALIUNDE
ALIVE
ALIVENESS
ALIVENESSES
ALIYA
ALIYAH
ALIYAHS
ALIYAS
ALIYOT
ALIYOTH
ALIZARI
ALIZARIN
ALIZARINE
ALIZARINES
ALIZARINS
ALIZARIS
ALKAHEST
ALKAHESTS
ALKALI
ALKALIES

ALKALIFIED
ALKALIFIES
ALKALIFY
ALKALIFYING
ALKALINE
ALKALIS
ALKALISE
ALKALISED
ALKALISES
ALKALISING
ALKALIZE
ALKALIZED
ALKALIZES
ALKALIZING
ALKALOID
ALKALOIDS
ALKALOSES
ALKALOSIS
ALKANE
ALKANES
ALKANET
ALKANETS
ALKENE
ALKENES
ALKIE
ALKIES
ALKY
ALKYD
ALKYDS
ALKYL
ALKYLS
ALKYNE
ALKYNES
ALL
ALLANTOIC
ALLANTOID
ALLANTOIDS
ALLANTOIS
ALLANTOISES
ALLATIVE
ALLATIVES
ALLAY
ALLAYED
ALLAYER
ALLAYERS
ALLAYING
ALLAYINGS
ALLAYMENT
ALLAYMENTS
ALLAYS
ALLCOMERS
ALLEDGE
ALLEDGED
ALLEDGES
ALLEDGING
ALLEE
ALLEES
ALLEGE
ALLEGED
ALLEGEDLY
ALLEGER
ALLEGERS
ALLEGES
ALLEGGE
ALLEGGED
ALLEGGES
ALLEGGING
ALLEGIANT
ALLEGING
ALLEGORIC
ALLEGORIES
ALLEGORY
ALLEGRO
ALLEGROS
ALLEL
ALLELE
ALLELES
ALLELS
ALLELUIA
ALLELUIAH
ALLELUIAHS
ALLELUIAS
ALLEMANDE
ALLEMANDES
ALLENARLY
ALLERGEN
ALLERGENS
ALLERGIC
ALLERGICS
ALLERGIES
ALLERGIST
ALLERGISTS
ALLERGY
ALLERION
ALLERIONS
ALLEVIATE
ALLEVIATED
ALLEVIATES
ALLEVIATING
ALLEY
ALLEYCAT
ALLEYCATS
ALLEYED
ALLEYS
ALLEYWAY
ALLEYWAYS
ALLHEAL
ALLHEALS
ALLIANCE
ALLIANCES
ALLICE
ALLICES
ALLICHOLIES
ALLICHOLY
ALLIED
ALLIES
ALLIGARTA
ALLIGARTAS
ALLIGATE
ALLIGATED
ALLIGATES
ALLIGATING
ALLIGATOR
ALLIGATORS
ALLIS
ALLISES
ALLIUM
ALLIUMS
ALLNESS
ALLNESSES
ALLNIGHT
ALLOCABLE
ALLOCARPIES
ALLOCARPY
ALLOCATE
ALLOCATED
ALLOCATES
ALLOCATING
ALLOD
ALLODIAL
ALLODIUM
ALLODIUMS
ALLODS
ALLOGAMIES
ALLOGAMY
ALLOGRAFT
ALLOGRAFTS
ALLOGRAPH
ALLOGRAPHS
ALLOMETRIES
ALLOMETRY
ALLOMORPH
ALLOMORPHS
ALLONGE
ALLONGES
ALLONS
ALLONYM
ALLONYMS
ALLOPATH
ALLOPATHIES
ALLOPATHS
ALLOPATHY
ALLOPHONE
ALLOPHONES
ALLOPLASM
ALLOPLASMS
ALLOSAUR
ALLOSAURS
ALLOSTERIES
ALLOSTERY
ALLOT
ALLOTMENT
ALLOTMENTS
ALLOTROPE
ALLOTROPES
ALLOTROPIES
ALLOTROPY
ALLOTS
ALLOTTED
ALLOTTEE
ALLOTTEES
ALLOTTERIES
ALLOTTERY
ALLOTTING
ALLOW
ALLOWABLE
ALLOWABLY
ALLOWANCE
ALLOWANCED
ALLOWANCES
ALLOWANCING
ALLOWED
ALLOWEDLY
ALLOWING
ALLOWS
ALLOY
ALLOYED
ALLOYING
ALLOYS
ALLS
ALLSEED
ALLSEEDS
ALLSORTS
ALLSPICE
ALLSPICES
ALLUDE
ALLUDED
ALLUDES
ALLUDING
ALLURE
ALLURED
ALLURER
ALLURERS
ALLURES
ALLURING
ALLUSION
ALLUSIONS
ALLUSIVE
ALLUVIA
ALLUVIAL
ALLUVION
ALLUVIONS
ALLUVIUM
ALLY
ALLYING
ALLYL
ALLYLS
ALMA
ALMAH
ALMAHS
ALMAIN
ALMAINS
ALMANAC
ALMANACS
ALMANDINE
ALMANDINES
ALMAS
ALME
ALMEH
ALMEHS
ALMERIES
ALMERY
ALMES
ALMIGHTY
ALMIRAH
ALMIRAHS
ALMOND
ALMONDS
ALMONER
ALMONERS
ALMONRIES
ALMONRY
ALMOST
ALMOUS
ALMS
ALMUCE
ALMUCES
ALMUG
ALMUGS
ALNAGE
ALNAGER
ALNAGERS
ALNAGES
ALOD
ALODIAL
ALODIUM
ALODIUMS
ALODS
ALOE
ALOED
ALOES
ALOETIC
ALOETICS
ALOFT
ALOGIA
ALOGIAS
ALOGICAL
ALOHA
ALONE
ALONELY
ALONENESS
ALONENESSES
ALONG
ALONGSIDE
ALONGST
ALOOF
ALOOFLY
ALOOFNESS
ALOOFNESSES
ALOPECIA
ALOPECIAS
ALOPECOID
ALOUD
ALOW
ALOWE
ALP
ALPACA
ALPACAS
ALPARGATA
ALPARGATAS
ALPEEN
ALPEENS
ALPENHORN
ALPENHORNS
ALPHA
ALPHABET
ALPHABETED
ALPHABETING
ALPHABETS
ALPHAS
ALPHASORT
ALPHASORTED
ALPHASORTING
ALPHASORTS
ALPHORN
ALPHORNS
ALPINE
ALPINES
ALPINISM
ALPINISMS

ALPINIST
ALPINISTS
ALPS
ALREADY
ALRIGHT
ALS
ALSIKE
ALSIKES
ALSO
ALSOON
ALSOONE
ALT
ALTAR
ALTARAGE
ALTARAGES
ALTARS
ALTARWISE
ALTER
ALTERABLE
ALTERANT
ALTERANTS
ALTERCATE
ALTERCATED
ALTERCATES
ALTERCATING
ALTERED
ALTERING
ALTERITIES
ALTERITY
ALTERN
ALTERNANT
ALTERNANTS
ALTERNAT
ALTERNATE
ALTERNATED
ALTERNATES
ALTERNATING
ALTERNATS
ALTERNE
ALTERNES
ALTERS
ALTESSE
ALTESSES
ALTEZA
ALTEZAS
ALTEZZA
ALTEZZAS
ALTHAEA
ALTHAEAS
ALTHEA
ALTHEAS
ALTHORN
ALTHORNS
ALTHOUGH
ALTIMETER
ALTIMETERS
ALTIMETRIES
ALTIMETRY
ALTISSIMO
ALTITUDE
ALTITUDES
ALTO
ALTOS
ALTRICES
ALTRICIAL
ALTRUISM
ALTRUISMS
ALTRUIST
ALTRUISTS
ALTS
ALUDEL
ALUDELS
ALULA
ALULAE
ALUM
ALUMINA
ALUMINAS
ALUMINATE
ALUMINATES
ALUMINISE
ALUMINISED
ALUMINISES
ALUMINISING
ALUMINIUM
ALUMINIUMS
ALUMINIZE
ALUMINIZED
ALUMINIZES
ALUMINIZING
ALUMINOUS
ALUMINUM
ALUMINUMS
ALUMISH
ALUMIUM
ALUMIUMS
ALUMNA
ALUMNAE
ALUMNI
ALUMNUS
ALUMS
ALUNITE
ALUNITES
ALURE
ALURES
ALVEARIES
ALVEARY
ALVEATED
ALVEOLAR
ALVEOLATE
ALVEOLE
ALVEOLES
ALVEOLI
ALVEOLUS
ALVINE
ALWAY
ALWAYS
ALYSSUM
ALYSSUMS
AM
AMABILE
AMADAVAT
AMADAVATS
AMADOU
AMADOUS
AMAH
AMAHS
AMAIN
AMALGAM
AMALGAMS
AMANDINE
AMANDINES
AMANITA
AMANITAS
AMARACUS
AMARACUSES
AMARANT
AMARANTH
AMARANTHS
AMARANTIN
AMARANTS
AMARETTO
AMARETTOS
AMARYLLID
AMARYLLIDS
AMARYLLIS
AMARYLLISES
AMASS
AMASSABLE
AMASSED
AMASSES
AMASSING
AMASSMENT
AMASSMENTS
AMATE
AMATED
AMATES
AMATEUR
AMATEURS
AMATING
AMATION
AMATIONS
AMATIVE
AMATOL
AMATOLS
AMATORIAL
AMATORIAN
AMATORY
AMAUROSES
AMAUROSIS
AMAUROTIC
AMAZE
AMAZED
AMAZEDLY
AMAZEMENT
AMAZEMENTS
AMAZES
AMAZING
AMAZINGLY
AMAZON
AMAZONIAN
AMAZONITE
AMAZONITES
AMAZONS
AMBAGE
AMBAGES
AMBAGIOUS
AMBAN
AMBANS
AMBASSAGE
AMBASSAGES
AMBASSIES
AMBASSY
AMBATCH
AMBATCHES
AMBER
AMBERED
AMBERGRIS
AMBERGRISES
AMBERITE
AMBERITES
AMBERJACK
AMBERJACKS
AMBEROID
AMBEROIDS
AMBEROUS
AMBERS
AMBERY
AMBIANCE
AMBIANCES
AMBIENCE
AMBIENCES
AMBIENT
AMBIENTS
AMBIGUITIES
AMBIGUITY
AMBIGUOUS
AMBIT
AMBITION
AMBITIONS
AMBITIOUS
AMBITS
AMBITTY
AMBIVERT
AMBIVERTS
AMBLE
AMBLED
AMBLER
AMBLERS
AMBLES
AMBLING
AMBLINGS
AMBLYOPIA
AMBLYOPIAS
AMBO
AMBONES
AMBOS
AMBRIES
AMBROID
AMBROIDS
AMBROSIA
AMBROSIAL
AMBROSIAN
AMBROSIAS
AMBROTYPE
AMBROTYPES
AMBRY
AMBULACRA
AMBULANCE
AMBULANCES
AMBULANT
AMBULANTS
AMBULATE
AMBULATED
AMBULATES
AMBULATING
AMBULATOR
AMBULATORS
AMBUSCADE
AMBUSCADED
AMBUSCADES
AMBUSCADING
AMBUSCADO
AMBUSCADOES
AMBUSCADOS
AMBUSH
AMBUSHED
AMBUSHES
AMBUSHING
AMEARST
AMEBA
AMEBAE
AMEBAS
AMEBIC
AMEER
AMEERS
AMEIOSES
AMEIOSIS
AMELCORN
AMELCORNS
AMELIA
AMELIAS
AMEN
AMENABLE
AMENABLY
AMENAGE
AMENAGED
AMENAGES
AMENAGING
AMENAUNCE
AMENAUNCES
AMEND
AMENDABLE
AMENDE
AMENDED
AMENDER
AMENDERS
AMENDES
AMENDING
AMENDMENT
AMENDMENTS
AMENDS
AMENE
AMENED
AMENING
AMENITIES
AMENITY
AMENS
AMENT
AMENTA
AMENTAL
AMENTIA
AMENTIAS
AMENTS
AMENTUM
AMERCE
AMERCED
AMERCES
AMERCING
AMERICIUM
AMERICIUMS

AMETHYST
AMETHYSTS
AMI
AMIABLE
AMIABLY
AMIANTHUS
AMIANTHUSES
AMIANTUS
AMIANTUSES
AMICABLE
AMICABLY
AMICE
AMICES
AMID
AMIDE
AMIDES
AMIDMOST
AMIDSHIPS
AMIDST
AMIE
AMIES
AMIGO
AMIGOS
AMILDAR
AMILDARS
AMINE
AMINES
AMIR
AMIRS
AMIS
AMISES
AMISS
AMISSES
AMISSIBLE
AMISSING
AMITIES
AMITOSES
AMITOSIS
AMITOTIC
AMITY
AMLA
AMLAS
AMMAN
AMMANS
AMMETER
AMMETERS
AMMIRAL
AMMIRALS
AMMO
AMMON
AMMONAL
AMMONALS
AMMONIA
AMMONIAC
AMMONIAS
AMMONITE
AMMONITES
AMMONIUM
AMMONIUMS
AMMONOID
AMMONOIDS
AMMONS
AMMOS
AMNESIA
AMNESIAC
AMNESIACS
AMNESIAS
AMNESIC
AMNESICS
AMNESTIED
AMNESTIES
AMNESTY
AMNESTYING
AMNIA
AMNIO
AMNION
AMNIOS
AMNIOTIC
AMNIOTOMIES
AMNIOTOMY
AMOEBA
AMOEBAE
AMOEBAEAN
AMOEBAS
AMOEBIC
AMOEBOID
AMOK
AMOMUM
AMOMUMS
AMONG
AMONGST
AMOOVE
AMOOVED
AMOOVES
AMOOVING
AMORAL
AMORALISM
AMORALISMS
AMORALIST
AMORALISTS
AMORANCE
AMORANCES
AMORANT
AMORCE
AMORCES
AMORET
AMORETS
AMORETTI
AMORETTO
AMORINI
AMORINO
AMORISM
AMORISMS
AMORIST
AMORISTS
AMORNINGS
AMOROSA
AMOROSAS
AMOROSITIES
AMOROSITY
AMOROSO
AMOROSOS
AMOROUS
AMOROUSLY
AMORPHISM
AMORPHISMS
AMORPHOUS
AMORT
AMORTISE
AMORTISED
AMORTISES
AMORTISING
AMORTIZE
AMORTIZED
AMORTIZES
AMORTIZING
AMOSITE
AMOSITES
AMOUNT
AMOUNTED
AMOUNTING
AMOUNTS
AMOUR
AMOURETTE
AMOURETTES
AMOURS
AMOVE
AMOVED
AMOVES
AMOVING
AMP
AMPASSIES
AMPASSY
AMPERAGE
AMPERAGES
AMPERE
AMPERES
AMPERSAND
AMPERSANDS
AMPERZAND
AMPERZANDS
AMPHIBIAN
AMPHIBIANS
AMPHIBOLE
AMPHIBOLES
AMPHIBOLIES
AMPHIBOLY
AMPHIGORIES
AMPHIGORY
AMPHIOXUS
AMPHIOXUSES
AMPHIPOD
AMPHIPODS
AMPHOLYTE
AMPHOLYTES
AMPHORA
AMPHORAE
AMPHORIC
AMPLE
AMPLENESS
AMPLENESSES
AMPLER
AMPLEST
AMPLEXUS
AMPLIFIED
AMPLIFIER
AMPLIFIERS
AMPLIFIES
AMPLIFY
AMPLIFYING
AMPLITUDE
AMPLITUDES
AMPLOSOME
AMPLOSOMES
AMPLY
AMPOULE
AMPOULES
AMPS
AMPUL
AMPULE
AMPULES
AMPULLA
AMPULLAE
AMPULS
AMPUTATE
AMPUTATED
AMPUTATES
AMPUTATING
AMPUTATOR
AMPUTATORS
AMPUTEE
AMPUTEES
AMRIT
AMRITA
AMRITAS
AMRITS
AMTMAN
AMTMANS
AMTRACK
AMTRACKS
AMUCK
AMULET
AMULETIC
AMULETS
AMUSABLE
AMUSE
AMUSED
AMUSEDLY
AMUSEMENT
AMUSEMENTS
AMUSER
AMUSERS
AMUSES
AMUSETTE
AMUSETTES
AMUSING
AMUSINGLY
AMUSIVE
AMYGDAL
AMYGDALA
AMYGDALAS
AMYGDALE
AMYGDALES
AMYGDALIN
AMYGDALINS
AMYGDALS
AMYGDULE
AMYGDULES
AMYL
AMYLASE
AMYLASES
AMYLENE
AMYLENES
AMYLOID
AMYLOIDAL
AMYLOIDS
AMYLOPSIN
AMYLOPSINS
AMYLS
AMYLUM
AMYLUMS
AMYTAL
AMYTALS
AN
ANA
ANABAS
ANABASES
ANABASIS
ANABATIC
ANABIOSES
ANABIOSIS
ANABIOTIC
ANABLEPS
ANABLEPSES
ANABOLIC
ANABOLISM
ANABOLISMS
ANABOLITE
ANABOLITES
ANABRANCH
ANABRANCHES
ANACHARIS
ANACHARISES
ANACONDA
ANACONDAS
ANACRUSES
ANACRUSIS
ANADEM
ANADEMS
ANAEMIA
ANAEMIAS
ANAEMIC
ANAEROBE
ANAEROBES
ANAEROBIC
ANAGLYPH
ANAGLYPHS
ANAGOGE
ANAGOGES
ANAGOGIC
ANAGOGIES
ANAGOGY
ANAGRAM
ANAGRAMMED
ANAGRAMMING
ANAGRAMS
ANAL
ANALCIME
ANALCIMES
ANALCITE
ANALCITES
ANALECTA
ANALECTIC
ANALECTS
ANALEMMA
ANALEMMAS
ANALEMMATA
ANALEPTIC
ANALEPTICS
ANALGESIA

ANALGESIAS
ANALGESIC
ANALGESICS
ANALLY
ANALOG
ANALOGA
ANALOGIC
ANALOGIES
ANALOGISE
ANALOGISED
ANALOGISES
ANALOGISING
ANALOGIST
ANALOGISTS
ANALOGIZE
ANALOGIZED
ANALOGIZES
ANALOGIZING
ANALOGON
ANALOGONS
ANALOGOUS
ANALOGS
ANALOGUE
ANALOGUES
ANALOGY
ANALYSAND
ANALYSANDS
ANALYSE
ANALYSED
ANALYSER
ANALYSERS
ANALYSES
ANALYSING
ANALYSIS
ANALYST
ANALYSTS
ANALYTIC
ANALYTICS
ANALYZE
ANALYZED
ANALYZER
ANALYZERS
ANALYZES
ANALYZING
ANAMNESES
ANAMNESIS
ANAN
ANANA
ANANAS
ANANASES
ANANDROUS
ANANKE
ANANKES
ANANTHOUS
ANAPAEST
ANAPAESTS
ANAPEST
ANAPESTS
ANAPHASE
ANAPHASES
ANAPHORA
ANAPHORAS
ANAPHORIC
ANAPLASTIES
ANAPLASTY
ANAPTYXES
ANAPTYXIS
ANARCH
ANARCHAL
ANARCHIAL
ANARCHIC
ANARCHIES
ANARCHISE
ANARCHISED
ANARCHISES
ANARCHISING
ANARCHISM
ANARCHISMS
ANARCHIST
ANARCHISTS
ANARCHIZE
ANARCHIZED
ANARCHIZES
ANARCHIZING
ANARCHS
ANARCHY
ANAS
ANASARCA
ANASARCAS
ANASTASES
ANASTASIS
ANASTATIC
ANATASE
ANATASES
ANATHEMA
ANATHEMAS
ANATOMIC
ANATOMIES
ANATOMISE
ANATOMISED
ANATOMISES
ANATOMISING
ANATOMIST
ANATOMISTS
ANATOMIZE
ANATOMIZED
ANATOMIZES
ANATOMIZING
ANATOMY
ANATROPIES
ANATROPY
ANATTA
ANATTAS
ANATTO
ANATTOS
ANAXIAL
ANBURIES
ANBURY
ANCE
ANCESTOR
ANCESTORS
ANCESTRAL
ANCESTRIES
ANCESTRY
ANCHOR
ANCHORAGE
ANCHORAGES
ANCHORED
ANCHORESS
ANCHORESSES
ANCHORET
ANCHORETS
ANCHORING
ANCHORITE
ANCHORITES
ANCHORS
ANCHOVETA
ANCHOVETAS
ANCHOVIES
ANCHOVY
ANCHYLOSE
ANCHYLOSED
ANCHYLOSES
ANCHYLOSING
ANCIENT
ANCIENTLY
ANCIENTRIES
ANCIENTRY
ANCIENTS
ANCILE
ANCILIA
ANCILLARIES
ANCILLARY
ANCIPITAL
ANCLE
ANCLES
ANCOME
ANCOMES
ANCON
ANCONES
ANCORA
ANCRESS
ANCRESSES
AND
ANDANTE
ANDANTES
ANDANTINO
ANDANTINOS
ANDESINE
ANDESINES
ANDESITE
ANDESITES
ANDESITIC
ANDIRON
ANDIRONS
ANDROECIA
ANDROGEN
ANDROGENS
ANDROGYNE
ANDROGYNES
ANDROGYNIES
ANDROGYNY
ANDROID
ANDROIDS
ANDROLOGIES
ANDROLOGY
ANDROMEDA
ANDROMEDAS
ANDS
ANDVILE
ANDVILES
ANE
ANEAR
ANEARED
ANEARING
ANEARS
ANEATH
ANECDOTAL
ANECDOTE
ANECDOTES
ANECHOIC
ANELACE
ANELACES
ANELE
ANELED
ANELES
ANELING
ANEMIA
ANEMIAS
ANEMIC
ANEMOGRAM
ANEMOGRAMS
ANEMOLOGIES
ANEMOLOGY
ANEMONE
ANEMONES
ANENT
ANERLY
ANEROID
ANEROIDS
ANES
ANESTRA
ANESTRI
ANESTRUM
ANESTRUS
ANETIC
ANEUPLOID
ANEUPLOIDS
ANEURIN
ANEURINS
ANEURISM
ANEURISMS
ANEURYSM
ANEURYSMS
ANEW
ANGARIES
ANGARY
ANGEKKOK
ANGEKKOKS
ANGEKOK
ANGEKOKS
ANGEL
ANGELHOOD
ANGELHOODS
ANGELIC
ANGELICA
ANGELICAL
ANGELICAS
ANGELS
ANGELUS
ANGELUSES
ANGER
ANGERED
ANGERING
ANGERLESS
ANGERLY
ANGERS
ANGICO
ANGICOS
ANGINA
ANGINAL
ANGINAS
ANGIOGRAM
ANGIOGRAMS
ANGIOMA
ANGIOMAS
ANGIOMATA
ANGKLUNG
ANGKLUNGS
ANGLE
ANGLED
ANGLER
ANGLERS
ANGLES
ANGLESITE
ANGLESITES
ANGLEWISE
ANGLEWORM
ANGLEWORMS
ANGLICE
ANGLICISE
ANGLICISED
ANGLICISES
ANGLICISING
ANGLICISM
ANGLICISMS
ANGLICIST
ANGLICISTS
ANGLICIZE
ANGLICIZED
ANGLICIZES
ANGLICIZING
ANGLIFIED
ANGLIFIES
ANGLIFY
ANGLIFYING
ANGLING
ANGLINGS
ANGLIST
ANGLISTS
ANGLOPHIL
ANGLOPHILS
ANGOLA
ANGOPHORA
ANGOPHORAS
ANGORA
ANGORAS
ANGRIER
ANGRIES
ANGRIEST
ANGRILY
ANGRINESS
ANGRINESSES
ANGRY
ANGST
ANGSTROM
ANGSTROMS
ANGSTS
ANGUIFORM
ANGUINE

ANGUIPED
ANGUIPEDE
ANGUISH
ANGUISHED
ANGUISHES
ANGUISHING
ANGULAR
ANGULATE
ANGULATED
ANHEDONIA
ANHEDONIAS
ANHEDONIC
ANHEDRAL
ANHUNGRED
ANHYDRIDE
ANHYDRIDES
ANHYDRITE
ANHYDRITES
ANHYDROUS
ANI
ANICONIC
ANICONISM
ANICONISMS
ANICONIST
ANICONISTS
ANICUT
ANICUTS
ANIGH
ANIGHT
ANIL
ANILE
ANILINE
ANILINES
ANILITIES
ANILITY
ANILS
ANIMA
ANIMAL
ANIMALIC
ANIMALISE
ANIMALISED
ANIMALISES
ANIMALISING
ANIMALISM
ANIMALISMS
ANIMALIST
ANIMALISTS
ANIMALITIES
ANIMALITY
ANIMALIZE
ANIMALIZED
ANIMALIZES
ANIMALIZING
ANIMALLY
ANIMALS
ANIMAS
ANIMATE
ANIMATED
ANIMATER
ANIMATERS
ANIMATES
ANIMATIC
ANIMATICS
ANIMATING
ANIMATION
ANIMATIONS
ANIMATISM
ANIMATISMS
ANIMATOR
ANIMATORS
ANIME
ANIMES
ANIMISM
ANIMISMS
ANIMIST
ANIMISTIC
ANIMISTS
ANIMOSITIES
ANIMOSITY
ANIMUS
ANIMUSES
ANION
ANIONIC
ANIONS
ANIS
ANISE
ANISEED
ANISEEDS
ANISES
ANISETTE
ANISETTES
ANKER
ANKERITE
ANKERITES
ANKERS
ANKH
ANKHS
ANKLE
ANKLED
ANKLES
ANKLET
ANKLETS
ANKLONG
ANKLONGS
ANKLUNG
ANKLUNGS
ANKUS
ANKUSES
ANKYLOSE
ANKYLOSED
ANKYLOSES
ANKYLOSING
ANKYLOSIS
ANLACE
ANLACES
ANLAGE
ANLAGEN
ANLAGES
ANN
ANNA
ANNAL
ANNALISE
ANNALISED
ANNALISES
ANNALISING
ANNALIST
ANNALISTS
ANNALIZE
ANNALIZED
ANNALIZES
ANNALIZING
ANNALS
ANNAS
ANNAT
ANNATES
ANNATS
ANNATTA
ANNATTAS
ANNATTO
ANNATTOS
ANNEAL
ANNEALED
ANNEALER
ANNEALERS
ANNEALING
ANNEALINGS
ANNEALS
ANNECTENT
ANNELID
ANNELIDS
ANNEX
ANNEXE
ANNEXED
ANNEXES
ANNEXING
ANNEXION
ANNEXIONS
ANNEXMENT
ANNEXMENTS
ANNEXURE
ANNEXURES
ANNICUT
ANNICUTS
ANNO
ANNOTATE
ANNOTATED
ANNOTATES
ANNOTATING
ANNOTATOR
ANNOTATORS
ANNOUNCE
ANNOUNCED
ANNOUNCER
ANNOUNCERS
ANNOUNCES
ANNOUNCING
ANNOY
ANNOYANCE
ANNOYANCES
ANNOYED
ANNOYER
ANNOYERS
ANNOYING
ANNOYS
ANNS
ANNUAL
ANNUALISE
ANNUALISED
ANNUALISES
ANNUALISING
ANNUALIZE
ANNUALIZED
ANNUALIZES
ANNUALIZING
ANNUALLY
ANNUALS
ANNUITANT
ANNUITANTS
ANNUITIES
ANNUITY
ANNUL
ANNULAR
ANNULARS
ANNULATE
ANNULATED
ANNULATES
ANNULET
ANNULETS
ANNULI
ANNULLED
ANNULLING
ANNULMENT
ANNULMENTS
ANNULOSE
ANNULS
ANNULUS
ANOA
ANOAS
ANODAL
ANODE
ANODES
ANODIC
ANODISE
ANODISED
ANODISES
ANODISING
ANODIZE
ANODIZED
ANODIZES
ANODIZING
ANODYNE
ANODYNES
ANOESES
ANOESIS
ANOESTRA
ANOESTRI
ANOESTRUM
ANOESTRUS
ANOETIC
ANOINT
ANOINTED
ANOINTER
ANOINTERS
ANOINTING
ANOINTS
ANOMALIES
ANOMALOUS
ANOMALY
ANOMIC
ANOMIE
ANOMIES
ANOMY
ANON
ANONYM
ANONYMA
ANONYMAS
ANONYMISE
ANONYMISED
ANONYMISES
ANONYMISING
ANONYMITIES
ANONYMITY
ANONYMIZE
ANONYMIZED
ANONYMIZES
ANONYMIZING
ANONYMOUS
ANONYMS
ANOPHELES
ANORAK
ANORAKS
ANORECTAL
ANORECTIC
ANORECTICS
ANORETIC
ANORETICS
ANOREXIA
ANOREXIAS
ANOREXIC
ANOREXICS
ANOREXIES
ANOREXY
ANORTHIC
ANORTHITE
ANORTHITES
ANOSMIA
ANOSMIAS
ANOTHER
ANOUGH
ANOUROUS
ANOVULANT
ANOVULANTS
ANOW
ANOXIA
ANOXIAS
ANOXIC
ANSATE
ANSATED
ANSERINE
ANSWER
ANSWERED
ANSWERER
ANSWERERS
ANSWERING
ANSWERS
ANT
ANTA
ANTACID
ANTACIDS
ANTAE
ANTAR
ANTARA
ANTARAS
ANTARS
ANTAS
ANTBEAR
ANTBEARS
ANTBIRD
ANTBIRDS
ANTE

ANTEATER
ANTEATERS
ANTECEDE
ANTECEDED
ANTECEDES
ANTECEDING
ANTECHOIR
ANTECHOIRS
ANTED
ANTEDATE
ANTEDATED
ANTEDATES
ANTEDATING
ANTEFIX
ANTEFIXA
ANTEFIXAL
ANTEFIXES
ANTEING
ANTELOPE
ANTELOPES
ANTELUCAN
ANTENATAL
ANTENATI
ANTENNA
ANTENNAE
ANTENNAL
ANTENNARY
ANTENNAS
ANTENNULE
ANTENNULES
ANTEPAST
ANTEPASTS
ANTERIOR
ANTEROOM
ANTEROOMS
ANTES
ANTEVERT
ANTEVERTED
ANTEVERTING
ANTEVERTS
ANTHELIA
ANTHELICES
ANTHELION
ANTHELIX
ANTHEM
ANTHEMED
ANTHEMIA
ANTHEMIC
ANTHEMING
ANTHEMION
ANTHEMS
ANTHER
ANTHERS
ANTHESES
ANTHESIS
ANTHOCARP
ANTHOCARPS
ANTHOCYAN
ANTHOCYANS
ANTHOID
ANTHOLOGIES
ANTHOLOGY
ANTHRACIC
ANTHRAX
ANTHRAXES
ANTHROPIC
ANTHURIUM
ANTHURIUMS
ANTI
ANTIAR
ANTIARS
ANTIBODIES
ANTIBODY
ANTIC
ANTICHLOR
ANTICHLORS
ANTICIVIC
ANTICIZE
ANTICIZED
ANTICIZES
ANTICIZING
ANTICK
ANTICKE
ANTICKED
ANTICKING
ANTICLINE
ANTICLINES
ANTICOUS
ANTICS
ANTIDOTAL
ANTIDOTE
ANTIDOTES
ANTIENT
ANTIENTS
ANTIGAY
ANTIGEN
ANTIGENIC
ANTIGENS
ANTIHELICES
ANTIHELIX
ANTIKNOCK
ANTIKNOCKS
ANTILOG
ANTILOGIES
ANTILOGS
ANTILOGY
ANTIMASK
ANTIMASKS
ANTIMONIC
ANTIMONIES
ANTIMONY
ANTING
ANTINGS
ANTINODAL
ANTINODE
ANTINODES
ANTINOISE
ANTINOMIC
ANTINOMIES
ANTINOMY
ANTIPAPAL
ANTIPASTO
ANTIPASTOS
ANTIPATHIES
ANTIPATHY
ANTIPHON
ANTIPHONIES
ANTIPHONS
ANTIPHONY
ANTIPODAL
ANTIPODE
ANTIPODES
ANTIPOLE
ANTIPOLES
ANTIPOPE
ANTIPOPES
ANTIQUARIES
ANTIQUARK
ANTIQUARKS
ANTIQUARY
ANTIQUATE
ANTIQUATED
ANTIQUATES
ANTIQUATING
ANTIQUE
ANTIQUED
ANTIQUELY
ANTIQUES
ANTIQUING
ANTIQUITIES
ANTIQUITY
ANTIRIOT
ANTIRUST
ANTIS
ANTISCIAN
ANTISCIANS
ANTISERA
ANTISERUM
ANTISERUMS
ANTISHIP
ANTISKID
ANTISPAST
ANTISPASTS
ANTISTAT
ANTISTATS
ANTITANK
ANTITHEFT
ANTITHET
ANTITHETS
ANTITOXIC
ANTITOXIN
ANTITOXINS
ANTITRADE
ANTITRADES
ANTITRAGI
ANTITRUST
ANTITYPAL
ANTITYPE
ANTITYPES
ANTITYPIC
ANTIVENIN
ANTIVENINS
ANTIVIRAL
ANTIVIRUS
ANTIWAR
ANTLER
ANTLERED
ANTLERS
ANTLIA
ANTLIAE
ANTLIATE
ANTLION
ANTLIONS
ANTONYM
ANTONYMIC
ANTONYMIES
ANTONYMS
ANTONYMY
ANTRA
ANTRE
ANTRES
ANTRORSE
ANTRUM
ANTS
ANTSIER
ANTSIEST
ANTSY
ANUCLEATE
ANURIA
ANURIAS
ANUROUS
ANUS
ANUSES
ANVIL
ANVILS
ANXIETIES
ANXIETY
ANXIOUS
ANXIOUSLY
ANY
ANYBODIES
ANYBODY
ANYHOW
ANYONE
ANYONES
ANYROAD
ANYTHING
ANYTHINGS
ANYTIME
ANYWAY
ANYWAYS
ANYWHEN
ANYWHERE
ANYWISE
ANZIANI
AORIST
AORISTIC
AORISTS
AORTA
AORTAE
AORTAL
AORTAS
AORTIC
AORTITIS
AORTITISES
AOUDAD
AOUDADS
APACE
APACHE
APACHES
APADANA
APADANAS
APAGE
APAGOGE
APAGOGES
APAGOGIC
APAID
APANAGE
APANAGED
APANAGES
APART
APARTHEID
APARTHEIDS
APARTMENT
APARTMENTS
APARTNESS
APARTNESSES
APATETIC
APATHATON
APATHATONS
APATHETIC
APATHIES
APATHY
APATITE
APATITES
APAY
APAYD
APAYING
APAYS
APE
APEAK
APED
APEDOM
APEDOMS
APEEK
APEHOOD
APEHOODS
APEMAN
APEMEN
APEPSIA
APEPSIAS
APEPSIES
APEPSY
APERCU
APERCUS
APERIENT
APERIENTS
APERIES
APERIODIC
APERITIF
APERITIFS
APERITIVE
APERITIVES
APERT
APERTNESS
APERTNESSES
APERTURE
APERTURES
APERY
APES
APETALIES
APETALOUS
APETALY
APEX
APEXES
APHAGIA
APHAGIAS
APHANITE
APHANITES
APHASIA

APHASIAC
APHASIACS
APHASIAS
APHASIC
APHELIA
APHELIAN
APHELION
APHERESES
APHERESIS
APHESES
APHESIS
APHETIC
APHETISE
APHETISED
APHETISES
APHETISING
APHETIZE
APHETIZED
APHETIZES
APHETIZING
APHICIDE
APHICIDES
APHID
APHIDES
APHIDIAN
APHIDIANS
APHIDIOUS
APHIDS
APHIS
APHONIA
APHONIAS
APHONIC
APHONIES
APHONOUS
APHONY
APHORISE
APHORISED
APHORISER
APHORISERS
APHORISES
APHORISING
APHORISM
APHORISMS
APHORIST
APHORISTS
APHORIZE
APHORIZED
APHORIZER
APHORIZERS
APHORIZES
APHORIZING
APHOTIC
APHTHA
APHTHAE
APHTHOUS
APHYLLIES
APHYLLOUS
APHYLLY
APIAN
APIARIAN
APIARIES
APIARIST
APIARISTS
APIARY
APICAL
APICALLY
APICES
APICIAN
APICULATE
APIECE
APING
APIOL
APIOLS
APISH
APISHLY
APISHNESS
APISHNESSES
APISM
APISMS
APIVOROUS
APLANAT
APLANATIC
APLANATS
APLASIA
APLASIAS
APLASTIC
APLENTY
APLITE
APLITES
APLOMB
APLOMBS
APLUSTRE
APLUSTRES
APNEA
APNEAS
APNOEA
APNOEAS
APOCOPATE
APOCOPATED
APOCOPATES
APOCOPATING
APOCOPE
APOCOPES
APOCRINE
APOCRYPHA
APOD
APODAL
APODE
APODES
APODICTIC
APODOSES
APODOSIS
APODOUS
APODS
APOENZYME
APOENZYMES
APOGAEIC
APOGAMIC
APOGAMIES
APOGAMOUS
APOGAMY
APOGEAL
APOGEAN
APOGEE
APOGEES
APOGRAPH
APOGRAPHS
APOLLO
APOLLOS
APOLOGIA
APOLOGIAS
APOLOGIES
APOLOGISE
APOLOGISED
APOLOGISES
APOLOGISING
APOLOGIST
APOLOGISTS
APOLOGIZE
APOLOGIZED
APOLOGIZES
APOLOGIZING
APOLOGUE
APOLOGUES
APOLOGY
APOMICTIC
APOMIXES
APOMIXIS
APOOP
APOPHASES
APOPHASIS
APOPHATIC
APOPHYGE
APOPHYGES
APOPHYSES
APOPHYSIS
APOPLEX
APOPLEXED
APOPLEXES
APOPLEXIES
APOPLEXING
APOPLEXY
APOPTOSES
APOPTOSIS
APOPTOTIC
APORIA
APORIAS
APORT
APOSITIA
APOSITIAS
APOSITIC
APOSPORIES
APOSPORY
APOSTASIES
APOSTASY
APOSTATE
APOSTATES
APOSTATIC
APOSTIL
APOSTILLE
APOSTILLES
APOSTILS
APOSTLE
APOSTLES
APOSTOLIC
APOTHECIA
APOTHEGM
APOTHEGMS
APOTHEM
APOTHEMS
APOZEM
APOZEMS
APPAID
APPAIR
APPAIRED
APPAIRING
APPAIRS
APPAL
APPALLED
APPALLING
APPALS
APPALTI
APPALTO
APPANAGE
APPANAGED
APPANAGES
APPARAT
APPARATS
APPARATUS
APPARATUSES
APPAREL
APPARELLED
APPARELLING
APPARELS
APPARENCIES
APPARENCY
APPARENT
APPARENTS
APPARITOR
APPARITORS
APPAY
APPAYD
APPAYING
APPAYS
APPEACH
APPEACHED
APPEACHES
APPEACHING
APPEAL
APPEALED
APPEALING
APPEALS
APPEAR
APPEARED
APPEARER
APPEARERS
APPEARING
APPEARS
APPEASE
APPEASED
APPEASER
APPEASERS
APPEASES
APPEASING
APPEL
APPELLANT
APPELLANTS
APPELLATE
APPELS
APPEND
APPENDAGE
APPENDAGES
APPENDANT
APPENDANTS
APPENDED
APPENDICES
APPENDING
APPENDIX
APPENDIXES
APPENDS
APPERIL
APPERILL
APPERILLS
APPERILS
APPERTAIN
APPERTAINED
APPERTAINING
APPERTAINS
APPESTAT
APPESTATS
APPETENCE
APPETENCES
APPETENCIES
APPETENCY
APPETENT
APPETIBLE
APPETISE
APPETISED
APPETISER
APPETISERS
APPETISES
APPETISING
APPETITE
APPETITES
APPETIZE
APPETIZED
APPETIZER
APPETIZERS
APPETIZES
APPETIZING
APPLAUD
APPLAUDED
APPLAUDER
APPLAUDERS
APPLAUDING
APPLAUDS
APPLAUSE
APPLAUSES
APPLE
APPLES
APPLET
APPLETS
APPLIABLE
APPLIANCE
APPLIANCES
APPLICANT
APPLICANTS
APPLICATE
APPLIED
APPLIER
APPLIERS
APPLIES
APPLIQUE
APPLIQUES
APPLY
APPLYING
APPOINT
APPOINTED
APPOINTEE
APPOINTEES

APPOINTING
APPOINTOR
APPOINTORS
APPOINTS
APPORT
APPORTION
APPORTIONED
APPORTIONING
APPORTIONS
APPORTS
APPOSE
APPOSED
APPOSER
APPOSERS
APPOSES
APPOSING
APPOSITE
APPRAISAL
APPRAISALS
APPRAISE
APPRAISED
APPRAISEE
APPRAISEES
APPRAISER
APPRAISERS
APPRAISES
APPRAISING
APPREHEND
APPREHENDED
APPREHENDING
APPREHENDS
APPRESS
APPRESSED
APPRESSES
APPRESSING
APPRISE
APPRISED
APPRISER
APPRISERS
APPRISES
APPRISING
APPRISINGS
APPRIZE
APPRIZED
APPRIZER
APPRIZERS
APPRIZES
APPRIZING
APPRIZINGS
APPROACH
APPROACHED
APPROACHES
APPROACHING
APPROBATE
APPROBATED
APPROBATES
APPROBATING
APPROOF
APPROOFS
APPROVAL
APPROVALS
APPROVE
APPROVED
APPROVER
APPROVERS
APPROVES
APPROVING
APPUI
APPUIED
APPUIS
APPULSE
APPULSES
APPUY
APPUYED
APPUYING
APPUYS
APRAXIA
APRAXIAS
APRES
APRICATE
APRICATED
APRICATES
APRICATING
APRICOCK
APRICOCKS
APRICOT
APRICOTS
APRIORISM
APRIORISMS
APRIORIST
APRIORISTS
APRIORITIES
APRIORITY
APRON
APRONED
APRONFUL
APRONFULS
APRONING
APRONS
APROPOS
APSARAS
APSARASES
APSE
APSES
APSIDAL
APSIDES
APSIDIOLE
APSIDIOLES
APSIS
APT
APTED
APTER
APTERAL
APTERIA
APTERISM
APTERISMS
APTERIUM
APTEROUS
APTERYX
APTERYXES
APTEST
APTING
APTITUDE
APTITUDES
APTLY
APTNESS
APTNESSES
APTOTE
APTOTES
APTOTIC
APTS
APYRETIC
APYREXIA
APYREXIAS
AQUA
AQUABATIC
AQUABATICS
AQUABOARD
AQUABOARDS
AQUACADE
AQUACADES
AQUADROME
AQUADROMES
AQUAE
AQUAFER
AQUAFERS
AQUALUNG
AQUALUNGS
AQUANAUT
AQUANAUTS
AQUAPHOBE
AQUAPHOBES
AQUAPLANE
AQUAPLANED
AQUAPLANES
AQUAPLANING
AQUAPLANINGS
AQUARELLE
AQUARELLES
AQUARIA
AQUARIAN
AQUARIANS
AQUARIIST
AQUARIISTS
AQUARIST
AQUARISTS
AQUARIUM
AQUARIUMS
AQUAROBIC
AQUAROBICS
AQUAS
AQUATIC
AQUATICS
AQUATINT
AQUATINTA
AQUATINTAS
AQUATINTED
AQUATINTING
AQUATINTS
AQUAVIT
AQUAVITS
AQUEDUCT
AQUEDUCTS
AQUEOUS
AQUIFER
AQUIFERS
AQUILEGIA
AQUILEGIAS
AQUILINE
AQUILON
AQUILONS
AQUIVER
AR
ARABA
ARABAS
ARABESQUE
ARABESQUES
ARABICA
ARABICAS
ARABIN
ARABINOSE
ARABINOSES
ARABINS
ARABIS
ARABISE
ARABISED
ARABISES
ARABISING
ARABIZE
ARABIZED
ARABIZES
ARABIZING
ARABLE
ARACEOUS
ARACHIS
ARACHISES
ARACHNID
ARACHNIDS
ARACHNOID
ARACHNOIDS
ARAGONITE
ARAGONITES
ARAISE
ARAISED
ARAISES
ARAISING
ARAK
ARAKS
ARALIA
ARALIAS
ARAME
ARAMES
ARANEID
ARANEIDS
ARANEOUS
ARAPAIMA
ARAPAIMAS
ARAPONGA
ARAPONGAS
ARAPUNGA
ARAPUNGAS
ARAR
ARAROBA
ARAROBAS
ARARS
ARAUCARIA
ARAUCARIAS
ARAYSE
ARAYSED
ARAYSES
ARAYSING
ARB
ARBA
ARBALEST
ARBALESTS
ARBALIST
ARBALISTS
ARBAS
ARBITER
ARBITERS
ARBITRAGE
ARBITRAGED
ARBITRAGES
ARBITRAGING
ARBITRAL
ARBITRARY
ARBITRATE
ARBITRATED
ARBITRATES
ARBITRATING
ARBITRESS
ARBITRESSES
ARBITRIUM
ARBITRIUMS
ARBLAST
ARBLASTER
ARBLASTERS
ARBLASTS
ARBOR
ARBOREAL
ARBOREOUS
ARBORES
ARBORET
ARBORETA
ARBORETS
ARBORETUM
ARBORIST
ARBORISTS
ARBOROUS
ARBORS
ARBOUR
ARBOURED
ARBOURS
ARBOVIRUS
ARBOVIRUSES
ARBS
ARBUTE
ARBUTES
ARBUTUS
ARBUTUSES
ARC
ARCADE
ARCADED
ARCADES
ARCADING
ARCADINGS
ARCANA
ARCANE
ARCANELY
ARCANIST
ARCANISTS
ARCANUM
ARCCOS
ARCCOSES
ARCED
ARCH
ARCHAEI
ARCHAEUS
ARCHAIC
ARCHAISE

ARCHAISED
ARCHAISER
ARCHAISERS
ARCHAISES
ARCHAISING
ARCHAISM
ARCHAISMS
ARCHAIST
ARCHAISTS
ARCHAIZE
ARCHAIZED
ARCHAIZER
ARCHAIZERS
ARCHAIZES
ARCHAIZING
ARCHANGEL
ARCHANGELS
ARCHDUCAL
ARCHDUCHIES
ARCHDUCHY
ARCHDUKE
ARCHDUKES
ARCHED
ARCHEI
ARCHER
ARCHERESS
ARCHERESSES
ARCHERIES
ARCHERS
ARCHERY
ARCHES
ARCHEST
ARCHETYPE
ARCHETYPES
ARCHEUS
ARCHIL
ARCHILOWE
ARCHILOWES
ARCHILS
ARCHIMAGE
ARCHIMAGES
ARCHING
ARCHITECT
ARCHITECTED
ARCHITECTING
ARCHITECTS
ARCHITYPE
ARCHITYPES
ARCHIVAL
ARCHIVE
ARCHIVED
ARCHIVES
ARCHIVING
ARCHIVIST
ARCHIVISTS
ARCHIVOLT
ARCHIVOLTS
ARCHLET
ARCHLETS
ARCHLUTE
ARCHLUTES
ARCHLY
ARCHNESS
ARCHNESSES
ARCHOLOGIES
ARCHOLOGY
ARCHON
ARCHONS
ARCHONTIC
ARCHWAY
ARCHWAYS
ARCHWISE
ARCING
ARCINGS
ARCKED
ARCKING
ARCKINGS
ARCO
ARCOLOGIES
ARCOLOGY
ARCS
ARCSECOND
ARCSECONDS
ARCSIN
ARCSINS
ARCTAN
ARCTANS
ARCTIC
ARCTICS
ARCTIID
ARCTIIDS
ARCTOID
ARCTOPHIL
ARCTOPHILS
ARCUATE
ARCUATED
ARCUATION
ARCUATIONS
ARCUS
ARCUSES
ARD
ARDEB
ARDEBS
ARDENCIES
ARDENCY
ARDENT
ARDENTLY
ARDOR
ARDORS
ARDOUR
ARDOURS
ARDRI
ARDRIGH
ARDRIGHS
ARDRIS
ARDS
ARDUOUS
ARDUOUSLY
ARE
AREA
AREACH
AREACHED
AREACHES
AREACHING
AREAD
AREADING
AREADS
AREAL
AREAR
AREAS
AREAWAY
AREAWAYS
ARECA
ARECAS
ARED
AREDD
AREDE
AREDES
AREDING
AREFIED
AREFIES
AREFY
AREFYING
AREG
ARENA
ARENAS
ARENATION
ARENATIONS
AREOLA
AREOLAE
AREOLAR
AREOLATE
AREOLATED
AREOLE
AREOLES
AREOMETER
AREOMETERS
AREOSTYLE
AREOSTYLES
ARERE
ARES
ARET
ARETE
ARETES
ARETS
ARETT
ARETTED
ARETTING
ARETTS
AREW
ARGAL
ARGALA
ARGALAS
ARGALI
ARGALIS
ARGAN
ARGAND
ARGANDS
ARGANS
ARGEMONE
ARGEMONES
ARGENT
ARGENTINE
ARGENTINES
ARGENTITE
ARGENTITES
ARGENTS
ARGHAN
ARGHANS
ARGIL
ARGILLITE
ARGILLITES
ARGILS
ARGININE
ARGININES
ARGOL
ARGOLS
ARGON
ARGONAUT
ARGONAUTS
ARGONS
ARGOSIES
ARGOSY
ARGOT
ARGOTS
ARGUABLE
ARGUABLY
ARGUE
ARGUED
ARGUER
ARGUERS
ARGUES
ARGUFIED
ARGUFIER
ARGUFIERS
ARGUFIES
ARGUFY
ARGUFYING
ARGUING
ARGULI
ARGULUS
ARGUMENT
ARGUMENTA
ARGUMENTS
ARGUS
ARGUSES
ARGUTE
ARGUTELY
ARGYLE
ARGYLES
ARGYRIA
ARGYRIAS
ARGYRITE
ARGYRITES
ARHYTHMIA
ARHYTHMIAS
ARHYTHMIC
ARIA
ARIAS
ARID
ARIDER
ARIDEST
ARIDITIES
ARIDITY
ARIDLY
ARIDNESS
ARIDNESSES
ARIEL
ARIELS
ARIETTA
ARIETTAS
ARIETTE
ARIETTES
ARIGHT
ARIL
ARILLARY
ARILLATE
ARILLATED
ARILLI
ARILLODE
ARILLODES
ARILLOID
ARILLUS
ARILS
ARIOSI
ARIOSO
ARIOSOS
ARIOT
ARIPPLE
ARIS
ARISE
ARISEN
ARISES
ARISH
ARISHES
ARISING
ARISTA
ARISTAE
ARISTAS
ARISTATE
ARISTO
ARISTOS
ARK
ARKED
ARKING
ARKITE
ARKITES
ARKOSE
ARKOSES
ARKS
ARLE
ARLED
ARLES
ARLING
ARM
ARMADA
ARMADAS
ARMADILLO
ARMADILLOS
ARMAMENT
ARMAMENTS
ARMATURE
ARMATURES
ARMBAND
ARMBANDS
ARMCHAIR
ARMCHAIRS
ARMED
ARMET
ARMETS
ARMFUL
ARMFULS
ARMGAUNT
ARMHOLE
ARMHOLES
ARMIES
ARMIGER
ARMIGERAL
ARMIGERO
ARMIGEROS

ARMIGERS
ARMIL
ARMILLA
ARMILLAE
ARMILLARY
ARMILLAS
ARMILS
ARMING
ARMISTICE
ARMISTICES
ARMLESS
ARMLET
ARMLETS
ARMLOCK
ARMLOCKED
ARMLOCKING
ARMLOCKS
ARMOIRE
ARMOIRES
ARMOR
ARMORIAL
ARMORIALS
ARMORIES
ARMORIST
ARMORISTS
ARMORS
ARMORY
ARMOUR
ARMOURED
ARMOURER
ARMOURERS
ARMOURIES
ARMOURS
ARMOURY
ARMOZEEN
ARMOZEENS
ARMOZINE
ARMOZINES
ARMPIT
ARMPITS
ARMS
ARMURE
ARMURES
ARMY
ARNA
ARNAS
ARNICA
ARNICAS
ARNOTTO
ARNOTTOS
ARNUT
ARNUTS
AROBA
AROBAS
AROID
AROIDS
AROINT
AROINTED
AROINTING
AROINTS
AROLLA
AROLLAS
AROMA
AROMAS
AROMATIC
AROMATICS
AROMATISE
AROMATISED
AROMATISES
AROMATISING
AROMATIZE
AROMATIZED
AROMATIZES
AROMATIZING
AROSE
AROUND
AROUSAL
AROUSALS
AROUSE
AROUSED
AROUSER
AROUSERS
AROUSES
AROUSING
AROW
AROYNT
AROYNTED
AROYNTING
AROYNTS
ARPEGGIO
ARPEGGIOS
ARPENT
ARPENTS
ARPILLERA
ARPILLERAS
ARQUEBUS
ARQUEBUSES
ARRACACHA
ARRACACHAS
ARRACK
ARRACKS
ARRAH
ARRAIGN
ARRAIGNED
ARRAIGNER
ARRAIGNERS
ARRAIGNING
ARRAIGNINGS
ARRAIGNS
ARRANGE
ARRANGED
ARRANGER
ARRANGERS
ARRANGES
ARRANGING
ARRANT
ARRANTLY
ARRAS
ARRASED
ARRASENE
ARRASENES
ARRASES
ARRAUGHT
ARRAY
ARRAYAL
ARRAYALS
ARRAYED
ARRAYER
ARRAYERS
ARRAYING
ARRAYMENT
ARRAYMENTS
ARRAYS
ARREAR
ARREARAGE
ARREARAGES
ARREARS
ARRECT
ARREEDE
ARREEDES
ARREEDING
ARREST
ARRESTED
ARRESTEE
ARRESTEES
ARRESTER
ARRESTERS
ARRESTING
ARRESTIVE
ARRESTOR
ARRESTORS
ARRESTS
ARRET
ARRETS
ARRIAGE
ARRIAGES
ARRIDE
ARRIDED
ARRIDES
ARRIDING
ARRIERE
ARRIERO
ARRIEROS
ARRIS
ARRISES
ARRISH
ARRISHES
ARRIVAL
ARRIVALS
ARRIVANCE
ARRIVANCES
ARRIVANCIES
ARRIVANCY
ARRIVE
ARRIVED
ARRIVES
ARRIVING
ARRIVISME
ARRIVISMES
ARRIVISTE
ARRIVISTES
ARROBA
ARROBAS
ARROGANCE
ARROGANCES
ARROGANT
ARROGATE
ARROGATED
ARROGATES
ARROGATING
ARROW
ARROWED
ARROWING
ARROWROOT
ARROWROOTS
ARROWS
ARROWWOOD
ARROWWOODS
ARROWY
ARROYO
ARROYOS
ARS
ARSE
ARSEHOLE
ARSEHOLES
ARSENAL
ARSENALS
ARSENATE
ARSENATES
ARSENIATE
ARSENIATES
ARSENIC
ARSENICAL
ARSENICS
ARSENIDE
ARSENIDES
ARSENIOUS
ARSENITE
ARSENITES
ARSES
ARSHEEN
ARSHEENS
ARSHIN
ARSHINE
ARSHINES
ARSHINS
ARSINE
ARSINES
ARSIS
ARSON
ARSONIST
ARSONISTS
ARSONITE
ARSONITES
ARSONS
ART
ARTAL
ARTEFACT
ARTEFACTS
ARTEL
ARTELS
ARTEMISIA
ARTEMISIAS
ARTERIAL
ARTERIES
ARTERIOLE
ARTERIOLES
ARTERITIS
ARTERITISES
ARTERY
ARTESIAN
ARTFUL
ARTFULLY
ARTHRITIC
ARTHRITICS
ARTHRITIS
ARTHRITISES
ARTHROPOD
ARTHROPODS
ARTHROSES
ARTHROSIS
ARTIC
ARTICHOKE
ARTICHOKES
ARTICLE
ARTICLED
ARTICLES
ARTICLING
ARTICS
ARTICULAR
ARTIER
ARTIES
ARTIEST
ARTIFACT
ARTIFACTS
ARTIFICE
ARTIFICER
ARTIFICERS
ARTIFICES
ARTILLERIES
ARTILLERY
ARTINESS
ARTINESSES
ARTISAN
ARTISANAL
ARTISANS
ARTIST
ARTISTE
ARTISTES
ARTISTIC
ARTISTRIES
ARTISTRY
ARTISTS
ARTLESS
ARTLESSLY
ARTS
ARTSIER
ARTSIES
ARTSIEST
ARTSMAN
ARTSMEN
ARTSY
ARTWORK
ARTWORKS
ARTY
ARUGULA
ARUGULAS
ARUM
ARUMS
ARVAL
ARVICOLE
ARVICOLES
ARVO
ARVOS
ARY
ARYBALLOS
ARYBALLOSES
ARYL
ARYLS
ARYTENOID

ARYTENOIDS
AS
ASAFETIDA
ASAFETIDAS
ASANA
ASANAS
ASAR
ASARUM
ASARUMS
ASBESTIC
ASBESTINE
ASBESTOS
ASBESTOSES
ASBESTOUS
ASCARID
ASCARIDES
ASCARIDS
ASCARIS
ASCAUNT
ASCEND
ASCENDANT
ASCENDANTS
ASCENDED
ASCENDENT
ASCENDENTS
ASCENDER
ASCENDERS
ASCENDING
ASCENDS
ASCENSION
ASCENSIONS
ASCENSIVE
ASCENT
ASCENTS
ASCERTAIN
ASCERTAINED
ASCERTAINING
ASCERTAINS
ASCESES
ASCESIS
ASCETIC
ASCETICAL
ASCETICS
ASCI
ASCIAN
ASCIANS
ASCIDIA
ASCIDIAN
ASCIDIANS
ASCIDIUM
ASCITES
ASCITIC
ASCITICAL
ASCLEPIAD
ASCLEPIADS
ASCLEPIAS
ASCLEPIASES
ASCONCE
ASCORBATE
ASCORBATES
ASCOSPORE
ASCOSPORES
ASCOT
ASCOTS
ASCRIBE
ASCRIBED
ASCRIBES
ASCRIBING
ASCUS
ASEISMIC
ASEITIES
ASEITY
ASEPALOUS
ASEPSES
ASEPSIS
ASEPTATE
ASEPTIC
ASEPTICS
ASEXUAL
ASEXUALLY
ASH
ASHAKE
ASHAME
ASHAMED
ASHAMEDLY
ASHAMES
ASHAMING
ASHEN
ASHERIES
ASHERY
ASHES
ASHET
ASHETS
ASHIER
ASHIEST
ASHINE
ASHIVER
ASHLAR
ASHLARED
ASHLARING
ASHLARINGS
ASHLARS
ASHLER
ASHLERED
ASHLERING
ASHLERINGS
ASHLERS
ASHORE
ASHRAM
ASHRAMA
ASHRAMAS
ASHRAMITE
ASHRAMITES
ASHRAMS
ASHY
ASIDE
ASIDES
ASINICO
ASINICOS
ASININE
ASININITIES
ASININITY
ASK
ASKANCE
ASKANCED
ASKANCES
ASKANCING
ASKANT
ASKANTED
ASKANTING
ASKANTS
ASKARI
ASKARIS
ASKED
ASKER
ASKERS
ASKESES
ASKESIS
ASKEW
ASKING
ASKLENT
ASKS
ASLAKE
ASLAKED
ASLAKES
ASLAKING
ASLANT
ASLEEP
ASLOPE
ASMEAR
ASMOULDER
ASOCIAL
ASP
ASPARAGUS
ASPARAGUSES
ASPARTAME
ASPARTAMES
ASPECT
ASPECTED
ASPECTING
ASPECTS
ASPECTUAL
ASPEN
ASPENS
ASPER
ASPERATE
ASPERATED
ASPERATES
ASPERATING
ASPERGE
ASPERGED
ASPERGER
ASPERGERS
ASPERGES
ASPERGILL
ASPERGILLS
ASPERGING
ASPERITIES
ASPERITY
ASPEROUS
ASPERS
ASPERSE
ASPERSED
ASPERSES
ASPERSING
ASPERSION
ASPERSIONS
ASPERSIVE
ASPERSOIR
ASPERSOIRS
ASPERSORIES
ASPERSORY
ASPHALT
ASPHALTED
ASPHALTER
ASPHALTERS
ASPHALTIC
ASPHALTING
ASPHALTS
ASPHALTUM
ASPHALTUMS
ASPHERIC
ASPHODEL
ASPHODELS
ASPHYXIA
ASPHYXIAL
ASPHYXIAS
ASPHYXIES
ASPHYXY
ASPIC
ASPICK
ASPICKS
ASPICS
ASPIDIA
ASPIDIOID
ASPIDIUM
ASPINE
ASPINES
ASPIRANT
ASPIRANTS
ASPIRATE
ASPIRATED
ASPIRATES
ASPIRATING
ASPIRATOR
ASPIRATORS
ASPIRE
ASPIRED
ASPIRES
ASPIRIN
ASPIRING
ASPIRINS
ASPLENIUM
ASPLENIUMS
ASPORT
ASPORTED
ASPORTING
ASPORTS
ASPOUT
ASPRAWL
ASPREAD
ASPROUT
ASPS
ASQUAT
ASQUINT
ASS
ASSAGAI
ASSAGAIED
ASSAGAIING
ASSAGAIS
ASSAI
ASSAIL
ASSAILANT
ASSAILANTS
ASSAILED
ASSAILER
ASSAILERS
ASSAILING
ASSAILS
ASSAIS
ASSART
ASSARTED
ASSARTING
ASSARTS
ASSASSIN
ASSASSINS
ASSAULT
ASSAULTED
ASSAULTER
ASSAULTERS
ASSAULTING
ASSAULTS
ASSAY
ASSAYABLE
ASSAYED
ASSAYER
ASSAYERS
ASSAYING
ASSAYINGS
ASSAYS
ASSEGAAI
ASSEGAAIED
ASSEGAAIING
ASSEGAAIS
ASSEGAI
ASSEGAIED
ASSEGAIING
ASSEGAIS
ASSEMBLE
ASSEMBLED
ASSEMBLER
ASSEMBLERS
ASSEMBLES
ASSEMBLIES
ASSEMBLING
ASSEMBLY
ASSENT
ASSENTED
ASSENTER
ASSENTERS
ASSENTING
ASSENTIVE
ASSENTOR
ASSENTORS
ASSENTS
ASSERT
ASSERTED
ASSERTER
ASSERTERS
ASSERTING
ASSERTION
ASSERTIONS
ASSERTIVE
ASSERTOR
ASSERTORS
ASSERTORY
ASSERTS
ASSES
ASSESS
ASSESSED

ASSESSES
ASSESSING
ASSESSOR
ASSESSORS
ASSET
ASSETS
ASSEVER
ASSEVERED
ASSEVERING
ASSEVERS
ASSHOLE
ASSHOLES
ASSIDUITIES
ASSIDUITY
ASSIDUOUS
ASSIEGE
ASSIEGED
ASSIEGES
ASSIEGING
ASSIENTO
ASSIENTOS
ASSIGN
ASSIGNAT
ASSIGNATS
ASSIGNED
ASSIGNEE
ASSIGNEES
ASSIGNING
ASSIGNOR
ASSIGNORS
ASSIGNS
ASSIST
ASSISTANT
ASSISTANTS
ASSISTED
ASSISTING
ASSISTS
ASSIZE
ASSIZED
ASSIZER
ASSIZERS
ASSIZES
ASSIZING
ASSOCIATE
ASSOCIATED
ASSOCIATES
ASSOCIATING
ASSOIL
ASSOILED
ASSOILING
ASSOILS
ASSOILZIE
ASSOILZIED
ASSOILZIEING
ASSOILZIES
ASSONANCE
ASSONANCES
ASSONANT
ASSONATE
ASSONATED
ASSONATES
ASSONATING
ASSORT
ASSORTED
ASSORTER
ASSORTERS
ASSORTING
ASSORTS
ASSOT
ASSOTS
ASSOTT
ASSOTTED
ASSOTTING
ASSUAGE
ASSUAGED
ASSUAGES
ASSUAGING
ASSUAGINGS
ASSUASIVE
ASSUETUDE
ASSUETUDES
ASSUMABLE
ASSUMABLY
ASSUME
ASSUMED
ASSUMEDLY
ASSUMES
ASSUMING
ASSUMINGS
ASSUMPSIT
ASSUMPSITS
ASSURABLE
ASSURANCE
ASSURANCES
ASSURE
ASSURED
ASSUREDLY
ASSUREDS
ASSURER
ASSURERS
ASSURES
ASSURGENT
ASSURING
ASSWAGE
ASSWAGED
ASSWAGES
ASSWAGING
ASTABLE
ASTARE
ASTART
ASTARTED
ASTARTING
ASTARTS
ASTATIC
ASTATINE
ASTATINES
ASTATKI
ASTATKIS
ASTEISM
ASTEISMS
ASTELIC
ASTELIES
ASTELY
ASTER
ASTERIA
ASTERIAS
ASTERID
ASTERIDS
ASTERISK
ASTERISKED
ASTERISKING
ASTERISKS
ASTERISM
ASTERISMS
ASTERN
ASTEROID
ASTEROIDS
ASTERS
ASTERT
ASTERTED
ASTERTING
ASTERTS
ASTHENIA
ASTHENIAS
ASTHENIC
ASTHENICS
ASTHMA
ASTHMAS
ASTHMATIC
ASTHORE
ASTHORES
ASTICHOUS
ASTIGMIA
ASTIGMIAS
ASTILBE
ASTILBES
ASTIR
ASTOMOUS
ASTONE
ASTONED
ASTONES
ASTONIED
ASTONIES
ASTONING
ASTONISH
ASTONISHED
ASTONISHES
ASTONISHING
ASTONY
ASTONYING
ASTOOP
ASTOUND
ASTOUNDED
ASTOUNDING
ASTOUNDS
ASTRADDLE
ASTRAGAL
ASTRAGALI
ASTRAGALS
ASTRAKHAN
ASTRAKHANS
ASTRAL
ASTRAND
ASTRANTIA
ASTRANTIAS
ASTRAY
ASTRICT
ASTRICTED
ASTRICTING
ASTRICTS
ASTRIDE
ASTRINGE
ASTRINGED
ASTRINGER
ASTRINGERS
ASTRINGES
ASTRINGING
ASTROCYTE
ASTROCYTES
ASTRODOME
ASTRODOMES
ASTROFELL
ASTROFELLS
ASTROID
ASTROIDS
ASTROLABE
ASTROLABES
ASTROLOGIES
ASTROLOGY
ASTRONAUT
ASTRONAUTS
ASTRONOMIES
ASTRONOMY
ASTROPHEL
ASTROPHELS
ASTRUT
ASTUCIOUS
ASTUCITIES
ASTUCITY
ASTUN
ASTUNNED
ASTUNNING
ASTUNS
ASTUTE
ASTUTELY
ASTUTER
ASTUTEST
ASTYLAR
ASUDDEN
ASUNDER
ASWARM
ASWAY
ASWIM
ASWING
ASWIRL
ASWOON
ASYLUM
ASYLUMS
ASYMMETRIES
ASYMMETRY
ASYMPTOTE
ASYMPTOTES
ASYNDETIC
ASYNDETON
ASYNDETONS
ASYNERGIA
ASYNERGIAS
ASYNERGIES
ASYNERGY
ASYSTOLE
ASYSTOLES
AT
ATABAL
ATABALS
ATABEG
ATABEGS
ATABEK
ATABEKS
ATABRIN
ATABRINS
ATACAMITE
ATACAMITES
ATACTIC
ATAGHAN
ATAGHANS
ATALAYA
ATALAYAS
ATAMAN
ATAMANS
ATAP
ATAPS
ATARACTIC
ATARACTICS
ATARAXIA
ATARAXIAS
ATARAXIC
ATARAXICS
ATARAXIES
ATARAXY
ATAVISM
ATAVISMS
ATAVISTIC
ATAXIA
ATAXIAS
ATAXIC
ATAXIES
ATAXY
ATCHIEVE
ATCHIEVED
ATCHIEVES
ATCHIEVING
ATE
ATEBRIN
ATEBRINS
ATELIER
ATELIERS
ATHANASIES
ATHANASY
ATHANOR
ATHANORS
ATHEISE
ATHEISED
ATHEISES
ATHEISING
ATHEISM
ATHEISMS
ATHEIST
ATHEISTIC
ATHEISTS
ATHEIZE
ATHEIZED
ATHEIZES
ATHEIZING
ATHELING
ATHELINGS
ATHEMATIC
ATHEOLOGIES
ATHEOLOGY
ATHEOUS
ATHERINE

ATHERINES
ATHEROMA
ATHEROMAS
ATHEROMATA
ATHETESES
ATHETESIS
ATHETISE
ATHETISED
ATHETISES
ATHETISING
ATHETIZE
ATHETIZED
ATHETIZES
ATHETIZING
ATHETOID
ATHETOSES
ATHETOSIC
ATHETOSIS
ATHETOTIC
ATHIRST
ATHLETA
ATHLETAS
ATHLETE
ATHLETES
ATHLETIC
ATHLETICS
ATHRILL
ATHROB
ATHROCYTE
ATHROCYTES
ATHWART
ATILT
ATIMIES
ATIMY
ATINGLE
ATISHOO
ATISHOOS
ATLAS
ATLASES
ATLATL
ATLATLS
ATMAN
ATMANS
ATMOLOGIES
ATMOLOGY
ATMOLYSE
ATMOLYSED
ATMOLYSES
ATMOLYSING
ATMOLYSIS
ATMOLYZE
ATMOLYZED
ATMOLYZES
ATMOLYZING
ATMOMETER
ATMOMETERS
ATOC
ATOCIA
ATOCIAS
ATOCS
ATOK
ATOKAL
ATOKE
ATOKES
ATOKOUS
ATOKS
ATOLL
ATOLLS
ATOM
ATOMIC
ATOMICAL
ATOMICITIES
ATOMICITY
ATOMIES
ATOMISE
ATOMISED
ATOMISER
ATOMISERS
ATOMISES
ATOMISING
ATOMISM
ATOMISMS
ATOMIST
ATOMISTIC
ATOMISTS
ATOMIZE
ATOMIZED
ATOMIZER
ATOMIZERS
ATOMIZES
ATOMIZING
ATOMS
ATOMY
ATONAL
ATONALISM
ATONALISMS
ATONALIST
ATONALISTS
ATONALITIES
ATONALITY
ATONE
ATONED
ATONEMENT
ATONEMENTS
ATONER
ATONERS
ATONES
ATONIC
ATONICITIES
ATONICITY
ATONIES
ATONING
ATONINGLY
ATONY
ATOP
ATOPIC
ATOPIES
ATOPY
ATRAMENT
ATRAMENTS
ATRAZINE
ATRAZINES
ATREMBLE
ATRESIA
ATRESIAS
ATRIA
ATRIAL
ATRIP
ATRIUM
ATRIUMS
ATROCIOUS
ATROCITIES
ATROCITY
ATROPHIED
ATROPHIES
ATROPHY
ATROPHYING
ATROPIA
ATROPIAS
ATROPIN
ATROPINE
ATROPINES
ATROPINS
ATROPISM
ATROPISMS
ATROPOUS
ATTABOY
ATTACH
ATTACHE
ATTACHED
ATTACHES
ATTACHING
ATTACK
ATTACKED
ATTACKER
ATTACKERS
ATTACKING
ATTACKS
ATTAIN
ATTAINDER
ATTAINDERS
ATTAINED
ATTAINING
ATTAINS
ATTAINT
ATTAINTED
ATTAINTING
ATTAINTS
ATTAP
ATTAPS
ATTAR
ATTARS
ATTASK
ATTASKED
ATTASKING
ATTASKS
ATTASKT
ATTEMPER
ATTEMPERED
ATTEMPERING
ATTEMPERS
ATTEMPT
ATTEMPTED
ATTEMPTER
ATTEMPTERS
ATTEMPTING
ATTEMPTS
ATTEND
ATTENDANT
ATTENDANTS
ATTENDED
ATTENDEE
ATTENDEES
ATTENDER
ATTENDERS
ATTENDING
ATTENDS
ATTENT
ATTENTAT
ATTENTATS
ATTENTION
ATTENTIONS
ATTENTIVE
ATTENTS
ATTENUANT
ATTENUANTS
ATTENUATE
ATTENUATED
ATTENUATES
ATTENUATING
ATTERCOP
ATTERCOPS
ATTEST
ATTESTED
ATTESTER
ATTESTERS
ATTESTING
ATTESTOR
ATTESTORS
ATTESTS
ATTIC
ATTICS
ATTIRE
ATTIRED
ATTIRES
ATTIRING
ATTIRINGS
ATTITUDE
ATTITUDES
ATTOLLENS
ATTOLLENT
ATTOLLENTS
ATTONCE
ATTONE
ATTONES
ATTORN
ATTORNED
ATTORNEY
ATTORNEYED
ATTORNEYING
ATTORNEYS
ATTORNING
ATTORNS
ATTRACT
ATTRACTED
ATTRACTING
ATTRACTOR
ATTRACTORS
ATTRACTS
ATTRAHENS
ATTRAHENT
ATTRAHENTS
ATTRAP
ATTRAPPED
ATTRAPPING
ATTRAPS
ATTRIBUTE
ATTRIBUTED
ATTRIBUTES
ATTRIBUTING
ATTRIST
ATTRISTED
ATTRISTING
ATTRISTS
ATTRIT
ATTRITE
ATTRITED
ATTRITES
ATTRITING
ATTRITION
ATTRITIONS
ATTRITS
ATTRITTED
ATTRITTING
ATTUENT
ATTUITE
ATTUITED
ATTUITES
ATTUITING
ATTUITION
ATTUITIONS
ATTUITIVE
ATTUNE
ATTUNED
ATTUNES
ATTUNING
ATWAIN
ATWEEL
ATWEEN
ATWITTER
ATWIXT
ATYPICAL
AUBADE
AUBADES
AUBERGE
AUBERGES
AUBERGINE
AUBERGINES
AUBRETIA
AUBRETIAS
AUBRIETA
AUBRIETAS
AUBRIETIA
AUBRIETIAS
AUBURN
AUCEPS
AUCEPSES
AUCTION
AUCTIONED
AUCTIONING
AUCTIONS
AUCTORIAL
AUCUBA
AUCUBAS
AUDACIOUS
AUDACITIES
AUDACITY
AUDIBLE
AUDIBLES
AUDIBLY

AUDIENCE
AUDIENCES
AUDIENCIA
AUDIENCIAS
AUDIENT
AUDIENTS
AUDILE
AUDILES
AUDIO
AUDIOGRAM
AUDIOGRAMS
AUDIOLOGIES
AUDIOLOGY
AUDIOPHIL
AUDIOPHILS
AUDIOS
AUDIOTAPE
AUDIOTAPES
AUDIPHONE
AUDIPHONES
AUDIT
AUDITED
AUDITING
AUDITION
AUDITIONED
AUDITIONING
AUDITIONS
AUDITIVE
AUDITOR
AUDITORIA
AUDITORIES
AUDITORS
AUDITORY
AUDITRESS
AUDITRESSES
AUDITS
AUF
AUFGABE
AUFGABES
AUFS
AUGER
AUGERS
AUGHT
AUGHTS
AUGITE
AUGITES
AUGITIC
AUGMENT
AUGMENTED
AUGMENTER
AUGMENTERS
AUGMENTING
AUGMENTOR
AUGMENTORS
AUGMENTS
AUGUR
AUGURAL
AUGURED
AUGURER
AUGURERS
AUGURIES
AUGURING
AUGURS
AUGURSHIP
AUGURSHIPS
AUGURY
AUGUST
AUGUSTE
AUGUSTER
AUGUSTES
AUGUSTEST
AUGUSTLY
AUGUSTS
AUK
AUKLET
AUKLETS
AUKS
AULA
AULARIAN
AULARIANS
AULAS
AULD
AULDER
AULDEST
AULIC
AULNAGE
AULNAGER
AULNAGERS
AULNAGES
AULOI
AULOS
AUMAIL
AUMAILED
AUMAILING
AUMAILS
AUMBRIES
AUMBRY
AUMIL
AUMILS
AUNE
AUNES
AUNT
AUNTER
AUNTERS
AUNTIE
AUNTIES
AUNTLIER
AUNTLIEST
AUNTLY
AUNTS
AUNTY
AURA
AURAE
AURAL
AURALLY
AURAS
AURATE
AURATED
AURATES
AUREATE
AUREI
AUREITIES
AUREITY
AURELIA
AURELIAN
AURELIANS
AURELIAS
AUREOLA
AUREOLAS
AUREOLE
AUREOLED
AUREOLES
AUREUS
AURIC
AURICLE
AURICLED
AURICLES
AURICULA
AURICULAR
AURICULAS
AURIFIED
AURIFIES
AURIFORM
AURIFY
AURIFYING
AURISCOPE
AURISCOPES
AURIST
AURISTS
AUROCHS
AUROCHSES
AURORA
AURORAE
AURORAL
AURORALLY
AURORAS
AUROREAN
AUROUS
AUSPICATE
AUSPICATED
AUSPICATES
AUSPICATING
AUSPICE
AUSPICES
AUSTENITE
AUSTENITES
AUSTERE
AUSTERELY
AUSTERER
AUSTEREST
AUSTERITIES
AUSTERITY
AUSTRAL
AUSTRALES
AUTACOID
AUTACOIDS
AUTARCHIC
AUTARCHIES
AUTARCHY
AUTARKIC
AUTARKIES
AUTARKIST
AUTARKISTS
AUTARKY
AUTEUR
AUTEURS
AUTHENTIC
AUTHOR
AUTHORED
AUTHORESS
AUTHORESSES
AUTHORIAL
AUTHORING
AUTHORINGS
AUTHORISE
AUTHORISED
AUTHORISES
AUTHORISH
AUTHORISING
AUTHORISM
AUTHORISMS
AUTHORITIES
AUTHORITY
AUTHORIZE
AUTHORIZED
AUTHORIZES
AUTHORIZING
AUTHORS
AUTISM
AUTISMS
AUTISTIC
AUTISTICS
AUTO
AUTOBAHN
AUTOBAHNS
AUTOBUS
AUTOBUSES
AUTOBUSSES
AUTOCADE
AUTOCADES
AUTOCAR
AUTOCARP
AUTOCARPS
AUTOCARS
AUTOCLAVE
AUTOCLAVED
AUTOCLAVES
AUTOCLAVING
AUTOCRACIES
AUTOCRACY
AUTOCRAT
AUTOCRATS
AUTOCRIME
AUTOCRIMES
AUTOCROSS
AUTOCROSSES
AUTOCUE
AUTOCUES
AUTOCYCLE
AUTOCYCLES
AUTODYNE
AUTOFLARE
AUTOFLARES
AUTOFOCUS
AUTOFOCUSES
AUTOGAMIC
AUTOGAMIES
AUTOGAMY
AUTOGENIC
AUTOGENICS
AUTOGENIES
AUTOGENY
AUTOGIRO
AUTOGIROS
AUTOGRAFT
AUTOGRAFTED
AUTOGRAFTING
AUTOGRAFTS
AUTOGRAPH
AUTOGRAPHED
AUTOGRAPHING
AUTOGRAPHS
AUTOGUIDE
AUTOGUIDES
AUTOGYRO
AUTOGYROS
AUTOHARP
AUTOHARPS
AUTOLATRIES
AUTOLATRY
AUTOLOGIES
AUTOLOGY
AUTOLYSE
AUTOLYSED
AUTOLYSES
AUTOLYSING
AUTOLYSIS
AUTOLYTIC
AUTOLYZE
AUTOLYZED
AUTOLYZES
AUTOLYZING
AUTOMAT
AUTOMATA
AUTOMATE
AUTOMATED
AUTOMATES
AUTOMATIC
AUTOMATICS
AUTOMATING
AUTOMATON
AUTOMATONS
AUTOMATS
AUTONOMIC
AUTONOMICS
AUTONOMIES
AUTONOMY
AUTONYM
AUTONYMS
AUTOPHAGIES
AUTOPHAGY
AUTOPHOBIES
AUTOPHOBY
AUTOPHONIES
AUTOPHONY
AUTOPILOT
AUTOPILOTS
AUTOPISTA
AUTOPISTAS
AUTOPOINT
AUTOPOINTS
AUTOPSIA
AUTOPSIAS
AUTOPSIED
AUTOPSIES
AUTOPSY
AUTOPSYING
AUTOPTIC
AUTOROUTE
AUTOROUTES

AUTOS
AUTOSCOPIES
AUTOSCOPY
AUTOSOMAL
AUTOSOME
AUTOSOMES
AUTOTELIC
AUTOTIMER
AUTOTIMERS
AUTOTOMIES
AUTOTOMY
AUTOTOXIN
AUTOTOXINS
AUTOTROPH
AUTOTROPHS
AUTOTYPE
AUTOTYPED
AUTOTYPES
AUTOTYPING
AUTOVAC
AUTOVACS
AUTUMN
AUTUMNAL
AUTUMNS
AUTUMNY
AUTUNITE
AUTUNITES
AUXESES
AUXESIS
AUXETIC
AUXETICS
AUXILIAR
AUXILIARIES
AUXILIARS
AUXILIARY
AUXIN
AUXINS
AUXOMETER
AUXOMETERS
AVA
AVADAVAT
AVADAVATS
AVAIL
AVAILABLE
AVAILABLY
AVAILE
AVAILED
AVAILES
AVAILFUL
AVAILING
AVAILS
AVAL
AVALANCHE
AVALANCHED
AVALANCHES
AVALANCHING
AVALE
AVALED
AVALES
AVALING
AVANT
AVANTI
AVARICE
AVARICES
AVAS
AVASCULAR
AVAST
AVATAR
AVATARS
AVAUNT
AVAUNTED
AVAUNTING
AVAUNTS
AVE
AVENGE
AVENGED
AVENGEFUL
AVENGER
AVENGERS
AVENGES
AVENGING
AVENIR
AVENIRS
AVENS
AVENSES
AVENTAIL
AVENTAILE
AVENTAILES
AVENTAILS
AVENTRE
AVENTRED
AVENTRES
AVENTRING
AVENTURE
AVENTURES
AVENUE
AVENUES
AVER
AVERAGE
AVERAGED
AVERAGES
AVERAGING
AVERMENT
AVERMENTS
AVERRED
AVERRING
AVERS
AVERSE
AVERSELY
AVERSION
AVERSIONS
AVERSIVE
AVERT
AVERTABLE
AVERTED
AVERTEDLY
AVERTIBLE
AVERTING
AVERTS
AVES
AVGAS
AVGASES
AVIAN
AVIARIES
AVIARIST
AVIARISTS
AVIARY
AVIATE
AVIATED
AVIATES
AVIATING
AVIATION
AVIATIONS
AVIATOR
AVIATORS
AVIATRESS
AVIATRESSES
AVIATRICES
AVIATRIX
AVIATRIXES
AVID
AVIDER
AVIDEST
AVIDIN
AVIDINS
AVIDITIES
AVIDITY
AVIDLY
AVIDNESS
AVIDNESSES
AVIETTE
AVIETTES
AVIFAUNA
AVIFAUNAE
AVIFAUNAS
AVIFORM
AVINE
AVION
AVIONIC
AVIONICS
AVIONS
AVISANDUM
AVISANDUMS
AVISE
AVISED
AVISEMENT
AVISEMENTS
AVISES
AVISING
AVISO
AVISOS
AVITAL
AVIZANDUM
AVIZANDUMS
AVIZE
AVIZED
AVIZEFULL
AVIZES
AVIZING
AVOCADO
AVOCADOS
AVOCATION
AVOCATIONS
AVOCET
AVOCETS
AVOID
AVOIDABLE
AVOIDANCE
AVOIDANCES
AVOIDED
AVOIDING
AVOIDS
AVOISION
AVOISIONS
AVOSET
AVOSETS
AVOUCH
AVOUCHED
AVOUCHES
AVOUCHING
AVOURE
AVOURES
AVOUTERER
AVOUTERERS
AVOUTRER
AVOUTRERS
AVOUTRIES
AVOUTRY
AVOW
AVOWABLE
AVOWAL
AVOWALS
AVOWED
AVOWEDLY
AVOWER
AVOWERS
AVOWING
AVOWRIES
AVOWRY
AVOWS
AVOYER
AVOYERS
AVULSE
AVULSED
AVULSES
AVULSING
AVULSION
AVULSIONS
AVUNCULAR
AVYZE
AVYZED
AVYZES
AVYZING
AW
AWA
AWAIT
AWAITED
AWAITING
AWAITS
AWAKE
AWAKED
AWAKEN
AWAKENED
AWAKENING
AWAKENINGS
AWAKENS
AWAKES
AWAKING
AWAKINGS
AWANTING
AWARD
AWARDED
AWARDING
AWARDS
AWARE
AWARENESS
AWARENESSES
AWARER
AWAREST
AWARN
AWARNED
AWARNING
AWARNS
AWASH
AWATCH
AWAVE
AWAY
AWAYES
AWAYS
AWDL
AWDLS
AWE
AWEARIED
AWEARY
AWED
AWEEL
AWEIGH
AWELESS
AWES
AWESOME
AWESOMELY
AWESTRIKE
AWESTRIKES
AWESTRIKING
AWESTRUCK
AWETO
AWETOS
AWFUL
AWFULLER
AWFULLEST
AWFULLY
AWFULNESS
AWFULNESSES
AWHAPE
AWHAPED
AWHAPES
AWHAPING
AWHEEL
AWHEELS
AWHILE
AWING
AWKWARD
AWKWARDER
AWKWARDEST
AWKWARDLY
AWL
AWLBIRD
AWLBIRDS
AWLS
AWMOUS
AWMRIE
AWMRIES
AWMRY
AWN
AWNED
AWNER
AWNERS
AWNIER
AWNIEST
AWNING

AWNINGS
AWNLESS
AWNS
AWNY
AWOKE
AWOKEN
AWORK
AWRACK
AWRONG
AWRY
AWSOME
AX
AXE
AXED
AXEL
AXELS
AXEMAN
AXEMEN
AXES
AXIAL
AXIALITIES
AXIALITY
AXIALLY
AXIL
AXILE
AXILLA
AXILLAE
AXILLAR
AXILLARY
AXILS
AXING
AXINITE
AXINITES
AXIOLOGIES
AXIOLOGY
AXIOM
AXIOMATIC
AXIOMATICS
AXIOMS
AXIS
AXISES
AXLE
AXLES
AXMAN
AXMEN
AXOID
AXOIDS
AXOLOTL
AXOLOTLS
AXON
AXONS
AXOPLASM
AXOPLASMS
AY
AYAH
AYAHS
AYAHUASCO
AYAHUASCOS
AYATOLLAH
AYATOLLAHS
AYE
AYELP
AYENBITE
AYENBITES
AYES
AYGRE
AYONT
AYRE
AYRES
AYRIE
AYRIES
AYS
AYU
AYURVEDA
AYURVEDAS
AYURVEDIC
AYUS
AYWORD
AYWORDS
AZALEA
AZALEAS
AZAN
AZANS
AZEOTROPE
AZEOTROPES
AZIDE
AZIDES
AZIMUTH
AZIMUTHAL
AZIMUTHS
AZINE
AZINES
AZIONE
AZIONES
AZOIC
AZOLLA
AZOLLAS
AZONAL
AZONIC
AZOTE
AZOTES
AZOTH
AZOTHS
AZOTIC
AZOTISE
AZOTISED
AZOTISES
AZOTISING
AZOTIZE
AZOTIZED
AZOTIZES
AZOTIZING
AZOTOUS
AZOTURIA
AZOTURIAS
AZULEJO
AZULEJOS
AZURE
AZUREAN
AZURES
AZURINE
AZURINES
AZURITE
AZURITES
AZURN
AZURY
AZYGIES
AZYGOS
AZYGOSES
AZYGOUS
AZYGY
AZYM
AZYME
AZYMES
AZYMITE
AZYMITES
AZYMOUS
AZYMS

B

BA
BAA
BAAED
BAAING
BAAINGS
BAAS
BAASES
BAASSKAP
BAASSKAPS
BABA
BABACO
BABACOOTE
BABACOOTES
BABACOS
BABAS
BABASSU
BABASSUS
BABBITT
BABBITTED
BABBITTING
BABBITTS
BABBLE
BABBLED
BABBLER
BABBLERS
BABBLES
BABBLIER
BABBLIEST
BABBLING
BABBLINGS
BABBLY
BABE
BABEL
BABELDOM
BABELDOMS
BABELISH
BABELISM
BABELISMS
BABELS
BABES
BABICHE
BABICHES
BABIED
BABIER
BABIES
BABIEST
BABIRUSA
BABIRUSAS
BABIRUSSA
BABIRUSSAS
BABLAH
BABLAHS
BABOO
BABOON
BABOONERIES
BABOONERY
BABOONISH
BABOONS
BABOOS
BABOOSH
BABOOSHES
BABOUCHE
BABOUCHES
BABU
BABUCHE
BABUCHES
BABUDOM
BABUDOMS
BABUISM
BABUISMS
BABUL
BABULS
BABUS
BABUSHKA
BABUSHKAS
BABY
BABYFOOD
BABYFOODS
BABYHOOD
BABYHOODS
BABYING
BABYISH
BAC
BACCA
BACCAE
BACCARA
BACCARAS
BACCARAT
BACCARATS
BACCARE
BACCAS
BACCATE
BACCHANAL
BACCHANALS
BACCHANT
BACCHANTE
BACCHANTES
BACCHANTS
BACCHIAC
BACCHIAN
BACCHIC
BACCHII
BACCHIUS
BACCIES
BACCIFORM
BACCO
BACCOES
BACCOS
BACCY
BACH
BACHARACH
BACHARACHS
BACHED
BACHELOR
BACHELORS
BACHES
BACHING
BACHS
BACILLAR
BACILLARY
BACILLI
BACILLUS
BACK
BACKACHE
BACKACHES
BACKARE
BACKBAND
BACKBANDS
BACKBEAT
BACKBEATS
BACKBIT
BACKBITE
BACKBITER
BACKBITERS
BACKBITES
BACKBITING
BACKBITINGS
BACKBITTEN
BACKBOND
BACKBONDS
BACKBONE
BACKBONED
BACKBONES
BACKCHAT
BACKCHATS
BACKCHATTED
BACKCHATTING
BACKCOURT
BACKCOURTS
BACKDOWN
BACKDOWNS
BACKDROP
BACKDROPS
BACKED
BACKER
BACKERS
BACKET
BACKETS
BACKFALL
BACKFALLS
BACKFIELD
BACKFILE
BACKFILES
BACKFILL
BACKFILLED
BACKFILLING
BACKFILLS
BACKFIRE
BACKFIRED
BACKFIRES
BACKFIRING
BACKFISCH
BACKFISCHES
BACKHAND
BACKHANDS
BACKHOE
BACKHOES
BACKING
BACKINGS
BACKLAND
BACKLANDS
BACKLASH
BACKLASHES
BACKLIFT
BACKLIFTS
BACKLIST
BACKLISTS
BACKLOG
BACKLOGS
BACKLOT
BACKLOTS
BACKMOST
BACKPACK
BACKPACKED
BACKPACKING
BACKPACKINGS
BACKPACKS
BACKPAY
BACKPAYS
BACKPIECE
BACKPIECES
BACKRA
BACKRAS
BACKROOM
BACKS
BACKSAW
BACKSAWS
BACKSET
BACKSETS
BACKSEY
BACKSEYS
BACKSHISH
BACKSHISHED
BACKSHISHES
BACKSHISHING
BACKSIDE
BACKSIDES
BACKSIGHT
BACKSIGHTS
BACKSLASH
BACKSLASHES
BACKSLID
BACKSLIDE
BACKSLIDES
BACKSLIDING
BACKSLIDINGS
BACKSPACE
BACKSPACED
BACKSPACES
BACKSPACING
BACKSPEER
BACKSPEERED
BACKSPEERING
BACKSPEERS
BACKSPEIR
BACKSPEIRED
BACKSPEIRING
BACKSPEIRS
BACKSPIN
BACKSPINS
BACKSTAGE
BACKSTALL
BACKSTALLS
BACKSTAYS
BACKSTOP
BACKSTOPS
BACKSWING
BACKSWINGS
BACKSWORD
BACKSWORDS
BACKTRACK
BACKTRACKED
BACKTRACKING
BACKTRACKINGS
BACKTRACKS
BACKVELD
BACKVELDS
BACKWARD
BACKWARDS
BACKWASH
BACKWASHED
BACKWASHES
BACKWASHING
BACKWATER
BACKWATERS
BACKWOODS
BACKWORD
BACKWORDS
BACKWORK
BACKWORKS

The Chambers Dictionary is the authority for many longer words; see *OSW* Introduction, page xii

BACKYARD
BACKYARDS
BACLAVA
BACLAVAS
BACON
BACONER
BACONERS
BACONS
BACS
BACTERIA
BACTERIAL
BACTERIAN
BACTERIC
BACTERISE
BACTERISED
BACTERISES
BACTERISING
BACTERIUM
BACTERIZE
BACTERIZED
BACTERIZES
BACTERIZING
BACTEROID
BACTEROIDS
BACULA
BACULINE
BACULITE
BACULITES
BACULUM
BACULUMS
BAD
BADASS
BADASSED
BADASSES
BADDIE
BADDIES
BADDISH
BADDY
BADE
BADGE
BADGED
BADGER
BADGERED
BADGERING
BADGERLY
BADGERS
BADGES
BADGING
BADINAGE
BADINAGES
BADIOUS
BADLANDS
BADLY
BADMAN
BADMASH
BADMASHES
BADMEN
BADMINTON
BADMINTONS
BADMOUTH
BADMOUTHED
BADMOUTHING
BADMOUTHS
BADNESS
BADNESSES
BADS
BAEL
BAELS
BAETYL
BAETYLS
BAFF
BAFFED
BAFFIES
BAFFING
BAFFLE
BAFFLED
BAFFLEGAB
BAFFLEGABS
BAFFLER
BAFFLERS
BAFFLES
BAFFLING
BAFFS
BAFFY
BAFT
BAFTS
BAG
BAGARRE
BAGARRES
BAGASSE
BAGASSES
BAGATELLE
BAGATELLES
BAGEL
BAGELS
BAGFUL
BAGFULS
BAGGAGE
BAGGAGES
BAGGED
BAGGIER
BAGGIES
BAGGIEST
BAGGILY
BAGGINESS
BAGGINESSES
BAGGING
BAGGINGS
BAGGIT
BAGGITS
BAGGY
BAGMAN
BAGMEN
BAGNIO
BAGNIOS
BAGPIPE
BAGPIPER
BAGPIPERS
BAGPIPES
BAGPIPING
BAGPIPINGS
BAGS
BAGUETTE
BAGUETTES
BAGUIO
BAGUIOS
BAGWASH
BAGWASHES
BAGWIG
BAGWIGS
BAH
BAHADA
BAHADAS
BAHT
BAHTS
BAHUT
BAHUTS
BAHUVRIHI
BAHUVRIHIS
BAIGNOIRE
BAIGNOIRES
BAIL
BAILABLE
BAILBOND
BAILBONDS
BAILED
BAILEE
BAILEES
BAILER
BAILERS
BAILEY
BAILEYS
BAILIE
BAILIES
BAILIFF
BAILIFFS
BAILING
BAILIWICK
BAILIWICKS
BAILLI
BAILLIAGE
BAILLIAGES
BAILLIE
BAILLIES
BAILLIS
BAILMENT
BAILMENTS
BAILOR
BAILORS
BAILS
BAILSMAN
BAILSMEN
BAININ
BAININS
BAINITE
BAINITES
BAIRN
BAIRNLIER
BAIRNLIEST
BAIRNLIKE
BAIRNLY
BAIRNS
BAISEMAIN
BAISEMAINS
BAIT
BAITED
BAITER
BAITERS
BAITFISH
BAITFISHES
BAITING
BAITINGS
BAITS
BAIZE
BAIZED
BAIZES
BAIZING
BAJADA
BAJADAS
BAJAN
BAJANS
BAJRA
BAJRAS
BAJREE
BAJREES
BAJRI
BAJRIS
BAJU
BAJUS
BAKE
BAKEAPPLE
BAKEAPPLES
BAKEBOARD
BAKEBOARDS
BAKED
BAKEHOUSE
BAKEHOUSES
BAKEMEAT
BAKEMEATS
BAKEN
BAKER
BAKERIES
BAKERS
BAKERY
BAKES
BAKESTONE
BAKESTONES
BAKEWARE
BAKEWARES
BAKHSHISH
BAKHSHISHED
BAKHSHISHES
BAKHSHISHING
BAKING
BAKINGS
BAKLAVA
BAKLAVAS
BAKSHEESH
BAKSHEESHED
BAKSHEESHES
BAKSHEESHING
BALACLAVA
BALACLAVAS
BALADIN
BALADINE
BALADINES
BALADINS
BALALAIKA
BALALAIKAS
BALANCE
BALANCED
BALANCER
BALANCERS
BALANCES
BALANCING
BALANITIS
BALANITISES
BALAS
BALASES
BALATA
BALATAS
BALBOA
BALBOAS
BALCONET
BALCONETS
BALCONIED
BALCONIES
BALCONY
BALD
BALDACHIN
BALDACHINS
BALDAQUIN
BALDAQUINS
BALDER
BALDEST
BALDICOOT
BALDICOOTS
BALDIER
BALDIES
BALDIEST
BALDING
BALDISH
BALDLY
BALDMONEY
BALDMONEYS
BALDNESS
BALDNESSES
BALDPATE
BALDPATED
BALDPATES
BALDRIC
BALDRICK
BALDRICKS
BALDRICS
BALDY
BALE
BALECTION
BALECTIONS
BALED
BALEEN
BALEENS
BALEFUL
BALEFULLY
BALER
BALERS
BALES
BALING
BALISTA
BALISTAE
BALISTAS
BALK
BALKANISE
BALKANISED
BALKANISES
BALKANISING
BALKANIZE
BALKANIZED
BALKANIZES
BALKANIZING
BALKED

BALKER
BALKERS
BALKIER
BALKIEST
BALKINESS
BALKINESSES
BALKING
BALKINGLY
BALKINGS
BALKLINE
BALKLINES
BALKS
BALKY
BALL
BALLABILE
BALLABILES
BALLABILI
BALLAD
BALLADE
BALLADED
BALLADEER
BALLADEERED
BALLADEERING
BALLADEERS
BALLADES
BALLADIN
BALLADINE
BALLADINES
BALLADING
BALLADINS
BALLADIST
BALLADISTS
BALLADRIES
BALLADRY
BALLADS
BALLAN
BALLANS
BALLANT
BALLANTED
BALLANTING
BALLANTS
BALLAST
BALLASTED
BALLASTING
BALLASTS
BALLAT
BALLATED
BALLATING
BALLATS
BALLCLAY
BALLCLAYS
BALLCOCK
BALLCOCKS
BALLED
BALLERINA
BALLERINAS
BALLERINE
BALLET
BALLETED
BALLETIC
BALLETING
BALLETS
BALLING
BALLINGS
BALLISTA
BALLISTAE
BALLISTAS
BALLISTIC
BALLISTICS
BALLIUM
BALLIUMS
BALLOCKS
BALLOCKSED
BALLOCKSES
BALLOCKSING
BALLON
BALLONET
BALLONETS
BALLONS
BALLOON
BALLOONED
BALLOONING
BALLOONINGS
BALLOONS
BALLOT
BALLOTED
BALLOTEE
BALLOTEES
BALLOTING
BALLOTS
BALLOW
BALLOWS
BALLPARK
BALLPOINT
BALLPOINTS
BALLROOM
BALLROOMS
BALLS
BALLSIER
BALLSIEST
BALLSY
BALLUP
BALLUPS
BALLY
BALLYHOO
BALLYHOOED
BALLYHOOING
BALLYHOOS
BALLYRAG
BALLYRAGGED
BALLYRAGGING
BALLYRAGS
BALM
BALMACAAN
BALMACAANS
BALMED
BALMIER
BALMIEST
BALMILY
BALMINESS
BALMINESSES
BALMING
BALMORAL
BALMORALS
BALMS
BALMY
BALNEAL
BALNEARIES
BALNEARY
BALONEY
BALONEYS
BALOO
BALOOS
BALSA
BALSAM
BALSAMED
BALSAMIC
BALSAMING
BALSAMS
BALSAMY
BALSAS
BALSAWOOD
BALSAWOODS
BALTHASAR
BALTHASARS
BALTHAZAR
BALTHAZARS
BALU
BALUS
BALUSTER
BALUSTERS
BALZARINE
BALZARINES
BAM
BAMBINI
BAMBINO
BAMBINOS
BAMBOO
BAMBOOS
BAMBOOZLE
BAMBOOZLED
BAMBOOZLES
BAMBOOZLING
BAMMED
BAMMER
BAMMERS
BAMMING
BAMPOT
BAMPOTS
BAMS
BAN
BANAL
BANALER
BANALEST
BANALISE
BANALISED
BANALISES
BANALISING
BANALITIES
BANALITY
BANALIZE
BANALIZED
BANALIZES
BANALIZING
BANALLY
BANANA
BANANAS
BANAUSIAN
BANAUSIC
BANC
BANCO
BANCOS
BANCS
BAND
BANDA
BANDAGE
BANDAGED
BANDAGES
BANDAGING
BANDALORE
BANDALORES
BANDANA
BANDANAS
BANDANNA
BANDANNAS
BANDAR
BANDARS
BANDAS
BANDBRAKE
BANDBRAKES
BANDEAU
BANDEAUX
BANDED
BANDELET
BANDELETS
BANDELIER
BANDELIERS
BANDEROL
BANDEROLE
BANDEROLES
BANDEROLS
BANDICOOT
BANDICOOTED
BANDICOOTING
BANDICOOTS
BANDIED
BANDIER
BANDIES
BANDIEST
BANDING
BANDINGS
BANDIT
BANDITRIES
BANDITRY
BANDITS
BANDITTI
BANDITTIS
BANDOBAST
BANDOBASTS
BANDOG
BANDOGS
BANDOLEER
BANDOLEERS
BANDOLEON
BANDOLEONS
BANDOLERO
BANDOLEROS
BANDOLIER
BANDOLIERS
BANDOLINE
BANDOLINED
BANDOLINES
BANDOLINING
BANDONEON
BANDONEONS
BANDONION
BANDONIONS
BANDOOK
BANDOOKS
BANDORA
BANDORAS
BANDORE
BANDORES
BANDROL
BANDROLS
BANDS
BANDSMAN
BANDSMEN
BANDSTAND
BANDSTANDS
BANDSTER
BANDSTERS
BANDURA
BANDURAS
BANDWAGON
BANDWAGONS
BANDWIDTH
BANDWIDTHS
BANDY
BANDYING
BANDYINGS
BANDYMAN
BANDYMEN
BANE
BANEBERRIES
BANEBERRY
BANED
BANEFUL
BANEFULLY
BANES
BANG
BANGED
BANGER
BANGERS
BANGING
BANGINGS
BANGLE
BANGLED
BANGLES
BANGS
BANGSRING
BANGSRINGS
BANGSTER
BANGSTERS
BANI
BANIA
BANIAN
BANIANS
BANIAS
BANING
BANISH
BANISHED
BANISHES
BANISHING
BANISTER
BANISTERS
BANJAX
BANJAXED
BANJAXES
BANJAXING

BANJO
BANJOES
BANJOIST
BANJOISTS
BANJOS
BANJULELE
BANJULELES
BANK
BANKABLE
BANKED
BANKER
BANKERLY
BANKERS
BANKET
BANKETS
BANKING
BANKINGS
BANKROLL
BANKROLLED
BANKROLLING
BANKROLLS
BANKRUPT
BANKRUPTED
BANKRUPTING
BANKRUPTS
BANKS
BANKSIA
BANKSIAS
BANKSMAN
BANKSMEN
BANLIEUE
BANLIEUES
BANNED
BANNER
BANNERALL
BANNERALLS
BANNERED
BANNERET
BANNERETS
BANNEROL
BANNEROLS
BANNERS
BANNING
BANNISTER
BANNISTERS
BANNOCK
BANNOCKS
BANNS
BANQUET
BANQUETED
BANQUETER
BANQUETERS
BANQUETING
BANQUETINGS
BANQUETS
BANQUETTE
BANQUETTES
BANS
BANSHEE
BANSHEES
BANT
BANTAM
BANTAMS
BANTED
BANTENG
BANTENGS
BANTER
BANTERED
BANTERER
BANTERERS
BANTERING
BANTERINGS
BANTERS
BANTING
BANTINGS
BANTLING
BANTLINGS
BANTS
BANTU
BANTUS
BANXRING
BANXRINGS
BANYAN
BANYANS
BANZAI
BANZAIS
BAOBAB
BAOBABS
BAP
BAPS
BAPTISE
BAPTISED
BAPTISES
BAPTISING
BAPTISM
BAPTISMAL
BAPTISMS
BAPTIST
BAPTISTRIES
BAPTISTRY
BAPTISTS
BAPTIZE
BAPTIZED
BAPTIZES
BAPTIZING
BAPU
BAPUS
BAR
BARACAN
BARACANS
BARAGOUIN
BARAGOUINS
BARASINGA
BARASINGAS
BARATHEA
BARATHEAS
BARATHRUM
BARATHRUMS
BARAZA
BARAZAS
BARB
BARBARIAN
BARBARIANS
BARBARIC
BARBARISE
BARBARISED
BARBARISES
BARBARISING
BARBARISM
BARBARISMS
BARBARITIES
BARBARITY
BARBARIZE
BARBARIZED
BARBARIZES
BARBARIZING
BARBAROUS
BARBASCO
BARBASCOS
BARBASTEL
BARBASTELS
BARBATE
BARBATED
BARBE
BARBECUE
BARBECUED
BARBECUES
BARBECUING
BARBED
BARBEL
BARBELS
BARBEQUE
BARBEQUED
BARBEQUES
BARBEQUING
BARBER
BARBERED
BARBERING
BARBERRIES
BARBERRY
BARBERS
BARBES
BARBET
BARBETS
BARBETTE
BARBETTES
BARBICAN
BARBICANS
BARBICEL
BARBICELS
BARBIE
BARBIES
BARBING
BARBITAL
BARBITALS
BARBITONE
BARBITONES
BARBOLA
BARBOLAS
BARBOTINE
BARBOTINES
BARBS
BARBULE
BARBULES
BARCA
BARCAROLE
BARCAROLES
BARCAS
BARCHAN
BARCHANE
BARCHANES
BARCHANS
BARD
BARDASH
BARDASHES
BARDED
BARDIC
BARDIER
BARDIEST
BARDING
BARDLING
BARDLINGS
BARDO
BARDOS
BARDS
BARDSHIP
BARDSHIPS
BARDY
BARE
BAREBACK
BAREBOAT
BAREBONE
BAREBONES
BARED
BAREFACED
BAREFOOT
BAREGE
BAREGES
BAREGINE
BAREGINES
BARELY
BARENESS
BARENESSES
BARER
BARES
BARESARK
BARESARKS
BAREST
BARF
BARFED
BARFING
BARFLIES
BARFLY
BARFS
BARFUL
BARGAIN
BARGAINED
BARGAINER
BARGAINERS
BARGAINING
BARGAINS
BARGANDER
BARGANDERS
BARGE
BARGED
BARGEE
BARGEES
BARGEESE
BARGELLO
BARGELLOS
BARGEMAN
BARGEMEN
BARGEPOLE
BARGEPOLES
BARGES
BARGEST
BARGESTS
BARGHAIST
BARGHAISTS
BARGHEST
BARGHESTS
BARGING
BARGOOSE
BARIC
BARILLA
BARILLAS
BARING
BARISH
BARITE
BARITES
BARITONE
BARITONES
BARIUM
BARIUMS
BARK
BARKAN
BARKANS
BARKED
BARKEEPER
BARKEEPERS
BARKEN
BARKENED
BARKENING
BARKENS
BARKER
BARKERS
BARKHAN
BARKHANS
BARKIER
BARKIEST
BARKING
BARKLESS
BARKS
BARKY
BARLEY
BARLEYS
BARM
BARMAID
BARMAIDS
BARMAN
BARMBRACK
BARMBRACKS
BARMEN
BARMIER
BARMIEST
BARMINESS
BARMINESSES
BARMKIN
BARMKINS
BARMS
BARMY
BARN
BARNACLE
BARNACLED
BARNACLES
BARNED
BARNEY
BARNEYS
BARNING
BARNS

BARNSTORM
BARNSTORMED
BARNSTORMING
BARNSTORMINGS
BARNSTORMS
BARNYARD
BARNYARDS
BAROCCO
BAROCCOS
BAROCK
BAROCKS
BAROGRAM
BAROGRAMS
BAROGRAPH
BAROGRAPHS
BAROMETER
BAROMETERS
BAROMETRIES
BAROMETRY
BAROMETZ
BAROMETZES
BARON
BARONAGE
BARONAGES
BARONESS
BARONESSES
BARONET
BARONETCIES
BARONETCY
BARONETS
BARONG
BARONGS
BARONIAL
BARONIES
BARONNE
BARONNES
BARONS
BARONY
BAROQUE
BAROQUES
BAROSCOPE
BAROSCOPES
BAROSTAT
BAROSTATS
BAROUCHE
BAROUCHES
BARP
BARPERSON
BARPERSONS
BARPS
BARQUE
BARQUES
BARRACAN
BARRACANS
BARRACE
BARRACES
BARRACK
BARRACKED
BARRACKER
BARRACKERS
BARRACKING
BARRACKINGS
BARRACKS
BARRACOON
BARRACOONS
BARRACUDA
BARRACUDAS
BARRAGE
BARRAGES
BARRANCA
BARRANCAS
BARRANCO
BARRANCOS
BARRAT
BARRATOR
BARRATORS
BARRATRIES
BARRATRY
BARRATS
BARRE
BARRED
BARREFULL
BARREL
BARRELAGE
BARRELAGES
BARRELFUL
BARRELFULS
BARRELLED
BARRELLING
BARRELS
BARREN
BARRENER
BARRENEST
BARRES
BARRET
BARRETS
BARRETTE
BARRETTER
BARRETTERS
BARRETTES
BARRICADE
BARRICADED
BARRICADES
BARRICADING
BARRICADO
BARRICADOED
BARRICADOES
BARRICADOING
BARRICADOS
BARRICO
BARRICOES
BARRICOS
BARRIER
BARRIERED
BARRIERING
BARRIERS
BARRING
BARRINGS
BARRIO
BARRIOS
BARRISTER
BARRISTERS
BARROW
BARROWS
BARRULET
BARRULETS
BARS
BARTENDER
BARTENDERS
BARTER
BARTERED
BARTERER
BARTERERS
BARTERING
BARTERS
BARTISAN
BARTISANS
BARTIZAN
BARTIZANS
BARTON
BARTONS
BARWOOD
BARWOODS
BARYE
BARYES
BARYON
BARYONS
BARYTA
BARYTAS
BARYTES
BARYTIC
BARYTON
BARYTONE
BARYTONES
BARYTONS
BAS
BASAL
BASALT
BASALTIC
BASALTS
BASAN
BASANITE
BASANITES
BASANS
BASCULE
BASCULES
BASE
BASEBALL
BASEBALLS
BASEBAND
BASEBOARD
BASEBOARDS
BASED
BASELARD
BASELARDS
BASELESS
BASELINER
BASELINERS
BASELY
BASEMAN
BASEMEN
BASEMENT
BASEMENTS
BASENESS
BASENESSES
BASENJI
BASENJIS
BASEPLATE
BASEPLATES
BASER
BASES
BASEST
BASH
BASHAW
BASHAWISM
BASHAWISMS
BASHAWS
BASHED
BASHER
BASHERS
BASHES
BASHFUL
BASHFULLY
BASHING
BASHINGS
BASHLESS
BASHLIK
BASHLIKS
BASHO
BASIC
BASICALLY
BASICITIES
BASICITY
BASICS
BASIDIA
BASIDIAL
BASIDIUM
BASIFIXED
BASIFUGAL
BASIL
BASILAR
BASILICA
BASILICAL
BASILICAN
BASILICAS
BASILICON
BASILICONS
BASILISK
BASILISKS
BASILS
BASIN
BASINET
BASINETS
BASINFUL
BASINFULS
BASING
BASINS
BASIPETAL
BASIS
BASK
BASKED
BASKET
BASKETFUL
BASKETFULS
BASKETRIES
BASKETRY
BASKETS
BASKING
BASKS
BASNET
BASNETS
BASOCHE
BASOCHES
BASON
BASONS
BASOPHIL
BASOPHILS
BASQUE
BASQUED
BASQUES
BASQUINE
BASQUINES
BASS
BASSE
BASSED
BASSER
BASSES
BASSEST
BASSET
BASSETED
BASSETING
BASSETS
BASSI
BASSIER
BASSIEST
BASSINET
BASSINETS
BASSING
BASSIST
BASSISTS
BASSO
BASSOON
BASSOONS
BASSOS
BASSWOOD
BASSWOODS
BASSY
BAST
BASTA
BASTARD
BASTARDIES
BASTARDLY
BASTARDS
BASTARDY
BASTE
BASTED
BASTER
BASTERS
BASTES
BASTIDE
BASTIDES
BASTILLE
BASTILLES
BASTINADE
BASTINADED
BASTINADES
BASTINADING
BASTINADO
BASTINADOED
BASTINADOES
BASTINADOING
BASTING
BASTINGS
BASTION
BASTIONED
BASTIONS
BASTLE
BASTLES
BASTO
BASTOS

BASTS
BASUCO
BASUCOS
BAT
BATABLE
BATATA
BATATAS
BATCH
BATCHED
BATCHES
BATCHING
BATCHINGS
BATE
BATEAU
BATEAUX
BATED
BATELESS
BATELEUR
BATELEURS
BATEMENT
BATEMENTS
BATES
BATFISH
BATFISHES
BATH
BATHCUBE
BATHCUBES
BATHE
BATHED
BATHER
BATHERS
BATHES
BATHETIC
BATHHOUSE
BATHHOUSES
BATHING
BATHMIC
BATHMISM
BATHMISMS
BATHOLITE
BATHOLITES
BATHOLITH
BATHOLITHS
BATHORSE
BATHORSES
BATHOS
BATHOSES
BATHROBE
BATHROBES
BATHROOM
BATHROOMS
BATHS
BATHTUB
BATHTUBS
BATHYAL
BATHYBIUS
BATHYBIUSES
BATHYLITE
BATHYLITES
BATHYLITH
BATHYLITHS
BATIK
BATIKS
BATING
BATISTE
BATISTES
BATLER
BATLERS
BATLET
BATLETS
BATMAN
BATMEN
BATOLOGIES
BATOLOGY
BATON
BATONED
BATONING
BATONS
BATOON
BATOONED
BATOONING
BATOONS
BATRACHIA
BATS
BATSMAN
BATSMEN
BATSWING
BATSWOMAN
BATSWOMEN
BATT
BATTA
BATTALIA
BATTALIAS
BATTALION
BATTALIONS
BATTAS
BATTED
BATTEL
BATTELED
BATTELER
BATTELERS
BATTELING
BATTELLED
BATTELLING
BATTELS
BATTEMENT
BATTEMENTS
BATTEN
BATTENED
BATTENING
BATTENINGS
BATTENS
BATTER
BATTERED
BATTERER
BATTERERS
BATTERIE
BATTERIES
BATTERING
BATTERO
BATTEROS
BATTERS
BATTERY
BATTIER
BATTIEST
BATTILL
BATTILLED
BATTILLING
BATTILLS
BATTING
BATTINGS
BATTLE
BATTLEBUS
BATTLEBUSES
BATTLEBUSSES
BATTLED
BATTLER
BATTLERS
BATTLES
BATTLING
BATTOLOGIES
BATTOLOGY
BATTS
BATTUE
BATTUES
BATTUTA
BATTUTAS
BATTY
BATWOMAN
BATWOMEN
BAUBLE
BAUBLES
BAUBLING
BAUCHLE
BAUCHLED
BAUCHLES
BAUCHLING
BAUD
BAUDEKIN
BAUDEKINS
BAUDRIC
BAUDRICK
BAUDRICKE
BAUDRICKES
BAUDRICKS
BAUDRICS
BAUDRONS
BAUDRONSES
BAUDS
BAUERA
BAUERAS
BAUHINIA
BAUHINIAS
BAUK
BAUKED
BAUKING
BAUKS
BAULK
BAULKED
BAULKING
BAULKS
BAUR
BAURS
BAUSOND
BAUXITE
BAUXITES
BAUXITIC
BAVARDAGE
BAVARDAGES
BAVIN
BAVINS
BAWBEE
BAWBEES
BAWBLE
BAWBLES
BAWCOCK
BAWCOCKS
BAWD
BAWDIER
BAWDIES
BAWDIEST
BAWDILY
BAWDINESS
BAWDINESSES
BAWDKIN
BAWDKINS
BAWDRIES
BAWDRY
BAWDS
BAWDY
BAWL
BAWLED
BAWLER
BAWLERS
BAWLEY
BAWLEYS
BAWLING
BAWLINGS
BAWLS
BAWN
BAWNS
BAWR
BAWRS
BAXTER
BAXTERS
BAY
BAYADERE
BAYADERES
BAYARD
BAYARDS
BAYBERRIES
BAYBERRY
BAYE
BAYED
BAYES
BAYING
BAYLE
BAYLES
BAYONET
BAYONETED
BAYONETING
BAYONETS
BAYOU
BAYOUS
BAYS
BAYT
BAYTED
BAYTING
BAYTS
BAZAAR
BAZAARS
BAZAR
BAZARS
BAZAZZ
BAZAZZES
BAZOOKA
BAZOOKAS
BAZOUKI
BAZOUKIS
BDELLIUM
BDELLIUMS
BE
BEACH
BEACHED
BEACHES
BEACHHEAD
BEACHHEADS
BEACHIER
BEACHIEST
BEACHING
BEACHY
BEACON
BEACONED
BEACONING
BEACONS
BEAD
BEADED
BEADIER
BEADIEST
BEADING
BEADINGS
BEADLE
BEADLEDOM
BEADLEDOMS
BEADLES
BEADMAN
BEADMEN
BEADS
BEADSMAN
BEADSMEN
BEADY
BEAGLE
BEAGLED
BEAGLER
BEAGLERS
BEAGLES
BEAGLING
BEAGLINGS
BEAK
BEAKED
BEAKER
BEAKERS
BEAKIER
BEAKIEST
BEAKS
BEAKY
BEAM
BEAMED
BEAMER
BEAMERS
BEAMIER
BEAMIEST
BEAMILY
BEAMINESS
BEAMINESSES
BEAMING
BEAMINGLY
BEAMINGS
BEAMISH
BEAMLESS

BEAMLET
BEAMLETS
BEAMS
BEAMY
BEAN
BEANBAG
BEANBAGS
BEANED
BEANERIES
BEANERY
BEANFEAST
BEANFEASTS
BEANIE
BEANIES
BEANING
BEANO
BEANOS
BEANPOLE
BEANPOLES
BEANS
BEANSTALK
BEANSTALKS
BEAR
BEARABLE
BEARABLY
BEARBINE
BEARBINES
BEARD
BEARDED
BEARDIE
BEARDIES
BEARDING
BEARDLESS
BEARDS
BEARE
BEARED
BEARER
BEARERS
BEARES
BEARING
BEARINGS
BEARISH
BEARISHLY
BEARNAISE
BEARNAISES
BEARS
BEARSKIN
BEARSKINS
BEARWARD
BEARWARDS
BEAST
BEASTHOOD
BEASTHOODS
BEASTIE
BEASTIES
BEASTILY
BEASTINGS
BEASTLIER
BEASTLIEST
BEASTLIKE
BEASTLY
BEASTS
BEAT
BEATABLE
BEATEN
BEATER
BEATERS
BEATH
BEATHED
BEATHING
BEATHS
BEATIFIC
BEATIFIED
BEATIFIES
BEATIFY
BEATIFYING
BEATING
BEATINGS
BEATITUDE
BEATITUDES
BEATNIK
BEATNIKS
BEATS
BEAU
BEAUFET
BEAUFETS
BEAUFFET
BEAUFFETS
BEAUFIN
BEAUFINS
BEAUISH
BEAUT
BEAUTEOUS
BEAUTIED
BEAUTIES
BEAUTIFIED
BEAUTIFIES
BEAUTIFUL
BEAUTIFY
BEAUTIFYING
BEAUTS
BEAUTY
BEAUTYING
BEAUX
BEAUXITE
BEAUXITES
BEAVER
BEAVERED
BEAVERIES
BEAVERS
BEAVERY
BEBEERINE
BEBEERINES
BEBEERU
BEBEERUS
BEBOP
BEBOPPED
BEBOPPING
BEBOPS
BEBUNG
BEBUNGS
BECALL
BECALLED
BECALLING
BECALLS
BECALM
BECALMED
BECALMING
BECALMS
BECAME
BECASSE
BECASSES
BECAUSE
BECCACCIA
BECCACCIAS
BECCAFICO
BECCAFICOS
BECHAMEL
BECHAMELS
BECHANCE
BECHANCED
BECHANCES
BECHANCING
BECHARM
BECHARMED
BECHARMING
BECHARMS
BECK
BECKE
BECKED
BECKES
BECKET
BECKETS
BECKING
BECKON
BECKONED
BECKONING
BECKONS
BECKS
BECLOUD
BECLOUDED
BECLOUDING
BECLOUDS
BECOME
BECOMES
BECOMING
BECQUEREL
BECQUERELS
BECURL
BECURLED
BECURLING
BECURLS
BED
BEDABBLE
BEDABBLED
BEDABBLES
BEDABBLING
BEDAD
BEDAGGLE
BEDAGGLED
BEDAGGLES
BEDAGGLING
BEDARKEN
BEDARKENED
BEDARKENING
BEDARKENS
BEDASH
BEDASHED
BEDASHES
BEDASHING
BEDAUB
BEDAUBED
BEDAUBING
BEDAUBS
BEDAWIN
BEDAWINS
BEDAZE
BEDAZED
BEDAZES
BEDAZING
BEDAZZLE
BEDAZZLED
BEDAZZLES
BEDAZZLING
BEDBUG
BEDBUGS
BEDCOVER
BEDCOVERS
BEDDABLE
BEDDED
BEDDER
BEDDERS
BEDDING
BEDDINGS
BEDE
BEDEAFEN
BEDEAFENED
BEDEAFENING
BEDEAFENS
BEDECK
BEDECKED
BEDECKING
BEDECKS
BEDEGUAR
BEDEGUARS
BEDEL
BEDELL
BEDELLS
BEDELS
BEDELSHIP
BEDELSHIPS
BEDEMAN
BEDEMEN
BEDERAL
BEDERALS
BEDES
BEDESMAN
BEDESMEN
BEDEVIL
BEDEVILLED
BEDEVILLING
BEDEVILS
BEDEW
BEDEWED
BEDEWING
BEDEWS
BEDFAST
BEDFELLOW
BEDFELLOWS
BEDIDE
BEDIGHT
BEDIGHTING
BEDIGHTS
BEDIM
BEDIMMED
BEDIMMING
BEDIMMINGS
BEDIMS
BEDIZEN
BEDIZENED
BEDIZENING
BEDIZENS
BEDLAM
BEDLAMISM
BEDLAMISMS
BEDLAMITE
BEDLAMITES
BEDLAMS
BEDMAKER
BEDMAKERS
BEDOUIN
BEDOUINS
BEDPAN
BEDPANS
BEDPOST
BEDPOSTS
BEDRAGGLE
BEDRAGGLED
BEDRAGGLES
BEDRAGGLING
BEDRAL
BEDRALS
BEDRENCH
BEDRENCHED
BEDRENCHES
BEDRENCHING
BEDRID
BEDRIDDEN
BEDRIGHT
BEDRIGHTS
BEDROCK
BEDROCKS
BEDROOM
BEDROOMS
BEDROP
BEDROPPED
BEDROPPING
BEDROPS
BEDROPT
BEDS
BEDSIDE
BEDSIDES
BEDSOCKS
BEDSORE
BEDSORES
BEDSPREAD
BEDSPREADS
BEDSTEAD
BEDSTEADS
BEDSTRAW
BEDSTRAWS
BEDTICK
BEDTICKS
BEDTIME
BEDTIMES
BEDUCK
BEDUCKED
BEDUCKING
BEDUCKS
BEDUIN

BEDUINS
BEDUNG
BEDUNGED
BEDUNGING
BEDUNGS
BEDUST
BEDUSTED
BEDUSTING
BEDUSTS
BEDWARD
BEDWARDS
BEDWARF
BEDWARFED
BEDWARFING
BEDWARFS
BEDYDE
BEDYE
BEDYED
BEDYEING
BEDYES
BEE
BEECH
BEECHEN
BEECHES
BEEF
BEEFALO
BEEFALOES
BEEFALOS
BEEFCAKE
BEEFCAKES
BEEFEATER
BEEFEATERS
BEEFED
BEEFIER
BEEFIEST
BEEFING
BEEFS
BEEFSTEAK
BEEFSTEAKS
BEEFY
BEEGAH
BEEGAHS
BEEHIVE
BEEHIVES
BEEKEEPER
BEEKEEPERS
BEELINE
BEELINES
BEEN
BEENAH
BEENAHS
BEEP
BEEPED
BEEPER
BEEPERS
BEEPING
BEEPS
BEER
BEERAGE
BEERAGES
BEERHALL
BEERHALLS
BEERIER
BEERIEST
BEERINESS
BEERINESSES
BEERS
BEERY
BEES
BEESOME
BEESTINGS
BEESWAX
BEESWAXED
BEESWAXES
BEESWAXING
BEESWING
BEESWINGS
BEET
BEETED
BEETING
BEETLE
BEETLED
BEETLES
BEETLING
BEETROOT
BEETROOTS
BEETS
BEEVES
BEFALL
BEFALLEN
BEFALLING
BEFALLS
BEFANA
BEFANAS
BEFELD
BEFELL
BEFFANA
BEFFANAS
BEFINNED
BEFIT
BEFITS
BEFITTED
BEFITTING
BEFLOWER
BEFLOWERED
BEFLOWERING
BEFLOWERS
BEFLUM
BEFLUMMED
BEFLUMMING
BEFLUMS
BEFOAM
BEFOAMED
BEFOAMING
BEFOAMS
BEFOG
BEFOGGED
BEFOGGING
BEFOGS
BEFOOL
BEFOOLED
BEFOOLING
BEFOOLS
BEFORE
BEFORTUNE
BEFORTUNED
BEFORTUNES
BEFORTUNING
BEFOUL
BEFOULED
BEFOULING
BEFOULS
BEFRIEND
BEFRIENDED
BEFRIENDING
BEFRIENDS
BEFRINGE
BEFRINGED
BEFRINGES
BEFRINGING
BEFUDDLE
BEFUDDLED
BEFUDDLES
BEFUDDLING
BEG
BEGAD
BEGAN
BEGAR
BEGARS
BEGAT
BEGEM
BEGEMMED
BEGEMMING
BEGEMS
BEGET
BEGETS
BEGETTER
BEGETTERS
BEGETTING
BEGGAR
BEGGARDOM
BEGGARDOMS
BEGGARED
BEGGARIES
BEGGARING
BEGGARLY
BEGGARS
BEGGARY
BEGGED
BEGGING
BEGGINGLY
BEGGINGS
BEGHARD
BEGHARDS
BEGIFT
BEGIFTED
BEGIFTING
BEGIFTS
BEGILD
BEGILDED
BEGILDING
BEGILDS
BEGILT
BEGIN
BEGINNE
BEGINNER
BEGINNERS
BEGINNES
BEGINNING
BEGINNINGS
BEGINS
BEGIRD
BEGIRDED
BEGIRDING
BEGIRDS
BEGIRT
BEGLAMOUR
BEGLAMOURED
BEGLAMOURING
BEGLAMOURS
BEGLERBEG
BEGLERBEGS
BEGLOOM
BEGLOOMED
BEGLOOMING
BEGLOOMS
BEGNAW
BEGNAWED
BEGNAWING
BEGNAWS
BEGO
BEGOES
BEGOING
BEGONE
BEGONIA
BEGONIAS
BEGORED
BEGORRA
BEGORRAH
BEGOT
BEGOTTEN
BEGRIME
BEGRIMED
BEGRIMES
BEGRIMING
BEGRUDGE
BEGRUDGED
BEGRUDGES
BEGRUDGING
BEGS
BEGUILE
BEGUILED
BEGUILER
BEGUILERS
BEGUILES
BEGUILING
BEGUIN
BEGUINAGE
BEGUINAGES
BEGUINE
BEGUINES
BEGUINS
BEGUM
BEGUMS
BEGUN
BEGUNK
BEGUNKED
BEGUNKING
BEGUNKS
BEHALF
BEHALVES
BEHAPPEN
BEHAPPENED
BEHAPPENING
BEHAPPENS
BEHATTED
BEHAVE
BEHAVED
BEHAVES
BEHAVING
BEHAVIOR
BEHAVIORS
BEHAVIOUR
BEHAVIOURS
BEHEAD
BEHEADAL
BEHEADALS
BEHEADED
BEHEADING
BEHEADINGS
BEHEADS
BEHELD
BEHEMOTH
BEHEMOTHS
BEHEST
BEHESTS
BEHIGHT
BEHIGHTING
BEHIGHTS
BEHIND
BEHINDS
BEHOLD
BEHOLDEN
BEHOLDER
BEHOLDERS
BEHOLDING
BEHOLDINGS
BEHOLDS
BEHOOF
BEHOOFS
BEHOOVE
BEHOOVED
BEHOOVES
BEHOOVING
BEHOTE
BEHOTES
BEHOTING
BEHOVE
BEHOVED
BEHOVEFUL
BEHOVELY
BEHOVES
BEHOVING
BEHOWL
BEHOWLED
BEHOWLING
BEHOWLS
BEIGE
BEIGEL
BEIGELS
BEIGES
BEIGNET
BEIGNETS
BEIN
BEING
BEINGLESS
BEINGNESS
BEINGNESSES
BEINGS
BEINKED

BEINNESS
BEINNESSES
BEJABERS
BEJADE
BEJADED
BEJADES
BEJADING
BEJANT
BEJANTS
BEJESUIT
BEJESUITED
BEJESUITING
BEJESUITS
BEJEWEL
BEJEWELLED
BEJEWELLING
BEJEWELS
BEKAH
BEKAHS
BEKISS
BEKISSED
BEKISSES
BEKISSING
BEKNAVE
BEKNAVED
BEKNAVES
BEKNAVING
BEKNOWN
BEL
BELABOR
BELABORED
BELABORING
BELABORS
BELABOUR
BELABOURED
BELABOURING
BELABOURS
BELACE
BELACED
BELACES
BELACING
BELAH
BELAHS
BELAMIES
BELAMOURE
BELAMOURES
BELAMY
BELATE
BELATED
BELATEDLY
BELATES
BELATING
BELAUD
BELAUDED
BELAUDING
BELAUDS
BELAY
BELAYED
BELAYING
BELAYS
BELCH
BELCHED
BELCHER
BELCHERS
BELCHES
BELCHING
BELDAM
BELDAME
BELDAMES
BELDAMS
BELEAGUER
BELEAGUERED
BELEAGUERING
BELEAGUERS
BELEE
BELEED
BELEEING
BELEES
BELEMNITE
BELEMNITES
BELFRIED
BELFRIES
BELFRY
BELGA
BELGARD
BELGARDS
BELGAS
BELIE
BELIED
BELIEF
BELIEFS
BELIER
BELIERS
BELIES
BELIEVE
BELIEVED
BELIEVER
BELIEVERS
BELIEVES
BELIEVING
BELIKE
BELITTLE
BELITTLED
BELITTLES
BELITTLING
BELIVE
BELL
BELLBIND
BELLBINDS
BELLCOTE
BELLCOTES
BELLE
BELLED
BELLES
BELLETER
BELLETERS
BELLHOP
BELLHOPS
BELLIBONE
BELLIBONES
BELLICOSE
BELLIED
BELLIES
BELLING
BELLMAN
BELLMEN
BELLOW
BELLOWED
BELLOWER
BELLOWERS
BELLOWING
BELLOWS
BELLPUSH
BELLPUSHES
BELLS
BELLWORT
BELLWORTS
BELLY
BELLYFUL
BELLYFULS
BELLYING
BELLYINGS
BELOMANCIES
BELOMANCY
BELONG
BELONGED
BELONGER
BELONGERS
BELONGING
BELONGINGS
BELONGS
BELOVE
BELOVED
BELOVEDS
BELOVES
BELOVING
BELOW
BELS
BELT
BELTED
BELTER
BELTERS
BELTING
BELTINGS
BELTMAN
BELTMEN
BELTS
BELTWAY
BELTWAYS
BELUGA
BELUGAS
BELVEDERE
BELVEDERES
BELYING
BEMA
BEMAD
BEMADDED
BEMADDING
BEMADS
BEMAS
BEMATA
BEMAUL
BEMAULED
BEMAULING
BEMAULS
BEMAZED
BEMBEX
BEMBEXES
BEMBIX
BEMBIXES
BEMEAN
BEMEANED
BEMEANING
BEMEANS
BEMEANT
BEMEDAL
BEMEDALLED
BEMEDALLING
BEMEDALS
BEMETE
BEMETED
BEMETES
BEMETING
BEMIRE
BEMIRED
BEMIRES
BEMIRING
BEMOAN
BEMOANED
BEMOANER
BEMOANERS
BEMOANING
BEMOANINGS
BEMOANS
BEMOCK
BEMOCKED
BEMOCKING
BEMOCKS
BEMOIL
BEMOILED
BEMOILING
BEMOILS
BEMONSTER
BEMONSTERED
BEMONSTERING
BEMONSTERS
BEMOUTH
BEMOUTHED
BEMOUTHING
BEMOUTHS
BEMUD
BEMUDDED
BEMUDDING
BEMUDDLE
BEMUDDLED
BEMUDDLES
BEMUDDLING
BEMUDS
BEMUFFLE
BEMUFFLED
BEMUFFLES
BEMUFFLING
BEMUSE
BEMUSED
BEMUSES
BEMUSING
BEN
BENAME
BENAMED
BENAMES
BENAMING
BENCH
BENCHED
BENCHER
BENCHERS
BENCHES
BENCHING
BENCHMARK
BENCHMARKS
BEND
BENDED
BENDEE
BENDER
BENDERS
BENDIER
BENDIEST
BENDING
BENDINGLY
BENDINGS
BENDLET
BENDLETS
BENDS
BENDWISE
BENDY
BENE
BENEATH
BENEDICT
BENEDIGHT
BENEFACT
BENEFACTED
BENEFACTING
BENEFACTS
BENEFIC
BENEFICE
BENEFICED
BENEFICES
BENEFIT
BENEFITED
BENEFITING
BENEFITS
BENEFITTED
BENEFITTING
BENEMPT
BENES
BENET
BENETS
BENETTED
BENETTING
BENGALINE
BENGALINES
BENI
BENIGHT
BENIGHTED
BENIGHTEN
BENIGHTENED
BENIGHTENING
BENIGHTENINGS
BENIGHTENS
BENIGHTER
BENIGHTERS
BENIGHTING
BENIGHTINGS
BENIGHTS
BENIGN
BENIGNANT
BENIGNER
BENIGNEST
BENIGNITIES
BENIGNITY
BENIGNLY

BENIS
BENISEED
BENISEEDS
BENISON
BENISONS
BENITIER
BENITIERS
BENJ
BENJAMIN
BENJAMINS
BENJES
BENNE
BENNES
BENNET
BENNETS
BENNI
BENNIES
BENNIS
BENNY
BENS
BENT
BENTHIC
BENTHOAL
BENTHONIC
BENTHOS
BENTHOSES
BENTIER
BENTIEST
BENTONITE
BENTONITES
BENTS
BENTWOOD
BENTWOODS
BENTY
BENUMB
BENUMBED
BENUMBING
BENUMBS
BENZAL
BENZALS
BENZENE
BENZENES
BENZIDINE
BENZIDINES
BENZIL
BENZILS
BENZINE
BENZINES
BENZOATE
BENZOATES
BENZOIC
BENZOIN
BENZOINS
BENZOL
BENZOLE
BENZOLES
BENZOLINE
BENZOLINES
BENZOLS
BENZOYL
BENZOYLS
BENZYL
BENZYLS
BEPAINT
BEPAINTED
BEPAINTING
BEPAINTS
BEPAT
BEPATCHED
BEPATS
BEPATTED
BEPATTING
BEPEARL
BEPEARLED
BEPEARLING
BEPEARLS
BEPELT
BEPELTED
BEPELTING
BEPELTS
BEPEPPER
BEPEPPERED
BEPEPPERING
BEPEPPERS
BEPESTER
BEPESTERED
BEPESTERING
BEPESTERS
BEPITIED
BEPITIES
BEPITY
BEPITYING
BEPLASTER
BEPLASTERED
BEPLASTERING
BEPLASTERS
BEPLUMED
BEPOMMEL
BEPOMMELLED
BEPOMMELLING
BEPOMMELS
BEPOWDER
BEPOWDERED
BEPOWDERING
BEPOWDERS
BEPRAISE
BEPRAISED
BEPRAISES
BEPRAISING
BEPROSE
BEPROSED
BEPROSES
BEPROSING
BEPUFF
BEPUFFED
BEPUFFING
BEPUFFS
BEQUEATH
BEQUEATHED
BEQUEATHING
BEQUEATHS
BEQUEST
BEQUESTS
BERATE
BERATED
BERATES
BERATING
BERAY
BERAYED
BERAYING
BERAYS
BERBERINE
BERBERINES
BERBERIS
BERBERISES
BERCEAU
BERCEAUX
BERCEUSE
BERCEUSES
BERDACHE
BERDACHES
BERDASH
BERDASHES
BERE
BEREAVE
BEREAVED
BEREAVEN
BEREAVES
BEREAVING
BEREFT
BERES
BERET
BERETS
BERG
BERGAMA
BERGAMAS
BERGAMASK
BERGAMASKS
BERGAMOT
BERGAMOTS
BERGANDER
BERGANDERS
BERGENIA
BERGENIAS
BERGERE
BERGERES
BERGFALL
BERGFALLS
BERGHAAN
BERGHAANS
BERGMEHL
BERGMEHLS
BERGOMASK
BERGOMASKS
BERGS
BERGYLT
BERGYLTS
BERIBERI
BERIBERIS
BERK
BERKELIUM
BERKELIUMS
BERKS
BERLEY
BERLEYS
BERLIN
BERLINE
BERLINES
BERLINS
BERM
BERMS
BEROB
BEROBBED
BEROBBING
BEROBS
BERRET
BERRETS
BERRIED
BERRIES
BERRY
BERRYING
BERRYINGS
BERSERK
BERSERKER
BERSERKERS
BERSERKLY
BERSERKS
BERTH
BERTHA
BERTHAGE
BERTHAGES
BERTHAS
BERTHE
BERTHED
BERTHES
BERTHING
BERTHS
BERYL
BERYLLIA
BERYLLIAS
BERYLLIUM
BERYLLIUMS
BERYLS
BESAINT
BESAINTED
BESAINTING
BESAINTS
BESANG
BESAT
BESAW
BESCATTER
BESCATTERED
BESCATTERING
BESCATTERS
BESCRAWL
BESCRAWLED
BESCRAWLING
BESCRAWLS
BESCREEN
BESCREENED
BESCREENING
BESCREENS
BESEE
BESEECH
BESEECHED
BESEECHER
BESEECHERS
BESEECHES
BESEECHING
BESEECHINGS
BESEEING
BESEEKE
BESEEKES
BESEEKING
BESEEM
BESEEMED
BESEEMING
BESEEMINGS
BESEEMLY
BESEEMS
BESEEN
BESEES
BESET
BESETMENT
BESETMENTS
BESETS
BESETTER
BESETTERS
BESETTING
BESHADOW
BESHADOWED
BESHADOWING
BESHADOWS
BESHAME
BESHAMED
BESHAMES
BESHAMING
BESHINE
BESHINES
BESHINING
BESHONE
BESHREW
BESHREWED
BESHREWING
BESHREWS
BESIDE
BESIDES
BESIEGE
BESIEGED
BESIEGER
BESIEGERS
BESIEGES
BESIEGING
BESIEGINGS
BESIGH
BESIGHED
BESIGHING
BESIGHS
BESING
BESINGING
BESINGS
BESIT
BESITS
BESITTING
BESLAVE
BESLAVED
BESLAVER
BESLAVERED
BESLAVERING
BESLAVERS
BESLAVES
BESLAVING
BESLOBBER
BESLOBBERED
BESLOBBERING
BESLOBBERS
BESLUBBER
BESLUBBERED
BESLUBBERING
BESLUBBERS

The Chambers Dictionary is the authority for many longer words; see *OSW* Introduction, page xii

BESMEAR
BESMEARED
BESMEARING
BESMEARS
BESMIRCH
BESMIRCHED
BESMIRCHES
BESMIRCHING
BESMUT
BESMUTCH
BESMUTCHED
BESMUTCHES
BESMUTCHING
BESMUTS
BESMUTTED
BESMUTTING
BESOGNIO
BESOGNIOS
BESOIN
BESOINS
BESOM
BESOMED
BESOMING
BESOMS
BESONIAN
BESONIANS
BESORT
BESORTED
BESORTING
BESORTS
BESOT
BESOTS
BESOTTED
BESOTTING
BESOUGHT
BESOULED
BESPAKE
BESPANGLE
BESPANGLED
BESPANGLES
BESPANGLING
BESPAT
BESPATE
BESPATTER
BESPATTERED
BESPATTERING
BESPATTERS
BESPEAK
BESPEAKING
BESPEAKS
BESPECKLE
BESPECKLED
BESPECKLES
BESPECKLING
BESPED
BESPEED
BESPEEDING
BESPEEDS
BESPICE
BESPICED
BESPICES
BESPICING
BESPIT
BESPITS
BESPITTING
BESPOKE
BESPOKEN
BESPORT
BESPORTED
BESPORTING
BESPORTS
BESPOT
BESPOTS
BESPOTTED
BESPOTTING
BESPOUT
BESPOUTED
BESPOUTING
BESPOUTS
BESPREAD
BESPREADING
BESPREADS
BESPRENT
BEST
BESTAD
BESTADDE
BESTAIN
BESTAINED
BESTAINING
BESTAINS
BESTAR
BESTARRED
BESTARRING
BESTARS
BESTEAD
BESTEADED
BESTEADING
BESTEADS
BESTED
BESTIAL
BESTIALS
BESTIARIES
BESTIARY
BESTICK
BESTICKING
BESTICKS
BESTILL
BESTILLED
BESTILLING
BESTILLS
BESTING
BESTIR
BESTIRRED
BESTIRRING
BESTIRS
BESTORM
BESTORMED
BESTORMING
BESTORMS
BESTOW
BESTOWAL
BESTOWALS
BESTOWED
BESTOWER
BESTOWERS
BESTOWING
BESTOWS
BESTREAK
BESTREAKED
BESTREAKING
BESTREAKS
BESTREW
BESTREWED
BESTREWING
BESTREWN
BESTREWS
BESTRID
BESTRIDDEN
BESTRIDE
BESTRIDES
BESTRIDING
BESTRODE
BESTROWN
BESTS
BESTUCK
BESTUD
BESTUDDED
BESTUDDING
BESTUDS
BESUITED
BESUNG
BET
BETA
BETACISM
BETACISMS
BETAINE
BETAINES
BETAKE
BETAKEN
BETAKES
BETAKING
BETAS
BETATRON
BETATRONS
BETE
BETED
BETEEM
BETEEME
BETEEMED
BETEEMES
BETEEMING
BETEEMS
BETEL
BETELS
BETES
BETH
BETHANKIT
BETHANKITS
BETHEL
BETHELS
BETHESDA
BETHESDAS
BETHINK
BETHINKING
BETHINKS
BETHOUGHT
BETHRALL
BETHRALLED
BETHRALLING
BETHRALLS
BETHS
BETHUMB
BETHUMBED
BETHUMBING
BETHUMBS
BETHUMP
BETHUMPED
BETHUMPING
BETHUMPS
BETHWACK
BETHWACKED
BETHWACKING
BETHWACKS
BETID
BETIDE
BETIDED
BETIDES
BETIDING
BETIGHT
BETIME
BETIMED
BETIMES
BETIMING
BETING
BETISE
BETISES
BETITLE
BETITLED
BETITLES
BETITLING
BETOIL
BETOILED
BETOILING
BETOILS
BETOKEN
BETOKENED
BETOKENING
BETOKENS
BETON
BETONIES
BETONS
BETONY
BETOOK
BETOSS
BETOSSED
BETOSSES
BETOSSING
BETRAY
BETRAYAL
BETRAYALS
BETRAYED
BETRAYER
BETRAYERS
BETRAYING
BETRAYS
BETREAD
BETREADING
BETREADS
BETRIM
BETRIMMED
BETRIMMING
BETRIMS
BETROD
BETRODDEN
BETROTH
BETROTHAL
BETROTHALS
BETROTHED
BETROTHEDS
BETROTHING
BETROTHS
BETS
BETTED
BETTER
BETTERED
BETTERING
BETTERINGS
BETTERS
BETTIES
BETTING
BETTINGS
BETTOR
BETTORS
BETTY
BETUMBLED
BETWEEN
BETWEENS
BETWIXT
BEURRE
BEURRES
BEVATRON
BEVATRONS
BEVEL
BEVELLED
BEVELLER
BEVELLERS
BEVELLING
BEVELLINGS
BEVELMENT
BEVELMENTS
BEVELS
BEVER
BEVERAGE
BEVERAGES
BEVERS
BEVIES
BEVUE
BEVUES
BEVVIED
BEVVIES
BEVVY
BEVY
BEWAIL
BEWAILED
BEWAILING
BEWAILINGS
BEWAILS
BEWARE
BEWARED
BEWARES
BEWARING
BEWEEP
BEWEEPING
BEWEEPS
BEWENT
BEWEPT
BEWET
BEWETS
BEWETTED
BEWETTING

BEWHORE
BEWHORED
BEWHORES
BEWHORING
BEWIG
BEWIGGED
BEWIGGING
BEWIGS
BEWILDER
BEWILDERED
BEWILDERING
BEWILDERS
BEWITCH
BEWITCHED
BEWITCHES
BEWITCHING
BEWRAY
BEWRAYED
BEWRAYING
BEWRAYS
BEY
BEYOND
BEYONDS
BEYS
BEZ
BEZANT
BEZANTS
BEZAZZ
BEZAZZES
BEZEL
BEZELS
BEZES
BEZIQUE
BEZIQUES
BEZOAR
BEZOARDIC
BEZOARS
BEZONIAN
BEZONIANS
BEZZLE
BEZZLED
BEZZLES
BEZZLING
BHAGEE
BHAGEES
BHAJAN
BHAJANS
BHAJEE
BHAJEES
BHAKTI
BHAKTIS
BHANG
BHANGRA
BHANGRAS
BHANGS
BHARAL
BHARALS
BHEESTIE
BHEESTIES
BHEESTY
BHEL
BHELS
BHINDI
BHINDIS
BHISTEE
BHISTEES
BHISTI
BHISTIS
BI
BIANNUAL
BIANNUALS
BIAS
BIASED
BIASES
BIASING
BIASINGS
BIASSED
BIASSES
BIASSING
BIATHLETE
BIATHLETES
BIATHLON
BIATHLONS
BIAXAL
BIAXIAL
BIB
BIBACIOUS
BIBATION
BIBATIONS
BIBBED
BIBBER
BIBBERS
BIBBING
BIBCOCK
BIBCOCKS
BIBELOT
BIBELOTS
BIBLE
BIBLES
BIBLICAL
BIBLICISM
BIBLICISMS
BIBLICIST
BIBLICISTS
BIBLIST
BIBLISTS
BIBS
BIBULOUS
BICAMERAL
BICARB
BICARBS
BICCIES
BICCY
BICE
BICEPS
BICEPSES
BICES
BICHORD
BICIPITAL
BICKER
BICKERED
BICKERING
BICKERS
BICOASTAL
BICONCAVE
BICONVEX
BICORN
BICORNE
BICORNES
BICORNS
BICUSPID
BICUSPIDS
BICYCLE
BICYCLED
BICYCLES
BICYCLING
BICYCLIST
BICYCLISTS
BID
BIDARKA
BIDARKAS
BIDDABLE
BIDDEN
BIDDER
BIDDERS
BIDDIES
BIDDING
BIDDINGS
BIDDY
BIDE
BIDED
BIDENT
BIDENTAL
BIDENTALS
BIDENTATE
BIDENTS
BIDES
BIDET
BIDETS
BIDING
BIDINGS
BIDON
BIDONS
BIDS
BIELD
BIELDED
BIELDIER
BIELDIEST
BIELDING
BIELDS
BIELDY
BIEN
BIENNIAL
BIENNIALS
BIER
BIERS
BIESTINGS
BIFACIAL
BIFARIOUS
BIFF
BIFFED
BIFFIN
BIFFING
BIFFINS
BIFFS
BIFID
BIFILAR
BIFOCAL
BIFOCALS
BIFOLD
BIFOLIATE
BIFORM
BIFURCATE
BIFURCATED
BIFURCATES
BIFURCATING
BIG
BIGA
BIGAE
BIGAMIES
BIGAMIST
BIGAMISTS
BIGAMOUS
BIGAMY
BIGARADE
BIGARADES
BIGENER
BIGENERIC
BIGENERS
BIGFEET
BIGFOOT
BIGG
BIGGED
BIGGER
BIGGEST
BIGGIE
BIGGIES
BIGGIN
BIGGING
BIGGINS
BIGGISH
BIGGS
BIGGY
BIGHA
BIGHAS
BIGHEADED
BIGHORN
BIGHORNS
BIGHT
BIGHTS
BIGMOUTH
BIGMOUTHS
BIGNESS
BIGNESSES
BIGNONIA
BIGNONIAS
BIGOT
BIGOTED
BIGOTRIES
BIGOTRY
BIGOTS
BIGS
BIGUANIDE
BIGUANIDES
BIGWIG
BIGWIGS
BIJECTION
BIJECTIONS
BIJOU
BIJOUX
BIJWONER
BIJWONERS
BIKE
BIKED
BIKER
BIKERS
BIKES
BIKEWAY
BIKEWAYS
BIKIE
BIKIES
BIKING
BIKINGS
BIKINI
BIKINIS
BILABIAL
BILABIALS
BILABIATE
BILANDER
BILANDERS
BILATERAL
BILBERRIES
BILBERRY
BILBO
BILBOES
BILBOS
BILE
BILES
BILGE
BILGED
BILGES
BILGIER
BILGIEST
BILGING
BILGY
BILHARZIA
BILHARZIAS
BILIAN
BILIANS
BILIARIES
BILIARY
BILIMBI
BILIMBING
BILIMBINGS
BILIMBIS
BILINGUAL
BILIOUS
BILIOUSLY
BILIRUBIN
BILIRUBINS
BILITERAL
BILK
BILKED
BILKER
BILKERS
BILKING
BILKS
BILL
BILLABONG
BILLABONGS
BILLBOARD
BILLBOARDS
BILLBOOK
BILLBOOKS
BILLED
BILLET
BILLETED
BILLETING
BILLETS
BILLFOLD

BILLFOLDS
BILLHEAD
BILLHEADS
BILLHOOK
BILLHOOKS
BILLIARD
BILLIARDS
BILLIE
BILLIES
BILLING
BILLINGS
BILLION
BILLIONS
BILLIONTH
BILLIONTHS
BILLMAN
BILLMEN
BILLON
BILLONS
BILLOW
BILLOWED
BILLOWIER
BILLOWIEST
BILLOWING
BILLOWS
BILLOWY
BILLS
BILLY
BILLYBOY
BILLYBOYS
BILLYCOCK
BILLYCOCKS
BILOBAR
BILOBATE
BILOBED
BILOBULAR
BILOCULAR
BILTONG
BILTONGS
BIMANAL
BIMANOUS
BIMANUAL
BIMBASHI
BIMBASHIS
BIMBETTE
BIMBETTES
BIMBO
BIMBOS
BIMODAL
BIMONTHLY
BIN
BINARIES
BINARY
BINATE
BINAURAL
BIND
BINDER
BINDERIES
BINDERS
BINDERY
BINDING
BINDINGS
BINDS
BINDWEED
BINDWEEDS
BINE
BINERVATE
BINES
BING
BINGE
BINGED
BINGEING
BINGER
BINGERS
BINGES
BINGHI
BINGHIS
BINGIES
BINGING
BINGLE
BINGLED
BINGLES
BINGLING
BINGO
BINGOS
BINGS
BINGY
BINK
BINKS
BINMAN
BINMEN
BINNACLE
BINNACLES
BINNED
BINNING
BINOCLE
BINOCLES
BINOCULAR
BINOCULARS
BINOMIAL
BINOMIALS
BINOMINAL
BINS
BINT
BINTS
BINTURONG
BINTURONGS
BIO
BIOASSAY
BIOASSAYS
BIOBLAST
BIOBLASTS
BIOCIDAL
BIOCIDE
BIOCIDES
BIODATA
BIOETHICS
BIOG
BIOGAS
BIOGASES
BIOGEN
BIOGENIC
BIOGENIES
BIOGENOUS
BIOGENS
BIOGENY
BIOGRAPH
BIOGRAPHED
BIOGRAPHIES
BIOGRAPHING
BIOGRAPHS
BIOGRAPHY
BIOGS
BIOHAZARD
BIOHAZARDS
BIOLOGIES
BIOLOGIST
BIOLOGISTS
BIOLOGY
BIOLYSES
BIOLYSIS
BIOMASS
BIOMASSES
BIOME
BIOMES
BIOMETRIC
BIOMETRICS
BIOMETRIES
BIOMETRY
BIOMINING
BIOMININGS
BIOMORPH
BIOMORPHS
BIONIC
BIONICS
BIONOMIC
BIONOMICS
BIONT
BIONTIC
BIONTS
BIOPARENT
BIOPARENTS
BIOPHOR
BIOPHORE
BIOPHORES
BIOPHORS
BIOPIC
BIOPICS
BIOPLASM
BIOPLASMS
BIOPLAST
BIOPLASTS
BIOPSIES
BIOPSY
BIOS
BIOSCOPE
BIOSCOPES
BIOSENSOR
BIOSENSORS
BIOSPHERE
BIOSPHERES
BIOSTABLE
BIOTA
BIOTAS
BIOTIC
BIOTIN
BIOTINS
BIOTITE
BIOTITES
BIOTOPE
BIOTOPES
BIOTYPE
BIOTYPES
BIPAROUS
BIPARTITE
BIPED
BIPEDAL
BIPEDS
BIPHASIC
BIPHENYL
BIPHENYLS
BIPINNATE
BIPLANE
BIPLANES
BIPOD
BIPODS
BIPOLAR
BIPYRAMID
BIPYRAMIDS
BIRAMOUS
BIRCH
BIRCHED
BIRCHEN
BIRCHES
BIRCHING
BIRD
BIRDBATH
BIRDBATHS
BIRDCAGE
BIRDCAGES
BIRDCALL
BIRDCALLS
BIRDED
BIRDER
BIRDERS
BIRDIE
BIRDIED
BIRDIEING
BIRDIES
BIRDING
BIRDINGS
BIRDLIKE
BIRDMAN
BIRDMEN
BIRDS
BIRDSEED
BIRDSEEDS
BIRDSHOT
BIRDSHOTS
BIRDSONG
BIRDSONGS
BIRDWING
BIRDWINGS
BIREME
BIREMES
BIRETTA
BIRETTAS
BIRIYANI
BIRIYANIS
BIRK
BIRKEN
BIRKIE
BIRKIER
BIRKIES
BIRKIEST
BIRKS
BIRL
BIRLE
BIRLED
BIRLER
BIRLERS
BIRLES
BIRLIEMAN
BIRLIEMEN
BIRLING
BIRLINGS
BIRLINN
BIRLINNS
BIRLS
BIRR
BIRRED
BIRRING
BIRRS
BIRSE
BIRSES
BIRSIER
BIRSIEST
BIRSLE
BIRSLED
BIRSLES
BIRSLING
BIRSY
BIRTH
BIRTHDAY
BIRTHDAYS
BIRTHDOM
BIRTHDOMS
BIRTHED
BIRTHING
BIRTHINGS
BIRTHMARK
BIRTHMARKS
BIRTHS
BIRTHWORT
BIRTHWORTS
BIRYANI
BIRYANIS
BIS
BISCACHA
BISCACHAS
BISCUIT
BISCUITS
BISCUITY
BISE
BISECT
BISECTED
BISECTING
BISECTION
BISECTIONS
BISECTOR
BISECTORS
BISECTS
BISERIAL
BISERRATE
BISES
BISEXUAL
BISEXUALS
BISH
BISHES
BISHOP

BISHOPDOM
BISHOPDOMS
BISHOPED
BISHOPESS
BISHOPESSES
BISHOPING
BISHOPRIC
BISHOPRICS
BISHOPS
BISK
BISKS
BISMAR
BISMARS
BISMILLAH
BISMUTH
BISMUTHS
BISON
BISONS
BISQUE
BISQUES
BISSON
BISTABLE
BISTER
BISTERS
BISTORT
BISTORTS
BISTOURIES
BISTOURY
BISTRE
BISTRED
BISTRES
BISTRO
BISTROS
BISULCATE
BIT
BITCH
BITCHED
BITCHERIES
BITCHERY
BITCHES
BITCHIER
BITCHIEST
BITCHILY
BITCHING
BITCHY
BITE
BITER
BITERS
BITES
BITESIZE
BITING
BITINGS
BITLESS
BITMAP
BITMAPS
BITO
BITONAL
BITOS
BITS
BITSIER
BITSIEST
BITSY
BITT
BITTACLE
BITTACLES
BITTE
BITTED
BITTEN
BITTER
BITTERER
BITTEREST
BITTERISH
BITTERLY
BITTERN
BITTERNS
BITTERS
BITTIE
BITTIER
BITTIES
BITTIEST
BITTING
BITTOCK
BITTOCKS
BITTOR
BITTORS
BITTOUR
BITTOURS
BITTS
BITTUR
BITTURS
BITTY
BITUMED
BITUMEN
BITUMENS
BIVALENCE
BIVALENCES
BIVALENCIES
BIVALENCY
BIVALENT
BIVALENTS
BIVALVE
BIVALVES
BIVARIANT
BIVARIANTS
BIVARIATE
BIVARIATES
BIVIA
BIVIOUS
BIVIUM
BIVOUAC
BIVOUACKED
BIVOUACKING
BIVOUACS
BIVVIED
BIVVIES
BIVVY
BIVVYING
BIZ
BIZARRE
BIZAZZ
BIZAZZES
BIZCACHA
BIZCACHAS
BIZONAL
BIZONE
BIZONES
BIZZES
BLAB
BLABBED
BLABBER
BLABBERS
BLABBING
BLABBINGS
BLABS
BLACK
BLACKBALL
BLACKBALLED
BLACKBALLING
BLACKBALLINGS
BLACKBALLS
BLACKBAND
BLACKBANDS
BLACKBIRD
BLACKBIRDS
BLACKBOY
BLACKBOYS
BLACKBUCK
BLACKBUCKS
BLACKCAP
BLACKCAPS
BLACKCOCK
BLACKCOCKS
BLACKED
BLACKEN
BLACKENED
BLACKENING
BLACKENS
BLACKER
BLACKEST
BLACKFACE
BLACKFACES
BLACKFISH
BLACKFISHES
BLACKGAME
BLACKGAMES
BLACKHEAD
BLACKHEADS
BLACKING
BLACKINGS
BLACKISH
BLACKJACK
BLACKJACKED
BLACKJACKING
BLACKJACKS
BLACKLEAD
BLACKLEADS
BLACKLEG
BLACKLEGGED
BLACKLEGGING
BLACKLEGS
BLACKLIST
BLACKLISTED
BLACKLISTING
BLACKLISTINGS
BLACKLISTS
BLACKLY
BLACKMAIL
BLACKMAILED
BLACKMAILING
BLACKMAILS
BLACKNESS
BLACKNESSES
BLACKOUT
BLACKOUTS
BLACKS
BLACKTOP
BLACKTOPS
BLACKWASH
BLACKWASHES
BLACKWOOD
BLACKWOODS
BLAD
BLADDED
BLADDER
BLADDERED
BLADDERS
BLADDERY
BLADDING
BLADE
BLADED
BLADES
BLADEWORK
BLADEWORKS
BLADS
BLAE
BLAEBERRIES
BLAEBERRY
BLAER
BLAES
BLAEST
BLAG
BLAGGED
BLAGGER
BLAGGERS
BLAGGING
BLAGS
BLAGUE
BLAGUES
BLAGUEUR
BLAGUEURS
BLAH
BLAHED
BLAHING
BLAHS
BLAIN
BLAINS
BLAISE
BLAIZE
BLAMABLE
BLAMABLY
BLAME
BLAMEABLE
BLAMEABLY
BLAMED
BLAMEFUL
BLAMELESS
BLAMES
BLAMING
BLANCH
BLANCHED
BLANCHES
BLANCHING
BLANCO
BLANCOED
BLANCOING
BLANCOS
BLAND
BLANDER
BLANDEST
BLANDISH
BLANDISHED
BLANDISHES
BLANDISHING
BLANDLY
BLANDNESS
BLANDNESSES
BLANDS
BLANK
BLANKED
BLANKER
BLANKEST
BLANKET
BLANKETED
BLANKETIES
BLANKETING
BLANKETINGS
BLANKETS
BLANKETY
BLANKIES
BLANKING
BLANKINGS
BLANKLY
BLANKNESS
BLANKNESSES
BLANKS
BLANKY
BLANQUET
BLANQUETS
BLARE
BLARED
BLARES
BLARING
BLARNEY
BLARNEYED
BLARNEYING
BLARNEYS
BLASE
BLASH
BLASHES
BLASHIER
BLASHIEST
BLASHY
BLASPHEME
BLASPHEMED
BLASPHEMES
BLASPHEMIES
BLASPHEMING
BLASPHEMY
BLAST
BLASTED
BLASTEMA
BLASTEMAS
BLASTEMATA
BLASTER
BLASTERS
BLASTING
BLASTINGS
BLASTMENT
BLASTMENTS
BLASTOID

BLASTOIDS
BLASTS
BLASTULA
BLASTULAE
BLASTULAR
BLASTULAS
BLAT
BLATANT
BLATANTLY
BLATE
BLATER
BLATEST
BLATHER
BLATHERED
BLATHERER
BLATHERERS
BLATHERING
BLATHERS
BLATS
BLATT
BLATTANT
BLATTED
BLATTER
BLATTERED
BLATTERING
BLATTERS
BLATTING
BLATTS
BLAUBOK
BLAUBOKS
BLAUD
BLAUDED
BLAUDING
BLAUDS
BLAWORT
BLAWORTS
BLAY
BLAYS
BLAZE
BLAZED
BLAZER
BLAZERED
BLAZERS
BLAZES
BLAZING
BLAZON
BLAZONED
BLAZONER
BLAZONERS
BLAZONING
BLAZONRIES
BLAZONRY
BLAZONS
BLEACH
BLEACHED
BLEACHER
BLEACHERIES
BLEACHERS
BLEACHERY
BLEACHES
BLEACHING
BLEACHINGS
BLEAK
BLEAKER
BLEAKEST
BLEAKLY
BLEAKNESS
BLEAKNESSES
BLEAKS
BLEAKY
BLEAR
BLEARED
BLEARER
BLEAREST
BLEAREYED
BLEARIER
BLEARIEST
BLEARILY
BLEARING
BLEARS
BLEARY
BLEAT
BLEATED
BLEATER
BLEATERS
BLEATING
BLEATINGS
BLEATS
BLEB
BLEBS
BLED
BLEE
BLEED
BLEEDER
BLEEDERS
BLEEDING
BLEEDINGS
BLEEDS
BLEEP
BLEEPED
BLEEPER
BLEEPERS
BLEEPING
BLEEPS
BLEES
BLEMISH
BLEMISHED
BLEMISHES
BLEMISHING
BLENCH
BLENCHED
BLENCHES
BLENCHING
BLEND
BLENDE
BLENDED
BLENDER
BLENDERS
BLENDES
BLENDING
BLENDINGS
BLENDS
BLENNIES
BLENNY
BLENT
BLESBOK
BLESBOKS
BLESS
BLESSED
BLESSEDER
BLESSEDEST
BLESSEDLY
BLESSES
BLESSING
BLESSINGS
BLEST
BLET
BLETHER
BLETHERED
BLETHERER
BLETHERERS
BLETHERING
BLETHERINGS
BLETHERS
BLETS
BLETTED
BLETTING
BLEUATRE
BLEW
BLEWART
BLEWARTS
BLEWITS
BLEWITSES
BLEY
BLEYS
BLIGHT
BLIGHTED
BLIGHTER
BLIGHTERS
BLIGHTIES
BLIGHTING
BLIGHTINGS
BLIGHTS
BLIGHTY
BLIMBING
BLIMBINGS
BLIMEY
BLIMP
BLIMPISH
BLIMPS
BLIMY
BLIN
BLIND
BLINDAGE
BLINDAGES
BLINDED
BLINDER
BLINDERS
BLINDEST
BLINDFISH
BLINDFISHES
BLINDFOLD
BLINDFOLDED
BLINDFOLDING
BLINDFOLDS
BLINDING
BLINDINGS
BLINDLESS
BLINDLY
BLINDNESS
BLINDNESSES
BLINDS
BLINDWORM
BLINDWORMS
BLINI
BLINIS
BLINK
BLINKARD
BLINKARDS
BLINKED
BLINKER
BLINKERED
BLINKERING
BLINKERS
BLINKING
BLINKS
BLINNED
BLINNING
BLINS
BLINTZ
BLINTZE
BLINTZES
BLIP
BLIPPED
BLIPPING
BLIPS
BLISS
BLISSES
BLISSFUL
BLISSLESS
BLIST
BLISTER
BLISTERED
BLISTERIER
BLISTERIEST
BLISTERING
BLISTERS
BLISTERY
BLITE
BLITES
BLITHE
BLITHELY
BLITHER
BLITHERED
BLITHERING
BLITHERS
BLITHEST
BLITZ
BLITZED
BLITZES
BLITZING
BLIVE
BLIZZARD
BLIZZARDS
BLIZZARDY
BLOAT
BLOATED
BLOATER
BLOATERS
BLOATING
BLOATINGS
BLOATS
BLOATWARE
BLOATWARES
BLOB
BLOBBED
BLOBBING
BLOBS
BLOC
BLOCK
BLOCKADE
BLOCKADED
BLOCKADES
BLOCKADING
BLOCKAGE
BLOCKAGES
BLOCKED
BLOCKER
BLOCKERS
BLOCKHEAD
BLOCKHEADS
BLOCKHOLE
BLOCKHOLES
BLOCKIER
BLOCKIEST
BLOCKING
BLOCKINGS
BLOCKISH
BLOCKS
BLOCKWORK
BLOCKWORKS
BLOCKY
BLOCS
BLOKE
BLOKEDOM
BLOKEDOMS
BLOKEISH
BLOKES
BLOKEY
BLOKIER
BLOKIEST
BLONCKET
BLOND
BLONDE
BLONDER
BLONDES
BLONDEST
BLONDS
BLOOD
BLOODED
BLOODHEAT
BLOODHEATS
BLOODIED
BLOODIER
BLOODIES
BLOODIEST
BLOODILY
BLOODING
BLOODLESS
BLOODLUST
BLOODLUSTS
BLOODROOT
BLOODROOTS
BLOODS
BLOODSHED
BLOODSHEDS
BLOODSHOT
BLOODWOOD
BLOODWOODS
BLOODY

BLOODYING
BLOOM
BLOOMED
BLOOMER
BLOOMERIES
BLOOMERS
BLOOMERY
BLOOMIER
BLOOMIEST
BLOOMING
BLOOMLESS
BLOOMS
BLOOMY
BLOOP
BLOOPED
BLOOPER
BLOOPERS
BLOOPING
BLOOPS
BLOOSME
BLOOSMED
BLOOSMES
BLOOSMING
BLORE
BLORES
BLOSSOM
BLOSSOMED
BLOSSOMING
BLOSSOMINGS
BLOSSOMS
BLOSSOMY
BLOT
BLOTCH
BLOTCHED
BLOTCHES
BLOTCHIER
BLOTCHIEST
BLOTCHING
BLOTCHINGS
BLOTCHY
BLOTS
BLOTTED
BLOTTER
BLOTTERS
BLOTTIER
BLOTTIEST
BLOTTING
BLOTTINGS
BLOTTO
BLOTTY
BLOUBOK
BLOUBOKS
BLOUSE
BLOUSED
BLOUSES
BLOUSING
BLOUSON
BLOUSONS
BLOW
BLOWBALL
BLOWBALLS
BLOWDOWN
BLOWDOWNS
BLOWED
BLOWER
BLOWERS
BLOWFISH
BLOWFISHES
BLOWFLIES
BLOWFLY
BLOWGUN
BLOWGUNS
BLOWHARD
BLOWHARDS
BLOWHOLE
BLOWHOLES
BLOWIE
BLOWIER
BLOWIES
BLOWIEST
BLOWING
BLOWJOB
BLOWJOBS
BLOWLAMP
BLOWLAMPS
BLOWN
BLOWPIPE
BLOWPIPES
BLOWS
BLOWSE
BLOWSED
BLOWSES
BLOWSIER
BLOWSIEST
BLOWSY
BLOWTORCH
BLOWTORCHES
BLOWY
BLOWZE
BLOWZED
BLOWZES
BLOWZIER
BLOWZIEST
BLOWZY
BLUB
BLUBBED
BLUBBER
BLUBBERED
BLUBBERING
BLUBBERS
BLUBBING
BLUBS
BLUCHER
BLUCHERS
BLUDE
BLUDES
BLUDGE
BLUDGED
BLUDGEON
BLUDGEONED
BLUDGEONING
BLUDGEONS
BLUDGER
BLUDGERS
BLUDGES
BLUDGING
BLUDIE
BLUDIER
BLUDIEST
BLUDY
BLUE
BLUEBACK
BLUEBACKS
BLUEBEARD
BLUEBEARDS
BLUEBELL
BLUEBELLS
BLUEBERRIES
BLUEBERRY
BLUEBIRD
BLUEBIRDS
BLUEBUCK
BLUEBUCKS
BLUECAP
BLUECAPS
BLUECOAT
BLUECOATS
BLUED
BLUEFISH
BLUEFISHES
BLUEGOWN
BLUEGOWNS
BLUEGRASS
BLUEGRASSES
BLUEING
BLUEINGS
BLUELY
BLUENESS
BLUENESSES
BLUENOSE
BLUENOSES
BLUEPRINT
BLUEPRINTED
BLUEPRINTING
BLUEPRINTS
BLUER
BLUES
BLUESIER
BLUESIEST
BLUEST
BLUESTONE
BLUESTONES
BLUESY
BLUETTE
BLUETTES
BLUEWEED
BLUEWEEDS
BLUEWING
BLUEWINGS
BLUEY
BLUEYS
BLUFF
BLUFFED
BLUFFER
BLUFFERS
BLUFFEST
BLUFFING
BLUFFLY
BLUFFNESS
BLUFFNESSES
BLUFFS
BLUGGIER
BLUGGIEST
BLUGGY
BLUID
BLUIDIER
BLUIDIEST
BLUIDS
BLUIDY
BLUIER
BLUIEST
BLUING
BLUINGS
BLUISH
BLUNDER
BLUNDERED
BLUNDERER
BLUNDERERS
BLUNDERING
BLUNDERINGS
BLUNDERS
BLUNGE
BLUNGED
BLUNGER
BLUNGERS
BLUNGES
BLUNGING
BLUNK
BLUNKED
BLUNKER
BLUNKERS
BLUNKING
BLUNKS
BLUNT
BLUNTED
BLUNTER
BLUNTEST
BLUNTING
BLUNTISH
BLUNTLY
BLUNTNESS
BLUNTNESSES
BLUNTS
BLUR
BLURB
BLURBED
BLURBING
BLURBS
BLURRED
BLURRING
BLURS
BLURT
BLURTED
BLURTING
BLURTINGS
BLURTS
BLUSH
BLUSHED
BLUSHER
BLUSHERS
BLUSHES
BLUSHET
BLUSHETS
BLUSHFUL
BLUSHING
BLUSHINGS
BLUSHLESS
BLUSTER
BLUSTERED
BLUSTERER
BLUSTERERS
BLUSTERIER
BLUSTERIEST
BLUSTERING
BLUSTERINGS
BLUSTERS
BLUSTERY
BLUSTROUS
BLUTWURST
BLUTWURSTS
BO
BOA
BOAK
BOAKED
BOAKING
BOAKS
BOAR
BOARD
BOARDED
BOARDER
BOARDERS
BOARDING
BOARDINGS
BOARDROOM
BOARDROOMS
BOARDS
BOARDWALK
BOARDWALKS
BOARFISH
BOARFISHES
BOARISH
BOARS
BOART
BOARTS
BOAS
BOAST
BOASTED
BOASTER
BOASTERS
BOASTFUL
BOASTING
BOASTINGS
BOASTLESS
BOASTS
BOAT
BOATBILL
BOATBILLS
BOATED
BOATEL
BOATELS
BOATER
BOATERS
BOATHOUSE
BOATHOUSES
BOATIE
BOATIES
BOATING
BOATINGS
BOATMAN
BOATMEN

BOATS
BOATSWAIN
BOATSWAINS
BOATTAIL
BOATTAILS
BOB
BOBA
BOBAC
BOBACS
BOBAK
BOBAKS
BOBAS
BOBBED
BOBBERIES
BOBBERY
BOBBIES
BOBBIN
BOBBINET
BOBBINETS
BOBBING
BOBBINS
BOBBISH
BOBBITT
BOBBITTED
BOBBITTING
BOBBITTS
BOBBLE
BOBBLED
BOBBLES
BOBBLIER
BOBBLIEST
BOBBLING
BOBBLY
BOBBY
BOBBYSOCK
BOBBYSOCKS
BOBCAT
BOBCATS
BOBOLINK
BOBOLINKS
BOBS
BOBSLED
BOBSLEDS
BOBSLEIGH
BOBSLEIGHS
BOBSTAYS
BOBTAIL
BOBTAILED
BOBTAILING
BOBTAILS
BOBWHEEL
BOBWHEELS
BOBWIG
BOBWIGS
BOCAGE
BOCAGES
BOCCA
BOCCAS
BOCHE
BOCHES
BOCK
BOCKED
BOCKING
BOCKS
BOD
BODACH
BODACHS
BODACIOUS
BODDLE
BODDLES
BODE
BODED
BODEFUL
BODEGA
BODEGAS
BODEGUERO
BODEGUEROS
BODEMENT
BODEMENTS
BODES
BODGE
BODGED
BODGER
BODGERS
BODGES
BODGIE
BODGIER
BODGIES
BODGIEST
BODGING
BODHRAN
BODHRANS
BODICE
BODICES
BODIED
BODIES
BODIKIN
BODIKINS
BODILESS
BODILY
BODING
BODINGS
BODKIN
BODKINS
BODLE
BODLES
BODRAG
BODRAGS
BODS
BODY
BODYGUARD
BODYGUARDS
BODYING
BODYLINE
BODYLINES
BODYSHELL
BODYSHELLS
BODYSUIT
BODYSUITS
BODYWORK
BODYWORKS
BOEREWORS
BOEREWORSES
BOFF
BOFFED
BOFFIN
BOFFING
BOFFINS
BOFFS
BOG
BOGAN
BOGANS
BOGBEAN
BOGBEANS
BOGEY
BOGEYED
BOGEYING
BOGEYISM
BOGEYISMS
BOGEYS
BOGGARD
BOGGARDS
BOGGART
BOGGARTS
BOGGED
BOGGIER
BOGGIEST
BOGGINESS
BOGGINESSES
BOGGING
BOGGLE
BOGGLED
BOGGLER
BOGGLERS
BOGGLES
BOGGLING
BOGGY
BOGIE
BOGIES
BOGLAND
BOGLANDS
BOGLE
BOGLES
BOGOAK
BOGOAKS
BOGONG
BOGONGS
BOGS
BOGUS
BOGY
BOGYISM
BOGYISMS
BOH
BOHEA
BOHEAS
BOHS
BOHUNK
BOHUNKS
BOIL
BOILED
BOILER
BOILERIES
BOILERS
BOILERY
BOILING
BOILINGS
BOILS
BOING
BOINGED
BOINGING
BOINGS
BOINK
BOINKED
BOINKING
BOINKS
BOK
BOKE
BOKED
BOKES
BOKING
BOKO
BOKOS
BOKS
BOLAS
BOLASES
BOLD
BOLDEN
BOLDENED
BOLDENING
BOLDENS
BOLDER
BOLDEST
BOLDLY
BOLDNESS
BOLDNESSES
BOLDS
BOLE
BOLECTION
BOLECTIONS
BOLERO
BOLEROS
BOLES
BOLETI
BOLETUS
BOLETUSES
BOLIDE
BOLIDES
BOLIVAR
BOLIVARES
BOLIVARS
BOLIVIANO
BOLIVIANOS
BOLIX
BOLIXED
BOLIXES
BOLIXING
BOLL
BOLLARD
BOLLARDS
BOLLED
BOLLEN
BOLLETRIE
BOLLETRIES
BOLLING
BOLLIX
BOLLIXED
BOLLIXES
BOLLIXING
BOLLOCK
BOLLOCKED
BOLLOCKING
BOLLOCKINGS
BOLLOCKS
BOLLOCKSED
BOLLOCKSES
BOLLOCKSING
BOLLS
BOLO
BOLOMETER
BOLOMETERS
BOLOMETRIES
BOLOMETRY
BOLONEY
BOLONEYS
BOLOS
BOLSHEVIK
BOLSHEVIKS
BOLSHIE
BOLSHIER
BOLSHIES
BOLSHIEST
BOLSHY
BOLSTER
BOLSTERED
BOLSTERING
BOLSTERINGS
BOLSTERS
BOLT
BOLTED
BOLTER
BOLTERS
BOLTHEAD
BOLTHEADS
BOLTHOLE
BOLTHOLES
BOLTING
BOLTINGS
BOLTS
BOLUS
BOLUSES
BOMA
BOMAS
BOMB
BOMBARD
BOMBARDED
BOMBARDING
BOMBARDON
BOMBARDONS
BOMBARDS
BOMBASINE
BOMBASINES
BOMBAST
BOMBASTED
BOMBASTIC
BOMBASTING
BOMBASTS
BOMBAX
BOMBAXES
BOMBAZINE
BOMBAZINES
BOMBE
BOMBED
BOMBER
BOMBERS
BOMBES
BOMBILATE
BOMBILATED
BOMBILATES
BOMBILATING
BOMBINATE

BOMBINATED
BOMBINATES
BOMBINATING
BOMBING
BOMBLET
BOMBLETS
BOMBO
BOMBORA
BOMBORAS
BOMBOS
BOMBS
BOMBSHELL
BOMBSHELLS
BOMBSITE
BOMBSITES
BOMBYCID
BOMBYCIDS
BON
BONA
BONAMANI
BONAMANO
BONAMIA
BONAMIAS
BONANZA
BONANZAS
BONASSUS
BONASSUSES
BONASUS
BONASUSES
BONBON
BONBONS
BONCE
BONCES
BOND
BONDAGE
BONDAGER
BONDAGERS
BONDAGES
BONDED
BONDER
BONDERS
BONDING
BONDINGS
BONDMAID
BONDMAIDS
BONDMAN
BONDMEN
BONDS
BONDSMAN
BONDSMEN
BONDSTONE
BONDSTONES
BONDUC
BONDUCS
BONDWOMAN
BONDWOMEN
BONE
BONED
BONEHEAD
BONEHEADS
BONELESS
BONER
BONERS
BONES
BONESET
BONESETS
BONEYARD
BONEYARDS
BONFIRE
BONFIRES
BONG
BONGED
BONGING
BONGO
BONGOS
BONGRACE
BONGRACES
BONGS
BONHOMIE
BONHOMIES
BONHOMMIE
BONHOMMIES
BONHOMOUS
BONIBELL
BONIBELLS
BONIE
BONIER
BONIEST
BONIFACE
BONIFACES
BONILASSE
BONILASSES
BONINESS
BONINESSES
BONING
BONINGS
BONISM
BONISMS
BONIST
BONISTS
BONITO
BONITOS
BONJOUR
BONK
BONKED
BONKERS
BONKING
BONKS
BONNE
BONNES
BONNET
BONNETED
BONNETING
BONNETS
BONNIBELL
BONNIBELLS
BONNIE
BONNIER
BONNIES
BONNIEST
BONNILY
BONNINESS
BONNINESSES
BONNY
BONSAI
BONSAIS
BONSELLA
BONSELLAS
BONSOIR
BONSPIEL
BONSPIELS
BONTEBOK
BONTEBOKS
BONUS
BONUSES
BONXIE
BONXIES
BONY
BONZA
BONZE
BONZER
BONZES
BOO
BOOB
BOOBED
BOOBIES
BOOBING
BOOBOO
BOOBOOK
BOOBOOKS
BOOBOOS
BOOBS
BOOBY
BOOBYISH
BOOBYISM
BOOBYISMS
BOODIE
BOODIED
BOODIES
BOODLE
BOODLES
BOODY
BOODYING
BOOED
BOOGIE
BOOGIED
BOOGIEING
BOOGIES
BOOH
BOOHED
BOOHING
BOOHS
BOOING
BOOK
BOOKABLE
BOOKCASE
BOOKCASES
BOOKED
BOOKFUL
BOOKIE
BOOKIER
BOOKIES
BOOKIEST
BOOKING
BOOKINGS
BOOKISH
BOOKLAND
BOOKLANDS
BOOKLESS
BOOKLET
BOOKLETS
BOOKLICE
BOOKLORE
BOOKLORES
BOOKLOUSE
BOOKMAKER
BOOKMAKERS
BOOKMAN
BOOKMARK
BOOKMARKS
BOOKMEN
BOOKPLATE
BOOKPLATES
BOOKREST
BOOKRESTS
BOOKS
BOOKSHELF
BOOKSHELVES
BOOKSHOP
BOOKSHOPS
BOOKSIE
BOOKSIER
BOOKSIEST
BOOKSTALL
BOOKSTALLS
BOOKSTAND
BOOKSTANDS
BOOKSTORE
BOOKSTORES
BOOKSY
BOOKWORK
BOOKWORKS
BOOKWORM
BOOKWORMS
BOOKY
BOOL
BOOLS
BOOM
BOOMED
BOOMER
BOOMERANG
BOOMERANGED
BOOMERANGING
BOOMERANGS
BOOMERS
BOOMING
BOOMINGS
BOOMLET
BOOMLETS
BOOMS
BOOMSLANG
BOOMSLANGS
BOON
BOONDOCKS
BOONG
BOONGS
BOONS
BOOR
BOORD
BOORDE
BOORDES
BOORDS
BOORISH
BOORISHLY
BOORKA
BOORKAS
BOORS
BOORTREE
BOORTREES
BOOS
BOOSE
BOOSED
BOOSES
BOOSING
BOOST
BOOSTED
BOOSTER
BOOSTERS
BOOSTING
BOOSTS
BOOT
BOOTABLE
BOOTBLACK
BOOTBLACKS
BOOTED
BOOTEE
BOOTEES
BOOTH
BOOTHOSE
BOOTHS
BOOTIES
BOOTIKIN
BOOTIKINS
BOOTING
BOOTLACE
BOOTLACES
BOOTLAST
BOOTLASTS
BOOTLEG
BOOTLEGGED
BOOTLEGGING
BOOTLEGGINGS
BOOTLEGS
BOOTLESS
BOOTLICK
BOOTLICKED
BOOTLICKING
BOOTLICKINGS
BOOTLICKS
BOOTMAKER
BOOTMAKERS
BOOTS
BOOTSTRAP
BOOTSTRAPPED
BOOTSTRAPPING
BOOTSTRAPS
BOOTY
BOOZE
BOOZED
BOOZER
BOOZERS
BOOZES
BOOZEY
BOOZIER
BOOZIEST
BOOZILY
BOOZINESS
BOOZINESSES
BOOZING
BOOZY

BOP
BOPPED
BOPPER
BOPPERS
BOPPING
BOPS
BOR
BORA
BORACHIO
BORACHIOS
BORACIC
BORACITE
BORACITES
BORAGE
BORAGES
BORAK
BORAKS
BORANE
BORANES
BORAS
BORATE
BORATES
BORAX
BORAXES
BORAZON
BORAZONS
BORD
BORDAR
BORDARS
BORDE
BORDEL
BORDELLO
BORDELLOS
BORDELS
BORDER
BORDEREAU
BORDEREAUX
BORDERED
BORDERER
BORDERERS
BORDERING
BORDERS
BORDES
BORDS
BORDURE
BORDURES
BORE
BOREAL
BORECOLE
BORECOLES
BORED
BOREDOM
BOREDOMS
BOREE
BOREEN
BOREENS
BOREES
BOREHOLE
BOREHOLES
BOREL
BORER
BORERS
BORES
BORGHETTO
BORGHETTOS
BORGO
BORGOS
BORIC
BORIDE
BORIDES
BORING
BORINGLY
BORINGS
BORN
BORNE
BORNITE
BORNITES
BORON
BORONIA
BORONIAS
BORONS
BOROUGH
BOROUGHS
BORREL
BORRELL
BORROW
BORROWED
BORROWER
BORROWERS
BORROWING
BORROWINGS
BORROWS
BORS
BORSCH
BORSCHES
BORSCHT
BORSCHTS
BORSTAL
BORSTALL
BORSTALLS
BORSTALS
BORT
BORTS
BORTSCH
BORTSCHES
BORZOI
BORZOIS
BOS
BOSBOK
BOSBOKS
BOSCAGE
BOSCAGES
BOSCHBOK
BOSCHBOKS
BOSCHE
BOSCHES
BOSCHVELD
BOSCHVELDS
BOSH
BOSHES
BOSHTA
BOSHTER
BOSK
BOSKAGE
BOSKAGES
BOSKER
BOSKET
BOSKETS
BOSKIER
BOSKIEST
BOSKINESS
BOSKINESSES
BOSKS
BOSKY
BOSOM
BOSOMED
BOSOMIER
BOSOMIEST
BOSOMING
BOSOMS
BOSOMY
BOSON
BOSONS
BOSQUET
BOSQUETS
BOSS
BOSSED
BOSSER
BOSSES
BOSSEST
BOSSIER
BOSSIEST
BOSSILY
BOSSINESS
BOSSINESSES
BOSSING
BOSSY
BOSTANGI
BOSTANGIS
BOSTON
BOSTONS
BOSTRYX
BOSTRYXES
BOSUN
BOSUNS
BOT
BOTANIC
BOTANICAL
BOTANICALS
BOTANIES
BOTANISE
BOTANISED
BOTANISES
BOTANISING
BOTANIST
BOTANISTS
BOTANIZE
BOTANIZED
BOTANIZES
BOTANIZING
BOTANY
BOTARGO
BOTARGOES
BOTARGOS
BOTCH
BOTCHED
BOTCHER
BOTCHERIES
BOTCHERS
BOTCHERY
BOTCHES
BOTCHIER
BOTCHIEST
BOTCHING
BOTCHINGS
BOTCHY
BOTEL
BOTELS
BOTFLIES
BOTFLY
BOTH
BOTHAN
BOTHANS
BOTHER
BOTHERED
BOTHERING
BOTHERS
BOTHIE
BOTHIES
BOTHOLE
BOTHOLES
BOTHY
BOTHYMAN
BOTHYMEN
BOTONE
BOTRYOID
BOTRYOSE
BOTS
BOTT
BOTTE
BOTTED
BOTTEGA
BOTTEGAS
BOTTES
BOTTIES
BOTTINE
BOTTINES
BOTTING
BOTTLE
BOTTLED
BOTTLEFUL
BOTTLEFULS
BOTTLER
BOTTLERS
BOTTLES
BOTTLING
BOTTOM
BOTTOMED
BOTTOMING
BOTTOMRIES
BOTTOMRY
BOTTOMS
BOTTONY
BOTTS
BOTTY
BOTULISM
BOTULISMS
BOUCHE
BOUCHEE
BOUCHEES
BOUCHES
BOUCLE
BOUCLES
BOUDERIE
BOUDERIES
BOUDOIR
BOUDOIRS
BOUFFANT
BOUGE
BOUGED
BOUGES
BOUGET
BOUGETS
BOUGH
BOUGHPOT
BOUGHPOTS
BOUGHS
BOUGHT
BOUGHTEN
BOUGHTS
BOUGIE
BOUGIES
BOUGING
BOUILLI
BOUILLIS
BOUILLON
BOUILLONS
BOUK
BOUKS
BOULDER
BOULDERS
BOULE
BOULES
BOULEVARD
BOULEVARDS
BOULLE
BOULLES
BOULT
BOULTED
BOULTER
BOULTERS
BOULTING
BOULTINGS
BOULTS
BOUN
BOUNCE
BOUNCED
BOUNCER
BOUNCERS
BOUNCES
BOUNCIER
BOUNCIEST
BOUNCILY
BOUNCING
BOUNCY
BOUND
BOUNDARIES
BOUNDARY
BOUNDED
BOUNDEN
BOUNDER
BOUNDERS
BOUNDING
BOUNDLESS
BOUNDS
BOUNED
BOUNING
BOUNS
BOUNTEOUS
BOUNTIES

BOUNTIFUL
BOUNTREE
BOUNTREES
BOUNTY
BOUNTYHED
BOUNTYHEDS
BOUQUET
BOUQUETS
BOURASQUE
BOURASQUES
BOURBON
BOURBONS
BOURD
BOURDER
BOURDERS
BOURDON
BOURDONS
BOURDS
BOURG
BOURGEOIS
BOURGEOISES
BOURGEON
BOURGEONED
BOURGEONING
BOURGEONS
BOURGS
BOURKHA
BOURKHAS
BOURLAW
BOURLAWS
BOURN
BOURNE
BOURNES
BOURNS
BOURREE
BOURREES
BOURSE
BOURSES
BOURSIER
BOURSIERS
BOURTREE
BOURTREES
BOUSE
BOUSED
BOUSES
BOUSIER
BOUSIEST
BOUSING
BOUSY
BOUT
BOUTADE
BOUTADES
BOUTIQUE
BOUTIQUES
BOUTON
BOUTONNE
BOUTONNEE
BOUTONS
BOUTS
BOUZOUKI
BOUZOUKIS
BOVATE
BOVATES
BOVID
BOVIDS
BOVINE
BOVINELY
BOVINES
BOVVER
BOVVERS
BOW
BOWAT
BOWATS
BOWBENT
BOWED
BOWEL
BOWELLED
BOWELLING
BOWELS
BOWER
BOWERED
BOWERIES
BOWERING
BOWERS
BOWERY
BOWES
BOWET
BOWETS
BOWFIN
BOWFINS
BOWGET
BOWGETS
BOWHEAD
BOWHEADS
BOWING
BOWINGS
BOWKNOT
BOWKNOTS
BOWL
BOWLDER
BOWLDERS
BOWLED
BOWLER
BOWLERS
BOWLFUL
BOWLFULS
BOWLINE
BOWLINES
BOWLING
BOWLINGS
BOWLS
BOWMAN
BOWMEN
BOWNE
BOWNED
BOWNES
BOWNING
BOWPOT
BOWPOTS
BOWR
BOWRS
BOWS
BOWSE
BOWSED
BOWSER
BOWSERS
BOWSES
BOWSHOT
BOWSHOTS
BOWSING
BOWSPRIT
BOWSPRITS
BOWSTRING
BOWSTRINGED
BOWSTRINGING
BOWSTRINGS
BOWSTRUNG
BOWWOW
BOWWOWS
BOWYANG
BOWYANGS
BOWYER
BOWYERS
BOX
BOXCAR
BOXCARS
BOXED
BOXEN
BOXER
BOXERCISE
BOXERCISES
BOXERS
BOXES
BOXFUL
BOXFULS
BOXIER
BOXIEST
BOXINESS
BOXINESSES
BOXING
BOXINGS
BOXKEEPER
BOXKEEPERS
BOXROOM
BOXROOMS
BOXWALLAH
BOXWALLAHS
BOXWOOD
BOXWOODS
BOXY
BOY
BOYAR
BOYARS
BOYAU
BOYAUX
BOYCOTT
BOYCOTTED
BOYCOTTER
BOYCOTTERS
BOYCOTTING
BOYCOTTS
BOYED
BOYFRIEND
BOYFRIENDS
BOYG
BOYGS
BOYHOOD
BOYHOODS
BOYING
BOYISH
BOYISHLY
BOYO
BOYOS
BOYS
BOZO
BOZOS
BOZZETTI
BOZZETTO
BRA
BRABBLE
BRABBLED
BRABBLES
BRABBLING
BRACCATE
BRACCIA
BRACCIO
BRACE
BRACED
BRACELET
BRACELETS
BRACER
BRACERS
BRACES
BRACH
BRACHES
BRACHET
BRACHETS
BRACHIA
BRACHIAL
BRACHIATE
BRACHIATED
BRACHIATES
BRACHIATING
BRACHIUM
BRACING
BRACK
BRACKEN
BRACKENS
BRACKET
BRACKETED
BRACKETING
BRACKETS
BRACKISH
BRACKS
BRACT
BRACTEAL
BRACTEATE
BRACTEATES
BRACTEOLE
BRACTEOLES
BRACTLESS
BRACTLET
BRACTLETS
BRACTS
BRAD
BRADAWL
BRADAWLS
BRADS
BRAE
BRAES
BRAG
BRAGGART
BRAGGARTS
BRAGGED
BRAGGING
BRAGLY
BRAGS
BRAID
BRAIDE
BRAIDED
BRAIDER
BRAIDEST
BRAIDING
BRAIDINGS
BRAIDS
BRAIL
BRAILED
BRAILING
BRAILLER
BRAILLERS
BRAILS
BRAIN
BRAINBOX
BRAINBOXES
BRAINCASE
BRAINCASES
BRAINED
BRAINIER
BRAINIEST
BRAINING
BRAINISH
BRAINLESS
BRAINPAN
BRAINPANS
BRAINS
BRAINSICK
BRAINWASH
BRAINWASHED
BRAINWASHES
BRAINWASHING
BRAINWASHINGS
BRAINY
BRAIRD
BRAIRDED
BRAIRDING
BRAIRDS
BRAISE
BRAISED
BRAISES
BRAISING
BRAIZE
BRAIZES
BRAKE
BRAKED
BRAKELESS
BRAKEMAN
BRAKEMEN
BRAKES
BRAKIER
BRAKIEST
BRAKING
BRAKY
BRALESS
BRAMBLE
BRAMBLED
BRAMBLES
BRAMBLIER
BRAMBLIEST
BRAMBLING
BRAMBLINGS

BRAMBLY
BRAME
BRAMES
BRAN
BRANCARD
BRANCARDS
BRANCH
BRANCHED
BRANCHER
BRANCHERIES
BRANCHERS
BRANCHERY
BRANCHES
BRANCHIA
BRANCHIAE
BRANCHIAL
BRANCHIER
BRANCHIEST
BRANCHING
BRANCHINGS
BRANCHLET
BRANCHLETS
BRANCHY
BRAND
BRANDADE
BRANDADES
BRANDED
BRANDER
BRANDERED
BRANDERING
BRANDERS
BRANDIED
BRANDIES
BRANDING
BRANDISE
BRANDISES
BRANDISH
BRANDISHED
BRANDISHES
BRANDISHING
BRANDLING
BRANDLINGS
BRANDRETH
BRANDRETHS
BRANDS
BRANDY
BRANGLE
BRANGLED
BRANGLES
BRANGLING
BRANGLINGS
BRANK
BRANKED
BRANKIER
BRANKIEST
BRANKING
BRANKS
BRANKY
BRANLE
BRANLES
BRANNIER
BRANNIEST
BRANNY
BRANS
BRANSLE
BRANSLES
BRANTLE
BRANTLES
BRAS
BRASERO
BRASEROS
BRASES
BRASH
BRASHED
BRASHER
BRASHES
BRASHEST
BRASHIER
BRASHIEST
BRASHING
BRASHY
BRASIER
BRASIERS
BRASS
BRASSARD
BRASSARDS
BRASSART
BRASSARTS
BRASSERIE
BRASSERIES
BRASSES
BRASSET
BRASSETS
BRASSICA
BRASSICAS
BRASSIE
BRASSIER
BRASSIERE
BRASSIERES
BRASSIES
BRASSIEST
BRASSILY
BRASSY
BRAST
BRASTING
BRASTS
BRAT
BRATCHET
BRATCHETS
BRATLING
BRATLINGS
BRATPACK
BRATS
BRATTICE
BRATTICED
BRATTICES
BRATTICING
BRATTICINGS
BRATTIER
BRATTIEST
BRATTISH
BRATTISHED
BRATTISHES
BRATTISHING
BRATTISHINGS
BRATTLE
BRATTLED
BRATTLES
BRATTLING
BRATTLINGS
BRATTY
BRATWURST
BRATWURSTS
BRAUNCH
BRAUNCHED
BRAUNCHES
BRAUNCHING
BRAUNITE
BRAUNITES
BRAVA
BRAVADO
BRAVADOED
BRAVADOES
BRAVADOING
BRAVADOS
BRAVE
BRAVED
BRAVELY
BRAVER
BRAVERIES
BRAVERY
BRAVES
BRAVEST
BRAVI
BRAVING
BRAVO
BRAVOES
BRAVOS
BRAVURA
BRAVURAS
BRAW
BRAWER
BRAWEST
BRAWL
BRAWLED
BRAWLER
BRAWLERS
BRAWLIER
BRAWLIEST
BRAWLING
BRAWLINGS
BRAWLS
BRAWLY
BRAWN
BRAWNED
BRAWNIER
BRAWNIEST
BRAWNS
BRAWNY
BRAWS
BRAXIES
BRAXY
BRAY
BRAYED
BRAYER
BRAYERS
BRAYING
BRAYS
BRAZE
BRAZED
BRAZELESS
BRAZEN
BRAZENED
BRAZENING
BRAZENLY
BRAZENRIES
BRAZENRY
BRAZENS
BRAZES
BRAZIER
BRAZIERS
BRAZIL
BRAZILEIN
BRAZILEINS
BRAZILIN
BRAZILINS
BRAZILS
BRAZING
BREACH
BREACHED
BREACHES
BREACHING
BREAD
BREADED
BREADHEAD
BREADHEADS
BREADING
BREADLINE
BREADLINES
BREADNUT
BREADNUTS
BREADROOM
BREADROOMS
BREADROOT
BREADROOTS
BREADS
BREADTH
BREADTHS
BREAK
BREAKABLE
BREAKABLES
BREAKAGE
BREAKAGES
BREAKAWAY
BREAKAWAYS
BREAKBACK
BREAKBEAT
BREAKBEATS
BREAKDOWN
BREAKDOWNS
BREAKER
BREAKERS
BREAKFAST
BREAKFASTED
BREAKFASTING
BREAKFASTS
BREAKING
BREAKINGS
BREAKNECK
BREAKS
BREAKTIME
BREAKTIMES
BREAM
BREAMED
BREAMING
BREAMS
BREARE
BREARES
BREASKIT
BREASKITS
BREAST
BREASTED
BREASTING
BREASTPIN
BREASTPINS
BREASTS
BREATH
BREATHE
BREATHED
BREATHER
BREATHERS
BREATHES
BREATHFUL
BREATHIER
BREATHIEST
BREATHILY
BREATHING
BREATHINGS
BREATHS
BREATHY
BRECCIA
BRECCIAS
BRECHAM
BRECHAMS
BRED
BREDE
BREDED
BREDES
BREDING
BREE
BREECH
BREECHED
BREECHES
BREECHING
BREECHINGS
BREED
BREEDER
BREEDERS
BREEDING
BREEDINGS
BREEDS
BREEKS
BREEM
BREER
BREERED
BREERING
BREERS
BREES
BREESE
BREESES
BREEZE
BREEZED
BREEZES
BREEZEWAY
BREEZEWAYS
BREEZIER
BREEZIEST
BREEZILY
BREEZING
BREEZY

BREGMA
BREGMATA
BREGMATIC
BREHON
BREHONS
BRELOQUE
BRELOQUES
BREME
BREN
BRENNE
BRENNES
BRENNING
BRENS
BRENT
BRENTER
BRENTEST
BRER
BRERE
BRERES
BRERS
BRETASCHE
BRETASCHES
BRETESSE
BRETESSES
BRETHREN
BRETON
BRETONS
BRETTICE
BRETTICED
BRETTICES
BRETTICING
BREVE
BREVES
BREVET
BREVETE
BREVETED
BREVETING
BREVETS
BREVETTED
BREVETTING
BREVIARIES
BREVIARY
BREVIATE
BREVIATES
BREVIER
BREVIERS
BREVITIES
BREVITY
BREW
BREWAGE
BREWAGES
BREWED
BREWER
BREWERIES
BREWERS
BREWERY
BREWING
BREWINGS
BREWIS
BREWISES
BREWPUB
BREWPUBS
BREWS
BREWSTER
BREWSTERS
BRIAR
BRIARED
BRIARS
BRIBE
BRIBED
BRIBER
BRIBERIES
BRIBERS
BRIBERY
BRIBES
BRIBING
BRICABRAC
BRICABRACS
BRICK
BRICKBAT
BRICKBATS
BRICKCLAY
BRICKCLAYS
BRICKED
BRICKEN
BRICKIE
BRICKIER
BRICKIES
BRICKIEST
BRICKING
BRICKINGS
BRICKLE
BRICKS
BRICKWALL
BRICKWALLS
BRICKWORK
BRICKWORKS
BRICKY
BRICKYARD
BRICKYARDS
BRICOLE
BRICOLES
BRIDAL
BRIDALS
BRIDE
BRIDECAKE
BRIDECAKES
BRIDED
BRIDEMAID
BRIDEMAIDS
BRIDEMAN
BRIDEMEN
BRIDES
BRIDESMAN
BRIDESMEN
BRIDEWELL
BRIDEWELLS
BRIDGABLE
BRIDGE
BRIDGED
BRIDGES
BRIDGING
BRIDGINGS
BRIDIE
BRIDIES
BRIDING
BRIDLE
BRIDLED
BRIDLER
BRIDLERS
BRIDLES
BRIDLING
BRIDOON
BRIDOONS
BRIEF
BRIEFCASE
BRIEFCASES
BRIEFED
BRIEFER
BRIEFEST
BRIEFING
BRIEFINGS
BRIEFLESS
BRIEFLY
BRIEFNESS
BRIEFNESSES
BRIEFS
BRIER
BRIERED
BRIERIER
BRIERIEST
BRIERS
BRIERY
BRIG
BRIGADE
BRIGADED
BRIGADES
BRIGADIER
BRIGADIERS
BRIGADING
BRIGALOW
BRIGALOWS
BRIGAND
BRIGANDRIES
BRIGANDRY
BRIGANDS
BRIGHT
BRIGHTEN
BRIGHTENED
BRIGHTENING
BRIGHTENS
BRIGHTER
BRIGHTEST
BRIGHTLY
BRIGS
BRIGUE
BRIGUED
BRIGUES
BRIGUING
BRIGUINGS
BRILL
BRILLER
BRILLEST
BRILLIANT
BRILLIANTED
BRILLIANTING
BRILLIANTS
BRILLS
BRIM
BRIMFUL
BRIMING
BRIMINGS
BRIMLESS
BRIMMED
BRIMMER
BRIMMERS
BRIMMING
BRIMS
BRIMSTONE
BRIMSTONES
BRIMSTONY
BRINDED
BRINDISI
BRINDISIS
BRINDLE
BRINDLED
BRINDLES
BRINE
BRINED
BRINES
BRING
BRINGER
BRINGERS
BRINGING
BRINGINGS
BRINGS
BRINIER
BRINIEST
BRININESS
BRININESSES
BRINING
BRINISH
BRINJAL
BRINJALS
BRINJARRIES
BRINJARRY
BRINK
BRINKMAN
BRINKMEN
BRINKS
BRINY
BRIO
BRIOCHE
BRIOCHES
BRIONIES
BRIONY
BRIOS
BRIQUET
BRIQUETS
BRIQUETTE
BRIQUETTED
BRIQUETTES
BRIQUETTING
BRISE
BRISES
BRISK
BRISKED
BRISKEN
BRISKENED
BRISKENING
BRISKENS
BRISKER
BRISKEST
BRISKET
BRISKETS
BRISKING
BRISKISH
BRISKLY
BRISKNESS
BRISKNESSES
BRISKS
BRISKY
BRISLING
BRISLINGS
BRISTLE
BRISTLED
BRISTLES
BRISTLIER
BRISTLIEST
BRISTLING
BRISTLY
BRISTOLS
BRISURE
BRISURES
BRIT
BRITCHES
BRITS
BRITSCHKA
BRITSCHKAS
BRITSKA
BRITSKAS
BRITTLE
BRITTLELY
BRITTLER
BRITTLES
BRITTLEST
BRITTLY
BRITZKA
BRITZKAS
BRITZSKA
BRITZSKAS
BRIZE
BRIZES
BRO
BROACH
BROACHED
BROACHER
BROACHERS
BROACHES
BROACHING
BROAD
BROADBAND
BROADBILL
BROADBILLS
BROADCAST
BROADCASTED
BROADCASTING
BROADCASTINGS
BROADCASTS
BROADEN
BROADENED
BROADENING
BROADENS
BROADER
BROADEST
BROADISH
BROADLOOM
BROADLY
BROADNESS
BROADNESSES

BROADS
BROADSIDE
BROADSIDES
BROADTAIL
BROADTAILS
BROADWAY
BROADWAYS
BROADWISE
BROCADE
BROCADED
BROCADES
BROCAGE
BROCAGES
BROCARD
BROCARDS
BROCATEL
BROCATELS
BROCCOLI
BROCCOLIS
BROCH
BROCHAN
BROCHANS
BROCHE
BROCHED
BROCHES
BROCHETTE
BROCHETTES
BROCHING
BROCHS
BROCHURE
BROCHURES
BROCK
BROCKAGE
BROCKAGES
BROCKED
BROCKET
BROCKETS
BROCKIT
BROCKRAM
BROCKRAMS
BROCKS
BROD
BRODDED
BRODDING
BRODEKIN
BRODEKINS
BRODKIN
BRODKINS
BRODS
BROG
BROGAN
BROGANS
BROGGED
BROGGING
BROGH
BROGHS
BROGS
BROGUE
BROGUEISH
BROGUES
BROGUISH
BROIDER
BROIDERED
BROIDERER
BROIDERERS
BROIDERIES
BROIDERING
BROIDERINGS
BROIDERS
BROIDERY
BROIL
BROILED
BROILER
BROILERS
BROILING
BROILS
BROKAGE
BROKAGES
BROKE
BROKED
BROKEN
BROKENLY
BROKER
BROKERAGE
BROKERAGES
BROKERED
BROKERIES
BROKERING
BROKERS
BROKERY
BROKES
BROKING
BROKINGS
BROLGA
BROLGAS
BROLLIES
BROLLY
BROMATE
BROMATES
BROMELAIN
BROMELAINS
BROMELIA
BROMELIAD
BROMELIADS
BROMELIAS
BROMELIN
BROMELINS
BROMIC
BROMIDE
BROMIDES
BROMIDIC
BROMINE
BROMINES
BROMINISM
BROMINISMS
BROMISM
BROMISMS
BROMMER
BROMMERS
BROMOFORM
BROMOFORMS
BRONCHI
BRONCHIA
BRONCHIAL
BRONCHO
BRONCHOS
BRONCHUS
BRONCO
BRONCOS
BROND
BRONDS
BRONDYRON
BRONDYRONS
BRONZE
BRONZED
BRONZEN
BRONZER
BRONZERS
BRONZES
BRONZIER
BRONZIEST
BRONZIFIED
BRONZIFIES
BRONZIFY
BRONZIFYING
BRONZING
BRONZINGS
BRONZITE
BRONZITES
BRONZY
BROO
BROOCH
BROOCHED
BROOCHES
BROOCHING
BROOD
BROODED
BROODER
BROODERS
BROODIER
BROODIEST
BROODING
BROODS
BROODY
BROOK
BROOKED
BROOKING
BROOKITE
BROOKITES
BROOKLET
BROOKLETS
BROOKLIME
BROOKLIMES
BROOKS
BROOKWEED
BROOKWEEDS
BROOL
BROOLS
BROOM
BROOMBALL
BROOMBALLS
BROOMED
BROOMIER
BROOMIEST
BROOMING
BROOMRAPE
BROOMRAPES
BROOMS
BROOMY
BROOS
BROOSE
BROOSES
BROS
BROSE
BROSES
BROTH
BROTHEL
BROTHELS
BROTHER
BROTHERLY
BROTHERS
BROTHS
BROUGH
BROUGHAM
BROUGHAMS
BROUGHS
BROUGHT
BROUHAHA
BROUHAHAS
BROUZE
BROUZES
BROW
BROWBAND
BROWBANDS
BROWBEAT
BROWBEATEN
BROWBEATING
BROWBEATINGS
BROWBEATS
BROWLESS
BROWN
BROWNED
BROWNER
BROWNEST
BROWNIE
BROWNIER
BROWNIES
BROWNIEST
BROWNING
BROWNINGS
BROWNISH
BROWNNESS
BROWNNESSES
BROWNOUT
BROWNOUTS
BROWNS
BROWNY
BROWS
BROWSE
BROWSED
BROWSER
BROWSERS
BROWSES
BROWSIER
BROWSIEST
BROWSING
BROWSINGS
BROWST
BROWSTS
BROWSY
BRRR
BRUCHID
BRUCHIDS
BRUCINE
BRUCINES
BRUCITE
BRUCITES
BRUCKLE
BRUHAHA
BRUHAHAS
BRUILZIE
BRUILZIES
BRUISE
BRUISED
BRUISER
BRUISERS
BRUISES
BRUISING
BRUISINGS
BRUIT
BRUITED
BRUITING
BRUITS
BRULE
BRULYIE
BRULYIES
BRULZIE
BRULZIES
BRUMAL
BRUMBIES
BRUMBY
BRUME
BRUMES
BRUMMAGEM
BRUMMAGEMS
BRUMMER
BRUMMERS
BRUMOUS
BRUNCH
BRUNCHES
BRUNET
BRUNETS
BRUNETTE
BRUNETTES
BRUNT
BRUNTED
BRUNTING
BRUNTS
BRUSH
BRUSHED
BRUSHER
BRUSHERS
BRUSHES
BRUSHIER
BRUSHIEST
BRUSHING
BRUSHINGS
BRUSHWOOD
BRUSHWOODS
BRUSHWORK
BRUSHWORKS
BRUSHY
BRUSQUE
BRUSQUELY
BRUSQUER
BRUSQUEST
BRUST
BRUSTING
BRUSTS
BRUT

BRUTAL
BRUTALISE
BRUTALISED
BRUTALISES
BRUTALISING
BRUTALISM
BRUTALISMS
BRUTALIST
BRUTALISTS
BRUTALITIES
BRUTALITY
BRUTALIZE
BRUTALIZED
BRUTALIZES
BRUTALIZING
BRUTALLY
BRUTE
BRUTED
BRUTELIKE
BRUTENESS
BRUTENESSES
BRUTER
BRUTERS
BRUTES
BRUTIFIED
BRUTIFIES
BRUTIFY
BRUTIFYING
BRUTING
BRUTINGS
BRUTISH
BRUTISHLY
BRUXISM
BRUXISMS
BRYOLOGIES
BRYOLOGY
BRYONIES
BRYONY
BRYOPHYTE
BRYOPHYTES
BUAT
BUATS
BUAZE
BUAZES
BUB
BUBA
BUBAL
BUBALINE
BUBALIS
BUBALISES
BUBALS
BUBAS
BUBBIES
BUBBLE
BUBBLED
BUBBLES
BUBBLIER
BUBBLIES
BUBBLIEST
BUBBLING
BUBBLY
BUBBY
BUBINGA
BUBINGAS
BUBO
BUBOES
BUBONIC
BUBS
BUBUKLE
BUBUKLES
BUCCAL
BUCCANEER
BUCCANEERED
BUCCANEERING
BUCCANEERINGS
BUCCANEERS
BUCCANIER
BUCCANIERED
BUCCANIERING
BUCCANIERS
BUCCINA
BUCCINAS
BUCELLAS
BUCELLASES
BUCHU
BUCHUS
BUCK
BUCKAROO
BUCKAROOS
BUCKAYRO
BUCKAYROS
BUCKBEAN
BUCKBEANS
BUCKBOARD
BUCKBOARDS
BUCKED
BUCKEEN
BUCKEENS
BUCKER
BUCKEROO
BUCKEROOS
BUCKERS
BUCKET
BUCKETED
BUCKETFUL
BUCKETFULS
BUCKETING
BUCKETINGS
BUCKETS
BUCKHORN
BUCKHORNS
BUCKHOUND
BUCKHOUNDS
BUCKIE
BUCKIES
BUCKING
BUCKINGS
BUCKISH
BUCKISHLY
BUCKLE
BUCKLED
BUCKLER
BUCKLERED
BUCKLERING
BUCKLERS
BUCKLES
BUCKLING
BUCKLINGS
BUCKO
BUCKOES
BUCKRA
BUCKRAKE
BUCKRAKES
BUCKRAM
BUCKRAMED
BUCKRAMING
BUCKRAMS
BUCKRAS
BUCKS
BUCKSAW
BUCKSAWS
BUCKSHEE
BUCKSHISH
BUCKSHISHED
BUCKSHISHES
BUCKSHISHING
BUCKSHOT
BUCKSHOTS
BUCKSKIN
BUCKSKINS
BUCKSOM
BUCKTEETH
BUCKTHORN
BUCKTHORNS
BUCKTOOTH
BUCKU
BUCKUS
BUCKWHEAT
BUCKWHEATS
BUCKYBALL
BUCKYBALLS
BUCOLIC
BUCOLICAL
BUCOLICS
BUD
BUDDED
BUDDHA
BUDDHAS
BUDDIER
BUDDIES
BUDDIEST
BUDDING
BUDDINGS
BUDDLE
BUDDLED
BUDDLEIA
BUDDLEIAS
BUDDLES
BUDDLING
BUDDY
BUDGE
BUDGED
BUDGER
BUDGEREE
BUDGERO
BUDGEROS
BUDGEROW
BUDGEROWS
BUDGERS
BUDGES
BUDGET
BUDGETARY
BUDGETED
BUDGETING
BUDGETS
BUDGIE
BUDGIES
BUDGING
BUDLESS
BUDMASH
BUDMASHES
BUDO
BUDOS
BUDS
BUDWORM
BUDWORMS
BUFF
BUFFA
BUFFALO
BUFFALOED
BUFFALOES
BUFFALOING
BUFFE
BUFFED
BUFFER
BUFFERED
BUFFERING
BUFFERS
BUFFET
BUFFETED
BUFFETING
BUFFETINGS
BUFFETS
BUFFI
BUFFING
BUFFINGS
BUFFO
BUFFOON
BUFFOONS
BUFFS
BUFO
BUFOS
BUG
BUGABOO
BUGABOOS
BUGBANE
BUGBANES
BUGBEAR
BUGBEARS
BUGGAN
BUGGANE
BUGGANES
BUGGANS
BUGGED
BUGGER
BUGGERED
BUGGERIES
BUGGERING
BUGGERS
BUGGERY
BUGGIER
BUGGIES
BUGGIEST
BUGGIN
BUGGING
BUGGINGS
BUGGINS
BUGGY
BUGHOUSE
BUGHOUSES
BUGLE
BUGLED
BUGLER
BUGLERS
BUGLES
BUGLET
BUGLETS
BUGLING
BUGLOSS
BUGLOSSES
BUGONG
BUGONGS
BUGS
BUGWORT
BUGWORTS
BUHL
BUHLS
BUHRSTONE
BUHRSTONES
BUIK
BUIKS
BUILD
BUILDED
BUILDER
BUILDERS
BUILDING
BUILDINGS
BUILDS
BUILT
BUIRDLIER
BUIRDLIEST
BUIRDLY
BUIST
BUISTED
BUISTING
BUISTS
BUKE
BUKES
BUKSHEE
BUKSHEES
BUKSHI
BUKSHIS
BULB
BULBAR
BULBED
BULBEL
BULBELS
BULBIL
BULBILS
BULBING
BULBOSITIES
BULBOSITY
BULBOUS
BULBOUSLY
BULBS
BULBUL
BULBULS
BULGE
BULGED
BULGER

BULGERS
BULGES
BULGHUR
BULGHURS
BULGIER
BULGIEST
BULGINE
BULGINES
BULGINESS
BULGINESSES
BULGING
BULGINGLY
BULGUR
BULGURS
BULGY
BULIMIA
BULIMIAS
BULIMIC
BULIMICS
BULIMIES
BULIMUS
BULIMUSES
BULIMY
BULK
BULKED
BULKER
BULKERS
BULKHEAD
BULKHEADS
BULKIER
BULKIEST
BULKILY
BULKINESS
BULKINESSES
BULKING
BULKS
BULKY
BULL
BULLA
BULLACE
BULLACES
BULLAE
BULLARIES
BULLARY
BULLATE
BULLBAR
BULLBARS
BULLBAT
BULLBATS
BULLDOG
BULLDOGGED
BULLDOGGING
BULLDOGS
BULLDOZE
BULLDOZED
BULLDOZER
BULLDOZERS
BULLDOZES
BULLDOZING
BULLDUST
BULLDUSTS
BULLED
BULLER
BULLERED
BULLERING
BULLERS
BULLET
BULLETIN
BULLETINS
BULLETRIE
BULLETRIES
BULLETS
BULLFIGHT
BULLFIGHTS
BULLFINCH
BULLFINCHES
BULLFROG
BULLFROGS
BULLGINE
BULLGINES
BULLHEAD
BULLHEADS
BULLIED
BULLIER
BULLIES
BULLIEST
BULLING
BULLINGS
BULLION
BULLIONS
BULLISH
BULLISHLY
BULLNOSE
BULLNOSES
BULLOCK
BULLOCKED
BULLOCKIES
BULLOCKING
BULLOCKS
BULLOCKY
BULLS
BULLSHIT
BULLSHITS
BULLSHITTED
BULLSHITTING
BULLSHITTINGS
BULLWHACK
BULLWHACKED
BULLWHACKING
BULLWHACKS
BULLWHIP
BULLWHIPPED
BULLWHIPPING
BULLWHIPS
BULLY
BULLYING
BULLYISM
BULLYISMS
BULLYRAG
BULLYRAGGED
BULLYRAGGING
BULLYRAGS
BULRUSH
BULRUSHES
BULRUSHY
BULSE
BULSES
BULWARK
BULWARKED
BULWARKING
BULWARKS
BUM
BUMALO
BUMALOTI
BUMALOTIS
BUMBAG
BUMBAGS
BUMBAZE
BUMBAZED
BUMBAZES
BUMBAZING
BUMBLE
BUMBLED
BUMBLER
BUMBLERS
BUMBLES
BUMBLING
BUMBLINGS
BUMBO
BUMBOS
BUMF
BUMFS
BUMKIN
BUMKINS
BUMMALO
BUMMALOTI
BUMMALOTIS
BUMMAREE
BUMMAREES
BUMMED
BUMMEL
BUMMELS
BUMMER
BUMMERS
BUMMEST
BUMMING
BUMMLE
BUMMLED
BUMMLES
BUMMLING
BUMMOCK
BUMMOCKS
BUMP
BUMPED
BUMPER
BUMPERED
BUMPERING
BUMPERS
BUMPH
BUMPHS
BUMPIER
BUMPIEST
BUMPILY
BUMPINESS
BUMPINESSES
BUMPING
BUMPINGS
BUMPKIN
BUMPKINS
BUMPOLOGIES
BUMPOLOGY
BUMPS
BUMPTIOUS
BUMPY
BUMS
BUMSUCKER
BUMSUCKERS
BUN
BUNA
BUNAS
BUNCE
BUNCED
BUNCES
BUNCH
BUNCHED
BUNCHES
BUNCHIER
BUNCHIEST
BUNCHING
BUNCHINGS
BUNCHY
BUNCING
BUNCO
BUNCOED
BUNCOING
BUNCOMBE
BUNCOMBES
BUNCOS
BUND
BUNDED
BUNDING
BUNDLE
BUNDLED
BUNDLES
BUNDLING
BUNDLINGS
BUNDOBUST
BUNDOBUSTS
BUNDOOK
BUNDOOKS
BUNDS
BUNDU
BUNDUS
BUNG
BUNGALOID
BUNGALOIDS
BUNGALOW
BUNGALOWS
BUNGED
BUNGEE
BUNGEES
BUNGEY
BUNGEYS
BUNGHOLE
BUNGHOLES
BUNGIE
BUNGIES
BUNGING
BUNGLE
BUNGLED
BUNGLER
BUNGLERS
BUNGLES
BUNGLING
BUNGLINGS
BUNGS
BUNGY
BUNIA
BUNIAS
BUNION
BUNIONS
BUNJE
BUNJEE
BUNJEES
BUNJES
BUNJIE
BUNJIES
BUNJY
BUNK
BUNKED
BUNKER
BUNKERED
BUNKERING
BUNKERS
BUNKHOUSE
BUNKHOUSES
BUNKING
BUNKO
BUNKOED
BUNKOING
BUNKOS
BUNKS
BUNKUM
BUNKUMS
BUNNIA
BUNNIAS
BUNNIES
BUNNY
BUNODONT
BUNRAKU
BUNRAKUS
BUNS
BUNSEN
BUNSENS
BUNT
BUNTAL
BUNTALS
BUNTED
BUNTER
BUNTERS
BUNTIER
BUNTIEST
BUNTING
BUNTINGS
BUNTLINE
BUNTLINES
BUNTS
BUNTY
BUNYA
BUNYAS
BUNYIP
BUNYIPS
BUONAMANI
BUONAMANO
BUOY
BUOYAGE
BUOYAGES
BUOYANCE
BUOYANCES
BUOYANCIES

BUOYANCY
BUOYANT
BUOYED
BUOYING
BUOYS
BUPLEVER
BUPLEVERS
BUPPIES
BUPPY
BUPRESTID
BUPRESTIDS
BUR
BURAN
BURANS
BURBLE
BURBLED
BURBLER
BURBLERS
BURBLES
BURBLING
BURBLINGS
BURBOT
BURBOTS
BURD
BURDASH
BURDASHES
BURDEN
BURDENED
BURDENING
BURDENOUS
BURDENS
BURDIE
BURDIES
BURDOCK
BURDOCKS
BURDS
BUREAU
BUREAUS
BUREAUX
BURET
BURETS
BURETTE
BURETTES
BURG
BURGAGE
BURGAGES
BURGANET
BURGANETS
BURGEE
BURGEES
BURGEON
BURGEONED
BURGEONING
BURGEONS
BURGER
BURGERS
BURGESS
BURGESSES
BURGH
BURGHAL
BURGHER
BURGHERS
BURGHS
BURGHUL
BURGHULS
BURGLAR
BURGLARED
BURGLARIES
BURGLARING
BURGLARS
BURGLARY
BURGLE
BURGLED
BURGLES
BURGLING
BURGONET
BURGONETS
BURGOO
BURGOOS
BURGRAVE
BURGRAVES
BURGS
BURGUNDIES
BURGUNDY
BURHEL
BURHELS
BURIAL
BURIALS
BURIED
BURIES
BURIN
BURINIST
BURINISTS
BURINS
BURITI
BURITIS
BURK
BURKA
BURKAS
BURKE
BURKED
BURKES
BURKING
BURKS
BURL
BURLAP
BURLAPS
BURLED
BURLER
BURLERS
BURLESQUE
BURLESQUED
BURLESQUES
BURLESQUING
BURLETTA
BURLETTAS
BURLEY
BURLEYS
BURLIER
BURLIEST
BURLINESS
BURLINESSES
BURLING
BURLS
BURLY
BURN
BURNED
BURNER
BURNERS
BURNET
BURNETS
BURNING
BURNINGLY
BURNINGS
BURNISH
BURNISHED
BURNISHER
BURNISHERS
BURNISHES
BURNISHING
BURNISHINGS
BURNOUS
BURNOUSE
BURNOUSES
BURNS
BURNSIDE
BURNSIDES
BURNT
BUROO
BUROOS
BURP
BURPED
BURPING
BURPS
BURQA
BURQAS
BURR
BURRAWANG
BURRAWANGS
BURRED
BURREL
BURRELL
BURRELLS
BURRELS
BURRHEL
BURRHELS
BURRIER
BURRIEST
BURRING
BURRITO
BURRITOS
BURRO
BURROS
BURROW
BURROWED
BURROWING
BURROWS
BURRS
BURRSTONE
BURRSTONES
BURRY
BURS
BURSA
BURSAE
BURSAL
BURSAR
BURSARIAL
BURSARIES
BURSARS
BURSARY
BURSE
BURSES
BURSIFORM
BURSITIS
BURSITISES
BURST
BURSTED
BURSTEN
BURSTER
BURSTERS
BURSTING
BURSTS
BURTHEN
BURTHENED
BURTHENING
BURTHENS
BURTON
BURTONS
BURWEED
BURWEEDS
BURY
BURYING
BUS
BUSBIES
BUSBOY
BUSBOYS
BUSBY
BUSED
BUSES
BUSGIRL
BUSGIRLS
BUSH
BUSHCRAFT
BUSHCRAFTS
BUSHED
BUSHEL
BUSHELLED
BUSHELLER
BUSHELLERS
BUSHELLING
BUSHELLINGS
BUSHELMAN
BUSHELMEN
BUSHELS
BUSHES
BUSHFIRE
BUSHFIRES
BUSHIDO
BUSHIDOS
BUSHIER
BUSHIES
BUSHIEST
BUSHINESS
BUSHINESSES
BUSHING
BUSHINGS
BUSHMAN
BUSHMEN
BUSHVELD
BUSHVELDS
BUSHWALK
BUSHWALKED
BUSHWALKING
BUSHWALKINGS
BUSHWALKS
BUSHWHACK
BUSHWHACKED
BUSHWHACKING
BUSHWHACKINGS
BUSHWHACKS
BUSHWOMAN
BUSHWOMEN
BUSHY
BUSIED
BUSIER
BUSIES
BUSIEST
BUSILY
BUSINESS
BUSINESSES
BUSING
BUSINGS
BUSK
BUSKED
BUSKER
BUSKERS
BUSKET
BUSKETS
BUSKIN
BUSKINED
BUSKING
BUSKINGS
BUSKINS
BUSKS
BUSKY
BUSMAN
BUSMEN
BUSS
BUSSED
BUSSES
BUSSING
BUSSINGS
BUSSU
BUSSUS
BUST
BUSTARD
BUSTARDS
BUSTED
BUSTEE
BUSTEES
BUSTER
BUSTERS
BUSTIER
BUSTIERS
BUSTIEST
BUSTING
BUSTINGS
BUSTLE
BUSTLED
BUSTLER
BUSTLERS
BUSTLES
BUSTLING
BUSTS
BUSTY
BUSY
BUSYBODIED
BUSYBODIES
BUSYBODY
BUSYBODYING

BUSYING
BUSYNESS
BUSYNESSES
BUT
BUTADIENE
BUTADIENES
BUTANE
BUTANES
BUTANOL
BUTANOLS
BUTCH
BUTCHER
BUTCHERED
BUTCHERIES
BUTCHERING
BUTCHERINGS
BUTCHERLY
BUTCHERS
BUTCHERY
BUTCHES
BUTCHEST
BUTCHING
BUTCHINGS
BUTE
BUTENE
BUTENES
BUTES
BUTLER
BUTLERAGE
BUTLERAGES
BUTLERED
BUTLERIES
BUTLERING
BUTLERS
BUTLERY
BUTMENT
BUTMENTS
BUTS
BUTT
BUTTE
BUTTED
BUTTER
BUTTERBUR
BUTTERBURS
BUTTERCUP
BUTTERCUPS
BUTTERED
BUTTERFLIES
BUTTERFLY
BUTTERIER
BUTTERIES
BUTTERIEST
BUTTERINE
BUTTERINES
BUTTERING
BUTTERNUT
BUTTERNUTS
BUTTERS
BUTTERY
BUTTES
BUTTIES
BUTTING
BUTTLE
BUTTLED
BUTTLES
BUTTLING
BUTTOCK
BUTTOCKED
BUTTOCKING
BUTTOCKS
BUTTON
BUTTONED
BUTTONING
BUTTONS
BUTTONY
BUTTRESS
BUTTRESSED
BUTTRESSES
BUTTRESSING
BUTTS
BUTTY
BUTTYMAN
BUTTYMEN
BUTYL
BUTYLENE
BUTYLENES
BUTYLS
BUTYRATE
BUTYRATES
BUTYRIC
BUVETTE
BUVETTES
BUXOM
BUXOMER
BUXOMEST
BUXOMNESS
BUXOMNESSES
BUY
BUYABLE
BUYABLES
BUYER
BUYERS
BUYING
BUYS
BUZZ
BUZZARD
BUZZARDS
BUZZED
BUZZER
BUZZERS
BUZZES
BUZZIER
BUZZIEST
BUZZING
BUZZINGLY
BUZZINGS
BUZZWORD
BUZZWORDS
BUZZY
BWANA
BWANAS
BWAZI
BWAZIS
BY
BYCATCH
BYCATCHES
BYCOKET
BYCOKETS
BYE
BYES
BYGONE
BYGONES
BYKE
BYKED
BYKES
BYKING
BYLANDER
BYLANDERS
BYLAW
BYLAWS
BYLINE
BYLINES
BYLIVE
BYNAME
BYNAMES
BYNEMPT
BYPASS
BYPASSED
BYPASSES
BYPASSING
BYPATH
BYPATHS
BYPLACE
BYPLACES
BYRE
BYREMAN
BYREMEN
BYRES
BYREWOMAN
BYREWOMEN
BYRLADY
BYRLAKIN
BYRLAW
BYRLAWS
BYRNIE
BYRNIES
BYROAD
BYROADS
BYROOM
BYROOMS
BYS
BYSSAL
BYSSI
BYSSINE
BYSSOID
BYSSUS
BYSSUSES
BYSTANDER
BYSTANDERS
BYTE
BYTES
BYTOWNITE
BYTOWNITES
BYWAY
BYWAYS
BYWONER
BYWONERS
BYWORD
BYWORDS
BYZANT
BYZANTS

C

CAATINGA
CAATINGAS
CAB
CABA
CABAL
CABALA
CABALAS
CABALETTA
CABALETTAS
CABALETTE
CABALISM
CABALISMS
CABALIST
CABALISTS
CABALLED
CABALLER
CABALLERO
CABALLEROS
CABALLERS
CABALLINE
CABALLING
CABALS
CABANA
CABANAS
CABARET
CABARETS
CABAS
CABBAGE
CABBAGED
CABBAGES
CABBAGING
CABBAGY
CABBALA
CABBALAS
CABBALISM
CABBALISMS
CABBALIST
CABBALISTS
CABBIE
CABBIES
CABBY
CABER
CABERS
CABIN
CABINED
CABINET
CABINETS
CABINING
CABINS
CABLE
CABLED
CABLEGRAM
CABLEGRAMS
CABLES
CABLET
CABLETS
CABLEWAY
CABLEWAYS
CABLING
CABLINGS
CABMAN
CABMEN
CABOB
CABOBBED
CABOBBING
CABOBS
CABOC
CABOCEER
CABOCEERS
CABOCHED
CABOCHON
CABOCHONS
CABOCS
CABOODLE
CABOODLES
CABOOSE
CABOOSES
CABOSHED
CABOTAGE
CABOTAGES
CABRE
CABRETTA
CABRETTAS
CABRIE
CABRIES
CABRIOLE
CABRIOLES
CABRIOLET
CABRIOLETS
CABRIT
CABRITS
CABS
CACAFOGO
CACAFOGOS
CACAFUEGO
CACAFUEGOS
CACAO
CACAOS
CACHAEMIA
CACHAEMIAS
CACHAEMIC
CACHALOT
CACHALOTS
CACHE
CACHECTIC
CACHED
CACHEPOT
CACHEPOTS
CACHES
CACHET
CACHETS
CACHEXIA
CACHEXIAS
CACHEXIES
CACHEXY
CACHING
CACHOLONG
CACHOLONGS
CACHOLOT
CACHOLOTS
CACHOU
CACHOUS
CACHUCHA
CACHUCHAS
CACIQUE
CACIQUES
CACIQUISM
CACIQUISMS
CACKLE
CACKLED
CACKLER
CACKLERS
CACKLES
CACKLING
CACODEMON
CACODEMONS
CACODOXIES
CACODOXY
CACODYL
CACODYLIC
CACODYLS
CACOEPIES
CACOEPY
CACOETHES
CACOLET
CACOLETS
CACOLOGIES
CACOLOGY
CACOMIXL
CACOMIXLS
CACOON
CACOONS
CACOPHONIES
CACOPHONY
CACOTOPIA
CACOTOPIAS
CACTI
CACTIFORM
CACTUS
CACTUSES
CACUMEN
CACUMINA
CACUMINAL
CAD
CADASTRAL
CADASTRE
CADASTRES
CADAVER
CADAVERIC
CADAVERS
CADDICE
CADDICES
CADDIE
CADDIED
CADDIES
CADDIS
CADDISES
CADDISH
CADDY
CADDYING
CADDYSS
CADDYSSES
CADE
CADEAU
CADEAUX
CADEE
CADEES
CADELLE
CADELLES
CADENCE
CADENCED
CADENCES
CADENCIES
CADENCY
CADENT
CADENTIAL
CADENZA
CADENZAS
CADES
CADET
CADETS
CADETSHIP
CADETSHIPS
CADGE
CADGED
CADGER
CADGERS
CADGES
CADGIER
CADGIEST
CADGING
CADGY
CADI
CADIE
CADIES
CADIS
CADMIUM
CADMIUMS
CADRANS
CADRANSES
CADRE
CADRES
CADS
CADUAC
CADUACS
CADUCEAN
CADUCEI
CADUCEUS
CADUCITIES
CADUCITY
CADUCOUS
CAECA
CAECAL
CAECILIAN
CAECILIANS
CAECITIS
CAECITISES
CAECUM
CAERULE
CAERULEAN
CAESAR
CAESARS
CAESE
CAESIOUS
CAESIUM
CAESIUMS
CAESTUS
CAESTUSES
CAESURA
CAESURAE
CAESURAL
CAESURAS
CAFARD
CAFARDS
CAFE
CAFES
CAFETERIA
CAFETERIAS
CAFETIERE
CAFETIERES
CAFF
CAFFEIN
CAFFEINE
CAFFEINES
CAFFEINS
CAFFEISM
CAFFEISMS
CAFFILA
CAFFILAS
CAFFS

CAFILA
CAFILAS
CAFTAN
CAFTANS
CAGE
CAGEBIRD
CAGEBIRDS
CAGED
CAGELING
CAGELINGS
CAGES
CAGEWORK
CAGEWORKS
CAGEY
CAGEYNESS
CAGEYNESSES
CAGIER
CAGIEST
CAGILY
CAGINESS
CAGINESSES
CAGING
CAGOT
CAGOTS
CAGOUL
CAGOULE
CAGOULES
CAGOULS
CAGY
CAGYNESS
CAGYNESSES
CAHIER
CAHIERS
CAHOOT
CAHOOTS
CAILLACH
CAILLACHS
CAILLE
CAILLEACH
CAILLEACHS
CAILLES
CAILLIACH
CAILLIACHS
CAIMAC
CAIMACAM
CAIMACAMS
CAIMACS
CAIMAN
CAIMANS
CAIN
CAINS
CAIQUE
CAIQUES
CAIRD
CAIRDS
CAIRN
CAIRNED
CAIRNGORM
CAIRNGORMS
CAIRNS
CAISSON
CAISSONS
CAITIFF
CAITIFFS
CAITIVE
CAITIVES
CAJEPUT
CAJEPUTS
CAJOLE
CAJOLED
CAJOLER
CAJOLERIES
CAJOLERS
CAJOLERY
CAJOLES
CAJOLING
CAJUN
CAJUPUT
CAJUPUTS
CAKE
CAKED
CAKES
CAKEWALK
CAKEWALKED
CAKEWALKING
CAKEWALKS
CAKEY
CAKIER
CAKIEST
CAKING
CAKINGS
CAKY
CALABASH
CALABASHES
CALABOOSE
CALABOOSES
CALABRESE
CALABRESES
CALADIUM
CALADIUMS
CALAMANCO
CALAMANCOES
CALAMANCOS
CALAMARI
CALAMARIES
CALAMARY
CALAMI
CALAMINE
CALAMINES
CALAMINT
CALAMINTS
CALAMITE
CALAMITES
CALAMITIES
CALAMITY
CALAMUS
CALANDO
CALANDRIA
CALANDRIAS
CALANTHE
CALANTHES
CALASH
CALASHES
CALATHEA
CALATHEAS
CALATHI
CALATHUS
CALAVANCE
CALAVANCES
CALCANEA
CALCANEAL
CALCANEAN
CALCANEI
CALCANEUM
CALCANEUS
CALCAR
CALCARATE
CALCARIA
CALCARINE
CALCARS
CALCEATE
CALCEATED
CALCEATES
CALCEATING
CALCED
CALCEDONIES
CALCEDONY
CALCES
CALCIC
CALCICOLE
CALCICOLES
CALCIFIC
CALCIFIED
CALCIFIES
CALCIFUGE
CALCIFUGES
CALCIFY
CALCIFYING
CALCIMINE
CALCIMINED
CALCIMINES
CALCIMINING
CALCINE
CALCINED
CALCINES
CALCINING
CALCITE
CALCITES
CALCIUM
CALCIUMS
CALCRETE
CALCRETES
CALCSPAR
CALCSPARS
CALCULAR
CALCULARY
CALCULATE
CALCULATED
CALCULATES
CALCULATING
CALCULI
CALCULOSE
CALCULOUS
CALCULUS
CALCULUSES
CALDARIA
CALDARIUM
CALDERA
CALDERAS
CALDRON
CALDRONS
CALEFIED
CALEFIES
CALEFY
CALEFYING
CALEMBOUR
CALEMBOURS
CALENDAR
CALENDARED
CALENDARING
CALENDARS
CALENDER
CALENDERED
CALENDERING
CALENDERINGS
CALENDERS
CALENDRER
CALENDRERS
CALENDRIC
CALENDRIES
CALENDRY
CALENDS
CALENDULA
CALENDULAS
CALENTURE
CALENTURES
CALF
CALFDOZER
CALFDOZERS
CALFLESS
CALFLICK
CALFLICKS
CALFS
CALFSKIN
CALFSKINS
CALIATOUR
CALIATOURS
CALIBER
CALIBERED
CALIBERS
CALIBRATE
CALIBRATED
CALIBRATES
CALIBRATING
CALIBRE
CALIBRED
CALIBRES
CALICES
CALICHE
CALICHES
CALICLE
CALICLES
CALICO
CALICOES
CALICOS
CALID
CALIDITIES
CALIDITY
CALIF
CALIFS
CALIGO
CALIGOES
CALIGOS
CALIMA
CALIMAS
CALIOLOGIES
CALIOLOGY
CALIPASH
CALIPASHES
CALIPEE
CALIPEES
CALIPER
CALIPERS
CALIPH
CALIPHAL
CALIPHATE
CALIPHATES
CALIPHS
CALISAYA
CALISAYAS
CALIVER
CALIVERS
CALIX
CALK
CALKED
CALKER
CALKERS
CALKIN
CALKING
CALKINS
CALKS
CALL
CALLA
CALLAN
CALLANS
CALLANT
CALLANTS
CALLAS
CALLED
CALLER
CALLERS
CALLET
CALLETS
CALLID
CALLIDITIES
CALLIDITY
CALLIGRAM
CALLIGRAMS
CALLING
CALLINGS
CALLIOPE
CALLIOPES
CALLIPER
CALLIPERED
CALLIPERING
CALLIPERS
CALLOSITIES
CALLOSITY
CALLOUS
CALLOUSLY
CALLOW
CALLOWER
CALLOWEST
CALLOWS
CALLS
CALLUNA
CALLUNAS
CALLUS
CALLUSES
CALM

CALMANT
CALMANTS
CALMATIVE
CALMATIVES
CALMED
CALMER
CALMEST
CALMIER
CALMIEST
CALMING
CALMLY
CALMNESS
CALMNESSES
CALMS
CALMSTONE
CALMSTONES
CALMY
CALOMEL
CALOMELS
CALORIC
CALORICS
CALORIE
CALORIES
CALORIFIC
CALORIST
CALORISTS
CALORY
CALOTTE
CALOTTES
CALOTYPE
CALOTYPES
CALOYER
CALOYERS
CALP
CALPA
CALPAC
CALPACK
CALPACKS
CALPACS
CALPAS
CALPS
CALQUE
CALQUED
CALQUES
CALQUING
CALTHA
CALTHAS
CALTHROP
CALTHROPS
CALTRAP
CALTRAPS
CALTROP
CALTROPS
CALUMBA
CALUMBAS
CALUMET
CALUMETS
CALUMNIES
CALUMNY
CALUTRON
CALUTRONS
CALVARIA
CALVARIAS
CALVARIES
CALVARY
CALVE
CALVED
CALVER
CALVERED
CALVERING
CALVERS
CALVES
CALVING
CALVITIES
CALX
CALXES
CALYCES
CALYCINAL
CALYCINE
CALYCLE
CALYCLED
CALYCLES
CALYCOID
CALYCULE
CALYCULES
CALYCULI
CALYCULUS
CALYPSO
CALYPSOS
CALYPTERA
CALYPTERAS
CALYPTRA
CALYPTRAS
CALYX
CALYXES
CALZONE
CALZONES
CALZONI
CAM
CAMAIEU
CAMAIEUX
CAMAN
CAMANACHD
CAMANACHDS
CAMANS
CAMARILLA
CAMARILLAS
CAMARON
CAMARONS
CAMAS
CAMASES
CAMASH
CAMASHES
CAMASS
CAMASSES
CAMBER
CAMBERED
CAMBERING
CAMBERINGS
CAMBERS
CAMBIA
CAMBIAL
CAMBIFORM
CAMBISM
CAMBISMS
CAMBIST
CAMBISTRIES
CAMBISTRY
CAMBISTS
CAMBIUM
CAMBIUMS
CAMBOGE
CAMBOGES
CAMBREL
CAMBRELS
CAMBRIC
CAMBRICS
CAMCORDER
CAMCORDERS
CAME
CAMEL
CAMELBACK
CAMELBACKS
CAMELEER
CAMELEERS
CAMELEON
CAMELEONS
CAMELID
CAMELIDS
CAMELINE
CAMELINES
CAMELISH
CAMELLIA
CAMELLIAS
CAMELOID
CAMELOIDS
CAMELOT
CAMELOTS
CAMELRIES
CAMELRY
CAMELS
CAMEO
CAMEOS
CAMERA
CAMERAE
CAMERAL
CAMERAMAN
CAMERAMEN
CAMERAS
CAMERATED
CAMES
CAMESE
CAMESES
CAMION
CAMIONS
CAMIS
CAMISADE
CAMISADES
CAMISADO
CAMISADOS
CAMISE
CAMISES
CAMISOLE
CAMISOLES
CAMLET
CAMLETS
CAMMED
CAMMING
CAMOGIE
CAMOGIES
CAMOMILE
CAMOMILES
CAMORRA
CAMORRAS
CAMOTE
CAMOTES
CAMOUFLET
CAMOUFLETS
CAMP
CAMPAGNA
CAMPAGNAS
CAMPAIGN
CAMPAIGNED
CAMPAIGNING
CAMPAIGNS
CAMPANA
CAMPANAS
CAMPANERO
CAMPANEROS
CAMPANILE
CAMPANILES
CAMPANILI
CAMPANIST
CAMPANISTS
CAMPANULA
CAMPANULAS
CAMPEADOR
CAMPEADORS
CAMPED
CAMPER
CAMPERS
CAMPESINO
CAMPESINOS
CAMPEST
CAMPFIRE
CAMPFIRES
CAMPHANE
CAMPHANES
CAMPHENE
CAMPHENES
CAMPHINE
CAMPHINES
CAMPHIRE
CAMPHIRES
CAMPHOR
CAMPHORIC
CAMPHORS
CAMPIER
CAMPIEST
CAMPING
CAMPION
CAMPIONS
CAMPLE
CAMPLED
CAMPLES
CAMPLING
CAMPLY
CAMPNESS
CAMPNESSES
CAMPO
CAMPODEID
CAMPODEIDS
CAMPOREE
CAMPOREES
CAMPOS
CAMPS
CAMPSITE
CAMPSITES
CAMPUS
CAMPUSES
CAMPY
CAMS
CAMSHAFT
CAMSHAFTS
CAMSHEUGH
CAMSHO
CAMSHOCH
CAMSTAIRY
CAMSTANE
CAMSTANES
CAMSTEARY
CAMSTONE
CAMSTONES
CAMUS
CAMUSES
CAMWOOD
CAMWOODS
CAN
CANADA
CANADAS
CANAIGRE
CANAIGRES
CANAILLE
CANAILLES
CANAKIN
CANAKINS
CANAL
CANALISE
CANALISED
CANALISES
CANALISING
CANALIZE
CANALIZED
CANALIZES
CANALIZING
CANALS
CANAPE
CANAPES
CANARD
CANARDS
CANARIED
CANARIES
CANARY
CANARYING
CANASTA
CANASTAS
CANASTER
CANASTERS
CANBANK
CANBANKS
CANCAN
CANCANS
CANCEL
CANCELEER
CANCELEERED
CANCELEERING
CANCELEERS
CANCELIER
CANCELIERED
CANCELIERING

CANCELIERS
CANCELLED
CANCELLI
CANCELLING
CANCELS
CANCER
CANCERATE
CANCERATED
CANCERATES
CANCERATING
CANCEROUS
CANCERS
CANCRINE
CANCROID
CANCROIDS
CANDELA
CANDELAS
CANDENT
CANDID
CANDIDA
CANDIDACIES
CANDIDACY
CANDIDAL
CANDIDAS
CANDIDATE
CANDIDATES
CANDIDER
CANDIDEST
CANDIDLY
CANDIE
CANDIED
CANDIES
CANDLE
CANDLED
CANDLENUT
CANDLENUTS
CANDLES
CANDLING
CANDOCK
CANDOCKS
CANDOR
CANDORS
CANDOUR
CANDOURS
CANDY
CANDYING
CANDYTUFT
CANDYTUFTS
CANE
CANEBRAKE
CANEBRAKES
CANED
CANEFRUIT
CANEFRUITS
CANEH
CANEHS
CANELLA
CANELLAS
CANELLINI
CANEPHOR
CANEPHORA
CANEPHORAS
CANEPHORE
CANEPHORES
CANEPHORS
CANES
CANESCENT
CANFIELD
CANFIELDS
CANFUL
CANFULS
CANG
CANGLE
CANGLED
CANGLES
CANGLING
CANGS
CANGUE
CANGUES
CANICULAR
CANID
CANIDS
CANIER
CANIEST
CANIKIN
CANIKINS
CANINE
CANINES
CANING
CANINGS
CANINITIES
CANINITY
CANISTER
CANISTERED
CANISTERING
CANISTERS
CANITIES
CANKER
CANKERED
CANKERING
CANKEROUS
CANKERS
CANKERY
CANN
CANNA
CANNABIC
CANNABIN
CANNABINS
CANNABIS
CANNABISES
CANNACH
CANNACHS
CANNAE
CANNAS
CANNED
CANNEL
CANNELS
CANNELURE
CANNELURES
CANNER
CANNERIES
CANNERS
CANNERY
CANNIBAL
CANNIBALS
CANNIER
CANNIEST
CANNIKIN
CANNIKINS
CANNILY
CANNINESS
CANNINESSES
CANNING
CANNON
CANNONADE
CANNONADED
CANNONADES
CANNONADING
CANNONED
CANNONEER
CANNONEERS
CANNONIER
CANNONIERS
CANNONING
CANNONRIES
CANNONRY
CANNONS
CANNOT
CANNS
CANNULA
CANNULAE
CANNULAR
CANNULAS
CANNULATE
CANNY
CANOE
CANOED
CANOEING
CANOEINGS
CANOEIST
CANOEISTS
CANOES
CANON
CANONESS
CANONESSES
CANONIC
CANONICAL
CANONICALS
CANONISE
CANONISED
CANONISES
CANONISING
CANONIST
CANONISTS
CANONIZE
CANONIZED
CANONIZES
CANONIZING
CANONRIES
CANONRY
CANONS
CANOODLE
CANOODLED
CANOODLES
CANOODLING
CANOPIED
CANOPIES
CANOPY
CANOPYING
CANOROUS
CANS
CANST
CANSTICK
CANSTICKS
CANT
CANTABANK
CANTABANKS
CANTABILE
CANTABILES
CANTALA
CANTALAS
CANTALOUP
CANTALOUPS
CANTAR
CANTARS
CANTATA
CANTATAS
CANTATE
CANTATES
CANTDOG
CANTDOGS
CANTED
CANTEEN
CANTEENS
CANTER
CANTERED
CANTERING
CANTERS
CANTEST
CANTHARI
CANTHARID
CANTHARIDES
CANTHARIDS
CANTHARIS
CANTHARUS
CANTHI
CANTHOOK
CANTHOOKS
CANTHUS
CANTICLE
CANTICLES
CANTICO
CANTICOED
CANTICOING
CANTICOS
CANTICOY
CANTICOYED
CANTICOYING
CANTICOYS
CANTICUM
CANTICUMS
CANTIER
CANTIEST
CANTILENA
CANTILENAS
CANTINA
CANTINAS
CANTINESS
CANTINESSES
CANTING
CANTINGS
CANTION
CANTIONS
CANTLE
CANTLED
CANTLES
CANTLET
CANTLETS
CANTLING
CANTO
CANTON
CANTONAL
CANTONED
CANTONING
CANTONISE
CANTONISED
CANTONISES
CANTONISING
CANTONIZE
CANTONIZED
CANTONIZES
CANTONIZING
CANTONS
CANTOR
CANTORIAL
CANTORIS
CANTORS
CANTOS
CANTRED
CANTREDS
CANTREF
CANTREFS
CANTRIP
CANTRIPS
CANTS
CANTUS
CANTY
CANULA
CANULAE
CANULAS
CANVAS
CANVASED
CANVASES
CANVASING
CANVASS
CANVASSED
CANVASSER
CANVASSERS
CANVASSES
CANVASSING
CANY
CANYON
CANYONS
CANZONA
CANZONAS
CANZONE
CANZONET
CANZONETS
CANZONI
CAP
CAPA
CAPABLE
CAPABLER
CAPABLEST
CAPABLY
CAPACIOUS
CAPACITIES
CAPACITOR
CAPACITORS
CAPACITY

CAPARISON
CAPARISONED
CAPARISONING
CAPARISONS
CAPAS
CAPE
CAPED
CAPELET
CAPELETS
CAPELIN
CAPELINE
CAPELINES
CAPELINS
CAPELLET
CAPELLETS
CAPELLINE
CAPELLINES
CAPER
CAPERED
CAPERER
CAPERERS
CAPERING
CAPERS
CAPES
CAPESKIN
CAPESKINS
CAPEWORK
CAPEWORKS
CAPI
CAPIAS
CAPIASES
CAPILLARIES
CAPILLARY
CAPING
CAPITA
CAPITAL
CAPITALLY
CAPITALS
CAPITAN
CAPITANI
CAPITANO
CAPITANOS
CAPITANS
CAPITATE
CAPITAYN
CAPITAYNS
CAPITELLA
CAPITULA
CAPITULAR
CAPITULARS
CAPITULUM
CAPIZ
CAPIZES
CAPLE
CAPLES
CAPLET
CAPLETS
CAPLIN
CAPLINS
CAPO
CAPOCCHIA
CAPOCCHIAS
CAPOEIRA
CAPOEIRAS
CAPON
CAPONIER
CAPONIERE
CAPONIERES
CAPONIERS
CAPONISE
CAPONISED
CAPONISES
CAPONISING
CAPONIZE
CAPONIZED
CAPONIZES
CAPONIZING
CAPONS
CAPORAL
CAPORALS
CAPOS
CAPOT
CAPOTASTO
CAPOTASTOS
CAPOTE
CAPOTES
CAPOTS
CAPOTTED
CAPOTTING
CAPOUCH
CAPOUCHES
CAPPED
CAPPER
CAPPERS
CAPPING
CAPPINGS
CAPRATE
CAPRATES
CAPRIC
CAPRICCI
CAPRICCIO
CAPRICCIOS
CAPRICE
CAPRICES
CAPRID
CAPRIDS
CAPRIFIED
CAPRIFIES
CAPRIFIG
CAPRIFIGS
CAPRIFOIL
CAPRIFOILS
CAPRIFOLE
CAPRIFOLES
CAPRIFORM
CAPRIFY
CAPRIFYING
CAPRINE
CAPRIOLE
CAPRIOLED
CAPRIOLES
CAPRIOLING
CAPROATE
CAPROATES
CAPROIC
CAPRYLATE
CAPRYLATES
CAPRYLIC
CAPS
CAPSAICIN
CAPSAICINS
CAPSICUM
CAPSICUMS
CAPSID
CAPSIDS
CAPSIZAL
CAPSIZALS
CAPSIZE
CAPSIZED
CAPSIZES
CAPSIZING
CAPSTAN
CAPSTANS
CAPSTONE
CAPSTONES
CAPSULAR
CAPSULARY
CAPSULATE
CAPSULE
CAPSULES
CAPSULISE
CAPSULISED
CAPSULISES
CAPSULISING
CAPSULIZE
CAPSULIZED
CAPSULIZES
CAPSULIZING
CAPTAIN
CAPTAINCIES
CAPTAINCY
CAPTAINED
CAPTAINING
CAPTAINRIES
CAPTAINRY
CAPTAINS
CAPTAN
CAPTANS
CAPTION
CAPTIONED
CAPTIONING
CAPTIONS
CAPTIOUS
CAPTIVATE
CAPTIVATED
CAPTIVATES
CAPTIVATING
CAPTIVE
CAPTIVED
CAPTIVES
CAPTIVING
CAPTIVITIES
CAPTIVITY
CAPTOR
CAPTORS
CAPTURE
CAPTURED
CAPTURER
CAPTURERS
CAPTURES
CAPTURING
CAPUCCIO
CAPUCCIOS
CAPUCHE
CAPUCHES
CAPUCHIN
CAPUCHINS
CAPUERA
CAPUERAS
CAPUL
CAPULS
CAPUT
CAPYBARA
CAPYBARAS
CAR
CARABAO
CARABAOS
CARABID
CARABIDS
CARABIN
CARABINE
CARABINER
CARABINERS
CARABINES
CARABINS
CARACAL
CARACALS
CARACARA
CARACARAS
CARACK
CARACKS
CARACOL
CARACOLE
CARACOLED
CARACOLES
CARACOLING
CARACOLLED
CARACOLLING
CARACOLS
CARACT
CARACTS
CARACUL
CARACULS
CARAFE
CARAFES
CARAMBA
CARAMBOLA
CARAMBOLAS
CARAMBOLE
CARAMBOLED
CARAMBOLES
CARAMBOLING
CARAMEL
CARAMELLED
CARAMELLING
CARAMELS
CARANGID
CARANGIDS
CARANGOID
CARANGOIDS
CARANNA
CARANNAS
CARAP
CARAPACE
CARAPACES
CARAPS
CARAT
CARATS
CARAUNA
CARAUNAS
CARAVAN
CARAVANCE
CARAVANCES
CARAVANED
CARAVANER
CARAVANERS
CARAVANING
CARAVANNED
CARAVANNING
CARAVANS
CARAVEL
CARAVELS
CARAWAY
CARAWAYS
CARB
CARBACHOL
CARBACHOLS
CARBAMATE
CARBAMATES
CARBAMIDE
CARBAMIDES
CARBANION
CARBANIONS
CARBARYL
CARBARYLS
CARBAZOLE
CARBAZOLES
CARBIDE
CARBIDES
CARBIES
CARBINE
CARBINEER
CARBINEERS
CARBINES
CARBINIER
CARBINIERS
CARBOLIC
CARBOLICS
CARBON
CARBONADE
CARBONADES
CARBONADO
CARBONADOED
CARBONADOES
CARBONADOING
CARBONADOS
CARBONARA
CARBONARAS
CARBONATE
CARBONATED
CARBONATES
CARBONATING
CARBONIC
CARBONISE
CARBONISED
CARBONISES
CARBONISING
CARBONIZE
CARBONIZED
CARBONIZES

CARBONIZING
CARBONS
CARBONYL
CARBONYLS
CARBOXYL
CARBOXYLS
CARBOY
CARBOYS
CARBS
CARBUNCLE
CARBUNCLES
CARBURATE
CARBURATED
CARBURATES
CARBURATING
CARBURET
CARBURETS
CARBURETTED
CARBURETTING
CARBURISE
CARBURISED
CARBURISES
CARBURISING
CARBURIZE
CARBURIZED
CARBURIZES
CARBURIZING
CARBY
CARCAJOU
CARCAJOUS
CARCAKE
CARCAKES
CARCANET
CARCANETS
CARCASE
CARCASED
CARCASES
CARCASING
CARCASS
CARCASSED
CARCASSES
CARCASSING
CARCERAL
CARCINOMA
CARCINOMAS
CARCINOMATA
CARD
CARDAMINE
CARDAMINES
CARDAMOM
CARDAMOMS
CARDAMON
CARDAMONS
CARDAMUM
CARDAMUMS
CARDBOARD
CARDBOARDS
CARDCASE
CARDCASES
CARDECU
CARDECUE
CARDECUES
CARDECUS
CARDED
CARDER
CARDERS
CARDI
CARDIAC
CARDIACAL
CARDIACS
CARDIALGIES
CARDIALGY
CARDIES
CARDIGAN
CARDIGANS
CARDINAL
CARDINALS
CARDING
CARDIOID
CARDIOIDS
CARDIS
CARDITIS
CARDITISES
CARDOON
CARDOONS
CARDPHONE
CARDPHONES
CARDPUNCH
CARDPUNCHES
CARDS
CARDUUS
CARDUUSES
CARDY
CARE
CARED
CAREEN
CAREENAGE
CAREENAGES
CAREENED
CAREENING
CAREENS
CAREER
CAREERED
CAREERING
CAREERISM
CAREERISMS
CAREERIST
CAREERISTS
CAREERS
CAREFREE
CAREFUL
CAREFULLY
CARELESS
CAREME
CAREMES
CARER
CARERS
CARES
CARESS
CARESSED
CARESSES
CARESSING
CARESSINGS
CARESSIVE
CARET
CARETAKE
CARETAKEN
CARETAKER
CARETAKERS
CARETAKES
CARETAKING
CARETOOK
CARETS
CAREWORN
CAREX
CARFARE
CARFARES
CARFAX
CARFAXES
CARFOX
CARFOXES
CARFUFFLE
CARFUFFLED
CARFUFFLES
CARFUFFLING
CARGEESE
CARGO
CARGOED
CARGOES
CARGOING
CARGOOSE
CARIACOU
CARIACOUS
CARIAMA
CARIAMAS
CARIBE
CARIBES
CARIBOU
CARIBOUS
CARICES
CARIERE
CARIERES
CARIES
CARILLON
CARILLONED
CARILLONING
CARILLONS
CARINA
CARINAE
CARINAS
CARINATE
CARING
CARIOCA
CARIOCAS
CARIOLE
CARIOLES
CARIOUS
CARITAS
CARITATES
CARJACK
CARJACKED
CARJACKER
CARJACKERS
CARJACKING
CARJACKINGS
CARJACKS
CARJACOU
CARJACOUS
CARK
CARKED
CARKING
CARKS
CARL
CARLINE
CARLINES
CARLING
CARLINGS
CARLISH
CARLOAD
CARLOADS
CARLOCK
CARLOCKS
CARLOT
CARLOTS
CARLS
CARMAN
CARMELITE
CARMELITES
CARMEN
CARMINE
CARMINES
CARNAGE
CARNAGES
CARNAHUBA
CARNAHUBAS
CARNAL
CARNALISE
CARNALISED
CARNALISES
CARNALISING
CARNALISM
CARNALISMS
CARNALIST
CARNALISTS
CARNALITIES
CARNALITY
CARNALIZE
CARNALIZED
CARNALIZES
CARNALIZING
CARNALLED
CARNALLING
CARNALLY
CARNALS
CARNATION
CARNATIONS
CARNAUBA
CARNAUBAS
CARNELIAN
CARNELIANS
CARNEOUS
CARNET
CARNETS
CARNEY
CARNEYED
CARNEYING
CARNEYS
CARNIED
CARNIER
CARNIES
CARNIEST
CARNIFEX
CARNIFEXES
CARNIFIED
CARNIFIES
CARNIFY
CARNIFYING
CARNIVAL
CARNIVALS
CARNIVORE
CARNIVORES
CARNOSE
CARNOSITIES
CARNOSITY
CARNOTITE
CARNOTITES
CARNY
CARNYING
CAROB
CAROBS
CAROCHE
CAROCHES
CAROL
CAROLI
CAROLLED
CAROLLER
CAROLLERS
CAROLLING
CAROLS
CAROLUS
CAROLUSES
CAROM
CAROMED
CAROMEL
CAROMELLED
CAROMELLING
CAROMELS
CAROMING
CAROMS
CAROTENE
CAROTENES
CAROTID
CAROTIN
CAROTINS
CAROUSAL
CAROUSALS
CAROUSE
CAROUSED
CAROUSEL
CAROUSELS
CAROUSER
CAROUSERS
CAROUSES
CAROUSING
CARP
CARPACCIO
CARPACCIOS
CARPAL
CARPALS
CARPARK
CARPARKS
CARPED
CARPEL
CARPELS
CARPENTER
CARPENTERED
CARPENTERING
CARPENTERS
CARPENTRIES
CARPENTRY

CARPER
CARPERS
CARPET
CARPETBAG
CARPETBAGS
CARPETED
CARPETING
CARPETINGS
CARPETS
CARPI
CARPING
CARPINGLY
CARPINGS
CARPOLOGIES
CARPOLOGY
CARPORT
CARPORTS
CARPS
CARPUS
CARR
CARRACK
CARRACKS
CARRACT
CARRACTS
CARRAGEEN
CARRAGEENS
CARRAT
CARRATS
CARRAWAY
CARRAWAYS
CARRECT
CARRECTS
CARREL
CARRELL
CARRELLS
CARRELS
CARRIAGE
CARRIAGES
CARRIED
CARRIER
CARRIERS
CARRIES
CARRIOLE
CARRIOLES
CARRION
CARRIONS
CARRITCH
CARRITCHES
CARRONADE
CARRONADES
CARROT
CARROTIER
CARROTIEST
CARROTS
CARROTY
CARROUSEL
CARROUSELS
CARRS
CARRY
CARRYALL
CARRYALLS
CARRYCOT
CARRYCOTS
CARRYING
CARRYTALE
CARRYTALES
CARS
CARSE
CARSES
CARSEY
CARSEYS
CART
CARTA
CARTAGE
CARTAGES
CARTAS
CARTE
CARTED
CARTEL
CARTELISE
CARTELISED
CARTELISES
CARTELISING
CARTELISM
CARTELISMS
CARTELIST
CARTELISTS
CARTELIZE
CARTELIZED
CARTELIZES
CARTELIZING
CARTELS
CARTER
CARTERS
CARTES
CARTILAGE
CARTILAGES
CARTING
CARTLOAD
CARTLOADS
CARTOGRAM
CARTOGRAMS
CARTOLOGIES
CARTOLOGY
CARTON
CARTONAGE
CARTONAGES
CARTONED
CARTONING
CARTONS
CARTOON
CARTOONED
CARTOONING
CARTOONS
CARTOUCH
CARTOUCHE
CARTOUCHES
CARTRIDGE
CARTRIDGES
CARTROAD
CARTROADS
CARTS
CARTULARIES
CARTULARY
CARTWAY
CARTWAYS
CARTWHEEL
CARTWHEELED
CARTWHEELING
CARTWHEELS
CARUCAGE
CARUCAGES
CARUCATE
CARUCATES
CARUNCLE
CARUNCLES
CARVACROL
CARVACROLS
CARVE
CARVED
CARVEL
CARVELS
CARVEN
CARVER
CARVERIES
CARVERS
CARVERY
CARVES
CARVIES
CARVING
CARVINGS
CARVY
CARYATIC
CARYATID
CARYATIDES
CARYATIDS
CARYOPSES
CARYOPSIDES
CARYOPSIS
CASA
CASAS
CASBAH
CASBAHS
CASCABEL
CASCABELS
CASCADE
CASCADED
CASCADES
CASCADING
CASCADURA
CASCADURAS
CASCARA
CASCARAS
CASCHROM
CASCHROMS
CASCO
CASCOS
CASE
CASEATION
CASEATIONS
CASEBOOK
CASEBOOKS
CASED
CASEIN
CASEINS
CASEMAKER
CASEMAKERS
CASEMAN
CASEMATE
CASEMATED
CASEMATES
CASEMEN
CASEMENT
CASEMENTS
CASEOUS
CASERN
CASERNE
CASERNES
CASERNS
CASES
CASEWORK
CASEWORKS
CASH
CASHAW
CASHAWS
CASHED
CASHES
CASHEW
CASHEWS
CASHIER
CASHIERED
CASHIERER
CASHIERERS
CASHIERING
CASHIERINGS
CASHIERS
CASHING
CASHLESS
CASHMERE
CASHMERES
CASHPOINT
CASHPOINTS
CASIMERE
CASIMERES
CASING
CASINGS
CASINO
CASINOS
CASK
CASKED
CASKET
CASKETS
CASKING
CASKS
CASKSTAND
CASKSTANDS
CASQUE
CASQUES
CASSAREEP
CASSAREEPS
CASSARIPE
CASSARIPES
CASSATA
CASSATAS
CASSATION
CASSATIONS
CASSAVA
CASSAVAS
CASSEROLE
CASSEROLED
CASSEROLES
CASSEROLING
CASSETTE
CASSETTES
CASSIA
CASSIAS
CASSIMERE
CASSIMERES
CASSINGLE
CASSINGLES
CASSINO
CASSINOS
CASSIS
CASSISES
CASSOCK
CASSOCKED
CASSOCKS
CASSONADE
CASSONADES
CASSONE
CASSONES
CASSOULET
CASSOULETS
CASSOWARIES
CASSOWARY
CAST
CASTANET
CASTANETS
CASTAWAY
CASTAWAYS
CASTE
CASTED
CASTELESS
CASTELLA
CASTELLAN
CASTELLANS
CASTELLUM
CASTELLUMS
CASTER
CASTERS
CASTES
CASTIGATE
CASTIGATED
CASTIGATES
CASTIGATING
CASTING
CASTINGS
CASTLE
CASTLED
CASTLES
CASTLING
CASTOCK
CASTOCKS
CASTOR
CASTOREUM
CASTOREUMS
CASTORIES
CASTORS
CASTORY
CASTRAL
CASTRATE
CASTRATED
CASTRATES
CASTRATI
CASTRATING
CASTRATO
CASTS
CASUAL
CASUALISE
CASUALISED

CASUALISES
CASUALISING
CASUALISM
CASUALISMS
CASUALIZE
CASUALIZED
CASUALIZES
CASUALIZING
CASUALLY
CASUALS
CASUALTIES
CASUALTY
CASUARINA
CASUARINAS
CASUIST
CASUISTIC
CASUISTRIES
CASUISTRY
CASUISTS
CAT
CATABASES
CATABASIS
CATABOLIC
CATACLASM
CATACLASMS
CATACLYSM
CATACLYSMS
CATACOMB
CATACOMBS
CATAFALCO
CATAFALCOES
CATALASE
CATALASES
CATALEPSIES
CATALEPSY
CATALEXES
CATALEXIS
CATALO
CATALOES
CATALOG
CATALOGED
CATALOGER
CATALOGERS
CATALOGING
CATALOGS
CATALOGUE
CATALOGUED
CATALOGUES
CATALOGUING
CATALOS
CATALPA
CATALPAS
CATALYSE
CATALYSED
CATALYSER
CATALYSERS
CATALYSES
CATALYSING
CATALYSIS
CATALYST
CATALYSTS
CATALYTIC
CATALYZE
CATALYZED
CATALYZER
CATALYZERS
CATALYZES
CATALYZING
CATAMARAN
CATAMARANS
CATAMENIA
CATAMITE
CATAMITES
CATAMOUNT
CATAMOUNTS
CATAPAN
CATAPANS
CATAPHYLL
CATAPHYLLS
CATAPLASM
CATAPLASMS
CATAPLEXIES
CATAPLEXY
CATAPULT
CATAPULTED
CATAPULTING
CATAPULTS
CATARACT
CATARACTS
CATARHINE
CATARRH
CATARRHAL
CATARRHS
CATASTA
CATASTAS
CATATONIA
CATATONIAS
CATATONIC
CATATONICS
CATATONIES
CATATONY
CATAWBA
CATAWBAS
CATBIRD
CATBIRDS
CATBOAT
CATBOATS
CATCALL
CATCALLED
CATCALLING
CATCALLS
CATCH
CATCHABLE
CATCHED
CATCHEN
CATCHER
CATCHERS
CATCHES
CATCHFLIES
CATCHFLY
CATCHIER
CATCHIEST
CATCHING
CATCHINGS
CATCHMENT
CATCHMENTS
CATCHPOLE
CATCHPOLES
CATCHPOLL
CATCHPOLLS
CATCHT
CATCHUP
CATCHUPS
CATCHWEED
CATCHWEEDS
CATCHWORD
CATCHWORDS
CATCHY
CATE
CATECHISE
CATECHISED
CATECHISES
CATECHISING
CATECHISINGS
CATECHISM
CATECHISMS
CATECHIST
CATECHISTS
CATECHIZE
CATECHIZED
CATECHIZES
CATECHIZING
CATECHIZINGS
CATECHOL
CATECHOLS
CATECHU
CATECHUS
CATEGORIC
CATEGORIES
CATEGORY
CATELOG
CATELOGS
CATENA
CATENAE
CATENANE
CATENANES
CATENARIES
CATENARY
CATENAS
CATENATE
CATENATED
CATENATES
CATENATING
CATER
CATERAN
CATERANS
CATERED
CATERER
CATERERS
CATERESS
CATERESSES
CATERING
CATERINGS
CATERS
CATERWAUL
CATERWAULED
CATERWAULING
CATERWAULINGS
CATERWAULS
CATES
CATFISH
CATFISHES
CATGUT
CATGUTS
CATHARISE
CATHARISED
CATHARISES
CATHARISING
CATHARIZE
CATHARIZED
CATHARIZES
CATHARIZING
CATHARSES
CATHARSIS
CATHARTIC
CATHARTICS
CATHEAD
CATHEADS
CATHECTIC
CATHEDRA
CATHEDRAL
CATHEDRALS
CATHEDRAS
CATHETER
CATHETERS
CATHETUS
CATHETUSES
CATHEXES
CATHEXIS
CATHISMA
CATHISMAS
CATHODAL
CATHODE
CATHODES
CATHODIC
CATHOLE
CATHOLES
CATHOLIC
CATHOOD
CATHOODS
CATHOUSE
CATHOUSES
CATION
CATIONS
CATKIN
CATKINS
CATLIKE
CATLING
CATLINGS
CATMINT
CATMINTS
CATNAP
CATNAPS
CATNEP
CATNEPS
CATNIP
CATNIPS
CATOPTRIC
CATOPTRICS
CATS
CATSKIN
CATSKINS
CATSUIT
CATSUITS
CATSUP
CATSUPS
CATTABU
CATTABUS
CATTALO
CATTALOES
CATTALOS
CATTED
CATTERIES
CATTERY
CATTIER
CATTIES
CATTIEST
CATTILY
CATTINESS
CATTINESSES
CATTING
CATTISH
CATTISHLY
CATTLE
CATTLEMAN
CATTLEMEN
CATTLEYA
CATTLEYAS
CATTY
CATWORKS
CATWORM
CATWORMS
CAUCHEMAR
CAUCHEMARS
CAUCUS
CAUCUSED
CAUCUSES
CAUCUSING
CAUDAD
CAUDAL
CAUDATE
CAUDATED
CAUDEX
CAUDEXES
CAUDICES
CAUDICLE
CAUDICLES
CAUDILLO
CAUDILLOS
CAUDLE
CAUDLED
CAUDLES
CAUDLING
CAUDRON
CAUDRONS
CAUF
CAUGHT
CAUK
CAUKER
CAUKERS
CAUKS
CAUL
CAULD
CAULDER
CAULDEST
CAULDRIFE
CAULDRON
CAULDRONS
CAULDS
CAULES

CAULICLE
CAULICLES
CAULICULI
CAULIFORM
CAULINARY
CAULINE
CAULIS
CAULK
CAULKED
CAULKER
CAULKERS
CAULKING
CAULKINGS
CAULKS
CAULOME
CAULOMES
CAULS
CAUM
CAUMED
CAUMING
CAUMS
CAUMSTONE
CAUMSTONES
CAUP
CAUPS
CAUSA
CAUSAE
CAUSAL
CAUSALITIES
CAUSALITY
CAUSALLY
CAUSATION
CAUSATIONS
CAUSATIVE
CAUSATIVES
CAUSE
CAUSED
CAUSELESS
CAUSEN
CAUSER
CAUSERIE
CAUSERIES
CAUSERS
CAUSES
CAUSEWAY
CAUSEWAYED
CAUSEWAYS
CAUSEY
CAUSEYED
CAUSEYS
CAUSING
CAUSTIC
CAUSTICS
CAUTEL
CAUTELOUS
CAUTELS
CAUTER
CAUTERANT
CAUTERANTS
CAUTERIES
CAUTERISE
CAUTERISED
CAUTERISES
CAUTERISING
CAUTERISM
CAUTERISMS
CAUTERIZE
CAUTERIZED
CAUTERIZES
CAUTERIZING
CAUTERS
CAUTERY
CAUTION
CAUTIONED
CAUTIONER
CAUTIONERS
CAUTIONING
CAUTIONRIES
CAUTIONRY
CAUTIONS
CAUTIOUS
CAUVES
CAVALCADE
CAVALCADED
CAVALCADES
CAVALCADING
CAVALIER
CAVALIERED
CAVALIERING
CAVALIERS
CAVALLA
CAVALLAS
CAVALLIES
CAVALLY
CAVALRIES
CAVALRY
CAVASS
CAVASSES
CAVATINA
CAVATINAS
CAVE
CAVEAT
CAVEATS
CAVED
CAVEL
CAVELS
CAVEMAN
CAVEMEN
CAVENDISH
CAVENDISHES
CAVER
CAVERN
CAVERNED
CAVERNING
CAVERNOUS
CAVERNS
CAVERS
CAVES
CAVESSON
CAVESSONS
CAVETTI
CAVETTO
CAVIAR
CAVIARE
CAVIARES
CAVIARIE
CAVIARIES
CAVIARS
CAVICORN
CAVICORNS
CAVIE
CAVIER
CAVIERS
CAVIES
CAVIL
CAVILLED
CAVILLER
CAVILLERS
CAVILLING
CAVILLINGS
CAVILS
CAVING
CAVINGS
CAVITATE
CAVITATED
CAVITATES
CAVITATING
CAVITIED
CAVITIES
CAVITY
CAVORT
CAVORTED
CAVORTING
CAVORTS
CAVY
CAW
CAWED
CAWING
CAWINGS
CAWK
CAWKER
CAWKERS
CAWKS
CAWS
CAXON
CAXONS
CAY
CAYENNE
CAYENNED
CAYENNES
CAYMAN
CAYMANS
CAYS
CAYUSE
CAYUSES
CAZIQUE
CAZIQUES
CEANOTHUS
CEANOTHUSES
CEAS
CEASE
CEASED
CEASELESS
CEASES
CEASING
CEASINGS
CEAZE
CEAZED
CEAZES
CEAZING
CEBADILLA
CEBADILLAS
CECA
CECAL
CECILS
CECITIES
CECITIS
CECITISES
CECITY
CECROPIA
CECROPIAS
CECUM
CEDAR
CEDARED
CEDARN
CEDARS
CEDARWOOD
CEDARWOODS
CEDE
CEDED
CEDES
CEDI
CEDILLA
CEDILLAS
CEDING
CEDIS
CEDRATE
CEDRATES
CEDRINE
CEDULA
CEDULAS
CEE
CEES
CEIL
CEILED
CEILI
CEILIDH
CEILIDHS
CEILING
CEILINGED
CEILINGS
CEILIS
CEILS
CEINTURE
CEINTURES
CEL
CELADON
CELADONS
CELANDINE
CELANDINES
CELEBRANT
CELEBRANTS
CELEBRATE
CELEBRATED
CELEBRATES
CELEBRATING
CELEBRITIES
CELEBRITY
CELERIAC
CELERIACS
CELERIES
CELERITIES
CELERITY
CELERY
CELESTA
CELESTAS
CELESTE
CELESTES
CELESTIAL
CELESTIALS
CELESTINE
CELESTINES
CELESTITE
CELESTITES
CELIAC
CELIACS
CELIBACIES
CELIBACY
CELIBATE
CELIBATES
CELL
CELLA
CELLAE
CELLAR
CELLARAGE
CELLARAGES
CELLARED
CELLARER
CELLARERS
CELLARET
CELLARETS
CELLARING
CELLARIST
CELLARISTS
CELLARMAN
CELLARMEN
CELLAROUS
CELLARS
CELLED
CELLIST
CELLISTS
CELLO
CELLOS
CELLOSE
CELLOSES
CELLPHONE
CELLPHONES
CELLS
CELLULAR
CELLULASE
CELLULASES
CELLULE
CELLULES
CELLULITE
CELLULITES
CELLULOID®
CELLULOIDS
CELLULOSE
CELLULOSES
CELOM
CELOMS
CELS
CELSITUDE
CELSITUDES
CELT
CELTS
CEMBALI
CEMBALIST
CEMBALISTS
CEMBALO

CEMBALOS
CEMBRA
CEMBRAS
CEMENT
CEMENTA
CEMENTED
CEMENTER
CEMENTERS
CEMENTING
CEMENTITE
CEMENTITES
CEMENTS
CEMENTUM
CEMETERIES
CEMETERY
CEMITARE
CEMITARES
CENACLE
CENACLES
CENDRE
CENOBITE
CENOBITES
CENOTAPH
CENOTAPHS
CENOTE
CENOTES
CENS
CENSE
CENSED
CENSER
CENSERS
CENSES
CENSING
CENSOR
CENSORED
CENSORIAL
CENSORIAN
CENSORING
CENSORS
CENSUAL
CENSURE
CENSURED
CENSURES
CENSURING
CENSUS
CENSUSED
CENSUSES
CENSUSING
CENT
CENTAGE
CENTAGES
CENTAL
CENTALS
CENTARE
CENTARES
CENTAUR
CENTAUREA
CENTAUREAS
CENTAURIES
CENTAURS
CENTAURY
CENTAVO
CENTAVOS
CENTENARIES
CENTENARY
CENTENIER
CENTENIERS
CENTER
CENTERED
CENTERING
CENTERINGS
CENTERS
CENTESES
CENTESIMO
CENTESIMOS
CENTESIS
CENTIARE
CENTIARES
CENTIGRAM
CENTIGRAMS
CENTIME
CENTIMES
CENTIMO
CENTIMOS
CENTINEL
CENTINELL
CENTINELLS
CENTINELS
CENTIPEDE
CENTIPEDES
CENTNER
CENTNERS
CENTO
CENTOIST
CENTOISTS
CENTONATE
CENTONEL
CENTONELL
CENTONELLS
CENTONELS
CENTONES
CENTONIST
CENTONISTS
CENTOS
CENTRA
CENTRAL
CENTRALLY
CENTRE
CENTRED
CENTREING
CENTREINGS
CENTRES
CENTRIC
CENTRICAL
CENTRIES
CENTRING
CENTRINGS
CENTRIOLE
CENTRIOLES
CENTRISM
CENTRISMS
CENTRIST
CENTRISTS
CENTRODE
CENTRODES
CENTROID
CENTROIDS
CENTRUM
CENTRUMS
CENTRY
CENTS
CENTUM
CENTUMS
CENTUMVIR
CENTUMVIRI
CENTUPLE
CENTUPLED
CENTUPLES
CENTUPLING
CENTURIAL
CENTURIES
CENTURION
CENTURIONS
CENTURY
CEORL
CEORLS
CEP
CEPACEOUS
CEPHALAD
CEPHALATE
CEPHALIC
CEPHALICS
CEPHALIN
CEPHALINS
CEPHALOUS
CEPS
CERACEOUS
CERAMAL
CERAMALS
CERAMIC
CERAMICS
CERAMIST
CERAMISTS
CERASIN
CERASINS
CERASTES
CERASTIUM
CERASTIUMS
CERATE
CERATED
CERATES
CERATITIS
CERATITISES
CERATODUS
CERATODUSES
CERATOID
CERBEREAN
CERBERIAN
CERCAL
CERCARIA
CERCARIAE
CERCARIAN
CERCI
CERCUS
CERE
CEREAL
CEREALIST
CEREALISTS
CEREALS
CEREBELLA
CEREBRA
CEREBRAL
CEREBRATE
CEREBRATED
CEREBRATES
CEREBRATING
CEREBRIC
CEREBRUM
CEREBRUMS
CERECLOTH
CERECLOTHS
CERED
CEREMENT
CEREMENTS
CEREMONIES
CEREMONY
CEREOUS
CERES
CERESIN
CERESINE
CERESINES
CERESINS
CEREUS
CEREUSES
CERGE
CERGES
CERIA
CERIAS
CERIC
CERING
CERIPH
CERIPHS
CERISE
CERISES
CERITE
CERITES
CERIUM
CERIUMS
CERMET
CERMETS
CERNE
CERNED
CERNES
CERNING
CERNUOUS
CEROGRAPH
CEROGRAPHS
CEROMANCIES
CEROMANCY
CEROON
CEROONS
CEROTYPE
CEROTYPES
CEROUS
CERRIAL
CERRIS
CERRISES
CERT
CERTAIN
CERTAINLY
CERTAINTIES
CERTAINTY
CERTES
CERTIFIED
CERTIFIER
CERTIFIERS
CERTIFIES
CERTIFY
CERTIFYING
CERTITUDE
CERTITUDES
CERTS
CERULE
CERULEAN
CERULEIN
CERULEINS
CERULEOUS
CERUMEN
CERUMENS
CERUSE
CERUSES
CERUSITE
CERUSITES
CERUSSITE
CERUSSITES
CERVELAT
CERVELATS
CERVICAL
CERVICES
CERVID
CERVIDS
CERVINE
CERVIX
CERVIXES
CESAREVNA
CESAREVNAS
CESIUM
CESIUMS
CESPITOSE
CESS
CESSATION
CESSATIONS
CESSE
CESSED
CESSER
CESSERS
CESSES
CESSING
CESSION
CESSIONS
CESSPIT
CESSPITS
CESSPOOL
CESSPOOLS
CESTI
CESTODE
CESTODES
CESTOID
CESTOIDS
CESTOS
CESTOSES
CESTUI
CESTUIS
CESTUS
CESURA
CESURAE
CESURAL
CESURAS
CESURE
CESURES

CETACEAN
CETACEANS
CETACEOUS
CETANE
CETANES
CETE
CETERACH
CETERACHS
CETES
CETOLOGIES
CETOLOGY
CETYL
CETYLS
CETYWALL
CETYWALLS
CEVADILLA
CEVADILLAS
CEVAPCICI
CEVICHE
CEVICHES
CEYLANITE
CEYLANITES
CEYLONITE
CEYLONITES
CH
CHA
CHABAZITE
CHABAZITES
CHABOUK
CHABOUKS
CHACE
CHACED
CHACES
CHACING
CHACK
CHACKED
CHACKING
CHACKS
CHACMA
CHACMAS
CHACO
CHACOES
CHACONNE
CHACONNES
CHACOS
CHAD
CHADAR
CHADARS
CHADDAR
CHADDARS
CHADDOR
CHADDORS
CHADOR
CHADORS
CHADS
CHAETA
CHAETAE
CHAETODON
CHAETODONS
CHAETOPOD
CHAETOPODS
CHAFE
CHAFED
CHAFER
CHAFERS
CHAFES
CHAFF
CHAFFED
CHAFFER
CHAFFERED
CHAFFERER
CHAFFERERS
CHAFFERIES
CHAFFERING
CHAFFERS
CHAFFERY
CHAFFIER
CHAFFIEST
CHAFFINCH
CHAFFINCHES
CHAFFING
CHAFFINGS
CHAFFRON
CHAFFRONS
CHAFFS
CHAFFY
CHAFING
CHAFT
CHAFTS
CHAGAN
CHAGANS
CHAGRIN
CHAGRINED
CHAGRINING
CHAGRINS
CHAI
CHAIN
CHAINE
CHAINED
CHAINES
CHAINING
CHAINLESS
CHAINLET
CHAINLETS
CHAINMAN
CHAINMEN
CHAINS
CHAINSAW
CHAINSAWS
CHAINSHOT
CHAINSHOTS
CHAINWORK
CHAINWORKS
CHAIR
CHAIRDAYS
CHAIRED
CHAIRING
CHAIRLIFT
CHAIRLIFTS
CHAIRMAN
CHAIRMEN
CHAIRS
CHAIS
CHAISE
CHAISES
CHAKRA
CHAKRAS
CHAL
CHALAN
CHALANED
CHALANING
CHALANS
CHALAZA
CHALAZAE
CHALAZAS
CHALAZIA
CHALAZION
CHALCID
CHALCIDS
CHALDER
CHALDERS
CHALDRON
CHALDRONS
CHALET
CHALETS
CHALICE
CHALICED
CHALICES
CHALK
CHALKED
CHALKFACE
CHALKFACES
CHALKIER
CHALKIEST
CHALKING
CHALKPIT
CHALKPITS
CHALKS
CHALKY
CHALLAH
CHALLAHS
CHALLAN
CHALLANED
CHALLANING
CHALLANS
CHALLENGE
CHALLENGED
CHALLENGES
CHALLENGING
CHALLIE
CHALLIES
CHALLIS
CHALLISES
CHALONE
CHALONES
CHALONIC
CHALS
CHALUMEAU
CHALUMEAUX
CHALUTZ
CHALUTZES
CHALUTZIM
CHALYBEAN
CHALYBITE
CHALYBITES
CHAM
CHAMADE
CHAMADES
CHAMBER
CHAMBERED
CHAMBERER
CHAMBERERS
CHAMBERING
CHAMBERINGS
CHAMBERS
CHAMBRAY
CHAMBRAYS
CHAMBRE
CHAMELEON
CHAMELEONS
CHAMELOT
CHAMELOTS
CHAMFER
CHAMFERED
CHAMFERING
CHAMFERS
CHAMFRAIN
CHAMFRAINS
CHAMFRON
CHAMFRONS
CHAMISAL
CHAMISALS
CHAMISE
CHAMISES
CHAMISO
CHAMISOS
CHAMLET
CHAMLETS
CHAMMIES
CHAMMY
CHAMOIS
CHAMOMILE
CHAMOMILES
CHAMP
CHAMPAC
CHAMPACS
CHAMPAGNE
CHAMPAGNES
CHAMPAIGN
CHAMPAIGNS
CHAMPAK
CHAMPAKS
CHAMPART
CHAMPARTS
CHAMPED
CHAMPERS
CHAMPERTIES
CHAMPERTY
CHAMPING
CHAMPION
CHAMPIONED
CHAMPIONING
CHAMPIONS
CHAMPLEVE
CHAMPLEVES
CHAMPS
CHAMS
CHANCE
CHANCED
CHANCEFUL
CHANCEL
CHANCELS
CHANCER
CHANCERIES
CHANCERS
CHANCERY
CHANCES
CHANCEY
CHANCIER
CHANCIEST
CHANCING
CHANCRE
CHANCRES
CHANCROID
CHANCROIDS
CHANCROUS
CHANCY
CHANDELLE
CHANDELLED
CHANDELLES
CHANDELLING
CHANDLER
CHANDLERIES
CHANDLERS
CHANDLERY
CHANGE
CHANGED
CHANGEFUL
CHANGER
CHANGERS
CHANGES
CHANGING
CHANK
CHANKS
CHANNEL
CHANNELER
CHANNELERS
CHANNELLED
CHANNELLING
CHANNELS
CHANNER
CHANNERS
CHANOYU
CHANOYUS
CHANSON
CHANSONS
CHANT
CHANTAGE
CHANTAGES
CHANTED
CHANTER
CHANTERS
CHANTEUSE
CHANTEUSES
CHANTEY
CHANTEYS
CHANTIE
CHANTIES
CHANTING
CHANTOR
CHANTORS
CHANTRESS
CHANTRESSES
CHANTRIES
CHANTRY
CHANTS
CHANTY
CHAOLOGIES
CHAOLOGY
CHAOS

CHAOSES
CHAOTIC
CHAP
CHAPARRAL
CHAPARRALS
CHAPATI
CHAPATIS
CHAPATTI
CHAPATTIS
CHAPBOOK
CHAPBOOKS
CHAPE
CHAPEAU
CHAPEAUX
CHAPEL
CHAPELESS
CHAPELRIES
CHAPELRY
CHAPELS
CHAPERON
CHAPERONE
CHAPERONED
CHAPERONES
CHAPERONING
CHAPERONS
CHAPES
CHAPESS
CHAPESSES
CHAPITER
CHAPITERS
CHAPKA
CHAPKAS
CHAPLAIN
CHAPLAINS
CHAPLESS
CHAPLET
CHAPLETED
CHAPLETS
CHAPMAN
CHAPMEN
CHAPPAL
CHAPPALS
CHAPPED
CHAPPESS
CHAPPESSES
CHAPPIE
CHAPPIER
CHAPPIES
CHAPPIEST
CHAPPING
CHAPPY
CHAPRASSI
CHAPRASSIES
CHAPRASSIS
CHAPRASSY
CHAPS
CHAPSTICK
CHAPSTICKS
CHAPTER
CHAPTERED
CHAPTERING
CHAPTERS
CHAPTREL
CHAPTRELS
CHAR
CHARA
CHARABANC
CHARABANCS
CHARACID
CHARACIDS
CHARACIN
CHARACINS
CHARACT
CHARACTER
CHARACTERED
CHARACTERING
CHARACTERS
CHARACTS
CHARADE
CHARADES
CHARANGO
CHARANGOS
CHARAS
CHARASES
CHARBROIL
CHARBROILED
CHARBROILING
CHARBROILS
CHARCOAL
CHARCOALED
CHARCOALING
CHARCOALS
CHARD
CHARDS
CHARE
CHARED
CHARES
CHARET
CHARETS
CHARGE
CHARGED
CHARGEFUL
CHARGER
CHARGERS
CHARGES
CHARGING
CHARGRILL
CHARGRILLED
CHARGRILLING
CHARGRILLS
CHARIER
CHARIEST
CHARILY
CHARINESS
CHARINESSES
CHARING
CHARIOT
CHARIOTED
CHARIOTING
CHARIOTS
CHARISM
CHARISMA
CHARISMAS
CHARISMS
CHARITIES
CHARITY
CHARIVARI
CHARIVARIS
CHARK
CHARKA
CHARKAS
CHARKED
CHARKHA
CHARKHAS
CHARKING
CHARKS
CHARLADIES
CHARLADY
CHARLATAN
CHARLATANS
CHARLEY
CHARLEYS
CHARLIE
CHARLIES
CHARLOCK
CHARLOCKS
CHARLOTTE
CHARLOTTES
CHARM
CHARMED
CHARMER
CHARMERS
CHARMEUSE
CHARMEUSES
CHARMFUL
CHARMING
CHARMLESS
CHARMS
CHARNECO
CHARNECOS
CHARNEL
CHARNELS
CHAROSET
CHAROSETH
CHAROSETHS
CHAROSETS
CHARPIE
CHARPIES
CHARPOY
CHARPOYS
CHARQUI
CHARQUIS
CHARR
CHARRED
CHARRIER
CHARRIEST
CHARRING
CHARRS
CHARRY
CHARS
CHART
CHARTA
CHARTAS
CHARTED
CHARTER
CHARTERED
CHARTERER
CHARTERERS
CHARTERING
CHARTERS
CHARTING
CHARTISM
CHARTISMS
CHARTIST
CHARTISTS
CHARTLESS
CHARTS
CHARWOMAN
CHARWOMEN
CHARY
CHAS
CHASE
CHASED
CHASEPORT
CHASEPORTS
CHASER
CHASERS
CHASES
CHASING
CHASINGS
CHASM
CHASMAL
CHASMED
CHASMIC
CHASMIER
CHASMIEST
CHASMS
CHASMY
CHASSE
CHASSEED
CHASSEING
CHASSEPOT
CHASSEPOTS
CHASSES
CHASSEUR
CHASSEURS
CHASSIS
CHASTE
CHASTELY
CHASTEN
CHASTENED
CHASTENER
CHASTENERS
CHASTENING
CHASTENS
CHASTER
CHASTEST
CHASTISE
CHASTISED
CHASTISES
CHASTISING
CHASTITIES
CHASTITY
CHASUBLE
CHASUBLES
CHAT
CHATEAU
CHATEAUX
CHATELAIN
CHATELAINS
CHATLINE
CHATLINES
CHATON
CHATONS
CHATOYANT
CHATS
CHATTA
CHATTAS
CHATTED
CHATTEL
CHATTELS
CHATTER
CHATTERED
CHATTERER
CHATTERERS
CHATTERING
CHATTERINGS
CHATTERS
CHATTI
CHATTIER
CHATTIES
CHATTIEST
CHATTING
CHATTIS
CHATTY
CHAUFE
CHAUFED
CHAUFER
CHAUFERS
CHAUFES
CHAUFF
CHAUFFED
CHAUFFER
CHAUFFERS
CHAUFFEUR
CHAUFFEURED
CHAUFFEURING
CHAUFFEURS
CHAUFFING
CHAUFFS
CHAUFING
CHAUMER
CHAUMERS
CHAUNCE
CHAUNCED
CHAUNCES
CHAUNCING
CHAUNGE
CHAUNGED
CHAUNGES
CHAUNGING
CHAUNT
CHAUNTED
CHAUNTER
CHAUNTERS
CHAUNTING
CHAUNTRIES
CHAUNTRY
CHAUNTS
CHAUSSES
CHAUVIN
CHAUVINS
CHAVE
CHAVENDER
CHAVENDERS
CHAW
CHAWBACON
CHAWBACONS
CHAWDRON
CHAWDRONS

CHAWED
CHAWING
CHAWS
CHAY
CHAYA
CHAYAS
CHAYOTE
CHAYOTES
CHAYROOT
CHAYROOTS
CHAYS
CHAZAN
CHAZANIM
CHAZANS
CHE
CHEAP
CHEAPEN
CHEAPENED
CHEAPENER
CHEAPENERS
CHEAPENING
CHEAPENS
CHEAPER
CHEAPEST
CHEAPIE
CHEAPIES
CHEAPLY
CHEAPNESS
CHEAPNESSES
CHEAPO
CHEAPS
CHEAPY
CHEAT
CHEATED
CHEATER
CHEATERIES
CHEATERS
CHEATERY
CHEATING
CHEATINGS
CHEATS
CHECHAKO
CHECHAKOES
CHECHAKOS
CHECHAQUA
CHECHAQUAS
CHECHAQUO
CHECHAQUOS
CHECHIA
CHECHIAS
CHECK
CHECKBOOK
CHECKBOOKS
CHECKED
CHECKER
CHECKERED
CHECKERS
CHECKING
CHECKLIST
CHECKLISTS
CHECKMATE
CHECKMATED
CHECKMATES
CHECKMATING
CHECKOUT
CHECKOUTS
CHECKRAIL
CHECKRAILS
CHECKREIN
CHECKREINS
CHECKROOM
CHECKROOMS
CHECKS
CHECKSUM
CHECKSUMS
CHECKY
CHEDDITE
CHEDDITES
CHEECHAKO
CHEECHAKOES
CHEECHAKOS
CHEEK
CHEEKBONE
CHEEKBONES
CHEEKED
CHEEKIER
CHEEKIEST
CHEEKILY
CHEEKING
CHEEKS
CHEEKY
CHEEP
CHEEPED
CHEEPER
CHEEPERS
CHEEPING
CHEEPS
CHEER
CHEERED
CHEERER
CHEERERS
CHEERFUL
CHEERFULLER
CHEERFULLEST
CHEERIER
CHEERIEST
CHEERILY
CHEERING
CHEERIO
CHEERIOS
CHEERLESS
CHEERLY
CHEERS
CHEERY
CHEESE
CHEESED
CHEESES
CHEESEVAT
CHEESEVATS
CHEESIER
CHEESIEST
CHEESING
CHEESY
CHEETAH
CHEETAHS
CHEEWINK
CHEEWINKS
CHEF
CHEFS
CHEILITIS
CHEILITISES
CHEKA
CHEKAS
CHEKIST
CHEKISTS
CHELA
CHELAE
CHELAS
CHELASHIP
CHELASHIPS
CHELATE
CHELATED
CHELATES
CHELATING
CHELATION
CHELATIONS
CHELATOR
CHELATORS
CHELICERA
CHELICERAE
CHELIFORM
CHELIPED
CHELIPEDS
CHELOID
CHELOIDAL
CHELOIDS
CHELONE
CHELONES
CHELONIAN
CHELONIANS
CHEMIC
CHEMICAL
CHEMICALS
CHEMICKED
CHEMICKING
CHEMICS
CHEMISE
CHEMISES
CHEMISM
CHEMISMS
CHEMIST
CHEMISTRIES
CHEMISTRY
CHEMISTS
CHEMITYPE
CHEMITYPES
CHEMITYPIES
CHEMITYPY
CHEMMIES
CHEMMY
CHEMOSTAT
CHEMOSTATS
CHEMURGIC
CHEMURGIES
CHEMURGY
CHENAR
CHENARS
CHENET
CHENETS
CHENILLE
CHENILLES
CHENIX
CHENIXES
CHENOPOD
CHENOPODS
CHEONGSAM
CHEONGSAMS
CHEQUE
CHEQUER
CHEQUERED
CHEQUERING
CHEQUERS
CHEQUES
CHEQUY
CHER
CHERALITE
CHERALITES
CHERE
CHERIMOYA
CHERIMOYAS
CHERISH
CHERISHED
CHERISHES
CHERISHING
CHERNOZEM
CHERNOZEMS
CHEROOT
CHEROOTS
CHERRIED
CHERRIER
CHERRIES
CHERRIEST
CHERRY
CHERRYING
CHERT
CHERTIER
CHERTIEST
CHERTS
CHERTY
CHERUB
CHERUBIC
CHERUBIM
CHERUBIMS
CHERUBIN
CHERUBINS
CHERUBS
CHERUP
CHERUPED
CHERUPING
CHERUPS
CHERVIL
CHERVILS
CHESIL
CHESILS
CHESNUT
CHESNUTS
CHESS
CHESSEL
CHESSELS
CHESSES
CHESSMAN
CHESSMEN
CHEST
CHESTED
CHESTFUL
CHESTFULS
CHESTIER
CHESTIEST
CHESTING
CHESTNUT
CHESTNUTS
CHESTS
CHESTY
CHETAH
CHETAHS
CHETNIK
CHETNIKS
CHEVALET
CHEVALETS
CHEVALIER
CHEVALIERS
CHEVELURE
CHEVELURES
CHEVEN
CHEVENS
CHEVEREL
CHEVERELS
CHEVERIL
CHEVERILS
CHEVERON
CHEVERONS
CHEVERYE
CHEVERYES
CHEVET
CHEVETS
CHEVIED
CHEVIES
CHEVILLE
CHEVILLES
CHEVIN
CHEVINS
CHEVRE
CHEVRES
CHEVRETTE
CHEVRETTES
CHEVRON
CHEVRONED
CHEVRONS
CHEVRONY
CHEVY
CHEVYING
CHEW
CHEWABLE
CHEWED
CHEWER
CHEWERS
CHEWET
CHEWETS
CHEWIE
CHEWIER
CHEWIES
CHEWIEST
CHEWING
CHEWINK
CHEWINKS
CHEWS
CHEWY
CHEZ
CHI
CHIACK

CHIACKED
CHIACKING
CHIACKINGS
CHIACKS
CHIAO
CHIAREZZA
CHIAREZZE
CHIASM
CHIASMA
CHIASMAS
CHIASMATA
CHIASMI
CHIASMS
CHIASMUS
CHIASTIC
CHIAUS
CHIAUSED
CHIAUSES
CHIAUSING
CHIBOL
CHIBOLS
CHIBOUK
CHIBOUKS
CHIBOUQUE
CHIBOUQUES
CHIC
CHICA
CHICANA
CHICANAS
CHICANE
CHICANED
CHICANER
CHICANERIES
CHICANERS
CHICANERY
CHICANES
CHICANING
CHICANINGS
CHICANO
CHICANOS
CHICAS
CHICCORIES
CHICCORY
CHICER
CHICEST
CHICH
CHICHA
CHICHAS
CHICHES
CHICHI
CHICHIS
CHICK
CHICKADEE
CHICKADEES
CHICKAREE
CHICKAREES
CHICKEN
CHICKENED
CHICKENING
CHICKENS
CHICKLING
CHICKLINGS
CHICKPEA
CHICKPEAS
CHICKS
CHICKWEED
CHICKWEEDS
CHICLE
CHICLES
CHICLY
CHICO
CHICON
CHICONS
CHICORIES
CHICORY
CHICOS
CHICS
CHID
CHIDDEN
CHIDE
CHIDED
CHIDER
CHIDERS
CHIDES
CHIDING
CHIDINGS
CHIDLINGS
CHIEF
CHIEFDOM
CHIEFDOMS
CHIEFER
CHIEFERIES
CHIEFERY
CHIEFESS
CHIEFESSES
CHIEFEST
CHIEFLESS
CHIEFLING
CHIEFLINGS
CHIEFLY
CHIEFRIES
CHIEFRY
CHIEFS
CHIEFSHIP
CHIEFSHIPS
CHIEFTAIN
CHIEFTAINS
CHIEL
CHIELD
CHIELDS
CHIELS
CHIFFON
CHIFFONS
CHIGGER
CHIGGERS
CHIGNON
CHIGNONS
CHIGOE
CHIGOES
CHIGRE
CHIGRES
CHIHUAHUA
CHIHUAHUAS
CHIK
CHIKARA
CHIKARAS
CHIKHOR
CHIKHORS
CHIKOR
CHIKORS
CHIKS
CHILBLAIN
CHILBLAINS
CHILD
CHILDBED
CHILDBEDS
CHILDE
CHILDED
CHILDER
CHILDHOOD
CHILDHOODS
CHILDING
CHILDISH
CHILDLESS
CHILDLIKE
CHILDLY
CHILDNESS
CHILDNESSES
CHILDREN
CHILDS
CHILE
CHILES
CHILI
CHILIAD
CHILIADS
CHILIAGON
CHILIAGONS
CHILIARCH
CHILIARCHS
CHILIASM
CHILIASMS
CHILIAST
CHILIASTS
CHILIOI
CHILIOIS
CHILIS
CHILL
CHILLADA
CHILLADAS
CHILLED
CHILLER
CHILLERS
CHILLEST
CHILLI
CHILLIER
CHILLIES
CHILLIEST
CHILLILY
CHILLING
CHILLINGS
CHILLIS
CHILLNESS
CHILLNESSES
CHILLS
CHILLUM
CHILLUMS
CHILLY
CHILOPOD
CHILOPODS
CHIMAERA
CHIMAERAS
CHIMB
CHIMBS
CHIME
CHIMED
CHIMER
CHIMERA
CHIMERAS
CHIMERE
CHIMERES
CHIMERIC
CHIMERID
CHIMERIDS
CHIMERISM
CHIMERISMS
CHIMERS
CHIMES
CHIMING
CHIMLEY
CHIMLEYS
CHIMNEY
CHIMNEYED
CHIMNEYING
CHIMNEYS
CHIMO
CHIMP
CHIMPS
CHIN
CHINA
CHINAMPA
CHINAMPAS
CHINAR
CHINAROOT
CHINAROOTS
CHINARS
CHINAS
CHINAWARE
CHINAWARES
CHINCAPIN
CHINCAPINS
CHINCH
CHINCHES
CHINCOUGH
CHINCOUGHS
CHINDIT
CHINDITS
CHINE
CHINED
CHINES
CHINESE
CHINING
CHINK
CHINKAPIN
CHINKAPINS
CHINKARA
CHINKARAS
CHINKED
CHINKIE
CHINKIER
CHINKIES
CHINKIEST
CHINKING
CHINKS
CHINKY
CHINLESS
CHINNED
CHINNING
CHINO
CHINOOK
CHINOOKS
CHINOS
CHINOVNIK
CHINOVNIKS
CHINS
CHINSTRAP
CHINSTRAPS
CHINTZ
CHINTZES
CHINTZIER
CHINTZIEST
CHINTZY
CHINWAG
CHINWAGGED
CHINWAGGING
CHINWAGS
CHIP
CHIPBOARD
CHIPBOARDS
CHIPMUCK
CHIPMUCKS
CHIPMUNK
CHIPMUNKS
CHIPOCHIA
CHIPOCHIAS
CHIPOLATA
CHIPOLATAS
CHIPPED
CHIPPER
CHIPPERS
CHIPPIE
CHIPPIER
CHIPPIES
CHIPPIEST
CHIPPING
CHIPPINGS
CHIPPY
CHIPS
CHIPSET
CHIPSETS
CHIRAGRA
CHIRAGRAS
CHIRAGRIC
CHIRAL
CHIRALITIES
CHIRALITY
CHIRIMOYA
CHIRIMOYAS
CHIRK
CHIRKED
CHIRKING
CHIRKS
CHIRL
CHIRLED
CHIRLING
CHIRLS
CHIRM
CHIRMED
CHIRMING
CHIRMS
CHIROLOGIES

CHIROLOGY
CHIRONOMIES
CHIRONOMY
CHIROPODIES
CHIROPODY
CHIRP
CHIRPED
CHIRPER
CHIRPERS
CHIRPIER
CHIRPIEST
CHIRPILY
CHIRPING
CHIRPS
CHIRPY
CHIRR
CHIRRE
CHIRRED
CHIRRES
CHIRRING
CHIRRS
CHIRRUP
CHIRRUPED
CHIRRUPING
CHIRRUPS
CHIRRUPY
CHIRT
CHIRTED
CHIRTING
CHIRTS
CHIS
CHISEL
CHISELLED
CHISELLER
CHISELLERS
CHISELLING
CHISELLINGS
CHISELS
CHIT
CHITAL
CHITALS
CHITCHAT
CHITCHATS
CHITCHATTED
CHITCHATTING
CHITIN
CHITINOID
CHITINOUS
CHITINS
CHITLINGS
CHITON
CHITONS
CHITS
CHITTED
CHITTER
CHITTERED
CHITTERING
CHITTERINGS
CHITTERS
CHITTIER
CHITTIES
CHITTIEST
CHITTING
CHITTY
CHIV
CHIVALRIC
CHIVALRIES
CHIVALRY
CHIVAREE
CHIVAREES
CHIVE
CHIVED
CHIVES
CHIVIED
CHIVIES
CHIVING
CHIVS
CHIVVED
CHIVVIED
CHIVVIES
CHIVVING
CHIVVY
CHIVVYING
CHIVY
CHIVYING
CHIYOGAMI
CHIYOGAMIS
CHIZ
CHIZZ
CHIZZED
CHIZZES
CHIZZING
CHLAMYDES
CHLAMYDIA
CHLAMYDIAS
CHLAMYS
CHLAMYSES
CHLOASMA
CHLOASMATA
CHLORACNE
CHLORACNES
CHLORAL
CHLORALS
CHLORATE
CHLORATES
CHLORDAN
CHLORDANE
CHLORDANES
CHLORDANS
CHLORELLA
CHLORELLAS
CHLORIC
CHLORIDE
CHLORIDES
CHLORIN
CHLORINE
CHLORINES
CHLORINS
CHLORITE
CHLORITES
CHLORITIC
CHLOROSES
CHLOROSIS
CHLOROTIC
CHLOROUS
CHOANA
CHOANAE
CHOBDAR
CHOBDARS
CHOC
CHOCCIER
CHOCCIES
CHOCCIEST
CHOCCY
CHOCHO
CHOCHOS
CHOCK
CHOCKED
CHOCKER
CHOCKING
CHOCKO
CHOCKOS
CHOCKS
CHOCO
CHOCOLATE
CHOCOLATES
CHOCOLATIER
CHOCOLATIEST
CHOCOLATY
CHOCOS
CHOCS
CHOCTAW
CHOCTAWS
CHODE
CHOENIX
CHOENIXES
CHOICE
CHOICEFUL
CHOICELY
CHOICER
CHOICES
CHOICEST
CHOIR
CHOIRBOY
CHOIRBOYS
CHOIRED
CHOIRGIRL
CHOIRGIRLS
CHOIRING
CHOIRMAN
CHOIRMEN
CHOIRS
CHOKE
CHOKEBORE
CHOKEBORES
CHOKECOIL
CHOKECOILS
CHOKED
CHOKEDAMP
CHOKEDAMPS
CHOKER
CHOKERS
CHOKES
CHOKEY
CHOKEYS
CHOKIDAR
CHOKIDARS
CHOKIER
CHOKIES
CHOKIEST
CHOKING
CHOKO
CHOKOS
CHOKRA
CHOKRAS
CHOKRI
CHOKRIS
CHOKY
CHOLAEMIA
CHOLAEMIAS
CHOLAEMIC
CHOLECYST
CHOLECYSTS
CHOLELITH
CHOLELITHS
CHOLEMIA
CHOLEMIAS
CHOLENT
CHOLENTS
CHOLER
CHOLERA
CHOLERAIC
CHOLERAS
CHOLERIC
CHOLERS
CHOLI
CHOLIAMB
CHOLIAMBS
CHOLIC
CHOLINE
CHOLINES
CHOLIS
CHOLTRIES
CHOLTRY
CHOMP
CHOMPED
CHOMPING
CHOMPS
CHON
CHONDRAL
CHONDRE
CHONDRES
CHONDRI
CHONDRIFIED
CHONDRIFIES
CHONDRIFY
CHONDRIFYING
CHONDRIN
CHONDRINS
CHONDRITE
CHONDRITES
CHONDROID
CHONDRULE
CHONDRULES
CHONDRUS
CHONS
CHOOF
CHOOFED
CHOOFING
CHOOFS
CHOOK
CHOOKIE
CHOOKIES
CHOOKS
CHOOM
CHOOMS
CHOOSE
CHOOSER
CHOOSERS
CHOOSES
CHOOSEY
CHOOSIER
CHOOSIEST
CHOOSING
CHOOSY
CHOP
CHOPHOUSE
CHOPHOUSES
CHOPIN
CHOPINE
CHOPINES
CHOPINS
CHOPLOGIC
CHOPLOGICS
CHOPPED
CHOPPER
CHOPPERS
CHOPPIER
CHOPPIEST
CHOPPING
CHOPPINGS
CHOPPY
CHOPS
CHOPSTICK
CHOPSTICKS
CHORAGI
CHORAGIC
CHORAGUS
CHORAGUSES
CHORAL
CHORALE
CHORALES
CHORALIST
CHORALISTS
CHORALLY
CHORALS
CHORD
CHORDA
CHORDAE
CHORDAL
CHORDATE
CHORDATES
CHORDEE
CHORDEES
CHORDING
CHORDINGS
CHORDS
CHORE
CHOREA
CHOREAS
CHOREE
CHOREES
CHOREGI
CHOREGIC
CHOREGUS
CHOREGUSES
CHOREIC
CHORES
CHOREUS
CHOREUSES

CHORIA
CHORIAL
CHORIAMB
CHORIAMBI
CHORIAMBS
CHORIC
CHORINE
CHORINES
CHORIOID
CHORIOIDS
CHORION
CHORIONIC
CHORISES
CHORISIS
CHORISM
CHORISMS
CHORIST
CHORISTER
CHORISTERS
CHORISTS
CHORIZO
CHORIZONT
CHORIZONTS
CHORIZOS
CHOROID
CHOROIDS
CHOROLOGIES
CHOROLOGY
CHORTLE
CHORTLED
CHORTLES
CHORTLING
CHORUS
CHORUSED
CHORUSES
CHORUSING
CHOSE
CHOSEN
CHOSES
CHOTA
CHOTT
CHOTTS
CHOU
CHOUGH
CHOUGHS
CHOULTRIES
CHOULTRY
CHOUNTER
CHOUNTERED
CHOUNTERING
CHOUNTERS
CHOUSE
CHOUSED
CHOUSES
CHOUSING
CHOUT
CHOUTS
CHOUX
CHOW
CHOWDER
CHOWDERS
CHOWKIDAR
CHOWKIDARS
CHOWRI
CHOWRIES
CHOWRIS
CHOWRY
CHOWS
CHRISM
CHRISMAL
CHRISMALS
CHRISMS
CHRISOM
CHRISOMS
CHRISTEN
CHRISTENED
CHRISTENING
CHRISTENINGS
CHRISTENS
CHRISTIE
CHRISTIES
CHRISTOM
CHRISTOMS
CHRISTY
CHROMA
CHROMAKEY
CHROMAKEYS
CHROMAS
CHROMATE
CHROMATES
CHROMATIC
CHROMATICS
CHROMATID
CHROMATIDS
CHROMATIN
CHROMATINS
CHROME
CHROMED
CHROMEL
CHROMELS
CHROMENE
CHROMENES
CHROMES
CHROMIC
CHROMIDIA
CHROMING
CHROMITE
CHROMITES
CHROMIUM
CHROMIUMS
CHROMO
CHROMOGEN
CHROMOGENS
CHROMOS
CHRONAXIE
CHRONAXIES
CHRONIC
CHRONICAL
CHRONICLE
CHRONICLED
CHRONICLES
CHRONICLING
CHRONICS
CHRONON
CHRONONS
CHRYSALID
CHRYSALIDES
CHRYSALIDS
CHRYSALIS
CHRYSALISES
CHRYSANTH
CHRYSANTHS
CHTHONIAN
CHTHONIC
CHUB
CHUBBIER
CHUBBIEST
CHUBBY
CHUBS
CHUCK
CHUCKED
CHUCKHOLE
CHUCKHOLES
CHUCKIE
CHUCKIES
CHUCKING
CHUCKLE
CHUCKLED
CHUCKLES
CHUCKLING
CHUCKLINGS
CHUCKS
CHUDDAH
CHUDDAHS
CHUDDAR
CHUDDARS
CHUDDIES
CHUDDY
CHUFA
CHUFAS
CHUFF
CHUFFED
CHUFFIER
CHUFFIEST
CHUFFING
CHUFFS
CHUFFY
CHUG
CHUGGED
CHUGGING
CHUGS
CHUKAR
CHUKARS
CHUKKA
CHUKKAS
CHUKKER
CHUKKERS
CHUKOR
CHUKORS
CHUM
CHUMLEY
CHUMLEYS
CHUMMAGE
CHUMMAGES
CHUMMED
CHUMMIER
CHUMMIES
CHUMMIEST
CHUMMING
CHUMMY
CHUMP
CHUMPING
CHUMPINGS
CHUMPS
CHUMS
CHUNDER
CHUNDERED
CHUNDERING
CHUNDERS
CHUNK
CHUNKIER
CHUNKIEST
CHUNKING
CHUNKINGS
CHUNKS
CHUNKY
CHUNNEL
CHUNNELS
CHUNNER
CHUNNERED
CHUNNERING
CHUNNERS
CHUNTER
CHUNTERED
CHUNTERING
CHUNTERS
CHUPATI
CHUPATIS
CHUPATTI
CHUPATTIS
CHUPPAH
CHUPPAHS
CHUPRASSIES
CHUPRASSY
CHURCH
CHURCHED
CHURCHES
CHURCHIER
CHURCHIEST
CHURCHING
CHURCHINGS
CHURCHISM
CHURCHISMS
CHURCHLIER
CHURCHLIEST
CHURCHLY
CHURCHMAN
CHURCHMEN
CHURCHWAY
CHURCHWAYS
CHURCHY
CHURIDARS
CHURINGA
CHURINGAS
CHURL
CHURLISH
CHURLS
CHURN
CHURNED
CHURNING
CHURNINGS
CHURNMILK
CHURNMILKS
CHURNS
CHURR
CHURRED
CHURRING
CHURRS
CHURRUS
CHURRUSES
CHUSE
CHUSES
CHUSING
CHUT
CHUTE
CHUTES
CHUTIST
CHUTISTS
CHUTNEY
CHUTNEYS
CHUTZPAH
CHUTZPAHS
CHYACK
CHYACKED
CHYACKING
CHYACKS
CHYLDE
CHYLE
CHYLES
CHYLIFIED
CHYLIFIES
CHYLIFY
CHYLIFYING
CHYLURIA
CHYLURIAS
CHYME
CHYMES
CHYMIFIED
CHYMIFIES
CHYMIFY
CHYMIFYING
CHYMISTRIES
CHYMISTRY
CHYMOUS
CHYND
CHYPRE
CHYPRES
CIABATTA
CIABATTAS
CIABATTE
CIAO
CIAOS
CIBATION
CIBATIONS
CIBOL
CIBOLS
CIBORIA
CIBORIUM
CICADA
CICADAS
CICALA
CICALAS
CICATRICE
CICATRICES
CICATRISE
CICATRISED
CICATRISES
CICATRISING
CICATRIX
CICATRIXES

CICATRIZE
CICATRIZED
CICATRIZES
CICATRIZING
CICELIES
CICELY
CICERO
CICERONE
CICERONED
CICERONEING
CICERONES
CICERONI
CICEROS
CICHLID
CICHLIDS
CICHLOID
CICINNUS
CICINNUSES
CICISBEI
CICISBEO
CICLATON
CICLATONS
CICLATOUN
CICLATOUNS
CICUTA
CICUTAS
CID
CIDARIS
CIDARISES
CIDE
CIDED
CIDER
CIDERKIN
CIDERKINS
CIDERS
CIDERY
CIDES
CIDING
CIDS
CIEL
CIELED
CIELING
CIELINGS
CIELS
CIERGE
CIERGES
CIG
CIGAR
CIGARETTE
CIGARETTES
CIGARILLO
CIGARILLOS
CIGARS
CIGGIE
CIGGIES
CIGGY
CIGS
CILANTRO
CILANTROS
CILIA
CILIARY
CILIATE
CILIATES
CILICE
CILICES
CILICIOUS
CILIOLATE
CILIUM
CILL
CILLS
CIMAR
CIMARS
CIMBALOM
CIMBALOMS
CIMELIA
CIMEX
CIMICES
CIMIER
CIMIERS
CIMINITE
CIMINITES
CIMOLITE
CIMOLITES
CINCH
CINCHED
CINCHES
CINCHING
CINCHINGS
CINCHONA
CINCHONAS
CINCHONIC
CINCINNUS
CINCINNUSES
CINCT
CINCTURE
CINCTURED
CINCTURES
CINCTURING
CINDER
CINDERED
CINDERING
CINDERS
CINDERY
CINEAST
CINEASTE
CINEASTES
CINEASTS
CINEMA
CINEMAS
CINEMATIC
CINEOL
CINEOLE
CINEOLES
CINEOLS
CINEPHILE
CINEPHILES
CINEPLEX
CINEPLEXES
CINERAMIC
CINERARIA
CINERARIAS
CINERARY
CINERATOR
CINERATORS
CINEREA
CINEREAL
CINEREAS
CINEREOUS
CINERIN
CINERINS
CINGULA
CINGULUM
CINNABAR
CINNABARS
CINNAMIC
CINNAMON
CINNAMONS
CINQUAIN
CINQUAINS
CINQUE
CINQUES
CION
CIONS
CIPHER
CIPHERED
CIPHERING
CIPHERINGS
CIPHERS
CIPOLIN
CIPOLINS
CIPOLLINO
CIPOLLINOS
CIPPI
CIPPUS
CIRCA
CIRCADIAN
CIRCAR
CIRCARS
CIRCINATE
CIRCITER
CIRCLE
CIRCLED
CIRCLER
CIRCLERS
CIRCLES
CIRCLET
CIRCLETS
CIRCLING
CIRCLINGS
CIRCLIP
CIRCLIPS
CIRCS
CIRCUIT
CIRCUITED
CIRCUITIES
CIRCUITING
CIRCUITRIES
CIRCUITRY
CIRCUITS
CIRCUITY
CIRCULAR
CIRCULARS
CIRCULATE
CIRCULATED
CIRCULATES
CIRCULATING
CIRCULATINGS
CIRCUS
CIRCUSES
CIRCUSSY
CIRCUSY
CIRE
CIRES
CIRL
CIRLS
CIRQUE
CIRQUES
CIRRATE
CIRRHOPOD
CIRRHOPODS
CIRRHOSES
CIRRHOSIS
CIRRHOTIC
CIRRI
CIRRIFORM
CIRRIPED
CIRRIPEDE
CIRRIPEDES
CIRRIPEDS
CIRROSE
CIRROUS
CIRRUS
CIRSOID
CISALPINE
CISCO
CISCOES
CISCOS
CISELEUR
CISELEURS
CISELURE
CISELURES
CISLUNAR
CISPADANE
CISPLATIN
CISPLATINS
CISSIER
CISSIES
CISSIEST
CISSOID
CISSOIDS
CISSUS
CISSUSES
CISSY
CIST
CISTED
CISTERN
CISTERNA
CISTERNAE
CISTERNS
CISTIC
CISTRON
CISTRONS
CISTS
CISTUS
CISTUSES
CISTVAEN
CISTVAENS
CIT
CITABLE
CITADEL
CITADELS
CITAL
CITALS
CITATION
CITATIONS
CITATORY
CITE
CITEABLE
CITED
CITER
CITERS
CITES
CITESS
CITESSES
CITHARA
CITHARAS
CITHARIST
CITHARISTS
CITHER
CITHERN
CITHERNS
CITHERS
CITIES
CITIFIED
CITIFIES
CITIFY
CITIFYING
CITIGRADE
CITING
CITIZEN
CITIZENRIES
CITIZENRY
CITIZENS
CITO
CITOLE
CITOLES
CITRANGE
CITRANGES
CITRATE
CITRATES
CITREOUS
CITRIC
CITRIN
CITRINE
CITRINES
CITRINS
CITRON
CITRONS
CITROUS
CITRUS
CITRUSES
CITS
CITTERN
CITTERNS
CITY
CITYFIED
CITYFIES
CITYFY
CITYFYING
CITYSCAPE
CITYSCAPES
CIVE
CIVES
CIVET
CIVETS
CIVIC
CIVICALLY
CIVICS
CIVIL
CIVILIAN

CIVILIANS
CIVILISE
CIVILISED
CIVILISER
CIVILISERS
CIVILISES
CIVILISING
CIVILIST
CIVILISTS
CIVILITIES
CIVILITY
CIVILIZE
CIVILIZED
CIVILIZER
CIVILIZERS
CIVILIZES
CIVILIZING
CIVILLY
CIVISM
CIVISMS
CIVVIES
CIVVY
CIZERS
CLABBER
CLABBERS
CLACHAN
CLACHANS
CLACK
CLACKBOX
CLACKBOXES
CLACKDISH
CLACKDISHES
CLACKED
CLACKER
CLACKERS
CLACKING
CLACKS
CLAD
CLADDED
CLADDER
CLADDERS
CLADDING
CLADDINGS
CLADE
CLADES
CLADISM
CLADISMS
CLADIST
CLADISTIC
CLADISTICS
CLADISTS
CLADODE
CLADODES
CLADOGRAM
CLADOGRAMS
CLADS
CLAES
CLAG
CLAGGED
CLAGGIER
CLAGGIEST
CLAGGING
CLAGGY
CLAGS
CLAIM
CLAIMABLE
CLAIMANT
CLAIMANTS
CLAIMED
CLAIMER
CLAIMERS
CLAIMING
CLAIMS
CLAM
CLAMANCIES
CLAMANCY
CLAMANT
CLAMANTLY
CLAMBAKE
CLAMBAKES
CLAMBE
CLAMBER
CLAMBERED
CLAMBERING
CLAMBERS
CLAME
CLAMES
CLAMMED
CLAMMIER
CLAMMIEST
CLAMMILY
CLAMMING
CLAMMY
CLAMOR
CLAMORED
CLAMORING
CLAMOROUS
CLAMORS
CLAMOUR
CLAMOURED
CLAMOURER
CLAMOURERS
CLAMOURING
CLAMOURS
CLAMP
CLAMPDOWN
CLAMPDOWNS
CLAMPED
CLAMPER
CLAMPERED
CLAMPERING
CLAMPERS
CLAMPING
CLAMPS
CLAMS
CLAMSHELL
CLAMSHELLS
CLAN
CLANG
CLANGBOX
CLANGBOXES
CLANGED
CLANGER
CLANGERS
CLANGING
CLANGINGS
CLANGOR
CLANGORED
CLANGORING
CLANGORS
CLANGOUR
CLANGOURED
CLANGOURING
CLANGOURS
CLANGS
CLANK
CLANKED
CLANKING
CLANKINGS
CLANKS
CLANNISH
CLANS
CLANSHIP
CLANSHIPS
CLANSMAN
CLANSMEN
CLAP
CLAPBOARD
CLAPBOARDS
CLAPBREAD
CLAPBREADS
CLAPDISH
CLAPDISHES
CLAPNET
CLAPNETS
CLAPPED
CLAPPER
CLAPPERED
CLAPPERING
CLAPPERINGS
CLAPPERS
CLAPPING
CLAPPINGS
CLAPS
CLAPTRAP
CLAPTRAPS
CLAQUE
CLAQUES
CLAQUEUR
CLAQUEURS
CLARAIN
CLARAINS
CLARENCE
CLARENCES
CLARENDON
CLARENDONS
CLARET
CLARETED
CLARETING
CLARETS
CLARIES
CLARIFIED
CLARIFIER
CLARIFIERS
CLARIFIES
CLARIFY
CLARIFYING
CLARINET
CLARINETS
CLARINI
CLARINO
CLARINOS
CLARION
CLARIONET
CLARIONETS
CLARIONS
CLARITIES
CLARITY
CLARKIA
CLARKIAS
CLARO
CLAROES
CLAROS
CLARSACH
CLARSACHS
CLART
CLARTED
CLARTIER
CLARTIEST
CLARTING
CLARTS
CLARTY
CLARY
CLASH
CLASHED
CLASHER
CLASHERS
CLASHES
CLASHING
CLASHINGS
CLASP
CLASPED
CLASPER
CLASPERS
CLASPING
CLASPINGS
CLASPS
CLASS
CLASSABLE
CLASSED
CLASSES
CLASSIBLE
CLASSIC
CLASSICAL
CLASSICS
CLASSIER
CLASSIEST
CLASSIFIC
CLASSIFIED
CLASSIFIES
CLASSIFY
CLASSIFYING
CLASSING
CLASSIS
CLASSISM
CLASSISMS
CLASSIST
CLASSLESS
CLASSMAN
CLASSMATE
CLASSMATES
CLASSMEN
CLASSROOM
CLASSROOMS
CLASSY
CLASTIC
CLASTS
CLAT
CLATCH
CLATCHED
CLATCHES
CLATCHING
CLATHRATE
CLATS
CLATTED
CLATTER
CLATTERED
CLATTERER
CLATTERERS
CLATTERING
CLATTERS
CLATTERY
CLATTING
CLAUCHT
CLAUCHTED
CLAUCHTING
CLAUCHTS
CLAUGHT
CLAUGHTED
CLAUGHTING
CLAUGHTS
CLAUSAL
CLAUSE
CLAUSES
CLAUSTRA
CLAUSTRAL
CLAUSTRUM
CLAUSULA
CLAUSULAE
CLAUSULAR
CLAUT
CLAUTED
CLAUTING
CLAUTS
CLAVATE
CLAVATED
CLAVATION
CLAVATIONS
CLAVE
CLAVECIN
CLAVECINS
CLAVER
CLAVERED
CLAVERING
CLAVERS
CLAVES
CLAVICLE
CLAVICLES
CLAVICORN
CLAVICORNS
CLAVICULA
CLAVICULAE
CLAVIE
CLAVIER
CLAVIERS
CLAVIES
CLAVIFORM
CLAVIGER
CLAVIGERS
CLAVIS

CLAVULATE
CLAW
CLAWBACK
CLAWBACKS
CLAWED
CLAWING
CLAWLESS
CLAWS
CLAY
CLAYED
CLAYEY
CLAYIER
CLAYIEST
CLAYING
CLAYISH
CLAYMORE
CLAYMORES
CLAYPAN
CLAYPANS
CLAYS
CLAYTONIA
CLAYTONIAS
CLEAN
CLEANED
CLEANER
CLEANERS
CLEANEST
CLEANING
CLEANINGS
CLEANLIER
CLEANLIEST
CLEANLY
CLEANNESS
CLEANNESSES
CLEANS
CLEANSE
CLEANSED
CLEANSER
CLEANSERS
CLEANSES
CLEANSING
CLEANSINGS
CLEANSKIN
CLEANSKINS
CLEAR
CLEARAGE
CLEARAGES
CLEARANCE
CLEARANCES
CLEARCOLE
CLEARCOLES
CLEARED
CLEARER
CLEARERS
CLEAREST
CLEARING
CLEARINGS
CLEARLY
CLEARNESS
CLEARNESSES
CLEARS
CLEARSKIN
CLEARSKINS
CLEARWAY
CLEARWAYS
CLEARWING
CLEARWINGS
CLEAT
CLEATED
CLEATING
CLEATS
CLEAVABLE
CLEAVAGE
CLEAVAGES
CLEAVE
CLEAVED
CLEAVER
CLEAVERS
CLEAVES
CLEAVING
CLEAVINGS
CLECHE
CLECK
CLECKED
CLECKING
CLECKINGS
CLECKS
CLEEK
CLEEKED
CLEEKING
CLEEKIT
CLEEKS
CLEEP
CLEEPED
CLEEPING
CLEEPS
CLEEVE
CLEEVES
CLEF
CLEFS
CLEFT
CLEFTS
CLEG
CLEGS
CLEIDOIC
CLEITHRAL
CLEM
CLEMATIS
CLEMATISES
CLEMENCIES
CLEMENCY
CLEMENT
CLEMENTLY
CLEMMED
CLEMMING
CLEMS
CLENCH
CLENCHED
CLENCHES
CLENCHING
CLEPE
CLEPED
CLEPES
CLEPING
CLEPSYDRA
CLEPSYDRAS
CLERECOLE
CLERECOLES
CLERGIES
CLERGY
CLERGYMAN
CLERGYMEN
CLERIC
CLERICAL
CLERICALS
CLERICATE
CLERICATES
CLERICITIES
CLERICITY
CLERICS
CLERIHEW
CLERIHEWS
CLERISIES
CLERISY
CLERK
CLERKDOM
CLERKDOMS
CLERKED
CLERKESS
CLERKESSES
CLERKING
CLERKISH
CLERKLIKE
CLERKLING
CLERKLINGS
CLERKLY
CLERKS
CLERKSHIP
CLERKSHIPS
CLERUCH
CLERUCHIA
CLERUCHIAS
CLERUCHIES
CLERUCHS
CLERUCHY
CLEUCH
CLEUCHS
CLEUGH
CLEUGHS
CLEVE
CLEVEITE
CLEVEITES
CLEVER
CLEVERER
CLEVEREST
CLEVERISH
CLEVERLY
CLEVES
CLEVIS
CLEVISES
CLEW
CLEWED
CLEWING
CLEWS
CLIANTHUS
CLIANTHUSES
CLICHE
CLICHEED
CLICHES
CLICK
CLICKED
CLICKER
CLICKERS
CLICKET
CLICKETED
CLICKETING
CLICKETS
CLICKING
CLICKINGS
CLICKS
CLIED
CLIENT
CLIENTAGE
CLIENTAGES
CLIENTAL
CLIENTELE
CLIENTELES
CLIENTS
CLIES
CLIFF
CLIFFED
CLIFFHANG
CLIFFHANGING
CLIFFHANGINGS
CLIFFHANGS
CLIFFHUNG
CLIFFIER
CLIFFIEST
CLIFFS
CLIFFY
CLIFT
CLIFTED
CLIFTIER
CLIFTIEST
CLIFTS
CLIFTY
CLIMACTIC
CLIMATAL
CLIMATE
CLIMATED
CLIMATES
CLIMATIC
CLIMATING
CLIMATISE
CLIMATISED
CLIMATISES
CLIMATISING
CLIMATIZE
CLIMATIZED
CLIMATIZES
CLIMATIZING
CLIMATURE
CLIMATURES
CLIMAX
CLIMAXED
CLIMAXES
CLIMAXING
CLIMB
CLIMBABLE
CLIMBED
CLIMBER
CLIMBERS
CLIMBING
CLIMBINGS
CLIMBS
CLIME
CLIMES
CLINAMEN
CLINAMENS
CLINCH
CLINCHED
CLINCHER
CLINCHERS
CLINCHES
CLINCHING
CLINE
CLINES
CLING
CLINGER
CLINGERS
CLINGFILM
CLINGFILMS
CLINGIER
CLINGIEST
CLINGING
CLINGS
CLINGY
CLINIC
CLINICAL
CLINICIAN
CLINICIANS
CLINICS
CLINIQUE
CLINIQUES
CLINK
CLINKED
CLINKER
CLINKERS
CLINKING
CLINKS
CLINOAXES
CLINOAXIS
CLINQUANT
CLINQUANTS
CLINT
CLINTS
CLIP
CLIPART
CLIPARTS
CLIPBOARD
CLIPBOARDS
CLIPE
CLIPED
CLIPES
CLIPING
CLIPPED
CLIPPER
CLIPPERS
CLIPPIE
CLIPPIES
CLIPPING
CLIPPINGS
CLIPS
CLIPT
CLIQUE
CLIQUES
CLIQUEY
CLIQUIER
CLIQUIEST
CLIQUISH

CLIQUISM
CLIQUISMS
CLIQUY
CLITELLA
CLITELLAR
CLITELLUM
CLITHRAL
CLITIC
CLITICS
CLITORAL
CLITORIS
CLITORISES
CLITTER
CLITTERED
CLITTERING
CLITTERS
CLIVERS
CLIVIA
CLIVIAS
CLOACA
CLOACAE
CLOACAL
CLOACALIN
CLOACINAL
CLOAK
CLOAKED
CLOAKING
CLOAKROOM
CLOAKROOMS
CLOAKS
CLOAM
CLOAMS
CLOBBER
CLOBBERED
CLOBBERING
CLOBBERS
CLOCHARD
CLOCHARDS
CLOCHE
CLOCHES
CLOCK
CLOCKED
CLOCKER
CLOCKERS
CLOCKING
CLOCKINGS
CLOCKS
CLOCKWISE
CLOCKWORK
CLOCKWORKS
CLOD
CLODDED
CLODDIER
CLODDIEST
CLODDING
CLODDISH
CLODDY
CLODLY
CLODPATE
CLODPATED
CLODPATES
CLODPOLE
CLODPOLES
CLODPOLL
CLODPOLLS
CLODS
CLOFF
CLOFFS
CLOG
CLOGDANCE
CLOGDANCES
CLOGGED
CLOGGER
CLOGGERS
CLOGGIER
CLOGGIEST
CLOGGING
CLOGGY
CLOGS
CLOISON
CLOISONNE
CLOISONNES
CLOISONS
CLOISTER
CLOISTERED
CLOISTERING
CLOISTERS
CLOISTRAL
CLOKE
CLOKED
CLOKES
CLOKING
CLOMB
CLOMP
CLOMPED
CLOMPING
CLOMPS
CLONAL
CLONALLY
CLONE
CLONED
CLONES
CLONIC
CLONICITIES
CLONICITY
CLONING
CLONK
CLONKED
CLONKING
CLONKS
CLONUS
CLONUSES
CLOOP
CLOOPS
CLOOT
CLOOTS
CLOP
CLOPPED
CLOPPING
CLOPS
CLOQUE
CLOQUES
CLOSE
CLOSED
CLOSEDOWN
CLOSEDOWNS
CLOSEHEAD
CLOSEHEADS
CLOSELY
CLOSENESS
CLOSENESSES
CLOSER
CLOSERS
CLOSES
CLOSEST
CLOSET
CLOSETED
CLOSETING
CLOSETS
CLOSING
CLOSINGS
CLOSURE
CLOSURED
CLOSURES
CLOSURING
CLOT
CLOTBUR
CLOTBURS
CLOTE
CLOTEBUR
CLOTEBURS
CLOTES
CLOTH
CLOTHE
CLOTHED
CLOTHES
CLOTHIER
CLOTHIERS
CLOTHING
CLOTHINGS
CLOTHS
CLOTPOLL
CLOTPOLLS
CLOTS
CLOTTED
CLOTTER
CLOTTERED
CLOTTERING
CLOTTERS
CLOTTIER
CLOTTIEST
CLOTTING
CLOTTINGS
CLOTTY
CLOTURE
CLOTURED
CLOTURES
CLOTURING
CLOU
CLOUD
CLOUDAGE
CLOUDAGES
CLOUDED
CLOUDIER
CLOUDIEST
CLOUDILY
CLOUDING
CLOUDINGS
CLOUDLAND
CLOUDLANDS
CLOUDLESS
CLOUDLET
CLOUDLETS
CLOUDS
CLOUDTOWN
CLOUDTOWNS
CLOUDY
CLOUGH
CLOUGHS
CLOUR
CLOURED
CLOURING
CLOURS
CLOUS
CLOUT
CLOUTED
CLOUTER
CLOUTERLY
CLOUTERS
CLOUTING
CLOUTS
CLOVE
CLOVEN
CLOVEPINK
CLOVEPINKS
CLOVER
CLOVERED
CLOVERS
CLOVERY
CLOVES
CLOW
CLOWDER
CLOWDERS
CLOWN
CLOWNED
CLOWNERIES
CLOWNERY
CLOWNING
CLOWNINGS
CLOWNISH
CLOWNS
CLOWS
CLOY
CLOYE
CLOYED
CLOYES
CLOYING
CLOYLESS
CLOYMENT
CLOYMENTS
CLOYS
CLOYSOME
CLOZE
CLUB
CLUBABLE
CLUBBABLE
CLUBBED
CLUBBER
CLUBBERS
CLUBBIER
CLUBBIEST
CLUBBING
CLUBBINGS
CLUBBISH
CLUBBISM
CLUBBISMS
CLUBBIST
CLUBBISTS
CLUBBY
CLUBHOUSE
CLUBHOUSES
CLUBLAND
CLUBLANDS
CLUBMAN
CLUBMEN
CLUBROOM
CLUBROOMS
CLUBROOT
CLUBROOTS
CLUBRUSH
CLUBRUSHES
CLUBS
CLUBWOMAN
CLUBWOMEN
CLUCK
CLUCKED
CLUCKIER
CLUCKIEST
CLUCKING
CLUCKS
CLUCKY
CLUDGIE
CLUDGIES
CLUE
CLUED
CLUEING
CLUELESS
CLUES
CLUING
CLUMBER
CLUMBERS
CLUMP
CLUMPED
CLUMPER
CLUMPERS
CLUMPIER
CLUMPIEST
CLUMPING
CLUMPS
CLUMPY
CLUMSIER
CLUMSIEST
CLUMSILY
CLUMSY
CLUNCH
CLUNCHES
CLUNG
CLUNK
CLUNKED
CLUNKIER
CLUNKIEST
CLUNKING
CLUNKS
CLUNKY
CLUPEID
CLUPEIDS
CLUPEOID
CLUPEOIDS
CLUSIA
CLUSIAS

CLUSTER
CLUSTERED
CLUSTERING
CLUSTERS
CLUSTERY
CLUTCH
CLUTCHED
CLUTCHES
CLUTCHING
CLUTTER
CLUTTERED
CLUTTERING
CLUTTERS
CLY
CLYING
CLYPE
CLYPEAL
CLYPEATE
CLYPED
CLYPEI
CLYPES
CLYPEUS
CLYPING
CLYSTER
CLYSTERS
CNEMIAL
CNIDA
CNIDAE
CNIDARIAN
CNIDARIANS
COACH
COACHDOG
COACHDOGS
COACHED
COACHEE
COACHEES
COACHER
COACHERS
COACHES
COACHIES
COACHING
COACHINGS
COACHLINE
COACHLINES
COACHLOAD
COACHLOADS
COACHMAN
COACHMEN
COACHWHIP
COACHWHIPS
COACHWOOD
COACHWOODS
COACHWORK
COACHWORKS
COACHY
COACT
COACTED
COACTING
COACTION
COACTIONS
COACTIVE
COACTS
COADAPTED
COADJUTOR
COADJUTORS
COADUNATE
COADUNATED
COADUNATES
COADUNATING
COAGULA
COAGULANT
COAGULANTS
COAGULASE
COAGULASES
COAGULATE
COAGULATED
COAGULATES
COAGULATING
COAGULUM
COAITA
COAITAS
COAL
COALBALL
COALBALLS
COALED
COALER
COALERS
COALESCE
COALESCED
COALESCES
COALESCING
COALFACE
COALFACES
COALFIELD
COALFIELDS
COALFISH
COALFISHES
COALHOUSE
COALHOUSES
COALIER
COALIEST
COALING
COALISE
COALISED
COALISES
COALISING
COALITION
COALITIONS
COALIZE
COALIZED
COALIZES
COALIZING
COALMAN
COALMEN
COALMINE
COALMINER
COALMINERS
COALMINES
COALPIT
COALPITS
COALS
COALTAR
COALTARS
COALY
COAMING
COAMINGS
COAPT
COAPTED
COAPTING
COAPTS
COARB
COARBS
COARCTATE
COARCTATED
COARCTATES
COARCTATING
COARSE
COARSELY
COARSEN
COARSENED
COARSENING
COARSENS
COARSER
COARSEST
COARSISH
COAST
COASTAL
COASTED
COASTER
COASTERS
COASTING
COASTINGS
COASTLINE
COASTLINES
COASTS
COASTWARD
COASTWARDS
COASTWISE
COAT
COATE
COATED
COATEE
COATEES
COATER
COATERS
COATES
COATI
COATING
COATINGS
COATIS
COATLESS
COATRACK
COATRACKS
COATS
COATSTAND
COATSTANDS
COAX
COAXED
COAXER
COAXERS
COAXES
COAXIAL
COAXIALLY
COAXING
COAXINGLY
COB
COBALAMIN
COBALAMINS
COBALT
COBALTIC
COBALTITE
COBALTITES
COBALTS
COBB
COBBED
COBBER
COBBERS
COBBIER
COBBIEST
COBBING
COBBLE
COBBLED
COBBLER
COBBLERIES
COBBLERS
COBBLERY
COBBLES
COBBLING
COBBLINGS
COBBS
COBBY
COBIA
COBIAS
COBLE
COBLES
COBLOAF
COBLOAVES
COBNUT
COBNUTS
COBRA
COBRAS
COBRIC
COBRIFORM
COBS
COBURG
COBURGS
COBWEB
COBWEBBED
COBWEBBIER
COBWEBBIEST
COBWEBBING
COBWEBBY
COBWEBS
COBZA
COBZAS
COCA
COCAINE
COCAINES
COCAINISE
COCAINISED
COCAINISES
COCAINISING
COCAINISM
COCAINISMS
COCAINIST
COCAINISTS
COCAINIZE
COCAINIZED
COCAINIZES
COCAINIZING
COCAS
COCCAL
COCCI
COCCID
COCCIDIA
COCCIDIUM
COCCIDS
COCCO
COCCOID
COCCOLITE
COCCOLITES
COCCOLITH
COCCOLITHS
COCCOS
COCCUS
COCCYGEAL
COCCYGES
COCCYGIAN
COCCYX
COCH
COCHES
COCHINEAL
COCHINEALS
COCHLEA
COCHLEAE
COCHLEAR
COCHLEARE
COCHLEARES
COCHLEARS
COCHLEATE
COCK
COCKADE
COCKADES
COCKATEEL
COCKATEELS
COCKATIEL
COCKATIELS
COCKATOO
COCKATOOS
COCKBIRD
COCKBIRDS
COCKBOAT
COCKBOATS
COCKED
COCKER
COCKERED
COCKEREL
COCKERELS
COCKERING
COCKERS
COCKET
COCKETS
COCKEYE
COCKEYED
COCKEYES
COCKFIGHT
COCKFIGHTS
COCKHORSE
COCKHORSES
COCKIER
COCKIES
COCKIEST
COCKILY
COCKINESS
COCKINESSES
COCKING
COCKLAIRD
COCKLAIRDS
COCKLE
COCKLEBUR

COCKLEBURS
COCKLED
COCKLEMAN
COCKLEMEN
COCKLES
COCKLING
COCKLOFT
COCKLOFTS
COCKMATCH
COCKMATCHES
COCKNEY
COCKNEYFIED
COCKNEYFIES
COCKNEYFY
COCKNEYFYING
COCKNEYS
COCKNIFIED
COCKNIFIES
COCKNIFY
COCKNIFYING
COCKPIT
COCKPITS
COCKROACH
COCKROACHES
COCKS
COCKSCOMB
COCKSCOMBS
COCKSFOOT
COCKSFOOTS
COCKSHIES
COCKSHOT
COCKSHOTS
COCKSHUT
COCKSHUTS
COCKSHY
COCKSIER
COCKSIEST
COCKSPUR
COCKSPURS
COCKSURE
COCKSWAIN
COCKSWAINED
COCKSWAINING
COCKSWAINS
COCKSY
COCKTAIL
COCKTAILS
COCKY
COCO
COCOA
COCOANUT
COCOANUTS
COCOAS
COCONUT
COCONUTS
COCOON
COCOONED
COCOONERIES
COCOONERY
COCOONING
COCOONINGS
COCOONS
COCOPAN
COCOPANS
COCOPLUM
COCOPLUMS
COCOS
COCOTTE
COCOTTES
COCTILE
COCTION
COCTIONS
COCULTURE
COCULTURED
COCULTURES
COCULTURING
COCUSWOOD
COCUSWOODS
COD
CODA
CODAS
CODDED
CODDER
CODDERS
CODDING
CODDLE
CODDLED
CODDLES
CODDLING
CODE
CODEBOOK
CODEBOOKS
CODED
CODEINE
CODEINES
CODER
CODERS
CODES
CODETTA
CODETTAS
CODEX
CODFISH
CODFISHES
CODGER
CODGERS
CODICES
CODICIL
CODICILS
CODIFIED
CODIFIER
CODIFIERS
CODIFIES
CODIFY
CODIFYING
CODILLA
CODILLAS
CODILLE
CODILLES
CODING
CODINGS
CODIST
CODISTS
CODLIN
CODLING
CODLINGS
CODLINS
CODON
CODONS
CODPIECE
CODPIECES
CODS
COED
COEDS
COEHORN
COEHORNS
COELIAC
COELIACS
COELOM
COELOMATE
COELOMATES
COELOME
COELOMES
COELOMIC
COELOMS
COELOSTAT
COELOSTATS
COEMPTION
COEMPTIONS
COENOBIA
COENOBITE
COENOBITES
COENOBIUM
COENOCYTE
COENOCYTES
COENOSARC
COENOSARCS
COENURI
COENURUS
COENZYME
COENZYMES
COEQUAL
COEQUALLY
COEQUALS
COERCE
COERCED
COERCES
COERCIBLE
COERCIBLY
COERCING
COERCION
COERCIONS
COERCIVE
COETERNAL
COEVAL
COEVALS
COEXIST
COEXISTED
COEXISTING
COEXISTS
COEXTEND
COEXTENDED
COEXTENDING
COEXTENDS
COFACTOR
COFACTORS
COFF
COFFED
COFFEE
COFFEES
COFFER
COFFERDAM
COFFERDAMS
COFFERED
COFFERING
COFFERS
COFFIN
COFFINED
COFFING
COFFINING
COFFINITE
COFFINITES
COFFINS
COFFLE
COFFLES
COFFRET
COFFRETS
COFFS
COFT
COG
COGENCE
COGENCES
COGENCIES
COGENCY
COGENER
COGENERS
COGENT
COGENTLY
COGGED
COGGER
COGGERS
COGGIE
COGGIES
COGGING
COGGINGS
COGGLE
COGGLED
COGGLES
COGGLIER
COGGLIEST
COGGLING
COGGLY
COGIE
COGIES
COGITABLE
COGITATE
COGITATED
COGITATES
COGITATING
COGNATE
COGNATES
COGNATION
COGNATIONS
COGNISANT
COGNISE
COGNISED
COGNISES
COGNISING
COGNITION
COGNITIONS
COGNITIVE
COGNIZANT
COGNIZE
COGNIZED
COGNIZES
COGNIZING
COGNOMEN
COGNOMENS
COGNOMINA
COGNOSCE
COGNOSCED
COGNOSCES
COGNOSCING
COGNOVIT
COGNOVITS
COGS
COGUE
COGUES
COGWHEEL
COGWHEELS
COHAB
COHABIT
COHABITED
COHABITEE
COHABITEES
COHABITING
COHABITOR
COHABITORS
COHABITS
COHABS
COHEIR
COHEIRESS
COHEIRESSES
COHEIRS
COHERE
COHERED
COHERENCE
COHERENCES
COHERENCIES
COHERENCY
COHERENT
COHERER
COHERERS
COHERES
COHERING
COHERITOR
COHERITORS
COHESIBLE
COHESION
COHESIONS
COHESIVE
COHIBIT
COHIBITED
COHIBITING
COHIBITS
COHO
COHOBATE
COHOBATED
COHOBATES
COHOBATING
COHOE
COHOES
COHOG
COHOGS
COHORN
COHORNS
COHORT
COHORTS
COHOS
COHUNE
COHUNES

The Chambers Dictionary is the authority for many longer words; see *OSW* Introduction, page xii

COHYPONYM
COHYPONYMS
COIF
COIFED
COIFFEUR
COIFFEURS
COIFFEUSE
COIFFEUSES
COIFFURE
COIFFURED
COIFFURES
COIFFURING
COIFING
COIFS
COIGN
COIGNE
COIGNED
COIGNES
COIGNING
COIGNS
COIL
COILED
COILING
COILS
COIN
COINAGE
COINAGES
COINCIDE
COINCIDED
COINCIDES
COINCIDING
COINED
COINER
COINERS
COINHERE
COINHERED
COINHERES
COINHERING
COINING
COININGS
COINS
COIR
COIRS
COISTREL
COISTRELS
COISTRIL
COISTRILS
COIT
COITAL
COITION
COITIONS
COITS
COITUS
COITUSES
COJOIN
COJOINED
COJOINING
COJOINS
COJONES
COKE
COKED
COKEHEAD
COKEHEADS
COKERNUT
COKERNUTS
COKES
COKESES
COKIER
COKIEST
COKING
COKY
COL
COLA
COLANDER
COLANDERS
COLAS
COLCANNON
COLCANNONS
COLCHICA
COLCHICUM
COLCHICUMS
COLCOTHAR
COLCOTHARS
COLD
COLDBLOOD
COLDBLOODS
COLDER
COLDEST
COLDHOUSE
COLDHOUSES
COLDISH
COLDLY
COLDNESS
COLDNESSES
COLDS
COLE
COLECTOMIES
COLECTOMY
COLES
COLESEED
COLESEEDS
COLESLAW
COLESLAWS
COLEUS
COLEUSES
COLEWORT
COLEWORTS
COLEY
COLEYS
COLIBRI
COLIBRIS
COLIC
COLICKIER
COLICKIEST
COLICKY
COLICS
COLIFORM
COLIFORMS
COLIN
COLINS
COLISEUM
COLISEUMS
COLITIS
COLITISES
COLL
COLLAGE
COLLAGEN
COLLAGENS
COLLAGES
COLLAGIST
COLLAGISTS
COLLAPSAR
COLLAPSARS
COLLAPSE
COLLAPSED
COLLAPSES
COLLAPSING
COLLAR
COLLARD
COLLARDS
COLLARED
COLLARING
COLLARS
COLLATE
COLLATED
COLLATES
COLLATING
COLLATION
COLLATIONS
COLLATIVE
COLLATOR
COLLATORS
COLLEAGUE
COLLEAGUED
COLLEAGUES
COLLEAGUING
COLLECT
COLLECTED
COLLECTING
COLLECTINGS
COLLECTOR
COLLECTORS
COLLECTS
COLLED
COLLEEN
COLLEENS
COLLEGE
COLLEGER
COLLEGERS
COLLEGES
COLLEGIA
COLLEGIAL
COLLEGIAN
COLLEGIANS
COLLEGIUM
COLLEGIUMS
COLLET
COLLETS
COLLICULI
COLLIDE
COLLIDED
COLLIDER
COLLIDERS
COLLIDES
COLLIDING
COLLIE
COLLIED
COLLIER
COLLIERIES
COLLIERS
COLLIERY
COLLIES
COLLIGATE
COLLIGATED
COLLIGATES
COLLIGATING
COLLIMATE
COLLIMATED
COLLIMATES
COLLIMATING
COLLINEAR
COLLING
COLLINGS
COLLINS
COLLINSES
COLLISION
COLLISIONS
COLLOCATE
COLLOCATED
COLLOCATES
COLLOCATING
COLLODION
COLLODIONS
COLLOGUE
COLLOGUED
COLLOGUES
COLLOGUING
COLLOID
COLLOIDAL
COLLOIDS
COLLOP
COLLOPS
COLLOQUE
COLLOQUED
COLLOQUES
COLLOQUIA
COLLOQUIED
COLLOQUIES
COLLOQUING
COLLOQUY
COLLOQUYING
COLLOTYPE
COLLOTYPES
COLLS
COLLUDE
COLLUDED
COLLUDER
COLLUDERS
COLLUDES
COLLUDING
COLLUSION
COLLUSIONS
COLLUSIVE
COLLUVIES
COLLY
COLLYING
COLLYRIA
COLLYRIUM
COLLYRIUMS
COLOBI
COLOBID
COLOBOMA
COLOBOMATA
COLOBUS
COLOBUSES
COLOCYNTH
COLOCYNTHS
COLOG
COLOGNE
COLOGNES
COLOGS
COLON
COLONEL
COLONELCIES
COLONELCY
COLONELS
COLONES
COLONIAL
COLONIALS
COLONIC
COLONICS
COLONIES
COLONISE
COLONISED
COLONISES
COLONISING
COLONIST
COLONISTS
COLONITIS
COLONITISES
COLONIZE
COLONIZED
COLONIZES
COLONIZING
COLONNADE
COLONNADES
COLONS
COLONY
COLOPHON
COLOPHONIES
COLOPHONS
COLOPHONY
COLOR
COLORANT
COLORANTS
COLORED
COLORIFIC
COLORING
COLORS
COLOSSAL
COLOSSEUM
COLOSSEUMS
COLOSSI
COLOSSUS
COLOSSUSES
COLOSTOMIES
COLOSTOMY
COLOSTRIC
COLOSTRUM
COLOSTRUMS
COLOTOMIES
COLOTOMY
COLOUR
COLOURANT
COLOURANTS
COLOURED
COLOUREDS
COLOURER
COLOURERS
COLOURFUL

COLOURING
COLOURINGS
COLOURISE
COLOURISED
COLOURISES
COLOURISING
COLOURIST
COLOURISTS
COLOURIZE
COLOURIZED
COLOURIZES
COLOURIZING
COLOURMAN
COLOURMEN
COLOURS
COLOURWAY
COLOURWAYS
COLOURY
COLS
COLT
COLTED
COLTER
COLTERS
COLTING
COLTISH
COLTS
COLTSFOOT
COLTSFOOTS
COLTWOOD
COLTWOODS
COLUBRIAD
COLUBRIADS
COLUBRID
COLUBRIDS
COLUBRINE
COLUGO
COLUGOS
COLUMBARIES
COLUMBARY
COLUMBATE
COLUMBATES
COLUMBIC
COLUMBINE
COLUMBINES
COLUMBITE
COLUMBITES
COLUMBIUM
COLUMBIUMS
COLUMEL
COLUMELLA
COLUMELLAE
COLUMELS
COLUMN
COLUMNAL
COLUMNAR
COLUMNED
COLUMNIST
COLUMNISTS
COLUMNS
COLURE
COLURES
COLZA
COLZAS
COMA
COMAE
COMAL
COMARB
COMARBS
COMART
COMARTS
COMAS
COMATE
COMATES
COMATOSE
COMATULID
COMATULIDS
COMB
COMBAT
COMBATANT
COMBATANTS
COMBATED
COMBATING
COMBATIVE
COMBATS
COMBE
COMBED
COMBER
COMBERS
COMBES
COMBI
COMBIER
COMBIES
COMBIEST
COMBINATE
COMBINE
COMBINED
COMBINES
COMBING
COMBINGS
COMBINING
COMBIS
COMBLE
COMBLES
COMBLESS
COMBO
COMBOS
COMBRETUM
COMBRETUMS
COMBS
COMBUST
COMBUSTED
COMBUSTING
COMBUSTOR
COMBUSTORS
COMBUSTS
COMBWISE
COMBY
COME
COMEBACK
COMEBACKS
COMEDDLE
COMEDDLED
COMEDDLES
COMEDDLING
COMEDIAN
COMEDIANS
COMEDIC
COMEDIES
COMEDO
COMEDOS
COMEDOWN
COMEDOWNS
COMEDY
COMELIER
COMELIEST
COMELY
COMER
COMERS
COMES
COMET
COMETARY
COMETHER
COMETHERS
COMETIC
COMETS
COMFIER
COMFIEST
COMFIT
COMFITS
COMFITURE
COMFITURES
COMFORT
COMFORTED
COMFORTER
COMFORTERS
COMFORTING
COMFORTS
COMFREY
COMFREYS
COMFY
COMIC
COMICAL
COMICALLY
COMICE
COMICES
COMICS
COMING
COMINGS
COMIQUE
COMIQUES
COMITADJI
COMITADJIS
COMITAL
COMITATUS
COMITATUSES
COMITIA
COMITIES
COMITY
COMMA
COMMAND
COMMANDED
COMMANDER
COMMANDERS
COMMANDING
COMMANDO
COMMANDOS
COMMANDS
COMMAS
COMMENCE
COMMENCED
COMMENCES
COMMENCING
COMMEND
COMMENDAM
COMMENDAMS
COMMENDED
COMMENDING
COMMENDS
COMMENSAL
COMMENSALS
COMMENT
COMMENTED
COMMENTER
COMMENTERS
COMMENTING
COMMENTOR
COMMENTORS
COMMENTS
COMMER
COMMERCE
COMMERCED
COMMERCES
COMMERCING
COMMERE
COMMERES
COMMERGE
COMMERGED
COMMERGES
COMMERGING
COMMERS
COMMIE
COMMIES
COMMINATE
COMMINATED
COMMINATES
COMMINATING
COMMINGLE
COMMINGLED
COMMINGLES
COMMINGLING
COMMINUTE
COMMINUTED
COMMINUTES
COMMINUTING
COMMIS
COMMISSAR
COMMISSARS
COMMIT
COMMITS
COMMITTAL
COMMITTALS
COMMITTED
COMMITTEE
COMMITTEES
COMMITTING
COMMIX
COMMIXED
COMMIXES
COMMIXING
COMMO
COMMODE
COMMODES
COMMODIFIED
COMMODIFIES
COMMODIFY
COMMODIFYING
COMMODITIES
COMMODITY
COMMODO
COMMODORE
COMMODORES
COMMON
COMMONAGE
COMMONAGES
COMMONED
COMMONER
COMMONERS
COMMONEST
COMMONEY
COMMONEYS
COMMONING
COMMONINGS
COMMONLY
COMMONS
COMMORANT
COMMORANTS
COMMOS
COMMOT
COMMOTE
COMMOTES
COMMOTION
COMMOTIONS
COMMOTS
COMMOVE
COMMOVED
COMMOVES
COMMOVING
COMMUNAL
COMMUNARD
COMMUNARDS
COMMUNE
COMMUNED
COMMUNES
COMMUNING
COMMUNINGS
COMMUNION
COMMUNIONS
COMMUNISE
COMMUNISED
COMMUNISES
COMMUNISING
COMMUNISM
COMMUNISMS
COMMUNIST
COMMUNISTS
COMMUNITIES
COMMUNITY
COMMUNIZE
COMMUNIZED
COMMUNIZES
COMMUNIZING
COMMUTATE
COMMUTATED
COMMUTATES
COMMUTATING
COMMUTE
COMMUTED
COMMUTER
COMMUTERS
COMMUTES

COMMUTING
COMMUTUAL
COMMY
COMODO
COMOSE
COMOUS
COMP
COMPACT
COMPACTED
COMPACTER
COMPACTEST
COMPACTING
COMPACTLY
COMPACTOR
COMPACTORS
COMPACTS
COMPADRE
COMPADRES
COMPAGE
COMPAGES
COMPAND
COMPANDED
COMPANDER
COMPANDERS
COMPANDING
COMPANDOR
COMPANDORS
COMPANDS
COMPANIED
COMPANIES
COMPANING
COMPANION
COMPANIONED
COMPANIONING
COMPANIONS
COMPANY
COMPANYING
COMPARE
COMPARED
COMPARES
COMPARING
COMPART
COMPARTED
COMPARTING
COMPARTS
COMPASS
COMPASSED
COMPASSES
COMPASSING
COMPASSINGS
COMPAST
COMPEAR
COMPEARED
COMPEARING
COMPEARS
COMPED
COMPEER
COMPEERED
COMPEERING
COMPEERS
COMPEL
COMPELLED
COMPELLER
COMPELLERS
COMPELLING
COMPELS
COMPEND
COMPENDIA
COMPENDS
COMPER
COMPERE
COMPERED
COMPERES
COMPERING
COMPERS
COMPESCE
COMPESCED
COMPESCES
COMPESCING
COMPETE
COMPETED
COMPETENT
COMPETES
COMPETING
COMPILE
COMPILED
COMPILER
COMPILERS
COMPILES
COMPILING
COMPING
COMPINGS
COMPITAL
COMPLAIN
COMPLAINED
COMPLAINING
COMPLAININGS
COMPLAINS
COMPLAINT
COMPLAINTS
COMPLEAT
COMPLECT
COMPLECTED
COMPLECTING
COMPLECTS
COMPLETE
COMPLETED
COMPLETER
COMPLETES
COMPLETEST
COMPLETING
COMPLEX
COMPLEXED
COMPLEXER
COMPLEXES
COMPLEXEST
COMPLEXING
COMPLEXLY
COMPLEXUS
COMPLEXUSES
COMPLIANT
COMPLICE
COMPLICES
COMPLIED
COMPLIER
COMPLIERS
COMPLIES
COMPLIN
COMPLINE
COMPLINES
COMPLINS
COMPLISH
COMPLISHED
COMPLISHES
COMPLISHING
COMPLOT
COMPLOTS
COMPLOTTED
COMPLOTTING
COMPLUVIA
COMPLY
COMPLYING
COMPO
COMPONE
COMPONENT
COMPONENTS
COMPONY
COMPORT
COMPORTED
COMPORTING
COMPORTS
COMPOS
COMPOSE
COMPOSED
COMPOSER
COMPOSERS
COMPOSES
COMPOSING
COMPOSITE
COMPOSITED
COMPOSITES
COMPOSITING
COMPOST
COMPOSTED
COMPOSTER
COMPOSTERS
COMPOSTING
COMPOSTS
COMPOSURE
COMPOSURES
COMPOT
COMPOTE
COMPOTES
COMPOTIER
COMPOTIERS
COMPOTS
COMPOUND
COMPOUNDED
COMPOUNDING
COMPOUNDS
COMPRADOR
COMPRADORS
COMPRESS
COMPRESSED
COMPRESSES
COMPRESSING
COMPRINT
COMPRINTED
COMPRINTING
COMPRINTS
COMPRISAL
COMPRISALS
COMPRISE
COMPRISED
COMPRISES
COMPRISING
COMPS
COMPT
COMPTABLE
COMPTED
COMPTER
COMPTERS
COMPTIBLE
COMPTING
COMPTROLL
COMPTROLLED
COMPTROLLING
COMPTROLLS
COMPTS
COMPULSE
COMPULSED
COMPULSES
COMPULSING
COMPUTANT
COMPUTANTS
COMPUTE
COMPUTED
COMPUTER
COMPUTERS
COMPUTES
COMPUTING
COMPUTIST
COMPUTISTS
COMRADE
COMRADELY
COMRADES
COMS
COMUS
COMUSES
CON
CONACRE
CONACRED
CONACRES
CONACRING
CONARIA
CONARIAL
CONARIUM
CONATION
CONATIONS
CONATIVE
CONATUS
CONCAUSE
CONCAUSES
CONCAVE
CONCAVED
CONCAVELY
CONCAVES
CONCAVING
CONCAVITIES
CONCAVITY
CONCEAL
CONCEALED
CONCEALER
CONCEALERS
CONCEALING
CONCEALS
CONCEDE
CONCEDED
CONCEDER
CONCEDERS
CONCEDES
CONCEDING
CONCEDO
CONCEIT
CONCEITED
CONCEITING
CONCEITS
CONCEITY
CONCEIVE
CONCEIVED
CONCEIVES
CONCEIVING
CONCENT
CONCENTER
CONCENTERED
CONCENTERING
CONCENTERS
CONCENTRE
CONCENTRED
CONCENTRES
CONCENTRING
CONCENTS
CONCENTUS
CONCEPT
CONCEPTI
CONCEPTS
CONCEPTUS
CONCEPTUSES
CONCERN
CONCERNED
CONCERNING
CONCERNS
CONCERT
CONCERTED
CONCERTI
CONCERTING
CONCERTO
CONCERTOS
CONCERTS
CONCETTI
CONCETTO
CONCH
CONCHA
CONCHAE
CONCHAL
CONCHATE
CONCHE
CONCHED
CONCHES
CONCHIE
CONCHIES
CONCHING
CONCHITIS
CONCHITISES
CONCHOID
CONCHOIDS
CONCHS
CONCHY
CONCIERGE
CONCIERGES

CONCILIAR
CONCISE
CONCISED
CONCISELY
CONCISER
CONCISES
CONCISEST
CONCISING
CONCISION
CONCISIONS
CONCLAVE
CONCLAVES
CONCLUDE
CONCLUDED
CONCLUDES
CONCLUDING
CONCOCT
CONCOCTED
CONCOCTER
CONCOCTERS
CONCOCTING
CONCOCTOR
CONCOCTORS
CONCOCTS
CONCOLOR
CONCORD
CONCORDAT
CONCORDATS
CONCORDED
CONCORDING
CONCORDS
CONCOURS
CONCOURSE
CONCOURSES
CONCREATE
CONCREATED
CONCREATES
CONCREATING
CONCRETE
CONCRETED
CONCRETES
CONCRETING
CONCREW
CONCREWED
CONCREWING
CONCREWS
CONCUBINE
CONCUBINES
CONCUPIES
CONCUPY
CONCUR
CONCURRED
CONCURRING
CONCURS
CONCUSS
CONCUSSED
CONCUSSES
CONCUSSING
CONCYCLIC
COND
CONDEMN
CONDEMNED
CONDEMNING
CONDEMNS
CONDENSE
CONDENSED
CONDENSER
CONDENSERS
CONDENSES
CONDENSING
CONDER
CONDERS
CONDIDDLE
CONDIDDLED
CONDIDDLES
CONDIDDLING
CONDIE
CONDIES
CONDIGN
CONDIGNLY
CONDIMENT
CONDIMENTED
CONDIMENTING
CONDIMENTS
CONDITION
CONDITIONED
CONDITIONING
CONDITIONINGS
CONDITIONS
CONDO
CONDOLE
CONDOLED
CONDOLENT
CONDOLES
CONDOLING
CONDOM
CONDOMS
CONDONE
CONDONED
CONDONES
CONDONING
CONDOR
CONDORS
CONDOS
CONDUCE
CONDUCED
CONDUCES
CONDUCING
CONDUCIVE
CONDUCT
CONDUCTED
CONDUCTI
CONDUCTING
CONDUCTOR
CONDUCTORS
CONDUCTS
CONDUCTUS
CONDUIT
CONDUITS
CONDYLAR
CONDYLE
CONDYLES
CONDYLOID
CONDYLOMA
CONDYLOMAS
CONDYLOMATA
CONE
CONED
CONES
CONEY
CONEYS
CONF
CONFAB
CONFABBED
CONFABBING
CONFABS
CONFECT
CONFECTED
CONFECTING
CONFECTS
CONFER
CONFEREE
CONFEREES
CONFERRED
CONFERRER
CONFERRERS
CONFERRING
CONFERS
CONFERVA
CONFERVAE
CONFERVAS
CONFESS
CONFESSED
CONFESSES
CONFESSING
CONFESSOR
CONFESSORS
CONFEST
CONFESTLY
CONFETTI
CONFIDANT
CONFIDANTS
CONFIDE
CONFIDED
CONFIDENT
CONFIDENTS
CONFIDER
CONFIDERS
CONFIDES
CONFIDING
CONFIGURE
CONFIGURED
CONFIGURES
CONFIGURING
CONFINE
CONFINED
CONFINER
CONFINERS
CONFINES
CONFINING
CONFIRM
CONFIRMED
CONFIRMEE
CONFIRMEES
CONFIRMER
CONFIRMERS
CONFIRMING
CONFIRMINGS
CONFIRMOR
CONFIRMORS
CONFIRMS
CONFISEUR
CONFISEURS
CONFIT
CONFITEOR
CONFITEORS
CONFITS
CONFITURE
CONFITURES
CONFIX
CONFIXED
CONFIXES
CONFIXING
CONFLATE
CONFLATED
CONFLATES
CONFLATING
CONFLICT
CONFLICTED
CONFLICTING
CONFLICTS
CONFLUENT
CONFLUENTS
CONFLUX
CONFLUXES
CONFOCAL
CONFORM
CONFORMAL
CONFORMED
CONFORMER
CONFORMERS
CONFORMING
CONFORMS
CONFOUND
CONFOUNDED
CONFOUNDING
CONFOUNDS
CONFRERE
CONFRERES
CONFRERIE
CONFRERIES
CONFRONT
CONFRONTE
CONFRONTED
CONFRONTING
CONFRONTS
CONFS
CONFUSE
CONFUSED
CONFUSES
CONFUSING
CONFUSION
CONFUSIONS
CONFUTE
CONFUTED
CONFUTES
CONFUTING
CONGA
CONGAED
CONGAING
CONGAS
CONGE
CONGEAL
CONGEALED
CONGEALING
CONGEALS
CONGED
CONGEE
CONGEED
CONGEEING
CONGEES
CONGEING
CONGENER
CONGENERS
CONGENIAL
CONGENIC
CONGER
CONGERIES
CONGERS
CONGES
CONGEST
CONGESTED
CONGESTING
CONGESTS
CONGIARIES
CONGIARY
CONGII
CONGIUS
CONGLOBE
CONGLOBED
CONGLOBES
CONGLOBING
CONGO
CONGOS
CONGOU
CONGOUS
CONGRATS
CONGREE
CONGREED
CONGREEING
CONGREES
CONGREET
CONGREETED
CONGREETING
CONGREETS
CONGRESS
CONGRESSED
CONGRESSES
CONGRESSING
CONGRUE
CONGRUED
CONGRUENT
CONGRUES
CONGRUING
CONGRUITIES
CONGRUITY
CONGRUOUS
CONIA
CONIAS
CONIC
CONICAL
CONICALLY
CONICS
CONIDIA
CONIDIAL
CONIDIUM
CONIES
CONIFER
CONIFERS
CONIFORM

CONIINE
CONIINES
CONIMA
CONIMAS
CONIN
CONINE
CONINES
CONING
CONINS
CONJECT
CONJECTED
CONJECTING
CONJECTS
CONJEE
CONJEED
CONJEEING
CONJEES
CONJOIN
CONJOINED
CONJOINING
CONJOINS
CONJOINT
CONJUGAL
CONJUGANT
CONJUGANTS
CONJUGATE
CONJUGATED
CONJUGATES
CONJUGATING
CONJUGATINGS
CONJUNCT
CONJURE
CONJURED
CONJURER
CONJURERS
CONJURES
CONJURIES
CONJURING
CONJURINGS
CONJUROR
CONJURORS
CONJURY
CONK
CONKED
CONKER
CONKERS
CONKIER
CONKIEST
CONKING
CONKS
CONKY
CONN
CONNATE
CONNATION
CONNATIONS
CONNATURE
CONNATURES
CONNE
CONNECT
CONNECTED
CONNECTER
CONNECTERS
CONNECTING
CONNECTOR
CONNECTORS
CONNECTS
CONNED
CONNER
CONNERS
CONNES
CONNEXION
CONNEXIONS
CONNEXIVE
CONNING
CONNINGS
CONNIVE
CONNIVED
CONNIVENT
CONNIVER
CONNIVERS
CONNIVES
CONNIVING
CONNOTATE
CONNOTATED
CONNOTATES
CONNOTATING
CONNOTE
CONNOTED
CONNOTES
CONNOTING
CONNOTIVE
CONNS
CONNUBIAL
CONODONT
CONODONTS
CONOID
CONOIDAL
CONOIDIC
CONOIDS
CONQUER
CONQUERED
CONQUERING
CONQUEROR
CONQUERORS
CONQUERS
CONQUEST
CONQUESTS
CONS
CONSCIENT
CONSCIOUS
CONSCIOUSES
CONSCRIBE
CONSCRIBED
CONSCRIBES
CONSCRIBING
CONSCRIPT
CONSCRIPTED
CONSCRIPTING
CONSCRIPTS
CONSEIL
CONSEILS
CONSENSUS
CONSENSUSES
CONSENT
CONSENTED
CONSENTING
CONSENTS
CONSERVE
CONSERVED
CONSERVER
CONSERVERS
CONSERVES
CONSERVING
CONSIDER
CONSIDERED
CONSIDERING
CONSIDERS
CONSIGN
CONSIGNED
CONSIGNEE
CONSIGNEES
CONSIGNER
CONSIGNERS
CONSIGNING
CONSIGNOR
CONSIGNORS
CONSIGNS
CONSIST
CONSISTED
CONSISTING
CONSISTS
CONSOCIES
CONSOLATE
CONSOLATED
CONSOLATES
CONSOLATING
CONSOLE
CONSOLED
CONSOLER
CONSOLERS
CONSOLES
CONSOLING
CONSOLS
CONSOLUTE
CONSOMME
CONSOMMES
CONSONANT
CONSONANTS
CONSONOUS
CONSORT
CONSORTED
CONSORTER
CONSORTERS
CONSORTIA
CONSORTING
CONSORTS
CONSPIRE
CONSPIRED
CONSPIRER
CONSPIRERS
CONSPIRES
CONSPIRING
CONSTABLE
CONSTABLES
CONSTANCIES
CONSTANCY
CONSTANT
CONSTANTS
CONSTATE
CONSTATED
CONSTATES
CONSTATING
CONSTER
CONSTERED
CONSTERING
CONSTERS
CONSTRAIN
CONSTRAINED
CONSTRAINING
CONSTRAINS
CONSTRICT
CONSTRICTED
CONSTRICTING
CONSTRICTS
CONSTRUCT
CONSTRUCTED
CONSTRUCTING
CONSTRUCTS
CONSTRUE
CONSTRUED
CONSTRUER
CONSTRUERS
CONSTRUES
CONSTRUING
CONSUL
CONSULAGE
CONSULAGES
CONSULAR
CONSULARS
CONSULATE
CONSULATES
CONSULS
CONSULT
CONSULTA
CONSULTAS
CONSULTED
CONSULTEE
CONSULTEES
CONSULTER
CONSULTERS
CONSULTING
CONSULTOR
CONSULTORS
CONSULTS
CONSUME
CONSUMED
CONSUMER
CONSUMERS
CONSUMES
CONSUMING
CONSUMINGS
CONSUMPT
CONSUMPTS
CONTACT
CONTACTED
CONTACTING
CONTACTOR
CONTACTORS
CONTACTS
CONTADINA
CONTADINAS
CONTADINE
CONTADINI
CONTADINO
CONTAGIA
CONTAGION
CONTAGIONS
CONTAGIUM
CONTAIN
CONTAINED
CONTAINER
CONTAINERS
CONTAINING
CONTAINS
CONTANGO
CONTANGOED
CONTANGOING
CONTANGOS
CONTE
CONTECK
CONTECKS
CONTEMN
CONTEMNED
CONTEMNER
CONTEMNERS
CONTEMNING
CONTEMNOR
CONTEMNORS
CONTEMNS
CONTEMPER
CONTEMPERED
CONTEMPERING
CONTEMPERS
CONTEMPT
CONTEMPTS
CONTEND
CONTENDED
CONTENDER
CONTENDERS
CONTENDING
CONTENDINGS
CONTENDS
CONTENT
CONTENTED
CONTENTING
CONTENTS
CONTES
CONTESSA
CONTESSAS
CONTEST
CONTESTED
CONTESTER
CONTESTERS
CONTESTING
CONTESTS
CONTEXT
CONTEXTS
CONTICENT
CONTINENT
CONTINENTS
CONTINUA
CONTINUAL
CONTINUE
CONTINUED
CONTINUER
CONTINUERS
CONTINUES
CONTINUING
CONTINUO
CONTINUOS

CONTINUUM
CONTINUUMS
CONTLINE
CONTLINES
CONTO
CONTORNO
CONTORNOS
CONTORT
CONTORTED
CONTORTING
CONTORTS
CONTOS
CONTOUR
CONTOURED
CONTOURING
CONTOURS
CONTRA
CONTRACT
CONTRACTED
CONTRACTING
CONTRACTS
CONTRAIL
CONTRAILS
CONTRAIR
CONTRALTI
CONTRALTO
CONTRALTOS
CONTRARIED
CONTRARIES
CONTRARY
CONTRARYING
CONTRAS
CONTRAST
CONTRASTED
CONTRASTING
CONTRASTS
CONTRASTY
CONTRAT
CONTRATE
CONTRATS
CONTRIST
CONTRISTED
CONTRISTING
CONTRISTS
CONTRITE
CONTRIVE
CONTRIVED
CONTRIVER
CONTRIVERS
CONTRIVES
CONTRIVING
CONTROL
CONTROLE
CONTROLLED
CONTROLLING
CONTROLS
CONTROUL
CONTROULED
CONTROULING
CONTROULS
CONTUMACIES
CONTUMACY
CONTUMELIES
CONTUMELY
CONTUND
CONTUNDED
CONTUNDING
CONTUNDS
CONTUSE
CONTUSED
CONTUSES
CONTUSING
CONTUSION
CONTUSIONS
CONTUSIVE
CONUNDRUM
CONUNDRUMS
CONURBAN
CONURBIA
CONURBIAS
CONURE
CONURES
CONVECTOR
CONVECTORS
CONVENE
CONVENED
CONVENER
CONVENERS
CONVENES
CONVENING
CONVENOR
CONVENORS
CONVENT
CONVENTED
CONVENTING
CONVENTS
CONVERGE
CONVERGED
CONVERGES
CONVERGING
CONVERSE
CONVERSED
CONVERSES
CONVERSING
CONVERT
CONVERTED
CONVERTER
CONVERTERS
CONVERTING
CONVERTOR
CONVERTORS
CONVERTS
CONVEX
CONVEXED
CONVEXES
CONVEXITIES
CONVEXITY
CONVEXLY
CONVEY
CONVEYAL
CONVEYALS
CONVEYED
CONVEYER
CONVEYERS
CONVEYING
CONVEYOR
CONVEYORS
CONVEYS
CONVICT
CONVICTED
CONVICTING
CONVICTS
CONVINCE
CONVINCED
CONVINCES
CONVINCING
CONVIVE
CONVIVED
CONVIVES
CONVIVIAL
CONVIVING
CONVO
CONVOCATE
CONVOCATED
CONVOCATES
CONVOCATING
CONVOKE
CONVOKED
CONVOKES
CONVOKING
CONVOLUTE
CONVOLVE
CONVOLVED
CONVOLVES
CONVOLVING
CONVOS
CONVOY
CONVOYED
CONVOYING
CONVOYS
CONVULSE
CONVULSED
CONVULSES
CONVULSING
CONY
COO
COOED
COOEE
COOEED
COOEEING
COOEES
COOEY
COOEYED
COOEYING
COOEYS
COOF
COOFS
COOING
COOINGLY
COOINGS
COOK
COOKABLE
COOKBOOK
COOKBOOKS
COOKED
COOKER
COOKERIES
COOKERS
COOKERY
COOKHOUSE
COOKHOUSES
COOKIE
COOKIES
COOKING
COOKMAID
COOKMAIDS
COOKOUT
COOKOUTS
COOKROOM
COOKROOMS
COOKS
COOKWARE
COOKWARES
COOKY
COOL
COOLABAH
COOLABAHS
COOLAMON
COOLAMONS
COOLANT
COOLANTS
COOLED
COOLER
COOLERS
COOLEST
COOLHOUSE
COOLHOUSES
COOLIBAH
COOLIBAHS
COOLIBAR
COOLIBARS
COOLIE
COOLIES
COOLING
COOLISH
COOLLY
COOLNESS
COOLNESSES
COOLS
COOLTH
COOLTHS
COOLY
COOM
COOMB
COOMBE
COOMBES
COOMBS
COOMED
COOMIER
COOMIEST
COOMING
COOMS
COOMY
COON
COONCAN
COONCANS
COONDOG
COONDOGS
COONHOUND
COONHOUNDS
COONS
COONSKIN
COONSKINS
COONTIE
COONTIES
COONTY
COOP
COOPED
COOPER
COOPERAGE
COOPERAGES
COOPERATE
COOPERATED
COOPERATES
COOPERATING
COOPERED
COOPERIES
COOPERING
COOPERINGS
COOPERS
COOPERY
COOPING
COOPS
COOPT
COOPTED
COOPTING
COOPTS
COORDINAL
COOS
COOSEN
COOSENED
COOSENING
COOSENS
COOSER
COOSERS
COOSIN
COOSINED
COOSINING
COOSINS
COOST
COOT
COOTIE
COOTIES
COOTIKIN
COOTIKINS
COOTS
COP
COPACETIC
COPAIBA
COPAIBAS
COPAIVA
COPAIVAS
COPAL
COPALS
COPARTNER
COPARTNERS
COPATAINE
COPATRIOT
COPATRIOTS
COPE
COPECK
COPECKS
COPED
COPEMATE
COPEMATES
COPEPOD
COPEPODS
COPER
COPERED
COPERING

COPERS
COPES
COPESTONE
COPESTONES
COPIED
COPIER
COPIERS
COPIES
COPILOT
COPILOTS
COPING
COPINGS
COPIOUS
COPIOUSLY
COPITA
COPITAS
COPLANAR
COPOLYMER
COPOLYMERS
COPPED
COPPER
COPPERAS
COPPERASES
COPPERED
COPPERING
COPPERINGS
COPPERISH
COPPERS
COPPERY
COPPICE
COPPICED
COPPICES
COPPICING
COPPICINGS
COPPIES
COPPIN
COPPING
COPPINS
COPPLE
COPPLES
COPPY
COPRA
COPRAS
COPRESENT
COPROLITE
COPROLITES
COPROLITH
COPROLITHS
COPROLOGIES
COPROLOGY
COPROSMA
COPROSMAS
COPROZOIC
COPS
COPSE
COPSED
COPSES
COPSEWOOD
COPSEWOODS
COPSHOP
COPSHOPS
COPSIER
COPSIEST
COPSING
COPSY
COPTER
COPTERS
COPULA
COPULAR
COPULAS
COPULATE
COPULATED
COPULATES
COPULATING
COPY
COPYBOOK
COPYBOOKS
COPYCAT
COPYCATS
COPYCATTED
COPYCATTING
COPYHOLD
COPYHOLDS
COPYING
COPYISM
COPYISMS
COPYIST
COPYISTS
COPYREAD
COPYREADING
COPYREADINGS
COPYREADS
COPYRIGHT
COPYRIGHTED
COPYRIGHTING
COPYRIGHTS
COQUET
COQUETRIES
COQUETRY
COQUETS
COQUETTE
COQUETTED
COQUETTES
COQUETTING
COQUILLA
COQUILLAS
COQUILLE
COQUILLES
COQUINA
COQUINAS
COQUITO
COQUITOS
COR
CORACLE
CORACLES
CORACOID
CORACOIDS
CORAGGIO
CORAGGIOS
CORAL
CORALLA
CORALLINE
CORALLINES
CORALLITE
CORALLITES
CORALLOID
CORALLUM
CORALROOT
CORALROOTS
CORALS
CORALWORT
CORALWORTS
CORAM
CORAMINE
CORAMINES
CORANACH
CORANACHS
CORANTO
CORANTOES
CORANTOS
CORBAN
CORBANS
CORBE
CORBEAU
CORBEAUS
CORBEIL
CORBEILLE
CORBEILLES
CORBEILS
CORBEL
CORBELED
CORBELING
CORBELINGS
CORBELLED
CORBELLING
CORBELLINGS
CORBELS
CORBES
CORBICULA
CORBICULAE
CORBIE
CORBIES
CORCASS
CORCASSES
CORD
CORDAGE
CORDAGES
CORDATE
CORDED
CORDIAL
CORDIALLY
CORDIALS
CORDIFORM
CORDINER
CORDINERS
CORDING
CORDINGS
CORDITE
CORDITES
CORDLESS
CORDOBA
CORDOBAS
CORDON
CORDONED
CORDONING
CORDONS
CORDOTOMIES
CORDOTOMY
CORDOVAN
CORDOVANS
CORDS
CORDUROY
CORDUROYS
CORDWAIN
CORDWAINS
CORDWOOD
CORDWOODS
CORDYLINE
CORDYLINES
CORE
CORED
COREGENT
COREGENTS
CORELESS
CORELLA
CORELLAS
COREOPSIS
COREOPSISES
CORER
CORERS
CORES
COREY
COREYS
CORF
CORFHOUSE
CORFHOUSES
CORGI
CORGIS
CORIA
CORIANDER
CORIANDERS
CORIES
CORING
CORIOUS
CORIUM
CORIUMS
CORIVAL
CORIVALLED
CORIVALLING
CORIVALRIES
CORIVALRY
CORIVALS
CORK
CORKAGE
CORKAGES
CORKBOARD
CORKBOARDS
CORKBORER
CORKBORERS
CORKED
CORKER
CORKERS
CORKIER
CORKIEST
CORKINESS
CORKINESSES
CORKING
CORKIR
CORKIRS
CORKS
CORKSCREW
CORKSCREWED
CORKSCREWING
CORKSCREWS
CORKTREE
CORKTREES
CORKWOOD
CORKWOODS
CORKY
CORM
CORMEL
CORMELS
CORMIDIA
CORMIDIUM
CORMORANT
CORMORANTS
CORMOUS
CORMS
CORMUS
CORMUSES
CORN
CORNACRE
CORNACRES
CORNAGE
CORNAGES
CORNBALL
CORNBALLS
CORNBORER
CORNBORERS
CORNBRAKE
CORNBRAKES
CORNBRASH
CORNBRASHES
CORNBREAD
CORNBREADS
CORNCRAKE
CORNCRAKES
CORNEA
CORNEAL
CORNEAS
CORNED
CORNEL
CORNELIAN
CORNELIANS
CORNELS
CORNEMUSE
CORNEMUSES
CORNEOUS
CORNER
CORNERED
CORNERING
CORNERS
CORNET
CORNETCIES
CORNETCY
CORNETIST
CORNETISTS
CORNETS
CORNETT
CORNETTI
CORNETTO
CORNETTS
CORNFIELD
CORNFIELDS
CORNFLAG
CORNFLAGS
CORNFLAKE
CORNFLAKES
CORNFLIES
CORNFLOUR

CORNFLOURS
CORNFLY
CORNHUSK
CORNHUSKS
CORNI
CORNICE
CORNICED
CORNICES
CORNICHE
CORNICHES
CORNICING
CORNICLE
CORNICLES
CORNICULA
CORNIER
CORNIEST
CORNIFIC
CORNIFORM
CORNING
CORNIST
CORNISTS
CORNLAND
CORNLANDS
CORNLOFT
CORNLOFTS
CORNMILL
CORNMILLS
CORNMOTH
CORNMOTHS
CORNO
CORNOPEAN
CORNOPEANS
CORNPIPE
CORNPIPES
CORNRENT
CORNRENTS
CORNROW
CORNROWS
CORNS
CORNSTALK
CORNSTALKS
CORNSTONE
CORNSTONES
CORNU
CORNUA
CORNUAL
CORNUTE
CORNUTED
CORNUTES
CORNUTING
CORNUTO
CORNUTOS
CORNWORM
CORNWORMS
CORNY
COROCORE
COROCORES
COROCORO
COROCOROS
CORODIES
CORODY
COROLLA
COROLLARIES
COROLLARY
COROLLAS
COROLLINE
CORONA
CORONACH
CORONACHS
CORONAE
CORONAL
CORONALS
CORONARIES
CORONARY
CORONAS
CORONATE
CORONATED
CORONER
CORONERS
CORONET
CORONETED
CORONETS
CORONIS
CORONISES
CORONIUM
CORONIUMS
CORONOID
COROZO
COROZOS
CORPORA
CORPORAL
CORPORALS
CORPORAS
CORPORASES
CORPORATE
CORPOREAL
CORPORIFIED
CORPORIFIES
CORPORIFY
CORPORIFYING
CORPOSANT
CORPOSANTS
CORPS
CORPSE
CORPSED
CORPSES
CORPSING
CORPULENT
CORPUS
CORPUSCLE
CORPUSCLES
CORRADE
CORRADED
CORRADES
CORRADING
CORRAL
CORRALLED
CORRALLING
CORRALS
CORRASION
CORRASIONS
CORRECT
CORRECTED
CORRECTER
CORRECTEST
CORRECTING
CORRECTLY
CORRECTOR
CORRECTORS
CORRECTS
CORRELATE
CORRELATED
CORRELATES
CORRELATING
CORRIDA
CORRIDAS
CORRIDOR
CORRIDORS
CORRIE
CORRIES
CORRIGENT
CORRIGENTS
CORRIVAL
CORRIVALLED
CORRIVALLING
CORRIVALS
CORRODE
CORRODED
CORRODENT
CORRODENTS
CORRODES
CORRODIES
CORRODING
CORRODY
CORROSION
CORROSIONS
CORROSIVE
CORROSIVES
CORRUGATE
CORRUGATED
CORRUGATES
CORRUGATING
CORRUPT
CORRUPTED
CORRUPTER
CORRUPTERS
CORRUPTEST
CORRUPTING
CORRUPTLY
CORRUPTS
CORS
CORSAC
CORSACS
CORSAGE
CORSAGES
CORSAIR
CORSAIRS
CORSE
CORSELET
CORSELETS
CORSES
CORSET
CORSETED
CORSETIER
CORSETIERS
CORSETING
CORSETRIES
CORSETRY
CORSETS
CORSIVE
CORSIVES
CORSLET
CORSLETED
CORSLETS
CORSNED
CORSNEDS
CORSO
CORSOS
CORTEGE
CORTEGES
CORTEX
CORTEXES
CORTICAL
CORTICATE
CORTICES
CORTICOID
CORTICOIDS
CORTILE
CORTILI
CORTISOL
CORTISOLS
CORTISONE
CORTISONES
CORUNDUM
CORUNDUMS
CORUSCANT
CORUSCATE
CORUSCATED
CORUSCATES
CORUSCATING
CORVEE
CORVEES
CORVES
CORVET
CORVETED
CORVETING
CORVETS
CORVETTE
CORVETTED
CORVETTES
CORVETTING
CORVID
CORVIDS
CORVINE
CORVUS
CORVUSES
CORY
CORYBANT
CORYBANTES
CORYBANTS
CORYDALIS
CORYDALISES
CORYLUS
CORYLUSES
CORYMB
CORYMBOSE
CORYMBS
CORYPHAEI
CORYPHE
CORYPHEE
CORYPHEES
CORYPHENE
CORYPHENES
CORYPHES
CORYZA
CORYZAS
COS
COSE
COSEC
COSECANT
COSECANTS
COSECH
COSECHS
COSECS
COSED
COSEISMAL
COSEISMIC
COSES
COSET
COSETS
COSH
COSHED
COSHER
COSHERED
COSHERER
COSHERERS
COSHERIES
COSHERING
COSHERINGS
COSHERS
COSHERY
COSHES
COSHING
COSIER
COSIERS
COSIES
COSIEST
COSILY
COSINE
COSINES
COSINESS
COSINESSES
COSING
COSMEA
COSMEAS
COSMESES
COSMESIS
COSMETIC
COSMETICS
COSMIC
COSMICAL
COSMISM
COSMISMS
COSMIST
COSMISTS
COSMOCRAT
COSMOCRATS
COSMOGENIES
COSMOGENY
COSMOGONIES
COSMOGONY
COSMOLOGIES
COSMOLOGY
COSMONAUT
COSMONAUTS
COSMORAMA
COSMORAMAS
COSMOS
COSMOSES
COSMOTRON

COSMOTRONS
COSPHERED
COSPONSOR
COSPONSORED
COSPONSORING
COSPONSORS
COSS
COSSES
COSSET
COSSETED
COSSETING
COSSETS
COSSIE
COSSIES
COST
COSTA
COSTAE
COSTAL
COSTALGIA
COSTALGIAS
COSTALS
COSTARD
COSTARDS
COSTATE
COSTATED
COSTE
COSTEAN
COSTEANED
COSTEANING
COSTEANINGS
COSTEANS
COSTED
COSTER
COSTERS
COSTES
COSTING
COSTIVE
COSTIVELY
COSTLIER
COSTLIEST
COSTLY
COSTMARIES
COSTMARY
COSTREL
COSTRELS
COSTS
COSTUME
COSTUMED
COSTUMER
COSTUMERS
COSTUMES
COSTUMIER
COSTUMIERS
COSTUMING
COSTUS
COSTUSES
COSY
COT
COTANGENT
COTANGENTS
COTE
COTEAU
COTEAUX
COTED
COTELETTE
COTELETTES
COTELINE
COTELINES
COTENANT
COTENANTS
COTERIE
COTERIES
COTES
COTH
COTHS
COTHURN
COTHURNI
COTHURNS
COTHURNUS
COTICULAR
COTIDAL
COTILLION
COTILLIONS
COTILLON
COTILLONS
COTING
COTINGA
COTINGAS
COTISE
COTISED
COTISES
COTISING
COTLAND
COTLANDS
COTQUEAN
COTQUEANS
COTS
COTT
COTTA
COTTABUS
COTTABUSES
COTTAGE
COTTAGED
COTTAGER
COTTAGERS
COTTAGES
COTTAGEY
COTTAGING
COTTAGINGS
COTTAR
COTTARS
COTTAS
COTTED
COTTER
COTTERS
COTTID
COTTIDS
COTTIER
COTTIERS
COTTISE
COTTISED
COTTISES
COTTISING
COTTOID
COTTON
COTTONADE
COTTONADES
COTTONED
COTTONING
COTTONS
COTTONY
COTTOWN
COTTOWNS
COTTS
COTTUS
COTTUSES
COTWAL
COTWALS
COTYLAE
COTYLE
COTYLEDON
COTYLEDONS
COTYLES
COTYLOID
COUCAL
COUCALS
COUCH
COUCHANT
COUCHE
COUCHED
COUCHEE
COUCHEES
COUCHES
COUCHETTE
COUCHETTES
COUCHING
COUCHINGS
COUDE
COUGAR
COUGARS
COUGH
COUGHED
COUGHER
COUGHERS
COUGHING
COUGHINGS
COUGHS
COUGUAR
COUGUARS
COULD
COULEE
COULEES
COULIS
COULISSE
COULISSES
COULOIR
COULOIRS
COULOMB
COULOMBS
COULTER
COULTERS
COUMARIC
COUMARIN
COUMARINS
COUNCIL
COUNCILOR
COUNCILORS
COUNCILS
COUNSEL
COUNSELLED
COUNSELLING
COUNSELLINGS
COUNSELOR
COUNSELORS
COUNSELS
COUNT
COUNTABLE
COUNTED
COUNTER
COUNTERED
COUNTERING
COUNTERS
COUNTESS
COUNTESSES
COUNTIES
COUNTING
COUNTLESS
COUNTLINE
COUNTLINES
COUNTRIES
COUNTROL
COUNTROLLED
COUNTROLLING
COUNTROLS
COUNTRY
COUNTS
COUNTSHIP
COUNTSHIPS
COUNTY
COUP
COUPE
COUPED
COUPEE
COUPEES
COUPER
COUPERS
COUPES
COUPING
COUPLE
COUPLED
COUPLEDOM
COUPLEDOMS
COUPLER
COUPLERS
COUPLES
COUPLET
COUPLETS
COUPLING
COUPLINGS
COUPON
COUPONS
COUPS
COUPURE
COUPURES
COUR
COURAGE
COURAGES
COURANT
COURANTE
COURANTES
COURANTS
COURB
COURBARIL
COURBARILS
COURBED
COURBETTE
COURBETTES
COURBING
COURBS
COURD
COURE
COURED
COURES
COURGETTE
COURGETTES
COURIER
COURIERS
COURING
COURLAN
COURLANS
COURS
COURSE
COURSED
COURSER
COURSERS
COURSES
COURSING
COURSINGS
COURT
COURTED
COURTEOUS
COURTESAN
COURTESANS
COURTESIED
COURTESIES
COURTESY
COURTESYING
COURTEZAN
COURTEZANS
COURTIER
COURTIERS
COURTING
COURTINGS
COURTLET
COURTLETS
COURTLIER
COURTLIEST
COURTLIKE
COURTLING
COURTLINGS
COURTLY
COURTROOM
COURTROOMS
COURTS
COURTSHIP
COURTSHIPS
COURTYARD
COURTYARDS
COUSCOUS
COUSCOUSES
COUSIN
COUSINAGE
COUSINAGES
COUSINLY
COUSINRIES
COUSINRY
COUSINS
COUTER
COUTERS
COUTH

COUTHER
COUTHEST
COUTHIE
COUTHIER
COUTHIEST
COUTHY
COUTIL
COUTILLE
COUTILLES
COUTILS
COUTURE
COUTURES
COUTURIER
COUTURIERS
COUVADE
COUVADES
COUVERT
COUVERTS
COVALENCIES
COVALENCY
COVALENT
COVARIANT
COVARIANTS
COVARIED
COVARIES
COVARY
COVARYING
COVE
COVED
COVELET
COVELETS
COVELLITE
COVELLITES
COVEN
COVENANT
COVENANTED
COVENANTING
COVENANTS
COVENS
COVENT
COVENTS
COVER
COVERAGE
COVERAGES
COVERALL
COVERALLS
COVERED
COVERING
COVERINGS
COVERLET
COVERLETS
COVERLID
COVERLIDS
COVERS
COVERSLIP
COVERSLIPS
COVERT
COVERTLY
COVERTS
COVERTURE
COVERTURES
COVES
COVET
COVETABLE
COVETED
COVETING
COVETISE
COVETISES
COVETOUS
COVETS
COVEY
COVEYS
COVIN
COVING
COVINGS
COVINOUS
COVINS
COVYNE
COVYNES
COW
COWAGE
COWAGES
COWAL
COWALS
COWAN
COWANS
COWARD
COWARDED
COWARDICE
COWARDICES
COWARDING
COWARDLY
COWARDREE
COWARDREES
COWARDRIES
COWARDRY
COWARDS
COWBANE
COWBANES
COWBELL
COWBELLS
COWBERRIES
COWBERRY
COWBIRD
COWBIRDS
COWBOY
COWBOYS
COWED
COWER
COWERED
COWERING
COWERS
COWFEEDER
COWFEEDERS
COWFISH
COWFISHES
COWGIRL
COWGIRLS
COWGRASS
COWGRASSES
COWHAGE
COWHAGES
COWHAND
COWHANDS
COWHEARD
COWHEARDS
COWHEEL
COWHEELS
COWHERB
COWHERBS
COWHERD
COWHERDS
COWHIDE
COWHIDED
COWHIDES
COWHIDING
COWHOUSE
COWHOUSES
COWING
COWISH
COWITCH
COWITCHES
COWL
COWLED
COWLICK
COWLICKS
COWLING
COWLINGS
COWLS
COWMAN
COWMEN
COWP
COWPAT
COWPATS
COWPEA
COWPEAS
COWPED
COWPING
COWPOKE
COWPOKES
COWPOX
COWPOXES
COWPS
COWRIE
COWRIES
COWRY
COWS
COWSHED
COWSHEDS
COWSLIP
COWSLIPS
COWTREE
COWTREES
COX
COXA
COXAE
COXAL
COXALGIA
COXALGIAS
COXCOMB
COXCOMBIC
COXCOMBRIES
COXCOMBRY
COXCOMBS
COXED
COXES
COXIER
COXIEST
COXINESS
COXINESSES
COXING
COXSWAIN
COXSWAINED
COXSWAINING
COXSWAINS
COXY
COY
COYED
COYER
COYEST
COYING
COYISH
COYISHLY
COYLY
COYNESS
COYNESSES
COYOTE
COYOTES
COYOTILLO
COYOTILLOS
COYPU
COYPUS
COYSTREL
COYSTRELS
COYSTRIL
COYSTRILS
COZ
COZE
COZED
COZEN
COZENAGE
COZENAGES
COZENED
COZENER
COZENERS
COZENING
COZENS
COZES
COZIER
COZIERS
COZIES
COZIEST
COZING
COZY
COZZES
CRAB
CRABBED
CRABBEDLY
CRABBER
CRABBERS
CRABBIER
CRABBIEST
CRABBILY
CRABBING
CRABBY
CRABLIKE
CRABS
CRABSTICK
CRABSTICKS
CRABWISE
CRACK
CRACKDOWN
CRACKDOWNS
CRACKED
CRACKER
CRACKERS
CRACKHEAD
CRACKHEADS
CRACKING
CRACKJAW
CRACKLE
CRACKLED
CRACKLES
CRACKLIER
CRACKLIEST
CRACKLING
CRACKLINGS
CRACKLY
CRACKNEL
CRACKNELS
CRACKPOT
CRACKPOTS
CRACKS
CRACKSMAN
CRACKSMEN
CRACOWE
CRACOWES
CRADLE
CRADLED
CRADLES
CRADLING
CRADLINGS
CRAFT
CRAFTED
CRAFTIER
CRAFTIEST
CRAFTILY
CRAFTING
CRAFTLESS
CRAFTS
CRAFTSMAN
CRAFTSMEN
CRAFTWORK
CRAFTWORKS
CRAFTY
CRAG
CRAGFAST
CRAGGED
CRAGGIER
CRAGGIEST
CRAGGY
CRAGS
CRAGSMAN
CRAGSMEN
CRAIG
CRAIGS
CRAKE
CRAKED
CRAKES
CRAKING
CRAM
CRAMBO
CRAMBOES
CRAME
CRAMES
CRAMESIES
CRAMESY
CRAMMABLE
CRAMMED
CRAMMER

CRAMMERS
CRAMMING
CRAMOISIES
CRAMOISY
CRAMP
CRAMPBARK
CRAMPBARKS
CRAMPED
CRAMPET
CRAMPETS
CRAMPIER
CRAMPIEST
CRAMPING
CRAMPIT
CRAMPITS
CRAMPON
CRAMPONS
CRAMPS
CRAMPY
CRAMS
CRAN
CRANAGE
CRANAGES
CRANBERRIES
CRANBERRY
CRANCH
CRANCHED
CRANCHES
CRANCHING
CRANE
CRANED
CRANEFLIES
CRANEFLY
CRANES
CRANIA
CRANIAL
CRANING
CRANIUM
CRANIUMS
CRANK
CRANKCASE
CRANKCASES
CRANKED
CRANKIER
CRANKIEST
CRANKILY
CRANKING
CRANKLE
CRANKLED
CRANKLES
CRANKLING
CRANKNESS
CRANKNESSES
CRANKS
CRANKY
CRANNIED
CRANNIES
CRANNOG
CRANNOGS
CRANNY
CRANNYING
CRANREUCH
CRANREUCHS
CRANS
CRANTS
CRANTSES
CRAP
CRAPE
CRAPES
CRAPIER
CRAPIEST
CRAPLE
CRAPLES
CRAPPED
CRAPPIER
CRAPPIEST
CRAPPING
CRAPPY
CRAPS
CRAPULENT
CRAPULOUS
CRAPY
CRARE
CRARES
CRASES
CRASH
CRASHED
CRASHES
CRASHING
CRASHLAND
CRASHLANDED
CRASHLANDING
CRASHLANDS
CRASHPAD
CRASHPADS
CRASIS
CRASS
CRASSER
CRASSEST
CRASSLY
CRASSNESS
CRASSNESSES
CRATCH
CRATCHES
CRATE
CRATED
CRATER
CRATERED
CRATERING
CRATEROUS
CRATERS
CRATES
CRATING
CRATON
CRATONS
CRATUR
CRATURS
CRAUNCH
CRAUNCHED
CRAUNCHES
CRAUNCHING
CRAVAT
CRAVATS
CRAVATTED
CRAVATTING
CRAVE
CRAVED
CRAVEN
CRAVENED
CRAVENING
CRAVENLY
CRAVENS
CRAVER
CRAVERS
CRAVES
CRAVING
CRAVINGS
CRAW
CRAWFISH
CRAWFISHED
CRAWFISHES
CRAWFISHING
CRAWL
CRAWLED
CRAWLER
CRAWLERS
CRAWLIER
CRAWLIEST
CRAWLING
CRAWLINGS
CRAWLS
CRAWLY
CRAWS
CRAYER
CRAYERS
CRAYFISH
CRAYFISHES
CRAYON
CRAYONED
CRAYONING
CRAYONS
CRAZE
CRAZED
CRAZES
CRAZIER
CRAZIES
CRAZIEST
CRAZILY
CRAZINESS
CRAZINESSES
CRAZING
CRAZY
CREACH
CREACHS
CREAGH
CREAGHS
CREAK
CREAKED
CREAKIER
CREAKIEST
CREAKILY
CREAKING
CREAKS
CREAKY
CREAM
CREAMED
CREAMER
CREAMERIES
CREAMERS
CREAMERY
CREAMIER
CREAMIEST
CREAMING
CREAMLAID
CREAMS
CREAMWARE
CREAMWARES
CREAMWOVE
CREAMY
CREANCE
CREANCES
CREANT
CREASE
CREASED
CREASER
CREASERS
CREASES
CREASIER
CREASIEST
CREASING
CREASOTE
CREASOTED
CREASOTES
CREASOTING
CREASY
CREATABLE
CREATE
CREATED
CREATES
CREATIC
CREATIN
CREATINE
CREATINES
CREATING
CREATINS
CREATION
CREATIONS
CREATIVE
CREATOR
CREATORS
CREATRESS
CREATRESSES
CREATRIX
CREATRIXES
CREATURAL
CREATURE
CREATURES
CRECHE
CRECHES
CRED
CREDAL
CREDENCE
CREDENCES
CREDENDA
CREDENDUM
CREDENT
CREDENZA
CREDENZAS
CREDIBLE
CREDIBLY
CREDIT
CREDITED
CREDITING
CREDITOR
CREDITORS
CREDITS
CREDO
CREDOS
CREDS
CREDULITIES
CREDULITY
CREDULOUS
CREE
CREED
CREEDAL
CREEDS
CREEING
CREEK
CREEKIER
CREEKIEST
CREEKS
CREEKY
CREEL
CREELS
CREEP
CREEPER
CREEPERED
CREEPERS
CREEPIE
CREEPIER
CREEPIES
CREEPIEST
CREEPING
CREEPS
CREEPY
CREES
CREESE
CREESED
CREESES
CREESH
CREESHED
CREESHES
CREESHIER
CREESHIEST
CREESHING
CREESHY
CREESING
CREMASTER
CREMASTERS
CREMATE
CREMATED
CREMATES
CREMATING
CREMATION
CREMATIONS
CREMATOR
CREMATORIES
CREMATORS
CREMATORY
CREME
CREMES
CREMOCARP
CREMOCARPS
CREMONA
CREMONAS
CREMOR
CREMORNE
CREMORNES
CREMORS
CREMOSIN

CREMSIN
CRENA
CRENAS
CRENATE
CRENATED
CRENATION
CRENATIONS
CRENATURE
CRENATURES
CRENEL
CRENELATE
CRENELATED
CRENELATES
CRENELATING
CRENELLE
CRENELLED
CRENELLES
CRENELLING
CRENELS
CRENULATE
CREODONT
CREODONTS
CREOLE
CREOLES
CREOLIAN
CREOLIANS
CREOLIST
CREOLISTS
CREOSOL
CREOSOLS
CREOSOTE
CREOSOTED
CREOSOTES
CREOSOTING
CREPANCE
CREPANCES
CREPE
CREPERIE
CREPERIES
CREPES
CREPEY
CREPIER
CREPIEST
CREPINESS
CREPINESSES
CREPITANT
CREPITATE
CREPITATED
CREPITATES
CREPITATING
CREPITUS
CREPITUSES
CREPOLINE
CREPOLINES
CREPON
CREPONS
CREPT
CREPUSCLE
CREPUSCLES
CREPY
CRESCENDO
CRESCENDOED
CRESCENDOING
CRESCENDOS
CRESCENT
CRESCENTS
CRESCIVE
CRESOL
CRESOLS
CRESS
CRESSES
CRESSET
CRESSETS
CREST
CRESTED
CRESTING
CRESTLESS
CRESTON
CRESTONS
CRESTS
CRESYLIC
CRETIC
CRETICS
CRETIN
CRETINISE
CRETINISED
CRETINISES
CRETINISING
CRETINISM
CRETINISMS
CRETINIZE
CRETINIZED
CRETINIZES
CRETINIZING
CRETINOID
CRETINOIDS
CRETINOUS
CRETINS
CRETISM
CRETISMS
CRETONNE
CRETONNES
CREUTZER
CREUTZERS
CREVASSE
CREVASSED
CREVASSES
CREVASSING
CREVETTE
CREVETTES
CREVICE
CREVICES
CREW
CREWE
CREWED
CREWEL
CREWELIST
CREWELISTS
CREWELLED
CREWELLING
CREWELS
CREWES
CREWING
CREWS
CRIANT
CRIB
CRIBBAGE
CRIBBAGES
CRIBBED
CRIBBING
CRIBBLE
CRIBBLED
CRIBBLES
CRIBBLING
CRIBELLA
CRIBELLAR
CRIBELLUM
CRIBLE
CRIBRATE
CRIBROSE
CRIBROUS
CRIBS
CRIBWORK
CRIBWORKS
CRICETID
CRICETIDS
CRICK
CRICKED
CRICKET
CRICKETED
CRICKETER
CRICKETERS
CRICKETING
CRICKETINGS
CRICKETS
CRICKEY
CRICKING
CRICKS
CRICKY
CRICOID
CRICOIDS
CRIED
CRIER
CRIERS
CRIES
CRIKEY
CRIM
CRIME
CRIMED
CRIMEFUL
CRIMELESS
CRIMEN
CRIMES
CRIMINA
CRIMINAL
CRIMINALS
CRIMINATE
CRIMINATED
CRIMINATES
CRIMINATING
CRIMINE
CRIMING
CRIMINI
CRIMINOUS
CRIMMER
CRIMMERS
CRIMP
CRIMPED
CRIMPER
CRIMPERS
CRIMPIER
CRIMPIEST
CRIMPING
CRIMPLE
CRIMPLED
CRIMPLES
CRIMPLING
CRIMPS
CRIMPY
CRIMS
CRIMSON
CRIMSONED
CRIMSONING
CRIMSONS
CRINAL
CRINATE
CRINATED
CRINE
CRINED
CRINES
CRINGE
CRINGED
CRINGER
CRINGERS
CRINGES
CRINGING
CRINGINGS
CRINGLE
CRINGLES
CRINING
CRINITE
CRINITES
CRINKLE
CRINKLED
CRINKLES
CRINKLIER
CRINKLIES
CRINKLIEST
CRINKLING
CRINKLY
CRINOID
CRINOIDAL
CRINOIDS
CRINOLINE
CRINOLINES
CRINOSE
CRINUM
CRINUMS
CRIOLLO
CRIOLLOS
CRIPES
CRIPPLE
CRIPPLED
CRIPPLES
CRIPPLING
CRIPPLINGS
CRISE
CRISES
CRISIS
CRISP
CRISPATE
CRISPED
CRISPER
CRISPERS
CRISPEST
CRISPIER
CRISPIEST
CRISPIN
CRISPING
CRISPINS
CRISPLY
CRISPNESS
CRISPNESSES
CRISPS
CRISPY
CRISSA
CRISSUM
CRISTA
CRISTAE
CRISTATE
CRIT
CRITERIA
CRITERION
CRITH
CRITHS
CRITIC
CRITICAL
CRITICISE
CRITICISED
CRITICISES
CRITICISING
CRITICISM
CRITICISMS
CRITICIZE
CRITICIZED
CRITICIZES
CRITICIZING
CRITICS
CRITIQUE
CRITIQUED
CRITIQUES
CRITIQUING
CRITS
CRITTER
CRITTERS
CRITTUR
CRITTURS
CRIVENS
CRIVVENS
CROAK
CROAKED
CROAKER
CROAKERS
CROAKIER
CROAKIEST
CROAKILY
CROAKING
CROAKINGS
CROAKS
CROAKY
CROC
CROCEATE
CROCEIN
CROCEINS
CROCEOUS
CROCHE
CROCHES
CROCHET
CROCHETED
CROCHETING

ROCHETINGS
ROCHETS
ROCK
ROCKED
ROCKERIES
ROCKERY
ROCKET
ROCKETS
ROCKING
ROCKS
ROCODILE
ROCODILES
ROCOITE
ROCOITES
ROCOSMIA
ROCOSMIAS
ROCS
ROCUS
ROCUSES
ROFT
ROFTER
ROFTERS
ROFTING
ROFTINGS
ROFTS
ROISSANT
ROISSANTS
ROMACK
ROMACKS
ROMB
ROMBED
ROMBING
ROMBS
ROME
ROMED
ROMES
ROMING
ROMLECH
ROMLECHS
ROMORNA
ROMORNAS
ROMORNE
ROMORNES
RONE
RONES
RONET
RONETS
RONIES
RONK
RONKER
RONKEST
RONY
RONYISM
RONYISMS
ROODLE
ROODLED
ROODLES
ROODLING
ROOK
ROOKBACK
ROOKBACKS
ROOKED
ROOKEDER
ROOKEDEST
CROOKEDLY
CROOKER
CROOKEST
CROOKING
CROOKS
CROON
CROONED
CROONER
CROONERS
CROONING
CROONINGS
CROONS
CROOVE
CROOVES
CROP
CROPBOUND
CROPFUL
CROPFULL
CROPFULS
CROPLAND
CROPLANDS
CROPPED
CROPPER
CROPPERS
CROPPIES
CROPPING
CROPPINGS
CROPPY
CROPS
CROPSICK
CROQUANTE
CROQUANTES
CROQUET
CROQUETED
CROQUETING
CROQUETS
CROQUETTE
CROQUETTES
CROQUIS
CRORE
CRORES
CROSIER
CROSIERED
CROSIERS
CROSS
CROSSBAND
CROSSBANDS
CROSSBAR
CROSSBARS
CROSSBEAM
CROSSBEAMS
CROSSBILL
CROSSBILLS
CROSSBIT
CROSSBITE
CROSSBITES
CROSSBITING
CROSSBITTEN
CROSSBOW
CROSSBOWS
CROSSBRED
CROSSBUCK
CROSSBUCKS
CROSSCUT
CROSSCUTS
CROSSCUTTING
CROSSCUTTINGS
CROSSE
CROSSED
CROSSER
CROSSES
CROSSEST
CROSSETTE
CROSSETTES
CROSSFALL
CROSSFALLS
CROSSFIRE
CROSSFIRES
CROSSFISH
CROSSFISHES
CROSSHEAD
CROSSHEADS
CROSSING
CROSSINGS
CROSSISH
CROSSJACK
CROSSJACKS
CROSSLET
CROSSLETS
CROSSLY
CROSSNESS
CROSSNESSES
CROSSOVER
CROSSOVERS
CROSSROAD
CROSSROADS
CROSSTIE
CROSSTIES
CROSSTOWN
CROSSTREE
CROSSTREES
CROSSWALK
CROSSWALKS
CROSSWAY
CROSSWAYS
CROSSWIND
CROSSWINDS
CROSSWISE
CROSSWORD
CROSSWORDS
CROSSWORT
CROSSWORTS
CROST
CROSTINI
CROSTINIS
CROTAL
CROTALA
CROTALINE
CROTALISM
CROTALISMS
CROTALS
CROTALUM
CROTCH
CROTCHED
CROTCHES
CROTCHET
CROTCHETIER
CROTCHETIEST
CROTCHETS
CROTCHETY
CROTON
CROTONS
CROTTLE
CROTTLES
CROUCH
CROUCHED
CROUCHES
CROUCHING
CROUP
CROUPADE
CROUPADES
CROUPE
CROUPED
CROUPER
CROUPERS
CROUPES
CROUPIER
CROUPIERS
CROUPIEST
CROUPING
CROUPON
CROUPONS
CROUPOUS
CROUPS
CROUPY
CROUSE
CROUSELY
CROUSTADE
CROUSTADES
CROUT
CROUTE
CROUTES
CROUTON
CROUTONS
CROUTS
CROW
CROWBAR
CROWBARS
CROWBERRIES
CROWBERRY
CROWD
CROWDED
CROWDER
CROWDERS
CROWDIE
CROWDIES
CROWDING
CROWDS
CROWED
CROWFOOT
CROWFOOTS
CROWING
CROWN
CROWNED
CROWNER
CROWNERS
CROWNET
CROWNETS
CROWNING
CROWNINGS
CROWNLESS
CROWNLET
CROWNLETS
CROWNS
CROWNWORK
CROWNWORKS
CROWS
CROZE
CROZES
CROZIER
CROZIERS
CRU
CRUBEEN
CRUBEENS
CRUCES
CRUCIAL
CRUCIAN
CRUCIANS
CRUCIATE
CRUCIBLE
CRUCIBLES
CRUCIFER
CRUCIFERS
CRUCIFIED
CRUCIFIER
CRUCIFIERS
CRUCIFIES
CRUCIFIX
CRUCIFIXES
CRUCIFORM
CRUCIFY
CRUCIFYING
CRUCK
CRUCKS
CRUD
CRUDDED
CRUDDIER
CRUDDIEST
CRUDDING
CRUDDLE
CRUDDLED
CRUDDLES
CRUDDLING
CRUDDY
CRUDE
CRUDELY
CRUDENESS
CRUDENESSES
CRUDER
CRUDES
CRUDEST
CRUDITES
CRUDITIES
CRUDITY
CRUDS
CRUDY
CRUE
CRUEL
CRUELLER
CRUELLEST
CRUELLS
CRUELLY
CRUELNESS
CRUELNESSES
CRUELS
CRUELTIES

CRUELTY
CRUES
CRUET
CRUETS
CRUISE
CRUISED
CRUISER
CRUISERS
CRUISES
CRUISEWAY
CRUISEWAYS
CRUISIE
CRUISIES
CRUISING
CRUIVE
CRUIVES
CRULLER
CRULLERS
CRUMB
CRUMBED
CRUMBIER
CRUMBIEST
CRUMBING
CRUMBLE
CRUMBLED
CRUMBLES
CRUMBLIER
CRUMBLIES
CRUMBLIEST
CRUMBLING
CRUMBLY
CRUMBS
CRUMBY
CRUMEN
CRUMENAL
CRUMENALS
CRUMENS
CRUMHORN
CRUMHORNS
CRUMMACK
CRUMMACKS
CRUMMIER
CRUMMIES
CRUMMIEST
CRUMMOCK
CRUMMOCKS
CRUMMY
CRUMP
CRUMPED
CRUMPER
CRUMPEST
CRUMPET
CRUMPETS
CRUMPIER
CRUMPIEST
CRUMPING
CRUMPLE
CRUMPLED
CRUMPLES
CRUMPLING
CRUMPLINGS
CRUMPS
CRUMPY
CRUNCH
CRUNCHED
CRUNCHES
CRUNCHIER
CRUNCHIEST
CRUNCHING
CRUNCHY
CRUNKLE
CRUNKLED
CRUNKLES
CRUNKLING
CRUOR
CRUORES
CRUPPER
CRUPPERS
CRURAL
CRUS
CRUSADE
CRUSADED
CRUSADER
CRUSADERS
CRUSADES
CRUSADING
CRUSADO
CRUSADOS
CRUSE
CRUSES
CRUSET
CRUSETS
CRUSH
CRUSHABLE
CRUSHED
CRUSHER
CRUSHERS
CRUSHES
CRUSHING
CRUSIAN
CRUSIANS
CRUSIE
CRUSIES
CRUST
CRUSTA
CRUSTAE
CRUSTAL
CRUSTATE
CRUSTATED
CRUSTED
CRUSTIER
CRUSTIES
CRUSTIEST
CRUSTILY
CRUSTING
CRUSTLESS
CRUSTS
CRUSTY
CRUSY
CRUTCH
CRUTCHED
CRUTCHES
CRUTCHING
CRUVE
CRUVES
CRUX
CRUXES
CRUZADO
CRUZADOES
CRUZADOS
CRUZEIRO
CRUZEIROS
CRWTH
CRWTHS
CRY
CRYBABIES
CRYBABY
CRYING
CRYINGS
CRYOGEN
CRYOGENIC
CRYOGENICS
CRYOGENIES
CRYOGENS
CRYOGENY
CRYOLITE
CRYOLITES
CRYOMETER
CRYOMETERS
CRYONIC
CRYONICS
CRYOPROBE
CRYOPROBES
CRYOSCOPE
CRYOSCOPES
CRYOSCOPIES
CRYOSCOPY
CRYOSTAT
CRYOSTATS
CRYOTRON
CRYOTRONS
CRYPT
CRYPTADIA
CRYPTAL
CRYPTIC
CRYPTICAL
CRYPTO
CRYPTOGAM
CRYPTOGAMS
CRYPTON
CRYPTONS
CRYPTONYM
CRYPTONYMS
CRYPTOS
CRYPTS
CRYSTAL
CRYSTALS
CSARDAS
CSARDASES
CTENE
CTENES
CTENIFORM
CTENOID
CUADRILLA
CUADRILLAS
CUB
CUBAGE
CUBAGES
CUBATURE
CUBATURES
CUBBED
CUBBIES
CUBBING
CUBBINGS
CUBBISH
CUBBY
CUBE
CUBEB
CUBEBS
CUBED
CUBES
CUBHOOD
CUBHOODS
CUBIC
CUBICA
CUBICAL
CUBICALLY
CUBICAS
CUBICLE
CUBICLES
CUBICS
CUBIFORM
CUBING
CUBISM
CUBISMS
CUBIST
CUBISTIC
CUBISTS
CUBIT
CUBITAL
CUBITS
CUBITUS
CUBITUSES
CUBLESS
CUBOID
CUBOIDAL
CUBOIDS
CUBS
CUCKOLD
CUCKOLDED
CUCKOLDING
CUCKOLDLY
CUCKOLDOM
CUCKOLDOMS
CUCKOLDRIES
CUCKOLDRY
CUCKOLDS
CUCKOO
CUCKOOS
CUCULLATE
CUCUMBER
CUCUMBERS
CUCURBIT
CUCURBITS
CUD
CUDBEAR
CUDBEARS
CUDDEEHIH
CUDDEEHIHS
CUDDEN
CUDDENS
CUDDIE
CUDDIES
CUDDIN
CUDDINS
CUDDLE
CUDDLED
CUDDLES
CUDDLIER
CUDDLIEST
CUDDLING
CUDDLY
CUDDY
CUDGEL
CUDGELLED
CUDGELLER
CUDGELLERS
CUDGELLING
CUDGELLINGS
CUDGELS
CUDS
CUDWEED
CUDWEEDS
CUE
CUED
CUEING
CUEIST
CUEISTS
CUES
CUESTA
CUESTAS
CUFF
CUFFED
CUFFIN
CUFFING
CUFFINS
CUFFLE
CUFFLED
CUFFLES
CUFFLING
CUFFO
CUFFS
CUFFUFFLE
CUFFUFFLES
CUIF
CUIFS
CUING
CUIRASS
CUIRASSED
CUIRASSES
CUIRASSING
CUISH
CUISHES
CUISINE
CUISINES
CUISINIER
CUISINIERS
CUISSE
CUISSER
CUISSERS
CUISSES
CUIT
CUITER
CUITERED
CUITERING
CUITERS
CUITIKIN
CUITIKINS
CUITS
CUITTLE

CUITTLED
CUITTLES
CUITTLING
CULCH
CULCHES
CULCHIE
CULCHIES
CULET
CULETS
CULEX
CULICES
CULICID
CULICIDS
CULICINE
CULICINES
CULINARY
CULL
CULLED
CULLENDER
CULLENDERS
CULLER
CULLERS
CULLET
CULLETS
CULLIED
CULLIES
CULLING
CULLINGS
CULLION
CULLIONLY
CULLIONS
CULLIS
CULLISES
CULLS
CULLY
CULLYING
CULLYISM
CULLYISMS
CULM
CULMED
CULMEN
CULMENS
CULMINANT
CULMINATE
CULMINATED
CULMINATES
CULMINATING
CULMING
CULMS
CULOTTE
CULOTTES
CULPABLE
CULPABLY
CULPATORY
CULPRIT
CULPRITS
CULT
CULTCH
CULTCHES
CULTER
CULTERS
CULTIC
CULTIGEN
CULTIGENS
CULTISH
CULTISM
CULTISMS
CULTIST
CULTISTS
CULTIVAR
CULTIVARS
CULTIVATE
CULTIVATED
CULTIVATES
CULTIVATING
CULTRATE
CULTRATED
CULTS
CULTURAL
CULTURE
CULTURED
CULTURES
CULTURING
CULTURIST
CULTURISTS
CULTUS
CULTUSES
CULVER
CULVERIN
CULVERINS
CULVERS
CULVERT
CULVERTS
CUM
CUMARIN
CUMARINS
CUMBENT
CUMBER
CUMBERED
CUMBERER
CUMBERERS
CUMBERING
CUMBERS
CUMBRANCE
CUMBRANCES
CUMBROUS
CUMEC
CUMECS
CUMIN
CUMINS
CUMMER
CUMMERS
CUMMIN
CUMMINS
CUMQUAT
CUMQUATS
CUMSHAW
CUMSHAWS
CUMULATE
CUMULATED
CUMULATES
CUMULATING
CUMULI
CUMULOSE
CUMULUS
CUNABULA
CUNCTATOR
CUNCTATORS
CUNDIES
CUNDY
CUNEAL
CUNEATE
CUNEATIC
CUNEIFORM
CUNEIFORMS
CUNETTE
CUNETTES
CUNJEVOI
CUNJEVOIS
CUNNER
CUNNERS
CUNNING
CUNNINGER
CUNNINGEST
CUNNINGLY
CUNNINGS
CUNT
CUNTS
CUP
CUPBEARER
CUPBEARERS
CUPBOARD
CUPBOARDED
CUPBOARDING
CUPBOARDS
CUPCAKE
CUPCAKES
CUPEL
CUPELED
CUPELING
CUPELLED
CUPELLING
CUPELS
CUPFUL
CUPFULS
CUPGALL
CUPGALLS
CUPHEAD
CUPHEADS
CUPID
CUPIDITIES
CUPIDITY
CUPIDS
CUPMAN
CUPMEN
CUPOLA
CUPOLAED
CUPOLAING
CUPOLAR
CUPOLAS
CUPOLATED
CUPPA
CUPPAS
CUPPED
CUPPER
CUPPERS
CUPPING
CUPPINGS
CUPREOUS
CUPRIC
CUPRITE
CUPRITES
CUPROUS
CUPS
CUPULAR
CUPULATE
CUPULE
CUPULES
CUR
CURABLE
CURACAO
CURACAOS
CURACIES
CURACOA
CURACOAS
CURACY
CURARA
CURARAS
CURARE
CURARES
CURARI
CURARINE
CURARINES
CURARIS
CURARISE
CURARISED
CURARISES
CURARISING
CURARIZE
CURARIZED
CURARIZES
CURARIZING
CURASSOW
CURASSOWS
CURAT
CURATE
CURATED
CURATES
CURATING
CURATIVE
CURATOR
CURATORS
CURATORY
CURATRIX
CURATRIXES
CURATS
CURB
CURBABLE
CURBED
CURBING
CURBLESS
CURBS
CURBSTONE
CURBSTONES
CURCH
CURCHES
CURCULIO
CURCULIOS
CURCUMA
CURCUMAS
CURCUMIN
CURCUMINE
CURCUMINES
CURCUMINS
CURD
CURDED
CURDIER
CURDIEST
CURDINESS
CURDINESSES
CURDING
CURDLE
CURDLED
CURDLES
CURDLING
CURDS
CURDY
CURE
CURED
CURELESS
CURER
CURERS
CURES
CURETTAGE
CURETTAGES
CURETTE
CURETTED
CURETTES
CURETTING
CURFEW
CURFEWS
CURFUFFLE
CURFUFFLED
CURFUFFLES
CURFUFFLING
CURIA
CURIAE
CURIALISM
CURIALISMS
CURIALIST
CURIALISTS
CURIAS
CURIE
CURIES
CURIET
CURIETS
CURING
CURIO
CURIOS
CURIOSA
CURIOSITIES
CURIOSITY
CURIOUS
CURIOUSER
CURIOUSLY
CURIUM
CURIUMS
CURL
CURLED
CURLER
CURLERS
CURLEW
CURLEWS
CURLICUE
CURLICUES
CURLIER
CURLIEST
CURLINESS
CURLINESSES
CURLING

CURLINGS
CURLPAPER
CURLPAPERS
CURLS
CURLY
CURN
CURNEY
CURNIER
CURNIEST
CURNS
CURNY
CURPEL
CURPELS
CURR
CURRACH
CURRACHS
CURRAGH
CURRAGHS
CURRAJONG
CURRAJONGS
CURRANT
CURRANTIER
CURRANTIEST
CURRANTS
CURRANTY
CURRAWONG
CURRAWONGS
CURRED
CURRENCIES
CURRENCY
CURRENT
CURRENTLY
CURRENTS
CURRICLE
CURRICLES
CURRICULA
CURRIE
CURRIED
CURRIER
CURRIERS
CURRIES
CURRING
CURRISH
CURRISHLY
CURRS
CURRY
CURRYCOMB
CURRYCOMBS
CURRYING
CURRYINGS
CURS
CURSAL
CURSE
CURSED
CURSEDER
CURSEDEST
CURSEDLY
CURSENARY
CURSER
CURSERS
CURSES
CURSI
CURSING
CURSINGS
CURSITOR
CURSITORS
CURSITORY
CURSIVE
CURSIVELY
CURSOR
CURSORARY
CURSORES
CURSORIAL
CURSORILY
CURSORS
CURSORY
CURST
CURSTNESS
CURSTNESSES
CURSUS
CURT
CURTAIL
CURTAILED
CURTAILING
CURTAILS
CURTAIN
CURTAINED
CURTAINING
CURTAINS
CURTAL
CURTALAX
CURTALAXE
CURTALAXES
CURTALS
CURTANA
CURTANAS
CURTATE
CURTATION
CURTATIONS
CURTAXE
CURTAXES
CURTER
CURTESIES
CURTEST
CURTESY
CURTILAGE
CURTILAGES
CURTLY
CURTNESS
CURTNESSES
CURTSEY
CURTSEYED
CURTSEYING
CURTSEYS
CURTSIED
CURTSIES
CURTSY
CURTSYING
CURULE
CURVATE
CURVATED
CURVATION
CURVATIONS
CURVATIVE
CURVATURE
CURVATURES
CURVE
CURVED
CURVES
CURVESOME
CURVET
CURVETED
CURVETING
CURVETS
CURVETTED
CURVETTING
CURVIER
CURVIEST
CURVIFORM
CURVING
CURVITAL
CURVITIES
CURVITY
CURVY
CUSCUS
CUSCUSES
CUSEC
CUSECS
CUSH
CUSHAT
CUSHATS
CUSHAW
CUSHAWS
CUSHES
CUSHIER
CUSHIEST
CUSHION
CUSHIONED
CUSHIONET
CUSHIONETS
CUSHIONING
CUSHIONS
CUSHIONY
CUSHY
CUSK
CUSKS
CUSP
CUSPATE
CUSPED
CUSPID
CUSPIDAL
CUSPIDATE
CUSPIDOR
CUSPIDORE
CUSPIDORES
CUSPIDORS
CUSPIDS
CUSPS
CUSS
CUSSED
CUSSER
CUSSERS
CUSSES
CUSSING
CUSSWORD
CUSSWORDS
CUSTARD
CUSTARDS
CUSTOCK
CUSTOCKS
CUSTODE
CUSTODES
CUSTODIAL
CUSTODIAN
CUSTODIANS
CUSTODIER
CUSTODIERS
CUSTODIES
CUSTODY
CUSTOM
CUSTOMARIES
CUSTOMARY
CUSTOMED
CUSTOMER
CUSTOMERS
CUSTOMISE
CUSTOMISED
CUSTOMISES
CUSTOMISING
CUSTOMIZE
CUSTOMIZED
CUSTOMIZES
CUSTOMIZING
CUSTOMS
CUSTOS
CUSTREL
CUSTRELS
CUSTUMARIES
CUSTUMARY
CUT
CUTANEOUS
CUTAWAY
CUTAWAYS
CUTBACK
CUTBACKS
CUTCH
CUTCHA
CUTCHERIES
CUTCHERRIES
CUTCHERRY
CUTCHERY
CUTCHES
CUTE
CUTELY
CUTENESS
CUTENESSES
CUTER
CUTES
CUTESIER
CUTESIEST
CUTEST
CUTESY
CUTEY
CUTEYS
CUTGLASS
CUTICLE
CUTICLES
CUTICULAR
CUTIE
CUTIES
CUTIKIN
CUTIKINS
CUTIN
CUTINISE
CUTINISED
CUTINISES
CUTINISING
CUTINIZE
CUTINIZED
CUTINIZES
CUTINIZING
CUTINS
CUTIS
CUTISES
CUTLASS
CUTLASSES
CUTLER
CUTLERIES
CUTLERS
CUTLERY
CUTLET
CUTLETS
CUTLINE
CUTLINES
CUTPURSE
CUTPURSES
CUTS
CUTTER
CUTTERS
CUTTIER
CUTTIES
CUTTIEST
CUTTING
CUTTINGS
CUTTLE
CUTTLES
CUTTO
CUTTOE
CUTTOES
CUTTY
CUTWORK
CUTWORKS
CUTWORM
CUTWORMS
CUVEE
CUVEES
CUVETTE
CUVETTES
CUZ
CUZZES
CWM
CWMS
CYAN
CYANAMIDE
CYANAMIDES
CYANATE
CYANATES
CYANIC
CYANIDE
CYANIDED
CYANIDES
CYANIDING
CYANIDINGS
CYANIN
CYANINE
CYANINES
CYANINS
CYANISE
CYANISED
CYANISES

CYANISING
CYANITE
CYANITES
CYANIZE
CYANIZED
CYANIZES
CYANIZING
CYANOGEN
CYANOGENS
CYANOSED
CYANOSES
CYANOSIS
CYANOTIC
CYANOTYPE
CYANOTYPES
CYANS
CYANURET
CYANURETS
CYATHI
CYATHIA
CYATHIUM
CYATHUS
CYBERCAFE
CYBERCAFES
CYBERNATE
CYBERNATED
CYBERNATES
CYBERNATING
CYBERPET
CYBERPETS
CYBERPUNK
CYBERPUNKS
CYBERSEX
CYBERSEXES
CYBORG
CYBORGS
CYBRID
CYBRIDS
CYCAD
CYCADS
CYCLAMATE
CYCLAMATES
CYCLAMEN
CYCLAMENS
CYCLE
CYCLED
CYCLER
CYCLERS
CYCLES
CYCLEWAY
CYCLEWAYS
CYCLIC
CYCLICAL
CYCLICISM
CYCLICISMS
CYCLICITIES
CYCLICITY
CYCLING
CYCLINGS
CYCLIST
CYCLISTS
CYCLIZINE
CYCLIZINES
CYCLO
CYCLOID
CYCLOIDAL
CYCLOIDS
CYCLOLITH
CYCLOLITHS
CYCLONE
CYCLONES
CYCLONIC
CYCLONITE
CYCLONITES
CYCLOPEAN
CYCLOPES
CYCLOPIAN
CYCLOPIC
CYCLOPS
CYCLORAMA
CYCLORAMAS
CYCLOS
CYCLOSES
CYCLOSIS
CYCLOTRON
CYCLOTRONS
CYCLUS
CYCLUSES
CYDER
CYDERS
CYESES
CYESIS
CYGNET
CYGNETS
CYLICES
CYLINDER
CYLINDERS
CYLINDRIC
CYLIX
CYMA
CYMAGRAPH
CYMAGRAPHS
CYMAR
CYMARS
CYMAS
CYMATIA
CYMATICS
CYMATIUM
CYMBAL
CYMBALIST
CYMBALISTS
CYMBALO
CYMBALOES
CYMBALOS
CYMBALS
CYMBIDIA
CYMBIDIUM
CYMBIDIUMS
CYMBIFORM
CYME
CYMES
CYMOGRAPH
CYMOGRAPHS
CYMOID
CYMOPHANE
CYMOPHANES
CYMOSE
CYMOUS
CYNANCHE
CYNANCHES
CYNEGETIC
CYNIC
CYNICAL
CYNICALLY
CYNICISM
CYNICISMS
CYNICS
CYNOMOLGI
CYNOSURE
CYNOSURES
CYPHER
CYPHERED
CYPHERING
CYPHERS
CYPRESS
CYPRESSES
CYPRIAN
CYPRIANS
CYPRID
CYPRIDES
CYPRIDS
CYPRINE
CYPRINID
CYPRINIDS
CYPRINOID
CYPRIS
CYPRUS
CYPRUSES
CYPSELA
CYPSELAE
CYST
CYSTEINE
CYSTEINES
CYSTIC
CYSTID
CYSTIDEAN
CYSTIDEANS
CYSTIDS
CYSTIFORM
CYSTINE
CYSTINES
CYSTITIS
CYSTITISES
CYSTOCARP
CYSTOCARPS
CYSTOCELE
CYSTOCELES
CYSTOID
CYSTOIDS
CYSTOLITH
CYSTOLITHS
CYSTOTOMIES
CYSTOTOMY
CYSTS
CYTASE
CYTASES
CYTE
CYTES
CYTISI
CYTISINE
CYTISINES
CYTISUS
CYTODE
CYTODES
CYTOID
CYTOKINE
CYTOKINES
CYTOKININ
CYTOKININS
CYTOLOGIES
CYTOLOGY
CYTOLYSES
CYTOLYSIS
CYTOMETER
CYTOMETERS
CYTOMETRIES
CYTOMETRY
CYTON
CYTONS
CYTOPENIA
CYTOPENIAS
CYTOPLASM
CYTOPLASMS
CYTOSINE
CYTOSINES
CYTOSOME
CYTOSOMES
CYTOTOXIC
CYTOTOXIN
CYTOTOXINS
CZAPKA
CZAPKAS
CZAR
CZARDAS
CZARDASES
CZARDOM
CZARDOMS
CZAREVICH
CZAREVICHES
CZAREVNA
CZAREVNAS
CZARINA
CZARINAS
CZARISM
CZARISMS
CZARIST
CZARISTS
CZARITSA
CZARITSAS
CZARS

D

DA
DAB
DABBED
DABBER
DABBERS
DABBING
DABBITIES
DABBITY
DABBLE
DABBLED
DABBLER
DABBLERS
DABBLES
DABBLING
DABBLINGS
DABCHICK
DABCHICKS
DABS
DABSTER
DABSTERS
DACE
DACES
DACHA
DACHAS
DACHSHUND
DACHSHUNDS
DACITE
DACITES
DACKER
DACKERED
DACKERING
DACKERS
DACOIT
DACOITAGE
DACOITAGES
DACOITIES
DACOITS
DACOITY
DACTYL
DACTYLAR
DACTYLIC
DACTYLIST
DACTYLISTS
DACTYLS
DAD
DADDED
DADDIES
DADDING
DADDLE
DADDLED
DADDLES
DADDLING
DADDOCK
DADDOCKS
DADDY
DADO
DADOED
DADOES
DADOING
DADOS
DADS
DAE
DAEDAL
DAEDALIAN
DAEDALIC
DAEING
DAEMON
DAEMONIC
DAEMONS
DAES
DAFF
DAFFED
DAFFIER
DAFFIES
DAFFIEST
DAFFING
DAFFINGS
DAFFODIL
DAFFODILS
DAFFS
DAFFY
DAFT
DAFTAR
DAFTARS
DAFTER
DAFTEST
DAFTIE
DAFTIES
DAFTLY
DAFTNESS
DAFTNESSES
DAG
DAGABA
DAGABAS
DAGGA
DAGGAS
DAGGED
DAGGER
DAGGERS
DAGGIER
DAGGIEST
DAGGING
DAGGINGS
DAGGLE
DAGGLED
DAGGLES
DAGGLING
DAGGY
DAGLOCK
DAGLOCKS
DAGO
DAGOBA
DAGOBAS
DAGOES
DAGOS
DAGS
DAGWOOD
DAGWOODS
DAH
DAHABEEAH
DAHABEEAHS
DAHABIEH
DAHABIEHS
DAHABIYAH
DAHABIYAHS
DAHABIYEH
DAHABIYEHS
DAHL
DAHLIA
DAHLIAS
DAHLS
DAHS
DAIDLE
DAIDLED
DAIDLES
DAIDLING
DAIKER
DAIKERED
DAIKERING
DAIKERS
DAIKON
DAIKONS
DAILIES
DAILY
DAIMEN
DAIMIO
DAIMIOS
DAIMON
DAIMONIC
DAIMONS
DAINE
DAINED
DAINES
DAINING
DAINT
DAINTIER
DAINTIES
DAINTIEST
DAINTILY
DAINTY
DAIQUIRI
DAIQUIRIS
DAIRIES
DAIRY
DAIRYING
DAIRYINGS
DAIRYMAID
DAIRYMAIDS
DAIRYMAN
DAIRYMEN
DAIS
DAISES
DAISIED
DAISIES
DAISY
DAK
DAKER
DAKERED
DAKERING
DAKERS
DAKOIT
DAKOITI
DAKOITIS
DAKOITS
DAKS
DAL
DALE
DALES
DALESMAN
DALESMEN
DALI
DALIS
DALLE
DALLES
DALLIANCE
DALLIANCES
DALLIED
DALLIER
DALLIERS
DALLIES
DALLOP
DALLOPS
DALLY
DALLYING
DALMAHOY
DALMAHOYS
DALMATIC
DALMATICS
DALS
DALT
DALTON
DALTONISM
DALTONISMS
DALTONS
DALTS
DAM
DAMAGE
DAMAGED
DAMAGES
DAMAGING
DAMAN
DAMANS
DAMAR
DAMARS
DAMASCENE
DAMASCENED
DAMASCENES
DAMASCENING
DAMASCENINGS
DAMASK
DAMASKED
DAMASKEEN
DAMASKEENED
DAMASKEENING
DAMASKEENS
DAMASKIN
DAMASKINED
DAMASKING
DAMASKINING
DAMASKINS
DAMASKS
DAMASQUIN
DAMASQUINED
DAMASQUINING
DAMASQUINS
DAMASSIN
DAMASSINS
DAMBOARD
DAMBOARDS
DAMBROD
DAMBRODS
DAME
DAMES
DAMFOOL
DAMMAR
DAMMARS
DAMME
DAMMED
DAMMER
DAMMERS
DAMMING
DAMMIT
DAMN
DAMNABLE
DAMNABLY
DAMNATION
DAMNATIONS
DAMNATORY
DAMNED
DAMNEDER

DAMNEDEST
DAMNIFIED
DAMNIFIES
DAMNIFY
DAMNIFYING
DAMNING
DAMNS
DAMOISEL
DAMOISELS
DAMOSEL
DAMOSELS
DAMOZEL
DAMOZELS
DAMP
DAMPED
DAMPEN
DAMPENED
DAMPENING
DAMPENS
DAMPER
DAMPERS
DAMPEST
DAMPIER
DAMPIEST
DAMPING
DAMPINGS
DAMPISH
DAMPLY
DAMPNESS
DAMPNESSES
DAMPS
DAMPY
DAMS
DAMSEL
DAMSELFLIES
DAMSELFLY
DAMSELS
DAMSON
DAMSONS
DAN
DANCE
DANCEABLE
DANCED
DANCER
DANCERS
DANCES
DANCETTE
DANCETTEE
DANCETTES
DANCETTY
DANCING
DANCINGS
DANDELION
DANDELIONS
DANDER
DANDERED
DANDERING
DANDERS
DANDIACAL
DANDIER
DANDIES
DANDIEST
DANDIFIED
DANDIFIES
DANDIFY
DANDIFYING
DANDILY
DANDIPRAT
DANDIPRATS
DANDLE
DANDLED
DANDLER
DANDLERS
DANDLES
DANDLING
DANDRIFF
DANDRIFFS
DANDRUFF
DANDRUFFS
DANDY
DANDYFUNK
DANDYFUNKS
DANDYISH
DANDYISM
DANDYISMS
DANDYPRAT
DANDYPRATS
DANEGELD
DANEGELDS
DANEGELT
DANEGELTS
DANELAGH
DANELAGHS
DANELAW
DANELAWS
DANG
DANGED
DANGER
DANGERED
DANGERING
DANGEROUS
DANGERS
DANGING
DANGLE
DANGLED
DANGLER
DANGLERS
DANGLES
DANGLIER
DANGLIEST
DANGLING
DANGLINGS
DANGLY
DANGS
DANIO
DANIOS
DANK
DANKER
DANKEST
DANKISH
DANKNESS
DANKNESSES
DANKS
DANNEBROG
DANNEBROGS
DANS
DANSEUR
DANSEURS
DANSEUSE
DANSEUSES
DANT
DANTED
DANTING
DANTON
DANTONED
DANTONING
DANTONS
DANTS
DAP
DAPHNE
DAPHNES
DAPHNID
DAPHNIDS
DAPPED
DAPPER
DAPPERER
DAPPEREST
DAPPERLY
DAPPERS
DAPPING
DAPPLE
DAPPLED
DAPPLES
DAPPLING
DAPS
DAPSONE
DAPSONES
DAQUIRI
DAQUIRIS
DARAF
DARAFS
DARBIES
DARCIES
DARCY
DARCYS
DARE
DARED
DAREFUL
DARES
DARG
DARGA
DARGAS
DARGLE
DARGLES
DARGS
DARI
DARIC
DARICS
DARING
DARINGLY
DARINGS
DARIOLE
DARIOLES
DARIS
DARK
DARKEN
DARKENED
DARKENING
DARKENS
DARKER
DARKEST
DARKEY
DARKEYS
DARKIE
DARKIES
DARKISH
DARKLE
DARKLED
DARKLES
DARKLING
DARKLINGS
DARKLY
DARKMANS
DARKNESS
DARKNESSES
DARKROOM
DARKROOMS
DARKS
DARKSOME
DARKY
DARLING
DARLINGS
DARN
DARNED
DARNEDER
DARNEDEST
DARNEL
DARNELS
DARNER
DARNERS
DARNING
DARNINGS
DARNS
DARRAIGN
DARRAIGNE
DARRAIGNED
DARRAIGNES
DARRAIGNING
DARRAIGNS
DARRAIN
DARRAINE
DARRAINED
DARRAINES
DARRAINING
DARRAINS
DARRAYN
DARRAYNED
DARRAYNING
DARRAYNS
DARRE
DARRED
DARRES
DARRING
DARSHAN
DARSHANS
DART
DARTBOARD
DARTBOARDS
DARTED
DARTER
DARTERS
DARTING
DARTINGLY
DARTLE
DARTLED
DARTLES
DARTLING
DARTRE
DARTRES
DARTROUS
DARTS
DARZI
DARZIS
DAS
DASH
DASHBOARD
DASHBOARDS
DASHED
DASHEEN
DASHEENS
DASHEKI
DASHEKIS
DASHER
DASHERS
DASHES
DASHIKI
DASHIKIS
DASHING
DASHINGLY
DASSIE
DASSIES
DASTARD
DASTARDIES
DASTARDLY
DASTARDS
DASTARDY
DASYPOD
DASYPODS
DASYURE
DASYURES
DATA
DATABANK
DATABANKS
DATABASE
DATABASES
DATABLE
DATABUS
DATABUSES
DATABUSSES
DATACOMMS
DATAGLOVE
DATAGLOVES
DATAL
DATALLER
DATALLERS
DATALS
DATARIA
DATARIAS
DATARIES
DATARY
DATE
DATEABLE
DATED
DATELESS
DATER
DATERS
DATES
DATING
DATINGS
DATIVAL

DATIVE
DATIVES
DATOLITE
DATOLITES
DATUM
DATURA
DATURAS
DATURINE
DATURINES
DAUB
DAUBE
DAUBED
DAUBER
DAUBERIES
DAUBERS
DAUBERY
DAUBES
DAUBIER
DAUBIEST
DAUBING
DAUBINGS
DAUBS
DAUBY
DAUD
DAUDED
DAUDING
DAUDS
DAUGHTER
DAUGHTERS
DAULT
DAULTS
DAUNDER
DAUNDERED
DAUNDERING
DAUNDERS
DAUNER
DAUNERED
DAUNERING
DAUNERS
DAUNT
DAUNTED
DAUNTER
DAUNTERS
DAUNTING
DAUNTLESS
DAUNTON
DAUNTONED
DAUNTONING
DAUNTONS
DAUNTS
DAUPHIN
DAUPHINE
DAUPHINES
DAUPHINS
DAUR
DAURED
DAURING
DAURS
DAUT
DAUTED
DAUTIE
DAUTIES
DAUTING
DAUTS
DAVEN
DAVENED
DAVENING
DAVENPORT
DAVENPORTS
DAVENS
DAVIDIA
DAVIDIAS
DAVIT
DAVITS
DAW
DAWBRIES
DAWBRY
DAWCOCK
DAWCOCKS
DAWD
DAWDED
DAWDING
DAWDLE
DAWDLED
DAWDLER
DAWDLERS
DAWDLES
DAWDLING
DAWDS
DAWED
DAWING
DAWISH
DAWK
DAWKS
DAWN
DAWNED
DAWNER
DAWNERED
DAWNERING
DAWNERS
DAWNING
DAWNINGS
DAWNS
DAWS
DAWT
DAWTED
DAWTIE
DAWTIES
DAWTING
DAWTS
DAY
DAYBREAK
DAYBREAKS
DAYDREAM
DAYDREAMED
DAYDREAMING
DAYDREAMS
DAYDREAMT
DAYGLO
DAYLIGHT
DAYLIGHTS
DAYLONG
DAYMARK
DAYMARKS
DAYNT
DAYS
DAYSACK
DAYSACKS
DAYSMAN
DAYSMEN
DAYSPRING
DAYSPRINGS
DAYSTAR
DAYSTARS
DAYTALE
DAYTALER
DAYTALERS
DAYTALES
DAYTIME
DAYTIMES
DAZE
DAZED
DAZEDLY
DAZER
DAZERS
DAZES
DAZING
DAZZLE
DAZZLED
DAZZLER
DAZZLERS
DAZZLES
DAZZLING
DAZZLINGS
DEACON
DEACONESS
DEACONESSES
DEACONRIES
DEACONRY
DEACONS
DEAD
DEADED
DEADEN
DEADENED
DEADENER
DEADENERS
DEADENING
DEADENINGS
DEADENS
DEADER
DEADERS
DEADEST
DEADHEAD
DEADHEADED
DEADHEADING
DEADHEADS
DEADHOUSE
DEADHOUSES
DEADING
DEADLIER
DEADLIEST
DEADLINE
DEADLINES
DEADLOCK
DEADLOCKED
DEADLOCKING
DEADLOCKS
DEADLY
DEADNESS
DEADNESSES
DEADPAN
DEADPANS
DEADS
DEADSTOCK
DEADSTOCKS
DEAF
DEAFEN
DEAFENED
DEAFENING
DEAFENINGS
DEAFENS
DEAFER
DEAFEST
DEAFLY
DEAFNESS
DEAFNESSES
DEAL
DEALBATE
DEALER
DEALERS
DEALFISH
DEALFISHES
DEALING
DEALINGS
DEALS
DEALT
DEAN
DEANER
DEANERIES
DEANERS
DEANERY
DEANS
DEANSHIP
DEANSHIPS
DEAR
DEARE
DEARED
DEARER
DEARES
DEAREST
DEARIE
DEARIES
DEARING
DEARLING
DEARLINGS
DEARLY
DEARN
DEARNESS
DEARNESSES
DEARNFUL
DEARNLY
DEARNS
DEARS
DEARTH
DEARTHS
DEARY
DEASIL
DEASILS
DEASIUL
DEASIULS
DEASOIL
DEASOILS
DEATH
DEATHFUL
DEATHIER
DEATHIEST
DEATHLESS
DEATHLIER
DEATHLIEST
DEATHLIKE
DEATHLY
DEATHS
DEATHSMAN
DEATHSMEN
DEATHWARD
DEATHWARDS
DEATHY
DEAVE
DEAVED
DEAVES
DEAVING
DEAW
DEAWIE
DEAWS
DEAWY
DEB
DEBACLE
DEBACLES
DEBAG
DEBAGGED
DEBAGGING
DEBAGGINGS
DEBAGS
DEBAR
DEBARK
DEBARKED
DEBARKING
DEBARKS
DEBARMENT
DEBARMENTS
DEBARRASS
DEBARRASSED
DEBARRASSES
DEBARRASSING
DEBARRED
DEBARRING
DEBARS
DEBASE
DEBASED
DEBASER
DEBASERS
DEBASES
DEBASING
DEBATABLE
DEBATE
DEBATED
DEBATEFUL
DEBATER
DEBATERS
DEBATES
DEBATING
DEBAUCH
DEBAUCHED
DEBAUCHEE
DEBAUCHEES
DEBAUCHER
DEBAUCHERS
DEBAUCHES
DEBAUCHING
DEBBIER

EBBIES
EBBIEST
EBBY
EBEL
EBELLED
EBELLING
EBELS
EBENTURE
EBENTURES
EBILE
EBILITIES
EBILITY
EBIT
EBITED
EBITING
EBITOR
EBITORS
EBITS
EBONAIR
EBOSH
EBOSHED
EBOSHES
EBOSHING
EBOSS
EBOSSED
EBOSSES
EBOSSING
EBOUCH
EBOUCHE
EBOUCHED
EBOUCHES
EBOUCHING
EBRIDE
EBRIDED
EBRIDES
EBRIDING
EBRIEF
EBRIEFED
EBRIEFING
EBRIEFINGS
EBRIEFS
EBRIS
EBRUISED
EBS
EBT
EBTED
EBTEE
EBTEES
EBTOR
EBTORS
EBTS
EBUG
EBUGGED
EBUGGING
EBUGS
EBUNK
EBUNKED
EBUNKING
EBUNKS
EBUS
EBUSSED
EBUSSES
EBUSSING
EBUT
DEBUTANT
DEBUTANTE
DEBUTANTES
DEBUTANTS
DEBUTED
DEBUTING
DEBUTS
DECACHORD
DECACHORDS
DECAD
DECADAL
DECADE
DECADENCE
DECADENCES
DECADENCIES
DECADENCY
DECADENT
DECADENTS
DECADES
DECADS
DECAFF
DECAFFS
DECAGON
DECAGONAL
DECAGONS
DECAGRAM
DECAGRAMS
DECAHEDRA
DECAL
DECALCIFIED
DECALCIFIES
DECALCIFY
DECALCIFYING
DECALITRE
DECALITRES
DECALOGUE
DECALOGUES
DECALS
DECAMETRE
DECAMETRES
DECAMP
DECAMPED
DECAMPING
DECAMPS
DECANAL
DECANE
DECANES
DECANI
DECANT
DECANTATE
DECANTATED
DECANTATES
DECANTATING
DECANTED
DECANTER
DECANTERS
DECANTING
DECANTS
DECAPOD
DECAPODAL
DECAPODAN
DECAPODS
DECARB
DECARBED
DECARBING
DECARBS
DECARE
DECARES
DECASTERE
DECASTERES
DECASTICH
DECASTICHS
DECASTYLE
DECASTYLES
DECATHLON
DECATHLONS
DECAUDATE
DECAUDATED
DECAUDATES
DECAUDATING
DECAY
DECAYED
DECAYING
DECAYS
DECCIE
DECCIES
DECEASE
DECEASED
DECEASES
DECEASING
DECEDENT
DECEDENTS
DECEIT
DECEITFUL
DECEITS
DECEIVE
DECEIVED
DECEIVER
DECEIVERS
DECEIVES
DECEIVING
DECEMVIR
DECEMVIRI
DECEMVIRS
DECENCIES
DECENCY
DECENNARIES
DECENNARY
DECENNIA
DECENNIAL
DECENNIUM
DECENNIUMS
DECENT
DECENTER
DECENTEST
DECENTLY
DECEPTION
DECEPTIONS
DECEPTIVE
DECEPTORY
DECERN
DECERNED
DECERNING
DECERNS
DECESSION
DECESSIONS
DECHEANCE
DECHEANCES
DECIARE
DECIARES
DECIBEL
DECIBELS
DECIDABLE
DECIDE
DECIDED
DECIDEDLY
DECIDER
DECIDERS
DECIDES
DECIDING
DECIDUA
DECIDUAE
DECIDUAL
DECIDUAS
DECIDUATE
DECIDUOUS
DECIGRAM
DECIGRAMS
DECILITER
DECILITERS
DECILITRE
DECILITRES
DECILLION
DECILLIONS
DECIMAL
DECIMALLY
DECIMALS
DECIMATE
DECIMATED
DECIMATES
DECIMATING
DECIMATOR
DECIMATORS
DECIME
DECIMES
DECIMETER
DECIMETERS
DECIMETRE
DECIMETRES
DECIPHER
DECIPHERED
DECIPHERING
DECIPHERS
DECISION
DECISIONS
DECISIVE
DECISORY
DECISTERE
DECISTERES
DECK
DECKCHAIR
DECKCHAIRS
DECKED
DECKER
DECKERS
DECKHOUSE
DECKHOUSES
DECKING
DECKINGS
DECKLE
DECKLED
DECKLES
DECKO
DECKOED
DECKOING
DECKOS
DECKS
DECLAIM
DECLAIMED
DECLAIMER
DECLAIMERS
DECLAIMING
DECLAIMINGS
DECLAIMS
DECLARANT
DECLARANTS
DECLARE
DECLARED
DECLARER
DECLARERS
DECLARES
DECLARING
DECLASS
DECLASSE
DECLASSED
DECLASSEE
DECLASSES
DECLASSING
DECLINAL
DECLINANT
DECLINATE
DECLINE
DECLINED
DECLINES
DECLINING
DECLIVITIES
DECLIVITY
DECLIVOUS
DECLUTCH
DECLUTCHED
DECLUTCHES
DECLUTCHING
DECO
DECOCT
DECOCTED
DECOCTING
DECOCTION
DECOCTIONS
DECOCTIVE
DECOCTS
DECOCTURE
DECOCTURES
DECODE
DECODED
DECODER
DECODERS
DECODES
DECODING
DECOHERER
DECOHERERS
DECOKE
DECOKED
DECOKES
DECOKING
DECOLLATE
DECOLLATED

DECOLLATES
DECOLLATING
DECOLLETE
DECOLOR
DECOLORED
DECOLORING
DECOLORS
DECOLOUR
DECOLOURED
DECOLOURING
DECOLOURS
DECOMPLEX
DECOMPOSE
DECOMPOSED
DECOMPOSES
DECOMPOSING
DECONGEST
DECONGESTED
DECONGESTING
DECONGESTS
DECONTROL
DECONTROLLED
DECONTROLLING
DECONTROLS
DECOR
DECORATE
DECORATED
DECORATES
DECORATING
DECORATOR
DECORATORS
DECOROUS
DECORS
DECORUM
DECORUMS
DECOUPAGE
DECOUPAGES
DECOUPLE
DECOUPLED
DECOUPLES
DECOUPLING
DECOUPLINGS
DECOY
DECOYED
DECOYING
DECOYS
DECREASE
DECREASED
DECREASES
DECREASING
DECREE
DECREED
DECREEING
DECREES
DECREET
DECREETS
DECREMENT
DECREMENTED
DECREMENTING
DECREMENTS
DECREPIT
DECRETAL
DECRETALS
DECRETIST
DECRETISTS
DECRETIVE
DECRETORY
DECREW
DECREWED
DECREWING
DECREWS
DECRIAL
DECRIALS
DECRIED
DECRIER
DECRIERS
DECRIES
DECROWN
DECROWNED
DECROWNING
DECROWNS
DECRY
DECRYING
DECRYPT
DECRYPTED
DECRYPTING
DECRYPTS
DECTET
DECTETS
DECUBITI
DECUBITUS
DECUMAN
DECUMANS
DECUMBENT
DECUPLE
DECUPLED
DECUPLES
DECUPLING
DECURIA
DECURIAS
DECURIES
DECURION
DECURIONS
DECURRENT
DECURSION
DECURSIONS
DECURSIVE
DECURVE
DECURVED
DECURVES
DECURVING
DECURY
DECUSSATE
DECUSSATED
DECUSSATES
DECUSSATING
DEDAL
DEDALIAN
DEDANS
DEDICANT
DEDICANTS
DEDICATE
DEDICATED
DEDICATEE
DEDICATEES
DEDICATES
DEDICATING
DEDICATOR
DEDICATORS
DEDIMUS
DEDIMUSES
DEDUCE
DEDUCED
DEDUCES
DEDUCIBLE
DEDUCING
DEDUCT
DEDUCTED
DEDUCTING
DEDUCTION
DEDUCTIONS
DEDUCTIVE
DEDUCTS
DEE
DEED
DEEDED
DEEDER
DEEDEST
DEEDFUL
DEEDIER
DEEDIEST
DEEDILY
DEEDING
DEEDLESS
DEEDS
DEEDY
DEEING
DEEJAY
DEEJAYED
DEEJAYING
DEEJAYS
DEEK
DEEM
DEEMED
DEEMING
DEEMS
DEEMSTER
DEEMSTERS
DEEN
DEENS
DEEP
DEEPEN
DEEPENED
DEEPENING
DEEPENS
DEEPER
DEEPEST
DEEPFELT
DEEPIE
DEEPIES
DEEPLY
DEEPMOST
DEEPNESS
DEEPNESSES
DEEPS
DEER
DEERBERRIES
DEERBERRY
DEERE
DEERHORN
DEERHORNS
DEERLET
DEERLETS
DEERSKIN
DEERSKINS
DEES
DEEV
DEEVE
DEEVED
DEEVES
DEEVING
DEEVS
DEF
DEFACE
DEFACED
DEFACER
DEFACERS
DEFACES
DEFACING
DEFAECATE
DEFAECATED
DEFAECATES
DEFAECATING
DEFALCATE
DEFALCATED
DEFALCATES
DEFALCATING
DEFAME
DEFAMED
DEFAMES
DEFAMING
DEFAMINGS
DEFAST
DEFASTE
DEFAT
DEFATS
DEFATTED
DEFATTING
DEFAULT
DEFAULTED
DEFAULTER
DEFAULTERS
DEFAULTING
DEFAULTS
DEFEAT
DEFEATED
DEFEATING
DEFEATISM
DEFEATISMS
DEFEATIST
DEFEATISTS
DEFEATS
DEFEATURE
DEFEATURED
DEFEATURES
DEFEATURING
DEFECATE
DEFECATED
DEFECATES
DEFECATING
DEFECATOR
DEFECATORS
DEFECT
DEFECTED
DEFECTING
DEFECTION
DEFECTIONS
DEFECTIVE
DEFECTIVES
DEFECTOR
DEFECTORS
DEFECTS
DEFENCE
DEFENCED
DEFENCES
DEFEND
DEFENDANT
DEFENDANTS
DEFENDED
DEFENDER
DEFENDERS
DEFENDING
DEFENDS
DEFENSE
DEFENSES
DEFENSIVE
DEFENSIVES
DEFER
DEFERABLE
DEFERENCE
DEFERENCES
DEFERENT
DEFERENTS
DEFERMENT
DEFERMENTS
DEFERRAL
DEFERRALS
DEFERRED
DEFERRER
DEFERRERS
DEFERRING
DEFERS
DEFFER
DEFFEST
DEFFLY
DEFIANCE
DEFIANCES
DEFIANT
DEFIANTLY
DEFICIENT
DEFICIENTS
DEFICIT
DEFICITS
DEFIED
DEFIER
DEFIERS
DEFIES
DEFILADE
DEFILADED
DEFILADES
DEFILADING
DEFILE
DEFILED
DEFILER
DEFILERS
DEFILES
DEFILING
DEFINABLE
DEFINABLY
DEFINE

DEFINED
DEFINER
DEFINERS
DEFINES
DEFINIENS
DEFINIENTIA
DEFINING
DEFINITE
DEFLATE
DEFLATED
DEFLATER
DEFLATERS
DEFLATES
DEFLATING
DEFLATION
DEFLATIONS
DEFLATOR
DEFLATORS
DEFLECT
DEFLECTED
DEFLECTING
DEFLECTOR
DEFLECTORS
DEFLECTS
DEFLEX
DEFLEXED
DEFLEXES
DEFLEXING
DEFLEXION
DEFLEXIONS
DEFLEXURE
DEFLEXURES
DEFLORATE
DEFLORATED
DEFLORATES
DEFLORATING
DEFLOWER
DEFLOWERED
DEFLOWERING
DEFLOWERS
DEFLUENT
DEFLUXION
DEFLUXIONS
DEFOLIANT
DEFOLIANTS
DEFOLIATE
DEFOLIATED
DEFOLIATES
DEFOLIATING
DEFORCE
DEFORCED
DEFORCES
DEFORCING
DEFOREST
DEFORESTED
DEFORESTING
DEFORESTS
DEFORM
DEFORMED
DEFORMER
DEFORMERS
DEFORMING
DEFORMITIES
DEFORMITY
DEFORMS
DEFOUL
DEFOULED
DEFOULING
DEFOULS
DEFRAG
DEFRAGGED
DEFRAGGING
DEFRAGS
DEFRAUD
DEFRAUDED
DEFRAUDER
DEFRAUDERS
DEFRAUDING
DEFRAUDS
DEFRAY
DEFRAYAL
DEFRAYALS
DEFRAYED
DEFRAYER
DEFRAYERS
DEFRAYING
DEFRAYS
DEFREEZE
DEFREEZES
DEFREEZING
DEFROCK
DEFROCKED
DEFROCKING
DEFROCKS
DEFROST
DEFROSTED
DEFROSTER
DEFROSTERS
DEFROSTING
DEFROSTS
DEFROZE
DEFROZEN
DEFT
DEFTER
DEFTEST
DEFTLY
DEFTNESS
DEFTNESSES
DEFUNCT
DEFUNCTS
DEFUSE
DEFUSED
DEFUSES
DEFUSING
DEFUZE
DEFUZED
DEFUZES
DEFUZING
DEFY
DEFYING
DEGAGE
DEGARNISH
DEGARNISHED
DEGARNISHES
DEGARNISHING
DEGAS
DEGASSED
DEGASSES
DEGASSING
DEGAUSS
DEGAUSSED
DEGAUSSES
DEGAUSSING
DEGENDER
DEGENDERED
DEGENDERING
DEGENDERS
DEGOUT
DEGOUTS
DEGRADE
DEGRADED
DEGRADES
DEGRADING
DEGRAS
DEGREASE
DEGREASED
DEGREASES
DEGREASING
DEGREE
DEGREES
DEGUM
DEGUMMED
DEGUMMING
DEGUMS
DEGUST
DEGUSTATE
DEGUSTATED
DEGUSTATES
DEGUSTATING
DEGUSTED
DEGUSTING
DEGUSTS
DEHISCE
DEHISCED
DEHISCENT
DEHISCES
DEHISCING
DEHORN
DEHORNED
DEHORNER
DEHORNERS
DEHORNING
DEHORNS
DEHORT
DEHORTED
DEHORTER
DEHORTERS
DEHORTING
DEHORTS
DEHYDRATE
DEHYDRATED
DEHYDRATES
DEHYDRATING
DEI
DEICIDAL
DEICIDE
DEICIDES
DEICTIC
DEICTICS
DEID
DEIDER
DEIDEST
DEIDS
DEIFIC
DEIFICAL
DEIFIED
DEIFIER
DEIFIERS
DEIFIES
DEIFORM
DEIFY
DEIFYING
DEIGN
DEIGNED
DEIGNING
DEIGNS
DEIL
DEILS
DEINOSAUR
DEINOSAURS
DEIPAROUS
DEISEAL
DEISEALS
DEISHEAL
DEISHEALS
DEISM
DEISMS
DEIST
DEISTIC
DEISTICAL
DEISTS
DEITIES
DEITY
DEIXES
DEIXIS
DEJECT
DEJECTA
DEJECTED
DEJECTING
DEJECTION
DEJECTIONS
DEJECTORY
DEJECTS
DEJEUNE
DEJEUNER
DEJEUNERS
DEJEUNES
DEKALOGIES
DEKALOGY
DEKKO
DEKKOED
DEKKOING
DEKKOS
DEL
DELAINE
DELAINES
DELAPSE
DELAPSED
DELAPSES
DELAPSING
DELAPSION
DELAPSIONS
DELATE
DELATED
DELATES
DELATING
DELATION
DELATIONS
DELATOR
DELATORS
DELAY
DELAYED
DELAYER
DELAYERS
DELAYING
DELAYS
DELE
DELEBLE
DELED
DELEGABLE
DELEGACIES
DELEGACY
DELEGATE
DELEGATED
DELEGATES
DELEGATING
DELEING
DELENDA
DELES
DELETE
DELETED
DELETES
DELETING
DELETION
DELETIONS
DELETIVE
DELETORY
DELF
DELFS
DELFT
DELFTS
DELI
DELIBATE
DELIBATED
DELIBATES
DELIBATING
DELIBLE
DELICACIES
DELICACY
DELICATE
DELICATES
DELICE
DELICES
DELICIOUS
DELICT
DELICTS
DELIGHT
DELIGHTED
DELIGHTING
DELIGHTS
DELIMIT
DELIMITED
DELIMITER
DELIMITERS
DELIMITING
DELIMITS
DELINEATE
DELINEATED
DELINEATES
DELINEATING

DELIQUIUM
DELIQUIUMS
DELIRIA
DELIRIANT
DELIRIOUS
DELIRIUM
DELIRIUMS
DELIS
DELIVER
DELIVERED
DELIVERER
DELIVERERS
DELIVERIES
DELIVERING
DELIVERLY
DELIVERS
DELIVERY
DELL
DELLS
DELOPE
DELOPED
DELOPES
DELOPING
DELOUSE
DELOUSED
DELOUSES
DELOUSING
DELPH
DELPHIC
DELPHIN
DELPHINIA
DELPHS
DELS
DELT
DELTA
DELTAIC
DELTAS
DELTOID
DELTOIDS
DELTS
DELUBRUM
DELUBRUMS
DELUDABLE
DELUDE
DELUDED
DELUDER
DELUDERS
DELUDES
DELUDING
DELUGE
DELUGED
DELUGES
DELUGING
DELUNDUNG
DELUNDUNGS
DELUSION
DELUSIONS
DELUSIVE
DELUSORY
DELVE
DELVED
DELVER
DELVERS
DELVES
DELVING
DEMAGOGIC
DEMAGOGIES
DEMAGOGUE
DEMAGOGUES
DEMAGOGY
DEMAIN
DEMAINE
DEMAINES
DEMAINS
DEMAN
DEMAND
DEMANDANT
DEMANDANTS
DEMANDED
DEMANDER
DEMANDERS
DEMANDING
DEMANDS
DEMANNED
DEMANNING
DEMANNINGS
DEMANS
DEMARCATE
DEMARCATED
DEMARCATES
DEMARCATING
DEMARCHE
DEMARCHES
DEMARK
DEMARKED
DEMARKING
DEMARKS
DEMAYNE
DEMAYNES
DEME
DEMEAN
DEMEANE
DEMEANED
DEMEANES
DEMEANING
DEMEANOR
DEMEANORS
DEMEANOUR
DEMEANOURS
DEMEANS
DEMENT
DEMENTATE
DEMENTATED
DEMENTATES
DEMENTATING
DEMENTED
DEMENTI
DEMENTIA
DEMENTIAS
DEMENTING
DEMENTIS
DEMENTS
DEMERARA
DEMERARAS
DEMERGE
DEMERGED
DEMERGER
DEMERGERS
DEMERGES
DEMERGING
DEMERIT
DEMERITS
DEMERSAL
DEMERSE
DEMERSED
DEMERSES
DEMERSING
DEMERSION
DEMERSIONS
DEMES
DEMESNE
DEMESNES
DEMIC
DEMIES
DEMIGOD
DEMIGODS
DEMIJOHN
DEMIJOHNS
DEMIPIQUE
DEMIPIQUES
DEMIREP
DEMIREPS
DEMISABLE
DEMISE
DEMISED
DEMISES
DEMISING
DEMISS
DEMISSION
DEMISSIONS
DEMISSIVE
DEMISSLY
DEMIST
DEMISTED
DEMISTER
DEMISTERS
DEMISTING
DEMISTS
DEMIT
DEMITASSE
DEMITASSES
DEMITS
DEMITTED
DEMITTING
DEMIURGE
DEMIURGES
DEMIURGIC
DEMIURGUS
DEMIURGUSES
DEMO
DEMOB
DEMOBBED
DEMOBBING
DEMOBS
DEMOCRACIES
DEMOCRACY
DEMOCRAT
DEMOCRATIES
DEMOCRATS
DEMOCRATY
DEMODE
DEMODED
DEMOLISH
DEMOLISHED
DEMOLISHES
DEMOLISHING
DEMOLOGIES
DEMOLOGY
DEMON
DEMONESS
DEMONESSES
DEMONIAC
DEMONIACS
DEMONIAN
DEMONIC
DEMONISE
DEMONISED
DEMONISES
DEMONISING
DEMONISM
DEMONISMS
DEMONIST
DEMONISTS
DEMONIZE
DEMONIZED
DEMONIZES
DEMONIZING
DEMONRIES
DEMONRY
DEMONS
DEMOS
DEMOSES
DEMOTE
DEMOTED
DEMOTES
DEMOTIC
DEMOTING
DEMOTION
DEMOTIONS
DEMOTIST
DEMOTISTS
DEMOUNT
DEMOUNTED
DEMOUNTING
DEMOUNTS
DEMPSTER
DEMPSTERS
DEMPT
DEMULCENT
DEMULCENTS
DEMULSIFIED
DEMULSIFIES
DEMULSIFY
DEMULSIFYING
DEMUR
DEMURE
DEMURED
DEMURELY
DEMURER
DEMURES
DEMUREST
DEMURING
DEMURRAGE
DEMURRAGES
DEMURRAL
DEMURRALS
DEMURRED
DEMURRER
DEMURRERS
DEMURRING
DEMURS
DEMY
DEMYSHIP
DEMYSHIPS
DEMYSTIFIED
DEMYSTIFIES
DEMYSTIFY
DEMYSTIFYING
DEN
DENARIES
DENARII
DENARIUS
DENARY
DENATURE
DENATURED
DENATURES
DENATURING
DENAY
DENAYED
DENAYING
DENAYS
DENAZIFIED
DENAZIFIES
DENAZIFY
DENAZIFYING
DENDRITE
DENDRITES
DENDRITIC
DENDROID
DENDRON
DENDRONS
DENE
DENES
DENET
DENETS
DENETTED
DENETTING
DENGUE
DENGUES
DENIABLE
DENIABLY
DENIAL
DENIALS
DENIED
DENIER
DENIERS
DENIES
DENIGRATE
DENIGRATED
DENIGRATES
DENIGRATING
DENIM
DENIMS
DENITRATE
DENITRATED
DENITRATES
DENITRATING
DENITRIFIED
DENITRIFIES
DENITRIFY

ENITRIFYING
ENIZEN
ENIZENED
ENIZENING
ENIZENS
ENNED
ENNET
ENNETS
ENNING
ENOTABLE
ENOTATE
ENOTATED
ENOTATES
ENOTATING
ENOTE
ENOTED
ENOTES
ENOTING
ENOUNCE
ENOUNCED
ENOUNCER
ENOUNCERS
ENOUNCES
ENOUNCING
ENS
ENSE
ENSELY
ENSENESS
ENSENESSES
ENSER
ENSEST
ENSIFIED
ENSIFIER
ENSIFIERS
ENSIFIES
ENSIFY
ENSIFYING
ENSITIES
ENSITY
ENT
ENTAL
ENTALIA
ENTALIUM
ENTALIUMS
ENTALS
ENTARIA
ENTARIAS
ENTARIES
ENTARY
ENTATE
ENTATED
ENTATION
ENTATIONS
ENTED
ENTEL
ENTELLE
ENTELLES
ENTELS
ENTEX
ENTEXES
ENTICLE
ENTICLES
ENTIFORM
ENTIL

DENTILS
DENTIN
DENTINE
DENTINES
DENTING
DENTINS
DENTIST
DENTISTRIES
DENTISTRY
DENTISTS
DENTITION
DENTITIONS
DENTOID
DENTS
DENTURE
DENTURES
DENUDATE
DENUDATED
DENUDATES
DENUDATING
DENUDE
DENUDED
DENUDES
DENUDING
DENY
DENYING
DENYINGLY
DEODAND
DEODANDS
DEODAR
DEODARS
DEODATE
DEODATES
DEODORANT
DEODORANTS
DEODORISE
DEODORISED
DEODORISES
DEODORISING
DEODORIZE
DEODORIZED
DEODORIZES
DEODORIZING
DEONTIC
DEONTICS
DEOXIDATE
DEOXIDATED
DEOXIDATES
DEOXIDATING
DEOXIDISE
DEOXIDISED
DEOXIDISES
DEOXIDISING
DEOXIDIZE
DEOXIDIZED
DEOXIDIZES
DEOXIDIZING
DEPAINT
DEPAINTED
DEPAINTING
DEPAINTS
DEPART
DEPARTED
DEPARTER

DEPARTERS
DEPARTING
DEPARTINGS
DEPARTS
DEPARTURE
DEPARTURES
DEPASTURE
DEPASTURED
DEPASTURES
DEPASTURING
DEPECHE
DEPECHES
DEPEINCT
DEPEINCTED
DEPEINCTING
DEPEINCTS
DEPEND
DEPENDANT
DEPENDANTS
DEPENDED
DEPENDENT
DEPENDENTS
DEPENDING
DEPENDS
DEPICT
DEPICTED
DEPICTER
DEPICTERS
DEPICTING
DEPICTION
DEPICTIONS
DEPICTIVE
DEPICTOR
DEPICTORS
DEPICTS
DEPICTURE
DEPICTURED
DEPICTURES
DEPICTURING
DEPILATE
DEPILATED
DEPILATES
DEPILATING
DEPILATOR
DEPILATORS
DEPLANE
DEPLANED
DEPLANES
DEPLANING
DEPLETE
DEPLETED
DEPLETES
DEPLETING
DEPLETION
DEPLETIONS
DEPLETIVE
DEPLETORY
DEPLORE
DEPLORED
DEPLORES
DEPLORING
DEPLOY
DEPLOYED
DEPLOYING

DEPLOYS
DEPLUME
DEPLUMED
DEPLUMES
DEPLUMING
DEPONE
DEPONED
DEPONENT
DEPONENTS
DEPONES
DEPONING
DEPORT
DEPORTED
DEPORTEE
DEPORTEES
DEPORTING
DEPORTS
DEPOSABLE
DEPOSAL
DEPOSALS
DEPOSE
DEPOSED
DEPOSER
DEPOSERS
DEPOSES
DEPOSING
DEPOSIT
DEPOSITED
DEPOSITING
DEPOSITOR
DEPOSITORS
DEPOSITS
DEPOT
DEPOTS
DEPRAVE
DEPRAVED
DEPRAVES
DEPRAVING
DEPRAVITIES
DEPRAVITY
DEPRECATE
DEPRECATED
DEPRECATES
DEPRECATING
DEPREDATE
DEPREDATED
DEPREDATES
DEPREDATING
DEPREHEND
DEPREHENDED
DEPREHENDING
DEPREHENDS
DEPRESS
DEPRESSED
DEPRESSES
DEPRESSING
DEPRESSOR
DEPRESSORS
DEPRIVAL
DEPRIVALS
DEPRIVE
DEPRIVED
DEPRIVES
DEPRIVING

DEPROGRAM
DEPROGRAMMED
DEPROGRAMMING
DEPROGRAMS
DEPSIDE
DEPSIDES
DEPTH
DEPTHLESS
DEPTHS
DEPURANT
DEPURANTS
DEPURATE
DEPURATED
DEPURATES
DEPURATING
DEPURATOR
DEPURATORS
DEPUTE
DEPUTED
DEPUTES
DEPUTIES
DEPUTING
DEPUTISE
DEPUTISED
DEPUTISES
DEPUTISING
DEPUTIZE
DEPUTIZED
DEPUTIZES
DEPUTIZING
DEPUTY
DERACINE
DERAIGN
DERAIGNED
DERAIGNING
DERAIGNS
DERAIL
DERAILED
DERAILER
DERAILERS
DERAILING
DERAILS
DERANGE
DERANGED
DERANGES
DERANGING
DERATE
DERATED
DERATES
DERATING
DERATINGS
DERATION
DERATIONED
DERATIONING
DERATIONS
DERAY
DERAYED
DERAYING
DERAYS
DERBIES
DERBY
DERE
DERED
DERELICT

DERELICTS
DERES
DERHAM
DERHAMS
DERIDE
DERIDED
DERIDER
DERIDERS
DERIDES
DERIDING
DERIG
DERIGGED
DERIGGING
DERIGS
DERING
DERISIBLE
DERISION
DERISIONS
DERISIVE
DERISORY
DERIVABLE
DERIVABLY
DERIVATE
DERIVATES
DERIVE
DERIVED
DERIVES
DERIVING
DERM
DERMA
DERMAL
DERMAS
DERMATIC
DERMATOID
DERMATOME
DERMATOMES
DERMIC
DERMIS
DERMISES
DERMOID
DERMOIDS
DERMS
DERN
DERNFUL
DERNIER
DERNLY
DERNS
DEROGATE
DEROGATED
DEROGATES
DEROGATING
DERRICK
DERRICKED
DERRICKING
DERRICKS
DERRIERE
DERRIERES
DERRIES
DERRINGER
DERRINGERS
DERRIS
DERRISES
DERRY
DERTH
DERTHS
DERV
DERVISH
DERVISHES
DERVS
DESALT
DESALTED
DESALTING
DESALTINGS
DESALTS
DESCALE
DESCALED
DESCALES
DESCALING
DESCANT
DESCANTED
DESCANTING
DESCANTS
DESCEND
DESCENDED
DESCENDER
DESCENDERS
DESCENDING
DESCENDINGS
DESCENDS
DESCENT
DESCENTS
DESCHOOL
DESCHOOLED
DESCHOOLING
DESCHOOLINGS
DESCHOOLS
DESCRIBE
DESCRIBED
DESCRIBER
DESCRIBERS
DESCRIBES
DESCRIBING
DESCRIED
DESCRIES
DESCRIVE
DESCRIVED
DESCRIVES
DESCRIVING
DESCRY
DESCRYING
DESECRATE
DESECRATED
DESECRATES
DESECRATING
DESELECT
DESELECTED
DESELECTING
DESELECTS
DESERT
DESERTED
DESERTER
DESERTERS
DESERTING
DESERTION
DESERTIONS
DESERTS
DESERVE
DESERVED
DESERVER
DESERVERS
DESERVES
DESERVING
DESEX
DESEXED
DESEXES
DESEXING
DESICCANT
DESICCANTS
DESICCATE
DESICCATED
DESICCATES
DESICCATING
DESIGN
DESIGNATE
DESIGNATED
DESIGNATES
DESIGNATING
DESIGNED
DESIGNER
DESIGNERS
DESIGNFUL
DESIGNING
DESIGNINGS
DESIGNS
DESILVER
DESILVERED
DESILVERING
DESILVERS
DESINE
DESINED
DESINENCE
DESINENCES
DESINENT
DESINES
DESINING
DESIPIENT
DESIRABLE
DESIRABLES
DESIRABLY
DESIRE
DESIRED
DESIRER
DESIRERS
DESIRES
DESIRING
DESIROUS
DESIST
DESISTED
DESISTING
DESISTS
DESK
DESKBOUND
DESKILL
DESKILLED
DESKILLING
DESKILLS
DESKS
DESKTOP
DESKTOPS
DESMAN
DESMANS
DESMID
DESMIDS
DESMINE
DESMINES
DESMODIUM
DESMODIUMS
DESMOID
DESMOIDS
DESMOSOME
DESMOSOMES
DESOEUVRE
DESOLATE
DESOLATED
DESOLATER
DESOLATERS
DESOLATES
DESOLATING
DESOLATOR
DESOLATORS
DESORB
DESORBED
DESORBING
DESORBS
DESPAIR
DESPAIRED
DESPAIRING
DESPAIRS
DESPATCH
DESPATCHED
DESPATCHES
DESPATCHING
DESPERADO
DESPERADOES
DESPERADOS
DESPERATE
DESPIGHT
DESPIGHTS
DESPISAL
DESPISALS
DESPISE
DESPISED
DESPISER
DESPISERS
DESPISES
DESPISING
DESPITE
DESPITES
DESPOIL
DESPOILED
DESPOILER
DESPOILERS
DESPOILING
DESPOILS
DESPOND
DESPONDED
DESPONDING
DESPONDINGS
DESPONDS
DESPOT
DESPOTAT
DESPOTATE
DESPOTATES
DESPOTATS
DESPOTIC
DESPOTISM
DESPOTISMS
DESPOTS
DESPUMATE
DESPUMATED
DESPUMATES
DESPUMATING
DESSE
DESSERT
DESSERTS
DESSES
DESTEMPER
DESTEMPERED
DESTEMPERING
DESTEMPERS
DESTINATE
DESTINATED
DESTINATES
DESTINATING
DESTINE
DESTINED
DESTINES
DESTINIES
DESTINING
DESTINY
DESTITUTE
DESTITUTED
DESTITUTES
DESTITUTING
DESTRIER
DESTRIERS
DESTROY
DESTROYED
DESTROYER
DESTROYERS
DESTROYING
DESTROYS
DESTRUCT
DESTRUCTED
DESTRUCTING
DESTRUCTS
DESUETUDE
DESUETUDES
DESULPHUR
DESULPHURED
DESULPHURING
DESULPHURS
DESULTORY
DESYATIN
DESYATINS
DESYNE
DESYNED
DESYNES
DESYNING
DETACH
DETACHED
DETACHES
DETACHING
DETAIL
DETAILED
DETAILING
DETAILS
DETAIN
DETAINED
DETAINEE

DETAINEES
DETAINER
DETAINERS
DETAINING
DETAINS
DETECT
DETECTED
DETECTING
DETECTION
DETECTIONS
DETECTIVE
DETECTIVES
DETECTOR
DETECTORS
DETECTS
DETENT
DETENTE
DETENTES
DETENTION
DETENTIONS
DETENTS
DETENU
DETENUE
DETENUES
DETENUS
DETER
DETERGE
DETERGED
DETERGENT
DETERGENTS
DETERGES
DETERGING
DETERMENT
DETERMENTS
DETERMINE
DETERMINED
DETERMINES
DETERMINING
DETERRED
DETERRENT
DETERRENTS
DETERRING
DETERS
DETERSION
DETERSIONS
DETERSIVE
DETERSIVES
DETEST
DETESTED
DETESTING
DETESTS
DETHRONE
DETHRONED
DETHRONER
DETHRONERS
DETHRONES
DETHRONING
DETHRONINGS
DETINUE
DETINUES
DETONATE
DETONATED
DETONATES
DETONATING
DETONATOR
DETONATORS
DETORSION
DETORSIONS
DETORT
DETORTED
DETORTING
DETORTION
DETORTIONS
DETORTS
DETOUR
DETOURED
DETOURING
DETOURS
DETOX
DETOXED
DETOXES
DETOXIFIED
DETOXIFIES
DETOXIFY
DETOXIFYING
DETOXING
DETRACT
DETRACTED
DETRACTING
DETRACTINGS
DETRACTOR
DETRACTORS
DETRACTS
DETRAIN
DETRAINED
DETRAINING
DETRAINS
DETRAQUE
DETRAQUEE
DETRAQUEES
DETRAQUES
DETRIMENT
DETRIMENTS
DETRITAL
DETRITION
DETRITIONS
DETRITUS
DETRUDE
DETRUDED
DETRUDES
DETRUDING
DETRUSION
DETRUSIONS
DETUNE
DETUNED
DETUNES
DETUNING
DEUCE
DEUCED
DEUCEDLY
DEUCES
DEUDDARN
DEUDDARNS
DEUS
DEUTERATE
DEUTERATED
DEUTERATES
DEUTERATING
DEUTERIDE
DEUTERIDES
DEUTERIUM
DEUTERIUMS
DEUTERON
DEUTERONS
DEUTON
DEUTONS
DEVA
DEVALL
DEVALLED
DEVALLING
DEVALLS
DEVALUATE
DEVALUATED
DEVALUATES
DEVALUATING
DEVALUE
DEVALUED
DEVALUES
DEVALUING
DEVAS
DEVASTATE
DEVASTATED
DEVASTATES
DEVASTATING
DEVEL
DEVELLED
DEVELLING
DEVELOP
DEVELOPE
DEVELOPED
DEVELOPER
DEVELOPERS
DEVELOPES
DEVELOPING
DEVELOPS
DEVELS
DEVEST
DEVESTED
DEVESTING
DEVESTS
DEVIANCE
DEVIANCES
DEVIANCIES
DEVIANCY
DEVIANT
DEVIANTS
DEVIATE
DEVIATED
DEVIATES
DEVIATING
DEVIATION
DEVIATIONS
DEVIATOR
DEVIATORS
DEVIATORY
DEVICE
DEVICEFUL
DEVICES
DEVIL
DEVILDOM
DEVILDOMS
DEVILED
DEVILESS
DEVILESSES
DEVILET
DEVILETS
DEVILING
DEVILINGS
DEVILISH
DEVILISM
DEVILISMS
DEVILKIN
DEVILKINS
DEVILLED
DEVILLING
DEVILMENT
DEVILMENTS
DEVILRIES
DEVILRY
DEVILS
DEVILSHIP
DEVILSHIPS
DEVILTRIES
DEVILTRY
DEVIOUS
DEVIOUSLY
DEVISABLE
DEVISAL
DEVISALS
DEVISE
DEVISED
DEVISEE
DEVISEES
DEVISER
DEVISERS
DEVISES
DEVISING
DEVISOR
DEVISORS
DEVITRIFIED
DEVITRIFIES
DEVITRIFY
DEVITRIFYING
DEVLING
DEVLINGS
DEVOICE
DEVOICED
DEVOICES
DEVOICING
DEVOID
DEVOIR
DEVOIRS
DEVOLVE
DEVOLVED
DEVOLVES
DEVOLVING
DEVONPORT
DEVONPORTS
DEVORE
DEVOT
DEVOTE
DEVOTED
DEVOTEDLY
DEVOTEE
DEVOTEES
DEVOTES
DEVOTING
DEVOTION
DEVOTIONS
DEVOTS
DEVOUR
DEVOURED
DEVOURER
DEVOURERS
DEVOURING
DEVOURS
DEVOUT
DEVOUTER
DEVOUTEST
DEVOUTLY
DEVVEL
DEVVELLED
DEVVELLING
DEVVELS
DEW
DEWAN
DEWANI
DEWANIS
DEWANNIES
DEWANNY
DEWANS
DEWAR
DEWARS
DEWATER
DEWATERED
DEWATERING
DEWATERINGS
DEWATERS
DEWED
DEWFULL
DEWIER
DEWIEST
DEWILY
DEWINESS
DEWINESSES
DEWING
DEWITT
DEWITTED
DEWITTING
DEWITTS
DEWLAP
DEWLAPPED
DEWLAPS
DEWLAPT
DEWPOINT
DEWPOINTS
DEWS
DEWY
DEXTER
DEXTERITIES
DEXTERITY
DEXTEROUS
DEXTERS
DEXTRAL
DEXTRALLY
DEXTRAN
DEXTRANS
DEXTRIN
DEXTRINE
DEXTRINES

DEXTRINS
DEXTRORSE
DEXTROSE
DEXTROSES
DEXTROUS
DEY
DEYS
DHAK
DHAKS
DHAL
DHALS
DHARMA
DHARMAS
DHARMSALA
DHARMSALAS
DHARNA
DHARNAS
DHOBI
DHOBIS
DHOL
DHOLE
DHOLES
DHOLL
DHOLLS
DHOLS
DHOOLIES
DHOOLY
DHOOTI
DHOOTIS
DHOTI
DHOTIS
DHOW
DHOWS
DHURRA
DHURRAS
DHURRIE
DHURRIES
DI
DIABASE
DIABASES
DIABASIC
DIABETES
DIABETIC
DIABETICS
DIABLE
DIABLERIE
DIABLERIES
DIABLERY
DIABLES
DIABOLIC
DIABOLISE
DIABOLISED
DIABOLISES
DIABOLISING
DIABOLISM
DIABOLISMS
DIABOLIST
DIABOLISTS
DIABOLIZE
DIABOLIZED
DIABOLIZES
DIABOLIZING
DIABOLO
DIABOLOGIES
DIABOLOGY
DIABOLOS
DIACHYLON
DIACHYLONS
DIACHYLUM
DIACHYLUMS
DIACID
DIACODION
DIACODIONS
DIACODIUM
DIACODIUMS
DIACONAL
DIACONATE
DIACONATES
DIACRITIC
DIACRITICS
DIACT
DIACTINAL
DIACTINE
DIACTINIC
DIADEM
DIADEMED
DIADEMS
DIADOCHI
DIADROM
DIADROMS
DIAERESES
DIAERESIS
DIAGLYPH
DIAGLYPHS
DIAGNOSE
DIAGNOSED
DIAGNOSES
DIAGNOSING
DIAGNOSIS
DIAGONAL
DIAGONALS
DIAGRAM
DIAGRAMS
DIAGRAPH
DIAGRAPHS
DIAGRID
DIAGRIDS
DIAL
DIALECT
DIALECTAL
DIALECTIC
DIALECTICS
DIALECTS
DIALED
DIALING
DIALIST
DIALISTS
DIALLAGE
DIALLAGES
DIALLAGIC
DIALLED
DIALLER
DIALLERS
DIALLING
DIALLINGS
DIALOG
DIALOGED
DIALOGIC
DIALOGING
DIALOGISE
DIALOGISED
DIALOGISES
DIALOGISING
DIALOGIST
DIALOGISTS
DIALOGITE
DIALOGITES
DIALOGIZE
DIALOGIZED
DIALOGIZES
DIALOGIZING
DIALOGS
DIALOGUE
DIALOGUED
DIALOGUES
DIALOGUING
DIALS
DIALYSE
DIALYSED
DIALYSER
DIALYSERS
DIALYSES
DIALYSING
DIALYSIS
DIALYTIC
DIALYZE
DIALYZED
DIALYZER
DIALYZERS
DIALYZES
DIALYZING
DIAMAGNET
DIAMAGNETS
DIAMANTE
DIAMANTES
DIAMETER
DIAMETERS
DIAMETRAL
DIAMETRIC
DIAMOND
DIAMONDED
DIAMONDS
DIAMYL
DIANDRIES
DIANDROUS
DIANDRY
DIANODAL
DIANOETIC
DIANTHUS
DIANTHUSES
DIAPASE
DIAPASES
DIAPASON
DIAPASONS
DIAPAUSE
DIAPAUSES
DIAPENTE
DIAPENTES
DIAPER
DIAPERED
DIAPERING
DIAPERINGS
DIAPERS
DIAPHONE
DIAPHONES
DIAPHRAGM
DIAPHRAGMS
DIAPHYSES
DIAPHYSIS
DIAPIR
DIAPIRIC
DIAPIRISM
DIAPIRISMS
DIAPIRS
DIAPYESES
DIAPYESIS
DIAPYETIC
DIAPYETICS
DIARCH
DIARCHAL
DIARCHIC
DIARCHIES
DIARCHY
DIARIAL
DIARIAN
DIARIES
DIARISE
DIARISED
DIARISES
DIARISING
DIARIST
DIARISTS
DIARIZE
DIARIZED
DIARIZES
DIARIZING
DIARRHEA
DIARRHEAL
DIARRHEAS
DIARRHEIC
DIARRHOEA
DIARRHOEAS
DIARY
DIASCOPE
DIASCOPES
DIASPORA
DIASPORAS
DIASPORE
DIASPORES
DIASTASE
DIASTASES
DIASTASIC
DIASTASIS
DIASTATIC
DIASTEMA
DIASTEMATA
DIASTER
DIASTERS
DIASTOLE
DIASTOLES
DIASTOLIC
DIASTYLE
DIASTYLES
DIATHERMIES
DIATHERMY
DIATHESES
DIATHESIS
DIATHETIC
DIATOM
DIATOMIC
DIATOMIST
DIATOMISTS
DIATOMITE
DIATOMITES
DIATOMS
DIATONIC
DIATRETUM
DIATRETUMS
DIATRIBE
DIATRIBES
DIATROPIC
DIAXON
DIAXONS
DIAZEPAM
DIAZEPAMS
DIAZEUXES
DIAZEUXIS
DIAZO
DIAZOES
DIAZOS
DIB
DIBASIC
DIBBED
DIBBER
DIBBERS
DIBBING
DIBBLE
DIBBLED
DIBBLER
DIBBLERS
DIBBLES
DIBBLING
DIBBS
DIBS
DIBUTYL
DICACIOUS
DICACITIES
DICACITY
DICAST
DICASTERIES
DICASTERY
DICASTIC
DICASTS
DICE
DICED
DICENTRA
DICENTRAS
DICER
DICERS
DICES
DICEY
DICH
DICHASIA
DICHASIAL
DICHASIUM
DICHOGAMIES
DICHOGAMY
DICHORD
DICHORDS
DICHOTOMIES

ICHOTOMY
CHROIC
ICHROISM
CHROISMS
ICHROITE
CHROITES
ICHROMAT
CHROMATS
ICHROMIC
CHT
ICHTED
CHTING
ICHTS
CIER
CIEST
ICING
ICINGS
ICK
ICKENS
ICKER
ICKERED
ICKERING
ICKERS
ICKEY
ICKEYS
ICKHEAD
ICKHEADS
ICKIE
ICKIER
ICKIES
ICKIEST
ICKS
ICKTIER
ICKTIEST
ICKTY
ICKY
ICLINISM
ICLINISMS
ICLINOUS
ICOT
ICOTS
ICROTIC
ICROTISM
ICROTISMS
ICROTOUS
ICT
ICTA
ICTATE
ICTATED
ICTATES
ICTATING
ICTATION
ICTATIONS
ICTATOR
ICTATORS
ICTATORY
ICTATRIX
ICTATRIXES
ICTATURE
ICTATURES
ICTED
ICTIER
ICTIEST
ICTING

DICTION
DICTIONS
DICTS
DICTUM
DICTY
DICTYOGEN
DICTYOGENS
DICYCLIC
DID
DIDACTIC
DIDACTICS
DIDACTYL
DIDACTYLS
DIDAKAI
DIDAKAIS
DIDAKEI
DIDAKEIS
DIDAPPER
DIDAPPERS
DIDDER
DIDDERED
DIDDERING
DIDDERS
DIDDICOY
DIDDICOYS
DIDDIER
DIDDIES
DIDDIEST
DIDDLE
DIDDLED
DIDDLER
DIDDLERS
DIDDLES
DIDDLING
DIDDY
DIDELPHIC
DIDELPHID
DIDELPHIDS
DIDICOI
DIDICOIS
DIDICOY
DIDICOYS
DIDO
DIDOES
DIDOS
DIDRACHM
DIDRACHMA
DIDRACHMAS
DIDRACHMS
DIDST
DIDYMIUM
DIDYMIUMS
DIDYMOUS
DIE
DIEB
DIEBACK
DIEBACKS
DIEBS
DIED
DIEDRAL
DIEDRALS
DIEDRE
DIEDRES
DIEGESES

DIEGESIS
DIELDRIN
DIELDRINS
DIELYTRA
DIELYTRAS
DIENE
DIENES
DIERESES
DIERESIS
DIES
DIESEL
DIESELISE
DIESELISED
DIESELISES
DIESELISING
DIESELIZE
DIESELIZED
DIESELIZES
DIESELIZING
DIESELS
DIESES
DIESIS
DIESTRUS
DIESTRUSES
DIET
DIETARIAN
DIETARIANS
DIETARIES
DIETARY
DIETED
DIETER
DIETERS
DIETETIC
DIETETICS
DIETHYL
DIETICIAN
DIETICIANS
DIETINE
DIETINES
DIETING
DIETIST
DIETISTS
DIETITIAN
DIETITIANS
DIETS
DIFFER
DIFFERED
DIFFERENT
DIFFERING
DIFFERS
DIFFICILE
DIFFICULT
DIFFIDENT
DIFFLUENT
DIFFORM
DIFFRACT
DIFFRACTED
DIFFRACTING
DIFFRACTS
DIFFUSE
DIFFUSED
DIFFUSELY
DIFFUSER
DIFFUSERS

DIFFUSES
DIFFUSING
DIFFUSION
DIFFUSIONS
DIFFUSIVE
DIG
DIGAMIES
DIGAMIST
DIGAMISTS
DIGAMMA
DIGAMMAS
DIGAMOUS
DIGAMY
DIGASTRIC
DIGEST
DIGESTED
DIGESTER
DIGESTERS
DIGESTING
DIGESTION
DIGESTIONS
DIGESTIVE
DIGESTIVES
DIGESTS
DIGGABLE
DIGGED
DIGGER
DIGGERS
DIGGING
DIGGINGS
DIGHT
DIGHTED
DIGHTING
DIGHTS
DIGIT
DIGITAL
DIGITALIN
DIGITALINS
DIGITALIS
DIGITALISES
DIGITALS
DIGITATE
DIGITATED
DIGITISE
DIGITISED
DIGITISER
DIGITISERS
DIGITISES
DIGITISING
DIGITIZE
DIGITIZED
DIGITIZER
DIGITIZERS
DIGITIZES
DIGITIZING
DIGITS
DIGLOT
DIGLOTS
DIGLYPH
DIGLYPHS
DIGNIFIED
DIGNIFIES
DIGNIFY
DIGNIFYING

DIGNITARIES
DIGNITARY
DIGNITIES
DIGNITY
DIGONAL
DIGRAPH
DIGRAPHS
DIGRESS
DIGRESSED
DIGRESSES
DIGRESSING
DIGS
DIGYNIAN
DIGYNOUS
DIHEDRA
DIHEDRAL
DIHEDRALS
DIHEDRON
DIHEDRONS
DIHYBRID
DIHYBRIDS
DIHYDRIC
DIKA
DIKAS
DIKAST
DIKASTS
DIKE
DIKED
DIKER
DIKERS
DIKES
DIKEY
DIKIER
DIKIEST
DIKING
DIKKOP
DIKKOPS
DIKTAT
DIKTATS
DILATABLE
DILATANCIES
DILATANCY
DILATANT
DILATATOR
DILATATORS
DILATE
DILATED
DILATER
DILATERS
DILATES
DILATING
DILATION
DILATIONS
DILATIVE
DILATOR
DILATORS
DILATORY
DILDO
DILDOE
DILDOES
DILDOS
DILEMMA
DILEMMAS
DILIGENCE

DILIGENCES
DILIGENT
DILL
DILLI
DILLIER
DILLIES
DILLIEST
DILLING
DILLINGS
DILLIS
DILLS
DILLY
DILUENT
DILUENTS
DILUTABLE
DILUTABLES
DILUTE
DILUTED
DILUTEE
DILUTEES
DILUTER
DILUTERS
DILUTES
DILUTING
DILUTION
DILUTIONS
DILUTOR
DILUTORS
DILUVIA
DILUVIAL
DILUVIAN
DILUVION
DILUVIONS
DILUVIUM
DILUVIUMS
DIM
DIMBLE
DIMBLES
DIME
DIMENSION
DIMENSIONED
DIMENSIONING
DIMENSIONS
DIMER
DIMERIC
DIMERISE
DIMERISED
DIMERISES
DIMERISING
DIMERISM
DIMERISMS
DIMERIZE
DIMERIZED
DIMERIZES
DIMERIZING
DIMEROUS
DIMERS
DIMES
DIMETER
DIMETERS
DIMETHYL
DIMETHYLS
DIMETRIC
DIMIDIATE
DIMIDIATED
DIMIDIATES
DIMIDIATING
DIMINISH
DIMINISHED
DIMINISHES
DIMINISHING
DIMINISHINGS
DIMISSORY
DIMITIES
DIMITY
DIMLY
DIMMED
DIMMER
DIMMERS
DIMMEST
DIMMING
DIMMISH
DIMNESS
DIMNESSES
DIMORPH
DIMORPHIC
DIMORPHS
DIMPLE
DIMPLED
DIMPLES
DIMPLIER
DIMPLIEST
DIMPLING
DIMPLY
DIMS
DIMWIT
DIMWITS
DIMYARIAN
DIN
DINAR
DINARCHIES
DINARCHY
DINARS
DINDLE
DINDLED
DINDLES
DINDLING
DINE
DINED
DINER
DINERS
DINES
DINETTE
DINETTES
DINFUL
DING
DINGBAT
DINGBATS
DINGE
DINGED
DINGER
DINGERS
DINGES
DINGESES
DINGEY
DINGEYS
DINGHIES
DINGHY
DINGIER
DINGIES
DINGIEST
DINGINESS
DINGINESSES
DINGING
DINGLE
DINGLES
DINGO
DINGOES
DINGS
DINGUS
DINGUSES
DINGY
DINIC
DINICS
DINING
DINK
DINKED
DINKER
DINKEST
DINKIER
DINKIES
DINKIEST
DINKING
DINKS
DINKUM
DINKY
DINMONT
DINMONTS
DINNED
DINNER
DINNERED
DINNERING
DINNERS
DINNING
DINNLE
DINNLED
DINNLES
DINNLING
DINO
DINOMANIA
DINOMANIAS
DINOS
DINOSAUR
DINOSAURS
DINOTHERE
DINOTHERES
DINS
DINT
DINTED
DINTING
DINTS
DIOCESAN
DIOCESANS
DIOCESE
DIOCESES
DIODE
DIODES
DIOECIOUS
DIOECISM
DIOECISMS
DIOESTRUS
DIOESTRUSES
DIOPSIDE
DIOPSIDES
DIOPTASE
DIOPTASES
DIOPTER
DIOPTERS
DIOPTRATE
DIOPTRE
DIOPTRES
DIOPTRIC
DIOPTRICS
DIORAMA
DIORAMAS
DIORAMIC
DIORISM
DIORISMS
DIORISTIC
DIORITE
DIORITES
DIORITIC
DIOSGENIN
DIOSGENINS
DIOTA
DIOTAS
DIOXAN
DIOXANE
DIOXANES
DIOXANS
DIOXIDE
DIOXIDES
DIOXIN
DIOXINS
DIP
DIPCHICK
DIPCHICKS
DIPEPTIDE
DIPEPTIDES
DIPHENYL
DIPHENYLS
DIPHONE
DIPHONES
DIPHTHONG
DIPHTHONGS
DIPHYSITE
DIPHYSITES
DIPLEGIA
DIPLEGIAS
DIPLEX
DIPLOE
DIPLOES
DIPLOGEN
DIPLOGENS
DIPLOID
DIPLOIDIES
DIPLOIDY
DIPLOMA
DIPLOMACIES
DIPLOMACY
DIPLOMAED
DIPLOMAING
DIPLOMAS
DIPLOMAT
DIPLOMATE
DIPLOMATED
DIPLOMATES
DIPLOMATING
DIPLOMATS
DIPLON
DIPLONS
DIPLONT
DIPLONTS
DIPLOPIA
DIPLOPIAS
DIPLOZOA
DIPLOZOON
DIPNOAN
DIPNOANS
DIPNOOUS
DIPODIES
DIPODY
DIPOLAR
DIPOLE
DIPOLES
DIPPED
DIPPER
DIPPERS
DIPPIER
DIPPIEST
DIPPING
DIPPINGS
DIPPY
DIPS
DIPSADES
DIPSAS
DIPSO
DIPSOS
DIPSTICK
DIPSTICKS
DIPTERA
DIPTERAL
DIPTERAN
DIPTERANS
DIPTERAS
DIPTERIST
DIPTERISTS
DIPTEROI
DIPTEROS
DIPTEROSES
DIPTEROUS
DIPTYCH
DIPTYCHS
DIRDAM
DIRDAMS
DIRDUM
DIRDUMS
DIRE
DIRECT
DIRECTED
DIRECTER
DIRECTEST
DIRECTING
DIRECTION
DIRECTIONS
DIRECTIVE
DIRECTIVES
DIRECTLY
DIRECTOR
DIRECTORIES

DIRECTORS
DIRECTORY
DIRECTRICES
DIRECTRIX
DIRECTRIXES
DIRECTS
DIREFUL
DIREFULLY
DIREMPT
DIREMPTED
DIREMPTING
DIREMPTS
DIRENESS
DIRENESSES
DIRER
DIREST
DIRGE
DIRGES
DIRHAM
DIRHAMS
DIRHEM
DIRHEMS
DIRIGE
DIRIGENT
DIRIGES
DIRIGIBLE
DIRIGIBLES
DIRIGISM
DIRIGISME
DIRIGISMES
DIRIGISMS
DIRIGISTE
DIRIMENT
DIRK
DIRKE
DIRKED
DIRKES
DIRKING
DIRKS
DIRL
DIRLED
DIRLING
DIRLS
DIRNDL
DIRNDLS
DIRT
DIRTED
DIRTIED
DIRTIER
DIRTIES
DIRTIEST
DIRTILY
DIRTINESS
DIRTINESSES
DIRTING
DIRTS
DIRTY
DIRTYING
DISA
DISABLE
DISABLED
DISABLES
DISABLING
DISABUSE
DISABUSED
DISABUSES
DISABUSING
DISACCORD
DISACCORDED
DISACCORDING
DISACCORDS
DISADORN
DISADORNED
DISADORNING
DISADORNS
DISAFFECT
DISAFFECTED
DISAFFECTING
DISAFFECTS
DISAFFIRM
DISAFFIRMED
DISAFFIRMING
DISAFFIRMS
DISAGREE
DISAGREED
DISAGREEING
DISAGREES
DISALLIED
DISALLIES
DISALLOW
DISALLOWED
DISALLOWING
DISALLOWS
DISALLY
DISALLYING
DISANCHOR
DISANCHORED
DISANCHORING
DISANCHORS
DISANNEX
DISANNEXED
DISANNEXES
DISANNEXING
DISANNUL
DISANNULLED
DISANNULLING
DISANNULLINGS
DISANNULS
DISANOINT
DISANOINTED
DISANOINTING
DISANOINTS
DISAPPEAR
DISAPPEARED
DISAPPEARING
DISAPPEARS
DISAPPLIED
DISAPPLIES
DISAPPLY
DISAPPLYING
DISARM
DISARMED
DISARMER
DISARMERS
DISARMING
DISARMS
DISARRAY
DISARRAYED
DISARRAYING
DISARRAYS
DISAS
DISASTER
DISASTERS
DISATTIRE
DISATTIRED
DISATTIRES
DISATTIRING
DISATTUNE
DISATTUNED
DISATTUNES
DISATTUNING
DISAVOUCH
DISAVOUCHED
DISAVOUCHES
DISAVOUCHING
DISAVOW
DISAVOWAL
DISAVOWALS
DISAVOWED
DISAVOWING
DISAVOWS
DISBAND
DISBANDED
DISBANDING
DISBANDS
DISBAR
DISBARK
DISBARKED
DISBARKING
DISBARKS
DISBARRED
DISBARRING
DISBARS
DISBELIEF
DISBELIEFS
DISBENCH
DISBENCHED
DISBENCHES
DISBENCHING
DISBODIED
DISBOSOM
DISBOSOMED
DISBOSOMING
DISBOSOMS
DISBOWEL
DISBOWELLED
DISBOWELLING
DISBOWELS
DISBRANCH
DISBRANCHED
DISBRANCHES
DISBRANCHING
DISBUD
DISBUDDED
DISBUDDING
DISBUDS
DISBURDEN
DISBURDENED
DISBURDENING
DISBURDENS
DISBURSAL
DISBURSALS
DISBURSE
DISBURSED
DISBURSES
DISBURSING
DISC
DISCAGE
DISCAGED
DISCAGES
DISCAGING
DISCAL
DISCALCED
DISCANDIE
DISCANDIED
DISCANDIES
DISCANDY
DISCANDYING
DISCANDYINGS
DISCANT
DISCANTED
DISCANTING
DISCANTS
DISCARD
DISCARDED
DISCARDING
DISCARDS
DISCASE
DISCASED
DISCASES
DISCASING
DISCED
DISCEPT
DISCEPTED
DISCEPTING
DISCEPTS
DISCERN
DISCERNED
DISCERNER
DISCERNERS
DISCERNING
DISCERNS
DISCERP
DISCERPED
DISCERPING
DISCERPS
DISCHARGE
DISCHARGED
DISCHARGES
DISCHARGING
DISCHURCH
DISCHURCHED
DISCHURCHES
DISCHURCHING
DISCIDE
DISCIDED
DISCIDES
DISCIDING
DISCINCT
DISCING
DISCIPLE
DISCIPLED
DISCIPLES
DISCIPLING
DISCLAIM
DISCLAIMED
DISCLAIMING
DISCLAIMS
DISCLOSE
DISCLOSED
DISCLOSES
DISCLOSING
DISCLOST
DISCO
DISCOBOLI
DISCOED
DISCOER
DISCOERS
DISCOID
DISCOIDAL
DISCOING
DISCOLOR
DISCOLORED
DISCOLORING
DISCOLORS
DISCOLOUR
DISCOLOURED
DISCOLOURING
DISCOLOURS
DISCOMFIT
DISCOMFITED
DISCOMFITING
DISCOMFITS
DISCOMMON
DISCOMMONED
DISCOMMONING
DISCOMMONS
DISCORD
DISCORDED
DISCORDING
DISCORDS
DISCOS
DISCOUNT
DISCOUNTED
DISCOUNTING
DISCOUNTS
DISCOURE
DISCOURED
DISCOURES
DISCOURING
DISCOURSE
DISCOURSED
DISCOURSES
DISCOURSING
DISCOVER
DISCOVERED
DISCOVERIES
DISCOVERING
DISCOVERS
DISCOVERT
DISCOVERY
DISCREDIT
DISCREDITED
DISCREDITING
DISCREDITS
DISCREET
DISCREETER
DISCREETEST
DISCRETE
DISCRETER

DISCRETEST
DISCROWN
DISCROWNED
DISCROWNING
DISCROWNS
DISCS
DISCUMBER
DISCUMBERED
DISCUMBERING
DISCUMBERS
DISCURE
DISCURED
DISCURES
DISCURING
DISCURSUS
DISCURSUSES
DISCUS
DISCUSES
DISCUSS
DISCUSSED
DISCUSSES
DISCUSSING
DISDAIN
DISDAINED
DISDAINING
DISDAINS
DISEASE
DISEASED
DISEASES
DISEASING
DISEDGE
DISEDGED
DISEDGES
DISEDGING
DISEMBARK
DISEMBARKED
DISEMBARKING
DISEMBARKS
DISEMBODIED
DISEMBODIES
DISEMBODY
DISEMBODYING
DISEMPLOY
DISEMPLOYED
DISEMPLOYING
DISEMPLOYS
DISENABLE
DISENABLED
DISENABLES
DISENABLING
DISENDOW
DISENDOWED
DISENDOWING
DISENDOWS
DISENGAGE
DISENGAGED
DISENGAGES
DISENGAGING
DISENROL
DISENROLLED
DISENROLLING
DISENROLS
DISENTAIL
DISENTAILED
DISENTAILING
DISENTAILS
DISENTOMB
DISENTOMBED
DISENTOMBING
DISENTOMBS
DISESTEEM
DISESTEEMED
DISESTEEMING
DISESTEEMS
DISEUR
DISEURS
DISEUSE
DISEUSES
DISFAME
DISFAMES
DISFAVOR
DISFAVORED
DISFAVORING
DISFAVORS
DISFAVOUR
DISFAVOURED
DISFAVOURING
DISFAVOURS
DISFIGURE
DISFIGURED
DISFIGURES
DISFIGURING
DISFLESH
DISFLESHED
DISFLESHES
DISFLESHING
DISFLUENT
DISFOREST
DISFORESTED
DISFORESTING
DISFORESTS
DISFORM
DISFORMED
DISFORMING
DISFORMS
DISFROCK
DISFROCKED
DISFROCKING
DISFROCKS
DISGAVEL
DISGAVELLED
DISGAVELLING
DISGAVELS
DISGEST
DISGESTED
DISGESTING
DISGESTS
DISGODDED
DISGORGE
DISGORGED
DISGORGES
DISGORGING
DISGOWN
DISGOWNED
DISGOWNING
DISGOWNS
DISGRACE
DISGRACED
DISGRACER
DISGRACERS
DISGRACES
DISGRACING
DISGRADE
DISGRADED
DISGRADES
DISGRADING
DISGUISE
DISGUISED
DISGUISER
DISGUISERS
DISGUISES
DISGUISING
DISGUISINGS
DISGUST
DISGUSTED
DISGUSTING
DISGUSTS
DISH
DISHABIT
DISHABITED
DISHABITING
DISHABITS
DISHABLE
DISHABLED
DISHABLES
DISHABLING
DISHALLOW
DISHALLOWED
DISHALLOWING
DISHALLOWS
DISHED
DISHELM
DISHELMED
DISHELMING
DISHELMS
DISHERIT
DISHERITED
DISHERITING
DISHERITS
DISHES
DISHEVEL
DISHEVELLED
DISHEVELLING
DISHEVELS
DISHFUL
DISHFULS
DISHIER
DISHIEST
DISHING
DISHINGS
DISHOME
DISHOMED
DISHOMES
DISHOMING
DISHONEST
DISHONOR
DISHONORED
DISHONORING
DISHONORS
DISHONOUR
DISHONOURED
DISHONOURING
DISHONOURS
DISHORN
DISHORNED
DISHORNING
DISHORNS
DISHORSE
DISHORSED
DISHORSES
DISHORSING
DISHOUSE
DISHOUSED
DISHOUSES
DISHOUSING
DISHTOWEL
DISHTOWELS
DISHUMOUR
DISHUMOURED
DISHUMOURING
DISHUMOURS
DISHWATER
DISHWATERS
DISHY
DISILLUDE
DISILLUDED
DISILLUDES
DISILLUDING
DISIMMURE
DISIMMURED
DISIMMURES
DISIMMURING
DISINFECT
DISINFECTED
DISINFECTING
DISINFECTS
DISINFEST
DISINFESTED
DISINFESTING
DISINFESTS
DISINHUME
DISINHUMED
DISINHUMES
DISINHUMING
DISINTER
DISINTERRED
DISINTERRING
DISINTERS
DISINURE
DISINURED
DISINURES
DISINURING
DISINVEST
DISINVESTED
DISINVESTING
DISINVESTS
DISJASKIT
DISJECT
DISJECTED
DISJECTING
DISJECTS
DISJOIN
DISJOINED
DISJOINING
DISJOINS
DISJOINT
DISJOINTED
DISJOINTING
DISJOINTS
DISJUNCT
DISJUNCTS
DISJUNE
DISJUNES
DISK
DISKED
DISKETTE
DISKETTES
DISKING
DISKLESS
DISKS
DISLEAF
DISLEAFED
DISLEAFING
DISLEAFS
DISLEAL
DISLEAVE
DISLEAVED
DISLEAVES
DISLEAVING
DISLIKE
DISLIKED
DISLIKEN
DISLIKENED
DISLIKENING
DISLIKENS
DISLIKES
DISLIKING
DISLIMB
DISLIMBED
DISLIMBING
DISLIMBS
DISLIMN
DISLIMNED
DISLIMNING
DISLIMNS
DISLINK
DISLINKED
DISLINKING
DISLINKS
DISLOAD
DISLOADED
DISLOADING
DISLOADS
DISLOCATE
DISLOCATED
DISLOCATES
DISLOCATING
DISLODGE
DISLODGED
DISLODGES
DISLODGING
DISLOIGN
DISLOIGNED
DISLOIGNING
DISLOIGNS
DISLOYAL
DISLUSTRE
DISLUSTRED
DISLUSTRES
DISLUSTRING

DISMAL
DISMALITIES
DISMALITY
DISMALLER
DISMALLEST
DISMALLY
DISMALS
DISMAN
DISMANNED
DISMANNING
DISMANS
DISMANTLE
DISMANTLED
DISMANTLES
DISMANTLING
DISMASK
DISMASKED
DISMASKING
DISMASKS
DISMAST
DISMASTED
DISMASTING
DISMASTS
DISMAY
DISMAYD
DISMAYED
DISMAYFUL
DISMAYING
DISMAYL
DISMAYLED
DISMAYLING
DISMAYLS
DISMAYS
DISME
DISMEMBER
DISMEMBERED
DISMEMBERING
DISMEMBERS
DISMES
DISMISS
DISMISSAL
DISMISSALS
DISMISSED
DISMISSES
DISMISSING
DISMODED
DISMOUNT
DISMOUNTED
DISMOUNTING
DISMOUNTS
DISNEST
DISNESTED
DISNESTING
DISNESTS
DISOBEY
DISOBEYED
DISOBEYING
DISOBEYS
DISOBLIGE
DISOBLIGED
DISOBLIGES
DISOBLIGING
DISORBED
DISORDER
DISORDERED
DISORDERING
DISORDERS
DISORIENT
DISORIENTED
DISORIENTING
DISORIENTS
DISOWN
DISOWNED
DISOWNER
DISOWNERS
DISOWNING
DISOWNS
DISPACE
DISPACED
DISPACES
DISPACING
DISPARAGE
DISPARAGED
DISPARAGES
DISPARAGING
DISPARATE
DISPARATES
DISPARITIES
DISPARITY
DISPARK
DISPARKED
DISPARKING
DISPARKS
DISPART
DISPARTED
DISPARTING
DISPARTS
DISPATCH
DISPATCHED
DISPATCHES
DISPATCHING
DISPATHIES
DISPATHY
DISPAUPER
DISPAUPERED
DISPAUPERING
DISPAUPERS
DISPEACE
DISPEACES
DISPEL
DISPELLED
DISPELLING
DISPELS
DISPENCE
DISPENCED
DISPENCES
DISPENCING
DISPEND
DISPENDED
DISPENDING
DISPENDS
DISPENSE
DISPENSED
DISPENSER
DISPENSERS
DISPENSES
DISPENSING
DISPEOPLE
DISPEOPLED
DISPEOPLES
DISPEOPLING
DISPERSAL
DISPERSALS
DISPERSE
DISPERSED
DISPERSER
DISPERSERS
DISPERSES
DISPERSING
DISPIRIT
DISPIRITED
DISPIRITING
DISPIRITS
DISPLACE
DISPLACED
DISPLACES
DISPLACING
DISPLANT
DISPLANTED
DISPLANTING
DISPLANTS
DISPLAY
DISPLAYED
DISPLAYER
DISPLAYERS
DISPLAYING
DISPLAYS
DISPLE
DISPLEASE
DISPLEASED
DISPLEASES
DISPLEASING
DISPLED
DISPLES
DISPLING
DISPLODE
DISPLODED
DISPLODES
DISPLODING
DISPLUME
DISPLUMED
DISPLUMES
DISPLUMING
DISPONDEE
DISPONDEES
DISPONE
DISPONED
DISPONEE
DISPONEES
DISPONER
DISPONERS
DISPONES
DISPONGE
DISPONGED
DISPONGES
DISPONGING
DISPONING
DISPORT
DISPORTED
DISPORTING
DISPORTS
DISPOSAL
DISPOSALS
DISPOSE
DISPOSED
DISPOSER
DISPOSERS
DISPOSES
DISPOSING
DISPOSINGS
DISPOST
DISPOSTED
DISPOSTING
DISPOSTS
DISPOSURE
DISPOSURES
DISPRAD
DISPRAISE
DISPRAISED
DISPRAISES
DISPRAISING
DISPREAD
DISPREADING
DISPREADS
DISPRED
DISPREDDEN
DISPREDDING
DISPREDS
DISPRISON
DISPRISONED
DISPRISONING
DISPRISONS
DISPRIZE
DISPRIZED
DISPRIZES
DISPRIZING
DISPROFIT
DISPROFITS
DISPROOF
DISPROOFS
DISPROOVE
DISPROOVED
DISPROOVES
DISPROOVING
DISPROVAL
DISPROVALS
DISPROVE
DISPROVED
DISPROVEN
DISPROVES
DISPROVING
DISPUNGE
DISPUNGED
DISPUNGES
DISPUNGING
DISPURSE
DISPURSED
DISPURSES
DISPURSING
DISPURVEY
DISPURVEYED
DISPURVEYING
DISPURVEYS
DISPUTANT
DISPUTANTS
DISPUTE
DISPUTED
DISPUTER
DISPUTERS
DISPUTES
DISPUTING
DISQUIET
DISQUIETED
DISQUIETING
DISQUIETS
DISRANK
DISRANKED
DISRANKING
DISRANKS
DISRATE
DISRATED
DISRATES
DISRATING
DISREGARD
DISREGARDED
DISREGARDING
DISREGARDS
DISRELISH
DISRELISHED
DISRELISHES
DISRELISHING
DISREPAIR
DISREPAIRS
DISREPUTE
DISREPUTES
DISROBE
DISROBED
DISROBES
DISROBING
DISROOT
DISROOTED
DISROOTING
DISROOTS
DISRUPT
DISRUPTED
DISRUPTER
DISRUPTERS
DISRUPTING
DISRUPTOR
DISRUPTORS
DISRUPTS
DISS
DISSAVING
DISSAVINGS
DISSEAT
DISSEATED
DISSEATING
DISSEATS
DISSECT
DISSECTED
DISSECTING
DISSECTINGS
DISSECTOR
DISSECTORS
DISSECTS
DISSED
DISSEISE
DISSEISED
DISSEISES
DISSEISIN

DISSEISING
DISSEISINS
DISSEISOR
DISSEISORS
DISSEIZE
DISSEIZED
DISSEIZES
DISSEIZIN
DISSEIZING
DISSEIZINS
DISSEIZOR
DISSEIZORS
DISSEMBLE
DISSEMBLED
DISSEMBLES
DISSEMBLIES
DISSEMBLING
DISSEMBLINGS
DISSEMBLY
DISSENT
DISSENTED
DISSENTER
DISSENTERS
DISSENTING
DISSENTS
DISSERT
DISSERTED
DISSERTING
DISSERTS
DISSERVE
DISSERVED
DISSERVES
DISSERVING
DISSES
DISSEVER
DISSEVERED
DISSEVERING
DISSEVERS
DISSHIVER
DISSHIVERED
DISSHIVERING
DISSHIVERS
DISSIDENT
DISSIDENTS
DISSIGHT
DISSIGHTS
DISSIMILE
DISSIMILES
DISSING
DISSIPATE
DISSIPATED
DISSIPATES
DISSIPATING
DISSOCIAL
DISSOLUTE
DISSOLUTES
DISSOLVE
DISSOLVED
DISSOLVES
DISSOLVING
DISSOLVINGS
DISSONANT
DISSUADE
DISSUADED
DISSUADER
DISSUADERS
DISSUADES
DISSUADING
DISSUNDER
DISSUNDERED
DISSUNDERING
DISSUNDERS
DISTAFF
DISTAFFS
DISTAIN
DISTAINED
DISTAINING
DISTAINS
DISTAL
DISTALLY
DISTANCE
DISTANCED
DISTANCES
DISTANCING
DISTANT
DISTANTLY
DISTASTE
DISTASTED
DISTASTES
DISTASTING
DISTEMPER
DISTEMPERED
DISTEMPERING
DISTEMPERS
DISTEND
DISTENDED
DISTENDING
DISTENDS
DISTENT
DISTHENE
DISTHENES
DISTHRONE
DISTHRONED
DISTHRONES
DISTHRONING
DISTICH
DISTICHAL
DISTICHS
DISTIL
DISTILL
DISTILLED
DISTILLER
DISTILLERS
DISTILLING
DISTILLINGS
DISTILLS
DISTILS
DISTINCT
DISTINCTER
DISTINCTEST
DISTINGUE
DISTORT
DISTORTED
DISTORTING
DISTORTS
DISTRACT
DISTRACTED
DISTRACTING
DISTRACTS
DISTRAIL
DISTRAILS
DISTRAIN
DISTRAINED
DISTRAINING
DISTRAINS
DISTRAINT
DISTRAINTS
DISTRAIT
DISTRAITE
DISTRESS
DISTRESSED
DISTRESSES
DISTRESSING
DISTRICT
DISTRICTED
DISTRICTING
DISTRICTS
DISTRUST
DISTRUSTED
DISTRUSTING
DISTRUSTS
DISTUNE
DISTUNED
DISTUNES
DISTUNING
DISTURB
DISTURBED
DISTURBER
DISTURBERS
DISTURBING
DISTURBS
DISTYLE
DISTYLES
DISUNION
DISUNIONS
DISUNITE
DISUNITED
DISUNITES
DISUNITIES
DISUNITING
DISUNITY
DISUSAGE
DISUSAGES
DISUSE
DISUSED
DISUSES
DISUSING
DISVALUE
DISVALUED
DISVALUES
DISVALUING
DISVOUCH
DISVOUCHED
DISVOUCHES
DISVOUCHING
DISYOKE
DISYOKED
DISYOKES
DISYOKING
DIT
DITA
DITAL
DITALS
DITAS
DITCH
DITCHED
DITCHER
DITCHERS
DITCHES
DITCHING
DITE
DITED
DITES
DITHECAL
DITHECOUS
DITHEISM
DITHEISMS
DITHEIST
DITHEISTS
DITHELETE
DITHELETES
DITHELISM
DITHELISMS
DITHER
DITHERED
DITHERER
DITHERERS
DITHERIER
DITHERIEST
DITHERING
DITHERS
DITHERY
DITHYRAMB
DITHYRAMBS
DITING
DITOKOUS
DITONE
DITONES
DITROCHEE
DITROCHEES
DITS
DITSIER
DITSIEST
DITSY
DITT
DITTANDER
DITTANDERS
DITTANIES
DITTANY
DITTAY
DITTAYS
DITTED
DITTIED
DITTIES
DITTING
DITTIT
DITTO
DITTOED
DITTOING
DITTOLOGIES
DITTOLOGY
DITTOS
DITTS
DITTY
DITTYING
DITZIER
DITZIEST
DITZY
DIURESES
DIURESIS
DIURETIC
DIURETICS
DIURNAL
DIURNALLY
DIURNALS
DIUTURNAL
DIV
DIVA
DIVAGATE
DIVAGATED
DIVAGATES
DIVAGATING
DIVALENCIES
DIVALENCY
DIVALENT
DIVALENTS
DIVAN
DIVANS
DIVAS
DIVE
DIVED
DIVELLENT
DIVER
DIVERGE
DIVERGED
DIVERGENT
DIVERGES
DIVERGING
DIVERS
DIVERSE
DIVERSED
DIVERSELY
DIVERSES
DIVERSIFIED
DIVERSIFIES
DIVERSIFY
DIVERSIFYING
DIVERSING
DIVERSION
DIVERSIONS
DIVERSITIES
DIVERSITY
DIVERSLY
DIVERT
DIVERTED
DIVERTING
DIVERTIVE
DIVERTS
DIVES
DIVEST
DIVESTED
DIVESTING
DIVESTS
DIVESTURE
DIVESTURES
DIVI
DIVIDABLE
DIVIDANT
DIVIDE
DIVIDED

IVIDEDLY
IVIDEND
IVIDENDS
IVIDER
IVIDERS
IVIDES
IVIDING
IVIDINGS
IVIDIVI
IVIDIVIS
IVIDUAL
IVIDUOUS
IVINATOR
IVINATORS
IVINE
IVINED
IVINELY
IVINER
IVINERS
IVINES
IVINEST
IVING
IVINGS
IVINIFIED
IVINIFIES
IVINIFY
IVINIFYING
IVINING
IVINISE
IVINISED
IVINISES
IVINISING
IVINITIES
IVINITY
IVINIZE
IVINIZED
IVINIZES
IVINIZING
IVIS
IVISIBLE
IVISIBLY
IVISIM
IVISION
IVISIONS
IVISIVE
IVISOR
IVISORS
IVORCE
IVORCED
IVORCEE
IVORCEES
IVORCER
IVORCERS
IVORCES
IVORCING
IVORCIVE
IVOT
IVOTS
IVS
IVULGATE
IVULGATED
IVULGATES
IVULGATING
IVULGE
DIVULGED
DIVULGES
DIVULGING
DIVULSION
DIVULSIONS
DIVULSIVE
DIVVIES
DIVVY
DIWAN
DIWANS
DIXI
DIXIE
DIXIES
DIXY
DIZAIN
DIZAINS
DIZEN
DIZENED
DIZENING
DIZENS
DIZYGOTIC
DIZZARD
DIZZARDS
DIZZIED
DIZZIER
DIZZIES
DIZZIEST
DIZZILY
DIZZINESS
DIZZINESSES
DIZZY
DIZZYING
DJEBEL
DJEBELS
DJELLABA
DJELLABAH
DJELLABAHS
DJELLABAS
DJIBBAH
DJIBBAHS
DJINN
DJINNI
DO
DOAB
DOABLE
DOABS
DOAT
DOATED
DOATER
DOATERS
DOATING
DOATINGS
DOATS
DOB
DOBBED
DOBBER
DOBBERS
DOBBIE
DOBBIES
DOBBIN
DOBBING
DOBBINS
DOBBY
DOBCHICK
DOBCHICKS
DOBHASH
DOBHASHES
DOBS
DOC
DOCENT
DOCENTS
DOCHMIAC
DOCHMII
DOCHMIUS
DOCHMIUSES
DOCHT
DOCIBLE
DOCILE
DOCILER
DOCILEST
DOCILITIES
DOCILITY
DOCIMASIES
DOCIMASY
DOCK
DOCKAGE
DOCKAGES
DOCKED
DOCKEN
DOCKENS
DOCKER
DOCKERS
DOCKET
DOCKETED
DOCKETING
DOCKETS
DOCKING
DOCKINGS
DOCKISE
DOCKISED
DOCKISES
DOCKISING
DOCKIZE
DOCKIZED
DOCKIZES
DOCKIZING
DOCKLAND
DOCKLANDS
DOCKS
DOCKSIDE
DOCKSIDES
DOCKYARD
DOCKYARDS
DOCQUET
DOCQUETED
DOCQUETING
DOCQUETS
DOCS
DOCTOR
DOCTORAL
DOCTORAND
DOCTORANDS
DOCTORATE
DOCTORATED
DOCTORATES
DOCTORATING
DOCTORED
DOCTORESS
DOCTORESSES
DOCTORIAL
DOCTORING
DOCTORLY
DOCTORS
DOCTRESS
DOCTRESSES
DOCTRINAL
DOCTRINE
DOCTRINES
DOCUDRAMA
DOCUDRAMAS
DOCUMENT
DOCUMENTED
DOCUMENTING
DOCUMENTS
DOD
DODDARD
DODDED
DODDER
DODDERED
DODDERER
DODDERERS
DODDERIER
DODDERIEST
DODDERING
DODDERS
DODDERY
DODDIER
DODDIES
DODDIEST
DODDING
DODDIPOLL
DODDIPOLLS
DODDLE
DODDLES
DODDY
DODDYPOLL
DODDYPOLLS
DODECAGON
DODECAGONS
DODGE
DODGED
DODGEMS
DODGER
DODGERIES
DODGERS
DODGERY
DODGES
DODGIER
DODGIEST
DODGING
DODGINGS
DODGY
DODKIN
DODKINS
DODMAN
DODMANS
DODO
DODOES
DODOS
DODS
DOE
DOEK
DOEKS
DOEN
DOER
DOERS
DOES
DOEST
DOETH
DOFF
DOFFED
DOFFER
DOFFERS
DOFFING
DOFFS
DOG
DOGARESSA
DOGARESSAS
DOGATE
DOGATES
DOGBANE
DOGBANES
DOGBERRIES
DOGBERRY
DOGBOLT
DOGBOLTS
DOGCART
DOGCARTS
DOGDAYS
DOGE
DOGEATE
DOGEATES
DOGES
DOGESHIP
DOGESHIPS
DOGFIGHT
DOGFIGHTS
DOGFISH
DOGFISHES
DOGFOX
DOGFOXES
DOGGED
DOGGEDER
DOGGEDEST
DOGGEDLY
DOGGER
DOGGEREL
DOGGERELS
DOGGERIES
DOGGERMAN
DOGGERMEN
DOGGERS
DOGGERY
DOGGESS
DOGGESSES
DOGGIE
DOGGIER
DOGGIES
DOGGIEST
DOGGINESS
DOGGINESSES
DOGGING
DOGGINGS
DOGGISH
DOGGISHLY
DOGGO

DOGGONE
DOGGONED
DOGGONEDER
DOGGONEDEST
DOGGONER
DOGGONEST
DOGGREL
DOGGRELS
DOGGY
DOGHOLE
DOGHOLES
DOGIE
DOGIES
DOGMA
DOGMAS
DOGMATIC
DOGMATICS
DOGMATISE
DOGMATISED
DOGMATISES
DOGMATISING
DOGMATISM
DOGMATISMS
DOGMATIST
DOGMATISTS
DOGMATIZE
DOGMATIZED
DOGMATIZES
DOGMATIZING
DOGMATORY
DOGS
DOGSBODIES
DOGSBODY
DOGSHIP
DOGSHIPS
DOGSHORES
DOGSKIN
DOGSKINS
DOGSLED
DOGSLEDS
DOGSLEEP
DOGSLEEPS
DOGTEETH
DOGTOOTH
DOGTOWN
DOGTOWNS
DOGTROT
DOGTROTS
DOGVANE
DOGVANES
DOGWOOD
DOGWOODS
DOGY
DOH
DOHS
DOHYO
DOHYOS
DOILED
DOILIES
DOILT
DOILTER
DOILTEST
DOILY
DOING
DOINGS
DOIT
DOITED
DOITIT
DOITKIN
DOITKINS
DOITS
DOJO
DOJOS
DOLCE
DOLCES
DOLDRUMS
DOLE
DOLED
DOLEFUL
DOLEFULLY
DOLENT
DOLERITE
DOLERITES
DOLERITIC
DOLES
DOLESOME
DOLIA
DOLICHOS
DOLICHOSES
DOLICHURI
DOLINA
DOLINAS
DOLINE
DOLINES
DOLING
DOLIUM
DOLL
DOLLAR
DOLLARED
DOLLARS
DOLLDOM
DOLLDOMS
DOLLED
DOLLHOOD
DOLLHOODS
DOLLIED
DOLLIER
DOLLIERS
DOLLIES
DOLLINESS
DOLLINESSES
DOLLING
DOLLISH
DOLLOP
DOLLOPS
DOLLS
DOLLY
DOLLYING
DOLMA
DOLMADES
DOLMAN
DOLMANS
DOLMAS
DOLMEN
DOLMENS
DOLOMITE
DOLOMITES
DOLOMITIC
DOLOR
DOLORIFIC
DOLOROSO
DOLOROUS
DOLORS
DOLOUR
DOLOURS
DOLPHIN
DOLPHINET
DOLPHINETS
DOLPHINS
DOLT
DOLTISH
DOLTISHLY
DOLTS
DOMAIN
DOMAINAL
DOMAINS
DOMAL
DOMANIAL
DOMATIA
DOMATIUM
DOME
DOMED
DOMES
DOMESTIC
DOMESTICS
DOMETT
DOMETTS
DOMICAL
DOMICIL
DOMICILE
DOMICILED
DOMICILES
DOMICILING
DOMICILS
DOMIER
DOMIEST
DOMINANCE
DOMINANCES
DOMINANCIES
DOMINANCY
DOMINANT
DOMINANTS
DOMINATE
DOMINATED
DOMINATES
DOMINATING
DOMINATOR
DOMINATORS
DOMINEE
DOMINEER
DOMINEERED
DOMINEERING
DOMINEERS
DOMINEES
DOMING
DOMINICAL
DOMINIE
DOMINIES
DOMINION
DOMINIONS
DOMINO
DOMINOES
DOMINOS
DOMY
DON
DONA
DONAH
DONAHS
DONARIES
DONARY
DONAS
DONATARIES
DONATARY
DONATE
DONATED
DONATES
DONATING
DONATION
DONATIONS
DONATISM
DONATISMS
DONATIVE
DONATIVES
DONATOR
DONATORIES
DONATORS
DONATORY
DONDER
DONDERED
DONDERING
DONDERS
DONE
DONEE
DONEES
DONENESS
DONENESSES
DONG
DONGA
DONGAS
DONGED
DONGING
DONGLE
DONGLES
DONGS
DONING
DONINGS
DONJON
DONJONS
DONKEY
DONKEYS
DONNARD
DONNART
DONNAT
DONNATS
DONNE
DONNED
DONNEE
DONNEES
DONNERD
DONNERED
DONNERT
DONNES
DONNING
DONNISH
DONNISM
DONNISMS
DONNOT
DONNOTS
DONOR
DONORS
DONS
DONSHIP
DONSHIPS
DONSIE
DONSIER
DONSIEST
DONUT
DONUTS
DONUTTED
DONUTTING
DONZEL
DONZELS
DOO
DOOB
DOOBS
DOOCOT
DOOCOTS
DOODAD
DOODADS
DOODAH
DOODAHS
DOODLE
DOODLEBUG
DOODLEBUGS
DOODLED
DOODLER
DOODLERS
DOODLES
DOODLING
DOOFER
DOOFERS
DOOK
DOOKED
DOOKET
DOOKETS
DOOKING
DOOKS
DOOL
DOOLALLY
DOOLE
DOOLES
DOOLIE
DOOLIES
DOOLS
DOOM
DOOMED
DOOMFUL
DOOMIER
DOOMIEST
DOOMING
DOOMS
DOOMSAYER
DOOMSAYERS
DOOMSDAY
DOOMSDAYS
DOOMSMAN
DOOMSMEN
DOOMSTER
DOOMSTERS
DOOMWATCH

OOMWATCHED
OOMWATCHES
OOMWATCHING
OOMWATCHINGS
OOMY
OONA
OONAS
OOR
OORBELL
OORBELLS
OORKNOB
OORKNOBS
OORKNOCK
OORKNOCKED
OORKNOCKING
OORKNOCKS
OORMAT
OORMATS
OORN
OORNAIL
OORNAILS
OORNS
OORPOST
OORPOSTS
OORS
OORSMAN
OORSMEN
OORSTEP
OORSTEPPED
OORSTEPPING
OORSTEPPINGS
OORSTEPS
OORSTONE
OORSTONES
OORSTOP
OORSTOPS
OORWAY
OORWAYS
OOS
OP
OPA
OPAMINE
OPAMINES
OPANT
OPANTS
OPAS
OPATTA
OPATTAS
OPE
OPED
OPER
OPERS
OPES
OPEY
OPIER
OPIEST
OPINESS
OPINESSES
OPING
OPINGS
OPPED
OPPER
OPPERS
OPPIE
DOPPIES
DOPPING
DOPPINGS
DOPS
DOPY
DOR
DORAD
DORADO
DORADOS
DORADS
DOREE
DOREES
DORHAWK
DORHAWKS
DORIDOID
DORIDOIDS
DORIES
DORISE
DORISED
DORISES
DORISING
DORIZE
DORIZED
DORIZES
DORIZING
DORK
DORKIER
DORKIEST
DORKS
DORKY
DORLACH
DORLACHS
DORM
DORMANCIES
DORMANCY
DORMANT
DORMANTS
DORMER
DORMERS
DORMICE
DORMIE
DORMIENT
DORMITION
DORMITIONS
DORMITIVE
DORMITIVES
DORMITORIES
DORMITORY
DORMOUSE
DORMS
DORMY
DORNICK
DORNICKS
DORONICUM
DORONICUMS
DORP
DORPS
DORR
DORRED
DORRING
DORRS
DORS
DORSA
DORSAL
DORSALLY
DORSALS
DORSE
DORSEL
DORSELS
DORSER
DORSERS
DORSES
DORSIFLEX
DORSUM
DORT
DORTED
DORTER
DORTERS
DORTIER
DORTIEST
DORTING
DORTOUR
DORTOURS
DORTS
DORTY
DORY
DOS
DOSAGE
DOSAGES
DOSE
DOSED
DOSEH
DOSEHS
DOSES
DOSH
DOSHES
DOSIMETER
DOSIMETERS
DOSIMETRIES
DOSIMETRY
DOSING
DOSIOLOGIES
DOSIOLOGY
DOSOLOGIES
DOSOLOGY
DOSS
DOSSAL
DOSSALS
DOSSED
DOSSEL
DOSSELS
DOSSER
DOSSERS
DOSSES
DOSSHOUSE
DOSSHOUSES
DOSSIER
DOSSIERS
DOSSIL
DOSSILS
DOSSING
DOST
DOT
DOTAGE
DOTAGES
DOTAL
DOTANT
DOTANTS
DOTARD
DOTARDS
DOTATION
DOTATIONS
DOTE
DOTED
DOTER
DOTERS
DOTES
DOTH
DOTIER
DOTIEST
DOTING
DOTINGLY
DOTINGS
DOTISH
DOTS
DOTTED
DOTTEREL
DOTTERELS
DOTTIER
DOTTIEST
DOTTINESS
DOTTINESSES
DOTTING
DOTTIPOLL
DOTTIPOLLS
DOTTLE
DOTTLED
DOTTLER
DOTTLES
DOTTLEST
DOTTREL
DOTTRELS
DOTTY
DOTY
DOUANE
DOUANES
DOUANIER
DOUANIERS
DOUAR
DOUARS
DOUBLE
DOUBLED
DOUBLER
DOUBLERS
DOUBLES
DOUBLET
DOUBLETON
DOUBLETONS
DOUBLETS
DOUBLING
DOUBLINGS
DOUBLOON
DOUBLOONS
DOUBLY
DOUBT
DOUBTABLE
DOUBTED
DOUBTER
DOUBTERS
DOUBTFUL
DOUBTFULS
DOUBTING
DOUBTINGS
DOUBTLESS
DOUBTS
DOUC
DOUCE
DOUCELY
DOUCENESS
DOUCENESSES
DOUCEPERE
DOUCEPERES
DOUCER
DOUCEST
DOUCET
DOUCETS
DOUCEUR
DOUCEURS
DOUCHE
DOUCHED
DOUCHES
DOUCHING
DOUCINE
DOUCINES
DOUCS
DOUGH
DOUGHIER
DOUGHIEST
DOUGHNUT
DOUGHNUTS
DOUGHNUTTED
DOUGHNUTTING
DOUGHNUTTINGS
DOUGHS
DOUGHT
DOUGHTIER
DOUGHTIEST
DOUGHTILY
DOUGHTY
DOUGHY
DOULEIA
DOULEIAS
DOUMA
DOUMAS
DOUP
DOUPS
DOUR
DOURA
DOURAS
DOURER
DOUREST
DOURINE
DOURINES
DOURLY
DOURNESS
DOURNESSES
DOUSE
DOUSED
DOUSER
DOUSERS
DOUSES
DOUSING
DOUT
DOUTED
DOUTER
DOUTERS

DOUTING
DOUTS
DOUZEPER
DOUZEPERS
DOVE
DOVECOT
DOVECOTS
DOVED
DOVEISH
DOVEKIE
DOVEKIES
DOVELET
DOVELETS
DOVELIKE
DOVER
DOVERED
DOVERING
DOVERS
DOVES
DOVETAIL
DOVETAILED
DOVETAILING
DOVETAILINGS
DOVETAILS
DOVIE
DOVIER
DOVIEST
DOVING
DOVISH
DOW
DOWABLE
DOWAGER
DOWAGERS
DOWAR
DOWARS
DOWD
DOWDIER
DOWDIES
DOWDIEST
DOWDILY
DOWDINESS
DOWDINESSES
DOWDS
DOWDY
DOWDYISH
DOWDYISM
DOWDYISMS
DOWED
DOWEL
DOWELLED
DOWELLING
DOWELLINGS
DOWELS
DOWER
DOWERED
DOWERING
DOWERLESS
DOWERS
DOWF
DOWFNESS
DOWFNESSES
DOWIE
DOWIER
DOWIEST
DOWING
DOWITCHER
DOWITCHERS
DOWL
DOWLAS
DOWLASES
DOWLE
DOWLES
DOWLNE
DOWLNES
DOWLNEY
DOWLS
DOWN
DOWNA
DOWNBEAT
DOWNBEATS
DOWNBOW
DOWNBOWS
DOWNBURST
DOWNBURSTS
DOWNCAST
DOWNCASTS
DOWNED
DOWNER
DOWNERS
DOWNFALL
DOWNFALLS
DOWNFLOW
DOWNFLOWS
DOWNFORCE
DOWNFORCES
DOWNGRADE
DOWNGRADED
DOWNGRADES
DOWNGRADING
DOWNHILL
DOWNHILLS
DOWNHOLE
DOWNIER
DOWNIEST
DOWNINESS
DOWNINESSES
DOWNING
DOWNLAND
DOWNLANDS
DOWNLOAD
DOWNLOADED
DOWNLOADING
DOWNLOADS
DOWNMOST
DOWNPIPE
DOWNPIPES
DOWNPLAY
DOWNPLAYED
DOWNPLAYING
DOWNPLAYS
DOWNPOUR
DOWNPOURS
DOWNRIGHT
DOWNRUSH
DOWNRUSHES
DOWNS
DOWNSHIFT
DOWNSHIFTED
DOWNSHIFTING
DOWNSHIFTS
DOWNSIDE
DOWNSIDES
DOWNSIZE
DOWNSIZED
DOWNSIZES
DOWNSIZING
DOWNSPOUT
DOWNSPOUTS
DOWNSTAGE
DOWNSTAIR
DOWNSTAIRS
DOWNSWING
DOWNSWINGS
DOWNTIME
DOWNTIMES
DOWNTREND
DOWNTRENDS
DOWNTURN
DOWNTURNS
DOWNWARD
DOWNWARDS
DOWNWIND
DOWNY
DOWP
DOWPS
DOWRIES
DOWRY
DOWS
DOWSE
DOWSED
DOWSER
DOWSERS
DOWSES
DOWSET
DOWSETS
DOWSING
DOWT
DOWTS
DOXIES
DOXOLOGIES
DOXOLOGY
DOXY
DOYEN
DOYENNE
DOYENNES
DOYENS
DOYLEY
DOYLEYS
DOYLIES
DOYLY
DOZE
DOZED
DOZEN
DOZENED
DOZENING
DOZENS
DOZENTH
DOZENTHS
DOZER
DOZERS
DOZES
DOZIER
DOZIEST
DOZINESS
DOZINESSES
DOZING
DOZINGS
DOZY
DRAB
DRABBED
DRABBER
DRABBERS
DRABBEST
DRABBET
DRABBETS
DRABBIER
DRABBIEST
DRABBING
DRABBISH
DRABBLE
DRABBLED
DRABBLER
DRABBLERS
DRABBLES
DRABBLING
DRABBLINGS
DRABBY
DRABETTE
DRABETTES
DRABLER
DRABLERS
DRABLY
DRABNESS
DRABNESSES
DRABS
DRACHM
DRACHMA
DRACHMAE
DRACHMAI
DRACHMAS
DRACHMS
DRACONE
DRACONES
DRACONIAN
DRACONIC
DRACONISM
DRACONISMS
DRACONTIC
DRAD
DRAFF
DRAFFIER
DRAFFIEST
DRAFFISH
DRAFFS
DRAFFY
DRAFT
DRAFTED
DRAFTEE
DRAFTEES
DRAFTER
DRAFTERS
DRAFTIER
DRAFTIEST
DRAFTING
DRAFTS
DRAFTSMAN
DRAFTSMEN
DRAFTY
DRAG
DRAGEE
DRAGEES
DRAGGED
DRAGGIER
DRAGGIEST
DRAGGING
DRAGGLE
DRAGGLED
DRAGGLES
DRAGGLING
DRAGGY
DRAGHOUND
DRAGHOUNDS
DRAGLINE
DRAGLINES
DRAGNET
DRAGNETS
DRAGOMAN
DRAGOMANS
DRAGON
DRAGONESS
DRAGONESSES
DRAGONET
DRAGONETS
DRAGONFLIES
DRAGONFLY
DRAGONISE
DRAGONISED
DRAGONISES
DRAGONISH
DRAGONISING
DRAGONISM
DRAGONISMS
DRAGONIZE
DRAGONIZED
DRAGONIZES
DRAGONIZING
DRAGONNE
DRAGONS
DRAGOON
DRAGOONED
DRAGOONING
DRAGOONS
DRAGS
DRAGSMAN
DRAGSMEN
DRAGSTER
DRAGSTERS
DRAIL
DRAILED
DRAILING
DRAILS
DRAIN
DRAINABLE
DRAINAGE
DRAINAGES
DRAINED
DRAINER
DRAINERS
DRAINING
DRAINPIPE

DRAINPIPES
DRAINS
DRAISENE
DRAISENES
DRAISINE
DRAISINES
DRAKE
DRAKES
DRAM
DRAMA
DRAMAS
DRAMATIC
DRAMATICS
DRAMATISE
DRAMATISED
DRAMATISES
DRAMATISING
DRAMATIST
DRAMATISTS
DRAMATIZE
DRAMATIZED
DRAMATIZES
DRAMATIZING
DRAMATURG
DRAMATURGS
DRAMMACH
DRAMMACHS
DRAMMED
DRAMMING
DRAMMOCK
DRAMMOCKS
DRAMS
DRANK
DRANT
DRANTED
DRANTING
DRANTS
DRAP
DRAPE
DRAPED
DRAPER
DRAPERIED
DRAPERIES
DRAPERS
DRAPERY
DRAPERYING
DRAPES
DRAPET
DRAPETS
DRAPIER
DRAPIERS
DRAPING
DRAPPED
DRAPPIE
DRAPPIES
DRAPPING
DRAPPY
DRAPS
DRASTIC
DRASTICS
DRAT
DRATCHELL
DRATCHELLS
DRATTED
DRAUGHT
DRAUGHTED
DRAUGHTER
DRAUGHTERS
DRAUGHTIER
DRAUGHTIEST
DRAUGHTING
DRAUGHTS
DRAUGHTY
DRAUNT
DRAUNTED
DRAUNTING
DRAUNTS
DRAVE
DRAW
DRAWABLE
DRAWBACK
DRAWBACKS
DRAWBAR
DRAWBARS
DRAWEE
DRAWEES
DRAWER
DRAWERS
DRAWING
DRAWINGS
DRAWL
DRAWLED
DRAWLER
DRAWLERS
DRAWLING
DRAWLS
DRAWN
DRAWS
DRAY
DRAYAGE
DRAYAGES
DRAYMAN
DRAYMEN
DRAYS
DRAZEL
DRAZELS
DREAD
DREADED
DREADER
DREADERS
DREADFUL
DREADING
DREADLESS
DREADLY
DREADS
DREAM
DREAMBOAT
DREAMBOATS
DREAMED
DREAMER
DREAMERIES
DREAMERS
DREAMERY
DREAMFUL
DREAMHOLE
DREAMHOLES
DREAMIER
DREAMIEST
DREAMILY
DREAMING
DREAMINGS
DREAMLESS
DREAMS
DREAMT
DREAMTIME
DREAMTIMES
DREAMY
DREAR
DREARE
DREARER
DREARES
DREAREST
DREARIER
DREARIEST
DREARILY
DREARING
DREARINGS
DREARS
DREARY
DRECK
DRECKIER
DRECKIEST
DRECKS
DRECKY
DREDGE
DREDGED
DREDGER
DREDGERS
DREDGES
DREDGING
DREE
DREED
DREEING
DREES
DREG
DREGGIER
DREGGIEST
DREGGY
DREGS
DREICH
DREICHER
DREICHEST
DREK
DREKS
DRENCH
DRENCHED
DRENCHER
DRENCHERS
DRENCHES
DRENCHING
DRENT
DREPANIUM
DREPANIUMS
DRERE
DRERES
DRERIHEAD
DRERIHEADS
DRESS
DRESSAGE
DRESSAGES
DRESSED
DRESSER
DRESSERS
DRESSES
DRESSIER
DRESSIEST
DRESSING
DRESSINGS
DRESSMADE
DRESSMAKE
DRESSMAKES
DRESSMAKING
DRESSMAKINGS
DRESSY
DREST
DREVILL
DREVILLS
DREW
DREY
DREYS
DRIB
DRIBBED
DRIBBER
DRIBBERS
DRIBBING
DRIBBLE
DRIBBLED
DRIBBLER
DRIBBLERS
DRIBBLES
DRIBBLET
DRIBBLETS
DRIBBLIER
DRIBBLIEST
DRIBBLING
DRIBBLY
DRIBLET
DRIBLETS
DRIBS
DRICE
DRICES
DRICKSIE
DRICKSIER
DRICKSIEST
DRIED
DRIER
DRIERS
DRIES
DRIEST
DRIFT
DRIFTAGE
DRIFTAGES
DRIFTED
DRIFTER
DRIFTERS
DRIFTIER
DRIFTIEST
DRIFTING
DRIFTLESS
DRIFTPIN
DRIFTPINS
DRIFTS
DRIFTWOOD
DRIFTWOODS
DRIFTY
DRILL
DRILLED
DRILLER
DRILLERS
DRILLING
DRILLINGS
DRILLS
DRILLSHIP
DRILLSHIPS
DRILY
DRINK
DRINKABLE
DRINKER
DRINKERS
DRINKING
DRINKINGS
DRINKS
DRIP
DRIPPED
DRIPPIER
DRIPPIEST
DRIPPING
DRIPPINGS
DRIPPY
DRIPS
DRISHEEN
DRISHEENS
DRIVABLE
DRIVE
DRIVEABLE
DRIVEL
DRIVELLED
DRIVELLER
DRIVELLERS
DRIVELLING
DRIVELS
DRIVEN
DRIVER
DRIVERS
DRIVES
DRIVEWAY
DRIVEWAYS
DRIVING
DRIZZLE
DRIZZLED
DRIZZLES
DRIZZLIER
DRIZZLIEST
DRIZZLING
DRIZZLY
DROGER
DROGERS
DROGHER
DROGHERS
DROGUE
DROGUES
DROGUET
DROGUETS
DROICH
DROICHIER
DROICHIEST
DROICHS
DROICHY
DROIL
DROILED

DROILING
DROILS
DROIT
DROITS
DROLE
DROLER
DROLES
DROLEST
DROLL
DROLLED
DROLLER
DROLLERIES
DROLLERY
DROLLEST
DROLLING
DROLLINGS
DROLLISH
DROLLNESS
DROLLNESSES
DROLLS
DROLLY
DROME
DROMEDARE
DROMEDARES
DROMEDARIES
DROMEDARY
DROMES
DROMIC
DROMICAL
DROMOI
DROMON
DROMOND
DROMONDS
DROMONS
DROMOS
DRONE
DRONED
DRONES
DRONGO
DRONGOES
DRONGOS
DRONIER
DRONIEST
DRONING
DRONINGLY
DRONISH
DRONISHLY
DRONY
DROOG
DROOGISH
DROOGS
DROOK
DROOKED
DROOKING
DROOKINGS
DROOKIT
DROOKS
DROOL
DROOLED
DROOLING
DROOLS
DROOME
DROOMES
DROOP
DROOPED
DROOPIER
DROOPIEST
DROOPILY
DROOPING
DROOPS
DROOPY
DROP
DROPFLIES
DROPFLY
DROPLET
DROPLETS
DROPOUT
DROPOUTS
DROPPED
DROPPER
DROPPERS
DROPPING
DROPPINGS
DROPPLE
DROPPLES
DROPS
DROPSICAL
DROPSIED
DROPSIES
DROPSTONE
DROPSTONES
DROPSY
DROPWISE
DROSERA
DROSERAS
DROSHKIES
DROSHKY
DROSKIES
DROSKY
DROSS
DROSSES
DROSSIER
DROSSIEST
DROSSY
DROSTDIES
DROSTDY
DROSTDYS
DROUGHT
DROUGHTIER
DROUGHTIEST
DROUGHTS
DROUGHTY
DROUK
DROUKED
DROUKING
DROUKINGS
DROUKIT
DROUKS
DROUTH
DROUTHIER
DROUTHIEST
DROUTHS
DROUTHY
DROVE
DROVER
DROVERS
DROVES
DROVING
DROVINGS
DROW
DROWN
DROWNDED
DROWNED
DROWNER
DROWNERS
DROWNING
DROWNINGS
DROWNS
DROWS
DROWSE
DROWSED
DROWSES
DROWSIER
DROWSIEST
DROWSIHED
DROWSIHEDS
DROWSILY
DROWSING
DROWSY
DRUB
DRUBBED
DRUBBING
DRUBBINGS
DRUBS
DRUCKEN
DRUDGE
DRUDGED
DRUDGER
DRUDGERIES
DRUDGERS
DRUDGERY
DRUDGES
DRUDGING
DRUDGISM
DRUDGISMS
DRUG
DRUGGED
DRUGGER
DRUGGERS
DRUGGET
DRUGGETS
DRUGGIE
DRUGGIER
DRUGGIES
DRUGGIEST
DRUGGING
DRUGGIST
DRUGGISTS
DRUGGY
DRUGS
DRUID
DRUIDESS
DRUIDESSES
DRUIDIC
DRUIDICAL
DRUIDISM
DRUIDISMS
DRUIDS
DRUM
DRUMBEAT
DRUMBEATS
DRUMBLE
DRUMBLED
DRUMBLES
DRUMBLING
DRUMFIRE
DRUMFIRES
DRUMFISH
DRUMFISHES
DRUMHEAD
DRUMHEADS
DRUMLIER
DRUMLIEST
DRUMLIN
DRUMLINS
DRUMLY
DRUMMED
DRUMMER
DRUMMERS
DRUMMING
DRUMMOCK
DRUMMOCKS
DRUMS
DRUMSTICK
DRUMSTICKS
DRUNK
DRUNKARD
DRUNKARDS
DRUNKEN
DRUNKENLY
DRUNKER
DRUNKEST
DRUNKS
DRUPE
DRUPEL
DRUPELET
DRUPELETS
DRUPELS
DRUPES
DRUSE
DRUSES
DRUSIER
DRUSIEST
DRUSY
DRUTHERS
DRUXIER
DRUXIEST
DRUXY
DRY
DRYAD
DRYADES
DRYADS
DRYBEAT
DRYBEATEN
DRYBEATING
DRYBEATS
DRYER
DRYERS
DRYING
DRYINGS
DRYISH
DRYLY
DRYMOUTH
DRYMOUTHS
DRYNESS
DRYNESSES
DRYSALTER
DRYSALTERS
DSO
DSOBO
DSOBOS
DSOMO
DSOMOS
DSOS
DUAD
DUADS
DUAL
DUALIN
DUALINS
DUALISM
DUALISMS
DUALIST
DUALISTIC
DUALISTS
DUALITIES
DUALITY
DUALLED
DUALLING
DUALLY
DUALS
DUAN
DUANS
DUAR
DUARCHIES
DUARCHY
DUARS
DUB
DUBBED
DUBBIN
DUBBING
DUBBINGS
DUBBINS
DUBIETIES
DUBIETY
DUBIOSITIES
DUBIOSITY
DUBIOUS
DUBIOUSLY
DUBITABLE
DUBITABLY
DUBITANCIES
DUBITANCY
DUBITATE
DUBITATED
DUBITATES
DUBITATING
DUBS
DUCAL
DUCALLY
DUCAT
DUCATOON
DUCATOONS
DUCATS
DUCDAME
DUCE
DUCES
DUCHESS
DUCHESSE
DUCHESSES
DUCHIES

DUCHY
DUCK
DUCKBILL
DUCKBILLS
DUCKED
DUCKER
DUCKERS
DUCKIER
DUCKIES
DUCKIEST
DUCKING
DUCKINGS
DUCKLING
DUCKLINGS
DUCKMOLE
DUCKMOLES
DUCKS
DUCKSHOVE
DUCKSHOVED
DUCKSHOVES
DUCKSHOVING
DUCKWEED
DUCKWEEDS
DUCKY
DUCT
DUCTED
DUCTILE
DUCTILITIES
DUCTILITY
DUCTING
DUCTLESS
DUCTS
DUD
DUDDER
DUDDERIES
DUDDERS
DUDDERY
DUDDIE
DUDDIER
DUDDIEST
DUDDY
DUDE
DUDEEN
DUDEENS
DUDES
DUDGEON
DUDGEONS
DUDHEEN
DUDHEENS
DUDISH
DUDISM
DUDISMS
DUDS
DUE
DUED
DUEFUL
DUEL
DUELLED
DUELLER
DUELLERS
DUELLING
DUELLINGS
DUELLIST
DUELLISTS
DUELLO
DUELLOS
DUELS
DUELSOME
DUENDE
DUENDES
DUENNA
DUENNAS
DUES
DUET
DUETS
DUETT
DUETTED
DUETTI
DUETTING
DUETTINO
DUETTINOS
DUETTIST
DUETTISTS
DUETTO
DUETTOS
DUETTS
DUFF
DUFFED
DUFFEL
DUFFELS
DUFFER
DUFFERDOM
DUFFERDOMS
DUFFERISM
DUFFERISMS
DUFFERS
DUFFEST
DUFFING
DUFFINGS
DUFFLE
DUFFLES
DUFFS
DUG
DUGONG
DUGONGS
DUGOUT
DUGOUTS
DUGS
DUIKER
DUIKERS
DUING
DUKE
DUKED
DUKEDOM
DUKEDOMS
DUKELING
DUKELINGS
DUKERIES
DUKERY
DUKES
DUKESHIP
DUKESHIPS
DUKING
DULCAMARA
DULCAMARAS
DULCET
DULCIAN
DULCIANA
DULCIANAS
DULCIANS
DULCIFIED
DULCIFIES
DULCIFY
DULCIFYING
DULCIMER
DULCIMERS
DULCITE
DULCITES
DULCITOL
DULCITOLS
DULCITUDE
DULCITUDES
DULCOSE
DULCOSES
DULE
DULES
DULIA
DULIAS
DULL
DULLARD
DULLARDS
DULLED
DULLER
DULLEST
DULLIER
DULLIEST
DULLING
DULLISH
DULLNESS
DULLNESSES
DULLS
DULLY
DULNESS
DULNESSES
DULOCRACIES
DULOCRACY
DULOSES
DULOSIS
DULOTIC
DULSE
DULSES
DULY
DUMA
DUMAIST
DUMAISTS
DUMAS
DUMB
DUMBED
DUMBER
DUMBEST
DUMBFOUND
DUMBFOUNDED
DUMBFOUNDING
DUMBFOUNDS
DUMBING
DUMBLY
DUMBNESS
DUMBNESSES
DUMBO
DUMBOS
DUMBS
DUMDUM
DUMDUMS
DUMFOUND
DUMFOUNDED
DUMFOUNDING
DUMFOUNDS
DUMKA
DUMKY
DUMMERER
DUMMERERS
DUMMIED
DUMMIER
DUMMIES
DUMMIEST
DUMMINESS
DUMMINESSES
DUMMY
DUMMYING
DUMOSE
DUMOSITIES
DUMOSITY
DUMOUS
DUMP
DUMPBIN
DUMPBINS
DUMPED
DUMPER
DUMPERS
DUMPIER
DUMPIES
DUMPIEST
DUMPINESS
DUMPINESSES
DUMPING
DUMPISH
DUMPISHLY
DUMPLE
DUMPLED
DUMPLES
DUMPLING
DUMPLINGS
DUMPS
DUMPSTER
DUMPSTERS
DUMPY
DUN
DUNCE
DUNCEDOM
DUNCEDOMS
DUNCERIES
DUNCERY
DUNCES
DUNCH
DUNCHED
DUNCHES
DUNCHING
DUNDER
DUNDERS
DUNE
DUNES
DUNG
DUNGAREE
DUNGAREES
DUNGED
DUNGEON
DUNGEONED
DUNGEONER
DUNGEONERS
DUNGEONING
DUNGEONS
DUNGIER
DUNGIEST
DUNGING
DUNGMERE
DUNGMERES
DUNGS
DUNGY
DUNITE
DUNITES
DUNK
DUNKED
DUNKER
DUNKERS
DUNKING
DUNKS
DUNLIN
DUNLINS
DUNNAGE
DUNNAGES
DUNNAKIN
DUNNAKINS
DUNNART
DUNNARTS
DUNNED
DUNNER
DUNNEST
DUNNIER
DUNNIES
DUNNIEST
DUNNING
DUNNINGS
DUNNISH
DUNNITE
DUNNITES
DUNNO
DUNNOCK
DUNNOCKS
DUNNY
DUNS
DUNSH
DUNSHED
DUNSHES
DUNSHING
DUNT
DUNTED
DUNTING
DUNTS
DUO
DUODECIMO
DUODECIMOS
DUODENA
DUODENAL
DUODENARY
DUODENUM
DUOLOGUE
DUOLOGUES
DUOMI
DUOMO
DUOMOS

DUOPOLIES
DUOPOLY
DUOS
DUOTONE
DUOTONES
DUP
DUPABLE
DUPATTA
DUPATTAS
DUPE
DUPED
DUPER
DUPERIES
DUPERS
DUPERY
DUPES
DUPING
DUPION
DUPIONS
DUPLE
DUPLET
DUPLETS
DUPLEX
DUPLEXER
DUPLEXERS
DUPLEXES
DUPLICAND
DUPLICANDS
DUPLICATE
DUPLICATED
DUPLICATES
DUPLICATING
DUPLICITIES
DUPLICITY
DUPLIED
DUPLIES
DUPLY
DUPLYING
DUPONDII
DUPONDIUS
DUPPED
DUPPIES
DUPPING
DUPPY
DUPS
DURA
DURABLE
DURABLES
DURABLY
DURAL
DURALS
DURALUMIN
DURALUMINS
DURAMEN
DURAMENS
DURANCE
DURANCES
DURANT
DURANTS
DURAS
DURATION
DURATIONS
DURBAR
DURBARS
DURDUM
DURDUMS
DURE
DURED
DUREFUL
DURES
DURESS
DURESSE
DURESSES
DURGAN
DURGANS
DURGIER
DURGIEST
DURGY
DURIAN
DURIANS
DURING
DURION
DURIONS
DURMAST
DURMASTS
DURN
DURNS
DURO
DUROS
DUROY
DUROYS
DURRA
DURRAS
DURRIE
DURRIES
DURST
DURUKULI
DURUKULIS
DURUM
DURUMS
DUSH
DUSHED
DUSHES
DUSHING
DUSK
DUSKED
DUSKEN
DUSKENED
DUSKENING
DUSKENS
DUSKER
DUSKEST
DUSKIER
DUSKIEST
DUSKILY
DUSKINESS
DUSKINESSES
DUSKING
DUSKISH
DUSKISHLY
DUSKLY
DUSKNESS
DUSKNESSES
DUSKS
DUSKY
DUST
DUSTBIN
DUSTBINS
DUSTCART
DUSTCARTS
DUSTED
DUSTER
DUSTERS
DUSTIER
DUSTIEST
DUSTILY
DUSTINESS
DUSTINESSES
DUSTING
DUSTLESS
DUSTMAN
DUSTMEN
DUSTPROOF
DUSTS
DUSTSHEET
DUSTSHEETS
DUSTY
DUTCH
DUTCHES
DUTEOUS
DUTEOUSLY
DUTIABLE
DUTIED
DUTIES
DUTIFUL
DUTIFULLY
DUTY
DUUMVIR
DUUMVIRAL
DUUMVIRI
DUUMVIRS
DUVET
DUVETINE
DUVETINES
DUVETS
DUVETYN
DUVETYNE
DUVETYNES
DUVETYNS
DUX
DUXELLES
DUXES
DUYKER
DUYKERS
DVANDVA
DVANDVAS
DVORNIK
DVORNIKS
DWALE
DWALES
DWALM
DWALMED
DWALMING
DWALMS
DWAM
DWAMMED
DWAMMING
DWAMS
DWANG
DWANGS
DWARF
DWARFED
DWARFER
DWARFEST
DWARFING
DWARFISH
DWARFISM
DWARFISMS
DWARFS
DWARVES
DWAUM
DWAUMED
DWAUMING
DWAUMS
DWEEB
DWEEBS
DWELL
DWELLED
DWELLER
DWELLERS
DWELLING
DWELLINGS
DWELLS
DWELT
DWILE
DWILES
DWINDLE
DWINDLED
DWINDLES
DWINDLING
DWINE
DWINED
DWINES
DWINING
DYABLE
DYAD
DYADIC
DYADS
DYARCHIES
DYARCHY
DYBBUK
DYBBUKIM
DYBBUKS
DYE
DYEABLE
DYED
DYEING
DYEINGS
DYELINE
DYELINES
DYER
DYERS
DYES
DYESTER
DYESTERS
DYESTUFF
DYESTUFFS
DYING
DYINGLY
DYINGNESS
DYINGNESSES
DYINGS
DYKE
DYKED
DYKES
DYKEY
DYKIER
DYKIEST
DYKING
DYNAMIC
DYNAMICAL
DYNAMICS
DYNAMISE
DYNAMISED
DYNAMISES
DYNAMISING
DYNAMISM
DYNAMISMS
DYNAMIST
DYNAMISTS
DYNAMITE
DYNAMITED
DYNAMITER
DYNAMITERS
DYNAMITES
DYNAMITING
DYNAMIZE
DYNAMIZED
DYNAMIZES
DYNAMIZING
DYNAMO
DYNAMOS
DYNAMOTOR
DYNAMOTORS
DYNAST
DYNASTIC
DYNASTIES
DYNASTS
DYNASTY
DYNATRON
DYNATRONS
DYNE
DYNES
DYNODE
DYNODES
DYSCHROA
DYSCHROAS
DYSCHROIA
DYSCHROIAS
DYSCRASIA
DYSCRASIAS
DYSENTERIES
DYSENTERY
DYSGENIC
DYSGENICS
DYSLECTIC
DYSLECTICS
DYSLEXIA
DYSLEXIAS
DYSLEXIC
DYSLEXICS
DYSLOGIES
DYSLOGY
DYSMELIA
DYSMELIAS
DYSMELIC
DYSODIL
DYSODILE
DYSODILES
DYSODILS

YSODYLE
YSODYLES
YSPATHIES
YSPATHY
YSPEPSIA
YSPEPSIAS
YSPEPSIES
YSPEPSY
YSPEPTIC
YSPEPTICS
YSPHAGIA
YSPHAGIAS
YSPHAGIC
YSPHAGIES
YSPHAGY
DYSPHASIA
DYSPHASIAS
DYSPHONIA
DYSPHONIAS
DYSPHONIC
DYSPHORIA
DYSPHORIAS
DYSPHORIC
DYSPLASIA
DYSPLASIAS
DYSPNEA
DYSPNEAL
DYSPNEAS
DYSPNEIC
DYSPNOEA
DYSPNOEAL
DYSPNOEAS
DYSPNOEIC
DYSPRAXIA
DYSPRAXIAS
DYSTECTIC
DYSTHESIA
DYSTHESIAS
DYSTHETIC
DYSTHYMIA
DYSTHYMIAS
DYSTHYMIC
DYSTOCIA
DYSTOCIAS
DYSTONIA
DYSTONIAS
DYSTONIC
DYSTOPIA
DYSTOPIAN
DYSTOPIAS
DYSTROPHIES
DYSTROPHY
DYSURIA
DYSURIAS
DYSURIC
DYSURIES
DYSURY
DYTISCID
DYTISCIDS
DYVOUR
DYVOURIES
DYVOURS
DYVOURY
DZEREN
DZERENS
DZHO
DZHOS
DZIGGETAI
DZIGGETAIS
DZO
DZOS

E

EA
EACH
EACHWHERE
EADISH
EADISHES
EAGER
EAGERER
EAGEREST
EAGERLY
EAGERNESS
EAGERNESSES
EAGERS
EAGLE
EAGLES
EAGLET
EAGLETS
EAGLEWOOD
EAGLEWOODS
EAGRE
EAGRES
EALDORMAN
EALDORMEN
EALE
EALES
EAN
EANED
EANING
EANLING
EANLINGS
EANS
EAR
EARACHE
EARACHES
EARBASH
EARBASHED
EARBASHES
EARBASHING
EARBOB
EARBOBS
EARCON
EARCONS
EARD
EARDED
EARDING
EARDROP
EARDROPS
EARDRUM
EARDRUMS
EARDS
EARED
EARFLAP
EARFLAPS
EARFUL
EARFULS
EARING
EARINGS
EARL
EARLAP
EARLAPS
EARLDOM
EARLDOMS
EARLESS
EARLIER
EARLIES
EARLIEST
EARLINESS
EARLINESSES
EARLOBE
EARLOBES
EARLOCK
EARLOCKS
EARLS
EARLY
EARMARK
EARMARKED
EARMARKING
EARMARKS
EARMUFFS
EARN
EARNED
EARNER
EARNERS
EARNEST
EARNESTLY
EARNESTS
EARNING
EARNINGS
EARNS
EARPHONE
EARPHONES
EARPICK
EARPICKS
EARPIECE
EARPIECES
EARPLUG
EARPLUGS
EARRING
EARRINGS
EARS
EARSHOT
EARSHOTS
EARST
EARTH
EARTHBORN
EARTHED
EARTHEN
EARTHFALL
EARTHFALLS
EARTHFAST
EARTHFLAX
EARTHFLAXES
EARTHIER
EARTHIEST
EARTHING
EARTHLIER
EARTHLIES
EARTHLIEST
EARTHLING
EARTHLINGS
EARTHLY
EARTHMAN
EARTHMEN
EARTHS
EARTHWARD
EARTHWARDS
EARTHWAX
EARTHWAXES
EARTHWOLF
EARTHWOLVES
EARTHWORK
EARTHWORKS
EARTHWORM
EARTHWORMS
EARTHY
EARWAX
EARWAXES
EARWIG
EARWIGGED
EARWIGGING
EARWIGGY
EARWIGS
EAS
EASE
EASED
EASEFUL
EASEL
EASELESS
EASELS
EASEMENT
EASEMENTS
EASES
EASIER
EASIEST
EASILY
EASINESS
EASINESSES
EASING
EASLE
EASLES
EASSEL
EASSIL
EAST
EASTBOUND
EASTED
EASTER
EASTERLIES
EASTERLY
EASTERN
EASTERNER
EASTERNERS
EASTING
EASTINGS
EASTLAND
EASTLIN
EASTLING
EASTLINGS
EASTLINS
EASTMOST
EASTS
EASTWARD
EASTWARDS
EASY
EAT
EATABLE
EATABLES
EATAGE
EATAGES
EATCHE
EATCHES
EATEN
EATER
EATERIES
EATERS
EATERY
EATH
EATHE
EATHLY
EATING
EATINGS
EATS
EAU
EAUS
EAUX
EAVES
EAVESDRIP
EAVESDRIPS
EAVESDROP
EAVESDROPPED
EAVESDROPPING
EAVESDROPPINGS
EAVESDROPS
EBAUCHE
EBAUCHES
EBB
EBBED
EBBING
EBBLESS
EBBS
EBBTIDE
EBBTIDES
EBENEZER
EBENEZERS
EBENISTE
EBENISTES
EBIONISE
EBIONISED
EBIONISES
EBIONISING
EBIONISM
EBIONISMS
EBIONITIC
EBIONIZE
EBIONIZED
EBIONIZES
EBIONIZING
EBON
EBONICS
EBONIES
EBONISE
EBONISED
EBONISES
EBONISING
EBONIST
EBONISTS
EBONITE
EBONITES
EBONIZE
EBONIZED
EBONIZES
EBONIZING
EBONS
EBONY
EBRIATE
EBRIATED
EBRIETIES
EBRIETY
EBRILLADE
EBRILLADES
EBRIOSE
EBRIOSITIES
EBRIOSITY
EBULLIENT
EBURNEAN
EBURNEOUS
ECAD
ECADS
ECARTE
ECARTES
ECAUDATE
ECBOLE

CBOLES
CBOLIC
CBOLICS
CCE
CCENTRIC
CCENTRICS
CCLESIA
CCLESIAE
CCLESIAL
CCO
CCRINE
CCRISES
CCRISIS
CCRITIC
CCRITICS
CDYSES
CDYSIAST
CDYSIASTS
CDYSIS
CH
CHAPPE
CHAPPES
CHE
CHED
CHELON
CHELONS
CHES
CHEVERIA
CHEVERIAS
CHIDNA
CHIDNAS
CHIDNINE
CHIDNINES
CHINATE
CHINATED
CHING
CHINI
CHINOID
CHINOIDS
CHINUS
CHINUSES
CHO
CHOED
CHOER
CHOERS
CHOES
CHOGRAM
CHOGRAMS
CHOIC
CHOING
CHOISE
CHOISED
CHOISES
CHOISING
CHOISM
CHOISMS
CHOIST
CHOISTS
CHOIZE
CHOIZED
CHOIZES
CHOIZING
CHOLALIA
CHOLALIAS

ECHOLESS
ECHT
ECLAIR
ECLAIRS
ECLAMPSIA
ECLAMPSIAS
ECLAMPSIES
ECLAMPSY
ECLAMPTIC
ECLAT
ECLATS
ECLECTIC
ECLECTICS
ECLIPSE
ECLIPSED
ECLIPSES
ECLIPSING
ECLIPTIC
ECLIPTICS
ECLOGITE
ECLOGITES
ECLOGUE
ECLOGUES
ECLOSE
ECLOSED
ECLOSES
ECLOSING
ECLOSION
ECLOSIONS
ECOCIDE
ECOCIDES
ECOD
ECOFREAK
ECOFREAKS
ECOLOGIC
ECOLOGIES
ECOLOGIST
ECOLOGISTS
ECOLOGY
ECONOMIC
ECONOMICS
ECONOMIES
ECONOMISE
ECONOMISED
ECONOMISES
ECONOMISING
ECONOMISM
ECONOMISMS
ECONOMIST
ECONOMISTS
ECONOMIZE
ECONOMIZED
ECONOMIZES
ECONOMIZING
ECONOMY
ECONUT
ECONUTS
ECOPHOBIA
ECOPHOBIAS
ECORCHE
ECORCHES
ECOSPHERE
ECOSPHERES
ECOSSAISE

ECOSSAISES
ECOSTATE
ECOSYSTEM
ECOSYSTEMS
ECOTOXIC
ECOTYPE
ECOTYPES
ECRASEUR
ECRASEURS
ECRITOIRE
ECRITOIRES
ECRU
ECRUS
ECSTASES
ECSTASIED
ECSTASIES
ECSTASIS
ECSTASISE
ECSTASISED
ECSTASISES
ECSTASISING
ECSTASIZE
ECSTASIZED
ECSTASIZES
ECSTASIZING
ECSTASY
ECSTASYING
ECSTATIC
ECSTATICS
ECTASES
ECTASIS
ECTHYMA
ECTHYMAS
ECTOBLAST
ECTOBLASTS
ECTOCRINE
ECTOCRINES
ECTODERM
ECTODERMS
ECTOGENIC
ECTOGENIES
ECTOGENY
ECTOMORPH
ECTOMORPHS
ECTOPHYTE
ECTOPHYTES
ECTOPIA
ECTOPIAS
ECTOPIC
ECTOPIES
ECTOPLASM
ECTOPLASMS
ECTOPY
ECTOSARC
ECTOSARCS
ECTOTHERM
ECTOTHERMS
ECTOZOA
ECTOZOAN
ECTOZOANS
ECTOZOIC
ECTOZOON
ECTROPIC
ECTROPION

ECTROPIONS
ECTROPIUM
ECTROPIUMS
ECTYPAL
ECTYPE
ECTYPES
ECU
ECUELLE
ECUELLES
ECUMENIC
ECUMENICS
ECUMENISM
ECUMENISMS
ECURIE
ECURIES
ECUS
ECZEMA
ECZEMAS
EDACIOUS
EDACITIES
EDACITY
EDAPHIC
EDDIED
EDDIES
EDDISH
EDDISHES
EDDO
EDDOES
EDDY
EDDYING
EDELWEISS
EDELWEISSES
EDEMA
EDEMAS
EDEMATA
EDEMATOSE
EDEMATOUS
EDENTAL
EDENTATE
EDENTATES
EDGE
EDGEBONE
EDGEBONES
EDGED
EDGELESS
EDGER
EDGERS
EDGES
EDGEWAYS
EDGEWISE
EDGIER
EDGIEST
EDGINESS
EDGINESSES
EDGING
EDGINGS
EDGY
EDH
EDHS
EDIBILITIES
EDIBILITY
EDIBLE
EDIBLES
EDICT

EDICTAL
EDICTALLY
EDICTS
EDIFICE
EDIFICES
EDIFICIAL
EDIFIED
EDIFIER
EDIFIERS
EDIFIES
EDIFY
EDIFYING
EDILE
EDILES
EDIT
EDITED
EDITING
EDITION
EDITIONS
EDITOR
EDITORIAL
EDITORIALS
EDITORS
EDITRESS
EDITRESSES
EDITS
EDUCABLE
EDUCATE
EDUCATED
EDUCATES
EDUCATING
EDUCATION
EDUCATIONS
EDUCATIVE
EDUCATOR
EDUCATORS
EDUCATORY
EDUCE
EDUCED
EDUCEMENT
EDUCEMENTS
EDUCES
EDUCIBLE
EDUCING
EDUCT
EDUCTION
EDUCTIONS
EDUCTOR
EDUCTORS
EDUCTS
EDUSKUNTA
EDUSKUNTAS
EE
EECH
EECHED
EECHES
EECHING
EEK
EEL
EELFARE
EELFARES
EELGRASS
EELGRASSES
EELIER

The Chambers Dictionary is the authority for many longer words; see *OSW* Introduction, page xii

EELIEST
EELPOUT
EELPOUTS
EELS
EELWORM
EELWORMS
EELWRACK
EELWRACKS
EELY
EEN
EERIE
EERIER
EERIEST
EERILY
EERINESS
EERINESSES
EERY
EEVEN
EEVENS
EEVN
EEVNING
EEVNINGS
EEVNS
EF
EFF
EFFABLE
EFFACE
EFFACED
EFFACES
EFFACING
EFFECT
EFFECTED
EFFECTER
EFFECTERS
EFFECTING
EFFECTIVE
EFFECTIVES
EFFECTOR
EFFECTORS
EFFECTS
EFFECTUAL
EFFED
EFFEIR
EFFEIRED
EFFEIRING
EFFEIRS
EFFENDI
EFFENDIS
EFFERE
EFFERED
EFFERENCE
EFFERENCES
EFFERENT
EFFERES
EFFERING
EFFETE
EFFETELY
EFFICACIES
EFFICACY
EFFICIENT
EFFICIENTS
EFFIERCE
EFFIERCED
EFFIERCES
EFFIERCING
EFFIGIES
EFFIGY
EFFING
EFFLUENCE
EFFLUENCES
EFFLUENT
EFFLUENTS
EFFLUVIA
EFFLUVIAL
EFFLUVIUM
EFFLUX
EFFLUXES
EFFLUXION
EFFLUXIONS
EFFORCE
EFFORCED
EFFORCES
EFFORCING
EFFORT
EFFORTFUL
EFFORTS
EFFRAIDE
EFFRAY
EFFRAYS
EFFS
EFFULGE
EFFULGED
EFFULGENT
EFFULGES
EFFULGING
EFFUSE
EFFUSED
EFFUSES
EFFUSING
EFFUSION
EFFUSIONS
EFFUSIVE
EFS
EFT
EFTEST
EFTS
EFTSOONS
EGAD
EGAL
EGALITIES
EGALITY
EGALLY
EGAREMENT
EGAREMENTS
EGENCE
EGENCES
EGENCIES
EGENCY
EGER
EGERS
EGEST
EGESTA
EGESTED
EGESTING
EGESTION
EGESTIONS
EGESTIVE
EGESTS
EGG
EGGAR
EGGARS
EGGCUP
EGGCUPS
EGGED
EGGER
EGGERIES
EGGERS
EGGERY
EGGHEAD
EGGHEADS
EGGIER
EGGIEST
EGGING
EGGLER
EGGLERS
EGGMASS
EGGMASSES
EGGNOG
EGGNOGS
EGGS
EGGSHELL
EGGSHELLS
EGGWASH
EGGWASHES
EGGY
EGIS
EGISES
EGLANTINE
EGLANTINES
EGLATERE
EGLATERES
EGMA
EGMAS
EGO
EGOISM
EGOISMS
EGOIST
EGOISTIC
EGOISTS
EGOITIES
EGOITY
EGOMANIA
EGOMANIAC
EGOMANIACS
EGOMANIAS
EGOS
EGOTHEISM
EGOTHEISMS
EGOTISE
EGOTISED
EGOTISES
EGOTISING
EGOTISM
EGOTISMS
EGOTIST
EGOTISTIC
EGOTISTS
EGOTIZE
EGOTIZED
EGOTIZES
EGOTIZING
EGREGIOUS
EGRESS
EGRESSES
EGRESSION
EGRESSIONS
EGRET
EGRETS
EH
EHED
EHING
EHS
EIDENT
EIDER
EIDERDOWN
EIDERDOWNS
EIDERS
EIDETIC
EIDETICS
EIDOGRAPH
EIDOGRAPHS
EIDOLA
EIDOLON
EIGENTONE
EIGENTONES
EIGHT
EIGHTEEN
EIGHTEENS
EIGHTFOIL
EIGHTFOILS
EIGHTFOLD
EIGHTFOOT
EIGHTH
EIGHTHLY
EIGHTHS
EIGHTIES
EIGHTIETH
EIGHTIETHS
EIGHTS
EIGHTSMAN
EIGHTSMEN
EIGHTSOME
EIGHTSOMES
EIGHTVO
EIGHTVOS
EIGHTY
EIGNE
EIK
EIKED
EIKING
EIKON
EIKONS
EIKS
EILD
EILDING
EILDINGS
EILDS
EINE
EIRACK
EIRACKS
EIRENIC
EIRENICON
EIRENICONS
EISEL
EISELL
EISELLS
EISELS
EITHER
EJACULATE
EJACULATED
EJACULATES
EJACULATING
EJECT
EJECTA
EJECTED
EJECTING
EJECTION
EJECTIONS
EJECTIVE
EJECTMENT
EJECTMENTS
EJECTOR
EJECTORS
EJECTS
EKE
EKED
EKES
EKING
EKISTIC
EKISTICS
EKKA
EKKAS
EKLOGITE
EKLOGITES
EKPHRASES
EKPHRASIS
EKPWELE
EKPWELES
EKUELE
EL
ELABORATE
ELABORATED
ELABORATES
ELABORATING
ELAEOLITE
ELAEOLITES
ELAN
ELANCE
ELANCED
ELANCES
ELANCING
ELAND
ELANDS
ELANET
ELANETS
ELANS
ELAPHINE
ELAPSE
ELAPSED
ELAPSES
ELAPSING
ELASTANCE
ELASTANCES
ELASTASE
ELASTASES
ELASTIC
ELASTICS
ELASTIN
ELASTINS
ELASTOMER

ELASTOMERS
ELATE
ELATED
ELATEDLY
ELATER
ELATERIN
ELATERINS
ELATERITE
ELATERITES
ELATERIUM
ELATERIUMS
ELATERS
ELATES
ELATING
ELATION
ELATIONS
ELATIVE
ELATIVES
ELBOW
ELBOWED
ELBOWING
ELBOWS
ELCHEE
ELCHEES
ELCHI
ELCHIS
ELD
ELDER
ELDERLIES
ELDERLY
ELDERS
ELDERSHIP
ELDERSHIPS
ELDEST
ELDIN
ELDING
ELDINGS
ELDINS
ELDRITCH
ELDS
ELECT
ELECTABLE
ELECTED
ELECTING
ELECTION
ELECTIONS
ELECTIVE
ELECTIVES
ELECTOR
ELECTORAL
ELECTORS
ELECTRESS
ELECTRESSES
ELECTRET
ELECTRETS
ELECTRIC
ELECTRICS
ELECTRIFIED
ELECTRIFIES
ELECTRIFY
ELECTRIFYING
ELECTRISE
ELECTRISED
ELECTRISES
ELECTRISING
ELECTRIZE
ELECTRIZED
ELECTRIZES
ELECTRIZING
ELECTRO
ELECTRODE
ELECTRODES
ELECTRON
ELECTRONS
ELECTROS
ELECTRUM
ELECTRUMS
ELECTS
ELECTUARIES
ELECTUARY
ELEGANCE
ELEGANCES
ELEGANCIES
ELEGANCY
ELEGANT
ELEGANTLY
ELEGIAC
ELEGIACAL
ELEGIACS
ELEGIAST
ELEGIASTS
ELEGIES
ELEGISE
ELEGISED
ELEGISES
ELEGISING
ELEGIST
ELEGISTS
ELEGIT
ELEGITS
ELEGIZE
ELEGIZED
ELEGIZES
ELEGIZING
ELEGY
ELEMENT
ELEMENTAL
ELEMENTALS
ELEMENTS
ELEMI
ELEMIS
ELENCH
ELENCHI
ELENCHS
ELENCHUS
ELENCTIC
ELEPHANT
ELEPHANTS
ELEUTHERI
ELEVATE
ELEVATED
ELEVATES
ELEVATING
ELEVATION
ELEVATIONS
ELEVATOR
ELEVATORS
ELEVATORY
ELEVEN
ELEVENS
ELEVENSES
ELEVENTH
ELEVENTHS
ELEVON
ELEVONS
ELF
ELFED
ELFHOOD
ELFHOODS
ELFIN
ELFING
ELFINS
ELFISH
ELFLAND
ELFLANDS
ELFLOCKS
ELFS
ELIAD
ELIADS
ELICIT
ELICITED
ELICITING
ELICITOR
ELICITORS
ELICITS
ELIDE
ELIDED
ELIDES
ELIDING
ELIGIBLE
ELIGIBLES
ELIGIBLY
ELIMINANT
ELIMINANTS
ELIMINATE
ELIMINATED
ELIMINATES
ELIMINATING
ELISION
ELISIONS
ELITE
ELITES
ELITISM
ELITISMS
ELITIST
ELITISTS
ELIXIR
ELIXIRS
ELK
ELKHOUND
ELKHOUNDS
ELKS
ELL
ELLAGIC
ELLIPSE
ELLIPSES
ELLIPSIS
ELLIPSOID
ELLIPSOIDS
ELLIPTIC
ELLOPS
ELLOPSES
ELLS
ELLWAND
ELLWANDS
ELM
ELMEN
ELMIER
ELMIEST
ELMS
ELMWOOD
ELMWOODS
ELMY
ELOCUTE
ELOCUTED
ELOCUTES
ELOCUTING
ELOCUTION
ELOCUTIONS
ELOCUTORY
ELOGE
ELOGES
ELOGIES
ELOGIST
ELOGISTS
ELOGIUM
ELOGIUMS
ELOGY
ELOIGN
ELOIGNED
ELOIGNER
ELOIGNERS
ELOIGNING
ELOIGNS
ELOIN
ELOINED
ELOINER
ELOINERS
ELOINING
ELOINMENT
ELOINMENTS
ELOINS
ELONGATE
ELONGATED
ELONGATES
ELONGATING
ELOPE
ELOPED
ELOPEMENT
ELOPEMENTS
ELOPER
ELOPERS
ELOPES
ELOPING
ELOPS
ELOPSES
ELOQUENCE
ELOQUENCES
ELOQUENT
ELPEE
ELPEES
ELS
ELSE
ELSEWHERE
ELSEWISE
ELSHIN
ELSHINS
ELSIN
ELSINS
ELT
ELTCHI
ELTCHIS
ELTS
ELUANT
ELUANTS
ELUATE
ELUATES
ELUCIDATE
ELUCIDATED
ELUCIDATES
ELUCIDATING
ELUDE
ELUDED
ELUDER
ELUDERS
ELUDES
ELUDIBLE
ELUDING
ELUENT
ELUENTS
ELUSION
ELUSIONS
ELUSIVE
ELUSIVELY
ELUSORY
ELUTE
ELUTED
ELUTES
ELUTING
ELUTION
ELUTIONS
ELUTOR
ELUTORS
ELUTRIATE
ELUTRIATED
ELUTRIATES
ELUTRIATING
ELUVIA
ELUVIAL
ELUVIUM
ELUVIUMS
ELVAN
ELVANITE
ELVANITES
ELVANS
ELVER
ELVERS
ELVES
ELVISH
ELYTRA
ELYTRAL
ELYTRON
ELYTRUM
EM
EMACIATE
EMACIATED
EMACIATES
EMACIATING
EMAIL
EMAILED

EMAILING
EMAILS
EMALANGENI
EMANANT
EMANATE
EMANATED
EMANATES
EMANATING
EMANATION
EMANATIONS
EMANATIST
EMANATISTS
EMANATIVE
EMANATORY
EMBACE
EMBACES
EMBACING
EMBAIL
EMBAILED
EMBAILING
EMBAILS
EMBALE
EMBALED
EMBALES
EMBALING
EMBALL
EMBALLED
EMBALLING
EMBALLINGS
EMBALLS
EMBALM
EMBALMED
EMBALMER
EMBALMERS
EMBALMING
EMBALMINGS
EMBALMS
EMBANK
EMBANKED
EMBANKER
EMBANKERS
EMBANKING
EMBANKS
EMBAR
EMBARGO
EMBARGOED
EMBARGOES
EMBARGOING
EMBARK
EMBARKED
EMBARKING
EMBARKS
EMBARRASS
EMBARRASSED
EMBARRASSES
EMBARRASSING
EMBARRED
EMBARRING
EMBARRINGS
EMBARS
EMBASE
EMBASED
EMBASES
EMBASING
EMBASSADE
EMBASSADES
EMBASSAGE
EMBASSAGES
EMBASSIES
EMBASSY
EMBASTE
EMBATHE
EMBATHED
EMBATHES
EMBATHING
EMBATTLE
EMBATTLED
EMBATTLES
EMBATTLING
EMBAY
EMBAYED
EMBAYING
EMBAYLD
EMBAYMENT
EMBAYMENTS
EMBAYS
EMBED
EMBEDDED
EMBEDDING
EMBEDDINGS
EMBEDMENT
EMBEDMENTS
EMBEDS
EMBELLISH
EMBELLISHED
EMBELLISHES
EMBELLISHING
EMBER
EMBERS
EMBEZZLE
EMBEZZLED
EMBEZZLER
EMBEZZLERS
EMBEZZLES
EMBEZZLING
EMBITTER
EMBITTERED
EMBITTERING
EMBITTERINGS
EMBITTERS
EMBLAZE
EMBLAZED
EMBLAZES
EMBLAZING
EMBLAZON
EMBLAZONED
EMBLAZONING
EMBLAZONS
EMBLEM
EMBLEMA
EMBLEMATA
EMBLEMED
EMBLEMING
EMBLEMISE
EMBLEMISED
EMBLEMISES
EMBLEMISING
EMBLEMIZE
EMBLEMIZED
EMBLEMIZES
EMBLEMIZING
EMBLEMS
EMBLIC
EMBLICS
EMBLOOM
EMBLOOMED
EMBLOOMING
EMBLOOMS
EMBLOSSOM
EMBLOSSOMED
EMBLOSSOMING
EMBLOSSOMS
EMBODIED
EMBODIES
EMBODY
EMBODYING
EMBOG
EMBOGGED
EMBOGGING
EMBOGS
EMBOGUE
EMBOGUED
EMBOGUES
EMBOGUING
EMBOIL
EMBOILED
EMBOILING
EMBOILS
EMBOLDEN
EMBOLDENED
EMBOLDENING
EMBOLDENS
EMBOLI
EMBOLIC
EMBOLIES
EMBOLISM
EMBOLISMS
EMBOLUS
EMBOLUSES
EMBOLY
EMBORDER
EMBORDERED
EMBORDERING
EMBORDERS
EMBOSCATA
EMBOSCATAS
EMBOSOM
EMBOSOMED
EMBOSOMING
EMBOSOMS
EMBOSS
EMBOSSED
EMBOSSER
EMBOSSERS
EMBOSSES
EMBOSSING
EMBOST
EMBOUND
EMBOUNDED
EMBOUNDING
EMBOUNDS
EMBOW
EMBOWED
EMBOWEL
EMBOWELLED
EMBOWELLING
EMBOWELS
EMBOWER
EMBOWERED
EMBOWERING
EMBOWERS
EMBOWING
EMBOWS
EMBOX
EMBOXED
EMBOXES
EMBOXING
EMBRACE
EMBRACED
EMBRACEOR
EMBRACEORS
EMBRACER
EMBRACERIES
EMBRACERS
EMBRACERY
EMBRACES
EMBRACING
EMBRACIVE
EMBRAID
EMBRAIDED
EMBRAIDING
EMBRAIDS
EMBRANGLE
EMBRANGLED
EMBRANGLES
EMBRANGLING
EMBRASOR
EMBRASORS
EMBRASURE
EMBRASURES
EMBRAVE
EMBRAVED
EMBRAVES
EMBRAVING
EMBRAZURE
EMBRAZURES
EMBREAD
EMBREADED
EMBREADING
EMBREADS
EMBREATHE
EMBREATHED
EMBREATHES
EMBREATHING
EMBREWE
EMBREWED
EMBREWES
EMBREWING
EMBRITTLE
EMBRITTLED
EMBRITTLES
EMBRITTLING
EMBROCATE
EMBROCATED
EMBROCATES
EMBROCATING
EMBROGLIO
EMBROGLIOS
EMBROIDER
EMBROIDERED
EMBROIDERING
EMBROIDERS
EMBROIL
EMBROILED
EMBROILING
EMBROILS
EMBROWN
EMBROWNED
EMBROWNING
EMBROWNS
EMBRUE
EMBRUED
EMBRUES
EMBRUING
EMBRUTE
EMBRUTED
EMBRUTES
EMBRUTING
EMBRYO
EMBRYOID
EMBRYOIDS
EMBRYON
EMBRYONAL
EMBRYONIC
EMBRYONS
EMBRYOS
EMBRYOTIC
EMBUS
EMBUSIED
EMBUSIES
EMBUSQUE
EMBUSQUES
EMBUSSED
EMBUSSES
EMBUSSING
EMBUSY
EMBUSYING
EMCEE
EMCEED
EMCEEING
EMCEES
EME
EMEER
EMEERS
EMEND
EMENDABLE
EMENDALS
EMENDATE
EMENDATED
EMENDATES
EMENDATING
EMENDATOR
EMENDATORS
EMENDED
EMENDING
EMENDS
EMERALD
EMERALDS
EMERAUDE
EMERAUDES

EMERGE
EMERGED
EMERGENCE
EMERGENCES
EMERGENCIES
EMERGENCY
EMERGENT
EMERGES
EMERGING
EMERIED
EMERIES
EMERITI
EMERITUS
EMERODS
EMERSED
EMERSION
EMERSIONS
EMERY
EMERYING
EMES
EMESES
EMESIS
EMETIC
EMETICAL
EMETICS
EMETIN
EMETINE
EMETINES
EMETINS
EMEU
EMEUS
EMEUTE
EMEUTES
EMICANT
EMICATE
EMICATED
EMICATES
EMICATING
EMICATION
EMICATIONS
EMICTION
EMICTIONS
EMICTORY
EMIGRANT
EMIGRANTS
EMIGRATE
EMIGRATED
EMIGRATES
EMIGRATING
EMIGRE
EMIGRES
EMINENCE
EMINENCES
EMINENCIES
EMINENCY
EMINENT
EMINENTLY
EMIR
EMIRATE
EMIRATES
EMIRS
EMISSARIES
EMISSARY
EMISSILE
EMISSION
EMISSIONS
EMISSIVE
EMIT
EMITS
EMITTED
EMITTER
EMITTERS
EMITTING
EMMA
EMMARBLE
EMMARBLED
EMMARBLES
EMMARBLING
EMMAS
EMMER
EMMERS
EMMESH
EMMESHED
EMMESHES
EMMESHING
EMMET
EMMETROPE
EMMETROPES
EMMETS
EMMEW
EMMEWED
EMMEWING
EMMEWS
EMMOVE
EMMOVED
EMMOVES
EMMOVING
EMOLLIATE
EMOLLIATED
EMOLLIATES
EMOLLIATING
EMOLLIENT
EMOLLIENTS
EMOLUMENT
EMOLUMENTS
EMONG
EMONGES
EMONGEST
EMONGST
EMOTE
EMOTED
EMOTES
EMOTICON
EMOTICONS
EMOTING
EMOTION
EMOTIONAL
EMOTIONS
EMOTIVE
EMOTIVISM
EMOTIVISMS
EMOVE
EMOVED
EMOVES
EMOVING
EMPACKET
EMPACKETED
EMPACKETING
EMPACKETS
EMPAESTIC
EMPAIRE
EMPAIRED
EMPAIRES
EMPAIRING
EMPALE
EMPALED
EMPALES
EMPALING
EMPANEL
EMPANELLED
EMPANELLING
EMPANELS
EMPANOPLIED
EMPANOPLIES
EMPANOPLY
EMPANOPLYING
EMPARE
EMPARED
EMPARES
EMPARING
EMPARL
EMPARLED
EMPARLING
EMPARLS
EMPART
EMPARTED
EMPARTING
EMPARTS
EMPATHIC
EMPATHIES
EMPATHISE
EMPATHISED
EMPATHISES
EMPATHISING
EMPATHIZE
EMPATHIZED
EMPATHIZES
EMPATHIZING
EMPATHY
EMPATRON
EMPATRONED
EMPATRONING
EMPATRONS
EMPAYRE
EMPAYRED
EMPAYRES
EMPAYRING
EMPEACH
EMPEACHED
EMPEACHES
EMPEACHING
EMPENNAGE
EMPENNAGES
EMPEOPLE
EMPEOPLED
EMPEOPLES
EMPEOPLING
EMPERCE
EMPERCED
EMPERCES
EMPERCING
EMPERIES
EMPERISE
EMPERISED
EMPERISES
EMPERISH
EMPERISHED
EMPERISHES
EMPERISHING
EMPERISING
EMPERIZE
EMPERIZED
EMPERIZES
EMPERIZING
EMPEROR
EMPERORS
EMPERY
EMPHASES
EMPHASIS
EMPHASISE
EMPHASISED
EMPHASISES
EMPHASISING
EMPHASIZE
EMPHASIZED
EMPHASIZES
EMPHASIZING
EMPHATIC
EMPHLYSES
EMPHLYSIS
EMPHYSEMA
EMPHYSEMAS
EMPIERCE
EMPIERCED
EMPIERCES
EMPIERCING
EMPIGHT
EMPIRE
EMPIRES
EMPIRIC
EMPIRICAL
EMPIRICS
EMPLACE
EMPLACED
EMPLACES
EMPLACING
EMPLANE
EMPLANED
EMPLANES
EMPLANING
EMPLASTER
EMPLASTERED
EMPLASTERING
EMPLASTERS
EMPLASTIC
EMPLASTICS
EMPLEACH
EMPLEACHED
EMPLEACHES
EMPLEACHING
EMPLECTON
EMPLECTONS
EMPLECTUM
EMPLECTUMS
EMPLONGE
EMPLONGED
EMPLONGES
EMPLONGING
EMPLOY
EMPLOYED
EMPLOYEE
EMPLOYEES
EMPLOYER
EMPLOYERS
EMPLOYING
EMPLOYS
EMPLUME
EMPLUMED
EMPLUMES
EMPLUMING
EMPOISON
EMPOISONED
EMPOISONING
EMPOISONS
EMPOLDER
EMPOLDERED
EMPOLDERING
EMPOLDERS
EMPORIA
EMPORIUM
EMPORIUMS
EMPOWER
EMPOWERED
EMPOWERING
EMPOWERS
EMPRESS
EMPRESSE
EMPRESSES
EMPRISE
EMPRISES
EMPTIED
EMPTIER
EMPTIERS
EMPTIES
EMPTIEST
EMPTILY
EMPTINESS
EMPTINESSES
EMPTION
EMPTIONAL
EMPTIONS
EMPTY
EMPTYING
EMPTYINGS
EMPTYSES
EMPTYSIS
EMPURPLE
EMPURPLED
EMPURPLES
EMPURPLING
EMPUSA
EMPUSAS
EMPUSE
EMPUSES
EMPYEMA
EMPYEMAS
EMPYEMATA
EMPYEMIC
EMPYESES
EMPYESIS

EMPYREAL
EMPYREAN
EMPYREANS
EMPYREUMA
EMPYREUMATA
EMS
EMU
EMULATE
EMULATED
EMULATES
EMULATING
EMULATION
EMULATIONS
EMULATIVE
EMULATOR
EMULATORS
EMULE
EMULED
EMULES
EMULGE
EMULGED
EMULGENCE
EMULGENCES
EMULGENT
EMULGES
EMULGING
EMULING
EMULOUS
EMULOUSLY
EMULSIFIED
EMULSIFIES
EMULSIFY
EMULSIFYING
EMULSIN
EMULSINS
EMULSION
EMULSIONS
EMULSIVE
EMULSOID
EMULSOIDS
EMULSOR
EMULSORS
EMUNCTION
EMUNCTIONS
EMUNCTORIES
EMUNCTORY
EMUNGE
EMUNGED
EMUNGES
EMUNGING
EMURE
EMURED
EMURES
EMURING
EMUS
EMYDES
EMYS
EN
ENABLE
ENABLED
ENABLER
ENABLERS
ENABLES
ENABLING
ENACT
ENACTED
ENACTING
ENACTION
ENACTIONS
ENACTIVE
ENACTMENT
ENACTMENTS
ENACTOR
ENACTORS
ENACTS
ENACTURE
ENACTURES
ENALLAGE
ENALLAGES
ENAMEL
ENAMELLED
ENAMELLER
ENAMELLERS
ENAMELLING
ENAMELLINGS
ENAMELS
ENAMOR
ENAMORADO
ENAMORADOS
ENAMORED
ENAMORING
ENAMORS
ENAMOUR
ENAMOURED
ENAMOURING
ENAMOURS
ENARCH
ENARCHED
ENARCHES
ENARCHING
ENARM
ENARMED
ENARMING
ENARMS
ENATE
ENATION
ENATIONS
ENAUNTER
ENCAENIA
ENCAENIAS
ENCAGE
ENCAGED
ENCAGES
ENCAGING
ENCALM
ENCALMED
ENCALMING
ENCALMS
ENCAMP
ENCAMPED
ENCAMPING
ENCAMPS
ENCANTHIS
ENCANTHISES
ENCARPUS
ENCARPUSES
ENCASE
ENCASED
ENCASES
ENCASH
ENCASHED
ENCASHES
ENCASHING
ENCASING
ENCAUSTIC
ENCAUSTICS
ENCAVE
ENCAVED
ENCAVES
ENCAVING
ENCEINTE
ENCEINTES
ENCHAFE
ENCHAFED
ENCHAFES
ENCHAFING
ENCHAIN
ENCHAINED
ENCHAINING
ENCHAINS
ENCHANT
ENCHANTED
ENCHANTER
ENCHANTERS
ENCHANTING
ENCHANTS
ENCHARGE
ENCHARGED
ENCHARGES
ENCHARGING
ENCHARM
ENCHARMED
ENCHARMING
ENCHARMS
ENCHASE
ENCHASED
ENCHASES
ENCHASING
ENCHEASON
ENCHEASONS
ENCHEER
ENCHEERED
ENCHEERING
ENCHEERS
ENCHILADA
ENCHILADAS
ENCHORIAL
ENCHORIC
ENCIERRO
ENCIERROS
ENCIPHER
ENCIPHERED
ENCIPHERING
ENCIPHERS
ENCIRCLE
ENCIRCLED
ENCIRCLES
ENCIRCLING
ENCIRCLINGS
ENCLASP
ENCLASPED
ENCLASPING
ENCLASPS
ENCLAVE
ENCLAVED
ENCLAVES
ENCLAVING
ENCLISES
ENCLISIS
ENCLITIC
ENCLITICS
ENCLOSE
ENCLOSED
ENCLOSER
ENCLOSERS
ENCLOSES
ENCLOSING
ENCLOSURE
ENCLOSURES
ENCLOTHE
ENCLOTHED
ENCLOTHES
ENCLOTHING
ENCLOUD
ENCLOUDED
ENCLOUDING
ENCLOUDS
ENCODE
ENCODED
ENCODES
ENCODING
ENCOLOUR
ENCOLOURED
ENCOLOURING
ENCOLOURS
ENCOLPION
ENCOLPIONS
ENCOLPIUM
ENCOLPIUMS
ENCOLURE
ENCOLURES
ENCOMIA
ENCOMIAST
ENCOMIASTS
ENCOMION
ENCOMIUM
ENCOMIUMS
ENCOMPASS
ENCOMPASSED
ENCOMPASSES
ENCOMPASSING
ENCORE
ENCORED
ENCORES
ENCORING
ENCOUNTER
ENCOUNTERED
ENCOUNTERING
ENCOUNTERS
ENCOURAGE
ENCOURAGED
ENCOURAGES
ENCOURAGING
ENCOURAGINGS
ENCRADLE
ENCRADLED
ENCRADLES
ENCRADLING
ENCRATIES
ENCRATY
ENCREASE
ENCREASED
ENCREASES
ENCREASING
ENCRIMSON
ENCRIMSONED
ENCRIMSONING
ENCRIMSONS
ENCRINAL
ENCRINIC
ENCRINITE
ENCRINITES
ENCROACH
ENCROACHED
ENCROACHES
ENCROACHING
ENCRUST
ENCRUSTED
ENCRUSTING
ENCRUSTS
ENCRYPT
ENCRYPTED
ENCRYPTING
ENCRYPTS
ENCUMBER
ENCUMBERED
ENCUMBERING
ENCUMBERS
ENCURTAIN
ENCURTAINED
ENCURTAINING
ENCURTAINS
ENCYCLIC
ENCYST
ENCYSTED
ENCYSTING
ENCYSTS
END
ENDAMAGE
ENDAMAGED
ENDAMAGES
ENDAMAGING
ENDAMOEBA
ENDAMOEBAE
ENDAMOEBAS
ENDANGER
ENDANGERED
ENDANGERING
ENDANGERS
ENDARCH
ENDART
ENDARTED
ENDARTING
ENDARTS
ENDEAR
ENDEARED
ENDEARING
ENDEARS
ENDEAVOR
ENDEAVORED

NDEAVORING
NDEAVORS
NDEAVOUR
NDEAVOURED
NDEAVOURING
NDEAVOURS
NDECAGON
NDECAGONS
NDED
NDEICTIC
NDEIXES
NDEIXIS
NDEIXISES
NDEMIAL
NDEMIC
NDEMICAL
NDEMICS
NDEMISM
NDEMISMS
NDENIZEN
NDENIZENED
NDENIZENING
NDENIZENS
NDERMIC
NDERON
NDERONS
NDEW
NDEWED
NDEWING
NDEWS
NDGAME
NDGAMES
NDING
NDINGS
NDIRON
NDIRONS
NDITE
NDITED
NDITES
NDITING
NDIVE
NDIVES
NDLANG
NDLESS
NDLESSLY
NDLONG
NDMOST
NDOBLAST
NDOBLASTS
NDOCARP
NDOCARPS
NDOCRINE
NDOCRINES
NDODERM
NDODERMS
NDODYNE
NDOGAMIC
NDOGAMIES
NDOGAMY
NDOGEN
NDOGENIC
NDOGENIES
NDOGENS
NDOGENY
ENDOLYMPH
ENDOLYMPHS
ENDOMIXES
ENDOMIXIS
ENDOMIXISES
ENDOMORPH
ENDOMORPHS
ENDOPHAGIES
ENDOPHAGY
ENDOPHYTE
ENDOPHYTES
ENDOPLASM
ENDOPLASMS
ENDORPHIN
ENDORPHINS
ENDORSE
ENDORSED
ENDORSEE
ENDORSEES
ENDORSER
ENDORSERS
ENDORSES
ENDORSING
ENDOSARC
ENDOSARCS
ENDOSCOPE
ENDOSCOPES
ENDOSCOPIES
ENDOSCOPY
ENDOSMOSE
ENDOSMOSES
ENDOSPERM
ENDOSPERMS
ENDOSPORE
ENDOSPORES
ENDOSS
ENDOSSED
ENDOSSES
ENDOSSING
ENDOSTEA
ENDOSTEAL
ENDOSTEUM
ENDOW
ENDOWED
ENDOWER
ENDOWERS
ENDOWING
ENDOWMENT
ENDOWMENTS
ENDOWS
ENDOZOA
ENDOZOIC
ENDOZOON
ENDS
ENDSHIP
ENDSHIPS
ENDUE
ENDUED
ENDUES
ENDUING
ENDUNGEON
ENDUNGEONED
ENDUNGEONING
ENDUNGEONS
ENDURABLE
ENDURABLY
ENDURANCE
ENDURANCES
ENDURE
ENDURED
ENDURER
ENDURERS
ENDURES
ENDURING
ENDURO
ENDUROS
ENDWAYS
ENDWISE
ENE
ENEMA
ENEMAS
ENEMATA
ENEMIES
ENEMY
ENERGETIC
ENERGETICS
ENERGIC
ENERGID
ENERGIDS
ENERGIES
ENERGISE
ENERGISED
ENERGISER
ENERGISERS
ENERGISES
ENERGISING
ENERGIZE
ENERGIZED
ENERGIZER
ENERGIZERS
ENERGIZES
ENERGIZING
ENERGUMEN
ENERGUMENS
ENERGY
ENERVATE
ENERVATED
ENERVATES
ENERVATING
ENERVE
ENERVED
ENERVES
ENERVING
ENES
ENEW
ENEWED
ENEWING
ENEWS
ENFACE
ENFACED
ENFACES
ENFACING
ENFANT
ENFANTS
ENFEEBLE
ENFEEBLED
ENFEEBLES
ENFEEBLING
ENFELON
ENFELONED
ENFELONING
ENFELONS
ENFEOFF
ENFEOFFED
ENFEOFFING
ENFEOFFS
ENFESTED
ENFETTER
ENFETTERED
ENFETTERING
ENFETTERS
ENFIERCE
ENFIERCED
ENFIERCES
ENFIERCING
ENFILADE
ENFILADED
ENFILADES
ENFILADING
ENFILED
ENFIRE
ENFIRED
ENFIRES
ENFIRING
ENFIX
ENFIXED
ENFIXES
ENFIXING
ENFLAME
ENFLAMED
ENFLAMES
ENFLAMING
ENFLESH
ENFLESHED
ENFLESHES
ENFLESHING
ENFLOWER
ENFLOWERED
ENFLOWERING
ENFLOWERS
ENFOLD
ENFOLDED
ENFOLDING
ENFOLDS
ENFORCE
ENFORCED
ENFORCER
ENFORCERS
ENFORCES
ENFORCING
ENFOREST
ENFORESTED
ENFORESTING
ENFORESTS
ENFORM
ENFORMED
ENFORMING
ENFORMS
ENFRAME
ENFRAMED
ENFRAMES
ENFRAMING
ENFREE
ENFREED
ENFREEDOM
ENFREEDOMED
ENFREEDOMING
ENFREEDOMS
ENFREEING
ENFREES
ENFREEZE
ENFREEZES
ENFREEZING
ENFROSEN
ENFROZE
ENFROZEN
ENG
ENGAGE
ENGAGED
ENGAGER
ENGAGERS
ENGAGES
ENGAGING
ENGAOL
ENGAOLED
ENGAOLING
ENGAOLS
ENGARLAND
ENGARLANDED
ENGARLANDING
ENGARLANDS
ENGENDER
ENGENDERED
ENGENDERING
ENGENDERS
ENGENDURE
ENGENDURES
ENGILD
ENGILDED
ENGILDING
ENGILDS
ENGILT
ENGINE
ENGINED
ENGINEER
ENGINEERED
ENGINEERING
ENGINEERINGS
ENGINEERS
ENGINER
ENGINERIES
ENGINERS
ENGINERY
ENGINES
ENGINING
ENGIRD
ENGIRDING
ENGIRDLE
ENGIRDLED
ENGIRDLES
ENGIRDLING
ENGIRDS
ENGIRT
ENGISCOPE
ENGISCOPES
ENGLOBE

The Chambers Dictionary is the authority for many longer words; see *OSW* Introduction, page xii

ENGLOBED
ENGLOBES
ENGLOBING
ENGLOOM
ENGLOOMED
ENGLOOMING
ENGLOOMS
ENGLUT
ENGLUTS
ENGLUTTED
ENGLUTTING
ENGOBE
ENGOBES
ENGORE
ENGORED
ENGORES
ENGORGE
ENGORGED
ENGORGES
ENGORGING
ENGORING
ENGOULED
ENGOUMENT
ENGOUMENTS
ENGRACE
ENGRACED
ENGRACES
ENGRACING
ENGRAFF
ENGRAFFED
ENGRAFFING
ENGRAFFS
ENGRAFT
ENGRAFTED
ENGRAFTING
ENGRAFTS
ENGRAIL
ENGRAILED
ENGRAILING
ENGRAILS
ENGRAIN
ENGRAINED
ENGRAINER
ENGRAINERS
ENGRAINING
ENGRAINS
ENGRAM
ENGRAMMA
ENGRAMMAS
ENGRAMS
ENGRASP
ENGRASPED
ENGRASPING
ENGRASPS
ENGRAVE
ENGRAVED
ENGRAVEN
ENGRAVER
ENGRAVERIES
ENGRAVERS
ENGRAVERY
ENGRAVES
ENGRAVING
ENGRAVINGS
ENGRENAGE
ENGRENAGES
ENGRIEVE
ENGRIEVED
ENGRIEVES
ENGRIEVING
ENGROOVE
ENGROOVED
ENGROOVES
ENGROOVING
ENGROSS
ENGROSSED
ENGROSSER
ENGROSSERS
ENGROSSES
ENGROSSING
ENGS
ENGUARD
ENGUARDED
ENGUARDING
ENGUARDS
ENGULF
ENGULFED
ENGULFING
ENGULFS
ENGULPH
ENGULPHED
ENGULPHING
ENGULPHS
ENGYSCOPE
ENGYSCOPES
ENHALO
ENHALOED
ENHALOES
ENHALOING
ENHALOS
ENHANCE
ENHANCED
ENHANCER
ENHANCERS
ENHANCES
ENHANCING
ENHANCIVE
ENHEARSE
ENHEARSED
ENHEARSES
ENHEARSING
ENHEARTEN
ENHEARTENED
ENHEARTENING
ENHEARTENS
ENHUNGER
ENHUNGERED
ENHUNGERING
ENHUNGERS
ENHYDRITE
ENHYDRITES
ENHYDROS
ENHYDROSES
ENHYDROUS
ENIAC
ENIACS
ENIGMA
ENIGMAS
ENIGMATIC
ENISLE
ENISLED
ENISLES
ENISLING
ENJAMB
ENJAMBED
ENJAMBING
ENJAMBS
ENJOIN
ENJOINED
ENJOINER
ENJOINERS
ENJOINING
ENJOINS
ENJOY
ENJOYABLE
ENJOYABLY
ENJOYED
ENJOYER
ENJOYERS
ENJOYING
ENJOYMENT
ENJOYMENTS
ENJOYS
ENKERNEL
ENKERNELLED
ENKERNELLING
ENKERNELS
ENKINDLE
ENKINDLED
ENKINDLES
ENKINDLING
ENLACE
ENLACED
ENLACES
ENLACING
ENLARD
ENLARDED
ENLARDING
ENLARDS
ENLARGE
ENLARGED
ENLARGEN
ENLARGENED
ENLARGENING
ENLARGENS
ENLARGER
ENLARGERS
ENLARGES
ENLARGING
ENLEVE
ENLIGHT
ENLIGHTED
ENLIGHTEN
ENLIGHTENED
ENLIGHTENING
ENLIGHTENS
ENLIGHTING
ENLIGHTS
ENLINK
ENLINKED
ENLINKING
ENLINKS
ENLIST
ENLISTED
ENLISTING
ENLISTS
ENLIT
ENLIVEN
ENLIVENED
ENLIVENER
ENLIVENERS
ENLIVENING
ENLIVENS
ENLOCK
ENLOCKED
ENLOCKING
ENLOCKS
ENLUMINE
ENLUMINED
ENLUMINES
ENLUMINING
ENMESH
ENMESHED
ENMESHES
ENMESHING
ENMEW
ENMEWED
ENMEWING
ENMEWS
ENMITIES
ENMITY
ENMOSSED
ENMOVE
ENMOVED
ENMOVES
ENMOVING
ENNAGE
ENNAGES
ENNEAD
ENNEADIC
ENNEADS
ENNEAGON
ENNEAGONS
ENNOBLE
ENNOBLED
ENNOBLES
ENNOBLING
ENNUI
ENNUIED
ENNUIS
ENNUYE
ENNUYED
ENNUYING
ENODAL
ENOKI
ENOKIS
ENOMOTIES
ENOMOTY
ENORM
ENORMITIES
ENORMITY
ENORMOUS
ENOSES
ENOSIS
ENOUGH
ENOUGHS
ENOUNCE
ENOUNCED
ENOUNCES
ENOUNCING
ENOW
ENPLANE
ENPLANED
ENPLANES
ENPLANING
ENPRINT
ENPRINTS
ENQUIRE
ENQUIRED
ENQUIRER
ENQUIRERS
ENQUIRES
ENQUIRIES
ENQUIRING
ENQUIRY
ENRACE
ENRACED
ENRACES
ENRACING
ENRAGE
ENRAGED
ENRAGES
ENRAGING
ENRANCKLE
ENRANCKLED
ENRANCKLES
ENRANCKLING
ENRANGE
ENRANGED
ENRANGES
ENRANGING
ENRANK
ENRANKED
ENRANKING
ENRANKS
ENRAPT
ENRAPTURE
ENRAPTURED
ENRAPTURES
ENRAPTURING
ENRAUNGE
ENRAUNGED
ENRAUNGES
ENRAUNGING
ENRAVISH
ENRAVISHED
ENRAVISHES
ENRAVISHING
ENRHEUM
ENRHEUMED
ENRHEUMING
ENRHEUMS
ENRICH
ENRICHED
ENRICHES
ENRICHING
ENRIDGED
ENRING
ENRINGED
ENRINGING

NRINGS
NRIVEN
NROBE
NROBED
NROBES
NROBING
NROL
NROLL
NROLLED
NROLLER
NROLLERS
NROLLING
NROLLS
NROLMENT
NROLMENTS
NROLS
NROOT
NROOTED
NROOTING
NROOTS
NROUGH
NROUGHED
NROUGHING
NROUGHS
NROUND
NROUNDED
NROUNDING
NROUNDS
NS
NSAMPLE
NSAMPLED
NSAMPLES
NSAMPLING
NSATE
NSCONCE
NSCONCED
NSCONCES
NSCONCING
NSEAL
NSEALED
NSEALING
NSEALS
NSEAM
NSEAMED
NSEAMING
NSEAMS
NSEAR
NSEARED
NSEARING
NSEARS
NSEMBLE
NSEMBLES
NSEW
NSEWED
NSEWING
NSEWS
NSHEATH
NSHEATHE
NSHEATHED
NSHEATHES
NSHEATHING
NSHEATHS
NSHELL
NSHELLED
ENSHELLING
ENSHELLS
ENSHELTER
ENSHELTERED
ENSHELTERING
ENSHELTERS
ENSHIELD
ENSHIELDED
ENSHIELDING
ENSHIELDS
ENSHRINE
ENSHRINED
ENSHRINES
ENSHRINING
ENSHROUD
ENSHROUDED
ENSHROUDING
ENSHROUDS
ENSIFORM
ENSIGN
ENSIGNCIES
ENSIGNCY
ENSIGNED
ENSIGNING
ENSIGNS
ENSILAGE
ENSILAGED
ENSILAGEING
ENSILAGES
ENSILAGING
ENSILE
ENSILED
ENSILES
ENSILING
ENSKIED
ENSKIES
ENSKY
ENSKYING
ENSLAVE
ENSLAVED
ENSLAVER
ENSLAVERS
ENSLAVES
ENSLAVING
ENSNARE
ENSNARED
ENSNARES
ENSNARING
ENSNARL
ENSNARLED
ENSNARLING
ENSNARLS
ENSORCELL
ENSORCELLED
ENSORCELLING
ENSORCELLS
ENSOUL
ENSOULED
ENSOULING
ENSOULS
ENSPHERE
ENSPHERED
ENSPHERES
ENSPHERING
ENSTAMP
ENSTAMPED
ENSTAMPING
ENSTAMPS
ENSTATITE
ENSTATITES
ENSTEEP
ENSTEEPED
ENSTEEPING
ENSTEEPS
ENSTYLE
ENSTYLED
ENSTYLES
ENSTYLING
ENSUE
ENSUED
ENSUES
ENSUING
ENSURE
ENSURED
ENSURER
ENSURERS
ENSURES
ENSURING
ENSWATHE
ENSWATHED
ENSWATHES
ENSWATHING
ENSWEEP
ENSWEEPING
ENSWEEPS
ENSWEPT
ENTAIL
ENTAILED
ENTAILER
ENTAILERS
ENTAILING
ENTAILS
ENTAME
ENTAMED
ENTAMES
ENTAMING
ENTAMOEBA
ENTAMOEBAE
ENTAMOEBAS
ENTANGLE
ENTANGLED
ENTANGLES
ENTANGLING
ENTASES
ENTASIS
ENTAYLE
ENTAYLED
ENTAYLES
ENTAYLING
ENTELECHIES
ENTELECHY
ENTELLUS
ENTELLUSES
ENTENDER
ENTENDERED
ENTENDERING
ENTENDERS
ENTENTE
ENTENTES
ENTER
ENTERA
ENTERABLE
ENTERAL
ENTERATE
ENTERED
ENTERER
ENTERERS
ENTERIC
ENTERICS
ENTERING
ENTERINGS
ENTERITIS
ENTERITISES
ENTERON
ENTERS
ENTERTAIN
ENTERTAINED
ENTERTAINING
ENTERTAININGS
ENTERTAINS
ENTERTAKE
ENTERTAKEN
ENTERTAKES
ENTERTAKING
ENTERTOOK
ENTETE
ENTETEE
ENTHALPIES
ENTHALPY
ENTHETIC
ENTHRAL
ENTHRALL
ENTHRALLED
ENTHRALLING
ENTHRALLS
ENTHRALS
ENTHRONE
ENTHRONED
ENTHRONES
ENTHRONING
ENTHUSE
ENTHUSED
ENTHUSES
ENTHUSING
ENTHYMEME
ENTHYMEMES
ENTIA
ENTICE
ENTICED
ENTICER
ENTICERS
ENTICES
ENTICING
ENTICINGS
ENTIRE
ENTIRELY
ENTIRES
ENTIRETIES
ENTIRETY
ENTITIES
ENTITLE
ENTITLED
ENTITLES
ENTITLING
ENTITY
ENTOBLAST
ENTOBLASTS
ENTODERM
ENTODERMS
ENTOIL
ENTOILED
ENTOILING
ENTOILS
ENTOMB
ENTOMBED
ENTOMBING
ENTOMBS
ENTOMIC
ENTOPHYTE
ENTOPHYTES
ENTOPIC
ENTOPTIC
ENTOPTICS
ENTOTIC
ENTOURAGE
ENTOURAGES
ENTOZOA
ENTOZOAL
ENTOZOIC
ENTOZOON
ENTRAIL
ENTRAILED
ENTRAILING
ENTRAILS
ENTRAIN
ENTRAINED
ENTRAINING
ENTRAINS
ENTRALL
ENTRALLES
ENTRAMMEL
ENTRAMMELLED
ENTRAMMELLING
ENTRAMMELS
ENTRANCE
ENTRANCED
ENTRANCES
ENTRANCING
ENTRANT
ENTRANTS
ENTRAP
ENTRAPPED
ENTRAPPER
ENTRAPPERS
ENTRAPPING
ENTRAPS
ENTREAT
ENTREATED
ENTREATIES
ENTREATING
ENTREATS
ENTREATY
ENTRECHAT
ENTRECHATS
ENTRECOTE
ENTRECOTES

ENTREE
ENTREES
ENTREMES
ENTREMETS
ENTRENCH
ENTRENCHED
ENTRENCHES
ENTRENCHING
ENTREPOT
ENTREPOTS
ENTRESOL
ENTRESOLS
ENTREZ
ENTRIES
ENTRISM
ENTRISMS
ENTRIST
ENTRISTS
ENTROLD
ENTROPIC
ENTROPIES
ENTROPION
ENTROPIONS
ENTROPIUM
ENTROPIUMS
ENTROPY
ENTRUST
ENTRUSTED
ENTRUSTING
ENTRUSTS
ENTRY
ENTRYISM
ENTRYISMS
ENTRYIST
ENTRYISTS
ENTWINE
ENTWINED
ENTWINES
ENTWINING
ENTWIST
ENTWISTED
ENTWISTING
ENTWISTS
ENUCLEATE
ENUCLEATED
ENUCLEATES
ENUCLEATING
ENUMERATE
ENUMERATED
ENUMERATES
ENUMERATING
ENUNCIATE
ENUNCIATED
ENUNCIATES
ENUNCIATING
ENURE
ENURED
ENUREMENT
ENUREMENTS
ENURES
ENURESES
ENURESIS
ENURETIC
ENURETICS
ENURING
ENVASSAL
ENVASSALLED
ENVASSALLING
ENVASSALS
ENVAULT
ENVAULTED
ENVAULTING
ENVAULTS
ENVEIGLE
ENVEIGLED
ENVEIGLES
ENVEIGLING
ENVELOP
ENVELOPE
ENVELOPED
ENVELOPES
ENVELOPING
ENVELOPS
ENVENOM
ENVENOMED
ENVENOMING
ENVENOMS
ENVERMEIL
ENVERMEILED
ENVERMEILING
ENVERMEILS
ENVIABLE
ENVIABLY
ENVIED
ENVIER
ENVIERS
ENVIES
ENVIOUS
ENVIOUSLY
ENVIRON
ENVIRONED
ENVIRONING
ENVIRONS
ENVISAGE
ENVISAGED
ENVISAGES
ENVISAGING
ENVISION
ENVISIONED
ENVISIONING
ENVISIONS
ENVOI
ENVOIS
ENVOY
ENVOYS
ENVOYSHIP
ENVOYSHIPS
ENVY
ENVYING
ENVYINGS
ENWALL
ENWALLED
ENWALLING
ENWALLOW
ENWALLOWED
ENWALLOWING
ENWALLOWS
ENWALLS
ENWHEEL
ENWHEELED
ENWHEELING
ENWHEELS
ENWIND
ENWINDING
ENWINDS
ENWOMB
ENWOMBED
ENWOMBING
ENWOMBS
ENWOUND
ENWRAP
ENWRAPPED
ENWRAPPING
ENWRAPPINGS
ENWRAPS
ENWREATHE
ENWREATHED
ENWREATHES
ENWREATHING
ENZIAN
ENZIANS
ENZONE
ENZONED
ENZONES
ENZONING
ENZOOTIC
ENZOOTICS
ENZYMATIC
ENZYME
ENZYMES
ENZYMIC
EOAN
EOLIENNE
EOLIENNES
EOLIPILE
EOLIPILES
EOLITH
EOLITHIC
EOLITHS
EON
EONISM
EONISMS
EONS
EORL
EORLS
EOSIN
EOSINS
EOTHEN
EPACRID
EPACRIDS
EPACRIS
EPACRISES
EPACT
EPACTS
EPAENETIC
EPAGOGE
EPAGOGES
EPAGOGIC
EPAINETIC
EPANODOS
EPANODOSES
EPARCH
EPARCHATE
EPARCHATES
EPARCHIES
EPARCHS
EPARCHY
EPATANT
EPAULE
EPAULES
EPAULET
EPAULETS
EPAULETTE
EPAULETTES
EPAXIAL
EPEDAPHIC
EPEE
EPEES
EPEIRA
EPEIRAS
EPEIRID
EPEIRIDS
EPEOLATRIES
EPEOLATRY
EPERDU
EPERDUE
EPERGNE
EPERGNES
EPHA
EPHAH
EPHAHS
EPHAS
EPHEBE
EPHEBES
EPHEBI
EPHEBIC
EPHEBOS
EPHEBUS
EPHEDRA
EPHEDRAS
EPHEDRINE
EPHEDRINES
EPHELIDES
EPHELIS
EPHEMERA
EPHEMERAE
EPHEMERAL
EPHEMERALS
EPHEMERAS
EPHEMERID
EPHEMERIDES
EPHEMERIDS
EPHEMERIS
EPHEMERON
EPHIALTES
EPHOD
EPHODS
EPHOR
EPHORALTIES
EPHORALTY
EPHORS
EPIBLAST
EPIBLASTS
EPIC
EPICAL
EPICALLY
EPICALYCES
EPICALYX
EPICALYXES
EPICANTHI
EPICARP
EPICARPS
EPICEDE
EPICEDES
EPICEDIA
EPICEDIAL
EPICEDIAN
EPICEDIUM
EPICENE
EPICENES
EPICENTER
EPICENTERS
EPICENTRE
EPICENTRES
EPICIER
EPICIERS
EPICISM
EPICISMS
EPICIST
EPICISTS
EPICLESES
EPICLESIS
EPICOTYL
EPICOTYLS
EPICRITIC
EPICS
EPICURE
EPICUREAN
EPICUREANS
EPICURES
EPICURISE
EPICURISED
EPICURISES
EPICURISING
EPICURISM
EPICURISMS
EPICURIZE
EPICURIZED
EPICURIZES
EPICURIZING
EPICYCLE
EPICYCLES
EPICYCLIC
EPIDEMIC
EPIDEMICS
EPIDERMAL
EPIDERMIC
EPIDERMIS
EPIDERMISES
EPIDOSITE
EPIDOSITES
EPIDOTE
EPIDOTES
EPIDOTIC
EPIDURAL
EPIDURALS
EPIFAUNA
EPIFAUNAE
EPIFAUNAS
EPIFOCAL

EPIGAEAL
EPIGAEAN
EPIGAEOUS
EPIGAMIC
EPIGEAL
EPIGEAN
EPIGENE
EPIGEOUS
EPIGON
EPIGONE
EPIGONES
EPIGONI
EPIGONS
EPIGRAM
EPIGRAMS
EPIGRAPH
EPIGRAPHED
EPIGRAPHIES
EPIGRAPHING
EPIGRAPHS
EPIGRAPHY
EPIGYNIES
EPIGYNOUS
EPIGYNY
EPILATE
EPILATED
EPILATES
EPILATING
EPILATION
EPILATIONS
EPILATOR
EPILATORS
EPILEPSIES
EPILEPSY
EPILEPTIC
EPILEPTICS
EPILOBIUM
EPILOBIUMS
EPILOG
EPILOGIC
EPILOGISE
EPILOGISED
EPILOGISES
EPILOGISING
EPILOGIST
EPILOGISTS
EPILOGIZE
EPILOGIZED
EPILOGIZES
EPILOGIZING
EPILOGS
EPILOGUE
EPILOGUES
EPIMER
EPIMERIC
EPIMERS
EPINASTIC
EPINASTIES
EPINASTY
EPINEURAL
EPINICIAN
EPINICION
EPINICIONS
EPINIKIAN
EPINIKION
EPINIKIONS
EPINOSIC
EPIPHANIC
EPIPHRAGM
EPIPHRAGMS
EPIPHYSES
EPIPHYSIS
EPIPHYTAL
EPIPHYTE
EPIPHYTES
EPIPHYTIC
EPIPLOIC
EPIPLOON
EPIPLOONS
EPIPOLIC
EPIPOLISM
EPIPOLISMS
EPIRRHEMA
EPIRRHEMAS
EPISCOPAL
EPISCOPE
EPISCOPES
EPISCOPIES
EPISCOPY
EPISEMON
EPISEMONS
EPISODAL
EPISODE
EPISODES
EPISODIAL
EPISODIC
EPISOME
EPISOMES
EPISPERM
EPISPERMS
EPISPORE
EPISPORES
EPISTASES
EPISTASIS
EPISTATIC
EPISTAXES
EPISTAXIS
EPISTAXISES
EPISTEMIC
EPISTEMICS
EPISTERNA
EPISTLE
EPISTLED
EPISTLER
EPISTLERS
EPISTLES
EPISTLING
EPISTOLER
EPISTOLERS
EPISTOLET
EPISTOLETS
EPISTOLIC
EPISTYLE
EPISTYLES
EPITAPH
EPITAPHED
EPITAPHER
EPITAPHERS
EPITAPHIC
EPITAPHING
EPITAPHS
EPITASES
EPITASIS
EPITAXIAL
EPITAXIES
EPITAXY
EPITHELIA
EPITHEM
EPITHEMA
EPITHEMATA
EPITHEMS
EPITHESES
EPITHESIS
EPITHET
EPITHETED
EPITHETIC
EPITHETING
EPITHETON
EPITHETONS
EPITHETS
EPITOME
EPITOMES
EPITOMIC
EPITOMISE
EPITOMISED
EPITOMISES
EPITOMISING
EPITOMIST
EPITOMISTS
EPITOMIZE
EPITOMIZED
EPITOMIZES
EPITOMIZING
EPITONIC
EPITOPE
EPITOPES
EPITRITE
EPITRITES
EPIZEUXES
EPIZEUXIS
EPIZEUXISES
EPIZOA
EPIZOAN
EPIZOANS
EPIZOIC
EPIZOON
EPIZOOTIC
EPIZOOTICS
EPOCH
EPOCHA
EPOCHAL
EPOCHAS
EPOCHS
EPODE
EPODES
EPODIC
EPONYM
EPONYMIC
EPONYMOUS
EPONYMS
EPOPEE
EPOPEES
EPOPOEIA
EPOPOEIAS
EPOPT
EPOPTS
EPOS
EPOSES
EPOXIDE
EPOXIDES
EPOXIES
EPOXY
EPRIS
EPRISE
EPROM
EPROMS
EPSILON
EPSILONS
EPSOMITE
EPSOMITES
EPUISE
EPUISEE
EPULARY
EPULATION
EPULATIONS
EPULIDES
EPULIS
EPULISES
EPULOTIC
EPULOTICS
EPURATE
EPURATED
EPURATES
EPURATING
EPURATION
EPURATIONS
EPYLLION
EPYLLIONS
EQUABLE
EQUABLY
EQUAL
EQUALISE
EQUALISED
EQUALISER
EQUALISERS
EQUALISES
EQUALISING
EQUALITIES
EQUALITY
EQUALIZE
EQUALIZED
EQUALIZER
EQUALIZERS
EQUALIZES
EQUALIZING
EQUALLED
EQUALLING
EQUALLY
EQUALNESS
EQUALNESSES
EQUALS
EQUANT
EQUANTS
EQUATE
EQUATED
EQUATES
EQUATING
EQUATION
EQUATIONS
EQUATOR
EQUATORS
EQUERRIES
EQUERRY
EQUID
EQUIDS
EQUINAL
EQUINE
EQUINIA
EQUINIAS
EQUINITIES
EQUINITY
EQUINOX
EQUINOXES
EQUIP
EQUIPAGE
EQUIPAGED
EQUIPAGES
EQUIPAGING
EQUIPE
EQUIPES
EQUIPMENT
EQUIPMENTS
EQUIPOISE
EQUIPOISED
EQUIPOISES
EQUIPOISING
EQUIPPED
EQUIPPING
EQUIPS
EQUISETA
EQUISETIC
EQUISETUM
EQUISETUMS
EQUITABLE
EQUITABLY
EQUITANT
EQUITIES
EQUITY
EQUIVALVE
EQUIVOCAL
EQUIVOKE
EQUIVOKES
EQUIVOQUE
EQUIVOQUES
ER
ERA
ERADIATE
ERADIATED
ERADIATES
ERADIATING
ERADICATE
ERADICATED
ERADICATES
ERADICATING
ERAS
ERASABLE
ERASE
ERASED
ERASEMENT
ERASEMENTS

ERASER
ERASERS
ERASES
ERASING
ERASION
ERASIONS
ERASURE
ERASURES
ERATHEM
ERATHEMS
ERBIA
ERBIAS
ERBIUM
ERBIUMS
ERE
ERECT
ERECTED
ERECTER
ERECTERS
ERECTILE
ERECTING
ERECTION
ERECTIONS
ERECTIVE
ERECTLY
ERECTNESS
ERECTNESSES
ERECTOR
ERECTORS
ERECTS
ERED
ERELONG
EREMIC
EREMITAL
EREMITE
EREMITES
EREMITIC
EREMITISM
EREMITISMS
ERENOW
EREPSIN
EREPSINS
ERES
ERETHISM
ERETHISMS
ERETHITIC
EREWHILE
ERF
ERG
ERGATANER
ERGATANERS
ERGATE
ERGATES
ERGATIVE
ERGATOID
ERGO
ERGODIC
ERGOGRAM
ERGOGRAMS
ERGOGRAPH
ERGOGRAPHS
ERGOMANIA
ERGOMANIAS
ERGOMETER
ERGOMETERS
ERGON
ERGONOMIC
ERGONOMICS
ERGONS
ERGOT
ERGOTISE
ERGOTISED
ERGOTISES
ERGOTISING
ERGOTISM
ERGOTISMS
ERGOTIZE
ERGOTIZED
ERGOTIZES
ERGOTIZING
ERGOTS
ERGS
ERIACH
ERIACHS
ERIC
ERICA
ERICAS
ERICK
ERICKS
ERICOID
ERICS
ERIGERON
ERIGERONS
ERING
ERINGO
ERINGOES
ERINGOS
ERINITE
ERINITES
ERIOMETER
ERIOMETERS
ERIONITE
ERIONITES
ERISTIC
ERISTICAL
ERK
ERKS
ERMELIN
ERMELINS
ERMINE
ERMINED
ERMINES
ERN
ERNE
ERNED
ERNES
ERNING
ERNS
ERODE
ERODED
ERODENT
ERODENTS
ERODES
ERODIBLE
ERODING
ERODIUM
ERODIUMS
EROGENIC
EROGENOUS
EROSE
EROSION
EROSIONS
EROSIVE
EROSTRATE
EROTEMA
EROTEMAS
EROTEME
EROTEMES
EROTESES
EROTESIS
EROTETIC
EROTIC
EROTICA
EROTICAL
EROTICISE
EROTICISED
EROTICISES
EROTICISING
EROTICISM
EROTICISMS
EROTICIST
EROTICISTS
EROTICIZE
EROTICIZED
EROTICIZES
EROTICIZING
EROTICS
EROTISM
EROTISMS
ERR
ERRABLE
ERRAND
ERRANDS
ERRANT
ERRANTLY
ERRANTRIES
ERRANTRY
ERRANTS
ERRATA
ERRATIC
ERRATICAL
ERRATICS
ERRATUM
ERRED
ERRHINE
ERRHINES
ERRING
ERRINGLY
ERRINGS
ERRONEOUS
ERROR
ERRORIST
ERRORISTS
ERRORS
ERRS
ERS
ERSATZ
ERSATZES
ERSES
ERST
ERSTWHILE
ERUCIFORM
ERUCT
ERUCTATE
ERUCTATED
ERUCTATES
ERUCTATING
ERUCTED
ERUCTING
ERUCTS
ERUDITE
ERUDITELY
ERUDITES
ERUDITION
ERUDITIONS
ERUMPENT
ERUPT
ERUPTED
ERUPTING
ERUPTION
ERUPTIONS
ERUPTIVE
ERUPTS
ERVALENTA
ERVALENTAS
ERVEN
ERYNGIUM
ERYNGIUMS
ERYNGO
ERYNGOES
ERYNGOS
ERYTHEMA
ERYTHEMAL
ERYTHEMAS
ERYTHRINA
ERYTHRINAS
ERYTHRISM
ERYTHRISMS
ERYTHRITE
ERYTHRITES
ES
ESCALADE
ESCALADED
ESCALADES
ESCALADING
ESCALADO
ESCALADOES
ESCALATE
ESCALATED
ESCALATES
ESCALATING
ESCALATOR
ESCALATORS
ESCALIER
ESCALIERS
ESCALLOP
ESCALLOPS
ESCALOP
ESCALOPE
ESCALOPED
ESCALOPES
ESCALOPING
ESCALOPS
ESCAPABLE
ESCAPADE
ESCAPADES
ESCAPADO
ESCAPADOES
ESCAPE
ESCAPED
ESCAPEE
ESCAPEES
ESCAPER
ESCAPERS
ESCAPES
ESCAPING
ESCAPISM
ESCAPISMS
ESCAPIST
ESCAPISTS
ESCARGOT
ESCARGOTS
ESCAROLE
ESCAROLES
ESCARP
ESCARPED
ESCARPING
ESCARPS
ESCHALOT
ESCHALOTS
ESCHAR
ESCHARS
ESCHEAT
ESCHEATED
ESCHEATING
ESCHEATOR
ESCHEATORS
ESCHEATS
ESCHEW
ESCHEWAL
ESCHEWALS
ESCHEWED
ESCHEWER
ESCHEWERS
ESCHEWING
ESCHEWS
ESCLANDRE
ESCLANDRES
ESCOLAR
ESCOLARS
ESCOPETTE
ESCOPETTES
ESCORT
ESCORTAGE
ESCORTAGES
ESCORTED
ESCORTING
ESCORTS
ESCOT
ESCOTS
ESCOTTED
ESCOTTING
ESCRIBANO
ESCRIBANOS
ESCRIBE
ESCRIBED
ESCRIBES
ESCRIBING
ESCROC
ESCROCS

ESCROL
ESCROLL
ESCROLLS
ESCROLS
ESCROW
ESCROWED
ESCROWING
ESCROWS
ESCUAGE
ESCUAGES
ESCUDO
ESCUDOS
ESCULENT
ESCULENTS
ESEMPLASIES
ESEMPLASY
ESILE
ESILES
ESKAR
ESKARS
ESKER
ESKERS
ESKIES
ESKY®
ESLOIN
ESLOINED
ESLOINING
ESLOINS
ESLOYNE
ESLOYNED
ESLOYNES
ESLOYNING
ESNE
ESNECIES
ESNECY
ESNES
ESOPHAGI
ESOPHAGUS
ESOTERIC
ESOTERICA
ESOTERIES
ESOTERISM
ESOTERISMS
ESOTERY
ESPADA
ESPADAS
ESPAGNOLE
ESPAGNOLES
ESPALIER
ESPALIERED
ESPALIERING
ESPALIERS
ESPARTO
ESPARTOS
ESPECIAL
ESPERANCE
ESPERANCES
ESPIAL
ESPIALS
ESPIED
ESPIEGLE
ESPIES
ESPIONAGE
ESPIONAGES
ESPLANADE
ESPLANADES
ESPOUSAL
ESPOUSALS
ESPOUSE
ESPOUSED
ESPOUSER
ESPOUSERS
ESPOUSES
ESPOUSING
ESPRESSO
ESPRESSOS
ESPRIT
ESPRITS
ESPUMOSO
ESPUMOSOS
ESPY
ESPYING
ESQUIRE
ESQUIRES
ESQUIRESS
ESQUIRESSES
ESQUISSE
ESQUISSES
ESS
ESSAY
ESSAYED
ESSAYER
ESSAYERS
ESSAYETTE
ESSAYETTES
ESSAYING
ESSAYISH
ESSAYIST
ESSAYISTS
ESSAYS
ESSE
ESSENCE
ESSENCES
ESSENTIAL
ESSENTIALS
ESSES
ESSIVE
ESSIVES
ESSOIN
ESSOINER
ESSOINERS
ESSOINS
ESSONITE
ESSONITES
ESSOYNE
ESSOYNES
EST
ESTABLISH
ESTABLISHED
ESTABLISHES
ESTABLISHING
ESTACADE
ESTACADES
ESTAFETTE
ESTAFETTES
ESTAMINET
ESTAMINETS
ESTANCIA
ESTANCIAS
ESTATE
ESTATED
ESTATES
ESTATING
ESTEEM
ESTEEMED
ESTEEMING
ESTEEMS
ESTER
ESTERIFIED
ESTERIFIES
ESTERIFY
ESTERIFYING
ESTERS
ESTHESIA
ESTHESIAS
ESTHETE
ESTHETES
ESTIMABLE
ESTIMABLY
ESTIMATE
ESTIMATED
ESTIMATES
ESTIMATING
ESTIMATOR
ESTIMATORS
ESTIVAL
ESTIVATE
ESTIVATED
ESTIVATES
ESTIVATING
ESTOC
ESTOCS
ESTOILE
ESTOILES
ESTOP
ESTOPPAGE
ESTOPPAGES
ESTOPPED
ESTOPPEL
ESTOPPELS
ESTOPPING
ESTOPS
ESTOVER
ESTOVERS
ESTRADE
ESTRADES
ESTRADIOL
ESTRADIOLS
ESTRAL
ESTRANGE
ESTRANGED
ESTRANGER
ESTRANGERS
ESTRANGES
ESTRANGING
ESTRAPADE
ESTRAPADES
ESTRAY
ESTRAYED
ESTRAYING
ESTRAYS
ESTREAT
ESTREATED
ESTREATING
ESTREATS
ESTREPE
ESTREPED
ESTREPES
ESTREPING
ESTRICH
ESTRICHES
ESTRIDGE
ESTRIDGES
ESTRILDID
ESTRILDIDS
ESTRO
ESTROGEN
ESTROGENS
ESTROS
ESTROUS
ESTRUM
ESTRUMS
ESTRUS
ESTRUSES
ESTS
ESTUARIAL
ESTUARIAN
ESTUARIES
ESTUARINE
ESTUARY
ESURIENCE
ESURIENCES
ESURIENCIES
ESURIENCY
ESURIENT
ETA
ETACISM
ETACISMS
ETAERIO
ETAERIOS
ETAGE
ETAGERE
ETAGERES
ETAGES
ETALAGE
ETALAGES
ETALON
ETALONS
ETAPE
ETAPES
ETAS
ETAT
ETATISME
ETATISMES
ETATISTE
ETATISTES
ETATS
ETCETERA
ETCETERAS
ETCH
ETCHANT
ETCHANTS
ETCHED
ETCHER
ETCHERS
ETCHES
ETCHING
ETCHINGS
ETEN
ETENS
ETERNAL
ETERNALLY
ETERNE
ETERNISE
ETERNISED
ETERNISES
ETERNISING
ETERNITIES
ETERNITY
ETERNIZE
ETERNIZED
ETERNIZES
ETERNIZING
ETESIAN
ETH
ETHAL
ETHALS
ETHANE
ETHANES
ETHANOL
ETHANOLS
ETHE
ETHENE
ETHENES
ETHER
ETHERCAP
ETHERCAPS
ETHEREAL
ETHEREOUS
ETHERIAL
ETHERIC
ETHERICAL
ETHERIFIED
ETHERIFIES
ETHERIFY
ETHERIFYING
ETHERION
ETHERIONS
ETHERISE
ETHERISED
ETHERISES
ETHERISING
ETHERISM
ETHERISMS
ETHERIST
ETHERISTS
ETHERIZE
ETHERIZED
ETHERIZES
ETHERIZING
ETHERS
ETHIC
ETHICAL
ETHICALLY
ETHICALS
ETHICISE
ETHICISED
ETHICISES
ETHICISING
ETHICISM

ETHICISMS
ETHICIST
ETHICISTS
ETHICIZE
ETHICIZED
ETHICIZES
ETHICIZING
ETHICS
ETHIOPS
ETHIOPSES
ETHMOID
ETHMOIDAL
ETHNARCH
ETHNARCHIES
ETHNARCHS
ETHNARCHY
ETHNIC
ETHNICAL
ETHNICISM
ETHNICISMS
ETHNICITIES
ETHNICITY
ETHNICS
ETHNOCIDE
ETHNOCIDES
ETHNOLOGIES
ETHNOLOGY
ETHOLOGIC
ETHOLOGIES
ETHOLOGY
ETHOS
ETHOSES
ETHS
ETHYL
ETHYLATE
ETHYLATED
ETHYLATES
ETHYLATING
ETHYLENE
ETHYLENES
ETHYLS
ETHYNE
ETHYNES
ETIOLATE
ETIOLATED
ETIOLATES
ETIOLATING
ETIOLIN
ETIOLINS
ETIOLOGIES
ETIOLOGY
ETIQUETTE
ETIQUETTES
ETNA
ETNAS
ETOILE
ETOILES
ETOURDI
ETOURDIE
ETRANGER
ETRANGERE
ETRANGERES
ETRANGERS
ETRENNE
ETRENNES
ETRIER
ETRIERS
ETTERCAP
ETTERCAPS
ETTIN
ETTINS
ETTLE
ETTLED
ETTLES
ETTLING
ETUDE
ETUDES
ETUI
ETUIS
ETWEE
ETWEES
ETYMA
ETYMIC
ETYMOLOGIES
ETYMOLOGY
ETYMON
ETYMONS
ETYPIC
ETYPICAL
EUCAIN
EUCAINE
EUCAINES
EUCAINS
EUCALYPT
EUCALYPTI
EUCALYPTS
EUCARYON
EUCARYONS
EUCARYOT
EUCARYOTE
EUCARYOTES
EUCARYOTS
EUCHARIS
EUCHARISES
EUCHLORIC
EUCHOLOGIES
EUCHOLOGY
EUCHRE
EUCHRED
EUCHRES
EUCHRING
EUCLASE
EUCLASES
EUCRITE
EUCRITES
EUCRITIC
EUCYCLIC
EUDAEMONIES
EUDAEMONY
EUDIALYTE
EUDIALYTES
EUGE
EUGENIA
EUGENIAS
EUGENIC
EUGENICS
EUGENISM
EUGENISMS
EUGENIST
EUGENISTS
EUGENOL
EUGENOLS
EUGH
EUGHEN
EUGHS
EUK
EUKARYON
EUKARYONS
EUKARYOT
EUKARYOTE
EUKARYOTES
EUKARYOTS
EUKED
EUKING
EUKS
EULACHAN
EULACHANS
EULACHON
EULACHONS
EULOGIA
EULOGIES
EULOGISE
EULOGISED
EULOGISES
EULOGISING
EULOGIST
EULOGISTS
EULOGIUM
EULOGIUMS
EULOGIZE
EULOGIZED
EULOGIZES
EULOGIZING
EULOGY
EUMELANIN
EUMELANINS
EUMERISM
EUMERISMS
EUNUCH
EUNUCHISE
EUNUCHISED
EUNUCHISES
EUNUCHISING
EUNUCHISM
EUNUCHISMS
EUNUCHIZE
EUNUCHIZED
EUNUCHIZES
EUNUCHIZING
EUNUCHOID
EUNUCHOIDS
EUNUCHS
EUOI
EUONYMIN
EUONYMINS
EUONYMUS
EUONYMUSES
EUOUAE
EUOUAES
EUPAD
EUPADS
EUPATRID
EUPATRIDAE
EUPATRIDS
EUPEPSIA
EUPEPSIAS
EUPEPSIES
EUPEPSY
EUPEPTIC
EUPHAUSID
EUPHAUSIDS
EUPHEMISE
EUPHEMISED
EUPHEMISES
EUPHEMISING
EUPHEMISM
EUPHEMISMS
EUPHEMIZE
EUPHEMIZED
EUPHEMIZES
EUPHEMIZING
EUPHENICS
EUPHOBIA
EUPHOBIAS
EUPHON
EUPHONIA
EUPHONIAS
EUPHONIC
EUPHONIES
EUPHONISE
EUPHONISED
EUPHONISES
EUPHONISING
EUPHONISM
EUPHONISMS
EUPHONIUM
EUPHONIUMS
EUPHONIZE
EUPHONIZED
EUPHONIZES
EUPHONIZING
EUPHONS
EUPHONY
EUPHORBIA
EUPHORBIAS
EUPHORIA
EUPHORIAS
EUPHORIC
EUPHORIES
EUPHORY
EUPHRASIES
EUPHRASY
EUPHROE
EUPHROES
EUPHUISE
EUPHUISED
EUPHUISES
EUPHUISING
EUPHUISM
EUPHUISMS
EUPHUIST
EUPHUISTS
EUPHUIZE
EUPHUIZED
EUPHUIZES
EUPHUIZING
EUREKA
EUREKAS
EURHYTHMIES
EURHYTHMY
EURIPI
EURIPUS
EURIPUSES
EURO
EUROPIUM
EUROPIUMS
EUROS
EURYTHERM
EURYTHERMS
EURYTHMIES
EURYTHMY
EUSOL
EUSOLS
EUSTACIES
EUSTACY
EUSTASIES
EUSTASY
EUSTATIC
EUSTYLE
EUSTYLES
EUTAXIES
EUTAXITE
EUTAXITES
EUTAXITIC
EUTAXY
EUTECTIC
EUTECTICS
EUTECTOID
EUTECTOIDS
EUTEXIA
EUTEXIAS
EUTHANASIES
EUTHANASY
EUTHENICS
EUTHENIST
EUTHENISTS
EUTHERIAN
EUTHERIANS
EUTRAPELIES
EUTRAPELY
EUTROPHIC
EUTROPHIES
EUTROPHY
EUTROPIC
EUTROPIES
EUTROPOUS
EUTROPY
EUXENITE
EUXENITES
EVACUANT
EVACUANTS
EVACUATE
EVACUATED
EVACUATES
EVACUATING
EVACUATOR
EVACUATORS
EVACUEE
EVACUEES
EVADABLE

EVADE
EVADED
EVADER
EVADERS
EVADES
EVADING
EVAGATION
EVAGATIONS
EVAGINATE
EVAGINATED
EVAGINATES
EVAGINATING
EVALUATE
EVALUATED
EVALUATES
EVALUATING
EVANESCE
EVANESCED
EVANESCES
EVANESCING
EVANGEL
EVANGELIC
EVANGELIES
EVANGELS
EVANGELY
EVANISH
EVANISHED
EVANISHES
EVANISHING
EVANITION
EVANITIONS
EVAPORATE
EVAPORATED
EVAPORATES
EVAPORATING
EVAPORITE
EVAPORITES
EVASIBLE
EVASION
EVASIONS
EVASIVE
EVASIVELY
EVE
EVECTION
EVECTIONS
EVEJAR
EVEJARS
EVEN
EVENED
EVENEMENT
EVENEMENTS
EVENER
EVENERS
EVENEST
EVENFALL
EVENFALLS
EVENING
EVENINGS
EVENLY
EVENNESS
EVENNESSES
EVENS
EVENSONG
EVENSONGS
EVENT
EVENTED
EVENTER
EVENTERS
EVENTFUL
EVENTIDE
EVENTIDES
EVENTING
EVENTINGS
EVENTRATE
EVENTRATED
EVENTRATES
EVENTRATING
EVENTS
EVENTUAL
EVENTUATE
EVENTUATED
EVENTUATES
EVENTUATING
EVER
EVERGLADE
EVERGLADES
EVERGREEN
EVERGREENS
EVERMORE
EVERSIBLE
EVERSION
EVERSIONS
EVERT
EVERTED
EVERTING
EVERTOR
EVERTORS
EVERTS
EVERY
EVERYBODY
EVERYDAY
EVERYDAYS
EVERYMAN
EVERYMEN
EVERYONE
EVERYWAY
EVERYWHEN
EVES
EVET
EVETS
EVHOE
EVICT
EVICTED
EVICTING
EVICTION
EVICTIONS
EVICTOR
EVICTORS
EVICTS
EVIDENCE
EVIDENCED
EVIDENCES
EVIDENCING
EVIDENT
EVIDENTLY
EVIDENTS
EVIL
EVILLER
EVILLEST
EVILLY
EVILNESS
EVILNESSES
EVILS
EVINCE
EVINCED
EVINCES
EVINCIBLE
EVINCIBLY
EVINCING
EVINCIVE
EVIRATE
EVIRATED
EVIRATES
EVIRATING
EVITABLE
EVITATE
EVITATED
EVITATES
EVITATING
EVITATION
EVITATIONS
EVITE
EVITED
EVITERNAL
EVITES
EVITING
EVOCABLE
EVOCATE
EVOCATED
EVOCATES
EVOCATING
EVOCATION
EVOCATIONS
EVOCATIVE
EVOCATOR
EVOCATORS
EVOCATORY
EVOE
EVOHE
EVOKE
EVOKED
EVOKER
EVOKERS
EVOKES
EVOKING
EVOLUE
EVOLUES
EVOLUTE
EVOLUTED
EVOLUTES
EVOLUTING
EVOLUTION
EVOLUTIONS
EVOLUTIVE
EVOLVABLE
EVOLVE
EVOLVED
EVOLVENT
EVOLVER
EVOLVERS
EVOLVES
EVOLVING
EVOVAE
EVOVAES
EVULGATE
EVULGATED
EVULGATES
EVULGATING
EVULSE
EVULSED
EVULSES
EVULSING
EVULSION
EVULSIONS
EVZONE
EVZONES
EWE
EWER
EWERS
EWES
EWEST
EWFTES
EWGHEN
EWHOW
EWK
EWKED
EWKING
EWKS
EWT
EWTS
EX
EXACT
EXACTABLE
EXACTED
EXACTER
EXACTERS
EXACTEST
EXACTING
EXACTION
EXACTIONS
EXACTLY
EXACTMENT
EXACTMENTS
EXACTNESS
EXACTNESSES
EXACTOR
EXACTORS
EXACTRESS
EXACTRESSES
EXACTS
EXALT
EXALTED
EXALTEDLY
EXALTING
EXALTS
EXAM
EXAMEN
EXAMENS
EXAMINANT
EXAMINANTS
EXAMINATE
EXAMINATES
EXAMINE
EXAMINED
EXAMINEE
EXAMINEES
EXAMINER
EXAMINERS
EXAMINES
EXAMINING
EXAMPLAR
EXAMPLARS
EXAMPLE
EXAMPLED
EXAMPLES
EXAMPLING
EXAMS
EXANIMATE
EXANTHEM
EXANTHEMA
EXANTHEMATA
EXANTHEMS
EXARATE
EXARATION
EXARATIONS
EXARCH
EXARCHAL
EXARCHATE
EXARCHATES
EXARCHIES
EXARCHIST
EXARCHISTS
EXARCHS
EXARCHY
EXCAMB
EXCAMBED
EXCAMBING
EXCAMBION
EXCAMBIONS
EXCAMBIUM
EXCAMBIUMS
EXCAMBS
EXCARNATE
EXCARNATED
EXCARNATES
EXCARNATING
EXCAUDATE
EXCAVATE
EXCAVATED
EXCAVATES
EXCAVATING
EXCAVATOR
EXCAVATORS
EXCEED
EXCEEDED
EXCEEDING
EXCEEDS
EXCEL
EXCELLED
EXCELLENT
EXCELLING
EXCELS
EXCELSIOR
EXCELSIORS
EXCENTRIC
EXCENTRICS
EXCEPT
EXCEPTANT
EXCEPTANTS
EXCEPTED

EXCEPTING
EXCEPTION
EXCEPTIONS
EXCEPTIVE
EXCEPTOR
EXCEPTORS
EXCEPTS
EXCERPT
EXCERPTA
EXCERPTED
EXCERPTING
EXCERPTINGS
EXCERPTOR
EXCERPTORS
EXCERPTS
EXCERPTUM
EXCESS
EXCESSES
EXCESSIVE
EXCHANGE
EXCHANGED
EXCHANGER
EXCHANGERS
EXCHANGES
EXCHANGING
EXCHEAT
EXCHEATS
EXCHEQUER
EXCHEQUERED
EXCHEQUERING
EXCHEQUERS
EXCIDE
EXCIDED
EXCIDES
EXCIDING
EXCIPIENT
EXCIPIENTS
EXCISABLE
EXCISE
EXCISED
EXCISEMAN
EXCISEMEN
EXCISES
EXCISING
EXCISION
EXCISIONS
EXCITABLE
EXCITANCIES
EXCITANCY
EXCITANT
EXCITANTS
EXCITE
EXCITED
EXCITEDLY
EXCITER
EXCITERS
EXCITES
EXCITING
EXCITON
EXCITONS
EXCITOR
EXCITORS
EXCLAIM
EXCLAIMED
EXCLAIMING
EXCLAIMS
EXCLAVE
EXCLAVES
EXCLOSURE
EXCLOSURES
EXCLUDE
EXCLUDED
EXCLUDEE
EXCLUDEES
EXCLUDER
EXCLUDERS
EXCLUDES
EXCLUDING
EXCLUSION
EXCLUSIONS
EXCLUSIVE
EXCLUSIVES
EXCLUSORY
EXCORIATE
EXCORIATED
EXCORIATES
EXCORIATING
EXCREMENT
EXCREMENTS
EXCRETA
EXCRETAL
EXCRETE
EXCRETED
EXCRETER
EXCRETERS
EXCRETES
EXCRETING
EXCRETION
EXCRETIONS
EXCRETIVE
EXCRETORIES
EXCRETORY
EXCUBANT
EXCUDIT
EXCULPATE
EXCULPATED
EXCULPATES
EXCULPATING
EXCURRENT
EXCURSE
EXCURSED
EXCURSES
EXCURSING
EXCURSION
EXCURSIONED
EXCURSIONING
EXCURSIONS
EXCURSIVE
EXCURSUS
EXCURSUSES
EXCUSABLE
EXCUSABLY
EXCUSAL
EXCUSALS
EXCUSE
EXCUSED
EXCUSER
EXCUSERS
EXCUSES
EXCUSING
EXCUSIVE
EXEAT
EXEATS
EXECRABLE
EXECRABLY
EXECRATE
EXECRATED
EXECRATES
EXECRATING
EXECUTANT
EXECUTANTS
EXECUTE
EXECUTED
EXECUTER
EXECUTERS
EXECUTES
EXECUTING
EXECUTION
EXECUTIONS
EXECUTIVE
EXECUTIVES
EXECUTOR
EXECUTORS
EXECUTORY
EXECUTRICES
EXECUTRIES
EXECUTRIX
EXECUTRIXES
EXECUTRY
EXEDRA
EXEDRAE
EXEEM
EXEEMED
EXEEMING
EXEEMS
EXEGESES
EXEGESIS
EXEGETE
EXEGETES
EXEGETIC
EXEGETICS
EXEGETIST
EXEGETISTS
EXEME
EXEMED
EXEMES
EXEMING
EXEMPLA
EXEMPLAR
EXEMPLARS
EXEMPLARY
EXEMPLE
EXEMPLES
EXEMPLIFIED
EXEMPLIFIES
EXEMPLIFY
EXEMPLIFYING
EXEMPLUM
EXEMPT
EXEMPTED
EXEMPTING
EXEMPTION
EXEMPTIONS
EXEMPTS
EXEQUATUR
EXEQUATURS
EXEQUIAL
EXEQUIES
EXEQUY
EXERCISE
EXERCISED
EXERCISER
EXERCISERS
EXERCISES
EXERCISING
EXERGONIC
EXERGUAL
EXERGUE
EXERGUES
EXERT
EXERTED
EXERTING
EXERTION
EXERTIONS
EXERTIVE
EXERTS
EXES
EXEUNT
EXFOLIATE
EXFOLIATED
EXFOLIATES
EXFOLIATING
EXHALABLE
EXHALANT
EXHALANTS
EXHALE
EXHALED
EXHALES
EXHALING
EXHAUST
EXHAUSTED
EXHAUSTER
EXHAUSTERS
EXHAUSTING
EXHAUSTS
EXHEDRA
EXHEDRAE
EXHIBIT
EXHIBITED
EXHIBITER
EXHIBITERS
EXHIBITING
EXHIBITOR
EXHIBITORS
EXHIBITS
EXHORT
EXHORTED
EXHORTER
EXHORTERS
EXHORTING
EXHORTS
EXHUMATE
EXHUMATED
EXHUMATES
EXHUMATING
EXHUME
EXHUMED
EXHUMER
EXHUMERS
EXHUMES
EXHUMING
EXIES
EXIGEANT
EXIGEANTE
EXIGENCE
EXIGENCES
EXIGENCIES
EXIGENCY
EXIGENT
EXIGENTLY
EXIGENTS
EXIGIBLE
EXIGUITIES
EXIGUITY
EXIGUOUS
EXILE
EXILED
EXILEMENT
EXILEMENTS
EXILES
EXILIAN
EXILIC
EXILING
EXILITIES
EXILITY
EXIMIOUS
EXINE
EXINES
EXIST
EXISTED
EXISTENCE
EXISTENCES
EXISTENT
EXISTING
EXISTS
EXIT
EXITANCE
EXITANCES
EXITED
EXITING
EXITS
EXOCARP
EXOCARPS
EXOCRINE
EXOCRINES
EXODE
EXODERM
EXODERMAL
EXODERMIS
EXODERMISES
EXODERMS
EXODES
EXODIC
EXODIST
EXODISTS
EXODUS
EXODUSES
EXOENZYME
EXOENZYMES
EXOERGIC

XOGAMIC
XOGAMIES
XOGAMOUS
XOGAMY
XOGEN
XOGENOUS
XOGENS
XOMION
XOMIONS
XOMIS
XOMISES
XON
XONERATE
XONERATED
XONERATES
XONERATING
XONIC
XONS
XONYM
XONYMS
XOPHAGIES
XOPHAGY
XOPLASM
XOPLASMS
XOPOD
XOPODITE
XOPODITES
XOPODS
XORABLE
XORATION
XORATIONS
XORCISE
XORCISED
XORCISER
XORCISERS
XORCISES
XORCISING
XORCISM
XORCISMS
XORCIST
XORCISTS
XORCIZE
XORCIZED
XORCIZER
XORCIZERS
XORCIZES
XORCIZING
XORDIA
XORDIAL
XORDIUM
XORDIUMS
XOSMOSE
XOSMOSES
XOSMOSIS
XOSMOTIC
XOSPHERE
XOSPHERES
XOSPORAL
XOSPORE
XOSPORES
XOSTOSES
XOSTOSIS
XOTERIC
XOTIC
EXOTICA
EXOTICISM
EXOTICISMS
EXOTICS
EXOTOXIC
EXOTOXIN
EXOTOXINS
EXPAND
EXPANDED
EXPANDER
EXPANDERS
EXPANDING
EXPANDOR
EXPANDORS
EXPANDS
EXPANSE
EXPANSES
EXPANSILE
EXPANSION
EXPANSIONS
EXPANSIVE
EXPAT
EXPATIATE
EXPATIATED
EXPATIATES
EXPATIATING
EXPATS
EXPECT
EXPECTANT
EXPECTANTS
EXPECTED
EXPECTER
EXPECTERS
EXPECTING
EXPECTINGS
EXPECTS
EXPEDIENT
EXPEDIENTS
EXPEDITE
EXPEDITED
EXPEDITER
EXPEDITERS
EXPEDITES
EXPEDITING
EXPEDITOR
EXPEDITORS
EXPEL
EXPELLANT
EXPELLANTS
EXPELLED
EXPELLEE
EXPELLEES
EXPELLENT
EXPELLENTS
EXPELLING
EXPELS
EXPEND
EXPENDED
EXPENDER
EXPENDERS
EXPENDING
EXPENDS
EXPENSE
EXPENSES
EXPENSIVE
EXPERT
EXPERTED
EXPERTING
EXPERTISE
EXPERTISED
EXPERTISES
EXPERTISING
EXPERTIZE
EXPERTIZED
EXPERTIZES
EXPERTIZING
EXPERTLY
EXPERTS
EXPIABLE
EXPIATE
EXPIATED
EXPIATES
EXPIATING
EXPIATION
EXPIATIONS
EXPIATOR
EXPIATORS
EXPIATORY
EXPIRABLE
EXPIRANT
EXPIRANTS
EXPIRE
EXPIRED
EXPIRES
EXPIRIES
EXPIRING
EXPIRY
EXPISCATE
EXPISCATED
EXPISCATES
EXPISCATING
EXPLAIN
EXPLAINED
EXPLAINER
EXPLAINERS
EXPLAINING
EXPLAINS
EXPLANT
EXPLANTED
EXPLANTING
EXPLANTS
EXPLETIVE
EXPLETIVES
EXPLETORY
EXPLICATE
EXPLICATED
EXPLICATES
EXPLICATING
EXPLICIT
EXPLICITS
EXPLODE
EXPLODED
EXPLODER
EXPLODERS
EXPLODES
EXPLODING
EXPLOIT
EXPLOITED
EXPLOITER
EXPLOITERS
EXPLOITING
EXPLOITS
EXPLORE
EXPLORED
EXPLORER
EXPLORERS
EXPLORES
EXPLORING
EXPLOSION
EXPLOSIONS
EXPLOSIVE
EXPLOSIVES
EXPO
EXPONENT
EXPONENTS
EXPONIBLE
EXPORT
EXPORTED
EXPORTER
EXPORTERS
EXPORTING
EXPORTS
EXPOS
EXPOSABLE
EXPOSAL
EXPOSALS
EXPOSE
EXPOSED
EXPOSER
EXPOSERS
EXPOSES
EXPOSING
EXPOSITOR
EXPOSITORS
EXPOSTURE
EXPOSTURES
EXPOSURE
EXPOSURES
EXPOUND
EXPOUNDED
EXPOUNDER
EXPOUNDERS
EXPOUNDING
EXPOUNDS
EXPRESS
EXPRESSED
EXPRESSES
EXPRESSING
EXPRESSLY
EXPRESSO
EXPRESSOS
EXPUGN
EXPUGNED
EXPUGNING
EXPUGNS
EXPULSE
EXPULSED
EXPULSES
EXPULSING
EXPULSION
EXPULSIONS
EXPULSIVE
EXPUNCT
EXPUNCTED
EXPUNCTING
EXPUNCTS
EXPUNGE
EXPUNGED
EXPUNGER
EXPUNGERS
EXPUNGES
EXPUNGING
EXPURGATE
EXPURGATED
EXPURGATES
EXPURGATING
EXPURGE
EXPURGED
EXPURGES
EXPURGING
EXQUISITE
EXQUISITES
EXSCIND
EXSCINDED
EXSCINDING
EXSCINDS
EXSECT
EXSECTED
EXSECTING
EXSECTION
EXSECTIONS
EXSECTS
EXSERT
EXSERTED
EXSERTILE
EXSERTING
EXSERTION
EXSERTIONS
EXSERTS
EXSICCANT
EXSICCATE
EXSICCATED
EXSICCATES
EXSICCATING
EXSUCCOUS
EXTANT
EXTASIES
EXTASY
EXTATIC
EXTEMPORE
EXTEMPORES
EXTEND
EXTENDANT
EXTENDED
EXTENDER
EXTENDERS
EXTENDING
EXTENDS
EXTENSE
EXTENSILE
EXTENSION
EXTENSIONS
EXTENSITIES
EXTENSITY
EXTENSIVE
EXTENSOR

EXTENSORS
EXTENT
EXTENTS
EXTENUATE
EXTENUATED
EXTENUATES
EXTENUATING
EXTENUATINGS
EXTERIOR
EXTERIORS
EXTERMINE
EXTERMINED
EXTERMINES
EXTERMINING
EXTERN
EXTERNAL
EXTERNALS
EXTERNAT
EXTERNATS
EXTERNE
EXTERNES
EXTERNS
EXTINCT
EXTINCTED
EXTINE
EXTINES
EXTIRP
EXTIRPATE
EXTIRPATED
EXTIRPATES
EXTIRPATING
EXTIRPED
EXTIRPING
EXTIRPS
EXTOL
EXTOLD
EXTOLLED
EXTOLLER
EXTOLLERS
EXTOLLING
EXTOLMENT
EXTOLMENTS
EXTOLS
EXTORSIVE
EXTORT
EXTORTED
EXTORTING
EXTORTION
EXTORTIONS
EXTORTIVE
EXTORTS
EXTRA
EXTRACT
EXTRACTED
EXTRACTING
EXTRACTOR
EXTRACTORS
EXTRACTS
EXTRADITE
EXTRADITED
EXTRADITES
EXTRADITING
EXTRADOS
EXTRADOSES
EXTRAIT
EXTRAITS
EXTRANET
EXTRANETS
EXTRAPOSE
EXTRAPOSED
EXTRAPOSES
EXTRAPOSING
EXTRAS
EXTRAUGHT
EXTRAVERT
EXTRAVERTED
EXTRAVERTING
EXTRAVERTS
EXTREAT
EXTREATS
EXTREME
EXTREMELY
EXTREMER
EXTREMES
EXTREMEST
EXTREMISM
EXTREMISMS
EXTREMIST
EXTREMISTS
EXTREMITIES
EXTREMITY
EXTRICATE
EXTRICATED
EXTRICATES
EXTRICATING
EXTRINSIC
EXTRORSAL
EXTRORSE
EXTROVERT
EXTROVERTED
EXTROVERTING
EXTROVERTS
EXTRUDE
EXTRUDED
EXTRUDER
EXTRUDERS
EXTRUDES
EXTRUDING
EXTRUSION
EXTRUSIONS
EXTRUSIVE
EXTRUSORY
EXUBERANT
EXUBERATE
EXUBERATED
EXUBERATES
EXUBERATING
EXUDATE
EXUDATES
EXUDATION
EXUDATIONS
EXUDATIVE
EXUDE
EXUDED
EXUDES
EXUDING
EXUL
EXULS
EXULT
EXULTANCE
EXULTANCES
EXULTANCIES
EXULTANCY
EXULTANT
EXULTED
EXULTING
EXULTS
EXURB
EXURBAN
EXURBIA
EXURBIAS
EXURBS
EXUVIAE
EXUVIAL
EXUVIATE
EXUVIATED
EXUVIATES
EXUVIATING
EYALET
EYALETS
EYAS
EYASES
EYE
EYEBALL
EYEBALLED
EYEBALLING
EYEBALLS
EYEBOLT
EYEBOLTS
EYEBRIGHT
EYEBRIGHTS
EYEBROW
EYEBROWED
EYEBROWING
EYEBROWS
EYED
EYEFUL
EYEFULS
EYEGLASS
EYEGLASSES
EYEHOOK
EYEHOOKS
EYEING
EYELASH
EYELASHES
EYELESS
EYELET
EYELETED
EYELETEER
EYELETEERS
EYELETING
EYELETS
EYELIAD
EYELIADS
EYELID
EYELIDS
EYELINER
EYELINERS
EYES
EYESHADE
EYESHADES
EYESHADOW
EYESHADOWS
EYESIGHT
EYESIGHTS
EYESORE
EYESORES
EYESTALK
EYESTALKS
EYESTRAIN
EYESTRAINS
EYING
EYLIAD
EYLIADS
EYNE
EYOT
EYOTS
EYRA
EYRAS
EYRE
EYRES
EYRIE
EYRIES
EYRY

F

FA
FAB
FABACEOUS
FABBER
FABBEST
FABLE
FABLED
FABLER
FABLERS
FABLES
FABLIAU
FABLIAUX
FABLING
FABLINGS
FABRIC
FABRICANT
FABRICANTS
FABRICATE
FABRICATED
FABRICATES
FABRICATING
FABRICKED
FABRICKING
FABRICS
FABULAR
FABULISE
FABULISED
FABULISES
FABULISING
FABULIST
FABULISTS
FABULIZE
FABULIZED
FABULIZES
FABULIZING
FABULOUS
FABURDEN
FABURDENS
FACADE
FACADES
FACE
FACED
FACELESS
FACEMAN
FACEMEN
FACER
FACERS
FACES
FACET
FACETE
FACETED
FACETIAE
FACETING
FACETIOUS
FACETS
FACIA
FACIAL
FACIALLY
FACIALS
FACIAS
FACIES
FACILE
FACILELY
FACILITIES
FACILITY
FACING
FACINGS
FACONNE
FACONNES
FACSIMILE
FACSIMILED
FACSIMILEING
FACSIMILES
FACT
FACTICE
FACTICES
FACTICITIES
FACTICITY
FACTION
FACTIONAL
FACTIONS
FACTIOUS
FACTIS
FACTISES
FACTITIVE
FACTIVE
FACTOID
FACTOIDS
FACTOR
FACTORAGE
FACTORAGES
FACTORED
FACTORIAL
FACTORIALS
FACTORIES
FACTORING
FACTORINGS
FACTORISE
FACTORISED
FACTORISES
FACTORISING
FACTORIZE
FACTORIZED
FACTORIZES
FACTORIZING
FACTORS
FACTORY
FACTOTUM
FACTOTUMS
FACTS
FACTUAL
FACTUM
FACTUMS
FACTURE
FACTURES
FACULA
FACULAE
FACULAR
FACULTIES
FACULTY
FACUNDITIES
FACUNDITY
FAD
FADABLE
FADAISE
FADAISES
FADDIER
FADDIEST
FADDINESS
FADDINESSES
FADDISH
FADDISM
FADDISMS
FADDIST
FADDISTS
FADDLE
FADDLED
FADDLES
FADDLING
FADDY
FADE
FADED
FADEDLY
FADEDNESS
FADEDNESSES
FADELESS
FADER
FADERS
FADES
FADEUR
FADEURS
FADGE
FADGED
FADGES
FADGING
FADIER
FADIEST
FADING
FADINGS
FADO
FADOS
FADS
FADY
FAECAL
FAECES
FAERIE
FAERIES
FAERY
FAFF
FAFFED
FAFFING
FAFFS
FAG
FAGACEOUS
FAGGED
FAGGERIES
FAGGERY
FAGGING
FAGGINGS
FAGGOT
FAGGOTED
FAGGOTING
FAGGOTINGS
FAGGOTS
FAGOT
FAGOTED
FAGOTING
FAGOTINGS
FAGOTS
FAGOTTI
FAGOTTIST
FAGOTTISTS
FAGOTTO
FAGS
FAH
FAHLBAND
FAHLBANDS
FAHLERZ
FAHLERZES
FAHLORE
FAHLORES
FAHS
FAIBLE
FAIBLES
FAIENCE
FAIENCES
FAIK
FAIKED
FAIKES
FAIKING
FAIKS
FAIL
FAILED
FAILING
FAILINGS
FAILLE
FAILLES
FAILS
FAILURE
FAILURES
FAIN
FAINE
FAINEANCE
FAINEANCES
FAINEANCIES
FAINEANCY
FAINEANT
FAINEANTS
FAINED
FAINER
FAINES
FAINEST
FAINING
FAINITES
FAINLY
FAINNESS
FAINNESSES
FAINS
FAINT
FAINTED
FAINTER
FAINTEST
FAINTIER
FAINTIEST
FAINTING
FAINTINGS
FAINTISH
FAINTLY
FAINTNESS
FAINTNESSES
FAINTS
FAINTY
FAIR
FAIRED
FAIRER
FAIREST
FAIRIES
FAIRILY
FAIRING
FAIRINGS
FAIRISH
FAIRLY
FAIRNESS
FAIRNESSES
FAIRS
FAIRWAY
FAIRWAYS
FAIRY
FAIRYDOM
FAIRYDOMS

FAIRYHOOD
FAIRYHOODS
FAIRYISM
FAIRYISMS
FAIRYLAND
FAIRYLANDS
FAIRYLIKE
FAIRYTALE
FAIRYTALES
FAITH
FAITHCURE
FAITHCURES
FAITHED
FAITHFUL
FAITHING
FAITHLESS
FAITHS
FAITOR
FAITORS
FAITOUR
FAITOURS
FAIX
FAJITAS
FAKE
FAKED
FAKEMENT
FAKEMENTS
FAKER
FAKERIES
FAKERS
FAKERY
FAKES
FAKING
FAKIR
FAKIRISM
FAKIRISMS
FAKIRS
FALAFEL
FALAFELS
FALAJ
FALANGISM
FALANGISMS
FALANGIST
FALANGISTS
FALBALA
FALBALAS
FALCADE
FALCADES
FALCATE
FALCATED
FALCATION
FALCATIONS
FALCES
FALCHION
FALCHIONS
FALCIFORM
FALCON
FALCONER
FALCONERS
FALCONET
FALCONETS
FALCONINE
FALCONRIES
FALCONRY
FALCONS
FALCULA
FALCULAS
FALCULATE
FALDAGE
FALDAGES
FALDERAL
FALDERALS
FALDETTA
FALDETTAS
FALDSTOOL
FALDSTOOLS
FALL
FALLACIES
FALLACY
FALLAL
FALLALERIES
FALLALERY
FALLALS
FALLEN
FALLER
FALLERS
FALLIBLE
FALLIBLY
FALLING
FALLINGS
FALLOUT
FALLOUTS
FALLOW
FALLOWED
FALLOWER
FALLOWEST
FALLOWING
FALLOWS
FALLS
FALSE
FALSED
FALSEHOOD
FALSEHOODS
FALSELY
FALSENESS
FALSENESSES
FALSER
FALSERS
FALSES
FALSEST
FALSETTO
FALSETTOS
FALSEWORK
FALSEWORKS
FALSIES
FALSIFIED
FALSIFIER
FALSIFIERS
FALSIFIES
FALSIFY
FALSIFYING
FALSING
FALSISH
FALSISM
FALSISMS
FALSITIES
FALSITY
FALTBOAT
FALTBOATS
FALTER
FALTERED
FALTERING
FALTERINGS
FALTERS
FALX
FAME
FAMED
FAMELESS
FAMES
FAMILIAL
FAMILIAR
FAMILIARS
FAMILIES
FAMILISM
FAMILISMS
FAMILY
FAMINE
FAMINES
FAMING
FAMISH
FAMISHED
FAMISHES
FAMISHING
FAMOUS
FAMOUSED
FAMOUSES
FAMOUSING
FAMOUSLY
FAMULUS
FAMULUSES
FAN
FANAL
FANALS
FANATIC
FANATICAL
FANATICS
FANCIABLE
FANCIED
FANCIER
FANCIERS
FANCIES
FANCIEST
FANCIFUL
FANCILESS
FANCY
FANCYING
FANCYWORK
FANCYWORKS
FAND
FANDANGLE
FANDANGLES
FANDANGO
FANDANGOES
FANDANGOS
FANDED
FANDING
FANDOM
FANDOMS
FANDS
FANE
FANES
FANFARADE
FANFARADES
FANFARE
FANFARED
FANFARES
FANFARING
FANFARON
FANFARONA
FANFARONAS
FANFARONS
FANFOLD
FANG
FANGED
FANGING
FANGLE
FANGLED
FANGLES
FANGLESS
FANGLING
FANGO
FANGOS
FANGS
FANION
FANIONS
FANK
FANKLE
FANKLED
FANKLES
FANKLING
FANKS
FANLIGHT
FANLIGHTS
FANNED
FANNEL
FANNELL
FANNELLS
FANNELS
FANNER
FANNERS
FANNIES
FANNING
FANNINGS
FANNY
FANON
FANONS
FANS
FANTAD
FANTADS
FANTAIL
FANTAILED
FANTAILS
FANTASIA
FANTASIAS
FANTASIED
FANTASIES
FANTASISE
FANTASISED
FANTASISES
FANTASISING
FANTASIST
FANTASISTS
FANTASIZE
FANTASIZED
FANTASIZES
FANTASIZING
FANTASM
FANTASMS
FANTASQUE
FANTASQUES
FANTAST
FANTASTIC
FANTASTICS
FANTASTRIES
FANTASTRY
FANTASTS
FANTASY
FANTASYING
FANTEEG
FANTEEGS
FANTIGUE
FANTIGUES
FANTOD
FANTODS
FANTOM
FANTOMS
FANTOOSH
FANZINE
FANZINES
FAP
FAQUIR
FAQUIRS
FAR
FARAD
FARADAY
FARADAYS
FARADIC
FARADISE
FARADISED
FARADISES
FARADISING
FARADISM
FARADISMS
FARADIZE
FARADIZED
FARADIZES
FARADIZING
FARADS
FARAND
FARANDINE
FARANDINES
FARANDOLE
FARANDOLES
FARAWAY
FARAWAYS
FARCE
FARCED
FARCES
FARCEUR
FARCEURS
FARCEUSE
FARCEUSES
FARCI
FARCICAL
FARCIED
FARCIES
FARCIFIED
FARCIFIES
FARCIFY
FARCIFYING

FARCIN
FARCING
FARCINGS
FARCINS
FARCY
FARD
FARDAGE
FARDAGES
FARDED
FARDEL
FARDELS
FARDEN
FARDENS
FARDING
FARDINGS
FARDS
FARE
FARED
FARES
FAREWELL
FAREWELLS
FARFET
FARINA
FARINAS
FARING
FARINOSE
FARL
FARLE
FARLES
FARLS
FARM
FARMED
FARMER
FARMERESS
FARMERESSES
FARMERIES
FARMERS
FARMERY
FARMHOUSE
FARMHOUSES
FARMING
FARMINGS
FARMOST
FARMS
FARMSTEAD
FARMSTEADS
FARMYARD
FARMYARDS
FARNESOL
FARNESOLS
FARNESS
FARNESSES
FARO
FAROS
FAROUCHE
FARRAGO
FARRAGOES
FARRAGOS
FARRAND
FARRANT
FARRED
FARREN
FARRENS
FARRIER
FARRIERIES
FARRIERS
FARRIERY
FARRING
FARROW
FARROWED
FARROWING
FARROWS
FARRUCA
FARRUCAS
FARS
FARSE
FARSED
FARSES
FARSING
FART
FARTED
FARTHEL
FARTHELS
FARTHER
FARTHEST
FARTHING
FARTHINGS
FARTING
FARTLEK
FARTLEKS
FARTS
FAS
FASCES
FASCI
FASCIA
FASCIAL
FASCIAS
FASCIATE
FASCIATED
FASCICLE
FASCICLED
FASCICLES
FASCICULE
FASCICULES
FASCICULI
FASCINATE
FASCINATED
FASCINATES
FASCINATING
FASCINE
FASCINES
FASCIO
FASCIOLA
FASCIOLAS
FASCIOLE
FASCIOLES
FASCISM
FASCISMI
FASCISMO
FASCISMS
FASCIST
FASCISTA
FASCISTI
FASCISTIC
FASCISTS
FASH
FASHED
FASHERIES
FASHERY
FASHES
FASHING
FASHION
FASHIONED
FASHIONER
FASHIONERS
FASHIONING
FASHIONS
FASHIOUS
FAST
FASTBACK
FASTBACKS
FASTBALL
FASTBALLS
FASTED
FASTEN
FASTENED
FASTENER
FASTENERS
FASTENING
FASTENINGS
FASTENS
FASTER
FASTERS
FASTEST
FASTI
FASTIGIUM
FASTIGIUMS
FASTING
FASTINGS
FASTISH
FASTLY
FASTNESS
FASTNESSES
FASTS
FASTUOUS
FAT
FATAL
FATALISM
FATALISMS
FATALIST
FATALISTS
FATALITIES
FATALITY
FATALLY
FATE
FATED
FATEFUL
FATEFULLY
FATES
FATHER
FATHERED
FATHERING
FATHERLY
FATHERS
FATHOM
FATHOMED
FATHOMING
FATHOMS
FATIDICAL
FATIGABLE
FATIGATE
FATIGATED
FATIGATES
FATIGATING
FATIGUE
FATIGUED
FATIGUES
FATIGUING
FATISCENT
FATLING
FATLINGS
FATLY
FATNESS
FATNESSES
FATS
FATSIA
FATSIAS
FATSO
FATSOES
FATSOS
FATSTOCK
FATSTOCKS
FATTED
FATTEN
FATTENED
FATTENER
FATTENERS
FATTENING
FATTENINGS
FATTENS
FATTER
FATTEST
FATTIER
FATTIES
FATTIEST
FATTINESS
FATTINESSES
FATTING
FATTISH
FATTISM
FATTISMS
FATTIST
FATTISTS
FATTRELS
FATTY
FATUITIES
FATUITOUS
FATUITY
FATUOUS
FATWA
FATWAED
FATWAH
FATWAHED
FATWAHING
FATWAHS
FATWAING
FATWAS
FAUBOURG
FAUBOURGS
FAUCAL
FAUCES
FAUCET
FAUCETS
FAUCHION
FAUCHIONS
FAUCHON
FAUCHONS
FAUCIAL
FAUGH
FAULCHIN
FAULCHINS
FAULCHION
FAULCHIONS
FAULT
FAULTED
FAULTFUL
FAULTIER
FAULTIEST
FAULTILY
FAULTING
FAULTLESS
FAULTS
FAULTY
FAUN
FAUNA
FAUNAE
FAUNAL
FAUNAS
FAUNIST
FAUNISTIC
FAUNISTS
FAUNS
FAURD
FAUSTIAN
FAUTEUIL
FAUTEUILS
FAUTOR
FAUTORS
FAUVETTE
FAUVETTES
FAUX
FAVE
FAVEL
FAVELA
FAVELAS
FAVELL
FAVEOLATE
FAVER
FAVEST
FAVISM
FAVISMS
FAVOR
FAVORABLE
FAVORABLY
FAVORED
FAVORER
FAVORERS
FAVORING
FAVORITE
FAVORITES
FAVORLESS
FAVORS
FAVOSE
FAVOUR
FAVOURED
FAVOURER
FAVOURERS
FAVOURING
FAVOURITE
FAVOURITES

FAVOURS
FAVOUS
FAVRILE
FAVRILES
FAVUS
FAVUSES
FAW
FAWN
FAWNED
FAWNER
FAWNERS
FAWNING
FAWNINGLY
FAWNINGS
FAWNS
FAWS
FAX
FAXED
FAXES
FAXING
FAY
FAYALITE
FAYALITES
FAYED
FAYENCE
FAYENCES
FAYER
FAYEST
FAYING
FAYNE
FAYNED
FAYNES
FAYNING
FAYRE
FAYRES
FAYS
FAZE
FAZED
FAZENDA
FAZENDAS
FAZES
FAZING
FEAGUE
FEAGUED
FEAGUES
FEAGUING
FEAL
FEALED
FEALING
FEALS
FEALTIES
FEALTY
FEAR
FEARE
FEARED
FEARES
FEARFUL
FEARFULLY
FEARING
FEARLESS
FEARS
FEARSOME
FEASIBLE
FEASIBLY
FEAST
FEASTED
FEASTER
FEASTERS
FEASTFUL
FEASTING
FEASTINGS
FEASTS
FEAT
FEATED
FEATEOUS
FEATHER
FEATHERED
FEATHERIER
FEATHERIEST
FEATHERING
FEATHERINGS
FEATHERS
FEATHERY
FEATING
FEATLY
FEATOUS
FEATS
FEATUOUS
FEATURE
FEATURED
FEATURELY
FEATURES
FEATURING
FEBLESSE
FEBLESSES
FEBRICITIES
FEBRICITY
FEBRICULA
FEBRICULAS
FEBRICULE
FEBRICULES
FEBRIFIC
FEBRIFUGE
FEBRIFUGES
FEBRILE
FEBRILITIES
FEBRILITY
FECAL
FECES
FECHT
FECHTER
FECHTERS
FECHTING
FECHTS
FECIAL
FECIT
FECK
FECKLESS
FECKLY
FECKS
FECULA
FECULAS
FECULENCE
FECULENCES
FECULENCIES
FECULENCY
FECULENT
FECUND
FECUNDATE
FECUNDATED
FECUNDATES
FECUNDATING
FECUNDITIES
FECUNDITY
FED
FEDARIE
FEDARIES
FEDAYEE
FEDAYEEN
FEDELINI
FEDELINIS
FEDERACIES
FEDERACY
FEDERAL
FEDERALS
FEDERARIE
FEDERARIES
FEDERARY
FEDERATE
FEDERATED
FEDERATES
FEDERATING
FEDORA
FEDORAS
FEDS
FEE
FEEBLE
FEEBLED
FEEBLER
FEEBLES
FEEBLEST
FEEBLING
FEEBLISH
FEEBLY
FEED
FEEDBACK
FEEDBACKS
FEEDER
FEEDERS
FEEDING
FEEDINGS
FEEDLOT
FEEDLOTS
FEEDS
FEEDSTOCK
FEEDSTOCKS
FEEDSTUFF
FEEDSTUFFS
FEEING
FEEL
FEELBAD
FEELBADS
FEELER
FEELERS
FEELGOOD
FEELGOODS
FEELING
FEELINGLY
FEELINGS
FEELS
FEER
FEERED
FEERIE
FEERIES
FEERIN
FEERING
FEERINGS
FEERINS
FEERS
FEES
FEESE
FEESED
FEESES
FEESING
FEET
FEETLESS
FEEZE
FEEZED
FEEZES
FEEZING
FEGARIES
FEGARY
FEGS
FEHM
FEHME
FEHMIC
FEIGN
FEIGNED
FEIGNEDLY
FEIGNING
FEIGNINGS
FEIGNS
FEIJOA
FEIJOAS
FEINT
FEINTED
FEINTER
FEINTEST
FEINTING
FEINTS
FEIS
FEISEANNA
FEISTIER
FEISTIEST
FEISTY
FELAFEL
FELAFELS
FELDGRAU
FELDGRAUS
FELDSHER
FELDSHERS
FELDSPAR
FELDSPARS
FELDSPATH
FELDSPATHS
FELICIA
FELICIAS
FELICIFIC
FELICITER
FELICITIES
FELICITY
FELID
FELIDS
FELINE
FELINES
FELINITIES
FELINITY
FELL
FELLA
FELLABLE
FELLAH
FELLAHEEN
FELLAHIN
FELLAHS
FELLAS
FELLATE
FELLATED
FELLATES
FELLATING
FELLATIO
FELLATION
FELLATIONS
FELLATIOS
FELLED
FELLER
FELLERS
FELLEST
FELLIES
FELLING
FELLNESS
FELLNESSES
FELLOE
FELLOES
FELLOW
FELLOWLY
FELLOWS
FELLS
FELLY
FELON
FELONIES
FELONIOUS
FELONOUS
FELONRIES
FELONRY
FELONS
FELONY
FELSIC
FELSITE
FELSITES
FELSITIC
FELSPAR
FELSPARS
FELSTONE
FELSTONES
FELT
FELTED
FELTER
FELTERED
FELTERING
FELTERS
FELTIER
FELTIEST
FELTING
FELTINGS
FELTS
FELTY
FELUCCA
FELUCCAS
FELWORT
FELWORTS

EMAL
EMALE
EMALES
EMALITIES
EMALITY
EMALS
EME
EMERALL
EMERALLS
EMES
EMETARIES
EMETARY
EMINAL
EMINEITIES
EMINEITY
EMININE
EMININES
EMINISE
EMINISED
EMINISES
EMINISING
EMINISM
EMINISMS
EMINIST
EMINISTS
EMINITIES
EMINITY
EMINIZE
EMINIZED
EMINIZES
EMINIZING
EMITER
EMITERS
EMME
EMMES
EMORA
EMORAL
EMUR
EMURS
EN
ENCE
ENCED
ENCELESS
ENCER
ENCERS
ENCES
ENCIBLE
ENCIBLES
ENCING
ENCINGS
END
ENDED
ENDER
ENDERS
ENDIER
ENDIEST
ENDING
ENDS
ENDY
ENESTRA
ENESTRAL
ENESTRALS
ENESTRAS
ENI
FENIS
FENITAR
FENITARS
FENKS
FENLAND
FENLANDS
FENMAN
FENMEN
FENNEC
FENNECS
FENNEL
FENNELS
FENNIER
FENNIES
FENNIEST
FENNISH
FENNY
FENS
FENT
FENTS
FENUGREEK
FENUGREEKS
FEOD
FEODAL
FEODARIES
FEODARY
FEODS
FEOFF
FEOFFED
FEOFFEE
FEOFFEES
FEOFFER
FEOFFERS
FEOFFING
FEOFFMENT
FEOFFMENTS
FEOFFOR
FEOFFORS
FEOFFS
FERACIOUS
FERACITIES
FERACITY
FERAL
FERALISED
FERALIZED
FERE
FERER
FERES
FEREST
FERETORIES
FERETORY
FERIAL
FERINE
FERITIES
FERITY
FERLIED
FERLIER
FERLIES
FERLIEST
FERLY
FERLYING
FERM
FERMATA
FERMATAS
FERMATE
FERMENT
FERMENTED
FERMENTING
FERMENTS
FERMI
FERMION
FERMIONS
FERMIS
FERMIUM
FERMIUMS
FERMS
FERN
FERNBIRD
FERNBIRDS
FERNERIES
FERNERY
FERNIER
FERNIEST
FERNING
FERNINGS
FERNS
FERNSHAW
FERNSHAWS
FERNTICLE
FERNTICLES
FERNY
FEROCIOUS
FEROCITIES
FEROCITY
FERRATE
FERRATES
FERREL
FERRELS
FERREOUS
FERRET
FERRETED
FERRETER
FERRETERS
FERRETING
FERRETS
FERRETY
FERRIAGE
FERRIAGES
FERRIC
FERRIED
FERRIES
FERRITE
FERRITES
FERRITIC
FERRITIN
FERRITINS
FERROTYPE
FERROTYPES
FERROUS
FERRUGO
FERRUGOS
FERRULE
FERRULES
FERRY
FERRYING
FERRYMAN
FERRYMEN
FERTILE
FERTILELY
FERTILER
FERTILEST
FERTILISE
FERTILISED
FERTILISES
FERTILISING
FERTILITIES
FERTILITY
FERTILIZE
FERTILIZED
FERTILIZES
FERTILIZING
FERULA
FERULAS
FERULE
FERULES
FERVENCIES
FERVENCY
FERVENT
FERVENTER
FERVENTEST
FERVENTLY
FERVID
FERVIDER
FERVIDEST
FERVIDITIES
FERVIDITY
FERVIDLY
FERVOROUS
FERVOUR
FERVOURS
FESCUE
FESCUES
FESS
FESSE
FESSED
FESSES
FESSING
FEST
FESTA
FESTAL
FESTALLY
FESTALS
FESTAS
FESTER
FESTERED
FESTERING
FESTERS
FESTILOGIES
FESTILOGY
FESTINATE
FESTINATED
FESTINATES
FESTINATING
FESTIVAL
FESTIVALS
FESTIVE
FESTIVELY
FESTIVITIES
FESTIVITY
FESTIVOUS
FESTOLOGIES
FESTOLOGY
FESTOON
FESTOONED
FESTOONING
FESTOONS
FESTS
FET
FETA
FETAL
FETAS
FETCH
FETCHED
FETCHES
FETCHING
FETE
FETED
FETES
FETIAL
FETICH
FETICHE
FETICHES
FETICHISE
FETICHISED
FETICHISES
FETICHISING
FETICHISM
FETICHISMS
FETICHIST
FETICHISTS
FETICHIZE
FETICHIZED
FETICHIZES
FETICHIZING
FETICIDAL
FETICIDE
FETICIDES
FETID
FETIDER
FETIDEST
FETIDNESS
FETIDNESSES
FETING
FETISH
FETISHES
FETISHISE
FETISHISED
FETISHISES
FETISHISING
FETISHISM
FETISHISMS
FETISHIST
FETISHISTS
FETISHIZE
FETISHIZED
FETISHIZES
FETISHIZING
FETLOCK
FETLOCKED
FETLOCKS
FETOR
FETORS
FETOSCOPIES
FETOSCOPY
FETS
FETT

FETTA
FETTAS
FETTED
FETTER
FETTERED
FETTERING
FETTERS
FETTING
FETTLE
FETTLED
FETTLER
FETTLERS
FETTLES
FETTLING
FETTLINGS
FETTS
FETTUCINE
FETTUCINES
FETTUCINI
FETTUCINIS
FETUS
FETUSES
FETWA
FETWAS
FEU
FEUAR
FEUARS
FEUD
FEUDAL
FEUDALISE
FEUDALISED
FEUDALISES
FEUDALISING
FEUDALISM
FEUDALISMS
FEUDALIST
FEUDALISTS
FEUDALITIES
FEUDALITY
FEUDALIZE
FEUDALIZED
FEUDALIZES
FEUDALIZING
FEUDALLY
FEUDARIES
FEUDARY
FEUDATORIES
FEUDATORY
FEUDED
FEUDING
FEUDINGS
FEUDIST
FEUDISTS
FEUDS
FEUED
FEUILLETE
FEUILLETES
FEUING
FEUS
FEUTRE
FEUTRED
FEUTRES
FEUTRING
FEVER
FEVERED
FEVERFEW
FEVERFEWS
FEVERING
FEVERISH
FEVEROUS
FEVERS
FEW
FEWER
FEWEST
FEWMET
FEWMETS
FEWNESS
FEWNESSES
FEWTER
FEWTERED
FEWTERING
FEWTERS
FEWTRILS
FEY
FEYED
FEYER
FEYEST
FEYING
FEYS
FEZ
FEZES
FEZZED
FEZZES
FIACRE
FIACRES
FIANCE
FIANCEE
FIANCEES
FIANCES
FIAR
FIARS
FIASCO
FIASCOES
FIASCOS
FIAT
FIATED
FIATING
FIATS
FIAUNT
FIAUNTS
FIB
FIBBED
FIBBER
FIBBERIES
FIBBERS
FIBBERY
FIBBING
FIBER
FIBERED
FIBERLESS
FIBERS
FIBRE
FIBRED
FIBRELESS
FIBRES
FIBRIFORM
FIBRIL
FIBRILLA
FIBRILLAE
FIBRILLAR
FIBRILLIN
FIBRILLINS
FIBRILS
FIBRIN
FIBRINOUS
FIBRINS
FIBRO
FIBROCYTE
FIBROCYTES
FIBROID
FIBROIDS
FIBROIN
FIBROINS
FIBROLINE
FIBROLINES
FIBROLITE
FIBROLITES
FIBROMA
FIBROMAS
FIBROMATA
FIBROS
FIBROSE
FIBROSED
FIBROSES
FIBROSING
FIBROSIS
FIBROTIC
FIBROUS
FIBS
FIBSTER
FIBSTERS
FIBULA
FIBULAE
FIBULAR
FIBULAS
FICHE
FICHES
FICHU
FICHUS
FICKLE
FICKLED
FICKLER
FICKLES
FICKLEST
FICKLING
FICO
FICOS
FICTILE
FICTION
FICTIONAL
FICTIONS
FICTIVE
FICTOR
FICTORS
FICUS
FICUSES
FID
FIDDIOUS
FIDDIOUSED
FIDDIOUSES
FIDDIOUSING
FIDDLE
FIDDLED
FIDDLER
FIDDLERS
FIDDLES
FIDDLEY
FIDDLEYS
FIDDLIER
FIDDLIEST
FIDDLING
FIDDLY
FIDEISM
FIDEISMS
FIDEIST
FIDEISTIC
FIDEISTS
FIDELITIES
FIDELITY
FIDGE
FIDGED
FIDGES
FIDGET
FIDGETED
FIDGETIER
FIDGETIEST
FIDGETING
FIDGETS
FIDGETY
FIDGING
FIDIBUS
FIDIBUSES
FIDS
FIDUCIAL
FIDUCIARIES
FIDUCIARY
FIE
FIEF
FIEFDOM
FIEFDOMS
FIEFS
FIELD
FIELDED
FIELDER
FIELDERS
FIELDFARE
FIELDFARES
FIELDING
FIELDINGS
FIELDMICE
FIELDS
FIELDSMAN
FIELDSMEN
FIELDVOLE
FIELDVOLES
FIELDWARD
FIELDWARDS
FIELDWORK
FIELDWORKS
FIEND
FIENDISH
FIENDS
FIENT
FIENTS
FIER
FIERCE
FIERCELY
FIERCER
FIERCEST
FIERE
FIERES
FIERIER
FIERIEST
FIERILY
FIERINESS
FIERINESSES
FIERY
FIEST
FIESTA
FIESTAS
FIFE
FIFED
FIFER
FIFERS
FIFES
FIFING
FIFTEEN
FIFTEENER
FIFTEENERS
FIFTEENS
FIFTEENTH
FIFTEENTHS
FIFTH
FIFTHLY
FIFTHS
FIFTIES
FIFTIETH
FIFTIETHS
FIFTY
FIFTYISH
FIG
FIGGED
FIGGERIES
FIGGERY
FIGGING
FIGHT
FIGHTABLE
FIGHTBACK
FIGHTBACKS
FIGHTER
FIGHTERS
FIGHTING
FIGHTINGS
FIGHTS
FIGMENT
FIGMENTS
FIGO
FIGOS
FIGS
FIGULINE
FIGULINES
FIGURABLE
FIGURAL
FIGURANT
FIGURANTE
FIGURANTES
FIGURANTS
FIGURATE
FIGURE
FIGURED

GURES
GURINE
GURINES
GURING
GURIST
GURISTS
GWORT
GWORTS
KE
KED
KERIES
KERY
KES
KIER
KIEST
KING
KISH
KY
L
LABEG
LABEGS
LACEOUS
LACER
LACERS
LAGREE
LAGREES
LAMENT
LAMENTS
LANDER
LANDERS
LAR
LARIA
LARIAL
LARIAS
LASSE
LASSES
LATORIES
LATORY
LATURE
LATURES
LAZER
LAZERS
LBERD
LBERDS
LBERT
LBERTS
LCH
LCHED
LCHER
LCHERS
LCHES
LCHING
LCHINGS
LE
LED
LEMOT
LEMOTS
LENAME
LENAMES
LER
LERS
LES
LET
LETS
FILFOT
FILFOTS
FILIAL
FILIALLY
FILIATE
FILIATED
FILIATES
FILIATING
FILIATION
FILIATIONS
FILIBEG
FILIBEGS
FILICIDE
FILICIDES
FILIFORM
FILIGRAIN
FILIGRAINS
FILIGRANE
FILIGRANES
FILIGREE
FILIGREED
FILIGREES
FILING
FILINGS
FILIOQUE
FILIOQUES
FILL
FILLE
FILLED
FILLER
FILLERS
FILLES
FILLET
FILLETED
FILLETING
FILLETS
FILLIBEG
FILLIBEGS
FILLIES
FILLING
FILLINGS
FILLIP
FILLIPED
FILLIPEEN
FILLIPEENS
FILLIPING
FILLIPS
FILLISTER
FILLISTERS
FILLS
FILLY
FILM
FILMABLE
FILMDOM
FILMDOMS
FILMED
FILMGOER
FILMGOERS
FILMIC
FILMIER
FILMIEST
FILMINESS
FILMINESSES
FILMING
FILMISH
FILMLAND
FILMLANDS
FILMS
FILMSET
FILMSETS
FILMSETTING
FILMSETTINGS
FILMY
FILO
FILOPLUME
FILOPLUMES
FILOPODIA
FILOS
FILOSE
FILOSELLE
FILOSELLES
FILS
FILTER
FILTERED
FILTERING
FILTERS
FILTH
FILTHIER
FILTHIEST
FILTHILY
FILTHS
FILTHY
FILTRABLE
FILTRATE
FILTRATED
FILTRATES
FILTRATING
FIMBLE
FIMBLES
FIMBRIA
FIMBRIAE
FIMBRIATE
FIMBRIATED
FIMBRIATES
FIMBRIATING
FIN
FINABLE
FINAGLE
FINAGLED
FINAGLES
FINAGLING
FINAL
FINALE
FINALES
FINALISE
FINALISED
FINALISES
FINALISING
FINALISM
FINALISMS
FINALIST
FINALISTS
FINALITIES
FINALITY
FINALIZE
FINALIZED
FINALIZES
FINALIZING
FINALLY
FINALS
FINANCE
FINANCED
FINANCES
FINANCIAL
FINANCIER
FINANCIERED
FINANCIERING
FINANCIERS
FINANCING
FINBACK
FINBACKS
FINCH
FINCHED
FINCHES
FIND
FINDER
FINDERS
FINDING
FINDINGS
FINDRAM
FINDRAMS
FINDS
FINE
FINED
FINEER
FINEERED
FINEERING
FINEERS
FINEISH
FINELESS
FINELY
FINENESS
FINENESSES
FINER
FINERIES
FINERS
FINERY
FINES
FINESSE
FINESSED
FINESSER
FINESSERS
FINESSES
FINESSING
FINESSINGS
FINEST
FINGAN
FINGANS
FINGER
FINGERED
FINGERING
FINGERINGS
FINGERS
FINGERTIP
FINGERTIPS
FINI
FINIAL
FINIALS
FINICAL
FINICALLY
FINICKETIER
FINICKETIEST
FINICKETY
FINICKIER
FINICKIEST
FINICKING
FINICKINGS
FINICKY
FINIKIN
FINING
FININGS
FINIS
FINISH
FINISHED
FINISHER
FINISHERS
FINISHES
FINISHING
FINISHINGS
FINITE
FINITELY
FINITUDE
FINITUDES
FINJAN
FINJANS
FINK
FINKED
FINKING
FINKS
FINLESS
FINNAC
FINNACK
FINNACKS
FINNACS
FINNAN
FINNANS
FINNED
FINNER
FINNERS
FINNESKO
FINNIER
FINNIEST
FINNOCHIO
FINNOCHIOS
FINNOCK
FINNOCKS
FINNSKO
FINNY
FINO
FINOCCHIO
FINOCCHIOS
FINOCHIO
FINOCHIOS
FINOS
FINS
FINSKO
FIORD
FIORDS
FIORIN
FIORINS
FIORITURA
FIORITURE
FIPPENCE
FIPPENCES
FIPPLE
FIPPLES

FIR
FIRE
FIREARM
FIREARMS
FIREBALL
FIREBALLS
FIREBOX
FIREBOXES
FIREBRAND
FIREBRANDS
FIREBRAT
FIREBRATS
FIREBRICK
FIREBRICKS
FIREBUG
FIREBUGS
FIRECREST
FIRECRESTS
FIRED
FIREDAMP
FIREDAMPS
FIREDOG
FIREDOGS
FIREFLIES
FIREFLOAT
FIREFLOATS
FIREFLY
FIREGUARD
FIREGUARDS
FIREHOUSE
FIREHOUSES
FIRELESS
FIRELIGHT
FIRELIGHTS
FIRELOCK
FIRELOCKS
FIREMAN
FIREMARK
FIREMARKS
FIREMEN
FIREPAN
FIREPANS
FIREPLACE
FIREPLACES
FIREPOT
FIREPOTS
FIREPROOF
FIREPROOFED
FIREPROOFING
FIREPROOFINGS
FIREPROOFS
FIRER
FIRERS
FIRES
FIRESHIP
FIRESHIPS
FIRESIDE
FIRESIDES
FIRESTONE
FIRESTONES
FIRETHORN
FIRETHORNS
FIREWALL
FIREWALLS
FIREWEED
FIREWEEDS
FIREWOMAN
FIREWOMEN
FIREWOOD
FIREWOODS
FIREWORK
FIREWORKS
FIREWORM
FIREWORMS
FIRING
FIRINGS
FIRK
FIRKED
FIRKIN
FIRKING
FIRKINS
FIRKS
FIRLOT
FIRLOTS
FIRM
FIRMAMENT
FIRMAMENTS
FIRMAN
FIRMANS
FIRMED
FIRMER
FIRMERS
FIRMEST
FIRMING
FIRMLESS
FIRMLY
FIRMNESS
FIRMNESSES
FIRMS
FIRMWARE
FIRMWARES
FIRN
FIRNS
FIRRIER
FIRRIEST
FIRRING
FIRRINGS
FIRRY
FIRS
FIRST
FIRSTLING
FIRSTLINGS
FIRSTLY
FIRSTS
FIRTH
FIRTHS
FISC
FISCAL
FISCALLY
FISCALS
FISCS
FISGIG
FISGIGS
FISH
FISHABLE
FISHBALL
FISHBALLS
FISHED
FISHER
FISHERIES
FISHERMAN
FISHERMEN
FISHERS
FISHERY
FISHES
FISHEYE
FISHEYES
FISHFUL
FISHGIG
FISHGIGS
FISHIER
FISHIEST
FISHIFIED
FISHIFIES
FISHIFY
FISHIFYING
FISHINESS
FISHINESSES
FISHING
FISHINGS
FISHSKIN
FISHSKINS
FISHWIFE
FISHWIVES
FISHY
FISHYBACK
FISHYBACKS
FISK
FISKED
FISKING
FISKS
FISNOMIE
FISNOMIES
FISSILE
FISSILITIES
FISSILITY
FISSION
FISSIONS
FISSIPED
FISSIPEDE
FISSIPEDES
FISSIPEDS
FISSIVE
FISSLE
FISSLED
FISSLES
FISSLING
FISSURE
FISSURED
FISSURES
FISSURING
FIST
FISTED
FISTFUL
FISTFULS
FISTIANA
FISTIC
FISTICAL
FISTICUFF
FISTICUFFS
FISTIER
FISTIEST
FISTING
FISTMELE
FISTMELES
FISTS
FISTULA
FISTULAE
FISTULAR
FISTULAS
FISTULOSE
FISTULOUS
FISTY
FIT
FITCH
FITCHE
FITCHEE
FITCHES
FITCHET
FITCHETS
FITCHEW
FITCHEWS
FITCHY
FITFUL
FITFULLY
FITLIER
FITLIEST
FITLY
FITMENT
FITMENTS
FITNESS
FITNESSES
FITS
FITT
FITTE
FITTED
FITTER
FITTERS
FITTES
FITTEST
FITTING
FITTINGLY
FITTINGS
FITTS
FIVE
FIVEFOLD
FIVEPENCE
FIVEPENCES
FIVEPENNY
FIVEPIN
FIVEPINS
FIVER
FIVERS
FIVES
FIX
FIXABLE
FIXATE
FIXATED
FIXATES
FIXATING
FIXATION
FIXATIONS
FIXATIVE
FIXATIVES
FIXATURE
FIXATURES
FIXED
FIXEDLY
FIXEDNESS
FIXEDNESSES
FIXER
FIXERS
FIXES
FIXING
FIXINGS
FIXITIES
FIXITY
FIXIVE
FIXTURE
FIXTURES
FIXURE
FIXURES
FIZ
FIZGIG
FIZGIGS
FIZZ
FIZZED
FIZZEN
FIZZENS
FIZZER
FIZZERS
FIZZES
FIZZGIG
FIZZGIGS
FIZZIER
FIZZIEST
FIZZING
FIZZINGS
FIZZLE
FIZZLED
FIZZLES
FIZZLING
FIZZY
FJORD
FJORDS
FLAB
FLABBIER
FLABBIEST
FLABBILY
FLABBY
FLABELLA
FLABELLUM
FLABELLUMS
FLABS
FLACCID
FLACCIDER
FLACCIDEST
FLACCIDLY
FLACK
FLACKER
FLACKERED
FLACKERING
FLACKERS
FLACKET
FLACKETS
FLACKS
FLACON
FLACONS
FLAFF
FLAFFED

FLAFFER
FLAFFERED
FLAFFERING
FLAFFERS
FLAFFING
FLAFFS
FLAG
FLAGELLA
FLAGELLUM
FLAGEOLET
FLAGEOLETS
FLAGGED
FLAGGIER
FLAGGIEST
FLAGGING
FLAGGINGS
FLAGGY
FLAGITATE
FLAGITATED
FLAGITATES
FLAGITATING
FLAGON
FLAGONS
FLAGPOLE
FLAGPOLES
FLAGRANCE
FLAGRANCES
FLAGRANCIES
FLAGRANCY
FLAGRANT
FLAGS
FLAGSHIP
FLAGSHIPS
FLAGSTAFF
FLAGSTAFFS
FLAGSTICK
FLAGSTICKS
FLAGSTONE
FLAGSTONES
FLAIL
FLAILED
FLAILING
FLAILS
FLAIR
FLAIRS
FLAK
FLAKE
FLAKED
FLAKES
FLAKIER
FLAKIES
FLAKIEST
FLAKINESS
FLAKINESSES
FLAKING
FLAKS
FLAKY
FLAM
FLAMBE
FLAMBEAU
FLAMBEAUS
FLAMBEAUX
FLAMBEED
FLAME
FLAMED
FLAMELESS
FLAMELET
FLAMELETS
FLAMEN
FLAMENCO
FLAMENCOS
FLAMENS
FLAMEOUT
FLAMEOUTS
FLAMES
FLAMFEW
FLAMFEWS
FLAMIER
FLAMIEST
FLAMINES
FLAMING
FLAMINGLY
FLAMINGO
FLAMINGOES
FLAMINGOS
FLAMM
FLAMMABLE
FLAMMED
FLAMMING
FLAMMS
FLAMMULE
FLAMMULES
FLAMS
FLAMY
FLAN
FLANCH
FLANCHED
FLANCHES
FLANCHING
FLANCHINGS
FLANERIE
FLANERIES
FLANEUR
FLANEURS
FLANGE
FLANGED
FLANGES
FLANGING
FLANK
FLANKED
FLANKER
FLANKERED
FLANKERING
FLANKERS
FLANKING
FLANKS
FLANNEL
FLANNELLED
FLANNELLING
FLANNELLY
FLANNELS
FLANNEN
FLANNENS
FLANS
FLAP
FLAPJACK
FLAPJACKS
FLAPPABLE
FLAPPED
FLAPPER
FLAPPERS
FLAPPIER
FLAPPIEST
FLAPPING
FLAPPINGS
FLAPPY
FLAPS
FLAPTRACK
FLAPTRACKS
FLARE
FLARED
FLARES
FLARIER
FLARIEST
FLARING
FLARINGLY
FLARY
FLASER
FLASERS
FLASH
FLASHBACK
FLASHBACKED
FLASHBACKING
FLASHBACKS
FLASHBULB
FLASHBULBS
FLASHCUBE
FLASHCUBES
FLASHED
FLASHER
FLASHERS
FLASHES
FLASHEST
FLASHGUN
FLASHGUNS
FLASHIER
FLASHIEST
FLASHILY
FLASHING
FLASHINGS
FLASHY
FLASK
FLASKET
FLASKETS
FLASKS
FLAT
FLATBACK
FLATBACKS
FLATBED
FLATBEDS
FLATBOAT
FLATBOATS
FLATFISH
FLATFISHES
FLATHEAD
FLATHEADS
FLATIRON
FLATIRONS
FLATLET
FLATLETS
FLATLING
FLATLINGS
FLATLONG
FLATLY
FLATMATE
FLATMATES
FLATNESS
FLATNESSES
FLATPACK
FLATPACKS
FLATS
FLATSHARE
FLATSHARES
FLATTED
FLATTEN
FLATTENED
FLATTENING
FLATTENS
FLATTER
FLATTERED
FLATTERER
FLATTERERS
FLATTERIES
FLATTERING
FLATTERS
FLATTERY
FLATTEST
FLATTIES
FLATTING
FLATTINGS
FLATTISH
FLATTY
FLATULENT
FLATUOUS
FLATUS
FLATUSES
FLATWARE
FLATWARES
FLATWAYS
FLATWISE
FLATWORM
FLATWORMS
FLAUGHT
FLAUGHTED
FLAUGHTER
FLAUGHTERED
FLAUGHTERING
FLAUGHTERS
FLAUGHTING
FLAUGHTS
FLAUNCH
FLAUNCHED
FLAUNCHES
FLAUNCHING
FLAUNCHINGS
FLAUNE
FLAUNES
FLAUNT
FLAUNTED
FLAUNTER
FLAUNTERS
FLAUNTIER
FLAUNTIEST
FLAUNTING
FLAUNTS
FLAUNTY
FLAUTIST
FLAUTISTS
FLAVIN
FLAVINE
FLAVINES
FLAVINS
FLAVONE
FLAVONES
FLAVOR
FLAVORED
FLAVORING
FLAVORINGS
FLAVOROUS
FLAVORS
FLAVOUR
FLAVOURED
FLAVOURING
FLAVOURINGS
FLAVOURS
FLAW
FLAWED
FLAWIER
FLAWIEST
FLAWING
FLAWLESS
FLAWN
FLAWNS
FLAWS
FLAWY
FLAX
FLAXEN
FLAXES
FLAXIER
FLAXIEST
FLAXY
FLAY
FLAYED
FLAYER
FLAYERS
FLAYING
FLAYS
FLEA
FLEAM
FLEAMS
FLEAPIT
FLEAPITS
FLEAS
FLEASOME
FLEAWORT
FLEAWORTS
FLECHE
FLECHES
FLECHETTE
FLECHETTES
FLECK
FLECKED
FLECKER
FLECKERED
FLECKERING
FLECKERS
FLECKING
FLECKLESS
FLECKS
FLECTION

FLECTIONS
FLED
FLEDGE
FLEDGED
FLEDGES
FLEDGIER
FLEDGIEST
FLEDGING
FLEDGLING
FLEDGLINGS
FLEDGY
FLEE
FLEECE
FLEECED
FLEECER
FLEECERS
FLEECES
FLEECH
FLEECHED
FLEECHES
FLEECHING
FLEECHINGS
FLEECIER
FLEECIEST
FLEECING
FLEECY
FLEEING
FLEER
FLEERED
FLEERER
FLEERERS
FLEERING
FLEERINGS
FLEERS
FLEES
FLEET
FLEETED
FLEETER
FLEETEST
FLEETING
FLEETLY
FLEETNESS
FLEETNESSES
FLEETS
FLEG
FLEGGED
FLEGGING
FLEGS
FLEME
FLEMES
FLEMING
FLEMISH
FLEMISHED
FLEMISHES
FLEMISHING
FLEMIT
FLENCH
FLENCHED
FLENCHES
FLENCHING
FLENSE
FLENSED
FLENSES
FLENSING
FLESH
FLESHED
FLESHER
FLESHERS
FLESHES
FLESHHOOD
FLESHHOODS
FLESHIER
FLESHIEST
FLESHING
FLESHINGS
FLESHLESS
FLESHLIER
FLESHLIEST
FLESHLING
FLESHLINGS
FLESHLY
FLESHMENT
FLESHMENTS
FLESHWORM
FLESHWORMS
FLESHY
FLETCH
FLETCHED
FLETCHER
FLETCHERS
FLETCHES
FLETCHING
FLETTON
FLETTONS
FLEURET
FLEURETS
FLEURETTE
FLEURETTES
FLEURON
FLEURONS
FLEURY
FLEW
FLEWED
FLEWS
FLEX
FLEXED
FLEXES
FLEXIBLE
FLEXIBLY
FLEXILE
FLEXING
FLEXION
FLEXIONS
FLEXITIME
FLEXITIMES
FLEXOR
FLEXORS
FLEXUOSE
FLEXUOUS
FLEXURAL
FLEXURE
FLEXURES
FLEY
FLEYED
FLEYING
FLEYS
FLIC
FLICHTER
FLICHTERED
FLICHTERING
FLICHTERS
FLICK
FLICKED
FLICKER
FLICKERED
FLICKERING
FLICKERS
FLICKING
FLICKS
FLICS
FLIER
FLIERS
FLIES
FLIEST
FLIGHT
FLIGHTED
FLIGHTIER
FLIGHTIEST
FLIGHTILY
FLIGHTING
FLIGHTS
FLIGHTY
FLIMP
FLIMPED
FLIMPING
FLIMPS
FLIMSIER
FLIMSIES
FLIMSIEST
FLIMSILY
FLIMSY
FLINCH
FLINCHED
FLINCHER
FLINCHERS
FLINCHES
FLINCHING
FLINCHINGS
FLINDER
FLINDERS
FLING
FLINGER
FLINGERS
FLINGING
FLINGS
FLINT
FLINTIER
FLINTIEST
FLINTIFIED
FLINTIFIES
FLINTIFY
FLINTIFYING
FLINTILY
FLINTLOCK
FLINTLOCKS
FLINTS
FLINTY
FLIP
FLIPPANCIES
FLIPPANCY
FLIPPANT
FLIPPED
FLIPPER
FLIPPERS
FLIPPEST
FLIPPING
FLIPS
FLIRT
FLIRTED
FLIRTIER
FLIRTIEST
FLIRTING
FLIRTINGS
FLIRTISH
FLIRTS
FLIRTY
FLISK
FLISKED
FLISKIER
FLISKIEST
FLISKING
FLISKS
FLISKY
FLIT
FLITCH
FLITCHES
FLITE
FLITED
FLITES
FLITING
FLITS
FLITT
FLITTED
FLITTER
FLITTERED
FLITTERING
FLITTERN
FLITTERNS
FLITTERS
FLITTING
FLITTINGS
FLIVVER
FLIVVERS
FLIX
FLIXED
FLIXES
FLIXING
FLOAT
FLOATABLE
FLOATAGE
FLOATAGES
FLOATANT
FLOATANTS
FLOATED
FLOATEL
FLOATELS
FLOATER
FLOATERS
FLOATIER
FLOATIEST
FLOATING
FLOATINGS
FLOATS
FLOATY
FLOCCI
FLOCCOSE
FLOCCULAR
FLOCCULE
FLOCCULES
FLOCCULI
FLOCCULUS
FLOCCUS
FLOCK
FLOCKED
FLOCKING
FLOCKS
FLOE
FLOES
FLOG
FLOGGED
FLOGGING
FLOGGINGS
FLOGS
FLOKATI
FLOKATIS
FLONG
FLONGS
FLOOD
FLOODED
FLOODGATE
FLOODGATES
FLOODING
FLOODINGS
FLOODLIT
FLOODMARK
FLOODMARKS
FLOODS
FLOODTIDE
FLOODTIDES
FLOODWALL
FLOODWALLS
FLOODWAY
FLOODWAYS
FLOOR
FLOORED
FLOORER
FLOORERS
FLOORHEAD
FLOORHEADS
FLOORING
FLOORINGS
FLOORS
FLOOSIE
FLOOSIES
FLOOSY
FLOOZIE
FLOOZIES
FLOOZY
FLOP
FLOPHOUSE
FLOPHOUSES
FLOPPED
FLOPPIER
FLOPPIES
FLOPPIEST
FLOPPILY
FLOPPING
FLOPPY
FLOPS
FLOPTICAL

FLOR
FLORA
FLORAE
FLORAL
FLORALLY
FLORAS
FLOREAT
FLOREATED
FLORENCE
FLORENCES
FLORET
FLORETS
FLORIATED
FLORID
FLORIDEAN
FLORIDEANS
FLORIDER
FLORIDEST
FLORIDITIES
FLORIDITY
FLORIDLY
FLORIER
FLORIEST
FLORIFORM
FLORIGEN
FLORIGENS
FLORIN
FLORINS
FLORIST
FLORISTIC
FLORISTICS
FLORISTRIES
FLORISTRY
FLORISTS
FLORS
FLORUIT
FLORUITED
FLORUITING
FLORUITS
FLORY
FLOSCULAR
FLOSCULE
FLOSCULES
FLOSH
FLOSHES
FLOSS
FLOSSED
FLOSSES
FLOSSIER
FLOSSIEST
FLOSSING
FLOSSINGS
FLOSSY
FLOTA
FLOTAGE
FLOTAGES
FLOTANT
FLOTAS
FLOTATION
FLOTATIONS
FLOTE
FLOTEL
FLOTELS
FLOTES
FLOTILLA
FLOTILLAS
FLOTSAM
FLOTSAMS
FLOUNCE
FLOUNCED
FLOUNCES
FLOUNCIER
FLOUNCIEST
FLOUNCING
FLOUNCINGS
FLOUNCY
FLOUNDER
FLOUNDERED
FLOUNDERING
FLOUNDERS
FLOUR
FLOURED
FLOURIER
FLOURIEST
FLOURING
FLOURISH
FLOURISHED
FLOURISHES
FLOURISHING
FLOURISHY
FLOURS
FLOURY
FLOUSE
FLOUSED
FLOUSES
FLOUSH
FLOUSHED
FLOUSHES
FLOUSHING
FLOUSING
FLOUT
FLOUTED
FLOUTING
FLOUTS
FLOW
FLOWAGE
FLOWAGES
FLOWED
FLOWER
FLOWERAGE
FLOWERAGES
FLOWERED
FLOWERER
FLOWERERS
FLOWERET
FLOWERETS
FLOWERIER
FLOWERIEST
FLOWERING
FLOWERINGS
FLOWERPOT
FLOWERPOTS
FLOWERS
FLOWERY
FLOWING
FLOWINGLY
FLOWMETER
FLOWMETERS
FLOWN
FLOWS
FLU
FLUATE
FLUATES
FLUB
FLUBBED
FLUBBING
FLUBS
FLUCTUANT
FLUCTUATE
FLUCTUATED
FLUCTUATES
FLUCTUATING
FLUE
FLUELLIN
FLUELLINS
FLUENCE
FLUENCES
FLUENCIES
FLUENCY
FLUENT
FLUENTLY
FLUENTS
FLUES
FLUEWORK
FLUEWORKS
FLUEY
FLUFF
FLUFFED
FLUFFIER
FLUFFIEST
FLUFFING
FLUFFS
FLUFFY
FLUGEL
FLUGELMAN
FLUGELMEN
FLUGELS
FLUID
FLUIDAL
FLUIDIC
FLUIDICS
FLUIDIFIED
FLUIDIFIES
FLUIDIFY
FLUIDIFYING
FLUIDISE
FLUIDISED
FLUIDISES
FLUIDISING
FLUIDITIES
FLUIDITY
FLUIDIZE
FLUIDIZED
FLUIDIZES
FLUIDIZING
FLUIDNESS
FLUIDNESSES
FLUIDS
FLUIER
FLUIEST
FLUKE
FLUKED
FLUKES
FLUKEY
FLUKIER
FLUKIEST
FLUKING
FLUKY
FLUME
FLUMES
FLUMMERIES
FLUMMERY
FLUMMOX
FLUMMOXED
FLUMMOXES
FLUMMOXING
FLUMP
FLUMPED
FLUMPING
FLUMPS
FLUNG
FLUNK
FLUNKED
FLUNKEY
FLUNKEYS
FLUNKIES
FLUNKING
FLUNKS
FLUNKY
FLUOR
FLUORESCE
FLUORESCED
FLUORESCES
FLUORESCING
FLUORIC
FLUORIDE
FLUORIDES
FLUORINE
FLUORINES
FLUORITE
FLUORITES
FLUOROSES
FLUOROSIS
FLUORS
FLUORSPAR
FLUORSPARS
FLURR
FLURRED
FLURRIED
FLURRIES
FLURRING
FLURRS
FLURRY
FLURRYING
FLUS
FLUSH
FLUSHED
FLUSHER
FLUSHERS
FLUSHES
FLUSHEST
FLUSHIER
FLUSHIEST
FLUSHING
FLUSHINGS
FLUSHNESS
FLUSHNESSES
FLUSHY
FLUSTER
FLUSTERED
FLUSTERING
FLUSTERS
FLUSTERY
FLUSTRATE
FLUSTRATED
FLUSTRATES
FLUSTRATING
FLUTE
FLUTED
FLUTER
FLUTERS
FLUTES
FLUTIER
FLUTIEST
FLUTINA
FLUTINAS
FLUTING
FLUTINGS
FLUTIST
FLUTISTS
FLUTTER
FLUTTERED
FLUTTERING
FLUTTERS
FLUTY
FLUVIAL
FLUVIATIC
FLUX
FLUXED
FLUXES
FLUXING
FLUXION
FLUXIONAL
FLUXIONS
FLUXIVE
FLY
FLYABLE
FLYAWAY
FLYBANE
FLYBANES
FLYBELT
FLYBELTS
FLYBLOW
FLYBLOWS
FLYBOAT
FLYBOATS
FLYBOOK
FLYBOOKS
FLYER
FLYERS
FLYEST
FLYING
FLYINGS
FLYLEAF
FLYLEAVES
FLYMAKER
FLYMAKERS
FLYOVER
FLYOVERS
FLYPAPER

FLYPAPERS
FLYPE
FLYPED
FLYPES
FLYPING
FLYPITCH
FLYPITCHES
FLYSCH
FLYSCHES
FLYTE
FLYTED
FLYTES
FLYTING
FLYTINGS
FLYTRAP
FLYTRAPS
FLYWAY
FLYWAYS
FLYWEIGHT
FLYWEIGHTS
FLYWHEEL
FLYWHEELS
FOAL
FOALED
FOALFOOT
FOALFOOTS
FOALING
FOALS
FOAM
FOAMED
FOAMIER
FOAMIEST
FOAMILY
FOAMINESS
FOAMINESSES
FOAMING
FOAMINGLY
FOAMINGS
FOAMLESS
FOAMS
FOAMY
FOB
FOBBED
FOBBING
FOBS
FOCACCIA
FOCACCIAS
FOCAL
FOCALISE
FOCALISED
FOCALISES
FOCALISING
FOCALIZE
FOCALIZED
FOCALIZES
FOCALIZING
FOCALLY
FOCI
FOCIMETER
FOCIMETERS
FOCUS
FOCUSED
FOCUSES
FOCUSING
FOCUSINGS
FOCUSSED
FOCUSSES
FOCUSSING
FODDER
FODDERED
FODDERER
FODDERERS
FODDERING
FODDERINGS
FODDERS
FOE
FOEDARIE
FOEDARIES
FOEDERATI
FOEHN
FOEHNS
FOEMAN
FOEMEN
FOEN
FOES
FOETAL
FOETICIDE
FOETICIDES
FOETID
FOETIDER
FOETIDEST
FOETOR
FOETORS
FOETUS
FOETUSES
FOG
FOGASH
FOGASHES
FOGBOUND
FOGEY
FOGEYDOM
FOGEYDOMS
FOGEYISH
FOGEYISM
FOGEYISMS
FOGEYS
FOGGAGE
FOGGAGES
FOGGED
FOGGER
FOGGERS
FOGGIER
FOGGIEST
FOGGILY
FOGGINESS
FOGGINESSES
FOGGING
FOGGY
FOGHORN
FOGHORNS
FOGIES
FOGLE
FOGLES
FOGLESS
FOGMAN
FOGMEN
FOGRAM
FOGRAMITE
FOGRAMITES
FOGRAMITIES
FOGRAMITY
FOGRAMS
FOGS
FOGY
FOGYDOM
FOGYDOMS
FOGYISH
FOGYISM
FOGYISMS
FOH
FOHN
FOHNS
FOHS
FOIBLE
FOIBLES
FOID
FOIDS
FOIL
FOILBORNE
FOILED
FOILING
FOILINGS
FOILS
FOIN
FOINED
FOINING
FOININGLY
FOINS
FOISON
FOISONS
FOIST
FOISTED
FOISTER
FOISTERS
FOISTING
FOISTS
FOLACIN
FOLACINS
FOLATE
FOLATES
FOLD
FOLDABLE
FOLDAWAY
FOLDBOAT
FOLDBOATS
FOLDED
FOLDER
FOLDEROL
FOLDEROLS
FOLDERS
FOLDING
FOLDINGS
FOLDS
FOLIA
FOLIAGE
FOLIAGED
FOLIAGES
FOLIAR
FOLIATE
FOLIATED
FOLIATES
FOLIATING
FOLIATION
FOLIATIONS
FOLIATURE
FOLIATURES
FOLIE
FOLIES
FOLIO
FOLIOED
FOLIOING
FOLIOLATE
FOLIOLE
FOLIOLES
FOLIOLOSE
FOLIOS
FOLIOSE
FOLIUM
FOLK
FOLKIE
FOLKIES
FOLKLAND
FOLKLANDS
FOLKLORE
FOLKLORES
FOLKLORIC
FOLKMOOT
FOLKMOOTS
FOLKS
FOLKSIER
FOLKSIEST
FOLKSY
FOLKWAY
FOLKWAYS
FOLLICLE
FOLLICLES
FOLLIED
FOLLIES
FOLLOW
FOLLOWED
FOLLOWER
FOLLOWERS
FOLLOWING
FOLLOWINGS
FOLLOWS
FOLLY
FOLLYING
FOMENT
FOMENTED
FOMENTER
FOMENTERS
FOMENTING
FOMENTS
FOMES
FOMITES
FON
FOND
FONDA
FONDANT
FONDANTS
FONDAS
FONDED
FONDER
FONDEST
FONDING
FONDLE
FONDLED
FONDLER
FONDLERS
FONDLES
FONDLING
FONDLINGS
FONDLY
FONDNESS
FONDNESSES
FONDS
FONDUE
FONDUES
FONE
FONLY
FONNED
FONNING
FONS
FONT
FONTAL
FONTANEL
FONTANELS
FONTANGE
FONTANGES
FONTICULI
FONTLET
FONTLETS
FONTS
FOOD
FOODFUL
FOODIE
FOODIES
FOODISM
FOODISMS
FOODLESS
FOODS
FOODSTUFF
FOODSTUFFS
FOODY
FOOL
FOOLED
FOOLERIES
FOOLERY
FOOLHARDIER
FOOLHARDIEST
FOOLHARDY
FOOLING
FOOLINGS
FOOLISH
FOOLISHER
FOOLISHEST
FOOLISHLY
FOOLPROOF
FOOLS
FOOLSCAP
FOOLSCAPS
FOOT
FOOTAGE
FOOTAGES
FOOTBALL
FOOTBALLS
FOOTBAR
FOOTBARS
FOOTBOARD
FOOTBOARDS

OOTBOY
OOTBOYS
OOTCLOTH
OOTCLOTHS
OOTED
OOTER
OOTERS
OOTFALL
OOTFALLS
OOTFAULT
OOTFAULTED
OOTFAULTING
OOTFAULTS
OOTGEAR
OOTGEARS
OOTHILL
OOTHILLS
OOTHOLD
OOTHOLDS
OOTIE
OOTIER
OOTIES
OOTIEST
OOTING
OOTINGS
OOTLE
OOTLED
OOTLES
OOTLESS
OOTLIGHT
OOTLIGHTS
OOTLING
OOTLINGS
OOTLOOSE
OOTMAN
OOTMARK
OOTMARKS
OOTMEN
OOTMUFF
OOTMUFFS
OOTNOTE
OOTNOTES
OOTPACE
OOTPACES
OOTPAD
OOTPADS
OOTPAGE
OOTPAGES
OOTPATH
OOTPATHS
OOTPLATE
OOTPLATES
OOTPOST
OOTPOSTS
OOTPRINT
OOTPRINTS
OOTRA
OOTRAS
OOTREST
OOTRESTS
OOTROT
OOTROTS
OOTRULE
OOTRULES
FOOTS
FOOTSLOG
FOOTSLOGGED
FOOTSLOGGING
FOOTSLOGGINGS
FOOTSLOGS
FOOTSORE
FOOTSTALK
FOOTSTALKS
FOOTSTEP
FOOTSTEPS
FOOTSTOOL
FOOTSTOOLS
FOOTWAY
FOOTWAYS
FOOTWEAR
FOOTWEARS
FOOTWELL
FOOTWELLS
FOOTWORK
FOOTWORKS
FOOTWORN
FOOTY
FOOZLE
FOOZLED
FOOZLER
FOOZLERS
FOOZLES
FOOZLING
FOOZLINGS
FOP
FOPLING
FOPLINGS
FOPPERIES
FOPPERY
FOPPISH
FOPPISHLY
FOPS
FOR
FORA
FORAGE
FORAGED
FORAGER
FORAGERS
FORAGES
FORAGING
FORAMEN
FORAMINA
FORAMINAL
FORANE
FORASMUCH
FORAY
FORAYED
FORAYER
FORAYERS
FORAYING
FORAYS
FORB
FORBAD
FORBADE
FORBEAR
FORBEARING
FORBEARS
FORBID
FORBIDDAL
FORBIDDALS
FORBIDDEN
FORBIDDER
FORBIDDERS
FORBIDDING
FORBIDDINGS
FORBIDS
FORBODE
FORBODES
FORBORE
FORBORNE
FORBS
FORBY
FORBYE
FORCAT
FORCATS
FORCE
FORCED
FORCEDLY
FORCEFUL
FORCELESS
FORCEMEAT
FORCEMEATS
FORCEPS
FORCEPSES
FORCER
FORCERS
FORCES
FORCIBLE
FORCIBLY
FORCING
FORCIPATE
FORCIPES
FORD
FORDABLE
FORDED
FORDID
FORDING
FORDO
FORDOES
FORDOING
FORDONE
FORDS
FORE
FOREANENT
FOREARM
FOREARMED
FOREARMING
FOREARMS
FOREBEAR
FOREBEARS
FOREBITT
FOREBITTS
FOREBODE
FOREBODED
FOREBODER
FOREBODERS
FOREBODES
FOREBODING
FOREBODINGS
FOREBRAIN
FOREBRAINS
FOREBY
FORECABIN
FORECABINS
FORECAR
FORECARS
FORECAST
FORECASTED
FORECASTING
FORECASTS
FORECLOSE
FORECLOSED
FORECLOSES
FORECLOSING
FORECLOTH
FORECLOTHS
FORECOURT
FORECOURTS
FOREDATE
FOREDATED
FOREDATES
FOREDATING
FOREDECK
FOREDECKS
FOREDOOM
FOREDOOMED
FOREDOOMING
FOREDOOMS
FOREFEEL
FOREFEELING
FOREFEELS
FOREFEET
FOREFELT
FOREFOOT
FOREFRONT
FOREFRONTS
FOREGLEAM
FOREGLEAMS
FOREGO
FOREGOER
FOREGOERS
FOREGOES
FOREGOING
FOREGOINGS
FOREGONE
FOREGUT
FOREGUTS
FOREHAND
FOREHANDS
FOREHEAD
FOREHEADS
FOREHENT
FOREHENTING
FOREHENTS
FOREIGN
FOREIGNER
FOREIGNERS
FOREJUDGE
FOREJUDGED
FOREJUDGES
FOREJUDGING
FOREKING
FOREKINGS
FOREKNEW
FOREKNOW
FOREKNOWING
FOREKNOWN
FOREKNOWS
FOREL
FORELAID
FORELAIN
FORELAND
FORELANDS
FORELAY
FORELAYING
FORELAYS
FORELEG
FORELEGS
FORELEND
FORELENDING
FORELENDS
FORELENT
FORELIE
FORELIES
FORELIFT
FORELIFTED
FORELIFTING
FORELIFTS
FORELIMB
FORELIMBS
FORELOCK
FORELOCKS
FORELS
FORELYING
FOREMAN
FOREMAST
FOREMASTS
FOREMEAN
FOREMEANING
FOREMEANS
FOREMEANT
FOREMEN
FOREMOST
FORENAME
FORENAMED
FORENAMES
FORENIGHT
FORENIGHTS
FORENOON
FORENOONS
FORENSIC
FORENSICS
FOREPART
FOREPARTS
FOREPAST
FOREPAW
FOREPAWS
FOREPEAK
FOREPEAKS
FOREPLAN
FOREPLANNED
FOREPLANNING
FOREPLANS
FOREPLAY
FOREPLAYS
FOREPOINT
FOREPOINTED
FOREPOINTING
FOREPOINTS
FORERAN

FOREREACH
FOREREACHED
FOREREACHES
FOREREACHING
FOREREAD
FOREREADING
FOREREADINGS
FOREREADS
FORERUN
FORERUNNING
FORERUNS
FORES
FORESAID
FORESAIL
FORESAILS
FORESAW
FORESAY
FORESAYING
FORESAYS
FORESEE
FORESEEING
FORESEEN
FORESEES
FORESHEW
FORESHEWED
FORESHEWING
FORESHEWN
FORESHEWS
FORESHIP
FORESHIPS
FORESHOCK
FORESHOCKS
FORESHORE
FORESHORES
FORESHOW
FORESHOWED
FORESHOWING
FORESHOWN
FORESHOWS
FORESIDE
FORESIDES
FORESIGHT
FORESIGHTS
FORESKIN
FORESKINS
FORESKIRT
FORESKIRTS
FORESLACK
FORESLACKED
FORESLACKING
FORESLACKS
FORESLOW
FORESLOWED
FORESLOWING
FORESLOWS
FORESPEAK
FORESPEAKING
FORESPEAKS
FORESPEND
FORESPENDING
FORESPENDS
FORESPENT
FORESPOKE
FORESPOKEN
FOREST
FORESTAGE
FORESTAGES
FORESTAIR
FORESTAIRS
FORESTAL
FORESTALL
FORESTALLED
FORESTALLING
FORESTALLINGS
FORESTALLS
FORESTAY
FORESTAYS
FORESTEAL
FORESTED
FORESTER
FORESTERS
FORESTINE
FORESTING
FORESTRIES
FORESTRY
FORESTS
FORETASTE
FORETASTED
FORETASTES
FORETASTING
FORETAUGHT
FORETEACH
FORETEACHES
FORETEACHING
FORETEETH
FORETELL
FORETELLING
FORETELLS
FORETHINK
FORETHINKING
FORETHINKS
FORETHOUGHT
FORETHOUGHTS
FORETIME
FORETIMES
FORETOKEN
FORETOKENED
FORETOKENING
FORETOKENINGS
FORETOKENS
FORETOLD
FORETOOTH
FORETOP
FORETOPS
FOREVER
FOREVERS
FOREWARD
FOREWARDS
FOREWARN
FOREWARNED
FOREWARNING
FOREWARNINGS
FOREWARNS
FOREWEIGH
FOREWEIGHED
FOREWEIGHING
FOREWEIGHS
FOREWENT
FOREWIND
FOREWINDS
FOREWING
FOREWINGS
FOREWOMAN
FOREWOMEN
FOREWORD
FOREWORDS
FORFAIR
FORFAIRED
FORFAIRING
FORFAIRN
FORFAIRS
FORFAITER
FORFAITERS
FORFAULT
FORFAULTS
FORFEIT
FORFEITED
FORFEITER
FORFEITERS
FORFEITING
FORFEITS
FORFEND
FORFENDED
FORFENDING
FORFENDS
FORFEX
FORFEXES
FORFICATE
FORGAT
FORGATHER
FORGATHERED
FORGATHERING
FORGATHERS
FORGAVE
FORGE
FORGEABLE
FORGED
FORGEMAN
FORGEMEN
FORGER
FORGERIES
FORGERS
FORGERY
FORGES
FORGET
FORGETFUL
FORGETIVE
FORGETS
FORGETTER
FORGETTERS
FORGETTING
FORGETTINGS
FORGING
FORGINGS
FORGIVE
FORGIVEN
FORGIVES
FORGIVING
FORGO
FORGOES
FORGOING
FORGONE
FORGOT
FORGOTTEN
FORHAILE
FORHAILED
FORHAILES
FORHAILING
FORHENT
FORHENTING
FORHENTS
FORHOO
FORHOOED
FORHOOIE
FORHOOIED
FORHOOIEING
FORHOOIES
FORHOOING
FORHOOS
FORHOW
FORHOWED
FORHOWING
FORHOWS
FORINSEC
FORINT
FORINTS
FORJASKIT
FORJESKIT
FORJUDGE
FORJUDGED
FORJUDGES
FORJUDGING
FORK
FORKED
FORKEDLY
FORKER
FORKERS
FORKFUL
FORKFULS
FORKHEAD
FORKHEADS
FORKIER
FORKIEST
FORKINESS
FORKINESSES
FORKING
FORKS
FORKTAIL
FORKTAILS
FORKY
FORLANA
FORLANAS
FORLEND
FORLENDING
FORLENDS
FORLENT
FORLESE
FORLESES
FORLESING
FORLORE
FORLORN
FORLORNER
FORLORNEST
FORLORNLY
FORLORNS
FORM
FORMABLE
FORMAL
FORMALIN
FORMALINS
FORMALISE
FORMALISED
FORMALISES
FORMALISING
FORMALISM
FORMALISMS
FORMALIST
FORMALISTS
FORMALITIES
FORMALITY
FORMALIZE
FORMALIZED
FORMALIZES
FORMALIZING
FORMALLY
FORMANT
FORMANTS
FORMAT
FORMATE
FORMATED
FORMATES
FORMATING
FORMATION
FORMATIONS
FORMATIVE
FORMATIVES
FORMATS
FORMATTED
FORMATTER
FORMATTERS
FORMATTING
FORME
FORMED
FORMER
FORMERLY
FORMERS
FORMES
FORMIATE
FORMIATES
FORMIC
FORMICANT
FORMICARIES
FORMICARY
FORMICATE
FORMING
FORMINGS
FORMLESS
FORMOL
FORMOLS
FORMS
FORMULA
FORMULAE
FORMULAIC
FORMULAR
FORMULARIES
FORMULARY
FORMULAS
FORMULATE
FORMULATED
FORMULATES

RMULATING
RMULISE
RMULISED
RMULISES
RMULISING
RMULISM
RMULISMS
RMULIST
RMULISTS
RMULIZE
RMULIZED
RMULIZES
RMULIZING
RMWORK
RMWORKS
RNENST
RNENT
RNICAL
RNICATE
RNICATED
RNICATES
RNICATING
RNICES
RNIX
RPET
RPETS
RPINE
RPINED
RPINES
RPINING
RPIT
RPITS
RRAD
RRADER
RRAY
RRAYED
RRAYING
RRAYS
RREN
RRIT
RSAID
RSAKE
RSAKEN
RSAKES
RSAKING
RSAKINGS
RSAY
RSAYING
RSAYS
RSLACK
RSLACKED
RSLACKING
RSLACKS
RSLOE
RSLOED
RSLOEING
RSLOES
RSLOW
RSLOWED
RSLOWING
RSLOWS
RSOOK
RSOOTH
RSPEAK

FORSPEAKING
FORSPEAKS
FORSPEND
FORSPENDING
FORSPENDS
FORSPENT
FORSPOKE
FORSPOKEN
FORSWATT
FORSWEAR
FORSWEARING
FORSWEARS
FORSWINK
FORSWINKED
FORSWINKING
FORSWINKS
FORSWONCK
FORSWORE
FORSWORN
FORSWUNK
FORSYTHIA
FORSYTHIAS
FORT
FORTALICE
FORTALICES
FORTE
FORTED
FORTES
FORTH
FORTHCAME
FORTHCOME
FORTHCOMES
FORTHCOMING
FORTHINK
FORTHINKING
FORTHINKS
FORTHOUGHT
FORTHWITH
FORTHY
FORTIES
FORTIETH
FORTIETHS
FORTIFIED
FORTIFIER
FORTIFIERS
FORTIFIES
FORTIFY
FORTIFYING
FORTILAGE
FORTILAGES
FORTING
FORTIS
FORTITUDE
FORTITUDES
FORTLET
FORTLETS
FORTNIGHT
FORTNIGHTS
FORTRESS
FORTRESSED
FORTRESSES
FORTRESSING
FORTS
FORTUITIES

FORTUITY
FORTUNATE
FORTUNE
FORTUNED
FORTUNES
FORTUNING
FORTUNIZE
FORTUNIZED
FORTUNIZES
FORTUNIZING
FORTY
FORTYISH
FORUM
FORUMS
FORWANDER
FORWANDERED
FORWANDERING
FORWANDERS
FORWARD
FORWARDED
FORWARDER
FORWARDERS
FORWARDEST
FORWARDING
FORWARDINGS
FORWARDLY
FORWARDS
FORWARN
FORWARNED
FORWARNING
FORWARNS
FORWASTE
FORWASTED
FORWASTES
FORWASTING
FORWEARIED
FORWEARIES
FORWEARY
FORWEARYING
FORWENT
FORWHY
FORWORN
FORZANDI
FORZANDO
FORZANDOS
FORZATI
FORZATO
FORZATOS
FOSS
FOSSA
FOSSAE
FOSSAS
FOSSE
FOSSED
FOSSES
FOSSETTE
FOSSETTES
FOSSICK
FOSSICKED
FOSSICKER
FOSSICKERS
FOSSICKING
FOSSICKINGS
FOSSICKS

FOSSIL
FOSSILISE
FOSSILISED
FOSSILISES
FOSSILISING
FOSSILIZE
FOSSILIZED
FOSSILIZES
FOSSILIZING
FOSSILS
FOSSOR
FOSSORIAL
FOSSORS
FOSSULA
FOSSULAE
FOSSULATE
FOSTER
FOSTERAGE
FOSTERAGES
FOSTERED
FOSTERER
FOSTERERS
FOSTERING
FOSTERINGS
FOSTERS
FOSTRESS
FOSTRESSES
FOTHER
FOTHERED
FOTHERING
FOTHERS
FOU
FOUAT
FOUATS
FOUD
FOUDRIE
FOUDRIES
FOUDS
FOUER
FOUEST
FOUET
FOUETS
FOUETTE
FOUETTES
FOUGADE
FOUGADES
FOUGASSE
FOUGASSES
FOUGHT
FOUGHTEN
FOUGHTIER
FOUGHTIEST
FOUGHTY
FOUL
FOULARD
FOULARDS
FOULDER
FOULDERED
FOULDERING
FOULDERS
FOULE
FOULED
FOULER
FOULES

FOULEST
FOULING
FOULLY
FOULMART
FOULMARTS
FOULNESS
FOULNESSES
FOULS
FOUMART
FOUMARTS
FOUND
FOUNDED
FOUNDER
FOUNDERED
FOUNDERING
FOUNDERS
FOUNDING
FOUNDINGS
FOUNDLING
FOUNDLINGS
FOUNDRESS
FOUNDRESSES
FOUNDRIES
FOUNDRY
FOUNDS
FOUNT
FOUNTAIN
FOUNTAINED
FOUNTAINING
FOUNTAINS
FOUNTFUL
FOUNTS
FOUR
FOURFOLD
FOURGON
FOURGONS
FOURPENCE
FOURPENCES
FOURPENNIES
FOURPENNY
FOURS
FOURSCORE
FOURSES
FOURSOME
FOURSOMES
FOURTEEN
FOURTEENS
FOURTH
FOURTHLY
FOURTHS
FOUS
FOUSSA
FOUSSAS
FOUSTIER
FOUSTIEST
FOUSTY
FOUTER
FOUTERED
FOUTERING
FOUTERS
FOUTH
FOUTHS
FOUTRA
FOUTRAS

FOUTRE
FOUTRED
FOUTRES
FOUTRING
FOVEA
FOVEAE
FOVEAL
FOVEATE
FOVEOLA
FOVEOLAE
FOVEOLAS
FOVEOLE
FOVEOLES
FOWL
FOWLED
FOWLER
FOWLERS
FOWLING
FOWLINGS
FOWLS
FOWTH
FOWTHS
FOX
FOXBERRIES
FOXBERRY
FOXED
FOXES
FOXGLOVE
FOXGLOVES
FOXHOLE
FOXHOLES
FOXHOUND
FOXHOUNDS
FOXIER
FOXIEST
FOXINESS
FOXINESSES
FOXING
FOXINGS
FOXSHARK
FOXSHARKS
FOXSHIP
FOXSHIPS
FOXTROT
FOXTROTS
FOXTROTTED
FOXTROTTING
FOXY
FOY
FOYER
FOYERS
FOYLE
FOYLED
FOYLES
FOYLING
FOYNE
FOYNED
FOYNES
FOYNING
FOYS
FOZIER
FOZIEST
FOZINESS
FOZINESSES
FOZY
FRA
FRAB
FRABBED
FRABBING
FRABBIT
FRABJOUS
FRABS
FRACAS
FRACK
FRACKING
FRACKINGS
FRACT
FRACTAL
FRACTALS
FRACTED
FRACTING
FRACTION
FRACTIONS
FRACTIOUS
FRACTS
FRACTURE
FRACTURED
FRACTURES
FRACTURING
FRAE
FRAENA
FRAENUM
FRAG
FRAGGED
FRAGGING
FRAGILE
FRAGILELY
FRAGILER
FRAGILEST
FRAGILITIES
FRAGILITY
FRAGMENT
FRAGMENTED
FRAGMENTING
FRAGMENTS
FRAGOR
FRAGORS
FRAGRANCE
FRAGRANCED
FRAGRANCES
FRAGRANCIES
FRAGRANCING
FRAGRANCY
FRAGRANT
FRAGS
FRAICHEUR
FRAICHEURS
FRAIL
FRAILER
FRAILEST
FRAILISH
FRAILLY
FRAILNESS
FRAILNESSES
FRAILS
FRAILTEE
FRAILTEES
FRAILTIES
FRAILTY
FRAIM
FRAIMS
FRAISE
FRAISED
FRAISES
FRAISING
FRAME
FRAMED
FRAMER
FRAMERS
FRAMES
FRAMEWORK
FRAMEWORKS
FRAMING
FRAMINGS
FRAMPAL
FRAMPLER
FRAMPLERS
FRAMPOLD
FRANC
FRANCHISE
FRANCHISED
FRANCHISES
FRANCHISING
FRANCIUM
FRANCIUMS
FRANCO
FRANCOLIN
FRANCOLINS
FRANCS
FRANGIBLE
FRANION
FRANIONS
FRANK
FRANKED
FRANKER
FRANKEST
FRANKING
FRANKLIN
FRANKLINS
FRANKLY
FRANKNESS
FRANKNESSES
FRANKS
FRANTIC
FRANTICLY
FRANZIER
FRANZIEST
FRANZY
FRAP
FRAPPANT
FRAPPE
FRAPPED
FRAPPEE
FRAPPES
FRAPPING
FRAPS
FRAS
FRASCATI
FRASCATIS
FRASS
FRASSES
FRATCH
FRATCHES
FRATCHETY
FRATCHIER
FRATCHIEST
FRATCHING
FRATCHY
FRATE
FRATER
FRATERIES
FRATERNAL
FRATERS
FRATERY
FRATI
FRATRIES
FRATRY
FRAU
FRAUD
FRAUDFUL
FRAUDS
FRAUDSMAN
FRAUDSMEN
FRAUDSTER
FRAUDSTERS
FRAUGHT
FRAUGHTED
FRAUGHTER
FRAUGHTEST
FRAUGHTING
FRAUGHTS
FRAULEIN
FRAULEINS
FRAUS
FRAUTAGE
FRAUTAGES
FRAY
FRAYED
FRAYING
FRAYINGS
FRAYS
FRAZIL
FRAZILS
FRAZZLE
FRAZZLED
FRAZZLES
FRAZZLING
FREAK
FREAKED
FREAKFUL
FREAKIER
FREAKIEST
FREAKING
FREAKISH
FREAKS
FREAKY
FRECKLE
FRECKLED
FRECKLES
FRECKLIER
FRECKLIEST
FRECKLING
FRECKLINGS
FRECKLY
FREDAINE
FREDAINES
FREE
FREEBASE
FREEBASED
FREEBASES
FREEBASING
FREEBEE
FREEBEES
FREEBIE
FREEBIES
FREEBOOTIES
FREEBOOTY
FREEBORN
FREED
FREEDMAN
FREEDMEN
FREEDOM
FREEDOMS
FREEHAND
FREEHOLD
FREEHOLDS
FREEING
FREELANCE
FREELANCED
FREELANCES
FREELANCING
FREELOAD
FREELOADED
FREELOADING
FREELOADINGS
FREELOADS
FREELY
FREEMAN
FREEMASON
FREEMASONS
FREEMEN
FREENESS
FREENESSES
FREEPHONE
FREEPHONES
FREER
FREERS
FREES
FREESHEET
FREESHEETS
FREESIA
FREESIAS
FREEST
FREESTONE
FREESTONES
FREESTYLE
FREESTYLES
FREET
FREETIER
FREETIEST
FREETS
FREETY
FREEWARE
FREEWARES
FREEWAY
FREEWAYS
FREEWHEEL
FREEWHEELED
FREEWHEELING
FREEWHEELING

FREEWHEELS
FREEWOMAN
FREEWOMEN
FREEZABLE
FREEZE
FREEZER
FREEZERS
FREEZES
FREEZING
FREEZINGS
FREIGHT
FREIGHTED
FREIGHTER
FREIGHTERS
FREIGHTING
FREIGHTS
FREIT
FREITIER
FREITIEST
FREITS
FREITY
FREMD
FREMDS
FREMIT
FREMITS
FREMITUS
FREMITUSES
FRENA
FRENCH
FRENETIC
FRENETICS
FRENNE
FRENULA
FRENULUM
FRENUM
FRENZICAL
FRENZIED
FRENZIES
FRENZY
FRENZYING
FREON
FREONS
FREQUENCE
FREQUENCES
FREQUENCIES
FREQUENCY
FREQUENT
FREQUENTED
FREQUENTER
FREQUENTERS
FREQUENTEST
FREQUENTING
FREQUENTS
FRERE
FRERES
FRESCADE
FRESCADES
FRESCO
FRESCOED
FRESCOER
FRESCOERS
FRESCOES
FRESCOING
FRESCOINGS
FRESCOIST
FRESCOISTS
FRESCOS
FRESH
FRESHED
FRESHEN
FRESHENED
FRESHENER
FRESHENERS
FRESHENING
FRESHENS
FRESHER
FRESHERS
FRESHES
FRESHEST
FRESHET
FRESHETS
FRESHING
FRESHISH
FRESHLY
FRESHMAN
FRESHMEN
FRESHNESS
FRESHNESSES
FRESNEL
FRESNELS
FRET
FRETFUL
FRETFULLY
FRETS
FRETSAW
FRETSAWS
FRETTED
FRETTIER
FRETTIEST
FRETTING
FRETTINGS
FRETTY
FRETWORK
FRETWORKS
FRIABLE
FRIAND
FRIANDE
FRIANDES
FRIANDS
FRIAR
FRIARBIRD
FRIARBIRDS
FRIARIES
FRIARLY
FRIARS
FRIARY
FRIBBLE
FRIBBLED
FRIBBLER
FRIBBLERS
FRIBBLES
FRIBBLING
FRIBBLISH
FRICADEL
FRICADELS
FRICASSEE
FRICASSEED
FRICASSEEING
FRICASSEES
FRICATIVE
FRICATIVES
FRICHT
FRICHTED
FRICHTING
FRICHTS
FRICTION
FRICTIONS
FRIDGE
FRIDGED
FRIDGES
FRIDGING
FRIED
FRIEDCAKE
FRIEDCAKES
FRIEND
FRIENDED
FRIENDING
FRIENDINGS
FRIENDLIER
FRIENDLIES
FRIENDLIEST
FRIENDLY
FRIENDS
FRIER
FRIERS
FRIES
FRIEZE
FRIEZED
FRIEZES
FRIEZING
FRIG
FRIGATE
FRIGATES
FRIGATOON
FRIGATOONS
FRIGES
FRIGGED
FRIGGER
FRIGGERS
FRIGGING
FRIGGINGS
FRIGHT
FRIGHTED
FRIGHTEN
FRIGHTENED
FRIGHTENING
FRIGHTENS
FRIGHTFUL
FRIGHTING
FRIGHTS
FRIGID
FRIGIDER
FRIGIDEST
FRIGIDITIES
FRIGIDITY
FRIGIDLY
FRIGOT
FRIGOTS
FRIGS
FRIJOL
FRIJOLE
FRIJOLES
FRIKKADEL
FRIKKADELS
FRILL
FRILLED
FRILLIER
FRILLIES
FRILLIEST
FRILLING
FRILLINGS
FRILLS
FRILLY
FRINGE
FRINGED
FRINGES
FRINGIER
FRINGIEST
FRINGING
FRINGY
FRIPON
FRIPONS
FRIPPER
FRIPPERER
FRIPPERERS
FRIPPERIES
FRIPPERS
FRIPPERY
FRIS
FRISEE
FRISEES
FRISES
FRISETTE
FRISETTES
FRISEUR
FRISEURS
FRISK
FRISKA
FRISKAS
FRISKED
FRISKER
FRISKERS
FRISKET
FRISKETS
FRISKFUL
FRISKIER
FRISKIEST
FRISKILY
FRISKING
FRISKINGS
FRISKS
FRISKY
FRISSON
FRISSONS
FRIST
FRISTED
FRISTING
FRISTS
FRISURE
FRISURES
FRIT
FRITFLIES
FRITFLY
FRITH
FRITHBORH
FRITHBORHS
FRITHGILD
FRITHGILDS
FRITHS
FRITS
FRITTED
FRITTER
FRITTERED
FRITTERER
FRITTERERS
FRITTERING
FRITTERS
FRITTING
FRITURE
FRITURES
FRIVOL
FRIVOLITIES
FRIVOLITY
FRIVOLLED
FRIVOLLING
FRIVOLOUS
FRIVOLS
FRIZ
FRIZE
FRIZES
FRIZING
FRIZZ
FRIZZANTE
FRIZZED
FRIZZES
FRIZZIER
FRIZZIEST
FRIZZING
FRIZZLE
FRIZZLED
FRIZZLES
FRIZZLIER
FRIZZLIEST
FRIZZLING
FRIZZLY
FRIZZY
FRO
FROCK
FROCKED
FROCKING
FROCKINGS
FROCKLESS
FROCKS
FROG
FROGBIT
FROGBITS
FROGGED
FROGGERIES
FROGGERY
FROGGIER
FROGGIEST
FROGGING
FROGGINGS
FROGGY
FROGLET
FROGLETS
FROGLING
FROGLINGS
FROGMAN
FROGMARCH

FROGMARCHED
FROGMARCHES
FROGMARCHING
FROGMEN
FROGMOUTH
FROGMOUTHS
FROGS
FROIDEUR
FROIDEURS
FROISE
FROISES
FROLIC
FROLICKED
FROLICKING
FROLICS
FROM
FROMENTIES
FROMENTY
FROND
FRONDAGE
FRONDAGES
FRONDED
FRONDENT
FRONDEUR
FRONDEURS
FRONDOSE
FRONDS
FRONT
FRONTAGE
FRONTAGER
FRONTAGERS
FRONTAGES
FRONTAL
FRONTALS
FRONTED
FRONTIER
FRONTIERED
FRONTIERING
FRONTIERS
FRONTING
FRONTLESS
FRONTLET
FRONTLETS
FRONTMAN
FRONTMEN
FRONTON
FRONTONS
FRONTOON
FRONTOONS
FRONTS
FRONTWARD
FRONTWARDS
FRONTWAYS
FRONTWISE
FRORE
FROREN
FRORN
FRORNE
FRORY
FROST
FROSTBIT
FROSTBITE
FROSTBITES
FROSTBITING
FROSTBITTEN
FROSTED
FROSTIER
FROSTIEST
FROSTILY
FROSTING
FROSTINGS
FROSTLESS
FROSTLIKE
FROSTS
FROSTWORK
FROSTWORKS
FROSTY
FROTH
FROTHED
FROTHERIES
FROTHERY
FROTHIER
FROTHIEST
FROTHILY
FROTHING
FROTHLESS
FROTHS
FROTHY
FROTTAGE
FROTTAGES
FROTTEUR
FROTTEURS
FROUGHIER
FROUGHIEST
FROUGHY
FROUNCE
FROUNCED
FROUNCES
FROUNCING
FROW
FROWARD
FROWARDLY
FROWARDS
FROWIE
FROWIER
FROWIEST
FROWN
FROWNED
FROWNING
FROWNS
FROWS
FROWSIER
FROWSIEST
FROWST
FROWSTED
FROWSTER
FROWSTERS
FROWSTIER
FROWSTIEST
FROWSTING
FROWSTS
FROWSTY
FROWSY
FROWY
FROWZIER
FROWZIEST
FROWZY
FROZE
FROZEN
FRUCTANS
FRUCTED
FRUCTIFIED
FRUCTIFIES
FRUCTIFY
FRUCTIFYING
FRUCTIVE
FRUCTOSE
FRUCTOSES
FRUCTUARIES
FRUCTUARY
FRUCTUATE
FRUCTUATED
FRUCTUATES
FRUCTUATING
FRUCTUOUS
FRUGAL
FRUGALIST
FRUGALISTS
FRUGALITIES
FRUGALITY
FRUGALLY
FRUICT
FRUICTS
FRUIT
FRUITAGE
FRUITAGES
FRUITCAKE
FRUITCAKES
FRUITED
FRUITER
FRUITERER
FRUITERERS
FRUITERIES
FRUITERS
FRUITERY
FRUITFUL
FRUITIER
FRUITIEST
FRUITING
FRUITINGS
FRUITION
FRUITIONS
FRUITIVE
FRUITLESS
FRUITLET
FRUITLETS
FRUITS
FRUITWOOD
FRUITWOODS
FRUITY
FRUMENTIES
FRUMENTY
FRUMP
FRUMPED
FRUMPIER
FRUMPIEST
FRUMPING
FRUMPISH
FRUMPLE
FRUMPLED
FRUMPLES
FRUMPLING
FRUMPS
FRUMPY
FRUSH
FRUSHED
FRUSHES
FRUSHING
FRUST
FRUSTA
FRUSTRATE
FRUSTRATED
FRUSTRATES
FRUSTRATING
FRUSTS
FRUSTULE
FRUSTULES
FRUSTUM
FRUSTUMS
FRUTEX
FRUTICES
FRUTICOSE
FRUTIFIED
FRUTIFIES
FRUTIFY
FRUTIFYING
FRY
FRYER
FRYERS
FRYING
FRYINGS
FUB
FUBBED
FUBBERIES
FUBBERY
FUBBIER
FUBBIEST
FUBBING
FUBBY
FUBS
FUBSIER
FUBSIEST
FUBSY
FUCHSIA
FUCHSIAS
FUCHSINE
FUCHSINES
FUCHSITE
FUCHSITES
FUCI
FUCK
FUCKED
FUCKER
FUCKERS
FUCKING
FUCKINGS
FUCKS
FUCOID
FUCOIDAL
FUCOIDS
FUCUS
FUCUSED
FUCUSES
FUD
FUDDLE
FUDDLED
FUDDLER
FUDDLERS
FUDDLES
FUDDLING
FUDDLINGS
FUDGE
FUDGED
FUDGES
FUDGING
FUDS
FUEL
FUELLED
FUELLER
FUELLERS
FUELLING
FUELS
FUERO
FUEROS
FUFF
FUFFED
FUFFIER
FUFFIEST
FUFFING
FUFFS
FUFFY
FUG
FUGACIOUS
FUGACITIES
FUGACITY
FUGAL
FUGALLY
FUGATO
FUGATOS
FUGGED
FUGGIER
FUGGIEST
FUGGING
FUGGY
FUGHETTA
FUGHETTAS
FUGIE
FUGIES
FUGITIVE
FUGITIVES
FUGLE
FUGLED
FUGLEMAN
FUGLEMEN
FUGLES
FUGLING
FUGS
FUGUE
FUGUES
FUGUIST
FUGUISTS
FULCRA
FULCRATE
FULCRUM
FULCRUMS
FULFIL
FULFILL
FULFILLED
FULFILLER
FULFILLERS

ULFILLING
ULFILLINGS
ULFILLS
ULFILS
ULGENCIES
ULGENCY
ULGENT
ULGENTLY
ULGID
ULGOR
ULGOROUS
ULGORS
ULGOUR
ULGOURS
ULGURAL
ULGURANT
ULGURATE
ULGURATED
ULGURATES
ULGURATING
ULGURITE
ULGURITES
ULGUROUS
ULHAM
ULHAMS
ULL
ULLAGE
ULLAGES
ULLAM
ULLAMS
ULLAN
ULLANS
ULLBACK
ULLBACKS
ULLED
ULLER
ULLERENE
ULLERENES
ULLERS
ULLEST
ULLING
ULLISH
ULLNESS
ULLNESSES
ULLS
ULLY
ULMAR
ULMARS
ULMINANT
ULMINANTS
ULMINATE
ULMINATED
ULMINATES
ULMINATING
ULMINE
FULMINED
FULMINES
FULMINING
FULMINOUS
FULNESS
FULNESSES
FULSOME
FULSOMELY
FULSOMER
FULSOMEST
FULVID
FULVOUS
FUM
FUMADO
FUMADOES
FUMADOS
FUMAGE
FUMAGES
FUMAROLE
FUMAROLES
FUMAROLIC
FUMATORIA
FUMATORIES
FUMATORY
FUMBLE
FUMBLED
FUMBLER
FUMBLERS
FUMBLES
FUMBLING
FUME
FUMED
FUMEROLE
FUMEROLES
FUMES
FUMET
FUMETS
FUMETTE
FUMETTES
FUMETTI
FUMETTO
FUMIER
FUMIEST
FUMIGANT
FUMIGANTS
FUMIGATE
FUMIGATED
FUMIGATES
FUMIGATING
FUMIGATOR
FUMIGATORS
FUMING
FUMITORIES
FUMITORY
FUMOSITIES
FUMOSITY
FUMOUS
FUMS
FUMY
FUN
FUNBOARD
FUNBOARDS
FUNCTION
FUNCTIONED
FUNCTIONING
FUNCTIONS
FUND
FUNDABLE
FUNDAMENT
FUNDAMENTS
FUNDED
FUNDER
FUNDERS
FUNDI
FUNDIE
FUNDIES
FUNDING
FUNDINGS
FUNDIS
FUNDLESS
FUNDS
FUNDUS
FUNDY
FUNEBRAL
FUNEBRE
FUNEBRIAL
FUNERAL
FUNERALS
FUNERARY
FUNEREAL
FUNEST
FUNFAIR
FUNFAIRS
FUNG
FUNGAL
FUNGI
FUNGIBLES
FUNGICIDE
FUNGICIDES
FUNGIFORM
FUNGOID
FUNGOIDAL
FUNGOSITIES
FUNGOSITY
FUNGOUS
FUNGS
FUNGUS
FUNGUSES
FUNICLE
FUNICLES
FUNICULAR
FUNICULI
FUNICULUS
FUNK
FUNKED
FUNKHOLE
FUNKHOLES
FUNKIA
FUNKIAS
FUNKIER
FUNKIEST
FUNKINESS
FUNKINESSES
FUNKING
FUNKS
FUNKY
FUNNED
FUNNEL
FUNNELLED
FUNNELLING
FUNNELS
FUNNER
FUNNEST
FUNNIER
FUNNIES
FUNNIEST
FUNNILY
FUNNINESS
FUNNINESSES
FUNNING
FUNNY
FUNS
FUNSTER
FUNSTERS
FUR
FURACIOUS
FURACITIES
FURACITY
FURAL
FURALS
FURAN
FURANE
FURANES
FURANS
FURBELOW
FURBELOWED
FURBELOWING
FURBELOWS
FURBISH
FURBISHED
FURBISHER
FURBISHERS
FURBISHES
FURBISHING
FURCAL
FURCATE
FURCATED
FURCATION
FURCATIONS
FURCULA
FURCULAE
FURCULAR
FURDER
FUREUR
FUREURS
FURFAIR
FURFAIRS
FURFUR
FURFURAL
FURFURALS
FURFURAN
FURFURANS
FURFUROL
FURFUROLE
FURFUROLES
FURFUROLS
FURFUROUS
FURFURS
FURIBUND
FURIES
FURIOSITIES
FURIOSITY
FURIOSO
FURIOSOS
FURIOUS
FURIOUSLY
FURL
FURLANA
FURLANAS
FURLED
FURLING
FURLONG
FURLONGS
FURLOUGH
FURLOUGHED
FURLOUGHING
FURLOUGHS
FURLS
FURMENTIES
FURMENTY
FURMETIES
FURMETY
FURMITIES
FURMITY
FURNACE
FURNACED
FURNACES
FURNACING
FURNIMENT
FURNIMENTS
FURNISH
FURNISHED
FURNISHER
FURNISHERS
FURNISHES
FURNISHING
FURNISHINGS
FURNITURE
FURNITURES
FUROL
FUROLE
FUROLES
FUROLS
FUROR
FURORE
FURORES
FURORS
FURPHIES
FURPHY
FURR
FURRED
FURRIER
FURRIERIES
FURRIERS
FURRIERY
FURRIES
FURRIEST
FURRINESS
FURRINESSES
FURRING
FURRINGS
FURROW
FURROWED
FURROWING
FURROWS
FURROWY
FURRS
FURRY
FURS
FURTH
FURTHER
FURTHERED
FURTHERER
FURTHERERS
FURTHERING

FURTHERS
FURTHEST
FURTIVE
FURTIVELY
FURUNCLE
FURUNCLES
FURY
FURZE
FURZES
FURZIER
FURZIEST
FURZY
FUSAIN
FUSAINS
FUSAROL
FUSAROLE
FUSAROLES
FUSAROLS
FUSC
FUSCOUS
FUSE
FUSED
FUSEE
FUSEES
FUSELAGE
FUSELAGES
FUSES
FUSHION
FUSHIONS
FUSIBLE
FUSIFORM
FUSIL
FUSILE
FUSILEER
FUSILEERS
FUSILIER
FUSILIERS
FUSILLADE
FUSILLADES
FUSILLI
FUSILS
FUSING
FUSION
FUSIONISM
FUSIONISMS
FUSIONIST
FUSIONISTS
FUSIONS
FUSS
FUSSED
FUSSER
FUSSERS
FUSSES
FUSSIER
FUSSIEST
FUSSILY
FUSSINESS
FUSSINESSES
FUSSING
FUSSY
FUST
FUSTED
FUSTET
FUSTETS
FUSTIAN
FUSTIANS
FUSTIC
FUSTICS
FUSTIER
FUSTIEST
FUSTIGATE
FUSTIGATED
FUSTIGATES
FUSTIGATING
FUSTILUGS
FUSTILY
FUSTINESS
FUSTINESSES
FUSTING
FUSTOC
FUSTOCS
FUSTS
FUSTY
FUTCHEL
FUTCHELS
FUTHARK
FUTHARKS
FUTHORC
FUTHORCS
FUTHORK
FUTHORKS
FUTILE
FUTILELY
FUTILER
FUTILEST
FUTILITIES
FUTILITY
FUTON
FUTONS
FUTTOCK
FUTTOCKS
FUTURE
FUTURES
FUTURISM
FUTURISMS
FUTURIST
FUTURISTS
FUTURITIES
FUTURITY
FUZE
FUZEE
FUZEES
FUZES
FUZZ
FUZZED
FUZZES
FUZZIER
FUZZIEST
FUZZILY
FUZZINESS
FUZZINESSES
FUZZING
FUZZLE
FUZZLED
FUZZLES
FUZZLING
FUZZY
FY
FYKE
FYKED
FYKES
FYKING
FYLE
FYLES
FYLFOT
FYLFOTS
FYNBOS
FYNBOSES
FYRD
FYRDS
FYTTE
FYTTES

G

AB
ABARDINE
ABARDINES
ABBARD
ABBARDS
ABBART
ABBARTS
ABBED
ABBER
ABBERS
ABBIER
ABBIEST
ABBING
ABBLE
ABBLED
ABBLER
ABBLERS
ABBLES
ABBLING
ABBLINGS
ABBRO
ABBROIC
ABBROID
ABBROS
ABBY
ABELLE
ABELLER
ABELLERS
ABELLES
ABERDINE
ABERDINES
ABFEST
ABFESTS
ABIES
ABION
ABIONADE
ABIONADES
ABIONAGE
ABIONAGES
ABIONED
ABIONS
ABLE
ABLED
ABLES
ABLET
ABLETS
ABNASH
ABNASHES
ABS
ABY
AD
ADABOUT
ADABOUTS
ADDED
GADDER
GADDERS
GADDING
GADE
GADES
GADFLIES
GADFLY
GADGE
GADGES
GADGET
GADGETEER
GADGETEERS
GADGETRIES
GADGETRY
GADGETS
GADGIE
GADGIES
GADI
GADIS
GADJE
GADJES
GADLING
GADLINGS
GADOID
GADOIDS
GADROON
GADROONED
GADROONS
GADS
GADSMAN
GADSMEN
GADSO
GADSOS
GADWALL
GADWALLS
GADZOOKS
GAE
GAED
GAELICISE
GAELICISED
GAELICISES
GAELICISING
GAELICISM
GAELICISMS
GAELICIZE
GAELICIZED
GAELICIZES
GAELICIZING
GAES
GAFF
GAFFE
GAFFED
GAFFER
GAFFERS
GAFFES
GAFFING
GAFFINGS
GAFFS
GAG
GAGA
GAGAKU
GAGAKUS
GAGE
GAGED
GAGES
GAGGED
GAGGER
GAGGERS
GAGGING
GAGGLE
GAGGLED
GAGGLES
GAGGLING
GAGGLINGS
GAGING
GAGMAN
GAGMEN
GAGS
GAGSTER
GAGSTERS
GAHNITE
GAHNITES
GAID
GAIDS
GAIETIES
GAIETY
GAIJIN
GAILLARD
GAILLARDE
GAILY
GAIN
GAINABLE
GAINED
GAINER
GAINERS
GAINEST
GAINFUL
GAINFULLY
GAINING
GAININGS
GAINLESS
GAINLIER
GAINLIEST
GAINLY
GAINS
GAINSAID
GAINSAY
GAINSAYER
GAINSAYERS
GAINSAYING
GAINSAYINGS
GAINSAYS
GAIR
GAIRFOWL
GAIRFOWLS
GAIRS
GAIT
GAITED
GAITER
GAITERS
GAITING
GAITS
GAITT
GAITTS
GAJO
GAJOS
GAL
GALA
GALABEA
GALABEAH
GALABEAHS
GALABEAS
GALABIA
GALABIAH
GALABIAHS
GALABIAS
GALACTIC
GALACTOSE
GALACTOSES
GALAGE
GALAGES
GALAGO
GALAGOS
GALAH
GALAHS
GALANGA
GALANGAL
GALANGALS
GALANGAS
GALANT
GALANTINE
GALANTINES
GALAPAGO
GALAPAGOS
GALAS
GALATEA
GALATEAS
GALAXIES
GALAXY
GALBANUM
GALBANUMS
GALDRAGON
GALDRAGONS
GALE
GALEA
GALEAE
GALEAS
GALEATE
GALEATED
GALENA
GALENAS
GALENGALE
GALENGALES
GALENITE
GALENITES
GALENOID
GALERE
GALERES
GALES
GALETTE
GALETTES
GALILEE
GALILEES
GALINGALE
GALINGALES
GALIONGEE
GALIONGEES
GALIOT
GALIOTS
GALIPOT
GALIPOTS
GALL
GALLABEA
GALLABEAH
GALLABEAHS
GALLABEAS
GALLABIA
GALLABIAH
GALLABIAHS
GALLABIAS
GALLABIEH
GALLABIEHS
GALLABIYA
GALLABIYAS
GALLANT
GALLANTER
GALLANTEST
GALLANTLY
GALLANTRIES
GALLANTRY
GALLANTS
GALLATE
GALLATES
GALLEASS
GALLEASSES
GALLED

GALLEON
GALLEONS
GALLERIA
GALLERIAS
GALLERIED
GALLERIES
GALLERY
GALLERYING
GALLET
GALLETED
GALLETING
GALLETS
GALLEY
GALLEYS
GALLFLIES
GALLFLY
GALLIARD
GALLIARDS
GALLIASS
GALLIASSES
GALLIC
GALLICISE
GALLICISED
GALLICISES
GALLICISING
GALLICISM
GALLICISMS
GALLICIZE
GALLICIZED
GALLICIZES
GALLICIZING
GALLIED
GALLIES
GALLINAZO
GALLINAZOS
GALLING
GALLINGLY
GALLINULE
GALLINULES
GALLIOT
GALLIOTS
GALLIPOT
GALLIPOTS
GALLISE
GALLISED
GALLISES
GALLISING
GALLISISE
GALLISISED
GALLISISES
GALLISISING
GALLISIZE
GALLISIZED
GALLISIZES
GALLISIZING
GALLIUM
GALLIUMS
GALLIVANT
GALLIVANTED
GALLIVANTING
GALLIVANTS
GALLIVAT
GALLIVATS
GALLIWASP
GALLIWASPS
GALLIZE
GALLIZED
GALLIZES
GALLIZING
GALLNUT
GALLNUTS
GALLON
GALLONAGE
GALLONAGES
GALLONS
GALLOON
GALLOONED
GALLOONS
GALLOP
GALLOPADE
GALLOPADED
GALLOPADES
GALLOPADING
GALLOPED
GALLOPER
GALLOPERS
GALLOPING
GALLOPS
GALLOW
GALLOWED
GALLOWING
GALLOWS
GALLOWSES
GALLS
GALLSTONE
GALLSTONES
GALLUMPH
GALLUMPHED
GALLUMPHING
GALLUMPHS
GALLUS
GALLUSES
GALLY
GALLYING
GALOCHE
GALOCHED
GALOCHES
GALOCHING
GALOOT
GALOOTS
GALOP
GALOPED
GALOPIN
GALOPING
GALOPINS
GALOPPED
GALOPPING
GALOPS
GALORE
GALOSH
GALOSHED
GALOSHES
GALOSHING
GALOWSES
GALRAVAGE
GALRAVAGED
GALRAVAGES
GALRAVAGING
GALS
GALTONIA
GALTONIAS
GALUMPH
GALUMPHED
GALUMPHER
GALUMPHERS
GALUMPHING
GALUMPHS
GALUT
GALUTH
GALUTHS
GALUTS
GALVANIC
GALVANISE
GALVANISED
GALVANISES
GALVANISING
GALVANISM
GALVANISMS
GALVANIST
GALVANISTS
GALVANIZE
GALVANIZED
GALVANIZES
GALVANIZING
GAM
GAMASH
GAMASHES
GAMAY
GAMAYS
GAMB
GAMBA
GAMBADO
GAMBADOED
GAMBADOES
GAMBADOING
GAMBADOS
GAMBAS
GAMBESON
GAMBESONS
GAMBET
GAMBETS
GAMBETTA
GAMBETTAS
GAMBIER
GAMBIERS
GAMBIR
GAMBIRS
GAMBIST
GAMBISTS
GAMBIT
GAMBITED
GAMBITING
GAMBITS
GAMBLE
GAMBLED
GAMBLER
GAMBLERS
GAMBLES
GAMBLING
GAMBLINGS
GAMBO
GAMBOGE
GAMBOGES
GAMBOGIAN
GAMBOGIC
GAMBOL
GAMBOLLED
GAMBOLLING
GAMBOLS
GAMBOS
GAMBREL
GAMBRELS
GAMBROON
GAMBROONS
GAMBS
GAME
GAMECOCK
GAMECOCKS
GAMED
GAMELAN
GAMELANS
GAMELY
GAMENESS
GAMENESSES
GAMER
GAMES
GAMESIER
GAMESIEST
GAMESOME
GAMEST
GAMESTER
GAMESTERS
GAMESY
GAMETAL
GAMETE
GAMETES
GAMETIC
GAMEY
GAMIC
GAMIER
GAMIEST
GAMIN
GAMINE
GAMINERIE
GAMINERIES
GAMINES
GAMINESS
GAMINESSES
GAMING
GAMINGS
GAMINS
GAMMA
GAMMADIA
GAMMADION
GAMMAS
GAMMATIA
GAMMATION
GAMME
GAMMED
GAMMER
GAMMERS
GAMMES
GAMMIER
GAMMIEST
GAMMING
GAMMOCK
GAMMOCKED
GAMMOCKING
GAMMOCKS
GAMMON
GAMMONED
GAMMONER
GAMMONERS
GAMMONING
GAMMONINGS
GAMMONS
GAMMY
GAMP
GAMPISH
GAMPS
GAMS
GAMUT
GAMUTS
GAMY
GAMYNESS
GAMYNESSES
GAN
GANCH
GANCHED
GANCHES
GANCHING
GANDER
GANDERISM
GANDERISMS
GANDERS
GANE
GANG
GANGBOARD
GANGBOARDS
GANGED
GANGER
GANGERS
GANGING
GANGINGS
GANGLAND
GANGLANDS
GANGLIA
GANGLIAR
GANGLIATE
GANGLIER
GANGLIEST
GANGLING
GANGLION
GANGLIONS
GANGLY
GANGPLANK
GANGPLANKS
GANGREL
GANGRELS
GANGRENE
GANGRENED
GANGRENES
GANGRENING
GANGS
GANGSMAN
GANGSMEN
GANGSTA
GANGSTAS
GANGSTER
GANGSTERS

ANGUE
ANGUES
ANGWAY
ANGWAYS
ANISTER
ANISTERS
ANJA
ANJAS
ANNET
ANNETRIES
ANNETRY
ANNETS
ANNISTER
ANNISTERS
ANOID
ANOIDS
ANOIN
ANOINE
ANOINES
ANOINS
ANSEY
ANSEYS
ANT
ANTED
ANTING
ANTLET
ANTLETS
ANTLINE
ANTLINES
ANTLOPE
ANTLOPES
ANTRIES
ANTRY
ANTS
AOL
AOLED
AOLER
AOLERESS
AOLERESSES
AOLERS
AOLING
AOLS
AP
APE
APED
APER
APERS
APES
APESEED
APESEEDS
APEWORM
APEWORMS
APING
APINGLY
APINGS
APO
APOS
APPED
APPIER
APPIEST
APPING
APPY
APS
AR
GARAGE
GARAGED
GARAGES
GARAGING
GARAGINGS
GARAGIST
GARAGISTE
GARAGISTES
GARAGISTS
GARB
GARBAGE
GARBAGES
GARBANZO
GARBANZOS
GARBE
GARBED
GARBES
GARBING
GARBLE
GARBLED
GARBLER
GARBLERS
GARBLES
GARBLING
GARBLINGS
GARBO
GARBOARD
GARBOARDS
GARBOIL
GARBOILS
GARBOLOGIES
GARBOLOGY
GARBOS
GARBS
GARBURE
GARBURES
GARCINIA
GARCINIAS
GARCON
GARCONS
GARDA
GARDAI
GARDANT
GARDANTS
GARDEN
GARDENED
GARDENER
GARDENERS
GARDENIA
GARDENIAS
GARDENING
GARDENINGS
GARDENS
GARDEROBE
GARDEROBES
GARDYLOO
GARDYLOOS
GARE
GAREFOWL
GAREFOWLS
GARFISH
GARFISHES
GARGANEY
GARGANEYS
GARGARISE
GARGARISED
GARGARISES
GARGARISING
GARGARISM
GARGARISMS
GARGARIZE
GARGARIZED
GARGARIZES
GARGARIZING
GARGET
GARGETS
GARGETY
GARGLE
GARGLED
GARGLES
GARGLING
GARGOYLE
GARGOYLES
GARIAL
GARIALS
GARIBALDI
GARIBALDIS
GARIGUE
GARIGUES
GARISH
GARISHED
GARISHES
GARISHING
GARISHLY
GARJAN
GARJANS
GARLAND
GARLANDED
GARLANDING
GARLANDRIES
GARLANDRY
GARLANDS
GARLIC
GARLICKIER
GARLICKIEST
GARLICKY
GARLICS
GARMENT
GARMENTED
GARMENTING
GARMENTS
GARNER
GARNERED
GARNERING
GARNERS
GARNET
GARNETS
GARNI
GARNISH
GARNISHED
GARNISHEE
GARNISHEED
GARNISHEEING
GARNISHEES
GARNISHER
GARNISHERS
GARNISHES
GARNISHING
GARNISHINGS
GARNISHRIES
GARNISHRY
GARNITURE
GARNITURES
GAROTTE
GAROTTED
GAROTTER
GAROTTERS
GAROTTES
GAROTTING
GAROTTINGS
GARPIKE
GARPIKES
GARRAN
GARRANS
GARRE
GARRED
GARRES
GARRET
GARRETED
GARRETEER
GARRETEERS
GARRETS
GARRIGUE
GARRIGUES
GARRING
GARRISON
GARRISONED
GARRISONING
GARRISONS
GARRON
GARRONS
GARROT
GARROTE
GARROTED
GARROTES
GARROTING
GARROTS
GARROTTE
GARROTTED
GARROTTER
GARROTTERS
GARROTTES
GARROTTING
GARROTTINGS
GARRULITIES
GARRULITY
GARRULOUS
GARRYA
GARRYAS
GARRYOWEN
GARRYOWENS
GARS
GART
GARTER
GARTERED
GARTERING
GARTERS
GARTH
GARTHS
GARUDA
GARUDAS
GARUM
GARUMS
GARVIE
GARVIES
GARVOCK
GARVOCKS
GAS
GASAHOL
GASAHOLS
GASALIER
GASALIERS
GASBAG
GASBAGS
GASCON
GASCONADE
GASCONADED
GASCONADES
GASCONADING
GASCONISM
GASCONISMS
GASCONS
GASEITIES
GASEITY
GASELIER
GASELIERS
GASEOUS
GASES
GASFIELD
GASFIELDS
GASH
GASHED
GASHER
GASHES
GASHEST
GASHFUL
GASHING
GASHLY
GASHOLDER
GASHOLDERS
GASIFIED
GASIFIER
GASIFIERS
GASIFIES
GASIFORM
GASIFY
GASIFYING
GASKET
GASKETS
GASKIN
GASKINS
GASLIGHT
GASLIGHTS
GASLIT
GASMAN
GASMEN
GASOGENE
GASOGENES
GASOHOL
GASOHOLS
GASOLENE
GASOLENES
GASOLIER
GASOLIERS
GASOLINE
GASOLINES

GASOMETER
GASOMETERS
GASOMETRIES
GASOMETRY
GASP
GASPED
GASPER
GASPEREAU
GASPEREAUS
GASPERS
GASPIER
GASPIEST
GASPINESS
GASPINESSES
GASPING
GASPINGLY
GASPINGS
GASPS
GASPY
GASSED
GASSER
GASSERS
GASSES
GASSIER
GASSIEST
GASSINESS
GASSINESSES
GASSING
GASSINGS
GASSY
GAST
GASTED
GASTER
GASTERS
GASTFULL
GASTING
GASTNESS
GASTNESSE
GASTNESSES
GASTRAEA
GASTRAEAS
GASTRAEUM
GASTRAEUMS
GASTRIC
GASTRIN
GASTRINS
GASTRITIS
GASTRITISES
GASTROPOD
GASTROPODS
GASTRULA
GASTRULAE
GASTRULAS
GASTS
GAT
GATE
GATEAU
GATEAUS
GATEAUX
GATECRASH
GATECRASHED
GATECRASHES
GATECRASHING
GATED
GATEFOLD
GATEFOLDS
GATEHOUSE
GATEHOUSES
GATELEG
GATELESS
GATEMAN
GATEMEN
GATEPOST
GATEPOSTS
GATES
GATEWAY
GATEWAYS
GATH
GATHER
GATHERED
GATHERER
GATHERERS
GATHERING
GATHERINGS
GATHERS
GATHS
GATING
GATINGS
GATS
GAU
GAUCHE
GAUCHER
GAUCHERIE
GAUCHERIES
GAUCHESCO
GAUCHEST
GAUCHO
GAUCHOS
GAUCIE
GAUCIER
GAUCIEST
GAUCY
GAUD
GAUDEAMUS
GAUDEAMUSES
GAUDED
GAUDERIES
GAUDERY
GAUDGIE
GAUDGIES
GAUDIER
GAUDIES
GAUDIEST
GAUDILY
GAUDINESS
GAUDINESSES
GAUDING
GAUDS
GAUDY
GAUFER
GAUFERS
GAUFFER
GAUFFERED
GAUFFERING
GAUFFERINGS
GAUFFERS
GAUFRE
GAUFRES
GAUGE
GAUGEABLE
GAUGED
GAUGER
GAUGERS
GAUGES
GAUGING
GAUGINGS
GAUJE
GAUJES
GAULEITER
GAULEITERS
GAULT
GAULTER
GAULTERS
GAULTS
GAUM
GAUMED
GAUMIER
GAUMIEST
GAUMING
GAUMLESS
GAUMS
GAUMY
GAUN
GAUNCH
GAUNCHED
GAUNCHES
GAUNCHING
GAUNT
GAUNTED
GAUNTER
GAUNTEST
GAUNTING
GAUNTLET
GAUNTLETS
GAUNTLY
GAUNTNESS
GAUNTNESSES
GAUNTREE
GAUNTREES
GAUNTRIES
GAUNTRY
GAUNTS
GAUP
GAUPED
GAUPER
GAUPERS
GAUPING
GAUPS
GAUPUS
GAUPUSES
GAUR
GAURS
GAUS
GAUSS
GAUSSES
GAUSSIAN
GAUZE
GAUZES
GAUZIER
GAUZIEST
GAUZINESS
GAUZINESSES
GAUZY
GAVAGE
GAVAGES
GAVE
GAVEL
GAVELKIND
GAVELKINDS
GAVELMAN
GAVELMEN
GAVELOCK
GAVELOCKS
GAVELS
GAVIAL
GAVIALS
GAVOTTE
GAVOTTES
GAWCIER
GAWCIEST
GAWCY
GAWD
GAWDS
GAWK
GAWKED
GAWKER
GAWKERS
GAWKIER
GAWKIES
GAWKIEST
GAWKIHOOD
GAWKIHOODS
GAWKINESS
GAWKINESSES
GAWKING
GAWKS
GAWKY
GAWP
GAWPED
GAWPER
GAWPERS
GAWPING
GAWPS
GAWPUS
GAWPUSES
GAWSIER
GAWSIEST
GAWSY
GAY
GAYAL
GAYALS
GAYER
GAYEST
GAYNESS
GAYNESSES
GAYS
GAYSOME
GAZAL
GAZALS
GAZANIA
GAZANIAS
GAZAR
GAZARS
GAZE
GAZEBO
GAZEBOES
GAZEBOS
GAZED
GAZEFUL
GAZELLE
GAZELLES
GAZEMENT
GAZEMENTS
GAZER
GAZERS
GAZES
GAZETTE
GAZETTED
GAZETTEER
GAZETTEERED
GAZETTEERING
GAZETTEERS
GAZETTES
GAZETTING
GAZIER
GAZIEST
GAZING
GAZOGENE
GAZOGENES
GAZON
GAZONS
GAZOO
GAZOOKA
GAZOOKAS
GAZOON
GAZOONS
GAZOOS
GAZPACHO
GAZPACHOS
GAZUMP
GAZUMPED
GAZUMPING
GAZUMPS
GAZUNDER
GAZUNDERED
GAZUNDERING
GAZUNDERS
GAZY
GEAL
GEALED
GEALING
GEALOUS
GEALOUSIES
GEALOUSY
GEALS
GEAN
GEANS
GEAR
GEARBOX
GEARBOXES
GEARE
GEARED
GEARES
GEARING
GEARINGS
GEARLESS
GEARS
GEARSHIFT
GEARSHIFTS
GEARWHEEL

GEARWHEELS
GEASON
GEAT
GEATS
GEBUR
GEBURS
GECK
GECKED
GECKING
GECKO
GECKOES
GECKOS
GECKS
GED
GEDDIT
GEDS
GEE
GEEBUNG
GEEBUNGS
GEECHEE
GEECHEES
GEED
GEEGAW
GEEGAWS
GEEING
GEEK
GEEKIER
GEEKIEST
GEEKS
GEEKY
GEEP
GEEPS
GEES
GEESE
GEEZER
GEEZERS
GEFUFFLE
GEFUFFLED
GEFUFFLES
GEFUFFLING
GEISHA
GEISHAS
GEIST
GEISTS
GEIT
GEITS
GEL
GELADA
GELADAS
GELASTIC
GELATI
GELATIN
GELATINE
GELATINES
GELATINS
GELATION
GELATIONS
GELATO
GELD
GELDED
GELDER
GELDERS
GELDING
GELDINGS
GELDS
GELID
GELIDER
GELIDEST
GELIDITIES
GELIDITY
GELIDLY
GELIDNESS
GELIDNESSES
GELIGNITE
GELIGNITES
GELLED
GELLIES
GELLING
GELLY
GELOSIES
GELOSY
GELS
GELSEMINE
GELSEMINES
GELSEMIUM
GELSEMIUMS
GELT
GELTS
GEM
GEMATRIA
GEMATRIAS
GEMEL
GEMELS
GEMFISH
GEMFISHES
GEMINATE
GEMINATED
GEMINATES
GEMINATING
GEMINI
GEMINIES
GEMINOUS
GEMINY
GEMMA
GEMMAE
GEMMAN
GEMMATE
GEMMATED
GEMMATES
GEMMATING
GEMMATION
GEMMATIONS
GEMMATIVE
GEMMED
GEMMEN
GEMMEOUS
GEMMERIES
GEMMERY
GEMMIER
GEMMIEST
GEMMING
GEMMOLOGIES
GEMMOLOGY
GEMMULE
GEMMULES
GEMMY
GEMOLOGIES
GEMOLOGY
GEMONY
GEMOT
GEMOTS
GEMS
GEMSBOK
GEMSBOKS
GEMSHORN
GEMSHORNS
GEMSTONE
GEMSTONES
GEMUTLICH
GEN
GENA
GENAL
GENAPPE
GENAPPES
GENAS
GENDARME
GENDARMES
GENDER
GENDERED
GENDERING
GENDERS
GENE
GENEALOGIES
GENEALOGY
GENERA
GENERABLE
GENERAL
GENERALE
GENERALIA
GENERALLED
GENERALLING
GENERALLY
GENERALS
GENERANT
GENERANTS
GENERATE
GENERATED
GENERATES
GENERATING
GENERATOR
GENERATORS
GENERIC
GENERICAL
GENERICS
GENEROUS
GENES
GENESES
GENESIS
GENET
GENETIC
GENETICAL
GENETICS
GENETRICES
GENETRIX
GENETRIXES
GENETS
GENETTE
GENETTES
GENEVA
GENEVAS
GENIAL
GENIALISE
GENIALISED
GENIALISES
GENIALISING
GENIALITIES
GENIALITY
GENIALIZE
GENIALIZED
GENIALIZES
GENIALIZING
GENIALLY
GENIC
GENIE
GENIES
GENII
GENIP
GENIPAP
GENIPAPS
GENIPS
GENISTA
GENISTAS
GENITAL
GENITALIA
GENITALIC
GENITALS
GENITIVAL
GENITIVE
GENITIVES
GENITOR
GENITORS
GENITRICES
GENITRIX
GENITRIXES
GENITURE
GENITURES
GENIUS
GENIUSES
GENIZAH
GENIZAHS
GENLOCK
GENLOCKS
GENNEL
GENNELS
GENNET
GENNETS
GENOA
GENOAS
GENOCIDAL
GENOCIDE
GENOCIDES
GENOM
GENOME
GENOMES
GENOMS
GENOTYPE
GENOTYPES
GENOTYPIC
GENRE
GENRES
GENS
GENSDARMES
GENT
GENTEEL
GENTEELER
GENTEELEST
GENTEELLY
GENTES
GENTIAN
GENTIANS
GENTIER
GENTIEST
GENTILE
GENTILES
GENTILIC
GENTILISE
GENTILISED
GENTILISES
GENTILISH
GENTILISING
GENTILISM
GENTILISMS
GENTILITIES
GENTILITY
GENTILIZE
GENTILIZED
GENTILIZES
GENTILIZING
GENTLE
GENTLED
GENTLEMAN
GENTLEMEN
GENTLER
GENTLES
GENTLEST
GENTLING
GENTLY
GENTOO
GENTOOS
GENTRICE
GENTRICES
GENTRIES
GENTRIFIED
GENTRIFIES
GENTRIFY
GENTRIFYING
GENTRY
GENTS
GENTY
GENU
GENUFLECT
GENUFLECTED
GENUFLECTING
GENUFLECTS
GENUINE
GENUINELY
GENUS
GENUSES
GEO
GEOCARPIC
GEOCARPIES
GEOCARPY
GEODE
GEODES
GEODESIC
GEODESICS
GEODESIES
GEODESIST
GEODESISTS
GEODESY

The Chambers Dictionary is the authority for many longer words; see *OSW* Introduction, page xii

GEODETIC
GEODETICS
GEODIC
GEOFACT
GEOFACTS
GEOGENIES
GEOGENY
GEOGNOSES
GEOGNOSIES
GEOGNOSIS
GEOGNOST
GEOGNOSTS
GEOGNOSY
GEOGONIC
GEOGONIES
GEOGONY
GEOGRAPHIES
GEOGRAPHY
GEOID
GEOIDAL
GEOIDS
GEOLATRIES
GEOLATRY
GEOLOGER
GEOLOGERS
GEOLOGIAN
GEOLOGIANS
GEOLOGIC
GEOLOGIES
GEOLOGISE
GEOLOGISED
GEOLOGISES
GEOLOGISING
GEOLOGIST
GEOLOGISTS
GEOLOGIZE
GEOLOGIZED
GEOLOGIZES
GEOLOGIZING
GEOLOGY
GEOMANCER
GEOMANCERS
GEOMANCIES
GEOMANCY
GEOMANT
GEOMANTIC
GEOMANTS
GEOMETER
GEOMETERS
GEOMETRIC
GEOMETRID
GEOMETRIDS
GEOMETRIES
GEOMETRY
GEOMYOID
GEOPHAGIES
GEOPHAGY
GEOPHILIC
GEOPHONE
GEOPHONES
GEOPHYTE
GEOPHYTES
GEOPHYTIC
GEOPONIC
GEOPONICS
GEORGETTE
GEORGETTES
GEORGIC
GEORGICS
GEOS
GEOSPHERE
GEOSPHERES
GEOSTATIC
GEOSTATICS
GEOTACTIC
GEOTAXES
GEOTAXIS
GEOTROPIC
GERAH
GERAHS
GERANIOL
GERANIOLS
GERANIUM
GERANIUMS
GERBE
GERBERA
GERBERAS
GERBES
GERBIL
GERBILLE
GERBILLES
GERBILS
GERE
GERENT
GERENTS
GERENUK
GERENUKS
GERES
GERFALCON
GERFALCONS
GERIATRIC
GERIATRICS
GERLE
GERLES
GERM
GERMAIN
GERMAINE
GERMAINES
GERMAINS
GERMAN
GERMANDER
GERMANDERS
GERMANE
GERMANELY
GERMANIUM
GERMANIUMS
GERMANS
GERMED
GERMEN
GERMENS
GERMICIDE
GERMICIDES
GERMIN
GERMINAL
GERMINANT
GERMINATE
GERMINATED
GERMINATES
GERMINATING
GERMING
GERMINS
GERMS
GERNE
GERNED
GERNES
GERNING
GERONTIC
GEROPIGA
GEROPIGAS
GERTCHA
GERUND
GERUNDIAL
GERUNDIVE
GERUNDIVES
GERUNDS
GESNERIA
GESNERIAS
GESSAMINE
GESSAMINES
GESSE
GESSED
GESSES
GESSING
GESSO
GESSOES
GEST
GESTALT
GESTALTS
GESTANT
GESTAPO
GESTAPOS
GESTATE
GESTATED
GESTATES
GESTATING
GESTATION
GESTATIONS
GESTATIVE
GESTATORY
GESTE
GESTES
GESTIC
GESTS
GESTURAL
GESTURE
GESTURED
GESTURES
GESTURING
GET
GETA
GETAS
GETAWAY
GETAWAYS
GETS
GETTABLE
GETTER
GETTERED
GETTERING
GETTERINGS
GETTERS
GETTING
GETTINGS
GEUM
GEUMS
GEWGAW
GEWGAWS
GEY
GEYAN
GEYER
GEYEST
GEYSER
GEYSERITE
GEYSERITES
GEYSERS
GHARIAL
GHARIALS
GHARRI
GHARRIES
GHARRIS
GHARRY
GHAST
GHASTED
GHASTFUL
GHASTFULL
GHASTING
GHASTLIER
GHASTLIEST
GHASTLY
GHASTNESS
GHASTNESSES
GHASTS
GHAT
GHATS
GHAUT
GHAUTS
GHAZAL
GHAZALS
GHAZEL
GHAZELS
GHAZI
GHAZIS
GHEE
GHEES
GHERAO
GHERAOED
GHERAOING
GHERAOS
GHERKIN
GHERKINS
GHESSE
GHESSED
GHESSES
GHESSING
GHEST
GHETTO
GHETTOES
GHETTOISE
GHETTOISED
GHETTOISES
GHETTOISING
GHETTOIZE
GHETTOIZED
GHETTOIZES
GHETTOIZING
GHETTOS
GHI
GHILGAI
GHILGAIS
GHILLIE
GHILLIED
GHILLIES
GHILLYING
GHIS
GHOST
GHOSTED
GHOSTIER
GHOSTIEST
GHOSTING
GHOSTINGS
GHOSTLIER
GHOSTLIEST
GHOSTLIKE
GHOSTLY
GHOSTS
GHOSTY
GHOUL
GHOULISH
GHOULS
GHYLL
GHYLLS
GI
GIAMBEUX
GIANT
GIANTESS
GIANTESSES
GIANTHOOD
GIANTHOODS
GIANTISM
GIANTISMS
GIANTLIER
GIANTLIEST
GIANTLY
GIANTRIES
GIANTRY
GIANTS
GIANTSHIP
GIANTSHIPS
GIAOUR
GIAOURS
GIB
GIBBED
GIBBER
GIBBERED
GIBBERING
GIBBERISH
GIBBERISHES
GIBBERS
GIBBET
GIBBETED
GIBBETING
GIBBETS
GIBBING
GIBBON
GIBBONS
GIBBOSE
GIBBOSITIES
GIBBOSITY
GIBBOUS
GIBBOUSLY
GIBBSITE

GIBBSITES
GIBE
GIBED
GIBEL
GIBELS
GIBER
GIBERS
GIBES
GIBING
GIBINGLY
GIBLET
GIBLETS
GIBS
GIBUS
GIBUSES
GID
GIDDAP
GIDDIED
GIDDIER
GIDDIES
GIDDIEST
GIDDILY
GIDDINESS
GIDDINESSES
GIDDUP
GIDDY
GIDDYING
GIDGEE
GIDGEES
GIDJEE
GIDJEES
GIDS
GIE
GIED
GIEING
GIEN
GIES
GIF
GIFT
GIFTED
GIFTEDLY
GIFTING
GIFTS
GIFTSHOP
GIFTSHOPS
GIG
GIGA
GIGABYTE
GIGABYTES
GIGAFLOP
GIGAFLOPS
GIGAHERTZ
GIGAHERTZES
GIGANTEAN
GIGANTIC
GIGANTISM
GIGANTISMS
GIGAS
GIGAWATT
GIGAWATTS
GIGGED
GIGGING
GIGGIT
GIGGITED
GIGGITING
GIGGITS
GIGGLE
GIGGLED
GIGGLER
GIGGLERS
GIGGLES
GIGGLIER
GIGGLIEST
GIGGLING
GIGGLINGS
GIGGLY
GIGLET
GIGLETS
GIGLOT
GIGLOTS
GIGMAN
GIGMANITIES
GIGMANITY
GIGMEN
GIGOLO
GIGOLOS
GIGOT
GIGOTS
GIGS
GIGUE
GIGUES
GILA
GILAS
GILBERT
GILBERTS
GILCUP
GILCUPS
GILD
GILDED
GILDEN
GILDER
GILDERS
GILDING
GILDINGS
GILDS
GILET
GILETS
GILGAI
GILGAIS
GILGIE
GILGIES
GILL
GILLAROO
GILLAROOS
GILLED
GILLET
GILLETS
GILLFLIRT
GILLFLIRTS
GILLIE
GILLIED
GILLIES
GILLING
GILLION
GILLIONS
GILLS
GILLY
GILLYING
GILLYVOR
GILLYVORS
GILPEY
GILPEYS
GILPIES
GILPY
GILRAVAGE
GILRAVAGED
GILRAVAGES
GILRAVAGING
GILSONITE
GILSONITES
GILT
GILTCUP
GILTCUPS
GILTS
GILTWOOD
GIMBAL
GIMBALS
GIMCRACK
GIMCRACKS
GIMLET
GIMLETED
GIMLETING
GIMLETS
GIMMAL
GIMMALLED
GIMMALS
GIMME
GIMMER
GIMMERS
GIMMES
GIMMICK
GIMMICKED
GIMMICKIER
GIMMICKIEST
GIMMICKING
GIMMICKRIES
GIMMICKRY
GIMMICKS
GIMMICKY
GIMMOR
GIMMORS
GIMP
GIMPED
GIMPIER
GIMPIEST
GIMPING
GIMPS
GIMPY
GIN
GING
GINGAL
GINGALL
GINGALLS
GINGALS
GINGELLIES
GINGELLY
GINGER
GINGERADE
GINGERADES
GINGERED
GINGERING
GINGERLY
GINGEROUS
GINGERS
GINGERY
GINGHAM
GINGHAMS
GINGILI
GINGILIS
GINGIVAL
GINGKO
GINGKOES
GINGLE
GINGLES
GINGLYMI
GINGLYMUS
GINGS
GINHOUSE
GINHOUSES
GINK
GINKGO
GINKGOES
GINKS
GINN
GINNED
GINNEL
GINNELS
GINNER
GINNERIES
GINNERS
GINNERY
GINNIER
GINNIEST
GINNING
GINNY
GINORMOUS
GINS
GINSENG
GINSENGS
GINSHOP
GINSHOPS
GIO
GIOCOSO
GIOS
GIP
GIPPIES
GIPPO
GIPPOS
GIPPY
GIPS
GIPSEN
GIPSENS
GIPSIED
GIPSIES
GIPSY
GIPSYING
GIRAFFE
GIRAFFES
GIRAFFID
GIRAFFINE
GIRAFFOID
GIRANDOLA
GIRANDOLAS
GIRANDOLE
GIRANDOLES
GIRASOL
GIRASOLE
GIRASOLES
GIRASOLS
GIRD
GIRDED
GIRDER
GIRDERS
GIRDING
GIRDINGS
GIRDLE
GIRDLED
GIRDLER
GIRDLERS
GIRDLES
GIRDLING
GIRDS
GIRKIN
GIRKINS
GIRL
GIRLHOOD
GIRLHOODS
GIRLIE
GIRLIES
GIRLISH
GIRLISHLY
GIRLOND
GIRLONDS
GIRLS
GIRLY
GIRN
GIRNED
GIRNEL
GIRNELS
GIRNER
GIRNERS
GIRNIE
GIRNIER
GIRNIEST
GIRNING
GIRNS
GIRO
GIRON
GIRONIC
GIRONS
GIROS
GIROSOL
GIROSOLS
GIRR
GIRRS
GIRT
GIRTED
GIRTH
GIRTHED
GIRTHING
GIRTHLINE
GIRTHLINES
GIRTHS
GIRTING
GIRTLINE
GIRTLINES
GIRTS
GIS
GISARME
GISARMES

GISM
GISMO
GISMOLOGIES
GISMOLOGY
GISMOS
GISMS
GIST
GISTS
GIT
GITANA
GITANAS
GITANO
GITANOS
GITE
GITES
GITS
GITTERN
GITTERNED
GITTERNING
GITTERNS
GIUST
GIUSTED
GIUSTING
GIUSTO
GIUSTS
GIVE
GIVEAWAY
GIVEAWAYS
GIVED
GIVEN
GIVENNESS
GIVENNESSES
GIVER
GIVERS
GIVES
GIVING
GIVINGS
GIZMO
GIZMOLOGIES
GIZMOLOGY
GIZMOS
GIZZ
GIZZARD
GIZZARDS
GIZZEN
GIZZENED
GIZZENING
GIZZENS
GIZZES
GJU
GJUS
GLABELLA
GLABELLAE
GLABELLAR
GLABRATE
GLABROUS
GLACE
GLACEED
GLACEING
GLACES
GLACIAL
GLACIALS
GLACIATE
GLACIATED
GLACIATES
GLACIATING
GLACIER
GLACIERS
GLACIS
GLACISES
GLAD
GLADDED
GLADDEN
GLADDENED
GLADDENING
GLADDENS
GLADDER
GLADDEST
GLADDIE
GLADDIES
GLADDING
GLADDON
GLADDONS
GLADE
GLADES
GLADFUL
GLADIATE
GLADIATOR
GLADIATORS
GLADIER
GLADIEST
GLADIOLE
GLADIOLES
GLADIOLI
GLADIOLUS
GLADIOLUSES
GLADIUS
GLADIUSES
GLADLY
GLADNESS
GLADNESSES
GLADS
GLADSOME
GLADY
GLAIK
GLAIKET
GLAIKIT
GLAIKS
GLAIR
GLAIRED
GLAIREOUS
GLAIRIER
GLAIRIEST
GLAIRIN
GLAIRING
GLAIRINS
GLAIRS
GLAIRY
GLAIVE
GLAIVED
GLAIVES
GLAM
GLAMOR
GLAMORED
GLAMORING
GLAMORISE
GLAMORISED
GLAMORISES
GLAMORISING
GLAMORIZE
GLAMORIZED
GLAMORIZES
GLAMORIZING
GLAMOROUS
GLAMORS
GLAMOUR
GLAMOURED
GLAMOURING
GLAMOURS
GLAMS
GLANCE
GLANCED
GLANCES
GLANCING
GLANCINGS
GLAND
GLANDERED
GLANDERS
GLANDES
GLANDS
GLANDULAR
GLANDULE
GLANDULES
GLANS
GLARE
GLAREAL
GLARED
GLAREOUS
GLARES
GLARIER
GLARIEST
GLARING
GLARINGLY
GLARY
GLASNOST
GLASNOSTS
GLASS
GLASSED
GLASSEN
GLASSES
GLASSFUL
GLASSFULS
GLASSIER
GLASSIEST
GLASSIFIED
GLASSIFIES
GLASSIFY
GLASSIFYING
GLASSILY
GLASSINE
GLASSINES
GLASSING
GLASSLIKE
GLASSMAN
GLASSMEN
GLASSWARE
GLASSWARES
GLASSWORK
GLASSWORKS
GLASSWORT
GLASSWORTS
GLASSY
GLAUCOMA
GLAUCOMAS
GLAUCOUS
GLAUM
GLAUMED
GLAUMING
GLAUMS
GLAUR
GLAURIER
GLAURIEST
GLAURS
GLAURY
GLAZE
GLAZED
GLAZEN
GLAZER
GLAZERS
GLAZES
GLAZIER
GLAZIERS
GLAZIEST
GLAZING
GLAZINGS
GLAZY
GLEAM
GLEAMED
GLEAMIER
GLEAMIEST
GLEAMING
GLEAMINGS
GLEAMS
GLEAMY
GLEAN
GLEANED
GLEANER
GLEANERS
GLEANING
GLEANINGS
GLEANS
GLEAVE
GLEAVES
GLEBE
GLEBES
GLEBOUS
GLEBY
GLED
GLEDE
GLEDES
GLEDGE
GLEDGED
GLEDGES
GLEDGING
GLEDS
GLEE
GLEED
GLEEDS
GLEEFUL
GLEEING
GLEEK
GLEEKED
GLEEKING
GLEEKS
GLEEMAN
GLEEMEN
GLEES
GLEESOME
GLEET
GLEETED
GLEETIER
GLEETIEST
GLEETING
GLEETS
GLEETY
GLEG
GLEGGER
GLEGGEST
GLEI
GLEIS
GLEN
GLENGARRIES
GLENGARRY
GLENOID
GLENOIDAL
GLENOIDS
GLENS
GLENT
GLENTED
GLENTING
GLENTS
GLEY
GLEYED
GLEYING
GLEYS
GLIA
GLIADIN
GLIADINE
GLIADINES
GLIADINS
GLIAL
GLIAS
GLIB
GLIBBED
GLIBBER
GLIBBERY
GLIBBEST
GLIBBING
GLIBLY
GLIBNESS
GLIBNESSES
GLIBS
GLID
GLIDDER
GLIDDERY
GLIDDEST
GLIDE
GLIDED
GLIDER
GLIDERS
GLIDES
GLIDING
GLIDINGLY
GLIDINGS
GLIFF
GLIFFING
GLIFFINGS
GLIFFS
GLIFT
GLIFTS

GLIKE
GLIKES
GLIM
GLIMMER
GLIMMERED
GLIMMERING
GLIMMERINGS
GLIMMERS
GLIMMERY
GLIMPSE
GLIMPSED
GLIMPSES
GLIMPSING
GLIMS
GLINT
GLINTED
GLINTING
GLINTS
GLIOMA
GLIOMAS
GLIOMATA
GLIOSES
GLIOSIS
GLISK
GLISKS
GLISSADE
GLISSADED
GLISSADES
GLISSADING
GLISSANDI
GLISSANDO
GLISSANDOS
GLISTEN
GLISTENED
GLISTENING
GLISTENS
GLISTER
GLISTERED
GLISTERING
GLISTERS
GLIT
GLITCH
GLITCHES
GLITS
GLITTER
GLITTERED
GLITTERIER
GLITTERIEST
GLITTERING
GLITTERINGS
GLITTERS
GLITTERY
GLITZ
GLITZES
GLITZIER
GLITZIEST
GLITZILY
GLITZY
GLOAMING
GLOAMINGS
GLOAT
GLOATED
GLOATER
GLOATERS
GLOATING
GLOATS
GLOB
GLOBAL
GLOBALISE
GLOBALISED
GLOBALISES
GLOBALISING
GLOBALISM
GLOBALISMS
GLOBALIZE
GLOBALIZED
GLOBALIZES
GLOBALIZING
GLOBALLY
GLOBATE
GLOBATED
GLOBBIER
GLOBBIEST
GLOBBY
GLOBE
GLOBED
GLOBES
GLOBIN
GLOBING
GLOBINS
GLOBOID
GLOBOIDS
GLOBOSE
GLOBOSES
GLOBOSITIES
GLOBOSITY
GLOBOUS
GLOBS
GLOBULAR
GLOBULE
GLOBULES
GLOBULET
GLOBULETS
GLOBULIN
GLOBULINS
GLOBULITE
GLOBULITES
GLOBULOUS
GLOBY
GLODE
GLOGG
GLOGGS
GLOIRE
GLOIRES
GLOM
GLOMERATE
GLOMERATED
GLOMERATES
GLOMERATING
GLOMERULE
GLOMERULES
GLOMERULI
GLOMMED
GLOMMING
GLOMS
GLONOIN
GLONOINS
GLOOM
GLOOMED
GLOOMFUL
GLOOMIER
GLOOMIEST
GLOOMILY
GLOOMING
GLOOMINGS
GLOOMS
GLOOMY
GLOOP
GLOOPED
GLOOPIER
GLOOPIEST
GLOOPING
GLOOPS
GLOOPY
GLOP
GLOPS
GLORIA
GLORIAS
GLORIED
GLORIES
GLORIFIED
GLORIFIES
GLORIFY
GLORIFYING
GLORIOLE
GLORIOLES
GLORIOSA
GLORIOSAS
GLORIOUS
GLORY
GLORYING
GLOSS
GLOSSA
GLOSSAE
GLOSSAL
GLOSSARIES
GLOSSARY
GLOSSAS
GLOSSATOR
GLOSSATORS
GLOSSED
GLOSSEME
GLOSSEMES
GLOSSER
GLOSSERS
GLOSSES
GLOSSIER
GLOSSIES
GLOSSIEST
GLOSSILY
GLOSSINA
GLOSSINAS
GLOSSING
GLOSSITIS
GLOSSITISES
GLOSSY
GLOTTAL
GLOTTIC
GLOTTIDES
GLOTTIS
GLOTTISES
GLOUT
GLOUTED
GLOUTING
GLOUTS
GLOVE
GLOVED
GLOVER
GLOVERS
GLOVES
GLOVING
GLOVINGS
GLOW
GLOWED
GLOWER
GLOWERED
GLOWERING
GLOWERS
GLOWING
GLOWINGLY
GLOWLAMP
GLOWLAMPS
GLOWS
GLOXINIA
GLOXINIAS
GLOZE
GLOZED
GLOZES
GLOZING
GLOZINGS
GLUCAGON
GLUCAGONS
GLUCINA
GLUCINAS
GLUCINIUM
GLUCINIUMS
GLUCINUM
GLUCINUMS
GLUCOSE
GLUCOSES
GLUCOSIC
GLUCOSIDE
GLUCOSIDES
GLUE
GLUED
GLUER
GLUERS
GLUES
GLUEY
GLUEYNESS
GLUEYNESSES
GLUG
GLUGGED
GLUGGING
GLUGS
GLUHWEIN
GLUHWEINS
GLUIER
GLUIEST
GLUING
GLUISH
GLUM
GLUME
GLUMELLA
GLUMELLAS
GLUMES
GLUMLY
GLUMMER
GLUMMEST
GLUMNESS
GLUMNESSES
GLUMPIER
GLUMPIEST
GLUMPISH
GLUMPS
GLUMPY
GLUON
GLUONS
GLUT
GLUTAEAL
GLUTAEI
GLUTAEUS
GLUTAMATE
GLUTAMATES
GLUTAMINE
GLUTAMINES
GLUTEAL
GLUTEI
GLUTELIN
GLUTELINS
GLUTEN
GLUTENOUS
GLUTENS
GLUTEUS
GLUTINOUS
GLUTS
GLUTTED
GLUTTING
GLUTTON
GLUTTONIES
GLUTTONS
GLUTTONY
GLYCERIA
GLYCERIAS
GLYCERIC
GLYCERIDE
GLYCERIDES
GLYCERIN
GLYCERINE
GLYCERINES
GLYCERINS
GLYCEROL
GLYCEROLS
GLYCERYL
GLYCERYLS
GLYCIN
GLYCINE
GLYCINES
GLYCINS
GLYCOCOLL
GLYCOCOLLS
GLYCOGEN
GLYCOGENS
GLYCOL
GLYCOLIC
GLYCOLLIC
GLYCOLS
GLYCONIC
GLYCONICS
GLYCOSE

GLYCOSES
GLYCOSIDE
GLYCOSIDES
GLYCOSYL
GLYCOSYLS
GLYPH
GLYPHIC
GLYPHS
GLYPTIC
GLYPTICS
GMELINITE
GMELINITES
GNAR
GNARL
GNARLED
GNARLIER
GNARLIEST
GNARLING
GNARLS
GNARLY
GNARR
GNARRED
GNARRING
GNARRS
GNARS
GNASH
GNASHED
GNASHER
GNASHERS
GNASHES
GNASHING
GNAT
GNATHAL
GNATHIC
GNATHITE
GNATHITES
GNATHONIC
GNATLING
GNATLINGS
GNATS
GNAW
GNAWED
GNAWER
GNAWERS
GNAWING
GNAWN
GNAWS
GNEISS
GNEISSES
GNEISSIC
GNEISSOID
GNEISSOSE
GNOCCHI
GNOCCHIS
GNOMAE
GNOME
GNOMES
GNOMIC
GNOMISH
GNOMIST
GNOMISTS
GNOMON
GNOMONIC
GNOMONICS
GNOMONS
GNOSES
GNOSIS
GNOSTIC
GNOSTICAL
GNU
GNUS
GO
GOA
GOAD
GOADED
GOADING
GOADS
GOADSMAN
GOADSMEN
GOADSTER
GOADSTERS
GOAF
GOAFS
GOAL
GOALBALL
GOALBALLS
GOALED
GOALIE
GOALIES
GOALING
GOALLESS
GOALMOUTH
GOALMOUTHS
GOALPOST
GOALPOSTS
GOALS
GOANNA
GOANNAS
GOARY
GOAS
GOAT
GOATEE
GOATEED
GOATEES
GOATFISH
GOATFISHES
GOATHERD
GOATHERDS
GOATIER
GOATIEST
GOATISH
GOATLING
GOATLINGS
GOATS
GOATSKIN
GOATSKINS
GOATWEED
GOATWEEDS
GOATY
GOB
GOBANG
GOBANGS
GOBBED
GOBBELINE
GOBBELINES
GOBBET
GOBBETS
GOBBI
GOBBING
GOBBLE
GOBBLED
GOBBLER
GOBBLERS
GOBBLES
GOBBLING
GOBBO
GOBIES
GOBIID
GOBIIDS
GOBIOID
GOBLET
GOBLETS
GOBLIN
GOBLINS
GOBO
GOBOES
GOBONY
GOBOS
GOBS
GOBSHITE
GOBSHITES
GOBURRA
GOBURRAS
GOBY
GOD
GODCHILD
GODCHILDREN
GODDAM
GODDAMN
GODDAMNED
GODDED
GODDEN
GODDENS
GODDESS
GODDESSES
GODDING
GODET
GODETIA
GODETIAS
GODETS
GODFATHER
GODFATHERS
GODHEAD
GODHEADS
GODHOOD
GODHOODS
GODLESS
GODLESSLY
GODLIER
GODLIEST
GODLIKE
GODLILY
GODLINESS
GODLINESSES
GODLING
GODLINGS
GODLY
GODMOTHER
GODMOTHERS
GODOWN
GODOWNS
GODPARENT
GODPARENTS
GODROON
GODROONED
GODROONS
GODS
GODSEND
GODSENDS
GODSHIP
GODSHIPS
GODSO
GODSON
GODSONS
GODSOS
GODSPEED
GODSPEEDS
GODWARD
GODWARDS
GODWIT
GODWITS
GOE
GOEL
GOELS
GOER
GOERS
GOES
GOETHITE
GOETHITES
GOETIC
GOETIES
GOETY
GOEY
GOFER
GOFERS
GOFF
GOFFED
GOFFER
GOFFERED
GOFFERING
GOFFERINGS
GOFFERS
GOFFING
GOFFS
GOGGLE
GOGGLED
GOGGLER
GOGGLERS
GOGGLES
GOGGLIER
GOGGLIEST
GOGGLING
GOGGLINGS
GOGGLY
GOGLET
GOGLETS
GOGO
GOIER
GOIEST
GOING
GOINGS
GOITER
GOITERS
GOITRE
GOITRED
GOITRES
GOITROUS
GOLD
GOLDARN
GOLDCREST
GOLDCRESTS
GOLDEN
GOLDENED
GOLDENER
GOLDENEST
GOLDENING
GOLDENLY
GOLDENROD
GOLDENRODS
GOLDENS
GOLDER
GOLDEST
GOLDEYE
GOLDEYES
GOLDFIELD
GOLDFIELDS
GOLDFINCH
GOLDFINCHES
GOLDFINNIES
GOLDFINNY
GOLDFISH
GOLDFISHES
GOLDIER
GOLDIEST
GOLDISH
GOLDLESS
GOLDMINER
GOLDMINERS
GOLDS
GOLDSINNIES
GOLDSINNY
GOLDSIZE
GOLDSIZES
GOLDSMITH
GOLDSMITHS
GOLDSPINK
GOLDSPINKS
GOLDSTICK
GOLDSTICKS
GOLDSTONE
GOLDSTONES
GOLDY
GOLE
GOLEM
GOLEMS
GOLES
GOLF
GOLFED
GOLFER
GOLFERS
GOLFIANA
GOLFIANAS
GOLFING
GOLFINGS
GOLFS
GOLIARD
GOLIARDIC
GOLIARDIES
GOLIARDS
GOLIARDY

GOLIAS
GOLIASED
GOLIASES
GOLIASING
GOLLAN
GOLLAND
GOLLANDS
GOLLANS
GOLLAR
GOLLARED
GOLLARING
GOLLARS
GOLLER
GOLLERED
GOLLERING
GOLLERS
GOLLIES
GOLLIWOG
GOLLIWOGS
GOLLOP
GOLLOPED
GOLLOPING
GOLLOPS
GOLLY
GOLLYWOG
GOLLYWOGS
GOLOMYNKA
GOLOMYNKAS
GOLOSH
GOLOSHED
GOLOSHES
GOLOSHING
GOLOSHOES
GOLP
GOLPE
GOLPES
GOLPS
GOMBEEN
GOMBEENS
GOMBO
GOMBOS
GOMBRO
GOMBROS
GOMERAL
GOMERALS
GOMERIL
GOMERILS
GOMOKU
GOMOKUS
GOMPA
GOMPAS
GOMPHOSES
GOMPHOSIS
GOMUTI
GOMUTIS
GOMUTO
GOMUTOS
GON
GONAD
GONADAL
GONADIAL
GONADIC
GONADS
GONDELAY
GONDELAYS
GONDOLA
GONDOLAS
GONDOLIER
GONDOLIERS
GONE
GONENESS
GONENESSES
GONER
GONERS
GONFALON
GONFALONS
GONFANON
GONFANONS
GONG
GONGED
GONGING
GONGS
GONGSTER
GONGSTERS
GONIA
GONIATITE
GONIATITES
GONIDIA
GONIDIAL
GONIDIC
GONIDIUM
GONION
GONK
GONKS
GONNA
GONOCOCCI
GONOCYTE
GONOCYTES
GONOPHORE
GONOPHORES
GONORRHEA
GONORRHEAS
GONS
GONYS
GONYSES
GONZO
GOO
GOOBER
GOOBERS
GOOD
GOODFACED
GOODIER
GOODIES
GOODIEST
GOODINESS
GOODINESSES
GOODISH
GOODLIER
GOODLIEST
GOODLY
GOODMAN
GOODMEN
GOODNESS
GOODNESSES
GOODNIGHT
GOODNIGHTS
GOODS
GOODSIRE
GOODSIRES
GOODTIME
GOODWIFE
GOODWILL
GOODWILLS
GOODWIVES
GOODY
GOODYEAR
GOODYEARS
GOOEY
GOOF
GOOFBALL
GOOFBALLS
GOOFED
GOOFIER
GOOFIEST
GOOFILY
GOOFINESS
GOOFINESSES
GOOFING
GOOFS
GOOFY
GOOGLE
GOOGLED
GOOGLES
GOOGLIES
GOOGLING
GOOGLY
GOOGOL
GOOGOLS
GOOIER
GOOIEST
GOOK
GOOKS
GOOL
GOOLD
GOOLDS
GOOLEY
GOOLEYS
GOOLIE
GOOLIES
GOOLS
GOOLY
GOON
GOONDA
GOONDAS
GOONEY
GOONEYS
GOONS
GOOP
GOOPIER
GOOPIEST
GOOPS
GOOPY
GOOR
GOOROO
GOOROOS
GOORS
GOOS
GOOSANDER
GOOSANDERS
GOOSE
GOOSED
GOOSEFOOT
GOOSEFOOTS
GOOSEGOB
GOOSEGOBS
GOOSEGOG
GOOSEGOGS
GOOSEHERD
GOOSEHERDS
GOOSERIES
GOOSERY
GOOSES
GOOSEY
GOOSEYS
GOOSIER
GOOSIES
GOOSIEST
GOOSING
GOOSY
GOPAK
GOPAKS
GOPHER
GOPHERED
GOPHERING
GOPHERS
GOPURA
GOPURAM
GOPURAMS
GOPURAS
GORAL
GORALS
GORAMIES
GORAMY
GORBLIMEY
GORBLIMY
GORCOCK
GORCOCKS
GORCROW
GORCROWS
GORE
GORED
GORES
GORGE
GORGED
GORGEOUS
GORGERIN
GORGERINS
GORGES
GORGET
GORGETS
GORGIA
GORGIAS
GORGING
GORGIO
GORGIOS
GORGON
GORGONEIA
GORGONIAN
GORGONIANS
GORGONISE
GORGONISED
GORGONISES
GORGONISING
GORGONIZE
GORGONIZED
GORGONIZES
GORGONIZING
GORGONS
GORIER
GORIEST
GORILLA
GORILLAS
GORILLIAN
GORILLINE
GORILLOID
GORILY
GORINESS
GORINESSES
GORING
GORINGS
GORM
GORMAND
GORMANDS
GORMED
GORMIER
GORMIEST
GORMING
GORMLESS
GORMS
GORMY
GORP
GORPED
GORPING
GORPS
GORSE
GORSEDD
GORSEDDS
GORSES
GORSIER
GORSIEST
GORSOON
GORSOONS
GORSY
GORY
GOS
GOSH
GOSHAWK
GOSHAWKS
GOSHT
GOSHTS
GOSLARITE
GOSLARITES
GOSLET
GOSLETS
GOSLING
GOSLINGS
GOSPEL
GOSPELISE
GOSPELISED
GOSPELISES
GOSPELISING
GOSPELIZE
GOSPELIZED
GOSPELIZES
GOSPELIZING
GOSPELLED
GOSPELLER
GOSPELLERS
GOSPELLING
GOSPELS

GOSPODAR
GOSPODARS
GOSSAMER
GOSSAMERS
GOSSAMERY
GOSSAN
GOSSANS
GOSSE
GOSSES
GOSSIB
GOSSIBS
GOSSIP
GOSSIPED
GOSSIPING
GOSSIPINGS
GOSSIPRIES
GOSSIPRY
GOSSIPS
GOSSIPY
GOSSOON
GOSSOONS
GOSSYPINE
GOSSYPOL
GOSSYPOLS
GOT
GOTHIC
GOTHICISE
GOTHICISED
GOTHICISES
GOTHICISING
GOTHICIZE
GOTHICIZED
GOTHICIZES
GOTHICIZING
GOTHITE
GOTHITES
GOTTA
GOTTEN
GOUACHE
GOUACHES
GOUGE
GOUGED
GOUGERE
GOUGERES
GOUGES
GOUGING
GOUJEERS
GOUJONS
GOUK
GOUKS
GOULASH
GOULASHES
GOURA
GOURAMI
GOURAMIS
GOURAS
GOURD
GOURDE
GOURDES
GOURDIER
GOURDIEST
GOURDS
GOURDY
GOURMAND
GOURMANDS
GOURMET
GOURMETS
GOUSTIER
GOUSTIEST
GOUSTROUS
GOUSTY
GOUT
GOUTFLIES
GOUTFLY
GOUTIER
GOUTIEST
GOUTINESS
GOUTINESSES
GOUTS
GOUTTE
GOUTTES
GOUTWEED
GOUTWEEDS
GOUTWORT
GOUTWORTS
GOUTY
GOV
GOVERN
GOVERNALL
GOVERNALLS
GOVERNED
GOVERNESS
GOVERNESSED
GOVERNESSES
GOVERNESSING
GOVERNING
GOVERNOR
GOVERNORS
GOVERNS
GOVS
GOWAN
GOWANED
GOWANS
GOWANY
GOWD
GOWDER
GOWDEST
GOWDS
GOWDSPINK
GOWDSPINKS
GOWF
GOWFED
GOWFER
GOWFERS
GOWFING
GOWFS
GOWK
GOWKS
GOWL
GOWLAN
GOWLAND
GOWLANDS
GOWLANS
GOWLED
GOWLING
GOWLS
GOWN
GOWNBOY
GOWNBOYS
GOWNED
GOWNING
GOWNMAN
GOWNMEN
GOWNS
GOWNSMAN
GOWNSMEN
GOWPEN
GOWPENFUL
GOWPENFULS
GOWPENS
GOY
GOYIM
GOYISCH
GOYISH
GOYS
GOZZAN
GOZZANS
GRAAL
GRAALS
GRAB
GRABBED
GRABBER
GRABBERS
GRABBING
GRABBLE
GRABBLED
GRABBLER
GRABBLERS
GRABBLES
GRABBLING
GRABEN
GRABENS
GRABS
GRACE
GRACED
GRACEFUL
GRACELESS
GRACES
GRACILE
GRACILITIES
GRACILITY
GRACING
GRACIOSO
GRACIOSOS
GRACIOUS
GRACIOUSES
GRACKLE
GRACKLES
GRAD
GRADABLE
GRADABLES
GRADATE
GRADATED
GRADATES
GRADATIM
GRADATING
GRADATION
GRADATIONS
GRADATORY
GRADDAN
GRADDANED
GRADDANING
GRADDANS
GRADE
GRADED
GRADELY
GRADER
GRADERS
GRADES
GRADIENT
GRADIENTS
GRADIN
GRADINE
GRADINES
GRADING
GRADINI
GRADINO
GRADINS
GRADS
GRADUAL
GRADUALLY
GRADUALS
GRADUAND
GRADUANDS
GRADUATE
GRADUATED
GRADUATES
GRADUATING
GRADUATOR
GRADUATORS
GRADUS
GRADUSES
GRAFF
GRAFFED
GRAFFING
GRAFFITI
GRAFFITIS
GRAFFITO
GRAFFS
GRAFT
GRAFTED
GRAFTER
GRAFTERS
GRAFTING
GRAFTINGS
GRAFTS
GRAIL
GRAILE
GRAILES
GRAILS
GRAIN
GRAINAGE
GRAINAGES
GRAINE
GRAINED
GRAINER
GRAINERS
GRAINES
GRAINIER
GRAINIEST
GRAINING
GRAININGS
GRAINS
GRAINY
GRAIP
GRAIPS
GRAITH
GRAITHED
GRAITHING
GRAITHLY
GRAITHS
GRAKLE
GRAKLES
GRALLOCH
GRALLOCHED
GRALLOCHING
GRALLOCHS
GRAM
GRAMA
GRAMARIES
GRAMARY
GRAMARYE
GRAMARYES
GRAMAS
GRAMASH
GRAMASHES
GRAME
GRAMERCIES
GRAMERCY
GRAMES
GRAMMA
GRAMMAR
GRAMMARS
GRAMMAS
GRAMMATIC
GRAMME
GRAMMES
GRAMOCHE
GRAMOCHES
GRAMPUS
GRAMPUSES
GRAMS
GRAN
GRANARIES
GRANARY
GRAND
GRANDAD
GRANDADDIES
GRANDADDY
GRANDADS
GRANDAM
GRANDAMS
GRANDDAD
GRANDDADS
GRANDE
GRANDEE
GRANDEES
GRANDER
GRANDEST
GRANDEUR
GRANDEURS
GRANDIOSE
GRANDLY
GRANDMA
GRANDMAMA
GRANDMAMAS
GRANDMAS
GRANDNESS
GRANDNESSES
GRANDPA

GRANDPAPA
GRANDPAPAS
GRANDPAS
GRANDS
GRANDSIRE
GRANDSIRES
GRANDSON
GRANDSONS
GRANFER
GRANFERS
GRANGE
GRANGER
GRANGERS
GRANGES
GRANITA
GRANITAS
GRANITE
GRANITES
GRANITIC
GRANITISE
GRANITISED
GRANITISES
GRANITISING
GRANITITE
GRANITITES
GRANITIZE
GRANITIZED
GRANITIZES
GRANITIZING
GRANITOID
GRANIVORE
GRANIVORES
GRANNAM
GRANNAMS
GRANNIE
GRANNIED
GRANNIEING
GRANNIES
GRANNY
GRANNYING
GRANOLA
GRANOLAS
GRANS
GRANT
GRANTABLE
GRANTED
GRANTEE
GRANTEES
GRANTER
GRANTERS
GRANTING
GRANTOR
GRANTORS
GRANTS
GRANULAR
GRANULARY
GRANULATE
GRANULATED
GRANULATES
GRANULATING
GRANULE
GRANULES
GRANULITE
GRANULITES
GRANULOMA
GRANULOMAS
GRANULOMATA
GRANULOSE
GRANULOUS
GRAPE
GRAPED
GRAPELESS
GRAPERIES
GRAPERY
GRAPES
GRAPESEED
GRAPESEEDS
GRAPESHOT
GRAPESHOTS
GRAPETREE
GRAPETREES
GRAPEVINE
GRAPEVINES
GRAPEY
GRAPH
GRAPHED
GRAPHEME
GRAPHEMES
GRAPHEMIC
GRAPHEMICS
GRAPHIC
GRAPHICAL
GRAPHICLY
GRAPHICS
GRAPHING
GRAPHITE
GRAPHITES
GRAPHITIC
GRAPHIUM
GRAPHIUMS
GRAPHS
GRAPIER
GRAPIEST
GRAPING
GRAPLE
GRAPLES
GRAPNEL
GRAPNELS
GRAPPA
GRAPPAS
GRAPPLE
GRAPPLED
GRAPPLES
GRAPPLING
GRAPY
GRASP
GRASPABLE
GRASPED
GRASPER
GRASPERS
GRASPING
GRASPLESS
GRASPS
GRASS
GRASSED
GRASSER
GRASSERS
GRASSES
GRASSHOOK
GRASSHOOKS
GRASSIER
GRASSIEST
GRASSING
GRASSINGS
GRASSLAND
GRASSLANDS
GRASSUM
GRASSUMS
GRASSY
GRASTE
GRAT
GRATE
GRATED
GRATEFUL
GRATER
GRATERS
GRATES
GRATICULE
GRATICULES
GRATIFIED
GRATIFIER
GRATIFIERS
GRATIFIES
GRATIFY
GRATIFYING
GRATIN
GRATINATE
GRATINATED
GRATINATES
GRATINATING
GRATINE
GRATINEE
GRATING
GRATINGLY
GRATINGS
GRATINS
GRATIS
GRATITUDE
GRATITUDES
GRATTOIR
GRATTOIRS
GRATUITIES
GRATUITY
GRATULANT
GRATULATE
GRATULATED
GRATULATES
GRATULATING
GRAUNCH
GRAUNCHED
GRAUNCHER
GRAUNCHERS
GRAUNCHES
GRAUNCHING
GRAUPEL
GRAUPELS
GRAVADLAX
GRAVADLAXES
GRAVAMEN
GRAVAMINA
GRAVE
GRAVED
GRAVEL
GRAVELESS
GRAVELLED
GRAVELLING
GRAVELLY
GRAVELS
GRAVELY
GRAVEN
GRAVENESS
GRAVENESSES
GRAVER
GRAVERS
GRAVES
GRAVEST
GRAVEYARD
GRAVEYARDS
GRAVID
GRAVIDITIES
GRAVIDITY
GRAVIES
GRAVING
GRAVINGS
GRAVITAS
GRAVITASES
GRAVITATE
GRAVITATED
GRAVITATES
GRAVITATING
GRAVITIES
GRAVITON
GRAVITONS
GRAVITY
GRAVLAX
GRAVLAXES
GRAVURE
GRAVURES
GRAVY
GRAY
GRAYED
GRAYER
GRAYEST
GRAYFLIES
GRAYFLY
GRAYING
GRAYLE
GRAYLES
GRAYLING
GRAYLINGS
GRAYS
GRAYWACKE
GRAYWACKES
GRAZE
GRAZED
GRAZER
GRAZERS
GRAZES
GRAZIER
GRAZIERS
GRAZING
GRAZINGS
GRAZIOSO
GREASE
GREASED
GREASER
GREASERS
GREASES
GREASIER
GREASIES
GREASIEST
GREASILY
GREASING
GREASY
GREAT
GREATCOAT
GREATCOATS
GREATEN
GREATENED
GREATENING
GREATENS
GREATER
GREATEST
GREATLY
GREATNESS
GREATNESSES
GREATS
GREAVE
GREAVED
GREAVES
GREAVING
GREBE
GREBES
GRECE
GRECES
GRECIAN
GRECIANS
GRECQUE
GRECQUES
GREE
GREECE
GREECES
GREED
GREEDIER
GREEDIEST
GREEDILY
GREEDS
GREEDY
GREEGREE
GREEGREES
GREEING
GREEKING
GREEKINGS
GREEN
GREENBACK
GREENBACKS
GREENED
GREENER
GREENERIES
GREENERS
GREENERY
GREENEST
GREENFLIES
GREENFLY
GREENGAGE
GREENGAGES
GREENHAND
GREENHANDS
GREENHORN
GREENHORNS

GREENIE
GREENIER
GREENIES
GREENIEST
GREENING
GREENINGS
GREENISH
GREENLET
GREENLETS
GREENLY
GREENMAIL
GREENMAILS
GREENNESS
GREENNESSES
GREENROOM
GREENROOMS
GREENS
GREENSAND
GREENSANDS
GREENTH
GREENTHS
GREENWASH
GREENWASHED
GREENWASHES
GREENWASHING
GREENWEED
GREENWEEDS
GREENWOOD
GREENWOODS
GREENY
GREES
GREESE
GREESES
GREESING
GREESINGS
GREET
GREETE
GREETED
GREETER
GREETERS
GREETES
GREETING
GREETINGS
GREETS
GREFFIER
GREFFIERS
GREGALE
GREGALES
GREGARIAN
GREGARINE
GREGARINES
GREGATIM
GREGE
GREGO
GREGOS
GREIGE
GREIN
GREINED
GREINING
GREINS
GREISEN
GREISENS
GREISLY
GREMIAL
GREMIALS
GREMLIN
GREMLINS
GREMOLATA
GREMOLATAS
GREN
GRENADE
GRENADES
GRENADIER
GRENADIERS
GRENADINE
GRENADINES
GRENNED
GRENNING
GRENS
GRESE
GRESES
GRESSING
GRESSINGS
GREVE
GREVES
GREW
GREWED
GREWHOUND
GREWHOUNDS
GREWING
GREWS
GREY
GREYBEARD
GREYBEARDS
GREYED
GREYER
GREYEST
GREYHEN
GREYHENS
GREYHOUND
GREYHOUNDS
GREYING
GREYINGS
GREYISH
GREYLY
GREYNESS
GREYNESSES
GREYS
GREYSTONE
GREYSTONES
GREYWACKE
GREYWACKES
GRIBBLE
GRIBBLES
GRICE
GRICER
GRICERS
GRICES
GRICING
GRICINGS
GRID
GRIDDER
GRIDDERS
GRIDDLE
GRIDDLES
GRIDE
GRIDED
GRIDELIN
GRIDELINS
GRIDES
GRIDING
GRIDIRON
GRIDIRONED
GRIDIRONING
GRIDIRONS
GRIDLOCK
GRIDLOCKS
GRIDS
GRIECE
GRIECED
GRIECES
GRIEF
GRIEFFUL
GRIEFLESS
GRIEFS
GRIESIE
GRIESLY
GRIESY
GRIEVANCE
GRIEVANCES
GRIEVE
GRIEVED
GRIEVER
GRIEVERS
GRIEVES
GRIEVING
GRIEVOUS
GRIFF
GRIFFE
GRIFFES
GRIFFIN
GRIFFINS
GRIFFON
GRIFFONS
GRIFFS
GRIFT
GRIFTED
GRIFTER
GRIFTERS
GRIFTING
GRIFTS
GRIG
GRIGGED
GRIGGING
GRIGRI
GRIGRIS
GRIGS
GRIKE
GRIKES
GRILL
GRILLADE
GRILLADES
GRILLAGE
GRILLAGES
GRILLE
GRILLED
GRILLES
GRILLING
GRILLINGS
GRILLS
GRILLWORK
GRILLWORKS
GRILSE
GRILSES
GRIM
GRIMACE
GRIMACED
GRIMACES
GRIMACING
GRIMALKIN
GRIMALKINS
GRIME
GRIMED
GRIMES
GRIMIER
GRIMIEST
GRIMILY
GRIMINESS
GRIMINESSES
GRIMING
GRIMLY
GRIMMER
GRIMMEST
GRIMNESS
GRIMNESSES
GRIMOIRE
GRIMOIRES
GRIMY
GRIN
GRIND
GRINDED
GRINDER
GRINDERIES
GRINDERS
GRINDERY
GRINDING
GRINDINGS
GRINDS
GRINGO
GRINGOS
GRINNED
GRINNER
GRINNERS
GRINNING
GRINS
GRIOT
GRIOTS
GRIP
GRIPE
GRIPED
GRIPER
GRIPERS
GRIPES
GRIPING
GRIPINGLY
GRIPLE
GRIPPE
GRIPPED
GRIPPER
GRIPPERS
GRIPPES
GRIPPIER
GRIPPIEST
GRIPPING
GRIPPLE
GRIPPLES
GRIPPY
GRIPS
GRIPSACK
GRIPSACKS
GRIPTAPE
GRIPTAPES
GRIS
GRISAILLE
GRISAILLES
GRISE
GRISED
GRISELY
GRISEOUS
GRISES
GRISETTE
GRISETTES
GRISGRIS
GRISING
GRISKIN
GRISKINS
GRISLED
GRISLIER
GRISLIEST
GRISLY
GRISON
GRISONS
GRIST
GRISTLE
GRISTLES
GRISTLIER
GRISTLIEST
GRISTLY
GRISTS
GRISY
GRIT
GRITH
GRITHS
GRITS
GRITSTONE
GRITSTONES
GRITTED
GRITTER
GRITTERS
GRITTEST
GRITTIER
GRITTIEST
GRITTING
GRITTY
GRIVET
GRIVETS
GRIZE
GRIZES
GRIZZLE
GRIZZLED
GRIZZLER
GRIZZLERS
GRIZZLES
GRIZZLIER
GRIZZLIES
GRIZZLIEST
GRIZZLING
GRIZZLY
GROAN
GROANED

GROANER
GROANERS
GROANFUL
GROANING
GROANINGS
GROANS
GROAT
GROATS
GROCER
GROCERIES
GROCERS
GROCERY
GROCKLE
GROCKLES
GRODIER
GRODIEST
GRODY
GROG
GROGGED
GROGGERIES
GROGGERY
GROGGIER
GROGGIEST
GROGGING
GROGGY
GROGRAM
GROGRAMS
GROGS
GROIN
GROINED
GROINING
GROININGS
GROINS
GROMA
GROMAS
GROMET
GROMETS
GROMMET
GROMMETS
GROMWELL
GROMWELLS
GRONE
GRONED
GRONEFULL
GRONES
GRONING
GROOF
GROOFS
GROOLIER
GROOLIEST
GROOLY
GROOM
GROOMED
GROOMING
GROOMS
GROOMSMAN
GROOMSMEN
GROOVE
GROOVED
GROOVER
GROOVERS
GROOVES
GROOVIER
GROOVIEST
GROOVING
GROOVY
GROPE
GROPED
GROPER
GROPERS
GROPES
GROPING
GROPINGLY
GROSBEAK
GROSBEAKS
GROSCHEN
GROSCHENS
GROSER
GROSERS
GROSERT
GROSERTS
GROSET
GROSETS
GROSGRAIN
GROSGRAINS
GROSS
GROSSART
GROSSARTS
GROSSED
GROSSER
GROSSES
GROSSEST
GROSSING
GROSSLY
GROSSNESS
GROSSNESSES
GROSSULAR
GROSSULARS
GROT
GROTESQUE
GROTESQUER
GROTESQUES
GROTESQUEST
GROTS
GROTTIER
GROTTIEST
GROTTO
GROTTOES
GROTTOS
GROTTY
GROUCH
GROUCHED
GROUCHES
GROUCHIER
GROUCHIEST
GROUCHILY
GROUCHING
GROUCHY
GROUF
GROUFS
GROUGH
GROUGHS
GROUND
GROUNDAGE
GROUNDAGES
GROUNDED
GROUNDEN
GROUNDER
GROUNDERS
GROUNDHOG
GROUNDHOGS
GROUNDING
GROUNDINGS
GROUNDMAN
GROUNDMEN
GROUNDNUT
GROUNDNUTS
GROUNDS
GROUNDSEL
GROUNDSELS
GROUP
GROUPABLE
GROUPAGE
GROUPAGES
GROUPED
GROUPER
GROUPERS
GROUPIE
GROUPIES
GROUPING
GROUPINGS
GROUPIST
GROUPISTS
GROUPLET
GROUPLETS
GROUPS
GROUPWARE
GROUPWARES
GROUPY
GROUSE
GROUSED
GROUSER
GROUSERS
GROUSES
GROUSEST
GROUSING
GROUT
GROUTED
GROUTER
GROUTERS
GROUTIER
GROUTIEST
GROUTING
GROUTINGS
GROUTS
GROUTY
GROVE
GROVEL
GROVELED
GROVELER
GROVELERS
GROVELING
GROVELLED
GROVELLER
GROVELLERS
GROVELLING
GROVELS
GROVES
GROVET
GROVETS
GROW
GROWABLE
GROWER
GROWERS
GROWING
GROWINGS
GROWL
GROWLED
GROWLER
GROWLERIES
GROWLERS
GROWLERY
GROWLIER
GROWLIEST
GROWLING
GROWLINGS
GROWLS
GROWLY
GROWN
GROWS
GROWTH
GROWTHIST
GROWTHISTS
GROWTHS
GROYNE
GROYNES
GRUB
GRUBBED
GRUBBER
GRUBBERS
GRUBBIER
GRUBBIEST
GRUBBING
GRUBBLE
GRUBBLED
GRUBBLES
GRUBBLING
GRUBBY
GRUBS
GRUBSTAKE
GRUBSTAKED
GRUBSTAKES
GRUBSTAKING
GRUDGE
GRUDGED
GRUDGEFUL
GRUDGES
GRUDGING
GRUDGINGS
GRUE
GRUED
GRUEING
GRUEL
GRUELING
GRUELINGS
GRUELLED
GRUELLING
GRUELLINGS
GRUELS
GRUES
GRUESOME
GRUESOMER
GRUESOMEST
GRUFE
GRUFES
GRUFF
GRUFFER
GRUFFEST
GRUFFISH
GRUFFLY
GRUFFNESS
GRUFFNESSES
GRUFTED
GRUING
GRUM
GRUMBLE
GRUMBLED
GRUMBLER
GRUMBLERS
GRUMBLES
GRUMBLIER
GRUMBLIEST
GRUMBLING
GRUMBLINGS
GRUMBLY
GRUME
GRUMES
GRUMLY
GRUMMER
GRUMMEST
GRUMMET
GRUMMETS
GRUMNESS
GRUMNESSES
GRUMOSE
GRUMOUS
GRUMP
GRUMPED
GRUMPH
GRUMPHED
GRUMPHIE
GRUMPHIES
GRUMPHING
GRUMPHS
GRUMPIER
GRUMPIEST
GRUMPILY
GRUMPING
GRUMPS
GRUMPY
GRUNGE
GRUNGES
GRUNGIER
GRUNGIEST
GRUNGY
GRUNION
GRUNIONS
GRUNT
GRUNTED
GRUNTER
GRUNTERS
GRUNTING
GRUNTINGS
GRUNTLE
GRUNTLED
GRUNTLES
GRUNTLING
GRUNTS
GRUPPETTI
GRUPPETTO

GRUTCH
GRUTCHED
GRUTCHES
GRUTCHING
GRUTTEN
GRYCE
GRYCES
GRYDE
GRYDED
GRYDES
GRYDING
GRYESLY
GRYESY
GRYFON
GRYFONS
GRYKE
GRYKES
GRYPE
GRYPES
GRYPHON
GRYPHONS
GRYPT
GRYSBOK
GRYSBOKS
GRYSELY
GRYSIE
GU
GUACAMOLE
GUACAMOLES
GUACHARO
GUACHAROS
GUACO
GUACOS
GUAIACUM
GUAIACUMS
GUAN
GUANA
GUANACO
GUANACOS
GUANAS
GUANAZOLO
GUANAZOLOS
GUANGO
GUANGOS
GUANINE
GUANINES
GUANO
GUANOS
GUANS
GUAR
GUARANA
GUARANAS
GUARANI
GUARANIES
GUARANIS
GUARANTEE
GUARANTEED
GUARANTEEING
GUARANTEES
GUARANTIED
GUARANTIES
GUARANTOR
GUARANTORS
GUARANTY
GUARANTYING
GUARD
GUARDABLE
GUARDAGE
GUARDAGES
GUARDANT
GUARDANTS
GUARDED
GUARDEDLY
GUARDEE
GUARDEES
GUARDIAN
GUARDIANS
GUARDING
GUARDLESS
GUARDRAIL
GUARDRAILS
GUARDROOM
GUARDROOMS
GUARDS
GUARDSHIP
GUARDSHIPS
GUARDSMAN
GUARDSMEN
GUARISH
GUARISHED
GUARISHES
GUARISHING
GUARS
GUAVA
GUAVAS
GUAYULE
GUAYULES
GUB
GUBBAH
GUBBAHS
GUBBINS
GUBBINSES
GUBS
GUCK
GUCKIER
GUCKIEST
GUCKS
GUCKY
GUDDLE
GUDDLED
GUDDLES
GUDDLING
GUDE
GUDEMAN
GUDEMEN
GUDES
GUDESIRE
GUDESIRES
GUDEWIFE
GUDEWIVES
GUDGEON
GUDGEONED
GUDGEONING
GUDGEONS
GUE
GUENON
GUENONS
GUERDON
GUERDONED
GUERDONING
GUERDONS
GUEREZA
GUEREZAS
GUERIDON
GUERIDONS
GUERILLA
GUERILLAS
GUERITE
GUERITES
GUERNSEY
GUERNSEYS
GUERRILLA
GUERRILLAS
GUES
GUESS
GUESSABLE
GUESSED
GUESSER
GUESSERS
GUESSES
GUESSING
GUESSINGS
GUESSWORK
GUESSWORKS
GUEST
GUESTED
GUESTEN
GUESTENED
GUESTENING
GUESTENS
GUESTING
GUESTS
GUESTWISE
GUFF
GUFFAW
GUFFAWED
GUFFAWING
GUFFAWS
GUFFIE
GUFFIES
GUFFS
GUGA
GUGAS
GUGGLE
GUGGLED
GUGGLES
GUGGLING
GUICHET
GUICHETS
GUID
GUIDABLE
GUIDAGE
GUIDAGES
GUIDANCE
GUIDANCES
GUIDE
GUIDEBOOK
GUIDEBOOKS
GUIDED
GUIDELESS
GUIDELINE
GUIDELINES
GUIDEPOST
GUIDEPOSTS
GUIDER
GUIDERS
GUIDES
GUIDESHIP
GUIDESHIPS
GUIDING
GUIDINGS
GUIDON
GUIDONS
GUIDS
GUILD
GUILDER
GUILDERS
GUILDHALL
GUILDHALLS
GUILDRIES
GUILDRY
GUILDS
GUILDSMAN
GUILDSMEN
GUILE
GUILED
GUILEFUL
GUILELESS
GUILER
GUILERS
GUILES
GUILING
GUILLEMOT
GUILLEMOTS
GUILLOCHE
GUILLOCHED
GUILLOCHES
GUILLOCHING
GUILT
GUILTIER
GUILTIEST
GUILTILY
GUILTLESS
GUILTS
GUILTY
GUIMBARD
GUIMBARDS
GUIMP
GUIMPED
GUIMPING
GUIMPS
GUINEA
GUINEAS
GUIPURE
GUIPURES
GUIRO
GUIROS
GUISARD
GUISARDS
GUISE
GUISED
GUISER
GUISERS
GUISES
GUISING
GUISINGS
GUITAR
GUITARIST
GUITARISTS
GUITARS
GUIZER
GUIZERS
GULA
GULAG
GULAGS
GULAR
GULAS
GULCH
GULCHED
GULCHES
GULCHING
GULDEN
GULDENS
GULE
GULES
GULF
GULFED
GULFIER
GULFIEST
GULFING
GULFS
GULFWEED
GULFWEEDS
GULFY
GULL
GULLABLE
GULLED
GULLER
GULLERIES
GULLERS
GULLERY
GULLET
GULLETS
GULLEY
GULLEYED
GULLEYING
GULLEYS
GULLIBLE
GULLIED
GULLIES
GULLING
GULLISH
GULLS
GULLY
GULLYING
GULOSITIES
GULOSITY
GULP
GULPED
GULPER
GULPERS
GULPH
GULPHS
GULPING
GULPS
GULY
GUM
GUMBO
GUMBOIL
GUMBOILS

GUMBOOT
GUMBOOTS
GUMBOS
GUMDROP
GUMDROPS
GUMMA
GUMMATA
GUMMATOUS
GUMMED
GUMMIER
GUMMIEST
GUMMINESS
GUMMINESSES
GUMMING
GUMMINGS
GUMMITE
GUMMITES
GUMMOSES
GUMMOSIS
GUMMOSITIES
GUMMOSITY
GUMMOUS
GUMMY
GUMNUT
GUMNUTS
GUMP
GUMPED
GUMPHION
GUMPHIONS
GUMPING
GUMPS
GUMPTION
GUMPTIONS
GUMPTIOUS
GUMS
GUMSHIELD
GUMSHIELDS
GUMSHOE
GUMSHOED
GUMSHOEING
GUMSHOES
GUN
GUNBOAT
GUNBOATS
GUNCOTTON
GUNCOTTONS
GUNDIES
GUNDY
GUNFIGHT
GUNFIGHTING
GUNFIGHTS
GUNFIRE
GUNFIRES
GUNFLINT
GUNFLINTS
GUNFOUGHT
GUNGE
GUNGES
GUNGIER
GUNGIEST
GUNGY
GUNHOUSE
GUNHOUSES
GUNITE
GUNITES
GUNK
GUNKS
GUNLAYER
GUNLAYERS
GUNLESS
GUNLOCK
GUNLOCKS
GUNMAKER
GUNMAKERS
GUNMAN
GUNMEN
GUNMETAL
GUNMETALS
GUNNAGE
GUNNAGES
GUNNED
GUNNEL
GUNNELS
GUNNER
GUNNERA
GUNNERAS
GUNNERIES
GUNNERS
GUNNERY
GUNNIES
GUNNING
GUNNINGS
GUNNY
GUNPLAY
GUNPLAYS
GUNPOINT
GUNPOINTS
GUNPORT
GUNPORTS
GUNPOWDER
GUNPOWDERS
GUNROOM
GUNROOMS
GUNRUNNER
GUNRUNNERS
GUNS
GUNSEL
GUNSELS
GUNSHIP
GUNSHIPS
GUNSHOT
GUNSHOTS
GUNSMITH
GUNSMITHS
GUNSTICK
GUNSTICKS
GUNSTOCK
GUNSTOCKS
GUNSTONE
GUNSTONES
GUNTER
GUNTERS
GUNWALE
GUNWALES
GUNYAH
GUNYAHS
GUP
GUPPIES
GUPPY
GUPS
GUR
GURAMI
GURAMIS
GURDWARA
GURDWARAS
GURGE
GURGES
GURGLE
GURGLED
GURGLES
GURGLING
GURGOYLE
GURGOYLES
GURJUN
GURJUNS
GURL
GURLED
GURLET
GURLETS
GURLIER
GURLIEST
GURLING
GURLS
GURLY
GURN
GURNARD
GURNARDS
GURNED
GURNET
GURNETS
GURNEY
GURNEYS
GURNING
GURNS
GURRAH
GURRAHS
GURRIES
GURRY
GURS
GURU
GURUDOM
GURUDOMS
GURUISM
GURUISMS
GURUS
GURUSHIP
GURUSHIPS
GUS
GUSH
GUSHED
GUSHER
GUSHERS
GUSHES
GUSHIER
GUSHIEST
GUSHING
GUSHINGLY
GUSHY
GUSLA
GUSLAR
GUSLARS
GUSLAS
GUSLE
GUSLES
GUSLI
GUSLIS
GUSSET
GUSSETED
GUSSETING
GUSSETS
GUSSIE
GUSSIES
GUST
GUSTABLE
GUSTABLES
GUSTATION
GUSTATIONS
GUSTATIVE
GUSTATORY
GUSTED
GUSTFUL
GUSTIE
GUSTIER
GUSTIEST
GUSTINESS
GUSTINESSES
GUSTING
GUSTO
GUSTOS
GUSTS
GUSTY
GUT
GUTBUCKET
GUTBUCKETS
GUTCHER
GUTCHERS
GUTFUL
GUTFULS
GUTLESS
GUTROT
GUTROTS
GUTS
GUTSED
GUTSER
GUTSERS
GUTSES
GUTSFUL
GUTSFULS
GUTSIER
GUTSIEST
GUTSINESS
GUTSINESSES
GUTSING
GUTSY
GUTTA
GUTTAE
GUTTAS
GUTTATE
GUTTATED
GUTTATES
GUTTATING
GUTTATION
GUTTATIONS
GUTTED
GUTTER
GUTTERED
GUTTERING
GUTTERINGS
GUTTERS
GUTTIER
GUTTIES
GUTTIEST
GUTTING
GUTTLE
GUTTLED
GUTTLES
GUTTLING
GUTTURAL
GUTTURALS
GUTTY
GUTZER
GUTZERS
GUV
GUVS
GUY
GUYED
GUYING
GUYLE
GUYLED
GUYLER
GUYLERS
GUYLES
GUYLING
GUYOT
GUYOTS
GUYS
GUYSE
GUYSES
GUZZLE
GUZZLED
GUZZLER
GUZZLERS
GUZZLES
GUZZLING
GWINIAD
GWINIADS
GWYNIAD
GWYNIADS
GYAL
GYALS
GYBE
GYBED
GYBES
GYBING
GYELD
GYELDS
GYLDEN
GYM
GYMBAL
GYMBALS
GYMKHANA
GYMKHANAS
GYMMAL
GYMMALS
GYMNASIA
GYMNASIAL
GYMNASIC
GYMNASIEN
GYMNASIUM
GYMNASIUMS

GYMNAST
GYMNASTIC
GYMNASTICS
GYMNASTS
GYMNIC
GYMNOSOPH
GYMNOSOPHS
GYMP
GYMPED
GYMPING
GYMPS
GYMS
GYNAE
GYNAECEUM
GYNAECEUMS
GYNAECIA
GYNAECIUM
GYNAECOID
GYNAES
GYNANDRIES
GYNANDRY
GYNECIA
GYNECIUM
GYNIE
GYNIES
GYNNEY
GYNNEYS
GYNNIES
GYNNY
GYNOCRACIES
GYNOCRACY
GYNOECIA
GYNOECIUM
GYNOPHORE
GYNOPHORES
GYNY
GYP
GYPPED
GYPPIE
GYPPIES
GYPPING
GYPPO
GYPPOS
GYPPY
GYPS
GYPSEOUS
GYPSIED
GYPSIES
GYPSUM
GYPSUMS
GYPSY
GYPSYDOM
GYPSYDOMS
GYPSYING
GYPSYISM
GYPSYISMS
GYPSYWORT
GYPSYWORTS
GYRAL
GYRALLY
GYRANT
GYRATE
GYRATED
GYRATES
GYRATING
GYRATION
GYRATIONS
GYRATORY
GYRE
GYRED
GYRES
GYRFALCON
GYRFALCONS
GYRI
GYRING
GYRO
GYROCAR
GYROCARS
GYRODYNE
GYRODYNES
GYROIDAL
GYROLITE
GYROLITES
GYROMANCIES
GYROMANCY
GYRON
GYRONIC
GYRONNY
GYRONS
GYROPLANE
GYROPLANES
GYROS
GYROSCOPE
GYROSCOPES
GYROSE
GYROSTAT
GYROSTATS
GYROUS
GYROVAGUE
GYROVAGUES
GYRUS
GYRUSES
GYTE
GYTES
GYTRASH
GYTRASHES
GYVE
GYVED
GYVES
GYVING

A
AAF
AAFS
AANEPOOT
AANEPOOTS
AAR
AARS
ABANERA
ABANERAS
ABDABS
ABERDINE
ABERDINES
ABERGEON
ABERGEONS
ABILABLE
ABILE
ABIT
ABITABLE
ABITABLY
ABITANS
ABITANT
ABITANTS
ABITAT
ABITATS
ABITED
ABITING
ABITS
ABITUAL
ABITUALS
ABITUATE
ABITUATED
ABITUATES
ABITUATING
ABITUDE
ABITUDES
ABITUE
ABITUES
ABITUS
ABLE
ABOOB
ABOOBS
ACEK
ACEKS
ACHIS
ACHURE
ACHURED
ACHURES
ACHURING
ACIENDA
ACIENDAS
ACK
ACKAMORE
ACKAMORES
ACKBERRIES
HACKBERRY
HACKBOLT
HACKBOLTS
HACKBUT
HACKBUTS
HACKED
HACKEE
HACKEES
HACKER
HACKERIES
HACKERS
HACKERY
HACKETTE
HACKETTES
HACKING
HACKINGS
HACKLE
HACKLED
HACKLER
HACKLERS
HACKLES
HACKLET
HACKLETS
HACKLIER
HACKLIEST
HACKLING
HACKLY
HACKNEY
HACKNEYED
HACKNEYING
HACKNEYS
HACKS
HACQUETON
HACQUETONS
HAD
HADAL
HADDEN
HADDIE
HADDIES
HADDING
HADDOCK
HADDOCKS
HADE
HADED
HADES
HADING
HADJ
HADJES
HADJI
HADJIS
HADROME
HADROMES
HADRON
HADRONIC
HADRONS
HADROSAUR
HADROSAURS
HADS
HADST
HAE
HAECCEITIES
HAECCEITY
HAEING
HAEM
HAEMAL
HAEMATIC
HAEMATIN
HAEMATINS
HAEMATITE
HAEMATITES
HAEMATOID
HAEMATOMA
HAEMATOMAS
HAEMIC
HAEMIN
HAEMINS
HAEMOCOEL
HAEMOCOELS
HAEMOCYTE
HAEMOCYTES
HAEMONIES
HAEMONY
HAEMOSTAT
HAEMOSTATS
HAEMS
HAEREMAI
HAET
HAETS
HAFF
HAFFET
HAFFETS
HAFFIT
HAFFITS
HAFFLIN
HAFFLINS
HAFFS
HAFNIUM
HAFNIUMS
HAFT
HAFTED
HAFTING
HAFTS
HAG
HAGBERRIES
HAGBERRY
HAGBOLT
HAGBOLTS
HAGBUT
HAGBUTS
HAGDEN
HAGDENS
HAGDON
HAGDONS
HAGDOWN
HAGDOWNS
HAGFISH
HAGFISHES
HAGG
HAGGARD
HAGGARDLY
HAGGARDS
HAGGED
HAGGING
HAGGIS
HAGGISES
HAGGISH
HAGGISHLY
HAGGLE
HAGGLED
HAGGLER
HAGGLERS
HAGGLES
HAGGLING
HAGGS
HAGIARCHIES
HAGIARCHY
HAGIOLOGIES
HAGIOLOGY
HAGLET
HAGLETS
HAGS
HAH
HAHNIUM
HAHNIUMS
HAICK
HAICKS
HAIDUK
HAIDUKS
HAIK
HAIKAI
HAIKS
HAIKU
HAIL
HAILED
HAILER
HAILERS
HAILIER
HAILIEST
HAILING
HAILS
HAILSHOT
HAILSHOTS
HAILSTONE
HAILSTONES
HAILY
HAIN
HAINCH
HAINCHED
HAINCHES
HAINCHING
HAINED
HAINING
HAININGS
HAINS
HAIQUE
HAIQUES
HAIR
HAIRBELL
HAIRBELLS
HAIRBRUSH
HAIRBRUSHES
HAIRCLOTH
HAIRCLOTHS
HAIRCUT
HAIRCUTS
HAIRDO
HAIRDOS
HAIRDRIER
HAIRDRIERS
HAIRDRYER
HAIRDRYERS
HAIRED
HAIRGRIP
HAIRGRIPS
HAIRIER
HAIRIEST
HAIRINESS
HAIRINESSES
HAIRING
HAIRLESS
HAIRLIKE
HAIRLINE
HAIRLINES
HAIRNET
HAIRNETS
HAIRPIECE
HAIRPIECES
HAIRPIN
HAIRPINS
HAIRS
HAIRSPRAY
HAIRSPRAYS
HAIRST
HAIRSTED
HAIRSTING
HAIRSTS

The Chambers Dictionary is the authority for many longer words; see *OSW* Introduction, page xii

HAIRSTYLE
HAIRSTYLES
HAIRY
HAITH
HAJ
HAJES
HAJI
HAJIS
HAJJ
HAJJES
HAJJI
HAJJIS
HAKA
HAKAM
HAKAMS
HAKAS
HAKE
HAKES
HAKIM
HAKIMS
HALAL
HALALLED
HALALLING
HALALS
HALATION
HALATIONS
HALAVAH
HALAVAHS
HALBERD
HALBERDS
HALBERT
HALBERTS
HALCYON
HALCYONS
HALE
HALED
HALENESS
HALENESSES
HALER
HALERS
HALES
HALEST
HALF
HALFA
HALFAS
HALFEN
HALFLIN
HALFLING
HALFLINGS
HALFLINS
HALFPACE
HALFPACES
HALFPENCE
HALFPENNIES
HALFPENNY
HALFS
HALFWAY
HALFWIT
HALFWITS
HALIBUT
HALIBUTS
HALICORE
HALICORES
HALIDE
HALIDES
HALIDOM
HALIDOMS
HALIEUTIC
HALIEUTICS
HALIMOT
HALIMOTE
HALIMOTES
HALIMOTS
HALING
HALIOTIS
HALITE
HALITES
HALITOSES
HALITOSIS
HALITOTIC
HALITOUS
HALITUS
HALITUSES
HALL
HALLAL
HALLALI
HALLALIS
HALLALLED
HALLALLING
HALLALOO
HALLALOOS
HALLALS
HALLAN
HALLANS
HALLIAN
HALLIANS
HALLIARD
HALLIARDS
HALLING
HALLINGS
HALLION
HALLIONS
HALLMARK
HALLMARKED
HALLMARKING
HALLMARKS
HALLO
HALLOA
HALLOAED
HALLOAING
HALLOAS
HALLOED
HALLOING
HALLOO
HALLOOED
HALLOOING
HALLOOS
HALLOS
HALLOUMI
HALLOUMIS
HALLOW
HALLOWED
HALLOWING
HALLOWS
HALLS
HALLSTAND
HALLSTANDS
HALLUCES
HALLUX
HALLWAY
HALLWAYS
HALLYON
HALLYONS
HALM
HALMA
HALMAS
HALMS
HALO
HALOBIONT
HALOBIONTS
HALOED
HALOES
HALOGEN
HALOGENS
HALOID
HALOIDS
HALOING
HALON
HALONS
HALOPHILE
HALOPHILES
HALOPHILIES
HALOPHILY
HALOPHOBE
HALOPHOBES
HALOPHYTE
HALOPHYTES
HALOS
HALOTHANE
HALOTHANES
HALSE
HALSED
HALSER
HALSERS
HALSES
HALSING
HALT
HALTED
HALTER
HALTERED
HALTERES
HALTERING
HALTERS
HALTING
HALTINGLY
HALTINGS
HALTS
HALVA
HALVAH
HALVAHS
HALVAS
HALVE
HALVED
HALVER
HALVERS
HALVES
HALVING
HALYARD
HALYARDS
HAM
HAMADRYAD
HAMADRYADES
HAMADRYADS
HAMAL
HAMALS
HAMAMELIS
HAMAMELISES
HAMARTIA
HAMARTIAS
HAMATE
HAMBLE
HAMBLED
HAMBLES
HAMBLING
HAMBURGER
HAMBURGERS
HAME
HAMED
HAMES
HAMEWITH
HAMFATTER
HAMFATTERED
HAMFATTERING
HAMFATTERS
HAMING
HAMLET
HAMLETS
HAMMAL
HAMMALS
HAMMAM
HAMMAMS
HAMMED
HAMMER
HAMMERED
HAMMERER
HAMMERERS
HAMMERING
HAMMERINGS
HAMMERKOP
HAMMERKOPS
HAMMERMAN
HAMMERMEN
HAMMERS
HAMMIER
HAMMIEST
HAMMILY
HAMMING
HAMMOCK
HAMMOCKS
HAMMY
HAMOSE
HAMOUS
HAMPER
HAMPERED
HAMPERING
HAMPERS
HAMPSTER
HAMPSTERS
HAMS
HAMSTER
HAMSTERS
HAMSTRING
HAMSTRINGED
HAMSTRINGING
HAMSTRINGS
HAMSTRUNG
HAMULAR
HAMULATE
HAMULI
HAMULUS
HAMZA
HAMZAH
HAMZAHS
HAMZAS
HAN
HANAP
HANAPER
HANAPERS
HANAPS
HANCE
HANCES
HANCH
HANCHED
HANCHES
HANCHING
HAND
HANDBAG
HANDBAGGED
HANDBAGGING
HANDBAGGINGS
HANDBAGS
HANDBALL
HANDBALLS
HANDBELL
HANDBELLS
HANDBILL
HANDBILLS
HANDBOOK
HANDBOOKS
HANDBRAKE
HANDBRAKES
HANDCAR
HANDCARS
HANDCART
HANDCARTS
HANDCLAP
HANDCLAPS
HANDCLASP
HANDCLASPS
HANDCRAFT
HANDCRAFTS
HANDCUFF
HANDCUFFED
HANDCUFFING
HANDCUFFS
HANDED
HANDER
HANDERS
HANDFAST
HANDFASTED
HANDFASTING
HANDFASTINGS
HANDFASTS
HANDFUL
HANDFULS
HANDGRIP
HANDGRIPS
HANDGUN
HANDGUNS
HANDHOLD

HANDHOLDS
HANDICAP
HANDICAPPED
HANDICAPPING
HANDICAPS
HANDIER
HANDIEST
HANDILY
HANDINESS
HANDINESSES
HANDING
HANDIWORK
HANDIWORKS
HANDJAR
HANDJARS
HANDLE
HANDLEBAR
HANDLEBARS
HANDLED
HANDLER
HANDLERS
HANDLES
HANDLESS
HANDLING
HANDLINGS
HANDLIST
HANDLISTS
HANDMADE
HANDMAID
HANDMAIDS
HANDOUT
HANDOUTS
HANDOVER
HANDOVERS
HANDPLAY
HANDPLAYS
HANDRAIL
HANDRAILS
HANDS
HANDSAW
HANDSAWS
HANDSEL
HANDSELLED
HANDSELLING
HANDSELS
HANDSET
HANDSETS
HANDSHAKE
HANDSHAKES
HANDSOME
HANDSOMER
HANDSOMEST
HANDSPIKE
HANDSPIKES
HANDSTAFF
HANDSTAFFS
HANDSTAND
HANDSTANDS
HANDSTAVES
HANDSTURN
HANDSTURNS
HANDTOWEL
HANDTOWELS
HANDWORK
HANDWORKS
HANDY
HANDYMAN
HANDYMEN
HANDYWORK
HANDYWORKS
HANEPOOT
HANEPOOTS
HANG
HANGABLE
HANGAR
HANGARS
HANGBIRD
HANGBIRDS
HANGDOG
HANGDOGS
HANGED
HANGER
HANGERS
HANGFIRE
HANGFIRES
HANGING
HANGINGS
HANGMAN
HANGMEN
HANGNAIL
HANGNAILS
HANGNEST
HANGNESTS
HANGOUT
HANGOUTS
HANGOVER
HANGOVERS
HANGS
HANJAR
HANJARS
HANK
HANKED
HANKER
HANKERED
HANKERING
HANKERINGS
HANKERS
HANKIE
HANKIES
HANKING
HANKS
HANKY
HANSEL
HANSELLED
HANSELLING
HANSELS
HANSOM
HANSOMS
HANTLE
HANTLES
HANUMAN
HANUMANS
HAOMA
HAOMAS
HAP
HAPHAZARD
HAPHAZARDS
HAPLESS
HAPLESSLY
HAPLOID
HAPLOIDIES
HAPLOIDY
HAPLOLOGIES
HAPLOLOGY
HAPLY
HAPPED
HAPPEN
HAPPENED
HAPPENING
HAPPENINGS
HAPPENS
HAPPIED
HAPPIER
HAPPIES
HAPPIEST
HAPPILY
HAPPINESS
HAPPINESSES
HAPPING
HAPPY
HAPPYING
HAPS
HAPTEN
HAPTENS
HAPTERON
HAPTERONS
HAPTIC
HAPTICS
HAQUETON
HAQUETONS
HARAM
HARAMBEE
HARAMBEES
HARAMS
HARANGUE
HARANGUED
HARANGUER
HARANGUERS
HARANGUES
HARANGUING
HARASS
HARASSED
HARASSER
HARASSERS
HARASSES
HARASSING
HARASSINGS
HARBINGER
HARBINGERED
HARBINGERING
HARBINGERS
HARBOR
HARBORAGE
HARBORAGES
HARBORED
HARBORER
HARBORERS
HARBORING
HARBORS
HARBOUR
HARBOURED
HARBOURER
HARBOURERS
HARBOURING
HARBOURS
HARD
HARDBACK
HARDBACKS
HARDBAG
HARDBAGS
HARDBAKE
HARDBAKES
HARDBALL
HARDBALLS
HARDBEAM
HARDBEAMS
HARDBOARD
HARDBOARDS
HARDEN
HARDENED
HARDENER
HARDENERS
HARDENING
HARDENINGS
HARDENS
HARDER
HARDEST
HARDFACE
HARDFACES
HARDGRASS
HARDGRASSES
HARDHACK
HARDHACKS
HARDHEAD
HARDHEADS
HARDIER
HARDIEST
HARDIHEAD
HARDIHEADS
HARDIHOOD
HARDIHOODS
HARDILY
HARDIMENT
HARDIMENTS
HARDINESS
HARDINESSES
HARDISH
HARDLINE
HARDLINER
HARDLINERS
HARDLY
HARDNESS
HARDNESSES
HARDNOSED
HARDOKE
HARDOKES
HARDPARTS
HARDS
HARDSHELL
HARDSHIP
HARDSHIPS
HARDTACK
HARDTACKS
HARDTOP
HARDTOPS
HARDWARE
HARDWARES
HARDWOOD
HARDWOODS
HARDY
HARE
HAREBELL
HAREBELLS
HARED
HAREEM
HAREEMS
HARELD
HARELDS
HAREM
HAREMS
HARES
HAREWOOD
HAREWOODS
HARICOT
HARICOTS
HARIGALDS
HARIGALS
HARIM
HARIMS
HARING
HARIOLATE
HARIOLATED
HARIOLATES
HARIOLATING
HARISH
HARK
HARKED
HARKEN
HARKENED
HARKENING
HARKENS
HARKING
HARKS
HARL
HARLED
HARLEQUIN
HARLEQUINED
HARLEQUINING
HARLEQUINS
HARLING
HARLINGS
HARLOT
HARLOTRIES
HARLOTRY
HARLOTS
HARLS
HARM
HARMALA
HARMALAS
HARMALIN
HARMALINE
HARMALINES
HARMALINS
HARMAN
HARMANS
HARMATTAN
HARMATTANS
HARMDOING
HARMDOINGS
HARMED

HARMEL
HARMELS
HARMFUL
HARMFULLY
HARMIN
HARMINE
HARMINES
HARMING
HARMINS
HARMLESS
HARMONIC
HARMONICA
HARMONICAS
HARMONICS
HARMONIES
HARMONISE
HARMONISED
HARMONISES
HARMONISING
HARMONIST
HARMONISTS
HARMONIUM
HARMONIUMS
HARMONIZE
HARMONIZED
HARMONIZES
HARMONIZING
HARMONY
HARMOST
HARMOSTIES
HARMOSTS
HARMOSTY
HARMOTOME
HARMOTOMES
HARMS
HARN
HARNESS
HARNESSED
HARNESSES
HARNESSING
HARNS
HARO
HAROS
HAROSET
HAROSETH
HAROSETHS
HAROSETS
HARP
HARPED
HARPER
HARPERS
HARPIES
HARPING
HARPINGS
HARPIST
HARPISTS
HARPOON
HARPOONED
HARPOONER
HARPOONERS
HARPOONING
HARPOONS
HARPS
HARPY
HARQUEBUS
HARQUEBUSES
HARRIDAN
HARRIDANS
HARRIED
HARRIER
HARRIERS
HARRIES
HARROW
HARROWED
HARROWING
HARROWS
HARRUMPH
HARRUMPHED
HARRUMPHING
HARRUMPHS
HARRY
HARRYING
HARSH
HARSHEN
HARSHENED
HARSHENING
HARSHENS
HARSHER
HARSHEST
HARSHLY
HARSHNESS
HARSHNESSES
HARSLET
HARSLETS
HART
HARTAL
HARTALS
HARTBEES
HARTBEESES
HARTELY
HARTEN
HARTENED
HARTENING
HARTENS
HARTLESSE
HARTS
HARTSHORN
HARTSHORNS
HARUSPEX
HARUSPICES
HARUSPICIES
HARUSPICY
HARVEST
HARVESTED
HARVESTER
HARVESTERS
HARVESTING
HARVESTS
HAS
HASH
HASHED
HASHEESH
HASHEESHES
HASHES
HASHIER
HASHIEST
HASHING
HASHISH
HASHISHES
HASHMARK
HASHMARKS
HASHY
HASK
HASKS
HASLET
HASLETS
HASP
HASPED
HASPING
HASPS
HASSAR
HASSARS
HASSLE
HASSLED
HASSLES
HASSLING
HASSOCK
HASSOCKS
HASSOCKY
HAST
HASTA
HASTATE
HASTATED
HASTE
HASTED
HASTEN
HASTENED
HASTENER
HASTENERS
HASTENING
HASTENS
HASTES
HASTIER
HASTIEST
HASTILY
HASTINESS
HASTINESSES
HASTING
HASTINGS
HASTY
HAT
HATABLE
HATBAND
HATBANDS
HATBOX
HATBOXES
HATBRUSH
HATBRUSHES
HATCH
HATCHBACK
HATCHBACKS
HATCHED
HATCHEL
HATCHELLED
HATCHELLING
HATCHELS
HATCHER
HATCHERIES
HATCHERS
HATCHERY
HATCHES
HATCHET
HATCHETS
HATCHETY
HATCHING
HATCHINGS
HATCHLING
HATCHLINGS
HATCHMENT
HATCHMENTS
HATCHWAY
HATCHWAYS
HATE
HATEABLE
HATED
HATEFUL
HATEFULLY
HATELESS
HATER
HATERENT
HATERENTS
HATERS
HATES
HATFUL
HATFULS
HATGUARD
HATGUARDS
HATH
HATING
HATLESS
HATPEG
HATPEGS
HATPIN
HATPINS
HATRACK
HATRACKS
HATRED
HATREDS
HATS
HATSTAND
HATSTANDS
HATTED
HATTER
HATTERED
HATTERING
HATTERS
HATTING
HATTINGS
HATTOCK
HATTOCKS
HAUBERK
HAUBERKS
HAUD
HAUDING
HAUDS
HAUGH
HAUGHS
HAUGHT
HAUGHTIER
HAUGHTIEST
HAUGHTILY
HAUGHTY
HAUL
HAULAGE
HAULAGES
HAULD
HAULDS
HAULED
HAULER
HAULERS
HAULIER
HAULIERS
HAULING
HAULM
HAULMS
HAULS
HAULST
HAULT
HAUNCH
HAUNCHED
HAUNCHES
HAUNCHING
HAUNT
HAUNTED
HAUNTER
HAUNTERS
HAUNTING
HAUNTINGS
HAUNTS
HAURIANT
HAURIENT
HAUSE
HAUSED
HAUSES
HAUSFRAU
HAUSFRAUS
HAUSING
HAUSTELLA
HAUSTORIA
HAUT
HAUTBOIS
HAUTBOY
HAUTBOYS
HAUTE
HAUTEUR
HAUTEURS
HAUYNE
HAUYNES
HAVE
HAVELOCK
HAVELOCKS
HAVEN
HAVENED
HAVENING
HAVENS
HAVEOUR
HAVEOURS
HAVER
HAVERED
HAVEREL
HAVERELS
HAVERING
HAVERINGS
HAVERS
HAVERSACK
HAVERSACKS
HAVERSINE
HAVERSINES
HAVES
HAVILDAR

HAVILDARS
HAVING
HAVINGS
HAVIOUR
HAVIOURS
HAVOC
HAVOCKED
HAVOCKING
HAVOCS
HAW
HAWBUCK
HAWBUCKS
HAWED
HAWFINCH
HAWFINCHES
HAWING
HAWK
HAWKBELL
HAWKBELLS
HAWKBIT
HAWKBITS
HAWKED
HAWKER
HAWKERS
HAWKEY
HAWKEYS
HAWKIE
HAWKIES
HAWKING
HAWKINGS
HAWKISH
HAWKISHLY
HAWKIT
HAWKLIKE
HAWKS
HAWKSBILL
HAWKSBILLS
HAWKWEED
HAWKWEEDS
HAWM
HAWMED
HAWMING
HAWMS
HAWS
HAWSE
HAWSED
HAWSEHOLE
HAWSEHOLES
HAWSEPIPE
HAWSEPIPES
HAWSER
HAWSERS
HAWSES
HAWSING
HAWTHORN
HAWTHORNS
HAY
HAYBAND
HAYBANDS
HAYBOX
HAYBOXES
HAYCOCK
HAYCOCKS
HAYED
HAYFIELD
HAYFIELDS
HAYFORK
HAYFORKS
HAYING
HAYINGS
HAYLE
HAYLES
HAYLOFT
HAYLOFTS
HAYMAKER
HAYMAKERS
HAYMAKING
HAYMAKINGS
HAYMOW
HAYMOWS
HAYRICK
HAYRICKS
HAYRIDE
HAYRIDES
HAYS
HAYSEED
HAYSEEDS
HAYSEL
HAYSELS
HAYSTACK
HAYSTACKS
HAYWARD
HAYWARDS
HAYWIRE
HAYWIRES
HAZAN
HAZANIM
HAZANS
HAZARD
HAZARDED
HAZARDING
HAZARDIZE
HAZARDIZES
HAZARDOUS
HAZARDRIES
HAZARDRY
HAZARDS
HAZE
HAZED
HAZEL
HAZELLY
HAZELNUT
HAZELNUTS
HAZELS
HAZER
HAZERS
HAZES
HAZIER
HAZIEST
HAZILY
HAZINESS
HAZINESSES
HAZING
HAZINGS
HAZY
HAZZAN
HAZZANIM
HAZZANS
HE
HEAD
HEADACHE
HEADACHES
HEADACHIER
HEADACHIEST
HEADACHY
HEADAGE
HEADAGES
HEADBAND
HEADBANDS
HEADBOARD
HEADBOARDS
HEADCASE
HEADCASES
HEADCHAIR
HEADCHAIRS
HEADCLOTH
HEADCLOTHS
HEADDRESS
HEADDRESSES
HEADED
HEADER
HEADERS
HEADFAST
HEADFASTS
HEADFRAME
HEADFRAMES
HEADGEAR
HEADGEARS
HEADHUNT
HEADHUNTED
HEADHUNTING
HEADHUNTINGS
HEADHUNTS
HEADIER
HEADIEST
HEADILY
HEADINESS
HEADINESSES
HEADING
HEADINGS
HEADLAMP
HEADLAMPS
HEADLAND
HEADLANDS
HEADLEASE
HEADLEASES
HEADLESS
HEADLIGHT
HEADLIGHTS
HEADLINE
HEADLINED
HEADLINER
HEADLINERS
HEADLINES
HEADLINING
HEADLOCK
HEADLOCKS
HEADLONG
HEADMAN
HEADMARK
HEADMARKS
HEADMEN
HEADMOST
HEADNOTE
HEADNOTES
HEADPEACE
HEADPEACES
HEADPHONE
HEADPHONES
HEADPIECE
HEADPIECES
HEADRACE
HEADRACES
HEADRAIL
HEADRAILS
HEADREACH
HEADREACHED
HEADREACHES
HEADREACHING
HEADREST
HEADRESTS
HEADRIG
HEADRIGS
HEADRING
HEADRINGS
HEADROOM
HEADROOMS
HEADROPE
HEADROPES
HEADS
HEADSCARF
HEADSCARVES
HEADSET
HEADSETS
HEADSHAKE
HEADSHAKES
HEADSHIP
HEADSHIPS
HEADSHOT
HEADSHOTS
HEADSMAN
HEADSMEN
HEADSTALL
HEADSTALLS
HEADSTICK
HEADSTICKS
HEADSTOCK
HEADSTOCKS
HEADSTONE
HEADSTONES
HEADWAY
HEADWAYS
HEADWORD
HEADWORDS
HEADWORK
HEADWORKS
HEADY
HEAL
HEALABLE
HEALD
HEALDED
HEALDING
HEALDS
HEALED
HEALER
HEALERS
HEALING
HEALINGLY
HEALINGS
HEALS
HEALSOME
HEALTH
HEALTHFUL
HEALTHIER
HEALTHIEST
HEALTHILY
HEALTHS
HEALTHY
HEAME
HEAP
HEAPED
HEAPIER
HEAPIEST
HEAPING
HEAPS
HEAPSTEAD
HEAPSTEADS
HEAPY
HEAR
HEARD
HEARDS
HEARE
HEARER
HEARERS
HEARES
HEARIE
HEARING
HEARINGS
HEARKEN
HEARKENED
HEARKENER
HEARKENERS
HEARKENING
HEARKENS
HEARS
HEARSAY
HEARSAYS
HEARSE
HEARSED
HEARSES
HEARSIER
HEARSIEST
HEARSING
HEARSY
HEART
HEARTACHE
HEARTACHES
HEARTBEAT
HEARTBEATS
HEARTBURN
HEARTBURNS
HEARTED
HEARTEN
HEARTENED
HEARTENING
HEARTENS
HEARTFELT
HEARTH
HEARTHS
HEARTIER

HEARTIES
HEARTIEST
HEARTIKIN
HEARTIKINS
HEARTILY
HEARTING
HEARTLAND
HEARTLANDS
HEARTLESS
HEARTLET
HEARTLETS
HEARTLING
HEARTLINGS
HEARTLY
HEARTPEA
HEARTPEAS
HEARTS
HEARTSEED
HEARTSEEDS
HEARTSOME
HEARTWOOD
HEARTWOODS
HEARTY
HEAST
HEASTE
HEASTES
HEASTS
HEAT
HEATED
HEATER
HEATERS
HEATH
HEATHBIRD
HEATHBIRDS
HEATHCOCK
HEATHCOCKS
HEATHEN
HEATHENRIES
HEATHENRY
HEATHENS
HEATHER
HEATHERIER
HEATHERIEST
HEATHERS
HEATHERY
HEATHIER
HEATHIEST
HEATHS
HEATHY
HEATING
HEATINGS
HEATS
HEATSPOT
HEATSPOTS
HEAUME
HEAUMES
HEAVE
HEAVED
HEAVEN
HEAVENLIER
HEAVENLIEST
HEAVENLY
HEAVENS
HEAVER
HEAVERS
HEAVES
HEAVIER
HEAVIES
HEAVIEST
HEAVILY
HEAVINESS
HEAVINESSES
HEAVING
HEAVINGS
HEAVY
HEBDOMAD
HEBDOMADS
HEBE
HEBEN
HEBENON
HEBENONS
HEBENS
HEBES
HEBETANT
HEBETATE
HEBETATED
HEBETATES
HEBETATING
HEBETUDE
HEBETUDES
HEBONA
HEBONAS
HECATOMB
HECATOMBS
HECH
HECHT
HECHTING
HECHTS
HECK
HECKLE
HECKLED
HECKLER
HECKLERS
HECKLES
HECKLING
HECKLINGS
HECKS
HECOGENIN
HECOGENINS
HECTARE
HECTARES
HECTIC
HECTICAL
HECTICS
HECTOGRAM
HECTOGRAMS
HECTOR
HECTORED
HECTORER
HECTORERS
HECTORING
HECTORINGS
HECTORISM
HECTORISMS
HECTORLY
HECTORS
HEDDLE
HEDDLED
HEDDLES
HEDDLING
HEDERAL
HEDERATED
HEDGE
HEDGEBILL
HEDGEBILLS
HEDGED
HEDGEHOG
HEDGEHOGS
HEDGEPIG
HEDGEPIGS
HEDGER
HEDGEROW
HEDGEROWS
HEDGERS
HEDGES
HEDGIER
HEDGIEST
HEDGING
HEDGINGS
HEDGY
HEDONIC
HEDONICS
HEDONISM
HEDONISMS
HEDONIST
HEDONISTS
HEDYPHANE
HEDYPHANES
HEED
HEEDED
HEEDFUL
HEEDFULLY
HEEDINESS
HEEDINESSES
HEEDING
HEEDLESS
HEEDS
HEEDY
HEEHAW
HEEHAWED
HEEHAWING
HEEHAWS
HEEL
HEELED
HEELER
HEELERS
HEELING
HEELINGS
HEELS
HEEZE
HEEZED
HEEZES
HEEZIE
HEEZIES
HEEZING
HEFT
HEFTE
HEFTED
HEFTIER
HEFTIEST
HEFTILY
HEFTINESS
HEFTINESSES
HEFTING
HEFTS
HEFTY
HEGEMONIC
HEGEMONIES
HEGEMONY
HEGIRA
HEGIRAS
HEID
HEIDS
HEIFER
HEIFERS
HEIGH
HEIGHT
HEIGHTEN
HEIGHTENED
HEIGHTENING
HEIGHTENS
HEIGHTS
HEIL
HEINOUS
HEINOUSLY
HEIR
HEIRDOM
HEIRDOMS
HEIRED
HEIRESS
HEIRESSES
HEIRING
HEIRLESS
HEIRLOOM
HEIRLOOMS
HEIRS
HEIRSHIP
HEIRSHIPS
HEIST
HEISTED
HEISTER
HEISTERS
HEISTING
HEISTS
HEJAB
HEJABS
HEJIRA
HEJIRAS
HEJRA
HEJRAS
HELCOID
HELD
HELE
HELED
HELENIUM
HELENIUMS
HELES
HELIAC
HELIACAL
HELIBORNE
HELIBUS
HELIBUSES
HELIBUSSES
HELICAL
HELICALLY
HELICES
HELICOID
HELICON
HELICONS
HELICTITE
HELICTITES
HELIDECK
HELIDECKS
HELIDROME
HELIDROMES
HELIMAN
HELIMEN
HELING
HELIODOR
HELIODORS
HELIOLOGIES
HELIOLOGY
HELIOSES
HELIOSIS
HELIOSTAT
HELIOSTATS
HELIOTYPE
HELIOTYPES
HELIOTYPIES
HELIOTYPY
HELIOZOAN
HELIOZOANS
HELIOZOIC
HELIPAD
HELIPADS
HELIPILOT
HELIPILOTS
HELIPORT
HELIPORTS
HELISCOOP
HELISCOOPS
HELISTOP
HELISTOPS
HELIUM
HELIUMS
HELIX
HELIXES
HELL
HELLEBORE
HELLEBORES
HELLED
HELLENISE
HELLENISED
HELLENISES
HELLENISING
HELLENIZE
HELLENIZED
HELLENIZES
HELLENIZING
HELLER
HELLERS
HELLFIRE
HELLFIRES
HELLHOUND
HELLHOUNDS
HELLICAT
HELLICATS
HELLIER
HELLIERS
HELLING

HELLION
HELLIONS
HELLISH
HELLISHLY
HELLO
HELLOED
HELLOING
HELLOS
HELLOVA
HELLS
HELLUVA
HELLWARD
HELLWARDS
HELM
HELMED
HELMET
HELMETED
HELMETS
HELMING
HELMINTH
HELMINTHS
HELMLESS
HELMS
HELMSMAN
HELMSMEN
HELOT
HELOTAGE
HELOTAGES
HELOTISM
HELOTISMS
HELOTRIES
HELOTRY
HELOTS
HELP
HELPABLE
HELPDESK
HELPDESKS
HELPED
HELPER
HELPERS
HELPFUL
HELPING
HELPINGS
HELPLESS
HELPLINE
HELPLINES
HELPMATE
HELPMATES
HELPMEET
HELPMEETS
HELPS
HELVE
HELVED
HELVES
HELVETIUM
HELVETIUMS
HELVING
HEM
HEMAL
HEME
HEMES
HEMIALGIA
HEMIALGIAS
HEMICYCLE
HEMICYCLES
HEMIHEDRIES
HEMIHEDRY
HEMINA
HEMINAS
HEMIOLA
HEMIOLAS
HEMIOLIA
HEMIOLIAS
HEMIOLIC
HEMIONE
HEMIONES
HEMIONUS
HEMIONUSES
HEMIOPIA
HEMIOPIAS
HEMIOPIC
HEMIOPSIA
HEMIOPSIAS
HEMISPACE
HEMISPACES
HEMISTICH
HEMISTICHS
HEMITROPE
HEMITROPES
HEMLOCK
HEMLOCKS
HEMMED
HEMMING
HEMP
HEMPEN
HEMPIER
HEMPIES
HEMPIEST
HEMPS
HEMPY
HEMS
HEN
HENBANE
HENBANES
HENCE
HENCHMAN
HENCHMEN
HEND
HENDED
HENDIADYS
HENDIADYSES
HENDING
HENDS
HENEQUEN
HENEQUENS
HENEQUIN
HENEQUINS
HENGE
HENGES
HENIQUIN
HENIQUINS
HENNA
HENNAED
HENNAS
HENNED
HENNER
HENNERIES
HENNERS
HENNERY
HENNIER
HENNIES
HENNIEST
HENNIN
HENNING
HENNINS
HENNY
HENOTIC
HENPECK
HENPECKED
HENPECKING
HENPECKS
HENRIES
HENRY
HENRYS
HENS
HENT
HENTING
HENTS
HEP
HEPAR
HEPARIN
HEPARINS
HEPARS
HEPATIC
HEPATICAL
HEPATICS
HEPATISE
HEPATISED
HEPATISES
HEPATISING
HEPATITE
HEPATITES
HEPATITIS
HEPATITISES
HEPATIZE
HEPATIZED
HEPATIZES
HEPATIZING
HEPPER
HEPPEST
HEPS
HEPSTER
HEPSTERS
HEPT
HEPTAD
HEPTADS
HEPTAGLOT
HEPTAGLOTS
HEPTAGON
HEPTAGONS
HEPTANE
HEPTANES
HEPTAPODIES
HEPTAPODY
HEPTARCH
HEPTARCHIES
HEPTARCHS
HEPTARCHY
HER
HERALD
HERALDED
HERALDIC
HERALDING
HERALDRIES
HERALDRY
HERALDS
HERB
HERBAGE
HERBAGED
HERBAGES
HERBAL
HERBALISM
HERBALISMS
HERBALIST
HERBALISTS
HERBALS
HERBAR
HERBARIA
HERBARIAN
HERBARIANS
HERBARIES
HERBARIUM
HERBARIUMS
HERBARS
HERBARY
HERBELET
HERBELETS
HERBICIDE
HERBICIDES
HERBIER
HERBIEST
HERBIST
HERBISTS
HERBIVORA
HERBIVORE
HERBIVORES
HERBIVORIES
HERBIVORY
HERBLESS
HERBLET
HERBLETS
HERBORISE
HERBORISED
HERBORISES
HERBORISING
HERBORIST
HERBORISTS
HERBORIZE
HERBORIZED
HERBORIZES
HERBORIZING
HERBOSE
HERBOUS
HERBS
HERBY
HERCOGAMIES
HERCOGAMY
HERCULEAN
HERCYNITE
HERCYNITES
HERD
HERDBOY
HERDBOYS
HERDED
HERDEN
HERDENS
HERDESS
HERDESSES
HERDIC
HERDICS
HERDING
HERDMAN
HERDMEN
HERDS
HERDSMAN
HERDSMEN
HERDWICK
HERDWICKS
HERE
HEREABOUT
HEREABOUTS
HEREAFTER
HEREAFTERS
HEREAT
HEREAWAY
HEREBY
HEREDITIES
HEREDITY
HEREFROM
HEREIN
HERENESS
HERENESSES
HEREOF
HEREON
HERESIES
HERESY
HERETIC
HERETICAL
HERETICS
HERETO
HEREUNDER
HEREUNTO
HEREUPON
HEREWITH
HERIED
HERIES
HERIOT
HERIOTS
HERISSE
HERISSON
HERISSONS
HERITABLE
HERITABLY
HERITAGE
HERITAGES
HERITOR
HERITORS
HERITRESS
HERITRESSES
HERITRICES
HERITRIX
HERITRIXES
HERKOGAMIES
HERKOGAMY
HERL
HERLING
HERLINGS
HERLS
HERM
HERMA

HERMAE
HERMANDAD
HERMANDADS
HERMETIC
HERMETICS
HERMIT
HERMITAGE
HERMITAGES
HERMITESS
HERMITESSES
HERMITS
HERMS
HERN
HERNIA
HERNIAE
HERNIAL
HERNIAS
HERNIATED
HERNS
HERNSHAW
HERNSHAWS
HERO
HEROE
HEROES
HEROIC
HEROICAL
HEROICLY
HEROICS
HEROIN
HEROINE
HEROINES
HEROINS
HEROISE
HEROISED
HEROISES
HEROISING
HEROISM
HEROISMS
HEROIZE
HEROIZED
HEROIZES
HEROIZING
HERON
HERONRIES
HERONRY
HERONS
HERONSEW
HERONSEWS
HERONSHAW
HERONSHAWS
HEROON
HEROONS
HEROSHIP
HEROSHIPS
HERPES
HERPESES
HERPETIC
HERPETOID
HERRIED
HERRIES
HERRIMENT
HERRIMENTS
HERRING
HERRINGER
HERRINGERS
HERRINGS
HERRY
HERRYING
HERRYMENT
HERRYMENTS
HERS
HERSALL
HERSALLS
HERSE
HERSED
HERSELF
HERSES
HERSHIP
HERSHIPS
HERSTORIES
HERSTORY
HERTZ
HERTZES
HERY
HERYE
HERYED
HERYES
HERYING
HES
HESITANCE
HESITANCES
HESITANCIES
HESITANCY
HESITANT
HESITATE
HESITATED
HESITATES
HESITATING
HESITATOR
HESITATORS
HESP
HESPED
HESPERID
HESPERIDS
HESPING
HESPS
HESSIAN
HESSIANS
HESSONITE
HESSONITES
HEST
HESTERNAL
HESTS
HET
HETAERA
HETAERAE
HETAERISM
HETAERISMS
HETAIRA
HETAIRAI
HETAIRAS
HETAIRIA
HETAIRIAS
HETAIRISM
HETAIRISMS
HETAIRIST
HETAIRISTS
HETE
HETERO
HETERODOX
HETERONYM
HETERONYMS
HETEROPOD
HETEROPODS
HETEROS
HETEROSES
HETEROSIS
HETEROTIC
HETES
HETHER
HETING
HETMAN
HETMANATE
HETMANATES
HETMANS
HETS
HEUCH
HEUCHS
HEUGH
HEUGHS
HEUREKA
HEUREKAS
HEURETIC
HEURETICS
HEURISM
HEURISMS
HEURISTIC
HEURISTICS
HEVEA
HEVEAS
HEW
HEWED
HEWER
HEWERS
HEWGH
HEWING
HEWINGS
HEWN
HEWS
HEX
HEXACHORD
HEXACHORDS
HEXACT
HEXACTS
HEXAD
HEXADIC
HEXADS
HEXAFOIL
HEXAFOILS
HEXAGLOT
HEXAGON
HEXAGONAL
HEXAGONS
HEXAGRAM
HEXAGRAMS
HEXAHEDRA
HEXAMETER
HEXAMETERS
HEXANE
HEXANES
HEXAPLA
HEXAPLAR
HEXAPLAS
HEXAPLOID
HEXAPLOIDS
HEXAPOD
HEXAPODIES
HEXAPODS
HEXAPODY
HEXARCH
HEXASTICH
HEXASTICHS
HEXASTYLE
HEXASTYLES
HEXED
HEXENE
HEXENES
HEXES
HEXING
HEXINGS
HEXOSE
HEXOSES
HEXYLENE
HEXYLENES
HEY
HEYDAY
HEYDAYS
HEYDUCK
HEYDUCKS
HEYED
HEYING
HEYS
HI
HIANT
HIATUS
HIATUSES
HIBACHI
HIBACHIS
HIBAKUSHA
HIBERNAL
HIBERNATE
HIBERNATED
HIBERNATES
HIBERNATING
HIBERNISE
HIBERNISED
HIBERNISES
HIBERNISING
HIBERNIZE
HIBERNIZED
HIBERNIZES
HIBERNIZING
HIBISCUS
HIBISCUSES
HIC
HICATEE
HICATEES
HICCATEE
HICCATEES
HICCOUGH
HICCOUGHED
HICCOUGHING
HICCOUGHS
HICCUP
HICCUPED
HICCUPING
HICCUPS
HICCUPY
HICK
HICKEY
HICKEYS
HICKORIES
HICKORY
HICKS
HICKWALL
HICKWALLS
HID
HIDAGE
HIDAGES
HIDALGA
HIDALGAS
HIDALGO
HIDALGOS
HIDDEN
HIDDENITE
HIDDENITES
HIDDENLY
HIDDER
HIDDERS
HIDE
HIDED
HIDEOSITIES
HIDEOSITY
HIDEOUS
HIDEOUSLY
HIDEOUT
HIDEOUTS
HIDER
HIDERS
HIDES
HIDING
HIDINGS
HIDLING
HIDLINGS
HIDLINS
HIDROSES
HIDROSIS
HIDROTIC
HIDROTICS
HIE
HIED
HIEING
HIELAMAN
HIELAMANS
HIEMAL
HIEMS
HIERACIUM
HIERACIUMS
HIERARCH
HIERARCHIES
HIERARCHS
HIERARCHY
HIERATIC
HIERATICA
HIERATICAS
HIEROCRAT
HIEROCRATS
HIERODULE
HIERODULES
HIEROGRAM

IEROGRAMS
IEROLOGIES
IEROLOGY
IERURGIES
IERURGY
IES
IGGLE
IGGLED
IGGLER
IGGLERS
IGGLES
IGGLING
IGGLINGS
IGH
IGHBALL
IGHBALLED
IGHBALLING
IGHBALLS
IGHBOY
IGHBOYS
IGHBROW
IGHBROWS
IGHCHAIR
IGHCHAIRS
IGHED
IGHER
IGHERED
IGHERING
IGHERS
IGHEST
IGHING
IGHISH
IGHJACK
IGHJACKED
IGHJACKING
IGHJACKS
IGHLAND
IGHLANDS
IGHLIGHT
IGHLIGHTED
IGHLIGHTING
IGHLIGHTS
IGHLY
IGHMAN
IGHMEN
IGHMOST
IGHNESS
IGHNESSES
IGHROAD
IGHROADS
IGHS
IGHT
IGHTAIL
IGHTAILED
IGHTAILING
IGHTAILS
IGHTH
IGHTHS
IGHTING
IGHTS
IGHWAY
IGHWAYS
IJAB
IJABS

HIJACK
HIJACKED
HIJACKER
HIJACKERS
HIJACKING
HIJACKS
HIJINKS
HIJRA
HIJRAH
HIJRAHS
HIJRAS
HIKE
HIKED
HIKER
HIKERS
HIKES
HIKING
HILA
HILAR
HILARIOUS
HILARITIES
HILARITY
HILCH
HILCHED
HILCHES
HILCHING
HILD
HILDING
HILDINGS
HILI
HILL
HILLED
HILLFOLK
HILLIER
HILLIEST
HILLINESS
HILLINESSES
HILLING
HILLMEN
HILLO
HILLOCK
HILLOCKS
HILLOCKY
HILLOED
HILLOING
HILLOS
HILLS
HILLSIDE
HILLSIDES
HILLTOP
HILLTOPS
HILLY
HILT
HILTED
HILTING
HILTS
HILUM
HILUS
HIM
HIMATIA
HIMATION
HIMATIONS
HIMBO
HIMBOS

HIMSELF
HIN
HIND
HINDBERRIES
HINDBERRY
HINDBRAIN
HINDBRAINS
HINDER
HINDERED
HINDERER
HINDERERS
HINDERING
HINDERS
HINDFEET
HINDFOOT
HINDHEAD
HINDHEADS
HINDLEG
HINDLEGS
HINDMOST
HINDRANCE
HINDRANCES
HINDS
HINDSIGHT
HINDSIGHTS
HINDWARD
HINDWING
HINDWINGS
HING
HINGE
HINGED
HINGES
HINGING
HINGS
HINNIED
HINNIES
HINNY
HINNYING
HINS
HINT
HINTED
HINTING
HINTINGLY
HINTS
HIP
HIPNESS
HIPNESSES
HIPPARCH
HIPPARCHS
HIPPED
HIPPEN
HIPPENS
HIPPER
HIPPEST
HIPPIATRIES
HIPPIATRY
HIPPIC
HIPPIE
HIPPIEDOM
HIPPIEDOMS
HIPPIER
HIPPIES
HIPPIEST
HIPPIN

HIPPING
HIPPINGS
HIPPINS
HIPPISH
HIPPO
HIPPOCRAS
HIPPOCRASES
HIPPODAME
HIPPODAMES
HIPPOLOGIES
HIPPOLOGY
HIPPOS
HIPPURIC
HIPPURITE
HIPPURITES
HIPPUS
HIPPUSES
HIPPY
HIPPYDOM
HIPPYDOMS
HIPS
HIPSTER
HIPSTERS
HIPT
HIRABLE
HIRAGANA
HIRAGANAS
HIRAGE
HIRAGES
HIRCINE
HIRCOSITIES
HIRCOSITY
HIRE
HIREABLE
HIREAGE
HIREAGES
HIRED
HIRELING
HIRELINGS
HIRER
HIRERS
HIRES
HIRING
HIRINGS
HIRLING
HIRLINGS
HIRPLE
HIRPLED
HIRPLES
HIRPLING
HIRRIENT
HIRRIENTS
HIRSEL
HIRSELLED
HIRSELLING
HIRSELS
HIRSLE
HIRSLED
HIRSLES
HIRSLING
HIRSTIE
HIRSUTE
HIRSUTISM
HIRSUTISMS

HIRUDIN
HIRUDINS
HIRUNDINE
HIS
HISH
HISHED
HISHES
HISHING
HISN
HISPID
HISPIDITIES
HISPIDITY
HISS
HISSED
HISSES
HISSING
HISSINGLY
HISSINGS
HIST
HISTAMINE
HISTAMINES
HISTED
HISTIDINE
HISTIDINES
HISTIE
HISTING
HISTIOID
HISTOGEN
HISTOGENIES
HISTOGENS
HISTOGENY
HISTOGRAM
HISTOGRAMS
HISTOID
HISTOLOGIES
HISTOLOGY
HISTONE
HISTONES
HISTORIAN
HISTORIANS
HISTORIC
HISTORIED
HISTORIES
HISTORIFIED
HISTORIFIES
HISTORIFY
HISTORIFYING
HISTORISM
HISTORISMS
HISTORY
HISTORYING
HISTRIO
HISTRION
HISTRIONS
HISTRIOS
HISTS
HIT
HITCH
HITCHED
HITCHER
HITCHERS
HITCHES
HITCHIER
HITCHIEST

HITCHILY
HITCHING
HITCHY
HITHE
HITHER
HITHERED
HITHERING
HITHERS
HITHERTO
HITHES
HITS
HITTER
HITTERS
HITTING
HIVE
HIVED
HIVELESS
HIVELIKE
HIVER
HIVERS
HIVES
HIVEWARD
HIVEWARDS
HIVING
HIYA
HIZEN
HIZENS
HIZZ
HIZZED
HIZZES
HIZZING
HO
HOA
HOACTZIN
HOACTZINS
HOAED
HOAING
HOAR
HOARD
HOARDED
HOARDER
HOARDERS
HOARDING
HOARDINGS
HOARDS
HOARED
HOARHEAD
HOARHEADS
HOARHOUND
HOARHOUNDS
HOARIER
HOARIEST
HOARILY
HOARINESS
HOARINESSES
HOARING
HOARS
HOARSE
HOARSELY
HOARSEN
HOARSENED
HOARSENING
HOARSENS
HOARSER
HOARSEST
HOARY
HOAS
HOAST
HOASTED
HOASTING
HOASTMAN
HOASTMEN
HOASTS
HOATZIN
HOATZINS
HOAX
HOAXED
HOAXER
HOAXERS
HOAXES
HOAXING
HOB
HOBBIES
HOBBISH
HOBBIT
HOBBITRIES
HOBBITRY
HOBBITS
HOBBLE
HOBBLED
HOBBLER
HOBBLERS
HOBBLES
HOBBLING
HOBBLINGS
HOBBY
HOBBYISM
HOBBYISMS
HOBBYIST
HOBBYISTS
HOBBYLESS
HOBDAY
HOBDAYED
HOBDAYING
HOBDAYS
HOBGOBLIN
HOBGOBLINS
HOBJOB
HOBJOBBED
HOBJOBBER
HOBJOBBERS
HOBJOBBING
HOBJOBBINGS
HOBJOBS
HOBNAIL
HOBNAILED
HOBNAILING
HOBNAILS
HOBNOB
HOBNOBBED
HOBNOBBING
HOBNOBBY
HOBNOBS
HOBO
HOBODOM
HOBODOMS
HOBOED
HOBOES
HOBOING
HOBOISM
HOBOISMS
HOBOS
HOBS
HOC
HOCK
HOCKED
HOCKER
HOCKERS
HOCKEY
HOCKEYS
HOCKING
HOCKS
HOCUS
HOCUSED
HOCUSES
HOCUSING
HOCUSSED
HOCUSSES
HOCUSSING
HOD
HODDED
HODDEN
HODDENS
HODDING
HODDLE
HODDLED
HODDLES
HODDLING
HODIERNAL
HODJA
HODJAS
HODMAN
HODMANDOD
HODMANDODS
HODMEN
HODOGRAPH
HODOGRAPHS
HODOMETER
HODOMETERS
HODOMETRIES
HODOMETRY
HODOSCOPE
HODOSCOPES
HODS
HOE
HOED
HOEDOWN
HOEDOWNS
HOEING
HOER
HOERS
HOES
HOG
HOGAN
HOGANS
HOGBACK
HOGBACKS
HOGEN
HOGENS
HOGG
HOGGED
HOGGER
HOGGEREL
HOGGERELS
HOGGERIES
HOGGERS
HOGGERY
HOGGET
HOGGETS
HOGGIN
HOGGING
HOGGINGS
HOGGINS
HOGGISH
HOGGISHLY
HOGGS
HOGH
HOGHOOD
HOGHOODS
HOGHS
HOGS
HOGSHEAD
HOGSHEADS
HOGTIE
HOGTIED
HOGTIES
HOGTYING
HOGWARD
HOGWARDS
HOGWASH
HOGWASHES
HOGWEED
HOGWEEDS
HOH
HOHED
HOHING
HOHS
HOI
HOICK
HOICKED
HOICKING
HOICKS
HOICKSED
HOICKSES
HOICKSING
HOIDEN
HOIDENS
HOIK
HOIKED
HOIKING
HOIKS
HOING
HOISE
HOISED
HOISES
HOISING
HOIST
HOISTED
HOISTER
HOISTERS
HOISTING
HOISTINGS
HOISTMAN
HOISTMEN
HOISTS
HOISTWAY
HOISTWAYS
HOKE
HOKED
HOKES
HOKEY
HOKI
HOKIER
HOKIEST
HOKING
HOKIS
HOKKU
HOKUM
HOKUMS
HOLD
HOLDBACK
HOLDBACKS
HOLDEN
HOLDER
HOLDERBAT
HOLDERBATS
HOLDERS
HOLDFAST
HOLDFASTS
HOLDING
HOLDINGS
HOLDOUT
HOLDOUTS
HOLDOVER
HOLDOVERS
HOLDS
HOLE
HOLED
HOLES
HOLESOM
HOLESOME
HOLEY
HOLIBUT
HOLIBUTS
HOLIDAY
HOLIDAYED
HOLIDAYING
HOLIDAYS
HOLIER
HOLIES
HOLIEST
HOLILY
HOLINESS
HOLINESSES
HOLING
HOLINGS
HOLISM
HOLISMS
HOLIST
HOLISTIC
HOLISTS
HOLLA
HOLLAND
HOLLANDS
HOLLAS
HOLLER
HOLLERED
HOLLERING
HOLLERS
HOLLIDAM

HOLLIDAMS
HOLLIES
HOLLO
HOLLOA
HOLLOAED
HOLLOAING
HOLLOAS
HOLLOED
HOLLOES
HOLLOING
HOLLOS
HOLLOW
HOLLOWARE
HOLLOWARES
HOLLOWED
HOLLOWER
HOLLOWEST
HOLLOWING
HOLLOWLY
HOLLOWS
HOLLY
HOLLYHOCK
HOLLYHOCKS
HOLM
HOLMIA
HOLMIAS
HOLMIC
HOLMIUM
HOLMIUMS
HOLMS
HOLOCAUST
HOLOCAUSTS
HOLOCRINE
HOLOGRAM
HOLOGRAMS
HOLOGRAPH
HOLOGRAPHED
HOLOGRAPHING
HOLOGRAPHS
HOLOHEDRA
HOLOPHOTE
HOLOPHOTES
HOLOPHYTE
HOLOPHYTES
HOLOPTIC
HOLOTYPE
HOLOTYPES
HOLOTYPIC
HOLOZOIC
HOLP
HOLPEN
HOLS
HOLSTER
HOLSTERED
HOLSTERS
HOLT
HOLTS
HOLY
HOLYDAM
HOLYDAME
HOLYDAMES
HOLYDAMS
HOLYSTONE
HOLYSTONED
HOLYSTONES
HOLYSTONING
HOMAGE
HOMAGED
HOMAGER
HOMAGERS
HOMAGES
HOMAGING
HOMALOID
HOMALOIDS
HOMBRE
HOMBRES
HOME
HOMEBOUND
HOMEBOY
HOMEBOYS
HOMEBUYER
HOMEBUYERS
HOMECRAFT
HOMECRAFTS
HOMED
HOMEFELT
HOMELAND
HOMELANDS
HOMELESS
HOMELIER
HOMELIEST
HOMELIKE
HOMELILY
HOMELY
HOMELYN
HOMELYNS
HOMEMAKER
HOMEMAKERS
HOMEOBOX
HOMEOMERIES
HOMEOMERY
HOMEOPATH
HOMEOPATHS
HOMEOSES
HOMEOSIS
HOMEOTIC
HOMEOWNER
HOMEOWNERS
HOMER
HOMERS
HOMES
HOMESICK
HOMESPUN
HOMESPUNS
HOMESTALL
HOMESTALLS
HOMESTEAD
HOMESTEADS
HOMEWARD
HOMEWARDS
HOMEWORK
HOMEWORKS
HOMEY
HOMICIDAL
HOMICIDE
HOMICIDES
HOMIER
HOMIEST
HOMILETIC
HOMILETICS
HOMILIES
HOMILIST
HOMILISTS
HOMILY
HOMING
HOMINGS
HOMINID
HOMINIDS
HOMINIES
HOMINOID
HOMINOIDS
HOMINY
HOMME
HOMMES
HOMMOCK
HOMMOCKS
HOMO
HOMODONT
HOMODYNE
HOMOEOBOX
HOMOEOSES
HOMOEOSIS
HOMOEOTIC
HOMOGAMIC
HOMOGAMIES
HOMOGAMY
HOMOGENIES
HOMOGENY
HOMOGRAFT
HOMOGRAFTS
HOMOGRAPH
HOMOGRAPHS
HOMOLOG
HOMOLOGIES
HOMOLOGS
HOMOLOGUE
HOMOLOGUES
HOMOLOGY
HOMOMORPH
HOMOMORPHS
HOMONYM
HOMONYMIC
HOMONYMIES
HOMONYMS
HOMONYMY
HOMOPHILE
HOMOPHILES
HOMOPHOBE
HOMOPHOBES
HOMOPHONE
HOMOPHONES
HOMOPHONIES
HOMOPHONY
HOMOPHYLIES
HOMOPHYLY
HOMOPLASIES
HOMOPLASY
HOMOPOLAR
HOMOS
HOMOTAXES
HOMOTAXIC
HOMOTAXIS
HOMOTONIC
HOMOTONIES
HOMOTONY
HOMOTYPAL
HOMOTYPE
HOMOTYPES
HOMOTYPIC
HOMOTYPIES
HOMOTYPY
HOMOUSIAN
HOMOUSIANS
HOMUNCLE
HOMUNCLES
HOMUNCULE
HOMUNCULES
HOMUNCULI
HOMY
HON
HONCHO
HONCHOS
HOND
HONDS
HONE
HONED
HONER
HONERS
HONES
HONEST
HONESTER
HONESTEST
HONESTIES
HONESTLY
HONESTY
HONEWORT
HONEWORTS
HONEY
HONEYBUN
HONEYBUNS
HONEYCOMB
HONEYCOMBED
HONEYCOMBING
HONEYCOMBINGS
HONEYCOMBS
HONEYED
HONEYING
HONEYLESS
HONEYMOON
HONEYMOONED
HONEYMOONING
HONEYMOONS
HONEYPOT
HONEYPOTS
HONEYS
HONG
HONGI
HONGING
HONGIS
HONGS
HONIED
HONING
HONK
HONKED
HONKER
HONKERS
HONKIE
HONKIES
HONKING
HONKS
HONKY
HONOR
HONORAND
HONORANDS
HONORARIA
HONORARIES
HONORARY
HONORED
HONORIFIC
HONORIFICS
HONORING
HONORS
HONOUR
HONOURED
HONOURER
HONOURERS
HONOURING
HONOURS
HONS
HOO
HOOCH
HOOCHES
HOOD
HOODED
HOODIE
HOODIES
HOODING
HOODLESS
HOODLUM
HOODLUMS
HOODMAN
HOODMEN
HOODOO
HOODOOED
HOODOOING
HOODOOS
HOODS
HOODWINK
HOODWINKED
HOODWINKING
HOODWINKS
HOOEY
HOOEYS
HOOF
HOOFBEAT
HOOFBEATS
HOOFED
HOOFER
HOOFERS
HOOFING
HOOFLESS
HOOFPRINT
HOOFPRINTS
HOOFROT
HOOFROTS
HOOFS
HOOK
HOOKA
HOOKAH
HOOKAHS

HOOKAS
HOOKED
HOOKER
HOOKERS
HOOKEY
HOOKEYS
HOOKIER
HOOKIES
HOOKIEST
HOOKING
HOOKS
HOOKY
HOOLACHAN
HOOLACHANS
HOOLEY
HOOLEYS
HOOLICAN
HOOLICANS
HOOLIER
HOOLIEST
HOOLIGAN
HOOLIGANS
HOOLOCK
HOOLOCKS
HOOLY
HOON
HOONS
HOOP
HOOPED
HOOPER
HOOPERS
HOOPING
HOOPOE
HOOPOES
HOOPS
HOORAH
HOORAHED
HOORAHING
HOORAHS
HOORAY
HOORAYED
HOORAYING
HOORAYS
HOORD
HOORDS
HOOROO
HOOSEGOW
HOOSEGOWS
HOOSGOW
HOOSGOWS
HOOSH
HOOSHED
HOOSHES
HOOSHING
HOOT
HOOTCH
HOOTCHES
HOOTED
HOOTER
HOOTERS
HOOTING
HOOTNANNIES
HOOTNANNY
HOOTS
HOOVE
HOOVED
HOOVEN
HOOVER
HOOVERED
HOOVERING
HOOVERS
HOOVES
HOOVING
HOP
HOPBIND
HOPBINDS
HOPBINE
HOPBINES
HOPDOG
HOPDOGS
HOPE
HOPED
HOPEFUL
HOPEFULLY
HOPEFULS
HOPELESS
HOPER
HOPERS
HOPES
HOPING
HOPINGLY
HOPLITE
HOPLITES
HOPLOLOGIES
HOPLOLOGY
HOPPED
HOPPER
HOPPERS
HOPPIER
HOPPIEST
HOPPING
HOPPINGS
HOPPLE
HOPPLED
HOPPLES
HOPPLING
HOPPY
HOPS
HOPSACK
HOPSACKS
HOPSCOTCH
HOPSCOTCHES
HORAL
HORARY
HORDE
HORDED
HORDEIN
HORDEINS
HORDEOLA
HORDEOLUM
HORDES
HORDING
HORDOCK
HORDOCKS
HORE
HOREHOUND
HOREHOUNDS
HORIZON
HORIZONS
HORKEY
HORKEYS
HORME
HORMES
HORMONAL
HORMONE
HORMONES
HORMONIC
HORN
HORNBEAK
HORNBEAKS
HORNBEAM
HORNBEAMS
HORNBILL
HORNBILLS
HORNBOOK
HORNBOOKS
HORNBUG
HORNBUGS
HORNED
HORNER
HORNERS
HORNET
HORNETS
HORNFELS
HORNFUL
HORNFULS
HORNGELD
HORNGELDS
HORNIER
HORNIEST
HORNINESS
HORNINESSES
HORNING
HORNINGS
HORNISH
HORNIST
HORNISTS
HORNITO
HORNITOS
HORNLESS
HORNLET
HORNLETS
HORNPIPE
HORNPIPES
HORNS
HORNSTONE
HORNSTONES
HORNTAIL
HORNTAILS
HORNWORK
HORNWORKS
HORNWORM
HORNWORMS
HORNWORT
HORNWORTS
HORNWRACK
HORNWRACKS
HORNY
HORNYHEAD
HORNYHEADS
HOROLOGE
HOROLOGER
HOROLOGERS
HOROLOGES
HOROLOGIC
HOROLOGIES
HOROLOGY
HOROMETRIES
HOROMETRY
HOROSCOPE
HOROSCOPES
HOROSCOPIES
HOROSCOPY
HORRENT
HORRIBLE
HORRIBLY
HORRID
HORRIDER
HORRIDEST
HORRIDLY
HORRIFIC
HORRIFIED
HORRIFIES
HORRIFY
HORRIFYING
HORROR
HORRORS
HORS
HORSE
HORSEBACK
HORSEBACKS
HORSECAR
HORSECARS
HORSED
HORSEFLIES
HORSEFLY
HORSEHAIR
HORSEHAIRS
HORSEHIDE
HORSEHIDES
HORSELESS
HORSEMAN
HORSEMEAT
HORSEMEATS
HORSEMEN
HORSEMINT
HORSEMINTS
HORSEPLAY
HORSEPLAYS
HORSEPOND
HORSEPONDS
HORSES
HORSESHOE
HORSESHOES
HORSETAIL
HORSETAILS
HORSEWAY
HORSEWAYS
HORSEWHIP
HORSEWHIPPED
HORSEWHIPPING
HORSEWHIPS
HORSEY
HORSIER
HORSIEST
HORSINESS
HORSINESSES
HORSING
HORSINGS
HORSON
HORSONS
HORST
HORSTS
HORSY
HORTATION
HORTATIONS
HORTATIVE
HORTATORY
HOS
HOSANNA
HOSANNAS
HOSE
HOSED
HOSEMAN
HOSEMEN
HOSEN
HOSEPIPE
HOSEPIPES
HOSES
HOSIER
HOSIERIES
HOSIERS
HOSIERY
HOSING
HOSPICE
HOSPICES
HOSPITAGE
HOSPITAGES
HOSPITAL
HOSPITALE
HOSPITALES
HOSPITALS
HOSPITIA
HOSPITIUM
HOSPODAR
HOSPODARS
HOSS
HOSSES
HOST
HOSTA
HOSTAGE
HOSTAGES
HOSTAS
HOSTED
HOSTEL
HOSTELER
HOSTELERS
HOSTELLER
HOSTELLERS
HOSTELRIES
HOSTELRY
HOSTELS
HOSTESS
HOSTESSED
HOSTESSES
HOSTESSING
HOSTILE
HOSTILELY
HOSTILITIES
HOSTILITY

HOSTING
HOSTINGS
HOSTLER
HOSTLERS
HOSTLESSE
HOSTRIES
HOSTRY
HOSTS
HOT
HOTBED
HOTBEDS
HOTCH
HOTCHED
HOTCHES
HOTCHING
HOTCHPOT
HOTCHPOTS
HOTE
HOTEL
HOTELIER
HOTELIERS
HOTELS
HOTEN
HOTFOOT
HOTHEAD
HOTHEADED
HOTHEADS
HOTHOUSE
HOTHOUSES
HOTLINE
HOTLINES
HOTLY
HOTNESS
HOTNESSES
HOTPOT
HOTPOTS
HOTS
HOTSHOT
HOTSHOTS
HOTTED
HOTTENTOT
HOTTENTOTS
HOTTER
HOTTERED
HOTTERING
HOTTERS
HOTTEST
HOTTIE
HOTTIES
HOTTING
HOTTINGS
HOTTISH
HOUDAH
HOUDAHS
HOUDAN
HOUDANS
HOUF
HOUFED
HOUFF
HOUFFED
HOUFFING
HOUFFS
HOUFING
HOUFS
HOUGH
HOUGHED
HOUGHING
HOUGHS
HOUMMOS
HOUMMOSES
HOUMUS
HOUMUSES
HOUND
HOUNDED
HOUNDING
HOUNDS
HOUR
HOURI
HOURIS
HOURLONG
HOURLY
HOURPLATE
HOURPLATES
HOURS
HOUSE
HOUSEBOAT
HOUSEBOATS
HOUSEBOY
HOUSEBOYS
HOUSECOAT
HOUSECOATS
HOUSED
HOUSEFLIES
HOUSEFLY
HOUSEFUL
HOUSEFULS
HOUSEHOLD
HOUSEHOLDS
HOUSEL
HOUSELESS
HOUSELLED
HOUSELLING
HOUSELLINGS
HOUSELS
HOUSEMAID
HOUSEMAIDS
HOUSEMAN
HOUSEMEN
HOUSEROOM
HOUSEROOMS
HOUSES
HOUSETOP
HOUSETOPS
HOUSEWIFE
HOUSEWIVES
HOUSEWORK
HOUSEWORKS
HOUSEY
HOUSIER
HOUSIEST
HOUSING
HOUSINGS
HOUSLING
HOUT
HOUTED
HOUTING
HOUTINGS
HOUTS
HOVE
HOVED
HOVEL
HOVELED
HOVELING
HOVELLED
HOVELLER
HOVELLERS
HOVELLING
HOVELS
HOVEN
HOVER
HOVERED
HOVERING
HOVERPORT
HOVERPORTS
HOVERS
HOVES
HOVING
HOW
HOWBE
HOWBEIT
HOWDAH
HOWDAHS
HOWDIE
HOWDIES
HOWDY
HOWE
HOWES
HOWEVER
HOWF
HOWFED
HOWFF
HOWFFED
HOWFFING
HOWFFS
HOWFING
HOWFS
HOWITZER
HOWITZERS
HOWK
HOWKED
HOWKER
HOWKERS
HOWKING
HOWKS
HOWL
HOWLED
HOWLER
HOWLERS
HOWLET
HOWLETS
HOWLING
HOWLINGS
HOWLS
HOWRE
HOWRES
HOWS
HOWSO
HOWSOEVER
HOWTOWDIE
HOWTOWDIES
HOWZAT
HOX
HOXED
HOXES
HOXING
HOY
HOYA
HOYAS
HOYDEN
HOYDENISH
HOYDENISM
HOYDENISMS
HOYDENS
HOYED
HOYING
HOYS
HUANACO
HUANACOS
HUAQUERO
HUAQUEROS
HUB
HUBBIES
HUBBUB
HUBBUBOO
HUBBUBOOS
HUBBUBS
HUBBY
HUBRIS
HUBRISES
HUBRISTIC
HUBS
HUCK
HUCKABACK
HUCKABACKS
HUCKLE
HUCKLES
HUCKS
HUCKSTER
HUCKSTERED
HUCKSTERIES
HUCKSTERING
HUCKSTERS
HUCKSTERY
HUDDEN
HUDDLE
HUDDLED
HUDDLES
HUDDLING
HUDDUP
HUE
HUED
HUELESS
HUER
HUERS
HUES
HUFF
HUFFED
HUFFIER
HUFFIEST
HUFFILY
HUFFINESS
HUFFINESSES
HUFFING
HUFFISH
HUFFISHLY
HUFFKIN
HUFFKINS
HUFFS
HUFFY
HUG
HUGE
HUGELY
HUGENESS
HUGENESSES
HUGEOUS
HUGEOUSLY
HUGER
HUGEST
HUGGABLE
HUGGED
HUGGING
HUGS
HUGY
HUH
HUI
HUIA
HUIAS
HUIS
HUISSIER
HUISSIERS
HUITAIN
HUITAINS
HULA
HULAS
HULE
HULES
HULK
HULKIER
HULKIEST
HULKING
HULKS
HULKY
HULL
HULLED
HULLIER
HULLIEST
HULLING
HULLO
HULLOED
HULLOING
HULLOS
HULLS
HULLY
HUM
HUMA
HUMAN
HUMANE
HUMANELY
HUMANER
HUMANEST
HUMANISE
HUMANISED
HUMANISES
HUMANISING
HUMANISM
HUMANISMS
HUMANIST
HUMANISTS
HUMANITIES
HUMANITY

HUMANIZE
HUMANIZED
HUMANIZES
HUMANIZING
HUMANKIND
HUMANKINDS
HUMANLIKE
HUMANLY
HUMANNESS
HUMANNESSES
HUMANOID
HUMANOIDS
HUMANS
HUMAS
HUMBLE
HUMBLED
HUMBLER
HUMBLES
HUMBLESSE
HUMBLESSES
HUMBLEST
HUMBLING
HUMBLINGS
HUMBLY
HUMBUG
HUMBUGGED
HUMBUGGER
HUMBUGGERS
HUMBUGGING
HUMBUGS
HUMBUZZ
HUMBUZZES
HUMDINGER
HUMDINGERS
HUMDRUM
HUMDRUMS
HUMECT
HUMECTANT
HUMECTANTS
HUMECTATE
HUMECTATED
HUMECTATES
HUMECTATING
HUMECTED
HUMECTING
HUMECTIVE
HUMECTIVES
HUMECTS
HUMEFIED
HUMEFIES
HUMEFY
HUMEFYING
HUMERAL
HUMERALS
HUMERI
HUMERUS
HUMF
HUMFED
HUMFING
HUMFS
HUMHUM
HUMHUMS
HUMIC
HUMID
HUMIDER
HUMIDEST
HUMIDIFIED
HUMIDIFIES
HUMIDIFY
HUMIDIFYING
HUMIDITIES
HUMIDITY
HUMIDLY
HUMIDNESS
HUMIDNESSES
HUMIDOR
HUMIDORS
HUMIFIED
HUMIFIES
HUMIFY
HUMIFYING
HUMILIANT
HUMILIATE
HUMILIATED
HUMILIATES
HUMILIATING
HUMILITIES
HUMILITY
HUMITE
HUMITES
HUMLIE
HUMLIES
HUMMABLE
HUMMAUM
HUMMAUMS
HUMMED
HUMMEL
HUMMELLED
HUMMELLER
HUMMELLERS
HUMMELLING
HUMMELS
HUMMER
HUMMERS
HUMMING
HUMMINGS
HUMMOCK
HUMMOCKED
HUMMOCKS
HUMMOCKY
HUMMUM
HUMMUMS
HUMMUS
HUMMUSES
HUMOGEN
HUMOGENS
HUMONGOUS
HUMOR
HUMORAL
HUMORALLY
HUMORED
HUMORESK
HUMORESKS
HUMORING
HUMORIST
HUMORISTS
HUMORLESS
HUMOROUS
HUMORS
HUMOUR
HUMOURED
HUMOURING
HUMOURS
HUMOUS
HUMP
HUMPBACK
HUMPBACKS
HUMPED
HUMPEN
HUMPENS
HUMPER
HUMPERS
HUMPH
HUMPHED
HUMPHING
HUMPHS
HUMPIER
HUMPIES
HUMPIEST
HUMPING
HUMPS
HUMPTIES
HUMPTY
HUMPY
HUMS
HUMSTRUM
HUMSTRUMS
HUMUNGOUS
HUMUS
HUMUSES
HUMUSY
HUNCH
HUNCHBACK
HUNCHBACKS
HUNCHED
HUNCHES
HUNCHING
HUNDRED
HUNDREDER
HUNDREDERS
HUNDREDOR
HUNDREDORS
HUNDREDS
HUNDREDTH
HUNDREDTHS
HUNG
HUNGER
HUNGERED
HUNGERFUL
HUNGERING
HUNGERLY
HUNGERS
HUNGRIER
HUNGRIEST
HUNGRILY
HUNGRY
HUNK
HUNKER
HUNKERED
HUNKERING
HUNKERS
HUNKIER
HUNKIES
HUNKIEST
HUNKS
HUNKSES
HUNKY
HUNT
HUNTED
HUNTER
HUNTERS
HUNTING
HUNTINGS
HUNTRESS
HUNTRESSES
HUNTS
HUNTSMAN
HUNTSMEN
HUP
HUPPAH
HUPPAHS
HUPPED
HUPPING
HUPS
HURCHEON
HURCHEONS
HURDEN
HURDENS
HURDIES
HURDLE
HURDLED
HURDLER
HURDLERS
HURDLES
HURDLING
HURDLINGS
HURDS
HURL
HURLBAT
HURLBATS
HURLED
HURLER
HURLERS
HURLEY
HURLEYS
HURLIES
HURLING
HURLINGS
HURLS
HURLY
HURRA
HURRAED
HURRAH
HURRAHED
HURRAHING
HURRAHS
HURRAING
HURRAS
HURRAY
HURRAYED
HURRAYING
HURRAYS
HURRICANE
HURRICANES
HURRICANO
HURRICANOES
HURRIED
HURRIEDLY
HURRIES
HURRY
HURRYING
HURRYINGS
HURST
HURSTS
HURT
HURTER
HURTERS
HURTFUL
HURTFULLY
HURTING
HURTLE
HURTLED
HURTLES
HURTLESS
HURTLING
HURTS
HUSBAND
HUSBANDED
HUSBANDING
HUSBANDLY
HUSBANDRIES
HUSBANDRY
HUSBANDS
HUSH
HUSHABIED
HUSHABIES
HUSHABY
HUSHABYING
HUSHED
HUSHER
HUSHERED
HUSHERING
HUSHERS
HUSHES
HUSHIER
HUSHIEST
HUSHING
HUSHY
HUSK
HUSKED
HUSKER
HUSKERS
HUSKIER
HUSKIES
HUSKIEST
HUSKILY
HUSKINESS
HUSKINESSES
HUSKING
HUSKINGS
HUSKS
HUSKY
HUSO
HUSOS
HUSS
HUSSAR
HUSSARS
HUSSES
HUSSIES
HUSSIF

USSIFS
USSY
USTINGS
USTLE
USTLED
USTLER
USTLERS
USTLES
USTLING
USTLINGS
USWIFE
USWIVES
UT
UTCH
UTCHED
UTCHES
UTCHING
UTIA
UTIAS
UTMENT
UTMENTS
UTS
UTTED
UTTING
UTTINGS
UTZPAH
UTZPAHS
UZOOR
UZOORS
UZZA
UZZAED
UZZAING
UZZAS
UZZIES
UZZY
WYL
WYLS
YACINE
YACINES
YACINTH
YACINTHS
YAENA
YAENAS
YALINE
YALINES
YALINISE
YALINISED
YALINISES
YALINISING
YALINIZE
YALINIZED
YALINIZES
YALINIZING
YALITE
YALITES
YALOID
YALONEMA
YALONEMAS
YBRID
YBRIDISE
YBRIDISED
YBRIDISES
YBRIDISING
YBRIDISM
HYBRIDISMS
HYBRIDITIES
HYBRIDITY
HYBRIDIZE
HYBRIDIZED
HYBRIDIZES
HYBRIDIZING
HYBRIDOMA
HYBRIDOMAS
HYBRIDOUS
HYBRIDS
HYBRIS
HYBRISES
HYDATHODE
HYDATHODES
HYDATID
HYDATIDS
HYDATOID
HYDRA
HYDRAEMIA
HYDRAEMIAS
HYDRANGEA
HYDRANGEAS
HYDRANT
HYDRANTH
HYDRANTHS
HYDRANTS
HYDRAS
HYDRATE
HYDRATED
HYDRATES
HYDRATING
HYDRATION
HYDRATIONS
HYDRAULIC
HYDRAULICKED
HYDRAULICKING
HYDRAULICS
HYDRAZINE
HYDRAZINES
HYDREMIA
HYDREMIAS
HYDRIA
HYDRIAE
HYDRIC
HYDRIDE
HYDRIDES
HYDRIODIC
HYDRO
HYDROCELE
HYDROCELES
HYDROFOIL
HYDROFOILS
HYDROGEN
HYDROGENS
HYDROID
HYDROIDS
HYDROLOGIES
HYDROLOGY
HYDROLYSE
HYDROLYSED
HYDROLYSES
HYDROLYSING
HYDROLYTE
HYDROLYTES
HYDROLYZE
HYDROLYZED
HYDROLYZES
HYDROLYZING
HYDROMEL
HYDROMELS
HYDRONAUT
HYDRONAUTS
HYDROPIC
HYDROPSIES
HYDROPSY
HYDROPTIC
HYDROPULT
HYDROPULTS
HYDROS
HYDROSKI
HYDROSKIS
HYDROSOMA
HYDROSOMATA
HYDROSOME
HYDROSOMES
HYDROSTAT
HYDROSTATS
HYDROUS
HYDROVANE
HYDROVANES
HYDROXIDE
HYDROXIDES
HYDROXY
HYDROXYL
HYDROXYLS
HYDROZOA
HYDROZOAN
HYDROZOANS
HYDROZOON
HYDYNE
HYDYNES
HYE
HYED
HYEING
HYEN
HYENA
HYENAS
HYENS
HYES
HYETAL
HYETOLOGIES
HYETOLOGY
HYGIENE
HYGIENES
HYGIENIC
HYGIENICS
HYGIENIST
HYGIENISTS
HYGRISTOR
HYGRISTORS
HYGRODEIK
HYGRODEIKS
HYGROLOGIES
HYGROLOGY
HYGROPHIL
HYGROSTAT
HYGROSTATS
HYING
HYKE
HYKES
HYLDING
HYLDINGS
HYLE
HYLEG
HYLEGS
HYLES
HYLIC
HYLICISM
HYLICISMS
HYLICIST
HYLICISTS
HYLISM
HYLISMS
HYLIST
HYLISTS
HYLOBATE
HYLOBATES
HYLOIST
HYLOISTS
HYLOPHYTE
HYLOPHYTES
HYLOZOISM
HYLOZOISMS
HYLOZOIST
HYLOZOISTS
HYMEN
HYMENAEAL
HYMENAEAN
HYMENAL
HYMENEAL
HYMENEALS
HYMENEAN
HYMENIA
HYMENIAL
HYMENIUM
HYMENIUMS
HYMENS
HYMN
HYMNAL
HYMNALS
HYMNARIES
HYMNARY
HYMNED
HYMNIC
HYMNING
HYMNIST
HYMNISTS
HYMNODIES
HYMNODIST
HYMNODISTS
HYMNODY
HYMNOLOGIES
HYMNOLOGY
HYMNS
HYNDE
HYNDES
HYOID
HYOSCINE
HYOSCINES
HYP
HYPALGIA
HYPALGIAS
HYPALLAGE
HYPALLAGES
HYPANTHIA
HYPATE
HYPATES
HYPE
HYPED
HYPER
HYPERBOLA
HYPERBOLAS
HYPERBOLE
HYPERBOLES
HYPERCUBE
HYPERCUBES
HYPEREMIA
HYPEREMIAS
HYPEREMIC
HYPERGAMIES
HYPERGAMY
HYPERLINK
HYPERLINKS
HYPERMART
HYPERMARTS
HYPERNYM
HYPERNYMIES
HYPERNYMS
HYPERNYMY
HYPERON
HYPERONS
HYPEROPIA
HYPEROPIAS
HYPERS
HYPERTEXT
HYPERTEXTS
HYPES
HYPHA
HYPHAE
HYPHAL
HYPHEN
HYPHENATE
HYPHENATED
HYPHENATES
HYPHENATING
HYPHENED
HYPHENIC
HYPHENING
HYPHENISE
HYPHENISED
HYPHENISES
HYPHENISING
HYPHENISM
HYPHENISMS
HYPHENIZE
HYPHENIZED
HYPHENIZES
HYPHENIZING
HYPHENS
HYPING
HYPINOSES
HYPINOSIS
HYPNIC
HYPNICS
HYPNOGENIES

HYPNOGENY
HYPNOID
HYPNOIDAL
HYPNOLOGIES
HYPNOLOGY
HYPNONE
HYPNONES
HYPNOSES
HYPNOSIS
HYPNOTEE
HYPNOTEES
HYPNOTIC
HYPNOTICS
HYPNOTISE
HYPNOTISED
HYPNOTISES
HYPNOTISING
HYPNOTISM
HYPNOTISMS
HYPNOTIST
HYPNOTISTS
HYPNOTIZE
HYPNOTIZED
HYPNOTIZES
HYPNOTIZING
HYPNOTOID
HYPNUM
HYPNUMS
HYPO
HYPOBLAST
HYPOBLASTS
HYPOBOLE
HYPOBOLES
HYPOCAUST
HYPOCAUSTS
HYPOCIST
HYPOCISTS
HYPOCOTYL
HYPOCOTYLS
HYPOCRISIES
HYPOCRISY
HYPOCRITE
HYPOCRITES
HYPODERM
HYPODERMA
HYPODERMAS
HYPODERMS
HYPOGAEA
HYPOGAEAL
HYPOGAEAN
HYPOGAEUM
HYPOGEA
HYPOGEAL
HYPOGEAN
HYPOGENE
HYPOGEOUS
HYPOGEUM
HYPOGYNIES
HYPOGYNY
HYPOID
HYPOMANIA
HYPOMANIAS
HYPOMANIC
HYPONASTIES
HYPONASTY
HYPONYM
HYPONYMIES
HYPONYMS
HYPONYMY
HYPOS
HYPOSTYLE
HYPOSTYLES
HYPOTAXES
HYPOTAXIS
HYPOTHEC
HYPOTHECS
HYPOTONIA
HYPOTONIAS
HYPOTONIC
HYPOXEMIA
HYPOXEMIAS
HYPOXEMIC
HYPOXIA
HYPOXIAS
HYPOXIC
HYPPED
HYPPING
HYPS
HYPURAL
HYRACES
HYRACOID
HYRAX
HYRAXES
HYSON
HYSONS
HYSSOP
HYSSOPS
HYSTERIA
HYSTERIAS
HYSTERIC
HYSTERICS
HYSTEROID
HYTHE
HYTHES

I

MB
MBI
MBIC
MBICS
MBIST
MBISTS
MBS
MBUS
MBUSES
NTHINE
TROGENIES
TROGENY
ERIS
ERISES
EX
EXES
CES
DEM
S
SES
UPROFEN
UPROFENS
E
EBALL
EBALLS
EBERG
EBERGS
EBLINK
EBLINKS
EBOAT
EBOATS
EBOUND
EBOX
EBOXES
ECAP
ECAPS
ED
EFIELD
EFIELDS
EPACK
EPACKS
ER
ERS
ES
ESTONE
ESTONES
H
HABOD
HED
HES
HING
HNEUMON
HNEUMONS
HNITE
ICHNITES
ICHNOLITE
ICHNOLITES
ICHNOLOGIES
ICHNOLOGY
ICHOR
ICHOROUS
ICHORS
ICHTHIC
ICHTHYIC
ICHTHYOID
ICHTHYOIDS
ICHTHYS
ICHTHYSES
ICICLE
ICICLES
ICIER
ICIEST
ICILY
ICINESS
ICINESSES
ICING
ICINGS
ICKER
ICKERS
ICKIER
ICKIEST
ICKY
ICON
ICONIC
ICONIFIED
ICONIFIES
ICONIFY
ICONIFYING
ICONISE
ICONISED
ICONISES
ICONISING
ICONIZE
ICONIZED
ICONIZES
ICONIZING
ICONOLOGIES
ICONOLOGY
ICONOSTAS
ICONOSTASES
ICONS
ICTAL
ICTERIC
ICTERICAL
ICTERICALS
ICTERICS
ICTERID
ICTERIDS
ICTERINE
ICTERUS
ICTERUSES
ICTIC
ICTUS
ICTUSES
ICY
ID
IDANT
IDANTS
IDE
IDEA
IDEAED
IDEAL
IDEALESS
IDEALISE
IDEALISED
IDEALISER
IDEALISERS
IDEALISES
IDEALISING
IDEALISM
IDEALISMS
IDEALIST
IDEALISTS
IDEALITIES
IDEALITY
IDEALIZE
IDEALIZED
IDEALIZER
IDEALIZERS
IDEALIZES
IDEALIZING
IDEALLESS
IDEALLY
IDEALOGUE
IDEALOGUES
IDEALS
IDEAS
IDEATE
IDEATED
IDEATES
IDEATING
IDEATION
IDEATIONS
IDEATIVE
IDEE
IDEES
IDEM
IDENTIC
IDENTICAL
IDENTIFIED
IDENTIFIES
IDENTIFY
IDENTIFYING
IDENTIKIT
IDENTIKITS
IDENTITIES
IDENTITY
IDEOGRAM
IDEOGRAMS
IDEOGRAPH
IDEOGRAPHS
IDEOLOGIC
IDEOLOGIES
IDEOLOGUE
IDEOLOGUES
IDEOLOGY
IDEOMOTOR
IDEOPHONE
IDEOPHONES
IDES
IDIOBLAST
IDIOBLASTS
IDIOCIES
IDIOCY
IDIOGRAPH
IDIOGRAPHS
IDIOLECT
IDIOLECTS
IDIOM
IDIOMATIC
IDIOMS
IDIOPATHIES
IDIOPATHY
IDIOPHONE
IDIOPHONES
IDIOPLASM
IDIOPLASMS
IDIOT
IDIOTCIES
IDIOTCY
IDIOTIC
IDIOTICAL
IDIOTICON
IDIOTICONS
IDIOTISH
IDIOTISM
IDIOTISMS
IDIOTS
IDLE
IDLED
IDLEHOOD
IDLEHOODS
IDLENESS
IDLENESSES
IDLER
IDLERS
IDLES
IDLESSE
IDLESSES
IDLEST
IDLING
IDLY
IDOCRASE
IDOCRASES
IDOL
IDOLA
IDOLATER
IDOLATERS
IDOLATOR
IDOLATORS
IDOLATRIES
IDOLATRY
IDOLISE
IDOLISED
IDOLISER
IDOLISERS
IDOLISES
IDOLISING
IDOLISM
IDOLISMS
IDOLIST
IDOLISTS
IDOLIZE
IDOLIZED
IDOLIZER
IDOLIZERS
IDOLIZES
IDOLIZING
IDOLS
IDOLUM
IDS
IDYL
IDYLL
IDYLLIAN
IDYLLIC
IDYLLIST
IDYLLISTS
IDYLLS
IDYLS
IF
IFF
IFFIER
IFFIEST
IFFINESS
IFFINESSES
IFFY
IFS
IGAD
IGAPO
IGAPOS

IGARAPE
IGARAPES
IGLOO
IGLOOS
IGNARO
IGNAROES
IGNAROS
IGNEOUS
IGNESCENT
IGNESCENTS
IGNITABLE
IGNITE
IGNITED
IGNITER
IGNITERS
IGNITES
IGNITIBLE
IGNITING
IGNITION
IGNITIONS
IGNITRON
IGNITRONS
IGNOBLE
IGNOBLER
IGNOBLEST
IGNOBLY
IGNOMIES
IGNOMINIES
IGNOMINY
IGNOMY
IGNORABLE
IGNORAMUS
IGNORAMUSES
IGNORANCE
IGNORANCES
IGNORANT
IGNORANTS
IGNORE
IGNORED
IGNORER
IGNORERS
IGNORES
IGNORING
IGUANA
IGUANAS
IGUANID
IGUANIDS
IGUANODON
IGUANODONS
IHRAM
IHRAMS
IJTIHAD
IJTIHADS
IKAT
IKATS
IKEBANA
IKEBANAS
IKON
IKONS
ILEA
ILEAC
ILEITIS
ILEITISES
ILEOSTOMIES
ILEOSTOMY
ILEUM
ILEUS
ILEUSES
ILEX
ILEXES
ILIA
ILIAC
ILIACUS
ILIACUSES
ILICES
ILIUM
ILK
ILKA
ILKADAY
ILKADAYS
ILKS
ILL
ILLAPSE
ILLAPSED
ILLAPSES
ILLAPSING
ILLATION
ILLATIONS
ILLATIVE
ILLATIVES
ILLEGAL
ILLEGALLY
ILLEGIBLE
ILLEGIBLY
ILLIAD
ILLIADS
ILLIBERAL
ILLICIT
ILLICITLY
ILLIMITED
ILLINIUM
ILLINIUMS
ILLIPE
ILLIPES
ILLIQUID
ILLISION
ILLISIONS
ILLITE
ILLITES
ILLNESS
ILLNESSES
ILLOGIC
ILLOGICAL
ILLOGICS
ILLS
ILLTH
ILLTHS
ILLUDE
ILLUDED
ILLUDES
ILLUDING
ILLUME
ILLUMED
ILLUMES
ILLUMINE
ILLUMINED
ILLUMINER
ILLUMINERS
ILLUMINES
ILLUMING
ILLUMINING
ILLUPI
ILLUPIS
ILLUSION
ILLUSIONS
ILLUSIVE
ILLUSORY
ILLUVIA
ILLUVIAL
ILLUVIUM
ILLUVIUMS
ILLY
ILMENITE
ILMENITES
IMAGE
IMAGEABLE
IMAGED
IMAGELESS
IMAGERIES
IMAGERY
IMAGES
IMAGINAL
IMAGINARY
IMAGINE
IMAGINED
IMAGINER
IMAGINERS
IMAGINES
IMAGING
IMAGINGS
IMAGINING
IMAGININGS
IMAGINIST
IMAGINISTS
IMAGISM
IMAGISMS
IMAGIST
IMAGISTIC
IMAGISTS
IMAGO
IMAGOES
IMAGOS
IMAM
IMAMATE
IMAMATES
IMAMS
IMARET
IMARETS
IMARI
IMARIS
IMAUM
IMAUMS
IMBALANCE
IMBALANCES
IMBAR
IMBARK
IMBARKED
IMBARKING
IMBARKS
IMBARRED
IMBARRING
IMBARS
IMBASE
IMBASED
IMBASES
IMBASING
IMBATHE
IMBATHED
IMBATHES
IMBATHING
IMBECILE
IMBECILES
IMBECILIC
IMBED
IMBEDDED
IMBEDDING
IMBEDS
IMBIBE
IMBIBED
IMBIBER
IMBIBERS
IMBIBES
IMBIBING
IMBITTER
IMBITTERED
IMBITTERING
IMBITTERS
IMBODIED
IMBODIES
IMBODY
IMBODYING
IMBORDER
IMBORDERED
IMBORDERING
IMBORDERS
IMBOSK
IMBOSKED
IMBOSKING
IMBOSKS
IMBOSOM
IMBOSOMED
IMBOSOMING
IMBOSOMS
IMBOSS
IMBOSSED
IMBOSSES
IMBOSSING
IMBOWER
IMBOWERED
IMBOWERING
IMBOWERS
IMBRANGLE
IMBRANGLED
IMBRANGLES
IMBRANGLING
IMBRAST
IMBREX
IMBRICATE
IMBRICATED
IMBRICATES
IMBRICATING
IMBRICES
IMBROGLIO
IMBROGLIOS
IMBROWN
IMBROWNED
IMBROWNING
IMBROWNS
IMBRUE
IMBRUED
IMBRUES
IMBRUING
IMBRUTE
IMBRUTED
IMBRUTES
IMBRUTING
IMBUE
IMBUED
IMBUES
IMBUING
IMBURSE
IMBURSED
IMBURSES
IMBURSING
IMIDAZOLE
IMIDAZOLES
IMIDE
IMIDES
IMIDIC
IMINE
IMINES
IMITABLE
IMITANCIES
IMITANCY
IMITANT
IMITANTS
IMITATE
IMITATED
IMITATES
IMITATING
IMITATION
IMITATIONS
IMITATIVE
IMITATOR
IMITATORS
IMMANACLE
IMMANACLED
IMMANACLES
IMMANACLING
IMMANE
IMMANELY
IMMANENCE
IMMANENCES
IMMANENCIES
IMMANENCY
IMMANENT
IMMANITIES
IMMANITY
IMMANTLE
IMMANTLED
IMMANTLES
IMMANTLING
IMMASK
IMMASKED
IMMASKING
IMMASKS
IMMATURE
IMMEDIACIES
IMMEDIACY
IMMEDIATE

IMMENSE
IMMENSELY
IMMENSER
IMMENSEST
IMMENSITIES
IMMENSITY
IMMERGE
IMMERGED
IMMERGES
IMMERGING
IMMERSE
IMMERSED
IMMERSES
IMMERSING
IMMERSION
IMMERSIONS
IMMESH
IMMESHED
IMMESHES
IMMESHING
IMMEW
IMMEWED
IMMEWING
IMMEWS
IMMIGRANT
IMMIGRANTS
IMMIGRATE
IMMIGRATED
IMMIGRATES
IMMIGRATING
IMMINENCE
IMMINENCES
IMMINENCIES
IMMINENCY
IMMINENT
IMMINGLE
IMMINGLED
IMMINGLES
IMMINGLING
IMMINUTE
IMMISSION
IMMISSIONS
IMMIT
IMMITS
IMMITTED
IMMITTING
IMMIX
IMMIXED
IMMIXES
IMMIXING
IMMIXTURE
IMMIXTURES
IMMOBILE
IMMODEST
IMMODESTIES
IMMODESTY
IMMOLATE
IMMOLATED
IMMOLATES
IMMOLATING
IMMOLATOR
IMMOLATORS
IMMOMENT
IMMORAL
IMMORALLY
IMMORTAL
IMMORTALS
IMMOVABLE
IMMOVABLES
IMMOVABLY
IMMUNE
IMMUNES
IMMUNISE
IMMUNISED
IMMUNISES
IMMUNISING
IMMUNITIES
IMMUNITY
IMMUNIZE
IMMUNIZED
IMMUNIZES
IMMUNIZING
IMMUNOGEN
IMMUNOGENS
IMMURE
IMMURED
IMMURES
IMMURING
IMMUTABLE
IMMUTABLY
IMP
IMPACABLE
IMPACT
IMPACTED
IMPACTING
IMPACTION
IMPACTIONS
IMPACTITE
IMPACTITES
IMPACTIVE
IMPACTS
IMPAINT
IMPAINTED
IMPAINTING
IMPAINTS
IMPAIR
IMPAIRED
IMPAIRER
IMPAIRERS
IMPAIRING
IMPAIRINGS
IMPAIRS
IMPALA
IMPALAS
IMPALE
IMPALED
IMPALES
IMPALING
IMPANATE
IMPANEL
IMPANELLED
IMPANELLING
IMPANELS
IMPANNEL
IMPANNELLED
IMPANNELLING
IMPANNELS
IMPARITIES
IMPARITY
IMPARK
IMPARKED
IMPARKING
IMPARKS
IMPARL
IMPARLED
IMPARLING
IMPARLS
IMPART
IMPARTED
IMPARTER
IMPARTERS
IMPARTIAL
IMPARTING
IMPARTS
IMPASSE
IMPASSES
IMPASSION
IMPASSIONED
IMPASSIONING
IMPASSIONS
IMPASSIVE
IMPASTE
IMPASTED
IMPASTES
IMPASTING
IMPASTO
IMPASTOED
IMPASTOS
IMPATIENS
IMPATIENT
IMPAVE
IMPAVED
IMPAVES
IMPAVID
IMPAVIDLY
IMPAVING
IMPAWN
IMPAWNED
IMPAWNING
IMPAWNS
IMPEACH
IMPEACHED
IMPEACHER
IMPEACHERS
IMPEACHES
IMPEACHING
IMPEARL
IMPEARLED
IMPEARLING
IMPEARLS
IMPECCANT
IMPED
IMPEDANCE
IMPEDANCES
IMPEDE
IMPEDED
IMPEDES
IMPEDING
IMPEL
IMPELLED
IMPELLENT
IMPELLENTS
IMPELLER
IMPELLERS
IMPELLING
IMPELS
IMPEND
IMPENDED
IMPENDENT
IMPENDING
IMPENDS
IMPENNATE
IMPERATOR
IMPERATORS
IMPERFECT
IMPERFECTS
IMPERIA
IMPERIAL
IMPERIALS
IMPERIL
IMPERILLED
IMPERILLING
IMPERILS
IMPERIOUS
IMPERIUM
IMPETICOS
IMPETICOSSED
IMPETICOSSES
IMPETICOSSING
IMPETIGINES
IMPETIGO
IMPETIGOS
IMPETRATE
IMPETRATED
IMPETRATES
IMPETRATING
IMPETUOUS
IMPETUS
IMPETUSES
IMPI
IMPIES
IMPIETIES
IMPIETY
IMPING
IMPINGE
IMPINGED
IMPINGENT
IMPINGES
IMPINGING
IMPIOUS
IMPIOUSLY
IMPIS
IMPISH
IMPISHLY
IMPLANT
IMPLANTED
IMPLANTING
IMPLANTS
IMPLATE
IMPLATED
IMPLATES
IMPLATING
IMPLEACH
IMPLEACHED
IMPLEACHES
IMPLEACHING
IMPLEAD
IMPLEADED
IMPLEADER
IMPLEADERS
IMPLEADING
IMPLEADS
IMPLEDGE
IMPLEDGED
IMPLEDGES
IMPLEDGING
IMPLEMENT
IMPLEMENTED
IMPLEMENTING
IMPLEMENTS
IMPLETE
IMPLETED
IMPLETES
IMPLETING
IMPLETION
IMPLETIONS
IMPLEX
IMPLEXES
IMPLEXION
IMPLEXIONS
IMPLICATE
IMPLICATED
IMPLICATES
IMPLICATING
IMPLICIT
IMPLIED
IMPLIEDLY
IMPLIES
IMPLODE
IMPLODED
IMPLODENT
IMPLODENTS
IMPLODES
IMPLODING
IMPLORE
IMPLORED
IMPLORER
IMPLORERS
IMPLORES
IMPLORING
IMPLOSION
IMPLOSIONS
IMPLOSIVE
IMPLOSIVES
IMPLUNGE
IMPLUNGED
IMPLUNGES
IMPLUNGING
IMPLUVIA
IMPLUVIUM
IMPLY
IMPLYING
IMPOCKET
IMPOCKETED
IMPOCKETING
IMPOCKETS
IMPOLDER
IMPOLDERED
IMPOLDERING
IMPOLDERS

IMPOLICIES
IMPOLICY
IMPOLITE
IMPOLITER
IMPOLITEST
IMPOLITIC
IMPONE
IMPONED
IMPONENT
IMPONENTS
IMPONES
IMPONING
IMPORT
IMPORTANT
IMPORTED
IMPORTER
IMPORTERS
IMPORTING
IMPORTS
IMPORTUNE
IMPORTUNED
IMPORTUNES
IMPORTUNING
IMPORTUNINGS
IMPOSABLE
IMPOSE
IMPOSED
IMPOSER
IMPOSERS
IMPOSES
IMPOSING
IMPOST
IMPOSTER
IMPOSTERS
IMPOSTOR
IMPOSTORS
IMPOSTS
IMPOSTUME
IMPOSTUMES
IMPOSTURE
IMPOSTURES
IMPOT
IMPOTENCE
IMPOTENCES
IMPOTENCIES
IMPOTENCY
IMPOTENT
IMPOTS
IMPOUND
IMPOUNDED
IMPOUNDER
IMPOUNDERS
IMPOUNDING
IMPOUNDS
IMPRECATE
IMPRECATED
IMPRECATES
IMPRECATING
IMPRECISE
IMPREGN
IMPREGNED
IMPREGNING
IMPREGNS
IMPRESA
IMPRESARI
IMPRESAS
IMPRESE
IMPRESES
IMPRESS
IMPRESSE
IMPRESSED
IMPRESSES
IMPRESSING
IMPREST
IMPRESTS
IMPRIMIS
IMPRINT
IMPRINTED
IMPRINTING
IMPRINTINGS
IMPRINTS
IMPRISON
IMPRISONED
IMPRISONING
IMPRISONS
IMPROBITIES
IMPROBITY
IMPROMPTU
IMPROMPTUS
IMPROPER
IMPROV
IMPROVE
IMPROVED
IMPROVER
IMPROVERS
IMPROVES
IMPROVING
IMPROVISE
IMPROVISED
IMPROVISES
IMPROVISING
IMPROVS
IMPRUDENT
IMPS
IMPSONITE
IMPSONITES
IMPUDENCE
IMPUDENCES
IMPUDENT
IMPUGN
IMPUGNED
IMPUGNER
IMPUGNERS
IMPUGNING
IMPUGNS
IMPULSE
IMPULSED
IMPULSES
IMPULSING
IMPULSION
IMPULSIONS
IMPULSIVE
IMPUNDULU
IMPUNDULUS
IMPUNITIES
IMPUNITY
IMPURE
IMPURELY
IMPURER
IMPUREST
IMPURITIES
IMPURITY
IMPURPLE
IMPURPLED
IMPURPLES
IMPURPLING
IMPUTABLE
IMPUTABLY
IMPUTE
IMPUTED
IMPUTER
IMPUTERS
IMPUTES
IMPUTING
IMSHI
IMSHY
IN
INABILITIES
INABILITY
INACTION
INACTIONS
INACTIVE
INAIDABLE
INAMORATA
INAMORATAS
INAMORATO
INAMORATOS
INANE
INANELY
INANENESS
INANENESSES
INANER
INANEST
INANIMATE
INANITIES
INANITION
INANITIONS
INANITY
INAPT
INAPTLY
INAPTNESS
INAPTNESSES
INARABLE
INARCH
INARCHED
INARCHES
INARCHING
INARM
INARMED
INARMING
INARMS
INAUDIBLE
INAUDIBLY
INAUGURAL
INAUGURALS
INAURATE
INBEING
INBEINGS
INBENT
INBOARD
INBORN
INBOUND
INBREAK
INBREAKS
INBREATHE
INBREATHED
INBREATHES
INBREATHING
INBRED
INBREED
INBREEDING
INBREEDINGS
INBREEDS
INBRING
INBRINGING
INBRINGINGS
INBRINGS
INBROUGHT
INBURNING
INBURST
INBURSTS
INBY
INBYE
INCAGE
INCAGED
INCAGES
INCAGING
INCAPABLE
INCAPABLES
INCAPABLY
INCARNATE
INCARNATED
INCARNATES
INCARNATING
INCASE
INCASED
INCASES
INCASING
INCAUTION
INCAUTIONS
INCAVE
INCAVED
INCAVES
INCAVI
INCAVING
INCAVO
INCEDE
INCEDED
INCEDES
INCEDING
INCENSE
INCENSED
INCENSER
INCENSERS
INCENSES
INCENSING
INCENSOR
INCENSORIES
INCENSORS
INCENSORY
INCENTIVE
INCENTIVES
INCENTRE
INCENTRES
INCEPT
INCEPTED
INCEPTING
INCEPTION
INCEPTIONS
INCEPTIVE
INCEPTIVES
INCEPTOR
INCEPTORS
INCEPTS
INCERTAIN
INCESSANT
INCEST
INCESTS
INCH
INCHASE
INCHASED
INCHASES
INCHASING
INCHED
INCHES
INCHING
INCHMEAL
INCHOATE
INCHOATED
INCHOATES
INCHOATING
INCHPIN
INCHPINS
INCIDENCE
INCIDENCES
INCIDENT
INCIDENTS
INCIPIENT
INCIPIT
INCISE
INCISED
INCISES
INCISING
INCISION
INCISIONS
INCISIVE
INCISOR
INCISORS
INCISORY
INCISURE
INCISURES
INCITANT
INCITANTS
INCITE
INCITED
INCITER
INCITERS
INCITES
INCITING
INCIVIL
INCIVISM
INCIVISMS
INCLASP
INCLASPED
INCLASPING
INCLASPS
INCLE
INCLEMENT
INCLES
INCLINE

INCLINED
INCLINES
INCLINING
INCLININGS
INCLIP
INCLIPPED
INCLIPPING
INCLIPS
INCLOSE
INCLOSED
INCLOSER
INCLOSERS
INCLOSES
INCLOSING
INCLOSURE
INCLOSURES
INCLUDE
INCLUDED
INCLUDES
INCLUDING
INCLUSION
INCLUSIONS
INCLUSIVE
INCOGNITO
INCOGNITOS
INCOME
INCOMER
INCOMERS
INCOMES
INCOMING
INCOMINGS
INCOMMODE
INCOMMODED
INCOMMODES
INCOMMODING
INCONDITE
INCONIE
INCONNU
INCONNUE
INCONNUES
INCONNUS
INCONY
INCORPSE
INCORPSED
INCORPSES
INCORPSING
INCORRECT
INCORRUPT
NCREASE
NCREASED
NCREASER
NCREASERS
NCREASES
NCREASING
NCREASINGS
NCREATE
NCREMATE
NCREMATED
NCREMATES
NCREMATING
NCREMENT
NCREMENTED
NCREMENTING
NCREMENTS
INCRETION
INCRETIONS
INCROSS
INCROSSED
INCROSSES
INCROSSING
INCRUST
INCRUSTED
INCRUSTING
INCRUSTS
INCUBATE
INCUBATED
INCUBATES
INCUBATING
INCUBATOR
INCUBATORS
INCUBI
INCUBOUS
INCUBUS
INCUBUSES
INCUDES
INCULCATE
INCULCATED
INCULCATES
INCULCATING
INCULPATE
INCULPATED
INCULPATES
INCULPATING
INCULT
INCUMBENT
INCUMBENTS
INCUNABLE
INCUNABLES
INCUR
INCURABLE
INCURABLES
INCURABLY
INCURIOUS
INCURRED
INCURRENT
INCURRING
INCURS
INCURSION
INCURSIONS
INCURSIVE
INCURVATE
INCURVATED
INCURVATES
INCURVATING
INCURVE
INCURVED
INCURVES
INCURVING
INCURVITIES
INCURVITY
INCUS
INCUSE
INCUSED
INCUSES
INCUSING
INCUT
INDABA
INDABAS
INDAGATE
INDAGATED
INDAGATES
INDAGATING
INDAGATOR
INDAGATORS
INDAMINE
INDAMINES
INDART
INDARTED
INDARTING
INDARTS
INDEBTED
INDECENCIES
INDECENCY
INDECENT
INDECENTER
INDECENTEST
INDECORUM
INDECORUMS
INDEED
INDELIBLE
INDELIBLY
INDEMNIFIED
INDEMNIFIES
INDEMNIFY
INDEMNIFYING
INDEMNITIES
INDEMNITY
INDENE
INDENES
INDENT
INDENTED
INDENTER
INDENTERS
INDENTING
INDENTION
INDENTIONS
INDENTS
INDENTURE
INDENTURED
INDENTURES
INDENTURING
INDEW
INDEWED
INDEWING
INDEWS
INDEX
INDEXAL
INDEXED
INDEXER
INDEXERS
INDEXES
INDEXICAL
INDEXING
INDEXINGS
INDEXLESS
INDICAN
INDICANS
INDICANT
INDICANTS
INDICATE
INDICATED
INDICATES
INDICATING
INDICATOR
INDICATORS
INDICES
INDICIA
INDICIAL
INDICIUM
INDICT
INDICTED
INDICTEE
INDICTEES
INDICTING
INDICTION
INDICTIONS
INDICTS
INDIE
INDIES
INDIGENCE
INDIGENCES
INDIGENCIES
INDIGENCY
INDIGENE
INDIGENES
INDIGENT
INDIGENTS
INDIGEST
INDIGESTS
INDIGN
INDIGNANT
INDIGNIFIED
INDIGNIFIES
INDIGNIFY
INDIGNIFYING
INDIGNITIES
INDIGNITY
INDIGO
INDIGOES
INDIGOS
INDIGOTIN
INDIGOTINS
INDIRECT
INDIRUBIN
INDIRUBINS
INDISPOSE
INDISPOSED
INDISPOSES
INDISPOSING
INDITE
INDITED
INDITER
INDITERS
INDITES
INDITING
INDIUM
INDIUMS
INDIVIDUA
INDOCIBLE
INDOCILE
INDOL
INDOLE
INDOLENCE
INDOLENCES
INDOLENCIES
INDOLENCY
INDOLENT
INDOLES
INDOLS
INDOOR
INDOORS
INDORSE
INDORSED
INDORSES
INDORSING
INDOXYL
INDOXYLS
INDRAFT
INDRAFTS
INDRAUGHT
INDRAUGHTS
INDRAWN
INDRENCH
INDRENCHED
INDRENCHES
INDRENCHING
INDRI
INDRIS
INDRISES
INDUBIOUS
INDUCE
INDUCED
INDUCER
INDUCERS
INDUCES
INDUCIAE
INDUCIBLE
INDUCING
INDUCT
INDUCTED
INDUCTEE
INDUCTEES
INDUCTILE
INDUCTING
INDUCTION
INDUCTIONS
INDUCTIVE
INDUCTOR
INDUCTORS
INDUCTS
INDUE
INDUED
INDUES
INDUING
INDULGE
INDULGED
INDULGENT
INDULGER
INDULGERS
INDULGES
INDULGING
INDULIN
INDULINE
INDULINES
INDULINS
INDULT
INDULTS
INDUMENTA
INDUNA
INDUNAS

INDURATE
INDURATED
INDURATES
INDURATING
INDUSIA
INDUSIAL
INDUSIATE
INDUSIUM
INDUSTRIES
INDUSTRY
INDUVIAE
INDUVIAL
INDUVIATE
INDWELL
INDWELLER
INDWELLERS
INDWELLING
INDWELLINGS
INDWELLS
INDWELT
INEARTH
INEARTHED
INEARTHING
INEARTHS
INEBRIANT
INEBRIANTS
INEBRIATE
INEBRIATED
INEBRIATES
INEBRIATING
INEBRIETIES
INEBRIETY
INEBRIOUS
INEDIBLE
INEDITED
INEFFABLE
INEFFABLY
INELASTIC
INELEGANT
INEPT
INEPTER
INEPTEST
INEPTLY
INEPTNESS
INEPTNESSES
INEQUABLE
INEQUITIES
INEQUITY
INERM
INERMOUS
INERRABLE
INERRABLY
INERRANCIES
INERRANCY
INERRANT
INERT
INERTER
INERTEST
INERTIA
INERTIAL
INERTIAS
INERTLY
INERTNESS
INERTNESSES
INERUDITE
INESSIVE
INESSIVES
INEXACT
INEXACTLY
INEXPERT
INFALL
INFALLS
INFAME
INFAMED
INFAMES
INFAMIES
INFAMING
INFAMISE
INFAMISED
INFAMISES
INFAMISING
INFAMIZE
INFAMIZED
INFAMIZES
INFAMIZING
INFAMOUS
INFAMY
INFANCIES
INFANCY
INFANT
INFANTA
INFANTAS
INFANTE
INFANTES
INFANTILE
INFANTINE
INFANTRIES
INFANTRY
INFANTS
INFARCT
INFARCTS
INFARE
INFARES
INFATUATE
INFATUATED
INFATUATES
INFATUATING
INFAUNA
INFAUNAE
INFAUNAL
INFAUNAS
INFAUST
INFECT
INFECTED
INFECTING
INFECTION
INFECTIONS
INFECTIVE
INFECTOR
INFECTORS
INFECTS
INFECUND
INFEFT
INFEFTED
INFEFTING
INFEFTS
INFELT
INFER
INFERABLE
INFERE
INFERENCE
INFERENCES
INFERIAE
INFERIOR
INFERIORS
INFERNAL
INFERNO
INFERNOS
INFERRED
INFERRING
INFERS
INFERTILE
INFEST
INFESTED
INFESTING
INFESTS
INFICETE
INFIDEL
INFIDELS
INFIELD
INFIELDER
INFIELDERS
INFIELDS
INFILL
INFILLED
INFILLING
INFILLINGS
INFILLS
INFIMUM
INFIMUMS
INFINITE
INFINITES
INFINITIES
INFINITY
INFIRM
INFIRMARIES
INFIRMARY
INFIRMER
INFIRMEST
INFIRMITIES
INFIRMITY
INFIRMLY
INFIX
INFIXED
INFIXES
INFIXING
INFLAME
INFLAMED
INFLAMER
INFLAMERS
INFLAMES
INFLAMING
INFLATE
INFLATED
INFLATES
INFLATING
INFLATION
INFLATIONS
INFLATIVE
INFLATOR
INFLATORS
INFLATUS
INFLATUSES
INFLECT
INFLECTED
INFLECTING
INFLECTS
INFLEXED
INFLEXION
INFLEXIONS
INFLEXURE
INFLEXURES
INFLICT
INFLICTED
INFLICTER
INFLICTERS
INFLICTING
INFLICTOR
INFLICTORS
INFLICTS
INFLOW
INFLOWING
INFLOWINGS
INFLOWS
INFLUENCE
INFLUENCED
INFLUENCES
INFLUENCING
INFLUENT
INFLUENTS
INFLUENZA
INFLUENZAS
INFLUX
INFLUXES
INFLUXION
INFLUXIONS
INFO
INFOBAHN
INFOBAHNS
INFOLD
INFOLDED
INFOLDING
INFOLDS
INFOMANIA
INFOMANIAS
INFORCE
INFORCED
INFORCES
INFORCING
INFORM
INFORMAL
INFORMANT
INFORMANTS
INFORMED
INFORMER
INFORMERS
INFORMING
INFORMS
INFORTUNE
INFORTUNES
INFOS
INFRA
INFRACT
INFRACTED
INFRACTING
INFRACTOR
INFRACTORS
INFRACTS
INFRARED
INFRAREDS
INFRINGE
INFRINGED
INFRINGES
INFRINGING
INFULA
INFULAE
INFURIATE
INFURIATED
INFURIATES
INFURIATING
INFUSCATE
INFUSE
INFUSED
INFUSER
INFUSERS
INFUSES
INFUSIBLE
INFUSING
INFUSION
INFUSIONS
INFUSIVE
INFUSORIA
INFUSORY
INGAN
INGANS
INGATE
INGATES
INGATHER
INGATHERED
INGATHERING
INGATHERINGS
INGATHERS
INGENER
INGENERS
INGENIOUS
INGENIUM
INGENIUMS
INGENU
INGENUE
INGENUES
INGENUITIES
INGENUITY
INGENUOUS
INGENUS
INGEST
INGESTA
INGESTED
INGESTING
INGESTION
INGESTIONS
INGESTIVE
INGESTS
INGINE
INGINES
INGLE
INGLENEUK
INGLENEUKS
INGLENOOK
INGLENOOKS
INGLES

INGLOBE
INGLOBED
INGLOBES
INGLOBING
INGLUVIAL
INGLUVIES
INGO
INGOES
INGOING
INGOINGS
INGOT
INGOTS
INGRAFT
INGRAFTED
INGRAFTING
INGRAFTS
INGRAIN
INGRAINED
INGRAINING
INGRAINS
INGRAM
INGRATE
INGRATELY
INGRATES
INGRESS
INGRESSES
INGROOVE
INGROOVED
INGROOVES
INGROOVING
INGROSS
INGROSSED
INGROSSES
INGROSSING
INGROUP
INGROUPS
INGROWING
INGROWN
INGROWTH
INGROWTHS
INGRUM
INGUINAL
INGULF
INGULFED
INGULFING
INGULFS
INGULPH
INGULPHED
INGULPHING
INGULPHS
INHABIT
INHABITED
INHABITER
INHABITERS
INHABITING
INHABITOR
INHABITORS
INHABITS
INHALANT
INHALANTS
INHALATOR
INHALATORS
INHALE
INHALED
INHALER
INHALERS
INHALES
INHALING
INHARMONIES
INHARMONY
INHAUL
INHAULER
INHAULERS
INHAULS
INHAUST
INHAUSTED
INHAUSTING
INHAUSTS
INHEARSE
INHEARSED
INHEARSES
INHEARSING
INHERCE
INHERCED
INHERCES
INHERCING
INHERE
INHERED
INHERENCE
INHERENCES
INHERENCIES
INHERENCY
INHERENT
INHERES
INHERING
INHERIT
INHERITED
INHERITING
INHERITOR
INHERITORS
INHERITS
INHESION
INHESIONS
INHIBIT
INHIBITED
INHIBITER
INHIBITERS
INHIBITING
INHIBITOR
INHIBITORS
INHIBITS
INHOLDER
INHOLDERS
INHOOP
INHOOPED
INHOOPING
INHOOPS
INHUMAN
INHUMANE
INHUMANLY
INHUMATE
INHUMATED
INHUMATES
INHUMATING
INHUME
INHUMED
INHUMER
INHUMERS
INHUMES
INHUMING
INIA
INIMICAL
INION
INIQUITIES
INIQUITY
INISLE
INISLED
INISLES
INISLING
INITIAL
INITIALED
INITIALING
INITIALLED
INITIALLING
INITIALLY
INITIALS
INITIATE
INITIATED
INITIATES
INITIATING
INITIATOR
INITIATORS
INJECT
INJECTED
INJECTING
INJECTION
INJECTIONS
INJECTOR
INJECTORS
INJECTS
INJELLIED
INJELLIES
INJELLY
INJELLYING
INJERA
INJERAS
INJOINT
INJOINTED
INJOINTING
INJOINTS
INJUNCT
INJUNCTED
INJUNCTING
INJUNCTS
INJURE
INJURED
INJURER
INJURERS
INJURES
INJURIES
INJURING
INJURIOUS
INJURY
INJUSTICE
INJUSTICES
INK
INKBERRIES
INKBERRY
INKED
INKER
INKERS
INKHOLDER
INKHOLDERS
INKHORN
INKHORNS
INKIER
INKIEST
INKINESS
INKINESSES
INKING
INKLE
INKLED
INKLES
INKLING
INKLINGS
INKPOT
INKPOTS
INKS
INKSPOT
INKSPOTS
INKSTAND
INKSTANDS
INKSTONE
INKSTONES
INKWELL
INKWELLS
INKY
INLACE
INLACED
INLACES
INLACING
INLAID
INLAND
INLANDER
INLANDERS
INLANDS
INLAY
INLAYER
INLAYERS
INLAYING
INLAYINGS
INLAYS
INLET
INLETS
INLIER
INLIERS
INLOCK
INLOCKED
INLOCKING
INLOCKS
INLY
INLYING
INMATE
INMATES
INMESH
INMESHED
INMESHES
INMESHING
INMOST
INN
INNARDS
INNATE
INNATELY
INNATIVE
INNED
INNER
INNERMOST
INNERS
INNERVATE
INNERVATED
INNERVATES
INNERVATING
INNERVE
INNERVED
INNERVES
INNERVING
INNERWEAR
INNERWEARS
INNING
INNINGS
INNKEEPER
INNKEEPERS
INNOCENCE
INNOCENCES
INNOCENCIES
INNOCENCY
INNOCENT
INNOCENTS
INNOCUITIES
INNOCUITY
INNOCUOUS
INNOVATE
INNOVATED
INNOVATES
INNOVATING
INNOVATOR
INNOVATORS
INNOXIOUS
INNS
INNUENDO
INNUENDOED
INNUENDOES
INNUENDOING
INNUENDOS
INNYARD
INNYARDS
INOCULA
INOCULATE
INOCULATED
INOCULATES
INOCULATING
INOCULUM
INOCULUMS
INODOROUS
INOPINATE
INORB
INORBED
INORBING
INORBS
INORGANIC
INORNATE
INOSITOL
INOSITOLS
INOTROPIC
INPAYMENT
INPAYMENTS
INPHASE
INPOURING
INPOURINGS
INPUT

INPUTS
INPUTTER
INPUTTERS
INPUTTING
INQILAB
INQILABS
INQUERE
INQUERED
INQUERES
INQUERING
INQUEST
INQUESTS
INQUIET
INQUIETED
INQUIETING
INQUIETLY
INQUIETS
INQUILINE
INQUILINES
INQUINATE
INQUINATED
INQUINATES
INQUINATING
INQUIRE
INQUIRED
INQUIRER
INQUIRERS
INQUIRES
INQUIRIES
INQUIRING
INQUIRY
INQUORATE
INRO
INROAD
INROADS
INRUSH
INRUSHES
INRUSHING
INRUSHINGS
INS
INSANE
INSANELY
INSANER
INSANEST
INSANIE
INSANIES
INSANITIES
INSANITY
INSATIATE
INSATIETIES
INSATIETY
INSCAPE
INSCAPES
INSCIENCE
INSCIENCES
INSCIENT
INSCONCE
INSCONCED
INSCONCES
INSCONCING
INSCRIBE
INSCRIBED
INSCRIBER
INSCRIBERS
INSCRIBES
INSCRIBING
INSCROLL
INSCROLLED
INSCROLLING
INSCROLLS
INSCULP
INSCULPED
INSCULPING
INSCULPS
INSCULPT
INSEAM
INSEAMED
INSEAMING
INSEAMS
INSECT
INSECTARIES
INSECTARY
INSECTILE
INSECTION
INSECTIONS
INSECTS
INSECURE
INSEEM
INSEEMED
INSEEMING
INSEEMS
INSELBERG
INSELBERGE
INSENSATE
INSERT
INSERTED
INSERTER
INSERTERS
INSERTING
INSERTION
INSERTIONS
INSERTS
INSET
INSETS
INSETTING
INSHALLAH
INSHEATHE
INSHEATHED
INSHEATHES
INSHEATHING
INSHELL
INSHELLED
INSHELLING
INSHELLS
INSHELTER
INSHELTERED
INSHELTERING
INSHELTERS
INSHIP
INSHIPPED
INSHIPPING
INSHIPS
INSHORE
INSHRINE
INSHRINED
INSHRINES
INSHRINING
INSIDE
INSIDER
INSIDERS
INSIDES
INSIDIOUS
INSIGHT
INSIGHTS
INSIGNE
INSIGNIA
INSIGNIAS
INSINCERE
INSINEW
INSINEWED
INSINEWING
INSINEWS
INSINUATE
INSINUATED
INSINUATES
INSINUATING
INSIPID
INSIPIDLY
INSIPIENT
INSIST
INSISTED
INSISTENT
INSISTING
INSISTS
INSNARE
INSNARED
INSNARES
INSNARING
INSOLATE
INSOLATED
INSOLATES
INSOLATING
INSOLE
INSOLENCE
INSOLENCES
INSOLENT
INSOLES
INSOLUBLE
INSOLUBLY
INSOLVENT
INSOLVENTS
INSOMNIA
INSOMNIAC
INSOMNIACS
INSOMNIAS
INSOMUCH
INSOOTH
INSOUL
INSOULED
INSOULING
INSOULS
INSPAN
INSPANNED
INSPANNING
INSPANS
INSPECT
INSPECTED
INSPECTING
INSPECTOR
INSPECTORS
INSPECTS
INSPHERE
INSPHERED
INSPHERES
INSPHERING
INSPIRE
INSPIRED
INSPIRER
INSPIRERS
INSPIRES
INSPIRING
INSPIRIT
INSPIRITED
INSPIRITING
INSPIRITS
INSTABLE
INSTAL
INSTALL
INSTALLED
INSTALLING
INSTALLS
INSTALS
INSTANCE
INSTANCED
INSTANCES
INSTANCIES
INSTANCING
INSTANCY
INSTANT
INSTANTLY
INSTANTS
INSTAR
INSTARRED
INSTARRING
INSTARS
INSTATE
INSTATED
INSTATES
INSTATING
INSTEAD
INSTEP
INSTEPS
INSTIGATE
INSTIGATED
INSTIGATES
INSTIGATING
INSTIL
INSTILL
INSTILLED
INSTILLING
INSTILLS
INSTILS
INSTINCT
INSTINCTS
INSTITUTE
INSTITUTED
INSTITUTES
INSTITUTING
INSTRESS
INSTRESSED
INSTRESSES
INSTRESSING
INSTRUCT
INSTRUCTED
INSTRUCTING
INSTRUCTS
INSUCKEN
INSULA
INSULAE
INSULAR
INSULARLY
INSULAS
INSULATE
INSULATED
INSULATES
INSULATING
INSULATOR
INSULATORS
INSULIN
INSULINS
INSULSE
INSULSITIES
INSULSITY
INSULT
INSULTANT
INSULTED
INSULTER
INSULTERS
INSULTING
INSULTS
INSURABLE
INSURANCE
INSURANCES
INSURANT
INSURANTS
INSURE
INSURED
INSUREDS
INSURER
INSURERS
INSURES
INSURGENT
INSURGENTS
INSURING
INSWATHE
INSWATHED
INSWATHES
INSWATHING
INSWING
INSWINGER
INSWINGERS
INSWINGS
INTACT
INTAGLIO
INTAGLIOED
INTAGLIOING
INTAGLIOS
INTAKE
INTAKES
INTARSIA
INTARSIAS
INTEGER
INTEGERS
INTEGRAL
INTEGRALS
INTEGRAND
INTEGRANDS
INTEGRANT
INTEGRATE
INTEGRATED

TEGRATES
TEGRATING
TEGRITIES
TEGRITY
TELLECT
TELLECTS
TENABLE
TEND
TENDANT
TENDANTS
TENDED
TENDEDS
TENDER
TENDERED
TENDERING
TENDERS
TENDING
TENDS
TENIBLE
TENSATE
TENSATED
TENSATES
TENSATING
TENSE
TENSELY
TENSER
TENSEST
TENSIFIED
TENSIFIES
TENSIFY
TENSIFYING
TENSION
TENSIONS
TENSITIES
TENSITY
TENSIVE
TENSIVES
TENT
TENTION
TENTIONS
TENTIVE
TENTLY
TENTS
TER
TERACT
TERACTED
TERACTING
TERACTS
TERBANK
TERBRED
TERCEDE
TERCEDED
TERCEDES
TERCEDING
TERCEPT
TERCEPTED
TERCEPTING
TERCEPTS
TERCITY
TERCOM
TERCOMS
TERCROP
TERCROPPED
TERCROPPING
INTERCROPS
INTERCUT
INTERCUTS
INTERCUTTING
INTERDASH
INTERDASHED
INTERDASHES
INTERDASHING
INTERDEAL
INTERDEALING
INTERDEALS
INTERDEALT
INTERDICT
INTERDICTED
INTERDICTING
INTERDICTS
INTERDINE
INTERDINED
INTERDINES
INTERDINING
INTERESS
INTERESSE
INTERESSED
INTERESSES
INTERESSING
INTEREST
INTERESTED
INTERESTING
INTERESTS
INTERFACE
INTERFACED
INTERFACES
INTERFACING
INTERFACINGS
INTERFERE
INTERFERED
INTERFERES
INTERFERING
INTERFLOW
INTERFLOWED
INTERFLOWING
INTERFLOWS
INTERFOLD
INTERFOLDED
INTERFOLDING
INTERFOLDS
INTERFUSE
INTERFUSED
INTERFUSES
INTERFUSING
INTERGREW
INTERGROW
INTERGROWING
INTERGROWN
INTERGROWS
INTERIM
INTERIMS
INTERIOR
INTERIORS
INTERJECT
INTERJECTED
INTERJECTING
INTERJECTS
INTERJOIN
INTERJOINED
INTERJOINING
INTERJOINS
INTERKNIT
INTERKNITS
INTERKNITTED
INTERKNITTING
INTERLACE
INTERLACED
INTERLACES
INTERLACING
INTERLAID
INTERLARD
INTERLARDED
INTERLARDING
INTERLARDS
INTERLAY
INTERLAYING
INTERLAYS
INTERLEAF
INTERLEAVES
INTERLINE
INTERLINED
INTERLINES
INTERLINING
INTERLININGS
INTERLINK
INTERLINKED
INTERLINKING
INTERLINKS
INTERLOCK
INTERLOCKED
INTERLOCKING
INTERLOCKS
INTERLOPE
INTERLOPED
INTERLOPES
INTERLOPING
INTERLUDE
INTERLUDED
INTERLUDES
INTERLUDING
INTERMENT
INTERMENTS
INTERMIT
INTERMITS
INTERMITTED
INTERMITTING
INTERMIX
INTERMIXED
INTERMIXES
INTERMIXING
INTERMURE
INTERMURED
INTERMURES
INTERMURING
INTERN
INTERNAL
INTERNALS
INTERNE
INTERNED
INTERNEE
INTERNEES
INTERNES
INTERNING
INTERNIST
INTERNISTS
INTERNODE
INTERNODES
INTERNS
INTERPAGE
INTERPAGED
INTERPAGES
INTERPAGING
INTERPLAY
INTERPLAYS
INTERPLED
INTERPONE
INTERPONED
INTERPONES
INTERPONING
INTERPOSE
INTERPOSED
INTERPOSES
INTERPOSING
INTERPRET
INTERPRETED
INTERPRETING
INTERPRETS
INTERRAIL
INTERRAILED
INTERRAILING
INTERRAILS
INTERRED
INTERREGES
INTERREX
INTERRING
INTERRUPT
INTERRUPTED
INTERRUPTING
INTERRUPTS
INTERS
INTERSECT
INTERSECTED
INTERSECTING
INTERSECTS
INTERSERT
INTERSERTED
INTERSERTING
INTERSERTS
INTERSEX
INTERSEXES
INTERTEXT
INTERTEXTS
INTERTIE
INTERTIES
INTERVAL
INTERVALE
INTERVALES
INTERVALS
INTERVEIN
INTERVEINED
INTERVEINING
INTERVEINS
INTERVENE
INTERVENED
INTERVENES
INTERVENING
INTERVIEW
INTERVIEWED
INTERVIEWING
INTERVIEWS
INTERWAR
INTERWIND
INTERWINDING
INTERWINDS
INTERWORK
INTERWORKED
INTERWORKING
INTERWORKS
INTERWOUND
INTERWOVE
INTERZONE
INTERZONES
INTESTACIES
INTESTACY
INTESTATE
INTESTATES
INTESTINE
INTESTINES
INTHRAL
INTHRALL
INTHRALLED
INTHRALLING
INTHRALLS
INTHRALS
INTI
INTIFADA
INTIFADAS
INTIL
INTIMA
INTIMACIES
INTIMACY
INTIMAE
INTIMATE
INTIMATED
INTIMATES
INTIMATING
INTIME
INTIMISM
INTIMISMS
INTIMIST
INTIMISTE
INTIMISTES
INTIMISTS
INTIMITIES
INTIMITY
INTINE
INTINES
INTIRE
INTIS
INTITULE
INTITULED
INTITULES
INTITULING
INTO
INTOED
INTOMB
INTOMBED
INTOMBING
INTOMBS
INTONACO

INTONACOS
INTONATE
INTONATED
INTONATES
INTONATING
INTONATOR
INTONATORS
INTONE
INTONED
INTONER
INTONERS
INTONES
INTONING
INTONINGS
INTORSION
INTORSIONS
INTORTED
INTORTION
INTORTIONS
INTOWN
INTRA
INTRADA
INTRADAS
INTRADOS
INTRADOSES
INTRANET
INTRANETS
INTRANT
INTRANTS
INTREAT
INTREATED
INTREATING
INTREATS
INTRENCH
INTRENCHED
INTRENCHES
INTRENCHING
INTREPID
INTRICACIES
INTRICACY
INTRICATE
INTRIGANT
INTRIGANTS
INTRIGUE
INTRIGUED
INTRIGUER
INTRIGUERS
INTRIGUES
INTRIGUING
INTRINCE
INTRINSIC
INTRO
INTRODUCE
INTRODUCED
INTRODUCES
INTRODUCING
INTROIT
INTROITS
INTROITUS
INTROITUSES
INTROJECT
INTROJECTED
INTROJECTING
INTROJECTS
INTROLD
INTROMIT
INTROMITS
INTROMITTED
INTROMITTING
INTRON
INTRONS
INTRORSE
INTROS
INTROVERT
INTROVERTED
INTROVERTING
INTROVERTS
INTRUDE
INTRUDED
INTRUDER
INTRUDERS
INTRUDES
INTRUDING
INTRUSION
INTRUSIONS
INTRUSIVE
INTRUSIVES
INTRUST
INTRUSTED
INTRUSTING
INTRUSTS
INTUBATE
INTUBATED
INTUBATES
INTUBATING
INTUIT
INTUITED
INTUITING
INTUITION
INTUITIONS
INTUITIVE
INTUITS
INTUMESCE
INTUMESCED
INTUMESCES
INTUMESCING
INTUSE
INTUSES
INTWINE
INTWINED
INTWINES
INTWINING
INTWIST
INTWISTED
INTWISTING
INTWISTS
INULA
INULAS
INULASE
INULASES
INULIN
INULINS
INUMBRATE
INUMBRATED
INUMBRATES
INUMBRATING
INUNCTION
INUNCTIONS
INUNDANT
INUNDATE
INUNDATED
INUNDATES
INUNDATING
INURBANE
INURE
INURED
INUREMENT
INUREMENTS
INURES
INURING
INURN
INURNED
INURNING
INURNS
INUSITATE
INUST
INUSTION
INUSTIONS
INUTILITIES
INUTILITY
INVADE
INVADED
INVADER
INVADERS
INVADES
INVADING
INVALID
INVALIDED
INVALIDING
INVALIDINGS
INVALIDLY
INVALIDS
INVARIANT
INVARIANTS
INVASION
INVASIONS
INVASIVE
INVEAGLE
INVEAGLED
INVEAGLES
INVEAGLING
INVECKED
INVECTED
INVECTIVE
INVECTIVES
INVEIGH
INVEIGHED
INVEIGHING
INVEIGHS
INVEIGLE
INVEIGLED
INVEIGLER
INVEIGLERS
INVEIGLES
INVEIGLING
INVENIT
INVENT
INVENTED
INVENTING
INVENTION
INVENTIONS
INVENTIVE
INVENTOR
INVENTORIED
INVENTORIES
INVENTORS
INVENTORY
INVENTORYING
INVENTS
INVERSE
INVERSELY
INVERSES
INVERSION
INVERSIONS
INVERSIVE
INVERT
INVERTASE
INVERTASES
INVERTED
INVERTER
INVERTERS
INVERTIN
INVERTING
INVERTINS
INVERTOR
INVERTORS
INVERTS
INVEST
INVESTED
INVESTING
INVESTOR
INVESTORS
INVESTS
INVEXED
INVIABLE
INVIDIOUS
INVIOLATE
INVIOUS
INVISIBLE
INVISIBLES
INVISIBLY
INVITE
INVITED
INVITEE
INVITEES
INVITER
INVITERS
INVITES
INVITING
INVITINGS
INVOICE
INVOICED
INVOICES
INVOICING
INVOKE
INVOKED
INVOKES
INVOKING
INVOLUCEL
INVOLUCELS
INVOLUCRA
INVOLUCRE
INVOLUCRES
INVOLUTE
INVOLUTED
INVOLUTES
INVOLUTING
INVOLVE
INVOLVED
INVOLVES
INVOLVING
INWALL
INWALLED
INWALLING
INWALLS
INWARD
INWARDLY
INWARDS
INWEAVE
INWEAVES
INWEAVING
INWICK
INWICKED
INWICKING
INWICKS
INWIND
INWINDING
INWINDS
INWIT
INWITH
INWITS
INWORK
INWORKED
INWORKING
INWORKINGS
INWORKS
INWORN
INWOUND
INWOVE
INWOVEN
INWRAP
INWRAPPED
INWRAPPING
INWRAPS
INWREATHE
INWREATHED
INWREATHES
INWREATHING
INWROUGHT
INYALA
INYALAS
IO
IODATE
IODATES
IODIC
IODIDE
IODIDES
IODINE
IODINES
IODISE
IODISED
IODISES
IODISING
IODISM
IODISMS
IODIZE
IODIZED
IODIZES
IODIZING
IODOFORM

IODOFORMS
IODOPHILE
IODOUS
IODURET
IODURETS
IODYRITE
IODYRITES
IOLITE
IOLITES
ION
IONIC
IONISE
IONISED
IONISER
IONISERS
IONISES
IONISING
IONIUM
IONIUMS
IONIZE
IONIZED
IONIZER
IONIZERS
IONIZES
IONIZING
IONOMER
IONOMERS
IONONE
IONONES
IONOPAUSE
IONOPAUSES
IONOPHORE
IONOPHORES
IONS
IOS
IOTA
IOTAS
IPECAC
IPECACS
IPOMOEA
IPOMOEAS
IPPON
IPPONS
IPRINDOLE
IPRINDOLES
IRACUND
IRADE
IRADES
IRASCIBLE
IRASCIBLY
IRATE
IRATELY
IRATER
IRATEST
IRE
IREFUL
IREFULLY
IRENIC
IRENICAL
IRENICISM
IRENICISMS
IRENICON
IRENICONS
IRENICS
IRENOLOGIES
IRENOLOGY
IRES
IRID
IRIDAL
IRIDEAL
IRIDES
IRIDIAL
IRIDIAN
IRIDIC
IRIDISE
IRIDISED
IRIDISES
IRIDISING
IRIDIUM
IRIDIUMS
IRIDIZE
IRIDIZED
IRIDIZES
IRIDIZING
IRIDOLOGIES
IRIDOLOGY
IRIDOTOMIES
IRIDOTOMY
IRIDS
IRIS
IRISATE
IRISATED
IRISATES
IRISATING
IRISATION
IRISATIONS
IRISCOPE
IRISCOPES
IRISED
IRISES
IRITIC
IRITIS
IRITISES
IRK
IRKED
IRKING
IRKS
IRKSOME
IRKSOMELY
IROKO
IROKOS
IRON
IRONBARK
IRONBARKS
IRONED
IRONER
IRONERS
IRONIC
IRONICAL
IRONIER
IRONIES
IRONIEST
IRONING
IRONINGS
IRONISE
IRONISED
IRONISES
IRONISING
IRONIST
IRONISTS
IRONIZE
IRONIZED
IRONIZES
IRONIZING
IRONS
IRONSMITH
IRONSMITHS
IRONSTONE
IRONSTONES
IRONWARE
IRONWARES
IRONWOOD
IRONWOODS
IRONWORK
IRONWORKS
IRONY
IRRADIANT
IRRADIATE
IRRADIATED
IRRADIATES
IRRADIATING
IRREALITIES
IRREALITY
IRREGULAR
IRREGULARS
IRRELATED
IRRIGABLE
IRRIGATE
IRRIGATED
IRRIGATES
IRRIGATING
IRRIGATOR
IRRIGATORS
IRRIGUOUS
IRRISION
IRRISIONS
IRRISORY
IRRITABLE
IRRITABLY
IRRITANCIES
IRRITANCY
IRRITANT
IRRITANTS
IRRITATE
IRRITATED
IRRITATES
IRRITATING
IRRITATOR
IRRITATORS
IRRUPT
IRRUPTED
IRRUPTING
IRRUPTION
IRRUPTIONS
IRRUPTIVE
IRRUPTS
IS
ISABEL
ISABELLA
ISABELLAS
ISABELS
ISAGOGE
ISAGOGES
ISAGOGIC
ISAGOGICS
ISALLOBAR
ISALLOBARS
ISATIN
ISATINE
ISATINES
ISATINS
ISCHAEMIA
ISCHAEMIAS
ISCHAEMIC
ISCHEMIA
ISCHEMIAS
ISCHEMIC
ISCHIA
ISCHIADIC
ISCHIAL
ISCHIATIC
ISCHIUM
ISCHURIA
ISCHURIAS
ISENERGIC
ISH
ISHES
ISINGLASS
ISINGLASSES
ISLAND
ISLANDED
ISLANDER
ISLANDERS
ISLANDING
ISLANDS
ISLE
ISLED
ISLEMAN
ISLEMEN
ISLES
ISLESMAN
ISLESMEN
ISLET
ISLETS
ISLING
ISM
ISMATIC
ISMATICAL
ISMS
ISO
ISOBAR
ISOBARE
ISOBARES
ISOBARIC
ISOBARS
ISOBASE
ISOBASES
ISOBATH
ISOBATHIC
ISOBATHS
ISOBRONT
ISOBRONTS
ISOCHASM
ISOCHASMS
ISOCHEIM
ISOCHEIMS
ISOCHIMAL
ISOCHIMALS
ISOCHIME
ISOCHIMES
ISOCHOR
ISOCHORE
ISOCHORES
ISOCHORIC
ISOCHORS
ISOCHRONE
ISOCHRONES
ISOCLINAL
ISOCLINALS
ISOCLINE
ISOCLINES
ISOCLINIC
ISOCLINICS
ISOCRACIES
ISOCRACY
ISOCRATIC
ISOCRYMAL
ISOCRYMALS
ISOCRYME
ISOCRYMES
ISOCYCLIC
ISODICA
ISODICON
ISODOMA
ISODOMON
ISODOMONS
ISODOMOUS
ISODOMUM
ISODONT
ISODONTAL
ISODONTALS
ISODONTS
ISOETES
ISOGAMETE
ISOGAMETES
ISOGAMIC
ISOGAMIES
ISOGAMOUS
ISOGAMY
ISOGENIES
ISOGENOUS
ISOGENY
ISOGLOSS
ISOGLOSSES
ISOGON
ISOGONAL
ISOGONALS
ISOGONIC
ISOGONICS
ISOGONS
ISOGRAM
ISOGRAMS
ISOHEL
ISOHELS
ISOHYET
ISOHYETAL
ISOHYETALS
ISOHYETS
ISOKONT
ISOKONTAN

ISOKONTANS
ISOKONTS
ISOLABLE
ISOLATE
ISOLATED
ISOLATES
ISOLATING
ISOLATION
ISOLATIONS
ISOLATIVE
ISOLATOR
ISOLATORS
ISOLINE
ISOLINES
ISOLOGOUS
ISOLOGUE
ISOLOGUES
ISOMER
ISOMERASE
ISOMERASES
ISOMERE
ISOMERES
ISOMERIC
ISOMERISE
ISOMERISED
ISOMERISES
ISOMERISING
ISOMERISM
ISOMERISMS
ISOMERIZE
ISOMERIZED
ISOMERIZES
ISOMERIZING
ISOMEROUS
ISOMERS
ISOMETRIC
ISOMETRICS
ISOMETRIES
ISOMETRY
ISOMORPH
ISOMORPHS
ISONIAZID
ISONIAZIDS
ISONOMIC
ISONOMIES
ISONOMOUS
ISONOMY
ISOPLETH
ISOPLETHS
ISOPOD
ISOPODAN
ISOPODOUS
ISOPODS
ISOPOLITIES
ISOPOLITY
ISOPRENE
ISOPRENES
ISOPROPYL
ISOPROPYLS
ISOS
ISOSCELES
ISOSPIN
ISOSPINS
ISOSPORIES
ISOSPORY
ISOSTASIES
ISOSTASY
ISOSTATIC
ISOSTERIC
ISOTACTIC
ISOTHERAL
ISOTHERALS
ISOTHERE
ISOTHERES
ISOTHERM
ISOTHERMS
ISOTONE
ISOTONES
ISOTONIC
ISOTOPE
ISOTOPES
ISOTOPIC
ISOTOPIES
ISOTOPY
ISOTRON
ISOTRONS
ISOTROPIC
ISOTROPIES
ISOTROPY
ISOTYPE
ISOTYPES
ISSEI
ISSEIS
ISSUABLE
ISSUABLY
ISSUANCE
ISSUANCES
ISSUANT
ISSUE
ISSUED
ISSUELESS
ISSUER
ISSUERS
ISSUES
ISSUING
ISTHMIAN
ISTHMUS
ISTHMUSES
ISTLE
ISTLES
IT
ITA
ITACISM
ITACISMS
ITALIC
ITALICISE
ITALICISED
ITALICISES
ITALICISING
ITALICIZE
ITALICIZED
ITALICIZES
ITALICIZING
ITALICS
ITAS
ITCH
ITCHED
ITCHES
ITCHIER
ITCHIEST
ITCHINESS
ITCHINESSES
ITCHING
ITCHWEED
ITCHWEEDS
ITCHY
ITEM
ITEMED
ITEMING
ITEMISE
ITEMISED
ITEMISES
ITEMISING
ITEMIZE
ITEMIZED
ITEMIZES
ITEMIZING
ITEMS
ITERANCE
ITERANCES
ITERANT
ITERATE
ITERATED
ITERATES
ITERATING
ITERATION
ITERATIONS
ITERATIVE
ITERUM
ITINERACIES
ITINERACY
ITINERANT
ITINERANTS
ITINERARIES
ITINERARY
ITINERATE
ITINERATED
ITINERATES
ITINERATING
ITS
ITSELF
IURE
IVIED
IVIES
IVORIED
IVORIES
IVORIST
IVORISTS
IVORY
IVRESSE
IVRESSES
IVY
IWIS
IXIA
IXIAS
IXODIASES
IXODIASIS
IXTLE
IXTLES
IZARD
IZARDS
IZVESTIA
IZVESTIAS
IZVESTIYA
IZVESTIYAS
IZZARD
IZZARDS
IZZAT
IZZATS

J

AB
ABBED
ABBER
ABBERED
ABBERER
ABBERERS
ABBERING
ABBERINGS
ABBERS
ABBING
ABBLE
ABBLED
ABBLES
ABBLING
ABERS
ABIRU
ABIRUS
ABORANDI
ABORANDIS
ABOT
ABOTS
ABS
ACAMAR
ACAMARS
ACANA
ACANAS
ACARANDA
ACARANDAS
ACCHUS
ACCHUSES
ACENT
ACINTH
ACINTHS
ACK
ACKAL
ACKALLED
ACKALLING
ACKALS
ACKAROO
ACKAROOED
ACKAROOING
ACKAROOS
ACKASS
ACKASSES
ACKBOOT
ACKBOOTED
ACKBOOTING
ACKBOOTS
ACKDAW
ACKDAWS
ACKED
ACKEEN
ACKEENS
ACKEROO
JACKEROOED
JACKEROOING
JACKEROOS
JACKET
JACKETED
JACKETING
JACKETS
JACKING
JACKKNIFE
JACKKNIFED
JACKKNIFES
JACKKNIFING
JACKKNIVES
JACKMAN
JACKMEN
JACKPOT
JACKPOTS
JACKS
JACKSHAFT
JACKSHAFTS
JACKSIE
JACKSIES
JACKSMITH
JACKSMITHS
JACKSY
JACOBIN
JACOBINS
JACOBUS
JACOBUSES
JACONET
JACONETS
JACQUARD
JACQUARDS
JACTATION
JACTATIONS
JACULATE
JACULATED
JACULATES
JACULATING
JACULATOR
JACULATORS
JACUZZI
JACUZZIS
JADE
JADED
JADEDLY
JADEITE
JADEITES
JADERIES
JADERY
JADES
JADING
JADISH
JAEGER
JAEGERS
JAG
JAGER
JAGERS
JAGGED
JAGGEDER
JAGGEDEST
JAGGEDLY
JAGGER
JAGGERIES
JAGGERS
JAGGERY
JAGGIER
JAGGIEST
JAGGING
JAGGY
JAGHIR
JAGHIRDAR
JAGHIRDARS
JAGHIRE
JAGHIRES
JAGHIRS
JAGIR
JAGIRS
JAGS
JAGUAR
JAGUARS
JAIL
JAILED
JAILER
JAILERESS
JAILERESSES
JAILERS
JAILHOUSE
JAILHOUSES
JAILING
JAILOR
JAILORESS
JAILORESSES
JAILORS
JAILS
JAK
JAKE
JAKES
JAKESES
JAKS
JALAP
JALAPENO
JALAPENOS
JALAPIC
JALAPIN
JALAPINS
JALAPS
JALOPIES
JALOPPIES
JALOPPY
JALOPY
JALOUSE
JALOUSED
JALOUSES
JALOUSIE
JALOUSIED
JALOUSIES
JALOUSING
JAM
JAMADAR
JAMADARS
JAMB
JAMBALAYA
JAMBALAYAS
JAMBE
JAMBEAU
JAMBEAUX
JAMBEE
JAMBEES
JAMBER
JAMBERS
JAMBES
JAMBEUX
JAMBIER
JAMBIERS
JAMBIYA
JAMBIYAH
JAMBIYAHS
JAMBIYAS
JAMBO
JAMBOK
JAMBOKKED
JAMBOKKING
JAMBOKS
JAMBOLAN
JAMBOLANA
JAMBOLANAS
JAMBOLANS
JAMBONE
JAMBONES
JAMBOOL
JAMBOOLS
JAMBOREE
JAMBOREES
JAMBOS
JAMBS
JAMBU
JAMBUL
JAMBULS
JAMBUS
JAMDANI
JAMDANIS
JAMES
JAMESES
JAMJAR
JAMJARS
JAMMED
JAMMER
JAMMERS
JAMMIER
JAMMIEST
JAMMING
JAMMY
JAMPAN
JAMPANEE
JAMPANEES
JAMPANI
JAMPANIS
JAMPANS
JAMPOT
JAMPOTS
JAMS
JANDAL®
JANDALS
JANE
JANES
JANGLE
JANGLED
JANGLER
JANGLERS
JANGLES
JANGLIER
JANGLIEST
JANGLING
JANGLINGS
JANGLY
JANISSARIES
JANISSARY
JANITOR
JANITORS
JANITRESS
JANITRESSES
JANITRIX
JANITRIXES
JANIZAR
JANIZARIES
JANIZARS
JANIZARY
JANKER
JANKERS
JANN
JANNOCK
JANNOCKS
JANNS
JANSKY
JANSKYS

JANTEE
JANTIER
JANTIES
JANTIEST
JANTY
JAP
JAPAN
JAPANNED
JAPANNER
JAPANNERS
JAPANNING
JAPANS
JAPE
JAPED
JAPER
JAPERS
JAPES
JAPING
JAPINGS
JAPONICA
JAPONICAS
JAPPED
JAPPING
JAPS
JAR
JARARACA
JARARACAS
JARARAKA
JARARAKAS
JARFUL
JARFULS
JARGON
JARGONED
JARGONEER
JARGONEERS
JARGONING
JARGONISE
JARGONISED
JARGONISES
JARGONISING
JARGONIST
JARGONISTS
JARGONIZE
JARGONIZED
JARGONIZES
JARGONIZING
JARGONS
JARGOON
JARGOONS
JARK
JARKMAN
JARKMEN
JARKS
JARL
JARLS
JAROOL
JAROOLS
JAROSITE
JAROSITES
JARRAH
JARRAHS
JARRED
JARRING
JARRINGLY
JARRINGS
JARS
JARTA
JARTAS
JARUL
JARULS
JARVEY
JARVEYS
JARVIE
JARVIES
JASEY
JASEYS
JASIES
JASMINE
JASMINES
JASP
JASPE
JASPER
JASPERISE
JASPERISED
JASPERISES
JASPERISING
JASPERIZE
JASPERIZED
JASPERIZES
JASPERIZING
JASPEROUS
JASPERS
JASPERY
JASPES
JASPIDEAN
JASPIS
JASPISES
JASPS
JASS
JASSES
JASY
JATAKA
JATAKAS
JATO
JATOS
JAUNCE
JAUNCED
JAUNCES
JAUNCING
JAUNDICE
JAUNDICED
JAUNDICES
JAUNDICING
JAUNSE
JAUNSED
JAUNSES
JAUNSING
JAUNT
JAUNTED
JAUNTEE
JAUNTIE
JAUNTIER
JAUNTIES
JAUNTIEST
JAUNTILY
JAUNTING
JAUNTS
JAUNTY
JAUP
JAUPED
JAUPING
JAUPS
JAVEL
JAVELIN
JAVELINS
JAVELS
JAW
JAWAN
JAWANS
JAWARI
JAWARIS
JAWBATION
JAWBATIONS
JAWBONE
JAWBONED
JAWBONES
JAWBONING
JAWBONINGS
JAWBOX
JAWBOXES
JAWED
JAWFALL
JAWFALLS
JAWHOLE
JAWHOLES
JAWING
JAWINGS
JAWS
JAY
JAYS
JAYWALK
JAYWALKED
JAYWALKER
JAYWALKERS
JAYWALKING
JAYWALKINGS
JAYWALKS
JAZERANT
JAZERANTS
JAZIES
JAZY
JAZZ
JAZZED
JAZZER
JAZZERS
JAZZES
JAZZIER
JAZZIEST
JAZZILY
JAZZINESS
JAZZINESSES
JAZZING
JAZZMAN
JAZZMEN
JAZZY
JEALOUS
JEALOUSE
JEALOUSED
JEALOUSES
JEALOUSIES
JEALOUSING
JEALOUSLY
JEALOUSY
JEAN
JEANETTE
JEANETTES
JEANS
JEAT
JEATS
JEBEL
JEBELS
JEE
JEED
JEEING
JEEL
JEELED
JEELIE
JEELIED
JEELIEING
JEELIES
JEELING
JEELS
JEELY
JEELYING
JEEPERS
JEEPNEY
JEEPNEYS
JEER
JEERED
JEERER
JEERERS
JEERING
JEERINGLY
JEERINGS
JEERS
JEES
JEFF
JEFFED
JEFFING
JEFFS
JEHAD
JEHADS
JEJUNA
JEJUNE
JEJUNELY
JEJUNITIES
JEJUNITY
JEJUNUM
JELAB
JELABS
JELL
JELLABA
JELLABAS
JELLED
JELLIED
JELLIES
JELLIFIED
JELLIFIES
JELLIFORM
JELLIFY
JELLIFYING
JELLING
JELLO
JELLOS
JELLS
JELLY
JELLYBEAN
JELLYBEANS
JELLYFISH
JELLYFISHES
JELLYING
JELUTONG
JELUTONGS
JEMADAR
JEMADARS
JEMIDAR
JEMIDARS
JEMIMA
JEMIMAS
JEMMIED
JEMMIER
JEMMIES
JEMMIEST
JEMMINESS
JEMMINESSES
JEMMY
JEMMYING
JENNET
JENNETING
JENNETINGS
JENNETS
JENNIES
JENNY
JEOFAIL
JEOFAILS
JEOPARD
JEOPARDED
JEOPARDER
JEOPARDERS
JEOPARDIED
JEOPARDIES
JEOPARDING
JEOPARDS
JEOPARDY
JEOPARDYING
JEQUIRITIES
JEQUIRITY
JERBIL
JERBILS
JERBOA
JERBOAS
JEREED
JEREEDS
JEREMIAD
JEREMIADS
JERFALCON
JERFALCONS
JERID
JERIDS
JERK
JERKED
JERKER
JERKERS
JERKIER
JERKIES
JERKIEST
JERKIN
JERKINESS
JERKINESSES
JERKING

ERKINGS
ERKINS
ERKS
ERKWATER
ERKWATERS
ERKY
EROBOAM
EROBOAMS
ERQUE
ERQUED
ERQUER
ERQUERS
ERQUES
ERQUING
ERQUINGS
ERRICAN
ERRICANS
ERRIES
ERRY
ERRYCAN
ERRYCANS
ERSEY
ERSEYS
ESS
ESSAMIES
ESSAMINE
ESSAMINES
ESSAMY
ESSANT
ESSED
ESSERANT
ESSERANTS
ESSES
ESSIE
ESSIES
EST
ESTBOOK
ESTBOOKS
ESTED
ESTEE
ESTEES
ESTER
ESTERS
ESTFUL
ESTING
ESTINGLY
ESTINGS
ESTS
ESUS
ET
ETE
ETES
ETFOIL
ETFOILS
ETLINER
ETLINERS
ETON
ETONS
ETPLANE
ETPLANES
ETS
ETSAM
ETSAMS
ETSOM
JETSOMS
JETSON
JETSONS
JETSTREAM
JETSTREAMS
JETTATURA
JETTATURAS
JETTED
JETTIED
JETTIER
JETTIES
JETTIEST
JETTINESS
JETTINESSES
JETTING
JETTISON
JETTISONED
JETTISONING
JETTISONS
JETTON
JETTONS
JETTY
JETTYING
JEU
JEUNE
JEUX
JEW
JEWED
JEWEL
JEWELFISH
JEWELFISHES
JEWELLED
JEWELLER
JEWELLERIES
JEWELLERS
JEWELLERY
JEWELLING
JEWELRIES
JEWELRY
JEWELS
JEWFISH
JEWFISHES
JEWING
JEWS
JEZAIL
JEZAILS
JHALA
JHALAS
JIAO
JIAOS
JIB
JIBBAH
JIBBAHS
JIBBED
JIBBER
JIBBERED
JIBBERING
JIBBERS
JIBBING
JIBBINGS
JIBE
JIBED
JIBER
JIBERS
JIBES
JIBING
JIBS
JICKAJOG
JICKAJOGGED
JICKAJOGGING
JICKAJOGS
JIFF
JIFFIES
JIFFS
JIFFY
JIG
JIGAJIG
JIGAJIGGED
JIGAJIGGING
JIGAJIGS
JIGAJOG
JIGAJOGGED
JIGAJOGGING
JIGAJOGS
JIGAMAREE
JIGAMAREES
JIGGED
JIGGER
JIGGERED
JIGGERING
JIGGERS
JIGGING
JIGGINGS
JIGGISH
JIGGLE
JIGGLED
JIGGLES
JIGGLIER
JIGGLIEST
JIGGLING
JIGGLY
JIGGUMBOB
JIGGUMBOBS
JIGJIG
JIGJIGGED
JIGJIGGING
JIGJIGS
JIGOT
JIGOTS
JIGS
JIGSAW
JIGSAWED
JIGSAWING
JIGSAWS
JIHAD
JIHADS
JILGIE
JILGIES
JILL
JILLAROO
JILLAROOS
JILLET
JILLETS
JILLFLIRT
JILLFLIRTS
JILLION
JILLIONS
JILLS
JILT
JILTED
JILTING
JILTS
JIMCRACK
JIMCRACKS
JIMINY
JIMJAM
JIMJAMS
JIMMIED
JIMMIES
JIMMY
JIMMYING
JIMP
JIMPER
JIMPEST
JIMPIER
JIMPIEST
JIMPLY
JIMPNESS
JIMPNESSES
JIMPY
JINGAL
JINGALS
JINGBANG
JINGBANGS
JINGLE
JINGLED
JINGLER
JINGLERS
JINGLES
JINGLET
JINGLETS
JINGLIER
JINGLIEST
JINGLING
JINGLY
JINGO
JINGOES
JINGOISH
JINGOISM
JINGOISMS
JINGOIST
JINGOISTS
JINJILI
JINJILIS
JINK
JINKED
JINKER
JINKERS
JINKING
JINKS
JINN
JINNEE
JINNI
JINNS
JINX
JINXED
JINXES
JINXING
JIPYAPA
JIPYAPAS
JIRBLE
JIRBLED
JIRBLES
JIRBLING
JIRD
JIRDS
JIRGA
JIRGAS
JIRKINET
JIRKINETS
JISM
JISMS
JISSOM
JISSOMS
JITNEY
JITNEYS
JITTER
JITTERBUG
JITTERBUGGED
JITTERBUGGING
JITTERBUGS
JITTERED
JITTERIER
JITTERIEST
JITTERING
JITTERS
JITTERY
JIVE
JIVED
JIVER
JIVERS
JIVES
JIVING
JIZ
JIZZ
JIZZES
JNANA
JNANAS
JO
JOANNA
JOANNAS
JOANNES
JOANNESES
JOB
JOBATION
JOBATIONS
JOBBED
JOBBER
JOBBERIES
JOBBERS
JOBBERY
JOBBIE
JOBBIES
JOBBING
JOBBINGS
JOBCENTRE
JOBCENTRES
JOBE
JOBED
JOBERNOWL
JOBERNOWLS
JOBES
JOBING
JOBLESS
JOBS
JOBSHARE

JOBSHARES
JOBSWORTH
JOBSWORTHS
JOCK
JOCKETTE
JOCKETTES
JOCKEY
JOCKEYED
JOCKEYING
JOCKEYISM
JOCKEYISMS
JOCKEYS
JOCKNEY
JOCKNEYS
JOCKO
JOCKOS
JOCKS
JOCKSTRAP
JOCKSTRAPS
JOCKTELEG
JOCKTELEGS
JOCO
JOCOSE
JOCOSELY
JOCOSITIES
JOCOSITY
JOCULAR
JOCULARLY
JOCULATOR
JOCULATORS
JOCUND
JOCUNDITIES
JOCUNDITY
JOCUNDLY
JODEL
JODELLED
JODELLING
JODELS
JODHPURS
JOE
JOES
JOEY
JOEYS
JOG
JOGGED
JOGGER
JOGGERS
JOGGING
JOGGINGS
JOGGLE
JOGGLED
JOGGLES
JOGGLING
JOGPANTS
JOGS
JOGTROT
JOGTROTS
JOHANNES
JOHANNESES
JOHN
JOHNNIE
JOHNNIES
JOHNNY
JOHNS
JOIN
JOINDER
JOINDERS
JOINED
JOINER
JOINERIES
JOINERS
JOINERY
JOINING
JOININGS
JOINS
JOINT
JOINTED
JOINTER
JOINTERS
JOINTING
JOINTLESS
JOINTLY
JOINTNESS
JOINTNESSES
JOINTRESS
JOINTRESSES
JOINTS
JOINTURE
JOINTURED
JOINTURES
JOINTURING
JOINTWORM
JOINTWORMS
JOIST
JOISTED
JOISTING
JOISTS
JOJOBA
JOJOBAS
JOKE
JOKED
JOKER
JOKERS
JOKES
JOKESMITH
JOKESMITHS
JOKESOME
JOKEY
JOKIER
JOKIEST
JOKING
JOKINGLY
JOKOL
JOKY
JOLE
JOLED
JOLES
JOLING
JOLL
JOLLED
JOLLEY
JOLLEYER
JOLLEYERS
JOLLEYING
JOLLEYINGS
JOLLEYS
JOLLIED
JOLLIER
JOLLIES
JOLLIEST
JOLLIFIED
JOLLIFIES
JOLLIFY
JOLLIFYING
JOLLILY
JOLLIMENT
JOLLIMENTS
JOLLINESS
JOLLINESSES
JOLLING
JOLLITIES
JOLLITY
JOLLS
JOLLY
JOLLYBOAT
JOLLYBOATS
JOLLYER
JOLLYERS
JOLLYHEAD
JOLLYHEADS
JOLLYING
JOLLYINGS
JOLT
JOLTED
JOLTER
JOLTERS
JOLTHEAD
JOLTHEADS
JOLTIER
JOLTIEST
JOLTING
JOLTINGLY
JOLTS
JOLTY
JOMO
JOMOS
JONCANOE
JONCANOES
JONGLEUR
JONGLEURS
JONQUIL
JONQUILS
JONTIES
JONTY
JOOK
JOOKED
JOOKERIES
JOOKERY
JOOKING
JOOKS
JOR
JORAM
JORAMS
JORDAN
JORDANS
JORDELOO
JORDELOOS
JORS
JORUM
JORUMS
JOSEPH
JOSEPHS
JOSH
JOSHED
JOSHER
JOSHERS
JOSHES
JOSHING
JOSKIN
JOSKINS
JOSS
JOSSER
JOSSERS
JOSSES
JOSTLE
JOSTLED
JOSTLES
JOSTLING
JOSTLINGS
JOT
JOTA
JOTAS
JOTS
JOTTED
JOTTER
JOTTERS
JOTTING
JOTTINGS
JOTUN
JOTUNN
JOTUNNS
JOTUNS
JOUAL
JOUALS
JOUGS
JOUISANCE
JOUISANCES
JOUK
JOUKED
JOUKERIES
JOUKERY
JOUKING
JOUKS
JOULE
JOULED
JOULES
JOULING
JOUNCE
JOUNCED
JOUNCES
JOUNCING
JOUR
JOURNAL
JOURNALLED
JOURNALLING
JOURNALS
JOURNEY
JOURNEYED
JOURNEYER
JOURNEYERS
JOURNEYING
JOURNEYS
JOURNO
JOURNOS
JOURS
JOUST
JOUSTED
JOUSTER
JOUSTERS
JOUSTING
JOUSTS
JOVIAL
JOVIALITIES
JOVIALITY
JOVIALLY
JOW
JOWAR
JOWARI
JOWARIS
JOWARS
JOWED
JOWING
JOWL
JOWLED
JOWLER
JOWLERS
JOWLIER
JOWLIEST
JOWLING
JOWLS
JOWLY
JOWS
JOY
JOYANCE
JOYANCES
JOYED
JOYFUL
JOYFULLER
JOYFULLEST
JOYFULLY
JOYING
JOYLESS
JOYLESSLY
JOYOUS
JOYOUSLY
JOYS
JUBA
JUBAS
JUBATE
JUBBAH
JUBBAHS
JUBE
JUBES
JUBILANCE
JUBILANCES
JUBILANCIES
JUBILANCY
JUBILANT
JUBILATE
JUBILATED
JUBILATES
JUBILATING
JUBILEE
JUBILEES
JUD
JUDAS
JUDASES
JUDDER
JUDDERED
JUDDERING

DDERS
DGE
DGED
DGEMENT
DGEMENTS
DGES
DGESHIP
DGESHIPS
DGING
DGMENT
DGMENTS
DICABLE
DICATOR
DICATORS
DICIAL
DICIARIES
DICIARY
DICIOUS
DIES
DO
DOGI
DOGIS
DOIST
DOISTS
DOKA
DOKAS
DOS
DS
DY
G
GA
GAL
GALS
GATE
GFUL
GFULS
GGED
GGING
GGINGS
GGINS
GGINSES
GGLE
GGLED
GGLER
GGLERIES
GGLERS
GGLERY
GGLES
GGLING
GGLINGS
GHEAD
GHEADS
GLET
GLETS
GS
JUGULAR
JUGULARS
JUGULATE
JUGULATED
JUGULATES
JUGULATING
JUGUM
JUICE
JUICED
JUICELESS
JUICER
JUICERS
JUICES
JUICIER
JUICIEST
JUICINESS
JUICINESSES
JUICING
JUICY
JUJU
JUJUBE
JUJUBES
JUJUS
JUKE
JUKED
JUKES
JUKING
JUKSKEI
JUKSKEIS
JULEP
JULEPS
JULIENNE
JULIENNED
JULIENNES
JULIENNING
JUMAR
JUMARRED
JUMARRING
JUMARS
JUMART
JUMARTS
JUMBAL
JUMBALS
JUMBIE
JUMBIES
JUMBLE
JUMBLED
JUMBLER
JUMBLERS
JUMBLES
JUMBLIER
JUMBLIEST
JUMBLING
JUMBLY
JUMBO
JUMBOISE
JUMBOISED
JUMBOISES
JUMBOISING
JUMBOIZE
JUMBOIZED
JUMBOIZES
JUMBOIZING
JUMBOS
JUMBUCK
JUMBUCKS
JUMBY
JUMELLE
JUMELLES
JUMP
JUMPABLE
JUMPED
JUMPER
JUMPERS
JUMPIER
JUMPIEST
JUMPILY
JUMPINESS
JUMPINESSES
JUMPING
JUMPS
JUMPY
JUNCATE
JUNCATES
JUNCO
JUNCOES
JUNCOS
JUNCTION
JUNCTIONS
JUNCTURE
JUNCTURES
JUNCUS
JUNCUSES
JUNEATING
JUNEATINGS
JUNGLE
JUNGLES
JUNGLI
JUNGLIER
JUNGLIEST
JUNGLIS
JUNGLIST
JUNGLISTS
JUNGLY
JUNIOR
JUNIORITIES
JUNIORITY
JUNIORS
JUNIPER
JUNIPERS
JUNK
JUNKANOO
JUNKANOOS
JUNKED
JUNKER
JUNKERS
JUNKET
JUNKETED
JUNKETEER
JUNKETEERS
JUNKETING
JUNKETINGS
JUNKETS
JUNKIE
JUNKIER
JUNKIES
JUNKIEST
JUNKINESS
JUNKINESSES
JUNKING
JUNKMAN
JUNKMEN
JUNKS
JUNKY
JUNTA
JUNTAS
JUNTO
JUNTOS
JUPATI
JUPATIS
JUPON
JUPONS
JURA
JURAL
JURALLY
JURANT
JURANTS
JURAT
JURATORY
JURATS
JURE
JURIDIC
JURIDICAL
JURIES
JURIST
JURISTIC
JURISTS
JUROR
JURORS
JURY
JURYMAN
JURYMAST
JURYMASTS
JURYMEN
JURYWOMAN
JURYWOMEN
JUS
JUSSIVE
JUSSIVES
JUST
JUSTED
JUSTER
JUSTEST
JUSTICE
JUSTICER
JUSTICERS
JUSTICES
JUSTICIAR
JUSTICIARS
JUSTIFIED
JUSTIFIER
JUSTIFIERS
JUSTIFIES
JUSTIFY
JUSTIFYING
JUSTING
JUSTLE
JUSTLED
JUSTLES
JUSTLING
JUSTLY
JUSTNESS
JUSTNESSES
JUSTS
JUT
JUTE
JUTES
JUTS
JUTTED
JUTTIED
JUTTIES
JUTTING
JUTTINGLY
JUTTY
JUTTYING
JUVE
JUVENAL
JUVENALS
JUVENILE
JUVENILES
JUVENILIA
JUVES
JUXTAPOSE
JUXTAPOSED
JUXTAPOSES
JUXTAPOSING
JYMOLD
JYNX
JYNXES

K

KA
KAAMA
KAAMAS
KABAB
KABABBED
KABABBING
KABABS
KABADDI
KABADDIS
KABALA
KABALAS
KABAYA
KABAYAS
KABBALA
KABBALAH
KABBALAHS
KABBALAS
KABELE
KABELES
KABELJOU
KABELJOUS
KABELJOUW
KABELJOUWS
KABOB
KABOBBED
KABOBBING
KABOBS
KABUKI
KABUKIS
KACCHA
KACCHAS
KACHA
KACHAHRI
KACHAHRIS
KACHCHA
KACHERI
KACHERIS
KACHINA
KACHINAS
KADE
KADES
KADI
KADIS
KAE
KAED
KAEING
KAES
KAFFIYEH
KAFFIYEHS
KAFILA
KAFILAS
KAFTAN
KAFTANS
KAGO
KAGOOL
KAGOOLS
KAGOS
KAGOUL
KAGOULE
KAGOULES
KAGOULS
KAHAL
KAHALS
KAHAWAI
KAHAWAIS
KAI
KAIAK
KAIAKED
KAIAKING
KAIAKS
KAID
KAIDS
KAIE
KAIES
KAIF
KAIFS
KAIKAI
KAIKAIS
KAIL
KAILS
KAILYAIRD
KAILYAIRDS
KAILYARD
KAILYARDS
KAIM
KAIMAKAM
KAIMAKAMS
KAIMS
KAIN
KAING
KAINITE
KAINITES
KAINS
KAIS
KAISER
KAISERDOM
KAISERDOMS
KAISERIN
KAISERINS
KAISERISM
KAISERISMS
KAISERS
KAIZEN
KAIZENS
KAJAWAH
KAJAWAHS
KAKA
KAKAPO
KAKAPOS
KAKAS
KAKEMONO
KAKEMONOS
KAKI
KAKIEMON
KAKIEMONS
KAKIS
KAKODYL
KAKODYLS
KALAMDAN
KALAMDANS
KALAMKARI
KALAMKARIS
KALANCHOE
KALANCHOES
KALE
KALENDAR
KALENDARED
KALENDARING
KALENDARS
KALENDS
KALES
KALI
KALIAN
KALIANS
KALIF
KALIFS
KALINITE
KALINITES
KALIS
KALIUM
KALIUMS
KALLITYPE
KALLITYPES
KALMIA
KALMIAS
KALONG
KALONGS
KALOTYPE
KALOTYPES
KALPA
KALPAK
KALPAKS
KALPAS
KALPIS
KALPISES
KALSOMINE®
KALSOMINED
KALSOMINES
KALSOMINING
KALUMPIT
KALUMPITS
KALYPTRA
KALYPTRAS
KAM
KAMA
KAMACITE
KAMACITES
KAMALA
KAMALAS
KAMAS
KAME
KAMEES
KAMEESES
KAMEEZ
KAMEEZES
KAMELA
KAMELAS
KAMERAD
KAMERADED
KAMERADING
KAMERADS
KAMES
KAMI
KAMICHI
KAMICHIS
KAMIK
KAMIKAZE
KAMIKAZES
KAMIKS
KAMILA
KAMILAS
KAMIS
KAMISES
KAMME
KAMPONG
KAMPONGS
KAMSEEN
KAMSEENS
KAMSIN
KAMSINS
KANA
KANAKA
KANAKAS
KANAS
KANDIES
KANDY
KANEH
KANEHS
KANG
KANGA
KANGAROO
KANGAROOED
KANGAROOING
KANGAROOS
KANGAS
KANGHA
KANGHAS
KANGS
KANJI
KANJIS
KANS
KANSES
KANT
KANTAR
KANTARS
KANTED
KANTELA
KANTELAS
KANTELE
KANTELES
KANTEN
KANTENS
KANTHA
KANTHAS
KANTIKOY
KANTIKOYED
KANTIKOYING
KANTIKOYS
KANTING
KANTS
KANZU
KANZUS
KAOLIANG
KAOLIANGS
KAOLIN
KAOLINE
KAOLINES
KAOLINISE
KAOLINISED
KAOLINISES
KAOLINISING
KAOLINITE
KAOLINITES
KAOLINIZE
KAOLINIZED
KAOLINIZES
KAOLINIZING
KAOLINS
KAON
KAONS
KAPOK
KAPOKS
KAPPA
KAPPAS
KAPUT
KAPUTT
KARA
KARABINER
KARABINERS
KARAISM

KARAISMS
KARAIT
KARAITS
KARAKA
KARAKAS
KARAKUL
KARAKULS
KARAOKE
KARAOKES
KARAS
KARAT
KARATE
KARATEIST
KARATEISTS
KARATEKA
KARATEKAS
KARATES
KARATS
KARITE
KARITES
KARK
KARKED
KARKING
KARKS
KARMA
KARMAS
KARMIC
KAROSS
KAROSSES
KARRI
KARRIS
KARSEY
KARSEYS
KARSIES
KARST
KARSTIC
KARSTIFIED
KARSTIFIES
KARSTIFY
KARSTIFYING
KARSTS
KARSY
KART
KARTER
KARTERS
KARTING
KARTINGS
KARTS
KARYOGAMIES
KARYOGAMY
KARYOGRAM
KARYOGRAMS
KARYOLOGIES
KARYOLOGY
KARYON
KARYONS
KARYOSOME
KARYOSOMES
KARYOTIN
KARYOTINS
KARYOTYPE
KARYOTYPED
KARYOTYPES
KARYOTYPING
KARZIES
KARZY
KAS
KASBAH
KASBAHS
KASHA
KASHAS
KASHMIR
KASHMIRS
KASHRUS
KASHRUSES
KASHRUT
KASHRUTH
KASHRUTHS
KASHRUTS
KAT
KATA
KATABASES
KATABASIS
KATABATIC
KATAKANA
KATAKANAS
KATANA
KATANAS
KATAS
KATHAK
KATHAKALI
KATHAKALIS
KATHAKS
KATHARSES
KATHARSIS
KATHODE
KATHODES
KATI
KATION
KATIONS
KATIPO
KATIPOS
KATIS
KATORGA
KATORGAS
KATS
KATTI
KATTIS
KATYDID
KATYDIDS
KAUGH
KAUGHS
KAURI
KAURIS
KAVA
KAVAS
KAVASS
KAVASSES
KAW
KAWED
KAWING
KAWS
KAY
KAYAK
KAYAKED
KAYAKING
KAYAKS
KAYLE
KAYLES
KAYO
KAYOED
KAYOES
KAYOING
KAYOINGS
KAYOS
KAYS
KAZATZKA
KAZATZKAS
KAZI
KAZIS
KAZOO
KAZOOS
KEA
KEAS
KEASAR
KEASARS
KEAVIE
KEAVIES
KEB
KEBAB
KEBABBED
KEBABBING
KEBABS
KEBBED
KEBBIE
KEBBIES
KEBBING
KEBBOCK
KEBBOCKS
KEBBUCK
KEBBUCKS
KEBELE
KEBELES
KEBLAH
KEBLAHS
KEBOB
KEBOBBED
KEBOBBING
KEBOBS
KEBS
KECK
KECKED
KECKING
KECKLE
KECKLED
KECKLES
KECKLING
KECKLINGS
KECKS
KECKSES
KECKSIES
KECKSY
KED
KEDDAH
KEDDAHS
KEDGE
KEDGED
KEDGER
KEDGEREE
KEDGEREES
KEDGERS
KEDGES
KEDGIER
KEDGIEST
KEDGING
KEDGY
KEDS
KEECH
KEECHES
KEEK
KEEKED
KEEKER
KEEKERS
KEEKING
KEEKS
KEEL
KEELAGE
KEELAGES
KEELBOAT
KEELBOATS
KEELED
KEELER
KEELERS
KEELHAUL
KEELHAULED
KEELHAULING
KEELHAULINGS
KEELHAULS
KEELIE
KEELIES
KEELING
KEELINGS
KEELIVINE
KEELIVINES
KEELMAN
KEELMEN
KEELS
KEELSON
KEELSONS
KEELYVINE
KEELYVINES
KEEN
KEENED
KEENER
KEENERS
KEENEST
KEENING
KEENINGS
KEENLY
KEENNESS
KEENNESSES
KEENS
KEEP
KEEPER
KEEPERS
KEEPING
KEEPINGS
KEEPNET
KEEPNETS
KEEPS
KEEPSAKE
KEEPSAKES
KEEPSAKY
KEESHOND
KEESHONDEN
KEESHONDS
KEEVE
KEEVES
KEF
KEFFEL
KEFFELS
KEFFIYEH
KEFFIYEHS
KEFIR
KEFIRS
KEFS
KEFUFFLE
KEFUFFLED
KEFUFFLES
KEFUFFLING
KEG
KEGS
KEIGHT
KEIR
KEIRS
KEISTER
KEISTERS
KEITLOA
KEITLOAS
KEKS
KEKSYE
KEKSYES
KELIM
KELIMS
KELL
KELLAUT
KELLAUTS
KELLIES
KELLS
KELLY
KELOID
KELOIDAL
KELOIDS
KELP
KELPER
KELPERS
KELPIE
KELPIES
KELPS
KELPY
KELSON
KELSONS
KELT
KELTER
KELTERS
KELTIE
KELTIES
KELTS
KELTY
KELVIN
KELVINS
KEMB
KEMBED
KEMBING
KEMBO
KEMBOED
KEMBOING
KEMBOS
KEMBS
KEMP

KEMPED
KEMPER
KEMPERS
KEMPING
KEMPINGS
KEMPLE
KEMPLES
KEMPS
KEMPT
KEN
KENAF
KENAFS
KENDO
KENDOS
KENNED
KENNEL
KENNELLED
KENNELLING
KENNELS
KENNER
KENNERS
KENNET
KENNETS
KENNING
KENNINGS
KENO
KENOS
KENOSES
KENOSIS
KENOTIC
KENS
KENSPECK
KENT
KENTED
KENTIA
KENTIAS
KENTING
KENTLEDGE
KENTLEDGES
KENTS
KEP
KEPHALIC
KEPHALICS
KEPHALIN
KEPHALINS
KEPHIR
KEPHIRS
KEPI
KEPIS
KEPPING
KEPPIT
KEPS
KEPT
KERAMIC
KERAMICS
KERATIN
KERATINS
KERATITIS
KERATITISES
KERATOID
KERATOSE
KERATOSES
KERATOSIS
KERB
KERBS
KERBSIDE
KERBSIDES
KERBSTONE
KERBSTONES
KERCHIEF
KERCHIEFED
KERCHIEFING
KERCHIEFS
KERF
KERFS
KERFUFFLE
KERFUFFLED
KERFUFFLES
KERFUFFLING
KERMES
KERMESITE
KERMESITES
KERMESSE
KERMESSES
KERMIS
KERMISES
KERN
KERNE
KERNED
KERNEL
KERNELLED
KERNELLING
KERNELLY
KERNELS
KERNES
KERNING
KERNINGS
KERNISH
KERNITE
KERNITES
KERNS
KEROGEN
KEROGENS
KEROSENE
KEROSENES
KEROSINE
KEROSINES
KERRIA
KERRIAS
KERSEY
KERSEYS
KERVE
KERVED
KERVES
KERVING
KERYGMA
KERYGMAS
KERYGMATA
KESAR
KESARS
KESH
KESHES
KEST
KESTING
KESTREL
KESTRELS
KESTS
KET
KETA
KETAMINE
KETAMINES
KETAS
KETCH
KETCHES
KETCHING
KETCHUP
KETCHUPS
KETONE
KETONES
KETONURIA
KETONURIAS
KETOSE
KETOSES
KETOSIS
KETS
KETTLE
KETTLEFUL
KETTLEFULS
KETTLES
KEVEL
KEVELS
KEX
KEXES
KEY
KEYBOARD
KEYBOARDED
KEYBOARDING
KEYBOARDS
KEYBUGLE
KEYBUGLES
KEYED
KEYHOLE
KEYHOLES
KEYING
KEYLESS
KEYLINE
KEYLINES
KEYNOTE
KEYNOTED
KEYNOTES
KEYNOTING
KEYPAD
KEYPADS
KEYPUNCH
KEYPUNCHED
KEYPUNCHES
KEYPUNCHING
KEYS
KEYSTONE
KEYSTONED
KEYSTONES
KEYSTONING
KEYSTROKE
KEYSTROKES
KEYWORD
KEYWORDS
KGOTLA
KGOTLAS
KHADDAR
KHADDARS
KHADI
KHADIS
KHAKI
KHAKIS
KHALAT
KHALATS
KHALIF
KHALIFA
KHALIFAH
KHALIFAHS
KHALIFAS
KHALIFAT
KHALIFATE
KHALIFATES
KHALIFATS
KHALIFS
KHAMSIN
KHAMSINS
KHAN
KHANATE
KHANATES
KHANGA
KHANGAS
KHANJAR
KHANJARS
KHANS
KHANSAMA
KHANSAMAH
KHANSAMAHS
KHANSAMAS
KHANUM
KHANUMS
KHARIF
KHARIFS
KHAT
KHATS
KHAYA
KHAYAS
KHEDA
KHEDAS
KHEDIVA
KHEDIVAL
KHEDIVAS
KHEDIVATE
KHEDIVATES
KHEDIVE
KHEDIVES
KHEDIVIAL
KHILAFAT
KHILAFATS
KHILAT
KHILATS
KHILIM
KHILIMS
KHODJA
KHODJAS
KHOJA
KHOJAS
KHOR
KHORS
KHOTBAH
KHOTBAHS
KHOTBEH
KHOTBEHS
KHUD
KHUDS
KHURTA
KHURTAS
KHUSKHUS
KHUSKHUSES
KHUTBAH
KHUTBAHS
KIANG
KIANGS
KIAUGH
KIAUGHS
KIBBLE
KIBBLED
KIBBLES
KIBBLING
KIBBUTZ
KIBBUTZIM
KIBE
KIBES
KIBITKA
KIBITKAS
KIBITZ
KIBITZED
KIBITZER
KIBITZERS
KIBITZES
KIBITZING
KIBLAH
KIBLAHS
KIBOSH
KIBOSHED
KIBOSHES
KIBOSHING
KICK
KICKABLE
KICKBACK
KICKBACKS
KICKBALL
KICKBALLS
KICKDOWN
KICKDOWNS
KICKED
KICKER
KICKERS
KICKING
KICKS
KICKSHAW
KICKSHAWS
KICKSHAWSES
KICKSTAND
KICKSTANDS
KID
KIDDED
KIDDER
KIDDERS
KIDDIED
KIDDIER
KIDDIERS
KIDDIES
KIDDING
KIDDLE
KIDDLES
KIDDO
KIDDOS
KIDDUSH

IDDUSHES
IDDY
IDDYING
IDDYWINK
IDDYWINKS
IDEL
IDELS
IDGE
IDGIE
IDGIER
IDGIEST
IDLET
IDLETS
IDLING
IDLINGS
IDNAP
IDNAPPED
IDNAPPER
IDNAPPERS
IDNAPPING
IDNAPS
IDNEY
IDNEYS
IDOLOGIES
IDOLOGY
IDS
IDSKIN
IDSKINS
IDSTAKES
IDULT
IDULTS
IDVID
IDVIDS
IER
IERIE
IERIES
IERS
IESERITE
IESERITES
IEVE
IEVES
IF
IFS
IGHT
IGHTS
IKE
IKES
IKOI
IKOIS
IKUMON
IKUMONS
IKUYU
IKUYUS
ILD
ILDERKIN
ILDERKINS
ILERG
ILERGS
ILEY
ILEYS
ILIM
ILIMS
ILL
ILLADAR
KILLADARS
KILLAS
KILLASES
KILLCOW
KILLCOWS
KILLCROP
KILLCROPS
KILLDEE
KILLDEER
KILLDEERS
KILLDEES
KILLED
KILLER
KILLERS
KILLICK
KILLICKS
KILLIFISH
KILLIFISHES
KILLING
KILLINGS
KILLJOY
KILLJOYS
KILLOCK
KILLOCKS
KILLOGIE
KILLOGIES
KILLS
KILLUT
KILLUTS
KILN
KILNED
KILNING
KILNS
KILO
KILOBAR
KILOBARS
KILOBIT
KILOBITS
KILOBYTE
KILOBYTES
KILOCYCLE
KILOCYCLES
KILOGRAM
KILOGRAMS
KILOGRAY
KILOGRAYS
KILOHERTZ
KILOHERTZES
KILOJOULE
KILOJOULES
KILOMETRE
KILOMETRES
KILOS
KILOTON
KILOTONS
KILOVOLT
KILOVOLTS
KILOWATT
KILOWATTS
KILP
KILPS
KILT
KILTED
KILTER
KILTERS
KILTIE
KILTIES
KILTING
KILTS
KILTY
KIMBO
KIMBOED
KIMBOING
KIMBOS
KIMCHI
KIMCHIS
KIMMER
KIMMERS
KIMONO
KIMONOS
KIN
KINA
KINAKINA
KINAKINAS
KINAS
KINASE
KINASES
KINCHIN
KINCHINS
KINCOB
KINCOBS
KIND
KINDA
KINDED
KINDER
KINDERS
KINDEST
KINDIES
KINDING
KINDLE
KINDLED
KINDLER
KINDLERS
KINDLES
KINDLESS
KINDLIER
KINDLIEST
KINDLILY
KINDLING
KINDLINGS
KINDLY
KINDNESS
KINDNESSES
KINDRED
KINDREDS
KINDS
KINDY
KINE
KINEMA
KINEMAS
KINEMATIC
KINEMATICS
KINESCOPE
KINESCOPES
KINESES
KINESICS
KINESIS
KINETIC
KINETICAL
KINETICS
KINFOLK
KINFOLKS
KING
KINGCRAFT
KINGCRAFTS
KINGCUP
KINGCUPS
KINGDOM
KINGDOMED
KINGDOMS
KINGED
KINGFISH
KINGFISHES
KINGHOOD
KINGHOODS
KINGING
KINGKLIP
KINGKLIPS
KINGLE
KINGLES
KINGLESS
KINGLET
KINGLETS
KINGLIER
KINGLIEST
KINGLING
KINGLINGS
KINGLY
KINGMAKER
KINGMAKERS
KINGPOST
KINGPOSTS
KINGS
KINGSHIP
KINGSHIPS
KINGWOOD
KINGWOODS
KININ
KININS
KINK
KINKAJOU
KINKAJOUS
KINKED
KINKIER
KINKIEST
KINKILY
KINKING
KINKLE
KINKLES
KINKS
KINKY
KINLESS
KINO
KINONE
KINONES
KINOS
KINRED
KINREDS
KINS
KINSFOLK
KINSFOLKS
KINSHIP
KINSHIPS
KINSMAN
KINSMEN
KINSWOMAN
KINSWOMEN
KINTLEDGE
KINTLEDGES
KIOSK
KIOSKS
KIP
KIPE
KIPES
KIPP
KIPPA
KIPPAGE
KIPPAGES
KIPPAS
KIPPED
KIPPER
KIPPERED
KIPPERER
KIPPERERS
KIPPERING
KIPPERS
KIPPING
KIPPS
KIPS
KIR
KIRBEH
KIRBEHS
KIRBIGRIP
KIRBIGRIPS
KIRIMON
KIRIMONS
KIRK
KIRKED
KIRKING
KIRKINGS
KIRKS
KIRKTON
KIRKTONS
KIRKWARD
KIRKYAIRD
KIRKYAIRDS
KIRKYARD
KIRKYARDS
KIRMESS
KIRMESSES
KIRN
KIRNS
KIRPAN
KIRPANS
KIRRI
KIRRIS
KIRS
KIRSCH
KIRSCHES
KIRTLE
KIRTLED
KIRTLES
KISAN
KISANS
KISH
KISHES

KISHKE
KISHKES
KISMET
KISMETS
KISS
KISSABLE
KISSAGRAM
KISSAGRAMS
KISSED
KISSEL
KISSELS
KISSER
KISSERS
KISSES
KISSING
KISSOGRAM
KISSOGRAMS
KIST
KISTED
KISTING
KISTS
KISTVAEN
KISTVAENS
KIT
KITCHEN
KITCHENED
KITCHENER
KITCHENERS
KITCHENING
KITCHENS
KITE
KITED
KITENGE
KITENGES
KITES
KITH
KITHARA
KITHARAS
KITHE
KITHED
KITHES
KITHING
KITHS
KITING
KITINGS
KITLING
KITLINGS
KITS
KITSCH
KITSCHES
KITSCHIER
KITSCHIEST
KITSCHILY
KITSCHY
KITTED
KITTEN
KITTENED
KITTENING
KITTENISH
KITTENS
KITTENY
KITTIES
KITTING
KITTIWAKE
KITTIWAKES
KITTLE
KITTLED
KITTLER
KITTLES
KITTLEST
KITTLIER
KITTLIEST
KITTLING
KITTLY
KITTUL
KITTULS
KITTY
KIVA
KIVAS
KIWI
KIWIS
KLANG
KLANGS
KLATCH
KLATCHES
KLATSCH
KLATSCHES
KLAVIER
KLAVIERS
KLAXON
KLAXONED
KLAXONING
KLAXONS
KLENDUSIC
KLEPHT
KLEPHTIC
KLEPHTISM
KLEPHTISMS
KLEPHTS
KLEZMER
KLEZMORIM
KLINKER
KLINKERS
KLINOSTAT
KLINOSTATS
KLIPDAS
KLIPDASES
KLONDIKE
KLONDIKED
KLONDIKER
KLONDIKERS
KLONDIKES
KLONDIKING
KLONDYKE
KLONDYKED
KLONDYKER
KLONDYKERS
KLONDYKES
KLONDYKING
KLOOCH
KLOOCHES
KLOOCHMAN
KLOOCHMANS
KLOOCHMEN
KLOOF
KLOOFS
KLOOTCH
KLOOTCHES
KLUDGE
KLUDGES
KLUTZ
KLUTZES
KLYSTRON
KLYSTRONS
KNACK
KNACKER
KNACKERED
KNACKERIES
KNACKERING
KNACKERS
KNACKERY
KNACKIER
KNACKIEST
KNACKISH
KNACKS
KNACKY
KNAG
KNAGGIER
KNAGGIEST
KNAGGY
KNAGS
KNAIDEL
KNAIDLOCH
KNAP
KNAPPED
KNAPPER
KNAPPERS
KNAPPING
KNAPPLE
KNAPPLED
KNAPPLES
KNAPPLING
KNAPS
KNAPSACK
KNAPSACKS
KNAPSCAL
KNAPSCALS
KNAPSCULL
KNAPSCULLS
KNAPSKULL
KNAPSKULLS
KNAPWEED
KNAPWEEDS
KNAR
KNARL
KNARLS
KNARRED
KNARRING
KNARS
KNAVE
KNAVERIES
KNAVERY
KNAVES
KNAVESHIP
KNAVESHIPS
KNAVISH
KNAVISHLY
KNAWEL
KNAWELS
KNEAD
KNEADED
KNEADER
KNEADERS
KNEADING
KNEADS
KNEE
KNEECAP
KNEECAPPED
KNEECAPPING
KNEECAPPINGS
KNEECAPS
KNEED
KNEEHOLE
KNEEHOLES
KNEEING
KNEEL
KNEELED
KNEELER
KNEELERS
KNEELING
KNEELS
KNEES
KNEIDLACH
KNELL
KNELLED
KNELLING
KNELLS
KNELT
KNEVELL
KNEVELLED
KNEVELLING
KNEVELLS
KNEW
KNICKER
KNICKERED
KNICKERS
KNICKS
KNIFE
KNIFED
KNIFELESS
KNIFES
KNIFING
KNIFINGS
KNIGHT
KNIGHTAGE
KNIGHTAGES
KNIGHTED
KNIGHTING
KNIGHTLIER
KNIGHTLIEST
KNIGHTLY
KNIGHTS
KNIPHOFIA
KNIPHOFIAS
KNISH
KNISHES
KNIT
KNITCH
KNITCHES
KNITS
KNITTED
KNITTER
KNITTERS
KNITTING
KNITTINGS
KNITTLE
KNITTLES
KNITWEAR
KNITWEARS
KNIVE
KNIVED
KNIVES
KNIVING
KNOB
KNOBBED
KNOBBER
KNOBBERS
KNOBBIER
KNOBBIEST
KNOBBLE
KNOBBLED
KNOBBLES
KNOBBLIER
KNOBBLIEST
KNOBBLING
KNOBBLY
KNOBBY
KNOBS
KNOCK
KNOCKED
KNOCKER
KNOCKERS
KNOCKING
KNOCKINGS
KNOCKOUT
KNOCKOUTS
KNOCKS
KNOLL
KNOLLED
KNOLLING
KNOLLS
KNOP
KNOPS
KNOSP
KNOSPS
KNOT
KNOTGRASS
KNOTGRASSES
KNOTLESS
KNOTS
KNOTTED
KNOTTER
KNOTTERS
KNOTTIER
KNOTTIEST
KNOTTING
KNOTTINGS
KNOTTY
KNOTWEED
KNOTWEEDS
KNOTWORK
KNOTWORKS
KNOUT
KNOUTED
KNOUTING
KNOUTS
KNOW
KNOWABLE
KNOWE
KNOWER

KNOWERS
KNOWES
KNOWHOW
KNOWHOWS
KNOWING
KNOWINGLY
KNOWLEDGE
KNOWLEDGED
KNOWLEDGES
KNOWLEDGING
KNOWN
KNOWNS
KNOWS
KNUB
KNUBBIER
KNUBBIEST
KNUBBLE
KNUBBLED
KNUBBLES
KNUBBLIER
KNUBBLIEST
KNUBBLING
KNUBBLY
KNUBBY
KNUBS
KNUCKLE
KNUCKLED
KNUCKLES
KNUCKLIER
KNUCKLIEST
KNUCKLING
KNUCKLY
KNUR
KNURL
KNURLED
KNURLIER
KNURLIEST
KNURLING
KNURLINGS
KNURLS
KNURLY
KNURR
KNURRS
KNURS
KNUT
KNUTS
KO
KOA
KOALA
KOALAS
KOAN
KOANS
KOAS
KOB
KOBAN
KOBANG
KOBANGS
KOBANS
KOBOLD
KOBOLDS
KOBS
KOFF
KOFFS
KOFTA
KOFTAS
KOFTGAR
KOFTGARI
KOFTGARIS
KOFTGARS
KOFTWORK
KOFTWORKS
KOHL
KOHLRABI
KOHLRABIS
KOHLS
KOI
KOINE
KOINES
KOKANEE
KOKANEES
KOKER
KOKERS
KOKRA
KOKRAS
KOKUM
KOKUMS
KOLA
KOLAS
KOLINSKIES
KOLINSKY
KOLKHOZ
KOLKHOZES
KOLO
KOLOS
KOMATIK
KOMATIKS
KOMBU
KOMBUS
KOMISSAR
KOMISSARS
KOMITAJI
KOMITAJIS
KON
KOND
KONFYT
KONFYTS
KONIMETER
KONIMETERS
KONIOLOGIES
KONIOLOGY
KONISCOPE
KONISCOPES
KONK
KONKED
KONKING
KONKS
KONNING
KONS
KOODOO
KOODOOS
KOOK
KOOKED
KOOKIE
KOOKIER
KOOKIEST
KOOKING
KOOKS
KOOKY
KOOLAH
KOOLAHS
KOORI
KOORIS
KOP
KOPASETIC
KOPECK
KOPECKS
KOPH
KOPHS
KOPJE
KOPJES
KOPPA
KOPPAS
KOPPIE
KOPPIES
KOPS
KORA
KORAS
KORE
KORERO
KOREROS
KORES
KORFBALL
KORFBALLS
KORKIR
KORKIRS
KORMA
KORMAS
KORORA
KORORAS
KORUNA
KORUNAS
KOS
KOSES
KOSHER
KOSHERED
KOSHERING
KOSHERS
KOSMOS
KOSMOSES
KOSS
KOSSES
KOTO
KOTOS
KOTOW
KOTOWED
KOTOWING
KOTOWS
KOTTABOS
KOTTABOSES
KOTWAL
KOTWALS
KOULAN
KOULANS
KOUMISS
KOUMISSES
KOUPREY
KOUPREYS
KOURBASH
KOURBASHED
KOURBASHES
KOURBASHING
KOUROI
KOUROS
KOUSKOUS
KOUSKOUSES
KOW
KOWHAI
KOWHAIS
KOWS
KOWTOW
KOWTOWED
KOWTOWING
KOWTOWS
KRAAL
KRAALED
KRAALING
KRAALS
KRAB
KRABS
KRAFT
KRAFTS
KRAIT
KRAITS
KRAKEN
KRAKENS
KRAKOWIAK
KRAKOWIAKS
KRAMERIA
KRAMERIAS
KRANG
KRANGS
KRANS
KRANSES
KRANTZ
KRANTZES
KRANZ
KRANZES
KRATER
KRATERS
KRAUT
KRAUTS
KREASOTE
KREASOTED
KREASOTES
KREASOTING
KREATINE
KREATINES
KREESE
KREESED
KREESES
KREESING
KREMLIN
KREMLINS
KRENG
KRENGS
KREOSOTE
KREOSOTED
KREOSOTES
KREOSOTING
KREPLACH
KREUTZER
KREUTZERS
KRILL
KRILLS
KRIMMER
KRIMMERS
KRIS
KRISED
KRISES
KRISING
KROMESKIES
KROMESKY
KRONA
KRONE
KRONEN
KRONER
KRONOR
KRONUR
KRULLER
KRULLERS
KRUMHORN
KRUMHORNS
KRUMMHORN
KRUMMHORNS
KRYOMETER
KRYOMETERS
KRYPSES
KRYPSIS
KRYPTON
KRYPTONS
KRYTRON
KRYTRONS
KSAR
KSARS
KUCHCHA
KUDOS
KUDOSES
KUDU
KUDUS
KUDZU
KUDZUS
KUFIYAH
KUFIYAHS
KUKRI
KUKRIS
KUKU
KUKUS
KULAK
KULAKS
KULAN
KULANS
KUMARA
KUMARAS
KUMARI
KUMARIS
KUMISS
KUMISSES
KUMMEL
KUMMELS
KUMQUAT
KUMQUATS
KUNKAR
KUNKARS
KUNKUR
KUNKURS
KUNZITE
KUNZITES
KURBASH
KURBASHED
KURBASHES

The Chambers Dictionary is the authority for many longer words; see *OSW* Introduction, page xii

KURBASHING
KURGAN
KURGANS
KURI
KURIS
KURRAJONG
KURRAJONGS
KURRE
KURRES
KURSAAL
KURSAALS
KURTA
KURTAS
KURTOSES
KURTOSIS
KURU
KURUS
KURVEY
KURVEYED
KURVEYING
KURVEYOR
KURVEYORS
KURVEYS
KUTCH
KUTCHA
KUTCHES
KUZU
KUZUS
KVASS
KVASSES
KVETCH
KVETCHED
KVETCHER
KVETCHERS
KVETCHES
KVETCHING
KWACHA
KWACHAS
KWANZA
KWANZAS
KWELA
KWELAS
KY
KYANG
KYANGS
KYANISE
KYANISED
KYANISES
KYANISING
KYANITE
KYANITES
KYANIZE
KYANIZED
KYANIZES
KYANIZING
KYAT
KYATS
KYBOSH
KYBOSHED
KYBOSHES
KYBOSHING
KYDST
KYE
KYLE
KYLES
KYLICES
KYLIE
KYLIES
KYLIN
KYLINS
KYLIX
KYLLOSES
KYLLOSIS
KYLOE
KYLOES
KYMOGRAM
KYMOGRAMS
KYMOGRAPH
KYMOGRAPHS
KYND
KYNDE
KYNDED
KYNDES
KYNDING
KYNDS
KYNE
KYOGEN
KYOGENS
KYPHOSES
KYPHOSIS
KYPHOTIC
KYRIELLE
KYRIELLES
KYTE
KYTES
KYTHE
KYTHED
KYTHES
KYTHING
KYU
KYUS

L

LA
LAAGER
LAAGERED
LAAGERING
LAAGERS
LAB
LABARA
LABARUM
LABARUMS
LABDA
LABDACISM
LABDACISMS
LABDANUM
LABDANUMS
LABDAS
LABEL
LABELLA
LABELLED
LABELLING
LABELLOID
LABELLUM
LABELS
LABIA
LABIAL
LABIALISE
LABIALISED
LABIALISES
LABIALISING
LABIALISM
LABIALISMS
LABIALIZE
LABIALIZED
LABIALIZES
LABIALIZING
LABIALLY
LABIALS
LABIATE
LABIATES
LABILE
LABILITIES
LABILITY
LABIS
LABISES
LABIUM
LABLAB
LABLABS
LABOR
LABORED
LABORING
LABORIOUS
LABORS
LABOUR
LABOURED
LABOURER
LABOURERS
LABOURING
LABOURISM
LABOURISMS
LABOURIST
LABOURISTS
LABOURS
LABRA
LABRET
LABRETS
LABRID
LABRIDS
LABROID
LABROIDS
LABROSE
LABRUM
LABRYS
LABRYSES
LABS
LABURNUM
LABURNUMS
LABYRINTH
LABYRINTHS
LAC
LACCOLITE
LACCOLITES
LACCOLITH
LACCOLITHS
LACE
LACEBARK
LACEBARKS
LACED
LACERABLE
LACERANT
LACERATE
LACERATED
LACERATES
LACERATING
LACERTIAN
LACERTINE
LACES
LACET
LACETS
LACEWING
LACEWINGS
LACEY
LACHES
LACHESES
LACHRYMAL
LACHRYMALS
LACIER
LACIEST
LACING
LACINGS
LACINIA
LACINIAE
LACINIATE
LACK
LACKADAY
LACKED
LACKER
LACKERED
LACKERING
LACKERS
LACKEY
LACKEYED
LACKEYING
LACKEYS
LACKING
LACKLAND
LACKLANDS
LACKS
LACMUS
LACMUSES
LACONIC
LACONICAL
LACONISM
LACONISMS
LACQUER
LACQUERED
LACQUERER
LACQUERERS
LACQUERING
LACQUERINGS
LACQUERS
LACQUEY
LACQUEYED
LACQUEYING
LACQUEYS
LACRIMAL
LACRIMALS
LACRIMOSO
LACROSSE
LACROSSES
LACRYMAL
LACRYMALS
LACS
LACTARIAN
LACTARIANS
LACTASE
LACTASES
LACTATE
LACTATED
LACTATES
LACTATING
LACTATION
LACTATIONS
LACTEAL
LACTEALS
LACTEOUS
LACTIC
LACTIFIC
LACTONE
LACTONES
LACTOSE
LACTOSES
LACUNA
LACUNAE
LACUNAL
LACUNAR
LACUNARIA
LACUNARS
LACUNARY
LACUNATE
LACUNOSE
LACY
LAD
LADANUM
LADANUMS
LADDER
LADDERED
LADDERING
LADDERS
LADDERY
LADDIE
LADDIES
LADDISH
LADE
LADED
LADEN
LADES
LADETTE
LADETTES
LADIES
LADIFIED
LADIFIES
LADIFY
LADIFYING
LADING
LADINGS
LADLE
LADLED
LADLEFUL
LADLEFULS
LADLES
LADLING
LADRONE
LADRONES
LADS
LADY
LADYBIRD
LADYBIRDS
LADYBUG
LADYBUGS
LADYCOW
LADYCOWS
LADYFIED
LADYFIES
LADYFLIES
LADYFLY
LADYFY
LADYFYING
LADYHOOD
LADYHOODS
LADYISH
LADYISM
LADYISMS
LADYKIN
LADYKINS
LADYLIKE
LADYSHIP
LADYSHIPS
LAER
LAERED
LAERING
LAERS
LAESIE
LAETARE
LAETARES
LAEVIGATE
LAEVIGATED
LAEVIGATES
LAEVIGATING
LAEVULOSE
LAEVULOSES
LAG
LAGAN
LAGANS
LAGENA
LAGENAS
LAGER
LAGERS
LAGGARD
LAGGARDS
LAGGED
LAGGEN
LAGGENS
LAGGER
LAGGERS
LAGGIN
LAGGING
LAGGINGLY
LAGGINGS
LAGGINS
LAGNAPPE
LAGNAPPES

LAGNIAPPE
LAGNIAPPES
LAGOMORPH
LAGOMORPHS
LAGOON
LAGOONAL
LAGOONS
LAGRIMOSO
LAGS
LAGUNE
LAGUNES
LAH
LAHAR
LAHARS
LAHS
LAIC
LAICAL
LAICISE
LAICISED
LAICISES
LAICISING
LAICITIES
LAICITY
LAICIZE
LAICIZED
LAICIZES
LAICIZING
LAICS
LAID
LAIDED
LAIDING
LAIDLY
LAIDS
LAIGH
LAIGHER
LAIGHEST
LAIGHS
LAIK
LAIKA
LAIKAS
LAIKED
LAIKER
LAIKERS
LAIKING
LAIKS
LAIN
LAIR
LAIRAGE
LAIRAGES
LAIRD
LAIRDS
LAIRDSHIP
LAIRDSHIPS
LAIRED
LAIRIER
LAIRIEST
LAIRING
LAIRISE
LAIRISED
LAIRISES
LAIRISING
LAIRIZE
LAIRIZED
LAIRIZES
LAIRIZING
LAIRS
LAIRY
LAISSE
LAISSES
LAITANCE
LAITANCES
LAITH
LAITIES
LAITY
LAKE
LAKED
LAKELAND
LAKELANDS
LAKELET
LAKELETS
LAKER
LAKERS
LAKES
LAKESIDE
LAKESIDES
LAKH
LAKHS
LAKIER
LAKIEST
LAKIN
LAKING
LAKINS
LAKISH
LAKY
LALANG
LALANGS
LALDIE
LALDIES
LALDY
LALLAN
LALLANS
LALLATION
LALLATIONS
LALLING
LALLINGS
LALLYGAG
LALLYGAGGED
LALLYGAGGING
LALLYGAGS
LAM
LAMA
LAMAISTIC
LAMANTIN
LAMANTINS
LAMAS
LAMASERAI
LAMASERAIS
LAMASERIES
LAMASERY
LAMB
LAMBADA
LAMBADAS
LAMBAST
LAMBASTE
LAMBASTED
LAMBASTES
LAMBASTING
LAMBASTS
LAMBDA
LAMBDAS
LAMBDOID
LAMBED
LAMBENCIES
LAMBENCY
LAMBENT
LAMBENTLY
LAMBER
LAMBERS
LAMBERT
LAMBERTS
LAMBIE
LAMBIES
LAMBING
LAMBITIVE
LAMBITIVES
LAMBKIN
LAMBKINS
LAMBLING
LAMBLINGS
LAMBOYS
LAMBS
LAMBSKIN
LAMBSKINS
LAME
LAMED
LAMELLA
LAMELLAE
LAMELLAR
LAMELLATE
LAMELLOID
LAMELLOSE
LAMELY
LAMENESS
LAMENESSES
LAMENT
LAMENTED
LAMENTING
LAMENTINGS
LAMENTS
LAMER
LAMES
LAMEST
LAMETER
LAMETERS
LAMIA
LAMIAE
LAMIAS
LAMIGER
LAMIGERS
LAMINA
LAMINABLE
LAMINAE
LAMINAR
LAMINARY
LAMINATE
LAMINATED
LAMINATES
LAMINATING
LAMINATOR
LAMINATORS
LAMING
LAMINGTON
LAMINGTONS
LAMINITIS
LAMINITISES
LAMINOSE
LAMISH
LAMITER
LAMITERS
LAMMED
LAMMER
LAMMERS
LAMMIE
LAMMIES
LAMMIGER
LAMMIGERS
LAMMING
LAMMINGS
LAMMY
LAMP
LAMPAD
LAMPADARIES
LAMPADARY
LAMPADIST
LAMPADISTS
LAMPADS
LAMPAS
LAMPASES
LAMPASSE
LAMPASSES
LAMPED
LAMPERN
LAMPERNS
LAMPERS
LAMPERSES
LAMPHOLE
LAMPHOLES
LAMPING
LAMPINGS
LAMPION
LAMPIONS
LAMPLIGHT
LAMPLIGHTS
LAMPOON
LAMPOONED
LAMPOONER
LAMPOONERS
LAMPOONING
LAMPOONS
LAMPPOST
LAMPPOSTS
LAMPREY
LAMPREYS
LAMPS
LAMPSHADE
LAMPSHADES
LAMPUKA
LAMPUKAS
LAMPUKI
LAMPUKIS
LAMS
LANA
LANAS
LANATE
LANCE
LANCED
LANCEGAY
LANCEGAYS
LANCELET
LANCELETS
LANCEOLAR
LANCER
LANCERS
LANCES
LANCET
LANCETED
LANCETS
LANCH
LANCHED
LANCHES
LANCHING
LANCIFORM
LANCINATE
LANCINATED
LANCINATES
LANCINATING
LANCING
LAND
LANDAMMAN
LANDAMMANS
LANDAU
LANDAULET
LANDAULETS
LANDAUS
LANDDAMNE
LANDDAMNED
LANDDAMNES
LANDDAMNING
LANDDROS
LANDDROSES
LANDDROST
LANDDROSTS
LANDE
LANDED
LANDER
LANDERS
LANDES
LANDFALL
LANDFALLS
LANDFILL
LANDFILLS
LANDFORCE
LANDFORCES
LANDFORM
LANDFORMS
LANDGRAVE
LANDGRAVES
LANDING
LANDINGS
LANDLADIES
LANDLADY
LANDLER
LANDLERS
LANDLESS
LANDLOPER
LANDLOPERS
LANDLORD
LANDLORDS
LANDMAN
LANDMARK

LANDMARKS
LANDMASS
LANDMASSES
LANDMEN
LANDOWNER
LANDOWNERS
LANDRACE
LANDRACES
LANDRAIL
LANDRAILS
LANDS
LANDSCAPE
LANDSCAPED
LANDSCAPES
LANDSCAPING
LANDSIDE
LANDSIDES
LANDSKIP
LANDSKIPPED
LANDSKIPPING
LANDSKIPS
LANDSLIDE
LANDSLIDES
LANDSLIP
LANDSLIPS
LANDSMAN
LANDSMEN
LANDWARD
LANDWARDS
LANDWIND
LANDWINDS
LANE
LANES
LANEWAY
LANEWAYS
LANG
LANGAHA
LANGAHAS
LANGER
LANGEST
LANGLAUF
LANGLAUFS
LANGOUSTE
LANGOUSTES
LANGRAGE
LANGRAGES
LANGREL
LANGRELS
LANGRIDGE
LANGRIDGES
LANGSPEL
LANGSPELS
LANGSPIEL
LANGSPIELS
LANGUAGE
LANGUAGED
LANGUAGES
LANGUAGING
LANGUE
LANGUED
LANGUES
LANGUET
LANGUETS
LANGUETTE
LANGUETTES
LANGUID
LANGUIDLY
LANGUISH
LANGUISHED
LANGUISHES
LANGUISHING
LANGUISHINGS
LANGUOR
LANGUORS
LANGUR
LANGURS
LANIARD
LANIARDS
LANIARY
LANK
LANKED
LANKER
LANKEST
LANKIER
LANKIEST
LANKILY
LANKINESS
LANKINESSES
LANKING
LANKLY
LANKNESS
LANKNESSES
LANKS
LANKY
LANNER
LANNERET
LANNERETS
LANNERS
LANOLIN
LANOLINE
LANOLINES
LANOLINS
LANOSE
LANT
LANTANA
LANTANAS
LANTERLOO
LANTERLOOS
LANTERN
LANTERNED
LANTERNING
LANTERNS
LANTHANUM
LANTHANUMS
LANTHORN
LANTHORNS
LANTS
LANTSKIP
LANTSKIPS
LANUGO
LANUGOS
LANX
LANYARD
LANYARDS
LAP
LAPDOG
LAPDOGS
LAPEL
LAPELLED
LAPELS
LAPFUL
LAPFULS
LAPHELD
LAPIDARIES
LAPIDARY
LAPIDATE
LAPIDATED
LAPIDATES
LAPIDATING
LAPIDEOUS
LAPIDIFIC
LAPIDIFIED
LAPIDIFIES
LAPIDIFY
LAPIDIFYING
LAPILLI
LAPIS
LAPISES
LAPJE
LAPJES
LAPPED
LAPPEL
LAPPELS
LAPPER
LAPPERED
LAPPERING
LAPPERS
LAPPET
LAPPETED
LAPPETS
LAPPIE
LAPPIES
LAPPING
LAPPINGS
LAPS
LAPSABLE
LAPSANG
LAPSANGS
LAPSE
LAPSED
LAPSES
LAPSING
LAPSTONE
LAPSTONES
LAPSTRAKE
LAPSTRAKES
LAPSTREAK
LAPSTREAKS
LAPSUS
LAPTOP
LAPTOPS
LAPWING
LAPWINGS
LAPWORK
LAPWORKS
LAQUEARIA
LAR
LARBOARD
LARBOARDS
LARCENER
LARCENERS
LARCENIES
LARCENIST
LARCENISTS
LARCENOUS
LARCENY
LARCH
LARCHEN
LARCHES
LARD
LARDALITE
LARDALITES
LARDED
LARDER
LARDERER
LARDERERS
LARDERS
LARDIER
LARDIEST
LARDING
LARDON
LARDONS
LARDOON
LARDOONS
LARDS
LARDY
LARE
LARES
LARGE
LARGELY
LARGEN
LARGENED
LARGENESS
LARGENESSES
LARGENING
LARGENS
LARGER
LARGES
LARGESS
LARGESSE
LARGESSES
LARGEST
LARGHETTO
LARGHETTOS
LARGISH
LARGITION
LARGITIONS
LARGO
LARGOS
LARIAT
LARIATS
LARINE
LARK
LARKED
LARKER
LARKERS
LARKIER
LARKIEST
LARKINESS
LARKINESSES
LARKING
LARKISH
LARKS
LARKSPUR
LARKSPURS
LARKY
LARMIER
LARMIERS
LARN
LARNAKES
LARNAX
LARNED
LARNING
LARNS
LAROID
LARRIGAN
LARRIGANS
LARRIKIN
LARRIKINS
LARRUP
LARRUPED
LARRUPING
LARRUPS
LARUM
LARUMS
LARVA
LARVAE
LARVAL
LARVATE
LARVATED
LARVICIDE
LARVICIDES
LARVIFORM
LARVIKITE
LARVIKITES
LARYNGAL
LARYNGEAL
LARYNGES
LARYNX
LARYNXES
LAS
LASAGNA
LASAGNAS
LASAGNE
LASAGNES
LASCAR
LASCARS
LASE
LASED
LASER
LASERS
LASERWORT
LASERWORTS
LASES
LASH
LASHED
LASHER
LASHERS
LASHES
LASHING
LASHINGS
LASHKAR
LASHKARS
LASING
LASINGS
LASKET
LASKETS
LASQUE
LASQUES
LASS

LASSES
LASSI
LASSIE
LASSIES
LASSIS
LASSITUDE
LASSITUDES
LASSLORN
LASSO
LASSOCK
LASSOCKS
LASSOED
LASSOES
LASSOING
LASSOS
LASSU
LASSUS
LAST
LASTAGE
LASTAGES
LASTED
LASTER
LASTERS
LASTING
LASTINGLY
LASTINGS
LASTLY
LASTS
LAT
LATCH
LATCHED
LATCHES
LATCHET
LATCHETS
LATCHING
LATCHKEY
LATCHKEYS
LATE
LATED
LATEEN
LATEENS
LATELY
LATEN
LATENCE
LATENCES
LATENCIES
LATENCY
LATENED
LATENESS
LATENESSES
LATENING
LATENS
LATENT
LATENTLY
LATER
LATERAL
LATERALLY
LATERALS
LATERITE
LATERITES
LATERITIC
LATESCENT
LATEST
LATESTS
LATEWAKE
LATEWAKES
LATEX
LATEXES
LATH
LATHE
LATHED
LATHEE
LATHEES
LATHEN
LATHER
LATHERED
LATHERIER
LATHERIEST
LATHERING
LATHERS
LATHERY
LATHES
LATHI
LATHIER
LATHIEST
LATHING
LATHINGS
LATHIS
LATHLIKE
LATHS
LATHY
LATHYRISM
LATHYRISMS
LATHYRUS
LATHYRUSES
LATICES
LATICLAVE
LATICLAVES
LATIFONDI
LATISH
LATITANCIES
LATITANCY
LATITANT
LATITAT
LATITATS
LATITUDE
LATITUDES
LATKE
LATKES
LATRANT
LATRATION
LATRATIONS
LATRIA
LATRIAS
LATRINE
LATRINES
LATROCINIES
LATROCINY
LATRON
LATRONS
LATS
LATTEN
LATTENS
LATTER
LATTERLY
LATTICE
LATTICED
LATTICES
LATTICING
LATTICINI
LATTICINO
LAUCH
LAUCHING
LAUCHS
LAUD
LAUDABLE
LAUDABLY
LAUDANUM
LAUDANUMS
LAUDATION
LAUDATIONS
LAUDATIVE
LAUDATIVES
LAUDATORIES
LAUDATORY
LAUDED
LAUDER
LAUDERS
LAUDING
LAUDS
LAUF
LAUFS
LAUGH
LAUGHABLE
LAUGHABLY
LAUGHED
LAUGHER
LAUGHERS
LAUGHFUL
LAUGHIER
LAUGHIEST
LAUGHING
LAUGHINGS
LAUGHS
LAUGHSOME
LAUGHTER
LAUGHTERS
LAUGHY
LAUNCE
LAUNCED
LAUNCES
LAUNCH
LAUNCHED
LAUNCHER
LAUNCHERS
LAUNCHES
LAUNCHING
LAUNCING
LAUND
LAUNDER
LAUNDERED
LAUNDERER
LAUNDERERS
LAUNDERING
LAUNDERS
LAUNDRESS
LAUNDRESSES
LAUNDRIES
LAUNDRY
LAUNDS
LAURA
LAURAS
LAUREATE
LAUREATED
LAUREATES
LAUREATING
LAUREL
LAURELLED
LAURELS
LAUWINE
LAUWINES
LAV
LAVA
LAVABO
LAVABOES
LAVABOS
LAVAFORM
LAVAGE
LAVAGES
LAVALIERE
LAVALIERES
LAVAS
LAVATERA
LAVATERAS
LAVATION
LAVATIONS
LAVATORIES
LAVATORY
LAVE
LAVED
LAVEER
LAVEERED
LAVEERING
LAVEERS
LAVEMENT
LAVEMENTS
LAVENDER
LAVENDERED
LAVENDERING
LAVENDERS
LAVER
LAVEROCK
LAVEROCKED
LAVEROCKING
LAVEROCKS
LAVERS
LAVES
LAVING
LAVISH
LAVISHED
LAVISHER
LAVISHES
LAVISHEST
LAVISHING
LAVISHLY
LAVOLT
LAVOLTA
LAVOLTAED
LAVOLTAING
LAVOLTAS
LAVOLTED
LAVOLTING
LAVOLTS
LAVRA
LAVRAS
LAVS
LAW
LAWED
LAWER
LAWEST
LAWFUL
LAWFULLY
LAWIN
LAWING
LAWINGS
LAWINS
LAWK
LAWKS
LAWLAND
LAWLANDS
LAWLESS
LAWLESSLY
LAWMAN
LAWMEN
LAWMONGER
LAWMONGERS
LAWN
LAWNIER
LAWNIEST
LAWNMOWER
LAWNMOWERS
LAWNS
LAWNY
LAWS
LAWSUIT
LAWSUITS
LAWYER
LAWYERLY
LAWYERS
LAX
LAXATIVE
LAXATIVES
LAXATOR
LAXATORS
LAXER
LAXES
LAXEST
LAXISM
LAXISMS
LAXIST
LAXISTS
LAXITIES
LAXITY
LAXLY
LAXNESS
LAXNESSES
LAY
LAYABOUT
LAYABOUTS
LAYAWAY
LAYAWAYS
LAYBACK
LAYBACKED
LAYBACKING
LAYBACKS
LAYER
LAYERED
LAYERING
LAYERINGS
LAYERS

AYETTE
AYETTES
AYING
AYINGS
AYLOCK
AYLOCKS
AYMAN
AYMEN
AYOUT
AYOUTS
AYPERSON
AYPERSONS
AYS
AYSTALL
AYSTALLS
AYTIME
AYTIMES
AYWOMAN
AYWOMEN
AZAR
AZARET
AZARETS
AZARETTO
AZARETTOS
AZARS
AZE
AZED
AZES
AZIER
AZIEST
AZILY
AZINESS
AZINESSES
AZING
AZO
AZOED
AZOES
AZOING
AZOS
AZULITE
AZULITES
AZURITE
AZURITES
AZY
AZZARONE
AZZARONI
AZZI
AZZO
EA
EACH
EACHATE
EACHATES
EACHED
EACHES
LEACHIER
LEACHIEST
LEACHING
LEACHINGS
LEACHOUR
LEACHOURS
LEACHTUB
LEACHTUBS
LEACHY
LEAD
LEADED
LEADEN
LEADENED
LEADENING
LEADENLY
LEADENS
LEADER
LEADERENE
LEADERENES
LEADERS
LEADIER
LEADIEST
LEADING
LEADINGS
LEADLESS
LEADS
LEADSMAN
LEADSMEN
LEADY
LEAF
LEAFAGE
LEAFAGES
LEAFBUD
LEAFBUDS
LEAFED
LEAFERIES
LEAFERY
LEAFIER
LEAFIEST
LEAFINESS
LEAFINESSES
LEAFING
LEAFLESS
LEAFLET
LEAFLETED
LEAFLETING
LEAFLETS
LEAFLETTED
LEAFLETTING
LEAFLIKE
LEAFS
LEAFY
LEAGUE
LEAGUED
LEAGUER
LEAGUERED
LEAGUERING
LEAGUERS
LEAGUES
LEAGUING
LEAK
LEAKAGE
LEAKAGES
LEAKED
LEAKER
LEAKERS
LEAKIER
LEAKIEST
LEAKINESS
LEAKINESSES
LEAKING
LEAKS
LEAKY
LEAL
LEALLY
LEALTIES
LEALTY
LEAM
LEAMED
LEAMING
LEAMS
LEAN
LEANED
LEANER
LEANEST
LEANING
LEANINGS
LEANLY
LEANNESS
LEANNESSES
LEANS
LEANT
LEANY
LEAP
LEAPED
LEAPER
LEAPEROUS
LEAPERS
LEAPING
LEAPOROUS
LEAPROUS
LEAPS
LEAPT
LEAR
LEARE
LEARED
LEARES
LEARIER
LEARIEST
LEARING
LEARN
LEARNABLE
LEARNED
LEARNEDLY
LEARNER
LEARNERS
LEARNING
LEARNINGS
LEARNS
LEARNT
LEARS
LEARY
LEAS
LEASABLE
LEASE
LEASEBACK
LEASEBACKS
LEASED
LEASEHOLD
LEASEHOLDS
LEASER
LEASERS
LEASES
LEASH
LEASHED
LEASHES
LEASHING
LEASING
LEASINGS
LEASOW
LEASOWE
LEASOWED
LEASOWES
LEASOWING
LEASOWS
LEAST
LEASTS
LEASTWAYS
LEASTWISE
LEASURE
LEASURES
LEAT
LEATHER
LEATHERED
LEATHERIER
LEATHERIEST
LEATHERING
LEATHERINGS
LEATHERN
LEATHERS
LEATHERY
LEATS
LEAVE
LEAVED
LEAVEN
LEAVENED
LEAVENING
LEAVENINGS
LEAVENOUS
LEAVENS
LEAVER
LEAVERS
LEAVES
LEAVIER
LEAVIEST
LEAVING
LEAVINGS
LEAVY
LEAZE
LEAZES
LEBBEK
LEBBEKS
LECANORA
LECANORAS
LECH
LECHED
LECHER
LECHERED
LECHERIES
LECHERING
LECHEROUS
LECHERS
LECHERY
LECHES
LECHING
LECHWE
LECHWES
LECITHIN
LECITHINS
LECTERN
LECTERNS
LECTIN
LECTINS
LECTION
LECTIONS
LECTOR
LECTORATE
LECTORATES
LECTORS
LECTRESS
LECTRESSES
LECTURE
LECTURED
LECTURER
LECTURERS
LECTURES
LECTURING
LECTURN
LECTURNS
LECYTHI
LECYTHUS
LED
LEDDEN
LEDDENS
LEDGE
LEDGER
LEDGERED
LEDGERING
LEDGERS
LEDGES
LEDGIER
LEDGIEST
LEDGY
LEDUM
LEDUMS
LEE
LEEAR
LEEARS
LEECH
LEECHDOM
LEECHDOMS
LEECHED
LEECHEE
LEECHEES
LEECHES
LEECHING
LEED
LEEING
LEEK
LEEKS
LEEP
LEEPED
LEEPING
LEEPS
LEER
LEERED
LEERIER
LEERIEST
LEERING
LEERINGLY
LEERINGS
LEERS
LEERY
LEES
LEESE
LEESES

LEESING
LEET
LEETLE
LEETS
LEEWARD
LEEWARDS
LEEWAY
LEEWAYS
LEFT
LEFTE
LEFTER
LEFTEST
LEFTIE
LEFTIES
LEFTISH
LEFTISM
LEFTISMS
LEFTIST
LEFTISTS
LEFTOVER
LEFTOVERS
LEFTS
LEFTWARD
LEFTWARDS
LEFTY
LEG
LEGACIES
LEGACY
LEGAL
LEGALESE
LEGALESES
LEGALISE
LEGALISED
LEGALISES
LEGALISING
LEGALISM
LEGALISMS
LEGALIST
LEGALISTS
LEGALITIES
LEGALITY
LEGALIZE
LEGALIZED
LEGALIZES
LEGALIZING
LEGALLY
LEGATARIES
LEGATARY
LEGATE
LEGATEE
LEGATEES
LEGATES
LEGATINE
LEGATION
LEGATIONS
LEGATO
LEGATOR
LEGATORS
LEGATOS
LEGEND
LEGENDARIES
LEGENDARY
LEGENDIST
LEGENDISTS
LEGENDRIES
LEGENDRY
LEGENDS
LEGER
LEGERING
LEGERINGS
LEGERITIES
LEGERITY
LEGERS
LEGES
LEGGE
LEGGED
LEGGER
LEGGERS
LEGGES
LEGGIER
LEGGIEST
LEGGINESS
LEGGINESSES
LEGGING
LEGGINGS
LEGGISM
LEGGISMS
LEGGY
LEGHORN
LEGHORNS
LEGIBLE
LEGIBLY
LEGION
LEGIONARIES
LEGIONARY
LEGIONED
LEGIONS
LEGISLATE
LEGISLATED
LEGISLATES
LEGISLATING
LEGIST
LEGISTS
LEGIT
LEGITIM
LEGITIMS
LEGLAN
LEGLANS
LEGLEN
LEGLENS
LEGLESS
LEGLET
LEGLETS
LEGLIN
LEGLINS
LEGROOM
LEGROOMS
LEGS
LEGUME
LEGUMES
LEGUMIN
LEGUMINS
LEGWEAR
LEGWEARS
LEGWORK
LEGWORKS
LEHR
LEHRJAHRE
LEHRS
LEI
LEIDGER
LEIDGERS
LEIGER
LEIGERS
LEIPOA
LEIPOAS
LEIR
LEIRED
LEIRING
LEIRS
LEIS
LEISH
LEISHER
LEISHEST
LEISLER
LEISLERS
LEISTER
LEISTERED
LEISTERING
LEISTERS
LEISURE
LEISURED
LEISURELY
LEISURES
LEISURING
LEITMOTIF
LEITMOTIFS
LEITMOTIV
LEITMOTIVS
LEK
LEKE
LEKKED
LEKKING
LEKKINGS
LEKS
LEKYTHOI
LEKYTHOS
LEMAN
LEMANS
LEME
LEMED
LEMEL
LEMELS
LEMES
LEMING
LEMMA
LEMMAS
LEMMATA
LEMMATISE
LEMMATISED
LEMMATISES
LEMMATISING
LEMMATIZE
LEMMATIZED
LEMMATIZES
LEMMATIZING
LEMMING
LEMMINGS
LEMON
LEMONADE
LEMONADES
LEMONED
LEMONFISH
LEMONFISHES
LEMONIER
LEMONIEST
LEMONING
LEMONS
LEMONY
LEMPIRA
LEMPIRAS
LEMUR
LEMURES
LEMURIAN
LEMURIANS
LEMURINE
LEMURINES
LEMUROID
LEMUROIDS
LEMURS
LEND
LENDER
LENDERS
LENDING
LENDINGS
LENDS
LENES
LENG
LENGED
LENGER
LENGEST
LENGING
LENGS
LENGTH
LENGTHEN
LENGTHENED
LENGTHENING
LENGTHENS
LENGTHFUL
LENGTHIER
LENGTHIEST
LENGTHILY
LENGTHS
LENGTHY
LENIENCE
LENIENCES
LENIENCIES
LENIENCY
LENIENT
LENIENTLY
LENIENTS
LENIFIED
LENIFIES
LENIFY
LENIFYING
LENIS
LENITIES
LENITION
LENITIONS
LENITIVE
LENITIVES
LENITY
LENO
LENOS
LENS
LENSES
LENSMAN
LENSMEN
LENT
LENTANDO
LENTEN
LENTI
LENTIC
LENTICEL
LENTICELS
LENTICLE
LENTICLES
LENTIFORM
LENTIGINES
LENTIGO
LENTIL
LENTILS
LENTISK
LENTISKS
LENTO
LENTOID
LENTOR
LENTORS
LENTOS
LENTOUS
LENVOY
LENVOYS
LEONE
LEONES
LEONINE
LEOPARD
LEOPARDS
LEOTARD
LEOTARDS
LEP
LEPER
LEPERS
LEPID
LEPIDOTE
LEPORINE
LEPPED
LEPPING
LEPRA
LEPRAS
LEPROSE
LEPROSERIES
LEPROSERY
LEPROSIES
LEPROSITIES
LEPROSITY
LEPROSY
LEPROUS
LEPS
LEPTA
LEPTOME
LEPTOMES
LEPTON
LEPTONIC
LEPTONS
LEPTOSOME
LEPTOSOMES
LEPTOTENE
LEPTOTENES
LERE
LERED

LERES
LERING
LERNAEAN
LERNEAN
LERP
LERPS
LES
LESBIAN
LESBIANS
LESBIC
LESBO
LESBOS
LESES
LESION
LESIONS
LESS
LESSEE
LESSEES
LESSEN
LESSENED
LESSENING
LESSENS
LESSER
LESSES
LESSON
LESSONED
LESSONING
LESSONINGS
LESSONS
LESSOR
LESSORS
LEST
LESTED
LESTING
LESTS
LET
LETCH
LETCHED
LETCHES
LETCHING
LETCHINGS
LETHAL
LETHALITIES
LETHALITY
LETHALLY
LETHARGIC
LETHARGIES
LETHARGY
LETHEAN
LETHEE
LETHEES
LETHIED
LETS
LETTABLE
LETTED
LETTER
LETTERBOX
LETTERBOXES
LETTERED
LETTERER
LETTERERS
LETTERING
LETTERINGS
LETTERN
LETTERNS
LETTERS
LETTING
LETTINGS
LETTRE
LETTRES
LETTUCE
LETTUCES
LEU
LEUCAEMIA
LEUCAEMIAS
LEUCAEMIC
LEUCH
LEUCHEN
LEUCIN
LEUCINE
LEUCINES
LEUCINS
LEUCITE
LEUCITES
LEUCITIC
LEUCOCYTE
LEUCOCYTES
LEUCOMA
LEUCOMAS
LEUCOSIN
LEUCOSINS
LEUCOTOME
LEUCOTOMES
LEUCOTOMIES
LEUCOTOMY
LEUGH
LEUGHEN
LEUKAEMIA
LEUKAEMIAS
LEUKEMIA
LEUKEMIAS
LEV
LEVA
LEVANT
LEVANTED
LEVANTER
LEVANTERS
LEVANTINE
LEVANTINES
LEVANTING
LEVANTS
LEVATOR
LEVATORS
LEVE
LEVEE
LEVEED
LEVEEING
LEVEES
LEVEL
LEVELLED
LEVELLER
LEVELLERS
LEVELLEST
LEVELLING
LEVELLINGS
LEVELS
LEVER
LEVERAGE
LEVERAGED
LEVERAGES
LEVERAGING
LEVERED
LEVERET
LEVERETS
LEVERING
LEVERS
LEVIABLE
LEVIATHAN
LEVIATHANS
LEVIED
LEVIES
LEVIGABLE
LEVIGATE
LEVIGATED
LEVIGATES
LEVIGATING
LEVIN
LEVINS
LEVIRATE
LEVIRATES
LEVIS
LEVITATE
LEVITATED
LEVITATES
LEVITATING
LEVITE
LEVITES
LEVITIC
LEVITICAL
LEVITIES
LEVITY
LEVULOSE
LEVULOSES
LEVY
LEVYING
LEW
LEWD
LEWDER
LEWDEST
LEWDLY
LEWDNESS
LEWDNESSES
LEWDSBIES
LEWDSBY
LEWDSTER
LEWDSTERS
LEWIS
LEWISES
LEWISIA
LEWISIAS
LEWISITE
LEWISITES
LEWISSON
LEWISSONS
LEX
LEXEME
LEXEMES
LEXES
LEXICAL
LEXICALLY
LEXICON
LEXICONS
LEXIGRAM
LEXIGRAMS
LEXIS
LEXISES
LEY
LEYS
LEZ
LEZES
LEZZ
LEZZES
LEZZIES
LEZZY
LI
LIABILITIES
LIABILITY
LIABLE
LIAISE
LIAISED
LIAISES
LIAISING
LIAISON
LIAISONS
LIANA
LIANAS
LIANE
LIANES
LIANG
LIANGS
LIANOID
LIAR
LIARD
LIARDS
LIARS
LIART
LIB
LIBANT
LIBATE
LIBATED
LIBATES
LIBATING
LIBATION
LIBATIONS
LIBATORY
LIBBARD
LIBBARDS
LIBBED
LIBBER
LIBBERS
LIBBING
LIBECCHIO
LIBECCHIOS
LIBECCIO
LIBECCIOS
LIBEL
LIBELANT
LIBELANTS
LIBELED
LIBELEE
LIBELEES
LIBELER
LIBELERS
LIBELING
LIBELINGS
LIBELLANT
LIBELLANTS
LIBELLED
LIBELLEE
LIBELLEES
LIBELLER
LIBELLERS
LIBELLING
LIBELLINGS
LIBELLOUS
LIBELOUS
LIBELS
LIBER
LIBERAL
LIBERALLY
LIBERALS
LIBERATE
LIBERATED
LIBERATES
LIBERATING
LIBERATOR
LIBERATORS
LIBERO
LIBEROS
LIBERS
LIBERTIES
LIBERTINE
LIBERTINES
LIBERTY
LIBIDINAL
LIBIDO
LIBIDOS
LIBKEN
LIBKENS
LIBRA
LIBRAE
LIBRAIRE
LIBRAIRES
LIBRAIRIE
LIBRAIRIES
LIBRARIAN
LIBRARIANS
LIBRARIES
LIBRARY
LIBRAS
LIBRATE
LIBRATED
LIBRATES
LIBRATING
LIBRATION
LIBRATIONS
LIBRATORY
LIBRETTI
LIBRETTO
LIBRETTOS
LIBS
LICE
LICENCE
LICENCED
LICENCES
LICENCING
LICENSE
LICENSED
LICENSEE
LICENSEES

LICENSER
LICENSERS
LICENSES
LICENSING
LICENSOR
LICENSORS
LICENSURE
LICENSURES
LICH
LICHANOS
LICHANOSES
LICHEE
LICHEES
LICHEN
LICHENED
LICHENIN
LICHENINS
LICHENISM
LICHENISMS
LICHENIST
LICHENISTS
LICHENOID
LICHENOSE
LICHENOUS
LICHENS
LICHES
LICHGATE
LICHGATES
LICHI
LICHIS
LICHT
LICHTED
LICHTER
LICHTEST
LICHTING
LICHTLIED
LICHTLIES
LICHTLY
LICHTLYING
LICHTS
LICHWAKE
LICHWAKES
LICHWAY
LICHWAYS
LICIT
LICITLY
LICK
LICKED
LICKER
LICKERISH
LICKERS
LICKING
LICKINGS
LICKPENNIES
LICKPENNY
LICKS
LICORICE
LICORICES
LICTOR
LICTORS
LID
LIDDED
LIDGER
LIDGERS
LIDLESS
LIDO
LIDOCAINE
LIDOCAINES
LIDOS
LIDS
LIE
LIED
LIEDER
LIEF
LIEFER
LIEFEST
LIEFS
LIEGE
LIEGEDOM
LIEGEDOMS
LIEGELESS
LIEGEMAN
LIEGEMEN
LIEGER
LIEGERS
LIEGES
LIEN
LIENAL
LIENS
LIENTERIC
LIENTERIES
LIENTERY
LIER
LIERNE
LIERNES
LIERS
LIES
LIEU
LIEUS
LIEVE
LIEVER
LIEVEST
LIFE
LIFEBELT
LIFEBELTS
LIFEBOAT
LIFEBOATS
LIFEBUOY
LIFEBUOYS
LIFEFUL
LIFEGUARD
LIFEGUARDS
LIFEHOLD
LIFELESS
LIFELIKE
LIFELINE
LIFELINES
LIFELONG
LIFER
LIFERS
LIFESOME
LIFESPAN
LIFESPANS
LIFESTYLE
LIFESTYLES
LIFETIME
LIFETIMES
LIFT
LIFTABLE
LIFTBACK
LIFTBACKS
LIFTED
LIFTER
LIFTERS
LIFTING
LIFTS
LIFULL
LIG
LIGAMENT
LIGAMENTS
LIGAN
LIGAND
LIGANDS
LIGANS
LIGASE
LIGASES
LIGATE
LIGATED
LIGATES
LIGATING
LIGATION
LIGATIONS
LIGATURE
LIGATURED
LIGATURES
LIGATURING
LIGER
LIGERS
LIGGE
LIGGED
LIGGEN
LIGGER
LIGGERS
LIGGES
LIGGING
LIGGINGS
LIGHT
LIGHTED
LIGHTEN
LIGHTENED
LIGHTENING
LIGHTENINGS
LIGHTENS
LIGHTER
LIGHTERS
LIGHTEST
LIGHTFUL
LIGHTING
LIGHTINGS
LIGHTISH
LIGHTLESS
LIGHTLIED
LIGHTLIES
LIGHTLY
LIGHTLYING
LIGHTNESS
LIGHTNESSES
LIGHTNING
LIGHTNINGS
LIGHTS
LIGHTSHIP
LIGHTSHIPS
LIGHTSOME
LIGNAGE
LIGNAGES
LIGNALOES
LIGNE
LIGNEOUS
LIGNES
LIGNIFIED
LIGNIFIES
LIGNIFORM
LIGNIFY
LIGNIFYING
LIGNIN
LIGNINS
LIGNITE
LIGNITES
LIGNITIC
LIGNOSE
LIGNOSES
LIGNUM
LIGNUMS
LIGROIN
LIGROINS
LIGS
LIGULA
LIGULAE
LIGULAR
LIGULAS
LIGULATE
LIGULE
LIGULES
LIGULOID
LIGURE
LIGURES
LIKABLE
LIKE
LIKEABLE
LIKED
LIKELIER
LIKELIEST
LIKELY
LIKEN
LIKENED
LIKENESS
LIKENESSES
LIKENING
LIKENS
LIKER
LIKERS
LIKES
LIKEWAKE
LIKEWAKES
LIKEWALK
LIKEWALKS
LIKEWISE
LIKIN
LIKING
LIKINGS
LIKINS
LILAC
LILACS
LILANGENI
LILIED
LILIES
LILL
LILLED
LILLING
LILLS
LILO
LILOS
LILT
LILTED
LILTING
LILTS
LILY
LIMA
LIMACEL
LIMACELS
LIMACEOUS
LIMACES
LIMACINE
LIMACON
LIMACONS
LIMAIL
LIMAILS
LIMAS
LIMATION
LIMATIONS
LIMAX
LIMB
LIMBATE
LIMBEC
LIMBECK
LIMBECKS
LIMBECS
LIMBED
LIMBER
LIMBERED
LIMBERING
LIMBERS
LIMBIC
LIMBING
LIMBLESS
LIMBMEAL
LIMBO
LIMBOS
LIMBOUS
LIMBS
LIME
LIMEADE
LIMEADES
LIMED
LIMEKILN
LIMEKILNS
LIMELIGHT
LIMELIGHTED
LIMELIGHTING
LIMELIGHTS
LIMELIT
LIMEN
LIMENS
LIMEPIT
LIMEPITS
LIMERICK
LIMERICKS
LIMES
LIMESTONE
LIMESTONES

LIMEWASH
LIMEWASHES
LIMEWATER
LIMEWATERS
LIMEY
LIMEYS
LIMIER
LIMIEST
LIMINAL
LIMINESS
LIMINESSES
LIMING
LIMINGS
LIMIT
LIMITABLE
LIMITARY
LIMITED
LIMITEDLY
LIMITEDS
LIMITER
LIMITERS
LIMITES
LIMITING
LIMITINGS
LIMITLESS
LIMITS
LIMMA
LIMMAS
LIMMER
LIMMERS
LIMN
LIMNAEID
LIMNAEIDS
LIMNED
LIMNER
LIMNERS
LIMNETIC
LIMNING
LIMNOLOGIES
LIMNOLOGY
LIMNS
LIMO
LIMONITE
LIMONITES
LIMONITIC
LIMOS
LIMOSES
LIMOSIS
LIMOUS
LIMOUSINE
LIMOUSINES
LIMP
LIMPED
LIMPER
LIMPEST
LIMPET
LIMPETS
LIMPID
LIMPIDITIES
LIMPIDITY
LIMPIDLY
LIMPING
LIMPINGLY
LIMPINGS
LIMPKIN
LIMPKINS
LIMPLY
LIMPNESS
LIMPNESSES
LIMPS
LIMULI
LIMULUS
LIMULUSES
LIMY
LIN
LINAC
LINACS
LINAGE
LINAGES
LINALOOL
LINALOOLS
LINCH
LINCHES
LINCHET
LINCHETS
LINCHPIN
LINCHPINS
LINCRUSTA
LINCRUSTAS
LINCTURE
LINCTURES
LINCTUS
LINCTUSES
LIND
LINDANE
LINDANES
LINDEN
LINDENS
LINDS
LINDWORM
LINDWORMS
LINE
LINEAGE
LINEAGES
LINEAL
LINEALITIES
LINEALITY
LINEALLY
LINEAMENT
LINEAMENTS
LINEAR
LINEARITIES
LINEARITY
LINEARLY
LINEATE
LINEATED
LINEATION
LINEATIONS
LINED
LINEMAN
LINEMEN
LINEN
LINENS
LINEOLATE
LINER
LINERS
LINES
LINESMAN
LINESMEN
LINEY
LING
LINGA
LINGAM
LINGAMS
LINGAS
LINGEL
LINGELS
LINGER
LINGERED
LINGERER
LINGERERS
LINGERIE
LINGERIES
LINGERING
LINGERINGS
LINGERS
LINGIER
LINGIEST
LINGLE
LINGLES
LINGO
LINGOES
LINGOT
LINGOTS
LINGS
LINGSTER
LINGSTERS
LINGUA
LINGUAE
LINGUAL
LINGUALLY
LINGUAS
LINGUINE
LINGUINI
LINGUIST
LINGUISTS
LINGULA
LINGULAE
LINGULAR
LINGULAS
LINGULATE
LINGY
LINHAY
LINHAYS
LINIER
LINIEST
LINIMENT
LINIMENTS
LININ
LINING
LININGS
LININS
LINISH
LINISHED
LINISHER
LINISHERS
LINISHES
LINISHING
LINISHINGS
LINK
LINKABLE
LINKAGE
LINKAGES
LINKBOY
LINKBOYS
LINKED
LINKER
LINKERS
LINKING
LINKMAN
LINKMEN
LINKS
LINKSTER
LINKSTERS
LINKWORK
LINKWORKS
LINN
LINNED
LINNET
LINNETS
LINNEY
LINNEYS
LINNIES
LINNING
LINNS
LINNY
LINO
LINOCUT
LINOCUTS
LINOLEUM
LINOLEUMS
LINOS
LINS
LINSANG
LINSANGS
LINSEED
LINSEEDS
LINSEY
LINSEYS
LINSTOCK
LINSTOCKS
LINT
LINTEL
LINTELLED
LINTELS
LINTER
LINTERS
LINTIE
LINTIER
LINTIES
LINTIEST
LINTS
LINTSEED
LINTSEEDS
LINTSTOCK
LINTSTOCKS
LINTWHITE
LINTWHITES
LINTY
LINY
LION
LIONCEL
LIONCELLE
LIONCELLES
LIONCELS
LIONEL
LIONELS
LIONESS
LIONESSES
LIONET
LIONETS
LIONISE
LIONISED
LIONISES
LIONISING
LIONISM
LIONISMS
LIONIZE
LIONIZED
LIONIZES
LIONIZING
LIONLIKE
LIONLY
LIONS
LIP
LIPARITE
LIPARITES
LIPASE
LIPASES
LIPECTOMIES
LIPECTOMY
LIPID
LIPIDE
LIPIDES
LIPIDS
LIPLESS
LIPLIKE
LIPOGRAM
LIPOGRAMS
LIPOID
LIPOIDS
LIPOMA
LIPOMATA
LIPOSOMAL
LIPOSOME
LIPOSOMES
LIPPED
LIPPEN
LIPPENED
LIPPENING
LIPPENS
LIPPIE
LIPPIER
LIPPIES
LIPPIEST
LIPPING
LIPPITUDE
LIPPITUDES
LIPPY
LIPS
LIPSTICK
LIPSTICKED
LIPSTICKING
LIPSTICKS
LIQUABLE
LIQUATE
LIQUATED
LIQUATES
LIQUATING
LIQUATION

LIQUATIONS
LIQUEFIED
LIQUEFIER
LIQUEFIERS
LIQUEFIES
LIQUEFY
LIQUEFYING
LIQUESCE
LIQUESCED
LIQUESCES
LIQUESCING
LIQUEUR
LIQUEURED
LIQUEURING
LIQUEURS
LIQUID
LIQUIDATE
LIQUIDATED
LIQUIDATES
LIQUIDATING
LIQUIDISE
LIQUIDISED
LIQUIDISES
LIQUIDISING
LIQUIDITIES
LIQUIDITY
LIQUIDIZE
LIQUIDIZED
LIQUIDIZES
LIQUIDIZING
LIQUIDLY
LIQUIDS
LIQUIDUS
LIQUIDUSES
LIQUOR
LIQUORED
LIQUORICE
LIQUORICES
LIQUORING
LIQUORISH
LIQUORS
LIRA
LIRAS
LIRE
LIRIPIPE
LIRIPIPES
LIRIPOOP
LIRIPOOPS
LIRK
LIRKED
LIRKING
LIRKS
LIS
LISK
LISKS
LISLE
LISLES
LISP
LISPED
LISPER
LISPERS
LISPING
LISPINGLY
LISPINGS
LISPOUND
LISPOUNDS
LISPS
LISPUND
LISPUNDS
LISSES
LISSOM
LISSOME
LISSOMELY
LISSOMLY
LIST
LISTED
LISTEL
LISTELS
LISTEN
LISTENED
LISTENER
LISTENERS
LISTENING
LISTENS
LISTER
LISTERIA
LISTERIAS
LISTERS
LISTETH
LISTFUL
LISTING
LISTINGS
LISTLESS
LISTS
LIT
LITANIES
LITANY
LITCHI
LITCHIS
LITE
LITED
LITER
LITERACIES
LITERACY
LITERAL
LITERALLY
LITERALS
LITERARY
LITERATE
LITERATES
LITERATI
LITERATIM
LITERATO
LITERATOR
LITERATORS
LITERATUS
LITEROSE
LITERS
LITES
LITH
LITHARGE
LITHARGES
LITHATE
LITHATES
LITHE
LITHED
LITHELY
LITHENESS
LITHENESSES
LITHER
LITHERLY
LITHES
LITHESOME
LITHEST
LITHIA
LITHIAS
LITHIASES
LITHIASIS
LITHIC
LITHING
LITHISTID
LITHISTIDS
LITHITE
LITHITES
LITHIUM
LITHIUMS
LITHO
LITHOCYST
LITHOCYSTS
LITHOID
LITHOIDAL
LITHOLOGIES
LITHOLOGY
LITHOPONE
LITHOPONES
LITHOS
LITHOTOME
LITHOTOMES
LITHOTOMIES
LITHOTOMY
LITHS
LITIGABLE
LITIGANT
LITIGANTS
LITIGATE
LITIGATED
LITIGATES
LITIGATING
LITIGIOUS
LITING
LITMUS
LITMUSES
LITOTES
LITRE
LITRES
LITTEN
LITTER
LITTERED
LITTERING
LITTERS
LITTERY
LITTLE
LITTLEANE
LITTLEANES
LITTLER
LITTLES
LITTLEST
LITTLIN
LITTLING
LITTLINGS
LITTLINS
LITTORAL
LITTORALS
LITURGIC
LITURGICS
LITURGIES
LITURGIST
LITURGISTS
LITURGY
LITUUS
LITUUSES
LIVABLE
LIVE
LIVEABLE
LIVED
LIVELIER
LIVELIEST
LIVELILY
LIVELOD
LIVELODS
LIVELONG
LIVELONGS
LIVELOOD
LIVELOODS
LIVELY
LIVEN
LIVENED
LIVENER
LIVENERS
LIVENING
LIVENS
LIVER
LIVERIED
LIVERIES
LIVERISH
LIVERS
LIVERWING
LIVERWINGS
LIVERWORT
LIVERWORTS
LIVERY
LIVERYMAN
LIVERYMEN
LIVES
LIVEST
LIVESTOCK
LIVESTOCKS
LIVEWARE
LIVEWARES
LIVID
LIVIDER
LIVIDEST
LIVIDITIES
LIVIDITY
LIVIDLY
LIVIDNESS
LIVIDNESSES
LIVING
LIVINGS
LIVOR
LIVORS
LIVRAISON
LIVRAISONS
LIVRE
LIVRES
LIXIVIA
LIXIVIAL
LIXIVIATE
LIXIVIATED
LIXIVIATES
LIXIVIATING
LIXIVIOUS
LIXIVIUM
LIXIVIUMS
LIZARD
LIZARDS
LLAMA
LLAMAS
LLANERO
LLANEROS
LLANO
LLANOS
LO
LOACH
LOACHES
LOAD
LOADED
LOADEN
LOADENED
LOADENING
LOADENS
LOADER
LOADERS
LOADING
LOADINGS
LOADS
LOADSTAR
LOADSTARS
LOADSTONE
LOADSTONES
LOAF
LOAFED
LOAFER
LOAFERISH
LOAFERS
LOAFING
LOAFINGS
LOAFS
LOAM
LOAMED
LOAMIER
LOAMIEST
LOAMINESS
LOAMINESSES
LOAMING
LOAMS
LOAMY
LOAN
LOANABLE
LOANBACK
LOANBACKS
LOANED
LOANING
LOANINGS
LOANS
LOAST
LOATH
LOATHE
LOATHED
LOATHER

OATHERS
OATHES
OATHEST
OATHFUL
OATHING
OATHINGS
OATHLY
OATHSOME
OATHY
OAVE
OAVED
OAVES
OAVING
OB
OBAR
OBATE
OBATION
OBATIONS
OBBED
OBBIED
OBBIES
OBBING
OBBY
OBBYER
OBBYERS
OBBYING
OBBYINGS
OBBYIST
OBBYISTS
OBE
OBECTOMIES
OBECTOMY
OBED
OBELET
OBELETS
OBELIA
OBELIAS
OBELINE
OBELINES
OBES
OBI
OBING
OBINGS
OBIPED
OBLOLLIES
OBLOLLY
OBO
OBOS
OBOSE
OBOTOMIES
OBOTOMY
OBS
OBSCOUSE
OBSCOUSES
OBSTER
OBSTERS
OBULAR
OBULATE
OBULATED
OBULE
OBULES
OBULI
OBULUS
OBUS
LOBWORM
LOBWORMS
LOCAL
LOCALE
LOCALES
LOCALISE
LOCALISED
LOCALISER
LOCALISERS
LOCALISES
LOCALISING
LOCALISM
LOCALISMS
LOCALIST
LOCALISTS
LOCALITIES
LOCALITY
LOCALIZE
LOCALIZED
LOCALIZER
LOCALIZERS
LOCALIZES
LOCALIZING
LOCALLY
LOCALS
LOCATABLE
LOCATE
LOCATED
LOCATES
LOCATING
LOCATION
LOCATIONS
LOCATIVE
LOCATIVES
LOCELLATE
LOCH
LOCHAN
LOCHANS
LOCHIA
LOCHIAL
LOCHS
LOCI
LOCK
LOCKABLE
LOCKAGE
LOCKAGES
LOCKAWAY
LOCKAWAYS
LOCKED
LOCKER
LOCKERS
LOCKET
LOCKETS
LOCKFAST
LOCKFUL
LOCKFULS
LOCKHOUSE
LOCKHOUSES
LOCKING
LOCKJAW
LOCKJAWS
LOCKMAN
LOCKMEN
LOCKOUT
LOCKOUTS
LOCKPICK
LOCKPICKS
LOCKRAM
LOCKRAMS
LOCKS
LOCKSMAN
LOCKSMEN
LOCKSMITH
LOCKSMITHS
LOCKSTEP
LOCKSTEPS
LOCO
LOCOED
LOCOES
LOCOFOCO
LOCOFOCOS
LOCOMAN
LOCOMEN
LOCOMOTE
LOCOMOTED
LOCOMOTES
LOCOMOTING
LOCOMOTOR
LOCOMOTORS
LOCOPLANT
LOCOPLANTS
LOCOS
LOCOWEED
LOCOWEEDS
LOCULAR
LOCULATE
LOCULE
LOCULES
LOCULI
LOCULUS
LOCUM
LOCUMS
LOCUPLETE
LOCUS
LOCUST
LOCUSTA
LOCUSTAE
LOCUSTED
LOCUSTING
LOCUSTS
LOCUTION
LOCUTIONS
LOCUTORIES
LOCUTORY
LOD
LODE
LODEN
LODENS
LODES
LODESMAN
LODESMEN
LODESTAR
LODESTARS
LODESTONE
LODESTONES
LODGE
LODGED
LODGEMENT
LODGEMENTS
LODGEPOLE
LODGEPOLES
LODGER
LODGERS
LODGES
LODGING
LODGINGS
LODGMENT
LODGMENTS
LODICULA
LODICULAE
LODICULE
LODICULES
LODS
LOESS
LOESSES
LOFT
LOFTED
LOFTER
LOFTERS
LOFTIER
LOFTIEST
LOFTILY
LOFTINESS
LOFTINESSES
LOFTING
LOFTS
LOFTY
LOG
LOGAN
LOGANIA
LOGANIAS
LOGANS
LOGAOEDIC
LOGARITHM
LOGARITHMS
LOGBOARD
LOGBOARDS
LOGBOOK
LOGBOOKS
LOGE
LOGES
LOGGAT
LOGGATS
LOGGED
LOGGER
LOGGERS
LOGGIA
LOGGIAS
LOGGIE
LOGGING
LOGGINGS
LOGIA
LOGIC
LOGICAL
LOGICALLY
LOGICIAN
LOGICIANS
LOGICISE
LOGICISED
LOGICISES
LOGICISING
LOGICISM
LOGICISMS
LOGICIST
LOGICISTS
LOGICIZE
LOGICIZED
LOGICIZES
LOGICIZING
LOGICS
LOGIE
LOGIER
LOGIES
LOGIEST
LOGIN
LOGINS
LOGION
LOGISTIC
LOGISTICS
LOGJUICE
LOGJUICES
LOGLINE
LOGLINES
LOGLOG
LOGLOGS
LOGO
LOGOFF
LOGOFFS
LOGOGRAM
LOGOGRAMS
LOGOGRAPH
LOGOGRAPHS
LOGOGRIPH
LOGOGRIPHS
LOGOMACHIES
LOGOMACHY
LOGON
LOGONS
LOGOPEDIC
LOGOPHILE
LOGOPHILES
LOGORRHEA
LOGORRHEAS
LOGOS
LOGOTHETE
LOGOTHETES
LOGOTYPE
LOGOTYPES
LOGOUT
LOGOUTS
LOGS
LOGWOOD
LOGWOODS
LOGY
LOID
LOIDED
LOIDING
LOIDS
LOIN
LOINCLOTH
LOINCLOTHS
LOINS
LOIPE
LOIPEN
LOIR
LOIRS

The Chambers Dictionary is the authority for many longer words; see *OSW* Introduction, page xii

LOITER
LOITERED
LOITERER
LOITERERS
LOITERING
LOITERINGS
LOITERS
LOKE
LOKES
LOKSHEN
LOLIGO
LOLIGOS
LOLIUM
LOLIUMS
LOLL
LOLLED
LOLLER
LOLLERS
LOLLIES
LOLLING
LOLLINGLY
LOLLIPOP
LOLLIPOPS
LOLLOP
LOLLOPED
LOLLOPING
LOLLOPS
LOLLS
LOLLY
LOLLYGAG
LOLLYGAGGED
LOLLYGAGGING
LOLLYGAGS
LOLOG
LOLOGS
LOMA
LOMAS
LOMATA
LOME
LOMED
LOMENT
LOMENTA
LOMENTS
LOMENTUM
LOMES
LOMING
LOMPISH
LONE
LONELIER
LONELIEST
LONELY
LONENESS
LONENESSES
LONER
LONERS
LONESOME
LONESOMES
LONG
LONGA
LONGAEVAL
LONGAN
LONGANS
LONGAS
LONGBOAT
LONGBOATS
LONGBOW
LONGBOWS
LONGCLOTH
LONGCLOTHS
LONGE
LONGED
LONGEING
LONGER
LONGERON
LONGERONS
LONGES
LONGEST
LONGEVAL
LONGEVITIES
LONGEVITY
LONGEVOUS
LONGHAND
LONGHANDS
LONGHORN
LONGHORNS
LONGHOUSE
LONGHOUSES
LONGICORN
LONGICORNS
LONGING
LONGINGLY
LONGINGS
LONGISH
LONGITUDE
LONGITUDES
LONGLY
LONGNESS
LONGNESSES
LONGS
LONGSHIP
LONGSHIPS
LONGSHORE
LONGSOME
LONGUEUR
LONGUEURS
LONGWALL
LONGWALLS
LONGWAYS
LONGWISE
LONICERA
LONICERAS
LOO
LOOBIER
LOOBIES
LOOBIEST
LOOBILY
LOOBY
LOOED
LOOF
LOOFA
LOOFAH
LOOFAHS
LOOFAS
LOOFFUL
LOOFFULS
LOOFS
LOOING
LOOK
LOOKED
LOOKER
LOOKERS
LOOKING
LOOKISM
LOOKISMS
LOOKOUT
LOOKOUTS
LOOKS
LOOM
LOOMED
LOOMING
LOOMS
LOON
LOONIE
LOONIER
LOONIES
LOONIEST
LOONINESS
LOONINESSES
LOONING
LOONINGS
LOONS
LOONY
LOOP
LOOPED
LOOPER
LOOPERS
LOOPHOLE
LOOPHOLED
LOOPHOLES
LOOPHOLING
LOOPIER
LOOPIEST
LOOPING
LOOPINGS
LOOPS
LOOPY
LOOR
LOORD
LOORDS
LOOS
LOOSE
LOOSED
LOOSELY
LOOSEN
LOOSENED
LOOSENER
LOOSENERS
LOOSENESS
LOOSENESSES
LOOSENING
LOOSENS
LOOSER
LOOSES
LOOSEST
LOOSING
LOOT
LOOTED
LOOTEN
LOOTER
LOOTERS
LOOTING
LOOTINGS
LOOTS
LOOVES
LOP
LOPE
LOPED
LOPER
LOPERS
LOPES
LOPGRASS
LOPGRASSES
LOPHODONT
LOPING
LOPPED
LOPPER
LOPPERED
LOPPERING
LOPPERS
LOPPING
LOPPINGS
LOPS
LOPSIDED
LOQUACITIES
LOQUACITY
LOQUAT
LOQUATS
LOQUITUR
LOR
LORAL
LORAN
LORANS
LORATE
LORAZEPAM
LORAZEPAMS
LORCHA
LORCHAS
LORD
LORDED
LORDING
LORDINGS
LORDKIN
LORDKINS
LORDLESS
LORDLIER
LORDLIEST
LORDLING
LORDLINGS
LORDLY
LORDOSES
LORDOSIS
LORDOTIC
LORDS
LORDSHIP
LORDSHIPS
LORDY
LORE
LOREL
LORELS
LORES
LORETTE
LORETTES
LORGNETTE
LORGNETTES
LORGNON
LORGNONS
LORIC
LORICA
LORICAE
LORICATE
LORICATED
LORICATES
LORICATING
LORICS
LORIES
LORIKEET
LORIKEETS
LORIMER
LORIMERS
LORINER
LORINERS
LORING
LORINGS
LORIOT
LORIOTS
LORIS
LORISES
LORN
LORRELL
LORRELLS
LORRIES
LORRY
LORY
LOS
LOSABLE
LOSE
LOSED
LOSEL
LOSELS
LOSEN
LOSER
LOSERS
LOSES
LOSH
LOSING
LOSINGLY
LOSINGS
LOSS
LOSSES
LOSSIER
LOSSIEST
LOSSMAKER
LOSSMAKERS
LOSSY
LOST
LOT
LOTA
LOTAH
LOTAHS
LOTAS
LOTE
LOTES
LOTH
LOTHEFULL
LOTHER
LOTHEST
LOTHFULL
LOTIC
LOTION
LOTIONS

OTO
OTOS
OTOSES
OTS
OTTED
OTTERIES
OTTERY
OTTING
OTTO
OTTOS
OTUS
OTUSES
OUCHE
OUCHELY
OUD
OUDEN
OUDENED
OUDENING
OUDENS
OUDER
OUDEST
OUDISH
OUDLY
OUDMOUTH
OUDMOUTHS
OUDNESS
OUDNESSES
OUGH
OUGHS
OUIS
OUN
OUND
OUNDED
OUNDER
OUNDERED
OUNDERING
OUNDERINGS
OUNDERS
OUNDING
OUNDS
OUNED
OUNGE
OUNGED
OUNGER
OUNGERS
OUNGES
OUNGING
OUNGINGS
OUNING
OUNS
OUP
OUPE
OUPED
OUPEN
OUPES
OUPING
OUPIT
OUPS
OUR
OURE
OURED
OURES
OURIER
OURIEST
LOURING
LOURINGLY
LOURINGS
LOURS
LOURY
LOUSE
LOUSED
LOUSES
LOUSIER
LOUSIEST
LOUSILY
LOUSINESS
LOUSINESSES
LOUSING
LOUSY
LOUT
LOUTED
LOUTING
LOUTISH
LOUTISHLY
LOUTS
LOUVER
LOUVERED
LOUVERS
LOUVRE
LOUVRED
LOUVRES
LOVABLE
LOVAGE
LOVAGES
LOVAT
LOVATS
LOVE
LOVEABLE
LOVEBIRD
LOVEBIRDS
LOVEBITE
LOVEBITES
LOVED
LOVELESS
LOVELIER
LOVELIES
LOVELIEST
LOVELIGHT
LOVELIGHTS
LOVELILY
LOVELOCK
LOVELOCKS
LOVELORN
LOVELY
LOVEMAKER
LOVEMAKERS
LOVER
LOVERED
LOVERLESS
LOVERLY
LOVERS
LOVES
LOVESICK
LOVESOME
LOVEY
LOVEYS
LOVING
LOVINGLY
LOVINGS
LOW
LOWAN
LOWANS
LOWBOY
LOWBOYS
LOWE
LOWED
LOWER
LOWERED
LOWERIER
LOWERIEST
LOWERING
LOWERINGS
LOWERMOST
LOWERS
LOWERY
LOWES
LOWEST
LOWING
LOWINGS
LOWLAND
LOWLANDER
LOWLANDERS
LOWLANDS
LOWLIER
LOWLIEST
LOWLIGHT
LOWLIGHTED
LOWLIGHTING
LOWLIGHTS
LOWLIHEAD
LOWLIHEADS
LOWLILY
LOWLINESS
LOWLINESSES
LOWLY
LOWN
LOWND
LOWNDED
LOWNDING
LOWNDS
LOWNE
LOWNED
LOWNES
LOWNESS
LOWNESSES
LOWNING
LOWNS
LOWS
LOWSE
LOWSER
LOWSES
LOWSEST
LOWSING
LOWSIT
LOWT
LOWTED
LOWTING
LOWTS
LOWVELD
LOWVELDS
LOX
LOXES
LOXODROME
LOXODROMES
LOXODROMIES
LOXODROMY
LOXYGEN
LOXYGENS
LOY
LOYAL
LOYALIST
LOYALISTS
LOYALLER
LOYALLEST
LOYALLY
LOYALTIES
LOYALTY
LOYS
LOZELL
LOZELLS
LOZEN
LOZENGE
LOZENGED
LOZENGES
LOZENGY
LOZENS
LUAU
LUAUS
LUBBARD
LUBBARDS
LUBBER
LUBBERLY
LUBBERS
LUBFISH
LUBFISHES
LUBRA
LUBRAS
LUBRIC
LUBRICAL
LUBRICANT
LUBRICANTS
LUBRICATE
LUBRICATED
LUBRICATES
LUBRICATING
LUBRICITIES
LUBRICITY
LUBRICOUS
LUCARNE
LUCARNES
LUCE
LUCENCIES
LUCENCY
LUCENT
LUCERN
LUCERNE
LUCERNES
LUCERNS
LUCES
LUCID
LUCIDER
LUCIDEST
LUCIDITIES
LUCIDITY
LUCIDLY
LUCIDNESS
LUCIDNESSES
LUCIFER
LUCIFERIN
LUCIFERINS
LUCIFERS
LUCIGEN
LUCIGENS
LUCK
LUCKEN
LUCKIE
LUCKIER
LUCKIES
LUCKIEST
LUCKILY
LUCKINESS
LUCKINESSES
LUCKLESS
LUCKS
LUCKY
LUCRATIVE
LUCRE
LUCRES
LUCTATION
LUCTATIONS
LUCUBRATE
LUCUBRATED
LUCUBRATES
LUCUBRATING
LUCULENT
LUCUMA
LUCUMAS
LUCUMO
LUCUMONES
LUCUMOS
LUD
LUDIC
LUDICALLY
LUDICROUS
LUDO
LUDOS
LUDS
LUDSHIP
LUDSHIPS
LUES
LUETIC
LUFF
LUFFA
LUFFAS
LUFFED
LUFFING
LUFFS
LUG
LUGE
LUGED
LUGEING
LUGEINGS
LUGER
LUGERS
LUGES
LUGGABLE
LUGGABLES
LUGGAGE
LUGGAGES
LUGGED

LUGGER
LUGGERS
LUGGIE
LUGGIES
LUGGING
LUGHOLE
LUGHOLES
LUGING
LUGINGS
LUGS
LUGSAIL
LUGSAILS
LUGWORM
LUGWORMS
LUIT
LUITEN
LUKE
LUKEWARM
LULIBUB
LULIBUBS
LULL
LULLABIED
LULLABIES
LULLABY
LULLABYING
LULLED
LULLING
LULLS
LULU
LULUS
LUM
LUMBAGO
LUMBAGOS
LUMBANG
LUMBANGS
LUMBAR
LUMBER
LUMBERED
LUMBERER
LUMBERERS
LUMBERING
LUMBERINGS
LUMBERLY
LUMBERMAN
LUMBERMEN
LUMBERS
LUMBRICAL
LUMBRICALS
LUMBRICI
LUMBRICUS
LUMBRICUSES
LUMEN
LUMENAL
LUMENS
LUMINA
LUMINAIRE
LUMINAIRES
LUMINAL
LUMINANCE
LUMINANCES
LUMINANT
LUMINANTS
LUMINARIES
LUMINARY
LUMINE
LUMINED
LUMINES
LUMINESCE
LUMINESCED
LUMINESCES
LUMINESCING
LUMINING
LUMINIST
LUMINISTS
LUMINOUS
LUMME
LUMMIER
LUMMIEST
LUMMOX
LUMMOXES
LUMMY
LUMP
LUMPED
LUMPEN
LUMPENLY
LUMPER
LUMPERS
LUMPFISH
LUMPFISHES
LUMPIER
LUMPIEST
LUMPILY
LUMPINESS
LUMPINESSES
LUMPING
LUMPISH
LUMPISHLY
LUMPKIN
LUMPKINS
LUMPS
LUMPY
LUMS
LUNA
LUNACIES
LUNACY
LUNANAUT
LUNANAUTS
LUNAR
LUNARIAN
LUNARIANS
LUNARIES
LUNARIST
LUNARISTS
LUNARNAUT
LUNARNAUTS
LUNARS
LUNARY
LUNAS
LUNATE
LUNATED
LUNATIC
LUNATICS
LUNATION
LUNATIONS
LUNCH
LUNCHED
LUNCHEON
LUNCHEONED
LUNCHEONING
LUNCHEONS
LUNCHER
LUNCHERS
LUNCHES
LUNCHING
LUNE
LUNES
LUNETTE
LUNETTES
LUNG
LUNGE
LUNGED
LUNGEING
LUNGES
LUNGFUL
LUNGFULS
LUNGI
LUNGIE
LUNGIES
LUNGING
LUNGIS
LUNGS
LUNGWORT
LUNGWORTS
LUNISOLAR
LUNITIDAL
LUNKER
LUNKERS
LUNKHEAD
LUNKHEADS
LUNT
LUNTED
LUNTING
LUNTS
LUNULA
LUNULAE
LUNULAR
LUNULATE
LUNULATED
LUNULE
LUNULES
LUNYIE
LUNYIES
LUPIN
LUPINE
LUPINES
LUPINS
LUPPEN
LUPULIN
LUPULINE
LUPULINIC
LUPULINS
LUPUS
LUPUSES
LUR
LURCH
LURCHED
LURCHER
LURCHERS
LURCHES
LURCHING
LURDAN
LURDANE
LURDANES
LURDANS
LURDEN
LURDENS
LURE
LURED
LURES
LURGI
LURGIES
LURGIS
LURGY
LURID
LURIDER
LURIDEST
LURIDLY
LURIDNESS
LURIDNESSES
LURING
LURK
LURKED
LURKER
LURKERS
LURKING
LURKINGS
LURKS
LURRIES
LURRY
LURS
LURVE
LURVES
LUSCIOUS
LUSH
LUSHED
LUSHER
LUSHERS
LUSHES
LUSHEST
LUSHIER
LUSHIEST
LUSHING
LUSHLY
LUSHNESS
LUSHNESSES
LUSHY
LUSK
LUSKED
LUSKING
LUSKISH
LUSKS
LUST
LUSTED
LUSTER
LUSTERED
LUSTERING
LUSTERS
LUSTFUL
LUSTFULLY
LUSTICK
LUSTIER
LUSTIEST
LUSTIHEAD
LUSTIHEADS
LUSTIHOOD
LUSTIHOODS
LUSTILY
LUSTINESS
LUSTINESSES
LUSTING
LUSTIQUE
LUSTLESS
LUSTRA
LUSTRAL
LUSTRATE
LUSTRATED
LUSTRATES
LUSTRATING
LUSTRE
LUSTRED
LUSTRES
LUSTRINE
LUSTRINES
LUSTRING
LUSTRINGS
LUSTROUS
LUSTRUM
LUSTRUMS
LUSTS
LUSTY
LUTANIST
LUTANISTS
LUTE
LUTEAL
LUTECIUM
LUTECIUMS
LUTED
LUTEIN
LUTEINISE
LUTEINISED
LUTEINISES
LUTEINISING
LUTEINIZE
LUTEINIZED
LUTEINIZES
LUTEINIZING
LUTEINS
LUTENIST
LUTENISTS
LUTEOLIN
LUTEOLINS
LUTEOLOUS
LUTEOUS
LUTER
LUTERS
LUTES
LUTESCENT
LUTETIUM
LUTETIUMS
LUTHERN
LUTHERNS
LUTHIER
LUTHIERS
LUTING
LUTINGS
LUTIST
LUTISTS
LUTTEN
LUTZ
LUTZES

JV
JVS
JVVIE
JVVIES
IVVY
JX
JXATE
JXATED
JXATES
JXATING
JXATION
JXATIONS
JXE
JXES
JXMETER
JXMETERS
JXURIANT
JXURIATE
JXURIATED
JXURIATES
JXURIATING
JXURIES
JXURIOUS
JXURIST
JXURISTS
JXURY
IZ
JZERN
JZERNS
LUZZES
LYAM
LYAMS
LYART
LYCEE
LYCEES
LYCEUM
LYCEUMS
LYCHEE
LYCHEES
LYCHGATE
LYCHGATES
LYCHNIS
LYCHNISES
LYCOPOD
LYCOPODS
LYDDITE
LYDDITES
LYE
LYES
LYFULL
LYING
LYINGLY
LYINGS
LYKEWAKE
LYKEWAKES
LYKEWALK
LYKEWALKS
LYM
LYME
LYMES
LYMITER
LYMITERS
LYMPH
LYMPHAD
LYMPHADS
LYMPHATIC
LYMPHATICS
LYMPHOID
LYMPHOMA
LYMPHOMAS
LYMPHOMATA
LYMPHS
LYMS
LYNAGE
LYNAGES
LYNCEAN
LYNCH
LYNCHED
LYNCHES
LYNCHET
LYNCHETS
LYNCHING
LYNCHPIN
LYNCHPINS
LYNE
LYNES
LYNX
LYNXES
LYOMEROUS
LYONNAISE
LYOPHIL
LYOPHILE
LYOPHILIC
LYOPHOBE
LYOPHOBIC
LYRATE
LYRATED
LYRE
LYRES
LYRIC
LYRICAL
LYRICALLY
LYRICISM
LYRICISMS
LYRICIST
LYRICISTS
LYRICON
LYRICONS
LYRICS
LYRIFORM
LYRISM
LYRISMS
LYRIST
LYRISTS
LYSE
LYSED
LYSERGIDE
LYSERGIDES
LYSES
LYSIGENIC
LYSIMETER
LYSIMETERS
LYSIN
LYSINE
LYSINES
LYSING
LYSINS
LYSIS
LYSOL
LYSOLS
LYSOSOME
LYSOSOMES
LYSOZYME
LYSOZYMES
LYSSA
LYSSAS
LYTE
LYTED
LYTES
LYTHE
LYTHES
LYTING
LYTTA
LYTTAE
LYTTAS

M

MA
MAA
MAAED
MAAING
MAAR
MAARS
MAAS
MAATJES
MAC
MACABRE
MACACO
MACACOS
MACADAM
MACADAMIA
MACADAMIAS
MACADAMS
MACAHUBA
MACAHUBAS
MACALLUM
MACALLUMS
MACAQUE
MACAQUES
MACARISE
MACARISED
MACARISES
MACARISING
MACARISM
MACARISMS
MACARIZE
MACARIZED
MACARIZES
MACARIZING
MACARONI
MACARONIC
MACARONICS
MACARONIES
MACARONIS
MACAROON
MACAROONS
MACASSAR
MACASSARS
MACAW
MACAWS
MACCHIE
MACE
MACED
MACEDOINE
MACEDOINES
MACER
MACERATE
MACERATED
MACERATES
MACERATING
MACERATOR
MACERATORS
MACERS
MACES
MACHAIR
MACHAIRS
MACHAN
MACHANS
MACHETE
MACHETES
MACHINATE
MACHINATED
MACHINATES
MACHINATING
MACHINE
MACHINED
MACHINERIES
MACHINERY
MACHINES
MACHINING
MACHINIST
MACHINISTS
MACHISMO
MACHISMOS
MACHMETER
MACHMETERS
MACHO
MACHOS
MACHREE
MACHREES
MACHZOR
MACHZORIM
MACING
MACINTOSH
MACINTOSHES
MACK
MACKEREL
MACKERELS
MACKINAW
MACKINAWS
MACKLE
MACKLED
MACKLES
MACKLING
MACKS
MACLE
MACLED
MACLES
MACON
MACONS
MACOYA
MACOYAS
MACRAME
MACRAMES
MACRAMI
MACRAMIS
MACRO
MACROBIAN
MACROCODE
MACROCODES
MACROCOPIES
MACROCOPY
MACROCOSM
MACROCOSMS
MACROCYTE
MACROCYTES
MACRODOME
MACRODOMES
MACROLOGIES
MACROLOGY
MACRON
MACRONS
MACROPOD
MACROPODS
MACROS
MACRURAL
MACRUROUS
MACS
MACTATION
MACTATIONS
MACULA
MACULAE
MACULAR
MACULATE
MACULATED
MACULATES
MACULATING
MACULE
MACULES
MACULOSE
MAD
MADAM
MADAME
MADAMED
MADAMING
MADAMS
MADAROSES
MADAROSIS
MADBRAIN
MADCAP
MADCAPS
MADDED
MADDEN
MADDENED
MADDENING
MADDENS
MADDER
MADDERS
MADDEST
MADDING
MADDINGLY
MADDOCK
MADDOCKS
MADE
MADEFIED
MADEFIES
MADEFY
MADEFYING
MADELEINE
MADELEINES
MADERISE
MADERISED
MADERISES
MADERISING
MADERIZE
MADERIZED
MADERIZES
MADERIZING
MADGE
MADGES
MADHOUSE
MADHOUSES
MADID
MADLING
MADLINGS
MADLY
MADMAN
MADMEN
MADNESS
MADNESSES
MADOQUA
MADOQUAS
MADRAS
MADRASA
MADRASAH
MADRASAHS
MADRASAS
MADRASES
MADRASSA
MADRASSAH
MADRASSAHS
MADRASSAS
MADREPORE
MADREPORES
MADRIGAL
MADRIGALS
MADRONA
MADRONAS
MADRONE
MADRONES
MADRONO
MADRONOS
MADS
MADWOMAN
MADWOMEN
MADWORT
MADWORTS
MADZOON
MADZOONS
MAE
MAELID
MAELIDS
MAELSTROM
MAELSTROMS
MAENAD
MAENADIC
MAENADS
MAESTOSO
MAESTRI
MAESTRO
MAESTROS
MAFFIA
MAFFIAS
MAFFICK
MAFFICKED
MAFFICKER
MAFFICKERS
MAFFICKING
MAFFICKINGS
MAFFICKS
MAFFLED
MAFFLIN
MAFFLING
MAFFLINGS
MAFFLINS
MAFIA
MAFIAS
MAFIC
MAFICS
MAFIOSI
MAFIOSO
MAG
MAGALOG
MAGALOGS
MAGAZINE
MAGAZINES
MAGDALEN
MAGDALENE
MAGDALENES
MAGDALENS
MAGE
MAGENTA
MAGENTAS
MAGES
MAGESHIP
MAGESHIPS
MAGG

AGGED
AGGING
AGGOT
AGGOTIER
AGGOTIEST
AGGOTS
AGGOTY
AGGS
AGI
AGIAN
AGIANISM
AGIANISMS
AGIANS
AGIC
AGICAL
AGICALLY
AGICIAN
AGICIANS
AGICKED
AGICKING
AGICS
AGILP
AGILPS
AGISM
AGISMS
AGISTER
AGISTERIES
AGISTERS
AGISTERY
AGISTRAL
AGISTRALS
AGLEV
AGMA
AGMAS
AGMATA
AGMATIC
AGNALIUM
AGNALIUMS
AGNATE
AGNATES
AGNES
AGNESES
AGNESIA
AGNESIAN
AGNESIAS
AGNESITE
AGNESITES
AGNESIUM
AGNESIUMS
AGNET
AGNETIC
AGNETICS
AGNETISE
AGNETISED
AGNETISES
AGNETISING
AGNETISM
AGNETISMS
AGNETIST
AGNETISTS
AGNETITE
AGNETITES
AGNETIZE
AGNETIZED

MAGNETIZES
MAGNETIZING
MAGNETO
MAGNETON
MAGNETONS
MAGNETOS
MAGNETRON
MAGNETRONS
MAGNETS
MAGNIFIC
MAGNIFICO
MAGNIFICOES
MAGNIFIED
MAGNIFIER
MAGNIFIERS
MAGNIFIES
MAGNIFY
MAGNIFYING
MAGNITUDE
MAGNITUDES
MAGNOLIA
MAGNOLIAS
MAGNON
MAGNONS
MAGNOX
MAGNOXES
MAGNUM
MAGNUMS
MAGOT
MAGOTS
MAGPIE
MAGPIES
MAGS
MAGSMAN
MAGSMEN
MAGUEY
MAGUEYS
MAGUS
MAGYAR
MAHARAJA
MAHARAJAH
MAHARAJAHS
MAHARAJAS
MAHARANEE
MAHARANEES
MAHARANI
MAHARANIS
MAHARISHI
MAHARISHIS
MAHATMA
MAHATMAS
MAHLSTICK
MAHLSTICKS
MAHMAL
MAHMALS
MAHOE
MAHOES
MAHOGANIES
MAHOGANY
MAHONIA
MAHONIAS
MAHOUT
MAHOUTS
MAHSEER

MAHSEERS
MAHSIR
MAHSIRS
MAHUA
MAHUAS
MAHWA
MAHWAS
MAHZOR
MAHZORIM
MAID
MAIDAN
MAIDANS
MAIDED
MAIDEN
MAIDENISH
MAIDENLY
MAIDENS
MAIDHOOD
MAIDHOODS
MAIDING
MAIDISH
MAIDISM
MAIDISMS
MAIDLESS
MAIDS
MAIEUTIC
MAIEUTICS
MAIGRE
MAIGRES
MAIK
MAIKO
MAIKOS
MAIKS
MAIL
MAILABLE
MAILBAG
MAILBAGS
MAILBOX
MAILBOXES
MAILE
MAILED
MAILER
MAILERS
MAILES
MAILGRAM
MAILGRAMMED
MAILGRAMMING
MAILGRAMS
MAILING
MAILINGS
MAILLOT
MAILLOTS
MAILMAN
MAILMEN
MAILMERGE
MAILMERGED
MAILMERGES
MAILMERGING
MAILROOM
MAILROOMS
MAILS
MAILSACK
MAILSACKS
MAILSHOT

MAILSHOTS
MAILSHOTTED
MAILSHOTTING
MAILVAN
MAILVANS
MAIM
MAIMED
MAIMING
MAIMINGS
MAIMS
MAIN
MAINBOOM
MAINBOOMS
MAINBRACE
MAINBRACES
MAINDOOR
MAINDOORS
MAINED
MAINER
MAINEST
MAINFRAME
MAINFRAMES
MAINING
MAINLAND
MAINLANDS
MAINLINE
MAINLINED
MAINLINER
MAINLINERS
MAINLINES
MAINLINING
MAINLININGS
MAINLY
MAINMAST
MAINMASTS
MAINOR
MAINORS
MAINOUR
MAINOURS
MAINPRISE
MAINPRISES
MAINS
MAINSAIL
MAINSAILS
MAINSHEET
MAINSHEETS
MAINSTAY
MAINSTAYS
MAINTAIN
MAINTAINED
MAINTAINING
MAINTAINS
MAINTOP
MAINTOPS
MAINYARD
MAINYARDS
MAIOLICA
MAIOLICAS
MAIR
MAIRE
MAIRES
MAIRS
MAISE
MAISES

MAIST
MAISTER
MAISTERED
MAISTERING
MAISTERS
MAISTRIES
MAISTRING
MAISTRINGS
MAISTRY
MAIZE
MAIZES
MAJESTIC
MAJESTIES
MAJESTY
MAJLIS
MAJLISES
MAJOLICA
MAJOLICAS
MAJOR
MAJORAT
MAJORATS
MAJORED
MAJORETTE
MAJORETTES
MAJORING
MAJORITIES
MAJORITY
MAJORS
MAJORSHIP
MAJORSHIPS
MAJUSCULE
MAJUSCULES
MAK
MAKABLE
MAKAR
MAKARS
MAKE
MAKEABLE
MAKEBATE
MAKEBATES
MAKELESS
MAKEOVER
MAKEOVERS
MAKER
MAKERS
MAKES
MAKESHIFT
MAKESHIFTS
MAKIMONO
MAKIMONOS
MAKING
MAKINGS
MAKO
MAKOS
MAKS
MAL
MALACHITE
MALACHITES
MALACIA
MALACIAS
MALADIES
MALADROIT
MALADY
MALAGUENA

MALAGUENAS
MALAISE
MALAISES
MALAMUTE
MALAMUTES
MALANDER
MALANDERS
MALAPERT
MALAR
MALARIA
MALARIAL
MALARIAN
MALARIAS
MALARIOUS
MALARKEY
MALARKEYS
MALARKIES
MALARKY
MALARS
MALATE
MALATES
MALAX
MALAXAGE
MALAXAGES
MALAXATE
MALAXATED
MALAXATES
MALAXATING
MALAXATOR
MALAXATORS
MALAXED
MALAXES
MALAXING
MALE
MALEATE
MALEATES
MALEDICT
MALEDICTED
MALEDICTING
MALEDICTS
MALEFFECT
MALEFFECTS
MALEFIC
MALEFICE
MALEFICES
MALEIC
MALEMUTE
MALEMUTES
MALENGINE
MALENGINES
MALES
MALFORMED
MALGRADO
MALGRE
MALGRED
MALGRES
MALGRING
MALI
MALIC
MALICE
MALICED
MALICES
MALICHO
MALICHOS
MALICING
MALICIOUS
MALIGN
MALIGNANT
MALIGNANTS
MALIGNED
MALIGNER
MALIGNERS
MALIGNING
MALIGNITIES
MALIGNITY
MALIGNLY
MALIGNS
MALIK
MALIKS
MALINGER
MALINGERED
MALINGERIES
MALINGERING
MALINGERS
MALINGERY
MALIS
MALISM
MALISMS
MALISON
MALISONS
MALIST
MALKIN
MALKINS
MALL
MALLAM
MALLAMS
MALLANDER
MALLANDERS
MALLARD
MALLARDS
MALLEABLE
MALLEATE
MALLEATED
MALLEATES
MALLEATING
MALLECHO
MALLECHOS
MALLED
MALLEE
MALLEES
MALLEI
MALLEMUCK
MALLEMUCKS
MALLENDER
MALLENDERS
MALLEOLAR
MALLEOLI
MALLEOLUS
MALLEOLUSES
MALLET
MALLETS
MALLEUS
MALLEUSES
MALLING
MALLOW
MALLOWS
MALLS
MALM
MALMAG
MALMAGS
MALMS
MALMSEY
MALMSEYS
MALMSTONE
MALMSTONES
MALODOUR
MALODOURS
MALONATE
MALONATES
MALS
MALSTICK
MALSTICKS
MALT
MALTALENT
MALTALENTS
MALTASE
MALTASES
MALTED
MALTHA
MALTHAS
MALTIER
MALTIEST
MALTING
MALTINGS
MALTMAN
MALTMEN
MALTOSE
MALTOSES
MALTREAT
MALTREATED
MALTREATING
MALTREATS
MALTS
MALTSTER
MALTSTERS
MALTWORM
MALTWORMS
MALTY
MALVA
MALVAS
MALVASIA
MALVASIAS
MALVESIE
MALVESIES
MALVOISIE
MALVOISIES
MAM
MAMA
MAMAS
MAMBA
MAMBAS
MAMBO
MAMBOED
MAMBOING
MAMBOS
MAMEE
MAMEES
MAMELON
MAMELONS
MAMELUCO
MAMELUCOS
MAMILLA
MAMILLAE
MAMILLAR
MAMILLARY
MAMILLATE
MAMMA
MAMMAE
MAMMAL
MAMMALIAN
MAMMALOGIES
MAMMALOGY
MAMMALS
MAMMARY
MAMMAS
MAMMATE
MAMMEE
MAMMEES
MAMMER
MAMMERED
MAMMERING
MAMMERS
MAMMET
MAMMETRIES
MAMMETRY
MAMMETS
MAMMIES
MAMMIFER
MAMMIFERS
MAMMIFORM
MAMMILLA
MAMMILLAE
MAMMOCK
MAMMOCKED
MAMMOCKING
MAMMOCKS
MAMMOGRAM
MAMMOGRAMS
MAMMON
MAMMONISH
MAMMONISM
MAMMONISMS
MAMMONIST
MAMMONISTS
MAMMONITE
MAMMONITES
MAMMONS
MAMMOTH
MAMMOTHS
MAMMY
MAMS
MAMSELLE
MAMSELLES
MAMZER
MAMZERIM
MAMZERS
MAN
MANA
MANACLE
MANACLED
MANACLES
MANACLING
MANAGE
MANAGED
MANAGER
MANAGERS
MANAGES
MANAGING
MANAKIN
MANAKINS
MANANA
MANANAS
MANAS
MANATEE
MANATEES
MANATI
MANATIS
MANCALA
MANCALAS
MANCANDO
MANCHE
MANCHES
MANCHET
MANCHETS
MANCIPATE
MANCIPATED
MANCIPATES
MANCIPATING
MANCIPLE
MANCIPLES
MANCUS
MANCUSES
MAND
MANDALA
MANDALAS
MANDAMUS
MANDAMUSES
MANDARIN
MANDARINE
MANDARINES
MANDARINS
MANDATARIES
MANDATARY
MANDATE
MANDATED
MANDATES
MANDATING
MANDATOR
MANDATORIES
MANDATORS
MANDATORY
MANDIBLE
MANDIBLES
MANDILION
MANDILIONS
MANDIOC
MANDIOCA
MANDIOCAS
MANDIOCCA
MANDIOCCAS
MANDIOCS
MANDIR
MANDIRA
MANDIRAS
MANDIRS
MANDOLA
MANDOLAS
MANDOLIN
MANDOLINE
MANDOLINES

MANDOLINS
MANDOM
MANDOMS
MANDORA
MANDORAS
MANDORLA
MANDORLAS
MANDRAKE
MANDRAKES
MANDREL
MANDRELS
MANDRIL
MANDRILL
MANDRILLS
MANDRILS
MANDUCATE
MANDUCATED
MANDUCATES
MANDUCATING
MANDYLION
MANDYLIONS
MANE
MANED
MANEGE
MANEGED
MANEGES
MANEGING
MANEH
MANEHS
MANELESS
MANENT
MANES
MANET
MANEUVER
MANEUVERED
MANEUVERING
MANEUVERS
MANFUL
MANFULLY
MANG
MANGA
MANGABEY
MANGABEYS
MANGAL
MANGALS
MANGANATE
MANGANATES
MANGANESE
MANGANESES
MANGANIC
MANGANITE
MANGANITES
MANGANOUS
MANGAS
MANGE
MANGED
MANGEL
MANGELS
MANGER
MANGERS
MANGES
MANGETOUT
MANGETOUTS
MANGEY
MANGIER
MANGIEST
MANGINESS
MANGINESSES
MANGING
MANGLE
MANGLED
MANGLER
MANGLERS
MANGLES
MANGLING
MANGO
MANGOES
MANGOLD
MANGOLDS
MANGONEL
MANGONELS
MANGOSTAN
MANGOSTANS
MANGOUSTE
MANGOUSTES
MANGROVE
MANGROVES
MANGS
MANGY
MANHANDLE
MANHANDLED
MANHANDLES
MANHANDLING
MANHOLE
MANHOLES
MANHOOD
MANHOODS
MANHUNT
MANHUNTS
MANI
MANIA
MANIAC
MANIACAL
MANIACS
MANIAS
MANIC
MANICALLY
MANICURE
MANICURED
MANICURES
MANICURING
MANIES
MANIFEST
MANIFESTED
MANIFESTING
MANIFESTO
MANIFESTOED
MANIFESTOES
MANIFESTOING
MANIFESTOS
MANIFESTS
MANIFOLD
MANIFOLDED
MANIFOLDING
MANIFOLDS
MANIFORM
MANIHOC
MANIHOCS
MANIKIN
MANIKINS
MANILA
MANILAS
MANILLA
MANILLAS
MANILLE
MANILLES
MANIOC
MANIOCS
MANIPLE
MANIPLES
MANIPLIES
MANIPULAR
MANIPULARS
MANIS
MANITO
MANITOS
MANITOU
MANITOUS
MANJACK
MANJACKS
MANKIER
MANKIEST
MANKIND
MANKINDS
MANKY
MANLIER
MANLIEST
MANLINESS
MANLINESSES
MANLY
MANNA
MANNAS
MANNED
MANNEQUIN
MANNEQUINS
MANNER
MANNERED
MANNERISM
MANNERISMS
MANNERIST
MANNERISTS
MANNERLY
MANNERS
MANNIKIN
MANNIKINS
MANNING
MANNISH
MANNITE
MANNITES
MANNITOL
MANNITOLS
MANNOSE
MANNOSES
MANO
MANOAO
MANOAOS
MANOEUVRE
MANOEUVRED
MANOEUVRES
MANOEUVRING
MANOMETER
MANOMETERS
MANOMETRIES
MANOMETRY
MANOR
MANORIAL
MANORS
MANOS
MANPACK
MANPACKS
MANPOWER
MANPOWERS
MANQUE
MANRED
MANREDS
MANRENT
MANRENTS
MANRIDER
MANRIDERS
MANRIDING
MANS
MANSARD
MANSARDS
MANSE
MANSES
MANSHIFT
MANSHIFTS
MANSION
MANSIONS
MANSONRIES
MANSONRY
MANSUETE
MANSWORN
MANTA
MANTAS
MANTEAU
MANTEAUS
MANTEAUX
MANTEEL
MANTEELS
MANTEL
MANTELET
MANTELETS
MANTELS
MANTIC
MANTICORA
MANTICORAS
MANTICORE
MANTICORES
MANTID
MANTIDS
MANTIES
MANTILLA
MANTILLAS
MANTIS
MANTISES
MANTISSA
MANTISSAS
MANTLE
MANTLED
MANTLES
MANTLET
MANTLETS
MANTLING
MANTLINGS
MANTO
MANTOES
MANTOS
MANTRA
MANTRAM
MANTRAMS
MANTRAP
MANTRAPS
MANTRAS
MANTUA
MANTUAS
MANTY
MANUAL
MANUALLY
MANUALS
MANUBRIA
MANUBRIAL
MANUBRIUM
MANUKA
MANUKAS
MANUL
MANULS
MANUMEA
MANUMEAS
MANUMIT
MANUMITS
MANUMITTED
MANUMITTING
MANURANCE
MANURANCES
MANURE
MANURED
MANURER
MANURERS
MANURES
MANURIAL
MANURING
MANURINGS
MANUS
MANY
MANYATA
MANYATAS
MANYATTA
MANYATTAS
MANYFOLD
MANYPLIES
MANZANITA
MANZANITAS
MANZELLO
MANZELLOS
MAORMOR
MAORMORS
MAP
MAPLE
MAPLES
MAPPED
MAPPEMOND
MAPPEMONDS
MAPPER
MAPPERIES
MAPPERS
MAPPERY
MAPPING
MAPPINGS
MAPPIST

MAPPISTS
MAPS
MAPSTICK
MAPSTICKS
MAPWISE
MAQUETTE
MAQUETTES
MAQUI
MAQUIS
MAQUISARD
MAQUISARDS
MAR
MARA
MARABOU
MARABOUS
MARABOUT
MARABOUTS
MARACA
MARACAS
MARAE
MARAES
MARAGING
MARAGINGS
MARAH
MARAHS
MARAS
MARASMIC
MARASMUS
MARASMUSES
MARATHON
MARATHONS
MARAUD
MARAUDED
MARAUDER
MARAUDERS
MARAUDING
MARAUDS
MARAVEDI
MARAVEDIS
MARBLE
MARBLED
MARBLER
MARBLERS
MARBLES
MARBLIER
MARBLIEST
MARBLING
MARBLINGS
MARBLY
MARC
MARCASITE
MARCASITES
MARCATO
MARCEL
MARCELLA
MARCELLAS
MARCELLED
MARCELLING
MARCELS
MARCH
MARCHED
MARCHER
MARCHERS
MARCHES
MARCHESA
MARCHESAS
MARCHESE
MARCHESES
MARCHESI
MARCHING
MARCHMAN
MARCHMEN
MARCHPANE
MARCHPANES
MARCONI
MARCONIED
MARCONIING
MARCONIS
MARCS
MARD
MARDIED
MARDIER
MARDIES
MARDIEST
MARDY
MARDYING
MARE
MAREMMA
MAREMMAS
MARES
MARESCHAL
MARESCHALS
MARG
MARGARIC
MARGARIN
MARGARINE
MARGARINES
MARGARINS
MARGARITA
MARGARITAS
MARGARITE
MARGARITES
MARGAY
MARGAYS
MARGE
MARGENT
MARGENTED
MARGENTING
MARGENTS
MARGES
MARGIN
MARGINAL
MARGINALS
MARGINATE
MARGINED
MARGINING
MARGINS
MARGOSA
MARGOSAS
MARGRAVE
MARGRAVES
MARGS
MARIA
MARIACHI
MARIACHIS
MARIALITE
MARIALITES
MARID
MARIDS
MARIES
MARIGOLD
MARIGOLDS
MARIGRAM
MARIGRAMS
MARIGRAPH
MARIGRAPHS
MARIHUANA
MARIHUANAS
MARIJUANA
MARIJUANAS
MARIMBA
MARIMBAS
MARINA
MARINADE
MARINADED
MARINADES
MARINADING
MARINAS
MARINATE
MARINATED
MARINATES
MARINATING
MARINE
MARINER
MARINERA
MARINERAS
MARINERS
MARINES
MARINIERE
MARIPOSA
MARIPOSAS
MARISCHAL
MARISCHALLED
MARISCHALLING
MARISCHALS
MARISH
MARISHES
MARITAGE
MARITAGES
MARITAL
MARITALLY
MARITIME
MARJORAM
MARJORAMS
MARK
MARKED
MARKEDLY
MARKER
MARKERS
MARKET
MARKETED
MARKETEER
MARKETEERS
MARKETER
MARKETERS
MARKETING
MARKETINGS
MARKETS
MARKHOR
MARKHORS
MARKING
MARKINGS
MARKKA
MARKKAA
MARKKAS
MARKMAN
MARKMEN
MARKS
MARKSMAN
MARKSMEN
MARL
MARLE
MARLED
MARLES
MARLIER
MARLIEST
MARLIN
MARLINE
MARLINES
MARLING
MARLINGS
MARLINS
MARLS
MARLSTONE
MARLSTONES
MARLY
MARM
MARMALADE
MARMALADES
MARMARISE
MARMARISED
MARMARISES
MARMARISING
MARMARIZE
MARMARIZED
MARMARIZES
MARMARIZING
MARMELISE
MARMELISED
MARMELISES
MARMELISING
MARMELIZE
MARMELIZED
MARMELIZES
MARMELIZING
MARMITE
MARMITES
MARMOREAL
MARMOSE
MARMOSES
MARMOSET
MARMOSETS
MARMOT
MARMOTS
MARMS
MAROCAIN
MAROCAINS
MARON
MARONS
MAROON
MAROONED
MAROONER
MAROONERS
MAROONING
MAROONINGS
MAROONS
MAROQUIN
MAROQUINS
MAROR
MARORS
MARPLOT
MARPLOTS
MARQUE
MARQUEE
MARQUEES
MARQUES
MARQUESS
MARQUESSES
MARQUETRIES
MARQUETRY
MARQUIS
MARQUISE
MARQUISES
MARRAM
MARRAMS
MARRED
MARRELS
MARRIAGE
MARRIAGES
MARRIED
MARRIER
MARRIERS
MARRIES
MARRING
MARROW
MARROWED
MARROWFAT
MARROWFATS
MARROWING
MARROWISH
MARROWS
MARROWSKIED
MARROWSKIES
MARROWSKY
MARROWSKYING
MARROWY
MARRUM
MARRUMS
MARRY
MARRYING
MARRYINGS
MARS
MARSH
MARSHAL
MARSHALCIES
MARSHALCY
MARSHALLED
MARSHALLING
MARSHALLINGS
MARSHALS
MARSHES
MARSHIER
MARSHIEST
MARSHLAND
MARSHLANDS
MARSHWORT
MARSHWORTS
MARSHY
MARSPORT
MARSPORTS

ARSQUAKE
ARSQUAKES
ARSUPIA
ARSUPIAL
ARSUPIALS
ARSUPIUM
ARSUPIUMS
ART
ARTAGON
ARTAGONS
ARTED
ARTEL
ARTELLED
ARTELLING
ARTELLO
ARTELLOS
ARTELS
ARTEN
ARTENS
ARTEXT
ARTEXTS
ARTIAL
ARTIALLY
ARTIN
ARTINET
ARTINETS
ARTING
ARTINI
ARTINIS
ARTINS
ARTLET
ARTLETS
ARTS
ARTYR
ARTYRDOM
ARTYRDOMS
ARTYRED
ARTYRIA
ARTYRIES
ARTYRING
ARTYRISE
ARTYRISED
ARTYRISES
ARTYRISING
ARTYRIUM
ARTYRIZE
ARTYRIZED
ARTYRIZES
ARTYRIZING
ARTYRS
ARTYRY
ARVEL
ARVELLED
ARVELLING
ARVELS
ARVER
ARVERED
ARVERING
ARVERS
ARXISANT
ARY
ARYBUD
ARYBUDS
ARZIPAN
MARZIPANS
MAS
MASA
MASALA
MASALAS
MASAS
MASCARA
MASCARAS
MASCARON
MASCARONS
MASCLE
MASCLED
MASCLES
MASCON
MASCONS
MASCOT
MASCOTS
MASCULINE
MASCULINES
MASCULY
MASE
MASED
MASER
MASERS
MASES
MASH
MASHALLAH
MASHED
MASHER
MASHERS
MASHES
MASHIE
MASHIER
MASHIES
MASHIEST
MASHING
MASHINGS
MASHLAM
MASHLAMS
MASHLIM
MASHLIMS
MASHLIN
MASHLINS
MASHLOCH
MASHLOCHS
MASHLUM
MASHLUMS
MASHMAN
MASHMEN
MASHUA
MASHUAS
MASHY
MASING
MASJID
MASJIDS
MASK
MASKED
MASKER
MASKERS
MASKING
MASKS
MASLIN
MASLINS
MASOCHISM
MASOCHISMS
MASOCHIST
MASOCHISTS
MASON
MASONED
MASONIC
MASONING
MASONRIED
MASONRIES
MASONRY
MASONS
MASOOLAH
MASOOLAHS
MASQUE
MASQUER
MASQUERS
MASQUES
MASS
MASSA
MASSACRE
MASSACRED
MASSACRES
MASSACRING
MASSAGE
MASSAGED
MASSAGES
MASSAGING
MASSAGIST
MASSAGISTS
MASSAS
MASSE
MASSED
MASSES
MASSETER
MASSETERS
MASSEUR
MASSEURS
MASSEUSE
MASSEUSES
MASSICOT
MASSICOTS
MASSIER
MASSIEST
MASSIF
MASSIFS
MASSINESS
MASSINESSES
MASSING
MASSIVE
MASSIVELY
MASSOOLA
MASSOOLAS
MASSY
MASSYMORE
MASSYMORES
MAST
MASTABA
MASTABAS
MASTED
MASTER
MASTERATE
MASTERATES
MASTERDOM
MASTERDOMS
MASTERED
MASTERFUL
MASTERIES
MASTERING
MASTERINGS
MASTERLY
MASTERS
MASTERY
MASTFUL
MASTHEAD
MASTHEADED
MASTHEADING
MASTHEADS
MASTHOUSE
MASTHOUSES
MASTIC
MASTICATE
MASTICATED
MASTICATES
MASTICATING
MASTICH
MASTICHS
MASTICOT
MASTICOTS
MASTICS
MASTIER
MASTIEST
MASTIFF
MASTIFFS
MASTING
MASTITIS
MASTITISES
MASTLESS
MASTODON
MASTODONS
MASTOID
MASTOIDAL
MASTOIDS
MASTS
MASTY
MASU
MASULA
MASULAS
MASURIUM
MASURIUMS
MASUS
MAT
MATACHIN
MATACHINA
MATACHINAS
MATACHINI
MATADOR
MATADORA
MATADORAS
MATADORE
MATADORES
MATADORS
MATAMATA
MATAMATAS
MATCH
MATCHABLE
MATCHBOX
MATCHBOXES
MATCHED
MATCHER
MATCHERS
MATCHES
MATCHING
MATCHLESS
MATCHLOCK
MATCHLOCKS
MATCHWOOD
MATCHWOODS
MATE
MATED
MATELASSE
MATELASSES
MATELESS
MATELOT
MATELOTE
MATELOTES
MATELOTS
MATER
MATERIAL
MATERIALS
MATERIEL
MATERIELS
MATERNAL
MATERNITIES
MATERNITY
MATERS
MATES
MATESHIP
MATESHIPS
MATEY
MATEYNESS
MATEYNESSES
MATFELON
MATFELONS
MATGRASS
MATGRASSES
MATH
MATHESES
MATHESIS
MATHS
MATICO
MATICOS
MATIER
MATIEST
MATILY
MATIN
MATINAL
MATINEE
MATINEES
MATINESS
MATINESSES
MATING
MATINS
MATJES
MATLO
MATLOS
MATLOW
MATLOWS
MATOKE
MATOKES
MATOOKE
MATOOKES
MATRASS

MATRASSES
MATRIARCH
MATRIARCHS
MATRIC
MATRICE
MATRICES
MATRICIDE
MATRICIDES
MATRICS
MATRICULA
MATRICULAS
MATRILINIES
MATRILINY
MATRIMONIES
MATRIMONY
MATRIX
MATRIXES
MATRON
MATRONAGE
MATRONAGES
MATRONAL
MATRONISE
MATRONISED
MATRONISES
MATRONISING
MATRONIZE
MATRONIZED
MATRONIZES
MATRONIZING
MATRONLY
MATRONS
MATROSS
MATROSSES
MATS
MATSURI
MATSURIS
MATT
MATTAMORE
MATTAMORES
MATTE
MATTED
MATTER
MATTERED
MATTERFUL
MATTERING
MATTERS
MATTERY
MATTES
MATTIE
MATTIES
MATTING
MATTINGS
MATTINS
MATTOCK
MATTOCKS
MATTOID
MATTOIDS
MATTRESS
MATTRESSES
MATURABLE
MATURATE
MATURATED
MATURATES
MATURATING
MATURE
MATURED
MATURELY
MATURER
MATURES
MATUREST
MATURING
MATURITIES
MATURITY
MATUTINAL
MATUTINE
MATWEED
MATWEEDS
MATY
MATZA
MATZAH
MATZAHS
MATZAS
MATZO
MATZOH
MATZOON
MATZOONS
MATZOS
MATZOT
MATZOTH
MAUD
MAUDLIN
MAUDS
MAUGRE
MAUGRED
MAUGRES
MAUGRING
MAUL
MAULED
MAULERS
MAULGRE
MAULGRED
MAULGRES
MAULGRING
MAULING
MAULS
MAULSTICK
MAULSTICKS
MAULVI
MAULVIS
MAUMET
MAUMETRIES
MAUMETRY
MAUMETS
MAUN
MAUND
MAUNDED
MAUNDER
MAUNDERED
MAUNDERER
MAUNDERERS
MAUNDERING
MAUNDERINGS
MAUNDERS
MAUNDIES
MAUNDING
MAUNDS
MAUNDY
MAUNGIER
MAUNGIEST
MAUNGY
MAUNNA
MAUSOLEAN
MAUSOLEUM
MAUSOLEUMS
MAUTHER
MAUTHERS
MAUVAIS
MAUVAISE
MAUVE
MAUVEIN
MAUVEINE
MAUVEINES
MAUVEINS
MAUVER
MAUVES
MAUVEST
MAUVIN
MAUVINE
MAUVINES
MAUVINS
MAVEN
MAVENS
MAVERICK
MAVERICKED
MAVERICKING
MAVERICKS
MAVIN
MAVINS
MAVIS
MAVISES
MAW
MAWBOUND
MAWK
MAWKIER
MAWKIEST
MAWKIN
MAWKINS
MAWKISH
MAWKISHLY
MAWKS
MAWKY
MAWMET
MAWMETRIES
MAWMETRY
MAWMETS
MAWPUS
MAWPUSES
MAWR
MAWRS
MAWS
MAWSEED
MAWSEEDS
MAWTHER
MAWTHERS
MAX
MAXES
MAXI
MAXILLA
MAXILLAE
MAXILLARIES
MAXILLARY
MAXILLULA
MAXILLULAE
MAXIM
MAXIMA
MAXIMAL
MAXIMALLY
MAXIMIN
MAXIMINS
MAXIMISE
MAXIMISED
MAXIMISES
MAXIMISING
MAXIMIST
MAXIMISTS
MAXIMIZE
MAXIMIZED
MAXIMIZES
MAXIMIZING
MAXIMS
MAXIMUM
MAXIS
MAXIXE
MAXIXES
MAXWELL
MAXWELLS
MAY
MAYA
MAYAS
MAYBE
MAYBES
MAYDAY
MAYDAYS
MAYED
MAYEST
MAYFLIES
MAYFLOWER
MAYFLOWERS
MAYFLY
MAYHAP
MAYHEM
MAYHEMS
MAYING
MAYINGS
MAYOR
MAYORAL
MAYORALTIES
MAYORALTY
MAYORESS
MAYORESSES
MAYORS
MAYORSHIP
MAYORSHIPS
MAYPOLE
MAYPOLES
MAYS
MAYST
MAYSTER
MAYSTERS
MAYWEED
MAYWEEDS
MAZARD
MAZARDS
MAZARINE
MAZARINES
MAZE
MAZED
MAZEFUL
MAZELTOV
MAZEMENT
MAZEMENTS
MAZER
MAZERS
MAZES
MAZHBI
MAZHBIS
MAZIER
MAZIEST
MAZILY
MAZINESS
MAZINESSES
MAZING
MAZOUT
MAZOUTS
MAZUMA
MAZUMAS
MAZURKA
MAZURKAS
MAZUT
MAZUTS
MAZY
MAZZARD
MAZZARDS
MBAQANGA
MBAQANGAS
MBIRA
MBIRAS
ME
MEACOCK
MEACOCKS
MEAD
MEADOW
MEADOWS
MEADOWY
MEADS
MEAGRE
MEAGRELY
MEAGRER
MEAGRES
MEAGREST
MEAL
MEALED
MEALER
MEALERS
MEALIE
MEALIER
MEALIES
MEALIEST
MEALINESS
MEALINESSES
MEALING
MEALS
MEALTIME
MEALTIMES
MEALWORM
MEALWORMS
MEALY
MEAN
MEANDER
MEANDERED

EANDERING
EANDERS
EANDRIAN
EANDROUS
EANE
EANED
EANER
EANES
EANEST
EANIE
EANIES
EANING
EANINGLY
EANINGS
EANLY
EANNESS
EANNESSES
EANS
EANT
EANTIME
EANTIMES
EANWHILE
EANWHILES
EANY
EARE
EARES
EARING
EASE
EASED
EASES
EASING
EASLE
EASLED
EASLES
EASLIER
EASLIEST
EASLING
EASLY
EASURE
EASURED
EASURER
EASURERS
EASURES
EASURING
EASURINGS
EAT
EATAL
EATBALL
EATBALLS
EATH
EATHE
EATHEAD
EATHEADS
EATHES
EATHS
EATIER
EATIEST
EATILY
EATINESS
EATINESSES
EATLESS
EATS
EATUS
EATUSES
MEATY
MEAWES
MEAZEL
MEAZELS
MEBOS
MEBOSES
MECHANIC
MECHANICS
MECHANISE
MECHANISED
MECHANISES
MECHANISING
MECHANISM
MECHANISMS
MECHANIST
MECHANISTS
MECHANIZE
MECHANIZED
MECHANIZES
MECHANIZING
MECONATE
MECONATES
MECONIC
MECONIN
MECONINS
MECONIUM
MECONIUMS
MEDACCA
MEDACCAS
MEDAEWART
MEDAEWARTS
MEDAKA
MEDAKAS
MEDAL
MEDALED
MEDALET
MEDALETS
MEDALING
MEDALIST
MEDALISTS
MEDALLED
MEDALLIC
MEDALLING
MEDALLION
MEDALLIONED
MEDALLIONING
MEDALLIONS
MEDALLIST
MEDALLISTS
MEDALS
MEDCINAL
MEDDLE
MEDDLED
MEDDLER
MEDDLERS
MEDDLES
MEDDLING
MEDDLINGS
MEDFLIES
MEDFLY
MEDIA
MEDIACIES
MEDIACY
MEDIAE
MEDIAEVAL
MEDIAL
MEDIALLY
MEDIALS
MEDIAN
MEDIANS
MEDIANT
MEDIANTS
MEDIATE
MEDIATED
MEDIATELY
MEDIATES
MEDIATING
MEDIATION
MEDIATIONS
MEDIATISE
MEDIATISED
MEDIATISES
MEDIATISING
MEDIATIVE
MEDIATIZE
MEDIATIZED
MEDIATIZES
MEDIATIZING
MEDIATOR
MEDIATORS
MEDIATORY
MEDIATRICES
MEDIATRIX
MEDIC
MEDICABLE
MEDICAID
MEDICAIDS
MEDICAL
MEDICALLY
MEDICALS
MEDICARE
MEDICARES
MEDICATE
MEDICATED
MEDICATES
MEDICATING
MEDICINAL
MEDICINE
MEDICINED
MEDICINER
MEDICINERS
MEDICINES
MEDICINING
MEDICK
MEDICKS
MEDICO
MEDICOS
MEDICS
MEDIEVAL
MEDII
MEDINA
MEDINAS
MEDIOCRE
MEDITATE
MEDITATED
MEDITATES
MEDITATING
MEDIUM
MEDIUMS
MEDIUS
MEDIUSES
MEDLAR
MEDLARS
MEDLE
MEDLED
MEDLES
MEDLEY
MEDLEYS
MEDLING
MEDRESSEH
MEDRESSEHS
MEDULLA
MEDULLAE
MEDULLAR
MEDULLARY
MEDULLAS
MEDULLATE
MEDUSA
MEDUSAE
MEDUSAN
MEDUSANS
MEDUSAS
MEDUSOID
MEDUSOIDS
MEED
MEEDS
MEEK
MEEKEN
MEEKENED
MEEKENING
MEEKENS
MEEKER
MEEKEST
MEEKLY
MEEKNESS
MEEKNESSES
MEEMIE
MEEMIES
MEER
MEERCAT
MEERCATS
MEERED
MEERING
MEERKAT
MEERKATS
MEERS
MEET
MEETER
MEETEST
MEETING
MEETINGS
MEETLY
MEETNESS
MEETNESSES
MEETS
MEG
MEGA
MEGABAR
MEGABARS
MEGABIT
MEGABITS
MEGABUCK
MEGABUCKS
MEGABYTE
MEGABYTES
MEGACITIES
MEGACITY
MEGACURIE
MEGACURIES
MEGACYCLE
MEGACYCLES
MEGADEATH
MEGADEATHS
MEGADOSE
MEGADOSES
MEGADYNE
MEGADYNES
MEGAFARAD
MEGAFARADS
MEGAFAUNA
MEGAFAUNAE
MEGAFAUNAS
MEGAFLOP
MEGAFLOPS
MEGAFLORA
MEGAFLORAE
MEGAFLORAS
MEGAFOG
MEGAFOGS
MEGAGAUSS
MEGAGAUSSES
MEGAHERTZ
MEGAHERTZES
MEGAJOULE
MEGAJOULES
MEGALITH
MEGALITHS
MEGAPHONE
MEGAPHONED
MEGAPHONES
MEGAPHONING
MEGAPODE
MEGAPODES
MEGARA
MEGARAD
MEGARADS
MEGARON
MEGARONS
MEGASCOPE
MEGASCOPES
MEGASPORE
MEGASPORES
MEGASS
MEGASSE
MEGASSES
MEGASTAR
MEGASTARS
MEGASTORE
MEGASTORES
MEGATON
MEGATONS
MEGAVOLT
MEGAVOLTS
MEGAWATT
MEGAWATTS
MEGILLAH

MEGILLAHS
MEGILLOTH
MEGILP
MEGILPS
MEGOHM
MEGOHMS
MEGRIM
MEGRIMS
MEGS
MEIN
MEINED
MEINEY
MEINEYS
MEINIE
MEINIES
MEINING
MEINS
MEINT
MEINY
MEIOFAUNA
MEIONITE
MEIONITES
MEIOSES
MEIOSIS
MEIOTIC
MEISHI
MEISHIS
MEISTER
MEISTERS
MEITH
MEITHS
MEJLIS
MEJLISES
MEKOMETER
MEKOMETERS
MEL
MELA
MELAMINE
MELAMINES
MELAMPODE
MELAMPODES
MELANGE
MELANGES
MELANIC
MELANIN
MELANINS
MELANISM
MELANISMS
MELANITE
MELANITES
MELANO
MELANOMA
MELANOMAS
MELANOMATA
MELANOS
MELANOSES
MELANOSIS
MELANOTIC
MELANOUS
MELANURIA
MELANURIAS
MELANURIC
MELAPHYRE
MELAPHYRES
MELAS
MELATONIN
MELATONINS
MELD
MELDED
MELDER
MELDERS
MELDING
MELDS
MELEE
MELEES
MELIC
MELICS
MELIK
MELIKS
MELILITE
MELILITES
MELILOT
MELILOTS
MELINITE
MELINITES
MELIORATE
MELIORATED
MELIORATES
MELIORATING
MELIORISM
MELIORISMS
MELIORIST
MELIORISTS
MELIORITIES
MELIORITY
MELISMA
MELISMAS
MELISMATA
MELL
MELLAY
MELLAYS
MELLED
MELLING
MELLITE
MELLITES
MELLITIC
MELLOW
MELLOWED
MELLOWER
MELLOWEST
MELLOWING
MELLOWLY
MELLOWS
MELLOWY
MELLS
MELOCOTON
MELOCOTONS
MELODEON
MELODEONS
MELODIC
MELODICA
MELODICAS
MELODICS
MELODIES
MELODION
MELODIONS
MELODIOUS
MELODISE
MELODISED
MELODISES
MELODISING
MELODIST
MELODISTS
MELODIZE
MELODIZED
MELODIZES
MELODIZING
MELODRAMA
MELODRAMAS
MELODRAME
MELODRAMES
MELODY
MELOMANIA
MELOMANIAS
MELOMANIC
MELON
MELONS
MELS
MELT
MELTDOWN
MELTDOWNS
MELTED
MELTIER
MELTIEST
MELTING
MELTINGLY
MELTINGS
MELTITH
MELTITHS
MELTON
MELTONS
MELTS
MELTY
MEMBER
MEMBERED
MEMBERS
MEMBRAL
MEMBRANE
MEMBRANES
MEME
MEMENTO
MEMENTOES
MEMENTOS
MEMES
MEMO
MEMOIR
MEMOIRISM
MEMOIRISMS
MEMOIRIST
MEMOIRISTS
MEMOIRS
MEMORABLE
MEMORABLY
MEMORANDA
MEMORIAL
MEMORIALS
MEMORIES
MEMORISE
MEMORISED
MEMORISES
MEMORISING
MEMORITER
MEMORIZE
MEMORIZED
MEMORIZES
MEMORIZING
MEMORY
MEMOS
MEN
MENACE
MENACED
MENACER
MENACERS
MENACES
MENACING
MENADIONE
MENADIONES
MENAGE
MENAGED
MENAGERIE
MENAGERIES
MENAGES
MENAGING
MENARCHE
MENARCHES
MEND
MENDACITIES
MENDACITY
MENDED
MENDER
MENDERS
MENDICANT
MENDICANTS
MENDICITIES
MENDICITY
MENDING
MENDINGS
MENDS
MENE
MENED
MENEER
MENEERS
MENES
MENFOLK
MENFOLKS
MENG
MENGE
MENGED
MENGES
MENGING
MENGS
MENHADEN
MENHADENS
MENHIR
MENHIRS
MENIAL
MENIALS
MENING
MENINGEAL
MENINGES
MENINX
MENISCI
MENISCOID
MENISCUS
MENISCUSES
MENOLOGIES
MENOLOGY
MENOMINEE
MENOMINEES
MENOMINI
MENOMINIS
MENOPAUSE
MENOPAUSES
MENOPOME
MENOPOMES
MENORAH
MENORAHS
MENORRHEA
MENORRHEAS
MENSAL
MENSCH
MENSCHES
MENSE
MENSED
MENSEFUL
MENSELESS
MENSES
MENSH
MENSHED
MENSHES
MENSHING
MENSING
MENSTRUA
MENSTRUAL
MENSTRUUM
MENSTRUUMS
MENSUAL
MENSURAL
MENSWEAR
MENSWEARS
MENT
MENTA
MENTAL
MENTALISM
MENTALISMS
MENTALIST
MENTALISTS
MENTALITIES
MENTALITY
MENTALLY
MENTATION
MENTATIONS
MENTEE
MENTEES
MENTHOL
MENTHOLS
MENTICIDE
MENTICIDES
MENTION
MENTIONED
MENTIONING
MENTIONS
MENTO
MENTOR
MENTORIAL
MENTORING
MENTORINGS
MENTORS
MENTOS
MENTUM

MENU
MENUISIER
MENUISIERS
MENUS
MENYIE
MENYIES
MEOW
MEOWED
MEOWING
MEOWS
MEPACRINE
MEPACRINES
MEPHITIC
MEPHITIS
MEPHITISES
MEPHITISM
MEPHITISMS
MERC
MERCAPTAN
MERCAPTANS
MERCAT
MERCATS
MERCENARIES
MERCENARY
MERCER
MERCERIES
MERCERISE
MERCERISED
MERCERISES
MERCERISING
MERCERIZE
MERCERIZED
MERCERIZES
MERCERIZING
MERCERS
MERCERY
MERCHANT
MERCHANTED
MERCHANTING
MERCHANTINGS
MERCHANTS
MERCHET
MERCHETS
MERCHILD
MERCHILDREN
MERCIABLE
MERCIES
MERCIFIDE
MERCIFIED
MERCIFIES
MERCIFUL
MERCIFY
MERCIFYING
MERCILESS
MERCS
MERCURATE
MERCURATED
MERCURATES
MERCURATING
MERCURIAL
MERCURIALS
MERCURIC
MERCURIES
MERCURISE
MERCURISED
MERCURISES
MERCURISING
MERCURIZE
MERCURIZED
MERCURIZES
MERCURIZING
MERCUROUS
MERCURY
MERCY
MERE
MERED
MEREL
MERELL
MERELLS
MERELS
MERELY
MERENGUE
MERENGUES
MERER
MERES
MERESMAN
MERESMEN
MEREST
MERESTONE
MERESTONES
MERFOLK
MERFOLKS
MERGANSER
MERGANSERS
MERGE
MERGED
MERGENCE
MERGENCES
MERGER
MERGERS
MERGES
MERGING
MERI
MERICARP
MERICARPS
MERIDIAN
MERIDIANS
MERIL
MERILS
MERIMAKE
MERIMAKES
MERING
MERINGUE
MERINGUES
MERINO
MERINOS
MERIS
MERISM
MERISMS
MERISTEM
MERISTEMS
MERISTIC
MERIT
MERITED
MERITING
MERITS
MERK
MERKIN
MERKINS
MERKS
MERL
MERLE
MERLES
MERLIN
MERLING
MERLINGS
MERLINS
MERLON
MERLONS
MERLS
MERMAID
MERMAIDEN
MERMAIDENS
MERMAIDS
MERMAN
MERMEN
MEROGONIES
MEROGONY
MEROISTIC
MEROME
MEROMES
MERONYM
MERONYMIES
MERONYMS
MERONYMY
MEROPIDAN
MEROPIDANS
MEROSOME
MEROSOMES
MEROZOITE
MEROZOITES
MERPEOPLE
MERPEOPLES
MERRIER
MERRIES
MERRIEST
MERRILY
MERRIMENT
MERRIMENTS
MERRINESS
MERRINESSES
MERRY
MERRYMAN
MERRYMEN
MERSALYL
MERSALYLS
MERSE
MERSES
MERSION
MERSIONS
MERYCISM
MERYCISMS
MES
MESA
MESAIL
MESAILS
MESAL
MESALLY
MESARAIC
MESARCH
MESAS
MESCAL
MESCALIN
MESCALINS
MESCALISM
MESCALISMS
MESCALS
MESCLUM
MESCLUMS
MESCLUN
MESCLUNS
MESDAMES
MESE
MESEL
MESELED
MESELS
MESENTERA
MESENTERIES
MESENTERY
MESES
MESETA
MESETAS
MESH
MESHED
MESHES
MESHIER
MESHIEST
MESHING
MESHINGS
MESHUGA
MESHUGAAS
MESHUGAASEN
MESHUGGA
MESHUGGE
MESHY
MESIAL
MESIALLY
MESIAN
MESIC
MESMERIC
MESMERISE
MESMERISED
MESMERISES
MESMERISING
MESMERISM
MESMERISMS
MESMERIST
MESMERISTS
MESMERIZE
MESMERIZED
MESMERIZES
MESMERIZING
MESNE
MESOBLAST
MESOBLASTS
MESOCARP
MESOCARPS
MESODERM
MESODERMS
MESOGLOEA
MESOGLOEAS
MESOLITE
MESOLITES
MESOMORPH
MESOMORPHS
MESON
MESONIC
MESONS
MESOPHYLL
MESOPHYLLS
MESOPHYTE
MESOPHYTES
MESOTRON
MESOTRONS
MESPRISE
MESPRISES
MESPRIZE
MESPRIZES
MESQUIN
MESQUINE
MESQUIT
MESQUITE
MESQUITES
MESQUITS
MESS
MESSAGE
MESSAGED
MESSAGES
MESSAGING
MESSAGINGS
MESSAN
MESSANS
MESSED
MESSENGER
MESSENGERED
MESSENGERING
MESSENGERS
MESSES
MESSIAH
MESSIAHS
MESSIANIC
MESSIAS
MESSIASES
MESSIER
MESSIEST
MESSIEURS
MESSILY
MESSINESS
MESSINESSES
MESSING
MESSMATE
MESSMATES
MESSUAGE
MESSUAGES
MESSY
MESTEE
MESTEES
MESTIZA
MESTIZAS
MESTIZO
MESTIZOS
MESTO
MET
METABASES
METABASIS
METABATIC
METABOLIC
METACARPI
METAGE
METAGES

METAIRIE
METAIRIES
METAL
METALED
METALING
METALIST
METALISTS
METALIZE
METALIZED
METALIZES
METALIZING
METALLED
METALLIC
METALLINE
METALLING
METALLINGS
METALLISE
METALLISED
METALLISES
METALLISING
METALLIST
METALLISTS
METALLIZE
METALLIZED
METALLIZES
METALLIZING
METALLOID
METALLOIDS
METALLY
METALS
METALWARE
METALWARES
METALWORK
METALWORKS
METAMER
METAMERE
METAMERES
METAMERIC
METAMERS
METANOIA
METANOIAS
METAPELET
METAPHASE
METAPHASES
METAPHOR
METAPHORS
METAPLASM
METAPLASMS
METAPLOT
METATARSI
METATE
METATES
METAYAGE
METAYAGES
METAYER
METAYERS
METAZOA
METAZOAN
METAZOANS
METAZOIC
METAZOON
METCAST
METCASTS
METE
METED
METEOR
METEORIC
METEORISM
METEORISMS
METEORIST
METEORISTS
METEORITE
METEORITES
METEOROID
METEOROIDS
METEOROUS
METEORS
METER
METERED
METERING
METERS
METES
METESTICK
METESTICKS
METEWAND
METEWANDS
METEYARD
METEYARDS
METHADON
METHADONE
METHADONES
METHADONS
METHANAL
METHANALS
METHANE
METHANES
METHANOL
METHANOLS
METHEGLIN
METHEGLINS
METHINK
METHINKETH
METHINKS
METHOD
METHODIC
METHODISE
METHODISED
METHODISES
METHODISING
METHODIST
METHODISTS
METHODIZE
METHODIZED
METHODIZES
METHODIZING
METHODS
METHOUGHT
METHS
METHYL
METHYLATE
METHYLATED
METHYLATES
METHYLATING
METHYLENE
METHYLENES
METHYLIC
METHYLS
METHYSES
METHYSIS
METHYSTIC
METIC
METICAL
METICALS
METICS
METIER
METIERS
METIF
METIFS
METING
METIS
METISSE
METISSES
METOL
METOLS
METONYM
METONYMIC
METONYMIES
METONYMS
METONYMY
METOPAE
METOPE
METOPES
METOPIC
METOPISM
METOPISMS
METOPON
METOPONS
METOPRYL
METOPRYLS
METRE
METRED
METRES
METRIC
METRICAL
METRICATE
METRICATED
METRICATES
METRICATING
METRICIAN
METRICIANS
METRICISE
METRICISED
METRICISES
METRICISING
METRICIST
METRICISTS
METRICIZE
METRICIZED
METRICIZES
METRICIZING
METRICS
METRIFIER
METRIFIERS
METRING
METRIST
METRISTS
METRITIS
METRITISES
METRO
METROLOGIES
METROLOGY
METRONOME
METRONOMES
METROPLEX
METROPLEXES
METROS
METS
METTLE
METTLED
METTLES
MEU
MEUNIERE
MEUS
MEUSE
MEUSED
MEUSES
MEUSING
MEVE
MEVED
MEVES
MEVING
MEW
MEWED
MEWING
MEWL
MEWLED
MEWLING
MEWLS
MEWS
MEWSED
MEWSES
MEWSING
MEYNT
MEZAIL
MEZAILS
MEZE
MEZEREON
MEZEREONS
MEZEREUM
MEZEREUMS
MEZES
MEZUZA
MEZUZAH
MEZUZAHS
MEZUZOTH
MEZZANINE
MEZZANINES
MEZZE
MEZZES
MEZZO
MEZZOS
MEZZOTINT
MEZZOTINTS
MGANGA
MGANGAS
MHO
MHORR
MHORRS
MHOS
MI
MIAOW
MIAOWED
MIAOWING
MIAOWS
MIASM
MIASMA
MIASMAL
MIASMAS
MIASMATA
MIASMATIC
MIASMIC
MIASMOUS
MIASMS
MIAUL
MIAULED
MIAULING
MIAULS
MICA
MICACEOUS
MICAS
MICATE
MICATED
MICATES
MICATING
MICE
MICELLA
MICELLAE
MICELLAR
MICELLE
MICELLES
MICHE
MICHED
MICHER
MICHERS
MICHES
MICHING
MICHINGS
MICK
MICKEY
MICKEYED
MICKEYING
MICKEYS
MICKIES
MICKLE
MICKLES
MICKS
MICKY
MICO
MICOS
MICRA
MICRO
MICROBAR
MICROBARS
MICROBE
MICROBES
MICROBIAL
MICROBIAN
MICROBIC
MICROBUS
MICROBUSES
MICROBUSSES
MICROCAR
MICROCARD
MICROCARDS
MICROCARS
MICROCHIP
MICROCHIPS
MICROCODE
MICROCODES
MICROCOPIED

CROCOPIES
CROCOPY
CROCOPYING
CROCOPYINGS
CROCOSM
CROCOSMS
CROCYTE
CROCYTES
CRODOT
CRODOTS
CROFILM
CROFILMED
CROFILMING
CROFILMS
CROFORM
CROFORMS
CROGRAM
CROGRAMS
CROLITE
CROLITES
CROLITH
CROLITHS
CROLOGIES
CROLOGY
CROMESH
CROMESHES
CRON
CRONS
CROPORE
CROPORES
CROPSIA
CROPSIAS
CROPUMP
CROPUMPS
CROPYLE
CROPYLES
CROS
CROSOME
CROSOMES
CROTOME
CROTOMES
CROTOMIES
CROTOMY
CROTONE
CROTONES
CROWAVE
CROWAVED
CROWAVES
CROWAVING
CROWIRE
CROWIRES
CRURGIES
CRURGY
CTION
CTIONS
CTURATE
CTURATED
CTURATES
CTURATING
D
DAIR
DAIRS
DBRAIN
DBRAINS
MIDDAY
MIDDAYS
MIDDEN
MIDDENS
MIDDEST
MIDDIES
MIDDLE
MIDDLED
MIDDLEMAN
MIDDLEMEN
MIDDLES
MIDDLING
MIDDLINGS
MIDDY
MIDFIELD
MIDFIELDS
MIDGE
MIDGES
MIDGET
MIDGETS
MIDI
MIDINETTE
MIDINETTES
MIDIRON
MIDIRONS
MIDIS
MIDLAND
MIDLANDS
MIDMOST
MIDMOSTS
MIDNIGHT
MIDNIGHTS
MIDNOON
MIDNOONS
MIDRIB
MIDRIBS
MIDRIFF
MIDRIFFS
MIDS
MIDSHIP
MIDSHIPS
MIDSIZE
MIDST
MIDSTREAM
MIDSTREAMS
MIDSTS
MIDSUMMER
MIDSUMMERS
MIDTERM
MIDTERMS
MIDWAY
MIDWAYS
MIDWIFE
MIDWIFED
MIDWIFERIES
MIDWIFERY
MIDWIFES
MIDWIFING
MIDWIVE
MIDWIVED
MIDWIVES
MIDWIVING
MIEN
MIENS
MIEVE
MIEVED
MIEVES
MIEVING
MIFF
MIFFED
MIFFIER
MIFFIEST
MIFFILY
MIFFINESS
MIFFINESSES
MIFFING
MIFFS
MIFFY
MIFTY
MIGHT
MIGHTEST
MIGHTFUL
MIGHTIER
MIGHTIEST
MIGHTILY
MIGHTS
MIGHTST
MIGHTY
MIGNON
MIGNONNE
MIGRAINE
MIGRAINES
MIGRANT
MIGRANTS
MIGRATE
MIGRATED
MIGRATES
MIGRATING
MIGRATION
MIGRATIONS
MIGRATOR
MIGRATORS
MIGRATORY
MIHRAB
MIHRABS
MIKADO
MIKADOS
MIKE
MIKES
MIKRA
MIKRON
MIKRONS
MIL
MILADI
MILADIES
MILADIS
MILADY
MILAGE
MILAGES
MILCH
MILD
MILDEN
MILDENED
MILDENING
MILDENS
MILDER
MILDEST
MILDEW
MILDEWED
MILDEWING
MILDEWS
MILDEWY
MILDLY
MILDNESS
MILDNESSES
MILDS
MILE
MILEAGE
MILEAGES
MILER
MILERS
MILES
MILESTONE
MILESTONES
MILFOIL
MILFOILS
MILIARIA
MILIARIAS
MILIARY
MILIEU
MILIEUS
MILIEUX
MILITANCIES
MILITANCY
MILITANT
MILITANTS
MILITAR
MILITARIA
MILITARIES
MILITARY
MILITATE
MILITATED
MILITATES
MILITATING
MILITIA
MILITIAS
MILK
MILKED
MILKEN
MILKER
MILKERS
MILKFISH
MILKFISHES
MILKIER
MILKIEST
MILKILY
MILKINESS
MILKINESSES
MILKING
MILKINGS
MILKLESS
MILKLIKE
MILKMAID
MILKMAIDS
MILKMAN
MILKMEN
MILKO
MILKOS
MILKS
MILKWOOD
MILKWOODS
MILKWORT
MILKWORTS
MILKY
MILL
MILLBOARD
MILLBOARDS
MILLDAM
MILLDAMS
MILLE
MILLED
MILLENARIES
MILLENARY
MILLENNIA
MILLEPED
MILLEPEDE
MILLEPEDES
MILLEPEDS
MILLEPORE
MILLEPORES
MILLER
MILLERITE
MILLERITES
MILLERS
MILLES
MILLET
MILLETS
MILLIARD
MILLIARDS
MILLIARE
MILLIARES
MILLIARIES
MILLIARY
MILLIBAR
MILLIBARS
MILLIEME
MILLIEMES
MILLIME
MILLIMES
MILLIMOLE
MILLIMOLES
MILLINER
MILLINERIES
MILLINERS
MILLINERY
MILLING
MILLINGS
MILLION
MILLIONS
MILLIONTH
MILLIONTHS
MILLIPED
MILLIPEDE
MILLIPEDES
MILLIPEDS
MILLIREM
MILLIREMS
MILLOCRAT
MILLOCRATS
MILLPOND
MILLPONDS
MILLRACE
MILLRACES
MILLRIND
MILLRINDS
MILLRUN

MILLRUNS
MILLS
MILLSCALE
MILLSCALES
MILLSTONE
MILLSTONES
MILLTAIL
MILLTAILS
MILO
MILOMETER
MILOMETERS
MILOR
MILORD
MILORDS
MILORS
MILOS
MILREIS
MILS
MILSEY
MILSEYS
MILT
MILTED
MILTER
MILTERS
MILTING
MILTONIA
MILTONIAS
MILTS
MILTZ
MILTZES
MILVINE
MIM
MIMBAR
MIMBARS
MIME
MIMED
MIMER
MIMERS
MIMES
MIMESES
MIMESIS
MIMESTER
MIMESTERS
MIMETIC
MIMETICAL
MIMETITE
MIMETITES
MIMIC
MIMICAL
MIMICKED
MIMICKER
MIMICKERS
MIMICKING
MIMICRIES
MIMICRY
MIMICS
MIMING
MIMMER
MIMMEST
MIMMICK
MIMMICKED
MIMMICKING
MIMMICKS
MIMOSA
MIMOSAS
MIMSEY
MIMSIER
MIMSIEST
MIMSY
MIMULUS
MIMULUSES
MINA
MINACIOUS
MINACITIES
MINACITY
MINAE
MINAR
MINARET
MINARETS
MINARS
MINAS
MINATORY
MINBAR
MINBARS
MINCE
MINCED
MINCEMEAT
MINCEMEATS
MINCER
MINCERS
MINCES
MINCEUR
MINCING
MINCINGLY
MINCINGS
MIND
MINDED
MINDER
MINDERS
MINDFUCK
MINDFUCKS
MINDFUL
MINDFULLY
MINDING
MINDINGS
MINDLESS
MINDS
MINDSET
MINDSETS
MINE
MINED
MINEFIELD
MINEFIELDS
MINEOLA
MINEOLAS
MINER
MINERAL
MINERALS
MINERS
MINES
MINESTONE
MINESTONES
MINETTE
MINETTES
MINEVER
MINEVERS
MING
MINGE
MINGED
MINGES
MINGIER
MINGIEST
MINGIN
MINGINESS
MINGINESSES
MINGING
MINGLE
MINGLED
MINGLER
MINGLERS
MINGLES
MINGLING
MINGLINGS
MINGS
MINGY
MINI
MINIATE
MINIATED
MINIATES
MINIATING
MINIATION
MINIATIONS
MINIATURE
MINIATURED
MINIATURES
MINIATURING
MINIBAR
MINIBARS
MINIBIKE
MINIBIKES
MINIBREAK
MINIBREAKS
MINIBUS
MINIBUSES
MINIBUSSES
MINICAB
MINICABS
MINICAM
MINICAMS
MINIDISK
MINIDISKS
MINIER
MINIEST
MINIFIED
MINIFIES
MINIFY
MINIFYING
MINIKIN
MINIKINS
MINIM
MINIMA
MINIMAL
MINIMAX
MINIMAXED
MINIMAXES
MINIMAXING
MINIMENT
MINIMENTS
MINIMISE
MINIMISED
MINIMISES
MINIMISING
MINIMISM
MINIMISMS
MINIMIST
MINIMISTS
MINIMIZE
MINIMIZED
MINIMIZES
MINIMIZING
MINIMS
MINIMUM
MINIMUS
MINIMUSES
MINING
MININGS
MINION
MINIONS
MINIPILL
MINIPILLS
MINIRUGBIES
MINIRUGBY
MINIS
MINISCULE
MINISCULES
MINISH
MINISHED
MINISHES
MINISHING
MINISKIRT
MINISKIRTS
MINISTER
MINISTERED
MINISTERING
MINISTERS
MINISTRIES
MINISTRY
MINIUM
MINIUMS
MINIVER
MINIVERS
MINIVET
MINIVETS
MINK
MINKE
MINKES
MINKS
MINNEOLA
MINNEOLAS
MINNICK
MINNICKED
MINNICKING
MINNICKS
MINNIE
MINNIES
MINNOCK
MINNOCKED
MINNOCKING
MINNOCKS
MINNOW
MINNOWS
MINO
MINOR
MINORED
MINORING
MINORITIES
MINORITY
MINORS
MINORSHIP
MINORSHIPS
MINOS
MINSHUKU
MINSHUKUS
MINSTER
MINSTERS
MINSTREL
MINSTRELS
MINT
MINTAGE
MINTAGES
MINTED
MINTER
MINTERS
MINTIER
MINTIEST
MINTING
MINTS
MINTY
MINUEND
MINUENDS
MINUET
MINUETS
MINUS
MINUSCULE
MINUSCULES
MINUSES
MINUTE
MINUTED
MINUTELY
MINUTEMAN
MINUTEMEN
MINUTER
MINUTES
MINUTEST
MINUTIA
MINUTIAE
MINUTING
MINUTIOSE
MINX
MINXES
MINY
MINYAN
MINYANIM
MINYANS
MIOMBO
MIOMBOS
MIOSES
MIOSIS
MIOTIC
MIOTICS
MIR
MIRABELLE
MIRABELLES
MIRABILIA
MIRABILIS
MIRABILISES
MIRABLE
MIRACIDIA
MIRACLE
MIRACLES

IRADOR
IRADORS
IRAGE
IRAGES
IRBANE
IRBANES
IRE
IRED
IREPOIX
IRES
IRI
IRIER
IRIEST
IRIFIC
IRIFICAL
IRIN
IRINESS
IRINESSES
IRING
IRINS
IRITI
IRITIS
IRK
IRKER
IRKEST
IRKS
IRLIER
IRLIEST
IRLIGOES
IRLITON
IRLITONS
IRLY
IRROR
IRRORED
IRRORING
IRRORS
IRS
IRTH
IRTHFUL
IRTHLESS
IRTHS
IRV
IRVED
IRVING
IRVS
IRY
IS
ISADVISE
ISADVISED
ISADVISES
ISADVISING
ISAIM
ISAIMED
ISAIMING
ISAIMS
ISALIGN
ISALIGNED
ISALIGNING
ISALIGNS
ISALLEGE
ISALLEGED
ISALLEGES
ISALLEGING
ISALLIED
MISALLIES
MISALLOT
MISALLOTS
MISALLOTTED
MISALLOTTING
MISALLY
MISALLYING
MISANDRIES
MISANDRY
MISAPPLIED
MISAPPLIES
MISAPPLY
MISAPPLYING
MISARRAY
MISARRAYS
MISASSIGN
MISASSIGNED
MISASSIGNING
MISASSIGNS
MISAUNTER
MISAUNTERS
MISAVISED
MISBECAME
MISBECOME
MISBECOMES
MISBECOMING
MISBEGOT
MISBEHAVE
MISBEHAVED
MISBEHAVES
MISBEHAVING
MISBELIEF
MISBELIEFS
MISBESEEM
MISBESEEMED
MISBESEEMING
MISBESEEMS
MISBESTOW
MISBESTOWED
MISBESTOWING
MISBESTOWS
MISBIRTH
MISBIRTHS
MISBORN
MISCALL
MISCALLED
MISCALLING
MISCALLS
MISCARRIED
MISCARRIES
MISCARRY
MISCARRYING
MISCAST
MISCASTING
MISCASTS
MISCEGEN
MISCEGENE
MISCEGENES
MISCEGENS
MISCEGINE
MISCEGINES
MISCHANCE
MISCHANCED
MISCHANCES
MISCHANCING
MISCHANCY
MISCHARGE
MISCHARGED
MISCHARGES
MISCHARGING
MISCHIEF
MISCHIEFED
MISCHIEFING
MISCHIEFS
MISCIBLE
MISCOLOR
MISCOLORED
MISCOLORING
MISCOLORS
MISCOLOUR
MISCOLOURED
MISCOLOURING
MISCOLOURS
MISCOPIED
MISCOPIES
MISCOPY
MISCOPYING
MISCOUNT
MISCOUNTED
MISCOUNTING
MISCOUNTS
MISCREANT
MISCREANTS
MISCREATE
MISCREDIT
MISCREDITED
MISCREDITING
MISCREDITS
MISCREED
MISCREEDS
MISCUE
MISCUED
MISCUEING
MISCUES
MISCUING
MISDATE
MISDATED
MISDATES
MISDATING
MISDEAL
MISDEALING
MISDEALS
MISDEALT
MISDEED
MISDEEDS
MISDEEM
MISDEEMED
MISDEEMING
MISDEEMINGS
MISDEEMS
MISDEMEAN
MISDEMEANED
MISDEMEANING
MISDEMEANS
MISDEMPT
MISDESERT
MISDESERTS
MISDIAL
MISDIALED
MISDIALING
MISDIALLED
MISDIALLING
MISDIALS
MISDID
MISDIET
MISDIETS
MISDIGHT
MISDIRECT
MISDIRECTED
MISDIRECTING
MISDIRECTS
MISDO
MISDOER
MISDOERS
MISDOES
MISDOING
MISDOINGS
MISDONE
MISDONNE
MISDOUBT
MISDOUBTED
MISDOUBTING
MISDOUBTS
MISDRAW
MISDRAWING
MISDRAWINGS
MISDRAWN
MISDRAWS
MISDREAD
MISDREADS
MISDREW
MISE
MISEASE
MISEASES
MISEMPLOY
MISEMPLOYED
MISEMPLOYING
MISEMPLOYS
MISENTRIES
MISENTRY
MISER
MISERABLE
MISERABLES
MISERABLY
MISERE
MISERERE
MISERERES
MISERES
MISERIES
MISERLIER
MISERLIEST
MISERLY
MISERS
MISERY
MISES
MISESTEEM
MISESTEEMED
MISESTEEMING
MISESTEEMS
MISFAITH
MISFAITHS
MISFALL
MISFALLEN
MISFALLING
MISFALLS
MISFALNE
MISFARE
MISFARED
MISFARES
MISFARING
MISFARINGS
MISFEASOR
MISFEASORS
MISFED
MISFEED
MISFEEDING
MISFEEDS
MISFEIGN
MISFEIGNED
MISFEIGNING
MISFEIGNS
MISFELL
MISFIELD
MISFIELDED
MISFIELDING
MISFIELDS
MISFILE
MISFILED
MISFILES
MISFILING
MISFIRE
MISFIRED
MISFIRES
MISFIRING
MISFIT
MISFITS
MISFITTED
MISFITTING
MISFORM
MISFORMED
MISFORMING
MISFORMS
MISGAVE
MISGIVE
MISGIVEN
MISGIVES
MISGIVING
MISGIVINGS
MISGO
MISGOES
MISGOING
MISGONE
MISGOTTEN
MISGOVERN
MISGOVERNED
MISGOVERNING
MISGOVERNS
MISGRAFF
MISGRAFT
MISGRAFTED
MISGRAFTING
MISGRAFTS
MISGROWTH
MISGROWTHS
MISGUGGLE
MISGUGGLED

MISGUGGLES
MISGUGGLING
MISGUIDE
MISGUIDED
MISGUIDER
MISGUIDERS
MISGUIDES
MISGUIDING
MISHANDLE
MISHANDLED
MISHANDLES
MISHANDLING
MISHANTER
MISHANTERS
MISHAP
MISHAPPED
MISHAPPEN
MISHAPPENED
MISHAPPENING
MISHAPPENS
MISHAPPING
MISHAPS
MISHAPT
MISHEAR
MISHEARD
MISHEARING
MISHEARS
MISHEGAAS
MISHEGAASEN
MISHIT
MISHITS
MISHITTING
MISHMASH
MISHMASHES
MISHMEE
MISHMEES
MISHMI
MISHMIS
MISINFORM
MISINFORMED
MISINFORMING
MISINFORMS
MISINTEND
MISINTENDED
MISINTENDING
MISINTENDS
MISJOIN
MISJOINED
MISJOINING
MISJOINS
MISJUDGE
MISJUDGED
MISJUDGES
MISJUDGING
MISKEN
MISKENNED
MISKENNING
MISKENS
MISKENT
MISKEY
MISKEYED
MISKEYING
MISKEYS
MISKNEW
MISKNOW
MISKNOWING
MISKNOWN
MISKNOWS
MISLAID
MISLAY
MISLAYING
MISLAYS
MISLEAD
MISLEADER
MISLEADERS
MISLEADING
MISLEADS
MISLEARED
MISLED
MISLEEKE
MISLEEKED
MISLEEKES
MISLEEKING
MISLETOE
MISLETOES
MISLIGHT
MISLIGHTED
MISLIGHTING
MISLIGHTS
MISLIKE
MISLIKED
MISLIKER
MISLIKERS
MISLIKES
MISLIKING
MISLIKINGS
MISLIPPEN
MISLIPPENED
MISLIPPENING
MISLIPPENS
MISLIT
MISLIVE
MISLIVED
MISLIVES
MISLIVING
MISLUCK
MISLUCKED
MISLUCKING
MISLUCKS
MISMADE
MISMAKE
MISMAKES
MISMAKING
MISMANAGE
MISMANAGED
MISMANAGES
MISMANAGING
MISMARRIED
MISMARRIES
MISMARRY
MISMARRYING
MISMATCH
MISMATCHED
MISMATCHES
MISMATCHING
MISMATE
MISMATED
MISMATES
MISMATING
MISMETRE
MISMETRED
MISMETRES
MISMETRING
MISNAME
MISNAMED
MISNAMES
MISNAMING
MISNOMER
MISNOMERED
MISNOMERING
MISNOMERS
MISO
MISOCLERE
MISOGAMIES
MISOGAMY
MISOGYNIES
MISOGYNY
MISOLOGIES
MISOLOGY
MISONEISM
MISONEISMS
MISONEIST
MISONEISTS
MISORDER
MISORDERED
MISORDERING
MISORDERS
MISOS
MISPICKEL
MISPICKELS
MISPLACE
MISPLACED
MISPLACES
MISPLACING
MISPLAY
MISPLAYED
MISPLAYING
MISPLAYS
MISPLEAD
MISPLEADED
MISPLEADING
MISPLEADINGS
MISPLEADS
MISPLEASE
MISPLEASED
MISPLEASES
MISPLEASING
MISPLED
MISPOINT
MISPOINTED
MISPOINTING
MISPOINTS
MISPRAISE
MISPRAISED
MISPRAISES
MISPRAISING
MISPRINT
MISPRINTED
MISPRINTING
MISPRINTS
MISPRISE
MISPRISED
MISPRISES
MISPRISING
MISPRIZE
MISPRIZED
MISPRIZES
MISPRIZING
MISPROUD
MISQUOTE
MISQUOTED
MISQUOTES
MISQUOTING
MISRATE
MISRATED
MISRATES
MISRATING
MISREAD
MISREADING
MISREADINGS
MISREADS
MISRECKON
MISRECKONED
MISRECKONING
MISRECKONINGS
MISRECKONS
MISREGARD
MISREGARDS
MISRELATE
MISRELATED
MISRELATES
MISRELATING
MISREPORT
MISREPORTED
MISREPORTING
MISREPORTS
MISROUTE
MISROUTED
MISROUTEING
MISROUTES
MISROUTING
MISRULE
MISRULED
MISRULES
MISRULING
MISS
MISSA
MISSABLE
MISSAE
MISSAID
MISSAL
MISSALS
MISSAW
MISSAY
MISSAYING
MISSAYINGS
MISSAYS
MISSED
MISSEE
MISSEEING
MISSEEM
MISSEEMED
MISSEEMING
MISSEEMINGS
MISSEEMS
MISSEEN
MISSEES
MISSEL
MISSELS
MISSEND
MISSENDING
MISSENDS
MISSENT
MISSES
MISSET
MISSETS
MISSETTING
MISSHAPE
MISSHAPED
MISSHAPEN
MISSHAPES
MISSHAPING
MISSHOOD
MISSHOODS
MISSIER
MISSIES
MISSIEST
MISSILE
MISSILERIES
MISSILERY
MISSILES
MISSILRIES
MISSILRY
MISSING
MISSINGLY
MISSION
MISSIONED
MISSIONER
MISSIONERS
MISSIONING
MISSIONS
MISSIS
MISSISES
MISSISH
MISSIVE
MISSIVES
MISSPEAK
MISSPEAKING
MISSPEAKS
MISSPELL
MISSPELLED
MISSPELLING
MISSPELLINGS
MISSPELLS
MISSPELT
MISSPEND
MISSPENDING
MISSPENDS
MISSPENT
MISSPOKE
MISSPOKEN
MISSTATE
MISSTATED
MISSTATES
MISSTATING
MISSTEP
MISSTEPPED
MISSTEPPING
MISSTEPS
MISSUIT

MISSUITED
MISSUITING
MISSUITS
MISSUS
MISSUSES
MISSY
MIST
MISTAKE
MISTAKEN
MISTAKES
MISTAKING
MISTAKINGS
MISTAUGHT
MISTEACH
MISTEACHES
MISTEACHING
MISTED
MISTELL
MISTELLING
MISTELLS
MISTEMPER
MISTEMPERED
MISTEMPERING
MISTEMPERS
MISTER
MISTERED
MISTERIES
MISTERING
MISTERM
MISTERMED
MISTERMING
MISTERMS
MISTERS
MISTERY
MISTFUL
MISTHINK
MISTHINKING
MISTHINKS
MISTHOUGHT
MISTHOUGHTS
MISTICO
MISTICOS
MISTIER
MISTIEST
MISTIGRIS
MISTIGRISES
MISTILY
MISTIME
MISTIMED
MISTIMES
MISTIMING
MISTINESS
MISTINESSES
MISTING
MISTINGS
MISTITLE
MISTITLED
MISTITLES
MISTITLING
MISTLE
MISTLED
MISTLES
MISTLETOE
MISTLETOES
MISTLING
MISTOLD
MISTOOK
MISTRAL
MISTRALS
MISTREAT
MISTREATED
MISTREATING
MISTREATS
MISTRESS
MISTRESSED
MISTRESSES
MISTRESSING
MISTRIAL
MISTRIALS
MISTRUST
MISTRUSTED
MISTRUSTING
MISTRUSTS
MISTRYST
MISTRYSTED
MISTRYSTING
MISTRYSTS
MISTS
MISTUNE
MISTUNED
MISTUNES
MISTUNING
MISTY
MISUSAGE
MISUSAGES
MISUSE
MISUSED
MISUSER
MISUSERS
MISUSES
MISUSING
MISUST
MISWEEN
MISWEENED
MISWEENING
MISWEENS
MISWEND
MISWENDING
MISWENDS
MISWENT
MISWORD
MISWORDED
MISWORDING
MISWORDINGS
MISWORDS
MISWRITE
MISWRITES
MISWRITING
MISWRITTEN
MISWROTE
MISYOKE
MISYOKED
MISYOKES
MISYOKING
MITCH
MITCHED
MITCHES
MITCHING
MITE
MITER
MITERED
MITERING
MITERS
MITES
MITHER
MITHERED
MITHERING
MITHERS
MITICIDAL
MITICIDE
MITICIDES
MITIER
MITIEST
MITIGABLE
MITIGANT
MITIGATE
MITIGATED
MITIGATES
MITIGATING
MITIGATOR
MITIGATORS
MITOGEN
MITOGENIC
MITOGENS
MITOSES
MITOSIS
MITOTIC
MITRAILLE
MITRAILLES
MITRAL
MITRE
MITRED
MITRES
MITRIFORM
MITRING
MITT
MITTEN
MITTENED
MITTENS
MITTIMUS
MITTIMUSES
MITTS
MITY
MITZVAH
MITZVAHS
MITZVOTH
MIURUS
MIURUSES
MIX
MIXABLE
MIXED
MIXEDLY
MIXEDNESS
MIXEDNESSES
MIXEN
MIXENS
MIXER
MIXERS
MIXES
MIXIER
MIXIEST
MIXING
MIXT
MIXTION
MIXTIONS
MIXTURE
MIXTURES
MIXY
MIZ
MIZEN
MIZENS
MIZMAZE
MIZMAZES
MIZZ
MIZZEN
MIZZENS
MIZZES
MIZZLE
MIZZLED
MIZZLES
MIZZLIER
MIZZLIEST
MIZZLING
MIZZLINGS
MIZZLY
MIZZONITE
MIZZONITES
MNA
MNAS
MNEME
MNEMES
MNEMIC
MNEMON
MNEMONIC
MNEMONICS
MNEMONIST
MNEMONISTS
MNEMONS
MO
MOA
MOAN
MOANED
MOANER
MOANERS
MOANFUL
MOANFULLY
MOANING
MOANS
MOAS
MOAT
MOATED
MOATING
MOATS
MOB
MOBBED
MOBBIE
MOBBIES
MOBBING
MOBBINGS
MOBBISH
MOBBLE
MOBBLED
MOBBLES
MOBBLING
MOBBY
MOBILE
MOBILES
MOBILISE
MOBILISED
MOBILISER
MOBILISERS
MOBILISES
MOBILISING
MOBILITIES
MOBILITY
MOBILIZE
MOBILIZED
MOBILIZER
MOBILIZERS
MOBILIZES
MOBILIZING
MOBLE
MOBLED
MOBLES
MOBLING
MOBOCRACIES
MOBOCRACY
MOBOCRAT
MOBOCRATS
MOBS
MOBSMAN
MOBSMEN
MOBSTER
MOBSTERS
MOCASSIN
MOCASSINS
MOCCASIN
MOCCASINS
MOCH
MOCHA
MOCHAS
MOCHELL
MOCHELLS
MOCHIE
MOCHIER
MOCHIEST
MOCHINESS
MOCHINESSES
MOCHS
MOCHY
MOCK
MOCKABLE
MOCKADO
MOCKADOES
MOCKAGE
MOCKAGES
MOCKED
MOCKER
MOCKERIES
MOCKERNUT
MOCKERNUTS
MOCKERS
MOCKERY
MOCKING
MOCKINGLY
MOCKINGS
MOCKS
MOCOCK
MOCOCKS
MOCUCK

MOCUCKS
MOCUDDUM
MOCUDDUMS
MOD
MODAL
MODALISM
MODALISMS
MODALIST
MODALISTS
MODALITIES
MODALITY
MODALLY
MODALS
MODE
MODEL
MODELED
MODELER
MODELERS
MODELING
MODELINGS
MODELLED
MODELLER
MODELLERS
MODELLI
MODELLING
MODELLINGS
MODELLO
MODELLOS
MODELS
MODEM
MODEMED
MODEMING
MODEMS
MODENA
MODENAS
MODER
MODERATE
MODERATED
MODERATES
MODERATING
MODERATO
MODERATOR
MODERATORS
MODERATOS
MODERN
MODERNER
MODERNEST
MODERNISE
MODERNISED
MODERNISES
MODERNISING
MODERNISM
MODERNISMS
MODERNIST
MODERNISTS
MODERNITIES
MODERNITY
MODERNIZE
MODERNIZED
MODERNIZES
MODERNIZING
MODERNLY
MODERNS
MODERS
MODES
MODEST
MODESTER
MODESTEST
MODESTIES
MODESTLY
MODESTY
MODI
MODICUM
MODICUMS
MODIFIED
MODIFIER
MODIFIERS
MODIFIES
MODIFY
MODIFYING
MODII
MODILLION
MODILLIONS
MODIOLAR
MODIOLI
MODIOLUS
MODIOLUSES
MODISH
MODISHLY
MODIST
MODISTE
MODISTES
MODISTS
MODIUS
MODIWORT
MODIWORTS
MODS
MODULAR
MODULATE
MODULATED
MODULATES
MODULATING
MODULATOR
MODULATORS
MODULE
MODULES
MODULI
MODULO
MODULUS
MODUS
MOE
MOELLON
MOELLONS
MOES
MOFETTE
MOFETTES
MOFUSSIL
MOFUSSILS
MOG
MOGGAN
MOGGANS
MOGGIE
MOGGIES
MOGGY
MOGS
MOGUL
MOGULED
MOGULS
MOHAIR
MOHAIRS
MOHAWK
MOHAWKS
MOHEL
MOHELS
MOHR
MOHRS
MOHUR
MOHURS
MOI
MOIDER
MOIDERED
MOIDERING
MOIDERS
MOIDORE
MOIDORES
MOIETIES
MOIETY
MOIL
MOILED
MOILER
MOILERS
MOILING
MOILS
MOINEAU
MOINEAUS
MOIRE
MOIRES
MOISER
MOISERS
MOIST
MOISTED
MOISTEN
MOISTENED
MOISTENING
MOISTENS
MOISTER
MOISTEST
MOISTIFIED
MOISTIFIES
MOISTIFY
MOISTIFYING
MOISTING
MOISTLY
MOISTNESS
MOISTNESSES
MOISTS
MOISTURE
MOISTURES
MOIT
MOITHER
MOITHERED
MOITHERING
MOITHERS
MOITS
MOJO
MOJOES
MOJOS
MOKADDAM
MOKADDAMS
MOKE
MOKES
MOKI
MOKIS
MOKO
MOKOS
MOLA
MOLAL
MOLALITIES
MOLALITY
MOLAR
MOLARITIES
MOLARITY
MOLARS
MOLAS
MOLASSES
MOLD
MOLDED
MOLDING
MOLDS
MOLDWARP
MOLDWARPS
MOLE
MOLECAST
MOLECASTS
MOLECULAR
MOLECULE
MOLECULES
MOLEHILL
MOLEHILLS
MOLEHUNT
MOLEHUNTS
MOLERAT
MOLERATS
MOLES
MOLESKIN
MOLESKINS
MOLEST
MOLESTED
MOLESTER
MOLESTERS
MOLESTFUL
MOLESTING
MOLESTS
MOLIES
MOLIMEN
MOLIMENS
MOLINE
MOLINES
MOLINET
MOLINETS
MOLL
MOLLA
MOLLAH
MOLLAHS
MOLLAS
MOLLIE
MOLLIES
MOLLIFIED
MOLLIFIER
MOLLIFIERS
MOLLIFIES
MOLLIFY
MOLLIFYING
MOLLITIES
MOLLS
MOLLUSC
MOLLUSCAN
MOLLUSCS
MOLLUSK
MOLLUSKAN
MOLLUSKS
MOLLY
MOLLYMAWK
MOLLYMAWKS
MOLOCH
MOLOCHISE
MOLOCHISED
MOLOCHISES
MOLOCHISING
MOLOCHIZE
MOLOCHIZED
MOLOCHIZES
MOLOCHIZING
MOLOCHS
MOLOSSI
MOLOSSUS
MOLT
MOLTED
MOLTEN
MOLTENLY
MOLTING
MOLTO
MOLTS
MOLY
MOLYBDATE
MOLYBDATES
MOLYBDIC
MOLYBDOUS
MOM
MOME
MOMENT
MOMENTA
MOMENTANY
MOMENTARY
MOMENTLY
MOMENTOUS
MOMENTS
MOMENTUM
MOMES
MOMMA
MOMMAS
MOMMET
MOMMETS
MOMMIES
MOMMY
MOMS
MOMZER
MOMZERIM
MOMZERS
MON
MONA
MONACHAL
MONACHISM
MONACHISMS
MONACHIST
MONACID
MONACT
MONACTINE
MONAD
MONADES

ONADIC
ONADICAL
ONADISM
ONADISMS
ONADNOCK
ONADNOCKS
ONADS
ONAL
ONALS
ONANDRIES
ONANDRY
ONARCH
ONARCHAL
ONARCHIC
ONARCHIES
ONARCHS
ONARCHY
ONARDA
ONARDAS
ONAS
ONASES
ONASTERIES
ONASTERY
ONASTIC
ONASTICS
ONATOMIC
ONAUL
ONAULS
ONAURAL
ONAXIAL
ONAXON
ONAXONIC
ONAXONS
ONAZITE
ONAZITES
ONDAIN
ONDAINE
ONDAINES
ONDAINS
ONDIAL
ONDO
ONECIOUS
ONER
ONERA
ONERGISM
ONERGISMS
ONERON
ONETARY
ONETH
ONETHS
ONETISE
ONETISED
ONETISES
ONETISING
ONETIZE
ONETIZED
ONETIZES
ONETIZING
ONEY
ONEYBAGS
ONEYED
ONEYER
ONEYERS
ONEYLESS

MONEYMAN
MONEYMEN
MONEYS
MONEYWORT
MONEYWORTS
MONG
MONGCORN
MONGCORNS
MONGER
MONGERIES
MONGERING
MONGERINGS
MONGERS
MONGERY
MONGOL
MONGOLISM
MONGOLISMS
MONGOLOID
MONGOLOIDS
MONGOLS
MONGOOSE
MONGOOSES
MONGREL
MONGRELLY
MONGRELS
MONGS
MONIAL
MONIALS
MONICKER
MONICKERS
MONIED
MONIES
MONIKER
MONIKERS
MONILIA
MONILIAS
MONIMENT
MONIMENTS
MONIPLIES
MONISM
MONISMS
MONIST
MONISTIC
MONISTS
MONITION
MONITIONS
MONITIVE
MONITOR
MONITORED
MONITORING
MONITORS
MONITORY
MONITRESS
MONITRESSES
MONK
MONKERIES
MONKERY
MONKEY
MONKEYED
MONKEYING
MONKEYISH
MONKEYISM
MONKEYISMS
MONKEYS

MONKFISH
MONKFISHES
MONKHOOD
MONKHOODS
MONKISH
MONKS
MONKSHOOD
MONKSHOODS
MONO
MONOACID
MONOAMINE
MONOAMINES
MONOBASIC
MONOCARP
MONOCARPS
MONOCEROS
MONOCEROSES
MONOCHORD
MONOCHORDS
MONOCLE
MONOCLED
MONOCLES
MONOCLINE
MONOCLINES
MONOCOQUE
MONOCOQUES
MONOCOT
MONOCOTS
MONOCRACIES
MONOCRACY
MONOCRAT
MONOCRATS
MONOCULAR
MONOCYTE
MONOCYTES
MONODIC
MONODICAL
MONODIES
MONODIST
MONODISTS
MONODONT
MONODRAMA
MONODRAMAS
MONODY
MONOECISM
MONOECISMS
MONOFIL
MONOFILS
MONOGAMIC
MONOGAMIES
MONOGAMY
MONOGENIC
MONOGENIES
MONOGENY
MONOGLOT
MONOGLOTS
MONOGONIES
MONOGONY
MONOGRAM
MONOGRAMS
MONOGRAPH
MONOGRAPHED
MONOGRAPHING
MONOGRAPHS

MONOGYNIES
MONOGYNY
MONOHULL
MONOHULLS
MONOKINI
MONOKINIS
MONOLATER
MONOLATERS
MONOLATRIES
MONOLATRY
MONOLAYER
MONOLAYERS
MONOLITH
MONOLITHS
MONOLOGIC
MONOLOGIES
MONOLOGUE
MONOLOGUES
MONOLOGY
MONOMACHIES
MONOMACHY
MONOMANIA
MONOMANIAS
MONOMARK
MONOMARKS
MONOMER
MONOMERIC
MONOMERS
MONOMETER
MONOMETERS
MONOMIAL
MONOMIALS
MONOMODE
MONOPHAGIES
MONOPHAGY
MONOPHASE
MONOPHONIES
MONOPHONY
MONOPITCH
MONOPLANE
MONOPLANES
MONOPOD
MONOPODE
MONOPODES
MONOPODIA
MONOPODS
MONOPOLE
MONOPOLES
MONOPOLIES
MONOPOLY
MONOPSONIES
MONOPSONY
MONOPTERA
MONOPTOTE
MONOPTOTES
MONOPULSE
MONOPULSES
MONORAIL
MONORAILS
MONORCHID
MONORHINE
MONORHYME
MONORHYMES
MONOS

MONOSES
MONOSIES
MONOSIS
MONOSTICH
MONOSTICHS
MONOSTYLE
MONOSY
MONOTINT
MONOTINTS
MONOTONE
MONOTONED
MONOTONES
MONOTONIC
MONOTONIES
MONOTONING
MONOTONY
MONOTREME
MONOTREMES
MONOTROCH
MONOTROCHS
MONOTYPE
MONOTYPES
MONOTYPIC
MONOXIDE
MONOXIDES
MONOXYLON
MONOXYLONS
MONSIEUR
MONSOON
MONSOONAL
MONSOONS
MONSTER
MONSTERA
MONSTERAS
MONSTERS
MONSTROUS
MONTAGE
MONTAGED
MONTAGES
MONTAGING
MONTANE
MONTANT
MONTANTO
MONTANTOS
MONTANTS
MONTARIA
MONTARIAS
MONTE
MONTEITH
MONTEITHS
MONTEM
MONTEMS
MONTERO
MONTEROS
MONTES
MONTH
MONTHLIES
MONTHLING
MONTHLINGS
MONTHLY
MONTHS
MONTICLE
MONTICLES
MONTICULE

MONTICULES
MONTIES
MONTRE
MONTRES
MONTURE
MONTURES
MONTY
MONUMENT
MONUMENTED
MONUMENTING
MONUMENTS
MONY
MONYPLIES
MONZONITE
MONZONITES
MOO
MOOCH
MOOCHED
MOOCHER
MOOCHERS
MOOCHES
MOOCHING
MOOD
MOODIED
MOODIER
MOODIES
MOODIEST
MOODILY
MOODINESS
MOODINESSES
MOODS
MOODY
MOODYING
MOOED
MOOI
MOOING
MOOK
MOOKS
MOOKTAR
MOOKTARS
MOOL
MOOLA
MOOLAH
MOOLAHS
MOOLAS
MOOLED
MOOLI
MOOLIES
MOOLING
MOOLIS
MOOLS
MOOLY
MOON
MOONBEAM
MOONBEAMS
MOONBLIND
MOONCALF
MOONCALVES
MOONED
MOONER
MOONERS
MOONEYE
MOONEYES
MOONFACE
MOONFACES
MOONIER
MOONIES
MOONIEST
MOONING
MOONISH
MOONLESS
MOONLET
MOONLETS
MOONLIGHT
MOONLIGHTED
MOONLIGHTING
MOONLIGHTINGS
MOONLIGHTS
MOONLIT
MOONPHASE
MOONPHASES
MOONQUAKE
MOONQUAKES
MOONRAKER
MOONRAKERS
MOONRISE
MOONRISES
MOONROCK
MOONROCKS
MOONROOF
MOONROOFS
MOONS
MOONSAIL
MOONSAILS
MOONSCAPE
MOONSCAPES
MOONSEED
MOONSEEDS
MOONSET
MOONSETS
MOONSHEE
MOONSHEES
MOONSHINE
MOONSHINES
MOONSHINY
MOONSHOT
MOONSHOTS
MOONSTONE
MOONSTONES
MOONWALK
MOONWALKED
MOONWALKING
MOONWALKS
MOONWORT
MOONWORTS
MOONY
MOOP
MOOPED
MOOPING
MOOPS
MOOR
MOORAGE
MOORAGES
MOORCOCK
MOORCOCKS
MOORED
MOORFOWL
MOORFOWLS
MOORHEN
MOORHENS
MOORIER
MOORIEST
MOORILL
MOORILLS
MOORING
MOORINGS
MOORISH
MOORLAND
MOORLANDS
MOORLOG
MOORLOGS
MOORMAN
MOORMEN
MOORS
MOORVA
MOORVAS
MOORY
MOOS
MOOSE
MOOSEYARD
MOOSEYARDS
MOOT
MOOTABLE
MOOTED
MOOTER
MOOTERS
MOOTEST
MOOTING
MOOTINGS
MOOTMAN
MOOTMEN
MOOTS
MOOVE
MOOVED
MOOVES
MOOVING
MOP
MOPANE
MOPANES
MOPANI
MOPANIS
MOPBOARD
MOPBOARDS
MOPE
MOPED
MOPEDS
MOPEHAWK
MOPEHAWKS
MOPER
MOPERS
MOPES
MOPEY
MOPHEAD
MOPHEADS
MOPIER
MOPIEST
MOPING
MOPINGLY
MOPISH
MOPISHLY
MOPOKE
MOPOKES
MOPPED
MOPPER
MOPPERS
MOPPET
MOPPETS
MOPPIER
MOPPIEST
MOPPING
MOPPY
MOPS
MOPSIES
MOPSTICK
MOPSTICKS
MOPSY
MOPUS
MOPUSES
MOPY
MOQUETTE
MOQUETTES
MOR
MORA
MORACEOUS
MORAINAL
MORAINE
MORAINES
MORAINIC
MORAL
MORALE
MORALES
MORALISE
MORALISED
MORALISER
MORALISERS
MORALISES
MORALISING
MORALISM
MORALISMS
MORALIST
MORALISTS
MORALITIES
MORALITY
MORALIZE
MORALIZED
MORALIZER
MORALIZERS
MORALIZES
MORALIZING
MORALL
MORALLED
MORALLER
MORALLERS
MORALLING
MORALLS
MORALLY
MORALS
MORAS
MORASS
MORASSES
MORASSY
MORAT
MORATORIA
MORATORY
MORATS
MORAY
MORAYS
MORBID
MORBIDER
MORBIDEST
MORBIDITIES
MORBIDITY
MORBIDLY
MORBIFIC
MORBILLI
MORBUS
MORBUSES
MORCEAU
MORCEAUX
MORDACITIES
MORDACITY
MORDANCIES
MORDANCY
MORDANT
MORDANTED
MORDANTING
MORDANTLY
MORDANTS
MORDENT
MORDENTS
MORE
MOREEN
MOREENS
MOREISH
MOREL
MORELLO
MORELLOS
MORELS
MORENDO
MOREOVER
MOREPORK
MOREPORKS
MORES
MORGANITE
MORGANITES
MORGAY
MORGAYS
MORGEN
MORGENS
MORGUE
MORGUES
MORIA
MORIAS
MORIBUND
MORICHE
MORICHES
MORION
MORIONS
MORISCO
MORISCOES
MORISCOS
MORISH
MORKIN
MORKINS
MORLING
MORLINGS
MORMAOR
MORMAORS
MORN
MORNAY

MORNAYS
MORNE
MORNED
MORNES
MORNING
MORNINGS
MORNS
MOROCCO
MOROCCOS
MORON
MORONIC
MORONS
MOROSE
MOROSELY
MOROSER
MOROSEST
MOROSITIES
MOROSITY
MORPH
MORPHEAN
MORPHED
MORPHEME
MORPHEMES
MORPHEMIC
MORPHEMICS
MORPHETIC
MORPHEW
MORPHEWS
MORPHIA
MORPHIAS
MORPHIC
MORPHINE
MORPHINES
MORPHING
MORPHINGS
MORPHO
MORPHOS
MORPHOSES
MORPHOSIS
MORPHOTIC
MORPHS
MORRA
MORRAS
MORRHUA
MORRHUAS
MORRICE
MORRICES
MORRION
MORRIONS
MORRIS
MORRISED
MORRISES
MORRISING
MORRO
MORROS
MORROW
MORROWS
MORS
MORSAL
MORSE
MORSEL
MORSELLED
MORSELLING
MORSELS
MORSES
MORSURE
MORSURES
MORT
MORTAL
MORTALISE
MORTALISED
MORTALISES
MORTALISING
MORTALITIES
MORTALITY
MORTALIZE
MORTALIZED
MORTALIZES
MORTALIZING
MORTALLY
MORTALS
MORTAR
MORTARED
MORTARING
MORTARS
MORTBELL
MORTBELLS
MORTCLOTH
MORTCLOTHS
MORTGAGE
MORTGAGED
MORTGAGEE
MORTGAGEES
MORTGAGER
MORTGAGERS
MORTGAGES
MORTGAGING
MORTGAGOR
MORTGAGORS
MORTICE
MORTICED
MORTICER
MORTICERS
MORTICES
MORTICIAN
MORTICIANS
MORTICING
MORTIFIC
MORTIFIED
MORTIFIER
MORTIFIERS
MORTIFIES
MORTIFY
MORTIFYING
MORTIFYINGS
MORTISE
MORTISED
MORTISER
MORTISERS
MORTISES
MORTISING
MORTLING
MORTLINGS
MORTMAIN
MORTMAINS
MORTS
MORTUARIES
MORTUARY
MORULA
MORULAE
MORULAR
MORWONG
MORWONGS
MOSAIC
MOSAICISM
MOSAICISMS
MOSAICIST
MOSAICISTS
MOSAICS
MOSCHATEL
MOSCHATELS
MOSE
MOSED
MOSES
MOSEY
MOSEYED
MOSEYING
MOSEYS
MOSHAV
MOSHAVIM
MOSHING
MOSHINGS
MOSING
MOSKONFYT
MOSKONFYTS
MOSLINGS
MOSQUE
MOSQUES
MOSQUITO
MOSQUITOES
MOSQUITOS
MOSS
MOSSBACK
MOSSBACKS
MOSSED
MOSSES
MOSSIE
MOSSIER
MOSSIES
MOSSIEST
MOSSINESS
MOSSINESSES
MOSSING
MOSSLAND
MOSSLANDS
MOSSPLANT
MOSSPLANTS
MOSSY
MOST
MOSTLY
MOSTS
MOSTWHAT
MOT
MOTE
MOTED
MOTEL
MOTELIER
MOTELIERS
MOTELS
MOTEN
MOTES
MOTET
MOTETS
MOTETT
MOTETTIST
MOTETTISTS
MOTETTS
MOTEY
MOTH
MOTHBALL
MOTHBALLED
MOTHBALLING
MOTHBALLS
MOTHED
MOTHER
MOTHERED
MOTHERING
MOTHERINGS
MOTHERLY
MOTHERS
MOTHERY
MOTHIER
MOTHIEST
MOTHPROOF
MOTHPROOFED
MOTHPROOFING
MOTHPROOFS
MOTHS
MOTHY
MOTIER
MOTIEST
MOTIF
MOTIFS
MOTILE
MOTILES
MOTILITIES
MOTILITY
MOTION
MOTIONAL
MOTIONED
MOTIONING
MOTIONIST
MOTIONISTS
MOTIONS
MOTIVATE
MOTIVATED
MOTIVATES
MOTIVATING
MOTIVATOR
MOTIVATORS
MOTIVE
MOTIVED
MOTIVES
MOTIVIC
MOTIVING
MOTIVITIES
MOTIVITY
MOTLEY
MOTLEYER
MOTLEYEST
MOTLEYS
MOTLIER
MOTLIEST
MOTMOT
MOTMOTS
MOTOCROSS
MOTOCROSSES
MOTOR
MOTORABLE
MOTORAIL
MOTORAILS
MOTORBIKE
MOTORBIKES
MOTORBOAT
MOTORBOATS
MOTORCADE
MOTORCADES
MOTORED
MOTORIAL
MOTORING
MOTORISE
MOTORISED
MOTORISES
MOTORISING
MOTORIST
MOTORISTS
MOTORIUM
MOTORIUMS
MOTORIZE
MOTORIZED
MOTORIZES
MOTORIZING
MOTORMAN
MOTORMEN
MOTORS
MOTORWAY
MOTORWAYS
MOTORY
MOTOSCAFI
MOTOSCAFO
MOTS
MOTSER
MOTSERS
MOTT
MOTTE
MOTTES
MOTTIER
MOTTIEST
MOTTLE
MOTTLED
MOTTLES
MOTTLING
MOTTLINGS
MOTTO
MOTTOED
MOTTOES
MOTTS
MOTTY
MOTU
MOTUCA
MOTUCAS
MOTUS
MOTZA
MOTZAS
MOU
MOUCH
MOUCHARD
MOUCHARDS
MOUCHED
MOUCHER

MOUCHERS
MOUCHES
MOUCHING
MOUCHOIR
MOUCHOIRS
MOUDIWART
MOUDIWARTS
MOUDIWORT
MOUDIWORTS
MOUE
MOUES
MOUFFLON
MOUFFLONS
MOUFLON
MOUFLONS
MOUGHT
MOUILLE
MOUJIK
MOUJIKS
MOULAGE
MOULAGES
MOULD
MOULDABLE
MOULDED
MOULDER
MOULDERED
MOULDERING
MOULDERS
MOULDIER
MOULDIEST
MOULDING
MOULDINGS
MOULDS
MOULDWARP
MOULDWARPS
MOULDY
MOULIN
MOULINET
MOULINETS
MOULINS
MOULS
MOULT
MOULTED
MOULTEN
MOULTING
MOULTINGS
MOULTS
MOUND
MOUNDED
MOUNDING
MOUNDS
MOUNSEER
MOUNSEERS
MOUNT
MOUNTAIN
MOUNTAINS
MOUNTANT
MOUNTANTS
MOUNTED
MOUNTER
MOUNTERS
MOUNTING
MOUNTINGS
MOUNTS
MOUP
MOUPED
MOUPING
MOUPS
MOURN
MOURNED
MOURNER
MOURNERS
MOURNFUL
MOURNING
MOURNINGS
MOURNIVAL
MOURNIVALS
MOURNS
MOUS
MOUSAKA
MOUSAKAS
MOUSE
MOUSED
MOUSEKIN
MOUSEKINS
MOUSER
MOUSERIES
MOUSERS
MOUSERY
MOUSES
MOUSEY
MOUSIE
MOUSIER
MOUSIES
MOUSIEST
MOUSING
MOUSINGS
MOUSLE
MOUSLED
MOUSLES
MOUSLING
MOUSME
MOUSMEE
MOUSMEES
MOUSMES
MOUSSAKA
MOUSSAKAS
MOUSSE
MOUSSES
MOUST
MOUSTACHE
MOUSTACHES
MOUSTED
MOUSTING
MOUSTS
MOUSY
MOUTAN
MOUTANS
MOUTER
MOUTERED
MOUTERER
MOUTERERS
MOUTERING
MOUTERS
MOUTH
MOUTHABLE
MOUTHED
MOUTHER
MOUTHERS
MOUTHFEEL
MOUTHFEELS
MOUTHFUL
MOUTHFULS
MOUTHIER
MOUTHIEST
MOUTHING
MOUTHLESS
MOUTHS
MOUTHWASH
MOUTHWASHES
MOUTHY
MOUTON
MOUTONS
MOVABLE
MOVABLES
MOVABLY
MOVE
MOVEABLE
MOVEABLES
MOVEABLY
MOVED
MOVELESS
MOVEMENT
MOVEMENTS
MOVER
MOVERS
MOVES
MOVIE
MOVIEGOER
MOVIEGOERS
MOVIELAND
MOVIELANDS
MOVIES
MOVING
MOVINGLY
MOW
MOWA
MOWAS
MOWBURN
MOWBURNED
MOWBURNING
MOWBURNS
MOWBURNT
MOWDIWART
MOWDIWARTS
MOWDIWORT
MOWDIWORTS
MOWED
MOWER
MOWERS
MOWING
MOWINGS
MOWN
MOWRA
MOWRAS
MOWS
MOXA
MOXAS
MOXIE
MOXIES
MOY
MOYA
MOYAS
MOYGASHEL
MOYGASHELS
MOYITIES
MOYITY
MOYL
MOYLE
MOYLED
MOYLES
MOYLING
MOYLS
MOYS
MOZ
MOZE
MOZED
MOZES
MOZETTA
MOZETTAS
MOZING
MOZZ
MOZZES
MOZZETTA
MOZZETTAS
MOZZIE
MOZZIES
MOZZLE
MOZZLES
MPRET
MPRETS
MRIDAMGAM
MRIDAMGAMS
MRIDANG
MRIDANGA
MRIDANGAM
MRIDANGAMS
MRIDANGAS
MRIDANGS
MU
MUCATE
MUCATES
MUCH
MUCHEL
MUCHELL
MUCHELLS
MUCHELS
MUCHES
MUCHLY
MUCHNESS
MUCHNESSES
MUCID
MUCIGEN
MUCIGENS
MUCILAGE
MUCILAGES
MUCIN
MUCINS
MUCK
MUCKED
MUCKENDER
MUCKENDERS
MUCKER
MUCKERED
MUCKERING
MUCKERS
MUCKHEAP
MUCKHEAPS
MUCKIER
MUCKIEST
MUCKINESS
MUCKINESSES
MUCKING
MUCKLE
MUCKLES
MUCKLUCK
MUCKLUCKS
MUCKS
MUCKSWEAT
MUCKSWEATS
MUCKY
MUCLUC
MUCLUCS
MUCOID
MUCOR
MUCORS
MUCOSA
MUCOSAE
MUCOSITIES
MUCOSITY
MUCOUS
MUCRO
MUCRONATE
MUCRONES
MUCROS
MUCULENT
MUCUS
MUCUSES
MUD
MUDBATH
MUDBATHS
MUDCAT
MUDCATS
MUDDED
MUDDER
MUDDERS
MUDDIED
MUDDIER
MUDDIES
MUDDIEST
MUDDILY
MUDDINESS
MUDDINESSES
MUDDING
MUDDLE
MUDDLED
MUDDLER
MUDDLERS
MUDDLES
MUDDLING
MUDDY
MUDDYING
MUDEJAR
MUDEJARES
MUDFISH
MUDFISHES
MUDFLAP
MUDFLAPS
MUDFLAT
MUDFLATS

MUDGE
MUDGED
MUDGER
MUDGERS
MUDGES
MUDGING
MUDGUARD
MUDGUARDS
MUDHOLE
MUDHOLES
MUDHOOK
MUDHOOKS
MUDIR
MUDIRIA
MUDIRIAS
MUDIRIEH
MUDIRIEHS
MUDIRS
MUDLARK
MUDLARKED
MUDLARKING
MUDLARKS
MUDLOGGER
MUDLOGGERS
MUDPACK
MUDPACKS
MUDPUPPIES
MUDPUPPY
MUDRA
MUDRAS
MUDS
MUDSCOW
MUDSCOWS
MUDSLIDE
MUDSLIDES
MUDSTONE
MUDSTONES
MUDWORT
MUDWORTS
MUEDDIN
MUEDDINS
MUENSTER
MUENSTERS
MUESLI
MUESLIS
MUEZZIN
MUEZZINS
MUFF
MUFFED
MUFFETTEE
MUFFETTEES
MUFFIN
MUFFINEER
MUFFINEERS
MUFFING
MUFFINS
MUFFISH
MUFFLE
MUFFLED
MUFFLER
MUFFLERS
MUFFLES
MUFFLING
MUFFS
MUFLON
MUFLONS
MUFTI
MUFTIS
MUG
MUGEARITE
MUGEARITES
MUGFUL
MUGFULS
MUGGED
MUGGEE
MUGGEES
MUGGER
MUGGERS
MUGGIER
MUGGIEST
MUGGINESS
MUGGINESSES
MUGGING
MUGGINGS
MUGGINS
MUGGINSES
MUGGISH
MUGGY
MUGS
MUGSHOT
MUGSHOTS
MUGWORT
MUGWORTS
MUGWUMP
MUGWUMPS
MUID
MUIDS
MUIL
MUILS
MUIR
MUIRBURN
MUIRBURNS
MUIRS
MUIST
MUISTED
MUISTING
MUISTS
MUJAHEDIN
MUJAHIDIN
MUJIK
MUJIKS
MUKHTAR
MUKHTARS
MUKLUK
MUKLUKS
MULATTA
MULATTAS
MULATTO
MULATTOES
MULATTOS
MULBERRIES
MULBERRY
MULCH
MULCHED
MULCHES
MULCHING
MULCT
MULCTED
MULCTING
MULCTS
MULE
MULES
MULETEER
MULETEERS
MULEY
MULEYS
MULGA
MULGAS
MULISH
MULISHLY
MULL
MULLAH
MULLAHS
MULLARKIES
MULLARKY
MULLED
MULLEIN
MULLEINS
MULLER
MULLERS
MULLET
MULLETS
MULLEY
MULLEYS
MULLIGAN
MULLIGANS
MULLING
MULLION
MULLIONED
MULLIONS
MULLOCK
MULLOCKS
MULLOWAY
MULLOWAYS
MULLS
MULMUL
MULMULL
MULMULLS
MULMULS
MULSE
MULSES
MULSH
MULSHED
MULSHES
MULSHING
MULTEITIES
MULTEITY
MULTIFID
MULTIFIL
MULTIFILS
MULTIFOIL
MULTIFOILS
MULTIFORM
MULTIFORMS
MULTIGYM
MULTIGYMS
MULTIHULL
MULTIHULLS
MULTIMODE
MULTIPACK
MULTIPACKS
MULTIPARA
MULTIPARAE
MULTIPARAS
MULTIPED
MULTIPEDE
MULTIPEDES
MULTIPEDS
MULTIPLE
MULTIPLES
MULTIPLET
MULTIPLETS
MULTIPLEX
MULTIPLEXED
MULTIPLEXES
MULTIPLEXING
MULTIPLIED
MULTIPLIES
MULTIPLY
MULTIPLYING
MULTITUDE
MULTITUDES
MULTIUSER
MULTUM
MULTUMS
MULTURE
MULTURED
MULTURER
MULTURERS
MULTURES
MULTURING
MUM
MUMBLE
MUMBLED
MUMBLER
MUMBLERS
MUMBLES
MUMBLING
MUMBLINGS
MUMCHANCE
MUMCHANCES
MUMM
MUMMED
MUMMER
MUMMERIES
MUMMERS
MUMMERY
MUMMIA
MUMMIAS
MUMMIED
MUMMIES
MUMMIFIED
MUMMIFIES
MUMMIFORM
MUMMIFY
MUMMIFYING
MUMMING
MUMMINGS
MUMMOCK
MUMMOCKS
MUMMS
MUMMY
MUMMYING
MUMP
MUMPED
MUMPER
MUMPERS
MUMPING
MUMPISH
MUMPISHLY
MUMPS
MUMPSIMUS
MUMPSIMUSES
MUMS
MUMSIER
MUMSIEST
MUMSY
MUN
MUNCH
MUNCHED
MUNCHER
MUNCHERS
MUNCHES
MUNCHING
MUNCHKIN
MUNCHKINS
MUNDANE
MUNDANELY
MUNDANER
MUNDANEST
MUNDANITIES
MUNDANITY
MUNDIC
MUNDICS
MUNDIFIED
MUNDIFIES
MUNDIFY
MUNDIFYING
MUNDUNGUS
MUNDUNGUSES
MUNGCORN
MUNGCORNS
MUNGO
MUNGOOSE
MUNGOOSES
MUNGOS
MUNICIPAL
MUNIFIED
MUNIFIES
MUNIFY
MUNIFYING
MUNIMENT
MUNIMENTS
MUNITE
MUNITED
MUNITES
MUNITING
MUNITION
MUNITIONED
MUNITIONING
MUNITIONS
MUNNION
MUNNIONS
MUNSHI
MUNSHIS
MUNSTER
MUNSTERS
MUNT
MUNTIN
MUNTING

MUNTINGS
MUNTINS
MUNTJAC
MUNTJACS
MUNTJAK
MUNTJAKS
MUNTS
MUNTU
MUNTUS
MUON
MUONIC
MUONIUM
MUONIUMS
MUONS
MUQADDAM
MUQADDAMS
MURAENA
MURAENAS
MURAGE
MURAGES
MURAL
MURALIST
MURALISTS
MURALS
MURDER
MURDERED
MURDEREE
MURDEREES
MURDERER
MURDERERS
MURDERESS
MURDERESSES
MURDERING
MURDEROUS
MURDERS
MURE
MURED
MURENA
MURENAS
MURES
MUREX
MUREXES
MURGEON
MURGEONED
MURGEONING
MURGEONS
MURIATE
MURIATED
MURIATES
MURIATIC
MURICATE
MURICATED
MURICES
MURIFORM
MURINE
MURINES
MURING
MURK
MURKER
MURKEST
MURKIER
MURKIEST
MURKILY
MURKINESS
MURKINESSES
MURKISH
MURKS
MURKSOME
MURKY
MURL
MURLAIN
MURLAINS
MURLAN
MURLANS
MURLED
MURLIER
MURLIEST
MURLIN
MURLING
MURLINS
MURLS
MURLY
MURMUR
MURMURED
MURMURER
MURMURERS
MURMURING
MURMURINGS
MURMUROUS
MURMURS
MURPHIES
MURPHY
MURRA
MURRAIN
MURRAINED
MURRAINS
MURRAM
MURRAMS
MURRAS
MURRAY
MURRAYS
MURRE
MURRELET
MURRELETS
MURREN
MURRENS
MURRES
MURREY
MURREYS
MURRHA
MURRHAS
MURRHINE
MURRIES
MURRIN
MURRINE
MURRINS
MURRION
MURRIONS
MURRY
MURTHER
MURTHERED
MURTHERER
MURTHERERS
MURTHERING
MURTHERS
MURVA
MURVAS
MUS
MUSACEOUS
MUSANG
MUSANGS
MUSCADEL
MUSCADELS
MUSCADIN
MUSCADINE
MUSCADINES
MUSCADINS
MUSCARINE
MUSCARINES
MUSCAT
MUSCATEL
MUSCATELS
MUSCATS
MUSCID
MUSCIDS
MUSCLE
MUSCLED
MUSCLEMAN
MUSCLEMEN
MUSCLES
MUSCLIER
MUSCLIEST
MUSCLING
MUSCLINGS
MUSCLY
MUSCOID
MUSCOLOGIES
MUSCOLOGY
MUSCONE
MUSCONES
MUSCOSE
MUSCOVADO
MUSCOVADOS
MUSCOVITE
MUSCOVITES
MUSCULAR
MUSCULOUS
MUSE
MUSED
MUSEFUL
MUSEFULLY
MUSEOLOGIES
MUSEOLOGY
MUSER
MUSERS
MUSES
MUSET
MUSETS
MUSETTE
MUSETTES
MUSEUM
MUSEUMS
MUSH
MUSHA
MUSHED
MUSHER
MUSHERS
MUSHES
MUSHIER
MUSHIEST
MUSHILY
MUSHINESS
MUSHINESSES
MUSHING
MUSHMOUTH
MUSHMOUTHS
MUSHROOM
MUSHROOMED
MUSHROOMING
MUSHROOMS
MUSHY
MUSIC
MUSICAL
MUSICALE
MUSICALES
MUSICALLY
MUSICALS
MUSICIAN
MUSICIANS
MUSICKED
MUSICKER
MUSICKERS
MUSICKING
MUSICS
MUSIMON
MUSIMONS
MUSING
MUSINGLY
MUSINGS
MUSIT
MUSITS
MUSIVE
MUSK
MUSKED
MUSKEG
MUSKEGS
MUSKET
MUSKETEER
MUSKETEERS
MUSKETOON
MUSKETOONS
MUSKETRIES
MUSKETRY
MUSKETS
MUSKIER
MUSKIEST
MUSKILY
MUSKINESS
MUSKINESSES
MUSKING
MUSKLE
MUSKLES
MUSKONE
MUSKONES
MUSKRAT
MUSKRATS
MUSKS
MUSKY
MUSLIN
MUSLINED
MUSLINET
MUSLINETS
MUSLINS
MUSMON
MUSMONS
MUSO
MUSOS
MUSQUASH
MUSQUASHES
MUSROL
MUSROLS
MUSS
MUSSE
MUSSED
MUSSEL
MUSSELLED
MUSSELS
MUSSES
MUSSIER
MUSSIEST
MUSSINESS
MUSSINESSES
MUSSING
MUSSITATE
MUSSITATED
MUSSITATES
MUSSITATING
MUSSY
MUST
MUSTACHE
MUSTACHES
MUSTACHIO
MUSTACHIOS
MUSTANG
MUSTANGS
MUSTARD
MUSTARDS
MUSTED
MUSTEE
MUSTEES
MUSTELINE
MUSTELINES
MUSTER
MUSTERED
MUSTERER
MUSTERERS
MUSTERING
MUSTERS
MUSTH
MUSTHS
MUSTIER
MUSTIEST
MUSTILY
MUSTINESS
MUSTINESSES
MUSTING
MUSTS
MUSTY
MUTABLE
MUTABLY
MUTAGEN
MUTAGENIC
MUTAGENS
MUTANDA
MUTANDUM
MUTANT
MUTANTS
MUTATE
MUTATED
MUTATES

MUTATING
MUTATION
MUTATIONS
MUTATIVE
MUTATORY
MUTCH
MUTCHES
MUTCHKIN
MUTCHKINS
MUTE
MUTED
MUTELY
MUTENESS
MUTENESSES
MUTER
MUTES
MUTEST
MUTI
MUTICOUS
MUTILATE
MUTILATED
MUTILATES
MUTILATING
MUTILATOR
MUTILATORS
MUTINE
MUTINED
MUTINEER
MUTINEERED
MUTINEERING
MUTINEERS
MUTINES
MUTING
MUTINIED
MUTINIES
MUTINING
MUTINOUS
MUTINY
MUTINYING
MUTIS
MUTISM
MUTISMS
MUTON
MUTONS
MUTOSCOPE
MUTOSCOPES
MUTT
MUTTER
MUTTERED
MUTTERER
MUTTERERS
MUTTERING
MUTTERINGS
MUTTERS
MUTTON
MUTTONS
MUTTONY
MUTTS
MUTUAL
MUTUALISE
MUTUALISED
MUTUALISES
MUTUALISING
MUTUALISM
MUTUALISMS
MUTUALITIES
MUTUALITY
MUTUALIZE
MUTUALIZED
MUTUALIZES
MUTUALIZING
MUTUALLY
MUTUALS
MUTUCA
MUTUCAS
MUTULE
MUTULES
MUTUUM
MUTUUMS
MUX
MUXED
MUXES
MUXING
MUZAKY
MUZHIK
MUZHIKS
MUZZIER
MUZZIEST
MUZZILY
MUZZINESS
MUZZINESSES
MUZZLE
MUZZLED
MUZZLER
MUZZLERS
MUZZLES
MUZZLING
MUZZY
MVULE
MVULES
MY
MYAL
MYALGIA
MYALGIAS
MYALGIC
MYALISM
MYALISMS
MYALL
MYALLS
MYCELIA
MYCELIAL
MYCELIUM
MYCETES
MYCETOMA
MYCETOMAS
MYCETOMATA
MYCOLOGIC
MYCOLOGIES
MYCOLOGY
MYCOPHAGIES
MYCOPHAGY
MYCORHIZA
MYCORHIZAS
MYCOSES
MYCOSIS
MYCOTIC
MYCOTOXIN
MYCOTOXINS
MYDRIASES
MYDRIASIS
MYDRIATIC
MYDRIATICS
MYELIN
MYELINS
MYELITIS
MYELITISES
MYELOID
MYELOMA
MYELOMAS
MYELOMATA
MYELON
MYELONS
MYGALE
MYGALES
MYIASES
MYIASIS
MYLODON
MYLODONS
MYLODONT
MYLODONTS
MYLOHYOID
MYLOHYOIDS
MYLONITE
MYLONITES
MYLONITIC
MYNA
MYNAH
MYNAHS
MYNAS
MYNHEER
MYNHEERS
MYOBLAST
MYOBLASTS
MYOFIBRIL
MYOFIBRILS
MYOGEN
MYOGENIC
MYOGENS
MYOGLOBIN
MYOGLOBINS
MYOGRAM
MYOGRAMS
MYOGRAPH
MYOGRAPHIES
MYOGRAPHS
MYOGRAPHY
MYOID
MYOLOGIES
MYOLOGIST
MYOLOGISTS
MYOLOGY
MYOMA
MYOMANCIES
MYOMANCY
MYOMANTIC
MYOMAS
MYOMATA
MYOPE
MYOPES
MYOPIA
MYOPIAS
MYOPIC
MYOPICS
MYOPS
MYOPSES
MYOSES
MYOSIN
MYOSINS
MYOSIS
MYOSITIS
MYOSITISES
MYOSOTE
MYOSOTES
MYOSOTIS
MYOSOTISES
MYOTONIA
MYOTONIAS
MYOTUBE
MYOTUBES
MYRBANE
MYRBANES
MYRIAD
MYRIADS
MYRIADTH
MYRIADTHS
MYRIAPOD
MYRIAPODS
MYRINGA
MYRINGAS
MYRIOPOD
MYRIOPODS
MYRIORAMA
MYRIORAMAS
MYRISTIC
MYRMECOID
MYRMIDON
MYRMIDONS
MYROBALAN
MYROBALANS
MYRRH
MYRRHIC
MYRRHINE
MYRRHOL
MYRRHOLS
MYRRHS
MYRTLE
MYRTLES
MYSELF
MYSTAGOGIES
MYSTAGOGY
MYSTERIES
MYSTERY
MYSTIC
MYSTICAL
MYSTICISM
MYSTICISMS
MYSTICS
MYSTIFIED
MYSTIFIER
MYSTIFIERS
MYSTIFIES
MYSTIFY
MYSTIFYING
MYSTIQUE
MYSTIQUES
MYTH
MYTHI
MYTHIC
MYTHICAL
MYTHICISE
MYTHICISED
MYTHICISES
MYTHICISING
MYTHICISM
MYTHICISMS
MYTHICIST
MYTHICISTS
MYTHICIZE
MYTHICIZED
MYTHICIZES
MYTHICIZING
MYTHISE
MYTHISED
MYTHISES
MYTHISING
MYTHISM
MYTHISMS
MYTHIST
MYTHISTS
MYTHIZE
MYTHIZED
MYTHIZES
MYTHIZING
MYTHOI
MYTHOLOGIES
MYTHOLOGY
MYTHOMANE
MYTHOMANES
MYTHOPOET
MYTHOPOETS
MYTHOS
MYTHS
MYTHUS
MYTILOID
MYXEDEMA
MYXEDEMAS
MYXEDEMIC
MYXOEDEMA
MYXOEDEMAS
MYXOMA
MYXOMATA
MYXOVIRUS
MYXOVIRUSES
MZEE
MZEES
MZUNGU
MZUNGUS

N

NA
NAAM
NAAMS
NAAN
NAANS
NAARTJE
NAARTJES
NAB
NABBED
NABBER
NABBERS
NABBING
NABK
NABKS
NABLA
NABLAS
NABOB
NABOBS
NABS
NACARAT
NACARATS
NACELLE
NACELLES
NACH
NACHE
NACHES
NACHO
NACHOS
NACHTMAAL
NACHTMAALS
NACKET
NACKETS
NACRE
NACRED
NACREOUS
NACRES
NACRITE
NACRITES
NACROUS
NADA
NADAS
NADIR
NADIRS
NAE
NAEBODIES
NAEBODY
NAETHING
NAETHINGS
NAEVE
NAEVES
NAEVI
NAEVOID
NAEVUS
NAFF
NAFFING
NAFFLY
NAFFNESS
NAFFNESSES
NAFFS
NAG
NAGA
NAGANA
NAGANAS
NAGAPIE
NAGAPIES
NAGARI
NAGARIS
NAGAS
NAGGED
NAGGER
NAGGERS
NAGGIER
NAGGIEST
NAGGING
NAGGY
NAGMAAL
NAGMAALS
NAGOR
NAGORS
NAGS
NAHAL
NAHALS
NAIAD
NAIADES
NAIADS
NAIANT
NAIF
NAIFER
NAIFEST
NAIK
NAIKS
NAIL
NAILED
NAILER
NAILERIES
NAILERS
NAILERY
NAILING
NAILINGS
NAILLESS
NAILS
NAIN
NAINSELL
NAINSELLS
NAINSOOK
NAINSOOKS
NAIRA
NAIRAS
NAISSANT
NAIVE
NAIVELY
NAIVENESS
NAIVENESSES
NAIVER
NAIVEST
NAIVETE
NAIVETES
NAIVETIES
NAIVETY
NAIVIST
NAKED
NAKEDER
NAKEDEST
NAKEDLY
NAKEDNESS
NAKEDNESSES
NAKER
NAKERS
NALA
NALAS
NALLA
NALLAH
NALLAHS
NALLAS
NALOXONE
NALOXONES
NAM
NAMABLE
NAMASKAR
NAMASKARS
NAMASTE
NAMASTES
NAME
NAMEABLE
NAMED
NAMELESS
NAMELY
NAMER
NAMERS
NAMES
NAMESAKE
NAMESAKES
NAMETAPE
NAMETAPES
NAMING
NAMINGS
NAMS
NAN
NANA
NANAS
NANCE
NANCES
NANCIES
NANCY
NANDINE
NANDINES
NANDOO
NANDOOS
NANDU
NANDUS
NANISM
NANISMS
NANKEEN
NANKEENS
NANKIN
NANKINS
NANNA
NANNAS
NANNIED
NANNIES
NANNY
NANNYGAI
NANNYGAIS
NANNYGHAI
NANNYGHAIS
NANNYING
NANNYISH
NANOGRAM
NANOGRAMS
NANOMETRE
NANOMETRES
NANS
NAOI
NAOS
NAOSES
NAP
NAPA
NAPALM
NAPALMED
NAPALMING
NAPALMS
NAPAS
NAPE
NAPERIES
NAPERY
NAPES
NAPHTHA
NAPHTHAS
NAPHTHENE
NAPHTHENES
NAPHTHOL
NAPHTHOLS
NAPIFORM
NAPKIN
NAPKINS
NAPLESS
NAPOLEON
NAPOLEONS
NAPOO
NAPOOED
NAPOOING
NAPOOS
NAPPA
NAPPAS
NAPPE
NAPPED
NAPPER
NAPPERS
NAPPES
NAPPIER
NAPPIES
NAPPIEST
NAPPINESS
NAPPINESSES
NAPPING
NAPPY
NAPRON
NAPRONS
NAPS
NARAS
NARASES
NARC
NARCEEN
NARCEENS
NARCEINE
NARCEINES
NARCISSI
NARCISSUS
NARCISSUSES
NARCO
NARCOS
NARCOSES
NARCOSIS
NARCOTIC
NARCOTICS
NARCOTINE
NARCOTINES
NARCOTISE
NARCOTISED
NARCOTISES
NARCOTISING
NARCOTISM
NARCOTISMS
NARCOTIST
NARCOTISTS
NARCOTIZE
NARCOTIZED
NARCOTIZES
NARCOTIZING
NARCS

NARD
NARDED
NARDING
NARDOO
NARDOOS
NARDS
NARE
NARES
NARGHILE
NARGHILES
NARGHILIES
NARGHILLIES
NARGHILLY
NARGHILY
NARGILE
NARGILEH
NARGILEHS
NARGILES
NARGILIES
NARGILLIES
NARGILLY
NARGILY
NARIAL
NARICORN
NARICORNS
NARINE
NARK
NARKED
NARKIER
NARKIEST
NARKING
NARKS
NARKY
NARQUOIS
NARRAS
NARRASES
NARRATE
NARRATED
NARRATES
NARRATING
NARRATION
NARRATIONS
NARRATIVE
NARRATIVES
NARRATOR
NARRATORS
NARRATORY
NARRE
NARROW
NARROWED
NARROWER
NARROWEST
NARROWING
NARROWINGS
NARROWLY
NARROWS
NARTHEX
NARTHEXES
NARTJIE
NARTJIES
NARWHAL
NARWHALS
NARY
NAS
NASAL
NASALISE
NASALISED
NASALISES
NASALISING
NASALITIES
NASALITY
NASALIZE
NASALIZED
NASALIZES
NASALIZING
NASALLY
NASALS
NASARD
NASARDS
NASCENCE
NASCENCES
NASCENCIES
NASCENCY
NASCENT
NASEBERRIES
NASEBERRY
NASHGAB
NASHGABS
NASION
NASIONS
NASTALIK
NASTALIKS
NASTIC
NASTIER
NASTIES
NASTIEST
NASTILY
NASTINESS
NASTINESSES
NASTY
NASUTE
NASUTES
NAT
NATAL
NATALITIES
NATALITY
NATANT
NATATION
NATATIONS
NATATORIA
NATATORY
NATCH
NATCHES
NATES
NATHELESS
NATHEMO
NATHEMORE
NATHLESS
NATIFORM
NATION
NATIONAL
NATIONALS
NATIONS
NATIVE
NATIVELY
NATIVES
NATIVISM
NATIVISMS
NATIVIST
NATIVISTS
NATIVITIES
NATIVITY
NATRIUM
NATRIUMS
NATROLITE
NATROLITES
NATRON
NATRONS
NATS
NATTER
NATTERED
NATTERER
NATTERERS
NATTERING
NATTERS
NATTERY
NATTIER
NATTIEST
NATTILY
NATTINESS
NATTINESSES
NATTY
NATURA
NATURAE
NATURAL
NATURALLY
NATURALS
NATURE
NATURED
NATURES
NATURING
NATURISM
NATURISMS
NATURIST
NATURISTS
NAUGHT
NAUGHTIER
NAUGHTIES
NAUGHTIEST
NAUGHTILY
NAUGHTS
NAUGHTY
NAUMACHIA
NAUMACHIAE
NAUMACHIAS
NAUMACHIES
NAUMACHY
NAUNT
NAUNTS
NAUPLII
NAUPLIOID
NAUPLIUS
NAUSEA
NAUSEANT
NAUSEANTS
NAUSEAS
NAUSEATE
NAUSEATED
NAUSEATES
NAUSEATING
NAUSEOUS
NAUTCH
NAUTCHES
NAUTIC
NAUTICAL
NAUTICS
NAUTILI
NAUTILUS
NAUTILUSES
NAVAID
NAVAIDS
NAVAL
NAVALISM
NAVALISMS
NAVARCH
NAVARCHIES
NAVARCHS
NAVARCHY
NAVARHO
NAVARHOS
NAVARIN
NAVARINS
NAVE
NAVEL
NAVELS
NAVELWORT
NAVELWORTS
NAVES
NAVETTE
NAVETTES
NAVEW
NAVEWS
NAVICERT
NAVICERTS
NAVICULA
NAVICULAR
NAVICULARS
NAVICULAS
NAVIES
NAVIGABLE
NAVIGABLY
NAVIGATE
NAVIGATED
NAVIGATES
NAVIGATING
NAVIGATOR
NAVIGATORS
NAVVIED
NAVVIES
NAVVY
NAVVYING
NAVY
NAWAB
NAWABS
NAY
NAYS
NAYTHLES
NAYWARD
NAYWARDS
NAYWORD
NAYWORDS
NAZE
NAZES
NAZIR
NAZIRS
NE
NEAFE
NEAFES
NEAFFE
NEAFFES
NEAL
NEALED
NEALING
NEALS
NEANIC
NEAP
NEAPED
NEAPING
NEAPS
NEAR
NEARED
NEARER
NEAREST
NEARING
NEARLY
NEARNESS
NEARNESSES
NEARS
NEARSIDE
NEARSIDES
NEAT
NEATEN
NEATENED
NEATENING
NEATENS
NEATER
NEATEST
NEATH
NEATLY
NEATNESS
NEATNESSES
NEB
NEBBED
NEBBICH
NEBBICHS
NEBBING
NEBBISH
NEBBISHE
NEBBISHER
NEBBISHERS
NEBBISHES
NEBBUK
NEBBUKS
NEBECK
NEBECKS
NEBEK
NEBEKS
NEBEL
NEBELS
NEBISH
NEBISHES
NEBRIS
NEBRISES
NEBS
NEBULA
NEBULAE
NEBULAR
NEBULAS
NEBULE
NEBULES

NEBULISE
NEBULISED
NEBULISER
NEBULISERS
NEBULISES
NEBULISING
NEBULIUM
NEBULIUMS
NEBULIZE
NEBULIZED
NEBULIZER
NEBULIZERS
NEBULIZES
NEBULIZING
NEBULOUS
NEBULY
NECESSARIES
NECESSARY
NECESSITIES
NECESSITY
NECK
NECKATEE
NECKATEES
NECKBAND
NECKBANDS
NECKBEEF
NECKBEEFS
NECKCLOTH
NECKCLOTHS
NECKED
NECKGEAR
NECKGEARS
NECKING
NECKINGS
NECKLACE
NECKLACED
NECKLACES
NECKLACING
NECKLACINGS
NECKLET
NECKLETS
NECKLINE
NECKLINES
NECKPIECE
NECKPIECES
NECKS
NECKTIE
NECKTIES
NECKVERSE
NECKVERSES
NECKWEAR
NECKWEARS
NECKWEED
NECKWEEDS
NECROLOGIES
NECROLOGY
NECROPHIL
NECROPHILS
NECROPSIES
NECROPSY
NECROSE
NECROSED
NECROSES
NECROSING
NECROSIS
NECROTIC
NECROTISE
NECROTISED
NECROTISES
NECROTISING
NECROTIZE
NECROTIZED
NECROTIZES
NECROTIZING
NECROTOMIES
NECROTOMY
NECTAR
NECTAREAL
NECTAREAN
NECTARED
NECTARIAL
NECTARIES
NECTARINE
NECTARINES
NECTAROUS
NECTARS
NECTARY
NED
NEDDIES
NEDDY
NEDS
NEE
NEED
NEEDED
NEEDER
NEEDERS
NEEDFIRE
NEEDFIRES
NEEDFUL
NEEDFULLY
NEEDIER
NEEDIEST
NEEDILY
NEEDINESS
NEEDINESSES
NEEDING
NEEDLE
NEEDLED
NEEDLEFUL
NEEDLEFULS
NEEDLER
NEEDLERS
NEEDLES
NEEDLESS
NEEDLIER
NEEDLIEST
NEEDLING
NEEDLY
NEEDMENT
NEEDMENTS
NEEDS
NEEDY
NEELD
NEELDS
NEELE
NEELES
NEEM
NEEMB
NEEMBS
NEEMS
NEEP
NEEPS
NEESBERRIES
NEESBERRY
NEESE
NEESED
NEESES
NEESING
NEEZE
NEEZED
NEEZES
NEEZING
NEF
NEFANDOUS
NEFARIOUS
NEFAST
NEFS
NEGATE
NEGATED
NEGATES
NEGATING
NEGATION
NEGATIONS
NEGATIVE
NEGATIVED
NEGATIVES
NEGATIVING
NEGATORY
NEGATRON
NEGATRONS
NEGLECT
NEGLECTED
NEGLECTER
NEGLECTERS
NEGLECTING
NEGLECTS
NEGLIGE
NEGLIGEE
NEGLIGEES
NEGLIGENT
NEGLIGES
NEGOCIANT
NEGOCIANTS
NEGOTIANT
NEGOTIANTS
NEGOTIATE
NEGOTIATED
NEGOTIATES
NEGOTIATING
NEGRESS
NEGRESSES
NEGRITUDE
NEGRITUDES
NEGRO
NEGROES
NEGROHEAD
NEGROHEADS
NEGROID
NEGROIDAL
NEGROIDS
NEGROISM
NEGROISMS
NEGROPHIL
NEGROPHILS
NEGUS
NEGUSES
NEIF
NEIFS
NEIGH
NEIGHBOR
NEIGHBORED
NEIGHBORING
NEIGHBORS
NEIGHBOUR
NEIGHBOURED
NEIGHBOURING
NEIGHBOURS
NEIGHED
NEIGHING
NEIGHS
NEIST
NEITHER
NEIVE
NEIVES
NEK
NEKS
NEKTON
NEKTONS
NELIES
NELIS
NELLIES
NELLY
NELSON
NELSONS
NELUMBIUM
NELUMBIUMS
NELUMBO
NELUMBOS
NEMATIC
NEMATODE
NEMATODES
NEMATOID
NEMERTEAN
NEMERTEANS
NEMERTIAN
NEMERTIANS
NEMERTINE
NEMERTINES
NEMESES
NEMESIA
NEMESIAS
NEMESIS
NEMN
NEMNED
NEMNING
NEMNS
NEMOPHILA
NEMOPHILAS
NEMORAL
NEMOROUS
NEMPT
NENE
NENES
NENNIGAI
NENNIGAIS
NENUPHAR
NENUPHARS
NEOBLAST
NEOBLASTS
NEODYMIUM
NEODYMIUMS
NEOLITH
NEOLITHS
NEOLOGIAN
NEOLOGIANS
NEOLOGIC
NEOLOGIES
NEOLOGISE
NEOLOGISED
NEOLOGISES
NEOLOGISING
NEOLOGISM
NEOLOGISMS
NEOLOGIST
NEOLOGISTS
NEOLOGIZE
NEOLOGIZED
NEOLOGIZES
NEOLOGIZING
NEOLOGY
NEOMYCIN
NEOMYCINS
NEON
NEONATAL
NEONATE
NEONATES
NEONOMIAN
NEONOMIANS
NEONS
NEOPAGAN
NEOPAGANS
NEOPHILE
NEOPHILES
NEOPHILIA
NEOPHILIAS
NEOPHOBE
NEOPHOBES
NEOPHOBIA
NEOPHOBIAS
NEOPHOBIC
NEOPHYTE
NEOPHYTES
NEOPHYTIC
NEOPILINA
NEOPILINAS
NEOPLASM
NEOPLASMS
NEOPRENE
NEOPRENES
NEOTEINIA
NEOTEINIAS
NEOTENIC
NEOTENIES
NEOTENOUS
NEOTENY
NEOTERIC
NEOTERICS
NEOTERISE
NEOTERISED
NEOTERISES

NEOTERISING
NEOTERISM
NEOTERISMS
NEOTERIST
NEOTERISTS
NEOTERIZE
NEOTERIZED
NEOTERIZES
NEOTERIZING
NEOTOXIN
NEOTOXINS
NEP
NEPENTHE
NEPENTHES
NEPER
NEPERS
NEPETA
NEPETAS
NEPHALISM
NEPHALISMS
NEPHALIST
NEPHALISTS
NEPHELINE
NEPHELINES
NEPHELITE
NEPHELITES
NEPHEW
NEPHEWS
NEPHOGRAM
NEPHOGRAMS
NEPHOLOGIES
NEPHOLOGY
NEPHRALGIES
NEPHRALGY
NEPHRIC
NEPHRIDIA
NEPHRITE
NEPHRITES
NEPHRITIC
NEPHRITICS
NEPHRITIS
NEPHRITISES
NEPHROID
NEPHRON
NEPHRONS
NEPHROSES
NEPHROSIS
NEPHROTIC
NEPIONIC
NEPIT
NEPITS
NEPOTIC
NEPOTISM
NEPOTISMS
NEPOTIST
NEPOTISTS
NEPS
NEPTUNIUM
NEPTUNIUMS
NERD
NERDIER
NERDIEST
NERDS
NERDY
NEREID
NEREIDES
NEREIDS
NERINE
NERINES
NERITE
NERITES
NERITIC
NERK
NERKA
NERKAS
NERKS
NEROLI
NEROLIS
NERVAL
NERVATE
NERVATION
NERVATIONS
NERVATURE
NERVATURES
NERVE
NERVED
NERVELESS
NERVELET
NERVELETS
NERVER
NERVERS
NERVES
NERVIER
NERVIEST
NERVILY
NERVINE
NERVINES
NERVINESS
NERVINESSES
NERVING
NERVOUS
NERVOUSLY
NERVULAR
NERVULE
NERVULES
NERVURE
NERVURES
NERVY
NESCIENCE
NESCIENCES
NESCIENT
NESH
NESHER
NESHEST
NESHNESS
NESHNESSES
NESS
NESSES
NEST
NESTED
NESTER
NESTERS
NESTFUL
NESTFULS
NESTING
NESTINGS
NESTLE
NESTLED
NESTLES
NESTLIKE
NESTLING
NESTLINGS
NESTS
NET
NETBALL
NETBALLS
NETE
NETES
NETFUL
NETFULS
NETHELESS
NETHER
NETIZEN
NETIZENS
NETS
NETSUKE
NETSUKES
NETT
NETTED
NETTIER
NETTIEST
NETTING
NETTINGS
NETTLE
NETTLED
NETTLES
NETTLIER
NETTLIEST
NETTLING
NETTLY
NETTS
NETTY
NETWORK
NETWORKED
NETWORKER
NETWORKERS
NETWORKING
NETWORKINGS
NETWORKS
NEUK
NEUKS
NEUM
NEUME
NEUMES
NEUMS
NEURAL
NEURALGIA
NEURALGIAS
NEURALGIC
NEURALLY
NEURATION
NEURATIONS
NEURILITIES
NEURILITY
NEURINE
NEURINES
NEURISM
NEURISMS
NEURITE
NEURITES
NEURITIC
NEURITICS
NEURITIS
NEURITISES
NEUROCHIP
NEUROCHIPS
NEUROGLIA
NEUROGLIAS
NEUROGRAM
NEUROGRAMS
NEUROLOGIES
NEUROLOGY
NEUROMA
NEUROMAS
NEUROMATA
NEURON
NEURONAL
NEURONE
NEURONES
NEURONIC
NEURONS
NEUROPATH
NEUROPATHS
NEUROPIL
NEUROPILS
NEUROSES
NEUROSIS
NEUROTIC
NEUROTICS
NEUROTOMIES
NEUROTOMY
NEUSTON
NEUSTONS
NEUTER
NEUTERED
NEUTERING
NEUTERS
NEUTRAL
NEUTRALLY
NEUTRALS
NEUTRETTO
NEUTRETTOS
NEUTRINO
NEUTRINOS
NEUTRON
NEUTRONS
NEVE
NEVEL
NEVELLED
NEVELLING
NEVELS
NEVER
NEVERMORE
NEVES
NEVI
NEVUS
NEW
NEWBIE
NEWBIES
NEWBORN
NEWCOME
NEWCOMER
NEWCOMERS
NEWED
NEWEL
NEWELL
NEWELLED
NEWELLS
NEWELS
NEWER
NEWEST
NEWFANGLE
NEWING
NEWISH
NEWISHLY
NEWLY
NEWMARKET
NEWMARKETS
NEWNESS
NEWNESSES
NEWS
NEWSAGENT
NEWSAGENTS
NEWSBOY
NEWSBOYS
NEWSCAST
NEWSCASTS
NEWSED
NEWSES
NEWSFLASH
NEWSFLASHES
NEWSGIRL
NEWSGIRLS
NEWSGROUP
NEWSGROUPS
NEWSHAWK
NEWSHAWKS
NEWSHOUND
NEWSHOUNDS
NEWSIER
NEWSIES
NEWSIEST
NEWSINESS
NEWSINESSES
NEWSING
NEWSLESS
NEWSMAN
NEWSMEN
NEWSPAPER
NEWSPAPERS
NEWSPEAK
NEWSPEAKS
NEWSPRINT
NEWSPRINTS
NEWSREEL
NEWSREELS
NEWSROOM
NEWSROOMS
NEWSTRADE
NEWSTRADES
NEWSWIRE
NEWSWIRES
NEWSWOMAN
NEWSWOMEN
NEWSY
NEWT
NEWTON
NEWTONS
NEWTS
NEXT

NEXTLY
NEXTNESS
NEXTNESSES
NEXTS
NEXUS
NGAIO
NGAIOS
NGANA
NGANAS
NGULTRUM
NGULTRUMS
NGWEE
NHANDU
NHANDUS
NIACIN
NIACINS
NIAISERIE
NIAISERIES
NIB
NIBBED
NIBBING
NIBBLE
NIBBLED
NIBBLER
NIBBLERS
NIBBLES
NIBBLING
NIBBLINGS
NIBLICK
NIBLICKS
NIBS
NICAD
NICADS
NICCOLITE
NICCOLITES
NICE
NICEISH
NICELY
NICENESS
NICENESSES
NICER
NICEST
NICETIES
NICETY
NICHE
NICHED
NICHER
NICHERED
NICHERING
NICHERS
NICHES
NICHING
NICISH
NICK
NICKAR
NICKARS
NICKED
NICKEL
NICKELED
NICKELIC
NICKELINE
NICKELINES
NICKELING
NICKELISE
NICKELISED
NICKELISES
NICKELISING
NICKELIZE
NICKELIZED
NICKELIZES
NICKELIZING
NICKELLED
NICKELLING
NICKELOUS
NICKELS
NICKER
NICKERED
NICKERING
NICKERS
NICKING
NICKNAME
NICKNAMED
NICKNAMES
NICKNAMING
NICKPOINT
NICKPOINTS
NICKS
NICKSTICK
NICKSTICKS
NICKUM
NICKUMS
NICOL
NICOLS
NICOMPOOP
NICOMPOOPS
NICOTIAN
NICOTIANA
NICOTIANAS
NICOTIANS
NICOTINE
NICOTINED
NICOTINES
NICOTINIC
NICTATE
NICTATED
NICTATES
NICTATING
NICTATION
NICTATIONS
NICTITATE
NICTITATED
NICTITATES
NICTITATING
NID
NIDAL
NIDAMENTA
NIDATION
NIDATIONS
NIDDERING
NIDDERINGS
NIDE
NIDERING
NIDERINGS
NIDERLING
NIDERLINGS
NIDES
NIDGET
NIDGETS
NIDI
NIDIFIED
NIDIFIES
NIDIFY
NIDIFYING
NIDING
NIDINGS
NIDOR
NIDOROUS
NIDORS
NIDS
NIDUS
NIE
NIECE
NIECES
NIED
NIEF
NIEFS
NIELLATED
NIELLI
NIELLIST
NIELLISTS
NIELLO
NIELLOED
NIELLOING
NIELLOS
NIES
NIEVE
NIEVEFUL
NIEVEFULS
NIEVES
NIFE
NIFES
NIFF
NIFFED
NIFFER
NIFFERED
NIFFERING
NIFFERS
NIFFIER
NIFFIEST
NIFFING
NIFFNAFF
NIFFNAFFED
NIFFNAFFING
NIFFNAFFS
NIFFS
NIFFY
NIFTIER
NIFTIEST
NIFTILY
NIFTINESS
NIFTINESSES
NIFTY
NIGELLA
NIGELLAS
NIGER
NIGERS
NIGGARD
NIGGARDED
NIGGARDING
NIGGARDLY
NIGGARDS
NIGGER
NIGGERDOM
NIGGERDOMS
NIGGERED
NIGGERING
NIGGERISH
NIGGERISM
NIGGERISMS
NIGGERS
NIGGERY
NIGGLE
NIGGLED
NIGGLER
NIGGLERS
NIGGLES
NIGGLIER
NIGGLIEST
NIGGLING
NIGGLINGS
NIGGLY
NIGH
NIGHED
NIGHEST
NIGHING
NIGHLY
NIGHNESS
NIGHNESSES
NIGHS
NIGHT
NIGHTBIRD
NIGHTBIRDS
NIGHTCAP
NIGHTCAPS
NIGHTCLUB
NIGHTCLUBS
NIGHTED
NIGHTFALL
NIGHTFALLS
NIGHTFIRE
NIGHTFIRES
NIGHTGEAR
NIGHTGEARS
NIGHTGOWN
NIGHTGOWNS
NIGHTHAWK
NIGHTHAWKS
NIGHTIE
NIGHTIES
NIGHTJAR
NIGHTJARS
NIGHTLESS
NIGHTLIFE
NIGHTLIFES
NIGHTLONG
NIGHTLY
NIGHTMARE
NIGHTMARES
NIGHTMARY
NIGHTS
NIGHTSPOT
NIGHTSPOTS
NIGHTWARD
NIGHTWEAR
NIGHTWEARS
NIGHTY
NIGRICANT
NIGRIFIED
NIGRIFIES
NIGRIFY
NIGRIFYING
NIGRITUDE
NIGRITUDES
NIGROSIN
NIGROSINE
NIGROSINES
NIGROSINS
NIHIL
NIHILISM
NIHILISMS
NIHILIST
NIHILISTS
NIHILITIES
NIHILITY
NIHILS
NIHONGA
NIHONGAS
NIKAU
NIKAUS
NIL
NILGAI
NILGAIS
NILGAU
NILGAUS
NILL
NILLED
NILLING
NILLS
NILS
NIM
NIMB
NIMBED
NIMBI
NIMBLE
NIMBLER
NIMBLESSE
NIMBLESSES
NIMBLEST
NIMBLY
NIMBS
NIMBUS
NIMBUSED
NIMBUSES
NIMBYISM
NIMBYISMS
NIMIETIES
NIMIETY
NIMIOUS
NIMMED
NIMMER
NIMMERS
NIMMING
NIMONIC
NIMS
NINCOM
NINCOMS
NINCUM
NINCUMS
NINE
NINEFOLD

NINEHOLES
NINEPENCE
NINEPENCES
NINEPENNIES
NINEPENNY
NINEPIN
NINEPINS
NINES
NINESCORE
NINESCORES
NINETEEN
NINETEENS
NINETIES
NINETIETH
NINETIETHS
NINETY
NINJA
NINJAS
NINJITSU
NINJITSUS
NINJUTSU
NINJUTSUS
NINNIES
NINNY
NINON
NINONS
NINTH
NINTHLY
NINTHS
NIOBATE
NIOBATES
NIOBIC
NIOBITE
NIOBITES
NIOBIUM
NIOBIUMS
NIOBOUS
NIP
NIPA
NIPAS
NIPCHEESE
NIPCHEESES
NIPPED
NIPPER
NIPPERED
NIPPERING
NIPPERKIN
NIPPERKINS
NIPPERS
NIPPIER
NIPPIEST
NIPPILY
NIPPINESS
NIPPINESSES
NIPPING
NIPPINGLY
NIPPLE
NIPPLED
NIPPLES
NIPPLING
NIPPY
NIPS
NIPTER
NIPTERS
NIRAMIAI
NIRAMIAIS
NIRL
NIRLED
NIRLIE
NIRLIER
NIRLIEST
NIRLING
NIRLIT
NIRLS
NIRLY
NIRVANA
NIRVANAS
NIS
NISBERRIES
NISBERRY
NISEI
NISEIS
NISI
NISSE
NISSES
NISUS
NIT
NITE
NITER
NITERIE
NITERIES
NITERS
NITERY
NITES
NITHING
NITHINGS
NITID
NITON
NITONS
NITRATE
NITRATED
NITRATES
NITRATINE
NITRATINES
NITRATING
NITRATION
NITRATIONS
NITRE
NITRES
NITRIC
NITRIDE
NITRIDED
NITRIDES
NITRIDING
NITRIDINGS
NITRIFIED
NITRIFIES
NITRIFY
NITRIFYING
NITRILE
NITRILES
NITRITE
NITRITES
NITROGEN
NITROGENS
NITROSO
NITROSYL
NITROUS
NITROXYL
NITROXYLS
NITRY
NITRYL
NITRYLS
NITS
NITTIER
NITTIEST
NITTY
NITWIT
NITWITS
NITWITTED
NIVAL
NIVEOUS
NIX
NIXED
NIXES
NIXIE
NIXIES
NIXING
NIXY
NIZAM
NIZAMS
NO
NOB
NOBBIER
NOBBIEST
NOBBILY
NOBBINESS
NOBBINESSES
NOBBLE
NOBBLED
NOBBLER
NOBBLERS
NOBBLES
NOBBLING
NOBBUT
NOBBY
NOBELIUM
NOBELIUMS
NOBILESSE
NOBILESSES
NOBILIARY
NOBILITIES
NOBILITY
NOBLE
NOBLEMAN
NOBLEMEN
NOBLENESS
NOBLENESSES
NOBLER
NOBLES
NOBLESSE
NOBLESSES
NOBLEST
NOBLY
NOBODIES
NOBODY
NOBS
NOCAKE
NOCAKES
NOCENT
NOCENTLY
NOCENTS
NOCHEL
NOCHELLED
NOCHELLING
NOCHELS
NOCK
NOCKED
NOCKET
NOCKETS
NOCKING
NOCKS
NOCTILIO
NOCTILIOS
NOCTILUCA
NOCTILUCAE
NOCTUA
NOCTUARIES
NOCTUARY
NOCTUAS
NOCTUID
NOCTUIDS
NOCTULE
NOCTULES
NOCTURN
NOCTURNAL
NOCTURNALS
NOCTURNE
NOCTURNES
NOCTURNS
NOCUOUS
NOCUOUSLY
NOD
NODAL
NODALISE
NODALISED
NODALISES
NODALISING
NODALITIES
NODALITY
NODALIZE
NODALIZED
NODALIZES
NODALIZING
NODALLY
NODATED
NODATION
NODATIONS
NODDED
NODDER
NODDERS
NODDIES
NODDING
NODDINGLY
NODDINGS
NODDLE
NODDLED
NODDLES
NODDLING
NODDY
NODE
NODES
NODI
NODICAL
NODOSE
NODOSITIES
NODOSITY
NODOUS
NODS
NODULAR
NODULATED
NODULE
NODULED
NODULES
NODULOSE
NODULOUS
NODUS
NOEL
NOELS
NOES
NOESES
NOESIS
NOETIC
NOG
NOGAKU
NOGG
NOGGED
NOGGIN
NOGGING
NOGGINGS
NOGGINS
NOGGS
NOGS
NOH
NOHOW
NOHOWISH
NOIL
NOILS
NOINT
NOINTED
NOINTING
NOINTS
NOISE
NOISED
NOISEFUL
NOISELESS
NOISES
NOISETTE
NOISETTES
NOISIER
NOISIEST
NOISILY
NOISINESS
NOISINESSES
NOISING
NOISOME
NOISOMELY
NOISY
NOLE
NOLES
NOLITION
NOLITIONS
NOLL
NOLLS
NOM
NOMA
NOMAD
NOMADE
NOMADES
NOMADIC

NOMADIES
NOMADISE
NOMADISED
NOMADISES
NOMADISING
NOMADISM
NOMADISMS
NOMADIZE
NOMADIZED
NOMADIZES
NOMADIZING
NOMADS
NOMADY
NOMARCH
NOMARCHIES
NOMARCHS
NOMARCHY
NOMAS
NOMBLES
NOMBRIL
NOMBRILS
NOME
NOMEN
NOMES
NOMIC
NOMINA
NOMINABLE
NOMINAL
NOMINALLY
NOMINALS
NOMINATE
NOMINATED
NOMINATES
NOMINATING
NOMINATOR
NOMINATORS
NOMINEE
NOMINEES
NOMISM
NOMISMS
NOMISTIC
NOMOCRACIES
NOMOCRACY
NOMOGENIES
NOMOGENY
NOMOGRAM
NOMOGRAMS
NOMOGRAPH
NOMOGRAPHS
NOMOI
NOMOLOGIES
NOMOLOGY
NOMOS
NOMOTHETE
NOMOTHETES
NOMS
NON
NONAGE
NONAGED
NONAGES
NONAGON
NONAGONAL
NONAGONS
NONANE
NONANES
NONARY
NONCE
NONCES
NONE
NONENTITIES
NONENTITY
NONES
NONESUCH
NONESUCHES
NONET
NONETS
NONETTE
NONETTES
NONETTI
NONETTO
NONETTOS
NONG
NONGS
NONILLION
NONILLIONS
NONJURING
NONJUROR
NONJURORS
NONNIES
NONNY
NONPAREIL
NONPAREILS
NONPAROUS
NONPLUS
NONPLUSED
NONPLUSES
NONPLUSING
NONPLUSSED
NONPLUSSES
NONPLUSSING
NONPOLAR
NONSENSE
NONSENSES
NONSUCH
NONSUCHES
NONSUIT
NONSUITED
NONSUITING
NONSUITS
NONUPLE
NONUPLET
NONUPLETS
NOODLE
NOODLED
NOODLEDOM
NOODLEDOMS
NOODLES
NOODLING
NOOK
NOOKIE
NOOKIER
NOOKIES
NOOKIEST
NOOKS
NOOKY
NOOLOGIES
NOOLOGY
NOOMETRIES
NOOMETRY
NOON
NOONDAY
NOONDAYS
NOONED
NOONER
NOONERS
NOONING
NOONINGS
NOONS
NOONTIDE
NOONTIDES
NOONTIME
NOONTIMES
NOOP
NOOPS
NOOSE
NOOSED
NOOSES
NOOSING
NOOSPHERE
NOOSPHERES
NOPAL
NOPALS
NOPE
NOR
NORI
NORIA
NORIAS
NORIMON
NORIMONS
NORIS
NORITE
NORITES
NORK
NORKS
NORLAND
NORLANDS
NORM
NORMA
NORMAL
NORMALCIES
NORMALCY
NORMALISE
NORMALISED
NORMALISES
NORMALISING
NORMALITIES
NORMALITY
NORMALIZE
NORMALIZED
NORMALIZES
NORMALIZING
NORMALLY
NORMALS
NORMAN
NORMANS
NORMAS
NORMATIVE
NORMS
NORSEL
NORSELLED
NORSELLER
NORSELLERS
NORSELLING
NORSELS
NORTENA
NORTENAS
NORTENO
NORTENOS
NORTH
NORTHED
NORTHER
NORTHERED
NORTHERING
NORTHERLIES
NORTHERLY
NORTHERN
NORTHERNS
NORTHERS
NORTHING
NORTHINGS
NORTHLAND
NORTHLANDS
NORTHMOST
NORTHS
NORTHWARD
NORTHWARDS
NORWARD
NORWARDS
NOS
NOSE
NOSEAN
NOSEANS
NOSEBAG
NOSEBAGS
NOSEBAND
NOSEBANDS
NOSEBLEED
NOSEBLEEDS
NOSED
NOSEDIVE
NOSEDIVED
NOSEDIVES
NOSEDIVING
NOSEGAY
NOSEGAYS
NOSELESS
NOSELITE
NOSELITES
NOSER
NOSERS
NOSES
NOSEY
NOSEYS
NOSH
NOSHED
NOSHER
NOSHERIES
NOSHERS
NOSHERY
NOSHES
NOSHING
NOSIER
NOSIES
NOSIEST
NOSILY
NOSINESS
NOSINESSES
NOSING
NOSINGS
NOSODE
NOSODES
NOSOLOGIES
NOSOLOGY
NOSTALGIA
NOSTALGIAS
NOSTALGIC
NOSTOC
NOSTOCS
NOSTOI
NOSTOLOGIES
NOSTOLOGY
NOSTOS
NOSTRIL
NOSTRILS
NOSTRUM
NOSTRUMS
NOSY
NOT
NOTA
NOTABILIA
NOTABLE
NOTABLES
NOTABLY
NOTAEUM
NOTAEUMS
NOTAL
NOTANDA
NOTANDUM
NOTAPHILIES
NOTAPHILY
NOTARIAL
NOTARIES
NOTARISE
NOTARISED
NOTARISES
NOTARISING
NOTARIZE
NOTARIZED
NOTARIZES
NOTARIZING
NOTARY
NOTATE
NOTATED
NOTATES
NOTATING
NOTATION
NOTATIONS
NOTCH
NOTCHBACK
NOTCHBACKS
NOTCHED
NOTCHEL
NOTCHELLED
NOTCHELLING
NOTCHELS
NOTCHER
NOTCHERS
NOTCHES
NOTCHIER
NOTCHIEST

NOTCHING
NOTCHINGS
NOTCHY
NOTE
NOTEBOOK
NOTEBOOKS
NOTECASE
NOTECASES
NOTED
NOTEDLY
NOTEDNESS
NOTEDNESSES
NOTELESS
NOTELET
NOTELETS
NOTEPAPER
NOTEPAPERS
NOTER
NOTERS
NOTES
NOTHING
NOTHINGS
NOTICE
NOTICED
NOTICES
NOTICING
NOTIFIED
NOTIFIER
NOTIFIERS
NOTIFIES
NOTIFY
NOTIFYING
NOTING
NOTION
NOTIONAL
NOTIONIST
NOTIONISTS
NOTIONS
NOTITIA
NOTITIAE
NOTITIAS
NOTOCHORD
NOTOCHORDS
NOTORIETIES
NOTORIETY
NOTORIOUS
NOTORNIS
NOTORNISES
NOTOUR
NOTT
NOTUM
NOUGAT
NOUGATS
NOUGHT
NOUGHTS
NOUL
NOULD
NOULDE
NOULE
NOULES
NOULS
NOUMENA
NOUMENAL
NOUMENON
NOUN
NOUNAL
NOUNIER
NOUNIEST
NOUNS
NOUNY
NOUP
NOUPS
NOURICE
NOURICES
NOURISH
NOURISHED
NOURISHER
NOURISHERS
NOURISHES
NOURISHING
NOURITURE
NOURITURES
NOURSLE
NOURSLED
NOURSLES
NOURSLING
NOUS
NOUSELL
NOUSELLED
NOUSELLING
NOUSELLS
NOUSES
NOUSLE
NOUSLED
NOUSLES
NOUSLING
NOUT
NOUVEAU
NOUVELLE
NOUVELLES
NOVA
NOVAE
NOVALIA
NOVAS
NOVATION
NOVATIONS
NOVEL
NOVELDOM
NOVELDOMS
NOVELESE
NOVELESES
NOVELETTE
NOVELETTES
NOVELISE
NOVELISED
NOVELISER
NOVELISERS
NOVELISES
NOVELISH
NOVELISING
NOVELISM
NOVELISMS
NOVELIST
NOVELISTS
NOVELIZE
NOVELIZED
NOVELIZER
NOVELIZERS
NOVELIZES
NOVELIZING
NOVELLA
NOVELLAE
NOVELLAS
NOVELLE
NOVELS
NOVELTIES
NOVELTY
NOVENA
NOVENARIES
NOVENARY
NOVENAS
NOVENNIAL
NOVERCAL
NOVERINT
NOVERINTS
NOVICE
NOVICES
NOVICIATE
NOVICIATES
NOVITIATE
NOVITIATES
NOVITIES
NOVITY
NOVODAMUS
NOVODAMUSES
NOVUM
NOVUMS
NOW
NOWADAYS
NOWAY
NOWAYS
NOWED
NOWHENCE
NOWHERE
NOWHERES
NOWHITHER
NOWISE
NOWL
NOWLS
NOWN
NOWNESS
NOWNESSES
NOWS
NOWT
NOWTS
NOWY
NOX
NOXAL
NOXES
NOXIOUS
NOXIOUSLY
NOY
NOYADE
NOYADES
NOYANCE
NOYANCES
NOYAU
NOYAUS
NOYED
NOYES
NOYESES
NOYING
NOYOUS
NOYS
NOYSOME
NOZZER
NOZZERS
NOZZLE
NOZZLES
NTH
NU
NUANCE
NUANCED
NUANCES
NUANCING
NUB
NUBBED
NUBBIER
NUBBIEST
NUBBIN
NUBBING
NUBBINS
NUBBLE
NUBBLED
NUBBLES
NUBBLIER
NUBBLIEST
NUBBLING
NUBBLY
NUBBY
NUBECULA
NUBECULAE
NUBIA
NUBIAS
NUBIFORM
NUBILE
NUBILITIES
NUBILITY
NUBILOUS
NUBS
NUCELLAR
NUCELLI
NUCELLUS
NUCHA
NUCHAE
NUCHAL
NUCLEAL
NUCLEAR
NUCLEASE
NUCLEASES
NUCLEATE
NUCLEATED
NUCLEATES
NUCLEATING
NUCLEATOR
NUCLEATORS
NUCLEI
NUCLEIDE
NUCLEIDES
NUCLEIN
NUCLEINS
NUCLEOLAR
NUCLEOLE
NUCLEOLES
NUCLEOLI
NUCLEOLUS
NUCLEON
NUCLEONS
NUCLEUS
NUCLIDE
NUCLIDES
NUCULE
NUCULES
NUDATION
NUDATIONS
NUDE
NUDELY
NUDENESS
NUDENESSES
NUDER
NUDES
NUDEST
NUDGE
NUDGED
NUDGER
NUDGERS
NUDGES
NUDGING
NUDICAUL
NUDIE
NUDIES
NUDISM
NUDISMS
NUDIST
NUDISTS
NUDITIES
NUDITY
NUDNIK
NUDNIKS
NUFF
NUFFIN
NUFFINS
NUFFS
NUGAE
NUGATORY
NUGGAR
NUGGARS
NUGGET
NUGGETS
NUGGETY
NUISANCE
NUISANCER
NUISANCERS
NUISANCES
NUKE
NUKED
NUKES
NUKING
NULL
NULLA
NULLAH
NULLAHS
NULLAS
NULLED
NULLIFIED
NULLIFIER
NULLIFIERS
NULLIFIES
NULLIFY
NULLIFYING

NULLING
NULLINGS
NULLIPARA
NULLIPARAE
NULLIPARAS
NULLIPORE
NULLIPORES
NULLITIES
NULLITY
NULLNESS
NULLNESSES
NULLS
NUMB
NUMBAT
NUMBATS
NUMBED
NUMBER
NUMBERED
NUMBERER
NUMBERERS
NUMBERING
NUMBERS
NUMBEST
NUMBING
NUMBINGLY
NUMBLES
NUMBLY
NUMBNESS
NUMBNESSES
NUMBS
NUMBSKULL
NUMBSKULLS
NUMDAH
NUMDAHS
NUMEN
NUMERABLE
NUMERABLY
NUMERACIES
NUMERACY
NUMERAIRE
NUMERAIRES
NUMERAL
NUMERALLY
NUMERALS
NUMERARY
NUMERATE
NUMERATED
NUMERATES
NUMERATING
NUMERATOR
NUMERATORS
NUMERIC
NUMERICAL
NUMEROUS
NUMINA
NUMINOUS
NUMINOUSES
NUMMARY
NUMMULAR
NUMMULARY
NUMMULINE
NUMMULITE
NUMMULITES
NUMNAH
NUMNAHS
NUMPTIES
NUMPTY
NUMSKULL
NUMSKULLS
NUN
NUNATAK
NUNATAKER
NUNATAKS
NUNCHAKU
NUNCHAKUS
NUNCHEON
NUNCHEONS
NUNCIO
NUNCIOS
NUNCLE
NUNCLES
NUNCUPATE
NUNCUPATED
NUNCUPATES
NUNCUPATING
NUNDINAL
NUNDINE
NUNDINES
NUNHOOD
NUNHOODS
NUNNATION
NUNNATIONS
NUNNERIES
NUNNERY
NUNNISH
NUNS
NUNSHIP
NUNSHIPS
NUPTIAL
NUPTIALS
NUR
NURAGHE
NURAGHI
NURAGHIC
NURD
NURDLE
NURDLED
NURDLES
NURDLING
NURDS
NURHAG
NURHAGS
NURL
NURLED
NURLING
NURLS
NURR
NURRS
NURS
NURSE
NURSED
NURSELIKE
NURSELING
NURSELINGS
NURSEMAID
NURSEMAIDED
NURSEMAIDING
NURSEMAIDS
NURSER
NURSERIES
NURSERS
NURSERY
NURSES
NURSING
NURSINGS
NURSLE
NURSLED
NURSLES
NURSLING
NURSLINGS
NURTURAL
NURTURANT
NURTURE
NURTURED
NURTURER
NURTURERS
NURTURES
NURTURING
NUS
NUT
NUTANT
NUTARIAN
NUTARIANS
NUTATE
NUTATED
NUTATES
NUTATING
NUTATION
NUTATIONS
NUTBUTTER
NUTBUTTERS
NUTCASE
NUTCASES
NUTGALL
NUTGALLS
NUTHATCH
NUTHATCHES
NUTHOUSE
NUTHOUSES
NUTJOBBER
NUTJOBBERS
NUTLET
NUTLETS
NUTLIKE
NUTMEAL
NUTMEALS
NUTMEG
NUTMEGGED
NUTMEGGING
NUTMEGGY
NUTMEGS
NUTPECKER
NUTPECKERS
NUTRIA
NUTRIAS
NUTRIENT
NUTRIENTS
NUTRIMENT
NUTRIMENTS
NUTRITION
NUTRITIONS
NUTRITIVE
NUTRITIVES
NUTS
NUTSHELL
NUTSHELLS
NUTTED
NUTTER
NUTTERIES
NUTTERS
NUTTERY
NUTTIER
NUTTIEST
NUTTILY
NUTTINESS
NUTTINESSES
NUTTING
NUTTINGS
NUTTY
NUTWOOD
NUTWOODS
NUZZER
NUZZERS
NUZZLE
NUZZLED
NUZZLES
NUZZLING
NY
NYAFF
NYAFFED
NYAFFING
NYAFFS
NYALA
NYALAS
NYANZA
NYANZAS
NYAS
NYASES
NYBBLE
NYBBLES
NYCTALOPES
NYCTALOPS
NYE
NYED
NYES
NYING
NYLGHAU
NYLGHAUS
NYLON
NYLONS
NYMPH
NYMPHAE
NYMPHAEA
NYMPHAEUM
NYMPHAEUMS
NYMPHAL
NYMPHALID
NYMPHALIDS
NYMPHEAN
NYMPHET
NYMPHETS
NYMPHIC
NYMPHICAL
NYMPHISH
NYMPHLIKE
NYMPHLY
NYMPHO
NYMPHOS
NYMPHS
NYS
NYSSA
NYSSAS
NYSTAGMIC
NYSTAGMUS
NYSTAGMUSES
NYSTATIN
NYSTATINS

O

OAF
OAFISH
OAFS
OAK
OAKEN
OAKENSHAW
OAKENSHAWS
OAKER
OAKERS
OAKIER
OAKIEST
OAKLEAF
OAKLEAVES
OAKLING
OAKLINGS
OAKS
OAKUM
OAKUMS
OAKY
OAR
OARAGE
OARAGES
OARED
OARIER
OARIEST
OARING
OARLESS
OARS
OARSMAN
OARSMEN
OARSWOMAN
OARSWOMEN
OARWEED
OARWEEDS
OARY
OASES
OASIS
OAST
OASTS
OAT
OATCAKE
OATCAKES
OATEN
OATER
OATERS
OATH
OATHABLE
OATHS
OATMEAL
OATMEALS
OATS
OAVES
OB
OBA
OBANG
OBANGS
OBAS
OBBLIGATI
OBBLIGATO
OBBLIGATOS
OBCONIC
OBCONICAL
OBCORDATE
OBDURACIES
OBDURACY
OBDURATE
OBDURATED
OBDURATES
OBDURATING
OBDURE
OBDURED
OBDURES
OBDURING
OBEAH
OBEAHED
OBEAHING
OBEAHISM
OBEAHISMS
OBEAHS
OBECHE
OBECHES
OBEDIENCE
OBEDIENCES
OBEDIENT
OBEISANCE
OBEISANCES
OBEISANT
OBEISM
OBEISMS
OBELI
OBELIA
OBELION
OBELISCAL
OBELISE
OBELISED
OBELISES
OBELISING
OBELISK
OBELISKS
OBELIZE
OBELIZED
OBELIZES
OBELIZING
OBELUS
OBESE
OBESENESS
OBESENESSES
OBESER
OBESEST
OBESITIES
OBESITY
OBEY
OBEYED
OBEYER
OBEYERS
OBEYING
OBEYS
OBFUSCATE
OBFUSCATED
OBFUSCATES
OBFUSCATING
OBI
OBIA
OBIAS
OBIED
OBIING
OBIISM
OBIISMS
OBIIT
OBIS
OBIT
OBITAL
OBITER
OBITS
OBITUAL
OBITUARIES
OBITUARY
OBJECT
OBJECTED
OBJECTIFIED
OBJECTIFIES
OBJECTIFY
OBJECTIFYING
OBJECTING
OBJECTION
OBJECTIONS
OBJECTIVE
OBJECTIVES
OBJECTOR
OBJECTORS
OBJECTS
OBJET
OBJETS
OBJURE
OBJURED
OBJURES
OBJURGATE
OBJURGATED
OBJURGATES
OBJURGATING
OBJURING
OBLAST
OBLASTS
OBLATE
OBLATES
OBLATION
OBLATIONS
OBLATORY
OBLIGANT
OBLIGANTS
OBLIGATE
OBLIGATED
OBLIGATES
OBLIGATI
OBLIGATING
OBLIGATO
OBLIGATOS
OBLIGE
OBLIGED
OBLIGEE
OBLIGEES
OBLIGES
OBLIGING
OBLIGOR
OBLIGORS
OBLIQUE
OBLIQUED
OBLIQUELY
OBLIQUER
OBLIQUES
OBLIQUEST
OBLIQUID
OBLIQUING
OBLIQUITIES
OBLIQUITY
OBLIVION
OBLIVIONS
OBLIVIOUS
OBLONG
OBLONGS
OBLOQUIES
OBLOQUY
OBNOXIOUS
OBO
OBOE
OBOES
OBOIST
OBOISTS
OBOL
OBOLARY
OBOLI
OBOLS
OBOLUS
OBOS
OBOVATE
OBOVATELY
OBOVOID
OBREPTION
OBREPTIONS
OBS
OBSCENE
OBSCENELY
OBSCENER
OBSCENEST
OBSCENITIES
OBSCENITY
OBSCURANT
OBSCURANTS
OBSCURE
OBSCURED
OBSCURELY
OBSCURER
OBSCURERS
OBSCURES
OBSCUREST
OBSCURING
OBSCURITIES
OBSCURITY
OBSECRATE
OBSECRATED
OBSECRATES
OBSECRATING
OBSEQUENT
OBSEQUIAL
OBSEQUIE
OBSEQUIES
OBSEQUY
OBSERVANT
OBSERVANTS
OBSERVE
OBSERVED
OBSERVER
OBSERVERS
OBSERVES
OBSERVING
OBSESS
OBSESSED
OBSESSES
OBSESSING
OBSESSION
OBSESSIONS
OBSESSIVE
OBSIDIAN
OBSIDIANS
OBSIGN
OBSIGNATE
OBSIGNATED
OBSIGNATES
OBSIGNATING
OBSIGNED

OBSIGNING
OBSIGNS
OBSOLESCE
OBSOLESCED
OBSOLESCES
OBSOLESCING
OBSOLETE
OBSTACLE
OBSTACLES
OBSTETRIC
OBSTETRICS
OBSTINACIES
OBSTINACY
OBSTINATE
OBSTRUCT
OBSTRUCTED
OBSTRUCTING
OBSTRUCTS
OBSTRUENT
OBSTRUENTS
OBTAIN
OBTAINED
OBTAINER
OBTAINERS
OBTAINING
OBTAINS
OBTECT
OBTECTED
OBTEMPER
OBTEMPERED
OBTEMPERING
OBTEMPERS
OBTEND
OBTENDED
OBTENDING
OBTENDS
OBTENTION
OBTENTIONS
OBTEST
OBTESTED
OBTESTING
OBTESTS
OBTRUDE
OBTRUDED
OBTRUDER
OBTRUDERS
OBTRUDES
OBTRUDING
OBTRUDINGS
OBTRUSION
OBTRUSIONS
OBTRUSIVE
OBTUND
OBTUNDED
OBTUNDENT
OBTUNDENTS
OBTUNDING
OBTUNDS
OBTURATE
OBTURATED
OBTURATES
OBTURATING
OBTURATOR
OBTURATORS
OBTUSE
OBTUSELY
OBTUSER
OBTUSEST
OBTUSITIES
OBTUSITY
OBUMBRATE
OBUMBRATED
OBUMBRATES
OBUMBRATING
OBVENTION
OBVENTIONS
OBVERSE
OBVERSELY
OBVERSES
OBVERSION
OBVERSIONS
OBVERT
OBVERTED
OBVERTING
OBVERTS
OBVIATE
OBVIATED
OBVIATES
OBVIATING
OBVIATION
OBVIATIONS
OBVIOUS
OBVIOUSLY
OBVOLUTE
OBVOLUTED
OBVOLVENT
OCA
OCARINA
OCARINAS
OCAS
OCCAM
OCCAMIES
OCCAMS
OCCAMY
OCCASION
OCCASIONED
OCCASIONING
OCCASIONS
OCCIDENT
OCCIDENTS
OCCIPITAL
OCCIPITALS
OCCIPUT
OCCIPUTS
OCCLUDE
OCCLUDED
OCCLUDENT
OCCLUDENTS
OCCLUDER
OCCLUDERS
OCCLUDES
OCCLUDING
OCCLUSAL
OCCLUSION
OCCLUSIONS
OCCLUSIVE
OCCLUSIVES
OCCLUSOR
OCCLUSORS
OCCULT
OCCULTED
OCCULTING
OCCULTISM
OCCULTISMS
OCCULTIST
OCCULTISTS
OCCULTLY
OCCULTS
OCCUPANCE
OCCUPANCES
OCCUPANCIES
OCCUPANCY
OCCUPANT
OCCUPANTS
OCCUPATE
OCCUPATED
OCCUPATES
OCCUPATING
OCCUPIED
OCCUPIER
OCCUPIERS
OCCUPIES
OCCUPY
OCCUPYING
OCCUR
OCCURRED
OCCURRENT
OCCURRENTS
OCCURRING
OCCURS
OCEAN
OCEANARIA
OCEANAUT
OCEANAUTS
OCEANIC
OCEANID
OCEANIDES
OCEANIDS
OCEANS
OCELLAR
OCELLATE
OCELLATED
OCELLI
OCELLUS
OCELOID
OCELOT
OCELOTS
OCH
OCHE
OCHER
OCHERED
OCHERING
OCHEROUS
OCHERS
OCHERY
OCHES
OCHIDORE
OCHIDORES
OCHLOCRAT
OCHLOCRATS
OCHONE
OCHRE
OCHREA
OCHREAE
OCHREATE
OCHRED
OCHREOUS
OCHRES
OCHREY
OCHRING
OCHROID
OCHROUS
OCHRY
OCKER
OCKERISM
OCKERISMS
OCKERS
OCOTILLO
OCOTILLOS
OCREA
OCREAE
OCREATE
OCTA
OCTACHORD
OCTACHORDS
OCTAD
OCTADIC
OCTADS
OCTAGON
OCTAGONAL
OCTAGONS
OCTAHEDRA
OCTAL
OCTALS
OCTAMETER
OCTAMETERS
OCTANE
OCTANES
OCTANT
OCTANTAL
OCTANTS
OCTAPLA
OCTAPLAS
OCTAPLOID
OCTAPLOIDS
OCTAPODIC
OCTAPODIES
OCTAPODY
OCTAROON
OCTAROONS
OCTAS
OCTASTICH
OCTASTICHS
OCTASTYLE
OCTASTYLES
OCTAVAL
OCTAVE
OCTAVES
OCTAVO
OCTAVOS
OCTENNIAL
OCTET
OCTETS
OCTETT
OCTETTE
OCTETTES
OCTETTS
OCTILLION
OCTILLIONS
OCTOFID
OCTOHEDRA
OCTONARIES
OCTONARII
OCTONARY
OCTOPI
OCTOPLOID
OCTOPLOIDS
OCTOPOD
OCTOPODES
OCTOPODS
OCTOPUS
OCTOPUSES
OCTOPUSH
OCTOPUSHES
OCTOROON
OCTOROONS
OCTOSTYLE
OCTOSTYLES
OCTROI
OCTROIS
OCTUOR
OCTUORS
OCTUPLE
OCTUPLED
OCTUPLES
OCTUPLET
OCTUPLETS
OCTUPLING
OCULAR
OCULARIST
OCULARISTS
OCULARLY
OCULARS
OCULATE
OCULATED
OCULI
OCULIST
OCULISTS
OCULUS
OD
ODA
ODAL
ODALIQUE
ODALIQUES
ODALISK
ODALISKS
ODALISQUE
ODALISQUES
ODALLER
ODALLERS
ODALS
ODAS
ODD
ODDBALL
ODDBALLS
ODDER
ODDEST
ODDISH
ODDITIES
ODDITY

DDLY
DDMENT
DDMENTS
DDNESS
DDNESSES
DDS
DDSMAN
DDSMEN
DE
DEA
DEON
DEONS
DES
DEUM
DEUMS
DIC
DIOUS
DIOUSLY
DISM
DISMS
DIST
DISTS
DIUM
DIUMS
DOGRAPH
DOGRAPHS
DOMETER
DOMETERS
DOMETRIES
DOMETRY
DONATIST
DONATISTS
DONTALGIES
DONTALGY
DONTIC
DONTIST
DONTISTS
DONTOID
DONTOMA
DONTOMAS
DONTOMATA
DOR
DORANT
DORANTS
DORATE
DOROUS
DOROUSLY
DORS
DOUR
DOURED
DOURLESS
DOURS
DS
DSO
DSOS
DYL
DYLE
DYLES
DYLISM
DYLISMS
DYLS
DYSSEY
DYSSEYS
DZOOKS
OE
OECIST
OECISTS
OECOLOGIES
OECOLOGY
OECUMENIC
OEDEMA
OEDEMAS
OEDEMATA
OEILLADE
OEILLADES
OENANTHIC
OENOLOGIES
OENOLOGY
OENOMANCIES
OENOMANCY
OENOMANIA
OENOMANIAS
OENOMEL
OENOMELS
OENOMETER
OENOMETERS
OENOPHIL
OENOPHILE
OENOPHILES
OENOPHILIES
OENOPHILS
OENOPHILY
OERLIKON
OERLIKONS
OERSTED
OERSTEDS
OES
OESOPHAGI
OESTRAL
OESTROGEN
OESTROGENS
OESTROUS
OESTRUM
OESTRUMS
OESTRUS
OESTRUSES
OEUVRE
OEUVRES
OF
OFAY
OFAYS
OFF
OFFAL
OFFALS
OFFBEAT
OFFBEATS
OFFCUT
OFFCUTS
OFFED
OFFENCE
OFFENCES
OFFEND
OFFENDED
OFFENDER
OFFENDERS
OFFENDING
OFFENDS
OFFENSE
OFFENSES
OFFENSIVE
OFFENSIVES
OFFER
OFFERABLE
OFFERED
OFFEREE
OFFEREES
OFFERER
OFFERERS
OFFERING
OFFERINGS
OFFEROR
OFFERORS
OFFERS
OFFERTORIES
OFFERTORY
OFFHAND
OFFHANDED
OFFICE
OFFICER
OFFICERED
OFFICERING
OFFICERS
OFFICES
OFFICIAL
OFFICIALS
OFFICIANT
OFFICIANTS
OFFICIATE
OFFICIATED
OFFICIATES
OFFICIATING
OFFICINAL
OFFICIOUS
OFFING
OFFINGS
OFFISH
OFFLINE
OFFLOAD
OFFLOADED
OFFLOADING
OFFLOADS
OFFPEAK
OFFPRINT
OFFPRINTS
OFFPUT
OFFPUTS
OFFS
OFFSADDLE
OFFSADDLED
OFFSADDLES
OFFSADDLING
OFFSCUM
OFFSCUMS
OFFSEASON
OFFSEASONS
OFFSET
OFFSETS
OFFSETTING
OFFSHOOT
OFFSHOOTS
OFFSHORE
OFFSIDE
OFFSIDER
OFFSIDERS
OFFSIDES
OFFSPRING
OFFSPRINGS
OFFTAKE
OFFTAKES
OFLAG
OFLAGS
OFT
OFTEN
OFTENER
OFTENEST
OFTENNESS
OFTENNESSES
OFTTIMES
OGAM
OGAMIC
OGAMS
OGDOAD
OGDOADS
OGEE
OGEES
OGGIN
OGGINS
OGHAM
OGHAMIC
OGHAMS
OGIVAL
OGIVE
OGIVES
OGLE
OGLED
OGLER
OGLERS
OGLES
OGLING
OGLINGS
OGMIC
OGRE
OGREISH
OGRES
OGRESS
OGRESSES
OGRISH
OH
OHM
OHMAGE
OHMAGES
OHMIC
OHMMETER
OHMMETERS
OHMS
OHO
OHONE
OHOS
OI
OIDIA
OIDIUM
OIK
OIKIST
OIKISTS
OIKS
OIL
OILCAN
OILCANS
OILCLOTH
OILCLOTHS
OILED
OILER
OILERIES
OILERS
OILERY
OILFIELD
OILFIELDS
OILIER
OILIEST
OILILY
OILINESS
OILINESSES
OILING
OILLET
OILLETS
OILMAN
OILMEN
OILNUT
OILNUTS
OILS
OILSKIN
OILSKINS
OILSTONE
OILSTONES
OILY
OINK
OINKED
OINKING
OINKS
OINT
OINTED
OINTING
OINTMENT
OINTMENTS
OINTS
OITICICA
OITICICAS
OJIME
OJIMES
OKAPI
OKAPIS
OKAY
OKAYED
OKAYING
OKAYS
OKE
OKES
OKIMONO
OKIMONOS
OKRA
OKRAS
OKTA
OKTAS
OLD
OLDEN
OLDENED
OLDENING
OLDENS
OLDER
OLDEST

OLDIE
OLDIES
OLDISH
OLDNESS
OLDNESSES
OLDS
OLDSQUAW
OLDSQUAWS
OLDSTER
OLDSTERS
OLDY
OLE
OLEACEOUS
OLEANDER
OLEANDERS
OLEARIA
OLEARIAS
OLEASTER
OLEASTERS
OLEATE
OLEATES
OLECRANAL
OLECRANON
OLECRANONS
OLEFIANT
OLEFIN
OLEFINE
OLEFINES
OLEFINS
OLEIC
OLEIN
OLEINS
OLENT
OLEO
OLEOGRAPH
OLEOGRAPHS
OLEOS
OLEUM
OLEUMS
OLFACT
OLFACTED
OLFACTING
OLFACTION
OLFACTIONS
OLFACTIVE
OLFACTORY
OLFACTS
OLIBANUM
OLIBANUMS
OLID
OLIGAEMIA
OLIGAEMIAS
OLIGARCH
OLIGARCHIES
OLIGARCHS
OLIGARCHY
OLIGIST
OLIGISTS
OLIGOPOLIES
OLIGOPOLY
OLIGURIA
OLIGURIAS
OLIO
OLIOS
OLIPHANT
OLIPHANTS
OLITORIES
OLITORY
OLIVARY
OLIVE
OLIVENITE
OLIVENITES
OLIVER
OLIVERS
OLIVES
OLIVET
OLIVETS
OLIVINE
OLIVINES
OLLA
OLLAMH
OLLAMHS
OLLAS
OLLAV
OLLAVS
OLM
OLMS
OLOGIES
OLOGY
OLOROSO
OLOROSOS
OLPAE
OLPE
OLPES
OLYCOOK
OLYCOOKS
OLYKOEK
OLYKOEKS
OLYMPIAD
OLYMPIADS
OLYMPICS
OM
OMADHAUN
OMADHAUNS
OMASA
OMASAL
OMASUM
OMBRE
OMBRELLA
OMBRELLAS
OMBRES
OMBROPHIL
OMBROPHILS
OMBU
OMBUDSMAN
OMBUDSMEN
OMBUS
OMEGA
OMEGAS
OMELET
OMELETS
OMELETTE
OMELETTES
OMEN
OMENED
OMENING
OMENS
OMENTA
OMENTAL
OMENTUM
OMER
OMERS
OMERTA
OMERTAS
OMICRON
OMICRONS
OMINOUS
OMINOUSLY
OMISSIBLE
OMISSION
OMISSIONS
OMISSIVE
OMIT
OMITS
OMITTANCE
OMITTANCES
OMITTED
OMITTER
OMITTERS
OMITTING
OMLAH
OMLAHS
OMMATEA
OMMATEUM
OMMATIDIA
OMNEITIES
OMNEITY
OMNIANA
OMNIBUS
OMNIBUSES
OMNIETIES
OMNIETY
OMNIFIC
OMNIFIED
OMNIFIES
OMNIFORM
OMNIFY
OMNIFYING
OMNIUM
OMNIUMS
OMNIVORE
OMNIVORES
OMNIVORIES
OMNIVORY
OMOHYOID
OMOHYOIDS
OMOPHAGIA
OMOPHAGIAS
OMOPHAGIC
OMOPHAGIES
OMOPHAGY
OMOPHORIA
OMOPLATE
OMOPLATES
OMPHACITE
OMPHACITES
OMPHALI
OMPHALIC
OMPHALOID
OMPHALOS
OMRAH
OMRAHS
OMS
ON
ONAGER
ONAGERS
ONANISM
ONANISMS
ONANIST
ONANISTIC
ONANISTS
ONBOARD
ONCE
ONCER
ONCERS
ONCES
ONCIDIUM
ONCIDIUMS
ONCOGEN
ONCOGENE
ONCOGENES
ONCOGENIC
ONCOGENS
ONCOLOGIES
ONCOLOGY
ONCOLYSES
ONCOLYSIS
ONCOLYTIC
ONCOLYTICS
ONCOME
ONCOMES
ONCOMETER
ONCOMETERS
ONCOMICE
ONCOMING
ONCOMINGS
ONCOMOUSE
ONCOST
ONCOSTMAN
ONCOSTMEN
ONCOSTS
ONCOTOMIES
ONCOTOMY
ONCUS
ONDATRA
ONDATRAS
ONDINE
ONDINES
ONDING
ONDINGS
ONE
ONEFOLD
ONEIRIC
ONELY
ONENESS
ONENESSES
ONER
ONEROUS
ONEROUSLY
ONERS
ONES
ONESELF
ONEYER
ONEYERS
ONEYRE
ONEYRES
ONFALL
ONFALLS
ONFLOW
ONFLOWS
ONGOING
ONGOINGS
ONION
ONIONED
ONIONIER
ONIONIEST
ONIONING
ONIONS
ONIONY
ONIRIC
ONISCOID
ONKUS
ONLIEST
ONLINE
ONLOOKER
ONLOOKERS
ONLOOKING
ONLY
ONNED
ONNING
ONOMASTIC
ONOMASTICS
ONRUSH
ONRUSHES
ONS
ONSET
ONSETS
ONSETTER
ONSETTERS
ONSETTING
ONSETTINGS
ONSHORE
ONSIDE
ONSIDES
ONSLAUGHT
ONSLAUGHTS
ONST
ONSTEAD
ONSTEADS
ONTO
ONTOGENIC
ONTOGENIES
ONTOGENY
ONTOLOGIC
ONTOLOGIES
ONTOLOGY
ONUS
ONUSES
ONWARD
ONWARDLY
ONWARDS
ONYCHA
ONYCHAS
ONYCHIA
ONYCHIAS
ONYCHITE
ONYCHITES
ONYCHITIS
ONYCHITISES
ONYCHIUM

NYCHIUMS
NYMOUS
NYX
NYXES
O
OBIT
OBITS
OCYTE
OCYTES
ODLES
ODLINS
OF
OFS
OFTISH
OFTISHES
OGAMIES
OGAMOUS
OGAMY
OGENESES
OGENESIS
OGENETIC
OGENIES
OGENY
OGONIA
OGONIAL
OGONIUM
OH
OHED
OHING
OHS
OIDAL
OLAKAN
OLAKANS
OLITE
OLITES
OLITIC
OLOGIES
OLOGIST
OLOGISTS
OLOGY
OLONG
OLONGS
OM
OMIAC
OMIACK
OMIACKS
OMIACS
OMIAK
OMIAKS
OMPAH
OMPAHED
OMPAHING
OMPAHS
OMPH
OMPHS
OMS
ON
ONS
ONT
ONTS
OP
OPED
OPHORON
OPHORONS
OOPHYTE
OOPHYTES
OOPING
OOPS
OOR
OORIAL
OORIALS
OORIE
OORIER
OORIEST
OOS
OOSE
OOSES
OOSIER
OOSIEST
OOSPHERE
OOSPHERES
OOSPORE
OOSPORES
OOSY
OOZE
OOZED
OOZES
OOZIER
OOZIEST
OOZILY
OOZINESS
OOZINESSES
OOZING
OOZY
OP
OPACITIES
OPACITY
OPACOUS
OPAH
OPAHS
OPAL
OPALED
OPALINE
OPALINES
OPALISED
OPALIZED
OPALS
OPAQUE
OPAQUED
OPAQUELY
OPAQUER
OPAQUES
OPAQUEST
OPAQUING
OPCODE
OPCODES
OPE
OPED
OPEN
OPENABLE
OPENED
OPENER
OPENERS
OPENEST
OPENING
OPENINGS
OPENLY
OPENNESS
OPENNESSES
OPENS
OPENWORK
OPENWORKS
OPEPE
OPEPES
OPERA
OPERABLE
OPERAND
OPERANDS
OPERANT
OPERANTS
OPERAS
OPERATE
OPERATED
OPERATES
OPERATIC
OPERATING
OPERATION
OPERATIONS
OPERATIVE
OPERATIVES
OPERATOR
OPERATORS
OPERCULA
OPERCULAR
OPERCULUM
OPERETTA
OPERETTAS
OPERON
OPERONS
OPEROSE
OPEROSELY
OPEROSITIES
OPEROSITY
OPES
OPHIDIAN
OPHIDIANS
OPHIOLITE
OPHIOLITES
OPHIOLOGIES
OPHIOLOGY
OPHITE
OPHITES
OPHITIC
OPHIURA
OPHIURAN
OPHIURANS
OPHIURAS
OPHIURID
OPHIURIDS
OPHIUROID
OPHIUROIDS
OPIATE
OPIATED
OPIATES
OPIATING
OPIFICER
OPIFICERS
OPINABLE
OPINE
OPINED
OPINES
OPING
OPINICUS
OPINICUSES
OPINING
OPINION
OPINIONED
OPINIONS
OPIOID
OPIUM
OPIUMISM
OPIUMISMS
OPIUMS
OPOBALSAM
OPOBALSAMS
OPODELDOC
OPODELDOCS
OPOPANAX
OPOPANAXES
OPORICE
OPORICES
OPOSSUM
OPOSSUMS
OPPIDAN
OPPIDANS
OPPILATE
OPPILATED
OPPILATES
OPPILATING
OPPO
OPPONENCIES
OPPONENCY
OPPONENT
OPPONENTS
OPPORTUNE
OPPOS
OPPOSABLE
OPPOSE
OPPOSED
OPPOSER
OPPOSERS
OPPOSES
OPPOSING
OPPOSITE
OPPOSITES
OPPRESS
OPPRESSED
OPPRESSES
OPPRESSING
OPPRESSOR
OPPRESSORS
OPPUGN
OPPUGNANT
OPPUGNANTS
OPPUGNED
OPPUGNER
OPPUGNERS
OPPUGNING
OPPUGNS
OPS
OPSIMATH
OPSIMATHIES
OPSIMATHS
OPSIMATHY
OPSOMANIA
OPSOMANIAS
OPSONIC
OPSONIN
OPSONINS
OPSONIUM
OPSONIUMS
OPT
OPTANT
OPTANTS
OPTATIVE
OPTATIVES
OPTED
OPTER
OPTERS
OPTIC
OPTICAL
OPTICALLY
OPTICIAN
OPTICIANS
OPTICS
OPTIMA
OPTIMAL
OPTIMALLY
OPTIMATE
OPTIMATES
OPTIME
OPTIMES
OPTIMISE
OPTIMISED
OPTIMISES
OPTIMISING
OPTIMISM
OPTIMISMS
OPTIMIST
OPTIMISTS
OPTIMIZE
OPTIMIZED
OPTIMIZES
OPTIMIZING
OPTIMUM
OPTING
OPTION
OPTIONAL
OPTIONS
OPTOLOGIES
OPTOLOGY
OPTOMETER
OPTOMETERS
OPTOMETRIES
OPTOMETRY
OPTOPHONE
OPTOPHONES
OPTRONICS
OPTS
OPULENCE
OPULENCES
OPULENT
OPULENTLY
OPULUS
OPULUSES
OPUNTIA
OPUNTIAS
OPUS
OPUSCLE
OPUSCLES

OPUSCULA
OPUSCULE
OPUSCULES
OPUSCULUM
OPUSES
OR
ORACH
ORACHE
ORACHES
ORACIES
ORACLE
ORACLED
ORACLES
ORACLING
ORACULAR
ORACULOUS
ORACY
ORAGIOUS
ORAL
ORALISM
ORALISMS
ORALITIES
ORALITY
ORALLY
ORALS
ORANG
ORANGE
ORANGEADE
ORANGEADES
ORANGER
ORANGERIES
ORANGERY
ORANGES
ORANGEST
ORANGEY
ORANGIER
ORANGIEST
ORANGS
ORANT
ORANTS
ORARIA
ORARIAN
ORARIANS
ORARION
ORARIONS
ORARIUM
ORARIUMS
ORATE
ORATED
ORATES
ORATING
ORATION
ORATIONS
ORATOR
ORATORIAL
ORATORIAN
ORATORIANS
ORATORIES
ORATORIO
ORATORIOS
ORATORS
ORATORY
ORATRESS
ORATRESSES
ORATRIX
ORATRIXES
ORB
ORBED
ORBICULAR
ORBIER
ORBIEST
ORBING
ORBIT
ORBITA
ORBITAL
ORBITALS
ORBITAS
ORBITED
ORBITER
ORBITERS
ORBITIES
ORBITING
ORBITS
ORBITY
ORBS
ORBY
ORC
ORCA
ORCAS
ORCEIN
ORCEINS
ORCHARD
ORCHARDS
ORCHAT
ORCHATS
ORCHEL
ORCHELLA
ORCHELLAS
ORCHELS
ORCHESES
ORCHESIS
ORCHESTIC
ORCHESTICS
ORCHESTRA
ORCHESTRAS
ORCHID
ORCHIDIST
ORCHIDISTS
ORCHIDS
ORCHIL
ORCHILLA
ORCHILLAS
ORCHILS
ORCHIS
ORCHISES
ORCHITIC
ORCHITIS
ORCHITISES
ORCIN
ORCINE
ORCINES
ORCINOL
ORCINOLS
ORCINS
ORCS
ORD
ORDAIN
ORDAINED
ORDAINER
ORDAINERS
ORDAINING
ORDAINS
ORDALIAN
ORDALIUM
ORDALIUMS
ORDEAL
ORDEALS
ORDER
ORDERED
ORDERER
ORDERERS
ORDERING
ORDERINGS
ORDERLESS
ORDERLIES
ORDERLY
ORDERS
ORDINAIRE
ORDINAIRES
ORDINAL
ORDINALS
ORDINANCE
ORDINANCES
ORDINAND
ORDINANDS
ORDINANT
ORDINANTS
ORDINAR
ORDINARIES
ORDINARS
ORDINARY
ORDINATE
ORDINATED
ORDINATES
ORDINATING
ORDINEE
ORDINEES
ORDNANCE
ORDNANCES
ORDS
ORDURE
ORDURES
ORDUROUS
ORE
OREAD
OREADES
OREADS
ORECROWE
ORECROWED
ORECROWES
ORECROWING
ORECTIC
OREGANO
OREGANOS
OREIDE
OREIDES
OREOLOGIES
OREOLOGY
OREPEARCH
OREPEARCHED
OREPEARCHES
OREPEARCHING
ORES
ORESTUNCK
OREWEED
OREWEEDS
OREXIS
OREXISES
ORF
ORFE
ORFES
ORFS
ORGAN
ORGANA
ORGANDIE
ORGANDIES
ORGANELLE
ORGANELLES
ORGANIC
ORGANICAL
ORGANISE
ORGANISED
ORGANISER
ORGANISERS
ORGANISES
ORGANISING
ORGANISM
ORGANISMS
ORGANIST
ORGANISTS
ORGANITIES
ORGANITY
ORGANIZE
ORGANIZED
ORGANIZER
ORGANIZERS
ORGANIZES
ORGANIZING
ORGANON
ORGANS
ORGANUM
ORGANZA
ORGANZAS
ORGANZINE
ORGANZINES
ORGASM
ORGASMED
ORGASMIC
ORGASMING
ORGASMS
ORGASTIC
ORGEAT
ORGEATS
ORGIA
ORGIAS
ORGIAST
ORGIASTIC
ORGIASTS
ORGIC
ORGIES
ORGILLOUS
ORGONE
ORGONES
ORGUE
ORGUES
ORGULOUS
ORGY
ORIBI
ORIBIS
ORICALCHE
ORICALCHES
ORICHALC
ORICHALCS
ORIEL
ORIELLED
ORIELS
ORIENCIES
ORIENCY
ORIENT
ORIENTAL
ORIENTALS
ORIENTATE
ORIENTATED
ORIENTATES
ORIENTATING
ORIENTED
ORIENTEER
ORIENTEERED
ORIENTEERING
ORIENTEERINGS
ORIENTEERS
ORIENTING
ORIENTS
ORIFEX
ORIFEXES
ORIFICE
ORIFICES
ORIFICIAL
ORIFLAMME
ORIFLAMMES
ORIGAMI
ORIGAMIS
ORIGAN
ORIGANE
ORIGANES
ORIGANS
ORIGANUM
ORIGANUMS
ORIGIN
ORIGINAL
ORIGINALS
ORIGINATE
ORIGINATED
ORIGINATES
ORIGINATING
ORIGINS
ORILLION
ORILLIONS
ORIOLE
ORIOLES
ORISON
ORISONS
ORLE
ORLEANS
ORLEANSES
ORLES
ORLOP
ORLOPS
ORMER
ORMERS

RMOLU
RMOLUS
RNAMENT
RNAMENTED
RNAMENTING
RNAMENTS
RNATE
RNATELY
RNATER
RNATEST
RNERY
RNIS
RNISES
RNITHIC
RNITHOID
ROGEN
ROGENIC
ROGENIES
ROGENS
ROGENY
ROGRAPHIES
ROGRAPHY
ROIDE
ROIDES
ROLOGIES
ROLOGIST
ROLOGISTS
ROLOGY
ROPESA
ROPESAS
ROROTUND
ROTUND
RPHAN
RPHANAGE
RPHANAGES
RPHANED
RPHANING
RPHANISM
RPHANISMS
RPHANS
RPHARION
RPHARIONS
RPHREY
RPHREYS
RPIMENT
RPIMENTS
RPIN
RPINE
RPINES
RPINS
RRA
RRERIES
RRERY
RRIS
RRISES
RS
RSEILLE
RSEILLES
RSELLIC
RT
RTANIQUE
RTANIQUES
RTHIAN
RTHICON
ORTHICONS
ORTHO
ORTHOAXES
ORTHOAXIS
ORTHODOX
ORTHODOXIES
ORTHODOXY
ORTHOEPIC
ORTHOEPIES
ORTHOEPY
ORTHOPEDIES
ORTHOPEDY
ORTHOPOD
ORTHOPODS
ORTHOPTIC
ORTHOPTICS
ORTHOS
ORTHOSES
ORTHOSIS
ORTHOTIC
ORTHOTICS
ORTHOTIST
ORTHOTISTS
ORTHOTONE
ORTHROS
ORTHROSES
ORTOLAN
ORTOLANS
ORTS
ORVAL
ORVALS
ORYX
ORYXES
ORZO
ORZOS
OS
OSCHEAL
OSCILLATE
OSCILLATED
OSCILLATES
OSCILLATING
OSCINE
OSCININE
OSCITANCIES
OSCITANCY
OSCITANT
OSCITATE
OSCITATED
OSCITATES
OSCITATING
OSCULA
OSCULANT
OSCULAR
OSCULATE
OSCULATED
OSCULATES
OSCULATING
OSCULE
OSCULES
OSCULUM
OSHAC
OSHACS
OSIER
OSIERED
OSIERIES
OSIERS
OSIERY
OSMATE
OSMATES
OSMETERIA
OSMIATE
OSMIATES
OSMIC
OSMIOUS
OSMIUM
OSMIUMS
OSMOMETER
OSMOMETERS
OSMOMETRIES
OSMOMETRY
OSMOSE
OSMOSED
OSMOSES
OSMOSING
OSMOSIS
OSMOTIC
OSMOUS
OSMUND
OSMUNDA
OSMUNDAS
OSMUNDS
OSNABURG
OSNABURGS
OSPREY
OSPREYS
OSSA
OSSARIUM
OSSARIUMS
OSSEIN
OSSEINS
OSSELET
OSSELETS
OSSEOUS
OSSETER
OSSETERS
OSSIA
OSSICLE
OSSICLES
OSSICULAR
OSSIFIC
OSSIFIED
OSSIFIES
OSSIFRAGA
OSSIFRAGAS
OSSIFRAGE
OSSIFRAGES
OSSIFY
OSSIFYING
OSSUARIES
OSSUARY
OSTEAL
OSTEITIS
OSTEITISES
OSTENSIVE
OSTENSORIES
OSTENSORY
OSTENT
OSTENTS
OSTEODERM
OSTEODERMS
OSTEOGEN
OSTEOGENIES
OSTEOGENS
OSTEOGENY
OSTEOID
OSTEOLOGIES
OSTEOLOGY
OSTEOMA
OSTEOMAS
OSTEOMATA
OSTEOPATH
OSTEOPATHS
OSTEOTOME
OSTEOTOMES
OSTEOTOMIES
OSTEOTOMY
OSTIA
OSTIAL
OSTIARIES
OSTIARY
OSTIATE
OSTINATO
OSTINATOS
OSTIOLATE
OSTIOLE
OSTIOLES
OSTIUM
OSTLER
OSTLERESS
OSTLERESSES
OSTLERS
OSTRACA
OSTRACEAN
OSTRACISE
OSTRACISED
OSTRACISES
OSTRACISING
OSTRACISM
OSTRACISMS
OSTRACIZE
OSTRACIZED
OSTRACIZES
OSTRACIZING
OSTRACOD
OSTRACODS
OSTRACON
OSTRAKA
OSTRAKON
OSTREGER
OSTREGERS
OSTRICH
OSTRICHES
OTAKU
OTALGIA
OTALGIAS
OTALGIES
OTALGY
OTARIES
OTARINE
OTARY
OTHER
OTHERNESS
OTHERNESSES
OTHERS
OTHERWISE
OTIC
OTIOSE
OTIOSITIES
OTIOSITY
OTITIS
OTITISES
OTOCYST
OTOCYSTS
OTOLITH
OTOLITHS
OTOLOGIES
OTOLOGIST
OTOLOGISTS
OTOLOGY
OTORRHOEA
OTORRHOEAS
OTOSCOPE
OTOSCOPES
OTTAR
OTTARS
OTTAVA
OTTAVAS
OTTAVINO
OTTAVINOS
OTTER
OTTERED
OTTERING
OTTERS
OTTO
OTTOMAN
OTTOMANS
OTTOS
OTTRELITE
OTTRELITES
OU
OUABAIN
OUABAINS
OUAKARI
OUAKARIS
OUBIT
OUBITS
OUBLIETTE
OUBLIETTES
OUCH
OUCHES
OUCHT
OUCHTS
OUD
OUDS
OUGHLIED
OUGHLIES
OUGHLY
OUGHLYING
OUGHT
OUGHTNESS
OUGHTNESSES
OUGHTS
OUGLIE
OUGLIED
OUGLIEING
OUGLIES

OUIJA
OUIJAS
OUISTITI
OUISTITIS
OUK
OUKS
OULACHON
OULACHONS
OULAKAN
OULAKANS
OULD
OULDER
OULDEST
OULK
OULKS
OULONG
OULONGS
OUNCE
OUNCES
OUNDY
OUP
OUPED
OUPH
OUPHE
OUPHES
OUPHS
OUPING
OUPS
OUR
OURALI
OURALIS
OURARI
OURARIS
OUREBI
OUREBIS
OURIE
OURIER
OURIEST
OURN
OUROBOROS
OUROBOROSES
OUROLOGIES
OUROLOGY
OUROSCOPIES
OUROSCOPY
OURS
OURSELF
OURSELVES
OUSEL
OUSELS
OUST
OUSTED
OUSTER
OUSTERS
OUSTING
OUSTITI
OUSTITIS
OUSTS
OUT
OUTAGE
OUTAGES
OUTATE
OUTBACK
OUTBACKER
OUTBACKERS
OUTBACKS
OUTBAR
OUTBARRED
OUTBARRING
OUTBARS
OUTBID
OUTBIDDING
OUTBIDS
OUTBOARD
OUTBOUND
OUTBOUNDS
OUTBOX
OUTBOXED
OUTBOXES
OUTBOXING
OUTBRAG
OUTBRAGGED
OUTBRAGGING
OUTBRAGS
OUTBRAVE
OUTBRAVED
OUTBRAVES
OUTBRAVING
OUTBREAK
OUTBREAKING
OUTBREAKS
OUTBRED
OUTBREED
OUTBREEDING
OUTBREEDINGS
OUTBREEDS
OUTBROKE
OUTBROKEN
OUTBURN
OUTBURNED
OUTBURNING
OUTBURNS
OUTBURNT
OUTBURST
OUTBURSTING
OUTBURSTS
OUTBY
OUTBYE
OUTCAST
OUTCASTE
OUTCASTED
OUTCASTES
OUTCASTING
OUTCASTS
OUTCLASS
OUTCLASSED
OUTCLASSES
OUTCLASSING
OUTCOME
OUTCOMES
OUTCRAFTIED
OUTCRAFTIES
OUTCRAFTY
OUTCRAFTYING
OUTCRIED
OUTCRIES
OUTCROP
OUTCROPPED
OUTCROPPING
OUTCROPS
OUTCROSS
OUTCROSSED
OUTCROSSES
OUTCROSSING
OUTCROSSINGS
OUTCRY
OUTCRYING
OUTDANCE
OUTDANCED
OUTDANCES
OUTDANCING
OUTDARE
OUTDARED
OUTDARES
OUTDARING
OUTDATE
OUTDATED
OUTDATES
OUTDATING
OUTDID
OUTDO
OUTDOES
OUTDOING
OUTDONE
OUTDOOR
OUTDOORS
OUTDOORSY
OUTDRANK
OUTDRINK
OUTDRINKING
OUTDRINKS
OUTDRIVE
OUTDRIVEN
OUTDRIVES
OUTDRIVING
OUTDROVE
OUTDRUNK
OUTDURE
OUTDURED
OUTDURES
OUTDURING
OUTDWELL
OUTDWELLED
OUTDWELLING
OUTDWELLS
OUTDWELT
OUTEAT
OUTEATEN
OUTEATING
OUTEATS
OUTED
OUTEDGE
OUTEDGES
OUTER
OUTERMOST
OUTERS
OUTERWEAR
OUTERWEARS
OUTFACE
OUTFACED
OUTFACES
OUTFACING
OUTFALL
OUTFALLS
OUTFIELD
OUTFIELDS
OUTFIGHT
OUTFIGHTING
OUTFIGHTS
OUTFIT
OUTFITS
OUTFITTED
OUTFITTER
OUTFITTERS
OUTFITTING
OUTFITTINGS
OUTFLANK
OUTFLANKED
OUTFLANKING
OUTFLANKS
OUTFLASH
OUTFLASHED
OUTFLASHES
OUTFLASHING
OUTFLEW
OUTFLIES
OUTFLING
OUTFLINGS
OUTFLOW
OUTFLOWED
OUTFLOWING
OUTFLOWINGS
OUTFLOWN
OUTFLOWS
OUTFLUSH
OUTFLUSHED
OUTFLUSHES
OUTFLUSHING
OUTFLY
OUTFLYING
OUTFOOT
OUTFOOTED
OUTFOOTING
OUTFOOTS
OUTFOUGHT
OUTFOX
OUTFOXED
OUTFOXES
OUTFOXING
OUTFROWN
OUTFROWNED
OUTFROWNING
OUTFROWNS
OUTGAS
OUTGASSED
OUTGASSES
OUTGASSING
OUTGASSINGS
OUTGATE
OUTGATES
OUTGAVE
OUTGIVE
OUTGIVEN
OUTGIVES
OUTGIVING
OUTGIVINGS
OUTGLARE
OUTGLARED
OUTGLARES
OUTGLARING
OUTGO
OUTGOER
OUTGOERS
OUTGOES
OUTGOING
OUTGOINGS
OUTGONE
OUTGREW
OUTGROW
OUTGROWING
OUTGROWN
OUTGROWS
OUTGROWTH
OUTGROWTHS
OUTGUARD
OUTGUARDS
OUTGUN
OUTGUNNED
OUTGUNNING
OUTGUNS
OUTGUSH
OUTGUSHED
OUTGUSHES
OUTGUSHING
OUTHAUL
OUTHAULER
OUTHAULERS
OUTHAULS
OUTHER
OUTHIRE
OUTHIRED
OUTHIRES
OUTHIRING
OUTHIT
OUTHITS
OUTHITTING
OUTHOUSE
OUTHOUSES
OUTHYRE
OUTHYRED
OUTHYRES
OUTHYRING
OUTING
OUTINGS
OUTJEST
OUTJESTED
OUTJESTING
OUTJESTS
OUTJET
OUTJETS
OUTJOCKEY
OUTJOCKEYED
OUTJOCKEYING
OUTJOCKEYS
OUTJUMP
OUTJUMPED
OUTJUMPING
OUTJUMPS
OUTJUT
OUTJUTS

OUTLAID
OUTLAIN
OUTLAND
OUTLANDER
OUTLANDERS
OUTLANDS
OUTLASH
OUTLASHES
OUTLAST
OUTLASTED
OUTLASTING
OUTLASTS
OUTLAUNCE
OUTLAUNCED
OUTLAUNCES
OUTLAUNCH
OUTLAUNCHED
OUTLAUNCHES
OUTLAUNCHING
OUTLAUNCING
OUTLAW
OUTLAWED
OUTLAWING
OUTLAWRIES
OUTLAWRY
OUTLAWS
OUTLAY
OUTLAYING
OUTLAYS
OUTLEAP
OUTLEAPED
OUTLEAPING
OUTLEAPS
OUTLEAPT
OUTLEARN
OUTLEARNED
OUTLEARNING
OUTLEARNS
OUTLEARNT
OUTLER
OUTLERS
OUTLET
OUTLETS
OUTLIE
OUTLIED
OUTLIER
OUTLIERS
OUTLIES
OUTLINE
OUTLINEAR
OUTLINED
OUTLINES
OUTLINING
OUTLIVE
OUTLIVED
OUTLIVES
OUTLIVING
OUTLOOK
OUTLOOKED
OUTLOOKING
OUTLOOKS
OUTLUSTRE
OUTLUSTRED
OUTLUSTRES
OUTLUSTRING
OUTLYING
OUTMAN
OUTMANNED
OUTMANNING
OUTMANS
OUTMANTLE
OUTMANTLED
OUTMANTLES
OUTMANTLING
OUTMARCH
OUTMARCHED
OUTMARCHES
OUTMARCHING
OUTMATCH
OUTMATCHED
OUTMATCHES
OUTMATCHING
OUTMODE
OUTMODED
OUTMODES
OUTMODING
OUTMOST
OUTMOVE
OUTMOVED
OUTMOVES
OUTMOVING
OUTNAME
OUTNAMED
OUTNAMES
OUTNAMING
OUTNESS
OUTNESSES
OUTNIGHT
OUTNIGHTED
OUTNIGHTING
OUTNIGHTS
OUTNUMBER
OUTNUMBERED
OUTNUMBERING
OUTNUMBERS
OUTPACE
OUTPACED
OUTPACES
OUTPACING
OUTPART
OUTPARTS
OUTPEEP
OUTPEEPED
OUTPEEPING
OUTPEEPS
OUTPEER
OUTPEERED
OUTPEERING
OUTPEERS
OUTPLACE
OUTPLACED
OUTPLACER
OUTPLACERS
OUTPLACES
OUTPLACING
OUTPLAY
OUTPLAYED
OUTPLAYING
OUTPLAYS
OUTPOINT
OUTPOINTED
OUTPOINTING
OUTPOINTS
OUTPORT
OUTPORTS
OUTPOST
OUTPOSTS
OUTPOUR
OUTPOURED
OUTPOURER
OUTPOURERS
OUTPOURING
OUTPOURINGS
OUTPOURS
OUTPOWER
OUTPOWERED
OUTPOWERING
OUTPOWERS
OUTPRAY
OUTPRAYED
OUTPRAYING
OUTPRAYS
OUTPRICE
OUTPRICED
OUTPRICES
OUTPRICING
OUTPRIZE
OUTPRIZED
OUTPRIZES
OUTPRIZING
OUTPUT
OUTPUTS
OUTPUTTING
OUTRACE
OUTRACED
OUTRACES
OUTRACING
OUTRAGE
OUTRAGED
OUTRAGES
OUTRAGING
OUTRAIGNE
OUTRAIGNED
OUTRAIGNES
OUTRAIGNING
OUTRAN
OUTRANCE
OUTRANCES
OUTRANK
OUTRANKED
OUTRANKING
OUTRANKS
OUTRATE
OUTRATED
OUTRATES
OUTRATING
OUTRE
OUTREACH
OUTREACHED
OUTREACHES
OUTREACHING
OUTRED
OUTREDDED
OUTREDDEN
OUTREDDENED
OUTREDDENING
OUTREDDENS
OUTREDDING
OUTREDS
OUTREIGN
OUTREIGNED
OUTREIGNING
OUTREIGNS
OUTRELIEF
OUTRELIEFS
OUTREMER
OUTREMERS
OUTRIDDEN
OUTRIDE
OUTRIDER
OUTRIDERS
OUTRIDES
OUTRIDING
OUTRIGGER
OUTRIGGERS
OUTRIGHT
OUTRIVAL
OUTRIVALLED
OUTRIVALLING
OUTRIVALS
OUTROAR
OUTROARED
OUTROARING
OUTROARS
OUTRODE
OUTROOP
OUTROOPER
OUTROOPERS
OUTROOPS
OUTROOT
OUTROOTED
OUTROOTING
OUTROOTS
OUTROPE
OUTROPER
OUTROPERS
OUTROPES
OUTRUN
OUTRUNNER
OUTRUNNERS
OUTRUNNING
OUTRUNS
OUTRUSH
OUTRUSHED
OUTRUSHES
OUTRUSHING
OUTS
OUTSAIL
OUTSAILED
OUTSAILING
OUTSAILS
OUTSAT
OUTSCOLD
OUTSCOLDED
OUTSCOLDING
OUTSCOLDS
OUTSCORN
OUTSCORNED
OUTSCORNING
OUTSCORNS
OUTSELL
OUTSELLING
OUTSELLS
OUTSET
OUTSETS
OUTSHINE
OUTSHINES
OUTSHINING
OUTSHONE
OUTSHOOT
OUTSHOOTING
OUTSHOOTS
OUTSHOT
OUTSHOTS
OUTSIDE
OUTSIDER
OUTSIDERS
OUTSIDES
OUTSIGHT
OUTSIGHTS
OUTSIT
OUTSITS
OUTSITTING
OUTSIZE
OUTSIZED
OUTSIZES
OUTSKIRTS
OUTSLEEP
OUTSLEEPING
OUTSLEEPS
OUTSLEPT
OUTSMART
OUTSMARTED
OUTSMARTING
OUTSMARTS
OUTSOAR
OUTSOARED
OUTSOARING
OUTSOARS
OUTSOLD
OUTSOLE
OUTSOLES
OUTSOURCE
OUTSOURCED
OUTSOURCES
OUTSOURCING
OUTSOURCINGS
OUTSPAN
OUTSPANNED
OUTSPANNING
OUTSPANS
OUTSPEAK
OUTSPEAKING
OUTSPEAKS
OUTSPEND
OUTSPENDING
OUTSPENDS
OUTSPENT
OUTSPOKE
OUTSPOKEN

OUTSPORT
OUTSPORTED
OUTSPORTING
OUTSPORTS
OUTSPRANG
OUTSPREAD
OUTSPREADING
OUTSPREADS
OUTSPRING
OUTSPRINGING
OUTSPRINGS
OUTSPRUNG
OUTSTAND
OUTSTANDING
OUTSTANDS
OUTSTARE
OUTSTARED
OUTSTARES
OUTSTARING
OUTSTAY
OUTSTAYED
OUTSTAYING
OUTSTAYS
OUTSTEP
OUTSTEPPED
OUTSTEPPING
OUTSTEPS
OUTSTOOD
OUTSTRAIN
OUTSTRAINED
OUTSTRAINING
OUTSTRAINS
OUTSTRIKE
OUTSTRIKES
OUTSTRIKING
OUTSTRIP
OUTSTRIPPED
OUTSTRIPPING
OUTSTRIPS
OUTSTRUCK
OUTSUM
OUTSUMMED
OUTSUMMING
OUTSUMS
OUTSWAM
OUTSWEAR
OUTSWEARING
OUTSWEARS
OUTSWELL
OUTSWELLED
OUTSWELLING
OUTSWELLS
OUTSWIM
OUTSWIMMING
OUTSWIMS
OUTSWING
OUTSWINGS
OUTSWOLLEN
OUTSWORE
OUTSWORN
OUTSWUM
OUTTAKE
OUTTAKEN
OUTTAKES
OUTTAKING
OUTTALK
OUTTALKED
OUTTALKING
OUTTALKS
OUTTELL
OUTTELLING
OUTTELLS
OUTTHINK
OUTTHINKING
OUTTHINKS
OUTTHOUGHT
OUTTOLD
OUTTONGUE
OUTTONGUED
OUTTONGUES
OUTTONGUING
OUTTOOK
OUTTOP
OUTTOPPED
OUTTOPPING
OUTTOPS
OUTTRAVEL
OUTTRAVELED
OUTTRAVELING
OUTTRAVELLED
OUTTRAVELLING
OUTTRAVELS
OUTTURN
OUTTURNS
OUTVALUE
OUTVALUED
OUTVALUES
OUTVALUING
OUTVENOM
OUTVENOMED
OUTVENOMING
OUTVENOMS
OUTVIE
OUTVIED
OUTVIES
OUTVOICE
OUTVOICED
OUTVOICES
OUTVOICING
OUTVOTE
OUTVOTED
OUTVOTER
OUTVOTERS
OUTVOTES
OUTVOTING
OUTVYING
OUTWALK
OUTWALKED
OUTWALKING
OUTWALKS
OUTWARD
OUTWARDLY
OUTWARDS
OUTWASH
OUTWASHES
OUTWATCH
OUTWATCHED
OUTWATCHES
OUTWATCHING
OUTWEAR
OUTWEARIED
OUTWEARIES
OUTWEARING
OUTWEARS
OUTWEARY
OUTWEARYING
OUTWEED
OUTWEEDED
OUTWEEDING
OUTWEEDS
OUTWEEP
OUTWEEPING
OUTWEEPS
OUTWEIGH
OUTWEIGHED
OUTWEIGHING
OUTWEIGHS
OUTWELL
OUTWELLED
OUTWELLING
OUTWELLS
OUTWENT
OUTWEPT
OUTWICK
OUTWICKED
OUTWICKING
OUTWICKS
OUTWIN
OUTWIND
OUTWINDING
OUTWINDS
OUTWING
OUTWINGED
OUTWINGING
OUTWINGS
OUTWINNING
OUTWINS
OUTWIT
OUTWITH
OUTWITS
OUTWITTED
OUTWITTING
OUTWON
OUTWORE
OUTWORK
OUTWORKER
OUTWORKERS
OUTWORKING
OUTWORKS
OUTWORN
OUTWORTH
OUTWORTHED
OUTWORTHING
OUTWORTHS
OUTWOUND
OUTWREST
OUTWRESTED
OUTWRESTING
OUTWRESTS
OUTWROUGHT
OUVERT
OUVERTE
OUVRAGE
OUVRAGES
OUVRIER
OUVRIERE
OUVRIERES
OUVRIERS
OUZEL
OUZELS
OUZO
OUZOS
OVA
OVAL
OVALBUMIN
OVALBUMINS
OVALLY
OVALS
OVARIAN
OVARIES
OVARIOLE
OVARIOLES
OVARIOUS
OVARITIS
OVARITISES
OVARY
OVATE
OVATED
OVATES
OVATING
OVATION
OVATIONS
OVATOR
OVATORS
OVEN
OVENS
OVENWARE
OVENWARES
OVENWOOD
OVENWOODS
OVER
OVERACT
OVERACTED
OVERACTING
OVERACTS
OVERAGE
OVERAGES
OVERALL
OVERALLED
OVERALLS
OVERARCH
OVERARCHED
OVERARCHES
OVERARCHING
OVERARM
OVERATE
OVERAWE
OVERAWED
OVERAWES
OVERAWING
OVERBEAR
OVERBEARING
OVERBEARS
OVERBEAT
OVERBEATEN
OVERBEATING
OVERBEATS
OVERBID
OVERBIDDING
OVERBIDDINGS
OVERBIDS
OVERBITE
OVERBITES
OVERBLEW
OVERBLOW
OVERBLOWING
OVERBLOWN
OVERBLOWS
OVERBOARD
OVERBOIL
OVERBOILED
OVERBOILING
OVERBOILS
OVERBOLD
OVERBOOK
OVERBOOKED
OVERBOOKING
OVERBOOKS
OVERBORE
OVERBORNE
OVERBOUGHT
OVERBOUND
OVERBOUNDED
OVERBOUNDING
OVERBOUNDS
OVERBRIM
OVERBRIMMED
OVERBRIMMING
OVERBRIMS
OVERBROW
OVERBROWED
OVERBROWING
OVERBROWS
OVERBUILD
OVERBUILDING
OVERBUILDS
OVERBUILT
OVERBULK
OVERBULKED
OVERBULKING
OVERBULKS
OVERBURN
OVERBURNED
OVERBURNING
OVERBURNS
OVERBURNT
OVERBUSIED
OVERBUSIES
OVERBUSY
OVERBUSYING
OVERBUY
OVERBUYING
OVERBUYS
OVERBY
OVERCALL
OVERCALLED
OVERCALLING
OVERCALLS
OVERCAME
OVERCARRIED

VERCARRIES
VERCARRY
VERCARRYING
VERCAST
VERCASTING
VERCASTINGS
VERCASTS
VERCATCH
VERCATCHES
VERCATCHING
VERCAUGHT
VERCHECK
VERCHECKS
VERCLAD
VERCLOUD
VERCLOUDED
VERCLOUDING
VERCLOUDS
VERCLOY
VERCLOYED
VERCLOYING
VERCLOYS
VERCOAT
VERCOATS
VERCOME
VERCOMES
VERCOMING
VERCOOK
VERCOOKED
VERCOOKING
VERCOOKS
VERCOUNT
VERCOUNTED
VERCOUNTING
VERCOUNTS
VERCOVER
VERCOVERED
VERCOVERING
VERCOVERS
VERCRAW
VERCRAWED
VERCRAWING
VERCRAWS
VERCROP
VERCROPPED
VERCROPPING
VERCROPS
VERCROW
VERCROWD
VERCROWDED
VERCROWDING
VERCROWDINGS
VERCROWDS
VERCROWED
VERCROWING
VERCROWS
VERDATED
VERDID
VERDIGHT
VERDO
VERDOER
VERDOERS
VERDOES
VERDOING
OVERDONE
OVERDOSE
OVERDOSED
OVERDOSES
OVERDOSING
OVERDRAFT
OVERDRAFTS
OVERDRAW
OVERDRAWING
OVERDRAWN
OVERDRAWS
OVERDRESS
OVERDRESSED
OVERDRESSES
OVERDRESSING
OVERDREW
OVERDRIVE
OVERDRIVEN
OVERDRIVES
OVERDRIVING
OVERDROVE
OVERDUE
OVERDUST
OVERDUSTED
OVERDUSTING
OVERDUSTS
OVERDYE
OVERDYED
OVERDYEING
OVERDYES
OVEREAT
OVEREATEN
OVEREATING
OVEREATS
OVERED
OVEREXERT
OVEREXERTED
OVEREXERTING
OVEREXERTS
OVEREYE
OVEREYED
OVEREYEING
OVEREYES
OVEREYING
OVERFALL
OVERFALLEN
OVERFALLING
OVERFALLS
OVERFAR
OVERFED
OVERFEED
OVERFEEDING
OVERFEEDS
OVERFELL
OVERFILL
OVERFILLED
OVERFILLING
OVERFILLS
OVERFINE
OVERFISH
OVERFISHED
OVERFISHES
OVERFISHING
OVERFLEW
OVERFLIES
OVERFLOW
OVERFLOWED
OVERFLOWING
OVERFLOWINGS
OVERFLOWN
OVERFLOWS
OVERFLUSH
OVERFLUSHES
OVERFLY
OVERFLYING
OVERFOLD
OVERFOLDED
OVERFOLDING
OVERFOLDS
OVERFOND
OVERFREE
OVERFULL
OVERFUND
OVERFUNDED
OVERFUNDING
OVERFUNDINGS
OVERFUNDS
OVERGALL
OVERGALLED
OVERGALLING
OVERGALLS
OVERGANG
OVERGANGING
OVERGANGS
OVERGAVE
OVERGET
OVERGETS
OVERGETTING
OVERGIVE
OVERGIVEN
OVERGIVES
OVERGIVING
OVERGLAZE
OVERGLAZED
OVERGLAZES
OVERGLAZING
OVERGLOOM
OVERGLOOMED
OVERGLOOMING
OVERGLOOMS
OVERGO
OVERGOES
OVERGOING
OVERGOINGS
OVERGONE
OVERGORGE
OVERGORGED
OVERGORGES
OVERGORGING
OVERGOT
OVERGRAIN
OVERGRAINED
OVERGRAINING
OVERGRAINS
OVERGRASS
OVERGRASSED
OVERGRASSES
OVERGRASSING
OVERGRAZE
OVERGRAZED
OVERGRAZES
OVERGRAZING
OVERGRAZINGS
OVERGREAT
OVERGREEN
OVERGREENED
OVERGREENING
OVERGREENS
OVERGREW
OVERGROW
OVERGROWING
OVERGROWN
OVERGROWS
OVERHAILE
OVERHAILED
OVERHAILES
OVERHAILING
OVERHAIR
OVERHAIRS
OVERHALE
OVERHALED
OVERHALES
OVERHALING
OVERHAND
OVERHANDED
OVERHANDING
OVERHANDS
OVERHANG
OVERHANGING
OVERHANGS
OVERHAPPY
OVERHASTE
OVERHASTES
OVERHASTY
OVERHAUL
OVERHAULED
OVERHAULING
OVERHAULS
OVERHEAD
OVERHEADS
OVERHEAR
OVERHEARD
OVERHEARING
OVERHEARS
OVERHEAT
OVERHEATED
OVERHEATING
OVERHEATINGS
OVERHEATS
OVERHELD
OVERHENT
OVERHENTING
OVERHENTS
OVERHIT
OVERHITS
OVERHITTING
OVERHOLD
OVERHOLDING
OVERHOLDS
OVERHUNG
OVERHYPE
OVERHYPED
OVERHYPES
OVERHYPING
OVERING
OVERINKED
OVERISSUE
OVERISSUED
OVERISSUES
OVERISSUING
OVERJOY
OVERJOYED
OVERJOYING
OVERJOYS
OVERJUMP
OVERJUMPED
OVERJUMPING
OVERJUMPS
OVERKEEP
OVERKEEPING
OVERKEEPS
OVERKEPT
OVERKEST
OVERKILL
OVERKILLS
OVERKIND
OVERKING
OVERKINGS
OVERKNEE
OVERLADE
OVERLADED
OVERLADEN
OVERLADES
OVERLADING
OVERLAID
OVERLAIN
OVERLAND
OVERLANDED
OVERLANDING
OVERLANDS
OVERLAP
OVERLAPPED
OVERLAPPING
OVERLAPS
OVERLARD
OVERLARDED
OVERLARDING
OVERLARDS
OVERLAY
OVERLAYING
OVERLAYINGS
OVERLAYS
OVERLEAF
OVERLEAP
OVERLEAPED
OVERLEAPING
OVERLEAPS
OVERLEAPT
OVERLEND
OVERLENDING
OVERLENDS
OVERLENT
OVERLIE
OVERLIER
OVERLIERS
OVERLIES

OVERLIVE
OVERLIVED
OVERLIVES
OVERLIVING
OVERLOAD
OVERLOADED
OVERLOADING
OVERLOADS
OVERLOCK
OVERLOCKED
OVERLOCKING
OVERLOCKINGS
OVERLOCKS
OVERLONG
OVERLOOK
OVERLOOKED
OVERLOOKING
OVERLOOKS
OVERLORD
OVERLORDED
OVERLORDING
OVERLORDS
OVERLOUD
OVERLUSTY
OVERLY
OVERLYING
OVERMAN
OVERMANNED
OVERMANNING
OVERMANS
OVERMAST
OVERMASTED
OVERMASTING
OVERMASTS
OVERMATCH
OVERMATCHED
OVERMATCHES
OVERMATCHING
OVERMEN
OVERMERRY
OVERMOUNT
OVERMOUNTED
OVERMOUNTING
OVERMOUNTS
OVERMUCH
OVERNAME
OVERNAMED
OVERNAMES
OVERNAMING
OVERNEAT
OVERNET
OVERNETS
OVERNETTED
OVERNETTING
OVERNICE
OVERNIGHT
OVERNIGHTS
OVERPAGE
OVERPAID
OVERPAINT
OVERPAINTED
OVERPAINTING
OVERPAINTS
OVERPART
OVERPARTED
OVERPARTING
OVERPARTS
OVERPASS
OVERPASSED
OVERPASSES
OVERPASSING
OVERPAST
OVERPAY
OVERPAYING
OVERPAYS
OVERPEDAL
OVERPEDALED
OVERPEDALING
OVERPEDALLED
OVERPEDALLING
OVERPEDALS
OVERPEER
OVERPEERED
OVERPEERING
OVERPEERS
OVERPERCH
OVERPERCHED
OVERPERCHES
OVERPERCHING
OVERPITCH
OVERPITCHED
OVERPITCHES
OVERPITCHING
OVERPLAST
OVERPLAY
OVERPLAYED
OVERPLAYING
OVERPLAYS
OVERPLIED
OVERPLIES
OVERPLUS
OVERPLUSES
OVERPLUSSES
OVERPLY
OVERPLYING
OVERPOISE
OVERPOISED
OVERPOISES
OVERPOISING
OVERPOST
OVERPOSTED
OVERPOSTING
OVERPOSTS
OVERPOWER
OVERPOWERED
OVERPOWERING
OVERPOWERS
OVERPRESS
OVERPRESSED
OVERPRESSES
OVERPRESSING
OVERPRICE
OVERPRICED
OVERPRICES
OVERPRICING
OVERPRINT
OVERPRINTED
OVERPRINTING
OVERPRINTS
OVERPRIZE
OVERPRIZED
OVERPRIZES
OVERPRIZING
OVERPROOF
OVERPROUD
OVERRACK
OVERRACKED
OVERRACKING
OVERRACKS
OVERRAKE
OVERRAKED
OVERRAKES
OVERRAKING
OVERRAN
OVERRANK
OVERRASH
OVERRATE
OVERRATED
OVERRATES
OVERRATING
OVERRAUGHT
OVERREACH
OVERREACHED
OVERREACHES
OVERREACHING
OVERREACT
OVERREACTED
OVERREACTING
OVERREACTS
OVERREAD
OVERREADING
OVERREADS
OVERRED
OVERREDDED
OVERREDDING
OVERREDS
OVERREN
OVERRENNING
OVERRENS
OVERRIDDEN
OVERRIDE
OVERRIDER
OVERRIDERS
OVERRIDES
OVERRIDING
OVERRIPE
OVERRIPEN
OVERRIPENED
OVERRIPENING
OVERRIPENS
OVERROAST
OVERROASTED
OVERROASTING
OVERROASTS
OVERRODE
OVERRUFF
OVERRUFFED
OVERRUFFING
OVERRUFFS
OVERRULE
OVERRULED
OVERRULER
OVERRULERS
OVERRULES
OVERRULING
OVERRULINGS
OVERRUN
OVERRUNNING
OVERRUNS
OVERS
OVERSAIL
OVERSAILED
OVERSAILING
OVERSAILS
OVERSAW
OVERSCORE
OVERSCORED
OVERSCORES
OVERSCORING
OVERSEA
OVERSEAS
OVERSEE
OVERSEEING
OVERSEEN
OVERSEER
OVERSEERS
OVERSEES
OVERSELL
OVERSELLING
OVERSELLS
OVERSET
OVERSETS
OVERSETTING
OVERSEW
OVERSEWED
OVERSEWING
OVERSEWN
OVERSEWS
OVERSEXED
OVERSHADE
OVERSHADED
OVERSHADES
OVERSHADING
OVERSHINE
OVERSHINES
OVERSHINING
OVERSHIRT
OVERSHIRTS
OVERSHOE
OVERSHOES
OVERSHONE
OVERSHOOT
OVERSHOOTING
OVERSHOOTS
OVERSHOT
OVERSIDE
OVERSIGHT
OVERSIGHTS
OVERSIZE
OVERSIZED
OVERSIZES
OVERSIZING
OVERSKIP
OVERSKIPPED
OVERSKIPPING
OVERSKIPS
OVERSKIRT
OVERSKIRTS
OVERSLEEP
OVERSLEEPING
OVERSLEEPS
OVERSLEPT
OVERSLIP
OVERSLIPPED
OVERSLIPPING
OVERSLIPS
OVERSMAN
OVERSMEN
OVERSOLD
OVERSOUL
OVERSOULS
OVERSOW
OVERSOWED
OVERSOWING
OVERSOWN
OVERSOWS
OVERSPEND
OVERSPENDING
OVERSPENDS
OVERSPENT
OVERSPILL
OVERSPILLS
OVERSPIN
OVERSPINS
OVERSTAFF
OVERSTAFFED
OVERSTAFFING
OVERSTAFFS
OVERSTAIN
OVERSTAINED
OVERSTAINING
OVERSTAINS
OVERSTAND
OVERSTANDING
OVERSTANDS
OVERSTANK
OVERSTARE
OVERSTARED
OVERSTARES
OVERSTARING
OVERSTATE
OVERSTATED
OVERSTATES
OVERSTATING
OVERSTAY
OVERSTAYED
OVERSTAYING
OVERSTAYS
OVERSTEER
OVERSTEERED
OVERSTEERING
OVERSTEERS
OVERSTEP
OVERSTEPPED
OVERSTEPPING
OVERSTEPS
OVERSTINK
OVERSTINKING
OVERSTINKS
OVERSTOCK

OVERSTOCKED
OVERSTOCKING
OVERSTOCKS
OVERSTOOD
OVERSTREW
OVERSTREWED
OVERSTREWING
OVERSTREWN
OVERSTREWS
OVERSTUDIED
OVERSTUDIES
OVERSTUDY
OVERSTUDYING
OVERSTUFF
OVERSTUFFED
OVERSTUFFING
OVERSTUFFS
OVERSTUNK
OVERSWAM
OVERSWAY
OVERSWAYED
OVERSWAYING
OVERSWAYS
OVERSWEAR
OVERSWEARING
OVERSWEARS
OVERSWELL
OVERSWELLED
OVERSWELLING
OVERSWELLS
OVERSWIM
OVERSWIMMING
OVERSWIMS
OVERSWOLLEN
OVERSWORE
OVERSWORN
OVERSWUM
OVERT
OVERTAKE
OVERTAKEN
OVERTAKES
OVERTAKING
OVERTALK
OVERTALKED
OVERTALKING
OVERTALKS
OVERTASK
OVERTASKED
OVERTASKING
OVERTASKS
OVERTAX
OVERTAXED
OVERTAXES
OVERTAXING
OVERTEEM
OVERTEEMED
OVERTEEMING
OVERTEEMS
OVERTHREW
OVERTHROW
OVERTHROWING
OVERTHROWN
OVERTHROWS
OVERTIME
OVERTIMED
OVERTIMER
OVERTIMERS
OVERTIMES
OVERTIMING
OVERTIRE
OVERTIRED
OVERTIRES
OVERTIRING
OVERTLY
OVERTOIL
OVERTOILED
OVERTOILING
OVERTOILS
OVERTONE
OVERTONES
OVERTOOK
OVERTOP
OVERTOPPED
OVERTOPPING
OVERTOPS
OVERTOWER
OVERTOWERED
OVERTOWERING
OVERTOWERS
OVERTRAIN
OVERTRAINED
OVERTRAINING
OVERTRAINS
OVERTRICK
OVERTRICKS
OVERTRIP
OVERTRIPPED
OVERTRIPPING
OVERTRIPS
OVERTRUMP
OVERTRUMPED
OVERTRUMPING
OVERTRUMPS
OVERTRUST
OVERTRUSTED
OVERTRUSTING
OVERTRUSTS
OVERTURE
OVERTURED
OVERTURES
OVERTURING
OVERTURN
OVERTURNED
OVERTURNING
OVERTURNS
OVERTYPE
OVERTYPED
OVERTYPES
OVERTYPING
OVERUSE
OVERUSED
OVERUSES
OVERUSING
OVERVALUE
OVERVALUED
OVERVALUES
OVERVALUING
OVERVEIL
OVERVEILED
OVERVEILING
OVERVEILS
OVERVIEW
OVERVIEWS
OVERWASH
OVERWASHES
OVERWATCH
OVERWATCHED
OVERWATCHES
OVERWATCHING
OVERWEAR
OVERWEARIED
OVERWEARIES
OVERWEARING
OVERWEARS
OVERWEARY
OVERWEARYING
OVERWEEN
OVERWEENED
OVERWEENING
OVERWEENINGS
OVERWEENS
OVERWEIGH
OVERWEIGHED
OVERWEIGHING
OVERWEIGHS
OVERWENT
OVERWHELM
OVERWHELMED
OVERWHELMING
OVERWHELMINGS
OVERWHELMS
OVERWIND
OVERWINDING
OVERWINDS
OVERWING
OVERWINGED
OVERWINGING
OVERWINGS
OVERWISE
OVERWORD
OVERWORDS
OVERWORE
OVERWORK
OVERWORKED
OVERWORKING
OVERWORKS
OVERWORN
OVERWOUND
OVERWREST
OVERWRESTED
OVERWRESTING
OVERWRESTS
OVERWRITE
OVERWRITES
OVERWRITING
OVERWRITTEN
OVERWROTE
OVERWROUGHT
OVERYEAR
OVERYEARED
OVERYEARING
OVERYEARS
OVIBOS
OVIBOSES
OVIBOVINE
OVICIDE
OVICIDES
OVIDUCAL
OVIDUCT
OVIDUCTAL
OVIDUCTS
OVIFEROUS
OVIFORM
OVIGEROUS
OVINE
OVIPARITIES
OVIPARITY
OVIPAROUS
OVIPOSIT
OVIPOSITED
OVIPOSITING
OVIPOSITS
OVIRAPTOR
OVIRAPTORS
OVISAC
OVISACS
OVIST
OVISTS
OVOID
OVOIDAL
OVOIDS
OVOLI
OVOLO
OVOTESTES
OVOTESTIS
OVULAR
OVULATE
OVULATED
OVULATES
OVULATING
OVULATION
OVULATIONS
OVULE
OVULES
OVUM
OW
OWCHE
OWCHES
OWE
OWED
OWELTIES
OWELTY
OWER
OWERBY
OWERLOUP
OWERLOUPEN
OWERLOUPING
OWERLOUPIT
OWERLOUPS
OWES
OWING
OWL
OWLED
OWLER
OWLERIES
OWLERS
OWLERY
OWLET
OWLETS
OWLIER
OWLIEST
OWLING
OWLISH
OWLS
OWLY
OWN
OWNED
OWNER
OWNERLESS
OWNERS
OWNERSHIP
OWNERSHIPS
OWNING
OWNS
OWRE
OWRECOME
OWRECOMES
OWRELAY
OWRELAYS
OWRES
OWREWORD
OWREWORDS
OWRIE
OWRIER
OWRIEST
OWSEN
OWT
OWTS
OX
OXALATE
OXALATES
OXALIC
OXALIS
OXALISES
OXAZINE
OXAZINES
OXBLOOD
OXBLOODS
OXEN
OXER
OXERS
OXFORD
OXFORDS
OXGANG
OXGANGS
OXGATE
OXGATES
OXHEAD
OXHEADS
OXIDANT
OXIDANTS
OXIDASE
OXIDASES
OXIDATE
OXIDATED
OXIDATES
OXIDATING
OXIDATION
OXIDATIONS
OXIDE

OXIDES
OXIDISE
OXIDISED
OXIDISER
OXIDISERS
OXIDISES
OXIDISING
OXIDIZE
OXIDIZED
OXIDIZER
OXIDIZERS
OXIDIZES
OXIDIZING
OXIME
OXIMES
OXIMETER
OXIMETERS
OXLAND
OXLANDS
OXLIP
OXLIPS
OXONIUM
OXONIUMS
OXSLIP
OXSLIPS
OXTAIL
OXTAILS
OXTER
OXTERED
OXTERING
OXTERS
OXYGEN
OXYGENATE
OXYGENATED
OXYGENATES
OXYGENATING
OXYGENISE
OXYGENISED
OXYGENISES
OXYGENISING
OXYGENIZE
OXYGENIZED
OXYGENIZES
OXYGENIZING
OXYGENOUS
OXYGENS
OXYMEL
OXYMELS
OXYMORON
OXYMORONS
OXYTOCIC
OXYTOCICS
OXYTOCIN
OXYTOCINS
OXYTONE
OXYTONES
OY
OYE
OYER
OYERS
OYES
OYESES
OYEZ
OYEZES
OYS
OYSTER
OYSTERS
OYSTRIGE
OYSTRIGES
OZAENA
OZAENAS
OZEKI
OZEKIS
OZOCERITE
OZOCERITES
OZOKERITE
OZOKERITES
OZONATION
OZONATIONS
OZONE
OZONES
OZONISE
OZONISED
OZONISER
OZONISERS
OZONISES
OZONISING
OZONIZE
OZONIZED
OZONIZER
OZONIZERS
OZONIZES
OZONIZING

P

PA
PABOUCHE
PABOUCHES
PABULAR
PABULOUS
PABULUM
PABULUMS
PACA
PACABLE
PACAS
PACATION
PACATIONS
PACE
PACED
PACEMAKER
PACEMAKERS
PACER
PACERS
PACES
PACEY
PACHA
PACHAK
PACHAKS
PACHALIC
PACHALICS
PACHAS
PACHINKO
PACHINKOS
PACHISI
PACHISIS
PACHYDERM
PACHYDERMS
PACIER
PACIEST
PACIFIC
PACIFICAL
PACIFIED
PACIFIER
PACIFIERS
PACIFIES
PACIFISM
PACIFISMS
PACIFIST
PACIFISTS
PACIFY
PACIFYING
PACING
PACK
PACKAGE
PACKAGED
PACKAGER
PACKAGERS
PACKAGES
PACKAGING
PACKAGINGS
PACKED
PACKER
PACKERS
PACKET
PACKETED
PACKETING
PACKETS
PACKFONG
PACKFONGS
PACKING
PACKINGS
PACKMAN
PACKMEN
PACKS
PACKSHEET
PACKSHEETS
PACKSTAFF
PACKSTAFFS
PACKWAY
PACKWAYS
PACO
PACOS
PACT
PACTA
PACTION
PACTIONAL
PACTIONED
PACTIONING
PACTIONS
PACTS
PACTUM
PACY
PAD
PADANG
PADANGS
PADAUK
PADAUKS
PADDED
PADDER
PADDERS
PADDIES
PADDING
PADDINGS
PADDLE
PADDLED
PADDLER
PADDLERS
PADDLES
PADDLING
PADDLINGS
PADDOCK
PADDOCKS
PADDY
PADELLA
PADELLAS
PADEMELON
PADEMELONS
PADERERO
PADEREROES
PADEREROS
PADISHAH
PADISHAHS
PADLE
PADLES
PADLOCK
PADLOCKED
PADLOCKING
PADLOCKS
PADMA
PADMAS
PADOUK
PADOUKS
PADRE
PADRES
PADRONE
PADRONI
PADS
PADSAW
PADSAWS
PADUASOY
PADUASOYS
PADYMELON
PADYMELONS
PAEAN
PAEANS
PAEDERAST
PAEDERASTS
PAEDEUTIC
PAEDEUTICS
PAEDIATRIES
PAEDIATRY
PAEDOLOGIES
PAEDOLOGY
PAELLA
PAELLAS
PAENULA
PAENULAE
PAENULAS
PAEON
PAEONIC
PAEONICS
PAEONIES
PAEONS
PAEONY
PAGAN
PAGANISE
PAGANISED
PAGANISES
PAGANISH
PAGANISING
PAGANISM
PAGANISMS
PAGANIZE
PAGANIZED
PAGANIZES
PAGANIZING
PAGANS
PAGE
PAGEANT
PAGEANTRIES
PAGEANTRY
PAGEANTS
PAGED
PAGEHOOD
PAGEHOODS
PAGER
PAGERS
PAGES
PAGINAL
PAGINATE
PAGINATED
PAGINATES
PAGINATING
PAGING
PAGINGS
PAGLE
PAGLES
PAGOD
PAGODA
PAGODAS
PAGODS
PAGRI
PAGRIS
PAGURIAN
PAGURIANS
PAGURID
PAGURIDS
PAH
PAHOEHOE
PAHOEHOES
PAHS
PAID
PAIDEUTIC
PAIDEUTICS
PAIDLE
PAIDLES
PAIGLE
PAIGLES
PAIK
PAIKED
PAIKING
PAIKS
PAIL
PAILFUL
PAILFULS
PAILLASSE
PAILLASSES
PAILLETTE
PAILLETTES
PAILLON
PAILLONS
PAILS
PAIN
PAINED
PAINFUL
PAINFULLER
PAINFULLEST
PAINFULLY
PAINIM
PAINIMS
PAINING
PAINLESS
PAINS
PAINT
PAINTABLE
PAINTBALL
PAINTBALLS
PAINTED
PAINTER
PAINTERLY
PAINTERS
PAINTIER
PAINTIEST
PAINTING
PAINTINGS
PAINTRESS
PAINTRESSES
PAINTS
PAINTURE
PAINTURES
PAINTY
PAIOCK
PAIOCKE
PAIOCKES
PAIOCKS
PAIR
PAIRE
PAIRED
PAIRES
PAIRIAL
PAIRIALS
PAIRING
PAIRINGS
PAIRS
PAIRWISE

PAIS
PAISA
PAISANO
PAISANOS
PAISAS
PAISE
PAISLEY
PAISLEYS
PAITRICK
PAITRICKS
PAJAMAS
PAJOCK
PAJOCKE
PAJOCKES
PAJOCKS
PAKAPOO
PAKAPOOS
PAKEHA
PAKEHAS
PAKFONG
PAKFONGS
PAKKA
PAKORA
PAKORAS
PAKTONG
PAKTONGS
PAL
PALABRA
PALABRAS
PALACE
PALACES
PALADIN
PALADINS
PALAESTRA
PALAESTRAE
PALAESTRAS
PALAFITTE
PALAFITTES
PALAGI
PALAGIS
PALAMA
PALAMAE
PALAMATE
PALAMINO
PALAMINOS
PALAMPORE
PALAMPORES
PALANKEEN
PALANKEENS
PALANQUIN
PALANQUINS
PALAS
PALASES
PALATABLE
PALATABLY
PALATAL
PALATALS
PALATE
PALATED
PALATES
PALATIAL
PALATINE
PALATINES
PALATING
PALAVER
PALAVERED
PALAVERER
PALAVERERS
PALAVERING
PALAVERS
PALAY
PALAYS
PALAZZI
PALAZZO
PALE
PALEA
PALEAE
PALEBUCK
PALEBUCKS
PALED
PALEFACE
PALEFACES
PALELY
PALEMPORE
PALEMPORES
PALENESS
PALENESSES
PALER
PALES
PALEST
PALESTRA
PALESTRAE
PALESTRAS
PALET
PALETOT
PALETOTS
PALETS
PALETTE
PALETTES
PALEWISE
PALFREY
PALFREYED
PALFREYS
PALIER
PALIEST
PALIFORM
PALILALIA
PALILALIAS
PALILLOGIES
PALILLOGY
PALIMONIES
PALIMONY
PALING
PALINGS
PALINODE
PALINODES
PALINODIES
PALINODY
PALISADE
PALISADED
PALISADES
PALISADING
PALISADO
PALISADOED
PALISADOES
PALISADOING
PALISH
PALKEE
PALKEES
PALKI
PALKIS
PALL
PALLA
PALLADIC
PALLADIUM
PALLADIUMS
PALLADOUS
PALLAE
PALLAH
PALLAHS
PALLED
PALLET
PALLETED
PALLETISE
PALLETISED
PALLETISES
PALLETISING
PALLETIZE
PALLETIZED
PALLETIZES
PALLETIZING
PALLETS
PALLIA
PALLIAL
PALLIARD
PALLIARDS
PALLIASSE
PALLIASSES
PALLIATE
PALLIATED
PALLIATES
PALLIATING
PALLID
PALLIDER
PALLIDEST
PALLIDITIES
PALLIDITY
PALLIDLY
PALLIER
PALLIEST
PALLING
PALLIUM
PALLONE
PALLONES
PALLOR
PALLORS
PALLS
PALLY
PALM
PALMAR
PALMARIAN
PALMARY
PALMATE
PALMATED
PALMATELY
PALMATION
PALMATIONS
PALMED
PALMER
PALMERS
PALMETTE
PALMETTES
PALMETTO
PALMETTOES
PALMETTOS
PALMFUL
PALMFULS
PALMHOUSE
PALMHOUSES
PALMIE
PALMIER
PALMIES
PALMIEST
PALMIET
PALMIETS
PALMING
PALMIPED
PALMIPEDE
PALMIPEDES
PALMIPEDS
PALMIST
PALMISTRIES
PALMISTRY
PALMISTS
PALMITATE
PALMITATES
PALMITIN
PALMITINS
PALMS
PALMTOP
PALMTOPS
PALMY
PALMYRA
PALMYRAS
PALOLO
PALOLOS
PALOMINO
PALOMINOS
PALOOKA
PALOOKAS
PALP
PALPABLE
PALPABLY
PALPAL
PALPATE
PALPATED
PALPATES
PALPATING
PALPATION
PALPATIONS
PALPEBRAL
PALPED
PALPI
PALPING
PALPITANT
PALPITATE
PALPITATED
PALPITATES
PALPITATING
PALPS
PALPUS
PALS
PALSGRAVE
PALSGRAVES
PALSIED
PALSIER
PALSIES
PALSIEST
PALSTAFF
PALSTAFFS
PALSTAVE
PALSTAVES
PALSY
PALSYING
PALTER
PALTERED
PALTERER
PALTERERS
PALTERING
PALTERS
PALTRIER
PALTRIEST
PALTRILY
PALTRY
PALUDAL
PALUDIC
PALUDINAL
PALUDINE
PALUDISM
PALUDISMS
PALUDOSE
PALUDOUS
PALUSTRAL
PALY
PAM
PAMPA
PAMPAS
PAMPASES
PAMPEAN
PAMPER
PAMPERED
PAMPERER
PAMPERERS
PAMPERING
PAMPERO
PAMPEROS
PAMPERS
PAMPHLET
PAMPHLETS
PAMS
PAN
PANACEA
PANACEAN
PANACEAS
PANACHAEA
PANACHAEAS
PANACHE
PANACHES
PANADA
PANADAS
PANAMA
PANAMAS
PANARIES
PANARY
PANATELLA
PANATELLAS
PANAX
PANAXES
PANCAKE
PANCAKED

PANCAKES
PANCAKING
PANCE
PANCES
PANCHAX
PANCHAXES
PANCHAYAT
PANCHAYATS
PANCHEON
PANCHEONS
PANCHION
PANCHIONS
PANCOSMIC
PANCRATIC
PANCREAS
PANCREASES
PAND
PANDA
PANDAR
PANDARED
PANDARING
PANDARS
PANDAS
PANDATION
PANDATIONS
PANDECT
PANDECTS
PANDEMIA
PANDEMIAN
PANDEMIAS
PANDEMIC
PANDEMICS
PANDER
PANDERED
PANDERESS
PANDERESSES
PANDERING
PANDERISM
PANDERISMS
PANDERLY
PANDEROUS
PANDERS
PANDIED
PANDIES
PANDIT
PANDITS
PANDOOR
PANDOORS
PANDORA
PANDORAS
PANDORE
PANDORES
PANDOUR
PANDOURS
PANDOWDIES
PANDOWDY
PANDS
PANDURA
PANDURAS
PANDURATE
PANDY
PANDYING
PANE
PANED
PANEGOISM
PANEGOISMS
PANEGYRIC
PANEGYRICS
PANEGYRIES
PANEGYRY
PANEITIES
PANEITY
PANEL
PANELLED
PANELLING
PANELLINGS
PANELLIST
PANELLISTS
PANELS
PANES
PANETTONE
PANETTONI
PANFUL
PANFULS
PANG
PANGA
PANGAMIC
PANGAMIES
PANGAMY
PANGAS
PANGED
PANGEN
PANGENE
PANGENES
PANGENS
PANGING
PANGLESS
PANGOLIN
PANGOLINS
PANGRAM
PANGRAMS
PANGS
PANHANDLE
PANHANDLED
PANHANDLES
PANHANDLING
PANIC
PANICK
PANICKED
PANICKIER
PANICKIEST
PANICKING
PANICKS
PANICKY
PANICLE
PANICLED
PANICLES
PANICS
PANIM
PANIMS
PANING
PANISC
PANISCS
PANISK
PANISKS
PANISLAM
PANISLAMS
PANLOGISM
PANLOGISMS
PANMICTIC
PANMIXIA
PANMIXIAS
PANMIXIS
PANMIXISES
PANNAGE
PANNAGES
PANNE
PANNED
PANNELLED
PANNES
PANNICK
PANNICKS
PANNICLE
PANNICLES
PANNIER
PANNIERED
PANNIERS
PANNIKEL
PANNIKELL
PANNIKELLS
PANNIKELS
PANNIKIN
PANNIKINS
PANNING
PANNINGS
PANNOSE
PANNUS
PANNUSES
PANOCHA
PANOCHAS
PANOISTIC
PANOPLIED
PANOPLIES
PANOPLY
PANOPTIC
PANORAMA
PANORAMAS
PANORAMIC
PANS
PANSEXUAL
PANSIED
PANSIES
PANSOPHIC
PANSOPHIES
PANSOPHY
PANSPERMIES
PANSPERMY
PANSY
PANT
PANTABLE
PANTABLES
PANTAGAMIES
PANTAGAMY
PANTALEON
PANTALEONS
PANTALETS
PANTALON
PANTALONS
PANTALOON
PANTALOONS
PANTED
PANTER
PANTERS
PANTHEISM
PANTHEISMS
PANTHEIST
PANTHEISTS
PANTHENOL
PANTHENOLS
PANTHER
PANTHERS
PANTIES
PANTIHOSE
PANTILE
PANTILED
PANTILES
PANTILING
PANTILINGS
PANTINE
PANTINES
PANTING
PANTINGLY
PANTINGS
PANTLER
PANTLERS
PANTO
PANTOFFLE
PANTOFFLES
PANTOFLE
PANTOFLES
PANTOMIME
PANTOMIMES
PANTON
PANTONS
PANTOS
PANTOUFLE
PANTOUFLES
PANTOUM
PANTOUMS
PANTRIES
PANTRY
PANTRYMAN
PANTRYMEN
PANTS
PANTUN
PANTUNS
PANZER
PANZERS
PAOLI
PAOLO
PAP
PAPA
PAPABLE
PAPACIES
PAPACY
PAPAIN
PAPAINS
PAPAL
PAPALISE
PAPALISED
PAPALISES
PAPALISING
PAPALISM
PAPALISMS
PAPALIST
PAPALISTS
PAPALIZE
PAPALIZED
PAPALIZES
PAPALIZING
PAPALLY
PAPARAZZI
PAPARAZZO
PAPAS
PAPAW
PAPAWS
PAPAYA
PAPAYAS
PAPE
PAPER
PAPERBACK
PAPERBACKED
PAPERBACKING
PAPERBACKS
PAPERED
PAPERER
PAPERERS
PAPERIER
PAPERIEST
PAPERING
PAPERINGS
PAPERLESS
PAPERS
PAPERWARE
PAPERWARES
PAPERWORK
PAPERWORKS
PAPERY
PAPES
PAPETERIE
PAPETERIES
PAPILIO
PAPILIOS
PAPILLA
PAPILLAE
PAPILLAR
PAPILLARY
PAPILLATE
PAPILLOMA
PAPILLOMAS
PAPILLOMATA
PAPILLON
PAPILLONS
PAPILLOSE
PAPILLOTE
PAPILLOTES
PAPILLOUS
PAPILLULE
PAPILLULES
PAPISH
PAPISHER
PAPISHERS
PAPISHES
PAPISM
PAPISMS
PAPIST
PAPISTIC
PAPISTRIES
PAPISTRY
PAPISTS

PAPOOSE
PAPOOSES
PAPPADOM
PAPPADOMS
PAPPED
PAPPIER
PAPPIES
PAPPIEST
PAPPING
PAPPOOSE
PAPPOOSES
PAPPOSE
PAPPOUS
PAPPUS
PAPPUSES
PAPPY
PAPRIKA
PAPRIKAS
PAPS
PAPULA
PAPULAE
PAPULAR
PAPULE
PAPULES
PAPULOSE
PAPULOUS
PAPYRI
PAPYRUS
PAR
PARA
PARABASES
PARABASIS
PARABEMA
PARABEMATA
PARABLE
PARABLED
PARABLES
PARABLING
PARABOLA
PARABOLAS
PARABOLE
PARABOLES
PARABOLIC
PARABRAKE
PARABRAKES
PARACHUTE
PARACHUTED
PARACHUTES
PARACHUTING
PARACLETE
PARACLETES
PARACME
PARACMES
PARACUSES
PARACUSIS
PARADE
PARADED
PARADES
PARADIGM
PARADIGMS
PARADING
PARADISAL
PARADISE
PARADISES
PARADISIC
PARADOR
PARADORES
PARADOS
PARADOSES
PARADOX
PARADOXAL
PARADOXER
PARADOXERS
PARADOXES
PARADOXIES
PARADOXY
PARADROP
PARADROPS
PARAFFIN
PARAFFINE
PARAFFINED
PARAFFINES
PARAFFINING
PARAFFINS
PARAFFINY
PARAFFLE
PARAFFLES
PARAFLE
PARAFLES
PARAFOIL
PARAFOILS
PARAGE
PARAGES
PARAGOGE
PARAGOGES
PARAGOGIC
PARAGOGUE
PARAGOGUES
PARAGON
PARAGONED
PARAGONING
PARAGONS
PARAGRAM
PARAGRAMS
PARAGRAPH
PARAGRAPHED
PARAGRAPHING
PARAGRAPHS
PARAKEET
PARAKEETS
PARALALIA
PARALALIAS
PARALEGAL
PARALEGALS
PARALEXIA
PARALEXIAS
PARALLAX
PARALLAXES
PARALLEL
PARALLELED
PARALLELING
PARALLELINGS
PARALLELS
PARALOGIA
PARALOGIAS
PARALOGIES
PARALOGY
PARALYSE
PARALYSED
PARALYSER
PARALYSERS
PARALYSES
PARALYSING
PARALYSIS
PARALYTIC
PARALYTICS
PARALYZE
PARALYZED
PARALYZER
PARALYZERS
PARALYZES
PARALYZING
PARAMATTA
PARAMATTAS
PARAMECIA
PARAMEDIC
PARAMEDICS
PARAMENT
PARAMENTS
PARAMESE
PARAMESES
PARAMETER
PARAMETERS
PARAMO
PARAMORPH
PARAMORPHS
PARAMOS
PARAMOUNT
PARAMOUNTS
PARAMOUR
PARAMOURS
PARANETE
PARANETES
PARANG
PARANGS
PARANOEA
PARANOEAS
PARANOEIC
PARANOEICS
PARANOIA
PARANOIAC
PARANOIACS
PARANOIAS
PARANOIC
PARANOICS
PARANOID
PARANYM
PARANYMPH
PARANYMPHS
PARANYMS
PARAPET
PARAPETED
PARAPETS
PARAPH
PARAPHED
PARAPHING
PARAPHS
PARAPODIA
PARAQUITO
PARAQUITOS
PARARHYME
PARARHYMES
PARAS
PARASANG
PARASANGS
PARASCEVE
PARASCEVES
PARASITE
PARASITES
PARASITIC
PARASOL
PARASOLS
PARATAXES
PARATAXIS
PARATHA
PARATHAS
PARATONIC
PARAVAIL
PARAVANE
PARAVANES
PARAVANT
PARAVAUNT
PARAZOA
PARAZOAN
PARAZOANS
PARAZOON
PARBOIL
PARBOILED
PARBOILING
PARBOILS
PARBREAK
PARBREAKED
PARBREAKING
PARBREAKS
PARBUCKLE
PARBUCKLED
PARBUCKLES
PARBUCKLING
PARCEL
PARCELLED
PARCELLING
PARCELS
PARCENARIES
PARCENARY
PARCENER
PARCENERS
PARCH
PARCHED
PARCHEDLY
PARCHEESI
PARCHEESIS
PARCHES
PARCHESI
PARCHESIS
PARCHING
PARCHMENT
PARCHMENTS
PARCIMONIES
PARCIMONY
PARCLOSE
PARCLOSES
PARD
PARDAL
PARDALE
PARDALES
PARDALIS
PARDALISES
PARDALS
PARDED
PARDI
PARDIE
PARDINE
PARDNER
PARDNERS
PARDON
PARDONED
PARDONER
PARDONERS
PARDONING
PARDONINGS
PARDONS
PARDS
PARDY
PARE
PARECIOUS
PARED
PAREGORIC
PAREGORICS
PAREIRA
PAREIRAS
PARELLA
PARELLAS
PARELLE
PARELLES
PARENESES
PARENESIS
PARENT
PARENTAGE
PARENTAGES
PARENTAL
PARENTED
PARENTING
PARENTINGS
PARENTS
PAREO
PAREOS
PARER
PARERGA
PARERGON
PARERS
PARES
PARESES
PARESIS
PARETIC
PAREU
PAREUS
PARFAIT
PARFAITS
PARFLECHE
PARFLECHES
PARGANA
PARGANAS
PARGASITE
PARGASITES
PARGE
PARGED
PARGES
PARGET
PARGETED
PARGETER

PARGETERS
PARGETING
PARGETINGS
PARGETS
PARGETTED
PARGETTING
PARGETTINGS
PARGING
PARHELIA
PARHELIC
PARHELION
PARHYPATE
PARHYPATES
PARIAH
PARIAHS
PARIAL
PARIALS
PARIETAL
PARIETALS
PARING
PARINGS
PARISCHAN
PARISCHANS
PARISH
PARISHEN
PARISHENS
PARISHES
PARISON
PARISONS
PARITIES
PARITOR
PARITORS
PARITY
PARK
PARKA
PARKAS
PARKED
PARKEE
PARKEES
PARKER
PARKERS
PARKI
PARKIE
PARKIER
PARKIES
PARKIEST
PARKIN
PARKING
PARKINGS
PARKINS
PARKIS
PARKISH
PARKLAND
PARKLANDS
PARKLIKE
PARKLY
PARKS
PARKWARD
PARKWARDS
PARKWAY
PARKWAYS
PARKY
PARLANCE
PARLANCES
PARLANDO
PARLAY
PARLAYED
PARLAYING
PARLAYS
PARLE
PARLED
PARLES
PARLEY
PARLEYED
PARLEYING
PARLEYS
PARLEYVOO
PARLEYVOOED
PARLEYVOOING
PARLEYVOOS
PARLIES
PARLING
PARLOR
PARLORS
PARLOUR
PARLOURS
PARLOUS
PARLY
PAROCHIAL
PAROCHIN
PAROCHINE
PAROCHINES
PAROCHINS
PARODIC
PARODICAL
PARODIED
PARODIES
PARODIST
PARODISTS
PARODY
PARODYING
PAROEMIA
PAROEMIAC
PAROEMIACS
PAROEMIAL
PAROEMIAS
PAROICOUS
PAROL
PAROLE
PAROLED
PAROLEE
PAROLEES
PAROLES
PAROLING
PARONYM
PARONYMIES
PARONYMS
PARONYMY
PAROQUET
PAROQUETS
PAROTIC
PAROTID
PAROTIDS
PAROTIS
PAROTISES
PAROTITIS
PAROTITISES
PAROUSIA
PAROUSIAS
PAROXYSM
PAROXYSMS
PARP
PARPANE
PARPANES
PARPED
PARPEN
PARPEND
PARPENDS
PARPENS
PARPENT
PARPENTS
PARPING
PARPOINT
PARPOINTS
PARPS
PARQUET
PARQUETED
PARQUETING
PARQUETRIES
PARQUETRY
PARQUETS
PARQUETTED
PARQUETTING
PARR
PARRAKEET
PARRAKEETS
PARRAL
PARRALS
PARREL
PARRELS
PARRHESIA
PARRHESIAS
PARRICIDE
PARRICIDES
PARRIED
PARRIES
PARRITCH
PARRITCHES
PARROCK
PARROCKED
PARROCKING
PARROCKS
PARROQUET
PARROQUETS
PARROT
PARROTED
PARROTER
PARROTERS
PARROTING
PARROTRIES
PARROTRY
PARROTS
PARROTY
PARRS
PARRY
PARRYING
PARS
PARSE
PARSEC
PARSECS
PARSED
PARSER
PARSERS
PARSES
PARSIMONIES
PARSIMONY
PARSING
PARSINGS
PARSLEY
PARSLEYS
PARSNEP
PARSNEPS
PARSNIP
PARSNIPS
PARSON
PARSONAGE
PARSONAGES
PARSONIC
PARSONISH
PARSONS
PART
PARTAKE
PARTAKEN
PARTAKER
PARTAKERS
PARTAKES
PARTAKING
PARTAKINGS
PARTAN
PARTANS
PARTED
PARTER
PARTERRE
PARTERRES
PARTERS
PARTI
PARTIAL
PARTIALLY
PARTIALS
PARTIBLE
PARTICLE
PARTICLES
PARTIED
PARTIES
PARTIM
PARTING
PARTINGS
PARTIS
PARTISAN
PARTISANS
PARTITA
PARTITAS
PARTITE
PARTITION
PARTITIONED
PARTITIONING
PARTITIONS
PARTITIVE
PARTITIVES
PARTITURA
PARTITURAS
PARTIZAN
PARTIZANS
PARTLET
PARTLETS
PARTLY
PARTNER
PARTNERED
PARTNERING
PARTNERS
PARTON
PARTONS
PARTOOK
PARTRIDGE
PARTRIDGES
PARTS
PARTURE
PARTURES
PARTWORK
PARTWORKS
PARTY
PARTYGOER
PARTYGOERS
PARTYING
PARTYISM
PARTYISMS
PARULIS
PARULISES
PARURE
PARURES
PARVENU
PARVENUS
PARVIS
PARVISE
PARVISES
PAS
PASCAL
PASCALS
PASCHAL
PASCUAL
PASEAR
PASEARED
PASEARING
PASEARS
PASEO
PASEOS
PASH
PASHA
PASHALIK
PASHALIKS
PASHAS
PASHED
PASHES
PASHIM
PASHIMS
PASHING
PASHM
PASHMINA
PASHMINAS
PASHMS
PASPALUM
PASPALUMS
PASPIES
PASPY
PASQUILER
PASQUILERS
PASS
PASSABLE
PASSABLY
PASSADE

PASSADES
PASSADO
PASSADOES
PASSADOS
PASSAGE
PASSAGED
PASSAGES
PASSAGING
PASSAMENT
PASSAMENTED
PASSAMENTING
PASSAMENTS
PASSANT
PASSATA
PASSATAS
PASSE
PASSED
PASSEE
PASSEMENT
PASSEMENTED
PASSEMENTING
PASSEMENTS
PASSENGER
PASSENGERS
PASSEPIED
PASSEPIEDS
PASSER
PASSERINE
PASSERINES
PASSERS
PASSES
PASSIBLE
PASSIBLY
PASSIM
PASSING
PASSINGS
PASSION
PASSIONAL
PASSIONALS
PASSIONED
PASSIONING
PASSIONS
PASSIVATE
PASSIVATED
PASSIVATES
PASSIVATING
PASSIVE
PASSIVELY
PASSIVES
PASSIVISM
PASSIVISMS
PASSIVIST
PASSIVISTS
PASSIVITIES
PASSIVITY
PASSKEY
PASSKEYS
PASSLESS
PASSMAN
PASSMEN
PASSMENT
PASSMENTED
PASSMENTING
PASSMENTS
PASSOUT
PASSOUTS
PASSPORT
PASSPORTS
PASSUS
PASSUSES
PASSWORD
PASSWORDS
PAST
PASTA
PASTANCE
PASTANCES
PASTAS
PASTE
PASTED
PASTEL
PASTELS
PASTER
PASTERN
PASTERNS
PASTERS
PASTES
PASTICCI
PASTICCIO
PASTICHE
PASTICHES
PASTIER
PASTIES
PASTIEST
PASTIL
PASTILLE
PASTILLES
PASTILS
PASTIME
PASTIMES
PASTINESS
PASTINESSES
PASTING
PASTINGS
PASTIS
PASTISES
PASTOR
PASTORAL
PASTORALE
PASTORALES
PASTORALI
PASTORALS
PASTORATE
PASTORATES
PASTORLY
PASTORS
PASTRAMI
PASTRAMIS
PASTRIES
PASTRY
PASTS
PASTURAGE
PASTURAGES
PASTURAL
PASTURE
PASTURED
PASTURES
PASTURING
PASTY
PAT
PATACA
PATACAS
PATAGIA
PATAGIAL
PATAGIUM
PATAMAR
PATAMARS
PATBALL
PATBALLS
PATCH
PATCHABLE
PATCHED
PATCHER
PATCHERIES
PATCHERS
PATCHERY
PATCHES
PATCHIER
PATCHIEST
PATCHILY
PATCHING
PATCHINGS
PATCHOCKE
PATCHOCKES
PATCHOULI
PATCHOULIES
PATCHOULIS
PATCHOULY
PATCHWORK
PATCHWORKS
PATCHY
PATE
PATED
PATELLA
PATELLAE
PATELLAR
PATELLAS
PATELLATE
PATEN
PATENCIES
PATENCY
PATENS
PATENT
PATENTED
PATENTEE
PATENTEES
PATENTING
PATENTLY
PATENTOR
PATENTORS
PATENTS
PATER
PATERA
PATERAE
PATERCOVE
PATERCOVES
PATERERO
PATEREROES
PATEREROS
PATERNAL
PATERNITIES
PATERNITY
PATERS
PATES
PATH
PATHED
PATHETIC
PATHETICS
PATHIC
PATHICS
PATHING
PATHLESS
PATHOGEN
PATHOGENIES
PATHOGENS
PATHOGENY
PATHOLOGIES
PATHOLOGY
PATHOS
PATHOSES
PATHS
PATHWAY
PATHWAYS
PATIBLE
PATIENCE
PATIENCES
PATIENT
PATIENTED
PATIENTER
PATIENTEST
PATIENTING
PATIENTLY
PATIENTS
PATIN
PATINA
PATINAS
PATINATED
PATINE
PATINED
PATINES
PATINS
PATIO
PATIOS
PATLY
PATNESS
PATNESSES
PATOIS
PATONCE
PATRIAL
PATRIALS
PATRIARCH
PATRIARCHS
PATRIATE
PATRIATED
PATRIATES
PATRIATING
PATRICIAN
PATRICIANS
PATRICIDE
PATRICIDES
PATRICK
PATRICKS
PATRICO
PATRICOES
PATRILINIES
PATRILINY
PATRIMONIES
PATRIMONY
PATRIOT
PATRIOTIC
PATRIOTS
PATRISTIC
PATRISTICS
PATROL
PATROLLED
PATROLLER
PATROLLERS
PATROLLING
PATROLMAN
PATROLMEN
PATROLOGIES
PATROLOGY
PATROLS
PATRON
PATRONAGE
PATRONAGED
PATRONAGES
PATRONAGING
PATRONAL
PATRONESS
PATRONESSES
PATRONISE
PATRONISED
PATRONISES
PATRONISING
PATRONIZE
PATRONIZED
PATRONIZES
PATRONIZING
PATRONNE
PATRONNES
PATRONS
PATROON
PATROONS
PATS
PATSIES
PATSY
PATTE
PATTED
PATTEE
PATTEN
PATTENED
PATTENING
PATTENS
PATTER
PATTERED
PATTERER
PATTERERS
PATTERING
PATTERN
PATTERNED
PATTERNING
PATTERNS
PATTERS
PATTES
PATTIES
PATTING
PATTLE
PATTLES
PATTY
PATULIN

PATULINS
PATULOUS
PATZER
PATZERS
PAUA
PAUAS
PAUCITIES
PAUCITY
PAUGHTIER
PAUGHTIEST
PAUGHTY
PAUL
PAULDRON
PAULDRONS
PAULOWNIA
PAULOWNIAS
PAULS
PAUNCE
PAUNCES
PAUNCH
PAUNCHED
PAUNCHES
PAUNCHIER
PAUNCHIEST
PAUNCHING
PAUNCHY
PAUPER
PAUPERESS
PAUPERESSES
PAUPERISE
PAUPERISED
PAUPERISES
PAUPERISING
PAUPERISM
PAUPERISMS
PAUPERIZE
PAUPERIZED
PAUPERIZES
PAUPERIZING
PAUPERS
PAUSAL
PAUSE
PAUSED
PAUSEFUL
PAUSELESS
PAUSER
PAUSERS
PAUSES
PAUSING
PAUSINGLY
PAUSINGS
PAVAGE
PAVAGES
PAVAN
PAVANE
PAVANES
PAVANS
PAVE
PAVED
PAVEMENT
PAVEMENTED
PAVEMENTING
PAVEMENTS
PAVEN
PAVENS
PAVER
PAVERS
PAVES
PAVID
PAVILION
PAVILIONED
PAVILIONING
PAVILIONS
PAVIN
PAVING
PAVINGS
PAVINS
PAVIOR
PAVIORS
PAVIOUR
PAVIOURS
PAVIS
PAVISE
PAVISES
PAVLOVA
PAVLOVAS
PAVONAZZO
PAVONAZZOS
PAVONE
PAVONES
PAVONIAN
PAVONINE
PAW
PAWA
PAWAS
PAWAW
PAWAWED
PAWAWING
PAWAWS
PAWED
PAWING
PAWK
PAWKIER
PAWKIEST
PAWKILY
PAWKINESS
PAWKINESSES
PAWKS
PAWKY
PAWL
PAWLS
PAWN
PAWNCE
PAWNCES
PAWNED
PAWNEE
PAWNEES
PAWNER
PAWNERS
PAWNING
PAWNS
PAWNSHOP
PAWNSHOPS
PAWPAW
PAWPAWS
PAWS
PAX
PAXES
PAXIUBA
PAXIUBAS
PAXWAX
PAXWAXES
PAY
PAYABLE
PAYBACK
PAYBACKS
PAYED
PAYEE
PAYEES
PAYER
PAYERS
PAYFONE
PAYFONES
PAYING
PAYINGS
PAYMASTER
PAYMASTERS
PAYMENT
PAYMENTS
PAYNIM
PAYNIMRIES
PAYNIMRY
PAYNIMS
PAYOLA
PAYOLAS
PAYROLL
PAYROLLS
PAYS
PAYSAGE
PAYSAGES
PAYSAGIST
PAYSAGISTS
PAYSD
PAYSLIP
PAYSLIPS
PAZAZZ
PAZAZZES
PEA
PEABERRIES
PEABERRY
PEACE
PEACEABLE
PEACEABLY
PEACED
PEACEFUL
PEACELESS
PEACENIK
PEACENIKS
PEACES
PEACETIME
PEACETIMES
PEACH
PEACHED
PEACHER
PEACHERS
PEACHES
PEACHIER
PEACHIEST
PEACHING
PEACHY
PEACING
PEACOCK
PEACOCKED
PEACOCKING
PEACOCKS
PEACOCKY
PEACOD
PEACODS
PEAFOWL
PEAFOWLS
PEAG
PEAGS
PEAK
PEAKED
PEAKIER
PEAKIEST
PEAKING
PEAKS
PEAKY
PEAL
PEALED
PEALING
PEALS
PEAN
PEANED
PEANING
PEANS
PEANUT
PEANUTS
PEAPOD
PEAPODS
PEAR
PEARCE
PEARCED
PEARCES
PEARCING
PEARE
PEARES
PEARL
PEARLED
PEARLER
PEARLERS
PEARLIER
PEARLIES
PEARLIEST
PEARLIN
PEARLING
PEARLINGS
PEARLINS
PEARLISED
PEARLITE
PEARLITES
PEARLITIC
PEARLIZED
PEARLS
PEARLWORT
PEARLWORTS
PEARLY
PEARMAIN
PEARMAINS
PEARS
PEARST
PEART
PEARTER
PEARTEST
PEARTLY
PEAS
PEASANT
PEASANTRIES
PEASANTRY
PEASANTS
PEASANTY
PEASCOD
PEASCODS
PEASE
PEASECOD
PEASECODS
PEASED
PEASES
PEASEWEEP
PEASEWEEPS
PEASING
PEASON
PEAT
PEATARIES
PEATARY
PEATERIES
PEATERY
PEATIER
PEATIEST
PEATMAN
PEATMEN
PEATS
PEATSHIP
PEATSHIPS
PEATY
PEAVEY
PEAVEYS
PEAVIES
PEAVY
PEAZE
PEAZED
PEAZES
PEAZING
PEBA
PEBAS
PEBBLE
PEBBLED
PEBBLES
PEBBLIER
PEBBLIEST
PEBBLING
PEBBLINGS
PEBBLY
PEBRINE
PEBRINES
PEC
PECAN
PECANS
PECCABLE
PECCANCIES
PECCANCY
PECCANT
PECCANTLY
PECCARIES
PECCARY
PECCAVI
PECCAVIS
PECH
PECHED

PECHING
PECHS
PECK
PECKE
PECKED
PECKER
PECKERS
PECKES
PECKING
PECKINGS
PECKISH
PECKS
PECS
PECTEN
PECTIC
PECTIN
PECTINAL
PECTINATE
PECTINEAL
PECTINES
PECTINS
PECTISE
PECTISED
PECTISES
PECTISING
PECTIZE
PECTIZED
PECTIZES
PECTIZING
PECTOLITE
PECTOLITES
PECTORAL
PECTORALS
PECTOSE
PECTOSES
PECULATE
PECULATED
PECULATES
PECULATING
PECULATOR
PECULATORS
PECULIA
PECULIAR
PECULIARS
PECULIUM
PECUNIARY
PECUNIOUS
PED
PEDAGOGIC
PEDAGOGICS
PEDAGOGIES
PEDAGOGUE
PEDAGOGUED
PEDAGOGUES
PEDAGOGUING
PEDAGOGY
PEDAL
PEDALED
PEDALIER
PEDALIERS
PEDALING
PEDALLED
PEDALLER
PEDALLERS
PEDALLING
PEDALLINGS
PEDALO
PEDALOES
PEDALOS
PEDALS
PEDANT
PEDANTIC
PEDANTISE
PEDANTISED
PEDANTISES
PEDANTISING
PEDANTISM
PEDANTISMS
PEDANTIZE
PEDANTIZED
PEDANTIZES
PEDANTIZING
PEDANTRIES
PEDANTRY
PEDANTS
PEDATE
PEDATELY
PEDATIFID
PEDDER
PEDDERS
PEDDLE
PEDDLED
PEDDLER
PEDDLERS
PEDDLES
PEDDLING
PEDDLINGS
PEDERAST
PEDERASTIES
PEDERASTS
PEDERASTY
PEDERERO
PEDEREROES
PEDEREROS
PEDESES
PEDESIS
PEDESTAL
PEDESTALLED
PEDESTALLING
PEDESTALS
PEDETIC
PEDICAB
PEDICABS
PEDICEL
PEDICELS
PEDICLE
PEDICLED
PEDICLES
PEDICULAR
PEDICULI
PEDICULUS
PEDICURE
PEDICURED
PEDICURES
PEDICURING
PEDIGREE
PEDIGREED
PEDIGREES
PEDIMENT
PEDIMENTS
PEDIPALP
PEDIPALPI
PEDIPALPS
PEDLAR
PEDLARIES
PEDLARS
PEDLARY
PEDOLOGIES
PEDOLOGY
PEDOMETER
PEDOMETERS
PEDRAIL
PEDRAILS
PEDRERO
PEDREROES
PEDREROS
PEDRO
PEDROS
PEDS
PEDUNCLE
PEDUNCLES
PEE
PEECE
PEECES
PEED
PEEING
PEEK
PEEKABO
PEEKABOO
PEEKABOOS
PEEKABOS
PEEKED
PEEKING
PEEKS
PEEL
PEELED
PEELER
PEELERS
PEELING
PEELINGS
PEELS
PEEN
PEENED
PEENGE
PEENGED
PEENGEING
PEENGES
PEENGING
PEENING
PEENS
PEEOY
PEEOYS
PEEP
PEEPE
PEEPED
PEEPER
PEEPERS
PEEPES
PEEPING
PEEPS
PEEPUL
PEEPULS
PEER
PEERAGE
PEERAGES
PEERED
PEERESS
PEERESSES
PEERIE
PEERIER
PEERIES
PEERIEST
PEERING
PEERLESS
PEERS
PEERY
PEES
PEESWEEP
PEESWEEPS
PEETWEET
PEETWEETS
PEEVE
PEEVED
PEEVER
PEEVERS
PEEVES
PEEVING
PEEVISH
PEEVISHLY
PEEWEE
PEEWEES
PEEWIT
PEEWITS
PEG
PEGASUS
PEGASUSES
PEGBOARD
PEGBOARDS
PEGGED
PEGGIES
PEGGING
PEGGINGS
PEGGY
PEGH
PEGHED
PEGHING
PEGHS
PEGMATITE
PEGMATITES
PEGS
PEIGNOIR
PEIGNOIRS
PEIN
PEINCT
PEINCTED
PEINCTING
PEINCTS
PEINED
PEINING
PEINS
PEIRASTIC
PEISE
PEISED
PEISES
PEISHWA
PEISHWAH
PEISHWAHS
PEISHWAS
PEISING
PEIZE
PEIZED
PEIZES
PEIZING
PEJORATE
PEJORATED
PEJORATES
PEJORATING
PEKAN
PEKANS
PEKE
PEKES
PEKOE
PEKOES
PELA
PELAGE
PELAGES
PELAGIAN
PELAGIANS
PELAGIC
PELAS
PELE
PELERINE
PELERINES
PELES
PELF
PELFS
PELHAM
PELHAMS
PELICAN
PELICANS
PELISSE
PELISSES
PELITE
PELITES
PELITIC
PELL
PELLACH
PELLACHS
PELLACK
PELLACKS
PELLAGRA
PELLAGRAS
PELLAGRIN
PELLAGRINS
PELLET
PELLETED
PELLETIFIED
PELLETIFIES
PELLETIFY
PELLETIFYING
PELLETING
PELLETISE
PELLETISED
PELLETISES
PELLETISING
PELLETIZE
PELLETIZED
PELLETIZES
PELLETIZING
PELLETS

PELLICLE
PELLICLES
PELLITORIES
PELLITORY
PELLOCK
PELLOCKS
PELLS
PELLUCID
PELMA
PELMANISM
PELMANISMS
PELMAS
PELMATIC
PELMET
PELMETS
PELOID
PELOIDS
PELOLOGIES
PELOLOGY
PELORIA
PELORIAS
PELORIC
PELORIES
PELORISED
PELORISM
PELORISMS
PELORIZED
PELORUS
PELORUSES
PELORY
PELOTA
PELOTAS
PELT
PELTA
PELTAE
PELTAS
PELTAST
PELTASTS
PELTATE
PELTED
PELTER
PELTERED
PELTERING
PELTERS
PELTING
PELTINGLY
PELTINGS
PELTRIES
PELTRY
PELTS
PELVES
PELVIC
PELVIFORM
PELVIS
PELVISES
PEMBROKE
PEMBROKES
PEMICAN
PEMICANS
PEMMICAN
PEMMICANS
PEMOLINE
PEMOLINES
PEMPHIGUS
PEMPHIGUSES
PEN
PENAL
PENALISE
PENALISED
PENALISES
PENALISING
PENALIZE
PENALIZED
PENALIZES
PENALIZING
PENALLY
PENALTIES
PENALTY
PENANCE
PENANCED
PENANCES
PENANCING
PENATES
PENCE
PENCEL
PENCELS
PENCES
PENCHANT
PENCHANTS
PENCIL
PENCILLED
PENCILLER
PENCILLERS
PENCILLING
PENCILLINGS
PENCILS
PENCRAFT
PENCRAFTS
PEND
PENDANT
PENDANTS
PENDED
PENDENCIES
PENDENCY
PENDENT
PENDENTLY
PENDENTS
PENDICLE
PENDICLER
PENDICLERS
PENDICLES
PENDING
PENDRAGON
PENDRAGONS
PENDS
PENDULAR
PENDULATE
PENDULATED
PENDULATES
PENDULATING
PENDULINE
PENDULOUS
PENDULUM
PENDULUMS
PENE
PENED
PENEPLAIN
PENEPLAINS
PENEPLANE
PENEPLANES
PENES
PENETRANT
PENETRANTS
PENETRATE
PENETRATED
PENETRATES
PENETRATING
PENFOLD
PENFOLDS
PENFUL
PENFULS
PENGUIN
PENGUINRIES
PENGUINRY
PENGUINS
PENHOLDER
PENHOLDERS
PENI
PENIAL
PENIE
PENIES
PENILE
PENILLION
PENING
PENINSULA
PENINSULAS
PENIS
PENISES
PENISTONE
PENISTONES
PENITENCE
PENITENCES
PENITENCIES
PENITENCY
PENITENT
PENITENTS
PENK
PENKNIFE
PENKNIVES
PENKS
PENLIGHT
PENLIGHTS
PENMAN
PENMEN
PENNA
PENNAE
PENNAL
PENNALISM
PENNALISMS
PENNALS
PENNANT
PENNANTS
PENNATE
PENNATULA
PENNATULAE
PENNATULAS
PENNE
PENNED
PENNEECH
PENNEECHS
PENNEECK
PENNEECKS
PENNER
PENNERS
PENNES
PENNIED
PENNIES
PENNIFORM
PENNILESS
PENNILL
PENNINE
PENNINES
PENNING
PENNINITE
PENNINITES
PENNON
PENNONCEL
PENNONCELS
PENNONED
PENNONS
PENNY
PENNYFEE
PENNYFEES
PENNYLAND
PENNYLANDS
PENOLOGIES
PENOLOGY
PENONCEL
PENONCELS
PENS
PENSEE
PENSEES
PENSEL
PENSELS
PENSIL
PENSILE
PENSILITIES
PENSILITY
PENSILS
PENSION
PENSIONED
PENSIONER
PENSIONERS
PENSIONING
PENSIONS
PENSIVE
PENSIVELY
PENSTEMON
PENSTEMONS
PENSTOCK
PENSTOCKS
PENSUM
PENSUMS
PENT
PENTACLE
PENTACLES
PENTACT
PENTACTS
PENTAD
PENTADIC
PENTADS
PENTAGON
PENTAGONS
PENTAGRAM
PENTAGRAMS
PENTALOGIES
PENTALOGY
PENTALPHA
PENTALPHAS
PENTAMERIES
PENTAMERY
PENTANE
PENTANES
PENTANGLE
PENTANGLES
PENTAPODIES
PENTAPODY
PENTARCH
PENTARCHIES
PENTARCHS
PENTARCHY
PENTATHLA
PENTEL®
PENTELS
PENTENE
PENTENES
PENTHIA
PENTHIAS
PENTHOUSE
PENTHOUSED
PENTHOUSES
PENTHOUSING
PENTICE
PENTICED
PENTICES
PENTICING
PENTISE
PENTISED
PENTISES
PENTISING
PENTODE
PENTODES
PENTOMIC
PENTOSAN
PENTOSANE
PENTOSANES
PENTOSANS
PENTOSE
PENTOSES
PENTOXIDE
PENTOXIDES
PENTROOF
PENTROOFS
PENTS
PENTYLENE
PENTYLENES
PENUCHE
PENUCHES
PENUCHI
PENUCHIS
PENUCHLE
PENUCHLES
PENULT
PENULTIMA
PENULTIMAS
PENULTS
PENUMBRA
PENUMBRAL
PENUMBRAS
PENURIES

PENURIOUS
PENURY
PENWOMAN
PENWOMEN
PEON
PEONAGE
PEONAGES
PEONIES
PEONISM
PEONISMS
PEONS
PEONY
PEOPLE
PEOPLED
PEOPLES
PEOPLING
PEP
PEPERINO
PEPERINOS
PEPEROMIA
PEPEROMIAS
PEPERONI
PEPERONIS
PEPFUL
PEPINO
PEPINOS
PEPLA
PEPLOS
PEPLOSES
PEPLUM
PEPLUMS
PEPLUS
PEPLUSES
PEPO
PEPOS
PEPPED
PEPPER
PEPPERED
PEPPERER
PEPPERERS
PEPPERIER
PEPPERIEST
PEPPERING
PEPPERINGS
PEPPERONI
PEPPERONIS
PEPPERS
PEPPERY
PEPPIER
PEPPIEST
PEPPING
PEPPY
PEPS
PEPSIN
PEPSINATE
PEPSINATED
PEPSINATES
PEPSINATING
PEPSINE
PEPSINES
PEPSINS
PEPTIC
PEPTICITIES
PEPTICITY
PEPTICS
PEPTIDASE
PEPTIDASES
PEPTIDE
PEPTIDES
PEPTISE
PEPTISED
PEPTISES
PEPTISING
PEPTIZE
PEPTIZED
PEPTIZES
PEPTIZING
PEPTONE
PEPTONES
PEPTONISE
PEPTONISED
PEPTONISES
PEPTONISING
PEPTONIZE
PEPTONIZED
PEPTONIZES
PEPTONIZING
PER
PERACUTE
PERAEA
PERAEON
PERAEONS
PERAEOPOD
PERAEOPODS
PERAI
PERAIS
PERCALE
PERCALES
PERCALINE
PERCALINES
PERCASE
PERCE
PERCEABLE
PERCEANT
PERCED
PERCEIVE
PERCEIVED
PERCEIVER
PERCEIVERS
PERCEIVES
PERCEIVING
PERCEIVINGS
PERCEN
PERCENTAL
PERCEPT
PERCEPTS
PERCES
PERCH
PERCHANCE
PERCHED
PERCHER
PERCHERON
PERCHERONS
PERCHERS
PERCHERY
PERCHES
PERCHING
PERCHINGS
PERCIFORM
PERCINE
PERCING
PERCOCT
PERCOID
PERCOLATE
PERCOLATED
PERCOLATES
PERCOLATING
PERCOLIN
PERCOLINS
PERCUSS
PERCUSSED
PERCUSSES
PERCUSSING
PERCUSSOR
PERCUSSORS
PERDENDO
PERDIE
PERDITION
PERDITIONS
PERDU
PERDUE
PERDUES
PERDURE
PERDURED
PERDURES
PERDURING
PERDUS
PERDY
PERE
PEREGAL
PEREGALS
PEREGRINE
PEREGRINES
PEREIA
PEREION
PEREIOPOD
PEREIOPODS
PEREIRA
PEREIRAS
PERENNATE
PERENNATED
PERENNATES
PERENNATING
PERENNIAL
PERENNIALS
PERENNITIES
PERENNITY
PERES
PERFAY
PERFECT
PERFECTA
PERFECTAS
PERFECTED
PERFECTER
PERFECTERS
PERFECTEST
PERFECTI
PERFECTING
PERFECTLY
PERFECTO
PERFECTOR
PERFECTORS
PERFECTOS
PERFECTS
PERFERVID
PERFERVOR
PERFERVORS
PERFET
PERFIDIES
PERFIDY
PERFORANS
PERFORANSES
PERFORANT
PERFORATE
PERFORATED
PERFORATES
PERFORATING
PERFORCE
PERFORM
PERFORMED
PERFORMER
PERFORMERS
PERFORMING
PERFORMINGS
PERFORMS
PERFUME
PERFUMED
PERFUMER
PERFUMERIES
PERFUMERS
PERFUMERY
PERFUMES
PERFUMING
PERFUMY
PERFUSATE
PERFUSATES
PERFUSE
PERFUSED
PERFUSES
PERFUSING
PERFUSION
PERFUSIONS
PERFUSIVE
PERGOLA
PERGOLAS
PERGUNNAH
PERGUNNAHS
PERHAPS
PERI
PERIAGUA
PERIAGUAS
PERIAKTOI
PERIAKTOS
PERIANTH
PERIANTHS
PERIAPT
PERIAPTS
PERIBLAST
PERIBLASTS
PERIBLEM
PERIBLEMS
PERIBOLI
PERIBOLOI
PERIBOLOS
PERIBOLUS
PERICARP
PERICARPS
PERICLASE
PERICLASES
PERICLINE
PERICLINES
PERICON
PERICONES
PERICOPE
PERICOPES
PERICRANIES
PERICRANY
PERICYCLE
PERICYCLES
PERIDERM
PERIDERMS
PERIDIA
PERIDIAL
PERIDINIA
PERIDIUM
PERIDIUMS
PERIDOT
PERIDOTE
PERIDOTES
PERIDOTIC
PERIDOTS
PERIDROME
PERIDROMES
PERIGEAL
PERIGEAN
PERIGEE
PERIGEES
PERIGON
PERIGONE
PERIGONES
PERIGONIA
PERIGONS
PERIGYNIES
PERIGYNY
PERIHELIA
PERIKARYA
PERIL
PERILLED
PERILLING
PERILOUS
PERILS
PERILUNE
PERILUNES
PERILYMPH
PERILYMPHS
PERIMETER
PERIMETERS
PERIMETRIES
PERIMETRY
PERIMORPH
PERIMORPHS
PERINAEUM
PERINAEUMS
PERINATAL
PERINEA
PERINEAL
PERINEUM
PERINEUMS
PERIOD
PERIODATE

PERIODATES
PERIODED
PERIODIC
PERIODING
PERIODS
PERIOST
PERIOSTEA
PERIOSTS
PERIOTIC
PERIOTICS
PERIPATUS
PERIPATUSES
PERIPETIA
PERIPETIAS
PERIPETIES
PERIPETY
PERIPHERIES
PERIPHERY
PERIPLAST
PERIPLASTS
PERIPLUS
PERIPLUSES
PERIPROCT
PERIPROCTS
PERIPTERIES
PERIPTERY
PERIQUE
PERIQUES
PERIS
PERISARC
PERISARCS
PERISCIAN
PERISCIANS
PERISCOPE
PERISCOPES
PERISH
PERISHED
PERISHER
PERISHERS
PERISHES
PERISHING
PERISPERM
PERISPERMS
PERISTOME
PERISTOMES
PERISTYLE
PERISTYLES
PERITI
PERITONEA
PERITRICH
PERITRICHA
PERITUS
PERIWIG
PERIWIGGED
PERIWIGGING
PERIWIGS
PERJINK
PERJURE
PERJURED
PERJURER
PERJURERS
PERJURES
PERJURIES
PERJURING
PERJUROUS
PERJURY
PERK
PERKED
PERKIER
PERKIEST
PERKILY
PERKIN
PERKINESS
PERKINESSES
PERKING
PERKINS
PERKS
PERKY
PERLITE
PERLITES
PERLITIC
PERLOUS
PERM
PERMALLOY
PERMALLOYS
PERMANENT
PERMEABLE
PERMEABLY
PERMEANCE
PERMEANCES
PERMEASE
PERMEASES
PERMEATE
PERMEATED
PERMEATES
PERMEATING
PERMED
PERMING
PERMIT
PERMITS
PERMITTED
PERMITTER
PERMITTERS
PERMITTING
PERMS
PERMUTATE
PERMUTATED
PERMUTATES
PERMUTATING
PERMUTE
PERMUTED
PERMUTES
PERMUTING
PERN
PERNANCIES
PERNANCY
PERNS
PERONE
PERONEAL
PERONES
PERONEUS
PERONEUSES
PERORATE
PERORATED
PERORATES
PERORATING
PEROVSKIA
PEROVSKIAS
PEROXIDE
PEROXIDED
PEROXIDES
PEROXIDING
PERPEND
PERPENDED
PERPENDING
PERPENDS
PERPENT
PERPENTS
PERPETUAL
PERPETUALS
PERPLEX
PERPLEXED
PERPLEXES
PERPLEXING
PERRADIAL
PERRADII
PERRADIUS
PERRIER
PERRIERS
PERRIES
PERRON
PERRONS
PERRUQUE
PERRUQUES
PERRY
PERSANT
PERSAUNT
PERSE
PERSECUTE
PERSECUTED
PERSECUTES
PERSECUTING
PERSEITIES
PERSEITY
PERSELINE
PERSELINES
PERSES
PERSEVERE
PERSEVERED
PERSEVERES
PERSEVERING
PERSICO
PERSICOS
PERSICOT
PERSICOTS
PERSIENNE
PERSIENNES
PERSIMMON
PERSIMMONS
PERSING
PERSIST
PERSISTED
PERSISTING
PERSISTS
PERSON
PERSONA
PERSONAE
PERSONAGE
PERSONAGES
PERSONAL
PERSONAS
PERSONATE
PERSONATED
PERSONATES
PERSONATING
PERSONATINGS
PERSONIFIED
PERSONIFIES
PERSONIFY
PERSONIFYING
PERSONISE
PERSONISED
PERSONISES
PERSONISING
PERSONIZE
PERSONIZED
PERSONIZES
PERSONIZING
PERSONNEL
PERSONNELS
PERSONS
PERSPIRE
PERSPIRED
PERSPIRES
PERSPIRING
PERST
PERSUADE
PERSUADED
PERSUADER
PERSUADERS
PERSUADES
PERSUADING
PERSUE
PERSUED
PERSUES
PERSUING
PERSWADE
PERSWADED
PERSWADES
PERSWADING
PERT
PERTAIN
PERTAINED
PERTAINING
PERTAINS
PERTAKE
PERTAKEN
PERTAKES
PERTAKING
PERTER
PERTEST
PERTHITE
PERTHITES
PERTHITIC
PERTINENT
PERTINENTS
PERTLY
PERTNESS
PERTNESSES
PERTOOK
PERTS
PERTURB
PERTURBED
PERTURBER
PERTURBERS
PERTURBING
PERTURBS
PERTUSATE
PERTUSE
PERTUSED
PERTUSION
PERTUSIONS
PERTUSSAL
PERTUSSIS
PERTUSSISES
PERUKE
PERUKED
PERUKES
PERUSAL
PERUSALS
PERUSE
PERUSED
PERUSER
PERUSERS
PERUSES
PERUSING
PERV
PERVADE
PERVADED
PERVADES
PERVADING
PERVASION
PERVASIONS
PERVASIVE
PERVE
PERVED
PERVERSE
PERVERSER
PERVERSEST
PERVERT
PERVERTED
PERVERTER
PERVERTERS
PERVERTING
PERVERTS
PERVES
PERVIATE
PERVIATED
PERVIATES
PERVIATING
PERVICACIES
PERVICACY
PERVING
PERVIOUS
PERVS
PESADE
PESADES
PESANT
PESANTE
PESANTS
PESAUNT
PESAUNTS
PESETA
PESETAS
PESEWA
PESEWAS
PESHWA
PESHWAS
PESKIER
PESKIEST

PESKILY
PESKY
PESO
PESOS
PESSARIES
PESSARY
PESSIMA
PESSIMAL
PESSIMISM
PESSIMISMS
PESSIMIST
PESSIMISTS
PESSIMUM
PEST
PESTER
PESTERED
PESTERER
PESTERERS
PESTERING
PESTEROUS
PESTERS
PESTFUL
PESTHOUSE
PESTHOUSES
PESTICIDE
PESTICIDES
PESTILENT
PESTLE
PESTLED
PESTLES
PESTLING
PESTO
PESTOLOGIES
PESTOLOGY
PESTOS
PESTS
PET
PETAL
PETALINE
PETALISM
PETALISMS
PETALLED
PETALODIES
PETALODY
PETALOID
PETALOUS
PETALS
PETANQUE
PETANQUES
PETAR
PETARA
PETARAS
PETARD
PETARDS
PETARIES
PETARS
PETARY
PETASUS
PETASUSES
PETAURINE
PETAURIST
PETAURISTS
PETCHARIES
PETCHARY
PETCOCK
PETCOCKS
PETECHIA
PETECHIAE
PETECHIAL
PETER
PETERED
PETERING
PETERMAN
PETERMEN
PETERS
PETERSHAM
PETERSHAMS
PETHER
PETHERS
PETHIDINE
PETHIDINES
PETILLANT
PETIOLAR
PETIOLATE
PETIOLE
PETIOLED
PETIOLES
PETIOLULE
PETIOLULES
PETIT
PETITE
PETITION
PETITIONED
PETITIONING
PETITIONINGS
PETITIONS
PETITORY
PETRARIES
PETRARY
PETRE
PETREL
PETRELS
PETRES
PETRIFIC
PETRIFIED
PETRIFIES
PETRIFY
PETRIFYING
PETROGRAM
PETROGRAMS
PETROL
PETROLAGE
PETROLAGES
PETROLEUM
PETROLEUMS
PETROLEUR
PETROLEURS
PETROLIC
PETROLLED
PETROLLING
PETROLOGIES
PETROLOGY
PETROLS
PETRONEL
PETRONELS
PETROSAL
PETROSALS
PETROUS
PETS
PETTED
PETTEDLY
PETTER
PETTERS
PETTICOAT
PETTICOATS
PETTIER
PETTIES
PETTIEST
PETTIFOG
PETTIFOGGED
PETTIFOGGING
PETTIFOGGINGS
PETTIFOGS
PETTILY
PETTINESS
PETTINESSES
PETTING
PETTINGS
PETTISH
PETTISHLY
PETTITOES
PETTLE
PETTLED
PETTLES
PETTLING
PETTY
PETULANCE
PETULANCES
PETULANCIES
PETULANCY
PETULANT
PETUNIA
PETUNIAS
PETUNTSE
PETUNTSES
PETUNTZE
PETUNTZES
PEW
PEWIT
PEWITS
PEWS
PEWTER
PEWTERER
PEWTERERS
PEWTERS
PEYOTE
PEYOTES
PEYOTISM
PEYOTISMS
PEYOTIST
PEYOTISTS
PEYSE
PEYSED
PEYSES
PEYSING
PEZANT
PEZANTS
PEZIZOID
PFENNIG
PFENNIGE
PFENNIGS
PFENNING
PFENNINGS
PH
PHACELIA
PHACELIAS
PHACOID
PHACOIDAL
PHACOLITE
PHACOLITES
PHACOLITH
PHACOLITHS
PHAEIC
PHAEISM
PHAEISMS
PHAENOGAM
PHAENOGAMS
PHAETON
PHAETONS
PHAGE
PHAGEDENA
PHAGEDENAS
PHAGES
PHAGOCYTE
PHAGOCYTES
PHALANGAL
PHALANGE
PHALANGER
PHALANGERS
PHALANGES
PHALANGID
PHALANGIDS
PHALANX
PHALANXES
PHALAROPE
PHALAROPES
PHALLI
PHALLIC
PHALLIN
PHALLINS
PHALLISM
PHALLISMS
PHALLOID
PHALLUS
PHALLUSES
PHANG
PHANGED
PHANGING
PHANGS
PHANSIGAR
PHANSIGARS
PHANTASIED
PHANTASIES
PHANTASIM
PHANTASIMS
PHANTASM
PHANTASMA
PHANTASMATA
PHANTASMS
PHANTASY
PHANTASYING
PHANTOM
PHANTOMS
PHANTOMY
PHANTOSME
PHANTOSMES
PHARAONIC
PHARE
PHARES
PHARISAIC
PHARMACIES
PHARMACY
PHAROS
PHAROSES
PHARYNGAL
PHARYNGES
PHARYNX
PHARYNXES
PHASE
PHASED
PHASELESS
PHASEOLIN
PHASEOLINS
PHASES
PHASIC
PHASING
PHASIS
PHASMID
PHASMIDS
PHAT
PHATIC
PHATTER
PHATTEST
PHEASANT
PHEASANTS
PHEAZAR
PHEAZARS
PHEER
PHEERE
PHEERES
PHEERS
PHEESE
PHEESED
PHEESES
PHEESING
PHEEZE
PHEEZED
PHEEZES
PHEEZING
PHELLEM
PHELLEMS
PHELLOGEN
PHELLOGENS
PHELLOID
PHELONION
PHELONIONS
PHENACITE
PHENACITES
PHENAKISM
PHENAKISMS
PHENAKITE
PHENAKITES
PHENATE
PHENATES
PHENE
PHENES
PHENETIC
PHENETICS
PHENGITE
PHENGITES

PHENIC
PHENOGAM
PHENOGAMS
PHENOL
PHENOLATE
PHENOLATES
PHENOLIC
PHENOLOGIES
PHENOLOGY
PHENOLS
PHENOM
PHENOMENA
PHENOMS
PHENOTYPE
PHENOTYPED
PHENOTYPES
PHENOTYPING
PHENYL
PHENYLIC
PHENYLS
PHEON
PHEONS
PHEROMONE
PHEROMONES
PHESE
PHESED
PHESES
PHESING
PHEW
PHI
PHIAL
PHIALLED
PHIALLING
PHIALS
PHILABEG
PHILABEGS
PHILAMOT
PHILAMOTS
PHILANDER
PHILANDERED
PHILANDERING
PHILANDERS
PHILATELIES
PHILATELY
PHILHORSE
PHILHORSES
PHILIBEG
PHILIBEGS
PHILIPPIC
PHILIPPICS
PHILLABEG
PHILLABEGS
PHILLIBEG
PHILLIBEGS
PHILOGYNIES
PHILOGYNY
PHILOLOGIES
PHILOLOGY
PHILOMATH
PHILOMATHS
PHILOMOT
PHILOMOTS
PHILOPENA
PHILOPENAS
PHILTER
PHILTERS
PHILTRE
PHILTRES
PHIMOSES
PHIMOSIS
PHINNOCK
PHINNOCKS
PHIS
PHISNOMIES
PHISNOMY
PHIZ
PHIZOG
PHIZOGS
PHIZZES
PHLEBITIS
PHLEBITISES
PHLEGM
PHLEGMIER
PHLEGMIEST
PHLEGMON
PHLEGMONS
PHLEGMS
PHLEGMY
PHLOEM
PHLOEMS
PHLOMIS
PHLOMISES
PHLOX
PHLOXES
PHLYCTENA
PHLYCTENAE
PHO
PHOBIA
PHOBIAS
PHOBIC
PHOBICS
PHOBISM
PHOBISMS
PHOBIST
PHOBISTS
PHOCA
PHOCAE
PHOCAS
PHOCINE
PHOEBE
PHOEBES
PHOENIX
PHOENIXES
PHOH
PHOHS
PHOLADES
PHOLAS
PHON
PHONAL
PHONATE
PHONATED
PHONATES
PHONATING
PHONATION
PHONATIONS
PHONATORY
PHONE
PHONECARD
PHONECARDS
PHONED
PHONEME
PHONEMES
PHONEMIC
PHONEMICS
PHONER
PHONERS
PHONES
PHONETIC
PHONETICS
PHONETISE
PHONETISED
PHONETISES
PHONETISING
PHONETISM
PHONETISMS
PHONETIST
PHONETISTS
PHONETIZE
PHONETIZED
PHONETIZES
PHONETIZING
PHONEY
PHONEYED
PHONEYING
PHONEYS
PHONIC
PHONICS
PHONIED
PHONIER
PHONIES
PHONIEST
PHONINESS
PHONINESSES
PHONING
PHONMETER
PHONMETERS
PHONOGRAM
PHONOGRAMS
PHONOLITE
PHONOLITES
PHONOLOGIES
PHONOLOGY
PHONON
PHONONS
PHONOPORE
PHONOPORES
PHONOTYPE
PHONOTYPED
PHONOTYPES
PHONOTYPIES
PHONOTYPING
PHONOTYPY
PHONS
PHONY
PHONYING
PHOOEY
PHORMINGES
PHORMINX
PHORMIUM
PHORMIUMS
PHOS
PHOSGENE
PHOSGENES
PHOSPHATE
PHOSPHATED
PHOSPHATES
PHOSPHATING
PHOSPHENE
PHOSPHENES
PHOSPHIDE
PHOSPHIDES
PHOSPHINE
PHOSPHINES
PHOSPHITE
PHOSPHITES
PHOSPHOR
PHOSPHORS
PHOT
PHOTIC
PHOTICS
PHOTINIA
PHOTINIAS
PHOTISM
PHOTISMS
PHOTO
PHOTOCELL
PHOTOCELLS
PHOTOCOPIED
PHOTOCOPIES
PHOTOCOPY
PHOTOCOPYING
PHOTOCOPYINGS
PHOTOED
PHOTOFIT
PHOTOFITS
PHOTOGEN
PHOTOGENE
PHOTOGENES
PHOTOGENIES
PHOTOGENS
PHOTOGENY
PHOTOGRAM
PHOTOGRAMS
PHOTOING
PHOTOLYSE
PHOTOLYSED
PHOTOLYSES
PHOTOLYSING
PHOTON
PHOTONICS
PHOTONS
PHOTOPHIL
PHOTOPHILS
PHOTOPIA
PHOTOPIAS
PHOTOPIC
PHOTOPSIA
PHOTOPSIAS
PHOTOPSIES
PHOTOPSY
PHOTOS
PHOTOTYPE
PHOTOTYPED
PHOTOTYPES
PHOTOTYPIES
PHOTOTYPING
PHOTOTYPY
PHOTS
PHRASAL
PHRASE
PHRASED
PHRASEMAN
PHRASEMEN
PHRASER
PHRASERS
PHRASES
PHRASIER
PHRASIEST
PHRASING
PHRASINGS
PHRASY
PHRATRIES
PHRATRY
PHREAK
PHREAKING
PHREAKINGS
PHREAKS
PHREATIC
PHRENESES
PHRENESIS
PHRENETIC
PHRENETICS
PHRENIC
PHRENISM
PHRENISMS
PHRENITIC
PHRENITIS
PHRENITISES
PHRENSIED
PHRENSIES
PHRENSY
PHRENSYING
PHRENTICK
PHS
PHTHALATE
PHTHALATES
PHTHALEIN
PHTHALEINS
PHTHALIC
PHTHALIN
PHTHALINS
PHTHISES
PHTHISIC
PHTHISICS
PHTHISIS
PHUT
PHUTS
PHUTTED
PHUTTING
PHYCOCYAN
PHYCOCYANS
PHYCOLOGIES
PHYCOLOGY
PHYLA
PHYLAE
PHYLARCH
PHYLARCHIES
PHYLARCHS
PHYLARCHY
PHYLE

PHYLETIC
PHYLLARIES
PHYLLARY
PHYLLITE
PHYLLITES
PHYLLO
PHYLLODE
PHYLLODES
PHYLLODIES
PHYLLODY
PHYLLOID
PHYLLOME
PHYLLOMES
PHYLLOPOD
PHYLLOPODS
PHYLLOS
PHYLOGENIES
PHYLOGENY
PHYLUM
PHYSALIA
PHYSALIAS
PHYSALIS
PHYSALISES
PHYSETER
PHYSETERS
PHYSIC
PHYSICAL
PHYSICALS
PHYSICIAN
PHYSICIANS
PHYSICISM
PHYSICISMS
PHYSICIST
PHYSICISTS
PHYSICKED
PHYSICKING
PHYSICKY
PHYSICS
PHYSIO
PHYSIOS
PHYSIQUE
PHYSIQUES
PHYTOGENIES
PHYTOGENY
PHYTOLOGIES
PHYTOLOGY
PHYTON
PHYTONS
PHYTOSES
PHYTOSIS
PHYTOTOMIES
PHYTOTOMY
PHYTOTRON
PHYTOTRONS
PI
PIA
PIACEVOLE
PIACULAR
PIAFFE
PIAFFED
PIAFFER
PIAFFERS
PIAFFES
PIAFFING
PIANETTE
PIANETTES
PIANINO
PIANINOS
PIANISM
PIANISMS
PIANIST
PIANISTE
PIANISTES
PIANISTIC
PIANISTS
PIANO
PIANOLIST
PIANOLISTS
PIANOS
PIARIST
PIARISTS
PIAS
PIASSABA
PIASSABAS
PIASSAVA
PIASSAVAS
PIASTRE
PIASTRES
PIAZZA
PIAZZAS
PIAZZIAN
PIBROCH
PIBROCHS
PIC
PICA
PICADOR
PICADORS
PICAMAR
PICAMARS
PICARIAN
PICARIANS
PICAROON
PICAROONS
PICAS
PICAYUNE
PICAYUNES
PICCADELL
PICCADELLS
PICCADILL
PICCADILLS
PICCANIN
PICCANINS
PICCIES
PICCOLO
PICCOLOS
PICCY
PICE
PICENE
PICENES
PICEOUS
PICHURIM
PICHURIMS
PICINE
PICK
PICKABACK
PICKABACKS
PICKADELL
PICKADELLS
PICKADILL
PICKADILLS
PICKAPACK
PICKAPACKS
PICKAXE
PICKAXES
PICKBACK
PICKBACKS
PICKED
PICKEER
PICKEERED
PICKEERER
PICKEERERS
PICKEERING
PICKEERS
PICKER
PICKEREL
PICKERELS
PICKERIES
PICKERS
PICKERY
PICKET
PICKETED
PICKETER
PICKETERS
PICKETING
PICKETS
PICKIER
PICKIEST
PICKING
PICKINGS
PICKLE
PICKLED
PICKLER
PICKLERS
PICKLES
PICKLING
PICKLOCK
PICKLOCKS
PICKMAW
PICKMAWS
PICKS
PICKY
PICNIC
PICNICKED
PICNICKER
PICNICKERS
PICNICKING
PICNICKY
PICNICS
PICOCURIE
PICOCURIES
PICOT
PICOTE
PICOTED
PICOTEE
PICOTEES
PICOTING
PICOTITE
PICOTITES
PICOTS
PICQUET
PICQUETED
PICQUETING
PICQUETS
PICRA
PICRAS
PICRATE
PICRATES
PICRIC
PICRITE
PICRITES
PICS
PICTARNIE
PICTARNIES
PICTOGRAM
PICTOGRAMS
PICTORIAL
PICTORIALS
PICTURAL
PICTURALS
PICTURE
PICTURED
PICTURES
PICTURING
PICUL
PICULS
PIDDLE
PIDDLED
PIDDLER
PIDDLERS
PIDDLES
PIDDLING
PIDDOCK
PIDDOCKS
PIDGEON
PIDGEONS
PIDGIN
PIDGINS
PIE
PIEBALD
PIEBALDS
PIECE
PIECED
PIECELESS
PIECEMEAL
PIECEMEALED
PIECEMEALING
PIECEMEALS
PIECEN
PIECENED
PIECENER
PIECENERS
PIECENING
PIECENS
PIECER
PIECERS
PIECES
PIECING
PIECRUST
PIECRUSTS
PIED
PIEDISH
PIEDISHES
PIEDMONT
PIEDMONTS
PIEDNESS
PIEDNESSES
PIEING
PIEMAN
PIEMEN
PIEND
PIENDS
PIEPOWDER
PIEPOWDERS
PIER
PIERAGE
PIERAGES
PIERCE
PIERCED
PIERCER
PIERCERS
PIERCES
PIERCING
PIERCINGS
PIERID
PIERIDINE
PIERIDS
PIERRETTE
PIERRETTES
PIERROT
PIERROTS
PIERS
PIERST
PIERT
PIES
PIET
PIETA
PIETAS
PIETIES
PIETISM
PIETISMS
PIETIST
PIETISTIC
PIETISTS
PIETS
PIETY
PIEZO
PIFFERARI
PIFFERARO
PIFFERO
PIFFEROS
PIFFLE
PIFFLED
PIFFLER
PIFFLERS
PIFFLES
PIFFLING
PIG
PIGBOAT
PIGBOATS
PIGEON
PIGEONED
PIGEONING
PIGEONRIES
PIGEONRY
PIGEONS
PIGFEED
PIGFEEDS
PIGGED
PIGGERIES
PIGGERY

PIGGIE
PIGGIER
PIGGIES
PIGGIEST
PIGGIN
PIGGING
PIGGINGS
PIGGINS
PIGGISH
PIGGISHLY
PIGGY
PIGGYBACK
PIGGYBACKS
PIGHEADED
PIGHT
PIGHTED
PIGHTING
PIGHTLE
PIGHTLES
PIGHTS
PIGLET
PIGLETS
PIGLING
PIGLINGS
PIGMAEAN
PIGMEAN
PIGMEAT
PIGMEATS
PIGMENT
PIGMENTAL
PIGMENTED
PIGMENTS
PIGMIES
PIGMOID
PIGMY
PIGNERATE
PIGNERATED
PIGNERATES
PIGNERATING
PIGNORATE
PIGNORATED
PIGNORATES
PIGNORATING
PIGNUT
PIGNUTS
PIGPEN
PIGPENS
PIGS
PIGSCONCE
PIGSCONCES
PIGSKIN
PIGSKINS
PIGSNEY
PIGSNEYS
PIGSNIE
PIGSNIES
PIGSNY
PIGSTIES
PIGSTY
PIGSWILL
PIGSWILLS
PIGTAIL
PIGTAILS
PIGWASH
PIGWASHES
PIGWEED
PIGWEEDS
PIKA
PIKAS
PIKE
PIKED
PIKELET
PIKELETS
PIKEMAN
PIKEMEN
PIKER
PIKERS
PIKES
PIKESTAFF
PIKESTAFFS
PIKING
PIKUL
PIKULS
PILA
PILAFF
PILAFFS
PILASTER
PILASTERS
PILAU
PILAUS
PILAW
PILAWS
PILCH
PILCHARD
PILCHARDS
PILCHER
PILCHERS
PILCHES
PILCORN
PILCORNS
PILCROW
PILCROWS
PILE
PILEA
PILEATE
PILEATED
PILED
PILEI
PILEOUS
PILER
PILERS
PILES
PILEUM
PILEUS
PILEWORK
PILEWORKS
PILEWORT
PILEWORTS
PILFER
PILFERAGE
PILFERAGES
PILFERED
PILFERER
PILFERERS
PILFERIES
PILFERING
PILFERINGS
PILFERS
PILFERY
PILGRIM
PILGRIMER
PILGRIMERS
PILGRIMS
PILHORSE
PILHORSES
PILI
PILIFORM
PILING
PILINGS
PILIS
PILL
PILLAGE
PILLAGED
PILLAGER
PILLAGERS
PILLAGES
PILLAGING
PILLAR
PILLARIST
PILLARISTS
PILLARS
PILLAU
PILLAUS
PILLED
PILLHEAD
PILLHEADS
PILLICOCK
PILLICOCKS
PILLING
PILLINGS
PILLION
PILLIONED
PILLIONING
PILLIONS
PILLOCK
PILLOCKS
PILLORIED
PILLORIES
PILLORISE
PILLORISED
PILLORISES
PILLORISING
PILLORIZE
PILLORIZED
PILLORIZES
PILLORIZING
PILLORY
PILLORYING
PILLOW
PILLOWED
PILLOWING
PILLOWS
PILLOWY
PILLS
PILLWORM
PILLWORMS
PILLWORT
PILLWORTS
PILOSE
PILOSITIES
PILOSITY
PILOT
PILOTAGE
PILOTAGES
PILOTED
PILOTING
PILOTIS
PILOTLESS
PILOTMAN
PILOTMEN
PILOTS
PILOUS
PILOW
PILOWS
PILSENER
PILSENERS
PILSNER
PILSNERS
PILULA
PILULAR
PILULAS
PILULE
PILULES
PILUM
PILUS
PIMENT
PIMENTO
PIMENTOS
PIMENTS
PIMIENTO
PIMIENTOS
PIMP
PIMPED
PIMPERNEL
PIMPERNELS
PIMPING
PIMPLE
PIMPLED
PIMPLES
PIMPLIER
PIMPLIEST
PIMPLY
PIMPS
PIN
PINA
PINACOID
PINACOIDS
PINAFORE
PINAFORED
PINAFORES
PINAKOID
PINAKOIDS
PINAS
PINASTER
PINASTERS
PINATA
PINATAS
PINBALL
PINBALLS
PINCASE
PINCASES
PINCER
PINCERED
PINCERING
PINCERS
PINCH
PINCHBECK
PINCHBECKS
PINCHCOCK
PINCHCOCKS
PINCHED
PINCHER
PINCHERS
PINCHES
PINCHFIST
PINCHFISTS
PINCHGUT
PINCHGUTS
PINCHING
PINCHINGS
PINDAREE
PINDAREES
PINDARI
PINDARIS
PINDER
PINDERS
PINDOWN
PINDOWNS
PINE
PINEAL
PINEAPPLE
PINEAPPLES
PINED
PINERIES
PINERY
PINES
PINETA
PINETUM
PINEWOOD
PINEWOODS
PINEY
PINFISH
PINFISHES
PINFOLD
PINFOLDED
PINFOLDING
PINFOLDS
PING
PINGED
PINGER
PINGERS
PINGING
PINGLE
PINGLED
PINGLER
PINGLERS
PINGLES
PINGLING
PINGO
PINGOES
PINGOS
PINGS
PINGUEFIED
PINGUEFIES
PINGUEFY
PINGUEFYING
PINGUID
PINGUIN
PINGUINS
PINHEAD

PINHEADS
PINHOLE
PINHOLES
PINHOOKER
PINHOOKERS
PINIER
PINIES
PINIEST
PINING
PINION
PINIONED
PINIONING
PINIONS
PINITE
PINITES
PINK
PINKED
PINKER
PINKERTON
PINKERTONS
PINKEST
PINKIE
PINKIER
PINKIES
PINKIEST
PINKINESS
PINKINESSES
PINKING
PINKINGS
PINKISH
PINKNESS
PINKNESSES
PINKO
PINKOES
PINKOS
PINKROOT
PINKROOTS
PINKS
PINKY
PINNA
PINNACE
PINNACES
PINNACLE
PINNACLED
PINNACLES
PINNACLING
PINNAE
PINNATE
PINNATED
PINNATELY
PINNED
PINNER
PINNERS
PINNET
PINNETS
PINNIE
PINNIES
PINNING
PINNINGS
PINNIPED
PINNIPEDE
PINNIPEDES
PINNIPEDS
PINNOCK
PINNOCKS
PINNOED
PINNULA
PINNULAS
PINNULATE
PINNULE
PINNULES
PINNY
PINOCHLE
PINOCHLES
PINOCLE
PINOCLES
PINOLE
PINOLES
PINON
PINONS
PINOT
PINOTS
PINPOINT
PINPOINTED
PINPOINTING
PINPOINTS
PINS
PINT
PINTA
PINTABLE
PINTABLES
PINTADO
PINTADOS
PINTAIL
PINTAILED
PINTAILS
PINTAS
PINTLE
PINTLES
PINTO
PINTOS
PINTS
PINXIT
PINY
PIOLET
PIOLETS
PION
PIONED
PIONEER
PIONEERED
PIONEERING
PIONEERS
PIONER
PIONERS
PIONEY
PIONEYS
PIONIC
PIONIES
PIONING
PIONINGS
PIONS
PIONY
PIOTED
PIOUS
PIOUSLY
PIOY
PIOYE
PIOYES
PIOYS
PIP
PIPA
PIPAGE
PIPAGES
PIPAL
PIPALS
PIPAS
PIPE
PIPECLAY
PIPECLAYED
PIPECLAYING
PIPECLAYS
PIPED
PIPEFISH
PIPEFISHES
PIPEFUL
PIPEFULS
PIPELESS
PIPELIKE
PIPELINE
PIPELINES
PIPER
PIPERIC
PIPERINE
PIPERINES
PIPERONAL
PIPERONALS
PIPERS
PIPES
PIPESTONE
PIPESTONES
PIPETTE
PIPETTED
PIPETTES
PIPETTING
PIPEWORK
PIPEWORKS
PIPEWORT
PIPEWORTS
PIPI
PIPIER
PIPIEST
PIPING
PIPINGS
PIPIS
PIPIT
PIPITS
PIPKIN
PIPKINS
PIPLESS
PIPPED
PIPPIER
PIPPIEST
PIPPIN
PIPPING
PIPPINS
PIPPY
PIPS
PIPSQUEAK
PIPSQUEAKS
PIPUL
PIPULS
PIPY
PIQUANCIES
PIQUANCY
PIQUANT
PIQUANTLY
PIQUE
PIQUED
PIQUES
PIQUET
PIQUETED
PIQUETING
PIQUETS
PIQUING
PIR
PIRACIES
PIRACY
PIRAGUA
PIRAGUAS
PIRAI
PIRAIS
PIRANA
PIRANAS
PIRANHA
PIRANHAS
PIRARUCU
PIRARUCUS
PIRATE
PIRATED
PIRATES
PIRATIC
PIRATICAL
PIRATING
PIRAYA
PIRAYAS
PIRL
PIRLICUE
PIRLICUED
PIRLICUES
PIRLICUING
PIRLS
PIRN
PIRNIE
PIRNIES
PIRNIT
PIRNS
PIROGUE
PIROGUES
PIROSHKI
PIROUETTE
PIROUETTED
PIROUETTES
PIROUETTING
PIROZHKI
PIRS
PIS
PISCARIES
PISCARY
PISCATOR
PISCATORS
PISCATORY
PISCATRIX
PISCATRIXES
PISCIFORM
PISCINA
PISCINAE
PISCINAS
PISCINE
PISCINES
PISE
PISES
PISH
PISHED
PISHES
PISHING
PISHOGUE
PISHOGUES
PISIFORM
PISIFORMS
PISKIES
PISKY
PISMIRE
PISMIRES
PISOLITE
PISOLITES
PISOLITIC
PISS
PISSED
PISSES
PISSHEAD
PISSHEADS
PISSING
PISSOIR
PISSOIRS
PISTACHIO
PISTACHIOS
PISTAREEN
PISTAREENS
PISTE
PISTES
PISTIL
PISTILS
PISTOL
PISTOLE
PISTOLEER
PISTOLEERS
PISTOLES
PISTOLET
PISTOLETS
PISTOLLED
PISTOLLING
PISTOLS
PISTON
PISTONS
PIT
PITA
PITAPAT
PITAPATS
PITAPATTED
PITAPATTING
PITARA
PITARAH
PITARAHS
PITARAS
PITAS
PITCH
PITCHED
PITCHER
PITCHERS
PITCHES

PITCHFORK
PITCHFORKED
PITCHFORKING
PITCHFORKS
PITCHIER
PITCHIEST
PITCHING
PITCHINGS
PITCHMAN
PITCHMEN
PITCHPINE
PITCHPINES
PITCHPIPE
PITCHPIPES
PITCHY
PITEOUS
PITEOUSLY
PITFALL
PITFALLS
PITH
PITHBALL
PITHBALLS
PITHEAD
PITHEADS
PITHECOID
PITHED
PITHFUL
PITHIER
PITHIEST
PITHILY
PITHINESS
PITHINESSES
PITHING
PITHLESS
PITHLIKE
PITHOI
PITHOS
PITHS
PITHY
PITIABLE
PITIABLY
PITIED
PITIER
PITIERS
PITIES
PITIFUL
PITIFULLY
PITILESS
PITMAN
PITMEN
PITON
PITONS
PITPROP
PITPROPS
PITS
PITTA
PITTANCE
PITTANCES
PITTAS
PITTED
PITTEN
PITTER
PITTERED
PITTERING
PITTERS
PITTING
PITTINGS
PITTITE
PITTITES
PITUITA
PITUITARY
PITUITAS
PITUITE
PITUITES
PITUITRIN
PITUITRINS
PITURI
PITURIS
PITY
PITYING
PITYINGLY
PITYROID
PIU
PIUM
PIUMS
PIUPIU
PIUPIUS
PIVOT
PIVOTAL
PIVOTALLY
PIVOTED
PIVOTER
PIVOTERS
PIVOTING
PIVOTINGS
PIVOTS
PIX
PIXEL
PIXELS
PIXES
PIXIE
PIXIES
PIXILATED
PIXY
PIZAZZ
PIZAZZES
PIZE
PIZES
PIZZA
PIZZAIOLA
PIZZAS
PIZZERIA
PIZZERIAS
PIZZICATO
PIZZICATOS
PIZZLE
PIZZLES
PLACABLE
PLACABLY
PLACARD
PLACARDED
PLACARDING
PLACARDS
PLACATE
PLACATED
PLACATES
PLACATING
PLACATION
PLACATIONS
PLACATORY
PLACCAT
PLACCATE
PLACCATES
PLACCATS
PLACE
PLACEBO
PLACEBOES
PLACEBOS
PLACED
PLACELESS
PLACEMAN
PLACEMEN
PLACEMENT
PLACEMENTS
PLACENTA
PLACENTAE
PLACENTAL
PLACENTALS
PLACENTAS
PLACER
PLACERS
PLACES
PLACET
PLACETS
PLACID
PLACIDER
PLACIDEST
PLACIDITIES
PLACIDITY
PLACIDLY
PLACING
PLACINGS
PLACIT
PLACITA
PLACITORY
PLACITS
PLACITUM
PLACK
PLACKET
PLACKETS
PLACKLESS
PLACKS
PLACODERM
PLACODERMS
PLACOID
PLAFOND
PLAFONDS
PLAGAL
PLAGE
PLAGES
PLAGIARIES
PLAGIARY
PLAGIUM
PLAGIUMS
PLAGUE
PLAGUED
PLAGUES
PLAGUEY
PLAGUIER
PLAGUIEST
PLAGUILY
PLAGUING
PLAGUY
PLAICE
PLAICES
PLAID
PLAIDED
PLAIDING
PLAIDINGS
PLAIDMAN
PLAIDMEN
PLAIDS
PLAIN
PLAINANT
PLAINANTS
PLAINED
PLAINER
PLAINEST
PLAINFUL
PLAINING
PLAININGS
PLAINISH
PLAINLY
PLAINNESS
PLAINNESSES
PLAINS
PLAINSMAN
PLAINSMEN
PLAINSONG
PLAINSONGS
PLAINT
PLAINTFUL
PLAINTIFF
PLAINTIFFS
PLAINTIVE
PLAINTS
PLAINWORK
PLAINWORKS
PLAISTER
PLAISTERS
PLAIT
PLAITED
PLAITER
PLAITERS
PLAITING
PLAITINGS
PLAITS
PLAN
PLANAR
PLANARIAN
PLANARIANS
PLANATION
PLANATIONS
PLANCH
PLANCHED
PLANCHES
PLANCHET
PLANCHETS
PLANCHING
PLANE
PLANED
PLANER
PLANERS
PLANES
PLANET
PLANETARY
PLANETIC
PLANETOID
PLANETOIDS
PLANETS
PLANGENCIES
PLANGENCY
PLANGENT
PLANING
PLANISH
PLANISHED
PLANISHER
PLANISHERS
PLANISHES
PLANISHING
PLANK
PLANKED
PLANKING
PLANKINGS
PLANKS
PLANKTON
PLANKTONS
PLANLESS
PLANNED
PLANNER
PLANNERS
PLANNING
PLANS
PLANT
PLANTA
PLANTABLE
PLANTAGE
PLANTAGES
PLANTAIN
PLANTAINS
PLANTAR
PLANTAS
PLANTED
PLANTER
PLANTERS
PLANTING
PLANTINGS
PLANTLESS
PLANTLET
PLANTLETS
PLANTLING
PLANTLINGS
PLANTS
PLANTSMAN
PLANTSMEN
PLANTULE
PLANTULES
PLANULA
PLANULAE
PLANULAR
PLANULOID
PLANURIA
PLANURIAS
PLANURIES
PLANURY
PLANXTIES
PLANXTY
PLAP
PLAPPED
PLAPPING

PLAPS
PLAQUE
PLAQUES
PLAQUETTE
PLAQUETTES
PLASH
PLASHED
PLASHES
PLASHET
PLASHETS
PLASHIER
PLASHIEST
PLASHING
PLASHINGS
PLASHY
PLASM
PLASMA
PLASMAS
PLASMATIC
PLASMIC
PLASMID
PLASMIDS
PLASMIN
PLASMINS
PLASMODIA
PLASMS
PLAST
PLASTE
PLASTER
PLASTERED
PLASTERER
PLASTERERS
PLASTERING
PLASTERINGS
PLASTERS
PLASTERY
PLASTIC
PLASTICKY
PLASTICS
PLASTID
PLASTIDS
PLASTIQUE
PLASTIQUES
PLASTISOL
PLASTISOLS
PLASTRAL
PLASTRON
PLASTRONS
PLAT
PLATAN
PLATANE
PLATANES
PLATANNA
PLATANNAS
PLATANS
PLATBAND
PLATBANDS
PLATE
PLATEASM
PLATEASMS
PLATEAU
PLATEAUED
PLATEAUING
PLATEAUS
PLATEAUX
PLATED
PLATEFUL
PLATEFULS
PLATELET
PLATELETS
PLATEMAN
PLATEMARK
PLATEMARKS
PLATEMEN
PLATEN
PLATENS
PLATER
PLATERS
PLATES
PLATFORM
PLATFORMED
PLATFORMING
PLATFORMINGS
PLATFORMS
PLATIER
PLATIEST
PLATINA
PLATINAS
PLATING
PLATINGS
PLATINIC
PLATINISE
PLATINISED
PLATINISES
PLATINISING
PLATINIZE
PLATINIZED
PLATINIZES
PLATINIZING
PLATINOID
PLATINOIDS
PLATINOUS
PLATINUM
PLATINUMS
PLATITUDE
PLATITUDES
PLATONIC
PLATONICS
PLATOON
PLATOONS
PLATS
PLATTED
PLATTER
PLATTERS
PLATTING
PLATTINGS
PLATY
PLATYPUS
PLATYPUSES
PLATYSMA
PLATYSMAS
PLAUDIT
PLAUDITE
PLAUDITS
PLAUSIBLE
PLAUSIBLY
PLAUSIVE
PLAUSTRAL
PLAY
PLAYA
PLAYABLE
PLAYAS
PLAYBACK
PLAYBACKS
PLAYBILL
PLAYBILLS
PLAYBOOK
PLAYBOOKS
PLAYBOY
PLAYBOYS
PLAYBUS®
PLAYBUSES
PLAYBUSSES
PLAYED
PLAYER
PLAYERS
PLAYFUL
PLAYFULLY
PLAYGIRL
PLAYGIRLS
PLAYGROUP
PLAYGROUPS
PLAYHOUSE
PLAYHOUSES
PLAYING
PLAYLET
PLAYLETS
PLAYMATE
PLAYMATES
PLAYPEN
PLAYPENS
PLAYROOM
PLAYROOMS
PLAYS
PLAYSOME
PLAYSUIT
PLAYSUITS
PLAYTHING
PLAYTHINGS
PLAYTIME
PLAYTIMES
PLAZA
PLAZAS
PLEA
PLEACH
PLEACHED
PLEACHES
PLEACHING
PLEAD
PLEADABLE
PLEADED
PLEADER
PLEADERS
PLEADING
PLEADINGS
PLEADS
PLEAED
PLEAING
PLEAS
PLEASANCE
PLEASANCES
PLEASANT
PLEASANTER
PLEASANTEST
PLEASE
PLEASED
PLEASEMAN
PLEASEMEN
PLEASER
PLEASERS
PLEASES
PLEASETH
PLEASING
PLEASINGS
PLEASURE
PLEASURED
PLEASURER
PLEASURERS
PLEASURES
PLEASURING
PLEAT
PLEATED
PLEATER
PLEATERS
PLEATING
PLEATS
PLEB
PLEBBIER
PLEBBIEST
PLEBBY
PLEBEAN
PLEBEIAN
PLEBEIANS
PLEBES
PLEBIFIED
PLEBIFIES
PLEBIFY
PLEBIFYING
PLEBS
PLECTRA
PLECTRE
PLECTRES
PLECTRON
PLECTRONS
PLECTRUM
PLECTRUMS
PLED
PLEDGE
PLEDGED
PLEDGEE
PLEDGEES
PLEDGEOR
PLEDGEORS
PLEDGER
PLEDGERS
PLEDGES
PLEDGET
PLEDGETS
PLEDGING
PLEDGOR
PLEDGORS
PLEIOMERIES
PLEIOMERY
PLENA
PLENARILY
PLENARTIES
PLENARTY
PLENARY
PLENILUNE
PLENILUNES
PLENIPO
PLENIPOES
PLENIPOS
PLENISH
PLENISHED
PLENISHES
PLENISHING
PLENISHINGS
PLENIST
PLENISTS
PLENITUDE
PLENITUDES
PLENTEOUS
PLENTIES
PLENTIFUL
PLENTY
PLENUM
PLENUMS
PLEON
PLEONASM
PLEONASMS
PLEONAST
PLEONASTE
PLEONASTES
PLEONASTS
PLEONEXIA
PLEONEXIAS
PLEONS
PLEOPOD
PLEOPODS
PLEROMA
PLEROMAS
PLEROME
PLEROMES
PLESH
PLESHES
PLESSOR
PLESSORS
PLETHORA
PLETHORAS
PLETHORIC
PLEUCH
PLEUCHS
PLEUGH
PLEUGHS
PLEURA
PLEURAE
PLEURAL
PLEURISIES
PLEURISY
PLEURITIC
PLEURITICS
PLEURITIS
PLEURITISES
PLEURON
PLEXIFORM
PLEXOR
PLEXORS
PLEXURE
PLEXURES

PLEXUS
PLEXUSES
PLIABLE
PLIABLY
PLIANCIES
PLIANCY
PLIANT
PLIANTLY
PLICA
PLICAE
PLICAL
PLICATE
PLICATED
PLICATELY
PLICATES
PLICATING
PLICATION
PLICATIONS
PLICATURE
PLICATURES
PLIE
PLIED
PLIER
PLIERS
PLIES
PLIGHT
PLIGHTED
PLIGHTER
PLIGHTERS
PLIGHTFUL
PLIGHTING
PLIGHTS
PLIM
PLIMMED
PLIMMING
PLIMS
PLIMSOLE
PLIMSOLES
PLIMSOLL
PLIMSOLLS
PLING
PLINGS
PLINK
PLINKED
PLINKING
PLINKS
PLINTH
PLINTHS
PLIOSAUR
PLIOSAURS
PLISKIE
PLISKIES
PLISSE
PLOAT
PLOATED
PLOATING
PLOATS
PLOD
PLODDED
PLODDER
PLODDERS
PLODDING
PLODDINGS
PLODS
PLOIDIES
PLOIDY
PLONG
PLONGD
PLONGE
PLONGED
PLONGES
PLONGING
PLONGS
PLONK
PLONKED
PLONKER
PLONKERS
PLONKIER
PLONKIEST
PLONKING
PLONKINGS
PLONKS
PLONKY
PLOOK
PLOOKIE
PLOOKIER
PLOOKIEST
PLOOKS
PLOP
PLOPPED
PLOPPING
PLOPS
PLOSION
PLOSIONS
PLOSIVE
PLOSIVES
PLOT
PLOTFUL
PLOTLESS
PLOTS
PLOTTED
PLOTTER
PLOTTERED
PLOTTERING
PLOTTERS
PLOTTIE
PLOTTIES
PLOTTING
PLOTTINGS
PLOTTY
PLOUGH
PLOUGHBOY
PLOUGHBOYS
PLOUGHED
PLOUGHER
PLOUGHERS
PLOUGHING
PLOUGHINGS
PLOUGHMAN
PLOUGHMEN
PLOUGHS
PLOUK
PLOUKIE
PLOUKIER
PLOUKIEST
PLOUKS
PLOUTER
PLOUTERED
PLOUTERING
PLOUTERS
PLOVER
PLOVERS
PLOVERY
PLOW
PLOWED
PLOWING
PLOWS
PLOWTER
PLOWTERED
PLOWTERING
PLOWTERS
PLOY
PLOYS
PLUCK
PLUCKED
PLUCKER
PLUCKERS
PLUCKIER
PLUCKIEST
PLUCKILY
PLUCKING
PLUCKS
PLUCKY
PLUFF
PLUFFED
PLUFFIER
PLUFFIEST
PLUFFING
PLUFFS
PLUFFY
PLUG
PLUGGED
PLUGGER
PLUGGERS
PLUGGING
PLUGGINGS
PLUGS
PLUM
PLUMAGE
PLUMAGED
PLUMAGES
PLUMATE
PLUMB
PLUMBAGO
PLUMBAGOS
PLUMBATE
PLUMBATES
PLUMBED
PLUMBEOUS
PLUMBER
PLUMBERIES
PLUMBERS
PLUMBERY
PLUMBIC
PLUMBING
PLUMBINGS
PLUMBISM
PLUMBISMS
PLUMBITE
PLUMBITES
PLUMBLESS
PLUMBOUS
PLUMBS
PLUMBUM
PLUMBUMS
PLUMCOT
PLUMCOTS
PLUMDAMAS
PLUMDAMASES
PLUME
PLUMED
PLUMELESS
PLUMELET
PLUMELETS
PLUMERIES
PLUMERY
PLUMES
PLUMIER
PLUMIEST
PLUMING
PLUMIPED
PLUMIST
PLUMISTS
PLUMMET
PLUMMETED
PLUMMETING
PLUMMETS
PLUMMIER
PLUMMIEST
PLUMMY
PLUMOSE
PLUMOUS
PLUMP
PLUMPED
PLUMPEN
PLUMPENED
PLUMPENING
PLUMPENS
PLUMPER
PLUMPERS
PLUMPEST
PLUMPIE
PLUMPIER
PLUMPIEST
PLUMPING
PLUMPISH
PLUMPLY
PLUMPNESS
PLUMPNESSES
PLUMPS
PLUMPY
PLUMS
PLUMULA
PLUMULAE
PLUMULAR
PLUMULATE
PLUMULE
PLUMULES
PLUMULOSE
PLUMY
PLUNDER
PLUNDERED
PLUNDERER
PLUNDERERS
PLUNDERING
PLUNDERS
PLUNGE
PLUNGED
PLUNGER
PLUNGERS
PLUNGES
PLUNGING
PLUNGINGS
PLUNK
PLUNKED
PLUNKER
PLUNKERS
PLUNKING
PLUNKS
PLURAL
PLURALISE
PLURALISED
PLURALISES
PLURALISING
PLURALISM
PLURALISMS
PLURALIST
PLURALISTS
PLURALITIES
PLURALITY
PLURALIZE
PLURALIZED
PLURALIZES
PLURALIZING
PLURALLY
PLURALS
PLURIPARA
PLURIPARAE
PLURIPARAS
PLURISIE
PLURISIES
PLUS
PLUSAGE
PLUSAGES
PLUSED
PLUSES
PLUSH
PLUSHER
PLUSHES
PLUSHEST
PLUSHIER
PLUSHIEST
PLUSHY
PLUSING
PLUSSAGE
PLUSSAGES
PLUSSED
PLUSSES
PLUSSING
PLUTEAL
PLUTEUS
PLUTEUSES
PLUTOCRAT
PLUTOCRATS
PLUTOLOGIES
PLUTOLOGY
PLUTON
PLUTONIC
PLUTONIUM
PLUTONIUMS

PLUTONOMIES
PLUTONOMY
PLUTONS
PLUVIAL
PLUVIALS
PLUVIOSE
PLUVIOUS
PLY
PLYING
PLYWOOD
PLYWOODS
PNEUMA
PNEUMAS
PNEUMATIC
PNEUMATICS
PNEUMONIA
PNEUMONIAS
PNEUMONIC
PNEUMONICS
PO
POA
POACEOUS
POACH
POACHED
POACHER
POACHERS
POACHES
POACHIER
POACHIEST
POACHING
POACHINGS
POACHY
POAKA
POAKAS
POAKE
POAKES
POAS
POCHARD
POCHARDS
POCHAY
POCHAYS
POCHETTE
POCHETTES
POCHOIR
POCHOIRS
POCK
POCKARD
POCKARDS
POCKED
POCKET
POCKETED
POCKETFUL
POCKETFULS
POCKETING
POCKETS
POCKIER
POCKIEST
POCKMANKIES
POCKMANKY
POCKMARK
POCKMARKS
POCKPIT
POCKPITS
POCKS
POCKY
POCO
POD
PODAGRA
PODAGRAL
PODAGRAS
PODAGRIC
PODAGROUS
PODAL
PODALIC
PODARGUS
PODARGUSES
PODDED
PODDIER
PODDIES
PODDIEST
PODDING
PODDY
PODESTA
PODESTAS
PODEX
PODEXES
PODGE
PODGES
PODGIER
PODGIEST
PODGINESS
PODGINESSES
PODGY
PODIA
PODIAL
PODIATRIES
PODIATRY
PODITE
PODITES
PODIUM
PODLEY
PODLEYS
PODOCARP
PODOCARPS
PODOLOGIES
PODOLOGY
PODS
PODSOL
PODSOLIC
PODSOLS
PODZOL
PODZOLS
POEM
POEMATIC
POEMS
POENOLOGIES
POENOLOGY
POESIED
POESIES
POESY
POESYING
POET
POETASTER
POETASTERS
POETASTRIES
POETASTRY
POETESS
POETESSES
POETIC
POETICAL
POETICALS
POETICISE
POETICISED
POETICISES
POETICISING
POETICISM
POETICISMS
POETICIZE
POETICIZED
POETICIZES
POETICIZING
POETICS
POETICULE
POETICULES
POETISE
POETISED
POETISES
POETISING
POETIZE
POETIZED
POETIZES
POETIZING
POETRESSE
POETRESSES
POETRIES
POETRY
POETS
POETSHIP
POETSHIPS
POFFLE
POFFLES
POGGE
POGGES
POGO
POGOED
POGOING
POGOS
POGROM
POGROMS
POH
POI
POIGNADO
POIGNADOES
POIGNANCIES
POIGNANCY
POIGNANT
POILU
POILUS
POINADO
POINADOES
POINCIANA
POINCIANAS
POIND
POINDED
POINDER
POINDERS
POINDING
POINDINGS
POINDS
POINT
POINTE
POINTED
POINTEDLY
POINTEL
POINTELS
POINTER
POINTERS
POINTES
POINTIER
POINTIEST
POINTILLE
POINTING
POINTINGS
POINTLESS
POINTS
POINTSMAN
POINTSMEN
POINTY
POIS
POISE
POISED
POISER
POISERS
POISES
POISING
POISON
POISONED
POISONER
POISONERS
POISONING
POISONOUS
POISONS
POISSON
POISSONS
POITREL
POITRELS
POKAL
POKALS
POKE
POKEBERRIES
POKEBERRY
POKED
POKEFUL
POKEFULS
POKER
POKERISH
POKERS
POKES
POKEWEED
POKEWEEDS
POKEY
POKEYS
POKIER
POKIES
POKIEST
POKING
POKY
POLACCA
POLACCAS
POLACRE
POLACRES
POLAR
POLARISE
POLARISED
POLARISER
POLARISERS
POLARISES
POLARISING
POLARITIES
POLARITY
POLARIZE
POLARIZED
POLARIZER
POLARIZERS
POLARIZES
POLARIZING
POLARON
POLARONS
POLARS
POLDER
POLDERED
POLDERING
POLDERS
POLE
POLECAT
POLECATS
POLED
POLEMARCH
POLEMARCHS
POLEMIC
POLEMICAL
POLEMICS
POLEMISE
POLEMISED
POLEMISES
POLEMISING
POLEMIST
POLEMISTS
POLEMIZE
POLEMIZED
POLEMIZES
POLEMIZING
POLENTA
POLENTAS
POLER
POLERS
POLES
POLEY
POLEYN
POLEYNS
POLEYS
POLIANITE
POLIANITES
POLICE
POLICED
POLICEMAN
POLICEMEN
POLICES
POLICIES
POLICING
POLICY
POLING
POLINGS
POLIO
POLIOS
POLISH
POLISHED
POLISHER
POLISHERS
POLISHES

OLISHING
OLISHINGS
OLITE
OLITELY
OLITER
OLITESSE
OLITESSES
OLITEST
OLITIC
OLITICAL
OLITICK
OLITICKED
OLITICKING
OLITICKINGS
OLITICKS
OLITICLY
OLITICO
OLITICOES
OLITICOS
OLITICS
OLITIES
OLITIQUE
OLITIQUES
OLITY
OLK
OLKA
OLKAS
OLKED
OLKING
OLKS
OLL
OLLACK
OLLACKS
OLLAN
OLLANS
OLLARD
OLLARDED
OLLARDING
OLLARDS
OLLED
OLLEN
OLLENED
OLLENING
OLLENS
OLLENT
OLLER
OLLERS
OLLEX
OLLICAL
OLLICES
OLLICIE
OLLICIES
OLLICY
OLLIES
OLLINATE
OLLINATED
OLLINATES
OLLINATING
OLLING
OLLINGS
OLLINIA
OLLINIC
OLLINIUM
OLLIWIG
POLLIWIGS
POLLIWOG
POLLIWOGS
POLLMAN
POLLMEN
POLLOCK
POLLOCKS
POLLS
POLLSTER
POLLSTERS
POLLUSION
POLLUSIONS
POLLUTANT
POLLUTANTS
POLLUTE
POLLUTED
POLLUTER
POLLUTERS
POLLUTES
POLLUTING
POLLUTION
POLLUTIONS
POLLUTIVE
POLLY
POLLYANNA
POLLYANNAS
POLLYWIG
POLLYWIGS
POLLYWOG
POLLYWOGS
POLO
POLOIDAL
POLOIST
POLOISTS
POLONAISE
POLONAISES
POLONIE
POLONIES
POLONISE
POLONISED
POLONISES
POLONISING
POLONISM
POLONISMS
POLONIUM
POLONIUMS
POLONIZE
POLONIZED
POLONIZES
POLONIZING
POLONY
POLOS
POLT
POLTED
POLTFEET
POLTFOOT
POLTING
POLTROON
POLTROONS
POLTS
POLVERINE
POLVERINES
POLY
POLYACID
POLYACT
POLYAMIDE
POLYAMIDES
POLYANDRIES
POLYANDRY
POLYARCH
POLYARCHIES
POLYARCHY
POLYAXIAL
POLYAXIALS
POLYAXON
POLYAXONS
POLYBASIC
POLYCONIC
POLYESTER
POLYESTERS
POLYGALA
POLYGALAS
POLYGAM
POLYGAMIC
POLYGAMIES
POLYGAMS
POLYGAMY
POLYGENE
POLYGENES
POLYGENIC
POLYGENIES
POLYGENY
POLYGLOT
POLYGLOTS
POLYGLOTT
POLYGLOTTS
POLYGON
POLYGONAL
POLYGONIES
POLYGONS
POLYGONUM
POLYGONUMS
POLYGONY
POLYGRAPH
POLYGRAPHS
POLYGYNIES
POLYGYNY
POLYHEDRA
POLYLEMMA
POLYLEMMAS
POLYMASTIES
POLYMASTY
POLYMATH
POLYMATHIES
POLYMATHS
POLYMATHY
POLYMER
POLYMERIC
POLYMERIES
POLYMERS
POLYMERY
POLYMORPH
POLYMORPHS
POLYNIA
POLYNIAS
POLYNYA
POLYNYAS
POLYOMA
POLYOMAS
POLYOMINO
POLYOMINOS
POLYONYM
POLYONYMIES
POLYONYMS
POLYONYMY
POLYP
POLYPARIES
POLYPARY
POLYPE
POLYPES
POLYPHAGIES
POLYPHAGY
POLYPHASE
POLYPHON
POLYPHONE
POLYPHONES
POLYPHONIES
POLYPHONS
POLYPHONY
POLYPI
POLYPIDE
POLYPIDES
POLYPIDOM
POLYPIDOMS
POLYPINE
POLYPITE
POLYPITES
POLYPLOID
POLYPOD
POLYPODIES
POLYPODS
POLYPODY
POLYPOID
POLYPOSES
POLYPOSIS
POLYPOUS
POLYPS
POLYPTYCH
POLYPTYCHS
POLYPUS
POLYS
POLYSEME
POLYSEMES
POLYSEMIES
POLYSEMY
POLYSOME
POLYSOMES
POLYSOMIES
POLYSOMY
POLYSTYLE
POLYTENE
POLYTHENE
POLYTHENES
POLYTONAL
POLYTYPIC
POLYURIA
POLYURIAS
POLYVINYL
POLYVINYLS
POLYWATER
POLYWATERS
POLYZOA
POLYZOAN
POLYZOANS
POLYZOARIES
POLYZOARY
POLYZOIC
POLYZONAL
POLYZOOID
POLYZOON
POM
POMACE
POMACEOUS
POMACES
POMADE
POMADED
POMADES
POMADING
POMANDER
POMANDERS
POMATO
POMATOES
POMATUM
POMATUMS
POMBE
POMBES
POME
POMELO
POMELOS
POMEROY
POMEROYS
POMES
POMFRET
POMFRETS
POMMEL
POMMELE
POMMELLED
POMMELLING
POMMELS
POMMETTY
POMMIES
POMMY
POMOERIUM
POMOERIUMS
POMOLOGIES
POMOLOGY
POMP
POMPADOUR
POMPADOURS
POMPANO
POMPANOS
POMPELO
POMPELOS
POMPEY
POMPEYED
POMPEYING
POMPEYS
POMPHOLYX
POMPHOLYXES
POMPIER
POMPION
POMPIONS
POMPOM
POMPOMS
POMPON
POMPONS

POMPOON
POMPOONS
POMPOSITIES
POMPOSITY
POMPOUS
POMPOUSLY
POMPS
POMROY
POMROYS
POMS
POMWATER
POMWATERS
PONCE
PONCEAU
PONCEAUS
PONCEAUX
PONCED
PONCES
PONCEY
PONCHO
PONCHOS
PONCIER
PONCIEST
PONCING
PONCY
POND
PONDAGE
PONDAGES
PONDED
PONDER
PONDERAL
PONDERATE
PONDERATED
PONDERATES
PONDERATING
PONDERED
PONDERER
PONDERERS
PONDERING
PONDEROUS
PONDERS
PONDING
PONDOK
PONDOKKIE
PONDOKKIES
PONDOKS
PONDS
PONDWEED
PONDWEEDS
PONE
PONENT
PONES
PONEY
PONEYS
PONG
PONGA
PONGAS
PONGED
PONGEE
PONGEES
PONGID
PONGIDS
PONGIER
PONGIEST
PONGING
PONGO
PONGOES
PONGOS
PONGS
PONGY
PONIARD
PONIARDED
PONIARDING
PONIARDS
PONIED
PONIES
PONK
PONKED
PONKING
PONKS
PONS
PONT
PONTAGE
PONTAGES
PONTAL
PONTES
PONTIANAC
PONTIANACS
PONTIANAK
PONTIANAKS
PONTIC
PONTIE
PONTIES
PONTIFEX
PONTIFF
PONTIFFS
PONTIFIC
PONTIFICE
PONTIFICES
PONTIFIED
PONTIFIES
PONTIFY
PONTIFYING
PONTIL
PONTILE
PONTILES
PONTILS
PONTLEVIS
PONTLEVISES
PONTON
PONTONEER
PONTONEERS
PONTONIER
PONTONIERS
PONTONS
PONTOON
PONTOONED
PONTOONER
PONTOONERS
PONTOONING
PONTOONS
PONTS
PONTY
PONY
PONYING
PONYSKIN
PONYSKINS
PONYTAIL
PONYTAILS
POO
POOCH
POOCHES
POOD
POODLE
POODLES
POODS
POOED
POOF
POOFIER
POOFIEST
POOFS
POOFTAH
POOFTAHS
POOFTER
POOFTERS
POOFY
POOGYE
POOGYEE
POOGYEES
POOGYES
POOH
POOING
POOJA
POOJAH
POOJAHS
POOJAS
POOK
POOKA
POOKAS
POOKING
POOKIT
POOKS
POOL
POOLED
POOLING
POOLS
POOLSIDE
POOLSIDES
POON
POONAC
POONACS
POONCE
POONCES
POONS
POONTANG
POONTANGS
POOP
POOPED
POOPING
POOPS
POOR
POORER
POOREST
POORHOUSE
POORHOUSES
POORI
POORIS
POORISH
POORLIER
POORLIEST
POORLY
POORNESS
POORNESSES
POORT
POORTITH
POORTITHS
POORTS
POORWILL
POORWILLS
POOS
POOT
POOTED
POOTER
POOTERS
POOTING
POOTS
POOVE
POOVERIES
POOVERY
POOVES
POOVIER
POOVIEST
POOVY
POP
POPADUM
POPADUMS
POPCORN
POPCORNS
POPE
POPEDOM
POPEDOMS
POPEHOOD
POPEHOODS
POPELING
POPELINGS
POPERIES
POPERIN
POPERINS
POPERY
POPES
POPESHIP
POPESHIPS
POPINJAY
POPINJAYS
POPISH
POPISHLY
POPJOY
POPJOYED
POPJOYING
POPJOYS
POPLAR
POPLARS
POPLIN
POPLINS
POPLITEAL
POPLITIC
POPOVER
POPOVERS
POPPA
POPPADUM
POPPADUMS
POPPAS
POPPED
POPPER
POPPERING
POPPERINGS
POPPERS
POPPET
POPPETS
POPPIED
POPPIER
POPPIES
POPPIEST
POPPING
POPPISH
POPPIT
POPPITS
POPPLE
POPPLED
POPPLES
POPPLIER
POPPLIEST
POPPLING
POPPLY
POPPY
POPPYCOCK
POPPYCOCKS
POPRIN
POPRINS
POPS
POPSIES
POPSY
POPULACE
POPULACES
POPULAR
POPULARLY
POPULARS
POPULATE
POPULATED
POPULATES
POPULATING
POPULISM
POPULISMS
POPULIST
POPULISTS
POPULOUS
PORAL
PORBEAGLE
PORBEAGLES
PORCELAIN
PORCELAINS
PORCH
PORCHES
PORCINE
PORCPISCE
PORCPISCES
PORCUPINE
PORCUPINES
PORE
PORED
PORER
PORERS
PORES
PORGE
PORGED
PORGES
PORGIE
PORGIES
PORGING
PORGY

PORIER
PORIEST
PORIFER
PORIFERAL
PORIFERAN
PORIFERS
PORINESS
PORINESSES
PORING
PORISM
PORISMS
PORISTIC
PORK
PORKER
PORKERS
PORKIER
PORKIES
PORKIEST
PORKLING
PORKLINGS
PORKS
PORKY
PORN
PORNO
PORNOMAG
PORNOMAGS
PORNOS
PORNS
POROGAMIC
POROGAMIES
POROGAMY
POROMERIC
POROSCOPE
POROSCOPES
POROSCOPIES
POROSCOPY
POROSE
POROSES
POROSIS
POROSITIES
POROSITY
POROUS
PORPESS
PORPESSE
PORPESSES
PORPHYRIA
PORPHYRIAS
PORPHYRIES
PORPHYRIN
PORPHYRINS
PORPHYRIO
PORPHYRIOS
PORPHYRY
PORPOISE
PORPOISED
PORPOISES
PORPOISING
PORPORATE
PORRECT
PORRECTED
PORRECTING
PORRECTS
PORRENGER
PORRENGERS
PORRIDGE
PORRIDGES
PORRIGO
PORRIGOS
PORRINGER
PORRINGERS
PORT
PORTA
PORTABLE
PORTABLES
PORTAGE
PORTAGES
PORTAGUE
PORTAGUES
PORTAL
PORTALS
PORTANCE
PORTANCES
PORTAS
PORTASES
PORTATE
PORTATILE
PORTATIVE
PORTATIVES
PORTED
PORTEND
PORTENDED
PORTENDING
PORTENDS
PORTENT
PORTENTS
PORTEOUS
PORTEOUSES
PORTER
PORTERAGE
PORTERAGES
PORTERESS
PORTERESSES
PORTERLY
PORTERS
PORTESS
PORTESSE
PORTESSES
PORTFOLIO
PORTFOLIOS
PORTHOLE
PORTHOLES
PORTHORS
PORTHORSES
PORTHOS
PORTHOSES
PORTHOUSE
PORTHOUSES
PORTICO
PORTICOED
PORTICOES
PORTICOS
PORTIER
PORTIERE
PORTIERES
PORTIEST
PORTIGUE
PORTIGUES
PORTING
PORTION
PORTIONED
PORTIONER
PORTIONERS
PORTIONING
PORTIONS
PORTLAND
PORTLANDS
PORTLAST
PORTLASTS
PORTLIER
PORTLIEST
PORTLY
PORTMAN
PORTMEN
PORTOISE
PORTOISES
PORTOLAN
PORTOLANI
PORTOLANO
PORTOLANOS
PORTOLANS
PORTOUS
PORTOUSES
PORTRAIT
PORTRAITED
PORTRAITING
PORTRAITS
PORTRAY
PORTRAYAL
PORTRAYALS
PORTRAYED
PORTRAYER
PORTRAYERS
PORTRAYING
PORTRAYS
PORTREEVE
PORTREEVES
PORTRESS
PORTRESSES
PORTS
PORTULACA
PORTULACAS
PORTULAN
PORTULANS
PORTY
PORWIGGLE
PORWIGGLES
PORY
POS
POSADA
POSADAS
POSAUNE
POSAUNES
POSE
POSEABLE
POSED
POSER
POSERS
POSES
POSEUR
POSEURS
POSEUSE
POSEUSES
POSEY
POSH
POSHED
POSHER
POSHES
POSHEST
POSHING
POSHLY
POSHNESS
POSHNESSES
POSHTEEN
POSHTEENS
POSIER
POSIES
POSIEST
POSIGRADE
POSING
POSINGLY
POSINGS
POSIT
POSITED
POSITING
POSITION
POSITIONED
POSITIONING
POSITIONS
POSITIVE
POSITIVES
POSITON
POSITONS
POSITRON
POSITRONS
POSITS
POSNET
POSNETS
POSOLOGIES
POSOLOGY
POSS
POSSE
POSSED
POSSER
POSSERS
POSSES
POSSESS
POSSESSED
POSSESSES
POSSESSING
POSSESSOR
POSSESSORS
POSSET
POSSETED
POSSETING
POSSETS
POSSIBLE
POSSIBLES
POSSIBLY
POSSIE
POSSIES
POSSING
POSSUM
POSSUMED
POSSUMING
POSSUMS
POST
POSTAGE
POSTAGES
POSTAL
POSTALLY
POSTALS
POSTBAG
POSTBAGS
POSTBOX
POSTBOXES
POSTBUS
POSTBUSES
POSTBUSSES
POSTCARD
POSTCARDED
POSTCARDING
POSTCARDS
POSTCAVA
POSTCAVAE
POSTCODE
POSTCODED
POSTCODES
POSTCODING
POSTDATE
POSTDATED
POSTDATES
POSTDATING
POSTED
POSTEEN
POSTEENS
POSTER
POSTERED
POSTERING
POSTERIOR
POSTERIORS
POSTERITIES
POSTERITY
POSTERN
POSTERNS
POSTERS
POSTFACE
POSTFACES
POSTFIX
POSTFIXED
POSTFIXES
POSTFIXING
POSTHASTE
POSTHASTES
POSTHORSE
POSTHORSES
POSTHOUSE
POSTHOUSES
POSTICHE
POSTICHES
POSTICOUS
POSTIE
POSTIES
POSTIL
POSTILION
POSTILIONS
POSTILLED
POSTILLER
POSTILLERS
POSTILLING
POSTILS

POSTING
POSTINGS
POSTLUDE
POSTLUDES
POSTMAN
POSTMARK
POSTMARKS
POSTMEN
POSTNASAL
POSTNATAL
POSTNATI
POSTORAL
POSTPONE
POSTPONED
POSTPONER
POSTPONERS
POSTPONES
POSTPONING
POSTPOSE
POSTPOSED
POSTPOSES
POSTPOSING
POSTRIDER
POSTRIDERS
POSTS
POSTULANT
POSTULANTS
POSTULATA
POSTULATE
POSTULATED
POSTULATES
POSTULATING
POSTURAL
POSTURE
POSTURED
POSTURER
POSTURERS
POSTURES
POSTURING
POSTURIST
POSTURISTS
POSTWAR
POSTWOMAN
POSTWOMEN
POSY
POT
POTABLE
POTABLES
POTAGE
POTAGER
POTAGERS
POTAGES
POTAMIC
POTASH
POTASHED
POTASHES
POTASHING
POTASS
POTASSA
POTASSAS
POTASSES
POTASSIC
POTASSIUM
POTASSIUMS
POTATION
POTATIONS
POTATO
POTATOES
POTATORY
POTBOY
POTBOYS
POTCH
POTCHE
POTCHED
POTCHER
POTCHERS
POTCHES
POTCHING
POTE
POTED
POTEEN
POTEENS
POTENCE
POTENCES
POTENCIES
POTENCY
POTENT
POTENTATE
POTENTATES
POTENTIAL
POTENTIALS
POTENTISE
POTENTISED
POTENTISES
POTENTISING
POTENTIZE
POTENTIZED
POTENTIZES
POTENTIZING
POTENTLY
POTENTS
POTES
POTFUL
POTFULS
POTGUN
POTGUNS
POTHECARIES
POTHECARY
POTHEEN
POTHEENS
POTHER
POTHERED
POTHERING
POTHERS
POTHERY
POTHOLE
POTHOLED
POTHOLER
POTHOLERS
POTHOLES
POTHOLING
POTHOLINGS
POTHOOK
POTHOOKS
POTHOUSE
POTHOUSES
POTICARIES
POTICARY
POTICHE
POTICHES
POTIN
POTING
POTINS
POTION
POTIONS
POTLACH
POTLACHES
POTLATCH
POTLATCHES
POTMAN
POTMEN
POTOMETER
POTOMETERS
POTOO
POTOOS
POTOROO
POTOROOS
POTPOURRI
POTPOURRIS
POTS
POTSHARD
POTSHARDS
POTSHARE
POTSHARES
POTSHERD
POTSHERDS
POTSHOP
POTSHOPS
POTSTONE
POTSTONES
POTT
POTTAGE
POTTAGES
POTTED
POTTER
POTTERED
POTTERER
POTTERERS
POTTERIES
POTTERING
POTTERINGS
POTTERS
POTTERY
POTTIER
POTTIES
POTTIEST
POTTINESS
POTTINESSES
POTTING
POTTINGAR
POTTINGARS
POTTINGER
POTTINGERS
POTTLE
POTTLES
POTTO
POTTOS
POTTS
POTTY
POUCH
POUCHED
POUCHES
POUCHFUL
POUCHFULS
POUCHIER
POUCHIEST
POUCHING
POUCHY
POUDER
POUDERS
POUDRE
POUDRES
POUF
POUFED
POUFFE
POUFFED
POUFFES
POUFFING
POUFING
POUFS
POUFTAH
POUFTAHS
POUFTER
POUFTERS
POUK
POUKE
POUKES
POUKING
POUKIT
POUKS
POULAINE
POULAINES
POULARD
POULARDS
POULDER
POULDERS
POULDRE
POULDRES
POULDRON
POULDRONS
POULE
POULES
POULP
POULPE
POULPES
POULPS
POULT
POULTER
POULTERER
POULTERERS
POULTERS
POULTFEET
POULTFOOT
POULTICE
POULTICED
POULTICES
POULTICING
POULTRIES
POULTRY
POULTS
POUNCE
POUNCED
POUNCES
POUNCET
POUNCETS
POUNCHING
POUNCING
POUND
POUNDAGE
POUNDAGES
POUNDAL
POUNDALS
POUNDED
POUNDER
POUNDERS
POUNDING
POUNDS
POUPE
POUPED
POUPES
POUPING
POUPT
POUR
POURABLE
POURBOIRE
POURBOIRES
POURED
POURER
POURERS
POURIE
POURIES
POURING
POURINGS
POURPOINT
POURPOINTS
POURS
POURSEW
POURSEWED
POURSEWING
POURSEWS
POURSUE
POURSUED
POURSUES
POURSUING
POURSUIT
POURSUITS
POURSUITT
POURSUITTS
POURTRAHED
POURTRAY
POURTRAYD
POURTRAYED
POURTRAYING
POURTRAYS
POUSOWDIE
POUSOWDIES
POUSSE
POUSSES
POUSSETTE
POUSSETTED
POUSSETTES
POUSSETTING
POUSSIN
POUSSINS
POUT
POUTED
POUTER
POUTERS
POUTHER
POUTHERED

POUTHERING
POUTHERS
POUTIER
POUTIEST
POUTING
POUTINGLY
POUTINGS
POUTS
POUTY
POVERTIES
POVERTY
POW
POWAN
POWANS
POWDER
POWDERED
POWDERIER
POWDERIEST
POWDERING
POWDERS
POWDERY
POWELLISE
POWELLISED
POWELLISES
POWELLISING
POWELLITE
POWELLITES
POWELLIZE
POWELLIZED
POWELLIZES
POWELLIZING
POWER
POWERBOAT
POWERBOATS
POWERED
POWERFUL
POWERING
POWERLESS
POWERPLAY
POWERPLAYS
POWERS
POWIN
POWINS
POWN
POWND
POWNDED
POWNDING
POWNDS
POWNEY
POWNEYS
POWNIE
POWNIES
POWNS
POWNY
POWRE
POWRED
POWRES
POWRING
POWS
POWSOWDIES
POWSOWDY
POWTER
POWTERED
POWTERING
POWTERS
POWWAW
POWWOW
POWWOWED
POWWOWING
POWWOWS
POX
POXED
POXES
POXIER
POXIEST
POXING
POXVIRUS
POXVIRUSES
POXY
POYNANT
POYNT
POYNTED
POYNTING
POYNTS
POYSE
POYSED
POYSES
POYSING
POYSON
POYSONED
POYSONING
POYSONS
POZ
POZZ
POZZIES
POZZOLANA
POZZOLANAS
POZZY
PRAAM
PRAAMS
PRABBLE
PRABBLES
PRACTIC
PRACTICAL
PRACTICALS
PRACTICE
PRACTICED
PRACTICES
PRACTICING
PRACTICK
PRACTICKS
PRACTICS
PRACTICUM
PRACTICUMS
PRACTIQUE
PRACTIQUES
PRACTISE
PRACTISED
PRACTISER
PRACTISERS
PRACTISES
PRACTISING
PRACTIVE
PRACTOLOL
PRACTOLOLS
PRAD
PRADS
PRAEAMBLE
PRAEAMBLES
PRAECAVA
PRAECAVAE
PRAECOCES
PRAEDIAL
PRAEDIALS
PRAEFECT
PRAEFECTS
PRAELUDIA
PRAENOMEN
PRAENOMENS
PRAENOMINA
PRAESES
PRAESIDIA
PRAETOR
PRAETORS
PRAGMATIC
PRAGMATICS
PRAHU
PRAHUS
PRAIRIE
PRAIRIED
PRAIRIES
PRAISE
PRAISEACH
PRAISEACHS
PRAISED
PRAISEFUL
PRAISER
PRAISERS
PRAISES
PRAISING
PRAISINGS
PRALINE
PRALINES
PRAM
PRAMS
PRANA
PRANAS
PRANAYAMA
PRANAYAMAS
PRANCE
PRANCED
PRANCER
PRANCERS
PRANCES
PRANCING
PRANCINGS
PRANCK
PRANCKE
PRANCKED
PRANCKES
PRANCKING
PRANCKS
PRANDIAL
PRANG
PRANGED
PRANGING
PRANGS
PRANK
PRANKED
PRANKFUL
PRANKIER
PRANKIEST
PRANKING
PRANKINGS
PRANKISH
PRANKLE
PRANKLED
PRANKLES
PRANKLING
PRANKS
PRANKSOME
PRANKSTER
PRANKSTERS
PRANKY
PRASE
PRASES
PRAT
PRATE
PRATED
PRATER
PRATERS
PRATES
PRATFALL
PRATFALLEN
PRATFALLING
PRATFALLS
PRATFELL
PRATIE
PRATIES
PRATING
PRATINGLY
PRATINGS
PRATIQUE
PRATIQUES
PRATS
PRATT
PRATTED
PRATTING
PRATTLE
PRATTLED
PRATTLER
PRATTLERS
PRATTLES
PRATTLING
PRATTS
PRATY
PRAU
PRAUNCE
PRAUNCED
PRAUNCES
PRAUNCING
PRAUS
PRAVITIES
PRAVITY
PRAWLE
PRAWLES
PRAWLIN
PRAWLINS
PRAWN
PRAWNED
PRAWNING
PRAWNS
PRAXES
PRAXIS
PRAY
PRAYED
PRAYER
PRAYERFUL
PRAYERS
PRAYING
PRAYINGLY
PRAYINGS
PRAYS
PRE
PREACE
PREACED
PREACES
PREACH
PREACHED
PREACHER
PREACHERS
PREACHES
PREACHIER
PREACHIEST
PREACHIFIED
PREACHIFIES
PREACHIFY
PREACHIFYING
PREACHILY
PREACHING
PREACHINGS
PREACHY
PREACING
PREAMBLE
PREAMBLED
PREAMBLES
PREAMBLING
PREAMP
PREAMPS
PREASE
PREASED
PREASES
PREASING
PREASSE
PREASSED
PREASSES
PREASSING
PREBEND
PREBENDAL
PREBENDS
PREBIOTIC
PREBORN
PRECAST
PRECATIVE
PRECATORY
PRECAVA
PRECAVAE
PRECEDE
PRECEDED
PRECEDENT
PRECEDENTS
PRECEDES
PRECEDING
PRECEESE
PRECENTOR
PRECENTORS
PRECEPIT
PRECEPITS
PRECEPT
PRECEPTOR

PRECEPTORS
PRECEPTS
PRECESS
PRECESSED
PRECESSES
PRECESSING
PRECIEUSE
PRECIEUSES
PRECINCT
PRECINCTS
PRECIOUS
PRECIOUSES
PRECIPICE
PRECIPICES
PRECIS
PRECISE
PRECISED
PRECISELY
PRECISER
PRECISES
PRECISEST
PRECISIAN
PRECISIANS
PRECISING
PRECISION
PRECISIONS
PRECISIVE
PRECLUDE
PRECLUDED
PRECLUDES
PRECLUDING
PRECOCIAL
PRECOCITIES
PRECOCITY
PRECOITAL
PRECONISE
PRECONISED
PRECONISES
PRECONISING
PRECONIZE
PRECONIZED
PRECONIZES
PRECONIZING
PRECOOK
PRECOOKED
PRECOOKING
PRECOOKS
PRECOOL
PRECOOLED
PRECOOLING
PRECOOLS
PRECURRER
PRECURRERS
PRECURSE
PRECURSES
PRECURSOR
PRECURSORS
PRECUT
PRECUTS
PRECUTTING
PREDACITIES
PREDACITY
PREDATE
PREDATED
PREDATES
PREDATING
PREDATION
PREDATIONS
PREDATIVE
PREDATOR
PREDATORS
PREDATORY
PREDAWN
PREDAWNS
PREDEFINE
PREDEFINED
PREDEFINES
PREDEFINING
PREDELLA
PREDELLAS
PREDESIGN
PREDESIGNED
PREDESIGNING
PREDESIGNS
PREDEVOTE
PREDIAL
PREDIALS
PREDICANT
PREDICANTS
PREDICATE
PREDICATED
PREDICATES
PREDICATING
PREDICT
PREDICTED
PREDICTER
PREDICTERS
PREDICTING
PREDICTOR
PREDICTORS
PREDICTS
PREDIED
PREDIES
PREDIGEST
PREDIGESTED
PREDIGESTING
PREDIGESTS
PREDIKANT
PREDIKANTS
PREDILECT
PREDOOM
PREDOOMED
PREDOOMING
PREDOOMS
PREDY
PREDYING
PREE
PREED
PREEING
PREEMIE
PREEMIES
PREEN
PREENED
PREENING
PREENS
PREES
PREEVE
PREEVED
PREEVES
PREEVING
PREFAB
PREFABS
PREFACE
PREFACED
PREFACES
PREFACIAL
PREFACING
PREFADE
PREFADED
PREFADES
PREFADING
PREFARD
PREFATORY
PREFECT
PREFECTS
PREFER
PREFERRED
PREFERRER
PREFERRERS
PREFERRING
PREFERS
PREFIGURE
PREFIGURED
PREFIGURES
PREFIGURING
PREFIX
PREFIXED
PREFIXES
PREFIXING
PREFIXION
PREFIXIONS
PREFLIGHT
PREFORM
PREFORMED
PREFORMING
PREFORMS
PREGGERS
PREGNABLE
PREGNANCE
PREGNANCES
PREGNANCIES
PREGNANCY
PREGNANT
PREHALLUCES
PREHALLUX
PREHEAT
PREHEATED
PREHEATING
PREHEATS
PREHEND
PREHENDED
PREHENDING
PREHENDS
PREHENSOR
PREHENSORS
PREHNITE
PREHNITES
PREHUMAN
PREIF
PREIFE
PREIFES
PREIFS
PREJINK
PREJUDGE
PREJUDGED
PREJUDGES
PREJUDGING
PREJUDICE
PREJUDICED
PREJUDICES
PREJUDICING
PREJUDIZE
PREJUDIZES
PRELACIES
PRELACY
PRELATE
PRELATES
PRELATESS
PRELATESSES
PRELATIAL
PRELATIC
PRELATIES
PRELATION
PRELATIONS
PRELATISE
PRELATISED
PRELATISES
PRELATISH
PRELATISING
PRELATISM
PRELATISMS
PRELATIST
PRELATISTS
PRELATIZE
PRELATIZED
PRELATIZES
PRELATIZING
PRELATURE
PRELATURES
PRELATY
PRELECT
PRELECTED
PRELECTING
PRELECTOR
PRELECTORS
PRELECTS
PRELIM
PRELIMS
PRELUDE
PRELUDED
PRELUDES
PRELUDI
PRELUDIAL
PRELUDING
PRELUDIO
PRELUSIVE
PRELUSORY
PREMATURE
PREMED
PREMEDIC
PREMEDICS
PREMEDS
PREMIA
PREMIE
PREMIER
PREMIERE
PREMIERED
PREMIERES
PREMIERING
PREMIERS
PREMIES
PREMISE
PREMISED
PREMISES
PREMISING
PREMISS
PREMISSES
PREMIUM
PREMIUMS
PREMIX
PREMIXED
PREMIXES
PREMIXING
PREMOLAR
PREMOLARS
PREMONISH
PREMONISHED
PREMONISHES
PREMONISHING
PREMORSE
PREMOSAIC
PREMOTION
PREMOTIONS
PREMOVE
PREMOVED
PREMOVES
PREMOVING
PREMY
PRENASAL
PRENASALS
PRENATAL
PRENOTIFIED
PRENOTIFIES
PRENOTIFY
PRENOTIFYING
PRENOTION
PRENOTIONS
PRENT
PRENTED
PRENTICE
PRENTICED
PRENTICES
PRENTICING
PRENTING
PRENTS
PRENUBILE
PRENZIE
PREOCCUPIED
PREOCCUPIES
PREOCCUPY
PREOCCUPYING
PREOCULAR
PREOPTION
PREOPTIONS
PREORAL
PREORDAIN
PREORDAINED
PREORDAINING
PREORDAINS
PREORDER

PREORDERED
PREORDERING
PREORDERS
PREP
PREPACK
PREPACKED
PREPACKING
PREPACKS
PREPAID
PREPARE
PREPARED
PREPARER
PREPARERS
PREPARES
PREPARING
PREPAY
PREPAYING
PREPAYS
PREPENSE
PREPENSED
PREPENSES
PREPENSING
PREPOLLEX
PREPOLLICES
PREPONE
PREPONED
PREPONES
PREPONING
PREPOSE
PREPOSED
PREPOSES
PREPOSING
PREPOSTOR
PREPOSTORS
PREPOTENT
PREPPED
PREPPIER
PREPPIES
PREPPIEST
PREPPILY
PREPPING
PREPPY
PREPS
PREPUCE
PREPUCES
PREPUTIAL
PREQUEL
PREQUELS
PRERECORD
PRERECORDED
PRERECORDING
PRERECORDS
PREROSION
PREROSIONS
PRERUPT
PRESA
PRESAGE
PRESAGED
PRESAGER
PRESAGERS
PRESAGES
PRESAGING
PRESBYOPE
PRESBYOPES
PRESBYOPIES
PRESBYOPY
PRESBYTE
PRESBYTER
PRESBYTERS
PRESBYTES
PRESBYTIC
PRESCHOOL
PRESCHOOLS
PRESCIENT
PRESCIND
PRESCINDED
PRESCINDING
PRESCINDS
PRESCIOUS
PRESCRIBE
PRESCRIBED
PRESCRIBES
PRESCRIBING
PRESCRIPT
PRESCRIPTS
PRESCUTA
PRESCUTUM
PRESE
PRESELECT
PRESELECTED
PRESELECTING
PRESELECTS
PRESENCE
PRESENCES
PRESENT
PRESENTED
PRESENTEE
PRESENTEES
PRESENTER
PRESENTERS
PRESENTING
PRESENTLY
PRESENTS
PRESERVE
PRESERVED
PRESERVER
PRESERVERS
PRESERVES
PRESERVING
PRESES
PRESET
PRESETS
PRESETTING
PRESIDE
PRESIDED
PRESIDENT
PRESIDENTS
PRESIDES
PRESIDIA
PRESIDIAL
PRESIDING
PRESIDIO
PRESIDIOS
PRESIDIUM
PRESIDIUMS
PRESS
PRESSED
PRESSER
PRESSERS
PRESSES
PRESSFAT
PRESSFATS
PRESSFUL
PRESSFULS
PRESSIE
PRESSIES
PRESSING
PRESSINGS
PRESSION
PRESSIONS
PRESSMAN
PRESSMARK
PRESSMARKS
PRESSMEN
PRESSOR
PRESSROOM
PRESSROOMS
PRESSURE
PRESSURED
PRESSURES
PRESSURING
PRESSWORK
PRESSWORKS
PREST
PRESTED
PRESTERNA
PRESTIGE
PRESTIGES
PRESTING
PRESTO
PRESTOS
PRESTS
PRESUME
PRESUMED
PRESUMER
PRESUMERS
PRESUMES
PRESUMING
PRETENCE
PRETENCES
PRETEND
PRETENDED
PRETENDER
PRETENDERS
PRETENDING
PRETENDS
PRETENSE
PRETENSES
PRETERIST
PRETERISTS
PRETERIT
PRETERITE
PRETERITES
PRETERITS
PRETERM
PRETERMIT
PRETERMITS
PRETERMITTED
PRETERMITTING
PRETEST
PRETESTED
PRETESTING
PRETESTS
PRETEXT
PRETEXTS
PRETOR
PRETORS
PRETTIED
PRETTIER
PRETTIES
PRETTIEST
PRETTIFIED
PRETTIFIES
PRETTIFY
PRETTIFYING
PRETTILY
PRETTY
PRETTYING
PRETTYISH
PRETTYISM
PRETTYISMS
PRETZEL
PRETZELS
PREVAIL
PREVAILED
PREVAILING
PREVAILS
PREVALENT
PREVE
PREVED
PREVENE
PREVENED
PREVENES
PREVENING
PREVENT
PREVENTED
PREVENTER
PREVENTERS
PREVENTING
PREVENTS
PREVERB
PREVERBAL
PREVERBS
PREVES
PREVIEW
PREVIEWED
PREVIEWING
PREVIEWS
PREVING
PREVIOUS
PREVISE
PREVISED
PREVISES
PREVISING
PREVISION
PREVISIONED
PREVISIONING
PREVISIONS
PREVUE
PREVUED
PREVUES
PREVUING
PREWARM
PREWARMED
PREWARMING
PREWARMS
PREWARN
PREWARNED
PREWARNING
PREWARNS
PREWYN
PREWYNS
PREX
PREXES
PREXIES
PREXY
PREY
PREYED
PREYFUL
PREYING
PREYS
PREZZIE
PREZZIES
PRIAL
PRIALS
PRIAPIC
PRIAPISM
PRIAPISMS
PRIBBLE
PRIBBLES
PRICE
PRICED
PRICELESS
PRICER
PRICERS
PRICES
PRICEY
PRICIER
PRICIEST
PRICINESS
PRICINESSES
PRICING
PRICK
PRICKED
PRICKER
PRICKERS
PRICKET
PRICKETS
PRICKING
PRICKINGS
PRICKLE
PRICKLED
PRICKLES
PRICKLIER
PRICKLIEST
PRICKLING
PRICKLINGS
PRICKLY
PRICKS
PRICKWOOD
PRICKWOODS
PRICY
PRIDE
PRIDED
PRIDEFUL
PRIDELESS
PRIDES
PRIDIAN
PRIDING
PRIED

PRIEF
PRIEFE
PRIEFES
PRIEFS
PRIER
PRIERS
PRIES
PRIEST
PRIESTED
PRIESTESS
PRIESTESSES
PRIESTING
PRIESTLIER
PRIESTLIEST
PRIESTLY
PRIESTS
PRIEVE
PRIEVED
PRIEVES
PRIEVING
PRIG
PRIGGED
PRIGGER
PRIGGERIES
PRIGGERS
PRIGGERY
PRIGGING
PRIGGINGS
PRIGGISH
PRIGGISM
PRIGGISMS
PRIGS
PRILL
PRILLED
PRILLING
PRILLS
PRIM
PRIMA
PRIMACIES
PRIMACY
PRIMAEVAL
PRIMAGE
PRIMAGES
PRIMAL
PRIMALITIES
PRIMALITY
PRIMALLY
PRIMARIES
PRIMARILY
PRIMARY
PRIMATAL
PRIMATE
PRIMATES
PRIMATIAL
PRIMATIC
PRIME
PRIMED
PRIMELY
PRIMENESS
PRIMENESSES
PRIMER
PRIMERO
PRIMEROS
PRIMERS
PRIMES
PRIMEUR
PRIMEURS
PRIMEVAL
PRIMINE
PRIMINES
PRIMING
PRIMINGS
PRIMIPARA
PRIMIPARAE
PRIMIPARAS
PRIMITIAE
PRIMITIAL
PRIMITIAS
PRIMITIVE
PRIMITIVES
PRIMLY
PRIMMED
PRIMMER
PRIMMERS
PRIMMEST
PRIMMING
PRIMNESS
PRIMNESSES
PRIMO
PRIMORDIA
PRIMOS
PRIMP
PRIMPED
PRIMPING
PRIMPS
PRIMROSE
PRIMROSED
PRIMROSES
PRIMROSING
PRIMROSY
PRIMS
PRIMSIE
PRIMSIER
PRIMSIEST
PRIMULA
PRIMULAS
PRIMULINE
PRIMULINES
PRIMUS
PRIMUSES
PRIMY
PRINCE
PRINCED
PRINCEDOM
PRINCEDOMS
PRINCEKIN
PRINCEKINS
PRINCELET
PRINCELETS
PRINCELIER
PRINCELIEST
PRINCELY
PRINCES
PRINCESS
PRINCESSE
PRINCESSES
PRINCING
PRINCIPAL
PRINCIPALS
PRINCIPIA
PRINCIPLE
PRINCIPLED
PRINCIPLES
PRINCIPLING
PRINCOCK
PRINCOCKS
PRINCOX
PRINCOXES
PRINK
PRINKED
PRINKING
PRINKS
PRINT
PRINTABLE
PRINTED
PRINTER
PRINTERS
PRINTHEAD
PRINTHEADS
PRINTING
PRINTINGS
PRINTLESS
PRINTOUT
PRINTOUTS
PRINTS
PRION
PRIONS
PRIOR
PRIORATE
PRIORATES
PRIORESS
PRIORESSES
PRIORIES
PRIORITIES
PRIORITY
PRIORS
PRIORSHIP
PRIORSHIPS
PRIORY
PRISAGE
PRISAGES
PRISE
PRISED
PRISER
PRISERS
PRISES
PRISING
PRISM
PRISMATIC
PRISMOID
PRISMOIDS
PRISMS
PRISMY
PRISON
PRISONED
PRISONER
PRISONERS
PRISONING
PRISONOUS
PRISONS
PRISSIER
PRISSIEST
PRISSY
PRISTANE
PRISTANES
PRISTINE
PRITHEE
PRIVACIES
PRIVACY
PRIVADO
PRIVADOES
PRIVADOS
PRIVATE
PRIVATEER
PRIVATEERED
PRIVATEERING
PRIVATEERINGS
PRIVATEERS
PRIVATELY
PRIVATER
PRIVATES
PRIVATEST
PRIVATION
PRIVATIONS
PRIVATISE
PRIVATISED
PRIVATISES
PRIVATISING
PRIVATIVE
PRIVATIVES
PRIVATIZE
PRIVATIZED
PRIVATIZES
PRIVATIZING
PRIVET
PRIVETS
PRIVIER
PRIVIES
PRIVIEST
PRIVILEGE
PRIVILEGED
PRIVILEGES
PRIVILEGING
PRIVILY
PRIVITIES
PRIVITY
PRIVY
PRIZABLE
PRIZE
PRIZED
PRIZEMAN
PRIZEMEN
PRIZER
PRIZERS
PRIZES
PRIZING
PRO
PROA
PROACTIVE
PROAS
PROB
PROBABLE
PROBABLES
PROBABLY
PROBALL
PROBAND
PROBANDS
PROBANG
PROBANGS
PROBATE
PROBATED
PROBATES
PROBATING
PROBATION
PROBATIONS
PROBATIVE
PROBATORY
PROBE
PROBEABLE
PROBED
PROBER
PROBERS
PROBES
PROBING
PROBIOTIC
PROBIOTICS
PROBIT
PROBITIES
PROBITS
PROBITY
PROBLEM
PROBLEMS
PROBOSCIDES
PROBOSCIS
PROBOSCISES
PROBS
PROCACITIES
PROCACITY
PROCAINE
PROCAINES
PROCARYON
PROCARYONS
PROCEDURE
PROCEDURES
PROCEED
PROCEEDED
PROCEEDER
PROCEEDERS
PROCEEDING
PROCEEDINGS
PROCEEDS
PROCERITIES
PROCERITY
PROCESS
PROCESSED
PROCESSES
PROCESSING
PROCESSOR
PROCESSORS
PROCIDENT
PROCINCT
PROCINCTS
PROCLAIM
PROCLAIMED
PROCLAIMING
PROCLAIMS
PROCLISES
PROCLISIS
PROCLITIC
PROCLITICS

PROCLIVE
PROCONSUL
PROCONSULS
PROCREANT
PROCREANTS
PROCREATE
PROCREATED
PROCREATES
PROCREATING
PROCTAL
PROCTITIS
PROCTITISES
PROCTOR
PROCTORS
PROCURACIES
PROCURACY
PROCURE
PROCURED
PROCURER
PROCURERS
PROCURES
PROCURESS
PROCURESSES
PROCUREUR
PROCUREURS
PROCURING
PROD
PRODDED
PRODDING
PRODIGAL
PRODIGALS
PRODIGIES
PRODIGY
PRODITOR
PRODITORS
PRODITORY
PRODNOSE
PRODNOSED
PRODNOSES
PRODNOSING
PRODROMAL
PRODROME
PRODROMES
PRODROMI
PRODROMIC
PRODROMUS
PRODS
PRODUCE
PRODUCED
PRODUCER
PRODUCERS
PRODUCES
PRODUCING
PRODUCT
PRODUCTS
PROEM
PROEMBRYO
PROEMBRYOS
PROEMIAL
PROEMS
PROENZYME
PROENZYMES
PROF
PROFACE
PROFANE
PROFANED
PROFANELY
PROFANER
PROFANERS
PROFANES
PROFANING
PROFANITIES
PROFANITY
PROFESS
PROFESSED
PROFESSES
PROFESSING
PROFESSOR
PROFESSORS
PROFFER
PROFFERED
PROFFERER
PROFFERERS
PROFFERING
PROFFERS
PROFILE
PROFILED
PROFILER
PROFILERS
PROFILES
PROFILING
PROFILINGS
PROFILIST
PROFILISTS
PROFIT
PROFITED
PROFITEER
PROFITEERED
PROFITEERING
PROFITEERINGS
PROFITEERS
PROFITER
PROFITERS
PROFITING
PROFITINGS
PROFITS
PROFLUENT
PROFORMA
PROFORMAS
PROFOUND
PROFOUNDER
PROFOUNDEST
PROFOUNDS
PROFS
PROFUSE
PROFUSELY
PROFUSER
PROFUSERS
PROFUSION
PROFUSIONS
PROG
PROGENIES
PROGENY
PROGERIA
PROGERIAS
PROGESTIN
PROGESTINS
PROGGED
PROGGING
PROGGINS
PROGGINSES
PROGNOSES
PROGNOSIS
PROGRADE
PROGRADED
PROGRADES
PROGRADING
PROGRAM
PROGRAMME
PROGRAMMED
PROGRAMMES
PROGRAMMING
PROGRAMMINGS
PROGRAMS
PROGRESS
PROGRESSED
PROGRESSES
PROGRESSING
PROGS
PROHIBIT
PROHIBITED
PROHIBITING
PROHIBITS
PROIGN
PROIGNED
PROIGNING
PROIGNS
PROIN
PROINE
PROINED
PROINES
PROINING
PROINS
PROJECT
PROJECTED
PROJECTING
PROJECTINGS
PROJECTOR
PROJECTORS
PROJECTS
PROKARYON
PROKARYONS
PROKARYOT
PROKARYOTS
PROKE
PROKED
PROKER
PROKERS
PROKES
PROKING
PROLACTIN
PROLACTINS
PROLAMIN
PROLAMINE
PROLAMINES
PROLAMINS
PROLAPSE
PROLAPSED
PROLAPSES
PROLAPSING
PROLAPSUS
PROLAPSUSES
PROLATE
PROLATED
PROLATELY
PROLATES
PROLATING
PROLATION
PROLATIONS
PROLATIVE
PROLE
PROLED
PROLEG
PROLEGS
PROLEPSES
PROLEPSIS
PROLEPTIC
PROLER
PROLERS
PROLES
PROLETARIES
PROLETARY
PROLICIDE
PROLICIDES
PROLIFIC
PROLINE
PROLINES
PROLING
PROLIX
PROLIXITIES
PROLIXITY
PROLIXLY
PROLL
PROLLED
PROLLER
PROLLERS
PROLLING
PROLLS
PROLOGISE
PROLOGISED
PROLOGISES
PROLOGISING
PROLOGIZE
PROLOGIZED
PROLOGIZES
PROLOGIZING
PROLOGUE
PROLOGUED
PROLOGUES
PROLOGUING
PROLONG
PROLONGE
PROLONGED
PROLONGER
PROLONGERS
PROLONGES
PROLONGING
PROLONGS
PROLUSION
PROLUSIONS
PROLUSORY
PROM
PROMACHOS
PROMACHOSES
PROMENADE
PROMENADED
PROMENADES
PROMENADING
PROMETAL
PROMETALS
PROMINENT
PROMISE
PROMISED
PROMISEE
PROMISEES
PROMISER
PROMISERS
PROMISES
PROMISING
PROMISOR
PROMISORS
PROMISSOR
PROMISSORS
PROMMER
PROMMERS
PROMO
PROMOS
PROMOTE
PROMOTED
PROMOTER
PROMOTERS
PROMOTES
PROMOTING
PROMOTION
PROMOTIONS
PROMOTIVE
PROMOTOR
PROMOTORS
PROMPT
PROMPTED
PROMPTER
PROMPTERS
PROMPTEST
PROMPTING
PROMPTINGS
PROMPTLY
PROMPTS
PROMPTURE
PROMPTURES
PROMS
PROMULGE
PROMULGED
PROMULGES
PROMULGING
PROMUSCES
PROMUSCIDES
PROMUSCIS
PRONAOI
PRONAOS
PRONATE
PRONATED
PRONATES
PRONATING
PRONATION
PRONATIONS
PRONATOR
PRONATORS
PRONE
PRONELY
PRONENESS

PRONENESSES
PRONER
PRONES
PRONEST
PRONEUR
PRONEURS
PRONG
PRONGBUCK
PRONGBUCKS
PRONGED
PRONGHORN
PRONGHORNS
PRONGING
PRONGS
PRONK
PRONKED
PRONKING
PRONKS
PRONOTA
PRONOTAL
PRONOTUM
PRONOUN
PRONOUNCE
PRONOUNCED
PRONOUNCES
PRONOUNCING
PRONOUNCINGS
PRONOUNS
PRONTO
PRONUCLEI
PRONUNCIO
PRONUNCIOS
PROO
PROOEMION
PROOEMIONS
PROOEMIUM
PROOEMIUMS
PROOF
PROOFED
PROOFING
PROOFINGS
PROOFLESS
PROOFREAD
PROOFREADING
PROOFREADINGS
PROOFREADS
PROOFS
PROOTIC
PROOTICS
PROP
PROPAGATE
PROPAGATED
PROPAGATES
PROPAGATING
PROPAGE
PROPAGED
PROPAGES
PROPAGING
PROPAGULA
PROPAGULE
PROPAGULES
PROPALE
PROPALED
PROPALES
PROPALING
PROPANE
PROPANES
PROPANOL
PROPANOLS
PROPEL
PROPELLED
PROPELLER
PROPELLERS
PROPELLING
PROPELS
PROPEND
PROPENDED
PROPENDING
PROPENDS
PROPENE
PROPENES
PROPENSE
PROPER
PROPERDIN
PROPERDINS
PROPERER
PROPEREST
PROPERLY
PROPERS
PROPERTIED
PROPERTIES
PROPERTY
PROPERTYING
PROPHAGE
PROPHAGES
PROPHASE
PROPHASES
PROPHECIES
PROPHECY
PROPHESIED
PROPHESIES
PROPHESY
PROPHESYING
PROPHESYINGS
PROPHET
PROPHETIC
PROPHETS
PROPHYLL
PROPHYLLS
PROPINE
PROPINED
PROPINES
PROPINING
PROPODEON
PROPODEONS
PROPODEUM
PROPODEUMS
PROPOLIS
PROPOLISES
PROPONE
PROPONED
PROPONENT
PROPONENTS
PROPONES
PROPONING
PROPOSAL
PROPOSALS
PROPOSE
PROPOSED
PROPOSER
PROPOSERS
PROPOSES
PROPOSING
PROPOUND
PROPOUNDED
PROPOUNDING
PROPOUNDS
PROPPANT
PROPPANTS
PROPPED
PROPPING
PROPRIETIES
PROPRIETY
PROPS
PROPTOSES
PROPTOSIS
PROPULSOR
PROPULSORS
PROPYL
PROPYLA
PROPYLAEA
PROPYLENE
PROPYLENES
PROPYLIC
PROPYLITE
PROPYLITES
PROPYLON
PROPYLS
PRORATE
PRORATED
PRORATES
PRORATING
PRORATION
PRORATIONS
PRORE
PRORECTOR
PRORECTORS
PRORES
PROROGATE
PROROGATED
PROROGATES
PROROGATING
PROROGUE
PROROGUED
PROROGUES
PROROGUING
PROS
PROSAIC
PROSAICAL
PROSAISM
PROSAISMS
PROSAIST
PROSAISTS
PROSATEUR
PROSATEURS
PROSCRIBE
PROSCRIBED
PROSCRIBES
PROSCRIBING
PROSCRIPT
PROSCRIPTS
PROSE
PROSECTOR
PROSECTORS
PROSECUTE
PROSECUTED
PROSECUTES
PROSECUTING
PROSED
PROSELYTE
PROSELYTED
PROSELYTES
PROSELYTING
PROSEMAN
PROSEMEN
PROSER
PROSERS
PROSES
PROSEUCHA
PROSEUCHAE
PROSEUCHE
PROSIER
PROSIEST
PROSIFIED
PROSIFIES
PROSIFY
PROSIFYING
PROSILY
PROSIMIAN
PROSIMIANS
PROSINESS
PROSINESSES
PROSING
PROSINGS
PROSIT
PROSO
PROSODIAL
PROSODIAN
PROSODIANS
PROSODIC
PROSODIES
PROSODIST
PROSODISTS
PROSODY
PROSOPON
PROSOPONS
PROSOS
PROSPECT
PROSPECTED
PROSPECTING
PROSPECTINGS
PROSPECTS
PROSPER
PROSPERED
PROSPERING
PROSPERS
PROSTATE
PROSTATES
PROSTATIC
PROSTRATE
PROSTRATED
PROSTRATES
PROSTRATING
PROSTYLE
PROSTYLES
PROSY
PROTAMINE
PROTAMINES
PROTANDRIES
PROTANDRY
PROTANOPE
PROTANOPES
PROTASES
PROTASIS
PROTATIC
PROTEA
PROTEAN
PROTEAS
PROTEASE
PROTEASES
PROTECT
PROTECTED
PROTECTING
PROTECTOR
PROTECTORS
PROTECTS
PROTEGE
PROTEGEE
PROTEGEES
PROTEGES
PROTEID
PROTEIDS
PROTEIN
PROTEINIC
PROTEINS
PROTEND
PROTENDED
PROTENDING
PROTENDS
PROTENSE
PROTENSES
PROTEOSE
PROTEOSES
PROTEST
PROTESTED
PROTESTER
PROTESTERS
PROTESTING
PROTESTOR
PROTESTORS
PROTESTS
PROTEUS
PROTEUSES
PROTHALLI
PROTHESES
PROTHESIS
PROTHETIC
PROTHORACES
PROTHORAX
PROTHORAXES
PROTHYL
PROTHYLE
PROTHYLES
PROTHYLS
PROTIST
PROTISTIC
PROTISTS
PROTIUM
PROTIUMS
PROTOAVIS

PROTOAVISES
PROTOCOL
PROTOCOLLED
PROTOCOLLING
PROTOCOLS
PROTOGINE
PROTOGINES
PROTOGYNIES
PROTOGYNY
PROTON
PROTONEMA
PROTONEMATA
PROTONIC
PROTONS
PROTORE
PROTORES
PROTOSTAR
PROTOSTARS
PROTOTYPE
PROTOTYPED
PROTOTYPES
PROTOTYPING
PROTOXIDE
PROTOXIDES
PROTOZOA
PROTOZOAL
PROTOZOAN
PROTOZOANS
PROTOZOIC
PROTOZOON
PROTRACT
PROTRACTED
PROTRACTING
PROTRACTS
PROTRUDE
PROTRUDED
PROTRUDES
PROTRUDING
PROTYL
PROTYLE
PROTYLES
PROTYLS
PROUD
PROUDER
PROUDEST
PROUDFUL
PROUDISH
PROUDLY
PROUDNESS
PROUDNESSES
PROUL
PROULED
PROULER
PROULERS
PROULING
PROULS
PROUSTITE
PROUSTITES
PROVABLE
PROVABLY
PROVAND
PROVANDS
PROVANT
PROVE
PROVEABLE
PROVEABLY
PROVED
PROVEDOR
PROVEDORE
PROVEDORES
PROVEDORS
PROVEN
PROVEND
PROVENDER
PROVENDERED
PROVENDERING
PROVENDERS
PROVENDS
PROVER
PROVERB
PROVERBED
PROVERBING
PROVERBS
PROVERS
PROVES
PROVIANT
PROVIANTS
PROVIDE
PROVIDED
PROVIDENT
PROVIDER
PROVIDERS
PROVIDES
PROVIDING
PROVIDOR
PROVIDORS
PROVINCE
PROVINCES
PROVINE
PROVINED
PROVINES
PROVING
PROVINGS
PROVINING
PROVIRAL
PROVIRUS
PROVIRUSES
PROVISION
PROVISIONED
PROVISIONING
PROVISIONS
PROVISO
PROVISOES
PROVISOR
PROVISORS
PROVISORY
PROVISOS
PROVOCANT
PROVOCANTS
PROVOKE
PROVOKED
PROVOKER
PROVOKERS
PROVOKES
PROVOKING
PROVOST
PROVOSTRIES
PROVOSTRY
PROVOSTS
PROW
PROWESS
PROWESSED
PROWESSES
PROWL
PROWLED
PROWLER
PROWLERS
PROWLING
PROWLINGS
PROWLS
PROWS
PROXIES
PROXIMAL
PROXIMATE
PROXIMITIES
PROXIMITY
PROXIMO
PROXY
PROYN
PROYNE
PROYNED
PROYNES
PROYNING
PROYNS
PROZYMITE
PROZYMITES
PRUDE
PRUDENCE
PRUDENCES
PRUDENT
PRUDENTLY
PRUDERIES
PRUDERY
PRUDES
PRUDISH
PRUDISHLY
PRUH
PRUINA
PRUINAS
PRUINE
PRUINES
PRUINOSE
PRUNE
PRUNED
PRUNELLA
PRUNELLAS
PRUNELLE
PRUNELLES
PRUNELLO
PRUNELLOS
PRUNER
PRUNERS
PRUNES
PRUNING
PRUNINGS
PRUNT
PRUNTED
PRUNTS
PRUNUS
PRUNUSES
PRURIENCE
PRURIENCES
PRURIENCIES
PRURIENCY
PRURIENT
PRURIGO
PRURIGOS
PRURITIC
PRURITUS
PRURITUSES
PRUSIK
PRUSIKED
PRUSIKING
PRUSIKS
PRUSSIATE
PRUSSIATES
PRUSSIC
PRY
PRYER
PRYERS
PRYING
PRYINGLY
PRYINGS
PRYS
PRYSE
PRYSED
PRYSES
PRYSING
PRYTANEA
PRYTANEUM
PRYTHEE
PSALM
PSALMIST
PSALMISTS
PSALMODIC
PSALMODIES
PSALMODY
PSALMS
PSALTER
PSALTERIA
PSALTERIES
PSALTERS
PSALTERY
PSALTRESS
PSALTRESSES
PSAMMITE
PSAMMITES
PSAMMITIC
PSCHENT
PSCHENTS
PSELLISM
PSELLISMS
PSEPHISM
PSEPHISMS
PSEPHITE
PSEPHITES
PSEPHITIC
PSEUD
PSEUDAXES
PSEUDAXIS
PSEUDERIES
PSEUDERY
PSEUDISH
PSEUDO
PSEUDONYM
PSEUDONYMS
PSEUDOPOD
PSEUDOPODS
PSEUDS
PSHAW
PSHAWED
PSHAWING
PSHAWS
PSI
PSILOCIN
PSILOCINS
PSILOSES
PSILOSIS
PSILOTIC
PSION
PSIONIC
PSIONICS
PSIONS
PSIS
PSOAS
PSOASES
PSOCID
PSOCIDS
PSORA
PSORALEN
PSORALENS
PSORAS
PSORIASES
PSORIASIS
PSORIATIC
PSORIC
PSST
PST
PSYCH
PSYCHE
PSYCHED
PSYCHES
PSYCHIC
PSYCHICAL
PSYCHICS
PSYCHING
PSYCHISM
PSYCHISMS
PSYCHIST
PSYCHISTS
PSYCHO
PSYCHOGAS
PSYCHOGASES
PSYCHOID
PSYCHOIDS
PSYCHOS
PSYCHOSES
PSYCHOSIS
PSYCHOTIC
PSYCHOTICS
PSYCHS
PSYLLA
PSYLLAS
PSYLLID
PSYLLIDS
PSYOP
PSYOPS
PSYWAR
PSYWARS
PTARMIC

PTARMICS
PTARMIGAN
PTARMIGANS
PTERIA
PTERIN
PTERINS
PTERION
PTEROPOD
PTEROPODS
PTEROSAUR
PTEROSAURS
PTERYGIA
PTERYGIAL
PTERYGIALS
PTERYGIUM
PTERYGOID
PTERYGOIDS
PTERYLA
PTERYLAE
PTILOSES
PTILOSIS
PTISAN
PTISANS
PTOMAINE
PTOMAINES
PTOSES
PTOSIS
PTYALIN
PTYALINS
PTYALISE
PTYALISED
PTYALISES
PTYALISING
PTYALISM
PTYALISMS
PTYALIZE
PTYALIZED
PTYALIZES
PTYALIZING
PTYXES
PTYXIS
PTYXISES
PUB
PUBERAL
PUBERTAL
PUBERTIES
PUBERTY
PUBES
PUBESCENT
PUBIC
PUBIS
PUBISES
PUBLIC
PUBLICAN
PUBLICANS
PUBLICISE
PUBLICISED
PUBLICISES
PUBLICISING
PUBLICIST
PUBLICISTS
PUBLICITIES
PUBLICITY
PUBLICIZE
PUBLICIZED
PUBLICIZES
PUBLICIZING
PUBLICLY
PUBLICS
PUBLISH
PUBLISHED
PUBLISHER
PUBLISHERS
PUBLISHES
PUBLISHING
PUBS
PUCCOON
PUCCOONS
PUCE
PUCELAGE
PUCELAGES
PUCELLE
PUCELLES
PUCER
PUCES
PUCEST
PUCK
PUCKA
PUCKER
PUCKERED
PUCKERING
PUCKERS
PUCKERY
PUCKFIST
PUCKFISTS
PUCKISH
PUCKLE
PUCKLES
PUCKS
PUD
PUDDEN
PUDDENING
PUDDENINGS
PUDDENS
PUDDER
PUDDERED
PUDDERING
PUDDERS
PUDDIES
PUDDING
PUDDINGS
PUDDINGY
PUDDLE
PUDDLED
PUDDLER
PUDDLERS
PUDDLES
PUDDLIER
PUDDLIEST
PUDDLING
PUDDLINGS
PUDDLY
PUDDOCK
PUDDOCKS
PUDDY
PUDENCIES
PUDENCY
PUDENDA
PUDENDAL
PUDENDOUS
PUDENDUM
PUDENT
PUDGE
PUDGES
PUDGIER
PUDGIEST
PUDGINESS
PUDGINESSES
PUDGY
PUDIBUND
PUDIC
PUDICITIES
PUDICITY
PUDOR
PUDORS
PUDS
PUDSEY
PUDSIER
PUDSIEST
PUDSY
PUDU
PUDUS
PUEBLO
PUEBLOS
PUER
PUERED
PUERILE
PUERILISM
PUERILISMS
PUERILITIES
PUERILITY
PUERING
PUERPERAL
PUERS
PUFF
PUFFBALL
PUFFBALLS
PUFFBIRD
PUFFBIRDS
PUFFED
PUFFER
PUFFERIES
PUFFERS
PUFFERY
PUFFIER
PUFFIEST
PUFFILY
PUFFIN
PUFFINESS
PUFFINESSES
PUFFING
PUFFINGLY
PUFFINGS
PUFFINS
PUFFS
PUFFY
PUFTALOON
PUFTALOONS
PUG
PUGGAREE
PUGGAREES
PUGGED
PUGGERIES
PUGGERY
PUGGIE
PUGGIER
PUGGIES
PUGGIEST
PUGGING
PUGGINGS
PUGGISH
PUGGLE
PUGGLED
PUGGLES
PUGGLING
PUGGREE
PUGGREES
PUGGY
PUGH
PUGIL
PUGILISM
PUGILISMS
PUGILIST
PUGILISTS
PUGILS
PUGNACITIES
PUGNACITY
PUGS
PUH
PUIR
PUIRER
PUIREST
PUISNE
PUISNES
PUISNY
PUISSANCE
PUISSANCES
PUISSANT
PUISSAUNT
PUJA
PUJAS
PUKE
PUKED
PUKEKO
PUKEKOS
PUKER
PUKERS
PUKES
PUKING
PUKKA
PUKU
PUKUS
PULA
PULAS
PULDRON
PULDRONS
PULE
PULED
PULER
PULERS
PULES
PULICIDE
PULICIDES
PULIER
PULIEST
PULING
PULINGLY
PULINGS
PULK
PULKA
PULKAS
PULKHA
PULKHAS
PULKS
PULL
PULLED
PULLER
PULLERS
PULLET
PULLETS
PULLEY
PULLEYS
PULLING
PULLOVER
PULLOVERS
PULLS
PULLULATE
PULLULATED
PULLULATES
PULLULATING
PULMO
PULMONARY
PULMONATE
PULMONATES
PULMONES
PULMONIC
PULMONICS
PULP
PULPBOARD
PULPBOARDS
PULPED
PULPER
PULPERS
PULPIER
PULPIEST
PULPIFIED
PULPIFIES
PULPIFY
PULPIFYING
PULPILY
PULPINESS
PULPINESSES
PULPING
PULPIT
PULPITED
PULPITEER
PULPITEERS
PULPITER
PULPITERS
PULPITRIES
PULPITRY
PULPITS
PULPITUM
PULPITUMS
PULPMILL
PULPMILLS
PULPOUS
PULPS
PULPSTONE
PULPSTONES

PULPWOOD
PULPWOODS
PULPY
PULQUE
PULQUES
PULSAR
PULSARS
PULSATE
PULSATED
PULSATES
PULSATILE
PULSATING
PULSATION
PULSATIONS
PULSATIVE
PULSATOR
PULSATORS
PULSATORY
PULSE
PULSED
PULSEJET
PULSEJETS
PULSELESS
PULSES
PULSIDGE
PULSIDGES
PULSIFIC
PULSING
PULSOJET
PULSOJETS
PULTAN
PULTANS
PULTON
PULTONS
PULTOON
PULTOONS
PULTUN
PULTUNS
PULTURE
PULTURES
PULU
PULUS
PULVER
PULVERED
PULVERINE
PULVERINES
PULVERING
PULVERISE
PULVERISED
PULVERISES
PULVERISING
PULVERIZE
PULVERIZED
PULVERIZES
PULVERIZING
PULVEROUS
PULVERS
PULVIL
PULVILIO
PULVILIOS
PULVILLAR
PULVILLE
PULVILLED
PULVILLES
PULVILLI
PULVILLING
PULVILLIO
PULVILLIOS
PULVILLUS
PULVILS
PULVINAR
PULVINARS
PULVINATE
PULVINI
PULVINULE
PULVINULES
PULVINUS
PULWAR
PULWARS
PULY
PUMA
PUMAS
PUMELO
PUMELOS
PUMICATE
PUMICATED
PUMICATES
PUMICATING
PUMICE
PUMICED
PUMICEOUS
PUMICES
PUMICING
PUMIE
PUMIES
PUMMEL
PUMMELLED
PUMMELLING
PUMMELS
PUMP
PUMPED
PUMPER
PUMPERS
PUMPHOOD
PUMPHOODS
PUMPING
PUMPION
PUMPIONS
PUMPKIN
PUMPKINS
PUMPS
PUMY
PUN
PUNA
PUNALUA
PUNALUAN
PUNALUAS
PUNAS
PUNCE
PUNCED
PUNCES
PUNCH
PUNCHED
PUNCHEON
PUNCHEONS
PUNCHER
PUNCHERS
PUNCHES
PUNCHIER
PUNCHIEST
PUNCHING
PUNCHY
PUNCING
PUNCTA
PUNCTATE
PUNCTATED
PUNCTATOR
PUNCTATORS
PUNCTILIO
PUNCTILIOS
PUNCTO
PUNCTOS
PUNCTUAL
PUNCTUATE
PUNCTUATED
PUNCTUATES
PUNCTUATING
PUNCTULE
PUNCTULES
PUNCTUM
PUNCTURE
PUNCTURED
PUNCTURER
PUNCTURERS
PUNCTURES
PUNCTURING
PUNDIT
PUNDITRIES
PUNDITRY
PUNDITS
PUNDONOR
PUNDONORES
PUNGA
PUNGAS
PUNGENCE
PUNGENCES
PUNGENCIES
PUNGENCY
PUNGENT
PUNGENTLY
PUNIER
PUNIEST
PUNILY
PUNINESS
PUNINESSES
PUNISH
PUNISHED
PUNISHER
PUNISHERS
PUNISHES
PUNISHING
PUNITION
PUNITIONS
PUNITIVE
PUNITORY
PUNK
PUNKA
PUNKAH
PUNKAHS
PUNKAS
PUNKER
PUNKEST
PUNKINESS
PUNKINESSES
PUNKS
PUNNED
PUNNER
PUNNERS
PUNNET
PUNNETS
PUNNING
PUNNINGLY
PUNNINGS
PUNS
PUNSTER
PUNSTERS
PUNT
PUNTED
PUNTEE
PUNTEES
PUNTER
PUNTERS
PUNTIES
PUNTING
PUNTO
PUNTOS
PUNTS
PUNTSMAN
PUNTSMEN
PUNTY
PUNY
PUP
PUPA
PUPAE
PUPAL
PUPARIA
PUPARIAL
PUPARIUM
PUPAS
PUPATE
PUPATED
PUPATES
PUPATING
PUPATION
PUPATIONS
PUPFISH
PUPFISHES
PUPIL
PUPILAGE
PUPILAGES
PUPILAR
PUPILARY
PUPILLAGE
PUPILLAGES
PUPILLAR
PUPILLARY
PUPILLATE
PUPILS
PUPILSHIP
PUPILSHIPS
PUPPED
PUPPET
PUPPETEER
PUPPETEERS
PUPPETRIES
PUPPETRY
PUPPETS
PUPPIED
PUPPIES
PUPPING
PUPPODUM
PUPPODUMS
PUPPY
PUPPYDOM
PUPPYDOMS
PUPPYHOOD
PUPPYHOODS
PUPPYING
PUPPYISH
PUPPYISM
PUPPYISMS
PUPS
PUPUNHA
PUPUNHAS
PUR
PURBLIND
PURCHASE
PURCHASED
PURCHASER
PURCHASERS
PURCHASES
PURCHASING
PURDAH
PURDAHED
PURDAHS
PURDONIUM
PURDONIUMS
PURE
PURED
PUREE
PUREED
PUREEING
PUREES
PURELY
PURENESS
PURENESSES
PURER
PURES
PUREST
PURFLE
PURFLED
PURFLES
PURFLING
PURFLINGS
PURFLY
PURGATION
PURGATIONS
PURGATIVE
PURGATIVES
PURGATORIES
PURGATORY
PURGE
PURGED
PURGER
PURGERS
PURGES
PURGING
PURGINGS
PURI
PURIFIED

PURIFIER
PURIFIERS
PURIFIES
PURIFY
PURIFYING
PURIM
PURIMS
PURIN
PURINE
PURINES
PURING
PURINS
PURIS
PURISM
PURISMS
PURIST
PURISTIC
PURISTS
PURITAN
PURITANIC
PURITANS
PURITIES
PURITY
PURL
PURLED
PURLER
PURLERS
PURLICUE
PURLICUED
PURLICUES
PURLICUING
PURLIEU
PURLIEUS
PURLIN
PURLINE
PURLINES
PURLING
PURLINGS
PURLINS
PURLOIN
PURLOINED
PURLOINER
PURLOINERS
PURLOINING
PURLOINS
PURLS
PURPIE
PURPIES
PURPLE
PURPLED
PURPLER
PURPLES
PURPLEST
PURPLIER
PURPLIEST
PURPLING
PURPLISH
PURPLY
PURPORT
PURPORTED
PURPORTING
PURPORTS
PURPOSE
PURPOSED
PURPOSELY
PURPOSES
PURPOSING
PURPOSIVE
PURPURA
PURPURAS
PURPURE
PURPUREAL
PURPURES
PURPURIC
PURPURIN
PURPURINS
PURPY
PURR
PURRED
PURRING
PURRINGLY
PURRINGS
PURRS
PURS
PURSE
PURSED
PURSEFUL
PURSEFULS
PURSER
PURSERS
PURSES
PURSEW
PURSEWED
PURSEWING
PURSEWS
PURSIER
PURSIEST
PURSINESS
PURSINESSES
PURSING
PURSLAIN
PURSLAINS
PURSLANE
PURSLANES
PURSUABLE
PURSUAL
PURSUALS
PURSUANCE
PURSUANCES
PURSUANT
PURSUE
PURSUED
PURSUER
PURSUERS
PURSUES
PURSUING
PURSUINGS
PURSUIT
PURSUITS
PURSY
PURTIER
PURTIEST
PURTRAID
PURTRAYD
PURTY
PURULENCE
PURULENCES
PURULENCIES
PURULENCY
PURULENT
PURVEY
PURVEYED
PURVEYING
PURVEYOR
PURVEYORS
PURVEYS
PURVIEW
PURVIEWS
PUS
PUSES
PUSH
PUSHED
PUSHER
PUSHERS
PUSHES
PUSHFUL
PUSHFULLY
PUSHIER
PUSHIEST
PUSHINESS
PUSHINESSES
PUSHING
PUSHINGLY
PUSHROD
PUSHRODS
PUSHY
PUSLE
PUSLED
PUSLES
PUSLING
PUSS
PUSSEL
PUSSELS
PUSSER
PUSSERS
PUSSES
PUSSIES
PUSSY
PUSSYFOOT
PUSSYFOOTED
PUSSYFOOTING
PUSSYFOOTS
PUSTULANT
PUSTULANTS
PUSTULAR
PUSTULATE
PUSTULATED
PUSTULATES
PUSTULATING
PUSTULE
PUSTULES
PUSTULOUS
PUT
PUTAMEN
PUTAMINA
PUTATIVE
PUTCHEON
PUTCHEONS
PUTCHER
PUTCHERS
PUTCHOCK
PUTCHOCKS
PUTCHUK
PUTCHUKS
PUTEAL
PUTEALS
PUTELI
PUTELIS
PUTID
PUTLOCK
PUTLOCKS
PUTLOG
PUTLOGS
PUTOIS
PUTREFIED
PUTREFIES
PUTREFY
PUTREFYING
PUTRID
PUTRIDER
PUTRIDEST
PUTRIDITIES
PUTRIDITY
PUTRIDLY
PUTS
PUTSCH
PUTSCHES
PUTSCHIST
PUTSCHISTS
PUTT
PUTTED
PUTTEE
PUTTEES
PUTTEN
PUTTER
PUTTERED
PUTTERING
PUTTERS
PUTTI
PUTTIE
PUTTIED
PUTTIER
PUTTIERS
PUTTIES
PUTTING
PUTTINGS
PUTTO
PUTTOCK
PUTTOCKS
PUTTS
PUTTY
PUTTYING
PUTURE
PUTURES
PUTZ
PUTZES
PUY
PUYS
PUZEL
PUZELS
PUZZEL
PUZZELS
PUZZLE
PUZZLED
PUZZLEDOM
PUZZLEDOMS
PUZZLER
PUZZLERS
PUZZLES
PUZZLING
PUZZOLANA
PUZZOLANAS
PYAEMIA
PYAEMIAS
PYAEMIC
PYAT
PYATS
PYCNIC
PYCNIDIA
PYCNIDIUM
PYCNITE
PYCNITES
PYCNON
PYCNONS
PYCNOSES
PYCNOSIS
PYE
PYEBALD
PYEBALDS
PYEING
PYELITIC
PYELITIS
PYELITISES
PYELOGRAM
PYELOGRAMS
PYEMIA
PYEMIAS
PYENGADU
PYENGADUS
PYES
PYET
PYETS
PYGAL
PYGALS
PYGARG
PYGARGS
PYGIDIA
PYGIDIAL
PYGIDIUM
PYGIDIUMS
PYGMAEAN
PYGMEAN
PYGMIES
PYGMOID
PYGMY
PYGOSTYLE
PYGOSTYLES
PYJAMAED
PYJAMAS
PYKNIC
PYKNOSOME
PYKNOSOMES
PYLON
PYLONS
PYLORIC
PYLORUS
PYLORUSES
PYNE
PYNED
PYNES

PYNING
PYOGENIC
PYOID
PYONER
PYONERS
PYONINGS
PYORRHOEA
PYORRHOEAS
PYOT
PYOTS
PYRACANTH
PYRACANTHS
PYRAL
PYRALID
PYRALIDS
PYRALIS
PYRALISES
PYRAMID
PYRAMIDAL
PYRAMIDED
PYRAMIDES
PYRAMIDIA
PYRAMIDIC
PYRAMIDING
PYRAMIDON
PYRAMIDONS
PYRAMIDS
PYRAMIS
PYRAMISES
PYRE
PYRENE
PYRENEITE
PYRENEITES
PYRENES
PYRENOID
PYRENOIDS
PYRES
PYRETHRIN
PYRETHRINS
PYRETHRUM
PYRETHRUMS
PYRETIC
PYREXIA
PYREXIAL
PYREXIAS
PYREXIC
PYRIDINE
PYRIDINES
PYRIDOXIN
PYRIDOXINS
PYRIFORM
PYRITE
PYRITES
PYRITIC
PYRITICAL
PYRITISE
PYRITISED
PYRITISES
PYRITISING
PYRITIZE
PYRITIZED
PYRITIZES
PYRITIZING
PYRITOUS
PYRO
PYROCLAST
PYROCLASTS
PYROGEN
PYROGENIC
PYROGENS
PYROLATER
PYROLATERS
PYROLATRIES
PYROLATRY
PYROLYSE
PYROLYSED
PYROLYSES
PYROLYSING
PYROLYSIS
PYROLYTIC
PYROLYZE
PYROLYZED
PYROLYZES
PYROLYZING
PYROMANCIES
PYROMANCY
PYROMANIA
PYROMANIAS
PYROMETER
PYROMETERS
PYROMETRIES
PYROMETRY
PYROPE
PYROPES
PYROPHONE
PYROPHONES
PYROPUS
PYROPUSES
PYROS
PYROSCOPE
PYROSCOPES
PYROSES
PYROSIS
PYROSOME
PYROSOMES
PYROSTAT
PYROSTATS
PYROXENE
PYROXENES
PYROXENIC
PYROXYLE
PYROXYLES
PYROXYLIC
PYROXYLIN
PYROXYLINS
PYRRHIC
PYRRHICS
PYRRHOUS
PYRROLE
PYRROLES
PYRUVATE
PYRUVATES
PYTHIUM
PYTHIUMS
PYTHON
PYTHONESS
PYTHONESSES
PYTHONIC
PYTHONS
PYURIA
PYURIAS
PYX
PYXED
PYXES
PYXIDES
PYXIDIA
PYXIDIUM
PYXING
PYXIS
PZAZZ
PZAZZES

Q

QABALAH
QABALAHS
QADI
QADIS
QAIMAQAM
QAIMAQAMS
QALAMDAN
QALAMDANS
QANAT
QANATS
QASIDA
QASIDAS
QAT
QATS
QAWWAL
QAWWALI
QAWWALIS
QAWWALS
QI
QIBLA
QIBLAS
QIGONG
QIGONGS
QINDAR
QINDARS
QINGHAOSU
QINGHAOSUS
QINTAR
QINTARS
QIS
QIVIUT
QIVIUTS
QOPH
QOPHS
QUA
QUACK
QUACKED
QUACKER
QUACKERIES
QUACKERS
QUACKERY
QUACKING
QUACKLE
QUACKLED
QUACKLES
QUACKLING
QUACKS
QUAD
QUADDED
QUADDING
QUADRANS
QUADRANT
QUADRANTES
QUADRANTS
QUADRAT
QUADRATE
QUADRATED
QUADRATES
QUADRATIC
QUADRATICS
QUADRATING
QUADRATS
QUADRATUS
QUADRATUSES
QUADRELLA
QUADRELLAS
QUADRIC
QUADRICS
QUADRIFID
QUADRIGA
QUADRIGAE
QUADRILLE
QUADRILLED
QUADRILLES
QUADRILLING
QUADROON
QUADROONS
QUADRUMAN
QUADRUMANS
QUADRUPED
QUADRUPEDS
QUADRUPLE
QUADRUPLED
QUADRUPLES
QUADRUPLIES
QUADRUPLING
QUADRUPLY
QUADS
QUAERE
QUAERED
QUAEREING
QUAERES
QUAERITUR
QUAESITUM
QUAESITUMS
QUAESTOR
QUAESTORS
QUAFF
QUAFFED
QUAFFER
QUAFFERS
QUAFFING
QUAFFS
QUAG
QUAGGA
QUAGGAS
QUAGGIER
QUAGGIEST
QUAGGY
QUAGMIRE
QUAGMIRED
QUAGMIRES
QUAGMIRIER
QUAGMIRIEST
QUAGMIRING
QUAGMIRY
QUAGS
QUAHAUG
QUAHAUGS
QUAHOG
QUAHOGS
QUAICH
QUAICHS
QUAIGH
QUAIGHS
QUAIL
QUAILED
QUAILING
QUAILINGS
QUAILS
QUAINT
QUAINTER
QUAINTEST
QUAINTLY
QUAIR
QUAIRS
QUAKE
QUAKED
QUAKER
QUAKERS
QUAKES
QUAKIER
QUAKIEST
QUAKINESS
QUAKINESSES
QUAKING
QUAKINGLY
QUAKINGS
QUAKY
QUALE
QUALIA
QUALIFIED
QUALIFIER
QUALIFIERS
QUALIFIES
QUALIFY
QUALIFYING
QUALIFYINGS
QUALITIED
QUALITIES
QUALITY
QUALM
QUALMIER
QUALMIEST
QUALMING
QUALMISH
QUALMLESS
QUALMS
QUALMY
QUAMASH
QUAMASHES
QUANDANG
QUANDANGS
QUANDARIES
QUANDARY
QUANDONG
QUANDONGS
QUANGO
QUANGOS
QUANNET
QUANNETS
QUANT
QUANTA
QUANTAL
QUANTED
QUANTIC
QUANTICAL
QUANTICS
QUANTIFIED
QUANTIFIES
QUANTIFY
QUANTIFYING
QUANTING
QUANTISE
QUANTISED
QUANTISES
QUANTISING
QUANTITIES
QUANTITY
QUANTIZE
QUANTIZED
QUANTIZES
QUANTIZING
QUANTONG
QUANTONGS
QUANTS
QUANTUM
QUARE
QUARENDEN
QUARENDENS
QUARENDER
QUARENDERS
QUARER
QUAREST
QUARK
QUARKS
QUARREL
QUARRELLED
QUARRELLING
QUARRELLINGS
QUARRELS
QUARRIED
QUARRIER
QUARRIERS
QUARRIES
QUARRY
QUARRYING
QUARRYMAN
QUARRYMEN
QUART
QUARTAN
QUARTANS
QUARTE
QUARTER
QUARTERED
QUARTERING
QUARTERINGS
QUARTERLIES
QUARTERLY
QUARTERN
QUARTERNS
QUARTERS
QUARTES
QUARTET
QUARTETS
QUARTETT
QUARTETTE
QUARTETTES
QUARTETTI
QUARTETTO
QUARTETTS
QUARTIC
QUARTICS
QUARTIER
QUARTIERS
QUARTILE
QUARTILES
QUARTO
QUARTOS
QUARTS
QUARTZ
QUARTZES
QUARTZIER
QUARTZIEST
QUARTZITE
QUARTZITES
QUARTZOSE
QUARTZY
QUASAR
QUASARS

UASH
UASHED
UASHEE
UASHEES
UASHES
UASHIE
UASHIES
UASHING
UASI
UASSIA
UASSIAS
UAT
UATCH
UATCHED
UATCHES
UATCHING
UATORZE
UATORZES
UATRAIN
UATRAINS
UATS
UAVER
UAVERED
UAVERER
UAVERERS
UAVERIER
UAVERIEST
UAVERING
UAVERINGS
UAVERS
UAVERY
UAY
UAYAGE
UAYAGES
UAYD
UAYS
UAYSIDE
UAYSIDES
UEACH
UEACHES
UEACHIER
UEACHIEST
UEACHY
UEAN
UEANS
UEASIER
UEASIEST
UEASILY
UEASY
UEAZIER
UEAZIEST
UEAZY
UEBRACHO
UEBRACHOS
UEECHIER
UEECHIEST
UEECHY
UEEN
UEENDOM
UEENDOMS
UEENED
UEENHOOD
UEENHOODS
UEENIE

QUEENIER
QUEENIES
QUEENIEST
QUEENING
QUEENINGS
QUEENITE
QUEENITES
QUEENLESS
QUEENLET
QUEENLETS
QUEENLIER
QUEENLIEST
QUEENLY
QUEENS
QUEENSHIP
QUEENSHIPS
QUEENY
QUEER
QUEERCORE
QUEERCORES
QUEERDOM
QUEERDOMS
QUEERED
QUEERER
QUEEREST
QUEERING
QUEERISH
QUEERITIES
QUEERITY
QUEERLY
QUEERNESS
QUEERNESSES
QUEERS
QUEEST
QUEESTS
QUEINT
QUELCH
QUELCHED
QUELCHES
QUELCHING
QUELEA
QUELEAS
QUELL
QUELLED
QUELLER
QUELLERS
QUELLING
QUELLS
QUEME
QUEMED
QUEMES
QUEMING
QUENA
QUENAS
QUENCH
QUENCHED
QUENCHER
QUENCHERS
QUENCHES
QUENCHING
QUENCHINGS
QUENELLE
QUENELLES
QUEP

QUERCETIN
QUERCETINS
QUERCETUM
QUERCETUMS
QUERIED
QUERIES
QUERIMONIES
QUERIMONY
QUERIST
QUERISTS
QUERN
QUERNS
QUERULOUS
QUERY
QUERYING
QUERYINGS
QUEST
QUESTANT
QUESTANTS
QUESTED
QUESTER
QUESTERS
QUESTING
QUESTINGS
QUESTION
QUESTIONED
QUESTIONING
QUESTIONINGS
QUESTIONS
QUESTOR
QUESTORS
QUESTRIST
QUESTRISTS
QUESTS
QUETCH
QUETCHED
QUETCHES
QUETCHING
QUETHE
QUETHES
QUETHING
QUETSCH
QUETSCHES
QUETZAL
QUETZALES
QUETZALS
QUEUE
QUEUED
QUEUEING
QUEUEINGS
QUEUES
QUEUING
QUEUINGS
QUEY
QUEYN
QUEYNIE
QUEYNIES
QUEYNS
QUEYS
QUIBBLE
QUIBBLED
QUIBBLER
QUIBBLERS
QUIBBLES

QUIBBLING
QUIBBLINGS
QUIBLIN
QUIBLINS
QUICH
QUICHE
QUICHED
QUICHES
QUICHING
QUICK
QUICKBEAM
QUICKBEAMS
QUICKEN
QUICKENED
QUICKENER
QUICKENERS
QUICKENING
QUICKENINGS
QUICKENS
QUICKER
QUICKEST
QUICKIE
QUICKIES
QUICKLIME
QUICKLIMES
QUICKLY
QUICKNESS
QUICKNESSES
QUICKS
QUICKSAND
QUICKSANDS
QUICKSET
QUICKSETS
QUICKSTEP
QUICKSTEPPED
QUICKSTEPPING
QUICKSTEPS
QUID
QUIDAM
QUIDAMS
QUIDDANIES
QUIDDANY
QUIDDIT
QUIDDITIES
QUIDDITS
QUIDDITY
QUIDDLE
QUIDDLED
QUIDDLER
QUIDDLERS
QUIDDLES
QUIDDLING
QUIDNUNC
QUIDNUNCS
QUIDS
QUIESCE
QUIESCED
QUIESCENT
QUIESCES
QUIESCING
QUIET
QUIETED
QUIETEN
QUIETENED

QUIETENING
QUIETENINGS
QUIETENS
QUIETER
QUIETERS
QUIETEST
QUIETING
QUIETINGS
QUIETISM
QUIETISMS
QUIETIST
QUIETISTS
QUIETIVE
QUIETIVES
QUIETLY
QUIETNESS
QUIETNESSES
QUIETS
QUIETSOME
QUIETUDE
QUIETUDES
QUIETUS
QUIETUSES
QUIFF
QUIFFS
QUIGHT
QUIGHTED
QUIGHTING
QUIGHTS
QUILL
QUILLAI
QUILLAIS
QUILLED
QUILLET
QUILLETS
QUILLING
QUILLINGS
QUILLMAN
QUILLMEN
QUILLON
QUILLONS
QUILLS
QUILLWORT
QUILLWORTS
QUILT
QUILTED
QUILTER
QUILTERS
QUILTING
QUILTINGS
QUILTS
QUIM
QUIMS
QUIN
QUINA
QUINARIES
QUINARY
QUINAS
QUINATE
QUINCE
QUINCES
QUINCHE
QUINCHED
QUINCHES

The Chambers Dictionary is the authority for many longer words; see *OSW* Introduction, page xii

QUINCHING
QUINCUNX
QUINCUNXES
QUINE
QUINELLA
QUINELLAS
QUINES
QUINIC
QUINIDINE
QUINIDINES
QUINIE
QUINIES
QUININE
QUININES
QUINNAT
QUINNATS
QUINOA
QUINOAS
QUINOID
QUINOIDAL
QUINOIDS
QUINOL
QUINOLINE
QUINOLINES
QUINOLONE
QUINOLONES
QUINOLS
QUINONE
QUINONES
QUINONOID
QUINQUINA
QUINQUINAS
QUINS
QUINSIED
QUINSIES
QUINSY
QUINT
QUINTA
QUINTAIN
QUINTAINS
QUINTAL
QUINTALS
QUINTAN
QUINTAS
QUINTE
QUINTES
QUINTET
QUINTETS
QUINTETT
QUINTETTE
QUINTETTES
QUINTETTI
QUINTETTO
QUINTETTS
QUINTIC
QUINTILE
QUINTILES
QUINTROON
QUINTROONS
QUINTS
QUINTUPLE
QUINTUPLED
QUINTUPLES
QUINTUPLING
QUINZE
QUINZES
QUIP
QUIPO
QUIPOS
QUIPPED
QUIPPING
QUIPPISH
QUIPS
QUIPSTER
QUIPSTERS
QUIPU
QUIPUS
QUIRE
QUIRED
QUIRES
QUIRING
QUIRISTER
QUIRISTERS
QUIRK
QUIRKED
QUIRKIER
QUIRKIEST
QUIRKILY
QUIRKING
QUIRKISH
QUIRKS
QUIRKY
QUIRT
QUIRTED
QUIRTING
QUIRTS
QUISLING
QUISLINGS
QUIST
QUISTS
QUIT
QUITCH
QUITCHED
QUITCHES
QUITCHING
QUITCLAIM
QUITCLAIMED
QUITCLAIMING
QUITCLAIMS
QUITE
QUITED
QUITES
QUITING
QUITS
QUITTAL
QUITTALS
QUITTANCE
QUITTANCED
QUITTANCES
QUITTANCING
QUITTED
QUITTER
QUITTERS
QUITTING
QUITTOR
QUITTORS
QUIVER
QUIVERED
QUIVERFUL
QUIVERFULS
QUIVERIER
QUIVERIEST
QUIVERING
QUIVERINGS
QUIVERISH
QUIVERS
QUIVERY
QUIXOTIC
QUIXOTISM
QUIXOTISMS
QUIXOTRIES
QUIXOTRY
QUIZ
QUIZZED
QUIZZER
QUIZZERIES
QUIZZERS
QUIZZERY
QUIZZES
QUIZZICAL
QUIZZIFIED
QUIZZIFIES
QUIZZIFY
QUIZZIFYING
QUIZZING
QUIZZINGS
QUOAD
QUOD
QUODDED
QUODDING
QUODLIBET
QUODLIBETS
QUODLIN
QUODLINS
QUODS
QUOIF
QUOIFED
QUOIFING
QUOIFS
QUOIN
QUOINED
QUOINING
QUOINS
QUOIST
QUOISTS
QUOIT
QUOITED
QUOITER
QUOITERS
QUOITING
QUOITS
QUOKKA
QUOKKAS
QUOLL
QUOLLS
QUONDAM
QUONK
QUONKED
QUONKING
QUONKS
QUOOKE
QUOP
QUOPPED
QUOPPING
QUOPS
QUORATE
QUORUM
QUORUMS
QUOTA
QUOTABLE
QUOTABLY
QUOTAS
QUOTATION
QUOTATIONS
QUOTATIVE
QUOTATIVES
QUOTE
QUOTED
QUOTER
QUOTERS
QUOTES
QUOTH
QUOTHA
QUOTIDIAN
QUOTIDIANS
QUOTIENT
QUOTIENTS
QUOTING
QUOTITION
QUOTITIONS
QUOTUM
QUOTUMS
QUYTE
QUYTED
QUYTES
QUYTING
QWERTIES
QWERTY
QWERTYS

R

RABANNA
RABANNAS
RABAT
RABATINE
RABATINES
RABATMENT
RABATMENTS
RABATO
RABATOES
RABATS
RABATTE
RABATTED
RABATTES
RABATTING
RABATTINGS
RABBET
RABBETED
RABBETING
RABBETS
RABBI
RABBIN
RABBINATE
RABBINATES
RABBINIC
RABBINISM
RABBINISMS
RABBINIST
RABBINISTS
RABBINITE
RABBINITES
RABBINS
RABBIS
RABBIT
RABBITED
RABBITER
RABBITERS
RABBITING
RABBITRIES
RABBITRY
RABBITS
RABBITY
RABBLE
RABBLED
RABBLER
RABBLERS
RABBLES
RABBLING
RABBLINGS
RABBONI
RABBONIS
RABI
RABIC
RABID
RABIDER
RABIDEST
RABIDITIES
RABIDITY
RABIDLY
RABIDNESS
RABIDNESSES
RABIES
RABIS
RACA
RACAHOUT
RACAHOUTS
RACCAHOUT
RACCAHOUTS
RACCOON
RACCOONS
RACE
RACECARD
RACECARDS
RACED
RACEGOER
RACEGOERS
RACEGOING
RACEGOINGS
RACEHORSE
RACEHORSES
RACEMATE
RACEMATES
RACEME
RACEMED
RACEMES
RACEMIC
RACEMISE
RACEMISED
RACEMISES
RACEMISING
RACEMISM
RACEMISMS
RACEMIZE
RACEMIZED
RACEMIZES
RACEMIZING
RACEMOSE
RACEPATH
RACEPATHS
RACER
RACERS
RACES
RACETRACK
RACETRACKS
RACEWAY
RACEWAYS
RACH
RACHE
RACHES
RACHIAL
RACHIDES
RACHIDIAL
RACHIDIAN
RACHILLA
RACHILLAS
RACHIS
RACHISES
RACHITIC
RACHITIS
RACHITISES
RACIAL
RACIALISM
RACIALISMS
RACIALIST
RACIALISTS
RACIALLY
RACIATION
RACIATIONS
RACIER
RACIEST
RACILY
RACINESS
RACINESSES
RACING
RACINGS
RACISM
RACISMS
RACIST
RACISTS
RACK
RACKED
RACKER
RACKERS
RACKET
RACKETED
RACKETEER
RACKETEERED
RACKETEERING
RACKETEERINGS
RACKETEERS
RACKETER
RACKETERS
RACKETIER
RACKETIEST
RACKETING
RACKETRIES
RACKETRY
RACKETS
RACKETT
RACKETTS
RACKETY
RACKING
RACKINGS
RACKS
RACKWORK
RACKWORKS
RACLETTE
RACLETTES
RACLOIR
RACLOIRS
RACON
RACONS
RACONTEUR
RACONTEURS
RACOON
RACOONS
RACQUET
RACQUETS
RACY
RAD
RADAR
RADARS
RADDER
RADDEST
RADDLE
RADDLED
RADDLEMAN
RADDLEMEN
RADDLES
RADDLING
RADDOCKE
RADDOCKES
RADE
RADGE
RADGER
RADGES
RADGEST
RADIAL
RADIALE
RADIALIA
RADIALISE
RADIALISED
RADIALISES
RADIALISING
RADIALITIES
RADIALITY
RADIALIZE
RADIALIZED
RADIALIZES
RADIALIZING
RADIALLY
RADIALS
RADIAN
RADIANCE
RADIANCES
RADIANCIES
RADIANCY
RADIANS
RADIANT
RADIANTLY
RADIANTS
RADIATA
RADIATAS
RADIATE
RADIATED
RADIATELY
RADIATES
RADIATING
RADIATION
RADIATIONS
RADIATIVE
RADIATOR
RADIATORS
RADIATORY
RADICAL
RADICALLY
RADICALS
RADICANT
RADICATE
RADICATED
RADICATES
RADICATING
RADICCHIO
RADICCHIOS
RADICEL
RADICELS
RADICES
RADICLE
RADICLES
RADICULAR
RADICULE
RADICULES
RADII
RADIO
RADIOED
RADIOGRAM
RADIOGRAMS
RADIOING
RADIOLOGIES
RADIOLOGY
RADIONICS
RADIOS
RADIOTHON
RADIOTHONS
RADISH
RADISHES
RADIUM
RADIUMS
RADIUS
RADIUSES
RADIX

RADOME
RADOMES
RADON
RADONS
RADS
RADULA
RADULAE
RADULAR
RADULATE
RADWASTE
RADWASTES
RAFALE
RAFALES
RAFF
RAFFIA
RAFFIAS
RAFFINATE
RAFFINATES
RAFFINOSE
RAFFINOSES
RAFFISH
RAFFISHLY
RAFFLE
RAFFLED
RAFFLER
RAFFLERS
RAFFLES
RAFFLING
RAFFS
RAFT
RAFTED
RAFTER
RAFTERED
RAFTERING
RAFTERINGS
RAFTERS
RAFTING
RAFTMAN
RAFTMEN
RAFTS
RAFTSMAN
RAFTSMEN
RAG
RAGA
RAGAS
RAGBAG
RAGBAGS
RAGBOLT
RAGBOLTS
RAGDE
RAGE
RAGED
RAGEE
RAGEES
RAGEFUL
RAGER
RAGERS
RAGES
RAGG
RAGGA
RAGGAS
RAGGED
RAGGEDER
RAGGEDEST
RAGGEDLY
RAGGEDY
RAGGEE
RAGGEES
RAGGERIES
RAGGERY
RAGGIER
RAGGIES
RAGGIEST
RAGGING
RAGGINGS
RAGGLE
RAGGLED
RAGGLES
RAGGLING
RAGGS
RAGGY
RAGHEAD
RAGHEADS
RAGI
RAGING
RAGINGLY
RAGINGS
RAGINI
RAGINIS
RAGIS
RAGLAN
RAGLANS
RAGMAN
RAGMANS
RAGMEN
RAGMENT
RAGMENTS
RAGOUT
RAGOUTED
RAGOUTING
RAGOUTS
RAGS
RAGSTONE
RAGSTONES
RAGTAG
RAGTAGS
RAGTIME
RAGTIMER
RAGTIMERS
RAGTIMES
RAGTOP
RAGTOPS
RAGULED
RAGULY
RAGWEED
RAGWEEDS
RAGWHEEL
RAGWHEELS
RAGWORK
RAGWORKS
RAGWORM
RAGWORMS
RAGWORT
RAGWORTS
RAH
RAHED
RAHING
RAHS
RAI
RAID
RAIDED
RAIDER
RAIDERS
RAIDING
RAIDS
RAIK
RAIKED
RAIKING
RAIKS
RAIL
RAILBED
RAILBEDS
RAILBUS
RAILBUSES
RAILBUSSES
RAILCARD
RAILCARDS
RAILE
RAILED
RAILER
RAILERS
RAILES
RAILHEAD
RAILHEADS
RAILING
RAILINGLY
RAILINGS
RAILLERIES
RAILLERY
RAILLESS
RAILLIES
RAILLY
RAILMAN
RAILMEN
RAILROAD
RAILROADED
RAILROADING
RAILROADS
RAILS
RAILWAY
RAILWAYS
RAILWOMAN
RAILWOMEN
RAIMENT
RAIMENTS
RAIN
RAINBAND
RAINBANDS
RAINBOW
RAINBOWED
RAINBOWS
RAINBOWY
RAINCHECK
RAINCHECKS
RAINCOAT
RAINCOATS
RAINDATE
RAINDATES
RAINDROP
RAINDROPS
RAINE
RAINED
RAINES
RAINFALL
RAINFALLS
RAINIER
RAINIEST
RAININESS
RAININESSES
RAINING
RAINLESS
RAINMAKER
RAINMAKERS
RAINPROOF
RAINPROOFED
RAINPROOFING
RAINPROOFS
RAINS
RAINSTORM
RAINSTORMS
RAINTIGHT
RAINWATER
RAINWATERS
RAINWEAR
RAINWEARS
RAINY
RAIRD
RAIRDS
RAIS
RAISABLE
RAISE
RAISEABLE
RAISED
RAISER
RAISERS
RAISES
RAISIN
RAISING
RAISINGS
RAISINS
RAISONNE
RAIT
RAITA
RAITAS
RAITED
RAITING
RAITS
RAIYAT
RAIYATS
RAJ
RAJA
RAJAH
RAJAHS
RAJAHSHIP
RAJAHSHIPS
RAJAS
RAJASHIP
RAJASHIPS
RAJES
RAKE
RAKED
RAKEE
RAKEES
RAKEHELL
RAKEHELLS
RAKEHELLY
RAKER
RAKERIES
RAKERS
RAKERY
RAKES
RAKESHAME
RAKESHAMES
RAKI
RAKING
RAKINGS
RAKIS
RAKISH
RAKISHLY
RAKSHAS
RAKSHASA
RAKSHASAS
RAKSHASES
RAKU
RAKUS
RALE
RALES
RALLIED
RALLIER
RALLIERS
RALLIES
RALLINE
RALLY
RALLYE
RALLYES
RALLYING
RALLYINGS
RALLYIST
RALLYISTS
RAM
RAMAKIN
RAMAKINS
RAMAL
RAMATE
RAMBLE
RAMBLED
RAMBLER
RAMBLERS
RAMBLES
RAMBLING
RAMBLINGS
RAMBUTAN
RAMBUTANS
RAMCAT
RAMCATS
RAMEAL
RAMEE
RAMEES
RAMEKIN
RAMEKINS
RAMEN
RAMENS
RAMENTA
RAMENTUM
RAMEOUS
RAMEQUIN
RAMEQUINS
RAMFEEZLE
RAMFEEZLED
RAMFEEZLES

RAMFEEZLING
RAMI
RAMIE
RAMIES
RAMIFIED
RAMIFIES
RAMIFORM
RAMIFY
RAMIFYING
RAMIN
RAMINS
RAMIS
RAMJET
RAMJETS
RAMMED
RAMMER
RAMMERS
RAMMIES
RAMMING
RAMMISH
RAMMY
RAMOSE
RAMOUS
RAMP
RAMPAGE
RAMPAGED
RAMPAGES
RAMPAGING
RAMPAGINGS
RAMPANCIES
RAMPANCY
RAMPANT
RAMPANTLY
RAMPART
RAMPARTED
RAMPARTING
RAMPARTS
RAMPAUGE
RAMPAUGED
RAMPAUGES
RAMPAUGING
RAMPED
RAMPER
RAMPERS
RAMPICK
RAMPICKED
RAMPICKS
RAMPIKE
RAMPIKES
RAMPING
RAMPINGS
RAMPION
RAMPIONS
RAMPIRE
RAMPIRED
RAMPIRES
RAMPS
RAMPSMAN
RAMPSMEN
RAMROD
RAMRODDED
RAMRODDING
RAMRODS
RAMS
RAMSON
RAMSONS
RAMSTAM
RAMULAR
RAMULI
RAMULOSE
RAMULOUS
RAMULUS
RAMUS
RAN
RANA
RANARIAN
RANARIUM
RANARIUMS
RANAS
RANCE
RANCED
RANCEL
RANCELS
RANCES
RANCH
RANCHED
RANCHER
RANCHERIA
RANCHERIAS
RANCHERIE
RANCHERIES
RANCHERO
RANCHEROS
RANCHERS
RANCHES
RANCHING
RANCHINGS
RANCHMAN
RANCHMEN
RANCHO
RANCHOS
RANCID
RANCIDER
RANCIDEST
RANCIDITIES
RANCIDITY
RANCING
RANCOR
RANCOROUS
RANCORS
RANCOUR
RANCOURS
RAND
RANDAN
RANDANS
RANDED
RANDEM
RANDEMS
RANDIE
RANDIER
RANDIES
RANDIEST
RANDING
RANDOM
RANDOMISE
RANDOMISED
RANDOMISES
RANDOMISING
RANDOMIZE
RANDOMIZED
RANDOMIZES
RANDOMIZING
RANDOMLY
RANDOMS
RANDON
RANDONS
RANDS
RANDY
RANEE
RANEES
RANG
RANGATIRA
RANGATIRAS
RANGE
RANGED
RANGELAND
RANGELANDS
RANGER
RANGERS
RANGES
RANGIER
RANGIEST
RANGINESS
RANGINESSES
RANGING
RANGOLI
RANGOLIS
RANGY
RANI
RANIFORM
RANINE
RANIS
RANK
RANKE
RANKED
RANKER
RANKERS
RANKES
RANKEST
RANKING
RANKINGS
RANKLE
RANKLED
RANKLES
RANKLING
RANKLY
RANKNESS
RANKNESSES
RANKS
RANSACK
RANSACKED
RANSACKER
RANSACKERS
RANSACKING
RANSACKS
RANSEL
RANSELS
RANSHAKLE
RANSHAKLED
RANSHAKLES
RANSHAKLING
RANSOM
RANSOMED
RANSOMER
RANSOMERS
RANSOMING
RANSOMS
RANT
RANTED
RANTER
RANTERISM
RANTERISMS
RANTERS
RANTING
RANTINGLY
RANTINGS
RANTIPOLE
RANTIPOLED
RANTIPOLES
RANTIPOLING
RANTS
RANULA
RANULAS
RANUNCULI
RANZEL
RANZELMAN
RANZELMEN
RANZELS
RAOULIA
RAOULIAS
RAP
RAPACIOUS
RAPACITIES
RAPACITY
RAPE
RAPED
RAPER
RAPERS
RAPES
RAPESEED
RAPESEEDS
RAPHANIA
RAPHANIAS
RAPHE
RAPHES
RAPHIA
RAPHIAS
RAPHIDE
RAPHIDES
RAPHIS
RAPID
RAPIDER
RAPIDEST
RAPIDITIES
RAPIDITY
RAPIDLY
RAPIDNESS
RAPIDNESSES
RAPIDS
RAPIER
RAPIERS
RAPINE
RAPINES
RAPING
RAPIST
RAPISTS
RAPLOCH
RAPLOCHS
RAPPAREE
RAPPAREES
RAPPED
RAPPEE
RAPPEES
RAPPEL
RAPPELLED
RAPPELLING
RAPPELLINGS
RAPPELS
RAPPER
RAPPERS
RAPPING
RAPPINGS
RAPPORT
RAPPORTS
RAPS
RAPT
RAPTLY
RAPTOR
RAPTORIAL
RAPTORS
RAPTURE
RAPTURED
RAPTURES
RAPTURING
RAPTURISE
RAPTURISED
RAPTURISES
RAPTURISING
RAPTURIST
RAPTURISTS
RAPTURIZE
RAPTURIZED
RAPTURIZES
RAPTURIZING
RAPTUROUS
RARE
RAREBIT
RAREBITS
RAREFIED
RAREFIES
RAREFY
RAREFYING
RARELY
RARENESS
RARENESSES
RARER
RAREST
RARING
RARITIES
RARITY
RAS
RASCAILLE
RASCAILLES
RASCAL
RASCALDOM
RASCALDOMS
RASCALISM
RASCALISMS
RASCALITIES
RASCALITY

RASCALLIEST
RASCALLY
RASCALS
RASCASSE
RASCASSES
RASCHEL
RASCHELS
RASE
RASED
RASES
RASH
RASHED
RASHER
RASHERS
RASHES
RASHEST
RASHING
RASHLY
RASHNESS
RASHNESSES
RASING
RASORIAL
RASP
RASPATORIES
RASPATORY
RASPBERRIES
RASPBERRY
RASPED
RASPER
RASPERS
RASPIER
RASPIEST
RASPING
RASPINGLY
RASPINGS
RASPS
RASPY
RASSE
RASSES
RAST
RASTA
RASTAFARI
RASTER
RASTERISE
RASTERISED
RASTERISES
RASTERISING
RASTERIZE
RASTERIZED
RASTERIZES
RASTERIZING
RASTERS
RASTRUM
RASTRUMS
RASURE
RASURES
RAT
RATA
RATABLE
RATABLY
RATAFIA
RATAFIAS
RATAN
RATANS
RATAPLAN
RATAPLANS
RATAS
RATBAG
RATBAGS
RATCH
RATCHED
RATCHES
RATCHET
RATCHETED
RATCHETING
RATCHETS
RATCHING
RATE
RATEABLE
RATEABLY
RATED
RATEL
RATELS
RATEPAYER
RATEPAYERS
RATER
RATERS
RATES
RATFINK
RATFINKS
RATH
RATHE
RATHER
RATHEREST
RATHERIPE
RATHERIPES
RATHERISH
RATHEST
RATHRIPE
RATHRIPES
RATHS
RATIFIED
RATIFIER
RATIFIERS
RATIFIES
RATIFY
RATIFYING
RATINE
RATINES
RATING
RATINGS
RATIO
RATION
RATIONAL
RATIONALE
RATIONALES
RATIONALS
RATIONED
RATIONING
RATIONS
RATIOS
RATITE
RATLIN
RATLINE
RATLINES
RATLING
RATLINGS
RATLINS
RATOO
RATOON
RATOONED
RATOONER
RATOONERS
RATOONING
RATOONS
RATOOS
RATPACK
RATPACKS
RATPROOF
RATS
RATSBANE
RATSBANES
RATTAN
RATTANS
RATTED
RATTEEN
RATTEENS
RATTEN
RATTENED
RATTENING
RATTENINGS
RATTENS
RATTER
RATTERIES
RATTERS
RATTERY
RATTIER
RATTIEST
RATTING
RATTINGS
RATTISH
RATTLE
RATTLEBAG
RATTLEBAGS
RATTLED
RATTLER
RATTLERS
RATTLES
RATTLIER
RATTLIEST
RATTLIN
RATTLINE
RATTLINES
RATTLING
RATTLINGS
RATTLINS
RATTLY
RATTON
RATTONS
RATTY
RATU
RATUS
RAUCID
RAUCLE
RAUCLER
RAUCLEST
RAUCOUS
RAUCOUSLY
RAUGHT
RAUN
RAUNCH
RAUNCHED
RAUNCHES
RAUNCHIER
RAUNCHIEST
RAUNCHILY
RAUNCHING
RAUNCHY
RAUNGE
RAUNGED
RAUNGES
RAUNGING
RAUNS
RAVAGE
RAVAGED
RAVAGER
RAVAGERS
RAVAGES
RAVAGING
RAVE
RAVED
RAVEL
RAVELIN
RAVELINS
RAVELLED
RAVELLING
RAVELLINGS
RAVELMENT
RAVELMENTS
RAVELS
RAVEN
RAVENED
RAVENER
RAVENERS
RAVENING
RAVENOUS
RAVENS
RAVER
RAVERS
RAVES
RAVIN
RAVINE
RAVINED
RAVINES
RAVING
RAVINGLY
RAVINGS
RAVINING
RAVINS
RAVIOLI
RAVIOLIS
RAVISH
RAVISHED
RAVISHER
RAVISHERS
RAVISHES
RAVISHING
RAW
RAWBONE
RAWBONED
RAWER
RAWEST
RAWHEAD
RAWHEADS
RAWHIDE
RAWHIDES
RAWING
RAWINGS
RAWISH
RAWLY
RAWN
RAWNESS
RAWNESSES
RAWNS
RAWS
RAX
RAXED
RAXES
RAXING
RAY
RAYAH
RAYAHS
RAYED
RAYING
RAYLE
RAYLED
RAYLES
RAYLESS
RAYLET
RAYLETS
RAYLING
RAYNE
RAYNES
RAYON
RAYONS
RAYS
RAZE
RAZED
RAZEE
RAZEED
RAZEEING
RAZEES
RAZES
RAZING
RAZMATAZ
RAZMATAZES
RAZOO
RAZOOS
RAZOR
RAZORABLE
RAZORS
RAZURE
RAZURES
RAZZ
RAZZED
RAZZES
RAZZIA
RAZZIAS
RAZZING
RAZZLE
RAZZLES
RE
REABSORB
REABSORBED
REABSORBING
REABSORBS
REACH
REACHABLE
REACHED
REACHER

REACHERS
REACHES
REACHING
REACHLESS
REACQUIRE
REACQUIRED
REACQUIRES
REACQUIRING
REACT
REACTANCE
REACTANCES
REACTANT
REACTANTS
REACTED
REACTING
REACTION
REACTIONS
REACTIVE
REACTOR
REACTORS
REACTS
REACTUATE
REACTUATED
REACTUATES
REACTUATING
READ
READABLE
READABLY
READAPT
READAPTED
READAPTING
READAPTS
READDRESS
READDRESSED
READDRESSES
READDRESSING
READER
READERS
READIED
READIER
READIES
READIEST
READILY
READINESS
READINESSES
READING
READINGS
READJUST
READJUSTED
READJUSTING
READJUSTS
READMIT
READMITS
READMITTED
READMITTING
READOPT
READOPTED
READOPTING
READOPTS
READS
READVANCE
READVANCED
READVANCES
READVANCING
READVISE
READVISED
READVISES
READVISING
READY
READYING
REAEDIFIED
REAEDIFIES
REAEDIFY
REAEDIFYE
REAEDIFYED
REAEDIFYES
REAEDIFYING
REAFFIRM
REAFFIRMED
REAFFIRMING
REAFFIRMS
REAGENCIES
REAGENCY
REAGENT
REAGENTS
REAK
REAKED
REAKING
REAKS
REAL
REALER
REALEST
REALGAR
REALGARS
REALIA
REALIGN
REALIGNED
REALIGNING
REALIGNS
REALISE
REALISED
REALISER
REALISERS
REALISES
REALISING
REALISM
REALISMS
REALIST
REALISTIC
REALISTS
REALITIES
REALITY
REALIZE
REALIZED
REALIZER
REALIZERS
REALIZES
REALIZING
REALLIE
REALLIED
REALLIES
REALLOT
REALLOTS
REALLOTTED
REALLOTTING
REALLY
REALLYING
REALM
REALMLESS
REALMS
REALNESS
REALNESSES
REALO
REALOS
REALS
REALTIE
REALTIES
REALTIME
REALTOR
REALTORS
REALTY
REAM
REAME
REAMED
REAMEND
REAMENDED
REAMENDING
REAMENDS
REAMER
REAMERS
REAMES
REAMIER
REAMIEST
REAMING
REAMS
REAMY
REAN
REANIMATE
REANIMATED
REANIMATES
REANIMATING
REANNEX
REANNEXED
REANNEXES
REANNEXING
REANS
REANSWER
REANSWERED
REANSWERING
REANSWERS
REAP
REAPED
REAPER
REAPERS
REAPING
REAPPAREL
REAPPARELLED
REAPPARELLING
REAPPARELS
REAPPEAR
REAPPEARED
REAPPEARING
REAPPEARS
REAPPLIED
REAPPLIES
REAPPLY
REAPPLYING
REAPPOINT
REAPPOINTED
REAPPOINTING
REAPPOINTS
REAPS
REAR
REARED
REARER
REARERS
REARGUARD
REARGUARDS
REARHORSE
REARHORSES
REARING
REARISE
REARISEN
REARISES
REARISING
REARLY
REARM
REARMED
REARMICE
REARMING
REARMOST
REARMOUSE
REARMS
REAROSE
REAROUSAL
REAROUSALS
REAROUSE
REAROUSED
REAROUSES
REAROUSING
REARRANGE
REARRANGED
REARRANGES
REARRANGING
REARREST
REARRESTED
REARRESTING
REARRESTS
REARS
REARWARD
REARWARDS
REASCEND
REASCENDED
REASCENDING
REASCENDS
REASCENT
REASCENTS
REASON
REASONED
REASONER
REASONERS
REASONING
REASONINGS
REASONS
REASSERT
REASSERTED
REASSERTING
REASSERTS
REASSESS
REASSESSED
REASSESSES
REASSESSING
REASSIGN
REASSIGNED
REASSIGNING
REASSIGNS
REASSUME
REASSUMED
REASSUMES
REASSUMING
REASSURE
REASSURED
REASSURER
REASSURERS
REASSURES
REASSURING
REAST
REASTED
REASTIER
REASTIEST
REASTING
REASTS
REASTY
REATA
REATAS
REATE
REATES
REATTACH
REATTACHED
REATTACHES
REATTACHING
REATTAIN
REATTAINED
REATTAINING
REATTAINS
REATTEMPT
REATTEMPTED
REATTEMPTING
REATTEMPTS
REAVE
REAVER
REAVERS
REAVES
REAVING
REAWAKE
REAWAKED
REAWAKEN
REAWAKENED
REAWAKENING
REAWAKENINGS
REAWAKENS
REAWAKES
REAWAKING
REAWOKE
REAWOKEN
REBACK
REBACKED
REBACKING
REBACKS
REBADGE
REBADGED
REBADGES
REBADGING
REBAPTISE
REBAPTISED
REBAPTISES
REBAPTISING
REBAPTISM
REBAPTISMS
REBAPTIZE

REBAPTIZED
REBAPTIZES
REBAPTIZING
REBATE
REBATED
REBATER
REBATERS
REBATES
REBATING
REBATO
REBATOES
REBBE
REBBES
REBBETZIN
REBBETZINS
REBEC
REBECK
REBECKS
REBECS
REBEL
REBELDOM
REBELDOMS
REBELLED
REBELLER
REBELLERS
REBELLING
REBELLION
REBELLIONS
REBELLOW
REBELLOWED
REBELLOWING
REBELLOWS
REBELS
REBID
REBIDDEN
REBIDDING
REBIDS
REBIND
REBINDING
REBINDS
REBIRTH
REBIRTHS
REBIT
REBITE
REBITES
REBITING
REBITTEN
REBLOOM
REBLOOMED
REBLOOMING
REBLOOMS
REBLOSSOM
REBLOSSOMED
REBLOSSOMING
REBLOSSOMS
REBOANT
REBOATION
REBOATIONS
REBOIL
REBOILED
REBOILING
REBOILS
REBOOT
REBOOTED
REBOOTING
REBOOTS
REBORE
REBORED
REBORES
REBORING
REBORN
REBORROW
REBORROWED
REBORROWING
REBORROWS
REBOUND
REBOUNDED
REBOUNDING
REBOUNDS
REBRACE
REBRACED
REBRACES
REBRACING
REBUFF
REBUFFED
REBUFFING
REBUFFS
REBUILD
REBUILDING
REBUILDS
REBUILT
REBUKABLE
REBUKE
REBUKED
REBUKEFUL
REBUKER
REBUKERS
REBUKES
REBUKING
REBURIAL
REBURIALS
REBURIED
REBURIES
REBURY
REBURYING
REBUS
REBUSES
REBUT
REBUTMENT
REBUTMENTS
REBUTS
REBUTTAL
REBUTTALS
REBUTTED
REBUTTER
REBUTTERS
REBUTTING
REBUTTON
REBUTTONED
REBUTTONING
REBUTTONS
REC
RECAL
RECALESCE
RECALESCED
RECALESCES
RECALESCING
RECALL
RECALLED
RECALLING
RECALLS
RECALMENT
RECALMENTS
RECALS
RECANT
RECANTED
RECANTER
RECANTERS
RECANTING
RECANTS
RECAP
RECAPPED
RECAPPING
RECAPS
RECAPTION
RECAPTIONS
RECAPTOR
RECAPTORS
RECAPTURE
RECAPTURED
RECAPTURES
RECAPTURING
RECAST
RECASTING
RECASTS
RECATCH
RECATCHES
RECATCHING
RECAUGHT
RECCE
RECCED
RECCEED
RECCEING
RECCES
RECCIED
RECCIES
RECCO
RECCOS
RECCY
RECCYING
RECEDE
RECEDED
RECEDES
RECEDING
RECEIPT
RECEIPTED
RECEIPTING
RECEIPTS
RECEIVAL
RECEIVALS
RECEIVE
RECEIVED
RECEIVER
RECEIVERS
RECEIVES
RECEIVING
RECEIVINGS
RECENCIES
RECENCY
RECENSE
RECENSED
RECENSES
RECENSING
RECENSION
RECENSIONS
RECENT
RECENTER
RECENTEST
RECENTLY
RECENTRE
RECENTRED
RECENTRES
RECENTRING
RECEPT
RECEPTION
RECEPTIONS
RECEPTIVE
RECEPTOR
RECEPTORS
RECEPTS
RECESS
RECESSED
RECESSES
RECESSING
RECESSION
RECESSIONS
RECESSIVE
RECESSIVES
RECHARGE
RECHARGED
RECHARGES
RECHARGING
RECHART
RECHARTED
RECHARTER
RECHARTERED
RECHARTERING
RECHARTERS
RECHARTING
RECHARTS
RECHATE
RECHATES
RECHAUFFE
RECHAUFFES
RECHEAT
RECHEATED
RECHEATING
RECHEATS
RECHECK
RECHECKED
RECHECKING
RECHECKS
RECHERCHE
RECHIE
RECHLESSE
RECIPE
RECIPES
RECIPIENT
RECIPIENTS
RECISION
RECISIONS
RECIT
RECITAL
RECITALS
RECITE
RECITED
RECITER
RECITERS
RECITES
RECITING
RECITS
RECK
RECKAN
RECKED
RECKING
RECKLESS
RECKLING
RECKLINGS
RECKON
RECKONED
RECKONER
RECKONERS
RECKONING
RECKONINGS
RECKONS
RECKS
RECLAIM
RECLAIMED
RECLAIMER
RECLAIMERS
RECLAIMING
RECLAIMS
RECLAME
RECLAMES
RECLIMB
RECLIMBED
RECLIMBING
RECLIMBS
RECLINATE
RECLINE
RECLINED
RECLINER
RECLINERS
RECLINES
RECLINING
RECLOSE
RECLOSED
RECLOSES
RECLOSING
RECLOTHE
RECLOTHED
RECLOTHES
RECLOTHING
RECLUSE
RECLUSELY
RECLUSES
RECLUSION
RECLUSIONS
RECLUSIVE
RECLUSORIES
RECLUSORY
RECODE
RECODED
RECODES
RECODING
RECOGNISE
RECOGNISED
RECOGNISES
RECOGNISING
RECOGNIZE

RECOGNIZED
RECOGNIZES
RECOGNIZING
RECOIL
RECOILED
RECOILER
RECOILERS
RECOILING
RECOILS
RECOIN
RECOINAGE
RECOINAGES
RECOINED
RECOINING
RECOINS
RECOLLECT
RECOLLECTED
RECOLLECTING
RECOLLECTS
RECOLLET
RECOLLETS
RECOMBINE
RECOMBINED
RECOMBINES
RECOMBINING
RECOMFORT
RECOMFORTED
RECOMFORTING
RECOMFORTS
RECOMMEND
RECOMMENDED
RECOMMENDING
RECOMMENDS
RECOMMIT
RECOMMITS
RECOMMITTED
RECOMMITTING
RECOMPACT
RECOMPACTED
RECOMPACTING
RECOMPACTS
RECOMPOSE
RECOMPOSED
RECOMPOSES
RECOMPOSING
RECONCILE
RECONCILED
RECONCILES
RECONCILING
RECONDITE
RECONFIRM
RECONFIRMED
RECONFIRMING
RECONFIRMS
RECONNECT
RECONNECTED
RECONNECTING
RECONNECTS
RECONQUER
RECONQUERED
RECONQUERING
RECONQUERS
RECONVENE
RECONVENED
RECONVENES
RECONVENING
RECONVERT
RECONVERTED
RECONVERTING
RECONVERTS
RECONVEY
RECONVEYED
RECONVEYING
RECONVEYS
RECORD
RECORDED
RECORDER
RECORDERS
RECORDING
RECORDINGS
RECORDIST
RECORDISTS
RECORDS
RECOUNT
RECOUNTAL
RECOUNTALS
RECOUNTED
RECOUNTING
RECOUNTS
RECOUP
RECOUPED
RECOUPING
RECOUPS
RECOURE
RECOURED
RECOURES
RECOURING
RECOURSE
RECOURSED
RECOURSES
RECOURSING
RECOVER
RECOVERED
RECOVEREE
RECOVEREES
RECOVERER
RECOVERERS
RECOVERIES
RECOVERING
RECOVEROR
RECOVERORS
RECOVERS
RECOVERY
RECOWER
RECOWERED
RECOWERING
RECOWERS
RECOYLE
RECOYLED
RECOYLES
RECOYLING
RECREANCE
RECREANCES
RECREANCIES
RECREANCY
RECREANT
RECREANTS
RECREATE
RECREATED
RECREATES
RECREATING
RECREMENT
RECREMENTS
RECROSS
RECROSSED
RECROSSES
RECROSSING
RECRUIT
RECRUITAL
RECRUITALS
RECRUITED
RECRUITER
RECRUITERS
RECRUITING
RECRUITS
RECS
RECTA
RECTAL
RECTALLY
RECTANGLE
RECTANGLES
RECTI
RECTIFIED
RECTIFIER
RECTIFIERS
RECTIFIES
RECTIFY
RECTIFYING
RECTION
RECTIONS
RECTITIC
RECTITIS
RECTITISES
RECTITUDE
RECTITUDES
RECTO
RECTOR
RECTORAL
RECTORATE
RECTORATES
RECTORESS
RECTORESSES
RECTORIAL
RECTORIALS
RECTORIES
RECTORS
RECTORY
RECTOS
RECTRESS
RECTRESSES
RECTRICES
RECTRIX
RECTUM
RECTUMS
RECTUS
RECUILE
RECUILED
RECUILES
RECUILING
RECULE
RECULED
RECULES
RECULING
RECUMBENT
RECUR
RECURE
RECURED
RECURES
RECURING
RECURRED
RECURRENT
RECURRING
RECURS
RECURSION
RECURSIONS
RECURSIVE
RECURVE
RECURVED
RECURVES
RECURVING
RECUSANCE
RECUSANCES
RECUSANCIES
RECUSANCY
RECUSANT
RECUSANTS
RECUSE
RECUSED
RECUSES
RECUSING
RECYCLATE
RECYCLATES
RECYCLE
RECYCLED
RECYCLES
RECYCLING
RECYCLIST
RECYCLISTS
RED
REDACT
REDACTED
REDACTING
REDACTION
REDACTIONS
REDACTOR
REDACTORS
REDACTS
REDAN
REDANS
REDARGUE
REDARGUED
REDARGUES
REDARGUING
REDATE
REDATED
REDATES
REDATING
REDBACK
REDBACKS
REDBELLIES
REDBELLY
REDBIRD
REDBIRDS
REDBREAST
REDBREASTS
REDBRICK
REDBUD
REDBUDS
REDCAP
REDCAPS
REDCOAT
REDCOATS
REDD
REDDEN
REDDENDA
REDDENDO
REDDENDOS
REDDENDUM
REDDENED
REDDENING
REDDENS
REDDER
REDDERS
REDDEST
REDDIER
REDDIEST
REDDING
REDDINGS
REDDISH
REDDLE
REDDLED
REDDLEMAN
REDDLEMEN
REDDLES
REDDLING
REDDS
REDDY
REDE
REDEAL
REDEALING
REDEALS
REDEALT
REDECRAFT
REDECRAFTS
REDEEM
REDEEMED
REDEEMER
REDEEMERS
REDEEMING
REDEEMS
REDEFINE
REDEFINED
REDEFINES
REDEFINING
REDELESS
REDELIVER
REDELIVERED
REDELIVERING
REDELIVERS
REDEPLOY
REDEPLOYED
REDEPLOYING
REDEPLOYS
REDES
REDESCEND
REDESCENDED
REDESCENDING
REDESCENDS
REDESIGN
REDESIGNED

REDESIGNING
REDESIGNS
REDEVELOP
REDEVELOPED
REDEVELOPING
REDEVELOPS
REDFISH
REDFISHES
REDHANDED
REDHEAD
REDHEADS
REDIA
REDIAE
REDIAL
REDIALED
REDIALING
REDIALLED
REDIALLING
REDIALS
REDID
REDING
REDINGOTE
REDINGOTES
REDIP
REDIPPED
REDIPPING
REDIPS
REDIRECT
REDIRECTED
REDIRECTING
REDIRECTS
REDISTIL
REDISTILLED
REDISTILLING
REDISTILS
REDIVIDE
REDIVIDED
REDIVIDES
REDIVIDING
REDIVIVUS
REDLEG
REDLEGS
REDLY
REDNECK
REDNECKS
REDNESS
REDNESSES
REDO
REDOES
REDOING
REDOLENCE
REDOLENCES
REDOLENCIES
REDOLENCY
REDOLENT
REDONE
REDOS
REDOUBLE
REDOUBLED
REDOUBLES
REDOUBLING
REDOUBT
REDOUBTED
REDOUBTING
REDOUBTS
REDOUND
REDOUNDED
REDOUNDING
REDOUNDINGS
REDOUNDS
REDOWA
REDOWAS
REDOX
REDPOLL
REDPOLLS
REDRAFT
REDRAFTED
REDRAFTING
REDRAFTS
REDRAW
REDRAWING
REDRAWN
REDRAWS
REDRESS
REDRESSED
REDRESSER
REDRESSERS
REDRESSES
REDRESSING
REDREW
REDRIVE
REDRIVEN
REDRIVES
REDRIVING
REDROOT
REDROOTS
REDROVE
REDS
REDSEAR
REDSHANK
REDSHANKS
REDSHARE
REDSHIRE
REDSHORT
REDSKIN
REDSKINS
REDSTART
REDSTARTS
REDSTREAK
REDSTREAKS
REDTOP
REDTOPS
REDUCE
REDUCED
REDUCER
REDUCERS
REDUCES
REDUCIBLE
REDUCING
REDUCTANT
REDUCTANTS
REDUCTASE
REDUCTASES
REDUCTION
REDUCTIONS
REDUCTIVE
REDUIT
REDUITS
REDUNDANT
REDUVIID
REDUVIIDS
REDWATER
REDWATERS
REDWING
REDWINGS
REDWOOD
REDWOODS
REE
REEBOK
REEBOKS
REECH
REECHED
REECHES
REECHIE
REECHIER
REECHIEST
REECHING
REECHY
REED
REEDBED
REEDBEDS
REEDE
REEDED
REEDEN
REEDER
REEDERS
REEDES
REEDIER
REEDIEST
REEDINESS
REEDINESSES
REEDING
REEDINGS
REEDLING
REEDLINGS
REEDMACE
REEDMACES
REEDS
REEDSTOP
REEDSTOPS
REEDY
REEF
REEFED
REEFER
REEFERS
REEFING
REEFINGS
REEFS
REEK
REEKED
REEKIE
REEKIER
REEKIEST
REEKING
REEKS
REEKY
REEL
REELED
REELER
REELERS
REELING
REELINGLY
REELINGS
REELMAN
REELMEN
REELS
REEN
REENS
REES
REEST
REESTED
REESTIER
REESTIEST
REESTING
REESTS
REESTY
REEVE
REEVED
REEVES
REEVING
REF
REFACE
REFACED
REFACES
REFACING
REFASHION
REFASHIONED
REFASHIONING
REFASHIONS
REFECT
REFECTED
REFECTING
REFECTION
REFECTIONS
REFECTORIES
REFECTORY
REFECTS
REFEL
REFELLED
REFELLING
REFELS
REFER
REFERABLE
REFEREE
REFEREED
REFEREEING
REFEREES
REFERENCE
REFERENCED
REFERENCES
REFERENCING
REFERENDA
REFERENT
REFERENTS
REFERRAL
REFERRALS
REFERRED
REFERRING
REFERS
REFFED
REFFING
REFFO
REFFOS
REFIGURE
REFIGURED
REFIGURES
REFIGURING
REFILL
REFILLED
REFILLING
REFILLS
REFINE
REFINED
REFINEDLY
REFINER
REFINERIES
REFINERS
REFINERY
REFINES
REFINING
REFININGS
REFIT
REFITMENT
REFITMENTS
REFITS
REFITTED
REFITTING
REFITTINGS
REFLAG
REFLAGGED
REFLAGGING
REFLAGS
REFLATE
REFLATED
REFLATES
REFLATING
REFLATION
REFLATIONS
REFLECT
REFLECTED
REFLECTER
REFLECTERS
REFLECTING
REFLECTOR
REFLECTORS
REFLECTS
REFLET
REFLETS
REFLEX
REFLEXED
REFLEXES
REFLEXING
REFLEXION
REFLEXIONS
REFLEXIVE
REFLEXLY
REFLOAT
REFLOATED
REFLOATING
REFLOATS
REFLOW
REFLOWED
REFLOWER
REFLOWERED
REFLOWERING
REFLOWERINGS
REFLOWERS
REFLOWING
REFLOWINGS
REFLOWS

REFLUENCE
REFLUENCES
REFLUENT
REFLUX
REFLUXED
REFLUXES
REFLUXING
REFOCUS
REFOCUSED
REFOCUSES
REFOCUSING
REFOCUSSED
REFOCUSSES
REFOCUSSING
REFOOT
REFOOTED
REFOOTING
REFOOTS
REFOREST
REFORESTED
REFORESTING
REFORESTS
REFORM
REFORMADE
REFORMADES
REFORMADO
REFORMADOES
REFORMADOS
REFORMAT
REFORMATS
REFORMATTED
REFORMATTING
REFORMED
REFORMER
REFORMERS
REFORMING
REFORMISM
REFORMISMS
REFORMIST
REFORMISTS
REFORMS
REFORTIFIED
REFORTIFIES
REFORTIFY
REFORTIFYING
REFOUND
REFOUNDED
REFOUNDER
REFOUNDERS
REFOUNDING
REFOUNDS
REFRACT
REFRACTED
REFRACTING
REFRACTOR
REFRACTORS
REFRACTS
REFRAIN
REFRAINED
REFRAINING
REFRAINS
REFRAME
REFRAMED
REFRAMES
REFRAMING
REFREEZE
REFREEZES
REFREEZING
REFRESH
REFRESHED
REFRESHEN
REFRESHENED
REFRESHENING
REFRESHENS
REFRESHER
REFRESHERS
REFRESHES
REFRESHING
REFRINGE
REFRINGED
REFRINGES
REFRINGING
REFROZE
REFROZEN
REFS
REFT
REFUEL
REFUELLED
REFUELLING
REFUELS
REFUGE
REFUGED
REFUGEE
REFUGEES
REFUGES
REFUGIA
REFUGING
REFUGIUM
REFULGENT
REFUND
REFUNDED
REFUNDER
REFUNDERS
REFUNDING
REFUNDS
REFURBISH
REFURBISHED
REFURBISHES
REFURBISHING
REFURNISH
REFURNISHED
REFURNISHES
REFURNISHING
REFUSABLE
REFUSAL
REFUSALS
REFUSE
REFUSED
REFUSENIK
REFUSENIKS
REFUSER
REFUSERS
REFUSES
REFUSING
REFUSION
REFUSIONS
REFUSNIK
REFUSNIKS
REFUTABLE
REFUTABLY
REFUTAL
REFUTALS
REFUTE
REFUTED
REFUTER
REFUTERS
REFUTES
REFUTING
REGAIN
REGAINED
REGAINER
REGAINERS
REGAINING
REGAINS
REGAL
REGALE
REGALED
REGALES
REGALIA
REGALIAN
REGALIAS
REGALING
REGALISM
REGALISMS
REGALIST
REGALISTS
REGALITIES
REGALITY
REGALLY
REGALS
REGAR
REGARD
REGARDANT
REGARDED
REGARDER
REGARDERS
REGARDFUL
REGARDING
REGARDS
REGARS
REGATHER
REGATHERED
REGATHERING
REGATHERS
REGATTA
REGATTAS
REGAVE
REGELATE
REGELATED
REGELATES
REGELATING
REGENCE
REGENCES
REGENCIES
REGENCY
REGENT
REGENTS
REGEST
REGESTS
REGGAE
REGGAES
REGGO
REGGOS
REGICIDAL
REGICIDE
REGICIDES
REGIE
REGIES
REGIME
REGIMEN
REGIMENS
REGIMENT
REGIMENTED
REGIMENTING
REGIMENTS
REGIMES
REGIMINAL
REGINA
REGINAE
REGINAL
REGINAS
REGION
REGIONAL
REGIONARY
REGIONS
REGISSEUR
REGISSEURS
REGISTER
REGISTERED
REGISTERING
REGISTERS
REGISTRAR
REGISTRARS
REGISTRIES
REGISTRY
REGIUS
REGIVE
REGIVEN
REGIVES
REGIVING
REGLET
REGLETS
REGMA
REGMATA
REGNAL
REGNANT
REGO
REGOLITH
REGOLITHS
REGORGE
REGORGED
REGORGES
REGORGING
REGOS
REGRADE
REGRADED
REGRADES
REGRADING
REGRANT
REGRANTED
REGRANTING
REGRANTS
REGRATE
REGRATED
REGRATER
REGRATERS
REGRATES
REGRATING
REGRATINGS
REGRATOR
REGRATORS
REGREDE
REGREDED
REGREDES
REGREDING
REGREET
REGREETED
REGREETING
REGREETS
REGRESS
REGRESSED
REGRESSES
REGRESSING
REGRET
REGRETFUL
REGRETS
REGRETTED
REGRETTING
REGRIND
REGRINDING
REGRINDS
REGROUND
REGROUP
REGROUPED
REGROUPING
REGROUPS
REGROWTH
REGROWTHS
REGUERDON
REGUERDONED
REGUERDONING
REGUERDONS
REGULA
REGULAE
REGULAR
REGULARLY
REGULARS
REGULATE
REGULATED
REGULATES
REGULATING
REGULATOR
REGULATORS
REGULINE
REGULISE
REGULISED
REGULISES
REGULISING
REGULIZE
REGULIZED
REGULIZES
REGULIZING
REGULO®
REGULOS
REGULUS
REGULUSES
REGUR
REGURS
REH
REHANDLE

REHANDLED
REHANDLES
REHANDLING
REHANDLINGS
REHANG
REHANGING
REHANGS
REHASH
REHASHED
REHASHES
REHASHING
REHEAR
REHEARD
REHEARING
REHEARINGS
REHEARS
REHEARSAL
REHEARSALS
REHEARSE
REHEARSED
REHEARSER
REHEARSERS
REHEARSES
REHEARSING
REHEARSINGS
REHEAT
REHEATED
REHEATER
REHEATERS
REHEATING
REHEATS
REHEEL
REHEELED
REHEELING
REHEELS
REHOBOAM
REHOBOAMS
REHOUSE
REHOUSED
REHOUSES
REHOUSING
REHOUSINGS
REHS
REHUNG
REHYDRATE
REHYDRATED
REHYDRATES
REHYDRATING
REIF
REIFIED
REIFIES
REIFS
REIFY
REIFYING
REIGN
REIGNED
REIGNING
REIGNS
REIK
REIKI
REIKIS
REIKS
REILLUME
REILLUMED
REILLUMES
REILLUMING
REIMBURSE
REIMBURSED
REIMBURSES
REIMBURSING
REIMPLANT
REIMPLANTED
REIMPLANTING
REIMPLANTS
REIMPORT
REIMPORTED
REIMPORTING
REIMPORTS
REIMPOSE
REIMPOSED
REIMPOSES
REIMPOSING
REIN
REINDEER
REINDEERS
REINED
REINETTE
REINETTES
REINFORCE
REINFORCED
REINFORCES
REINFORCING
REINFORM
REINFORMED
REINFORMING
REINFORMS
REINFUND
REINFUNDED
REINFUNDING
REINFUNDS
REINFUSE
REINFUSED
REINFUSES
REINFUSING
REINHABIT
REINHABITED
REINHABITING
REINHABITS
REINING
REINLESS
REINS
REINSERT
REINSERTED
REINSERTING
REINSERTS
REINSMAN
REINSMEN
REINSPECT
REINSPECTED
REINSPECTING
REINSPECTS
REINSPIRE
REINSPIRED
REINSPIRES
REINSPIRING
REINSTALL
REINSTALLED
REINSTALLING
REINSTALLS
REINSTATE
REINSTATED
REINSTATES
REINSTATING
REINSURE
REINSURED
REINSURER
REINSURERS
REINSURES
REINSURING
REINTER
REINTERRED
REINTERRING
REINTERS
REINVEST
REINVESTED
REINVESTING
REINVESTS
REINVOLVE
REINVOLVED
REINVOLVES
REINVOLVING
REIRD
REIRDS
REIS
REISES
REISSUE
REISSUED
REISSUES
REISSUING
REIST
REISTAFEL
REISTAFELS
REISTED
REISTING
REISTS
REITER
REITERANT
REITERATE
REITERATED
REITERATES
REITERATING
REITERS
REIVE
REIVER
REIVERS
REIVES
REIVING
REJECT
REJECTED
REJECTER
REJECTERS
REJECTING
REJECTION
REJECTIONS
REJECTIVE
REJECTOR
REJECTORS
REJECTS
REJIG
REJIGGED
REJIGGER
REJIGGERED
REJIGGERING
REJIGGERS
REJIGGING
REJIGS
REJOICE
REJOICED
REJOICER
REJOICERS
REJOICES
REJOICING
REJOICINGS
REJOIN
REJOINDER
REJOINDERS
REJOINED
REJOINING
REJOINS
REJON
REJONEO
REJONEOS
REJONES
REJOURN
REJOURNED
REJOURNING
REJOURNS
REJUDGE
REJUDGED
REJUDGES
REJUDGING
REKE
REKED
REKES
REKINDLE
REKINDLED
REKINDLES
REKINDLING
REKING
RELACHE
RELACHES
RELAID
RELAPSE
RELAPSED
RELAPSER
RELAPSERS
RELAPSES
RELAPSING
RELATE
RELATED
RELATER
RELATERS
RELATES
RELATING
RELATION
RELATIONS
RELATIVAL
RELATIVE
RELATIVES
RELATOR
RELATORS
RELAUNCH
RELAUNCHED
RELAUNCHES
RELAUNCHING
RELAX
RELAXANT
RELAXANTS
RELAXED
RELAXES
RELAXIN
RELAXING
RELAXINS
RELAY
RELAYED
RELAYING
RELAYS
RELEASE
RELEASED
RELEASEE
RELEASEES
RELEASER
RELEASERS
RELEASES
RELEASING
RELEASOR
RELEASORS
RELEGABLE
RELEGATE
RELEGATED
RELEGATES
RELEGATING
RELENT
RELENTED
RELENTING
RELENTINGS
RELENTS
RELET
RELETS
RELETTING
RELEVANCE
RELEVANCES
RELEVANCIES
RELEVANCY
RELEVANT
RELIABLE
RELIABLY
RELIANCE
RELIANCES
RELIANT
RELIC
RELICS
RELICT
RELICTS
RELIDE
RELIE
RELIED
RELIEF
RELIEFS
RELIER
RELIERS
RELIES
RELIEVE
RELIEVED
RELIEVER
RELIEVERS
RELIEVES
RELIEVING
RELIEVO
RELIEVOS

RELIGHT
RELIGHTED
RELIGHTING
RELIGHTS
RELIGIEUX
RELIGION
RELIGIONS
RELIGIOSE
RELIGIOSO
RELIGIOUS
RELIGIOUSES
RELINE
RELINED
RELINES
RELINING
RELIQUARIES
RELIQUARY
RELIQUE
RELIQUES
RELIQUIAE
RELISH
RELISHED
RELISHES
RELISHING
RELIT
RELIVE
RELIVED
RELIVER
RELIVERED
RELIVERING
RELIVERS
RELIVES
RELIVING
RELLISH
RELLISHED
RELLISHES
RELLISHING
RELOAD
RELOADED
RELOADING
RELOADS
RELOCATE
RELOCATED
RELOCATES
RELOCATING
RELUCENT
RELUCT
RELUCTANT
RELUCTATE
RELUCTATED
RELUCTATES
RELUCTATING
RELUCTED
RELUCTING
RELUCTS
RELUME
RELUMED
RELUMES
RELUMINE
RELUMINED
RELUMINES
RELUMING
RELUMINING
RELY
RELYING
REM
REMADE
REMADES
REMAIN
REMAINDER
REMAINDERED
REMAINDERING
REMAINDERS
REMAINED
REMAINING
REMAINS
REMAKE
REMAKES
REMAKING
REMAN
REMAND
REMANDED
REMANDING
REMANDS
REMANENCE
REMANENCES
REMANENCIES
REMANENCY
REMANENT
REMANENTS
REMANET
REMANETS
REMANIE
REMANIES
REMANNED
REMANNING
REMANS
REMARK
REMARKED
REMARKER
REMARKERS
REMARKING
REMARKS
REMARQUE
REMARQUED
REMARQUES
REMARRIED
REMARRIES
REMARRY
REMARRYING
REMASTER
REMASTERED
REMASTERING
REMASTERS
REMATCH
REMATCHED
REMATCHES
REMATCHING
REMBLAI
REMBLAIS
REMBLE
REMBLED
REMBLES
REMBLING
REMEAD
REMEADED
REMEADING
REMEADS
REMEASURE
REMEASURED
REMEASURES
REMEASURING
REMEDE
REMEDED
REMEDES
REMEDIAL
REMEDIAT
REMEDIATE
REMEDIED
REMEDIES
REMEDING
REMEDY
REMEDYING
REMEID
REMEIDED
REMEIDING
REMEIDS
REMEMBER
REMEMBERED
REMEMBERING
REMEMBERS
REMEN
REMENS
REMERCIED
REMERCIES
REMERCY
REMERCYING
REMERGE
REMERGED
REMERGES
REMERGING
REMEX
REMIGATE
REMIGATED
REMIGATES
REMIGATING
REMIGES
REMIGIAL
REMIGRATE
REMIGRATED
REMIGRATES
REMIGRATING
REMIND
REMINDED
REMINDER
REMINDERS
REMINDFUL
REMINDING
REMINDS
REMINISCE
REMINISCED
REMINISCES
REMINISCING
REMINT
REMINTED
REMINTING
REMINTS
REMISE
REMISED
REMISES
REMISING
REMISS
REMISSION
REMISSIONS
REMISSIVE
REMISSLY
REMISSORY
REMIT
REMITMENT
REMITMENTS
REMITS
REMITTAL
REMITTALS
REMITTED
REMITTEE
REMITTEES
REMITTENT
REMITTER
REMITTERS
REMITTING
REMITTOR
REMITTORS
REMIX
REMIXED
REMIXES
REMIXING
REMNANT
REMNANTS
REMODEL
REMODELED
REMODELING
REMODELLED
REMODELLING
REMODELS
REMODIFIED
REMODIFIES
REMODIFY
REMODIFYING
REMONTANT
REMONTANTS
REMORA
REMORAS
REMORSE
REMORSES
REMOTE
REMOTELY
REMOTER
REMOTES
REMOTEST
REMOTION
REMOTIONS
REMOUD
REMOULADE
REMOULADES
REMOULD
REMOULDED
REMOULDING
REMOULDS
REMOUNT
REMOUNTED
REMOUNTING
REMOUNTS
REMOVABLE
REMOVABLY
REMOVAL
REMOVALS
REMOVE
REMOVED
REMOVER
REMOVERS
REMOVES
REMOVING
REMS
REMUAGE
REMUAGES
REMUDA
REMUDAS
REMUEUR
REMUEURS
REMURMUR
REMURMURED
REMURMURING
REMURMURS
REN
RENAGUE
RENAGUED
RENAGUES
RENAGUING
RENAL
RENAME
RENAMED
RENAMES
RENAMING
RENASCENT
RENAY
RENAYED
RENAYING
RENAYS
RENCONTRE
RENCONTRES
REND
RENDER
RENDERED
RENDERER
RENDERERS
RENDERING
RENDERINGS
RENDERS
RENDING
RENDITION
RENDITIONS
RENDS
RENDZINA
RENDZINAS
RENEGADE
RENEGADED
RENEGADES
RENEGADING
RENEGADO
RENEGADOS
RENEGATE
RENEGATES
RENEGE
RENEGED
RENEGER
RENEGERS
RENEGES
RENEGING
RENEGUE
RENEGUED

RENEGUER
RENEGUERS
RENEGUES
RENEGUING
RENEW
RENEWABLE
RENEWABLES
RENEWAL
RENEWALS
RENEWED
RENEWER
RENEWERS
RENEWING
RENEWINGS
RENEWS
RENEY
RENEYED
RENEYING
RENEYS
RENFIERST
RENFORCE
RENFORCED
RENFORCES
RENFORCING
RENFORST
RENGA
RENGAS
RENIED
RENIES
RENIFORM
RENIG
RENIGGED
RENIGGING
RENIGS
RENIN
RENINS
RENITENCIES
RENITENCY
RENITENT
RENMINBI
RENMINBIS
RENNE
RENNED
RENNES
RENNET
RENNETS
RENNIN
RENNING
RENNINGS
RENNINS
RENOUNCE
RENOUNCED
RENOUNCER
RENOUNCERS
RENOUNCES
RENOUNCING
RENOVATE
RENOVATED
RENOVATES
RENOVATING
RENOVATOR
RENOVATORS
RENOWN
RENOWNED
RENOWNER
RENOWNERS
RENOWNING
RENOWNS
RENS
RENT
RENTABLE
RENTAL
RENTALLER
RENTALLERS
RENTALS
RENTE
RENTED
RENTER
RENTERS
RENTES
RENTIER
RENTIERS
RENTING
RENTS
RENUMBER
RENUMBERED
RENUMBERING
RENUMBERS
RENVERSE
RENVERSED
RENVERSES
RENVERSING
RENVERST
RENVOI
RENVOIS
RENVOY
RENVOYS
RENY
RENYING
REOCCUPIED
REOCCUPIES
REOCCUPY
REOCCUPYING
REOFFEND
REOFFENDED
REOFFENDING
REOFFENDS
REOPEN
REOPENED
REOPENER
REOPENERS
REOPENING
REOPENS
REORDAIN
REORDAINED
REORDAINING
REORDAINS
REORDER
REORDERED
REORDERING
REORDERS
REORIENT
REORIENTED
REORIENTING
REORIENTS
REP
REPACK
REPACKAGE
REPACKAGED
REPACKAGES
REPACKAGING
REPACKED
REPACKING
REPACKS
REPAID
REPAINT
REPAINTED
REPAINTING
REPAINTINGS
REPAINTS
REPAIR
REPAIRED
REPAIRER
REPAIRERS
REPAIRING
REPAIRMAN
REPAIRMEN
REPAIRS
REPAND
REPAPER
REPAPERED
REPAPERING
REPAPERS
REPARABLE
REPARABLY
REPARTEE
REPARTEED
REPARTEEING
REPARTEES
REPASS
REPASSAGE
REPASSAGES
REPASSED
REPASSES
REPASSING
REPAST
REPASTED
REPASTING
REPASTS
REPASTURE
REPASTURES
REPAY
REPAYABLE
REPAYING
REPAYMENT
REPAYMENTS
REPAYS
REPEAL
REPEALED
REPEALER
REPEALERS
REPEALING
REPEALS
REPEAT
REPEATED
REPEATER
REPEATERS
REPEATING
REPEATINGS
REPEATS
REPECHAGE
REPECHAGES
REPEL
REPELLANT
REPELLANTS
REPELLED
REPELLENT
REPELLENTS
REPELLER
REPELLERS
REPELLING
REPELS
REPENT
REPENTANT
REPENTANTS
REPENTED
REPENTER
REPENTERS
REPENTING
REPENTS
REPEOPLE
REPEOPLED
REPEOPLES
REPEOPLING
REPERCUSS
REPERCUSSED
REPERCUSSES
REPERCUSSING
REPERTORIES
REPERTORY
REPERUSAL
REPERUSALS
REPERUSE
REPERUSED
REPERUSES
REPERUSING
REPETEND
REPETENDS
REPHRASE
REPHRASED
REPHRASES
REPHRASING
REPINE
REPINED
REPINER
REPINERS
REPINES
REPINING
REPININGS
REPIQUE
REPIQUED
REPIQUES
REPIQUING
REPLA
REPLACE
REPLACED
REPLACER
REPLACERS
REPLACES
REPLACING
REPLAN
REPLANNED
REPLANNING
REPLANS
REPLANT
REPLANTED
REPLANTING
REPLANTS
REPLAY
REPLAYED
REPLAYING
REPLAYS
REPLENISH
REPLENISHED
REPLENISHES
REPLENISHING
REPLETE
REPLETED
REPLETES
REPLETING
REPLETION
REPLETIONS
REPLEVIED
REPLEVIES
REPLEVIN
REPLEVINED
REPLEVINING
REPLEVINS
REPLEVY
REPLEVYING
REPLICA
REPLICAS
REPLICATE
REPLICATED
REPLICATES
REPLICATING
REPLICON
REPLICONS
REPLIED
REPLIER
REPLIERS
REPLIES
REPLUM
REPLY
REPLYING
REPO
REPOINT
REPOINTED
REPOINTING
REPOINTS
REPOMAN
REPOMEN
REPONE
REPONED
REPONES
REPONING
REPORT
REPORTAGE
REPORTAGES
REPORTED
REPORTER
REPORTERS
REPORTING
REPORTINGS
REPORTS
REPOS
REPOSAL
REPOSALL
REPOSALLS
REPOSALS

REPOSE
REPOSED
REPOSEDLY
REPOSEFUL
REPOSES
REPOSING
REPOSIT
REPOSITED
REPOSITING
REPOSITOR
REPOSITORS
REPOSITS
REPOSSESS
REPOSSESSED
REPOSSESSES
REPOSSESSING
REPOST
REPOSTED
REPOSTING
REPOSTS
REPOSURE
REPOSURES
REPOT
REPOTS
REPOTTED
REPOTTING
REPOTTINGS
REPOUSSE
REPOUSSES
REPP
REPPED
REPPING
REPPINGS
REPPS
REPREEVE
REPREEVED
REPREEVES
REPREEVING
REPREHEND
REPREHENDED
REPREHENDING
REPREHENDS
REPRESENT
REPRESENTED
REPRESENTING
REPRESENTS
REPRESS
REPRESSED
REPRESSES
REPRESSING
REPRESSOR
REPRESSORS
REPRIEFE
REPRIEFES
REPRIEVAL
REPRIEVALS
REPRIEVE
REPRIEVED
REPRIEVES
REPRIEVING
REPRIMAND
REPRIMANDED
REPRIMANDING
REPRIMANDS
REPRIME
REPRIMED
REPRIMES
REPRIMING
REPRINT
REPRINTED
REPRINTING
REPRINTS
REPRISAL
REPRISALS
REPRISE
REPRISED
REPRISES
REPRISING
REPRIVE
REPRIVED
REPRIVES
REPRIVING
REPRIZE
REPRIZED
REPRIZES
REPRIZING
REPRO
REPROACH
REPROACHED
REPROACHES
REPROACHING
REPROBACIES
REPROBACY
REPROBATE
REPROBATED
REPROBATES
REPROBATING
REPROCESS
REPROCESSED
REPROCESSES
REPROCESSING
REPRODUCE
REPRODUCED
REPRODUCES
REPRODUCING
REPROGRAM
REPROGRAMMED
REPROGRAMMING
REPROGRAMS
REPROOF
REPROOFED
REPROOFING
REPROOFS
REPROS
REPROVAL
REPROVALS
REPROVE
REPROVED
REPROVER
REPROVERS
REPROVES
REPROVING
REPROVINGS
REPRYVE
REPRYVED
REPRYVES
REPRYVING
REPS
REPTANT
REPTATION
REPTATIONS
REPTILE
REPTILES
REPTILIAN
REPTILOID
REPUBLIC
REPUBLICS
REPUBLISH
REPUBLISHED
REPUBLISHES
REPUBLISHING
REPUDIATE
REPUDIATED
REPUDIATES
REPUDIATING
REPUGN
REPUGNANT
REPUGNED
REPUGNING
REPUGNS
REPULP
REPULPED
REPULPING
REPULPS
REPULSE
REPULSED
REPULSES
REPULSING
REPULSION
REPULSIONS
REPULSIVE
REPUNIT
REPUNITS
REPURE
REPURED
REPURES
REPURIFIED
REPURIFIES
REPURIFY
REPURIFYING
REPURING
REPUTABLE
REPUTABLY
REPUTE
REPUTED
REPUTEDLY
REPUTES
REPUTING
REPUTINGS
REQUERE
REQUERED
REQUERES
REQUERING
REQUEST
REQUESTED
REQUESTER
REQUESTERS
REQUESTING
REQUESTS
REQUICKEN
REQUICKENED
REQUICKENING
REQUICKENS
REQUIEM
REQUIEMS
REQUIGHT
REQUIGHTED
REQUIGHTING
REQUIGHTS
REQUIRE
REQUIRED
REQUIRER
REQUIRERS
REQUIRES
REQUIRING
REQUIRINGS
REQUISITE
REQUISITES
REQUIT
REQUITAL
REQUITALS
REQUITE
REQUITED
REQUITER
REQUITERS
REQUITES
REQUITING
REQUITS
REQUITTED
REQUITTING
REQUOTE
REQUOTED
REQUOTES
REQUOTING
REQUOYLE
REQUOYLED
REQUOYLES
REQUOYLING
RERADIATE
RERADIATED
RERADIATES
RERADIATING
RERAIL
RERAILED
RERAILING
RERAILS
RERAN
REREAD
REREADING
REREADS
REREBRACE
REREBRACES
REREDORSE
REREDORSES
REREDOS
REREDOSES
REREDOSSE
REREDOSSES
REREMICE
REREMOUSE
REREVISE
REREVISED
REREVISES
REREVISING
REREWARD
REREWARDS
REROUTE
REROUTED
REROUTEING
REROUTES
REROUTING
RERUN
RERUNNING
RERUNS
RES
RESAID
RESALE
RESALES
RESALGAR
RESALGARS
RESALUTE
RESALUTED
RESALUTES
RESALUTING
RESAT
RESAY
RESAYING
RESAYS
RESCALE
RESCALED
RESCALES
RESCALING
RESCIND
RESCINDED
RESCINDING
RESCINDS
RESCORE
RESCORED
RESCORES
RESCORING
RESCRIPT
RESCRIPTED
RESCRIPTING
RESCRIPTS
RESCUABLE
RESCUE
RESCUED
RESCUER
RESCUERS
RESCUES
RESCUING
RESEAL
RESEALED
RESEALING
RESEALS
RESEARCH
RESEARCHED
RESEARCHES
RESEARCHING
RESEAT
RESEATED
RESEATING
RESEATS
RESEAU
RESEAUS
RESEAUX
RESECT
RESECTED
RESECTING
RESECTION

RESECTIONS
RESECTS
RESEDA
RESEDAS
RESEIZE
RESEIZED
RESEIZES
RESEIZING
RESELECT
RESELECTED
RESELECTING
RESELECTS
RESELL
RESELLING
RESELLS
RESEMBLE
RESEMBLED
RESEMBLER
RESEMBLERS
RESEMBLES
RESEMBLING
RESENT
RESENTED
RESENTER
RESENTERS
RESENTFUL
RESENTING
RESENTIVE
RESENTS
RESERPINE
RESERPINES
RESERVE
RESERVED
RESERVES
RESERVING
RESERVIST
RESERVISTS
RESERVOIR
RESERVOIRED
RESERVOIRING
RESERVOIRS
RESES
RESET
RESETS
RESETTED
RESETTER
RESETTERS
RESETTING
RESETTLE
RESETTLED
RESETTLES
RESETTLING
RESHAPE
RESHAPED
RESHAPES
RESHAPING
RESHIP
RESHIPPED
RESHIPPING
RESHIPS
RESHUFFLE
RESHUFFLED
RESHUFFLES
RESHUFFLING
RESIANCE
RESIANCES
RESIANT
RESIANTS
RESIDE
RESIDED
RESIDENCE
RESIDENCES
RESIDENCIES
RESIDENCY
RESIDENT
RESIDENTS
RESIDER
RESIDERS
RESIDES
RESIDING
RESIDUA
RESIDUAL
RESIDUALS
RESIDUARY
RESIDUE
RESIDUES
RESIDUOUS
RESIDUUM
RESIGN
RESIGNED
RESIGNER
RESIGNERS
RESIGNING
RESIGNS
RESILE
RESILED
RESILES
RESILIENT
RESILING
RESIN
RESINATA
RESINATAS
RESINATE
RESINATES
RESINED
RESINER
RESINERS
RESINIFIED
RESINIFIES
RESINIFY
RESINIFYING
RESINING
RESINISE
RESINISED
RESINISES
RESINISING
RESINIZE
RESINIZED
RESINIZES
RESINIZING
RESINOID
RESINOIDS
RESINOSES
RESINOSIS
RESINOUS
RESINS
RESIST
RESISTANT
RESISTANTS
RESISTED
RESISTENT
RESISTENTS
RESISTING
RESISTIVE
RESISTOR
RESISTORS
RESISTS
RESIT
RESITS
RESITTING
RESKEW
RESKEWED
RESKEWING
RESKEWS
RESKILL
RESKILLED
RESKILLING
RESKILLS
RESKUE
RESKUED
RESKUES
RESKUING
RESNATRON
RESNATRONS
RESOLD
RESOLE
RESOLED
RESOLES
RESOLING
RESOLUBLE
RESOLUTE
RESOLUTES
RESOLVE
RESOLVED
RESOLVENT
RESOLVENTS
RESOLVER
RESOLVERS
RESOLVES
RESOLVING
RESONANCE
RESONANCES
RESONANT
RESONATE
RESONATED
RESONATES
RESONATING
RESONATOR
RESONATORS
RESORB
RESORBED
RESORBENT
RESORBING
RESORBS
RESORCIN
RESORCINS
RESORT
RESORTED
RESORTER
RESORTERS
RESORTING
RESORTS
RESOUND
RESOUNDED
RESOUNDING
RESOUNDS
RESOURCE
RESOURCED
RESOURCES
RESOURCING
RESPEAK
RESPEAKING
RESPEAKS
RESPECT
RESPECTED
RESPECTER
RESPECTERS
RESPECTING
RESPECTS
RESPELL
RESPELLED
RESPELLING
RESPELLS
RESPELT
RESPIRE
RESPIRED
RESPIRES
RESPIRING
RESPITE
RESPITED
RESPITES
RESPITING
RESPLEND
RESPLENDED
RESPLENDING
RESPLENDS
RESPOKE
RESPOKEN
RESPOND
RESPONDED
RESPONDER
RESPONDERS
RESPONDING
RESPONDS
RESPONSA
RESPONSE
RESPONSER
RESPONSERS
RESPONSES
RESPONSOR
RESPONSORS
RESPONSUM
RESPONSUMS
RESPRAY
RESPRAYED
RESPRAYING
RESPRAYS
RESSALDAR
RESSALDARS
REST
RESTAFF
RESTAFFED
RESTAFFING
RESTAFFS
RESTAGE
RESTAGED
RESTAGES
RESTAGING
RESTART
RESTARTED
RESTARTER
RESTARTERS
RESTARTING
RESTARTS
RESTATE
RESTATED
RESTATES
RESTATING
RESTED
RESTEM
RESTEMMED
RESTEMMING
RESTEMS
RESTER
RESTERS
RESTFUL
RESTFULLER
RESTFULLEST
RESTFULLY
RESTIER
RESTIEST
RESTIFF
RESTIFORM
RESTING
RESTINGS
RESTITUTE
RESTITUTED
RESTITUTES
RESTITUTING
RESTIVE
RESTIVELY
RESTLESS
RESTOCK
RESTOCKED
RESTOCKING
RESTOCKS
RESTORE
RESTORED
RESTORER
RESTORERS
RESTORES
RESTORING
RESTRAIN
RESTRAINED
RESTRAINING
RESTRAININGS
RESTRAINS
RESTRAINT
RESTRAINTS
RESTRICT
RESTRICTED
RESTRICTING
RESTRICTS
RESTRING
RESTRINGE
RESTRINGED
RESTRINGEING
RESTRINGES
RESTRINGING
RESTRINGS

ESTRUNG
ESTS
ESTY
ESTYLE
ESTYLED
ESTYLES
ESTYLING
ESUBMIT
ESUBMITS
ESUBMITTED
ESUBMITTING
ESULT
ESULTANT
ESULTANTS
ESULTED
ESULTFUL
ESULTING
ESULTS
ESUMABLE
ESUME
ESUMED
ESUMES
ESUMING
ESUPINE
ESURFACE
ESURFACED
ESURFACES
ESURFACING
ESURGE
ESURGED
ESURGENT
ESURGES
ESURGING
ESURRECT
ESURRECTED
ESURRECTING
ESURRECTS
ESURVEY
ESURVEYED
ESURVEYING
ESURVEYS
ET
ETABLE
ETABLES
ETAIL
ETAILED
ETAILER
ETAILERS
ETAILING
ETAILS
ETAIN
ETAINED
ETAINER
ETAINERS
ETAINING
ETAINS
ETAKE
ETAKEN
ETAKER
ETAKERS
ETAKES
ETAKING
ETAKINGS
ETALIATE
RETALIATED
RETALIATES
RETALIATING
RETAMA
RETAMAS
RETARD
RETARDANT
RETARDANTS
RETARDATE
RETARDATES
RETARDED
RETARDER
RETARDERS
RETARDING
RETARDS
RETCH
RETCHED
RETCHES
RETCHING
RETCHLESS
RETE
RETELL
RETELLER
RETELLERS
RETELLING
RETELLS
RETENE
RETENES
RETENTION
RETENTIONS
RETENTIVE
RETES
RETEXTURE
RETEXTURED
RETEXTURES
RETEXTURING
RETHINK
RETHINKING
RETHINKS
RETHOUGHT
RETIAL
RETIARII
RETIARIUS
RETIARIUSES
RETIARY
RETICELLA
RETICELLAS
RETICENCE
RETICENCES
RETICENCIES
RETICENCY
RETICENT
RETICLE
RETICLES
RETICULAR
RETICULE
RETICULES
RETICULUM
RETICULUMS
RETIE
RETIED
RETIES
RETIFORM
RETILE
RETILED
RETILES
RETILING
RETIME
RETIMED
RETIMES
RETIMING
RETINA
RETINAE
RETINAL
RETINAS
RETINITE
RETINITES
RETINITIS
RETINITISES
RETINOID
RETINOIDS
RETINOL
RETINOLS
RETINUE
RETINUES
RETINULA
RETINULAE
RETINULAR
RETIRACIES
RETIRACY
RETIRAL
RETIRALS
RETIRE
RETIRED
RETIREDLY
RETIREE
RETIREES
RETIRER
RETIRERS
RETIRES
RETIRING
RETITLE
RETITLED
RETITLES
RETITLING
RETOLD
RETOOK
RETOOL
RETOOLED
RETOOLING
RETOOLS
RETORSION
RETORSIONS
RETORT
RETORTED
RETORTER
RETORTERS
RETORTING
RETORTION
RETORTIONS
RETORTIVE
RETORTS
RETOUCH
RETOUCHED
RETOUCHER
RETOUCHERS
RETOUCHES
RETOUCHING
RETOUR
RETOURED
RETOURING
RETOURS
RETRACE
RETRACED
RETRACES
RETRACING
RETRACT
RETRACTED
RETRACTING
RETRACTOR
RETRACTORS
RETRACTS
RETRAICT
RETRAICTS
RETRAIN
RETRAINED
RETRAINING
RETRAINS
RETRAIT
RETRAITE
RETRAITES
RETRAITS
RETRAITT
RETRAITTS
RETRAL
RETRALLY
RETRATE
RETRATED
RETRATES
RETRATING
RETREAD
RETREADED
RETREADING
RETREADS
RETREAT
RETREATED
RETREATING
RETREATS
RETREE
RETREES
RETRENCH
RETRENCHED
RETRENCHES
RETRENCHING
RETRIAL
RETRIALS
RETRIBUTE
RETRIBUTED
RETRIBUTES
RETRIBUTING
RETRIED
RETRIES
RETRIEVAL
RETRIEVALS
RETRIEVE
RETRIEVED
RETRIEVER
RETRIEVERS
RETRIEVES
RETRIEVING
RETRIEVINGS
RETRIM
RETRIMMED
RETRIMMING
RETRIMS
RETRO
RETROACT
RETROACTED
RETROACTING
RETROACTS
RETROCEDE
RETROCEDED
RETROCEDES
RETROCEDING
RETROD
RETRODDEN
RETROFIT
RETROFITS
RETROFITTED
RETROFITTING
RETROFITTINGS
RETROFLEX
RETROJECT
RETROJECTED
RETROJECTING
RETROJECTS
RETRORSE
RETROS
RETROUSSE
RETROVERT
RETROVERTED
RETROVERTING
RETROVERTS
RETRY
RETRYING
RETS
RETSINA
RETSINAS
RETTED
RETTERIES
RETTERY
RETTING
RETUND
RETUNDED
RETUNDING
RETUNDS
RETUNE
RETUNED
RETUNES
RETUNING
RETURF
RETURFED
RETURFING
RETURFS
RETURN
RETURNED
RETURNEE
RETURNEES
RETURNER
RETURNERS
RETURNIK
RETURNIKS
RETURNING
RETURNS
RETUSE
RETYING

REUNIFIED
REUNIFIES
REUNIFY
REUNIFYING
REUNION
REUNIONS
REUNITE
REUNITED
REUNITES
REUNITING
REURGE
REURGED
REURGES
REURGING
REUSABLE
REUSE
REUSED
REUSES
REUSING
REUTTER
REUTTERED
REUTTERING
REUTTERS
REV
REVALENTA
REVALENTAS
REVALUE
REVALUED
REVALUES
REVALUING
REVAMP
REVAMPED
REVAMPING
REVAMPS
REVANCHE
REVANCHES
REVEAL
REVEALED
REVEALER
REVEALERS
REVEALING
REVEALINGS
REVEALS
REVEILLE
REVEILLES
REVEL
REVELATOR
REVELATORS
REVELLED
REVELLER
REVELLERS
REVELLING
REVELLINGS
REVELRIES
REVELRY
REVELS
REVENANT
REVENANTS
REVENGE
REVENGED
REVENGER
REVENGERS
REVENGES
REVENGING
REVENGINGS
REVENGIVE
REVENUE
REVENUED
REVENUES
REVERABLE
REVERB
REVERBED
REVERBING
REVERBS
REVERE
REVERED
REVERENCE
REVERENCED
REVERENCES
REVERENCING
REVEREND
REVERENDS
REVERENT
REVERER
REVERERS
REVERES
REVERIE
REVERIES
REVERING
REVERIST
REVERISTS
REVERS
REVERSAL
REVERSALS
REVERSE
REVERSED
REVERSELY
REVERSER
REVERSERS
REVERSES
REVERSI
REVERSING
REVERSINGS
REVERSION
REVERSIONS
REVERSIS
REVERSISES
REVERSO
REVERSOS
REVERT
REVERTED
REVERTING
REVERTIVE
REVERTS
REVERY
REVEST
REVESTED
REVESTING
REVESTRIES
REVESTRY
REVESTS
REVET
REVETMENT
REVETMENTS
REVETS
REVETTED
REVETTING
REVEUR
REVEURS
REVEUSE
REVEUSES
REVICTUAL
REVICTUALLED
REVICTUALLING
REVICTUALS
REVIE
REVIED
REVIES
REVIEW
REVIEWAL
REVIEWALS
REVIEWED
REVIEWER
REVIEWERS
REVIEWING
REVIEWS
REVILE
REVILED
REVILER
REVILERS
REVILES
REVILING
REVILINGS
REVISABLE
REVISAL
REVISALS
REVISE
REVISED
REVISER
REVISERS
REVISES
REVISING
REVISION
REVISIONS
REVISIT
REVISITED
REVISITING
REVISITS
REVISOR
REVISORS
REVISORY
REVIVABLE
REVIVABLY
REVIVAL
REVIVALS
REVIVE
REVIVED
REVIVER
REVIVERS
REVIVES
REVIVIFIED
REVIVIFIES
REVIVIFY
REVIVIFYING
REVIVING
REVIVINGS
REVIVOR
REVIVORS
REVOCABLE
REVOCABLY
REVOKABLE
REVOKE
REVOKED
REVOKES
REVOKING
REVOLT
REVOLTED
REVOLTER
REVOLTERS
REVOLTING
REVOLTS
REVOLUTE
REVOLVE
REVOLVED
REVOLVER
REVOLVERS
REVOLVES
REVOLVING
REVOLVINGS
REVS
REVUE
REVUES
REVULSION
REVULSIONS
REVULSIVE
REVVED
REVVING
REVYING
REW
REWARD
REWARDED
REWARDER
REWARDERS
REWARDFUL
REWARDING
REWARDS
REWAREWA
REWAREWAS
REWEIGH
REWEIGHED
REWEIGHING
REWEIGHS
REWIND
REWINDING
REWINDS
REWIRE
REWIRED
REWIRES
REWIRING
REWORD
REWORDED
REWORDING
REWORDS
REWORK
REWORKED
REWORKING
REWORKS
REWOUND
REWRAP
REWRAPPED
REWRAPPING
REWRAPS
REWRITE
REWRITES
REWRITING
REWRITTEN
REWROTE
REWS
REWTH
REWTHS
REX
REYNARD
REYNARDS
REZ
REZONE
REZONED
REZONES
REZONING
REZZES
RHABDOID
RHABDOIDS
RHABDOM
RHABDOMS
RHABDUS
RHABDUSES
RHACHIDES
RHACHIS
RHACHISES
RHACHITIS
RHACHITISES
RHAGADES
RHAMPHOID
RHAPHE
RHAPHES
RHAPHIDE
RHAPHIDES
RHAPHIS
RHAPONTIC
RHAPONTICS
RHAPSODE
RHAPSODES
RHAPSODIC
RHAPSODIES
RHAPSODY
RHATANIES
RHATANY
RHEA
RHEAS
RHEMATIC
RHENIUM
RHENIUMS
RHEOCHORD
RHEOCHORDS
RHEOCORD
RHEOCORDS
RHEOLOGIC
RHEOLOGIES
RHEOLOGY
RHEOMETER
RHEOMETERS
RHEOSTAT
RHEOSTATS
RHEOTAXES
RHEOTAXIS
RHEOTOME
RHEOTOMES
RHEOTROPE
RHEOTROPES
RHESUS
RHESUSES

HETOR
HETORIC
HETORICS
HETORISE
HETORISED
HETORISES
HETORISING
HETORIZE
HETORIZED
HETORIZES
HETORIZING
HETORS
HEUM
HEUMATIC
HEUMATICS
HEUMATIZ
HEUMATIZES
HEUMED
HEUMIER
HEUMIEST
HEUMS
HEUMY
HEXES
HEXIS
HEXISES
HIES
HIME
HIMES
HINAL
HINE
HINES
HINITIS
HINITISES
HINO
HINOLITH
HINOLITHS
HINOLOGIES
HINOLOGY
HINOS
HIPIDATE
HIPIDION
HIPIDIONS
HIPIDIUM
HIPIDIUMS
HIZIC
HIZINE
HIZINES
HIZOBIA
HIZOBIUM
HIZOCARP
HIZOCARPS
HIZOCAUL
HIZOCAULS
HIZOID
HIZOIDAL
HIZOIDS
HIZOME
HIZOMES
HIZOPI
HIZOPOD
HIZOPODS
HIZOPUS
HIZOPUSES
HO
RHODAMINE
RHODAMINES
RHODANATE
RHODANATES
RHODANIC
RHODANISE
RHODANISED
RHODANISES
RHODANISING
RHODANIZE
RHODANIZED
RHODANIZES
RHODANIZING
RHODIC
RHODIE
RHODIES
RHODIUM
RHODIUMS
RHODOLITE
RHODOLITES
RHODONITE
RHODONITES
RHODOPSIN
RHODOPSINS
RHODORA
RHODORAS
RHODOUS
RHODY
RHOEADINE
RHOEADINES
RHOMB
RHOMBI
RHOMBIC
RHOMBOI
RHOMBOID
RHOMBOIDS
RHOMBOS
RHOMBS
RHOMBUS
RHOMBUSES
RHONCHAL
RHONCHI
RHONCHIAL
RHONCHUS
RHONE
RHONES
RHOPALIC
RHOPALISM
RHOPALISMS
RHOS
RHOTACISE
RHOTACISED
RHOTACISES
RHOTACISING
RHOTACISM
RHOTACISMS
RHOTACIZE
RHOTACIZED
RHOTACIZES
RHOTACIZING
RHOTIC
RHUBARB
RHUBARBS
RHUBARBY
RHUMB
RHUMBA
RHUMBAED
RHUMBAING
RHUMBAS
RHUMBS
RHUS
RHUSES
RHY
RHYME
RHYMED
RHYMELESS
RHYMER
RHYMERS
RHYMES
RHYMESTER
RHYMESTERS
RHYMING
RHYMIST
RHYMISTS
RHYNE
RHYNES
RHYOLITE
RHYOLITES
RHYOLITIC
RHYTA
RHYTHM
RHYTHMAL
RHYTHMED
RHYTHMI
RHYTHMIC
RHYTHMICS
RHYTHMISE
RHYTHMISED
RHYTHMISES
RHYTHMISING
RHYTHMIST
RHYTHMISTS
RHYTHMIZE
RHYTHMIZED
RHYTHMIZES
RHYTHMIZING
RHYTHMS
RHYTHMUS
RHYTHMUSES
RHYTINA
RHYTINAS
RHYTON
RIA
RIAL
RIALS
RIANCIES
RIANCY
RIANT
RIAS
RIATA
RIATAS
RIB
RIBALD
RIBALDRIES
RIBALDRY
RIBALDS
RIBAND
RIBANDS
RIBATTUTA
RIBATTUTAS
RIBAUD
RIBAUDRED
RIBAUDRIES
RIBAUDRY
RIBAUDS
RIBBAND
RIBBANDS
RIBBED
RIBBIER
RIBBIEST
RIBBING
RIBBINGS
RIBBON
RIBBONED
RIBBONING
RIBBONRIES
RIBBONRY
RIBBONS
RIBBONY
RIBBY
RIBCAGE
RIBCAGES
RIBIBE
RIBIBES
RIBIBLE
RIBIBLES
RIBLESS
RIBLET
RIBLETS
RIBLIKE
RIBOSE
RIBOSES
RIBOSOMAL
RIBOSOME
RIBOSOMES
RIBOZYME
RIBOZYMES
RIBS
RIBSTON
RIBSTONE
RIBSTONES
RIBSTONS
RIBWORK
RIBWORKS
RIBWORT
RIBWORTS
RICE
RICED
RICER
RICERCAR
RICERCARE
RICERCARES
RICERCARS
RICERCATA
RICERCATAS
RICERS
RICES
RICEY
RICH
RICHED
RICHEN
RICHENED
RICHENING
RICHENS
RICHER
RICHES
RICHESSE
RICHESSES
RICHEST
RICHING
RICHLY
RICHNESS
RICHNESSES
RICHT
RICHTED
RICHTER
RICHTEST
RICHTING
RICHTS
RICIER
RICIEST
RICIN
RICING
RICINS
RICK
RICKED
RICKER
RICKERS
RICKETIER
RICKETIEST
RICKETILY
RICKETS
RICKETTIER
RICKETTIEST
RICKETTY
RICKETY
RICKING
RICKLE
RICKLES
RICKLY
RICKS
RICKSHA
RICKSHAS
RICKSHAW
RICKSHAWS
RICKSTAND
RICKSTANDS
RICKSTICK
RICKSTICKS
RICKYARD
RICKYARDS
RICOCHET
RICOCHETED
RICOCHETING
RICOCHETS
RICOCHETTED
RICOCHETTING
RICOTTA
RICOTTAS
RICTAL
RICTUS
RICTUSES
RICY
RID
RIDABLE
RIDDANCE

RIDDANCES
RIDDED
RIDDEN
RIDDER
RIDDERS
RIDDING
RIDDLE
RIDDLED
RIDDLER
RIDDLERS
RIDDLES
RIDDLING
RIDDLINGS
RIDE
RIDEABLE
RIDENT
RIDER
RIDERED
RIDERLESS
RIDERS
RIDES
RIDGE
RIDGEBACK
RIDGEBACKS
RIDGED
RIDGEL
RIDGELS
RIDGER
RIDGERS
RIDGES
RIDGEWAY
RIDGEWAYS
RIDGIER
RIDGIEST
RIDGIL
RIDGILS
RIDGING
RIDGINGS
RIDGLING
RIDGLINGS
RIDGY
RIDICULE
RIDICULED
RIDICULER
RIDICULERS
RIDICULES
RIDICULING
RIDING
RIDINGS
RIDOTTO
RIDOTTOS
RIDS
RIEL
RIELS
RIEM
RIEMPIE
RIEMPIES
RIEMS
RIEVE
RIEVER
RIEVERS
RIEVES
RIEVING
RIFE
RIFELY
RIFENESS
RIFENESSES
RIFER
RIFEST
RIFF
RIFFLE
RIFFLED
RIFFLER
RIFFLERS
RIFFLES
RIFFLING
RIFFS
RIFLE
RIFLED
RIFLEMAN
RIFLEMEN
RIFLER
RIFLERS
RIFLES
RIFLING
RIFLINGS
RIFT
RIFTE
RIFTED
RIFTIER
RIFTIEST
RIFTING
RIFTLESS
RIFTS
RIFTY
RIG
RIGADOON
RIGADOONS
RIGATONI
RIGATONIS
RIGG
RIGGALD
RIGGALDS
RIGGED
RIGGER
RIGGERS
RIGGING
RIGGINGS
RIGGISH
RIGGS
RIGHT
RIGHTABLE
RIGHTED
RIGHTEN
RIGHTENED
RIGHTENING
RIGHTENS
RIGHTEOUS
RIGHTER
RIGHTERS
RIGHTEST
RIGHTFUL
RIGHTING
RIGHTINGS
RIGHTISH
RIGHTIST
RIGHTISTS
RIGHTLESS
RIGHTLY
RIGHTNESS
RIGHTNESSES
RIGHTO
RIGHTOS
RIGHTS
RIGHTSIZE
RIGHTSIZED
RIGHTSIZES
RIGHTSIZING
RIGHTWARD
RIGHTWARDS
RIGID
RIGIDER
RIGIDEST
RIGIDIFIED
RIGIDIFIES
RIGIDIFY
RIGIDIFYING
RIGIDISE
RIGIDISED
RIGIDISES
RIGIDISING
RIGIDITIES
RIGIDITY
RIGIDIZE
RIGIDIZED
RIGIDIZES
RIGIDIZING
RIGIDLY
RIGIDNESS
RIGIDNESSES
RIGIDS
RIGLIN
RIGLING
RIGLINGS
RIGLINS
RIGMAROLE
RIGMAROLES
RIGOL
RIGOLL
RIGOLLS
RIGOLS
RIGOR
RIGORISM
RIGORISMS
RIGORIST
RIGORISTS
RIGOROUS
RIGORS
RIGOUR
RIGOURS
RIGS
RIGWIDDIE
RIGWIDDIES
RIGWOODIE
RIGWOODIES
RIJSTAFEL
RIJSTAFELS
RIKISHI
RILE
RILED
RILES
RILEY
RILIER
RILIEST
RILIEVI
RILIEVO
RILING
RILL
RILLE
RILLED
RILLES
RILLET
RILLETS
RILLETTES
RILLING
RILLMARK
RILLMARKS
RILLS
RIM
RIMA
RIMAE
RIME
RIMED
RIMER
RIMERS
RIMES
RIMIER
RIMIEST
RIMING
RIMLESS
RIMMED
RIMMING
RIMMINGS
RIMOSE
RIMOUS
RIMS
RIMU
RIMUS
RIMY
RIN
RIND
RINDED
RINDIER
RINDIEST
RINDING
RINDLESS
RINDS
RINDY
RINE
RINES
RING
RINGBIT
RINGBITS
RINGBONE
RINGBONES
RINGED
RINGENT
RINGER
RINGERS
RINGGIT
RINGGITS
RINGHALS
RINGHALSES
RINGING
RINGINGLY
RINGINGS
RINGLESS
RINGLET
RINGLETED
RINGLETS
RINGMAN
RINGMEN
RINGS
RINGSIDE
RINGSIDER
RINGSIDERS
RINGSIDES
RINGSTAND
RINGSTANDS
RINGSTER
RINGSTERS
RINGTAIL
RINGTAILS
RINGWAY
RINGWAYS
RINGWISE
RINGWORK
RINGWORKS
RINGWORM
RINGWORMS
RINK
RINKED
RINKHALS
RINKHALSES
RINKING
RINKS
RINNING
RINS
RINSABLE
RINSE
RINSEABLE
RINSED
RINSER
RINSERS
RINSES
RINSIBLE
RINSING
RINSINGS
RIOT
RIOTED
RIOTER
RIOTERS
RIOTING
RIOTINGS
RIOTISE
RIOTISES
RIOTIZE
RIOTIZES
RIOTOUS
RIOTOUSLY
RIOTRIES
RIOTRY
RIOTS
RIP
RIPARIAL
RIPARIAN
RIPARIANS
RIPE
RIPECK
RIPECKS

RIPED
RIPELY
RIPEN
RIPENED
RIPENESS
RIPENESSES
RIPENING
RIPENS
RIPER
RIPERS
RIPES
RIPEST
RIPIENI
RIPIENIST
RIPIENISTS
RIPIENO
RIPIENOS
RIPING
RIPOSTE
RIPOSTED
RIPOSTES
RIPOSTING
RIPP
RIPPED
RIPPER
RIPPERS
RIPPIER
RIPPIERS
RIPPING
RIPPINGLY
RIPPLE
RIPPLED
RIPPLER
RIPPLERS
RIPPLES
RIPPLET
RIPPLETS
RIPPLIER
RIPPLIEST
RIPPLING
RIPPLINGS
RIPPLY
RIPPS
RIPRAP
RIPRAPS
RIPS
RIPSTOP
RIPT
RIPTIDE
RIPTIDES
RISALDAR
RISALDARS
RISE
RISEN
RISER
RISERS
RISES
RISHI
RISHIS
RISIBLE
RISING
RISINGS
RISK
RISKED
RISKER
RISKERS
RISKFUL
RISKIER
RISKIEST
RISKILY
RISKINESS
RISKINESSES
RISKING
RISKS
RISKY
RISOLUTO
RISOTTO
RISOTTOS
RISP
RISPED
RISPETTI
RISPETTO
RISPING
RISPINGS
RISPS
RISQUE
RISQUES
RISSOLE
RISSOLES
RISUS
RISUSES
RIT
RITE
RITELESS
RITENUTO
RITENUTOS
RITES
RITORNEL
RITORNELL
RITORNELLS
RITORNELS
RITS
RITT
RITTED
RITTER
RITTERS
RITTING
RITTS
RITUAL
RITUALISE
RITUALISED
RITUALISES
RITUALISING
RITUALISM
RITUALISMS
RITUALIST
RITUALISTS
RITUALIZE
RITUALIZED
RITUALIZES
RITUALIZING
RITUALLY
RITUALS
RITZIER
RITZIEST
RITZY
RIVA
RIVAGE
RIVAGES
RIVAL
RIVALESS
RIVALESSES
RIVALISE
RIVALISED
RIVALISES
RIVALISING
RIVALITIES
RIVALITY
RIVALIZE
RIVALIZED
RIVALIZES
RIVALIZING
RIVALLED
RIVALLESS
RIVALLING
RIVALRIES
RIVALRY
RIVALS
RIVALSHIP
RIVALSHIPS
RIVAS
RIVE
RIVED
RIVEL
RIVELLED
RIVELLING
RIVELS
RIVEN
RIVER
RIVERAIN
RIVERAINS
RIVERBANK
RIVERBANKS
RIVERED
RIVERET
RIVERETS
RIVERINE
RIVERLESS
RIVERLIKE
RIVERMAN
RIVERMEN
RIVERS
RIVERSIDE
RIVERSIDES
RIVERWAY
RIVERWAYS
RIVERWEED
RIVERWEEDS
RIVERY
RIVES
RIVET
RIVETED
RIVETER
RIVETERS
RIVETING
RIVETINGS
RIVETS
RIVETTED
RIVETTING
RIVIERA
RIVIERAS
RIVIERE
RIVIERES
RIVING
RIVLIN
RIVLINS
RIVO
RIVOS
RIVULET
RIVULETS
RIYAL
RIYALS
RIZ
RIZA
RIZARD
RIZARDS
RIZAS
RIZZAR
RIZZARED
RIZZARING
RIZZARS
RIZZART
RIZZARTS
RIZZER
RIZZERED
RIZZERING
RIZZERS
RIZZOR
RIZZORED
RIZZORING
RIZZORS
ROACH
ROACHED
ROACHES
ROACHING
ROAD
ROADBLOCK
ROADBLOCKS
ROADCRAFT
ROADCRAFTS
ROADHOUSE
ROADHOUSES
ROADIE
ROADIES
ROADING
ROADINGS
ROADLESS
ROADMAN
ROADMEN
ROADS
ROADSHOW
ROADSHOWS
ROADSIDE
ROADSIDES
ROADSMAN
ROADSMEN
ROADSTEAD
ROADSTEADS
ROADSTER
ROADSTERS
ROADWAY
ROADWAYS
ROADWORKS
ROAM
ROAMED
ROAMER
ROAMERS
ROAMING
ROAMINGS
ROAMS
ROAN
ROANS
ROAR
ROARED
ROARER
ROARERS
ROARIE
ROARIER
ROARIEST
ROARING
ROARINGLY
ROARINGS
ROARS
ROARY
ROAST
ROASTED
ROASTER
ROASTERS
ROASTING
ROASTINGS
ROASTS
ROATE
ROATED
ROATES
ROATING
ROB
ROBALO
ROBALOS
ROBBED
ROBBER
ROBBERIES
ROBBERS
ROBBERY
ROBBING
ROBE
ROBED
ROBES
ROBIN
ROBING
ROBINGS
ROBINIA
ROBINIAS
ROBINS
ROBLE
ROBLES
ROBORANT
ROBORANTS
ROBOT
ROBOTIC
ROBOTICS
ROBOTISE
ROBOTISED
ROBOTISES
ROBOTISING
ROBOTIZE
ROBOTIZED
ROBOTIZES
ROBOTIZING
ROBOTS
ROBS

ROBURITE
ROBURITES
ROBUST
ROBUSTA
ROBUSTAS
ROBUSTER
ROBUSTEST
ROBUSTLY
ROC
ROCAILLE
ROCAILLES
ROCAMBOLE
ROCAMBOLES
ROCH
ROCHES
ROCHET
ROCHETS
ROCK
ROCKAWAY
ROCKAWAYS
ROCKCRESS
ROCKCRESSES
ROCKED
ROCKER
ROCKERIES
ROCKERS
ROCKERY
ROCKET
ROCKETED
ROCKETEER
ROCKETEERS
ROCKETER
ROCKETERS
ROCKETING
ROCKETRIES
ROCKETRY
ROCKETS
ROCKFISH
ROCKFISHES
ROCKIER
ROCKIERS
ROCKIEST
ROCKILY
ROCKINESS
ROCKINESSES
ROCKING
ROCKINGS
ROCKLAY
ROCKLAYS
ROCKLING
ROCKLINGS
ROCKS
ROCKWATER
ROCKWATERS
ROCKWEED
ROCKWEEDS
ROCKWORK
ROCKWORKS
ROCKY
ROCOCO
ROCOCOS
ROCQUET
ROCQUETS
ROCS
ROD
RODDED
RODDING
RODDINGS
RODE
RODED
RODENT
RODENTS
RODEO
RODEOS
RODES
RODEWAY
RODEWAYS
RODFISHER
RODFISHERS
RODGERSIA
RODGERSIAS
RODING
RODINGS
RODLESS
RODLIKE
RODMAN
RODMEN
RODS
RODSMAN
RODSMEN
RODSTER
RODSTERS
ROE
ROEBUCK
ROEBUCKS
ROED
ROEMER
ROEMERS
ROENTGEN
ROENTGENS
ROES
ROESTONE
ROESTONES
ROGATION
ROGATIONS
ROGATORY
ROGER
ROGERED
ROGERING
ROGERINGS
ROGERS
ROGUE
ROGUED
ROGUERIES
ROGUERY
ROGUES
ROGUESHIP
ROGUESHIPS
ROGUING
ROGUISH
ROGUISHLY
ROGUY
ROIL
ROILED
ROILIER
ROILIEST
ROILING
ROILS
ROILY
ROIN
ROINED
ROINING
ROINISH
ROINS
ROIST
ROISTED
ROISTER
ROISTERED
ROISTERER
ROISTERERS
ROISTERING
ROISTERINGS
ROISTERS
ROISTING
ROISTS
ROJI
ROJIS
ROK
ROKE
ROKED
ROKELAY
ROKELAYS
ROKER
ROKERS
ROKES
ROKIER
ROKIEST
ROKING
ROKKAKU
ROKS
ROKY
ROLAG
ROLAGS
ROLE
ROLES
ROLFER
ROLFERS
ROLFING
ROLFINGS
ROLL
ROLLABLE
ROLLED
ROLLER
ROLLERS
ROLLICK
ROLLICKED
ROLLICKING
ROLLICKINGS
ROLLICKS
ROLLING
ROLLINGS
ROLLMOP
ROLLMOPS
ROLLOCK
ROLLOCKS
ROLLOUT
ROLLOUTS
ROLLS
ROM
ROMA
ROMAGE
ROMAGES
ROMAIKA
ROMAIKAS
ROMAL
ROMALS
ROMAN
ROMANCE
ROMANCED
ROMANCER
ROMANCERS
ROMANCES
ROMANCING
ROMANCINGS
ROMANS
ROMANTIC
ROMANTICS
ROMAS
ROMAUNT
ROMAUNTS
ROMNEYA
ROMNEYAS
ROMP
ROMPED
ROMPER
ROMPERS
ROMPING
ROMPINGLY
ROMPISH
ROMPISHLY
ROMPS
RONCADOR
RONCADORS
RONDACHE
RONDACHES
RONDAVEL
RONDAVELS
RONDE
RONDEAU
RONDEAUX
RONDEL
RONDELS
RONDES
RONDINO
RONDINOS
RONDO
RONDOS
RONDURE
RONDURES
RONE
RONEO
RONEOED
RONEOING
RONEOS
RONES
RONG
RONGGENG
RONGGENGS
RONNE
RONNING
RONT
RONTE
RONTES
RONTGEN
RONTGENS
RONTS
RONYON
RONYONS
ROO
ROOD
ROODS
ROOF
ROOFED
ROOFER
ROOFERS
ROOFIER
ROOFIEST
ROOFING
ROOFINGS
ROOFLESS
ROOFLIKE
ROOFS
ROOFSCAPE
ROOFSCAPES
ROOFTOP
ROOFTOPS
ROOFTREE
ROOFTREES
ROOFY
ROOINEK
ROOINEKS
ROOK
ROOKED
ROOKERIES
ROOKERY
ROOKIE
ROOKIER
ROOKIES
ROOKIEST
ROOKING
ROOKISH
ROOKS
ROOKY
ROOM
ROOMED
ROOMER
ROOMERS
ROOMETTE
ROOMETTES
ROOMFUL
ROOMFULS
ROOMIE
ROOMIER
ROOMIES
ROOMIEST
ROOMILY
ROOMINESS
ROOMINESSES
ROOMING
ROOMS
ROOMSOME
ROOMY
ROON
ROONS
ROOP
ROOPED
ROOPIER
ROOPIEST
ROOPING
ROOPIT

ROOPS
ROOPY
ROOS
ROOSA
ROOSAS
ROOSE
ROOSED
ROOSES
ROOSING
ROOST
ROOSTED
ROOSTER
ROOSTERS
ROOSTING
ROOSTS
ROOT
ROOTAGE
ROOTAGES
ROOTED
ROOTEDLY
ROOTER
ROOTERS
ROOTHOLD
ROOTHOLDS
ROOTIER
ROOTIES
ROOTIEST
ROOTING
ROOTINGS
ROOTLE
ROOTLED
ROOTLES
ROOTLESS
ROOTLET
ROOTLETS
ROOTLIKE
ROOTLING
ROOTS
ROOTSIER
ROOTSIEST
ROOTSTOCK
ROOTSTOCKS
ROOTSY
ROOTY
ROPABLE
ROPE
ROPEABLE
ROPED
ROPER
ROPERIES
ROPERS
ROPERY
ROPES
ROPEWAY
ROPEWAYS
ROPEWORK
ROPEWORKS
ROPEY
ROPIER
ROPIEST
ROPILY
ROPINESS
ROPINESSES
ROPING
ROPINGS
ROPY
ROQUE
ROQUES
ROQUET
ROQUETED
ROQUETING
ROQUETS
ROQUETTE
ROQUETTES
RORAL
RORE
RORES
RORIC
RORID
RORIE
RORIER
RORIEST
RORQUAL
RORQUALS
RORT
RORTED
RORTER
RORTERS
RORTIER
RORTIEST
RORTING
RORTS
RORTY
RORY
ROSACE
ROSACEA
ROSACEAS
ROSACEOUS
ROSACES
ROSAKER
ROSAKERS
ROSALIA
ROSALIAS
ROSARIAN
ROSARIANS
ROSARIES
ROSARIUM
ROSARIUMS
ROSARY
ROSCID
ROSE
ROSEAL
ROSEATE
ROSEBAY
ROSEBAYS
ROSEBOWL
ROSEBOWLS
ROSEBUD
ROSEBUDS
ROSEBUSH
ROSEBUSHES
ROSED
ROSEFINCH
ROSEFINCHES
ROSEFISH
ROSEFISHES
ROSEHIP
ROSEHIPS
ROSELESS
ROSELIKE
ROSELLA
ROSELLAS
ROSELLE
ROSELLES
ROSEMARIES
ROSEMARY
ROSEOLA
ROSEOLAS
ROSERIES
ROSERY
ROSES
ROSET
ROSETED
ROSETING
ROSETS
ROSETTE
ROSETTED
ROSETTES
ROSETTY
ROSETY
ROSEWATER
ROSEWATERS
ROSEWOOD
ROSEWOODS
ROSIED
ROSIER
ROSIERE
ROSIERES
ROSIERS
ROSIES
ROSIEST
ROSILY
ROSIN
ROSINATE
ROSINATES
ROSINED
ROSINESS
ROSINESSES
ROSING
ROSINING
ROSINS
ROSINY
ROSIT
ROSITED
ROSITING
ROSITS
ROSMARINE
ROSMARINES
ROSOGLIO
ROSOGLIOS
ROSOLIO
ROSOLIOS
ROSSER
ROSSERS
ROST
ROSTED
ROSTELLAR
ROSTELLUM
ROSTELLUMS
ROSTER
ROSTERED
ROSTERING
ROSTERINGS
ROSTERS
ROSTING
ROSTRA
ROSTRAL
ROSTRATE
ROSTRATED
ROSTRUM
ROSTRUMS
ROSTS
ROSULA
ROSULAS
ROSULATE
ROSY
ROSYING
ROT
ROTA
ROTAL
ROTAPLANE
ROTAPLANES
ROTARIES
ROTARY
ROTAS
ROTATABLE
ROTATE
ROTATED
ROTATES
ROTATING
ROTATION
ROTATIONS
ROTATIVE
ROTATOR
ROTATORS
ROTATORY
ROTAVATE
ROTAVATED
ROTAVATES
ROTAVATING
ROTAVATOR
ROTAVATORS
ROTAVIRUS
ROTAVIRUSES
ROTCH
ROTCHE
ROTCHES
ROTCHIE
ROTCHIES
ROTE
ROTED
ROTENONE
ROTENONES
ROTES
ROTGRASS
ROTGRASSES
ROTGUT
ROTGUTS
ROTHER
ROTHERS
ROTI
ROTIFER
ROTIFERAL
ROTIFERS
ROTING
ROTIS
ROTL
ROTLS
ROTOGRAPH
ROTOGRAPHED
ROTOGRAPHING
ROTOGRAPHS
ROTOLO
ROTOLOS
ROTOR
ROTORS
ROTOVATE
ROTOVATED
ROTOVATES
ROTOVATING
ROTOVATOR
ROTOVATORS
ROTS
ROTTAN
ROTTANS
ROTTED
ROTTEN
ROTTENER
ROTTENEST
ROTTENLY
ROTTENS
ROTTER
ROTTERS
ROTTING
ROTULA
ROTULAS
ROTUND
ROTUNDA
ROTUNDAS
ROTUNDATE
ROTUNDED
ROTUNDER
ROTUNDEST
ROTUNDING
ROTUNDITIES
ROTUNDITY
ROTUNDLY
ROTUNDS
ROTURIER
ROTURIERS
ROUBLE
ROUBLES
ROUCOU
ROUCOUS
ROUE
ROUES
ROUGE
ROUGED
ROUGES
ROUGH
ROUGHAGE
ROUGHAGES
ROUGHCAST
ROUGHCASTED
ROUGHCASTING
ROUGHCASTS
ROUGHED
ROUGHEN
ROUGHENED
ROUGHENING

ROUGHENS
ROUGHER
ROUGHERS
ROUGHEST
ROUGHIE
ROUGHIES
ROUGHING
ROUGHISH
ROUGHLY
ROUGHNECK
ROUGHNECKED
ROUGHNECKING
ROUGHNECKS
ROUGHNESS
ROUGHNESSES
ROUGHS
ROUGHSHOD
ROUGHT
ROUGHY
ROUGING
ROUILLE
ROUILLES
ROUL
ROULADE
ROULADES
ROULE
ROULEAU
ROULEAUS
ROULEAUX
ROULES
ROULETTE
ROULETTES
ROULS
ROUM
ROUMING
ROUMINGS
ROUMS
ROUNCE
ROUNCES
ROUNCEVAL
ROUNCEVALS
ROUNCIES
ROUNCY
ROUND
ROUNDARCH
ROUNDED
ROUNDEL
ROUNDELAY
ROUNDELAYS
ROUNDELS
ROUNDER
ROUNDERS
ROUNDEST
ROUNDHAND
ROUNDHANDS
ROUNDING
ROUNDINGS
ROUNDISH
ROUNDLE
ROUNDLES
ROUNDLET
ROUNDLETS
ROUNDLY
ROUNDNESS
ROUNDNESSES
ROUNDS
ROUNDSMAN
ROUNDSMEN
ROUNDURE
ROUNDURES
ROUNDWORM
ROUNDWORMS
ROUP
ROUPED
ROUPIER
ROUPIEST
ROUPING
ROUPIT
ROUPS
ROUPY
ROUSANT
ROUSE
ROUSED
ROUSEMENT
ROUSEMENTS
ROUSER
ROUSERS
ROUSES
ROUSING
ROUSINGLY
ROUSSETTE
ROUSSETTES
ROUST
ROUSTED
ROUSTER
ROUSTERS
ROUSTING
ROUSTS
ROUT
ROUTE
ROUTED
ROUTEING
ROUTEMAN
ROUTEMEN
ROUTER
ROUTERS
ROUTES
ROUTH
ROUTHIE
ROUTHIER
ROUTHIEST
ROUTHS
ROUTINE
ROUTINEER
ROUTINEERS
ROUTINELY
ROUTINES
ROUTING
ROUTINGS
ROUTINISE
ROUTINISED
ROUTINISES
ROUTINISING
ROUTINISM
ROUTINISMS
ROUTINIST
ROUTINISTS
ROUTINIZE
ROUTINIZED
ROUTINIZES
ROUTINIZING
ROUTOUS
ROUTOUSLY
ROUTS
ROUX
ROVE
ROVED
ROVER
ROVERS
ROVES
ROVING
ROVINGLY
ROVINGS
ROW
ROWABLE
ROWAN
ROWANS
ROWBOAT
ROWBOATS
ROWDEDOW
ROWDEDOWS
ROWDIER
ROWDIES
ROWDIEST
ROWDILY
ROWDINESS
ROWDINESSES
ROWDY
ROWDYDOW
ROWDYDOWS
ROWDYISH
ROWDYISM
ROWDYISMS
ROWED
ROWEL
ROWELLED
ROWELLING
ROWELS
ROWEN
ROWENS
ROWER
ROWERS
ROWING
ROWINGS
ROWLOCK
ROWLOCKS
ROWME
ROWMES
ROWND
ROWNDED
ROWNDELL
ROWNDELLS
ROWNDING
ROWNDS
ROWS
ROWT
ROWTED
ROWTH
ROWTHS
ROWTING
ROWTS
ROYAL
ROYALET
ROYALETS
ROYALISE
ROYALISED
ROYALISES
ROYALISING
ROYALISM
ROYALISMS
ROYALIST
ROYALISTS
ROYALIZE
ROYALIZED
ROYALIZES
ROYALIZING
ROYALLER
ROYALLEST
ROYALLY
ROYALS
ROYALTIES
ROYALTY
ROYNE
ROYNED
ROYNES
ROYNING
ROYNISH
ROYST
ROYSTED
ROYSTER
ROYSTERED
ROYSTERER
ROYSTERERS
ROYSTERING
ROYSTERS
ROYSTING
ROYSTS
ROZELLE
ROZELLES
ROZET
ROZETED
ROZETING
ROZETS
ROZIT
ROZITED
ROZITING
ROZITS
ROZZER
ROZZERS
RUANA
RUANAS
RUB
RUBAI
RUBAIYAT
RUBATI
RUBATO
RUBATOS
RUBBED
RUBBER
RUBBERED
RUBBERIER
RUBBERIEST
RUBBERING
RUBBERISE
RUBBERISED
RUBBERISES
RUBBERISING
RUBBERIZE
RUBBERIZED
RUBBERIZES
RUBBERIZING
RUBBERS
RUBBERY
RUBBET
RUBBING
RUBBINGS
RUBBISH
RUBBISHED
RUBBISHES
RUBBISHING
RUBBISHLY
RUBBISHY
RUBBIT
RUBBLE
RUBBLES
RUBBLIER
RUBBLIEST
RUBBLY
RUBDOWN
RUBDOWNS
RUBE
RUBEFIED
RUBEFIES
RUBEFY
RUBEFYING
RUBELLA
RUBELLAN
RUBELLANS
RUBELLAS
RUBELLITE
RUBELLITES
RUBEOLA
RUBEOLAS
RUBES
RUBESCENT
RUBICELLE
RUBICELLES
RUBICON
RUBICONED
RUBICONING
RUBICONS
RUBICUND
RUBIDIUM
RUBIDIUMS
RUBIED
RUBIER
RUBIES
RUBIEST
RUBIFIED
RUBIFIES
RUBIFY
RUBIFYING
RUBIN
RUBINE
RUBINEOUS
RUBINES
RUBINS
RUBIOUS
RUBLE
RUBLES

RUBOUT
RUBOUTS
RUBRIC
RUBRICAL
RUBRICATE
RUBRICATED
RUBRICATES
RUBRICATING
RUBRICIAN
RUBRICIANS
RUBRICS
RUBS
RUBSTONE
RUBSTONES
RUBY
RUBYING
RUC
RUCHE
RUCHED
RUCHES
RUCHING
RUCHINGS
RUCK
RUCKED
RUCKING
RUCKLE
RUCKLED
RUCKLES
RUCKLING
RUCKS
RUCKSACK
RUCKSACKS
RUCKSEAT
RUCKSEATS
RUCKUS
RUCKUSES
RUCOLA
RUCOLAS
RUCS
RUCTATION
RUCTATIONS
RUCTION
RUCTIONS
RUD
RUDAS
RUDASES
RUDBECKIA
RUDBECKIAS
RUDD
RUDDED
RUDDER
RUDDERS
RUDDIED
RUDDIER
RUDDIES
RUDDIEST
RUDDILY
RUDDINESS
RUDDINESSES
RUDDING
RUDDLE
RUDDLED
RUDDLEMAN
RUDDLEMEN
RUDDLES
RUDDLING
RUDDOCK
RUDDOCKS
RUDDS
RUDDY
RUDDYING
RUDE
RUDELY
RUDENESS
RUDENESSES
RUDER
RUDERAL
RUDERALS
RUDERIES
RUDERY
RUDES
RUDESBIES
RUDESBY
RUDEST
RUDIE
RUDIES
RUDIMENT
RUDIMENTS
RUDISH
RUDS
RUE
RUED
RUEFUL
RUEFULLY
RUEING
RUEINGS
RUELLE
RUELLES
RUELLIA
RUELLIAS
RUES
RUFESCENT
RUFF
RUFFE
RUFFED
RUFFES
RUFFIAN
RUFFIANED
RUFFIANING
RUFFIANLY
RUFFIANS
RUFFIN
RUFFING
RUFFINS
RUFFLE
RUFFLED
RUFFLER
RUFFLERS
RUFFLES
RUFFLING
RUFFLINGS
RUFFS
RUFIYAA
RUFIYAAS
RUFOUS
RUG
RUGATE
RUGBIES
RUGBY
RUGELACH
RUGGED
RUGGEDER
RUGGEDEST
RUGGEDISE
RUGGEDISED
RUGGEDISES
RUGGEDISING
RUGGEDIZE
RUGGEDIZED
RUGGEDIZES
RUGGEDIZING
RUGGEDLY
RUGGELACH
RUGGER
RUGGERS
RUGGIER
RUGGIEST
RUGGING
RUGGINGS
RUGGY
RUGOSE
RUGOSELY
RUGOSITIES
RUGOSITY
RUGOUS
RUGS
RUGULOSE
RUIN
RUINABLE
RUINATE
RUINATED
RUINATES
RUINATING
RUINATION
RUINATIONS
RUINED
RUINER
RUINERS
RUING
RUINGS
RUINING
RUININGS
RUINOUS
RUINOUSLY
RUINS
RUKH
RUKHS
RULABLE
RULE
RULED
RULELESS
RULER
RULERED
RULERING
RULERS
RULERSHIP
RULERSHIPS
RULES
RULESSE
RULIER
RULIEST
RULING
RULINGS
RULLION
RULLIONS
RULLOCK
RULLOCKS
RULY
RUM
RUMAL
RUMALS
RUMBA
RUMBAED
RUMBAING
RUMBAS
RUMBELOW
RUMBELOWS
RUMBLE
RUMBLED
RUMBLER
RUMBLERS
RUMBLES
RUMBLIER
RUMBLIEST
RUMBLING
RUMBLINGS
RUMBLY
RUMBO
RUMBOS
RUME
RUMEN
RUMES
RUMINA
RUMINANT
RUMINANTS
RUMINATE
RUMINATED
RUMINATES
RUMINATING
RUMINATOR
RUMINATORS
RUMKIN
RUMKINS
RUMLY
RUMMAGE
RUMMAGED
RUMMAGER
RUMMAGERS
RUMMAGES
RUMMAGING
RUMMER
RUMMERS
RUMMEST
RUMMIER
RUMMIES
RUMMIEST
RUMMILY
RUMMINESS
RUMMINESSES
RUMMISH
RUMMY
RUMNESS
RUMNESSES
RUMOR
RUMORED
RUMORING
RUMOROUS
RUMORS
RUMOUR
RUMOURED
RUMOURER
RUMOURERS
RUMOURING
RUMOURS
RUMP
RUMPED
RUMPIES
RUMPING
RUMPLE
RUMPLED
RUMPLES
RUMPLESS
RUMPLING
RUMPS
RUMPUS
RUMPUSES
RUMPY
RUMS
RUN
RUNABOUT
RUNABOUTS
RUNAGATE
RUNAGATES
RUNAROUND
RUNAROUNDS
RUNAWAY
RUNAWAYS
RUNBACK
RUNBACKS
RUNCH
RUNCHES
RUNCIBLE
RUNCINATE
RUND
RUNDALE
RUNDALES
RUNDLE
RUNDLED
RUNDLES
RUNDLET
RUNDLETS
RUNDOWN
RUNDOWNS
RUNDS
RUNE
RUNECRAFT
RUNECRAFTS
RUNED
RUNES
RUNFLAT
RUNG
RUNGS
RUNIC
RUNKLE
RUNKLED
RUNKLES
RUNKLING
RUNLET
RUNLETS
RUNNABLE

RUNNEL
RUNNELS
RUNNER
RUNNERS
RUNNET
RUNNETS
RUNNIER
RUNNIEST
RUNNING
RUNNINGLY
RUNNINGS
RUNNION
RUNNIONS
RUNNY
RUNRIG
RUNRIGS
RUNS
RUNT
RUNTED
RUNTIER
RUNTIEST
RUNTISH
RUNTS
RUNTY
RUNWAY
RUNWAYS
RUPEE
RUPEES
RUPIA
RUPIAH
RUPIAHS
RUPIAS
RUPTURE
RUPTURED
RUPTURES
RUPTURING
RURAL
RURALISE
RURALISED
RURALISES
RURALISING
RURALISM
RURALISMS
RURALIST
RURALISTS
RURALITIES
RURALITY
RURALIZE
RURALIZED
RURALIZES
RURALIZING
RURALLY
RURALNESS
RURALNESSES
RURALS
RURP
RURPS
RURU
RURUS
RUSA
RUSALKA
RUSALKAS
RUSAS
RUSCUS
RUSCUSES
RUSE
RUSES
RUSH
RUSHED
RUSHEE
RUSHEES
RUSHEN
RUSHER
RUSHERS
RUSHES
RUSHIER
RUSHIEST
RUSHINESS
RUSHINESSES
RUSHING
RUSHLIGHT
RUSHLIGHTS
RUSHLIKE
RUSHY
RUSINE
RUSK
RUSKS
RUSMA
RUSMAS
RUSSEL
RUSSELS
RUSSET
RUSSETED
RUSSETING
RUSSETINGS
RUSSETS
RUSSETY
RUSSIA
RUSSIAS
RUST
RUSTED
RUSTIC
RUSTICAL
RUSTICALS
RUSTICATE
RUSTICATED
RUSTICATES
RUSTICATING
RUSTICIAL
RUSTICISE
RUSTICISED
RUSTICISES
RUSTICISING
RUSTICISM
RUSTICISMS
RUSTICITIES
RUSTICITY
RUSTICIZE
RUSTICIZED
RUSTICIZES
RUSTICIZING
RUSTICS
RUSTIER
RUSTIEST
RUSTILY
RUSTINESS
RUSTINESSES
RUSTING
RUSTINGS
RUSTLE
RUSTLED
RUSTLER
RUSTLERS
RUSTLES
RUSTLESS
RUSTLING
RUSTLINGS
RUSTRE
RUSTRED
RUSTRES
RUSTS
RUSTY
RUT
RUTABAGA
RUTABAGAS
RUTACEOUS
RUTH
RUTHENIC
RUTHENIUM
RUTHENIUMS
RUTHFUL
RUTHFULLY
RUTHLESS
RUTHS
RUTILANT
RUTILATED
RUTILE
RUTILES
RUTIN
RUTINS
RUTS
RUTTED
RUTTER
RUTTERS
RUTTIER
RUTTIEST
RUTTING
RUTTINGS
RUTTISH
RUTTY
RYA
RYAL
RYALS
RYAS
RYBAT
RYBATS
RYBAUDRYE
RYBAUDRYES
RYBAULD
RYBAULDS
RYE
RYEBREAD
RYEBREADS
RYEFLOUR
RYEFLOURS
RYEPECK
RYEPECKS
RYES
RYFE
RYKE
RYKED
RYKES
RYKING
RYMME
RYMMED
RYMMES
RYMMING
RYND
RYNDS
RYOKAN
RYOKANS
RYOT
RYOTS
RYOTWARI
RYOTWARIS
RYPE
RYPECK
RYPECKS
RYPER

S

SAB
SABADILLA
SABADILLAS
SABATON
SABATONS
SABBAT
SABBATIC
SABBATICS
SABBATINE
SABBATISE
SABBATISED
SABBATISES
SABBATISING
SABBATISM
SABBATISMS
SABBATIZE
SABBATIZED
SABBATIZES
SABBATIZING
SABBATS
SABELLA
SABELLAS
SABER
SABERED
SABERING
SABERS
SABIN
SABINS
SABKHA
SABKHAH
SABKHAHS
SABKHAS
SABKHAT
SABKHATS
SABLE
SABLED
SABLES
SABLING
SABOT
SABOTAGE
SABOTAGED
SABOTAGES
SABOTAGING
SABOTEUR
SABOTEURS
SABOTIER
SABOTIERS
SABOTS
SABRA
SABRAS
SABRE
SABRED
SABRES
SABREUR
SABREURS
SABRING
SABS
SABULINE
SABULOSE
SABULOUS
SABURRA
SABURRAL
SABURRAS
SAC
SACATON
SACATONS
SACCADE
SACCADES
SACCADIC
SACCATE
SACCHARIC
SACCHARIN
SACCHARINS
SACCHARUM
SACCHARUMS
SACCIFORM
SACCOI
SACCOS
SACCOSES
SACCULAR
SACCULATE
SACCULE
SACCULES
SACCULI
SACCULUS
SACELLA
SACELLUM
SACHEM
SACHEMDOM
SACHEMDOMS
SACHEMIC
SACHEMS
SACHET
SACHETS
SACK
SACKAGE
SACKAGES
SACKBUT
SACKBUTS
SACKCLOTH
SACKCLOTHS
SACKED
SACKER
SACKERS
SACKFUL
SACKFULS
SACKING
SACKINGS
SACKLESS
SACKS
SACLESS
SACLIKE
SACQUE
SACQUES
SACRA
SACRAL
SACRALGIA
SACRALGIAS
SACRALISE
SACRALISED
SACRALISES
SACRALISING
SACRALIZE
SACRALIZED
SACRALIZES
SACRALIZING
SACRAMENT
SACRAMENTED
SACRAMENTING
SACRAMENTS
SACRARIA
SACRARIUM
SACRED
SACREDLY
SACRIFICE
SACRIFICED
SACRIFICES
SACRIFICING
SACRIFIDE
SACRIFIED
SACRIFIES
SACRIFY
SACRIFYING
SACRILEGE
SACRILEGES
SACRING
SACRINGS
SACRIST
SACRISTAN
SACRISTANS
SACRISTIES
SACRISTS
SACRISTY
SACRUM
SACS
SAD
SADDEN
SADDENED
SADDENING
SADDENS
SADDER
SADDEST
SADDHU
SADDHUS
SADDISH
SADDLE
SADDLEBAG
SADDLEBAGS
SADDLEBOW
SADDLEBOWS
SADDLED
SADDLER
SADDLERIES
SADDLERS
SADDLERY
SADDLES
SADDLING
SADDO
SADDOS
SADE
SADES
SADHE
SADHES
SADHU
SADHUS
SADIRON
SADIRONS
SADISM
SADISMS
SADIST
SADISTIC
SADISTS
SADLY
SADNESS
SADNESSES
SADZA
SADZAS
SAE
SAECULUM
SAECULUMS
SAETER
SAETERS
SAFARI
SAFARIED
SAFARIING
SAFARIS
SAFARIST
SAFARISTS
SAFE
SAFED
SAFEGUARD
SAFEGUARDED
SAFEGUARDING
SAFEGUARDS
SAFELY
SAFENESS
SAFENESSES
SAFER
SAFES
SAFEST
SAFETIES
SAFETY
SAFETYMAN
SAFETYMEN
SAFFIAN
SAFFIANS
SAFFLOWER
SAFFLOWERS
SAFFRON
SAFFRONED
SAFFRONS
SAFFRONY
SAFING
SAFRANIN
SAFRANINE
SAFRANINES
SAFRANINS
SAFROLE
SAFROLES
SAFRONAL
SAFRONALS
SAG
SAGA
SAGACIOUS
SAGACITIES
SAGACITY
SAGAMAN
SAGAMEN
SAGAMORE
SAGAMORES
SAGAPENUM
SAGAPENUMS
SAGAS
SAGATHIES
SAGATHY
SAGE
SAGEBRUSH
SAGEBRUSHES
SAGELY
SAGENE
SAGENES
SAGENESS
SAGENESSES
SAGENITE
SAGENITES
SAGENITIC
SAGER
SAGES
SAGEST
SAGGAR

The Chambers Dictionary is the authority for many longer words; see *OSW* Introduction, page xii

SAGGARD
SAGGARDS
SAGGARS
SAGGED
SAGGER
SAGGERS
SAGGIER
SAGGIEST
SAGGING
SAGGINGS
SAGGY
SAGIER
SAGIEST
SAGINATE
SAGINATED
SAGINATES
SAGINATING
SAGITTA
SAGITTAL
SAGITTARIES
SAGITTARY
SAGITTAS
SAGITTATE
SAGO
SAGOIN
SAGOINS
SAGOS
SAGOUIN
SAGOUINS
SAGS
SAGUARO
SAGUAROS
SAGUIN
SAGUINS
SAGUM
SAGY
SAHIB
SAHIBA
SAHIBAH
SAHIBAHS
SAHIBAS
SAHIBS
SAI
SAIBLING
SAIBLINGS
SAIC
SAICE
SAICES
SAICK
SAICKS
SAICS
SAID
SAIDEST
SAIDS
SAIDST
SAIGA
SAIGAS
SAIKEI
SAIKEIS
SAIKLESS
SAIL
SAILABLE
SAILBOARD
SAILBOARDS
SAILCLOTH
SAILCLOTHS
SAILED
SAILER
SAILERS
SAILFISH
SAILFISHES
SAILING
SAILINGS
SAILLESS
SAILOR
SAILORING
SAILORINGS
SAILORLY
SAILORS
SAILPLANE
SAILPLANED
SAILPLANES
SAILPLANING
SAILROOM
SAILROOMS
SAILS
SAIM
SAIMIRI
SAIMIRIS
SAIMS
SAIN
SAINE
SAINED
SAINFOIN
SAINFOINS
SAINING
SAINS
SAINT
SAINTDOM
SAINTDOMS
SAINTED
SAINTESS
SAINTESSES
SAINTFOIN
SAINTFOINS
SAINTHOOD
SAINTHOODS
SAINTING
SAINTISH
SAINTISM
SAINTISMS
SAINTLIER
SAINTLIEST
SAINTLIKE
SAINTLING
SAINTLINGS
SAINTLY
SAINTS
SAINTSHIP
SAINTSHIPS
SAIQUE
SAIQUES
SAIR
SAIRED
SAIRER
SAIREST
SAIRING
SAIRS
SAIS
SAIST
SAITH
SAITHE
SAITHES
SAITHS
SAJOU
SAJOUS
SAKE
SAKER
SAKERET
SAKERETS
SAKERS
SAKES
SAKI
SAKIA
SAKIAS
SAKIEH
SAKIEHS
SAKIS
SAKIYEH
SAKIYEHS
SAKKOI
SAKKOS
SAKKOSES
SAKSAUL
SAKSAULS
SAL
SALAAM
SALAAMED
SALAAMING
SALAAMS
SALABLE
SALABLY
SALACIOUS
SALACITIES
SALACITY
SALAD
SALADE
SALADES
SALADING
SALADINGS
SALADS
SALAL
SALALS
SALAMI
SALAMIS
SALAMON
SALAMONS
SALANGANE
SALANGANES
SALARIAT
SALARIATS
SALARIED
SALARIES
SALARY
SALARYING
SALARYMAN
SALARYMEN
SALBAND
SALBANDS
SALCHOW
SALCHOWS
SALE
SALEABLE
SALEABLY
SALEP
SALEPS
SALERATUS
SALERATUSES
SALERING
SALERINGS
SALEROOM
SALEROOMS
SALES
SALESMAN
SALESMEN
SALESROOM
SALESROOMS
SALET
SALETS
SALEWD
SALEYARD
SALEYARDS
SALFERN
SALFERNS
SALIAUNCE
SALIAUNCES
SALIC
SALICES
SALICET
SALICETA
SALICETS
SALICETUM
SALICETUMS
SALICIN
SALICINE
SALICINES
SALICINS
SALICYLIC
SALIENCE
SALIENCES
SALIENCIES
SALIENCY
SALIENT
SALIENTLY
SALIENTS
SALIFIED
SALIFIES
SALIFY
SALIFYING
SALIGOT
SALIGOTS
SALIMETER
SALIMETERS
SALINA
SALINAS
SALINE
SALINES
SALINITIES
SALINITY
SALIVA
SALIVAL
SALIVARY
SALIVAS
SALIVATE
SALIVATED
SALIVATES
SALIVATING
SALIX
SALLAD
SALLADS
SALLAL
SALLALS
SALLE
SALLEE
SALLEES
SALLES
SALLET
SALLETS
SALLIED
SALLIES
SALLOW
SALLOWED
SALLOWER
SALLOWEST
SALLOWING
SALLOWISH
SALLOWS
SALLOWY
SALLY
SALLYING
SALLYPORT
SALLYPORTS
SALMI
SALMIS
SALMON
SALMONET
SALMONETS
SALMONID
SALMONIDS
SALMONOID
SALMONOIDS
SALMONS
SALON
SALONS
SALOON
SALOONS
SALOOP
SALOOPS
SALOP
SALOPIAN
SALOPS
SALP
SALPA
SALPAE
SALPAS
SALPIAN
SALPIANS
SALPICON
SALPICONS
SALPIFORM
SALPINGES
SALPINX
SALPINXES
SALPS
SALS
SALSA
SALSAED
SALSAING
SALSAS
SALSE

SALSES
SALSIFIES
SALSIFY
SALT
SALTANDO
SALTANT
SALTANTS
SALTATE
SALTATED
SALTATES
SALTATING
SALTATION
SALTATIONS
SALTATO
SALTATORY
SALTBOX
SALTBOXES
SALTBUSH
SALTBUSHES
SALTCAT
SALTCATS
SALTCHUCK
SALTCHUCKS
SALTED
SALTER
SALTERN
SALTERNS
SALTERS
SALTEST
SALTFISH
SALTFISHES
SALTIER
SALTIERS
SALTIEST
SALTILY
SALTINESS
SALTINESSES
SALTING
SALTINGS
SALTIRE
SALTIRES
SALTISH
SALTISHLY
SALTLESS
SALTLY
SALTNESS
SALTNESSES
SALTO
SALTOED
SALTOING
SALTOS
SALTPETER
SALTPETERS
SALTPETRE
SALTPETRES
SALTS
SALTUS
SALTUSES
SALTWATER
SALTWORKS
SALTWORT
SALTWORTS
SALTY
SALUBRITIES
SALUBRITY
SALUE
SALUED
SALUES
SALUING
SALUKI
SALUKIS
SALUTARY
SALUTE
SALUTED
SALUTER
SALUTERS
SALUTES
SALUTING
SALVABLE
SALVAGE
SALVAGED
SALVAGES
SALVAGING
SALVARSAN
SALVARSANS
SALVATION
SALVATIONS
SALVATORIES
SALVATORY
SALVE
SALVED
SALVER
SALVERS
SALVES
SALVETE
SALVETES
SALVIA
SALVIAS
SALVIFIC
SALVING
SALVINGS
SALVO
SALVOES
SALVOR
SALVORS
SALVOS
SAM
SAMA
SAMAAN
SAMAANS
SAMADHI
SAMADHIS
SAMAN
SAMANS
SAMARA
SAMARAS
SAMARIUM
SAMARIUMS
SAMAS
SAMBA
SAMBAED
SAMBAING
SAMBAL
SAMBALS
SAMBAR
SAMBARS
SAMBAS
SAMBO
SAMBOS
SAMBUCA
SAMBUCAS
SAMBUR
SAMBURS
SAME
SAMEKH
SAMEKHS
SAMEL
SAMELY
SAMEN
SAMENESS
SAMENESSES
SAMES
SAMEY
SAMFOO
SAMFOOS
SAMFU
SAMFUS
SAMIEL
SAMIELS
SAMIER
SAMIEST
SAMISEN
SAMISENS
SAMITE
SAMITES
SAMITI
SAMITIS
SAMIZDAT
SAMIZDATS
SAMLET
SAMLETS
SAMLOR
SAMLORS
SAMNITIS
SAMNITISES
SAMOSA
SAMOSAS
SAMOVAR
SAMOVARS
SAMP
SAMPAN
SAMPANS
SAMPHIRE
SAMPHIRES
SAMPI
SAMPIRE
SAMPIRES
SAMPIS
SAMPLE
SAMPLED
SAMPLER
SAMPLERIES
SAMPLERS
SAMPLERY
SAMPLES
SAMPLING
SAMPLINGS
SAMPS
SAMSARA
SAMSARAS
SAMSHOO
SAMSHOOS
SAMSHU
SAMSHUS
SAMURAI
SAN
SANATIVE
SANATORIA
SANATORY
SANBENITO
SANBENITOS
SANCAI
SANCAIS
SANCHO
SANCHOS
SANCTA
SANCTIFIED
SANCTIFIES
SANCTIFY
SANCTIFYING
SANCTIFYINGS
SANCTION
SANCTIONED
SANCTIONING
SANCTIONS
SANCTITIES
SANCTITY
SANCTUARIES
SANCTUARY
SANCTUM
SANCTUMS
SAND
SANDAL
SANDALLED
SANDALS
SANDARAC
SANDARACH
SANDARACHS
SANDARACS
SANDBAG
SANDBAGGED
SANDBAGGING
SANDBAGS
SANDBANK
SANDBANKS
SANDBLAST
SANDBLASTED
SANDBLASTING
SANDBLASTINGS
SANDBLASTS
SANDBOX
SANDBOXES
SANDBOY
SANDBOYS
SANDED
SANDER
SANDERS
SANDERSES
SANDFLIES
SANDFLY
SANDGLASS
SANDGLASSES
SANDHEAP
SANDHEAPS
SANDHI
SANDHILL
SANDHILLS
SANDHIS
SANDIER
SANDIEST
SANDINESS
SANDINESSES
SANDING
SANDINGS
SANDIVER
SANDIVERS
SANDLING
SANDLINGS
SANDMAN
SANDMEN
SANDPAPER
SANDPAPERED
SANDPAPERING
SANDPAPERS
SANDPIPER
SANDPIPERS
SANDPIT
SANDPITS
SANDPUMP
SANDPUMPS
SANDS
SANDSHOE
SANDSHOES
SANDSPOUT
SANDSPOUTS
SANDSTONE
SANDSTONES
SANDSTORM
SANDSTORMS
SANDWICH
SANDWICHED
SANDWICHES
SANDWICHING
SANDWORM
SANDWORMS
SANDWORT
SANDWORTS
SANDY
SANE
SANELY
SANENESS
SANENESSES
SANER
SANEST
SANG
SANGAR
SANGAREE
SANGAREES
SANGARS
SANGFROID
SANGFROIDS
SANGLIER
SANGLIERS
SANGOMA
SANGOMAS
SANGRIA
SANGRIAS
SANGS
SANGUIFIED
SANGUIFIES

SANGUIFY
SANGUIFYING
SANGUINE
SANGUINED
SANGUINES
SANGUINING
SANICLE
SANICLES
SANIDINE
SANIDINES
SANIES
SANIFIED
SANIFIES
SANIFY
SANIFYING
SANIOUS
SANITARIA
SANITARY
SANITATE
SANITATED
SANITATES
SANITATING
SANITIES
SANITISE
SANITISED
SANITISES
SANITISING
SANITIZE
SANITIZED
SANITIZES
SANITIZING
SANITY
SANJAK
SANJAKS
SANK
SANKO
SANKOS
SANNIE
SANNIES
SANNUP
SANNUPS
SANNYASI
SANNYASIN
SANNYASINS
SANNYASIS
SANPAN
SANPANS
SANS
SANSA
SANSAS
SANSEI
SANSEIS
SANSERIF
SANSERIFS
SANT
SANTAL
SANTALIN
SANTALINS
SANTALS
SANTIR
SANTIRS
SANTOLINA
SANTOLINAS
SANTON
SANTONICA
SANTONICAS
SANTONIN
SANTONINS
SANTONS
SANTOUR
SANTOURS
SANTS
SANTUR
SANTURS
SAOUARI
SAOUARIS
SAP
SAPAJOU
SAPAJOUS
SAPAN
SAPANS
SAPANWOOD
SAPANWOODS
SAPEGO
SAPEGOES
SAPELE
SAPELES
SAPFUL
SAPHEAD
SAPHEADED
SAPHEADS
SAPHENA
SAPHENAS
SAPHENOUS
SAPID
SAPIDITIES
SAPIDITY
SAPIDLESS
SAPIDNESS
SAPIDNESSES
SAPIENCE
SAPIENCES
SAPIENT
SAPIENTLY
SAPLESS
SAPLING
SAPLINGS
SAPODILLA
SAPODILLAS
SAPOGENIN
SAPOGENINS
SAPONARIA
SAPONARIAS
SAPONIFIED
SAPONIFIES
SAPONIFY
SAPONIFYING
SAPONIN
SAPONINS
SAPONITE
SAPONITES
SAPOR
SAPORIFIC
SAPOROUS
SAPORS
SAPOTA
SAPOTAS
SAPPAN
SAPPANS
SAPPED
SAPPER
SAPPERS
SAPPHIC
SAPPHICS
SAPPHIRE
SAPPHIRED
SAPPHIRES
SAPPHISM
SAPPHISMS
SAPPHIST
SAPPHISTS
SAPPIER
SAPPIEST
SAPPINESS
SAPPINESSES
SAPPING
SAPPLE
SAPPLED
SAPPLES
SAPPLING
SAPPY
SAPRAEMIA
SAPRAEMIAS
SAPRAEMIC
SAPROBE
SAPROBES
SAPROLITE
SAPROLITES
SAPROPEL
SAPROPELS
SAPROZOIC
SAPS
SAPSAGO
SAPSAGOS
SAPSUCKER
SAPSUCKERS
SAPUCAIA
SAPUCAIAS
SAPWOOD
SAPWOODS
SAR
SARABAND
SARABANDE
SARABANDES
SARABANDS
SARAFAN
SARAFANS
SARANGI
SARANGIS
SARAPE
SARAPES
SARBACANE
SARBACANES
SARCASM
SARCASMS
SARCASTIC
SARCENET
SARCENETS
SARCOCARP
SARCOCARPS
SARCODE
SARCODES
SARCODIC
SARCOID
SARCOIDS
SARCOLOGIES
SARCOLOGY
SARCOMA
SARCOMAS
SARCOMATA
SARCOMERE
SARCOMERES
SARCONET
SARCONETS
SARCOPTIC
SARCOUS
SARD
SARDANA
SARDANAS
SARDEL
SARDELLE
SARDELLES
SARDELS
SARDINE
SARDINES
SARDIUS
SARDIUSES
SARDONIAN
SARDONIC
SARDONYX
SARDONYXES
SARDS
SARED
SAREE
SAREES
SARGASSO
SARGASSOS
SARGASSUM
SARGASSUMS
SARGE
SARGES
SARGO
SARGOS
SARGOSES
SARGUS
SARGUSES
SARI
SARIN
SARING
SARINS
SARIS
SARK
SARKIER
SARKIEST
SARKING
SARKINGS
SARKS
SARKY
SARMENT
SARMENTA
SARMENTS
SARMENTUM
SARNEY
SARNEYS
SARNIE
SARNIES
SAROD
SARODS
SARONG
SARONGS
SARONIC
SAROS
SAROSES
SARPANCH
SARPANCHES
SARRASIN
SARRASINS
SARRAZIN
SARRAZINS
SARS
SARSDEN
SARSDENS
SARSEN
SARSENET
SARSENETS
SARSENS
SARSNET
SARSNETS
SARTOR
SARTORIAL
SARTORIAN
SARTORII
SARTORIUS
SARTORIUSES
SARTORS
SARUS
SARUSES
SASARARA
SASARARAS
SASH
SASHAY
SASHAYED
SASHAYING
SASHAYS
SASHED
SASHES
SASHIMI
SASHIMIS
SASHING
SASIN
SASINE
SASINES
SASINS
SASKATOON
SASKATOONS
SASQUATCH
SASQUATCHES
SASS
SASSABIES
SASSABY
SASSAFRAS
SASSAFRASES
SASSARARA
SASSARARAS
SASSE
SASSED
SASSES
SASSIER
SASSIEST
SASSING

SASSOLIN
SASSOLINS
SASSOLITE
SASSOLITES
SASSY
SASTRUGA
SASTRUGI
SAT
SATANG
SATANIC
SATANICAL
SATANISM
SATANISMS
SATANITIES
SATANITY
SATARA
SATARAS
SATAY
SATAYS
SATCHEL
SATCHELS
SATE
SATED
SATEDNESS
SATEDNESSES
SATEEN
SATEENS
SATELESS
SATELLES
SATELLITE
SATELLITED
SATELLITES
SATELLITING
SATES
SATI
SATIABLE
SATIATE
SATIATED
SATIATES
SATIATING
SATIATION
SATIATIONS
SATIETIES
SATIETY
SATIN
SATINED
SATINET
SATINETS
SATINETTA
SATINETTAS
SATINETTE
SATINETTES
SATING
SATINING
SATINS
SATINWOOD
SATINWOODS
SATINY
SATIRE
SATIRES
SATIRIC
SATIRICAL
SATIRISE
SATIRISED
SATIRISES
SATIRISING
SATIRIST
SATIRISTS
SATIRIZE
SATIRIZED
SATIRIZES
SATIRIZING
SATIS
SATISFICE
SATISFICED
SATISFICES
SATISFICING
SATISFICINGS
SATISFIED
SATISFIER
SATISFIERS
SATISFIES
SATISFY
SATISFYING
SATIVE
SATORI
SATORIS
SATRAP
SATRAPAL
SATRAPIES
SATRAPS
SATRAPY
SATSUMA
SATSUMAS
SATURABLE
SATURANT
SATURANTS
SATURATE
SATURATED
SATURATES
SATURATING
SATURATOR
SATURATORS
SATURNIC
SATURNIID
SATURNIIDS
SATURNINE
SATURNISM
SATURNISMS
SATURNIST
SATURNISTS
SATYR
SATYRA
SATYRAL
SATYRALS
SATYRAS
SATYRESS
SATYRESSES
SATYRIC
SATYRICAL
SATYRID
SATYRIDS
SATYRISK
SATYRISKS
SATYRS
SAUBA
SAUBAS
SAUCE
SAUCEBOX
SAUCEBOXES
SAUCED
SAUCEPAN
SAUCEPANS
SAUCER
SAUCERFUL
SAUCERFULS
SAUCERS
SAUCES
SAUCH
SAUCHS
SAUCIER
SAUCIEST
SAUCILY
SAUCINESS
SAUCINESSES
SAUCING
SAUCISSE
SAUCISSES
SAUCISSON
SAUCISSONS
SAUCY
SAUFGARD
SAUFGARDS
SAUGER
SAUGERS
SAUGH
SAUGHS
SAUL
SAULGE
SAULGES
SAULIE
SAULIES
SAULS
SAULT
SAULTS
SAUNA
SAUNAS
SAUNT
SAUNTED
SAUNTER
SAUNTERED
SAUNTERER
SAUNTERERS
SAUNTERING
SAUNTERINGS
SAUNTERS
SAUNTING
SAUNTS
SAUREL
SAURELS
SAURIAN
SAURIANS
SAURIES
SAUROID
SAUROPOD
SAUROPODS
SAURY
SAUSAGE
SAUSAGES
SAUT
SAUTE
SAUTED
SAUTEED
SAUTEEING
SAUTEES
SAUTEING
SAUTES
SAUTING
SAUTOIR
SAUTOIRS
SAUTS
SAVABLE
SAVAGE
SAVAGED
SAVAGEDOM
SAVAGEDOMS
SAVAGELY
SAVAGER
SAVAGERIES
SAVAGERY
SAVAGES
SAVAGEST
SAVAGING
SAVAGISM
SAVAGISMS
SAVANNA
SAVANNAH
SAVANNAHS
SAVANNAS
SAVANT
SAVANTS
SAVARIN
SAVARINS
SAVATE
SAVATES
SAVE
SAVED
SAVEGARD
SAVEGARDED
SAVEGARDING
SAVEGARDS
SAVELOY
SAVELOYS
SAVER
SAVERS
SAVES
SAVEY
SAVEYED
SAVEYING
SAVEYS
SAVIN
SAVINE
SAVINES
SAVING
SAVINGLY
SAVINGS
SAVINS
SAVIOUR
SAVIOURS
SAVOR
SAVORED
SAVORIES
SAVORING
SAVOROUS
SAVORS
SAVORY
SAVOUR
SAVOURED
SAVOURIES
SAVOURILY
SAVOURING
SAVOURLY
SAVOURS
SAVOURY
SAVOY
SAVOYARD
SAVOYARDS
SAVOYS
SAVVEY
SAVVEYED
SAVVEYING
SAVVEYS
SAVVIED
SAVVIER
SAVVIES
SAVVIEST
SAVVY
SAVVYING
SAW
SAWAH
SAWAHS
SAWBILL
SAWBILLS
SAWBLADE
SAWBLADES
SAWBONES
SAWBUCK
SAWBUCKS
SAWDER
SAWDERED
SAWDERING
SAWDERS
SAWDUST
SAWDUSTED
SAWDUSTING
SAWDUSTS
SAWDUSTY
SAWED
SAWER
SAWERS
SAWFISH
SAWFISHES
SAWHORSE
SAWHORSES
SAWING
SAWINGS
SAWMILL
SAWMILLS
SAWN
SAWNEY
SAWNEYS
SAWPIT
SAWPITS
SAWS
SAWSHARK
SAWSHARKS
SAWTEETH
SAWTOOTH
SAWYER
SAWYERS

SAX
SAXATILE
SAXAUL
SAXAULS
SAXES
SAXHORN
SAXHORNS
SAXIFRAGE
SAXIFRAGES
SAXITOXIN
SAXITOXINS
SAXONIES
SAXONITE
SAXONITES
SAXONY
SAXOPHONE
SAXOPHONES
SAY
SAYABLE
SAYED
SAYER
SAYERS
SAYEST
SAYID
SAYIDS
SAYING
SAYINGS
SAYNE
SAYON
SAYONARA
SAYONARAS
SAYONS
SAYS
SAYST
SAYYID
SAYYIDS
SAZ
SAZERAC®
SAZERACS
SAZES
SAZHEN
SAZHENS
SAZZES
SBIRRI
SBIRRO
SCAB
SCABBARD
SCABBARDED
SCABBARDING
SCABBARDS
SCABBED
SCABBIER
SCABBIEST
SCABBING
SCABBLE
SCABBLED
SCABBLES
SCABBLING
SCABBY
SCABIES
SCABIOUS
SCABIOUSES
SCABLANDS
SCABRID
SCABROUS
SCABS
SCAD
SCADS
SCAFF
SCAFFIE
SCAFFIES
SCAFFOLD
SCAFFOLDED
SCAFFOLDING
SCAFFOLDINGS
SCAFFOLDS
SCAFFS
SCAG
SCAGLIA
SCAGLIAS
SCAGLIOLA
SCAGLIOLAS
SCAGS
SCAIL
SCAILED
SCAILING
SCAILS
SCAITH
SCAITHED
SCAITHING
SCAITHS
SCALA
SCALABLE
SCALADE
SCALADES
SCALADO
SCALADOS
SCALAE
SCALAR
SCALARS
SCALAWAG
SCALAWAGS
SCALD
SCALDED
SCALDER
SCALDERS
SCALDFISH
SCALDFISHES
SCALDHEAD
SCALDHEADS
SCALDIC
SCALDING
SCALDINGS
SCALDINI
SCALDINO
SCALDS
SCALDSHIP
SCALDSHIPS
SCALE
SCALED
SCALELESS
SCALELIKE
SCALENE
SCALENI
SCALENUS
SCALER
SCALERS
SCALES
SCALEWORK
SCALEWORKS
SCALIER
SCALIEST
SCALINESS
SCALINESSES
SCALING
SCALINGS
SCALL
SCALLAWAG
SCALLAWAGS
SCALLED
SCALLIES
SCALLION
SCALLIONS
SCALLOP
SCALLOPED
SCALLOPING
SCALLOPS
SCALLS
SCALLY
SCALLYWAG
SCALLYWAGS
SCALP
SCALPED
SCALPEL
SCALPELS
SCALPER
SCALPERS
SCALPING
SCALPINGS
SCALPINS
SCALPLESS
SCALPRUM
SCALPRUMS
SCALPS
SCALY
SCAM
SCAMBLE
SCAMBLED
SCAMBLER
SCAMBLERS
SCAMBLES
SCAMBLING
SCAMBLINGS
SCAMEL
SCAMELS
SCAMMED
SCAMMING
SCAMMONIES
SCAMMONY
SCAMP
SCAMPED
SCAMPER
SCAMPERED
SCAMPERING
SCAMPERS
SCAMPI
SCAMPING
SCAMPINGS
SCAMPIS
SCAMPISH
SCAMPS
SCAMS
SCAN
SCAND
SCANDAL
SCANDALLED
SCANDALLING
SCANDALS
SCANDENT
SCANDIUM
SCANDIUMS
SCANNED
SCANNER
SCANNERS
SCANNING
SCANNINGS
SCANS
SCANSION
SCANSIONS
SCANT
SCANTED
SCANTER
SCANTEST
SCANTIER
SCANTIES
SCANTIEST
SCANTILY
SCANTING
SCANTITIES
SCANTITY
SCANTLE
SCANTLED
SCANTLES
SCANTLING
SCANTLINGS
SCANTLY
SCANTNESS
SCANTNESSES
SCANTS
SCANTY
SCAPA
SCAPAED
SCAPAING
SCAPAS
SCAPE
SCAPED
SCAPEGOAT
SCAPEGOATED
SCAPEGOATING
SCAPEGOATINGS
SCAPEGOATS
SCAPELESS
SCAPEMENT
SCAPEMENTS
SCAPES
SCAPHOID
SCAPHOIDS
SCAPHOPOD
SCAPHOPODS
SCAPI
SCAPING
SCAPOLITE
SCAPOLITES
SCAPPLE
SCAPPLED
SCAPPLES
SCAPPLING
SCAPULA
SCAPULAE
SCAPULAR
SCAPULARIES
SCAPULARS
SCAPULARY
SCAPULAS
SCAPUS
SCAR
SCARAB
SCARABAEI
SCARABEE
SCARABEES
SCARABOID
SCARABOIDS
SCARABS
SCARCE
SCARCELY
SCARCER
SCARCEST
SCARCITIES
SCARCITY
SCARE
SCARECROW
SCARECROWS
SCARED
SCAREDER
SCAREDEST
SCARER
SCARERS
SCARES
SCAREY
SCARF
SCARFED
SCARFING
SCARFINGS
SCARFISH
SCARFISHES
SCARFS
SCARFSKIN
SCARFSKINS
SCARFWISE
SCARIER
SCARIEST
SCARIFIED
SCARIFIER
SCARIFIERS
SCARIFIES
SCARIFY
SCARIFYING
SCARING
SCARIOUS
SCARLESS
SCARLET
SCARLETED
SCARLETING
SCARLETS
SCARMOGE
SCARMOGES
SCARP
SCARPA
SCARPAED
SCARPAING

SCARPAS
SCARPED
SCARPER
SCARPERED
SCARPERING
SCARPERS
SCARPETTI
SCARPETTO
SCARPH
SCARPHED
SCARPHING
SCARPHS
SCARPINES
SCARPING
SCARPINGS
SCARPS
SCARRE
SCARRED
SCARRES
SCARRIER
SCARRIEST
SCARRING
SCARRINGS
SCARRY
SCARS
SCART
SCARTED
SCARTH
SCARTHS
SCARTING
SCARTS
SCARVES
SCARY
SCAT
SCATCH
SCATCHES
SCATH
SCATHE
SCATHED
SCATHEFUL
SCATHES
SCATHING
SCATHS
SCATOLE
SCATOLES
SCATOLOGIES
SCATOLOGY
SCATS
SCATT
SCATTED
SCATTER
SCATTERED
SCATTERER
SCATTERERS
SCATTERING
SCATTERINGS
SCATTERS
SCATTERY
SCATTIER
SCATTIEST
SCATTING
SCATTINGS
SCATTS
SCATTY
SCAUD
SCAUDED
SCAUDING
SCAUDS
SCAUP
SCAUPED
SCAUPER
SCAUPERS
SCAUPING
SCAUPS
SCAUR
SCAURED
SCAURIES
SCAURING
SCAURS
SCAURY
SCAVAGE
SCAVAGER
SCAVAGERS
SCAVAGES
SCAVENGE
SCAVENGED
SCAVENGER
SCAVENGERED
SCAVENGERING
SCAVENGERINGS
SCAVENGERS
SCAVENGES
SCAVENGING
SCAVENGINGS
SCAW
SCAWS
SCAWTITE
SCAWTITES
SCAZON
SCAZONS
SCAZONTES
SCAZONTIC
SCAZONTICS
SCEAT
SCEATT
SCEATTAS
SCEDULE
SCEDULED
SCEDULES
SCEDULING
SCELERAT
SCELERATE
SCELERATES
SCELERATS
SCENA
SCENARIES
SCENARIO
SCENARIOS
SCENARISE
SCENARISED
SCENARISES
SCENARISING
SCENARIST
SCENARISTS
SCENARIZE
SCENARIZED
SCENARIZES
SCENARIZING
SCENARY
SCEND
SCENDED
SCENDING
SCENDS
SCENE
SCENED
SCENEMAN
SCENEMEN
SCENERIES
SCENERY
SCENES
SCENIC
SCENICAL
SCENING
SCENT
SCENTED
SCENTFUL
SCENTING
SCENTINGS
SCENTLESS
SCENTS
SCEPSIS
SCEPSISES
SCEPTER
SCEPTERED
SCEPTERS
SCEPTIC
SCEPTICAL
SCEPTICS
SCEPTRAL
SCEPTRE
SCEPTRED
SCEPTRES
SCEPTRY
SCERNE
SCERNED
SCERNES
SCERNING
SCHANSE
SCHANSES
SCHANTZE
SCHANTZES
SCHANZE
SCHANZES
SCHAPPE
SCHAPPED
SCHAPPEING
SCHAPPES
SCHAPSKA
SCHAPSKAS
SCHECHITA
SCHECHITAS
SCHEDULE
SCHEDULED
SCHEDULER
SCHEDULERS
SCHEDULES
SCHEDULING
SCHEELITE
SCHEELITES
SCHELLUM
SCHELLUMS
SCHELM
SCHELMS
SCHEMA
SCHEMATA
SCHEMATIC
SCHEME
SCHEMED
SCHEMER
SCHEMERS
SCHEMES
SCHEMING
SCHEMINGS
SCHERZI
SCHERZO
SCHERZOS
SCHIAVONE
SCHIAVONES
SCHIEDAM
SCHIEDAMS
SCHILLER
SCHILLERS
SCHILLING
SCHILLINGS
SCHIMMEL
SCHIMMELS
SCHISM
SCHISMA
SCHISMAS
SCHISMS
SCHIST
SCHISTOSE
SCHISTOUS
SCHISTS
SCHIZO
SCHIZOID
SCHIZOIDS
SCHIZONT
SCHIZONTS
SCHIZOPOD
SCHIZOPODS
SCHIZOS
SCHLAGER
SCHLAGERS
SCHLEMIEL
SCHLEMIELS
SCHLEMIHL
SCHLEMIHLS
SCHLEP
SCHLEPP
SCHLEPPED
SCHLEPPER
SCHLEPPERS
SCHLEPPIER
SCHLEPPIEST
SCHLEPPING
SCHLEPPS
SCHLEPPY
SCHLEPS
SCHLICH
SCHLICHS
SCHLIEREN
SCHLOCK
SCHLOCKER
SCHLOCKERS
SCHLOCKIER
SCHLOCKIEST
SCHLOCKS
SCHLOCKY
SCHLOSS
SCHLOSSES
SCHMALTZ
SCHMALTZES
SCHMALTZIER
SCHMALTZIEST
SCHMALTZY
SCHMECK
SCHMECKS
SCHMELZ
SCHMELZES
SCHMO
SCHMOCK
SCHMOCKS
SCHMOE
SCHMOES
SCHMOOZ
SCHMOOZE
SCHMOOZED
SCHMOOZES
SCHMOOZING
SCHMUCK
SCHMUCKS
SCHMUTTER
SCHMUTTERS
SCHNAPPER
SCHNAPPERS
SCHNAPPS
SCHNAPPSES
SCHNAPS
SCHNAPSES
SCHNAUZER
SCHNAUZERS
SCHNECKE
SCHNECKEN
SCHNELL
SCHNITZEL
SCHNITZELS
SCHNOOK
SCHNOOKS
SCHNORKEL
SCHNORKELS
SCHNORR
SCHNORRED
SCHNORRER
SCHNORRERS
SCHNORRING
SCHNORRS
SCHNOZZLE
SCHNOZZLES
SCHOLAR
SCHOLARCH
SCHOLARCHS
SCHOLARLIER
SCHOLARLIEST
SCHOLARLY
SCHOLARS
SCHOLIA
SCHOLIAST
SCHOLIASTS
SCHOLION

SCHOLIUM
SCHOOL
SCHOOLBAG
SCHOOLBAGS
SCHOOLBOY
SCHOOLBOYS
SCHOOLDAY
SCHOOLDAYS
SCHOOLE
SCHOOLED
SCHOOLERIES
SCHOOLERY
SCHOOLES
SCHOOLING
SCHOOLINGS
SCHOOLMAN
SCHOOLMEN
SCHOOLS
SCHOONER
SCHOONERS
SCHORL
SCHORLS
SCHOUT
SCHOUTS
SCHTICK
SCHTICKS
SCHTIK
SCHTIKS
SCHTOOK
SCHTOOKS
SCHTOOM
SCHTUCK
SCHTUCKS
SCHUIT
SCHUITS
SCHUSS
SCHUSSED
SCHUSSES
SCHUSSING
SCHUYT
SCHUYTS
SCHWA
SCHWAS
SCIAENID
SCIAENIDS
SCIAENOID
SCIAENOIDS
SCIAMACHIES
SCIAMACHY
SCIARID
SCIARIDS
SCIATIC
SCIATICA
SCIATICAL
SCIATICAS
SCIENCE
SCIENCED
SCIENCES
SCIENT
SCIENTER
SCIENTIAL
SCIENTISE
SCIENTISED
SCIENTISES
SCIENTISING
SCIENTISM
SCIENTISMS
SCIENTIST
SCIENTISTS
SCIENTIZE
SCIENTIZED
SCIENTIZES
SCIENTIZING
SCILICET
SCILLA
SCILLAS
SCIMITAR
SCIMITARS
SCINCOID
SCINCOIDS
SCINTILLA
SCINTILLAS
SCIOLISM
SCIOLISMS
SCIOLIST
SCIOLISTS
SCIOLOUS
SCIOLTO
SCION
SCIONS
SCIOSOPHIES
SCIOSOPHY
SCIROC
SCIROCCO
SCIROCCOS
SCIROCS
SCIRRHOID
SCIRRHOUS
SCIRRHUS
SCIRRHUSES
SCISSEL
SCISSELS
SCISSIL
SCISSILE
SCISSILS
SCISSION
SCISSIONS
SCISSOR
SCISSORED
SCISSORER
SCISSORERS
SCISSORING
SCISSORS
SCISSURE
SCISSURES
SCIURINE
SCIURINES
SCIUROID
SCLAFF
SCLAFFED
SCLAFFING
SCLAFFS
SCLATE
SCLATED
SCLATES
SCLATING
SCLAUNDER
SCLAUNDERS
SCLAVE
SCLAVES
SCLERA
SCLERAL
SCLERAS
SCLERE
SCLEREID
SCLEREIDE
SCLEREIDES
SCLEREIDS
SCLEREMA
SCLEREMAS
SCLERES
SCLERITE
SCLERITES
SCLERITIS
SCLERITISES
SCLEROID
SCLEROMA
SCLEROMAS
SCLEROMATA
SCLEROSAL
SCLEROSE
SCLEROSED
SCLEROSES
SCLEROSING
SCLEROSIS
SCLEROTAL
SCLEROTALS
SCLEROTIA
SCLEROTIC
SCLEROTICS
SCLEROTIN
SCLEROTINS
SCLEROUS
SCLIFF
SCLIFFS
SCLIM
SCLIMMED
SCLIMMING
SCLIMS
SCOFF
SCOFFED
SCOFFER
SCOFFERS
SCOFFING
SCOFFINGS
SCOFFLAW
SCOFFLAWS
SCOFFS
SCOG
SCOGGED
SCOGGING
SCOGS
SCOINSON
SCOINSONS
SCOLD
SCOLDED
SCOLDER
SCOLDERS
SCOLDING
SCOLDINGS
SCOLDS
SCOLECES
SCOLECID
SCOLECIDS
SCOLECITE
SCOLECITES
SCOLECOID
SCOLEX
SCOLIA
SCOLICES
SCOLIOMA
SCOLIOMAS
SCOLION
SCOLIOSES
SCOLIOSIS
SCOLIOTIC
SCOLLOP
SCOLLOPED
SCOLLOPING
SCOLLOPS
SCOLYTID
SCOLYTIDS
SCOLYTOID
SCOLYTOIDS
SCOMBRID
SCOMBRIDS
SCOMBROID
SCOMBROIDS
SCOMFISH
SCOMFISHED
SCOMFISHES
SCOMFISHING
SCONCE
SCONCED
SCONCES
SCONCHEON
SCONCHEONS
SCONCING
SCONE
SCONES
SCONTION
SCONTIONS
SCOOG
SCOOGED
SCOOGING
SCOOGS
SCOOP
SCOOPED
SCOOPER
SCOOPERS
SCOOPFUL
SCOOPFULS
SCOOPING
SCOOPINGS
SCOOPS
SCOOT
SCOOTED
SCOOTER
SCOOTERS
SCOOTING
SCOOTS
SCOP
SCOPA
SCOPAE
SCOPAS
SCOPATE
SCOPE
SCOPED
SCOPELID
SCOPELIDS
SCOPELOID
SCOPELOIDS
SCOPES
SCOPING
SCOPULA
SCOPULAS
SCOPULATE
SCORBUTIC
SCORCH
SCORCHED
SCORCHER
SCORCHERS
SCORCHES
SCORCHING
SCORCHINGS
SCORDATO
SCORE
SCORECARD
SCORECARDS
SCORED
SCORELINE
SCORELINES
SCORER
SCORERS
SCORES
SCORIA
SCORIAC
SCORIAE
SCORIFIED
SCORIFIER
SCORIFIERS
SCORIFIES
SCORIFY
SCORIFYING
SCORING
SCORINGS
SCORIOUS
SCORN
SCORNED
SCORNER
SCORNERS
SCORNFUL
SCORNING
SCORNINGS
SCORNS
SCORODITE
SCORODITES
SCORPER
SCORPERS
SCORPIOID
SCORPIOIDS
SCORPION
SCORPIONS
SCORRENDO
SCORSE
SCORSED
SCORSER
SCORSERS
SCORSES
SCORSING

SCOT
SCOTCH
SCOTCHED
SCOTCHES
SCOTCHING
SCOTER
SCOTERS
SCOTIA
SCOTIAS
SCOTOMA
SCOTOMAS
SCOTOMATA
SCOTOMIA
SCOTOMIAS
SCOTOMIES
SCOTOMY
SCOTOPIA
SCOTOPIAS
SCOTOPIC
SCOTS
SCOUG
SCOUGED
SCOUGING
SCOUGS
SCOUNDREL
SCOUNDRELS
SCOUP
SCOUPED
SCOUPING
SCOUPS
SCOUR
SCOURED
SCOURER
SCOURERS
SCOURGE
SCOURGED
SCOURGER
SCOURGERS
SCOURGES
SCOURGING
SCOURIE
SCOURIES
SCOURING
SCOURINGS
SCOURS
SCOURSE
SCOURSED
SCOURSES
SCOURSING
SCOUSE
SCOUSER
SCOUSERS
SCOUSES
SCOUT
SCOUTED
SCOUTER
SCOUTERS
SCOUTH
SCOUTHER
SCOUTHERED
SCOUTHERING
SCOUTHERINGS
SCOUTHERS
SCOUTHERY
SCOUTHS
SCOUTING
SCOUTINGS
SCOUTS
SCOW
SCOWDER
SCOWDERED
SCOWDERING
SCOWDERINGS
SCOWDERS
SCOWL
SCOWLED
SCOWLING
SCOWLS
SCOWP
SCOWPED
SCOWPING
SCOWPS
SCOWRER
SCOWRERS
SCOWRIE
SCOWRIES
SCOWS
SCOWTH
SCOWTHER
SCOWTHERED
SCOWTHERING
SCOWTHERS
SCOWTHS
SCRAB
SCRABBED
SCRABBING
SCRABBLE
SCRABBLED
SCRABBLER
SCRABBLERS
SCRABBLES
SCRABBLING
SCRABS
SCRAE
SCRAES
SCRAG
SCRAGGED
SCRAGGIER
SCRAGGIEST
SCRAGGILY
SCRAGGING
SCRAGGLIER
SCRAGGLIEST
SCRAGGLY
SCRAGGY
SCRAGS
SCRAICH
SCRAICHED
SCRAICHING
SCRAICHS
SCRAIGH
SCRAIGHED
SCRAIGHING
SCRAIGHS
SCRAM
SCRAMB
SCRAMBED
SCRAMBING
SCRAMBLE
SCRAMBLED
SCRAMBLER
SCRAMBLERS
SCRAMBLES
SCRAMBLING
SCRAMBLINGS
SCRAMBS
SCRAMJET
SCRAMJETS
SCRAMMED
SCRAMMING
SCRAMS
SCRAN
SCRANCH
SCRANCHED
SCRANCHES
SCRANCHING
SCRANNEL
SCRANNIER
SCRANNIEST
SCRANNY
SCRANS
SCRAP
SCRAPBOOK
SCRAPBOOKS
SCRAPE
SCRAPED
SCRAPEGUT
SCRAPEGUTS
SCRAPER
SCRAPERS
SCRAPES
SCRAPHEAP
SCRAPHEAPS
SCRAPIE
SCRAPIES
SCRAPING
SCRAPINGS
SCRAPPED
SCRAPPIER
SCRAPPIEST
SCRAPPILY
SCRAPPING
SCRAPPLE
SCRAPPLES
SCRAPPY
SCRAPS
SCRAPYARD
SCRAPYARDS
SCRAT
SCRATCH
SCRATCHED
SCRATCHER
SCRATCHERS
SCRATCHES
SCRATCHIER
SCRATCHIEST
SCRATCHING
SCRATCHINGS
SCRATCHY
SCRATS
SCRATTED
SCRATTING
SCRATTLE
SCRATTLED
SCRATTLES
SCRATTLING
SCRAUCH
SCRAUCHED
SCRAUCHING
SCRAUCHS
SCRAUGH
SCRAUGHED
SCRAUGHING
SCRAUGHS
SCRAW
SCRAWL
SCRAWLED
SCRAWLER
SCRAWLERS
SCRAWLIER
SCRAWLIEST
SCRAWLING
SCRAWLINGS
SCRAWLS
SCRAWLY
SCRAWM
SCRAWMED
SCRAWMING
SCRAWMS
SCRAWNIER
SCRAWNIEST
SCRAWNY
SCRAWS
SCRAY
SCRAYE
SCRAYES
SCRAYS
SCREAK
SCREAKED
SCREAKIER
SCREAKIEST
SCREAKING
SCREAKS
SCREAKY
SCREAM
SCREAMED
SCREAMER
SCREAMERS
SCREAMING
SCREAMS
SCREE
SCREECH
SCREECHED
SCREECHER
SCREECHERS
SCREECHES
SCREECHIER
SCREECHIEST
SCREECHING
SCREECHY
SCREED
SCREEDED
SCREEDER
SCREEDERS
SCREEDING
SCREEDINGS
SCREEDS
SCREEN
SCREENED
SCREENER
SCREENERS
SCREENING
SCREENINGS
SCREENS
SCREES
SCREEVE
SCREEVED
SCREEVER
SCREEVERS
SCREEVES
SCREEVING
SCREEVINGS
SCREICH
SCREICHED
SCREICHING
SCREICHS
SCREIGH
SCREIGHED
SCREIGHING
SCREIGHS
SCREW
SCREWBALL
SCREWBALLS
SCREWED
SCREWER
SCREWERS
SCREWIER
SCREWIEST
SCREWING
SCREWINGS
SCREWS
SCREWTOP
SCREWTOPS
SCREWY
SCRIBABLE
SCRIBAL
SCRIBBLE
SCRIBBLED
SCRIBBLER
SCRIBBLERS
SCRIBBLES
SCRIBBLIER
SCRIBBLIEST
SCRIBBLING
SCRIBBLINGS
SCRIBBLY
SCRIBE
SCRIBED
SCRIBER
SCRIBERS
SCRIBES
SCRIBING
SCRIBINGS
SCRIBISM
SCRIBISMS
SCRIECH
SCRIECHED
SCRIECHING
SCRIECHS
SCRIED

SCRIENE
SCRIENES
SCRIES
SCRIEVE
SCRIEVED
SCRIEVES
SCRIEVING
SCRIGGLE
SCRIGGLED
SCRIGGLES
SCRIGGLIER
SCRIGGLIEST
SCRIGGLING
SCRIGGLY
SCRIKE
SCRIKED
SCRIKES
SCRIKING
SCRIM
SCRIMMAGE
SCRIMMAGED
SCRIMMAGES
SCRIMMAGING
SCRIMP
SCRIMPED
SCRIMPIER
SCRIMPIEST
SCRIMPILY
SCRIMPING
SCRIMPLY
SCRIMPS
SCRIMPY
SCRIMS
SCRIMSHAW
SCRIMSHAWED
SCRIMSHAWING
SCRIMSHAWS
SCRIMURE
SCRIMURES
SCRINE
SCRINES
SCRIP
SCRIPPAGE
SCRIPPAGES
SCRIPS
SCRIPT
SCRIPTED
SCRIPTING
SCRIPTORY
SCRIPTS
SCRIPTURE
SCRIPTURES
SCRITCH
SCRITCHED
SCRITCHES
SCRITCHING
SCRIVE
SCRIVED
SCRIVENER
SCRIVENERS
SCRIVES
SCRIVING
SCROBE
SCROBES
SCROD
SCRODDLED
SCRODS
SCROFULA
SCROFULAS
SCROG
SCROGGIE
SCROGGIER
SCROGGIEST
SCROGGY
SCROGS
SCROLL
SCROLLED
SCROLLING
SCROLLS
SCROOGE
SCROOGED
SCROOGES
SCROOGING
SCROOP
SCROOPED
SCROOPING
SCROOPS
SCROTA
SCROTAL
SCROTUM
SCROTUMS
SCROUGE
SCROUGED
SCROUGER
SCROUGERS
SCROUGES
SCROUGING
SCROUNGE
SCROUNGED
SCROUNGER
SCROUNGERS
SCROUNGES
SCROUNGING
SCROUNGINGS
SCROW
SCROWDGE
SCROWDGED
SCROWDGES
SCROWDGING
SCROWL
SCROWLE
SCROWLED
SCROWLES
SCROWLING
SCROWLS
SCROWS
SCROYLE
SCROYLES
SCRUB
SCRUBBED
SCRUBBER
SCRUBBERS
SCRUBBIER
SCRUBBIEST
SCRUBBING
SCRUBBINGS
SCRUBBY
SCRUBLAND
SCRUBLANDS
SCRUBS
SCRUFF
SCRUFFIER
SCRUFFIEST
SCRUFFS
SCRUFFY
SCRUM
SCRUMDOWN
SCRUMDOWNS
SCRUMMAGE
SCRUMMAGED
SCRUMMAGES
SCRUMMAGING
SCRUMMED
SCRUMMIER
SCRUMMIEST
SCRUMMING
SCRUMMY
SCRUMP
SCRUMPED
SCRUMPIES
SCRUMPING
SCRUMPOX
SCRUMPOXES
SCRUMPS
SCRUMPY
SCRUMS
SCRUNCH
SCRUNCHED
SCRUNCHES
SCRUNCHIER
SCRUNCHIES
SCRUNCHIEST
SCRUNCHING
SCRUNCHY
SCRUNT
SCRUNTIER
SCRUNTIEST
SCRUNTS
SCRUNTY
SCRUPLE
SCRUPLED
SCRUPLER
SCRUPLERS
SCRUPLES
SCRUPLING
SCRUTABLE
SCRUTATOR
SCRUTATORS
SCRUTINIES
SCRUTINY
SCRUTO
SCRUTOIRE
SCRUTOIRES
SCRUTOS
SCRUZE
SCRUZED
SCRUZES
SCRUZING
SCRY
SCRYDE
SCRYER
SCRYERS
SCRYING
SCRYINGS
SCRYNE
SCRYNES
SCUBA
SCUBAS
SCUCHIN
SCUCHINS
SCUCHION
SCUCHIONS
SCUD
SCUDDALER
SCUDDALERS
SCUDDED
SCUDDER
SCUDDERS
SCUDDING
SCUDDLE
SCUDDLED
SCUDDLES
SCUDDLING
SCUDI
SCUDLER
SCUDLERS
SCUDO
SCUDS
SCUFF
SCUFFED
SCUFFING
SCUFFLE
SCUFFLED
SCUFFLER
SCUFFLERS
SCUFFLES
SCUFFLING
SCUFFS
SCUFT
SCUFTS
SCUG
SCUGGED
SCUGGING
SCUGS
SCUL
SCULK
SCULKED
SCULKING
SCULKS
SCULL
SCULLE
SCULLED
SCULLER
SCULLERIES
SCULLERS
SCULLERY
SCULLES
SCULLING
SCULLINGS
SCULLION
SCULLIONS
SCULLS
SCULP
SCULPED
SCULPIN
SCULPING
SCULPINS
SCULPS
SCULPSIT
SCULPT
SCULPTED
SCULPTING
SCULPTOR
SCULPTORS
SCULPTS
SCULPTURE
SCULPTURED
SCULPTURES
SCULPTURING
SCULPTURINGS
SCULS
SCUM
SCUMBAG
SCUMBAGS
SCUMBER
SCUMBERED
SCUMBERING
SCUMBERS
SCUMBLE
SCUMBLED
SCUMBLES
SCUMBLING
SCUMBLINGS
SCUMFISH
SCUMFISHED
SCUMFISHES
SCUMFISHING
SCUMMED
SCUMMER
SCUMMERS
SCUMMIER
SCUMMIEST
SCUMMING
SCUMMINGS
SCUMMY
SCUMS
SCUNCHEON
SCUNCHEONS
SCUNGE
SCUNGED
SCUNGES
SCUNGIER
SCUNGIEST
SCUNGING
SCUNGY
SCUNNER
SCUNNERED
SCUNNERING
SCUNNERS
SCUP
SCUPPAUG
SCUPPAUGS
SCUPPER
SCUPPERED
SCUPPERING
SCUPPERS
SCUPS
SCUR
SCURF
SCURFIER

SCURFIEST
SCURFS
SCURFY
SCURRED
SCURRIED
SCURRIER
SCURRIERS
SCURRIES
SCURRIL
SCURRILE
SCURRING
SCURRIOUR
SCURRIOURS
SCURRY
SCURRYING
SCURS
SCURVIER
SCURVIES
SCURVIEST
SCURVILY
SCURVY
SCUSE
SCUSED
SCUSES
SCUSING
SCUT
SCUTA
SCUTAGE
SCUTAGES
SCUTAL
SCUTATE
SCUTCH
SCUTCHED
SCUTCHEON
SCUTCHEONS
SCUTCHER
SCUTCHERS
SCUTCHES
SCUTCHING
SCUTCHINGS
SCUTE
SCUTELLA
SCUTELLAR
SCUTELLUM
SCUTES
SCUTIFORM
SCUTIGER
SCUTIGERS
SCUTS
SCUTTER
SCUTTERED
SCUTTERING
SCUTTERS
SCUTTLE
SCUTTLED
SCUTTLER
SCUTTLERS
SCUTTLES
SCUTTLING
SCUTUM
SCUZZ
SCUZZBALL
SCUZZBALLS
SCUZZES
SCUZZIER
SCUZZIEST
SCUZZY
SCYBALA
SCYBALOUS
SCYBALUM
SCYE
SCYES
SCYPHI
SCYPHUS
SCYTALE
SCYTALES
SCYTHE
SCYTHED
SCYTHEMAN
SCYTHEMEN
SCYTHER
SCYTHERS
SCYTHES
SCYTHING
SDAINE
SDAINED
SDAINES
SDAINING
SDAYN
SDAYNED
SDAYNING
SDAYNS
SDEIGN
SDEIGNE
SDEIGNED
SDEIGNES
SDEIGNING
SDEIGNS
SDEIN
SDEINED
SDEINING
SDEINS
SEA
SEABANK
SEABANKS
SEABED
SEABEDS
SEABIRD
SEABIRDS
SEABLITE
SEABLITES
SEABOARD
SEABOARDS
SEABORNE
SEABOTTLE
SEABOTTLES
SEACOAST
SEACOASTS
SEACOCK
SEACOCKS
SEACRAFT
SEACRAFTS
SEACUNNIES
SEACUNNY
SEADROME
SEADROMES
SEAFARER
SEAFARERS
SEAFARING
SEAFARINGS
SEAFOLK
SEAFOLKS
SEAFOOD
SEAFOODS
SEAFOWL
SEAFOWLS
SEAFRONT
SEAFRONTS
SEAGULL
SEAGULLS
SEAHAWK
SEAHAWKS
SEAHOG
SEAHOGS
SEAHORSE
SEAHORSES
SEAHOUND
SEAHOUNDS
SEAKALE
SEAKALES
SEAL
SEALANT
SEALANTS
SEALCH
SEALCHS
SEALED
SEALER
SEALERIES
SEALERS
SEALERY
SEALGH
SEALGHS
SEALINE
SEALINES
SEALING
SEALINGS
SEALPOINT
SEALPOINTS
SEALS
SEALSKIN
SEALSKINS
SEALWAX
SEALWAXES
SEALYHAM
SEALYHAMS
SEAM
SEAMAID
SEAMAIDS
SEAMAN
SEAMANLY
SEAMARK
SEAMARKS
SEAME
SEAMED
SEAMEN
SEAMER
SEAMERS
SEAMES
SEAMIER
SEAMIEST
SEAMINESS
SEAMINESSES
SEAMING
SEAMLESS
SEAMOUNT
SEAMOUNTS
SEAMS
SEAMSET
SEAMSETS
SEAMSTER
SEAMSTERS
SEAMY
SEAN
SEANCE
SEANCES
SEANED
SEANING
SEANNACHIES
SEANNACHY
SEANS
SEAPLANE
SEAPLANES
SEAPORT
SEAPORTS
SEAQUAKE
SEAQUAKES
SEAQUARIA
SEAR
SEARAT
SEARATS
SEARCE
SEARCED
SEARCES
SEARCH
SEARCHED
SEARCHER
SEARCHERS
SEARCHES
SEARCHING
SEARCING
SEARE
SEARED
SEARER
SEAREST
SEARING
SEARINGS
SEARNESS
SEARNESSES
SEARS
SEAS
SEASCAPE
SEASCAPES
SEASE
SEASED
SEASES
SEASHELL
SEASHELLS
SEASHORE
SEASHORES
SEASICK
SEASICKER
SEASICKEST
SEASIDE
SEASIDES
SEASING
SEASON
SEASONAL
SEASONED
SEASONER
SEASONERS
SEASONING
SEASONINGS
SEASONS
SEASPEAK
SEASPEAKS
SEASURE
SEASURES
SEAT
SEATED
SEATER
SEATERS
SEATING
SEATINGS
SEATLESS
SEATS
SEAWARD
SEAWARDLY
SEAWARDS
SEAWARE
SEAWARES
SEAWATER
SEAWATERS
SEAWAY
SEAWAYS
SEAWEED
SEAWEEDS
SEAWIFE
SEAWIVES
SEAWOMAN
SEAWOMEN
SEAWORM
SEAWORMS
SEAWORTHY
SEAZE
SEAZED
SEAZES
SEAZING
SEBACEOUS
SEBACIC
SEBATE
SEBATES
SEBESTEN
SEBESTENS
SEBIFIC
SEBUM
SEBUMS
SEBUNDIES
SEBUNDY
SEC
SECANT
SECANTLY
SECANTS
SECATEURS
SECCO
SECCOS
SECEDE
SECEDED
SECEDER
SECEDERS
SECEDES

SECEDING
SECERN
SECERNED
SECERNENT
SECERNENTS
SECERNING
SECERNS
SECESH
SECESHER
SECESHERS
SECESHES
SECESSION
SECESSIONS
SECKEL
SECKELS
SECKLE
SECKLES
SECLUDE
SECLUDED
SECLUDES
SECLUDING
SECLUSION
SECLUSIONS
SECLUSIVE
SECO
SECODONT
SECODONTS
SECOND
SECONDARIES
SECONDARY
SECONDE
SECONDED
SECONDEE
SECONDEES
SECONDER
SECONDERS
SECONDES
SECONDI
SECONDING
SECONDLY
SECONDO
SECONDS
SECRECIES
SECRECY
SECRET
SECRETA
SECRETAGE
SECRETAGES
SECRETARIES
SECRETARY
SECRETE
SECRETED
SECRETES
SECRETIN
SECRETING
SECRETINS
SECRETION
SECRETIONS
SECRETIVE
SECRETLY
SECRETORY
SECRETS
SECS
SECT
SECTARIAL
SECTARIAN
SECTARIANS
SECTARIES
SECTARY
SECTATOR
SECTATORS
SECTILE
SECTILITIES
SECTILITY
SECTION
SECTIONAL
SECTIONED
SECTIONING
SECTIONS
SECTOR
SECTORAL
SECTORED
SECTORIAL
SECTORIALS
SECTORING
SECTORISE
SECTORISED
SECTORISES
SECTORISING
SECTORIZE
SECTORIZED
SECTORIZES
SECTORIZING
SECTORS
SECTS
SECULAR
SECULARLY
SECULARS
SECULUM
SECULUMS
SECUND
SECUNDINE
SECUNDINES
SECUNDUM
SECURABLE
SECURANCE
SECURANCES
SECURE
SECURED
SECURELY
SECURER
SECURERS
SECURES
SECUREST
SECURING
SECURITAN
SECURITANS
SECURITIES
SECURITY
SED
SEDAN
SEDANS
SEDATE
SEDATED
SEDATELY
SEDATER
SEDATES
SEDATEST
SEDATING
SEDATION
SEDATIONS
SEDATIVE
SEDATIVES
SEDENT
SEDENTARY
SEDERUNT
SEDERUNTS
SEDES
SEDGE
SEDGED
SEDGELAND
SEDGELANDS
SEDGES
SEDGIER
SEDGIEST
SEDGY
SEDILE
SEDILIA
SEDIMENT
SEDIMENTED
SEDIMENTING
SEDIMENTS
SEDITION
SEDITIONS
SEDITIOUS
SEDUCE
SEDUCED
SEDUCER
SEDUCERS
SEDUCES
SEDUCING
SEDUCINGS
SEDUCTION
SEDUCTIONS
SEDUCTIVE
SEDUCTOR
SEDUCTORS
SEDULITIES
SEDULITY
SEDULOUS
SEDUM
SEDUMS
SEE
SEEABLE
SEECATCH
SEECATCHIE
SEED
SEEDBED
SEEDBEDS
SEEDBOX
SEEDBOXES
SEEDCAKE
SEEDCAKES
SEEDCASE
SEEDCASES
SEEDED
SEEDER
SEEDERS
SEEDIER
SEEDIEST
SEEDILY
SEEDINESS
SEEDINESSES
SEEDING
SEEDINGS
SEEDLESS
SEEDLIKE
SEEDLING
SEEDLINGS
SEEDLIP
SEEDLIPS
SEEDNESS
SEEDNESSES
SEEDS
SEEDSMAN
SEEDSMEN
SEEDY
SEEING
SEEINGS
SEEK
SEEKER
SEEKERS
SEEKING
SEEKS
SEEL
SEELD
SEELED
SEELIER
SEELIEST
SEELING
SEELINGS
SEELS
SEELY
SEEM
SEEMED
SEEMER
SEEMERS
SEEMING
SEEMINGLY
SEEMINGS
SEEMLESS
SEEMLIER
SEEMLIEST
SEEMLIHED
SEEMLIHEDS
SEEMLY
SEEMLYHED
SEEMLYHEDS
SEEMS
SEEN
SEEP
SEEPAGE
SEEPAGES
SEEPED
SEEPIER
SEEPIEST
SEEPING
SEEPS
SEEPY
SEER
SEERESS
SEERESSES
SEERS
SEES
SEESAW
SEESAWED
SEESAWING
SEESAWS
SEETHE
SEETHED
SEETHER
SEETHERS
SEETHES
SEETHING
SEETHINGS
SEEWING
SEG
SEGAR
SEGARS
SEGGAR
SEGGARS
SEGHOL
SEGHOLATE
SEGHOLATES
SEGHOLS
SEGMENT
SEGMENTAL
SEGMENTED
SEGMENTING
SEGMENTS
SEGNO
SEGNOS
SEGO
SEGOL
SEGOLATE
SEGOLATES
SEGOLS
SEGOS
SEGREANT
SEGREGATE
SEGREGATED
SEGREGATES
SEGREGATING
SEGS
SEGUE
SEGUED
SEGUEING
SEGUES
SEI
SEICENTO
SEICENTOS
SEICHE
SEICHES
SEIF
SEIFS
SEIGNEUR
SEIGNEURS
SEIGNIOR
SEIGNIORIES
SEIGNIORS
SEIGNIORY
SEIGNORAL
SEIGNORIES
SEIGNORY
SEIK
SEIKER
SEIKEST
SEIL
SEILED
SEILING

SEILS
SEINE
SEINED
SEINER
SEINERS
SEINES
SEINING
SEININGS
SEIR
SEIRS
SEIS
SEISE
SEISED
SEISES
SEISIN
SEISING
SEISINS
SEISM
SEISMAL
SEISMIC
SEISMICAL
SEISMISM
SEISMISMS
SEISMS
SEITEN
SEITENS
SEITIES
SEITY
SEIZABLE
SEIZE
SEIZED
SEIZER
SEIZERS
SEIZES
SEIZIN
SEIZING
SEIZINGS
SEIZINS
SEIZURE
SEIZURES
SEJANT
SEJEANT
SEKOS
SEKOSES
SEKT
SEKTS
SEL
SELACHIAN
SELACHIANS
SELADANG
SELADANGS
SELAH
SELAHS
SELCOUTH
SELD
SELDOM
SELDSEEN
SELDSHOWN
SELE
SELECT
SELECTED
SELECTEE
SELECTEES
SELECTING
SELECTION
SELECTIONS
SELECTIVE
SELECTOR
SELECTORS
SELECTS
SELENATE
SELENATES
SELENIAN
SELENIC
SELENIDE
SELENIDES
SELENIOUS
SELENITE
SELENITES
SELENITIC
SELENIUM
SELENIUMS
SELENOUS
SELES
SELF
SELFED
SELFHEAL
SELFHEALS
SELFHOOD
SELFHOODS
SELFING
SELFINGS
SELFISH
SELFISHLY
SELFISM
SELFISMS
SELFIST
SELFISTS
SELFLESS
SELFNESS
SELFNESSES
SELFS
SELICTAR
SELICTARS
SELKIE
SELKIES
SELL
SELLA
SELLABLE
SELLAE
SELLAS
SELLE
SELLER
SELLERS
SELLES
SELLING
SELLOTAPE
SELLOTAPED
SELLOTAPES
SELLOTAPING
SELLS
SELS
SELTZER
SELTZERS
SELVA
SELVAGE
SELVAGED
SELVAGEE
SELVAGEES
SELVAGES
SELVAGING
SELVAS
SELVEDGE
SELVEDGED
SELVEDGES
SELVEDGING
SELVES
SEMANTEME
SEMANTEMES
SEMANTIC
SEMANTICS
SEMANTIDE
SEMANTIDES
SEMANTRA
SEMANTRON
SEMAPHORE
SEMAPHORED
SEMAPHORES
SEMAPHORING
SEMATIC
SEMBLABLE
SEMBLABLES
SEMBLABLY
SEMBLANCE
SEMBLANCES
SEMBLANT
SEMBLANTS
SEMBLE
SEMBLED
SEMBLES
SEMBLING
SEME
SEMEE
SEMEED
SEMEIA
SEMEION
SEMEIOTIC
SEMEIOTICS
SEMEME
SEMEMES
SEMEN
SEMENS
SEMESTER
SEMESTERS
SEMESTRAL
SEMI
SEMIANGLE
SEMIANGLES
SEMIBOLD
SEMIBOLDS
SEMIBREVE
SEMIBREVES
SEMIBULL
SEMIBULLS
SEMICOLON
SEMICOLONS
SEMICOMA
SEMICOMAS
SEMIE
SEMIES
SEMIFINAL
SEMIFINALS
SEMIFLUID
SEMIFLUIDS
SEMILUNAR
SEMILUNE
SEMILUNES
SEMINAL
SEMINALLY
SEMINAR
SEMINARIES
SEMINARS
SEMINARY
SEMINATE
SEMINATED
SEMINATES
SEMINATING
SEMIOLOGIES
SEMIOLOGY
SEMIOTIC
SEMIOTICS
SEMIPED
SEMIPEDS
SEMIPLUME
SEMIPLUMES
SEMIS
SEMISES
SEMISOLID
SEMISOLIDS
SEMITAR
SEMITARS
SEMITAUR
SEMITAURS
SEMITONE
SEMITONES
SEMITONIC
SEMIVOWEL
SEMIVOWELS
SEMMIT
SEMMITS
SEMOLINA
SEMOLINAS
SEMPER
SEMPLE
SEMPLER
SEMPLEST
SEMPLICE
SEMPRE
SEMPSTER
SEMPSTERS
SEMSEM
SEMSEMS
SEMUNCIA
SEMUNCIAE
SEMUNCIAL
SEMUNCIAS
SEN
SENA
SENARIES
SENARII
SENARIUS
SENARY
SENAS
SENATE
SENATES
SENATOR
SENATORS
SEND
SENDAL
SENDALS
SENDED
SENDER
SENDERS
SENDING
SENDINGS
SENDS
SENECIO
SENECIOS
SENEGA
SENEGAS
SENESCENT
SENESCHAL
SENESCHALS
SENGREEN
SENGREENS
SENILE
SENILELY
SENILITIES
SENILITY
SENIOR
SENIORITIES
SENIORITY
SENIORS
SENNA
SENNACHIE
SENNACHIES
SENNAS
SENNET
SENNETS
SENNIGHT
SENNIGHTS
SENNIT
SENNITS
SENS
SENSA
SENSATE
SENSATION
SENSATIONS
SENSE
SENSED
SENSEFUL
SENSELESS
SENSES
SENSIBLE
SENSIBLER
SENSIBLES
SENSIBLEST
SENSIBLY
SENSILE
SENSILLA
SENSILLUM
SENSING
SENSINGS
SENSISM
SENSISMS
SENSIST
SENSISTS
SENSITISE
SENSITISED
SENSITISES

SENSITISING
SENSITIVE
SENSITIVES
SENSITIZE
SENSITIZED
SENSITIZES
SENSITIZING
SENSOR
SENSORIA
SENSORIAL
SENSORILY
SENSORIUM
SENSORIUMS
SENSORS
SENSORY
SENSUAL
SENSUALLY
SENSUM
SENSUOUS
SENT
SENTED
SENTENCE
SENTENCED
SENTENCER
SENTENCERS
SENTENCES
SENTENCING
SENTIENCE
SENTIENCES
SENTIENCIES
SENTIENCY
SENTIENT
SENTIENTS
SENTIMENT
SENTIMENTS
SENTINEL
SENTINELLED
SENTINELLING
SENTINELS
SENTING
SENTRIES
SENTRY
SENTS
SENVIES
SENVY
SENZA
SEPAD
SEPADDED
SEPADDING
SEPADS
SEPAL
SEPALINE
SEPALODIES
SEPALODY
SEPALOID
SEPALOUS
SEPALS
SEPARABLE
SEPARABLY
SEPARATA
SEPARATE
SEPARATED
SEPARATES
SEPARATING
SEPARATOR
SEPARATORS
SEPARATUM
SEPARATUMS
SEPHEN
SEPHENS
SEPIA
SEPIAS
SEPIMENT
SEPIMENTS
SEPIOLITE
SEPIOLITES
SEPIOST
SEPIOSTS
SEPIUM
SEPIUMS
SEPMAG
SEPOY
SEPOYS
SEPPUKU
SEPPUKUS
SEPS
SEPSES
SEPSIS
SEPT
SEPTA
SEPTAL
SEPTARIA
SEPTARIAN
SEPTARIUM
SEPTATE
SEPTATION
SEPTATIONS
SEPTEMFID
SEPTEMVIR
SEPTEMVIRI
SEPTEMVIRS
SEPTENARIES
SEPTENARY
SEPTENNIA
SEPTET
SEPTETS
SEPTETTE
SEPTETTES
SEPTIC
SEPTICITIES
SEPTICITY
SEPTIFORM
SEPTIMAL
SEPTIME
SEPTIMES
SEPTIMOLE
SEPTIMOLES
SEPTLEVA
SEPTLEVAS
SEPTS
SEPTUM
SEPTUOR
SEPTUORS
SEPTUPLE
SEPTUPLED
SEPTUPLES
SEPTUPLET
SEPTUPLETS
SEPTUPLING
SEPULCHER
SEPULCHERED
SEPULCHERING
SEPULCHERS
SEPULCHRE
SEPULCHRED
SEPULCHRES
SEPULCHRING
SEPULTURE
SEPULTURED
SEPULTURES
SEPULTURING
SEQUACITIES
SEQUACITY
SEQUEL
SEQUELA
SEQUELAE
SEQUELS
SEQUENCE
SEQUENCED
SEQUENCER
SEQUENCERS
SEQUENCES
SEQUENCING
SEQUENCINGS
SEQUENT
SEQUENTS
SEQUESTER
SEQUESTERED
SEQUESTERING
SEQUESTERS
SEQUESTRA
SEQUIN
SEQUINED
SEQUINNED
SEQUINS
SEQUOIA
SEQUOIAS
SERA
SERAC
SERACS
SERAFILE
SERAFILES
SERAFIN
SERAFINS
SERAGLIO
SERAGLIOS
SERAI
SERAIL
SERAILS
SERAIS
SERAL
SERANG
SERANGS
SERAPE
SERAPES
SERAPH
SERAPHIC
SERAPHIM
SERAPHIMS
SERAPHIN
SERAPHINE
SERAPHINES
SERAPHINS
SERAPHS
SERASKIER
SERASKIERS
SERDAB
SERDABS
SERE
SERED
SEREIN
SEREINS
SERENADE
SERENADED
SERENADER
SERENADERS
SERENADES
SERENADING
SERENATA
SERENATAS
SERENATE
SERENATES
SERENE
SERENED
SERENELY
SERENER
SERENES
SERENEST
SERENING
SERENITIES
SERENITY
SERER
SERES
SEREST
SERF
SERFAGE
SERFAGES
SERFDOM
SERFDOMS
SERFHOOD
SERFHOODS
SERFISH
SERFLIKE
SERFS
SERFSHIP
SERFSHIPS
SERGE
SERGEANCIES
SERGEANCY
SERGEANT
SERGEANTS
SERGES
SERIAL
SERIALISE
SERIALISED
SERIALISES
SERIALISING
SERIALISM
SERIALISMS
SERIALIST
SERIALISTS
SERIALITIES
SERIALITY
SERIALIZE
SERIALIZED
SERIALIZES
SERIALIZING
SERIALLY
SERIALS
SERIATE
SERIATED
SERIATELY
SERIATES
SERIATIM
SERIATING
SERIATION
SERIATIONS
SERIC
SERICEOUS
SERICIN
SERICINS
SERICITE
SERICITES
SERICITIC
SERICON
SERICONS
SERIEMA
SERIEMAS
SERIES
SERIF
SERIFS
SERIGRAPH
SERIGRAPHS
SERIN
SERINE
SERINES
SERINETTE
SERINETTES
SERING
SERINGA
SERINGAS
SERINS
SERIOUS
SERIOUSLY
SERIPH
SERIPHS
SERJEANCIES
SERJEANCY
SERJEANT
SERJEANTIES
SERJEANTS
SERJEANTY
SERK
SERKALI
SERKALIS
SERKS
SERMON
SERMONED
SERMONEER
SERMONEERS
SERMONER
SERMONERS
SERMONET
SERMONETS
SERMONIC
SERMONING
SERMONINGS
SERMONISE
SERMONISED
SERMONISES

SERMONISING
SERMONIZE
SERMONIZED
SERMONIZES
SERMONIZING
SERMONS
SEROLOGIES
SEROLOGY
SERON
SERONS
SEROON
SEROONS
SEROPUS
SEROPUSES
SEROSA
SEROSAE
SEROSAS
SEROSITIES
SEROSITY
SEROTINAL
SEROTINE
SEROTINES
SEROTONIN
SEROTONINS
SEROTYPE
SEROTYPED
SEROTYPES
SEROTYPING
SEROTYPINGS
SEROUS
SEROW
SEROWS
SERPENT
SERPENTRIES
SERPENTRY
SERPENTS
SERPIGINES
SERPIGO
SERPIGOES
SERPULA
SERPULAE
SERPULITE
SERPULITES
SERR
SERRA
SERRAE
SERRAN
SERRANID
SERRANIDS
SERRANOID
SERRANOIDS
SERRANS
SERRAS
SERRATE
SERRATED
SERRATES
SERRATI
SERRATING
SERRATION
SERRATIONS
SERRATURE
SERRATURES
SERRATUS
SERRATUSES
SERRE
SERRED
SERREFILE
SERREFILES
SERRES
SERRICORN
SERRIED
SERRIES
SERRING
SERRS
SERRULATE
SERRY
SERRYING
SERUEWE
SERUEWED
SERUEWES
SERUEWING
SERUM
SERUMS
SERVAL
SERVALS
SERVANT
SERVANTED
SERVANTING
SERVANTRIES
SERVANTRY
SERVANTS
SERVE
SERVED
SERVER
SERVERIES
SERVERS
SERVERY
SERVES
SERVEWE
SERVEWED
SERVEWES
SERVEWING
SERVICE
SERVICED
SERVICES
SERVICING
SERVIENT
SERVIETTE
SERVIETTES
SERVILE
SERVILELY
SERVILES
SERVILISM
SERVILISMS
SERVILITIES
SERVILITY
SERVING
SERVINGS
SERVITOR
SERVITORS
SERVITUDE
SERVITUDES
SERVO
SESAME
SESAMES
SESAMOID
SESAMOIDS
SESE
SESELI
SESELIS
SESEY
SESS
SESSA
SESSES
SESSILE
SESSION
SESSIONAL
SESSIONS
SESSPOOL
SESSPOOLS
SESTERCE
SESTERCES
SESTERTIA
SESTET
SESTETS
SESTETT
SESTETTE
SESTETTES
SESTETTO
SESTETTOS
SESTETTS
SESTINA
SESTINAS
SESTINE
SESTINES
SESTON
SESTONS
SET
SETA
SETACEOUS
SETAE
SETBACK
SETBACKS
SETIFORM
SETLINE
SETLINES
SETNESS
SETNESSES
SETON
SETONS
SETOSE
SETS
SETSCREW
SETSCREWS
SETT
SETTEE
SETTEES
SETTER
SETTERED
SETTERING
SETTERS
SETTING
SETTINGS
SETTLE
SETTLED
SETTLER
SETTLERS
SETTLES
SETTLING
SETTLINGS
SETTLOR
SETTLORS
SETTS
SETUALE
SETUALES
SETULE
SETULES
SETULOSE
SETULOUS
SETWALL
SETWALLS
SEVEN
SEVENFOLD
SEVENS
SEVENTEEN
SEVENTEENS
SEVENTH
SEVENTHLY
SEVENTHS
SEVENTIES
SEVENTY
SEVER
SEVERABLE
SEVERAL
SEVERALLY
SEVERALS
SEVERALTIES
SEVERALTY
SEVERANCE
SEVERANCES
SEVERE
SEVERED
SEVERELY
SEVERER
SEVEREST
SEVERIES
SEVERING
SEVERITIES
SEVERITY
SEVERS
SEVERY
SEVRUGA
SEVRUGAS
SEW
SEWAGE
SEWAGES
SEWED
SEWEL
SEWELLEL
SEWELLELS
SEWELS
SEWEN
SEWENS
SEWER
SEWERAGE
SEWERAGES
SEWERED
SEWERING
SEWERINGS
SEWERS
SEWIN
SEWING
SEWINGS
SEWINS
SEWN
SEWS
SEX
SEXED
SEXENNIAL
SEXER
SEXERS
SEXES
SEXFID
SEXFOIL
SEXFOILS
SEXIER
SEXIEST
SEXINESS
SEXINESSES
SEXING
SEXISM
SEXISMS
SEXIST
SEXISTS
SEXLESS
SEXOLOGIES
SEXOLOGY
SEXPERT
SEXPERTS
SEXPOT
SEXPOTS
SEXT
SEXTAN
SEXTANS
SEXTANSES
SEXTANT
SEXTANTAL
SEXTANTS
SEXTET
SEXTETS
SEXTETT
SEXTETTE
SEXTETTES
SEXTETTS
SEXTILE
SEXTILES
SEXTOLET
SEXTOLETS
SEXTON
SEXTONESS
SEXTONESSES
SEXTONS
SEXTS
SEXTUOR
SEXTUORS
SEXTUPLE
SEXTUPLED
SEXTUPLES
SEXTUPLET
SEXTUPLETS
SEXTUPLING
SEXUAL
SEXUALISE
SEXUALISED
SEXUALISES
SEXUALISING
SEXUALISM
SEXUALISMS
SEXUALIST
SEXUALISTS

SEXUALITIES
SEXUALITY
SEXUALIZE
SEXUALIZED
SEXUALIZES
SEXUALIZING
SEXUALLY
SEXVALENT
SEXY
SEY
SEYEN
SEYENS
SEYS
SEYSURE
SEYSURES
SEZ
SFERICS
SFORZANDI
SFORZANDO
SFORZANDOS
SFORZATI
SFORZATO
SFORZATOS
SFUMATO
SFUMATOS
SGRAFFITI
SGRAFFITO
SH
SHABBIER
SHABBIEST
SHABBILY
SHABBLE
SHABBLES
SHABBY
SHABRACK
SHABRACKS
SHACK
SHACKLE
SHACKLED
SHACKLES
SHACKLING
SHACKO
SHACKOES
SHACKOS
SHACKS
SHAD
SHADBERRIES
SHADBERRY
SHADBLOW
SHADBLOWS
SHADBUSH
SHADBUSHES
SHADDOCK
SHADDOCKS
SHADE
SHADED
SHADELESS
SHADES
SHADIER
SHADIEST
SHADILY
SHADINESS
SHADINESSES
SHADING
SHADINGS
SHADOOF
SHADOOFS
SHADOW
SHADOWED
SHADOWER
SHADOWERS
SHADOWIER
SHADOWIEST
SHADOWING
SHADOWINGS
SHADOWS
SHADOWY
SHADS
SHADUF
SHADUFS
SHADY
SHAFT
SHAFTED
SHAFTER
SHAFTERS
SHAFTING
SHAFTINGS
SHAFTLESS
SHAFTS
SHAG
SHAGGED
SHAGGIER
SHAGGIEST
SHAGGILY
SHAGGING
SHAGGY
SHAGPILE
SHAGREEN
SHAGREENS
SHAGROON
SHAGROONS
SHAGS
SHAH
SHAHS
SHAIKH
SHAIKHS
SHAIRN
SHAIRNS
SHAITAN
SHAITANS
SHAKABLE
SHAKE
SHAKEABLE
SHAKED
SHAKEDOWN
SHAKEDOWNS
SHAKEN
SHAKER
SHAKERS
SHAKES
SHAKIER
SHAKIEST
SHAKILY
SHAKINESS
SHAKINESSES
SHAKING
SHAKINGS
SHAKO
SHAKOES
SHAKOS
SHAKT
SHAKUDO
SHAKUDOS
SHAKY
SHALE
SHALED
SHALES
SHALIER
SHALIEST
SHALING
SHALL
SHALLI
SHALLIS
SHALLON
SHALLONS
SHALLOON
SHALLOONS
SHALLOP
SHALLOPS
SHALLOT
SHALLOTS
SHALLOW
SHALLOWED
SHALLOWER
SHALLOWEST
SHALLOWING
SHALLOWINGS
SHALLOWLY
SHALLOWS
SHALM
SHALMS
SHALOM
SHALOT
SHALOTS
SHALT
SHALWAR
SHALWARS
SHALY
SHAM
SHAMA
SHAMABLE
SHAMAN
SHAMANIC
SHAMANISM
SHAMANISMS
SHAMANIST
SHAMANISTS
SHAMANS
SHAMAS
SHAMATEUR
SHAMATEURS
SHAMBA
SHAMBAS
SHAMBLE
SHAMBLED
SHAMBLES
SHAMBLIER
SHAMBLIEST
SHAMBLING
SHAMBLINGS
SHAMBLY
SHAMBOLIC
SHAME
SHAMEABLE
SHAMED
SHAMEFAST
SHAMEFUL
SHAMELESS
SHAMER
SHAMERS
SHAMES
SHAMIANA
SHAMIANAH
SHAMIANAHS
SHAMIANAS
SHAMING
SHAMISEN
SHAMISENS
SHAMMASH
SHAMMASHIM
SHAMMED
SHAMMER
SHAMMERS
SHAMMES
SHAMMIES
SHAMMING
SHAMMOSIM
SHAMMY
SHAMOY
SHAMOYED
SHAMOYING
SHAMOYS
SHAMPOO
SHAMPOOED
SHAMPOOER
SHAMPOOERS
SHAMPOOING
SHAMPOOS
SHAMROCK
SHAMROCKS
SHAMS
SHAMUS
SHAMUSES
SHAN
SHANACHIE
SHANACHIES
SHAND
SHANDIES
SHANDRIES
SHANDRY
SHANDS
SHANDY
SHANGHAI
SHANGHAIED
SHANGHAIING
SHANGHAIS
SHANK
SHANKBONE
SHANKBONES
SHANKED
SHANKING
SHANKS
SHANNIES
SHANNY
SHANS
SHANTEY
SHANTEYS
SHANTIES
SHANTUNG
SHANTUNGS
SHANTY
SHANTYMAN
SHANTYMEN
SHAPABLE
SHAPE
SHAPEABLE
SHAPED
SHAPELESS
SHAPELIER
SHAPELIEST
SHAPELY
SHAPEN
SHAPER
SHAPERS
SHAPES
SHAPING
SHAPINGS
SHAPS
SHARD
SHARDED
SHARDS
SHARE
SHARECROP
SHARECROPPED
SHARECROPPING
SHARECROPS
SHARED
SHAREMAN
SHAREMEN
SHARER
SHARERS
SHARES
SHARESMAN
SHARESMEN
SHAREWARE
SHAREWARES
SHARIA
SHARIAS
SHARIAT
SHARIATS
SHARIF
SHARIFS
SHARING
SHARINGS
SHARK
SHARKED
SHARKER
SHARKERS
SHARKING
SHARKINGS
SHARKS
SHARKSKIN
SHARKSKINS
SHARN
SHARNIER
SHARNIEST
SHARNS
SHARNY
SHARP
SHARPED

SHARPEN
SHARPENED
SHARPENER
SHARPENERS
SHARPENING
SHARPENS
SHARPER
SHARPERS
SHARPEST
SHARPIE
SHARPIES
SHARPING
SHARPINGS
SHARPISH
SHARPLY
SHARPNESS
SHARPNESSES
SHARPS
SHASH
SHASHED
SHASHES
SHASHING
SHASHLICK
SHASHLICKS
SHASHLIK
SHASHLIKS
SHASTER
SHASTERS
SHASTRA
SHASTRAS
SHAT
SHATTER
SHATTERED
SHATTERING
SHATTERS
SHATTERY
SHAUCHLE
SHAUCHLED
SHAUCHLES
SHAUCHLIER
SHAUCHLIEST
SHAUCHLING
SHAUCHLY
SHAVE
SHAVED
SHAVELING
SHAVELINGS
SHAVEN
SHAVER
SHAVERS
SHAVES
SHAVIE
SHAVIES
SHAVING
SHAVINGS
SHAW
SHAWL
SHAWLED
SHAWLEY
SHAWLEYS
SHAWLIE
SHAWLIES
SHAWLING
SHAWLINGS
SHAWLLESS
SHAWLS
SHAWM
SHAWMS
SHAWS
SHAY
SHAYA
SHAYAS
SHAYS
SHCHI
SHCHIS
SHE
SHEA
SHEADING
SHEADINGS
SHEAF
SHEAFED
SHEAFIER
SHEAFIEST
SHEAFING
SHEAFS
SHEAFY
SHEAL
SHEALED
SHEALING
SHEALINGS
SHEALS
SHEAR
SHEARED
SHEARER
SHEARERS
SHEARING
SHEARINGS
SHEARLEG
SHEARLEGS
SHEARLING
SHEARLINGS
SHEARMAN
SHEARMEN
SHEARS
SHEAS
SHEATFISH
SHEATFISHES
SHEATH
SHEATHE
SHEATHED
SHEATHES
SHEATHIER
SHEATHIEST
SHEATHING
SHEATHINGS
SHEATHS
SHEATHY
SHEAVE
SHEAVED
SHEAVES
SHEAVING
SHEBANG
SHEBANGS
SHEBEEN
SHEBEENED
SHEBEENER
SHEBEENERS
SHEBEENING
SHEBEENINGS
SHEBEENS
SHECHITA
SHECHITAH
SHECHITAHS
SHECHITAS
SHED
SHEDDER
SHEDDERS
SHEDDING
SHEDDINGS
SHEDS
SHEEL
SHEELED
SHEELING
SHEELS
SHEEN
SHEENED
SHEENIER
SHEENIES
SHEENIEST
SHEENING
SHEENS
SHEENY
SHEEP
SHEEPCOTE
SHEEPCOTES
SHEEPDOG
SHEEPDOGS
SHEEPFOLD
SHEEPFOLDS
SHEEPIER
SHEEPIEST
SHEEPISH
SHEEPO
SHEEPOS
SHEEPSKIN
SHEEPSKINS
SHEEPWALK
SHEEPWALKS
SHEEPY
SHEER
SHEERED
SHEERER
SHEEREST
SHEERING
SHEERLEG
SHEERLEGS
SHEERLY
SHEERS
SHEET
SHEETED
SHEETIER
SHEETIEST
SHEETING
SHEETINGS
SHEETS
SHEETY
SHEHITA
SHEHITAH
SHEHITAHS
SHEHITAS
SHEIK
SHEIKDOM
SHEIKDOMS
SHEIKH
SHEIKHA
SHEIKHAS
SHEIKHDOM
SHEIKHDOMS
SHEIKHS
SHEIKS
SHEILA
SHEILAS
SHEILING
SHEILINGS
SHEKEL
SHEKELS
SHELDDUCK
SHELDDUCKS
SHELDRAKE
SHELDRAKES
SHELDUCK
SHELDUCKS
SHELF
SHELFED
SHELFIER
SHELFIEST
SHELFING
SHELFLIKE
SHELFROOM
SHELFROOMS
SHELFS
SHELFY
SHELL
SHELLAC
SHELLACKED
SHELLACKING
SHELLACKINGS
SHELLACS
SHELLBACK
SHELLBACKS
SHELLBARK
SHELLBARKS
SHELLDUCK
SHELLDUCKS
SHELLED
SHELLER
SHELLERS
SHELLFIRE
SHELLFIRES
SHELLFISH
SHELLFISHES
SHELLFUL
SHELLFULS
SHELLIER
SHELLIEST
SHELLING
SHELLINGS
SHELLS
SHELLWORK
SHELLWORKS
SHELLY
SHELTER
SHELTERED
SHELTERER
SHELTERERS
SHELTERING
SHELTERINGS
SHELTERS
SHELTERY
SHELTIE
SHELTIES
SHELTY
SHELVE
SHELVED
SHELVES
SHELVIER
SHELVIEST
SHELVING
SHELVINGS
SHELVY
SHEMOZZLE
SHEMOZZLED
SHEMOZZLES
SHEMOZZLING
SHEND
SHENDING
SHENDS
SHENT
SHEOL
SHEOLS
SHEPHERD
SHEPHERDED
SHEPHERDING
SHEPHERDS
SHERBET
SHERBETS
SHERD
SHERDS
SHERE
SHEREEF
SHEREEFS
SHERIA
SHERIAS
SHERIAT
SHERIATS
SHERIF
SHERIFF
SHERIFFS
SHERIFIAN
SHERIFS
SHERLOCK
SHERLOCKS
SHERPA
SHERPAS
SHERRIES
SHERRIS
SHERRISES
SHERRY
SHERWANI
SHERWANIS
SHES
SHET
SHETLAND
SHETS
SHETTING
SHEUCH
SHEUCHED
SHEUCHING
SHEUCHS
SHEUGH

SHEUGHED
SHEUGHING
SHEUGHS
SHEVA
SHEVAS
SHEW
SHEWBREAD
SHEWBREADS
SHEWED
SHEWEL
SHEWELS
SHEWING
SHEWN
SHEWS
SHIATSU
SHIATSUS
SHIATZU
SHIATZUS
SHIBAH
SHIBAHS
SHIBUICHI
SHIBUICHIS
SHICKER
SHICKERED
SHICKERS
SHICKSA
SHICKSAS
SHIDDER
SHIDDERS
SHIED
SHIEL
SHIELD
SHIELDED
SHIELDER
SHIELDERS
SHIELDING
SHIELDINGS
SHIELDS
SHIELDUCK
SHIELDUCKS
SHIELED
SHIELING
SHIELINGS
SHIELS
SHIER
SHIERS
SHIES
SHIEST
SHIFT
SHIFTED
SHIFTER
SHIFTERS
SHIFTIER
SHIFTIEST
SHIFTILY
SHIFTING
SHIFTINGS
SHIFTLESS
SHIFTS
SHIFTY
SHIGELLA
SHIGELLAS
SHIITAKE
SHIKAR
SHIKAREE
SHIKAREES
SHIKARI
SHIKARIS
SHIKARS
SHIKSA
SHIKSAS
SHIKSE
SHIKSES
SHILL
SHILLABER
SHILLABERS
SHILLALAH
SHILLALAHS
SHILLED
SHILLING
SHILLINGS
SHILLS
SHILPIT
SHILY
SHIM
SHIMAAL
SHIMAALS
SHIMMED
SHIMMER
SHIMMERED
SHIMMERING
SHIMMERINGS
SHIMMERS
SHIMMERY
SHIMMEY
SHIMMEYS
SHIMMIED
SHIMMIES
SHIMMING
SHIMMY
SHIMMYING
SHIMOZZLE
SHIMOZZLES
SHIMS
SHIN
SHINBONE
SHINBONES
SHINDIES
SHINDIG
SHINDIGS
SHINDY
SHINE
SHINED
SHINELESS
SHINER
SHINERS
SHINES
SHINESS
SHINESSES
SHINGLE
SHINGLED
SHINGLER
SHINGLERS
SHINGLES
SHINGLIER
SHINGLIEST
SHINGLING
SHINGLINGS
SHINGLY
SHINIER
SHINIES
SHINIEST
SHININESS
SHININESSES
SHINING
SHININGLY
SHINNE
SHINNED
SHINNES
SHINNIED
SHINNIES
SHINNING
SHINNY
SHINNYING
SHINS
SHINTIES
SHINTY
SHINY
SHIP
SHIPBOARD
SHIPBOARDS
SHIPFUL
SHIPFULS
SHIPLAP
SHIPLAPPED
SHIPLAPPING
SHIPLAPS
SHIPLESS
SHIPLOAD
SHIPLOADS
SHIPMAN
SHIPMATE
SHIPMATES
SHIPMEN
SHIPMENT
SHIPMENTS
SHIPPED
SHIPPEN
SHIPPENS
SHIPPER
SHIPPERS
SHIPPING
SHIPPINGS
SHIPPO
SHIPPON
SHIPPONS
SHIPPOS
SHIPPOUND
SHIPPOUNDS
SHIPS
SHIPSHAPE
SHIPWAY
SHIPWAYS
SHIPWORM
SHIPWORMS
SHIPWRECK
SHIPWRECKED
SHIPWRECKING
SHIPWRECKS
SHIPYARD
SHIPYARDS
SHIR
SHIRALEE
SHIRALEES
SHIRE
SHIREMAN
SHIREMEN
SHIRES
SHIRK
SHIRKED
SHIRKER
SHIRKERS
SHIRKING
SHIRKS
SHIRR
SHIRRA
SHIRRALEE
SHIRRALEES
SHIRRAS
SHIRRED
SHIRRING
SHIRRINGS
SHIRRS
SHIRS
SHIRT
SHIRTBAND
SHIRTBANDS
SHIRTED
SHIRTIER
SHIRTIEST
SHIRTILY
SHIRTING
SHIRTINGS
SHIRTLESS
SHIRTS
SHIRTY
SHIT
SHITE
SHITED
SHITES
SHITHEAD
SHITHEADS
SHITHOLE
SHITHOLES
SHITING
SHITS
SHITTAH
SHITTAHS
SHITTED
SHITTIER
SHITTIEST
SHITTIM
SHITTIMS
SHITTING
SHITTY
SHIV
SHIVAH
SHIVAHS
SHIVAREE
SHIVAREES
SHIVE
SHIVER
SHIVERED
SHIVERER
SHIVERERS
SHIVERIER
SHIVERIEST
SHIVERING
SHIVERINGS
SHIVERS
SHIVERY
SHIVES
SHIVOO
SHIVOOS
SHIVS
SHIVVED
SHIVVING
SHLEMIEL
SHLEMIELS
SHLEP
SHLEPPED
SHLEPPER
SHLEPPERS
SHLEPPING
SHLEPS
SHLIMAZEL
SHLIMAZELS
SHLOCK
SHLOCKS
SHMALTZ
SHMALTZES
SHMALTZIER
SHMALTZIEST
SHMALTZY
SHMEK
SHMEKS
SHMO
SHMOCK
SHMOCKS
SHMOES
SHMOOSE
SHMOOSED
SHMOOSES
SHMOOSING
SHMOOZE
SHMOOZED
SHMOOZES
SHMOOZING
SHMUCK
SHMUCKS
SHOAL
SHOALED
SHOALER
SHOALEST
SHOALIER
SHOALIEST
SHOALING
SHOALINGS
SHOALNESS
SHOALNESSES
SHOALS
SHOALWISE
SHOALY
SHOAT
SHOATS
SHOCHET
SHOCHETIM
SHOCK
SHOCKABLE
SHOCKED

SHOCKER
SHOCKERS
SHOCKING
SHOCKS
SHOD
SHODDIER
SHODDIES
SHODDIEST
SHODDILY
SHODDY
SHODER
SHODERS
SHOE
SHOEBILL
SHOEBILLS
SHOEBLACK
SHOEBLACKS
SHOED
SHOEHORN
SHOEHORNED
SHOEHORNING
SHOEHORNS
SHOEING
SHOEINGS
SHOELACE
SHOELACES
SHOELESS
SHOEMAKER
SHOEMAKERS
SHOER
SHOERS
SHOES
SHOESHINE
SHOESHINES
SHOETREE
SHOETREES
SHOFAR
SHOFARS
SHOFROTH
SHOG
SHOGGED
SHOGGING
SHOGGLE
SHOGGLED
SHOGGLES
SHOGGLIER
SHOGGLIEST
SHOGGLING
SHOGGLY
SHOGI
SHOGIS
SHOGS
SHOGUN
SHOGUNAL
SHOGUNATE
SHOGUNATES
SHOGUNS
SHOJI
SHOJIS
SHOLA
SHOLAS
SHOLOM
SHONE
SHONEEN
SHONEENS
SHONKIER
SHONKIEST
SHONKY
SHOO
SHOOED
SHOOFLIES
SHOOFLY
SHOOGIE
SHOOGIED
SHOOGIEING
SHOOGIES
SHOOGLE
SHOOGLED
SHOOGLES
SHOOGLIER
SHOOGLIEST
SHOOGLING
SHOOGLY
SHOOING
SHOOK
SHOOKS
SHOOL
SHOOLE
SHOOLED
SHOOLES
SHOOLING
SHOOLS
SHOON
SHOOS
SHOOT
SHOOTABLE
SHOOTER
SHOOTERS
SHOOTING
SHOOTINGS
SHOOTIST
SHOOTISTS
SHOOTS
SHOP
SHOPBOARD
SHOPBOARDS
SHOPE
SHOPFRONT
SHOPFRONTS
SHOPFUL
SHOPFULS
SHOPHAR
SHOPHARS
SHOPHROTH
SHOPMAN
SHOPMEN
SHOPPED
SHOPPER
SHOPPERS
SHOPPIER
SHOPPIEST
SHOPPING
SHOPPINGS
SHOPPY
SHOPS
SHOPWORN
SHORAN
SHORANS
SHORE
SHOREBIRD
SHOREBIRDS
SHORED
SHORELESS
SHORELINE
SHORELINES
SHOREMAN
SHOREMEN
SHORER
SHORERS
SHORES
SHORESMAN
SHORESMEN
SHOREWARD
SHOREWARDS
SHOREWEED
SHOREWEEDS
SHORING
SHORINGS
SHORN
SHORT
SHORTAGE
SHORTAGES
SHORTARM
SHORTCAKE
SHORTCAKES
SHORTED
SHORTEN
SHORTENED
SHORTENER
SHORTENERS
SHORTENING
SHORTENINGS
SHORTENS
SHORTER
SHORTEST
SHORTFALL
SHORTFALLS
SHORTGOWN
SHORTGOWNS
SHORTHAND
SHORTHANDS
SHORTHOLD
SHORTHORN
SHORTHORNS
SHORTIE
SHORTIES
SHORTING
SHORTISH
SHORTLY
SHORTNESS
SHORTNESSES
SHORTS
SHORTSTOP
SHORTSTOPS
SHORTY
SHOT
SHOTE
SHOTES
SHOTFIRER
SHOTFIRERS
SHOTGUN
SHOTGUNS
SHOTHOLE
SHOTHOLES
SHOTMAKER
SHOTMAKERS
SHOTPROOF
SHOTPUT
SHOTPUTS
SHOTS
SHOTT
SHOTTE
SHOTTED
SHOTTEN
SHOTTES
SHOTTING
SHOTTLE
SHOTTLES
SHOTTS
SHOUGH
SHOUGHS
SHOULD
SHOULDER
SHOULDERED
SHOULDERING
SHOULDERINGS
SHOULDERS
SHOULDEST
SHOULDST
SHOUT
SHOUTED
SHOUTER
SHOUTERS
SHOUTHER
SHOUTHERED
SHOUTHERING
SHOUTHERS
SHOUTING
SHOUTINGS
SHOUTLINE
SHOUTLINES
SHOUTS
SHOVE
SHOVED
SHOVEL
SHOVELER
SHOVELERS
SHOVELFUL
SHOVELFULS
SHOVELLED
SHOVELLER
SHOVELLERS
SHOVELLING
SHOVELS
SHOVER
SHOVERS
SHOVES
SHOVING
SHOW
SHOWBIZ
SHOWBIZZES
SHOWBIZZY
SHOWBOAT
SHOWBOATED
SHOWBOATING
SHOWBOATS
SHOWBOX
SHOWBOXES
SHOWBREAD
SHOWBREADS
SHOWCASE
SHOWCASED
SHOWCASES
SHOWCASING
SHOWDOWN
SHOWDOWNS
SHOWED
SHOWER
SHOWERED
SHOWERFUL
SHOWERIER
SHOWERIEST
SHOWERING
SHOWERINGS
SHOWERS
SHOWERY
SHOWGHE
SHOWGHES
SHOWGIRL
SHOWGIRLS
SHOWIER
SHOWIEST
SHOWILY
SHOWINESS
SHOWINESSES
SHOWING
SHOWINGS
SHOWMAN
SHOWMANLY
SHOWMEN
SHOWN
SHOWPIECE
SHOWPIECES
SHOWPLACE
SHOWPLACES
SHOWROOM
SHOWROOMS
SHOWS
SHOWY
SHOWYARD
SHOWYARDS
SHOYU
SHOYUS
SHRADDHA
SHRADDHAS
SHRANK
SHRAPNEL
SHRAPNELS
SHRED
SHREDDED
SHREDDER
SHREDDERS
SHREDDIER
SHREDDIEST
SHREDDING
SHREDDINGS
SHREDDY
SHREDLESS
SHREDS
SHREEK

SHREEKED
SHREEKING
SHREEKS
SHREIK
SHREIKED
SHREIKING
SHREIKS
SHREW
SHREWD
SHREWDER
SHREWDEST
SHREWDIE
SHREWDIES
SHREWDLY
SHREWED
SHREWING
SHREWISH
SHREWMICE
SHREWS
SHRIECH
SHRIECHED
SHRIECHES
SHRIECHING
SHRIEK
SHRIEKED
SHRIEKER
SHRIEKERS
SHRIEKING
SHRIEKINGS
SHRIEKS
SHRIEVAL
SHRIEVE
SHRIEVED
SHRIEVES
SHRIEVING
SHRIFT
SHRIFTS
SHRIGHT
SHRIGHTS
SHRIKE
SHRIKED
SHRIKES
SHRIKING
SHRILL
SHRILLED
SHRILLER
SHRILLEST
SHRILLIER
SHRILLIEST
SHRILLING
SHRILLINGS
SHRILLS
SHRILLY
SHRIMP
SHRIMPED
SHRIMPER
SHRIMPERS
SHRIMPIER
SHRIMPIEST
SHRIMPING
SHRIMPINGS
SHRIMPS
SHRIMPY
SHRINAL
SHRINE
SHRINED
SHRINES
SHRINING
SHRINK
SHRINKAGE
SHRINKAGES
SHRINKER
SHRINKERS
SHRINKING
SHRINKS
SHRITCH
SHRITCHED
SHRITCHES
SHRITCHING
SHRIVE
SHRIVED
SHRIVEL
SHRIVELED
SHRIVELING
SHRIVELLED
SHRIVELLING
SHRIVELS
SHRIVEN
SHRIVER
SHRIVERS
SHRIVES
SHRIVING
SHRIVINGS
SHROFF
SHROFFAGE
SHROFFAGES
SHROFFED
SHROFFING
SHROFFS
SHROUD
SHROUDED
SHROUDIER
SHROUDIEST
SHROUDING
SHROUDINGS
SHROUDS
SHROUDY
SHROVE
SHROVED
SHROVES
SHROVING
SHROW
SHROWD
SHROWED
SHROWING
SHROWS
SHRUB
SHRUBBED
SHRUBBERIES
SHRUBBERY
SHRUBBIER
SHRUBBIEST
SHRUBBING
SHRUBBY
SHRUBLESS
SHRUBLIKE
SHRUBS
SHRUG
SHRUGGED
SHRUGGING
SHRUGS
SHRUNK
SHRUNKEN
SHTCHI
SHTCHIS
SHTETEL
SHTETELACH
SHTETELS
SHTETL
SHTETLACH
SHTETLS
SHTICK
SHTICKS
SHTOOK
SHTOOKS
SHTOOM
SHTUCK
SHTUCKS
SHTUM
SHTUMM
SHTUP
SHTUPPED
SHTUPPING
SHTUPS
SHUBUNKIN
SHUBUNKINS
SHUCK
SHUCKED
SHUCKER
SHUCKERS
SHUCKING
SHUCKINGS
SHUCKS
SHUDDER
SHUDDERED
SHUDDERING
SHUDDERINGS
SHUDDERS
SHUDDERY
SHUFFLE
SHUFFLED
SHUFFLER
SHUFFLERS
SHUFFLES
SHUFFLING
SHUFFLINGS
SHUFTI
SHUFTIES
SHUFTIS
SHUFTY
SHUL
SHULE
SHULED
SHULES
SHULING
SHULN
SHULS
SHUN
SHUNLESS
SHUNNABLE
SHUNNED
SHUNNER
SHUNNERS
SHUNNING
SHUNS
SHUNT
SHUNTED
SHUNTER
SHUNTERS
SHUNTING
SHUNTINGS
SHUNTS
SHURA
SHURAS
SHUSH
SHUSHED
SHUSHES
SHUSHING
SHUT
SHUTDOWN
SHUTDOWNS
SHUTE
SHUTES
SHUTS
SHUTTER
SHUTTERED
SHUTTERING
SHUTTERINGS
SHUTTERS
SHUTTING
SHUTTLE
SHUTTLED
SHUTTLES
SHUTTLING
SHWA
SHWAS
SHY
SHYER
SHYERS
SHYEST
SHYING
SHYISH
SHYLY
SHYNESS
SHYNESSES
SHYSTER
SHYSTERS
SI
SIAL
SIALIC
SIALOGRAM
SIALOGRAMS
SIALOID
SIALOLITH
SIALOLITHS
SIALON
SIALONS
SIALS
SIAMANG
SIAMANGS
SIAMESE
SIAMESED
SIAMESES
SIAMESING
SIAMEZE
SIAMEZED
SIAMEZES
SIAMEZING
SIB
SIBB
SIBBS
SIBILANCE
SIBILANCES
SIBILANCIES
SIBILANCY
SIBILANT
SIBILANTS
SIBILATE
SIBILATED
SIBILATES
SIBILATING
SIBILATOR
SIBILATORS
SIBILOUS
SIBLING
SIBLINGS
SIBS
SIBSHIP
SIBSHIPS
SIBYL
SIBYLIC
SIBYLLIC
SIBYLLINE
SIBYLS
SIC
SICCAN
SICCAR
SICCATIVE
SICCATIVES
SICCED
SICCING
SICCITIES
SICCITY
SICE
SICES
SICH
SICILIANA
SICILIANE
SICILIANO
SICILIANOS
SICK
SICKBED
SICKBEDS
SICKED
SICKEN
SICKENED
SICKENER
SICKENERS
SICKENING
SICKENINGS
SICKENS
SICKER
SICKERLY
SICKEST
SICKIE
SICKIES
SICKING
SICKISH
SICKISHLY
SICKLE

SICKLED
SICKLEMAN
SICKLEMEN
SICKLEMIA
SICKLEMIAS
SICKLES
SICKLIED
SICKLIER
SICKLIES
SICKLIEST
SICKLILY
SICKLY
SICKLYING
SICKNESS
SICKNESSES
SICKNURSE
SICKNURSES
SICKO
SICKOS
SICKROOM
SICKROOMS
SICKS
SICLIKE
SICS
SIDA
SIDALCEA
SIDALCEAS
SIDAS
SIDDHA
SIDDHAS
SIDDHI
SIDDHIS
SIDDUR
SIDDURIM
SIDE
SIDEARM
SIDEARMS
SIDEBAND
SIDEBANDS
SIDEBAR
SIDEBARS
SIDEBOARD
SIDEBOARDS
SIDEBONES
SIDEBURNS
SIDECAR
SIDECARS
SIDED
SIDEKICK
SIDEKICKS
SIDELIGHT
SIDELIGHTS
SIDELINE
SIDELINED
SIDELINES
SIDELING
SIDELINING
SIDELOCK
SIDELOCKS
SIDELONG
SIDEMAN
SIDEMEN
SIDENOTE
SIDENOTES
SIDEPATH
SIDEPATHS
SIDER
SIDERAL
SIDERATE
SIDERATED
SIDERATES
SIDERATING
SIDEREAL
SIDERITE
SIDERITES
SIDERITIC
SIDEROAD
SIDEROADS
SIDEROSES
SIDEROSIS
SIDERS
SIDES
SIDESHOOT
SIDESHOOTS
SIDESHOW
SIDESHOWS
SIDESLIP
SIDESLIPPED
SIDESLIPPING
SIDESLIPS
SIDESMAN
SIDESMEN
SIDESTEP
SIDESTEPPED
SIDESTEPPING
SIDESTEPS
SIDESWIPE
SIDESWIPED
SIDESWIPES
SIDESWIPING
SIDETRACK
SIDETRACKED
SIDETRACKING
SIDETRACKS
SIDEWALK
SIDEWALKS
SIDEWALL
SIDEWALLS
SIDEWARD
SIDEWARDS
SIDEWAYS
SIDEWISE
SIDHA
SIDHAS
SIDING
SIDINGS
SIDLE
SIDLED
SIDLES
SIDLING
SIEGE
SIEGED
SIEGER
SIEGERS
SIEGES
SIEGING
SIELD
SIEMENS
SIEN
SIENNA
SIENNAS
SIENS
SIENT
SIENTS
SIERRA
SIERRAN
SIERRAS
SIESTA
SIESTAS
SIETH
SIETHS
SIEVE
SIEVED
SIEVERT
SIEVERTS
SIEVES
SIEVING
SIFAKA
SIFAKAS
SIFFLE
SIFFLED
SIFFLES
SIFFLEUR
SIFFLEURS
SIFFLEUSE
SIFFLEUSES
SIFFLING
SIFT
SIFTED
SIFTER
SIFTERS
SIFTING
SIFTINGLY
SIFTINGS
SIFTS
SIGH
SIGHED
SIGHER
SIGHERS
SIGHFUL
SIGHING
SIGHINGLY
SIGHS
SIGHT
SIGHTABLE
SIGHTED
SIGHTER
SIGHTERS
SIGHTING
SIGHTINGS
SIGHTLESS
SIGHTLIER
SIGHTLIEST
SIGHTLINE
SIGHTLINES
SIGHTLY
SIGHTS
SIGHTSAW
SIGHTSEE
SIGHTSEEING
SIGHTSEEINGS
SIGHTSEEN
SIGHTSEER
SIGHTSEERS
SIGHTSEES
SIGHTSMAN
SIGHTSMEN
SIGIL
SIGILLARY
SIGILLATE
SIGILS
SIGISBEI
SIGISBEO
SIGLA
SIGMA
SIGMAS
SIGMATE
SIGMATED
SIGMATES
SIGMATIC
SIGMATING
SIGMATION
SIGMATIONS
SIGMATISM
SIGMATISMS
SIGMATRON
SIGMATRONS
SIGMOID
SIGMOIDAL
SIGN
SIGNAGE
SIGNAGES
SIGNAL
SIGNALED
SIGNALER
SIGNALERS
SIGNALING
SIGNALINGS
SIGNALISE
SIGNALISED
SIGNALISES
SIGNALISING
SIGNALIZE
SIGNALIZED
SIGNALIZES
SIGNALIZING
SIGNALLED
SIGNALLER
SIGNALLERS
SIGNALLING
SIGNALLINGS
SIGNALLY
SIGNALMAN
SIGNALMEN
SIGNALS
SIGNARIES
SIGNARY
SIGNATORIES
SIGNATORY
SIGNATURE
SIGNATURES
SIGNBOARD
SIGNBOARDS
SIGNED
SIGNER
SIGNERS
SIGNET
SIGNETED
SIGNETING
SIGNETS
SIGNEUR
SIGNEURIE
SIGNEURIES
SIGNIEUR
SIGNIEURS
SIGNIFICS
SIGNIFIED
SIGNIFIER
SIGNIFIERS
SIGNIFIES
SIGNIFY
SIGNIFYING
SIGNING
SIGNINGS
SIGNIOR
SIGNIORS
SIGNLESS
SIGNOR
SIGNORA
SIGNORE
SIGNORES
SIGNORI
SIGNORIA
SIGNORIAL
SIGNORIAS
SIGNORIES
SIGNORINA
SIGNORINE
SIGNORINI
SIGNORINO
SIGNORS
SIGNORY
SIGNPOST
SIGNPOSTED
SIGNPOSTING
SIGNPOSTS
SIGNS
SIJO
SIJOS
SIKA
SIKAS
SIKE
SIKES
SIKORSKIES
SIKORSKY
SILAGE
SILAGED
SILAGEING
SILAGES
SILAGING
SILANE
SILANES
SILASTIC
SILASTICS
SILD
SILDS
SILE
SILED
SILEN
SILENCE

SILENCED
SILENCER
SILENCERS
SILENCES
SILENCING
SILENE
SILENES
SILENI
SILENS
SILENT
SILENTER
SILENTEST
SILENTLY
SILENTS
SILENUS
SILER
SILERS
SILES
SILESIA
SILESIAS
SILEX
SILEXES
SILICA
SILICAS
SILICATE
SILICATED
SILICATES
SILICATING
SILICEOUS
SILICIC
SILICIDE
SILICIDES
SILICIFIED
SILICIFIES
SILICIFY
SILICIFYING
SILICIOUS
SILICIUM
SILICIUMS
SILICLE
SILICLES
SILICON
SILICONE
SILICONES
SILICONS
SILICOSES
SILICOSIS
SILICOTIC
SILICOTICS
SILICULA
SILICULAS
SILICULE
SILICULES
SILING
SILIQUA
SILIQUAS
SILIQUE
SILIQUES
SILIQUOSE
SILK
SILKED
SILKEN
SILKENED
SILKENING
SILKENS
SILKIE
SILKIER
SILKIES
SILKIEST
SILKILY
SILKINESS
SILKINESSES
SILKING
SILKS
SILKTAIL
SILKTAILS
SILKWEED
SILKWEEDS
SILKWORM
SILKWORMS
SILKY
SILL
SILLABUB
SILLABUBS
SILLADAR
SILLADARS
SILLER
SILLERS
SILLIER
SILLIES
SILLIEST
SILLILY
SILLINESS
SILLINESSES
SILLOCK
SILLOCKS
SILLS
SILLY
SILO
SILOED
SILOING
SILOS
SILPHIA
SILPHIUM
SILPHIUMS
SILT
SILTATION
SILTATIONS
SILTED
SILTIER
SILTIEST
SILTING
SILTS
SILTSTONE
SILTSTONES
SILTY
SILURID
SILURIDS
SILURIST
SILURISTS
SILUROID
SILVA
SILVAE
SILVAN
SILVANS
SILVAS
SILVATIC
SILVER
SILVERED
SILVERIER
SILVERIEST
SILVERING
SILVERINGS
SILVERISE
SILVERISED
SILVERISES
SILVERISING
SILVERIZE
SILVERIZED
SILVERIZES
SILVERIZING
SILVERLY
SILVERN
SILVERS
SILVERY
SIM
SIMA
SIMAR
SIMAROUBA
SIMAROUBAS
SIMARRE
SIMARRES
SIMARS
SIMARUBA
SIMARUBAS
SIMAS
SIMAZINE
SIMAZINES
SIMI
SIMIAL
SIMIAN
SIMIANS
SIMILAR
SIMILARLY
SIMILE
SIMILES
SIMILISE
SIMILISED
SIMILISES
SIMILISING
SIMILIZE
SIMILIZED
SIMILIZES
SIMILIZING
SIMILOR
SIMILORS
SIMIOUS
SIMIS
SIMITAR
SIMITARS
SIMKIN
SIMKINS
SIMMER
SIMMERED
SIMMERING
SIMMERS
SIMNEL
SIMNELS
SIMONIAC
SIMONIACS
SIMONIES
SIMONIOUS
SIMONIST
SIMONISTS
SIMONY
SIMOOM
SIMOOMS
SIMOON
SIMOONS
SIMORG
SIMORGS
SIMP
SIMPAI
SIMPAIS
SIMPATICO
SIMPER
SIMPERED
SIMPERER
SIMPERERS
SIMPERING
SIMPERS
SIMPKIN
SIMPKINS
SIMPLE
SIMPLED
SIMPLER
SIMPLERS
SIMPLES
SIMPLESSE
SIMPLESSES
SIMPLEST
SIMPLETON
SIMPLETONS
SIMPLEX
SIMPLICES
SIMPLIFIED
SIMPLIFIES
SIMPLIFY
SIMPLIFYING
SIMPLING
SIMPLINGS
SIMPLISM
SIMPLISMS
SIMPLIST
SIMPLISTE
SIMPLISTS
SIMPLY
SIMPS
SIMS
SIMUL
SIMULACRA
SIMULACRE
SIMULACRES
SIMULANT
SIMULANTS
SIMULAR
SIMULARS
SIMULATE
SIMULATED
SIMULATES
SIMULATING
SIMULATOR
SIMULATORS
SIMULCAST
SIMULCASTED
SIMULCASTING
SIMULCASTS
SIMULIUM
SIMULIUMS
SIMULS
SIMURG
SIMURGH
SIMURGHS
SIMURGS
SIN
SINAPISM
SINAPISMS
SINCE
SINCERE
SINCERELY
SINCERER
SINCEREST
SINCERITIES
SINCERITY
SINCIPITA
SINCIPUT
SINCIPUTS
SIND
SINDED
SINDING
SINDINGS
SINDON
SINDONS
SINDS
SINE
SINECURE
SINECURES
SINED
SINES
SINEW
SINEWED
SINEWIER
SINEWIEST
SINEWING
SINEWLESS
SINEWS
SINEWY
SINFONIA
SINFONIAS
SINFUL
SINFULLY
SING
SINGABLE
SINGALONG
SINGALONGS
SINGE
SINGED
SINGEING
SINGER
SINGERS
SINGES
SINGING
SINGINGLY
SINGINGS
SINGLE
SINGLED
SINGLES
SINGLET
SINGLETON
SINGLETONS

NGLETS
NGLING
NGLINGS
NGLY
NGS
NGSONG
NGSONGED
NGSONGING
NGSONGS
NGSPIEL
NGSPIELS
NGULAR
NGULARS
NGULT
NGULTS
NGULTUS
NGULTUSES
NICAL
NICISE
NICISED
NICISES
NICISING
NICIZE
NICIZED
NICIZES
NICIZING
NING
NISTER
NISTRAL
NISTRALS
NK
NKAGE
NKAGES
NKER
NKERS
NKHOLE
NKHOLES
NKIER
NKIEST
NKING
NKINGS
NKS
NKY
NLESS
NLESSLY
NNED
NNER
NNERED
NNERING
NNERS
NNET
NNETS
NNING
NNINGIA
NNINGIAS
NOPIA
NOPIAS
NOPIS
NOPISES
NOPITE
NOPITES
NS
NSYNE
NTER

SINTERED
SINTERING
SINTERS
SINTERY
SINUATE
SINUATED
SINUATELY
SINUATION
SINUATIONS
SINUITIS
SINUITISES
SINUOSE
SINUOSITIES
SINUOSITY
SINUOUS
SINUOUSLY
SINUS
SINUSES
SINUSITIS
SINUSITISES
SINUSOID
SINUSOIDS
SIP
SIPE
SIPED
SIPES
SIPHON
SIPHONAGE
SIPHONAGES
SIPHONAL
SIPHONATE
SIPHONED
SIPHONET
SIPHONETS
SIPHONIC
SIPHONING
SIPHONS
SIPHUNCLE
SIPHUNCLES
SIPING
SIPPED
SIPPER
SIPPERS
SIPPET
SIPPETS
SIPPING
SIPPLE
SIPPLED
SIPPLES
SIPPLING
SIPS
SIR
SIRCAR
SIRCARS
SIRDAR
SIRDARS
SIRE
SIRED
SIREN
SIRENIAN
SIRENIANS
SIRENIC
SIRENISE
SIRENISED

SIRENISES
SIRENISING
SIRENIZE
SIRENIZED
SIRENIZES
SIRENIZING
SIRENS
SIRES
SIRGANG
SIRGANGS
SIRI
SIRIASES
SIRIASIS
SIRIH
SIRIHS
SIRING
SIRIS
SIRKAR
SIRKARS
SIRLOIN
SIRLOINS
SIRNAME
SIRNAMED
SIRNAMES
SIRNAMING
SIROC
SIROCCO
SIROCCOS
SIROCS
SIRRAH
SIRRAHS
SIRRED
SIRREE
SIRREES
SIRRING
SIRS
SIRUP
SIRUPED
SIRUPING
SIRUPS
SIRVENTE
SIRVENTES
SIS
SISAL
SISALS
SISERARIES
SISERARY
SISES
SISKIN
SISKINS
SISS
SISSERARIES
SISSERARY
SISSES
SISSIER
SISSIES
SISSIEST
SISSIFIED
SISSOO
SISSOOS
SISSY
SIST
SISTED
SISTER

SISTERED
SISTERING
SISTERLY
SISTERS
SISTING
SISTRA
SISTRUM
SISTS
SIT
SITAR
SITARS
SITATUNGA
SITATUNGAS
SITCOM
SITCOMS
SITE
SITED
SITES
SITFAST
SITFASTS
SITH
SITHE
SITHED
SITHEN
SITHENCE
SITHENS
SITHES
SITHING
SITING
SITIOLOGIES
SITIOLOGY
SITOLOGIES
SITOLOGY
SITREP
SITREPS
SITS
SITTAR
SITTARS
SITTER
SITTERS
SITTINE
SITTING
SITTINGS
SITUATE
SITUATED
SITUATES
SITUATING
SITUATION
SITUATIONS
SITULA
SITULAE
SITUS
SITUTUNGA
SITUTUNGAS
SITZKRIEG
SITZKRIEGS
SIVER
SIVERS
SIWASH
SIWASHES
SIX
SIXAIN
SIXAINE
SIXAINES

SIXAINS
SIXER
SIXERS
SIXES
SIXFOLD
SIXPENCE
SIXPENCES
SIXPENNIES
SIXPENNY
SIXSCORE
SIXSCORES
SIXTE
SIXTEEN
SIXTEENER
SIXTEENERS
SIXTEENMO
SIXTEENMOS
SIXTEENS
SIXTEENTH
SIXTEENTHS
SIXTES
SIXTH
SIXTHLY
SIXTHS
SIXTIES
SIXTIETH
SIXTIETHS
SIXTY
SIZABLE
SIZAR
SIZARS
SIZARSHIP
SIZARSHIPS
SIZE
SIZEABLE
SIZED
SIZEISM
SIZEISMS
SIZEIST
SIZEISTS
SIZEL
SIZELS
SIZER
SIZERS
SIZES
SIZIER
SIZIEST
SIZINESS
SIZINESSES
SIZING
SIZINGS
SIZISM
SIZISMS
SIZIST
SIZISTS
SIZY
SIZZLE
SIZZLED
SIZZLER
SIZZLERS
SIZZLES
SIZZLING
SIZZLINGS
SJAMBOK

SJAMBOKKED
SJAMBOKKING
SJAMBOKS
SKA
SKAG
SKAGS
SKAIL
SKAILED
SKAILING
SKAILS
SKAITH
SKAITHED
SKAITHING
SKAITHS
SKALD
SKALDIC
SKALDS
SKALDSHIP
SKALDSHIPS
SKANK
SKANKED
SKANKING
SKANKINGS
SKANKS
SKART
SKARTH
SKARTHS
SKARTS
SKAS
SKAT
SKATE
SKATED
SKATEPARK
SKATEPARKS
SKATER
SKATERS
SKATES
SKATING
SKATINGS
SKATOLE
SKATOLES
SKATS
SKATT
SKATTS
SKAW
SKAWS
SKEAN
SKEANS
SKEAR
SKEARED
SKEARIER
SKEARIEST
SKEARING
SKEARS
SKEARY
SKEDADDLE
SKEDADDLED
SKEDADDLES
SKEDADDLING
SKEECHAN
SKEECHANS
SKEELIER
SKEELIEST
SKEELY
SKEER
SKEERED
SKEERIER
SKEERIEST
SKEERING
SKEERS
SKEERY
SKEESICKS
SKEET
SKEETER
SKEETERS
SKEETS
SKEG
SKEGG
SKEGGER
SKEGGERS
SKEGGS
SKEGS
SKEIGH
SKEIGHER
SKEIGHEST
SKEIN
SKEINS
SKELDER
SKELDERED
SKELDERING
SKELDERS
SKELETAL
SKELETON
SKELETONS
SKELF
SKELFS
SKELL
SKELLIE
SKELLIED
SKELLIER
SKELLIES
SKELLIEST
SKELLOCH
SKELLOCHED
SKELLOCHING
SKELLOCHS
SKELLS
SKELLUM
SKELLUMS
SKELLY
SKELLYING
SKELM
SKELMS
SKELP
SKELPED
SKELPING
SKELPINGS
SKELPS
SKELTER
SKELTERED
SKELTERING
SKELTERS
SKELUM
SKELUMS
SKENE
SKENES
SKEO
SKEOS
SKEP
SKEPFUL
SKEPFULS
SKEPPED
SKEPPING
SKEPS
SKEPSIS
SKEPSISES
SKEPTIC
SKEPTICAL
SKEPTICS
SKER
SKERRED
SKERRICK
SKERRICKS
SKERRIES
SKERRING
SKERRY
SKERS
SKETCH
SKETCHED
SKETCHER
SKETCHERS
SKETCHES
SKETCHIER
SKETCHIEST
SKETCHILY
SKETCHING
SKETCHY
SKEW
SKEWBACK
SKEWBACKS
SKEWBALD
SKEWBALDS
SKEWED
SKEWER
SKEWERED
SKEWERING
SKEWERS
SKEWEST
SKEWING
SKEWNESS
SKEWNESSES
SKEWS
SKI
SKIABLE
SKIAGRAM
SKIAGRAMS
SKIAGRAPH
SKIAGRAPHS
SKIAMACHIES
SKIAMACHY
SKIASCOPIES
SKIASCOPY
SKIATRON
SKIATRONS
SKIBOB
SKIBOBBED
SKIBOBBING
SKIBOBBINGS
SKIBOBS
SKID
SKIDDED
SKIDDER
SKIDDERS
SKIDDING
SKIDOO
SKIDOOS
SKIDPAN
SKIDPANS
SKIDPROOF
SKIDS
SKIED
SKIER
SKIERS
SKIES
SKIEY
SKIEYER
SKIEYEST
SKIFF
SKIFFED
SKIFFING
SKIFFLE
SKIFFLES
SKIFFS
SKIING
SKIINGS
SKIJORING
SKIJORINGS
SKILFUL
SKILFULLY
SKILL
SKILLED
SKILLESS
SKILLET
SKILLETS
SKILLFUL
SKILLIER
SKILLIES
SKILLIEST
SKILLING
SKILLINGS
SKILLION
SKILLIONS
SKILLS
SKILLY
SKIM
SKIMMED
SKIMMER
SKIMMERS
SKIMMIA
SKIMMIAS
SKIMMING
SKIMMINGS
SKIMP
SKIMPED
SKIMPIER
SKIMPIEST
SKIMPILY
SKIMPING
SKIMPS
SKIMPY
SKIMS
SKIN
SKINCARE
SKINCARES
SKINFLICK
SKINFLICKS
SKINFLINT
SKINFLINTS
SKINFOOD
SKINFOODS
SKINFUL
SKINFULS
SKINHEAD
SKINHEADS
SKINK
SKINKED
SKINKER
SKINKERS
SKINKING
SKINKS
SKINLESS
SKINNED
SKINNER
SKINNERS
SKINNIER
SKINNIEST
SKINNING
SKINNY
SKINS
SKINT
SKINTER
SKINTEST
SKIO
SKIOS
SKIP
SKIPJACK
SKIPJACKS
SKIPPED
SKIPPER
SKIPPERED
SKIPPERING
SKIPPERINGS
SKIPPERS
SKIPPET
SKIPPETS
SKIPPIER
SKIPPIEST
SKIPPING
SKIPPINGS
SKIPPY
SKIPS
SKIRL
SKIRLED
SKIRLING
SKIRLINGS
SKIRLS
SKIRMISH
SKIRMISHED
SKIRMISHES
SKIRMISHING
SKIRMISHINGS
SKIRR
SKIRRED
SKIRRET
SKIRRETS
SKIRRING
SKIRRS
SKIRT
SKIRTED
SKIRTER

RTERS
RTING
RTINGS
RTLESS
RTS
S
T
TE
TED
TES
TING
TS
TTER
TTERED
TTERING
TTERS
TTISH
TTLE
TTLED
TTLES
TTLING
VE
VED
VER
VERED
VERING
VERS
VES
VIE
VIER
VIEST
VING
VINGS
VVIED
VVIES
VVY
VVYING
VY
LATE
LATED
LATES
LATING
LENT
LENTED
LENTING
LENTS
LIFF
LIFFS
LIM
LIMMED
LIMMING
LIMS
OAL
OFF
OFFED
OFFING
OFFS
OKIAAN
OKIAANS
OL
OLIA
OLION
OLLIE
OLLIES

SKOLLY
SKOOSH
SKOOSHED
SKOOSHES
SKOOSHING
SKRAN
SKRANS
SKREEN
SKREENS
SKREIGH
SKREIGHED
SKREIGHING
SKREIGHS
SKRIECH
SKRIECHED
SKRIECHING
SKRIECHS
SKRIED
SKRIEGH
SKRIEGHED
SKRIEGHING
SKRIEGHS
SKRIES
SKRIK
SKRIKS
SKRIMMAGE
SKRIMMAGED
SKRIMMAGES
SKRIMMAGING
SKRIMP
SKRIMPED
SKRIMPING
SKRIMPS
SKRUMP
SKRUMPED
SKRUMPING
SKRUMPS
SKRY
SKRYER
SKRYERS
SKRYING
SKUA
SKUAS
SKUDLER
SKUDLERS
SKUG
SKUGGED
SKUGGING
SKUGS
SKULK
SKULKED
SKULKER
SKULKERS
SKULKING
SKULKINGS
SKULKS
SKULL
SKULLCAP
SKULLCAPS
SKULLS
SKULPIN
SKULPINS
SKUMMER
SKUMMERED

SKUMMERING
SKUMMERS
SKUNK
SKUNKBIRD
SKUNKBIRDS
SKUNKED
SKUNKING
SKUNKS
SKURRIED
SKURRIES
SKURRY
SKURRYING
SKUTTLE
SKUTTLED
SKUTTLES
SKUTTLING
SKY
SKYBORN
SKYCLAD
SKYDIVER
SKYDIVERS
SKYER
SKYERS
SKYEY
SKYHOOK
SKYHOOKS
SKYIER
SKYIEST
SKYING
SKYISH
SKYJACK
SKYJACKED
SKYJACKER
SKYJACKERS
SKYJACKING
SKYJACKINGS
SKYJACKS
SKYLAB
SKYLABS
SKYLARK
SKYLARKED
SKYLARKER
SKYLARKERS
SKYLARKING
SKYLARKINGS
SKYLARKS
SKYLIGHT
SKYLIGHTS
SKYLINE
SKYLINES
SKYMAN
SKYMEN
SKYR
SKYRE
SKYRED
SKYRES
SKYRING
SKYROCKET
SKYROCKETED
SKYROCKETING
SKYROCKETS
SKYRS
SKYSAIL
SKYSAILS

SKYSCAPE
SKYSCAPES
SKYTE
SKYTED
SKYTES
SKYTING
SKYWARD
SKYWARDS
SKYWAY
SKYWAYS
SLAB
SLABBED
SLABBER
SLABBERED
SLABBERER
SLABBERERS
SLABBERING
SLABBERS
SLABBERY
SLABBIER
SLABBIEST
SLABBING
SLABBY
SLABS
SLABSTONE
SLABSTONES
SLACK
SLACKED
SLACKEN
SLACKENED
SLACKENING
SLACKENINGS
SLACKENS
SLACKER
SLACKERS
SLACKEST
SLACKING
SLACKLY
SLACKNESS
SLACKNESSES
SLACKS
SLADANG
SLADANGS
SLADE
SLADES
SLAE
SLAES
SLAG
SLAGGED
SLAGGIER
SLAGGIEST
SLAGGING
SLAGGY
SLAGS
SLAID
SLAIN
SLAINTE
SLAIRG
SLAIRGED
SLAIRGING
SLAIRGS
SLAISTER
SLAISTERED
SLAISTERIES

SLAISTERING
SLAISTERS
SLAISTERY
SLAKE
SLAKED
SLAKELESS
SLAKES
SLAKING
SLALOM
SLALOMED
SLALOMING
SLALOMS
SLAM
SLAMMAKIN
SLAMMAKINS
SLAMMED
SLAMMER
SLAMMERS
SLAMMING
SLAMMINGS
SLAMS
SLANDER
SLANDERED
SLANDERER
SLANDERERS
SLANDERING
SLANDERS
SLANE
SLANES
SLANG
SLANGED
SLANGER
SLANGERS
SLANGIER
SLANGIEST
SLANGILY
SLANGING
SLANGINGS
SLANGISH
SLANGS
SLANGULAR
SLANGY
SLANT
SLANTED
SLANTING
SLANTLY
SLANTS
SLANTWAYS
SLANTWISE
SLAP
SLAPHEAD
SLAPHEADS
SLAPJACK
SLAPJACKS
SLAPPED
SLAPPER
SLAPPERS
SLAPPING
SLAPS
SLAPSHOT
SLAPSHOTS
SLAPSTICK
SLAPSTICKS
SLASH

SLASHED
SLASHER
SLASHERS
SLASHES
SLASHING
SLASHINGS
SLAT
SLATCH
SLATCHES
SLATE
SLATED
SLATER
SLATERS
SLATES
SLATHER
SLATHERED
SLATHERING
SLATHERS
SLATIER
SLATIEST
SLATINESS
SLATINESSES
SLATING
SLATINGS
SLATS
SLATTED
SLATTER
SLATTERED
SLATTERING
SLATTERN
SLATTERNS
SLATTERS
SLATTERY
SLATTING
SLATY
SLAUGHTER
SLAUGHTERED
SLAUGHTERING
SLAUGHTERS
SLAVE
SLAVED
SLAVER
SLAVERED
SLAVERER
SLAVERERS
SLAVERIES
SLAVERING
SLAVERS
SLAVERY
SLAVES
SLAVEY
SLAVEYS
SLAVING
SLAVISH
SLAVISHLY
SLAVOCRAT
SLAVOCRATS
SLAW
SLAWS
SLAY
SLAYED
SLAYER
SLAYERS
SLAYING
SLAYS
SLEAVE
SLEAVED
SLEAVES
SLEAVING
SLEAZE
SLEAZEBAG
SLEAZEBAGS
SLEAZES
SLEAZIER
SLEAZIEST
SLEAZILY
SLEAZY
SLED
SLEDDED
SLEDDING
SLEDDINGS
SLEDED
SLEDGE
SLEDGED
SLEDGER
SLEDGERS
SLEDGES
SLEDGING
SLEDGINGS
SLEDS
SLEE
SLEECH
SLEECHES
SLEECHIER
SLEECHIEST
SLEECHY
SLEEK
SLEEKED
SLEEKEN
SLEEKENED
SLEEKENING
SLEEKENS
SLEEKER
SLEEKERS
SLEEKEST
SLEEKIER
SLEEKIEST
SLEEKING
SLEEKINGS
SLEEKIT
SLEEKLY
SLEEKNESS
SLEEKNESSES
SLEEKS
SLEEKY
SLEEP
SLEEPER
SLEEPERS
SLEEPERY
SLEEPIER
SLEEPIEST
SLEEPILY
SLEEPING
SLEEPINGS
SLEEPLESS
SLEEPOUT
SLEEPOUTS
SLEEPOVER
SLEEPOVERS
SLEEPRY
SLEEPS
SLEEPSUIT
SLEEPSUITS
SLEEPY
SLEER
SLEEST
SLEET
SLEETED
SLEETIER
SLEETIEST
SLEETING
SLEETS
SLEETY
SLEEVE
SLEEVED
SLEEVEEN
SLEEVEENS
SLEEVER
SLEEVERS
SLEEVES
SLEEVING
SLEEVINGS
SLEEZIER
SLEEZIEST
SLEEZY
SLEIDED
SLEIGH
SLEIGHED
SLEIGHER
SLEIGHERS
SLEIGHING
SLEIGHINGS
SLEIGHS
SLEIGHT
SLEIGHTS
SLENDER
SLENDERER
SLENDEREST
SLENDERLY
SLENTER
SLENTERS
SLEPT
SLEUTH
SLEUTHED
SLEUTHING
SLEUTHS
SLEW
SLEWED
SLEWING
SLEWS
SLEY
SLEYS
SLICE
SLICED
SLICER
SLICERS
SLICES
SLICING
SLICINGS
SLICK
SLICKED
SLICKEN
SLICKENED
SLICKENING
SLICKENS
SLICKER
SLICKERED
SLICKERS
SLICKEST
SLICKING
SLICKINGS
SLICKLY
SLICKNESS
SLICKNESSES
SLICKS
SLID
SLIDDEN
SLIDDER
SLIDDERED
SLIDDERING
SLIDDERS
SLIDDERY
SLIDE
SLIDED
SLIDER
SLIDERS
SLIDES
SLIDING
SLIDINGLY
SLIDINGS
SLIER
SLIEST
SLIGHT
SLIGHTED
SLIGHTER
SLIGHTEST
SLIGHTING
SLIGHTISH
SLIGHTLY
SLIGHTS
SLILY
SLIM
SLIME
SLIMEBALL
SLIMEBALLS
SLIMED
SLIMES
SLIMIER
SLIMIEST
SLIMILY
SLIMINESS
SLIMINESSES
SLIMING
SLIMLINE
SLIMLY
SLIMMED
SLIMMER
SLIMMERS
SLIMMEST
SLIMMING
SLIMMINGS
SLIMMISH
SLIMNESS
SLIMNESSES
SLIMS
SLIMSIER
SLIMSIEST
SLIMSY
SLIMY
SLING
SLINGBACK
SLINGBACKS
SLINGER
SLINGERS
SLINGING
SLINGS
SLINGSHOT
SLINGSHOTS
SLINK
SLINKER
SLINKERS
SLINKIER
SLINKIEST
SLINKING
SLINKS
SLINKSKIN
SLINKSKINS
SLINKWEED
SLINKWEEDS
SLINKY
SLINTER
SLINTERS
SLIP
SLIPCASE
SLIPCASES
SLIPE
SLIPES
SLIPFORM
SLIPKNOT
SLIPKNOTS
SLIPPAGE
SLIPPAGES
SLIPPED
SLIPPER
SLIPPERED
SLIPPERIER
SLIPPERIEST
SLIPPERING
SLIPPERS
SLIPPERY
SLIPPIER
SLIPPIEST
SLIPPING
SLIPPY
SLIPRAIL
SLIPRAILS
SLIPS
SLIPSHOD
SLIPSLOP
SLIPSLOPS
SLIPT
SLIPWARE
SLIPWARES
SLIPWAY
SLIPWAYS
SLISH
SLISHES
SLIT
SLITHER
SLITHERED

SLITHERIER
SLITHERIEST
SLITHERING
SLITHERS
SLITHERY
SLITS
SLITTER
SLITTERS
SLITTING
SLIVE
SLIVED
SLIVEN
SLIVER
SLIVERED
SLIVERING
SLIVERS
SLIVES
SLIVING
SLIVOVIC
SLIVOVICA
SLIVOVICAS
SLIVOVICES
SLIVOVITZ
SLIVOVITZES
SLIVOWITZ
SLIVOWITZES
SLOAN
SLOANS
SLOB
SLOBBER
SLOBBERED
SLOBBERIER
SLOBBERIEST
SLOBBERING
SLOBBERS
SLOBBERY
SLOBBIER
SLOBBIEST
SLOBBISH
SLOBBY
SLOBLAND
SLOBLANDS
SLOBS
SLOCKEN
SLOCKENED
SLOCKENING
SLOCKENS
SLOE
SLOEBUSH
SLOEBUSHES
SLOES
SLOETHORN
SLOETHORNS
SLOETREE
SLOETREES
SLOG
SLOGAN
SLOGANEER
SLOGANEERED
SLOGANEERING
SLOGANEERINGS
SLOGANEERS
SLOGANISE
SLOGANISED
SLOGANISES
SLOGANISING
SLOGANISINGS
SLOGANIZE
SLOGANIZED
SLOGANIZES
SLOGANIZING
SLOGANIZINGS
SLOGANS
SLOGGED
SLOGGER
SLOGGERS
SLOGGING
SLOGS
SLOID
SLOIDS
SLOKEN
SLOKENED
SLOKENING
SLOKENS
SLOOM
SLOOMED
SLOOMIER
SLOOMIEST
SLOOMING
SLOOMS
SLOOMY
SLOOP
SLOOPS
SLOOSH
SLOOSHED
SLOOSHES
SLOOSHING
SLOOT
SLOOTS
SLOP
SLOPE
SLOPED
SLOPES
SLOPEWISE
SLOPIER
SLOPIEST
SLOPING
SLOPINGLY
SLOPPED
SLOPPIER
SLOPPIEST
SLOPPILY
SLOPPING
SLOPPY
SLOPS
SLOPWORK
SLOPWORKS
SLOPY
SLOSH
SLOSHED
SLOSHES
SLOSHIER
SLOSHIEST
SLOSHING
SLOSHINGS
SLOSHY
SLOT
SLOTH
SLOTHED
SLOTHFUL
SLOTHING
SLOTHS
SLOTS
SLOTTED
SLOTTER
SLOTTERS
SLOTTING
SLOUCH
SLOUCHED
SLOUCHER
SLOUCHERS
SLOUCHES
SLOUCHIER
SLOUCHIEST
SLOUCHING
SLOUCHY
SLOUGH
SLOUGHED
SLOUGHIER
SLOUGHIEST
SLOUGHING
SLOUGHS
SLOUGHY
SLOVE
SLOVEN
SLOVENLIER
SLOVENLIEST
SLOVENLY
SLOVENRIES
SLOVENRY
SLOVENS
SLOW
SLOWBACK
SLOWBACKS
SLOWCOACH
SLOWCOACHES
SLOWED
SLOWER
SLOWEST
SLOWING
SLOWINGS
SLOWISH
SLOWLY
SLOWNESS
SLOWNESSES
SLOWPOKE
SLOWPOKES
SLOWS
SLOWWORM
SLOWWORMS
SLOYD
SLOYDS
SLUB
SLUBB
SLUBBED
SLUBBER
SLUBBERED
SLUBBERING
SLUBBERINGS
SLUBBERS
SLUBBIER
SLUBBIEST
SLUBBING
SLUBBINGS
SLUBBS
SLUBBY
SLUBS
SLUDGE
SLUDGES
SLUDGIER
SLUDGIEST
SLUDGY
SLUE
SLUED
SLUEING
SLUES
SLUG
SLUGFEST
SLUGFESTS
SLUGGABED
SLUGGABEDS
SLUGGARD
SLUGGARDS
SLUGGED
SLUGGER
SLUGGERS
SLUGGING
SLUGGISH
SLUGHORN
SLUGHORNE
SLUGHORNES
SLUGHORNS
SLUGS
SLUICE
SLUICED
SLUICES
SLUICIER
SLUICIEST
SLUICING
SLUICY
SLUING
SLUIT
SLUITS
SLUM
SLUMBER
SLUMBERED
SLUMBERER
SLUMBERERS
SLUMBERING
SLUMBERINGS
SLUMBERS
SLUMBERY
SLUMBROUS
SLUMBRY
SLUMLORD
SLUMLORDS
SLUMMED
SLUMMER
SLUMMERS
SLUMMIER
SLUMMIEST
SLUMMING
SLUMMINGS
SLUMMOCK
SLUMMOCKED
SLUMMOCKING
SLUMMOCKS
SLUMMY
SLUMP
SLUMPED
SLUMPIER
SLUMPIEST
SLUMPING
SLUMPS
SLUMPY
SLUMS
SLUNG
SLUNK
SLUR
SLURB
SLURBS
SLURP
SLURPED
SLURPER
SLURPERS
SLURPING
SLURPS
SLURRED
SLURRIES
SLURRING
SLURRY
SLURS
SLUSE
SLUSES
SLUSH
SLUSHED
SLUSHES
SLUSHIER
SLUSHIEST
SLUSHING
SLUSHY
SLUT
SLUTS
SLUTTERIES
SLUTTERY
SLUTTISH
SLY
SLYBOOTS
SLYER
SLYEST
SLYISH
SLYLY
SLYNESS
SLYNESSES
SLYPE
SLYPES
SMA
SMACK
SMACKED
SMACKER
SMACKERS
SMACKING
SMACKINGS
SMACKS
SMAIK
SMAIKS
SMALL
SMALLAGE
SMALLAGES
SMALLED

SMALLER
SMALLEST
SMALLING
SMALLISH
SMALLNESS
SMALLNESSES
SMALLPOX
SMALLPOXES
SMALLS
SMALLSAT
SMALLSATS
SMALM
SMALMED
SMALMILY
SMALMING
SMALMS
SMALMY
SMALT
SMALTI
SMALTITE
SMALTITES
SMALTO
SMALTOS
SMALTS
SMARAGD
SMARAGDS
SMARM
SMARMED
SMARMIER
SMARMIEST
SMARMILY
SMARMING
SMARMS
SMARMY
SMART
SMARTARSE
SMARTARSES
SMARTASS
SMARTASSES
SMARTED
SMARTEN
SMARTENED
SMARTENING
SMARTENS
SMARTER
SMARTEST
SMARTIE
SMARTIES
SMARTING
SMARTISH
SMARTLY
SMARTNESS
SMARTNESSES
SMARTS
SMARTWEED
SMARTWEEDS
SMARTY
SMASH
SMASHED
SMASHER
SMASHEROO
SMASHEROOS
SMASHERS
SMASHES
SMASHING
SMASHINGS
SMATCH
SMATCHED
SMATCHES
SMATCHING
SMATTER
SMATTERED
SMATTERER
SMATTERERS
SMATTERING
SMATTERINGS
SMATTERS
SMEAR
SMEARED
SMEARIER
SMEARIEST
SMEARILY
SMEARING
SMEARS
SMEARY
SMEATH
SMEATHS
SMECTIC
SMECTITE
SMECTITES
SMEDDUM
SMEDDUMS
SMEE
SMEECH
SMEECHED
SMEECHES
SMEECHING
SMEEK
SMEEKED
SMEEKING
SMEEKS
SMEES
SMEETH
SMEETHS
SMEGMA
SMEGMAS
SMELL
SMELLED
SMELLER
SMELLERS
SMELLIER
SMELLIEST
SMELLING
SMELLINGS
SMELLS
SMELLY
SMELT
SMELTED
SMELTER
SMELTERIES
SMELTERS
SMELTERY
SMELTING
SMELTINGS
SMELTS
SMEUSE
SMEUSES
SMEW
SMEWS
SMICKER
SMICKERED
SMICKERING
SMICKERINGS
SMICKERS
SMICKET
SMICKETS
SMICKLY
SMIDDIED
SMIDDIES
SMIDDY
SMIDDYING
SMIDGEN
SMIDGENS
SMIDGEON
SMIDGEONS
SMIDGIN
SMIDGINS
SMIGHT
SMIGHTING
SMIGHTS
SMILAX
SMILAXES
SMILE
SMILED
SMILEFUL
SMILELESS
SMILER
SMILERS
SMILES
SMILET
SMILETS
SMILEY
SMILEYS
SMILING
SMILINGLY
SMILINGS
SMILODON
SMILODONS
SMIR
SMIRCH
SMIRCHED
SMIRCHES
SMIRCHING
SMIRK
SMIRKED
SMIRKIER
SMIRKIEST
SMIRKING
SMIRKS
SMIRKY
SMIRR
SMIRRED
SMIRRIER
SMIRRIEST
SMIRRING
SMIRRS
SMIRRY
SMIRS
SMIT
SMITE
SMITER
SMITERS
SMITES
SMITH
SMITHED
SMITHERIES
SMITHERS
SMITHERY
SMITHIED
SMITHIES
SMITHING
SMITHS
SMITHY
SMITHYING
SMITING
SMITS
SMITTED
SMITTEN
SMITTING
SMITTLE
SMOCK
SMOCKED
SMOCKING
SMOCKINGS
SMOCKS
SMOG
SMOGGIER
SMOGGIEST
SMOGGY
SMOGS
SMOILE
SMOILED
SMOILES
SMOILING
SMOKABLE
SMOKE
SMOKEBUSH
SMOKEBUSHES
SMOKED
SMOKEHOOD
SMOKEHOODS
SMOKELESS
SMOKER
SMOKERS
SMOKES
SMOKETREE
SMOKETREES
SMOKIER
SMOKIES
SMOKIEST
SMOKILY
SMOKINESS
SMOKINESSES
SMOKING
SMOKINGS
SMOKO
SMOKOS
SMOKY
SMOLDER
SMOLDERED
SMOLDERING
SMOLDERS
SMOLT
SMOLTS
SMOOCH
SMOOCHED
SMOOCHES
SMOOCHING
SMOOR
SMOORED
SMOORING
SMOORS
SMOOT
SMOOTED
SMOOTH
SMOOTHED
SMOOTHEN
SMOOTHENED
SMOOTHENING
SMOOTHENS
SMOOTHER
SMOOTHERS
SMOOTHEST
SMOOTHIE
SMOOTHIES
SMOOTHING
SMOOTHINGS
SMOOTHISH
SMOOTHLY
SMOOTHS
SMOOTING
SMOOTS
SMORBROD
SMORBRODS
SMORE
SMORED
SMORES
SMORING
SMORZANDO
SMORZATO
SMOTE
SMOTHER
SMOTHERED
SMOTHERER
SMOTHERERS
SMOTHERING
SMOTHERINGS
SMOTHERS
SMOTHERY
SMOUCH
SMOUCHED
SMOUCHES
SMOUCHING
SMOULDER
SMOULDERED
SMOULDERING
SMOULDERINGS
SMOULDERS
SMOULDRY
SMOUSE
SMOUSED
SMOUSER
SMOUSERS
SMOUSES
SMOUSING
SMOUT
SMOUTED
SMOUTING
SMOUTS
SMOWT

SMOWTS
SMOYLE
SMOYLED
SMOYLES
SMOYLING
SMUDGE
SMUDGED
SMUDGER
SMUDGERS
SMUDGES
SMUDGIER
SMUDGIEST
SMUDGILY
SMUDGING
SMUDGY
SMUG
SMUGGED
SMUGGER
SMUGGEST
SMUGGING
SMUGGLE
SMUGGLED
SMUGGLER
SMUGGLERS
SMUGGLES
SMUGGLING
SMUGGLINGS
SMUGLY
SMUGNESS
SMUGNESSES
SMUGS
SMUR
SMURRED
SMURRIER
SMURRIEST
SMURRING
SMURRY
SMURS
SMUT
SMUTCH
SMUTCHED
SMUTCHES
SMUTCHING
SMUTS
SMUTTED
SMUTTIER
SMUTTIEST
SMUTTILY
SMUTTING
SMUTTY
SMYTRIE
SMYTRIES
SNAB
SNABBLE
SNABBLED
SNABBLES
SNABBLING
SNABS
SNACK
SNACKED
SNACKING
SNACKS
SNAFFLE
SNAFFLED
SNAFFLES
SNAFFLING
SNAFU
SNAFUS
SNAG
SNAGGED
SNAGGIER
SNAGGIEST
SNAGGING
SNAGGY
SNAGS
SNAIL
SNAILED
SNAILERIES
SNAILERY
SNAILIER
SNAILIEST
SNAILING
SNAILS
SNAILY
SNAKE
SNAKEBIRD
SNAKEBIRDS
SNAKEBITE
SNAKEBITES
SNAKED
SNAKELIKE
SNAKEROOT
SNAKEROOTS
SNAKES
SNAKESKIN
SNAKESKINS
SNAKEWEED
SNAKEWEEDS
SNAKEWISE
SNAKEWOOD
SNAKEWOODS
SNAKIER
SNAKIEST
SNAKILY
SNAKINESS
SNAKINESSES
SNAKING
SNAKISH
SNAKY
SNAP
SNAPHANCE
SNAPHANCES
SNAPPED
SNAPPER
SNAPPERED
SNAPPERING
SNAPPERS
SNAPPIER
SNAPPIEST
SNAPPILY
SNAPPING
SNAPPINGS
SNAPPISH
SNAPPY
SNAPS
SNAPSHOT
SNAPSHOTS
SNAR
SNARE
SNARED
SNARER
SNARERS
SNARES
SNARIER
SNARIEST
SNARING
SNARINGS
SNARK
SNARKS
SNARL
SNARLED
SNARLER
SNARLERS
SNARLIER
SNARLIEST
SNARLING
SNARLINGS
SNARLS
SNARLY
SNARRED
SNARRING
SNARS
SNARY
SNASH
SNASHED
SNASHES
SNASHING
SNASTE
SNASTES
SNATCH
SNATCHED
SNATCHER
SNATCHERS
SNATCHES
SNATCHIER
SNATCHIEST
SNATCHILY
SNATCHING
SNATCHY
SNATH
SNATHE
SNATHES
SNATHS
SNAZZIER
SNAZZIEST
SNAZZY
SNEAD
SNEADS
SNEAK
SNEAKED
SNEAKER
SNEAKERS
SNEAKEUP
SNEAKEUPS
SNEAKIER
SNEAKIEST
SNEAKILY
SNEAKING
SNEAKISH
SNEAKS
SNEAKSBIES
SNEAKSBY
SNEAKY
SNEAP
SNEAPED
SNEAPING
SNEAPS
SNEATH
SNEATHS
SNEB
SNEBBE
SNEBBED
SNEBBES
SNEBBING
SNEBS
SNECK
SNECKED
SNECKING
SNECKS
SNED
SNEDDED
SNEDDING
SNEDS
SNEE
SNEED
SNEEING
SNEER
SNEERED
SNEERER
SNEERERS
SNEERIER
SNEERIEST
SNEERING
SNEERINGS
SNEERS
SNEERY
SNEES
SNEESH
SNEESHAN
SNEESHANS
SNEESHES
SNEESHIN
SNEESHING
SNEESHINGS
SNEESHINS
SNEEZE
SNEEZED
SNEEZER
SNEEZERS
SNEEZES
SNEEZIER
SNEEZIEST
SNEEZING
SNEEZINGS
SNEEZY
SNELL
SNELLED
SNELLER
SNELLEST
SNELLING
SNELLS
SNELLY
SNIB
SNIBBED
SNIBBING
SNIBS
SNICK
SNICKED
SNICKER
SNICKERED
SNICKERING
SNICKERS
SNICKET
SNICKETS
SNICKING
SNICKS
SNIDE
SNIDELY
SNIDENESS
SNIDENESSES
SNIDER
SNIDES
SNIDEST
SNIES
SNIFF
SNIFFED
SNIFFER
SNIFFERS
SNIFFIER
SNIFFIEST
SNIFFILY
SNIFFING
SNIFFINGS
SNIFFLE
SNIFFLED
SNIFFLER
SNIFFLERS
SNIFFLES
SNIFFLING
SNIFFS
SNIFFY
SNIFT
SNIFTED
SNIFTER
SNIFTERED
SNIFTERING
SNIFTERS
SNIFTIER
SNIFTIEST
SNIFTING
SNIFTS
SNIFTY
SNIG
SNIGGED
SNIGGER
SNIGGERED
SNIGGERER
SNIGGERERS
SNIGGERING
SNIGGERINGS
SNIGGERS
SNIGGING
SNIGGLE
SNIGGLED
SNIGGLER
SNIGGLERS
SNIGGLES
SNIGGLING
SNIGGLINGS
SNIGS

SNIP
SNIPE
SNIPED
SNIPEFISH
SNIPEFISHES
SNIPER
SNIPERS
SNIPES
SNIPIER
SNIPIEST
SNIPING
SNIPINGS
SNIPPED
SNIPPER
SNIPPERS
SNIPPET
SNIPPETIER
SNIPPETIEST
SNIPPETS
SNIPPETY
SNIPPIER
SNIPPIEST
SNIPPING
SNIPPINGS
SNIPPY
SNIPS
SNIPY
SNIRT
SNIRTLE
SNIRTLED
SNIRTLES
SNIRTLING
SNIRTS
SNITCH
SNITCHED
SNITCHER
SNITCHERS
SNITCHES
SNITCHING
SNIVEL
SNIVELLED
SNIVELLER
SNIVELLERS
SNIVELLING
SNIVELLY
SNIVELS
SNOB
SNOBBERIES
SNOBBERY
SNOBBIER
SNOBBIEST
SNOBBISH
SNOBBISM
SNOBBISMS
SNOBBY
SNOBLING
SNOBLINGS
SNOBS
SNOD
SNODDED
SNODDER
SNODDEST
SNODDING
SNODDIT
SNODS
SNOEK
SNOEKS
SNOG
SNOGGED
SNOGGING
SNOGS
SNOKE
SNOKED
SNOKES
SNOKING
SNOOD
SNOODED
SNOODING
SNOODS
SNOOK
SNOOKED
SNOOKER
SNOOKERED
SNOOKERING
SNOOKERS
SNOOKING
SNOOKS
SNOOL
SNOOLED
SNOOLING
SNOOLS
SNOOP
SNOOPED
SNOOPER
SNOOPERS
SNOOPIER
SNOOPIEST
SNOOPING
SNOOPS
SNOOPY
SNOOT
SNOOTED
SNOOTFUL
SNOOTFULS
SNOOTIER
SNOOTIEST
SNOOTILY
SNOOTING
SNOOTS
SNOOTY
SNOOZE
SNOOZED
SNOOZER
SNOOZERS
SNOOZES
SNOOZIER
SNOOZIEST
SNOOZING
SNOOZLE
SNOOZLED
SNOOZLES
SNOOZLING
SNOOZY
SNORE
SNORED
SNORER
SNORERS
SNORES
SNORING
SNORINGS
SNORKEL
SNORKELER
SNORKELERS
SNORKELS
SNORT
SNORTED
SNORTER
SNORTERS
SNORTIER
SNORTIEST
SNORTING
SNORTINGS
SNORTS
SNORTY
SNOT
SNOTS
SNOTTED
SNOTTER
SNOTTERED
SNOTTERIES
SNOTTERING
SNOTTERS
SNOTTERY
SNOTTIE
SNOTTIER
SNOTTIES
SNOTTIEST
SNOTTILY
SNOTTING
SNOTTY
SNOUT
SNOUTED
SNOUTIER
SNOUTIEST
SNOUTING
SNOUTS
SNOUTY
SNOW
SNOWBALL
SNOWBALLED
SNOWBALLING
SNOWBALLS
SNOWBERRIES
SNOWBERRY
SNOWBIRD
SNOWBIRDS
SNOWBLINK
SNOWBLINKS
SNOWBOARD
SNOWBOARDS
SNOWBOOT
SNOWBOOTS
SNOWBOUND
SNOWBUSH
SNOWBUSHES
SNOWCAP
SNOWCAPS
SNOWDRIFT
SNOWDRIFTS
SNOWDROP
SNOWDROPS
SNOWED
SNOWFALL
SNOWFALLS
SNOWFIELD
SNOWFIELDS
SNOWFLAKE
SNOWFLAKES
SNOWFLECK
SNOWFLECKS
SNOWFLICK
SNOWFLICKS
SNOWIER
SNOWIEST
SNOWILY
SNOWINESS
SNOWINESSES
SNOWING
SNOWISH
SNOWK
SNOWKED
SNOWKING
SNOWKS
SNOWLESS
SNOWLIKE
SNOWLINE
SNOWLINES
SNOWMAN
SNOWMEN
SNOWS
SNOWSCAPE
SNOWSCAPES
SNOWSHOE
SNOWSHOED
SNOWSHOEING
SNOWSHOES
SNOWSLIP
SNOWSLIPS
SNOWSTORM
SNOWSTORMS
SNOWY
SNUB
SNUBBE
SNUBBED
SNUBBER
SNUBBERS
SNUBBES
SNUBBIER
SNUBBIEST
SNUBBING
SNUBBINGS
SNUBBISH
SNUBBY
SNUBS
SNUCK
SNUDGE
SNUDGED
SNUDGES
SNUDGING
SNUFF
SNUFFBOX
SNUFFBOXES
SNUFFED
SNUFFER
SNUFFERS
SNUFFIER
SNUFFIEST
SNUFFING
SNUFFINGS
SNUFFLE
SNUFFLED
SNUFFLER
SNUFFLERS
SNUFFLES
SNUFFLIER
SNUFFLIEST
SNUFFLING
SNUFFLINGS
SNUFFLY
SNUFFS
SNUFFY
SNUG
SNUGGED
SNUGGER
SNUGGERIES
SNUGGERY
SNUGGEST
SNUGGING
SNUGGLE
SNUGGLED
SNUGGLES
SNUGGLING
SNUGLY
SNUGNESS
SNUGNESSES
SNUGS
SNUSH
SNUSHED
SNUSHES
SNUSHING
SNUZZLE
SNUZZLED
SNUZZLES
SNUZZLING
SNY
SNYE
SNYES
SO
SOAK
SOAKAGE
SOAKAGES
SOAKAWAY
SOAKAWAYS
SOAKED
SOAKEN
SOAKER
SOAKERS
SOAKING
SOAKINGLY
SOAKINGS
SOAKS
SOAP
SOAPBARK
SOAPBARKS
SOAPBERRIES
SOAPBERRY
SOAPBOX
SOAPBOXES
SOAPED
SOAPER

SOAPERS
SOAPIE
SOAPIER
SOAPIES
SOAPIEST
SOAPILY
SOAPINESS
SOAPINESSES
SOAPING
SOAPLAND
SOAPLANDS
SOAPLESS
SOAPROOT
SOAPROOTS
SOAPS
SOAPSTONE
SOAPSTONES
SOAPSUDS
SOAPWORT
SOAPWORTS
SOAPY
SOAR
SOARAWAY
SOARE
SOARED
SOARER
SOARERS
SOARES
SOARING
SOARINGLY
SOARINGS
SOARS
SOB
SOBBED
SOBBING
SOBBINGLY
SOBBINGS
SOBEIT
SOBER
SOBERED
SOBERER
SOBEREST
SOBERING
SOBERISE
SOBERISED
SOBERISES
SOBERISING
SOBERIZE
SOBERIZED
SOBERIZES
SOBERIZING
SOBERLY
SOBERNESS
SOBERNESSES
SOBERS
SOBOLE
SOBOLES
SOBRIETIES
SOBRIETY
SOBRIQUET
SOBRIQUETS
SOBS
SOC
SOCA
SOCAGE
SOCAGER
SOCAGERS
SOCAGES
SOCAS
SOCCAGE
SOCCAGES
SOCCER
SOCCERS
SOCIABLE
SOCIABLES
SOCIABLY
SOCIAL
SOCIALISE
SOCIALISED
SOCIALISES
SOCIALISING
SOCIALISM
SOCIALISMS
SOCIALIST
SOCIALISTS
SOCIALITE
SOCIALITES
SOCIALITIES
SOCIALITY
SOCIALIZE
SOCIALIZED
SOCIALIZES
SOCIALIZING
SOCIALLY
SOCIALS
SOCIATE
SOCIATES
SOCIATION
SOCIATIONS
SOCIATIVE
SOCIETAL
SOCIETIES
SOCIETY
SOCIOGRAM
SOCIOGRAMS
SOCIOLECT
SOCIOLECTS
SOCIOLOGIES
SOCIOLOGY
SOCIOPATH
SOCIOPATHS
SOCK
SOCKED
SOCKET
SOCKETED
SOCKETING
SOCKETS
SOCKETTE
SOCKETTES
SOCKEYE
SOCKEYES
SOCKING
SOCKO
SOCKS
SOCLE
SOCLES
SOCMAN
SOCMEN
SOCS
SOD
SODA
SODAIC
SODAIN
SODAINE
SODALITE
SODALITES
SODALITIES
SODALITY
SODAMIDE
SODAMIDES
SODAS
SODBUSTER
SODBUSTERS
SODDED
SODDEN
SODDENED
SODDENING
SODDENS
SODDIER
SODDIEST
SODDING
SODDY
SODGER
SODGERS
SODIC
SODIUM
SODIUMS
SODOMIES
SODOMISE
SODOMISED
SODOMISES
SODOMISING
SODOMITE
SODOMITES
SODOMITIC
SODOMIZE
SODOMIZED
SODOMIZES
SODOMIZING
SODOMY
SODS
SOEVER
SOFA
SOFAR
SOFARS
SOFAS
SOFFIONI
SOFFIT
SOFFITS
SOFT
SOFTA
SOFTAS
SOFTBACK
SOFTBACKS
SOFTBALL
SOFTBALLS
SOFTCOVER
SOFTCOVERS
SOFTED
SOFTEN
SOFTENED
SOFTENER
SOFTENERS
SOFTENING
SOFTENINGS
SOFTENS
SOFTER
SOFTEST
SOFTHEAD
SOFTHEADS
SOFTIE
SOFTIES
SOFTING
SOFTISH
SOFTLING
SOFTLINGS
SOFTLY
SOFTNESS
SOFTNESSES
SOFTPASTE
SOFTS
SOFTWARE
SOFTWARES
SOFTWOOD
SOFTWOODS
SOFTY
SOG
SOGER
SOGERS
SOGGED
SOGGIER
SOGGIEST
SOGGILY
SOGGINESS
SOGGINESSES
SOGGING
SOGGINGS
SOGGY
SOGS
SOH
SOHO
SOHS
SOIGNE
SOIGNEE
SOIL
SOILAGE
SOILAGES
SOILED
SOILIER
SOILIEST
SOILINESS
SOILINESSES
SOILING
SOILINGS
SOILLESS
SOILS
SOILURE
SOILURES
SOILY
SOIREE
SOIREES
SOJA
SOJAS
SOJOURN
SOJOURNED
SOJOURNER
SOJOURNERS
SOJOURNING
SOJOURNINGS
SOJOURNS
SOKAH
SOKAHS
SOKAIYA
SOKE
SOKEMAN
SOKEMANRIES
SOKEMANRY
SOKEMEN
SOKEN
SOKENS
SOKES
SOL
SOLA
SOLACE
SOLACED
SOLACES
SOLACING
SOLACIOUS
SOLAH
SOLAHS
SOLAN
SOLANDER
SOLANDERS
SOLANINE
SOLANINES
SOLANO
SOLANOS
SOLANS
SOLANUM
SOLANUMS
SOLAR
SOLARIA
SOLARISE
SOLARISED
SOLARISES
SOLARISING
SOLARISM
SOLARISMS
SOLARIST
SOLARISTS
SOLARIUM
SOLARIUMS
SOLARIZE
SOLARIZED
SOLARIZES
SOLARIZING
SOLARS
SOLAS
SOLATIA
SOLATION
SOLATIONS
SOLATIUM
SOLD
SOLDADO
SOLDADOS
SOLDAN
SOLDANS
SOLDE
SOLDER
SOLDERED

SOLDERER
SOLDERERS
SOLDERING
SOLDERINGS
SOLDERS
SOLDES
SOLDI
SOLDIER
SOLDIERED
SOLDIERIES
SOLDIERING
SOLDIERINGS
SOLDIERLY
SOLDIERS
SOLDIERY
SOLDO
SOLDS
SOLE
SOLECISE
SOLECISED
SOLECISES
SOLECISING
SOLECISM
SOLECISMS
SOLECIST
SOLECISTS
SOLECIZE
SOLECIZED
SOLECIZES
SOLECIZING
SOLED
SOLEIN
SOLELY
SOLEMN
SOLEMNER
SOLEMNESS
SOLEMNESSES
SOLEMNEST
SOLEMNIFIED
SOLEMNIFIES
SOLEMNIFY
SOLEMNIFYING
SOLEMNISE
SOLEMNISED
SOLEMNISES
SOLEMNISING
SOLEMNITIES
SOLEMNITY
SOLEMNIZE
SOLEMNIZED
SOLEMNIZES
SOLEMNIZING
SOLEMNLY
SOLENESS
SOLENESSES
SOLENETTE
SOLENETTES
SOLENODON
SOLENODONS
SOLENOID
SOLENOIDS
SOLEPLATE
SOLEPLATES
SOLER
SOLERA
SOLERAS
SOLERS
SOLES
SOLEUS
SOLEUSES
SOLFATARA
SOLFATARAS
SOLFEGE
SOLFEGES
SOLFEGGI
SOLFEGGIO
SOLFEGGIOS
SOLFERINO
SOLFERINOS
SOLGEL
SOLI
SOLICIT
SOLICITED
SOLICITIES
SOLICITING
SOLICITINGS
SOLICITOR
SOLICITORS
SOLICITS
SOLICITY
SOLID
SOLIDAGO
SOLIDAGOS
SOLIDARE
SOLIDARES
SOLIDARY
SOLIDATE
SOLIDATED
SOLIDATES
SOLIDATING
SOLIDER
SOLIDEST
SOLIDI
SOLIDIFIED
SOLIDIFIES
SOLIDIFY
SOLIDIFYING
SOLIDISH
SOLIDISM
SOLIDISMS
SOLIDIST
SOLIDISTS
SOLIDITIES
SOLIDITY
SOLIDLY
SOLIDNESS
SOLIDNESSES
SOLIDS
SOLIDUM
SOLIDUMS
SOLIDUS
SOLILOQUIES
SOLILOQUY
SOLING
SOLION
SOLIONS
SOLIPED
SOLIPEDS
SOLIPSISM
SOLIPSISMS
SOLIPSIST
SOLIPSISTS
SOLITAIRE
SOLITAIRES
SOLITARIES
SOLITARY
SOLITO
SOLITON
SOLITONS
SOLITUDE
SOLITUDES
SOLIVE
SOLIVES
SOLLAR
SOLLARS
SOLLER
SOLLERET
SOLLERETS
SOLLERS
SOLO
SOLOED
SOLOING
SOLOIST
SOLOISTS
SOLONCHAK
SOLONCHAKS
SOLONETS
SOLONETSES
SOLONETZ
SOLONETZES
SOLOS
SOLPUGID
SOLPUGIDS
SOLS
SOLSTICE
SOLSTICES
SOLUBLE
SOLUM
SOLUMS
SOLUS
SOLUTE
SOLUTES
SOLUTION
SOLUTIONED
SOLUTIONING
SOLUTIONS
SOLUTIVE
SOLVABLE
SOLVATE
SOLVATED
SOLVATES
SOLVATING
SOLVATION
SOLVATIONS
SOLVE
SOLVED
SOLVENCIES
SOLVENCY
SOLVENT
SOLVENTS
SOLVER
SOLVERS
SOLVES
SOLVING
SOMA
SOMAN
SOMANS
SOMAS
SOMASCOPE
SOMASCOPES
SOMATA
SOMATIC
SOMATISM
SOMATISMS
SOMATIST
SOMATISTS
SOMBER
SOMBERED
SOMBERER
SOMBEREST
SOMBERING
SOMBERS
SOMBRE
SOMBRED
SOMBRELY
SOMBRER
SOMBRERO
SOMBREROS
SOMBRES
SOMBREST
SOMBRING
SOMBROUS
SOME
SOMEBODIES
SOMEBODY
SOMEDAY
SOMEDEAL
SOMEDELE
SOMEGATE
SOMEHOW
SOMEONE
SOMEONES
SOMEPLACE
SOMERSET
SOMERSETS
SOMERSETTED
SOMERSETTING
SOMETHING
SOMETHINGS
SOMETIME
SOMETIMES
SOMEWAY
SOMEWAYS
SOMEWHAT
SOMEWHATS
SOMEWHEN
SOMEWHERE
SOMEWHILE
SOMEWHILES
SOMEWHY
SOMEWISE
SOMITAL
SOMITE
SOMITES
SOMITIC
SOMMELIER
SOMMELIERS
SOMNIAL
SOMNIATE
SOMNIATED
SOMNIATES
SOMNIATING
SOMNIFIC
SOMNOLENT
SON
SONANCE
SONANCES
SONANCIES
SONANCY
SONANT
SONANTS
SONAR
SONARS
SONATA
SONATAS
SONATINA
SONATINAS
SONCE
SONCES
SONDAGE
SONDAGES
SONDE
SONDELI
SONDELIS
SONDES
SONE
SONERI
SONERIS
SONES
SONG
SONGBIRD
SONGBIRDS
SONGBOOK
SONGBOOKS
SONGCRAFT
SONGCRAFTS
SONGFEST
SONGFESTS
SONGFUL
SONGFULLY
SONGLESS
SONGLIKE
SONGMAN
SONGMEN
SONGS
SONGSMITH
SONGSMITHS
SONGSTER
SONGSTERS
SONIC
SONICS
SONLESS
SONNE
SONNES
SONNET
SONNETARY
SONNETED
SONNETEER
SONNETEERS
SONNETING

SONNETISE
SONNETISED
SONNETISES
SONNETISING
SONNETIZE
SONNETIZED
SONNETIZES
SONNETIZING
SONNETS
SONNIES
SONNY
SONOBUOY
SONOBUOYS
SONOGRAM
SONOGRAMS
SONOGRAPH
SONOGRAPHS
SONORANT
SONORANTS
SONORITIES
SONORITY
SONOROUS
SONS
SONSE
SONSES
SONSHIP
SONSHIPS
SONSIE
SONSIER
SONSIEST
SONSY
SONTAG
SONTAGS
SONTIES
SOOGEE
SOOGEED
SOOGEEING
SOOGEES
SOOGIE
SOOGIED
SOOGIEING
SOOGIES
SOOJEY
SOOJEYS
SOOK
SOOKS
SOOLE
SOOLED
SOOLES
SOOLING
SOOM
SOOMED
SOOMING
SOOMS
SOON
SOONER
SOONEST
SOOP
SOOPED
SOOPING
SOOPINGS
SOOPS
SOOPSTAKE
SOOT
SOOTE
SOOTED
SOOTERKIN
SOOTERKINS
SOOTES
SOOTFLAKE
SOOTFLAKES
SOOTH
SOOTHE
SOOTHED
SOOTHER
SOOTHERED
SOOTHERING
SOOTHERS
SOOTHES
SOOTHEST
SOOTHFAST
SOOTHFUL
SOOTHING
SOOTHINGS
SOOTHLICH
SOOTHLY
SOOTHS
SOOTHSAID
SOOTHSAY
SOOTHSAYING
SOOTHSAYINGS
SOOTHSAYS
SOOTIER
SOOTIEST
SOOTILY
SOOTINESS
SOOTINESSES
SOOTING
SOOTLESS
SOOTS
SOOTY
SOP
SOPH
SOPHERIC
SOPHERIM
SOPHISM
SOPHISMS
SOPHIST
SOPHISTER
SOPHISTERS
SOPHISTIC
SOPHISTRIES
SOPHISTRY
SOPHISTS
SOPHOMORE
SOPHOMORES
SOPHS
SOPITE
SOPITED
SOPITES
SOPITING
SOPOR
SOPORIFIC
SOPORIFICS
SOPOROSE
SOPOROUS
SOPORS
SOPPED
SOPPIER
SOPPIEST
SOPPILY
SOPPINESS
SOPPINESSES
SOPPING
SOPPINGS
SOPPY
SOPRA
SOPRANI
SOPRANINI
SOPRANINO
SOPRANINOS
SOPRANIST
SOPRANISTS
SOPRANO
SOPRANOS
SOPS
SORA
SORAGE
SORAGES
SORAL
SORAS
SORB
SORBARIA
SORBARIAS
SORBATE
SORBATES
SORBED
SORBENT
SORBENTS
SORBET
SORBETS
SORBING
SORBITE
SORBITES
SORBITIC
SORBITISE
SORBITISED
SORBITISES
SORBITISING
SORBITIZE
SORBITIZED
SORBITIZES
SORBITIZING
SORBITOL
SORBITOLS
SORBS
SORBUS
SORBUSES
SORCERER
SORCERERS
SORCERESS
SORCERESSES
SORCERIES
SORCEROUS
SORCERY
SORD
SORDA
SORDID
SORDIDER
SORDIDEST
SORDIDLY
SORDINI
SORDINO
SORDO
SORDS
SORE
SORED
SOREDIA
SOREDIAL
SOREDIATE
SOREDIUM
SOREE
SOREES
SOREHEAD
SOREHEADS
SOREHON
SOREHONS
SOREL
SORELL
SORELLS
SORELS
SORELY
SORENESS
SORENESSES
SORER
SORES
SOREST
SOREX
SOREXES
SORGHO
SORGHOS
SORGHUM
SORGHUMS
SORGO
SORGOS
SORI
SORICINE
SORICOID
SORING
SORITES
SORITIC
SORITICAL
SORN
SORNED
SORNER
SORNERS
SORNING
SORNINGS
SORNS
SOROBAN
SOROBANS
SOROCHE
SOROCHES
SORORAL
SORORATE
SORORATES
SORORIAL
SORORISE
SORORISED
SORORISES
SORORISING
SORORITIES
SORORITY
SORORIZE
SORORIZED
SORORIZES
SORORIZING
SOROSES
SOROSIS
SOROSISES
SORPTION
SORPTIONS
SORRA
SORRAS
SORREL
SORRELS
SORRIER
SORRIEST
SORRILY
SORRINESS
SORRINESSES
SORROW
SORROWED
SORROWER
SORROWERS
SORROWFUL
SORROWING
SORROWINGS
SORROWS
SORRY
SORRYISH
SORT
SORTABLE
SORTANCE
SORTANCES
SORTATION
SORTATIONS
SORTED
SORTER
SORTERS
SORTES
SORTIE
SORTIED
SORTIEING
SORTIES
SORTILEGE
SORTILEGES
SORTILEGIES
SORTILEGY
SORTING
SORTINGS
SORTITION
SORTITIONS
SORTMENT
SORTMENTS
SORTS
SORUS
SOS
SOSS
SOSSED
SOSSES
SOSSING
SOSSINGS
SOSTENUTO
SOT
SOTERIAL
SOTS
SOTTED
SOTTING
SOTTINGS

SOTTISH
SOTTISHLY
SOTTISIER
SOTTISIERS
SOU
SOUARI
SOUARIS
SOUBISE
SOUBISES
SOUBRETTE
SOUBRETTES
SOUCE
SOUCED
SOUCES
SOUCHONG
SOUCHONGS
SOUCING
SOUCT
SOUFFLE
SOUFFLES
SOUGH
SOUGHED
SOUGHING
SOUGHS
SOUGHT
SOUK
SOUKOUS
SOUKOUSES
SOUKS
SOUL
SOULDAN
SOULDANS
SOULDIER
SOULDIERED
SOULDIERING
SOULDIERS
SOULED
SOULFUL
SOULFULLY
SOULLESS
SOULS
SOUM
SOUMED
SOUMING
SOUMINGS
SOUMS
SOUND
SOUNDBITE
SOUNDBITES
SOUNDCARD
SOUNDCARDS
SOUNDED
SOUNDER
SOUNDERS
SOUNDEST
SOUNDING
SOUNDINGS
SOUNDLESS
SOUNDLY
SOUNDMAN
SOUNDMEN
SOUNDNESS
SOUNDNESSES
SOUNDS
SOUP
SOUPCON
SOUPCONS
SOUPER
SOUPERS
SOUPIER
SOUPIEST
SOUPLE
SOUPLED
SOUPLES
SOUPLING
SOUPS
SOUPSPOON
SOUPSPOONS
SOUPY
SOUR
SOURCE
SOURCED
SOURCES
SOURCING
SOURCINGS
SOURDINE
SOURDINES
SOURDOUGH
SOURDOUGHS
SOURED
SOURER
SOUREST
SOURING
SOURINGS
SOURISH
SOURISHLY
SOURLY
SOURNESS
SOURNESSES
SOUROCK
SOUROCKS
SOURPUSS
SOURPUSSES
SOURS
SOURSE
SOURSES
SOURSOP
SOURSOPS
SOUS
SOUSE
SOUSED
SOUSES
SOUSING
SOUSINGS
SOUSLIK
SOUSLIKS
SOUT
SOUTACHE
SOUTACHES
SOUTANE
SOUTANES
SOUTAR
SOUTARS
SOUTENEUR
SOUTENEURS
SOUTER
SOUTERLY
SOUTERS
SOUTH
SOUTHED
SOUTHER
SOUTHERED
SOUTHERING
SOUTHERLY
SOUTHERN
SOUTHERNS
SOUTHERS
SOUTHING
SOUTHINGS
SOUTHLAND
SOUTHLANDS
SOUTHMOST
SOUTHPAW
SOUTHPAWS
SOUTHRON
SOUTHRONS
SOUTHS
SOUTHSAID
SOUTHSAY
SOUTHSAYING
SOUTHSAYS
SOUTHWARD
SOUTHWARDS
SOUTS
SOUVENIR
SOUVENIRED
SOUVENIRING
SOUVENIRS
SOUVLAKI
SOUVLAKIA
SOV
SOVENANCE
SOVENANCES
SOVEREIGN
SOVEREIGNS
SOVIET
SOVIETIC
SOVIETISE
SOVIETISED
SOVIETISES
SOVIETISING
SOVIETISM
SOVIETISMS
SOVIETIZE
SOVIETIZED
SOVIETIZES
SOVIETIZING
SOVIETS
SOVRAN
SOVRANLY
SOVRANS
SOVRANTIES
SOVRANTY
SOVS
SOW
SOWANS
SOWAR
SOWARREE
SOWARREES
SOWARRIES
SOWARRY
SOWARS
SOWBACK
SOWBACKS
SOWBREAD
SOWBREADS
SOWCE
SOWCED
SOWCES
SOWCING
SOWED
SOWENS
SOWER
SOWERS
SOWF
SOWFED
SOWFF
SOWFFED
SOWFFING
SOWFFS
SOWFING
SOWFS
SOWING
SOWINGS
SOWL
SOWLE
SOWLED
SOWLES
SOWLING
SOWLS
SOWM
SOWMED
SOWMING
SOWMS
SOWN
SOWND
SOWNDED
SOWNDING
SOWNDS
SOWNE
SOWNES
SOWP
SOWPS
SOWS
SOWSE
SOWSED
SOWSES
SOWSING
SOWSSE
SOWSSED
SOWSSES
SOWSSING
SOWTER
SOWTERS
SOWTH
SOWTHED
SOWTHING
SOWTHS
SOX
SOY
SOYA
SOYAS
SOYLE
SOYLES
SOYS
SOZZLE
SOZZLED
SOZZLES
SOZZLIER
SOZZLIEST
SOZZLING
SOZZLY
SPA
SPACE
SPACED
SPACELESS
SPACEMAN
SPACEMEN
SPACER
SPACERS
SPACES
SPACESHIP
SPACESHIPS
SPACESUIT
SPACESUITS
SPACEY
SPACIAL
SPACIER
SPACIEST
SPACING
SPACINGS
SPACIOUS
SPACY
SPADASSIN
SPADASSINS
SPADE
SPADED
SPADEFISH
SPADEFISHES
SPADEFUL
SPADEFULS
SPADELIKE
SPADEMAN
SPADEMEN
SPADER
SPADERS
SPADES
SPADESMAN
SPADESMEN
SPADEWORK
SPADEWORKS
SPADGER
SPADGERS
SPADICES
SPADILLE
SPADILLES
SPADILLIO
SPADILLIOS
SPADILLO
SPADILLOS
SPADING
SPADIX
SPADO
SPADOES
SPADONES
SPADOS
SPADROON
SPADROONS
SPAE
SPAED

SPAEING
SPAEMAN
SPAEMEN
SPAER
SPAERS
SPAES
SPAEWIFE
SPAEWIVES
SPAG
SPAGERIC
SPAGERICS
SPAGERIST
SPAGERISTS
SPAGHETTI
SPAGHETTIS
SPAGIRIC
SPAGIRICS
SPAGIRIST
SPAGIRISTS
SPAGS
SPAGYRIC
SPAGYRICS
SPAGYRIST
SPAGYRISTS
SPAHEE
SPAHEES
SPAHI
SPAHIS
SPAIN
SPAINED
SPAING
SPAINGS
SPAINING
SPAINS
SPAIRGE
SPAIRGED
SPAIRGES
SPAIRGING
SPAKE
SPALD
SPALDS
SPALE
SPALES
SPALL
SPALLE
SPALLED
SPALLES
SPALLING
SPALLINGS
SPALLS
SPALPEEN
SPALPEENS
SPALT
SPALTED
SPALTING
SPALTS
SPAM
SPAMMED
SPAMMER
SPAMMERS
SPAMMIER
SPAMMIEST
SPAMMING
SPAMMINGS
SPAMMY
SPAMS
SPAN
SPANAEMIA
SPANAEMIAS
SPANAEMIC
SPANCEL
SPANCELLED
SPANCELLING
SPANCELS
SPANDEX
SPANDEXES
SPANDREL
SPANDRELS
SPANDRIL
SPANDRILS
SPANE
SPANED
SPANES
SPANG
SPANGED
SPANGHEW
SPANGHEWED
SPANGHEWING
SPANGHEWS
SPANGING
SPANGLE
SPANGLED
SPANGLER
SPANGLERS
SPANGLES
SPANGLET
SPANGLETS
SPANGLIER
SPANGLIEST
SPANGLING
SPANGLINGS
SPANGLY
SPANGS
SPANIEL
SPANIELLED
SPANIELLING
SPANIELS
SPANING
SPANK
SPANKED
SPANKER
SPANKERS
SPANKING
SPANKINGS
SPANKS
SPANLESS
SPANNED
SPANNER
SPANNERS
SPANNING
SPANS
SPANSULE
SPANSULES
SPAR
SPARABLE
SPARABLES
SPARAXIS
SPARAXISES
SPARD
SPARE
SPARED
SPARELESS
SPARELY
SPARENESS
SPARENESSES
SPARER
SPARERS
SPARES
SPAREST
SPARGE
SPARGED
SPARGER
SPARGERS
SPARGES
SPARGING
SPARID
SPARIDS
SPARING
SPARINGLY
SPARK
SPARKE
SPARKED
SPARKES
SPARKIE
SPARKIER
SPARKIES
SPARKIEST
SPARKING
SPARKISH
SPARKLE
SPARKLED
SPARKLER
SPARKLERS
SPARKLES
SPARKLESS
SPARKLET
SPARKLETS
SPARKLIER
SPARKLIES
SPARKLIEST
SPARKLING
SPARKLINGS
SPARKLY
SPARKS
SPARKY
SPARLING
SPARLINGS
SPAROID
SPAROIDS
SPARRE
SPARRED
SPARRER
SPARRERS
SPARRES
SPARRIER
SPARRIEST
SPARRING
SPARRINGS
SPARROW
SPARROWS
SPARRY
SPARS
SPARSE
SPARSEDLY
SPARSELY
SPARSER
SPARSEST
SPARSITIES
SPARSITY
SPART
SPARTAN
SPARTANS
SPARTEINE
SPARTEINES
SPARTERIE
SPARTERIES
SPARTH
SPARTHE
SPARTHES
SPARTHS
SPARTS
SPAS
SPASM
SPASMATIC
SPASMED
SPASMIC
SPASMING
SPASMODIC
SPASMS
SPASTIC
SPASTICS
SPAT
SPATE
SPATES
SPATFALL
SPATFALLS
SPATHE
SPATHED
SPATHES
SPATHIC
SPATHOSE
SPATIAL
SPATIALLY
SPATLESE
SPATLESEN
SPATLESES
SPATS
SPATTED
SPATTEE
SPATTEES
SPATTER
SPATTERED
SPATTERING
SPATTERS
SPATTING
SPATULA
SPATULAR
SPATULAS
SPATULATE
SPATULE
SPATULES
SPAUL
SPAULD
SPAULDS
SPAULS
SPAVIE
SPAVIES
SPAVIN
SPAVINED
SPAVINS
SPAW
SPAWL
SPAWLED
SPAWLING
SPAWLS
SPAWN
SPAWNED
SPAWNER
SPAWNERS
SPAWNIER
SPAWNIEST
SPAWNING
SPAWNINGS
SPAWNS
SPAWNY
SPAWS
SPAY
SPAYAD
SPAYADS
SPAYD
SPAYDS
SPAYED
SPAYING
SPAYS
SPAZZ
SPAZZED
SPAZZES
SPAZZING
SPEAK
SPEAKABLE
SPEAKEASIES
SPEAKEASY
SPEAKER
SPEAKERS
SPEAKING
SPEAKINGS
SPEAKOUT
SPEAKOUTS
SPEAKS
SPEAL
SPEALS
SPEAN
SPEANED
SPEANING
SPEANS
SPEAR
SPEARED
SPEARFISH
SPEARFISHES
SPEARHEAD
SPEARHEADED
SPEARHEADING
SPEARHEADS
SPEARIER
SPEARIEST
SPEARING
SPEARMAN
SPEARMEN
SPEARMINT
SPEARMINTS

SPEARS
SPEARWORT
SPEARWORTS
SPEARY
SPEAT
SPEATS
SPEC
SPECCIES
SPECCY
SPECIAL
SPECIALLY
SPECIALS
SPECIALTIES
SPECIALTY
SPECIATE
SPECIATED
SPECIATES
SPECIATING
SPECIE
SPECIES
SPECIFIC
SPECIFICS
SPECIFIED
SPECIFIES
SPECIFY
SPECIFYING
SPECIMEN
SPECIMENS
SPECIOUS
SPECK
SPECKED
SPECKIER
SPECKIEST
SPECKING
SPECKLE
SPECKLED
SPECKLES
SPECKLESS
SPECKLING
SPECKS
SPECKY
SPECS
SPECTACLE
SPECTACLES
SPECTATE
SPECTATED
SPECTATES
SPECTATING
SPECTATOR
SPECTATORS
SPECTER
SPECTERS
SPECTRA
SPECTRAL
SPECTRE
SPECTRES
SPECTRUM
SPECULA
SPECULAR
SPECULATE
SPECULATED
SPECULATES
SPECULATING
SPECULUM
SPED
SPEECH
SPEECHED
SPEECHES
SPEECHFUL
SPEECHIFIED
SPEECHIFIES
SPEECHIFY
SPEECHIFYING
SPEECHING
SPEED
SPEEDBALL
SPEEDBALLS
SPEEDBOAT
SPEEDBOATS
SPEEDED
SPEEDER
SPEEDERS
SPEEDFUL
SPEEDIER
SPEEDIEST
SPEEDILY
SPEEDING
SPEEDINGS
SPEEDLESS
SPEEDO
SPEEDOS
SPEEDS
SPEEDSTER
SPEEDSTERS
SPEEDWAY
SPEEDWAYS
SPEEDWELL
SPEEDWELLS
SPEEDY
SPEEL
SPEELED
SPEELER
SPEELERS
SPEELING
SPEELS
SPEER
SPEERED
SPEERING
SPEERINGS
SPEERS
SPEIR
SPEIRED
SPEIRING
SPEIRINGS
SPEIRS
SPEISS
SPEISSES
SPEK
SPEKBOOM
SPEKBOOMS
SPEKS
SPELAEAN
SPELD
SPELDED
SPELDER
SPELDERED
SPELDERING
SPELDERS
SPELDIN
SPELDING
SPELDINGS
SPELDINS
SPELDRIN
SPELDRING
SPELDRINGS
SPELDRINS
SPELDS
SPELEAN
SPELK
SPELKS
SPELL
SPELLABLE
SPELLBIND
SPELLBINDING
SPELLBINDS
SPELLBOUND
SPELLDOWN
SPELLDOWNS
SPELLED
SPELLER
SPELLERS
SPELLFUL
SPELLICAN
SPELLICANS
SPELLING
SPELLINGS
SPELLS
SPELT
SPELTER
SPELTERS
SPELTS
SPELUNKER
SPELUNKERS
SPENCE
SPENCER
SPENCERS
SPENCES
SPEND
SPENDABLE
SPENDALL
SPENDALLS
SPENDER
SPENDERS
SPENDING
SPENDINGS
SPENDS
SPENT
SPEOS
SPEOSES
SPERLING
SPERLINGS
SPERM
SPERMARIA
SPERMARIES
SPERMARY
SPERMATIA
SPERMATIC
SPERMATICS
SPERMATID
SPERMATIDS
SPERMIC
SPERMOUS
SPERMS
SPERRE
SPERRED
SPERRES
SPERRING
SPERSE
SPERSED
SPERSES
SPERSING
SPERST
SPERTHE
SPERTHES
SPET
SPETCH
SPETCHES
SPETS
SPETSNAZ
SPETSNAZES
SPETTING
SPETZNAZ
SPETZNAZES
SPEW
SPEWED
SPEWER
SPEWERS
SPEWIER
SPEWIEST
SPEWINESS
SPEWINESSES
SPEWING
SPEWS
SPEWY
SPHACELUS
SPHACELUSES
SPHAER
SPHAERE
SPHAERES
SPHAERITE
SPHAERITES
SPHAERS
SPHAGNOUS
SPHAGNUM
SPHAGNUMS
SPHEAR
SPHEARE
SPHEARES
SPHEARS
SPHENDONE
SPHENDONES
SPHENE
SPHENES
SPHENIC
SPHENODON
SPHENODONS
SPHENOID
SPHENOIDS
SPHERAL
SPHERE
SPHERED
SPHERES
SPHERIC
SPHERICAL
SPHERICS
SPHERIER
SPHERIEST
SPHERING
SPHEROID
SPHEROIDS
SPHERULAR
SPHERULE
SPHERULES
SPHERY
SPHINCTER
SPHINCTERS
SPHINGES
SPHINGID
SPHINGIDS
SPHINX
SPHINXES
SPHYGMIC
SPHYGMOID
SPHYGMUS
SPHYGMUSES
SPIAL
SPIALS
SPIC
SPICA
SPICAE
SPICAS
SPICATE
SPICATED
SPICCATO
SPICCATOS
SPICE
SPICEBUSH
SPICEBUSHES
SPICED
SPICER
SPICERIES
SPICERS
SPICERY
SPICES
SPICIER
SPICIEST
SPICILEGE
SPICILEGES
SPICILY
SPICINESS
SPICINESSES
SPICING
SPICK
SPICKER
SPICKEST
SPICKNEL
SPICKNELS
SPICKS
SPICS
SPICULA
SPICULAE
SPICULAR
SPICULATE
SPICULE
SPICULES
SPICULUM
SPICY
SPIDE
SPIDER
SPIDERIER

SPIDERIEST
SPIDERMAN
SPIDERMEN
SPIDERS
SPIDERY
SPIE
SPIED
SPIEL
SPIELED
SPIELER
SPIELERS
SPIELING
SPIELS
SPIES
SPIFF
SPIFFIER
SPIFFIEST
SPIFFING
SPIFFY
SPIGHT
SPIGHTED
SPIGHTING
SPIGHTS
SPIGNEL
SPIGNELS
SPIGOT
SPIGOTS
SPIK
SPIKE
SPIKED
SPIKEFISH
SPIKEFISHES
SPIKELET
SPIKELETS
SPIKENARD
SPIKENARDS
SPIKERIES
SPIKERY
SPIKES
SPIKIER
SPIKIEST
SPIKILY
SPIKINESS
SPIKINESSES
SPIKING
SPIKS
SPIKY
SPILE
SPILED
SPILES
SPILIKIN
SPILIKINS
SPILING
SPILINGS
SPILITE
SPILITES
SPILITIC
SPILL
SPILLAGE
SPILLAGES
SPILLED
SPILLER
SPILLERS
SPILLIKIN
SPILLIKINS
SPILLING
SPILLINGS
SPILLOVER
SPILLOVERS
SPILLS
SPILLWAY
SPILLWAYS
SPILOSITE
SPILOSITES
SPILT
SPILTH
SPILTHS
SPIN
SPINA
SPINACENE
SPINACENES
SPINACH
SPINACHES
SPINAE
SPINAGE
SPINAGES
SPINAL
SPINAR
SPINARS
SPINAS
SPINATE
SPINDLE
SPINDLED
SPINDLES
SPINDLIER
SPINDLIEST
SPINDLING
SPINDLINGS
SPINDLY
SPINDRIFT
SPINDRIFTS
SPINE
SPINED
SPINEL
SPINELESS
SPINELS
SPINES
SPINET
SPINETS
SPINETTE
SPINETTES
SPINIER
SPINIEST
SPINIFEX
SPINIFEXES
SPINIFORM
SPININESS
SPININESSES
SPINK
SPINKS
SPINNAKER
SPINNAKERS
SPINNER
SPINNERET
SPINNERETS
SPINNERIES
SPINNERS
SPINNERY
SPINNET
SPINNETS
SPINNEY
SPINNEYS
SPINNIES
SPINNING
SPINNINGS
SPINNY
SPINODE
SPINODES
SPINOSE
SPINOSITIES
SPINOSITY
SPINOUS
SPINOUT
SPINOUTS
SPINS
SPINSTER
SPINSTERS
SPINTEXT
SPINTEXTS
SPINTO
SPINULATE
SPINULE
SPINULES
SPINULOSE
SPINULOUS
SPINY
SPIRACLE
SPIRACLES
SPIRACULA
SPIRAEA
SPIRAEAS
SPIRAL
SPIRALISM
SPIRALISMS
SPIRALIST
SPIRALISTS
SPIRALITIES
SPIRALITY
SPIRALLED
SPIRALLING
SPIRALLY
SPIRALS
SPIRANT
SPIRANTS
SPIRASTER
SPIRASTERS
SPIRATED
SPIRATION
SPIRATIONS
SPIRE
SPIREA
SPIREAS
SPIRED
SPIRELESS
SPIREME
SPIREMES
SPIRES
SPIREWISE
SPIRIC
SPIRICS
SPIRIER
SPIRIEST
SPIRILLA
SPIRILLAR
SPIRILLUM
SPIRING
SPIRIT
SPIRITED
SPIRITFUL
SPIRITING
SPIRITINGS
SPIRITISM
SPIRITISMS
SPIRITIST
SPIRITISTS
SPIRITOSO
SPIRITOUS
SPIRITS
SPIRITUAL
SPIRITUALS
SPIRITUEL
SPIRITUS
SPIRITUSES
SPIRITY
SPIRLING
SPIRLINGS
SPIROGRAM
SPIROGRAMS
SPIROGYRA
SPIROGYRAS
SPIROID
SPIRT
SPIRTED
SPIRTING
SPIRTLE
SPIRTLES
SPIRTS
SPIRY
SPIT
SPITAL
SPITALS
SPITCHER
SPITE
SPITED
SPITEFUL
SPITEFULLER
SPITEFULLEST
SPITES
SPITFIRE
SPITFIRES
SPITING
SPITS
SPITTED
SPITTEN
SPITTER
SPITTERS
SPITTING
SPITTINGS
SPITTLE
SPITTLES
SPITTOON
SPITTOONS
SPITZ
SPITZES
SPIV
SPIVS
SPIVVERIES
SPIVVERY
SPIVVIER
SPIVVIEST
SPIVVY
SPLASH
SPLASHED
SPLASHER
SPLASHERS
SPLASHES
SPLASHIER
SPLASHIEST
SPLASHILY
SPLASHING
SPLASHINGS
SPLASHY
SPLAT
SPLATCH
SPLATCHED
SPLATCHES
SPLATCHING
SPLATS
SPLATTED
SPLATTER
SPLATTERED
SPLATTERING
SPLATTERS
SPLATTING
SPLATTINGS
SPLAY
SPLAYED
SPLAYING
SPLAYS
SPLEEN
SPLEENFUL
SPLEENISH
SPLEENS
SPLEENY
SPLENDENT
SPLENDID
SPLENDIDER
SPLENDIDEST
SPLENDOR
SPLENDORS
SPLENDOUR
SPLENDOURS
SPLENETIC
SPLENETICS
SPLENIA
SPLENIAL
SPLENIC
SPLENII
SPLENITIS
SPLENITISES
SPLENIUM
SPLENIUMS
SPLENIUS
SPLENIUSES
SPLENT
SPLENTS
SPLEUCHAN
SPLEUCHANS
SPLICE
SPLICED

SPLICER
SPLICERS
SPLICES
SPLICING
SPLIFF
SPLIFFS
SPLINE
SPLINED
SPLINES
SPLINING
SPLINT
SPLINTED
SPLINTER
SPLINTERED
SPLINTERIER
SPLINTERIEST
SPLINTERING
SPLINTERS
SPLINTERY
SPLINTING
SPLINTS
SPLIT
SPLITS
SPLITTED
SPLITTER
SPLITTERS
SPLITTING
SPLODGE
SPLODGED
SPLODGES
SPLODGIER
SPLODGIEST
SPLODGILY
SPLODGING
SPLODGY
SPLORE
SPLORES
SPLOSH
SPLOSHED
SPLOSHES
SPLOSHING
SPLOTCH
SPLOTCHED
SPLOTCHES
SPLOTCHIER
SPLOTCHIEST
SPLOTCHING
SPLOTCHY
SPLURGE
SPLURGED
SPLURGES
SPLURGIER
SPLURGIEST
SPLURGING
SPLURGY
SPLUTTER
SPLUTTERED
SPLUTTERING
SPLUTTERINGS
SPLUTTERS
SPLUTTERY
SPODE
SPODES
SPODIUM
SPODIUMS
SPODOGRAM
SPODOGRAMS
SPODUMENE
SPODUMENES
SPOFFISH
SPOFFY
SPOIL
SPOILAGE
SPOILAGES
SPOILED
SPOILER
SPOILERS
SPOILFIVE
SPOILFIVES
SPOILFUL
SPOILING
SPOILS
SPOILSMAN
SPOILSMEN
SPOILT
SPOKE
SPOKED
SPOKEN
SPOKES
SPOKESMAN
SPOKESMEN
SPOKEWISE
SPOLIATE
SPOLIATED
SPOLIATES
SPOLIATING
SPOLIATOR
SPOLIATORS
SPONDAIC
SPONDEE
SPONDEES
SPONDULIX
SPONDYL
SPONDYLS
SPONGE
SPONGEBAG
SPONGEBAGS
SPONGED
SPONGEOUS
SPONGER
SPONGERS
SPONGES
SPONGIER
SPONGIEST
SPONGILY
SPONGIN
SPONGING
SPONGINS
SPONGIOSE
SPONGIOUS
SPONGOID
SPONGY
SPONSAL
SPONSALIA
SPONSIBLE
SPONSING
SPONSINGS
SPONSION
SPONSIONS
SPONSON
SPONSONS
SPONSOR
SPONSORED
SPONSORING
SPONSORS
SPONTOON
SPONTOONS
SPOOF
SPOOFED
SPOOFER
SPOOFERIES
SPOOFERS
SPOOFERY
SPOOFING
SPOOFS
SPOOK
SPOOKED
SPOOKERIES
SPOOKERY
SPOOKIER
SPOOKIEST
SPOOKILY
SPOOKING
SPOOKISH
SPOOKS
SPOOKY
SPOOL
SPOOLED
SPOOLER
SPOOLERS
SPOOLING
SPOOLS
SPOOM
SPOOMED
SPOOMING
SPOOMS
SPOON
SPOONBAIT
SPOONBAITS
SPOONBILL
SPOONBILLS
SPOONED
SPOONEY
SPOONEYS
SPOONFED
SPOONFUL
SPOONFULS
SPOONHOOK
SPOONHOOKS
SPOONIER
SPOONIES
SPOONIEST
SPOONILY
SPOONING
SPOONS
SPOONWAYS
SPOONWISE
SPOONY
SPOOR
SPOORED
SPOORER
SPOORERS
SPOORING
SPOORS
SPOOT
SPOOTS
SPORADIC
SPORANGIA
SPORE
SPORES
SPORIDESM
SPORIDESMS
SPORIDIA
SPORIDIAL
SPORIDIUM
SPOROCARP
SPOROCARPS
SPOROCYST
SPOROCYSTS
SPOROGENIES
SPOROGENY
SPOROPHYL
SPOROPHYLS
SPOROZOAN
SPOROZOANS
SPORRAN
SPORRANS
SPORT
SPORTABLE
SPORTANCE
SPORTANCES
SPORTED
SPORTER
SPORTERS
SPORTFUL
SPORTIER
SPORTIEST
SPORTILY
SPORTING
SPORTIVE
SPORTLESS
SPORTS
SPORTSMAN
SPORTSMEN
SPORTY
SPORULAR
SPORULATE
SPORULATED
SPORULATES
SPORULATING
SPORULE
SPORULES
SPOSH
SPOSHES
SPOSHIER
SPOSHIEST
SPOSHY
SPOT
SPOTLESS
SPOTLIGHT
SPOTLIGHTED
SPOTLIGHTING
SPOTLIGHTS
SPOTLIT
SPOTS
SPOTTED
SPOTTER
SPOTTERS
SPOTTIER
SPOTTIEST
SPOTTILY
SPOTTING
SPOTTINGS
SPOTTY
SPOUSAGE
SPOUSAGES
SPOUSAL
SPOUSALS
SPOUSE
SPOUSED
SPOUSES
SPOUSING
SPOUT
SPOUTED
SPOUTER
SPOUTERS
SPOUTIER
SPOUTIEST
SPOUTING
SPOUTINGS
SPOUTLESS
SPOUTS
SPOUTY
SPRACK
SPRACKLE
SPRACKLED
SPRACKLES
SPRACKLING
SPRAD
SPRAG
SPRAGGED
SPRAGGING
SPRAGS
SPRAICKLE
SPRAICKLED
SPRAICKLES
SPRAICKLING
SPRAID
SPRAIN
SPRAINED
SPRAINING
SPRAINS
SPRAINT
SPRAINTS
SPRANG
SPRANGLE
SPRANGLED
SPRANGLES
SPRANGLING
SPRAT
SPRATS
SPRATTLE
SPRATTLED
SPRATTLES
SPRATTLING
SPRAUCHLE
SPRAUCHLED
SPRAUCHLES
SPRAUCHLING
SPRAUNCIER

SPRAUNCIEST
SPRAUNCY
SPRAWL
SPRAWLED
SPRAWLER
SPRAWLERS
SPRAWLIER
SPRAWLIEST
SPRAWLING
SPRAWLS
SPRAWLY
SPRAY
SPRAYED
SPRAYER
SPRAYERS
SPRAYEY
SPRAYIER
SPRAYIEST
SPRAYING
SPRAYS
SPREAD
SPREADER
SPREADERS
SPREADING
SPREADINGS
SPREADS
SPREAGH
SPREAGHS
SPREATHE
SPREATHED
SPREATHES
SPREATHING
SPREAZE
SPREAZED
SPREAZES
SPREAZING
SPRECHERIES
SPRECHERY
SPRECKLED
SPRED
SPREDD
SPREDDE
SPREDDEN
SPREDDES
SPREDDING
SPREDDS
SPREDS
SPREE
SPREED
SPREEING
SPREES
SPREETHE
SPREETHED
SPREETHES
SPREETHING
SPREEZE
SPREEZED
SPREEZES
SPREEZING
SPRENT
SPREW
SPREWS
SPRIG
SPRIGGED
SPRIGGIER
SPRIGGIEST
SPRIGGING
SPRIGGY
SPRIGHT
SPRIGHTED
SPRIGHTING
SPRIGHTLIER
SPRIGHTLIEST
SPRIGHTLY
SPRIGHTS
SPRIGS
SPRING
SPRINGAL
SPRINGALD
SPRINGALDS
SPRINGALS
SPRINGBOK
SPRINGBOKS
SPRINGE
SPRINGED
SPRINGER
SPRINGERS
SPRINGES
SPRINGIER
SPRINGIEST
SPRINGILY
SPRINGING
SPRINGINGS
SPRINGLE
SPRINGLES
SPRINGLET
SPRINGLETS
SPRINGS
SPRINGY
SPRINKLE
SPRINKLED
SPRINKLER
SPRINKLERS
SPRINKLES
SPRINKLING
SPRINKLINGS
SPRINT
SPRINTED
SPRINTER
SPRINTERS
SPRINTING
SPRINTINGS
SPRINTS
SPRIT
SPRITE
SPRITEFUL
SPRITELIER
SPRITELIEST
SPRITELY
SPRITES
SPRITS
SPRITSAIL
SPRITSAILS
SPRITZ
SPRITZED
SPRITZER
SPRITZERS
SPRITZES
SPRITZIG
SPRITZIGS
SPRITZING
SPROCKET
SPROCKETS
SPROD
SPRODS
SPROG
SPROGS
SPRONG
SPROUT
SPROUTED
SPROUTING
SPROUTINGS
SPROUTS
SPRUCE
SPRUCED
SPRUCELY
SPRUCER
SPRUCES
SPRUCEST
SPRUCING
SPRUE
SPRUES
SPRUG
SPRUGS
SPRUIK
SPRUIKED
SPRUIKER
SPRUIKERS
SPRUIKING
SPRUIKS
SPRUIT
SPRUITS
SPRUNG
SPRUSH
SPRUSHED
SPRUSHES
SPRUSHING
SPRY
SPRYER
SPRYEST
SPRYLY
SPRYNESS
SPRYNESSES
SPUD
SPUDDED
SPUDDIER
SPUDDIEST
SPUDDING
SPUDDINGS
SPUDDY
SPUDS
SPUE
SPUED
SPUEING
SPUES
SPUILZIE
SPUILZIED
SPUILZIEING
SPUILZIES
SPUING
SPULE
SPULEBANE
SPULEBANES
SPULEBONE
SPULEBONES
SPULES
SPULYE
SPULYED
SPULYEING
SPULYES
SPULYIE
SPULYIED
SPULYIEING
SPULYIES
SPULZIE
SPULZIED
SPULZIEING
SPULZIES
SPUMANTE
SPUMANTES
SPUME
SPUMED
SPUMES
SPUMIER
SPUMIEST
SPUMING
SPUMOUS
SPUMY
SPUN
SPUNGE
SPUNGES
SPUNK
SPUNKED
SPUNKIE
SPUNKIER
SPUNKIES
SPUNKIEST
SPUNKING
SPUNKS
SPUNKY
SPUNYARN
SPUNYARNS
SPUR
SPURGE
SPURGES
SPURIAE
SPURIOUS
SPURLESS
SPURLING
SPURLINGS
SPURN
SPURNE
SPURNED
SPURNER
SPURNERS
SPURNES
SPURNING
SPURNINGS
SPURNS
SPURRED
SPURRER
SPURRERS
SPURREY
SPURREYS
SPURRIER
SPURRIERS
SPURRIES
SPURRIEST
SPURRING
SPURRINGS
SPURRY
SPURS
SPURT
SPURTED
SPURTING
SPURTLE
SPURTLES
SPURTS
SPURWAY
SPURWAYS
SPUTA
SPUTNIK
SPUTNIKS
SPUTTER
SPUTTERED
SPUTTERER
SPUTTERERS
SPUTTERING
SPUTTERINGS
SPUTTERS
SPUTTERY
SPUTUM
SPY
SPYAL
SPYALS
SPYGLASS
SPYGLASSES
SPYHOLE
SPYHOLES
SPYING
SPYINGS
SPYMASTER
SPYMASTERS
SPYPLANE
SPYPLANES
SPYRE
SPYRES
SQUAB
SQUABASH
SQUABASHED
SQUABASHES
SQUABASHING
SQUABBED
SQUABBER
SQUABBEST
SQUABBIER
SQUABBIEST
SQUABBING
SQUABBISH
SQUABBLE
SQUABBLED
SQUABBLER
SQUABBLERS
SQUABBLES
SQUABBLING
SQUABBY
SQUABS
SQUACCO
SQUACCOS
SQUAD

SQUADDIE
SQUADDIES
SQUADDY
SQUADRON
SQUADRONE
SQUADRONED
SQUADRONES
SQUADRONING
SQUADRONS
SQUADS
SQUAIL
SQUAILED
SQUAILER
SQUAILERS
SQUAILING
SQUAILINGS
SQUAILS
SQUALENE
SQUALENES
SQUALID
SQUALIDER
SQUALIDEST
SQUALIDLY
SQUALL
SQUALLED
SQUALLER
SQUALLERS
SQUALLIER
SQUALLIEST
SQUALLING
SQUALLINGS
SQUALLS
SQUALLY
SQUALOID
SQUALOR
SQUALORS
SQUAMA
SQUAMAE
SQUAMATE
SQUAME
SQUAMELLA
SQUAMELLAS
SQUAMES
SQUAMOSAL
SQUAMOSALS
SQUAMOSE
SQUAMOUS
SQUAMULA
SQUAMULAS
SQUAMULE
SQUAMULES
SQUANDER
SQUANDERED
SQUANDERING
SQUANDERINGS
SQUANDERS
SQUARE
SQUARED
SQUARELY
SQUARER
SQUARERS
SQUARES
SQUAREST
SQUARIAL
SQUARIALS
SQUARING
SQUARINGS
SQUARISH
SQUARROSE
SQUARSON
SQUARSONS
SQUASH
SQUASHED
SQUASHER
SQUASHERS
SQUASHES
SQUASHIER
SQUASHIEST
SQUASHILY
SQUASHING
SQUASHY
SQUAT
SQUATNESS
SQUATNESSES
SQUATS
SQUATTED
SQUATTER
SQUATTERED
SQUATTERING
SQUATTERS
SQUATTEST
SQUATTIER
SQUATTIEST
SQUATTING
SQUATTLE
SQUATTLED
SQUATTLES
SQUATTLING
SQUATTY
SQUAW
SQUAWK
SQUAWKED
SQUAWKER
SQUAWKERS
SQUAWKIER
SQUAWKIEST
SQUAWKING
SQUAWKINGS
SQUAWKS
SQUAWKY
SQUAWMAN
SQUAWMEN
SQUAWS
SQUEAK
SQUEAKED
SQUEAKER
SQUEAKERIES
SQUEAKERS
SQUEAKERY
SQUEAKIER
SQUEAKIEST
SQUEAKILY
SQUEAKING
SQUEAKINGS
SQUEAKS
SQUEAKY
SQUEAL
SQUEALED
SQUEALER
SQUEALERS
SQUEALING
SQUEALINGS
SQUEALS
SQUEAMISH
SQUEEGEE
SQUEEGEED
SQUEEGEEING
SQUEEGEES
SQUEEZE
SQUEEZED
SQUEEZER
SQUEEZERS
SQUEEZES
SQUEEZIER
SQUEEZIEST
SQUEEZING
SQUEEZINGS
SQUEEZY
SQUEG
SQUEGGED
SQUEGGER
SQUEGGERS
SQUEGGING
SQUEGGINGS
SQUEGS
SQUELCH
SQUELCHED
SQUELCHER
SQUELCHERS
SQUELCHES
SQUELCHIER
SQUELCHIEST
SQUELCHING
SQUELCHINGS
SQUELCHY
SQUIB
SQUIBBED
SQUIBBING
SQUIBBINGS
SQUIBS
SQUID
SQUIDDED
SQUIDDING
SQUIDGE
SQUIDGED
SQUIDGES
SQUIDGIER
SQUIDGIEST
SQUIDGING
SQUIDGY
SQUIDS
SQUIER
SQUIERS
SQUIFF
SQUIFFER
SQUIFFERS
SQUIFFIER
SQUIFFIEST
SQUIFFY
SQUIGGLE
SQUIGGLED
SQUIGGLES
SQUIGGLIER
SQUIGGLIEST
SQUIGGLING
SQUIGGLY
SQUILGEE
SQUILGEED
SQUILGEEING
SQUILGEES
SQUILL
SQUILLA
SQUILLAS
SQUILLS
SQUINANCIES
SQUINANCY
SQUINCH
SQUINCHES
SQUINIED
SQUINIES
SQUINNIED
SQUINNIES
SQUINNY
SQUINNYING
SQUINT
SQUINTED
SQUINTER
SQUINTERS
SQUINTEST
SQUINTING
SQUINTINGS
SQUINTS
SQUINY
SQUINYING
SQUIRAGE
SQUIRAGES
SQUIRALTIES
SQUIRALTY
SQUIRARCH
SQUIRARCHS
SQUIRE
SQUIREAGE
SQUIREAGES
SQUIRED
SQUIREDOM
SQUIREDOMS
SQUIREEN
SQUIREENS
SQUIRELY
SQUIRES
SQUIRESS
SQUIRESSES
SQUIRING
SQUIRM
SQUIRMED
SQUIRMIER
SQUIRMIEST
SQUIRMING
SQUIRMS
SQUIRMY
SQUIRR
SQUIRRED
SQUIRREL
SQUIRRELLED
SQUIRRELLING
SQUIRRELS
SQUIRRELY
SQUIRRING
SQUIRRS
SQUIRT
SQUIRTED
SQUIRTER
SQUIRTERS
SQUIRTING
SQUIRTINGS
SQUIRTS
SQUISH
SQUISHED
SQUISHES
SQUISHIER
SQUISHIEST
SQUISHING
SQUISHY
SQUIT
SQUITCH
SQUITCHES
SQUITS
SQUIZ
SQUIZZES
SRADDHA
SRADDHAS
ST
STAB
STABBED
STABBER
STABBERS
STABBING
STABBINGS
STABILATE
STABILATES
STABILE
STABILES
STABILISE
STABILISED
STABILISES
STABILISING
STABILITIES
STABILITY
STABILIZE
STABILIZED
STABILIZES
STABILIZING
STABLE
STABLEBOY
STABLEBOYS
STABLED
STABLEMAN
STABLEMEN
STABLER
STABLERS
STABLES
STABLEST
STABLING
STABLINGS
STABLISH
STABLISHED
STABLISHES
STABLISHING
STABLY
STABS

STACCATO
STACCATOS
STACHYS
STACHYSES
STACK
STACKED
STACKER
STACKERS
STACKET
STACKETS
STACKING
STACKINGS
STACKROOM
STACKROOMS
STACKS
STACKYARD
STACKYARDS
STACTE
STACTES
STADDA
STADDAS
STADDLE
STADDLES
STADE
STADES
STADIA
STADIAL
STADIALS
STADIAS
STADIUM
STADIUMS
STAFF
STAFFAGE
STAFFAGES
STAFFED
STAFFER
STAFFERS
STAFFING
STAFFROOM
STAFFROOMS
STAFFS
STAG
STAGE
STAGED
STAGER
STAGERIES
STAGERS
STAGERY
STAGES
STAGEY
STAGGARD
STAGGARDS
STAGGED
STAGGER
STAGGERED
STAGGERER
STAGGERERS
STAGGERING
STAGGERINGS
STAGGERS
STAGGING
STAGHOUND
STAGHOUNDS
STAGIER
STAGIEST
STAGILY
STAGINESS
STAGINESSES
STAGING
STAGINGS
STAGNANCIES
STAGNANCY
STAGNANT
STAGNATE
STAGNATED
STAGNATES
STAGNATING
STAGS
STAGY
STAID
STAIDER
STAIDEST
STAIDLY
STAIDNESS
STAIDNESSES
STAIG
STAIGS
STAIN
STAINED
STAINER
STAINERS
STAINING
STAININGS
STAINLESS
STAINS
STAIR
STAIRCASE
STAIRCASED
STAIRCASES
STAIRCASING
STAIRCASINGS
STAIRED
STAIRFOOT
STAIRFOOTS
STAIRHEAD
STAIRHEADS
STAIRLIFT
STAIRLIFTS
STAIRS
STAIRWAY
STAIRWAYS
STAIRWELL
STAIRWELLS
STAIRWISE
STAIRWORK
STAIRWORKS
STAITH
STAITHE
STAITHES
STAITHS
STAKE
STAKED
STAKES
STAKING
STALACTIC
STALAG
STALAGS
STALE
STALED
STALELY
STALEMATE
STALEMATED
STALEMATES
STALEMATING
STALENESS
STALENESSES
STALER
STALES
STALEST
STALING
STALK
STALKED
STALKER
STALKERS
STALKIER
STALKIEST
STALKING
STALKINGS
STALKLESS
STALKO
STALKOES
STALKS
STALKY
STALL
STALLAGE
STALLAGES
STALLED
STALLING
STALLINGS
STALLION
STALLIONS
STALLMAN
STALLMEN
STALLS
STALWART
STALWARTS
STALWORTH
STALWORTHS
STAMEN
STAMENED
STAMENS
STAMINA
STAMINAL
STAMINAS
STAMINATE
STAMINEAL
STAMINODE
STAMINODES
STAMINODIES
STAMINODY
STAMINOID
STAMMEL
STAMMELS
STAMMER
STAMMERED
STAMMERER
STAMMERERS
STAMMERING
STAMMERINGS
STAMMERS
STAMNOI
STAMNOS
STAMP
STAMPED
STAMPEDE
STAMPEDED
STAMPEDES
STAMPEDING
STAMPEDO
STAMPEDOED
STAMPEDOING
STAMPEDOS
STAMPER
STAMPERS
STAMPING
STAMPINGS
STAMPS
STANCE
STANCES
STANCH
STANCHED
STANCHEL
STANCHELLED
STANCHELLING
STANCHELS
STANCHER
STANCHERED
STANCHERING
STANCHERS
STANCHES
STANCHEST
STANCHING
STANCHINGS
STANCHION
STANCHIONED
STANCHIONING
STANCHIONS
STANCHLY
STANCK
STAND
STANDARD
STANDARDS
STANDEE
STANDEES
STANDEN
STANDER
STANDERS
STANDGALE
STANDGALES
STANDING
STANDINGS
STANDISH
STANDISHES
STANDOFF
STANDOUT
STANDOUTS
STANDPIPE
STANDPIPES
STANDS
STANE
STANED
STANES
STANG
STANGED
STANGING
STANGS
STANHOPE
STANHOPES
STANIEL
STANIELS
STANING
STANK
STANKS
STANNARIES
STANNARY
STANNATE
STANNATES
STANNATOR
STANNATORS
STANNEL
STANNELS
STANNIC
STANNITE
STANNITES
STANNOUS
STANYEL
STANYELS
STANZA
STANZAIC
STANZAS
STANZE
STANZES
STANZO
STANZOES
STANZOS
STAP
STAPEDES
STAPEDIAL
STAPEDII
STAPEDIUS
STAPEDIUSES
STAPELIA
STAPELIAS
STAPES
STAPH
STAPHS
STAPLE
STAPLED
STAPLER
STAPLERS
STAPLES
STAPLING
STAPPED
STAPPING
STAPPLE
STAPPLES
STAPS
STAR
STARAGEN
STARAGENS
STARBOARD
STARBOARDED
STARBOARDING
STARBOARDS
STARCH
STARCHED
STARCHER
STARCHERS
STARCHES
STARCHIER

STARCHIEST
STARCHILY
STARCHING
STARCHY
STARDOM
STARDOMS
STARDRIFT
STARDRIFTS
STARDUST
STARDUSTS
STARE
STARED
STARER
STARERS
STARES
STARETS
STARETSES
STARETZ
STARETZES
STARFISH
STARFISHES
STARGAZER
STARGAZERS
STARING
STARINGLY
STARINGS
STARK
STARKED
STARKEN
STARKENED
STARKENING
STARKENS
STARKER
STARKERS
STARKEST
STARKING
STARKLY
STARKNESS
STARKNESSES
STARKS
STARLESS
STARLET
STARLETS
STARLIGHT
STARLIGHTS
STARLIKE
STARLING
STARLINGS
STARLIT
STARN
STARNED
STARNIE
STARNIES
STARNING
STARNS
STAROSTA
STAROSTAS
STAROSTIES
STAROSTY
STARR
STARRED
STARRIER
STARRIEST
STARRILY
STARRING
STARRINGS
STARRS
STARRY
STARS
STARSHINE
STARSHINES
STARSPOT
STARSPOTS
STARSTONE
STARSTONES
START
STARTED
STARTER
STARTERS
STARTFUL
STARTING
STARTINGS
STARTISH
STARTLE
STARTLED
STARTLER
STARTLERS
STARTLES
STARTLING
STARTLINGS
STARTLISH
STARTLY
STARTS
STARVE
STARVED
STARVES
STARVING
STARVINGS
STARWORT
STARWORTS
STASES
STASH
STASHED
STASHES
STASHIE
STASHIES
STASHING
STASIDION
STASIDIONS
STASIMA
STASIMON
STASIS
STATABLE
STATAL
STATANT
STATE
STATED
STATEDLY
STATEHOOD
STATEHOODS
STATELESS
STATELIER
STATELIEST
STATELILY
STATELY
STATEMENT
STATEMENTED
STATEMENTING
STATEMENTINGS
STATEMENTS
STATER
STATEROOM
STATEROOMS
STATERS
STATES
STATESIDE
STATESMAN
STATESMEN
STATEWIDE
STATIC
STATICAL
STATICE
STATICES
STATICS
STATIM
STATING
STATION
STATIONAL
STATIONED
STATIONER
STATIONERS
STATIONING
STATIONS
STATISM
STATISMS
STATIST
STATISTIC
STATISTICS
STATISTS
STATIVE
STATOCYST
STATOCYSTS
STATOLITH
STATOLITHS
STATOR
STATORS
STATUA
STATUARIES
STATUARY
STATUAS
STATUE
STATUED
STATUES
STATUETTE
STATUETTES
STATURE
STATURED
STATURES
STATUS
STATUSES
STATUTE
STATUTES
STATUTORY
STAUNCH
STAUNCHED
STAUNCHER
STAUNCHERS
STAUNCHES
STAUNCHEST
STAUNCHING
STAUNCHINGS
STAUNCHLY
STAVE
STAVED
STAVES
STAVING
STAW
STAWED
STAWING
STAWS
STAY
STAYAWAY
STAYAWAYS
STAYED
STAYER
STAYERS
STAYING
STAYLESS
STAYMAKER
STAYMAKERS
STAYNE
STAYNED
STAYNES
STAYNING
STAYRE
STAYRES
STAYS
STAYSAIL
STAYSAILS
STEAD
STEADED
STEADFAST
STEADICAM®
STEADICAMS
STEADIED
STEADIER
STEADIES
STEADIEST
STEADILY
STEADING
STEADINGS
STEADS
STEADY
STEADYING
STEAK
STEAKS
STEAL
STEALE
STEALED
STEALER
STEALERS
STEALES
STEALING
STEALINGS
STEALS
STEALT
STEALTH
STEALTHED
STEALTHIER
STEALTHIEST
STEALTHING
STEALTHINGS
STEALTHS
STEALTHY
STEAM
STEAMBOAT
STEAMBOATS
STEAMED
STEAMER
STEAMERS
STEAMIE
STEAMIER
STEAMIES
STEAMIEST
STEAMILY
STEAMING
STEAMINGS
STEAMS
STEAMSHIP
STEAMSHIPS
STEAMY
STEAN
STEANE
STEANED
STEANES
STEANING
STEANINGS
STEANS
STEAPSIN
STEAPSINS
STEAR
STEARAGE
STEARAGES
STEARATE
STEARATES
STEARD
STEARE
STEARED
STEARES
STEARIC
STEARIN
STEARINE
STEARINES
STEARING
STEARINS
STEARS
STEARSMAN
STEARSMEN
STEATITE
STEATITES
STEATITIC
STEATOMA
STEATOMAS
STEATOSES
STEATOSIS
STED
STEDD
STEDDE
STEDDED
STEDDES
STEDDIED
STEDDIES
STEDDING
STEDDS
STEDDY
STEDDYING
STEDE
STEDED
STEDES
STEDFAST

STEDING
STEDS
STEED
STEEDED
STEEDIED
STEEDIES
STEEDING
STEEDS
STEEDY
STEEDYING
STEEK
STEEKING
STEEKIT
STEEKS
STEEL
STEELBOW
STEELBOWS
STEELD
STEELED
STEELIER
STEELIEST
STEELING
STEELINGS
STEELMAN
STEELMEN
STEELS
STEELWARE
STEELWARES
STEELWORK
STEELWORKS
STEELY
STEELYARD
STEELYARDS
STEEM
STEEMED
STEEMING
STEEMS
STEEN
STEENBOK
STEENBOKS
STEENBRAS
STEENBRASES
STEENED
STEENING
STEENINGS
STEENKIRK
STEENKIRKS
STEENS
STEEP
STEEPED
STEEPEN
STEEPENED
STEEPENING
STEEPENS
STEEPER
STEEPERS
STEEPEST
STEEPEUP
STEEPIER
STEEPIEST
STEEPING
STEEPISH
STEEPLE
STEEPLED
STEEPLES
STEEPLY
STEEPNESS
STEEPNESSES
STEEPS
STEEPUP
STEEPY
STEER
STEERABLE
STEERAGE
STEERAGES
STEERED
STEERER
STEERERS
STEERIES
STEERING
STEERINGS
STEERLING
STEERLINGS
STEERS
STEERSMAN
STEERSMEN
STEERY
STEEVE
STEEVED
STEEVELY
STEEVER
STEEVES
STEEVEST
STEEVING
STEEVINGS
STEGNOSES
STEGNOSIS
STEGNOTIC
STEGODON
STEGODONS
STEGODONT
STEGODONTS
STEGOSAUR
STEGOSAURS
STEIL
STEILS
STEIN
STEINBOCK
STEINBOCKS
STEINED
STEINING
STEININGS
STEINKIRK
STEINKIRKS
STEINS
STELA
STELAE
STELAR
STELE
STELENE
STELES
STELL
STELLAR
STELLATE
STELLATED
STELLED
STELLERID
STELLERIDS
STELLIFIED
STELLIFIES
STELLIFY
STELLIFYING
STELLIFYINGS
STELLING
STELLION
STELLIONS
STELLS
STELLULAR
STEM
STEMBOK
STEMBOKS
STEMBUCK
STEMBUCKS
STEME
STEMED
STEMES
STEMING
STEMLESS
STEMLET
STEMLETS
STEMMA
STEMMATA
STEMME
STEMMED
STEMMER
STEMMERS
STEMMES
STEMMING
STEMMINGS
STEMPEL
STEMPELS
STEMPLE
STEMPLES
STEMS
STEMSON
STEMSONS
STEN
STENCH
STENCHED
STENCHES
STENCHIER
STENCHIEST
STENCHING
STENCHY
STENCIL
STENCILED
STENCILING
STENCILLED
STENCILLING
STENCILLINGS
STENCILS
STEND
STENDED
STENDING
STENDS
STENGAH
STENGAHS
STENLOCK
STENLOCKS
STENNED
STENNING
STENOPAIC
STENOSED
STENOSES
STENOSIS
STENOTIC
STENOTYPIES
STENOTYPY
STENS
STENT
STENTED
STENTING
STENTOR
STENTORS
STENTOUR
STENTOURS
STENTS
STEP
STEPBAIRN
STEPBAIRNS
STEPCHILD
STEPCHILDREN
STEPDAME
STEPDAMES
STEPHANE
STEPHANES
STEPNEY
STEPNEYS
STEPPE
STEPPED
STEPPER
STEPPERS
STEPPES
STEPPING
STEPS
STEPSON
STEPSONS
STEPT
STEPWISE
STERADIAN
STERADIANS
STERCORAL
STERCULIA
STERCULIAS
STERE
STEREO
STEREOME
STEREOMES
STEREOS
STERES
STERIC
STERIGMA
STERIGMATA
STERILANT
STERILANTS
STERILE
STERILISE
STERILISED
STERILISES
STERILISING
STERILITIES
STERILITY
STERILIZE
STERILIZED
STERILIZES
STERILIZING
STERLET
STERLETS
STERLING
STERLINGS
STERN
STERNA
STERNAGE
STERNAGES
STERNAL
STERNEBRA
STERNEBRAE
STERNED
STERNER
STERNEST
STERNFAST
STERNFASTS
STERNING
STERNITE
STERNITES
STERNITIC
STERNLY
STERNMOST
STERNNESS
STERNNESSES
STERNPORT
STERNPORTS
STERNPOST
STERNPOSTS
STERNS
STERNSON
STERNSONS
STERNUM
STERNUMS
STERNWARD
STERNWARDS
STERNWAY
STERNWAYS
STEROID
STEROIDS
STEROL
STEROLS
STERVE
STERVED
STERVES
STERVING
STET
STETS
STETTED
STETTING
STEVEDORE
STEVEDORED
STEVEDORES
STEVEDORING
STEVEN
STEVENS
STEW
STEWARD
STEWARDRIES
STEWARDRY
STEWARDS
STEWARTRIES
STEWARTRY
STEWED
STEWER

STEWERS
STEWIER
STEWIEST
STEWING
STEWINGS
STEWPAN
STEWPANS
STEWPOND
STEWPONDS
STEWPOT
STEWPOTS
STEWS
STEWY
STEY
STEYER
STEYEST
STHENIC
STIBBLE
STIBBLER
STIBBLERS
STIBBLES
STIBIAL
STIBINE
STIBINES
STIBIUM
STIBIUMS
STIBNITE
STIBNITES
STICCADO
STICCADOES
STICCADOS
STICCATO
STICCATOES
STICCATOS
STICH
STICHARIA
STICHERA
STICHERON
STICHIC
STICHIDIA
STICHOI
STICHOS
STICHS
STICK
STICKED
STICKER
STICKERED
STICKERING
STICKERS
STICKFUL
STICKFULS
STICKIED
STICKIER
STICKIES
STICKIEST
STICKILY
STICKING
STICKINGS
STICKIT
STICKJAW
STICKJAWS
STICKLE
STICKLED
STICKLER
STICKLERS
STICKLES
STICKLING
STICKS
STICKWORK
STICKWORKS
STICKY
STICKYING
STICTION
STICTIONS
STIDDIE
STIDDIED
STIDDIEING
STIDDIES
STIDDYING
STIE
STIED
STIES
STIEVE
STIEVELY
STIEVER
STIEVEST
STIFF
STIFFED
STIFFEN
STIFFENED
STIFFENER
STIFFENERS
STIFFENING
STIFFENINGS
STIFFENS
STIFFER
STIFFEST
STIFFIE
STIFFIES
STIFFING
STIFFISH
STIFFLY
STIFFNESS
STIFFNESSES
STIFFS
STIFFWARE
STIFFWARES
STIFFY
STIFLE
STIFLED
STIFLER
STIFLERS
STIFLES
STIFLING
STIFLINGS
STIGMA
STIGMAS
STIGMATA
STIGMATIC
STIGMATICS
STIGME
STIGMES
STILB
STILBENE
STILBENES
STILBITE
STILBITES
STILBS
STILE
STILED
STILES
STILET
STILETS
STILETTO
STILETTOED
STILETTOING
STILETTOS
STILING
STILL
STILLAGE
STILLAGES
STILLBORN
STILLED
STILLER
STILLERS
STILLEST
STILLIER
STILLIEST
STILLING
STILLINGS
STILLION
STILLIONS
STILLNESS
STILLNESSES
STILLROOM
STILLROOMS
STILLS
STILLY
STILT
STILTBIRD
STILTBIRDS
STILTED
STILTEDLY
STILTER
STILTERS
STILTIER
STILTIEST
STILTING
STILTINGS
STILTISH
STILTS
STILTY
STIME
STIMED
STIMES
STIMIE
STIMIED
STIMIES
STIMING
STIMULANT
STIMULANTS
STIMULATE
STIMULATED
STIMULATES
STIMULATING
STIMULI
STIMULUS
STIMY
STIMYING
STING
STINGAREE
STINGAREES
STINGBULL
STINGBULLS
STINGED
STINGER
STINGERS
STINGFISH
STINGFISHES
STINGIER
STINGIEST
STINGILY
STINGING
STINGINGS
STINGLESS
STINGO
STINGOS
STINGS
STINGY
STINK
STINKARD
STINKARDS
STINKER
STINKERS
STINKHORN
STINKHORNS
STINKING
STINKINGS
STINKO
STINKS
STINKWOOD
STINKWOODS
STINT
STINTED
STINTEDLY
STINTER
STINTERS
STINTIER
STINTIEST
STINTING
STINTINGS
STINTLESS
STINTS
STINTY
STIPA
STIPAS
STIPE
STIPEL
STIPELS
STIPEND
STIPENDS
STIPES
STIPITATE
STIPITES
STIPPLE
STIPPLED
STIPPLER
STIPPLERS
STIPPLES
STIPPLING
STIPPLINGS
STIPULAR
STIPULARY
STIPULATE
STIPULATED
STIPULATES
STIPULATING
STIPULE
STIPULED
STIPULES
STIR
STIRABOUT
STIRABOUTS
STIRE
STIRED
STIRES
STIRING
STIRK
STIRKS
STIRLESS
STIRP
STIRPES
STIRPS
STIRRA
STIRRAH
STIRRAHS
STIRRAS
STIRRE
STIRRED
STIRRER
STIRRERS
STIRRES
STIRRING
STIRRINGS
STIRRUP
STIRRUPS
STIRS
STISHIE
STISHIES
STITCH
STITCHED
STITCHER
STITCHERIES
STITCHERS
STITCHERY
STITCHES
STITCHING
STITCHINGS
STITHIED
STITHIES
STITHY
STITHYING
STIVE
STIVED
STIVER
STIVERS
STIVES
STIVIER
STIVIEST
STIVING
STIVY
STOA
STOAE
STOAI
STOAS
STOAT
STOATS
STOB
STOBS
STOCCADO

STOCCADOS
STOCCATA
STOCCATAS
STOCIOUS
STOCK
STOCKADE
STOCKADED
STOCKADES
STOCKADING
STOCKED
STOCKER
STOCKERS
STOCKFISH
STOCKFISHES
STOCKHORN
STOCKHORNS
STOCKIER
STOCKIEST
STOCKILY
STOCKINET
STOCKINETS
STOCKING
STOCKINGS
STOCKIST
STOCKISTS
STOCKLESS
STOCKLIST
STOCKLISTS
STOCKLOCK
STOCKLOCKS
STOCKMAN
STOCKMEN
STOCKPILE
STOCKPILED
STOCKPILES
STOCKPILING
STOCKPILINGS
STOCKPOT
STOCKPOTS
STOCKROOM
STOCKROOMS
STOCKS
STOCKTAKE
STOCKTAKEN
STOCKTAKES
STOCKTAKING
STOCKTAKINGS
STOCKTOOK
STOCKWORK
STOCKWORKS
STOCKY
STOCKYARD
STOCKYARDS
STODGE
STODGED
STODGER
STODGERS
STODGES
STODGIER
STODGIEST
STODGILY
STODGING
STODGY
STOEP
STOEPS
STOGEY
STOGEYS
STOGIE
STOGIES
STOGY
STOIC
STOICAL
STOICALLY
STOICISM
STOICISMS
STOICS
STOIT
STOITED
STOITER
STOITERED
STOITERING
STOITERS
STOITING
STOITS
STOKE
STOKED
STOKEHOLD
STOKEHOLDS
STOKEHOLE
STOKEHOLES
STOKER
STOKERS
STOKES
STOKING
STOLE
STOLED
STOLEN
STOLES
STOLID
STOLIDER
STOLIDEST
STOLIDITIES
STOLIDITY
STOLIDLY
STOLLEN
STOLLENS
STOLN
STOLON
STOLONS
STOMA
STOMACH
STOMACHAL
STOMACHED
STOMACHER
STOMACHERS
STOMACHIC
STOMACHICS
STOMACHING
STOMACHS
STOMACHY
STOMAL
STOMATA
STOMATAL
STOMATIC
STOMODAEA
STOMODEA
STOMODEUM
STOMODEUMS
STOMP
STOMPED
STOMPER
STOMPERS
STOMPING
STOMPS
STOND
STONDS
STONE
STONEBOAT
STONEBOATS
STONECAST
STONECASTS
STONECHAT
STONECHATS
STONECROP
STONECROPS
STONED
STONEFISH
STONEFISHES
STONEFLIES
STONEFLY
STONEHAND
STONEHANDS
STONELESS
STONEN
STONER
STONERAG
STONERAGS
STONERAW
STONERAWS
STONERN
STONERS
STONES
STONESHOT
STONESHOTS
STONEWALL
STONEWALLED
STONEWALLING
STONEWALLINGS
STONEWALLS
STONEWARE
STONEWARES
STONEWORK
STONEWORKS
STONEWORT
STONEWORTS
STONG
STONIED
STONIER
STONIES
STONIEST
STONILY
STONINESS
STONINESSES
STONING
STONINGS
STONK
STONKER
STONKERED
STONKERING
STONKERS
STONKING
STONKS
STONN
STONNE
STONNED
STONNES
STONNING
STONNS
STONY
STONYING
STOOD
STOODEN
STOOGE
STOOGED
STOOGES
STOOGING
STOOK
STOOKED
STOOKER
STOOKERS
STOOKING
STOOKS
STOOL
STOOLBALL
STOOLBALLS
STOOLED
STOOLIE
STOOLIES
STOOLING
STOOLS
STOOP
STOOPE
STOOPED
STOOPER
STOOPERS
STOOPES
STOOPING
STOOPS
STOOR
STOORS
STOOSHIE
STOOSHIES
STOP
STOPBANK
STOPBANKS
STOPCOCK
STOPCOCKS
STOPE
STOPED
STOPES
STOPGAP
STOPGAPS
STOPING
STOPINGS
STOPLESS
STOPLIGHT
STOPLIGHTS
STOPOFF
STOPOFFS
STOPOVER
STOPOVERS
STOPPAGE
STOPPAGES
STOPPED
STOPPER
STOPPERED
STOPPERING
STOPPERS
STOPPING
STOPPINGS
STOPPLE
STOPPLED
STOPPLES
STOPPLING
STOPS
STOPWATCH
STOPWATCHES
STORABLE
STORAGE
STORAGES
STORAX
STORAXES
STORE
STORED
STOREMAN
STOREMEN
STORER
STOREROOM
STOREROOMS
STORERS
STORES
STOREY
STOREYED
STOREYS
STORGE
STORGES
STORIATED
STORIED
STORIES
STORIETTE
STORIETTES
STORING
STORK
STORKS
STORM
STORMBIRD
STORMBIRDS
STORMED
STORMFUL
STORMIER
STORMIEST
STORMILY
STORMING
STORMINGS
STORMLESS
STORMS
STORMY
STORNELLI
STORNELLO
STORY
STORYBOOK
STORYBOOKS
STORYETTE
STORYETTES
STORYING
STORYINGS
STORYLINE
STORYLINES
STOSS
STOSSES

STOT
STOTINKA
STOTINKI
STOTIOUS
STOTS
STOTTED
STOTTER
STOTTERS
STOTTING
STOUN
STOUND
STOUNDED
STOUNDING
STOUNDS
STOUNING
STOUNS
STOUP
STOUPS
STOUR
STOURIER
STOURIEST
STOURS
STOURY
STOUSH
STOUSHED
STOUSHES
STOUSHING
STOUT
STOUTEN
STOUTENED
STOUTENING
STOUTENS
STOUTER
STOUTEST
STOUTH
STOUTHRIE
STOUTHRIES
STOUTHS
STOUTISH
STOUTLY
STOUTNESS
STOUTNESSES
STOUTS
STOVAINE
STOVAINES
STOVE
STOVED
STOVEPIPE
STOVEPIPES
STOVER
STOVERS
STOVES
STOVIES
STOVING
STOVINGS
STOW
STOWAGE
STOWAGES
STOWAWAY
STOWAWAYS
STOWDOWN
STOWDOWNS
STOWED
STOWER
STOWERS
STOWING
STOWINGS
STOWLINS
STOWN
STOWND
STOWNDED
STOWNDING
STOWNDS
STOWNLINS
STOWRE
STOWRES
STOWS
STRABISM
STRABISMS
STRAD
STRADDLE
STRADDLED
STRADDLES
STRADDLING
STRADIOT
STRADIOTS
STRADS
STRAE
STRAES
STRAFE
STRAFED
STRAFES
STRAFF
STRAFFED
STRAFFING
STRAFFS
STRAFING
STRAG
STRAGGLE
STRAGGLED
STRAGGLER
STRAGGLERS
STRAGGLES
STRAGGLIER
STRAGGLIEST
STRAGGLING
STRAGGLINGS
STRAGGLY
STRAGS
STRAICHT
STRAICHTER
STRAICHTEST
STRAIGHT
STRAIGHTER
STRAIGHTEST
STRAIGHTS
STRAIK
STRAIKED
STRAIKING
STRAIKS
STRAIN
STRAINED
STRAINER
STRAINERS
STRAINING
STRAININGS
STRAINS
STRAINT
STRAINTS
STRAIT
STRAITED
STRAITEN
STRAITENED
STRAITENING
STRAITENS
STRAITER
STRAITEST
STRAITING
STRAITLY
STRAITS
STRAKE
STRAKES
STRAMACON
STRAMACONS
STRAMASH
STRAMASHED
STRAMASHES
STRAMASHING
STRAMAZON
STRAMAZONS
STRAMMEL
STRAMMELS
STRAMP
STRAMPED
STRAMPING
STRAMPS
STRAND
STRANDED
STRANDING
STRANDS
STRANGE
STRANGELY
STRANGER
STRANGERED
STRANGERING
STRANGERS
STRANGEST
STRANGLE
STRANGLED
STRANGLER
STRANGLERS
STRANGLES
STRANGLING
STRANGURIES
STRANGURY
STRAP
STRAPLESS
STRAPLINE
STRAPLINES
STRAPPADO
STRAPPADOED
STRAPPADOING
STRAPPADOS
STRAPPED
STRAPPER
STRAPPERS
STRAPPIER
STRAPPIEST
STRAPPING
STRAPPINGS
STRAPPY
STRAPS
STRAPWORT
STRAPWORTS
STRASS
STRASSES
STRATA
STRATAGEM
STRATAGEMS
STRATEGIC
STRATEGICS
STRATEGIES
STRATEGY
STRATH
STRATHS
STRATI
STRATIFIED
STRATIFIES
STRATIFY
STRATIFYING
STRATONIC
STRATOSE
STRATOUS
STRATUM
STRATUS
STRAUCHT
STRAUCHTED
STRAUCHTER
STRAUCHTEST
STRAUCHTING
STRAUCHTS
STRAUGHT
STRAUGHTED
STRAUGHTER
STRAUGHTEST
STRAUGHTING
STRAUGHTS
STRAUNGE
STRAVAIG
STRAVAIGED
STRAVAIGING
STRAVAIGS
STRAW
STRAWED
STRAWEN
STRAWIER
STRAWIEST
STRAWING
STRAWLESS
STRAWLIKE
STRAWN
STRAWS
STRAWWORM
STRAWWORMS
STRAWY
STRAY
STRAYED
STRAYER
STRAYERS
STRAYING
STRAYINGS
STRAYLING
STRAYLINGS
STRAYS
STREAK
STREAKED
STREAKER
STREAKERS
STREAKIER
STREAKIEST
STREAKILY
STREAKING
STREAKINGS
STREAKS
STREAKY
STREAM
STREAMED
STREAMER
STREAMERS
STREAMIER
STREAMIEST
STREAMING
STREAMINGS
STREAMLET
STREAMLETS
STREAMS
STREAMY
STREEK
STREEKED
STREEKING
STREEKS
STREEL
STREELED
STREELING
STREELS
STREET
STREETAGE
STREETAGES
STREETBOY
STREETBOYS
STREETCAR
STREETCARS
STREETED
STREETFUL
STREETFULS
STREETIER
STREETIEST
STREETS
STREETY
STREIGHT
STREIGHTS
STREIGNE
STREIGNED
STREIGNES
STREIGNING
STRELITZ
STRELITZES
STRELITZI
STRENE
STRENES
STRENGTH
STRENGTHS
STRENUITIES
STRENUITY
STRENUOUS
STREP
STREPENT
STREPS
STRESS
STRESSED

STRESSES
STRESSFUL
STRESSING
STRESSOR
STRESSORS
STRETCH
STRETCHED
STRETCHER
STRETCHERED
STRETCHERING
STRETCHERS
STRETCHES
STRETCHIER
STRETCHIEST
STRETCHING
STRETCHY
STRETTA
STRETTE
STRETTI
STRETTO
STREW
STREWAGE
STREWAGES
STREWED
STREWER
STREWERS
STREWING
STREWINGS
STREWMENT
STREWMENTS
STREWN
STREWS
STREWTH
STRIA
STRIAE
STRIATA
STRIATE
STRIATED
STRIATES
STRIATING
STRIATION
STRIATIONS
STRIATUM
STRIATUMS
STRIATURE
STRIATURES
STRICH
STRICHES
STRICKEN
STRICKLE
STRICKLED
STRICKLES
STRICKLING
STRICT
STRICTER
STRICTEST
STRICTISH
STRICTLY
STRICTURE
STRICTURES
STRIDDEN
STRIDDLE
STRIDDLED
STRIDDLES
STRIDDLING
STRIDE
STRIDENCE
STRIDENCES
STRIDENCIES
STRIDENCY
STRIDENT
STRIDES
STRIDING
STRIDLING
STRIDOR
STRIDORS
STRIFE
STRIFEFUL
STRIFES
STRIFT
STRIFTS
STRIG
STRIGA
STRIGAE
STRIGATE
STRIGGED
STRIGGING
STRIGIL
STRIGILS
STRIGINE
STRIGOSE
STRIGS
STRIKE
STRIKEOUT
STRIKEOUTS
STRIKER
STRIKERS
STRIKES
STRIKING
STRIKINGS
STRING
STRINGED
STRINGENT
STRINGER
STRINGERS
STRINGIER
STRINGIEST
STRINGILY
STRINGING
STRINGINGS
STRINGS
STRINGY
STRINKLE
STRINKLED
STRINKLES
STRINKLING
STRINKLINGS
STRIP
STRIPE
STRIPED
STRIPES
STRIPEY
STRIPIER
STRIPIEST
STRIPING
STRIPINGS
STRIPLING
STRIPLINGS
STRIPPED
STRIPPER
STRIPPERS
STRIPPING
STRIPPINGS
STRIPS
STRIPY
STRIVE
STRIVED
STRIVEN
STRIVER
STRIVERS
STRIVES
STRIVING
STRIVINGS
STROAM
STROAMED
STROAMING
STROAMS
STROBE
STROBED
STROBES
STROBIC
STROBILA
STROBILAE
STROBILE
STROBILES
STROBILI
STROBILUS
STROBING
STROBINGS
STRODDLE
STRODDLED
STRODDLES
STRODDLING
STRODE
STRODLE
STRODLED
STRODLES
STRODLING
STROKE
STROKED
STROKEN
STROKER
STROKERS
STROKES
STROKING
STROKINGS
STROLL
STROLLED
STROLLER
STROLLERS
STROLLING
STROLLINGS
STROLLS
STROMA
STROMATA
STROMATIC
STROMB
STROMBS
STROMBUS
STROMBUSES
STROND
STRONDS
STRONG
STRONGARM
STRONGARMED
STRONGARMING
STRONGARMS
STRONGBOX
STRONGBOXES
STRONGER
STRONGEST
STRONGISH
STRONGLY
STRONGMAN
STRONGMEN
STRONGYL
STRONGYLE
STRONGYLES
STRONGYLS
STRONTIA
STRONTIAN
STRONTIANS
STRONTIAS
STRONTIUM
STRONTIUMS
STROOK
STROOKE
STROOKEN
STROOKES
STROP
STROPHE
STROPHES
STROPHIC
STROPPED
STROPPIER
STROPPIEST
STROPPING
STROPPY
STROPS
STROSSERS
STROUD
STROUDING
STROUDINGS
STROUDS
STROUP
STROUPACH
STROUPACHS
STROUPAN
STROUPANS
STROUPS
STROUT
STROUTED
STROUTING
STROUTS
STROVE
STROW
STROWED
STROWER
STROWERS
STROWING
STROWINGS
STROWN
STROWS
STROY
STROYED
STROYING
STROYS
STRUCK
STRUCTURE
STRUCTURED
STRUCTURES
STRUCTURING
STRUDEL
STRUDELS
STRUGGLE
STRUGGLED
STRUGGLER
STRUGGLERS
STRUGGLES
STRUGGLING
STRUGGLINGS
STRUM
STRUMA
STRUMAE
STRUMATIC
STRUMITIS
STRUMITISES
STRUMMED
STRUMMEL
STRUMMELS
STRUMMING
STRUMOSE
STRUMOUS
STRUMPET
STRUMPETED
STRUMPETING
STRUMPETS
STRUMS
STRUNG
STRUNT
STRUNTED
STRUNTING
STRUNTS
STRUT
STRUTS
STRUTTED
STRUTTER
STRUTTERS
STRUTTING
STRUTTINGS
STRYCHNIA
STRYCHNIAS
STRYCHNIC
STUB
STUBBED
STUBBIER
STUBBIES
STUBBIEST
STUBBING
STUBBLE
STUBBLED
STUBBLES
STUBBLIER
STUBBLIEST
STUBBLY
STUBBORN
STUBBORNED
STUBBORNER
STUBBORNEST
STUBBORNING

STUBBORNS
STUBBY
STUBS
STUCCO
STUCCOED
STUCCOER
STUCCOERS
STUCCOING
STUCCOS
STUCK
STUCKS
STUD
STUDBOOK
STUDBOOKS
STUDDED
STUDDEN
STUDDING
STUDDINGS
STUDDLE
STUDDLES
STUDENT
STUDENTRIES
STUDENTRY
STUDENTS
STUDFARM
STUDFARMS
STUDIED
STUDIEDLY
STUDIER
STUDIERS
STUDIES
STUDIO
STUDIOS
STUDIOUS
STUDS
STUDWORK
STUDWORKS
STUDY
STUDYING
STUFF
STUFFED
STUFFER
STUFFERS
STUFFIER
STUFFIEST
STUFFILY
STUFFING
STUFFINGS
STUFFS
STUFFY
STUGGIER
STUGGIEST
STUGGY
STULL
STULLS
STULM
STULMS
STULTIFIED
STULTIFIES
STULTIFY
STULTIFYING
STUM
STUMBLE
STUMBLED
STUMBLER
STUMBLERS
STUMBLES
STUMBLIER
STUMBLIEST
STUMBLING
STUMBLY
STUMER
STUMERS
STUMM
STUMMED
STUMMEL
STUMMELS
STUMMING
STUMP
STUMPAGE
STUMPAGES
STUMPED
STUMPER
STUMPERS
STUMPIER
STUMPIES
STUMPIEST
STUMPILY
STUMPING
STUMPS
STUMPY
STUMS
STUN
STUNG
STUNK
STUNKARD
STUNNED
STUNNER
STUNNERS
STUNNING
STUNNINGS
STUNS
STUNSAIL
STUNSAILS
STUNT
STUNTED
STUNTING
STUNTMAN
STUNTMEN
STUNTS
STUPA
STUPAS
STUPE
STUPED
STUPEFIED
STUPEFIER
STUPEFIERS
STUPEFIES
STUPEFY
STUPEFYING
STUPENT
STUPES
STUPID
STUPIDER
STUPIDEST
STUPIDITIES
STUPIDITY
STUPIDLY
STUPIDS
STUPING
STUPOR
STUPOROUS
STUPORS
STUPRATE
STUPRATED
STUPRATES
STUPRATING
STURDIED
STURDIER
STURDIES
STURDIEST
STURDILY
STURDY
STURE
STURGEON
STURGEONS
STURMER
STURMERS
STURNINE
STURNOID
STURNUS
STURNUSES
STURT
STURTED
STURTING
STURTS
STUSHIE
STUSHIES
STUTTER
STUTTERED
STUTTERER
STUTTERERS
STUTTERING
STUTTERINGS
STUTTERS
STY
STYE
STYED
STYES
STYING
STYLAR
STYLATE
STYLE
STYLEBOOK
STYLEBOOKS
STYLED
STYLELESS
STYLES
STYLET
STYLETS
STYLI
STYLIFORM
STYLING
STYLISE
STYLISED
STYLISES
STYLISH
STYLISHLY
STYLISING
STYLIST
STYLISTIC
STYLISTICS
STYLISTS
STYLITE
STYLITES
STYLIZE
STYLIZED
STYLIZES
STYLIZING
STYLO
STYLOBATE
STYLOBATES
STYLOID
STYLOIDS
STYLOLITE
STYLOLITES
STYLOS
STYLUS
STYLUSES
STYME
STYMED
STYMES
STYMIE
STYMIED
STYMIEING
STYMIES
STYMING
STYPSIS
STYPSISES
STYPTIC
STYPTICAL
STYPTICS
STYRAX
STYRAXES
STYRE
STYRED
STYRENE
STYRENES
STYRES
STYRING
STYROFOAM
STYROFOAMS
STYTE
STYTED
STYTES
STYTING
SUABILITIES
SUABILITY
SUABLE
SUABLY
SUASIBLE
SUASION
SUASIONS
SUASIVE
SUASIVELY
SUASORY
SUAVE
SUAVELY
SUAVER
SUAVEST
SUAVITIES
SUAVITY
SUB
SUBABBOT
SUBABBOTS
SUBACID
SUBACIDLY
SUBACRID
SUBACT
SUBACTED
SUBACTING
SUBACTION
SUBACTIONS
SUBACTS
SUBACUTE
SUBADAR
SUBADARS
SUBADULT
SUBADULTS
SUBAERIAL
SUBAGENCIES
SUBAGENCY
SUBAGENT
SUBAGENTS
SUBAH
SUBAHDAR
SUBAHDARIES
SUBAHDARS
SUBAHDARY
SUBAHS
SUBAHSHIP
SUBAHSHIPS
SUBALPINE
SUBALTERN
SUBALTERNS
SUBAPICAL
SUBAQUA
SUBARCTIC
SUBAREA
SUBAREAS
SUBARID
SUBASTRAL
SUBATOM
SUBATOMIC
SUBATOMICS
SUBATOMS
SUBAUDIO
SUBAURAL
SUBBASAL
SUBBASE
SUBBASES
SUBBED
SUBBIE
SUBBIES
SUBBING
SUBBINGS
SUBBRANCH
SUBBRANCHES
SUBBREED
SUBBREEDS
SUBBUREAU
SUBBUREAUS
SUBBUREAUX
SUBBY
SUBCANTOR
SUBCANTORS
SUBCASTE
SUBCASTES
SUBCAUDAL
SUBCAVITIES

SUBCAVITY
SUBCELLAR
SUBCELLARS
SUBCHIEF
SUBCHIEFS
SUBCHORD
SUBCHORDS
SUBCLAIM
SUBCLAIMS
SUBCLASS
SUBCLASSES
SUBCLAUSE
SUBCLAUSES
SUBCLIMAX
SUBCLIMAXES
SUBCOOL
SUBCORTEX
SUBCORTEXES
SUBCORTICES
SUBCOSTA
SUBCOSTAE
SUBCOSTAL
SUBCOSTALS
SUBCRUST
SUBCRUSTS
SUBDEACON
SUBDEACONS
SUBDEAN
SUBDEANS
SUBDERMAL
SUBDEW
SUBDEWED
SUBDEWING
SUBDEWS
SUBDIVIDE
SUBDIVIDED
SUBDIVIDES
SUBDIVIDING
SUBDOLOUS
SUBDORSAL
SUBDUABLE
SUBDUAL
SUBDUALS
SUBDUCE
SUBDUCED
SUBDUCES
SUBDUCING
SUBDUCT
SUBDUCTED
SUBDUCTING
SUBDUCTS
SUBDUE
SUBDUED
SUBDUEDLY
SUBDUER
SUBDUERS
SUBDUES
SUBDUING
SUBDUPLE
SUBDURAL
SUBEDAR
SUBEDARS
SUBEDIT
SUBEDITED
SUBEDITING
SUBEDITOR
SUBEDITORS
SUBEDITS
SUBENTIRE
SUBEQUAL
SUBER
SUBERATE
SUBERATES
SUBERECT
SUBEREOUS
SUBERIC
SUBERIN
SUBERINS
SUBERISE
SUBERISED
SUBERISES
SUBERISING
SUBERIZE
SUBERIZED
SUBERIZES
SUBERIZING
SUBEROSE
SUBEROUS
SUBERS
SUBFAMILIES
SUBFAMILY
SUBFEU
SUBFEUED
SUBFEUING
SUBFEUS
SUBFIELD
SUBFIELDS
SUBFLOOR
SUBFLOORS
SUBFRAME
SUBFRAMES
SUBFUSC
SUBFUSCS
SUBFUSK
SUBFUSKS
SUBGENERA
SUBGENRE
SUBGENRES
SUBGENUS
SUBGENUSES
SUBGOAL
SUBGOALS
SUBGRADE
SUBGRADES
SUBGROUP
SUBGROUPS
SUBGUM
SUBGUMS
SUBHEAD
SUBHEADS
SUBHEDRAL
SUBHUMAN
SUBHUMID
SUBIMAGINES
SUBIMAGO
SUBIMAGOS
SUBINCISE
SUBINCISED
SUBINCISES
SUBINCISING
SUBITISE
SUBITISED
SUBITISES
SUBITISING
SUBITIZE
SUBITIZED
SUBITIZES
SUBITIZING
SUBITO
SUBJACENT
SUBJECT
SUBJECTED
SUBJECTING
SUBJECTS
SUBJOIN
SUBJOINED
SUBJOINING
SUBJOINS
SUBJUGATE
SUBJUGATED
SUBJUGATES
SUBJUGATING
SUBLATE
SUBLATED
SUBLATES
SUBLATING
SUBLATION
SUBLATIONS
SUBLEASE
SUBLEASED
SUBLEASES
SUBLEASING
SUBLESSEE
SUBLESSEES
SUBLESSOR
SUBLESSORS
SUBLET
SUBLETHAL
SUBLETS
SUBLETTER
SUBLETTERS
SUBLETTING
SUBLETTINGS
SUBLIMATE
SUBLIMATED
SUBLIMATES
SUBLIMATING
SUBLIME
SUBLIMED
SUBLIMELY
SUBLIMER
SUBLIMES
SUBLIMEST
SUBLIMING
SUBLIMINGS
SUBLIMISE
SUBLIMISED
SUBLIMISES
SUBLIMISING
SUBLIMITIES
SUBLIMITY
SUBLIMIZE
SUBLIMIZED
SUBLIMIZES
SUBLIMIZING
SUBLINEAR
SUBLUNAR
SUBLUNARY
SUBLUNATE
SUBMAN
SUBMARINE
SUBMARINED
SUBMARINES
SUBMARINING
SUBMATRICES
SUBMATRIX
SUBMATRIXES
SUBMEN
SUBMENTA
SUBMENTAL
SUBMENTUM
SUBMERGE
SUBMERGED
SUBMERGES
SUBMERGING
SUBMERSE
SUBMERSED
SUBMERSES
SUBMERSING
SUBMICRON
SUBMICRONS
SUBMISS
SUBMISSLY
SUBMIT
SUBMITS
SUBMITTED
SUBMITTER
SUBMITTERS
SUBMITTING
SUBMITTINGS
SUBMUCOSA
SUBMUCOSAE
SUBMUCOUS
SUBNEURAL
SUBNIVEAL
SUBNIVEAN
SUBNORMAL
SUBNORMALS
SUBOCTAVE
SUBOCTAVES
SUBOCULAR
SUBOFFICE
SUBOFFICES
SUBORDER
SUBORDERS
SUBORN
SUBORNED
SUBORNER
SUBORNERS
SUBORNING
SUBORNS
SUBOVATE
SUBOXIDE
SUBOXIDES
SUBPHYLA
SUBPHYLUM
SUBPLOT
SUBPLOTS
SUBPOENA
SUBPOENAED
SUBPOENAING
SUBPOENAS
SUBPOLAR
SUBPOTENT
SUBPRIOR
SUBPRIORS
SUBREGION
SUBREGIONS
SUBRING
SUBRINGS
SUBROGATE
SUBROGATED
SUBROGATES
SUBROGATING
SUBS
SUBSACRAL
SUBSAMPLE
SUBSAMPLED
SUBSAMPLES
SUBSAMPLING
SUBSCHEMA
SUBSCHEMATA
SUBSCRIBE
SUBSCRIBED
SUBSCRIBES
SUBSCRIBING
SUBSCRIBINGS
SUBSCRIPT
SUBSCRIPTS
SUBSEA
SUBSECIVE
SUBSELLIA
SUBSERE
SUBSERES
SUBSERIES
SUBSERVE
SUBSERVED
SUBSERVES
SUBSERVING
SUBSET
SUBSETS
SUBSHRUB
SUBSHRUBS
SUBSIDE
SUBSIDED
SUBSIDES
SUBSIDIES
SUBSIDING
SUBSIDISE
SUBSIDISED
SUBSIDISES
SUBSIDISING
SUBSIDIZE
SUBSIDIZED
SUBSIDIZES
SUBSIDIZING
SUBSIDY
SUBSIST
SUBSISTED
SUBSISTING

SUBSISTS
SUBSIZAR
SUBSIZARS
SUBSOIL
SUBSOILED
SUBSOILER
SUBSOILERS
SUBSOILING
SUBSOILINGS
SUBSOILS
SUBSOLAR
SUBSONG
SUBSONGS
SUBSONIC
SUBSTAGE
SUBSTAGES
SUBSTANCE
SUBSTANCES
SUBSTATE
SUBSTATES
SUBSTRACT
SUBSTRACTED
SUBSTRACTING
SUBSTRACTS
SUBSTRATA
SUBSTRATE
SUBSTRATES
SUBSTRUCT
SUBSTRUCTED
SUBSTRUCTING
SUBSTRUCTS
SUBSTYLAR
SUBSTYLE
SUBSTYLES
SUBSULTUS
SUBSULTUSES
SUBSUME
SUBSUMED
SUBSUMES
SUBSUMING
SUBSYSTEM
SUBSYSTEMS
SUBTACK
SUBTACKS
SUBTEEN
SUBTEENS
SUBTENANT
SUBTENANTS
SUBTEND
SUBTENDED
SUBTENDING
SUBTENDS
SUBTENSE
SUBTENSES
SUBTENURE
SUBTENURES
SUBTEXT
SUBTEXTS
SUBTIDAL
SUBTIL
SUBTILE
SUBTILER
SUBTILEST
SUBTILISE
SUBTILISED
SUBTILISES
SUBTILISING
SUBTILIZE
SUBTILIZED
SUBTILIZES
SUBTILIZING
SUBTITLE
SUBTITLED
SUBTITLES
SUBTITLING
SUBTLE
SUBTLER
SUBTLEST
SUBTLETIES
SUBTLETY
SUBTLY
SUBTONIC
SUBTONICS
SUBTOPIA
SUBTOPIAN
SUBTOPIAS
SUBTORRID
SUBTOTAL
SUBTOTALLED
SUBTOTALLING
SUBTOTALS
SUBTRACT
SUBTRACTED
SUBTRACTING
SUBTRACTS
SUBTRIBE
SUBTRIBES
SUBTRIST
SUBTROPIC
SUBTROPICS
SUBTRUDE
SUBTRUDED
SUBTRUDES
SUBTRUDING
SUBTYPE
SUBTYPES
SUBUCULA
SUBUCULAS
SUBULATE
SUBUNIT
SUBUNITS
SUBURB
SUBURBAN
SUBURBANS
SUBURBIA
SUBURBIAS
SUBURBS
SUBURSINE
SUBVASSAL
SUBVASSALS
SUBVERSAL
SUBVERSALS
SUBVERSE
SUBVERSED
SUBVERSES
SUBVERSING
SUBVERST
SUBVERT
SUBVERTED
SUBVERTER
SUBVERTERS
SUBVERTING
SUBVERTS
SUBVIRAL
SUBVOCAL
SUBWARDEN
SUBWARDENS
SUBWAY
SUBWAYS
SUBWOOFER
SUBWOOFERS
SUBZERO
SUBZONAL
SUBZONE
SUBZONES
SUCCADE
SUCCADES
SUCCAH
SUCCAHS
SUCCEED
SUCCEEDED
SUCCEEDER
SUCCEEDERS
SUCCEEDING
SUCCEEDS
SUCCENTOR
SUCCENTORS
SUCCES
SUCCESS
SUCCESSES
SUCCESSOR
SUCCESSORS
SUCCI
SUCCINATE
SUCCINATES
SUCCINCT
SUCCINCTER
SUCCINCTEST
SUCCINIC
SUCCINITE
SUCCINITES
SUCCINYL
SUCCINYLS
SUCCISE
SUCCOR
SUCCORED
SUCCORIES
SUCCORING
SUCCORS
SUCCORY
SUCCOS
SUCCOSE
SUCCOT
SUCCOTASH
SUCCOTASHES
SUCCOTH
SUCCOUR
SUCCOURED
SUCCOURER
SUCCOURERS
SUCCOURING
SUCCOURS
SUCCOUS
SUCCUBA
SUCCUBAE
SUCCUBAS
SUCCUBI
SUCCUBINE
SUCCUBOUS
SUCCUBUS
SUCCUBUSES
SUCCULENT
SUCCULENTS
SUCCUMB
SUCCUMBED
SUCCUMBING
SUCCUMBS
SUCCURSAL
SUCCURSALS
SUCCUS
SUCCUSS
SUCCUSSED
SUCCUSSES
SUCCUSSING
SUCH
SUCHLIKE
SUCHNESS
SUCHNESSES
SUCHWISE
SUCK
SUCKED
SUCKEN
SUCKENER
SUCKENERS
SUCKENS
SUCKER
SUCKERED
SUCKERING
SUCKERS
SUCKET
SUCKETS
SUCKING
SUCKINGS
SUCKLE
SUCKLED
SUCKLER
SUCKLERS
SUCKLES
SUCKLING
SUCKLINGS
SUCKS
SUCRASE
SUCRASES
SUCRE
SUCRES
SUCRIER
SUCRIERS
SUCROSE
SUCROSES
SUCTION
SUCTIONS
SUCTORIAL
SUCTORIAN
SUCTORIANS
SUCURUJU
SUCURUJUS
SUD
SUDAMEN
SUDAMINA
SUDAMINAL
SUDARIA
SUDARIES
SUDARIUM
SUDARY
SUDATE
SUDATED
SUDATES
SUDATING
SUDATION
SUDATIONS
SUDATORIA
SUDATORIES
SUDATORY
SUDD
SUDDEN
SUDDENLY
SUDDENTIES
SUDDENTY
SUDDER
SUDDERS
SUDDS
SUDOR
SUDORAL
SUDORIFIC
SUDORIFICS
SUDOROUS
SUDORS
SUDS
SUDSED
SUDSER
SUDSERS
SUDSES
SUDSIER
SUDSIEST
SUDSING
SUDSY
SUE
SUEABLE
SUED
SUEDE
SUEDED
SUEDES
SUEDETTE
SUEDETTES
SUEDING
SUER
SUERS
SUES
SUET
SUETIER
SUETIEST
SUETS
SUETTIER
SUETTIEST
SUETTY
SUETY
SUFFECT
SUFFER
SUFFERED
SUFFERER

SUFFERERS
SUFFERING
SUFFERINGS
SUFFERS
SUFFETE
SUFFETES
SUFFICE
SUFFICED
SUFFICER
SUFFICERS
SUFFICES
SUFFICING
SUFFIX
SUFFIXAL
SUFFIXED
SUFFIXES
SUFFIXING
SUFFIXION
SUFFIXIONS
SUFFLATE
SUFFLATED
SUFFLATES
SUFFLATING
SUFFOCATE
SUFFOCATED
SUFFOCATES
SUFFOCATING
SUFFOCATINGS
SUFFRAGAN
SUFFRAGANS
SUFFRAGE
SUFFRAGES
SUFFUSE
SUFFUSED
SUFFUSES
SUFFUSING
SUFFUSION
SUFFUSIONS
SUFFUSIVE
SUGAR
SUGARALLIES
SUGARALLY
SUGARCANE
SUGARCANES
SUGARED
SUGARIER
SUGARIEST
SUGARING
SUGARINGS
SUGARLESS
SUGARLOAF
SUGARLOAVES
SUGARPLUM
SUGARPLUMS
SUGARS
SUGARY
SUGGEST
SUGGESTED
SUGGESTER
SUGGESTERS
SUGGESTING
SUGGESTS
SUGGING
SUGGINGS
SUI
SUICIDAL
SUICIDE
SUICIDES
SUID
SUIDIAN
SUIDIANS
SUIDS
SUILLINE
SUING
SUINGS
SUINT
SUINTS
SUIT
SUITABLE
SUITABLY
SUITCASE
SUITCASES
SUITE
SUITED
SUITES
SUITING
SUITINGS
SUITOR
SUITORED
SUITORING
SUITORS
SUITRESS
SUITRESSES
SUITS
SUIVANTE
SUIVANTES
SUIVEZ
SUJEE
SUJEES
SUK
SUKH
SUKHS
SUKIYAKI
SUKIYAKIS
SUKKAH
SUKKAHS
SUKKOS
SUKKOT
SUKKOTH
SUKS
SULCAL
SULCALISE
SULCALISED
SULCALISES
SULCALISING
SULCALIZE
SULCALIZED
SULCALIZES
SULCALIZING
SULCATE
SULCATED
SULCATION
SULCATIONS
SULCI
SULCUS
SULFA
SULFAS
SULFATASE
SULFATASES
SULFATE
SULFATED
SULFATES
SULFATIC
SULFATING
SULFATION
SULFATIONS
SULFIDE
SULFIDES
SULFINYL
SULFINYLS
SULFITE
SULFITES
SULFONATE
SULFONATED
SULFONATES
SULFONATING
SULFONE
SULFONES
SULFONIUM
SULFONIUMS
SULFUR
SULFURATE
SULFURATED
SULFURATES
SULFURATING
SULFURED
SULFURIC
SULFURING
SULFURS
SULK
SULKED
SULKIER
SULKIES
SULKIEST
SULKILY
SULKINESS
SULKINESSES
SULKING
SULKS
SULKY
SULLAGE
SULLAGES
SULLEN
SULLENER
SULLENEST
SULLENLY
SULLIED
SULLIES
SULLY
SULLYING
SULPHA
SULPHAS
SULPHATE
SULPHATED
SULPHATES
SULPHATIC
SULPHATING
SULPHIDE
SULPHIDES
SULPHINYL
SULPHINYLS
SULPHITE
SULPHITES
SULPHONE
SULPHONES
SULPHUR
SULPHURED
SULPHURET
SULPHURETED
SULPHURETING
SULPHURETS
SULPHURETTED
SULPHURETTING
SULPHURIC
SULPHURING
SULPHURS
SULPHURY
SULTAN
SULTANA
SULTANAS
SULTANATE
SULTANATES
SULTANESS
SULTANESSES
SULTANIC
SULTANS
SULTRIER
SULTRIEST
SULTRILY
SULTRY
SULU
SULUS
SUM
SUMAC
SUMACH
SUMACHS
SUMACS
SUMATRA
SUMATRAS
SUMLESS
SUMMA
SUMMAE
SUMMAND
SUMMANDS
SUMMAR
SUMMARIES
SUMMARILY
SUMMARISE
SUMMARISED
SUMMARISES
SUMMARISING
SUMMARIST
SUMMARISTS
SUMMARIZE
SUMMARIZED
SUMMARIZES
SUMMARIZING
SUMMARY
SUMMAT
SUMMATE
SUMMATED
SUMMATES
SUMMATING
SUMMATION
SUMMATIONS
SUMMATIVE
SUMMATS
SUMMED
SUMMER
SUMMERED
SUMMERIER
SUMMERIEST
SUMMERING
SUMMERINGS
SUMMERLY
SUMMERS
SUMMERSET
SUMMERSETS
SUMMERSETTED
SUMMERSETTING
SUMMERY
SUMMING
SUMMINGS
SUMMIST
SUMMISTS
SUMMIT
SUMMITAL
SUMMITEER
SUMMITEERS
SUMMITRIES
SUMMITRY
SUMMITS
SUMMON
SUMMONED
SUMMONER
SUMMONERS
SUMMONING
SUMMONS
SUMMONSED
SUMMONSES
SUMMONSING
SUMO
SUMOS
SUMOTORI
SUMOTORIS
SUMP
SUMPH
SUMPHISH
SUMPHS
SUMPIT
SUMPITAN
SUMPITANS
SUMPITS
SUMPS
SUMPSIMUS
SUMPSIMUSES
SUMPTER
SUMPTERS
SUMPTUARY
SUMPTUOUS
SUMS
SUN
SUNBAKE
SUNBAKED
SUNBAKES
SUNBAKING
SUNBATH
SUNBATHE
SUNBATHED
SUNBATHER

SUNBATHERS
SUNBATHES
SUNBATHING
SUNBATHINGS
SUNBATHS
SUNBEAM
SUNBEAMED
SUNBEAMS
SUNBEAMY
SUNBEAT
SUNBEATEN
SUNBED
SUNBEDS
SUNBELT
SUNBELTS
SUNBERRIES
SUNBERRY
SUNBIRD
SUNBIRDS
SUNBLIND
SUNBLINDS
SUNBLOCK
SUNBLOCKS
SUNBOW
SUNBOWS
SUNBRIGHT
SUNBURN
SUNBURNED
SUNBURNING
SUNBURNS
SUNBURNT
SUNBURST
SUNBURSTS
SUNDAE
SUNDAES
SUNDARI
SUNDARIS
SUNDECK
SUNDECKS
SUNDER
SUNDERED
SUNDERER
SUNDERERS
SUNDERING
SUNDERINGS
SUNDERS
SUNDEW
SUNDEWS
SUNDIAL
SUNDIALS
SUNDOG
SUNDOGS
SUNDOWN
SUNDOWNER
SUNDOWNERS
SUNDOWNS
SUNDRA
SUNDRAS
SUNDRESS
SUNDRESSES
SUNDRI
SUNDRIES
SUNDRIS
SUNDROPS
SUNDRY
SUNFAST
SUNFISH
SUNFISHES
SUNFLOWER
SUNFLOWERS
SUNG
SUNGAR
SUNGARS
SUNGLASS
SUNGLASSES
SUNGLOW
SUNGLOWS
SUNHAT
SUNHATS
SUNK
SUNKEN
SUNKET
SUNKETS
SUNKIE
SUNKIES
SUNKS
SUNLAMP
SUNLAMPS
SUNLESS
SUNLIGHT
SUNLIGHTS
SUNLIKE
SUNLIT
SUNN
SUNNED
SUNNIER
SUNNIEST
SUNNILY
SUNNINESS
SUNNINESSES
SUNNING
SUNNS
SUNNY
SUNPROOF
SUNRAY
SUNRAYS
SUNRISE
SUNRISES
SUNRISING
SUNRISINGS
SUNROOF
SUNROOFS
SUNS
SUNSCREEN
SUNSCREENS
SUNSET
SUNSETS
SUNSHADE
SUNSHADES
SUNSHINE
SUNSHINES
SUNSHINY
SUNSPOT
SUNSPOTS
SUNSTONE
SUNSTONES
SUNSTROKE
SUNSTROKES
SUNSTRUCK
SUNSUIT
SUNSUITS
SUNTAN
SUNTANNED
SUNTANS
SUNTRAP
SUNTRAPS
SUNUP
SUNUPS
SUNWARD
SUNWARDS
SUNWISE
SUP
SUPAWN
SUPAWNS
SUPE
SUPER
SUPERABLE
SUPERABLY
SUPERADD
SUPERADDED
SUPERADDING
SUPERADDS
SUPERATE
SUPERATED
SUPERATES
SUPERATING
SUPERB
SUPERBER
SUPERBEST
SUPERBITIES
SUPERBITY
SUPERBLY
SUPERBOLD
SUPERBRAT
SUPERBRATS
SUPERBUG
SUPERBUGS
SUPERCOIL
SUPERCOILS
SUPERCOLD
SUPERCOOL
SUPERCOOLED
SUPERCOOLING
SUPERCOOLS
SUPEREGO
SUPEREGOS
SUPERETTE
SUPERETTES
SUPERFAST
SUPERFINE
SUPERFIT
SUPERFLUX
SUPERFLUXES
SUPERFUSE
SUPERFUSED
SUPERFUSES
SUPERFUSING
SUPERGENE
SUPERGENES
SUPERGLUE
SUPERGLUED
SUPERGLUES
SUPERGLUING
SUPERGUN
SUPERGUNS
SUPERHEAT
SUPERHEATED
SUPERHEATING
SUPERHEATS
SUPERHERO
SUPERHEROES
SUPERHIVE
SUPERHIVES
SUPERIOR
SUPERIORS
SUPERJET
SUPERJETS
SUPERLOO
SUPERLOOS
SUPERMAN
SUPERMART
SUPERMARTS
SUPERMEN
SUPERMINI
SUPERMINIS
SUPERNAL
SUPERNOVA
SUPERNOVAE
SUPERNOVAS
SUPERPLUS
SUPERPLUSES
SUPERPOSE
SUPERPOSED
SUPERPOSES
SUPERPOSING
SUPERRICH
SUPERS
SUPERSAFE
SUPERSALT
SUPERSALTS
SUPERSEDE
SUPERSEDED
SUPERSEDES
SUPERSEDING
SUPERSELL
SUPERSELLS
SUPERSOFT
SUPERSPIES
SUPERSPY
SUPERSTAR
SUPERSTARS
SUPERTAX
SUPERTAXES
SUPERTHIN
SUPERVENE
SUPERVENED
SUPERVENES
SUPERVENING
SUPERVISE
SUPERVISED
SUPERVISES
SUPERVISING
SUPERWAIF
SUPERWAIFS
SUPES
SUPINATE
SUPINATED
SUPINATES
SUPINATING
SUPINATOR
SUPINATORS
SUPINE
SUPINELY
SUPINES
SUPPAWN
SUPPAWNS
SUPPEAGO
SUPPEAGOES
SUPPED
SUPPER
SUPPERED
SUPPERING
SUPPERS
SUPPING
SUPPLANT
SUPPLANTED
SUPPLANTING
SUPPLANTS
SUPPLE
SUPPLED
SUPPLELY
SUPPLER
SUPPLES
SUPPLEST
SUPPLIAL
SUPPLIALS
SUPPLIANT
SUPPLIANTS
SUPPLICAT
SUPPLICATS
SUPPLIED
SUPPLIER
SUPPLIERS
SUPPLIES
SUPPLING
SUPPLY
SUPPLYING
SUPPORT
SUPPORTED
SUPPORTER
SUPPORTERS
SUPPORTING
SUPPORTINGS
SUPPORTS
SUPPOSAL
SUPPOSALS
SUPPOSE
SUPPOSED
SUPPOSER
SUPPOSERS
SUPPOSES
SUPPOSING
SUPPOSINGS
SUPPRESS
SUPPRESSED
SUPPRESSES
SUPPRESSING
SUPPURATE
SUPPURATED
SUPPURATES

SUPPURATING
SUPREMACIES
SUPREMACY
SUPREME
SUPREMELY
SUPREMER
SUPREMES
SUPREMEST
SUPREMITIES
SUPREMITY
SUPREMO
SUPREMOS
SUPS
SUQ
SUQS
SUR
SURA
SURAH
SURAHS
SURAL
SURAMIN
SURAMINS
SURANCE
SURANCES
SURAS
SURAT
SURATS
SURBAHAR
SURBAHARS
SURBASE
SURBASED
SURBASES
SURBATE
SURBATED
SURBATES
SURBATING
SURBED
SURBEDDED
SURBEDDING
SURBEDS
SURBET
SURCEASE
SURCEASED
SURCEASES
SURCEASING
SURCHARGE
SURCHARGED
SURCHARGES
SURCHARGING
SURCINGLE
SURCINGLED
SURCINGLES
SURCINGLING
SURCOAT
SURCOATS
SURCULI
SURCULOSE
SURCULUS
SURCULUSES
SURD
SURDITIES
SURDITY
SURDS
SURE
SURED
SURELY
SURENESS
SURENESSES
SURER
SURES
SUREST
SURETIED
SURETIES
SURETY
SURETYING
SURF
SURFACE
SURFACED
SURFACER
SURFACERS
SURFACES
SURFACING
SURFACINGS
SURFBIRD
SURFBIRDS
SURFBOARD
SURFBOARDS
SURFED
SURFEIT
SURFEITED
SURFEITER
SURFEITERS
SURFEITING
SURFEITINGS
SURFEITS
SURFER
SURFERS
SURFFISH
SURFFISHES
SURFICIAL
SURFIE
SURFIER
SURFIES
SURFIEST
SURFING
SURFINGS
SURFMAN
SURFMEN
SURFPERCH
SURFPERCHES
SURFS
SURFY
SURGE
SURGED
SURGEFUL
SURGELESS
SURGENT
SURGEON
SURGEONCIES
SURGEONCY
SURGEONS
SURGERIES
SURGERY
SURGES
SURGICAL
SURGIER
SURGIEST
SURGING
SURGINGS
SURGY
SURICATE
SURICATES
SURING
SURLIER
SURLIEST
SURLILY
SURLINESS
SURLINESSES
SURLOIN
SURLOINS
SURLY
SURMASTER
SURMASTERS
SURMISAL
SURMISALS
SURMISE
SURMISED
SURMISER
SURMISERS
SURMISES
SURMISING
SURMISINGS
SURMOUNT
SURMOUNTED
SURMOUNTING
SURMOUNTINGS
SURMOUNTS
SURMULLET
SURMULLETS
SURNAME
SURNAMED
SURNAMES
SURNAMING
SURPASS
SURPASSED
SURPASSES
SURPASSING
SURPLICE
SURPLICED
SURPLICES
SURPLUS
SURPLUSES
SURPRISAL
SURPRISALS
SURPRISE
SURPRISED
SURPRISER
SURPRISERS
SURPRISES
SURPRISING
SURPRISINGS
SURQUEDIES
SURQUEDRIES
SURQUEDRY
SURQUEDY
SURRA
SURRAS
SURREAL
SURREBUT
SURREBUTS
SURREBUTTED
SURREBUTTING
SURREINED
SURREJOIN
SURREJOINED
SURREJOINING
SURREJOINS
SURRENDER
SURRENDERED
SURRENDERING
SURRENDERS
SURRENDRIES
SURRENDRY
SURREY
SURREYS
SURROGACIES
SURROGACY
SURROGATE
SURROGATES
SURROUND
SURROUNDED
SURROUNDING
SURROUNDINGS
SURROUNDS
SURROYAL
SURROYALS
SURTAX
SURTAXED
SURTAXES
SURTAXING
SURTITLE
SURTITLES
SURTOUT
SURTOUTS
SURUCUCU
SURUCUCUS
SURVEILLE
SURVEILLED
SURVEILLES
SURVEILLING
SURVEW
SURVEWE
SURVEWED
SURVEWES
SURVEWING
SURVEWS
SURVEY
SURVEYAL
SURVEYALS
SURVEYED
SURVEYING
SURVEYINGS
SURVEYOR
SURVEYORS
SURVEYS
SURVIEW
SURVIEWED
SURVIEWING
SURVIEWS
SURVIVAL
SURVIVALS
SURVIVE
SURVIVED
SURVIVES
SURVIVING
SURVIVOR
SURVIVORS
SUS
SUSCEPTOR
SUSCEPTORS
SUSCITATE
SUSCITATED
SUSCITATES
SUSCITATING
SUSES
SUSHI
SUSHIS
SUSLIK
SUSLIKS
SUSPECT
SUSPECTED
SUSPECTING
SUSPECTS
SUSPENCE
SUSPEND
SUSPENDED
SUSPENDER
SUSPENDERS
SUSPENDING
SUSPENDS
SUSPENS
SUSPENSE
SUSPENSER
SUSPENSERS
SUSPENSES
SUSPENSOR
SUSPENSORS
SUSPICION
SUSPICIONED
SUSPICIONING
SUSPICIONS
SUSPIRE
SUSPIRED
SUSPIRES
SUSPIRING
SUSS
SUSSARARA
SUSSARARAS
SUSSED
SUSSES
SUSSING
SUSTAIN
SUSTAINED
SUSTAINER
SUSTAINERS
SUSTAINING
SUSTAININGS
SUSTAINS
SUSTINENT
SUSURRANT
SUSURRATE
SUSURRATED
SUSURRATES
SUSURRATING
SUSURRUS
SUSURRUSES
SUTILE
SUTLER
SUTLERIES
SUTLERS

SUTLERY
SUTOR
SUTORIAL
SUTORIAN
SUTORS
SUTRA
SUTRAS
SUTTEE
SUTTEEISM
SUTTEEISMS
SUTTEES
SUTTLE
SUTTLED
SUTTLES
SUTTLETIE
SUTTLETIES
SUTTLING
SUTTLY
SUTURAL
SUTURALLY
SUTURE
SUTURED
SUTURES
SUTURING
SUVERSED
SUZERAIN
SUZERAINS
SVASTIKA
SVASTIKAS
SVELTE
SVELTER
SVELTEST
SWAB
SWABBED
SWABBER
SWABBERS
SWABBIES
SWABBING
SWABBY
SWABS
SWACK
SWAD
SWADDIES
SWADDLE
SWADDLED
SWADDLER
SWADDLERS
SWADDLES
SWADDLING
SWADDY
SWADS
SWAG
SWAGE
SWAGED
SWAGES
SWAGGED
SWAGGER
SWAGGERED
SWAGGERER
SWAGGERERS
SWAGGERING
SWAGGERINGS
SWAGGERS
SWAGGIE
SWAGGIES
SWAGGING
SWAGING
SWAGMAN
SWAGMEN
SWAGS
SWAGSHOP
SWAGSHOPS
SWAGSMAN
SWAGSMEN
SWAIN
SWAINING
SWAININGS
SWAINISH
SWAINS
SWALE
SWALED
SWALES
SWALIER
SWALIEST
SWALING
SWALINGS
SWALLET
SWALLETS
SWALLOW
SWALLOWED
SWALLOWER
SWALLOWERS
SWALLOWING
SWALLOWS
SWALY
SWAM
SWAMI
SWAMIS
SWAMP
SWAMPED
SWAMPER
SWAMPERS
SWAMPIER
SWAMPIEST
SWAMPING
SWAMPLAND
SWAMPLANDS
SWAMPS
SWAMPY
SWAN
SWANG
SWANHERD
SWANHERDS
SWANK
SWANKED
SWANKER
SWANKERS
SWANKEST
SWANKEY
SWANKEYS
SWANKIE
SWANKIER
SWANKIES
SWANKIEST
SWANKING
SWANKPOT
SWANKPOTS
SWANKS
SWANKY
SWANLIKE
SWANNED
SWANNERIES
SWANNERY
SWANNIER
SWANNIEST
SWANNING
SWANNINGS
SWANNY
SWANS
SWANSDOWN
SWANSDOWNS
SWANSKIN
SWANSKINS
SWAP
SWAPPED
SWAPPER
SWAPPERS
SWAPPING
SWAPPINGS
SWAPS
SWAPT
SWAPTION
SWAPTIONS
SWARAJ
SWARAJES
SWARAJISM
SWARAJISMS
SWARAJIST
SWARAJISTS
SWARD
SWARDED
SWARDIER
SWARDIEST
SWARDING
SWARDS
SWARDY
SWARE
SWARF
SWARFED
SWARFING
SWARFS
SWARM
SWARMED
SWARMER
SWARMERS
SWARMING
SWARMINGS
SWARMS
SWART
SWARTH
SWARTHIER
SWARTHIEST
SWARTHS
SWARTHY
SWARTNESS
SWARTNESSES
SWARTY
SWARVE
SWARVED
SWARVES
SWARVING
SWASH
SWASHED
SWASHER
SWASHERS
SWASHES
SWASHIER
SWASHIEST
SWASHING
SWASHINGS
SWASHWORK
SWASHWORKS
SWASHY
SWASTIKA
SWASTIKAS
SWAT
SWATCH
SWATCHES
SWATH
SWATHE
SWATHED
SWATHES
SWATHIER
SWATHIEST
SWATHING
SWATHS
SWATHY
SWATS
SWATTED
SWATTER
SWATTERED
SWATTERING
SWATTERS
SWATTING
SWATTINGS
SWAY
SWAYBACK
SWAYBACKS
SWAYED
SWAYER
SWAYERS
SWAYING
SWAYINGS
SWAYL
SWAYLED
SWAYLING
SWAYLINGS
SWAYLS
SWAYS
SWAZZLE
SWAZZLES
SWEAL
SWEALED
SWEALING
SWEALINGS
SWEALS
SWEAR
SWEARD
SWEARDS
SWEARER
SWEARERS
SWEARING
SWEARINGS
SWEARS
SWEAT
SWEATED
SWEATER
SWEATERS
SWEATIER
SWEATIEST
SWEATING
SWEATINGS
SWEATS
SWEATSUIT
SWEATSUITS
SWEATY
SWEDE
SWEDES
SWEE
SWEED
SWEEING
SWEEL
SWEELED
SWEELING
SWEELS
SWEENEY
SWEENEYS
SWEENIES
SWEENY
SWEEP
SWEEPBACK
SWEEPBACKS
SWEEPER
SWEEPERS
SWEEPIER
SWEEPIEST
SWEEPING
SWEEPINGS
SWEEPS
SWEEPY
SWEER
SWEERED
SWEERT
SWEES
SWEET
SWEETCORN
SWEETCORNS
SWEETED
SWEETEN
SWEETENED
SWEETENER
SWEETENERS
SWEETENING
SWEETENINGS
SWEETENS
SWEETER
SWEETEST
SWEETFISH
SWEETFISHES
SWEETIE
SWEETIES
SWEETING
SWEETINGS
SWEETISH
SWEETLY
SWEETMEAL
SWEETMEAT
SWEETMEATS
SWEETNESS
SWEETNESSES

SWEETPEA
SWEETPEAS
SWEETS
SWEETSOP
SWEETSOPS
SWEETWOOD
SWEETWOODS
SWEETY
SWEIR
SWEIRNESS
SWEIRNESSES
SWEIRT
SWELCHIE
SWELCHIES
SWELL
SWELLDOM
SWELLDOMS
SWELLED
SWELLER
SWELLERS
SWELLEST
SWELLING
SWELLINGS
SWELLISH
SWELLS
SWELT
SWELTED
SWELTER
SWELTERED
SWELTERING
SWELTERINGS
SWELTERS
SWELTING
SWELTRIER
SWELTRIEST
SWELTRY
SWELTS
SWEPT
SWEPTBACK
SWEPTWING
SWERF
SWERFED
SWERFING
SWERFS
SWERVE
SWERVED
SWERVER
SWERVERS
SWERVES
SWERVING
SWERVINGS
SWEVEN
SWEVENS
SWEY
SWEYED
SWEYING
SWEYS
SWIDDEN
SWIDDENS
SWIES
SWIFT
SWIFTED
SWIFTER
SWIFTERS
SWIFTEST
SWIFTING
SWIFTLET
SWIFTLETS
SWIFTLY
SWIFTNESS
SWIFTNESSES
SWIFTS
SWIG
SWIGGED
SWIGGER
SWIGGERS
SWIGGING
SWIGS
SWILL
SWILLED
SWILLER
SWILLERS
SWILLING
SWILLINGS
SWILLS
SWIM
SWIMMABLE
SWIMMER
SWIMMERET
SWIMMERETS
SWIMMERS
SWIMMIER
SWIMMIEST
SWIMMING
SWIMMINGS
SWIMMY
SWIMS
SWIMSUIT
SWIMSUITS
SWIMWEAR
SWIMWEARS
SWINDGE
SWINDGED
SWINDGES
SWINDGING
SWINDLE
SWINDLED
SWINDLER
SWINDLERS
SWINDLES
SWINDLING
SWINDLINGS
SWINE
SWINEHERD
SWINEHERDS
SWINEHOOD
SWINEHOODS
SWINERIES
SWINERY
SWING
SWINGBEAT
SWINGBEATS
SWINGBOAT
SWINGBOATS
SWINGE
SWINGED
SWINGEING
SWINGER
SWINGERS
SWINGES
SWINGIER
SWINGIEST
SWINGING
SWINGINGS
SWINGISM
SWINGISMS
SWINGLE
SWINGLED
SWINGLES
SWINGLING
SWINGLINGS
SWINGS
SWINGTREE
SWINGTREES
SWINGY
SWINISH
SWINISHLY
SWINK
SWINKED
SWINKING
SWINKS
SWIPE
SWIPED
SWIPER
SWIPERS
SWIPES
SWIPEY
SWIPIER
SWIPIEST
SWIPING
SWIPPLE
SWIPPLES
SWIRE
SWIRES
SWIRL
SWIRLED
SWIRLIER
SWIRLIEST
SWIRLING
SWIRLS
SWIRLY
SWISH
SWISHED
SWISHER
SWISHERS
SWISHES
SWISHEST
SWISHIER
SWISHIEST
SWISHING
SWISHINGS
SWISHY
SWISSING
SWISSINGS
SWITCH
SWITCHED
SWITCHEL
SWITCHELS
SWITCHES
SWITCHIER
SWITCHIEST
SWITCHING
SWITCHINGS
SWITCHMAN
SWITCHMEN
SWITCHY
SWITH
SWITHER
SWITHERED
SWITHERING
SWITHERS
SWITS
SWITSES
SWIVE
SWIVED
SWIVEL
SWIVELLED
SWIVELLING
SWIVELS
SWIVES
SWIVET
SWIVETS
SWIVING
SWIZ
SWIZZED
SWIZZES
SWIZZING
SWIZZLE
SWIZZLED
SWIZZLES
SWIZZLING
SWOB
SWOBBED
SWOBBER
SWOBBERS
SWOBBING
SWOBS
SWOLLEN
SWOLN
SWONE
SWONES
SWOON
SWOONED
SWOONING
SWOONINGS
SWOONS
SWOOP
SWOOPED
SWOOPING
SWOOPS
SWOOSH
SWOOSHED
SWOOSHES
SWOOSHING
SWOP
SWOPPED
SWOPPER
SWOPPERS
SWOPPING
SWOPPINGS
SWOPS
SWOPT
SWORD
SWORDED
SWORDER
SWORDERS
SWORDFISH
SWORDFISHES
SWORDING
SWORDLESS
SWORDLIKE
SWORDMAN
SWORDMEN
SWORDPLAY
SWORDPLAYS
SWORDS
SWORDSMAN
SWORDSMEN
SWORE
SWORN
SWOT
SWOTS
SWOTTED
SWOTTER
SWOTTERS
SWOTTING
SWOTTINGS
SWOUN
SWOUND
SWOUNDED
SWOUNDING
SWOUNDS
SWOUNE
SWOUNED
SWOUNES
SWOUNING
SWOUNS
SWOWND
SWOWNDS
SWOWNE
SWOWNES
SWOZZLE
SWOZZLES
SWUM
SWUNG
SWY
SYBARITE
SYBARITES
SYBARITIC
SYBBE
SYBBES
SYBIL
SYBILS
SYBO
SYBOE
SYBOES
SYBOTIC
SYBOTISM
SYBOTISMS
SYBOW
SYBOWS
SYCAMINE
SYCAMINES
SYCAMORE
SYCAMORES
SYCE
SYCEE
SYCEES
SYCES
SYCOMORE

SYCOMORES
SYCONIA
SYCONIUM
SYCOPHANT
SYCOPHANTS
SYCOSES
SYCOSIS
SYE
SYED
SYEING
SYEN
SYENITE
SYENITES
SYENITIC
SYENS
SYES
SYKE
SYKER
SYKES
SYLLABARIES
SYLLABARY
SYLLABI
SYLLABIC
SYLLABICS
SYLLABIFIED
SYLLABIFIES
SYLLABIFY
SYLLABIFYING
SYLLABISE
SYLLABISED
SYLLABISES
SYLLABISING
SYLLABISM
SYLLABISMS
SYLLABIZE
SYLLABIZED
SYLLABIZES
SYLLABIZING
SYLLABLE
SYLLABLED
SYLLABLES
SYLLABLING
SYLLABUB
SYLLABUBS
SYLLABUS
SYLLABUSES
SYLLEPSES
SYLLEPSIS
SYLLEPTIC
SYLLOGISE
SYLLOGISED
SYLLOGISES
SYLLOGISING
SYLLOGISM
SYLLOGISMS
SYLLOGIZE
SYLLOGIZED
SYLLOGIZES
SYLLOGIZING
SYLPH
SYLPHID
SYLPHIDE
SYLPHIDES
SYLPHIDS
SYLPHIER
SYLPHIEST
SYLPHINE
SYLPHISH
SYLPHS
SYLPHY
SYLVA
SYLVAE
SYLVAN
SYLVANER
SYLVANERS
SYLVANITE
SYLVANITES
SYLVANS
SYLVAS
SYLVATIC
SYLVIA
SYLVIAS
SYLVIINE
SYLVINE
SYLVINES
SYLVINITE
SYLVINITES
SYLVITE
SYLVITES
SYMAR
SYMARS
SYMBION
SYMBIONS
SYMBIONT
SYMBIONTS
SYMBIOSES
SYMBIOSIS
SYMBIOTIC
SYMBOL
SYMBOLE
SYMBOLES
SYMBOLIC
SYMBOLICS
SYMBOLISE
SYMBOLISED
SYMBOLISES
SYMBOLISING
SYMBOLISM
SYMBOLISMS
SYMBOLIST
SYMBOLISTS
SYMBOLIZE
SYMBOLIZED
SYMBOLIZES
SYMBOLIZING
SYMBOLLED
SYMBOLLING
SYMBOLOGIES
SYMBOLOGY
SYMBOLS
SYMITAR
SYMITARE
SYMITARES
SYMITARS
SYMMETRAL
SYMMETRIC
SYMMETRIES
SYMMETRY
SYMPATHIES
SYMPATHIN
SYMPATHINS
SYMPATHY
SYMPATRIC
SYMPHILE
SYMPHILES
SYMPHILIES
SYMPHILY
SYMPHONIC
SYMPHONIES
SYMPHONY
SYMPHYSES
SYMPHYSIS
SYMPHYTIC
SYMPLAST
SYMPLASTS
SYMPLOCE
SYMPLOCES
SYMPODIA
SYMPODIAL
SYMPODIUM
SYMPOSIA
SYMPOSIAC
SYMPOSIAL
SYMPOSIUM
SYMPTOM
SYMPTOMS
SYMPTOSES
SYMPTOSIS
SYMPTOTIC
SYNAGOGAL
SYNAGOGUE
SYNAGOGUES
SYNANDRIA
SYNANGIA
SYNANGIUM
SYNANTHIC
SYNANTHIES
SYNANTHY
SYNAPHEA
SYNAPHEAS
SYNAPHEIA
SYNAPHEIAS
SYNAPSE
SYNAPSES
SYNAPSIS
SYNAPTASE
SYNAPTASES
SYNAPTE
SYNAPTES
SYNAPTIC
SYNARCHIES
SYNARCHY
SYNASTRIES
SYNASTRY
SYNAXARIA
SYNAXES
SYNAXIS
SYNC
SYNCARP
SYNCARPIES
SYNCARPS
SYNCARPY
SYNCED
SYNCH
SYNCHED
SYNCHING
SYNCHRO
SYNCHRONIES
SYNCHRONY
SYNCHROS
SYNCHS
SYNCHYSES
SYNCHYSIS
SYNCING
SYNCLINAL
SYNCLINALS
SYNCLINE
SYNCLINES
SYNCOPAL
SYNCOPATE
SYNCOPATED
SYNCOPATES
SYNCOPATING
SYNCOPE
SYNCOPES
SYNCOPIC
SYNCOPTIC
SYNCRETIC
SYNCS
SYNCYTIA
SYNCYTIAL
SYNCYTIUM
SYND
SYNDACTYL
SYNDED
SYNDESES
SYNDESIS
SYNDET
SYNDETIC
SYNDETS
SYNDIC
SYNDICAL
SYNDICATE
SYNDICATED
SYNDICATES
SYNDICATING
SYNDICS
SYNDING
SYNDINGS
SYNDROME
SYNDROMES
SYNDROMIC
SYNDS
SYNE
SYNECHIA
SYNECHIAS
SYNECTIC
SYNECTICS
SYNED
SYNEDRIA
SYNEDRIAL
SYNEDRION
SYNEDRIUM
SYNERESES
SYNERESIS
SYNERGIC
SYNERGID
SYNERGIDS
SYNERGIES
SYNERGISE
SYNERGISED
SYNERGISES
SYNERGISING
SYNERGISM
SYNERGISMS
SYNERGIST
SYNERGISTS
SYNERGIZE
SYNERGIZED
SYNERGIZES
SYNERGIZING
SYNERGY
SYNES
SYNESES
SYNESIS
SYNFUEL
SYNFUELS
SYNGAMIC
SYNGAMIES
SYNGAMOUS
SYNGAMY
SYNGAS
SYNGASES
SYNGENEIC
SYNGRAPH
SYNGRAPHS
SYNING
SYNIZESES
SYNIZESIS
SYNKARYON
SYNKARYONS
SYNOD
SYNODAL
SYNODALS
SYNODIC
SYNODICAL
SYNODS
SYNODSMAN
SYNODSMEN
SYNOECETE
SYNOECETES
SYNOECISE
SYNOECISED
SYNOECISES
SYNOECISING
SYNOECISM
SYNOECISMS
SYNOECIZE
SYNOECIZED
SYNOECIZES
SYNOECIZING
SYNOEKETE
SYNOEKETES
SYNOICOUS
SYNONYM
SYNONYMIC
SYNONYMIES
SYNONYMS
SYNONYMY
SYNOPSES

SYNOPSIS
SYNOPSISE
SYNOPSISED
SYNOPSISES
SYNOPSISING
SYNOPSIZE
SYNOPSIZED
SYNOPSIZES
SYNOPSIZING
SYNOPTIC
SYNOPTIST
SYNOPTISTS
SYNOVIA
SYNOVIAL
SYNOVIAS
SYNOVITIC
SYNOVITIS
SYNOVITISES
SYNROC
SYNROCS
SYNTACTIC
SYNTAGM
SYNTAGMA
SYNTAGMATA
SYNTAGMS
SYNTAN
SYNTANS
SYNTAX
SYNTAXES
SYNTECTIC
SYNTEXIS
SYNTEXISES
SYNTH
SYNTHESES
SYNTHESIS
SYNTHETIC
SYNTHETICS
SYNTHON
SYNTHONS
SYNTHRONI
SYNTHS
SYNTONIC
SYNTONIES
SYNTONIN
SYNTONINS
SYNTONISE
SYNTONISED
SYNTONISES
SYNTONISING
SYNTONIZE
SYNTONIZED
SYNTONIZES
SYNTONIZING
SYNTONOUS
SYNTONY
SYPE
SYPED
SYPES
SYPHER
SYPHERED
SYPHERING
SYPHERS
SYPHILIS
SYPHILISE
SYPHILISED
SYPHILISES
SYPHILISING
SYPHILIZE
SYPHILIZED
SYPHILIZES
SYPHILIZING
SYPHILOID
SYPHILOMA
SYPHILOMAS
SYPHON
SYPHONED
SYPHONING
SYPHONS
SYPING
SYRAH
SYRAHS
SYREN
SYRENS
SYRINGA
SYRINGAS
SYRINGE
SYRINGEAL
SYRINGED
SYRINGES
SYRINGING
SYRINX
SYRINXES
SYRLYE
SYRPHID
SYRPHIDS
SYRTES
SYRTIS
SYRUP
SYRUPED
SYRUPIER
SYRUPIEST
SYRUPING
SYRUPS
SYRUPY
SYSOP
SYSOPS
SYSSITIA
SYSSITIAS
SYSTALTIC
SYSTEM
SYSTEMED
SYSTEMIC
SYSTEMISE
SYSTEMISED
SYSTEMISES
SYSTEMISING
SYSTEMIZE
SYSTEMIZED
SYSTEMIZES
SYSTEMIZING
SYSTEMS
SYSTOLE
SYSTOLES
SYSTOLIC
SYSTYLE
SYSTYLES
SYTHE
SYTHES
SYVER
SYVERS
SYZYGIAL
SYZYGIES
SYZYGY

T

TA
TAB
TABANID
TABANIDS
TABARD
TABARDS
TABARET
TABARETS
TABASHEER
TABASHEERS
TABASHIR
TABASHIRS
TABBED
TABBIED
TABBIES
TABBINET
TABBINETS
TABBING
TABBOULEH
TABBOULEHS
TABBY
TABBYHOOD
TABBYHOODS
TABBYING
TABEFIED
TABEFIES
TABEFY
TABEFYING
TABELLION
TABELLIONS
TABERD
TABERDAR
TABERDARS
TABERDS
TABES
TABESCENT
TABETIC
TABETICS
TABI
TABID
TABINET
TABINETS
TABIS
TABLA
TABLAS
TABLATURE
TABLATURES
TABLE
TABLEAU
TABLEAUX
TABLED
TABLEFUL
TABLEFULS
TABLELAND
TABLELANDS
TABLES
TABLET
TABLETED
TABLETING
TABLETOP
TABLETOPS
TABLETS
TABLEWARE
TABLEWARES
TABLEWISE
TABLIER
TABLIERS
TABLING
TABLINGS
TABLOID
TABLOIDS
TABLOIDY
TABOGGAN
TABOGGANED
TABOGGANING
TABOGGANS
TABOO
TABOOED
TABOOING
TABOOS
TABOR
TABORED
TABORER
TABORERS
TABORET
TABORETS
TABORIN
TABORING
TABORINS
TABORS
TABOUR
TABOURED
TABOURET
TABOURETS
TABOURIN
TABOURING
TABOURINS
TABOURS
TABRERE
TABRERES
TABRET
TABRETS
TABS
TABU
TABUED
TABUING
TABULA
TABULAE
TABULAR
TABULARLY
TABULATE
TABULATED
TABULATES
TABULATING
TABULATOR
TABULATORS
TABUN
TABUNS
TABUS
TACAHOUT
TACAHOUTS
TACAMAHAC
TACAMAHACS
TACAN
TACANS
TACE
TACES
TACET
TACH
TACHE
TACHES
TACHINID
TACHINIDS
TACHISM
TACHISME
TACHISMES
TACHISMS
TACHIST
TACHISTE
TACHISTES
TACHISTS
TACHO
TACHOGRAM
TACHOGRAMS
TACHOS
TACHYLITE
TACHYLITES
TACHYLYTE
TACHYLYTES
TACHYON
TACHYONS
TACHYPNEA
TACHYPNEAS
TACIT
TACITLY
TACITNESS
TACITNESSES
TACITURN
TACK
TACKED
TACKER
TACKERS
TACKET
TACKETS
TACKETY
TACKIER
TACKIES
TACKIEST
TACKILY
TACKINESS
TACKINESSES
TACKING
TACKINGS
TACKLE
TACKLED
TACKLER
TACKLERS
TACKLES
TACKLING
TACKLINGS
TACKS
TACKSMAN
TACKSMEN
TACKY
TACMAHACK
TACMAHACKS
TACO
TACONITE
TACONITES
TACOS
TACT
TACTFUL
TACTFULLY
TACTIC
TACTICAL
TACTICIAN
TACTICIANS
TACTICITIES
TACTICITY
TACTICS
TACTILE
TACTILIST
TACTILISTS
TACTILITIES
TACTILITY
TACTION
TACTIONS
TACTISM
TACTISMS
TACTLESS
TACTS
TACTUAL
TACTUALLY
TAD
TADDIE
TADDIES
TADPOLE
TADPOLES
TADS
TADVANCE
TAE
TAED
TAEDIUM
TAEDIUMS
TAEING
TAEL
TAELS
TAENIA
TAENIAE
TAENIAS
TAENIASES
TAENIASIS
TAENIATE
TAENIOID
TAES
TAFFEREL
TAFFERELS
TAFFETA
TAFFETAS
TAFFETASES
TAFFETIES
TAFFETY
TAFFIA
TAFFIAS
TAFFIES
TAFFRAIL
TAFFRAILS
TAFFY
TAFIA
TAFIAS
TAG
TAGETES
TAGGED
TAGGEE
TAGGEES
TAGGER
TAGGERS
TAGGIER
TAGGIEST
TAGGING
TAGGINGS
TAGGY
TAGHAIRM
TAGHAIRMS
TAGLIONI
TAGLIONIS
TAGMA
TAGMATA
TAGMEME
TAGMEMES

TAGMEMIC
TAGMEMICS
TAGRAG
TAGRAGS
TAGS
TAGUAN
TAGUANS
TAHA
TAHAS
TAHINA
TAHINAS
TAHINI
TAHINIS
TAHR
TAHRS
TAHSIL
TAHSILDAR
TAHSILDARS
TAHSILS
TAI
TAIAHA
TAIAHAS
TAIGA
TAIGAS
TAIGLE
TAIGLED
TAIGLES
TAIGLING
TAIL
TAILARD
TAILARDS
TAILBACK
TAILBACKS
TAILBOARD
TAILBOARDS
TAILED
TAILERON
TAILERONS
TAILGATE
TAILGATED
TAILGATER
TAILGATERS
TAILGATES
TAILGATING
TAILING
TAILINGS
TAILLE
TAILLES
TAILLESS
TAILLEUR
TAILLEURS
TAILLIE
TAILLIES
TAILOR
TAILORED
TAILORESS
TAILORESSES
TAILORING
TAILORINGS
TAILORS
TAILPIECE
TAILPIECES
TAILPIPE
TAILPIPED
TAILPIPES
TAILPIPING
TAILPLANE
TAILPLANES
TAILRACE
TAILRACES
TAILS
TAILSKID
TAILSKIDS
TAILSPIN
TAILSPINS
TAILSTOCK
TAILSTOCKS
TAILWHEEL
TAILWHEELS
TAILYE
TAILYES
TAILZIE
TAILZIES
TAINT
TAINTED
TAINTING
TAINTLESS
TAINTS
TAINTURE
TAINTURES
TAIPAN
TAIPANS
TAIRA
TAIRAS
TAIS
TAISCH
TAISCHES
TAISH
TAISHES
TAIT
TAITS
TAIVER
TAIVERED
TAIVERING
TAIVERS
TAIVERT
TAJ
TAJES
TAJINE
TAJINES
TAK
TAKA
TAKABLE
TAKAHE
TAKAHES
TAKAMAKA
TAKAMAKAS
TAKAS
TAKE
TAKEABLE
TAKEAWAY
TAKEAWAYS
TAKEN
TAKEOUT
TAKEOUTS
TAKEOVER
TAKEOVERS
TAKER
TAKERS
TAKES
TAKHI
TAKHIS
TAKI
TAKIER
TAKIEST
TAKIN
TAKING
TAKINGLY
TAKINGS
TAKINS
TAKIS
TAKS
TAKY
TALA
TALAK
TALAKS
TALANT
TALANTS
TALAPOIN
TALAPOINS
TALAQ
TALAQS
TALAR
TALARIA
TALARS
TALAS
TALAUNT
TALAUNTS
TALAYOT
TALAYOTS
TALBOT
TALBOTS
TALBOTYPE
TALBOTYPES
TALC
TALCED
TALCIER
TALCIEST
TALCING
TALCKED
TALCKIER
TALCKIEST
TALCKING
TALCKY
TALCOSE
TALCOUS
TALCS
TALCUM
TALCUMS
TALCY
TALE
TALEA
TALEAE
TALEFUL
TALEGALLA
TALEGALLAS
TALENT
TALENTED
TALENTS
TALER
TALERS
TALES
TALESMAN
TALESMEN
TALI
TALIGRADE
TALION
TALIONIC
TALIONS
TALIPAT
TALIPATS
TALIPED
TALIPEDS
TALIPES
TALIPOT
TALIPOTS
TALISMAN
TALISMANS
TALK
TALKABLE
TALKATHON
TALKATHONS
TALKATIVE
TALKBACK
TALKBACKS
TALKED
TALKER
TALKERS
TALKFEST
TALKFESTS
TALKIE
TALKIER
TALKIES
TALKIEST
TALKING
TALKINGS
TALKS
TALKY
TALL
TALLAGE
TALLAGED
TALLAGES
TALLAGING
TALLAT
TALLATS
TALLBOY
TALLBOYS
TALLENT
TALLENTS
TALLER
TALLEST
TALLET
TALLETS
TALLIABLE
TALLIATE
TALLIATED
TALLIATES
TALLIATING
TALLIED
TALLIER
TALLIERS
TALLIES
TALLISH
TALLITH
TALLITHIM
TALLITHS
TALLNESS
TALLNESSES
TALLOT
TALLOTS
TALLOW
TALLOWED
TALLOWING
TALLOWISH
TALLOWS
TALLOWY
TALLY
TALLYING
TALLYMAN
TALLYMEN
TALLYSHOP
TALLYSHOPS
TALMA
TALMAS
TALMUD
TALMUDS
TALON
TALONED
TALONS
TALOOKA
TALOOKAS
TALPA
TALPAE
TALPAS
TALUK
TALUKA
TALUKAS
TALUKDAR
TALUKDARS
TALUKS
TALUS
TALUSES
TALWEG
TALWEGS
TAM
TAMABLE
TAMAL
TAMALE
TAMALES
TAMALS
TAMANDU
TAMANDUA
TAMANDUAS
TAMANDUS
TAMANOIR
TAMANOIRS
TAMANU
TAMANUS
TAMARA
TAMARACK
TAMARACKS
TAMARAO
TAMARAOS
TAMARAS
TAMARAU
TAMARAUS
TAMARI
TAMARILLO
TAMARILLOS
TAMARIN

TAMARIND
TAMARINDS
TAMARINS
TAMARIS
TAMARISK
TAMARISKS
TAMASHA
TAMASHAS
TAMBAC
TAMBACS
TAMBER
TAMBERS
TAMBOUR
TAMBOURA
TAMBOURAS
TAMBOURED
TAMBOURIN
TAMBOURING
TAMBOURINS
TAMBOURS
TAMBURA
TAMBURAS
TAMBURIN
TAMBURINS
TAME
TAMEABLE
TAMED
TAMELESS
TAMELY
TAMENESS
TAMENESSES
TAMER
TAMERS
TAMES
TAMEST
TAMIN
TAMINE
TAMINES
TAMING
TAMINGS
TAMINS
TAMIS
TAMISE
TAMISES
TAMMAR
TAMMARS
TAMMIES
TAMMY
TAMOXIFEN
TAMOXIFENS
TAMP
TAMPED
TAMPER
TAMPERED
TAMPERER
TAMPERERS
TAMPERING
TAMPERINGS
TAMPERS
TAMPING
TAMPINGS
TAMPION
TAMPIONS
TAMPON
TAMPONADE
TAMPONADES
TAMPONAGE
TAMPONAGES
TAMPONED
TAMPONING
TAMPONS
TAMPS
TAMS
TAMWORTH
TAMWORTHS
TAN
TANA
TANADAR
TANADARS
TANAGER
TANAGERS
TANAGRA
TANAGRAS
TANAGRINE
TANAISTE
TANAISTES
TANALISED
TANALIZED
TANAS
TANBARK
TANBARKS
TANDEM
TANDEMS
TANDOOR
TANDOORI
TANDOORIS
TANDOORS
TANE
TANG
TANGA
TANGAS
TANGED
TANGELO
TANGELOS
TANGENCIES
TANGENCY
TANGENT
TANGENTS
TANGERINE
TANGERINES
TANGHIN
TANGHININ
TANGHININS
TANGHINS
TANGI
TANGIBLE
TANGIBLES
TANGIBLY
TANGIE
TANGIER
TANGIES
TANGIEST
TANGING
TANGIS
TANGLE
TANGLED
TANGLER
TANGLERS
TANGLES
TANGLIER
TANGLIEST
TANGLING
TANGLINGS
TANGLY
TANGO
TANGOED
TANGOING
TANGOIST
TANGOISTS
TANGOS
TANGRAM
TANGRAMS
TANGS
TANGUN
TANGUNS
TANGY
TANH
TANHS
TANIST
TANISTRIES
TANISTRY
TANISTS
TANIWHA
TANIWHAS
TANK
TANKA
TANKAGE
TANKAGES
TANKARD
TANKARDS
TANKAS
TANKED
TANKER
TANKERS
TANKFUL
TANKFULS
TANKIA
TANKIAS
TANKIES
TANKING
TANKINGS
TANKS
TANKY
TANLING
TANLINGS
TANNA
TANNABLE
TANNAGE
TANNAGES
TANNAH
TANNAHS
TANNAS
TANNATE
TANNATES
TANNED
TANNER
TANNERIES
TANNERS
TANNERY
TANNEST
TANNIC
TANNIN
TANNING
TANNINGS
TANNINS
TANNOY
TANNOYED
TANNOYING
TANNOYS
TANREC
TANRECS
TANS
TANSIES
TANSY
TANTALATE
TANTALATES
TANTALIC
TANTALISE
TANTALISED
TANTALISES
TANTALISING
TANTALISINGS
TANTALISM
TANTALISMS
TANTALITE
TANTALITES
TANTALIZE
TANTALIZED
TANTALIZES
TANTALIZING
TANTALIZINGS
TANTALOUS
TANTALUM
TANTALUMS
TANTALUS
TANTALUSES
TANTARA
TANTARARA
TANTARARAS
TANTARAS
TANTI
TANTIVIES
TANTIVY
TANTO
TANTONIES
TANTONY
TANTRA
TANTRAS
TANTRIC
TANTRUM
TANTRUMS
TANYARD
TANYARDS
TAOISEACH
TAOISEACHS
TAP
TAPA
TAPACOLO
TAPACOLOS
TAPACULO
TAPACULOS
TAPADERA
TAPADERAS
TAPADERO
TAPADEROS
TAPAS
TAPE
TAPEABLE
TAPED
TAPELESS
TAPELIKE
TAPELINE
TAPELINES
TAPEN
TAPENADE
TAPENADES
TAPER
TAPERED
TAPERER
TAPERERS
TAPERING
TAPERINGS
TAPERNESS
TAPERNESSES
TAPERS
TAPERWISE
TAPES
TAPESTRIED
TAPESTRIES
TAPESTRY
TAPESTRYING
TAPET
TAPETA
TAPETAL
TAPETI
TAPETIS
TAPETS
TAPETUM
TAPEWORM
TAPEWORMS
TAPHONOMIES
TAPHONOMY
TAPING
TAPIOCA
TAPIOCAS
TAPIR
TAPIROID
TAPIRS
TAPIS
TAPISES
TAPIST
TAPISTS
TAPLASH
TAPLASHES
TAPPA
TAPPABLE
TAPPAS
TAPPED
TAPPER
TAPPERS
TAPPET
TAPPETS
TAPPICE
TAPPICED
TAPPICES
TAPPICING
TAPPING
TAPPINGS
TAPPIT
TAPROOM

TAPROOMS
TAPROOT
TAPROOTS
TAPS
TAPSMAN
TAPSMEN
TAPSTER
TAPSTERS
TAPSTRY
TAPU
TAPUED
TAPUING
TAPUS
TAQUERIA
TAQUERIAS
TAR
TARA
TARAKIHI
TARAKIHIS
TARAND
TARANDS
TARANTARA
TARANTARAED
TARANTARAING
TARANTARAS
TARANTAS
TARANTASES
TARANTASS
TARANTASSES
TARANTISM
TARANTISMS
TARANTULA
TARANTULAS
TARAS
TARAXACUM
TARAXACUMS
TARBOGGIN
TARBOGGINED
TARBOGGINING
TARBOGGINS
TARBOOSH
TARBOOSHES
TARBOUSH
TARBOUSHES
TARBOY
TARBOYS
TARBUSH
TARBUSHES
TARCEL
TARCELS
TARDIED
TARDIER
TARDIES
TARDIEST
TARDILY
TARDINESS
TARDINESSES
TARDIVE
TARDY
TARDYING
TARE
TARED
TARES
TARGE
TARGED
TARGES
TARGET
TARGETED
TARGETEER
TARGETEERS
TARGETING
TARGETS
TARGING
TARIFF
TARIFFED
TARIFFING
TARIFFS
TARING
TARINGS
TARLATAN
TARLATANS
TARMAC
TARMACKED
TARMACKING
TARMACS
TARN
TARNAL
TARNALLY
TARNATION
TARNISH
TARNISHED
TARNISHER
TARNISHERS
TARNISHES
TARNISHING
TARNS
TARO
TAROC
TAROCS
TAROK
TAROKS
TAROS
TAROT
TAROTS
TARP
TARPAN
TARPANS
TARPAULIN
TARPAULINS
TARPON
TARPONS
TARPS
TARRAGON
TARRAGONS
TARRAS
TARRASES
TARRE
TARRED
TARRES
TARRIANCE
TARRIANCES
TARRIED
TARRIER
TARRIERS
TARRIES
TARRIEST
TARRINESS
TARRINESSES
TARRING
TARRINGS
TARROCK
TARROCKS
TARROW
TARROWED
TARROWING
TARROWS
TARRY
TARRYING
TARS
TARSAL
TARSALGIA
TARSALGIAS
TARSALS
TARSEL
TARSELS
TARSI
TARSIA
TARSIAS
TARSIER
TARSIERS
TARSIOID
TARSIPED
TARSIPEDS
TARSUS
TART
TARTAN
TARTANA
TARTANAS
TARTANE
TARTANED
TARTANES
TARTANRIES
TARTANRY
TARTANS
TARTAR
TARTARE
TARTARES
TARTARIC
TARTARISE
TARTARISED
TARTARISES
TARTARISING
TARTARIZE
TARTARIZED
TARTARIZES
TARTARIZING
TARTARLY
TARTARS
TARTER
TARTEST
TARTIER
TARTIEST
TARTINE
TARTINES
TARTINESS
TARTINESSES
TARTISH
TARTLET
TARTLETS
TARTLY
TARTNESS
TARTNESSES
TARTRATE
TARTRATES
TARTS
TARTY
TARWEED
TARWEEDS
TARWHINE
TARWHINES
TASAR
TASARS
TASER
TASERED
TASERING
TASERS
TASH
TASHED
TASHES
TASHING
TASIMETER
TASIMETERS
TASK
TASKED
TASKER
TASKERS
TASKING
TASKINGS
TASKS
TASLET
TASLETS
TASS
TASSE
TASSEL
TASSELED
TASSELING
TASSELL
TASSELLED
TASSELLING
TASSELLINGS
TASSELLS
TASSELLY
TASSELS
TASSES
TASSET
TASSETS
TASSIE
TASSIES
TASSWAGE
TASTABLE
TASTE
TASTED
TASTEFUL
TASTELESS
TASTER
TASTERS
TASTES
TASTEVIN
TASTEVINS
TASTIER
TASTIEST
TASTILY
TASTINESS
TASTINESSES
TASTING
TASTINGS
TASTY
TAT
TATAMI
TATAMIS
TATE
TATER
TATERS
TATES
TATH
TATHED
TATHING
TATHS
TATIE
TATIES
TATLER
TATLERS
TATOU
TATOUAY
TATOUAYS
TATOUS
TATS
TATT
TATTED
TATTER
TATTERED
TATTERING
TATTERS
TATTERY
TATTIE
TATTIER
TATTIES
TATTIEST
TATTILY
TATTINESS
TATTINESSES
TATTING
TATTINGS
TATTLE
TATTLED
TATTLER
TATTLERS
TATTLES
TATTLING
TATTLINGS
TATTOO
TATTOOED
TATTOOER
TATTOOERS
TATTOOING
TATTOOIST
TATTOOISTS
TATTOOS
TATTOW
TATTOWED
TATTOWING
TATTOWS
TATTS
TATTY
TATU
TATUED
TATUING
TATUS
TAU
TAUBE

TAUBES
TAUGHT
TAULD
TAUNT
TAUNTED
TAUNTER
TAUNTERS
TAUNTING
TAUNTINGS
TAUNTS
TAUPE
TAUPES
TAUPIE
TAUPIES
TAUREAN
TAURIC
TAURIFORM
TAURINE
TAURINES
TAUS
TAUT
TAUTED
TAUTEN
TAUTENED
TAUTENING
TAUTENS
TAUTER
TAUTEST
TAUTING
TAUTIT
TAUTLY
TAUTNESS
TAUTNESSES
TAUTOG
TAUTOGS
TAUTOLOGIES
TAUTOLOGY
TAUTOMER
TAUTOMERS
TAUTONYM
TAUTONYMS
TAUTS
TAVA
TAVAH
TAVAHS
TAVAS
TAVER
TAVERED
TAVERING
TAVERN
TAVERNA
TAVERNAS
TAVERNER
TAVERNERS
TAVERNS
TAVERS
TAVERT
TAW
TAWA
TAWAS
TAWDRIER
TAWDRIES
TAWDRIEST
TAWDRILY
TAWDRY
TAWED
TAWER
TAWERIES
TAWERS
TAWERY
TAWIE
TAWIER
TAWIEST
TAWING
TAWINGS
TAWNEY
TAWNEYS
TAWNIER
TAWNIES
TAWNIEST
TAWNINESS
TAWNINESSES
TAWNY
TAWPIE
TAWPIES
TAWS
TAWSE
TAWSES
TAWT
TAWTED
TAWTIE
TAWTIER
TAWTIEST
TAWTING
TAWTS
TAX
TAXA
TAXABLE
TAXABLY
TAXACEOUS
TAXAMETER
TAXAMETERS
TAXATION
TAXATIONS
TAXATIVE
TAXED
TAXER
TAXERS
TAXES
TAXI
TAXIARCH
TAXIARCHS
TAXICAB
TAXICABS
TAXIDERMIES
TAXIDERMY
TAXIED
TAXIES
TAXIING
TAXIMAN
TAXIMEN
TAXIMETER
TAXIMETERS
TAXING
TAXINGS
TAXIS
TAXIWAY
TAXIWAYS
TAXLESS
TAXMAN
TAXMEN
TAXOL
TAXOLS
TAXON
TAXONOMER
TAXONOMERS
TAXONOMIC
TAXONOMIES
TAXONOMY
TAXOR
TAXORS
TAXYING
TAY
TAYASSUID
TAYASSUIDS
TAYBERRIES
TAYBERRY
TAYRA
TAYRAS
TAYS
TAZZA
TAZZAS
TAZZE
TCHICK
TCHICKED
TCHICKING
TCHICKS
TE
TEA
TEABERRIES
TEABERRY
TEABOARD
TEABOARDS
TEACH
TEACHABLE
TEACHER
TEACHERLY
TEACHERS
TEACHES
TEACHIE
TEACHING
TEACHINGS
TEACHLESS
TEACUP
TEACUPFUL
TEACUPFULS
TEACUPS
TEAD
TEADE
TEADES
TEADS
TEAED
TEAGLE
TEAGLED
TEAGLES
TEAGLING
TEAING
TEAK
TEAKS
TEAL
TEALS
TEAM
TEAMED
TEAMER
TEAMERS
TEAMING
TEAMINGS
TEAMS
TEAMSTER
TEAMSTERS
TEAMWISE
TEAMWORK
TEAMWORKS
TEAPOT
TEAPOTS
TEAPOY
TEAPOYS
TEAR
TEARABLE
TEARAWAY
TEARAWAYS
TEARER
TEARERS
TEARFUL
TEARFULLY
TEARIER
TEARIEST
TEARING
TEARLESS
TEARS
TEARSHEET
TEARSHEETS
TEARY
TEAS
TEASE
TEASED
TEASEL
TEASELED
TEASELER
TEASELERS
TEASELING
TEASELINGS
TEASELLED
TEASELLER
TEASELLERS
TEASELLING
TEASELLINGS
TEASELS
TEASER
TEASERS
TEASES
TEASING
TEASINGLY
TEASINGS
TEASPOON
TEASPOONS
TEAT
TEATED
TEATIME
TEATIMES
TEATS
TEAZE
TEAZED
TEAZEL
TEAZELED
TEAZELING
TEAZELLED
TEAZELLING
TEAZELS
TEAZES
TEAZING
TEAZLE
TEAZLED
TEAZLES
TEAZLING
TEBBAD
TEBBADS
TECH
TECHIE
TECHIER
TECHIES
TECHIEST
TECHILY
TECHINESS
TECHINESSES
TECHNIC
TECHNICAL
TECHNICS
TECHNIQUE
TECHNIQUES
TECHNO
TECHNOPOP
TECHNOPOPS
TECHNOS
TECHS
TECHY
TECKEL
TECKELS
TECTA
TECTIFORM
TECTONIC
TECTONICS
TECTORIAL
TECTRICES
TECTRIX
TECTUM
TED
TEDDED
TEDDER
TEDDERS
TEDDIE
TEDDIES
TEDDING
TEDDY
TEDESCA
TEDESCHE
TEDESCHI
TEDESCO
TEDIER
TEDIEST
TEDIOSITIES
TEDIOSITY
TEDIOUS
TEDIOUSLY
TEDISOME
TEDIUM
TEDIUMS
TEDS
TEDY
TEE

TEED
TEEING
TEEL
TEELS
TEEM
TEEMED
TEEMER
TEEMERS
TEEMFUL
TEEMING
TEEMLESS
TEEMS
TEEN
TEENAGE
TEENAGED
TEENAGER
TEENAGERS
TEEND
TEENDED
TEENDING
TEENDS
TEENE
TEENED
TEENES
TEENIER
TEENIEST
TEENING
TEENS
TEENSIER
TEENSIEST
TEENSY
TEENTIER
TEENTIEST
TEENTSIER
TEENTSIEST
TEENTSY
TEENTY
TEENY
TEEPEE
TEEPEES
TEER
TEERED
TEERING
TEERS
TEES
TEETER
TEETERED
TEETERING
TEETERS
TEETH
TEETHE
TEETHED
TEETHES
TEETHING
TEETHINGS
TEETOTAL
TEETOTALS
TEETOTUM
TEETOTUMS
TEF
TEFF
TEFFS
TEFILLAH
TEFILLIN
TEFS
TEG
TEGG
TEGGS
TEGMEN
TEGMENTA
TEGMENTAL
TEGMENTUM
TEGMINA
TEGS
TEGU
TEGUEXIN
TEGUEXINS
TEGULA
TEGULAE
TEGULAR
TEGULARLY
TEGULATED
TEGUMENT
TEGUMENTS
TEGUS
TEHR
TEHRS
TEIL
TEILS
TEIND
TEINDED
TEINDING
TEINDS
TEKNONYMIES
TEKNONYMY
TEKTITE
TEKTITES
TEL
TELA
TELAE
TELAMON
TELAMONES
TELARY
TELD
TELECAST
TELECASTED
TELECASTING
TELECASTS
TELECHIR
TELECHIRS
TELECINE
TELECINES
TELECOM
TELECOMS
TELEDU
TELEDUS
TELEFAX
TELEFAXED
TELEFAXES
TELEFAXING
TELEFILM
TELEFILMS
TELEGA
TELEGAS
TELEGENIC
TELEGONIC
TELEGONIES
TELEGONY
TELEGRAM
TELEGRAMS
TELEGRAPH
TELEGRAPHED
TELEGRAPHING
TELEGRAPHS
TELEMARK
TELEMARKED
TELEMARKING
TELEMARKS
TELEMATIC
TELEMATICS
TELEMETER
TELEMETERED
TELEMETERING
TELEMETERS
TELEMETRIES
TELEMETRY
TELEOLOGIES
TELEOLOGY
TELEONOMIES
TELEONOMY
TELEOSAUR
TELEOSAURS
TELEOST
TELEOSTS
TELEPATH
TELEPATHED
TELEPATHIES
TELEPATHING
TELEPATHS
TELEPATHY
TELEPHEME
TELEPHEMES
TELEPHONE
TELEPHONED
TELEPHONES
TELEPHONIES
TELEPHONING
TELEPHONY
TELEPHOTO
TELEPLAY
TELEPLAYS
TELEPOINT
TELEPOINTS
TELEPORT
TELEPORTED
TELEPORTING
TELEPORTS
TELERGIC
TELERGIES
TELERGY
TELESALE
TELESALES
TELESCOPE
TELESCOPED
TELESCOPES
TELESCOPIES
TELESCOPING
TELESCOPY
TELESEME
TELESEMES
TELESES
TELESIS
TELESM
TELESMS
TELESTIC
TELESTICH
TELESTICHS
TELETEX
TELETEXES
TELETEXT
TELETEXTS
TELETHON
TELETHONS
TELETRON
TELETRONS
TELEVIEW
TELEVIEWED
TELEVIEWING
TELEVIEWS
TELEVISE
TELEVISED
TELEVISER
TELEVISERS
TELEVISES
TELEVISING
TELEVISOR
TELEVISORS
TELEX
TELEXED
TELEXES
TELEXING
TELFER
TELFERAGE
TELFERAGES
TELFERED
TELFERIC
TELFERING
TELFERS
TELIA
TELIAL
TELIC
TELIUM
TELL
TELLABLE
TELLAR
TELLARED
TELLARING
TELLARS
TELLEN
TELLENS
TELLER
TELLERED
TELLERING
TELLERS
TELLIES
TELLIN
TELLING
TELLINGLY
TELLINGS
TELLINOID
TELLINS
TELLS
TELLTALE
TELLTALES
TELLURAL
TELLURATE
TELLURATES
TELLURIAN
TELLURIANS
TELLURIC
TELLURIDE
TELLURIDES
TELLURION
TELLURIONS
TELLURISE
TELLURISED
TELLURISES
TELLURISING
TELLURITE
TELLURITES
TELLURIUM
TELLURIUMS
TELLURIZE
TELLURIZED
TELLURIZES
TELLURIZING
TELLUROUS
TELLUS
TELLUSES
TELLY
TELNET
TELNETS
TELOMERE
TELOMERES
TELOPHASE
TELOPHASES
TELOS
TELOSES
TELPHER
TELPHERED
TELPHERIC
TELPHERING
TELPHERS
TELS
TELSON
TELSONS
TELT
TEMAZEPAM
TEMAZEPAMS
TEMBLOR
TEMBLORES
TEMBLORS
TEME
TEMED
TEMENE
TEMENOS
TEMERITIES
TEMERITY
TEMEROUS
TEMES
TEMP
TEMPED
TEMPEH
TEMPEHS
TEMPER
TEMPERA
TEMPERAS
TEMPERATE
TEMPERATED
TEMPERATES

TEMPERATING
TEMPERED
TEMPERER
TEMPERERS
TEMPERING
TEMPERINGS
TEMPERS
TEMPEST
TEMPESTED
TEMPESTING
TEMPESTS
TEMPI
TEMPING
TEMPLAR
TEMPLARS
TEMPLATE
TEMPLATES
TEMPLE
TEMPLED
TEMPLES
TEMPLET
TEMPLETS
TEMPO
TEMPORAL
TEMPORALS
TEMPORARIES
TEMPORARY
TEMPORE
TEMPORISE
TEMPORISED
TEMPORISES
TEMPORISING
TEMPORISINGS
TEMPORIZE
TEMPORIZED
TEMPORIZES
TEMPORIZING
TEMPORIZINGS
TEMPOS
TEMPS
TEMPT
TEMPTABLE
TEMPTED
TEMPTER
TEMPTERS
TEMPTING
TEMPTINGS
TEMPTRESS
TEMPTRESSES
TEMPTS
TEMPURA
TEMPURAS
TEMS
TEMSE
TEMSED
TEMSES
TEMSING
TEMULENCE
TEMULENCES
TEMULENCIES
TEMULENCY
TEMULENT
TEN
TENABLE
TENACE
TENACES
TENACIOUS
TENACITIES
TENACITY
TENACULA
TENACULUM
TENAIL
TENAILLE
TENAILLES
TENAILLON
TENAILLONS
TENAILS
TENANCIES
TENANCY
TENANT
TENANTED
TENANTING
TENANTRIES
TENANTRY
TENANTS
TENCH
TENCHES
TEND
TENDANCE
TENDANCES
TENDED
TENDENCE
TENDENCES
TENDENCIES
TENDENCY
TENDENZ
TENDENZEN
TENDER
TENDERED
TENDERER
TENDERERS
TENDEREST
TENDERING
TENDERINGS
TENDERISE
TENDERISED
TENDERISES
TENDERISING
TENDERIZE
TENDERIZED
TENDERIZES
TENDERIZING
TENDERLY
TENDERS
TENDING
TENDINOUS
TENDON
TENDONS
TENDRE
TENDRES
TENDRIL
TENDRILS
TENDRON
TENDRONS
TENDS
TENE
TENEBRAE
TENEBRIO
TENEBRIOS
TENEBRISM
TENEBRISMS
TENEBRIST
TENEBRISTS
TENEBRITIES
TENEBRITY
TENEBROSE
TENEBROUS
TENEMENT
TENEMENTS
TENENDUM
TENENDUMS
TENES
TENESMUS
TENESMUSES
TENET
TENETS
TENFOLD
TENIA
TENIAE
TENIAS
TENIOID
TENNE
TENNER
TENNERS
TENNES
TENNIES
TENNIS
TENNISES
TENNO
TENNOS
TENNY
TENON
TENONED
TENONER
TENONERS
TENONING
TENONS
TENOR
TENORIST
TENORISTS
TENORITE
TENORITES
TENOROON
TENOROONS
TENORS
TENOTOMIES
TENOTOMY
TENOUR
TENOURS
TENPENCE
TENPENCES
TENPENNY
TENPINS
TENREC
TENRECS
TENS
TENSE
TENSED
TENSELESS
TENSELY
TENSENESS
TENSENESSES
TENSER
TENSES
TENSEST
TENSIBLE
TENSILE
TENSILITIES
TENSILITY
TENSING
TENSION
TENSIONAL
TENSIONED
TENSIONING
TENSIONS
TENSITIES
TENSITY
TENSIVE
TENSON
TENSONS
TENSOR
TENSORS
TENT
TENTACLE
TENTACLED
TENTACLES
TENTACULA
TENTAGE
TENTAGES
TENTATION
TENTATIONS
TENTATIVE
TENTATIVES
TENTED
TENTER
TENTERED
TENTERING
TENTERS
TENTFUL
TENTFULS
TENTH
TENTHLY
TENTHS
TENTIE
TENTIER
TENTIEST
TENTIGO
TENTIGOS
TENTING
TENTINGS
TENTLESS
TENTORIA
TENTORIAL
TENTORIUM
TENTORIUMS
TENTS
TENTWISE
TENTY
TENUE
TENUES
TENUIOUS
TENUIS
TENUITIES
TENUITY
TENUOUS
TENUOUSLY
TENURABLE
TENURE
TENURED
TENURES
TENURIAL
TENUTO
TENUTOS
TENZON
TENZONS
TEOCALLI
TEOCALLIS
TEOSINTE
TEOSINTES
TEPAL
TEPALS
TEPEE
TEPEES
TEPEFIED
TEPEFIES
TEPEFY
TEPEFYING
TEPHIGRAM
TEPHIGRAMS
TEPHILLAH
TEPHILLIN
TEPHRA
TEPHRAS
TEPHRITE
TEPHRITES
TEPHRITIC
TEPHROITE
TEPHROITES
TEPID
TEPIDARIA
TEPIDER
TEPIDEST
TEPIDITIES
TEPIDITY
TEPIDLY
TEPIDNESS
TEPIDNESSES
TEQUILA
TEQUILAS
TEQUILLA
TEQUILLAS
TERAFLOP
TERAI
TERAIS
TERAKIHI
TERAKIHIS
TERAPH
TERAPHIM
TERAPHIMS
TERAS
TERATA
TERATISM
TERATISMS
TERATOGEN
TERATOGENS
TERATOID
TERATOMA
TERATOMATA
TERBIC
TERBIUM

TERBIUMS
TERCE
TERCEL
TERCELET
TERCELETS
TERCELS
TERCES
TERCET
TERCETS
TERCIO
TERCIOS
TEREBENE
TEREBENES
TEREBINTH
TEREBINTHS
TEREBRA
TEREBRAE
TEREBRANT
TEREBRANTS
TEREBRAS
TEREBRATE
TEREBRATED
TEREBRATES
TEREBRATING
TEREDINES
TEREDO
TEREDOS
TEREFA
TEREFAH
TEREK
TEREKS
TERES
TERETE
TERETES
TERF
TERFE
TERFES
TERFS
TERGA
TERGAL
TERGITE
TERGITES
TERGUM
TERIYAKI
TERIYAKIS
TERM
TERMAGANT
TERMAGANTS
TERMED
TERMER
TERMERS
TERMINAL
TERMINALS
TERMINATE
TERMINATED
TERMINATES
TERMINATING
TERMINER
TERMINERS
TERMING
TERMINI
TERMINISM
TERMINISMS
TERMINIST
TERMINISTS
TERMINUS
TERMINUSES
TERMITARIES
TERMITARY
TERMITE
TERMITES
TERMLESS
TERMLIES
TERMLY
TERMOR
TERMORS
TERMS
TERN
TERNAL
TERNARIES
TERNARY
TERNATE
TERNATELY
TERNE
TERNED
TERNES
TERNING
TERNION
TERNIONS
TERNS
TERPENE
TERPENES
TERPENOID
TERPENOIDS
TERPINEOL
TERPINEOLS
TERRA
TERRACE
TERRACED
TERRACES
TERRACING
TERRACINGS
TERRAE
TERRAFORM
TERRAFORMED
TERRAFORMING
TERRAFORMINGS
TERRAFORMS
TERRAIN
TERRAINS
TERRAMARA
TERRAMARE
TERRAMARES
TERRANE
TERRANES
TERRAPIN
TERRAPINS
TERRARIA
TERRARIUM
TERRARIUMS
TERRAS
TERRASES
TERRAZZO
TERRAZZOS
TERREEN
TERREENS
TERRELLA
TERRELLAS
TERRENE
TERRENELY
TERRENES
TERRET
TERRETS
TERRIBLE
TERRIBLES
TERRIBLY
TERRICOLE
TERRICOLES
TERRIER
TERRIERS
TERRIES
TERRIFIC
TERRIFIED
TERRIFIER
TERRIFIERS
TERRIFIES
TERRIFY
TERRIFYING
TERRINE
TERRINES
TERRIT
TERRITORIES
TERRITORY
TERRITS
TERROR
TERRORFUL
TERRORISE
TERRORISED
TERRORISES
TERRORISING
TERRORISM
TERRORISMS
TERRORIST
TERRORISTS
TERRORIZE
TERRORIZED
TERRORIZES
TERRORIZING
TERRORS
TERRY
TERSE
TERSELY
TERSENESS
TERSENESSES
TERSER
TERSEST
TERSION
TERSIONS
TERTIA
TERTIAL
TERTIALS
TERTIAN
TERTIANS
TERTIARIES
TERTIARY
TERTIAS
TERTIUS
TERTIUSES
TERTS
TERVALENT
TERZETTA
TERZETTAS
TERZETTI
TERZETTO
TERZETTOS
TES
TESLA
TESLAS
TESSELLA
TESSELLAE
TESSELLAR
TESSERA
TESSERACT
TESSERACTS
TESSERAE
TESSERAL
TESSITURA
TESSITURAS
TEST
TESTA
TESTABLE
TESTACIES
TESTACY
TESTAE
TESTAMENT
TESTAMENTS
TESTAMUR
TESTAMURS
TESTATE
TESTATION
TESTATIONS
TESTATOR
TESTATORS
TESTATRICES
TESTATRIX
TESTATRIXES
TESTATUM
TESTATUMS
TESTE
TESTED
TESTEE
TESTEES
TESTER
TESTERN
TESTERNED
TESTERNING
TESTERNS
TESTERS
TESTES
TESTICLE
TESTICLES
TESTIER
TESTIEST
TESTIFIED
TESTIFIER
TESTIFIERS
TESTIFIES
TESTIFY
TESTIFYING
TESTILY
TESTIMONIED
TESTIMONIES
TESTIMONY
TESTIMONYING
TESTINESS
TESTINESSES
TESTING
TESTINGS
TESTIS
TESTON
TESTONS
TESTOON
TESTOONS
TESTRIL
TESTRILL
TESTRILLS
TESTRILS
TESTS
TESTUDINES
TESTUDO
TESTUDOS
TESTY
TETANAL
TETANIC
TETANICS
TETANIES
TETANISE
TETANISED
TETANISES
TETANISING
TETANIZE
TETANIZED
TETANIZES
TETANIZING
TETANOID
TETANUS
TETANUSES
TETANY
TETCHIER
TETCHIEST
TETCHILY
TETCHY
TETE
TETES
TETHER
TETHERED
TETHERING
TETHERS
TETRA
TETRACID
TETRACT
TETRACTS
TETRAD
TETRADIC
TETRADITE
TETRADITES
TETRADS
TETRAGON
TETRAGONS
TETRAGRAM
TETRAGRAMS
TETRALOGIES
TETRALOGY
TETRAPLA
TETRAPLAS
TETRAPOD
TETRAPODIES
TETRAPODS
TETRAPODY
TETRARCH

TETRARCHIES
TETRARCHS
TETRARCHY
TETRAS
TETRAXON
TETRAXONS
TETRODE
TETRODES
TETRONAL
TETRONALS
TETROXIDE
TETROXIDES
TETRYL
TETRYLS
TETTER
TETTERED
TETTERING
TETTEROUS
TETTERS
TETTIX
TETTIXES
TEUCH
TEUCHAT
TEUCHATS
TEUCHER
TEUCHEST
TEUCHTER
TEUCHTERS
TEUGH
TEUGHER
TEUGHEST
TEW
TEWART
TEWARTS
TEWED
TEWEL
TEWELS
TEWHIT
TEWHITS
TEWING
TEWIT
TEWITS
TEWS
TEXAS
TEXASES
TEXT
TEXTBOOK
TEXTBOOKS
TEXTILE
TEXTILES
TEXTLESS
TEXTORIAL
TEXTPHONE
TEXTPHONES
TEXTS
TEXTUAL
TEXTUALLY
TEXTUARIES
TEXTUARY
TEXTURAL
TEXTURE
TEXTURED
TEXTURES
TEXTURING
TEXTURISE
TEXTURISED
TEXTURISES
TEXTURISING
TEXTURIZE
TEXTURIZED
TEXTURIZES
TEXTURIZING
THACK
THACKS
THAE
THAGI
THAGIS
THAIM
THAIRM
THAIRMS
THALAMI
THALAMIC
THALAMUS
THALASSIC
THALER
THALERS
THALIAN
THALLI
THALLIC
THALLINE
THALLIUM
THALLIUMS
THALLOID
THALLOUS
THALLUS
THALLUSES
THALWEG
THALWEGS
THAN
THANA
THANADAR
THANADARS
THANAGE
THANAGES
THANAH
THANAHS
THANAS
THANATISM
THANATISMS
THANATIST
THANATISTS
THANATOID
THANE
THANEDOM
THANEDOMS
THANEHOOD
THANEHOODS
THANES
THANESHIP
THANESHIPS
THANK
THANKED
THANKEE
THANKER
THANKERS
THANKFUL
THANKING
THANKINGS
THANKLESS
THANKS
THANKYOU
THANKYOUS
THANNA
THANNAH
THANNAHS
THANNAS
THANS
THAR
THARS
THAT
THATAWAY
THATCH
THATCHED
THATCHER
THATCHERS
THATCHES
THATCHING
THATCHINGS
THATCHT
THATNESS
THATNESSES
THAUMATIN
THAUMATINS
THAW
THAWED
THAWER
THAWERS
THAWIER
THAWIEST
THAWING
THAWINGS
THAWLESS
THAWS
THAWY
THE
THEACEOUS
THEANDRIC
THEARCHIC
THEARCHIES
THEARCHY
THEATER
THEATERS
THEATRAL
THEATRE
THEATRES
THEATRIC
THEATRICS
THEAVE
THEAVES
THEBAINE
THEBAINES
THECA
THECAE
THECAL
THECATE
THECODONT
THECODONTS
THEE
THEED
THEEING
THEEK
THEEKED
THEEKING
THEEKS
THEES
THEFT
THEFTBOOT
THEFTBOOTS
THEFTS
THEFTUOUS
THEGITHER
THEGN
THEGNS
THEIC
THEICS
THEINE
THEINES
THEIR
THEIRS
THEISM
THEISMS
THEIST
THEISTIC
THEISTS
THELEMENT
THELEMENTS
THELF
THELVES
THELYTOKIES
THELYTOKY
THEM
THEMA
THEMATA
THEMATIC
THEME
THEMED
THEMELESS
THEMES
THEMING
THEMSELF
THEMSELVES
THEN
THENABOUT
THENABOUTS
THENAR
THENARS
THENCE
THENS
THEOCRACIES
THEOCRACY
THEOCRASIES
THEOCRASY
THEOCRAT
THEOCRATS
THEODICIES
THEODICY
THEOGONIC
THEOGONIES
THEOGONY
THEOLOGER
THEOLOGERS
THEOLOGIC
THEOLOGIES
THEOLOGUE
THEOLOGUES
THEOLOGY
THEOMACHIES
THEOMACHY
THEOMANCIES
THEOMANCY
THEOMANIA
THEOMANIAS
THEONOMIES
THEONOMY
THEOPATHIES
THEOPATHY
THEOPHAGIES
THEOPHAGY
THEOPHANIES
THEOPHANY
THEORBIST
THEORBISTS
THEORBO
THEORBOS
THEOREM
THEOREMS
THEORETIC
THEORETICS
THEORIC
THEORICS
THEORIES
THEORIQUE
THEORIQUES
THEORISE
THEORISED
THEORISER
THEORISERS
THEORISES
THEORISING
THEORIST
THEORISTS
THEORIZE
THEORIZED
THEORIZER
THEORIZERS
THEORIZES
THEORIZING
THEORY
THEOSOPH
THEOSOPHIES
THEOSOPHS
THEOSOPHY
THEOTOKOI
THEOTOKOS
THEOW
THEOWS
THERALITE
THERALITES
THERAPIES
THERAPIST
THERAPISTS
THERAPSID
THERAPSIDS
THERAPY
THERBLIG
THERBLIGS
THERE
THEREAT
THEREAWAY
THEREBY

THEREFOR
THEREFORE
THEREFROM
THEREIN
THEREINTO
THERENESS
THERENESSES
THEREOF
THEREON
THEREOUT
THERES
THERETO
THEREUNTO
THEREUPON
THEREWITH
THERIAC
THERIACA
THERIACAL
THERIACAS
THERIACS
THERIAN
THERIANS
THERM
THERMAE
THERMAL
THERMALLY
THERMALS
THERMIC
THERMICAL
THERMIDOR
THERMION
THERMIONS
THERMITE
THERMITES
THERMOTIC
THERMOTICS
THERMS
THEROID
THEROLOGIES
THEROLOGY
THEROPOD
THEROPODS
THESAURI
THESAURUS
THESAURUSES
THESE
THESES
THESIS
THESPIAN
THESPIANS
THETA
THETAS
THETCH
THETCHED
THETCHES
THETCHING
THETE
THETES
THETHER
THETIC
THETICAL
THEURGIC
THEURGIES
THEURGIST
THEURGISTS
THEURGY
THEW
THEWED
THEWES
THEWIER
THEWIEST
THEWLESS
THEWS
THEWY
THEY
THIAMIN
THIAMINE
THIAMINES
THIAMINS
THIASUS
THIASUSES
THIAZIDE
THIAZIDES
THIAZINE
THIAZINES
THIBET
THIBETS
THIBLE
THIBLES
THICK
THICKED
THICKEN
THICKENED
THICKENER
THICKENERS
THICKENING
THICKENINGS
THICKENS
THICKER
THICKEST
THICKET
THICKETED
THICKETS
THICKETY
THICKHEAD
THICKHEADS
THICKING
THICKISH
THICKLY
THICKNESS
THICKNESSES
THICKO
THICKOES
THICKOS
THICKS
THICKSET
THICKSETS
THICKSKIN
THICKSKINS
THICKY
THIEF
THIEVE
THIEVED
THIEVERIES
THIEVERY
THIEVES
THIEVING
THIEVINGS
THIEVISH
THIG
THIGGER
THIGGERS
THIGGING
THIGGINGS
THIGGIT
THIGH
THIGHBONE
THIGHBONES
THIGHS
THIGS
THILK
THILL
THILLER
THILLERS
THILLS
THIMBLE
THIMBLED
THIMBLES
THIMBLING
THIN
THINE
THING
THINGAMIES
THINGAMY
THINGHOOD
THINGHOODS
THINGIER
THINGIES
THINGIEST
THINGNESS
THINGNESSES
THINGS
THINGUMMIES
THINGUMMY
THINGY
THINK
THINKABLE
THINKER
THINKERS
THINKING
THINKINGS
THINKS
THINLY
THINNED
THINNER
THINNERS
THINNESS
THINNESSES
THINNEST
THINNING
THINNINGS
THINNISH
THINS
THIOL
THIOLS
THIOPHEN
THIOPHENE
THIOPHENES
THIOPHENS
THIOPHIL
THIOUREA
THIOUREAS
THIR
THIRAM
THIRAMS
THIRD
THIRDED
THIRDING
THIRDINGS
THIRDLY
THIRDS
THIRDSMAN
THIRDSMEN
THIRL
THIRLAGE
THIRLAGES
THIRLED
THIRLING
THIRLS
THIRST
THIRSTED
THIRSTER
THIRSTERS
THIRSTFUL
THIRSTIER
THIRSTIEST
THIRSTILY
THIRSTING
THIRSTS
THIRSTY
THIRTEEN
THIRTEENS
THIRTIES
THIRTIETH
THIRTIETHS
THIRTY
THIRTYISH
THIS
THISNESS
THISNESSES
THISTLE
THISTLES
THISTLIER
THISTLIEST
THISTLY
THITHER
THIVEL
THIVELS
THLIPSES
THLIPSIS
THO
THOFT
THOFTS
THOLE
THOLED
THOLES
THOLI
THOLING
THOLOBATE
THOLOBATES
THOLOI
THOLOS
THOLUS
THON
THONDER
THONG
THONGED
THONGS
THORACAL
THORACES
THORACIC
THORAX
THORAXES
THORIA
THORIAS
THORITE
THORITES
THORIUM
THORIUMS
THORN
THORNBACK
THORNBACKS
THORNBILL
THORNBILLS
THORNBUSH
THORNBUSHES
THORNED
THORNIER
THORNIEST
THORNING
THORNLESS
THORNS
THORNSET
THORNTREE
THORNTREES
THORNY
THORON
THORONS
THOROUGH
THOROUGHER
THOROUGHEST
THOROUGHS
THORP
THORPE
THORPES
THORPS
THOSE
THOTHER
THOU
THOUGH
THOUGHT
THOUGHTED
THOUGHTEN
THOUGHTS
THOUING
THOUS
THOUSAND
THOUSANDS
THOWEL
THOWELS
THOWL
THOWLESS
THOWLS
THRAE
THRALDOM
THRALDOMS
THRALL
THRALLDOM
THRALLDOMS
THRALLED

THRALLING
THRALLS
THRANG
THRANGED
THRANGING
THRANGS
THRAPPLE
THRAPPLED
THRAPPLES
THRAPPLING
THRASH
THRASHED
THRASHER
THRASHERS
THRASHES
THRASHING
THRASHINGS
THRASONIC
THRAVE
THRAVES
THRAW
THRAWARD
THRAWART
THRAWING
THRAWN
THRAWS
THREAD
THREADED
THREADEN
THREADER
THREADERS
THREADFIN
THREADFINS
THREADIER
THREADIEST
THREADING
THREADS
THREADY
THREAP
THREAPING
THREAPIT
THREAPS
THREAT
THREATED
THREATEN
THREATENED
THREATENING
THREATENINGS
THREATENS
THREATFUL
THREATING
THREATS
THREAVE
THREAVES
THREE
THREEFOLD
THREENESS
THREENESSES
THREEP
THREEPING
THREEPIT
THREEPS
THREES
THREESOME
THREESOMES
THRENE
THRENES
THRENETIC
THRENODE
THRENODES
THRENODIC
THRENODIES
THRENODY
THRENOS
THRENOSES
THREONINE
THREONINES
THRESH
THRESHED
THRESHEL
THRESHELS
THRESHER
THRESHERS
THRESHES
THRESHING
THRESHINGS
THRESHOLD
THRESHOLDS
THRETTIES
THRETTY
THREW
THRICE
THRID
THRIDACE
THRIDACES
THRIDDED
THRIDDING
THRIDS
THRIFT
THRIFTIER
THRIFTIEST
THRIFTILY
THRIFTS
THRIFTY
THRILL
THRILLANT
THRILLED
THRILLER
THRILLERS
THRILLIER
THRILLIEST
THRILLING
THRILLS
THRILLY
THRIMSA
THRIMSAS
THRIPS
THRIPSES
THRISSEL
THRISSELS
THRIST
THRISTED
THRISTING
THRISTLE
THRISTLES
THRISTS
THRISTY
THRIVE
THRIVED
THRIVEN
THRIVER
THRIVERS
THRIVES
THRIVING
THRIVINGS
THRO
THROAT
THROATED
THROATIER
THROATIEST
THROATILY
THROATS
THROATY
THROB
THROBBED
THROBBING
THROBBINGS
THROBLESS
THROBS
THROE
THROED
THROEING
THROES
THROMBI
THROMBIN
THROMBINS
THROMBOSE
THROMBOSED
THROMBOSES
THROMBOSING
THROMBUS
THRONE
THRONED
THRONES
THRONG
THRONGED
THRONGFUL
THRONGING
THRONGINGS
THRONGS
THRONING
THROPPLE
THROPPLED
THROPPLES
THROPPLING
THROSTLE
THROSTLES
THROTTLE
THROTTLED
THROTTLER
THROTTLERS
THROTTLES
THROTTLING
THROTTLINGS
THROUGH
THROUGHLY
THROVE
THROW
THROWAWAY
THROWAWAYS
THROWBACK
THROWBACKS
THROWE
THROWER
THROWERS
THROWES
THROWING
THROWINGS
THROWN
THROWS
THROWSTER
THROWSTERS
THRU
THRUM
THRUMMED
THRUMMER
THRUMMERS
THRUMMIER
THRUMMIEST
THRUMMING
THRUMMINGS
THRUMMY
THRUMS
THRUSH
THRUSHES
THRUST
THRUSTED
THRUSTER
THRUSTERS
THRUSTING
THRUSTINGS
THRUSTS
THRUTCH
THRUTCHED
THRUTCHES
THRUTCHING
THRUWAY
THRUWAYS
THRYMSA
THRYMSAS
THUD
THUDDED
THUDDING
THUDS
THUG
THUGGEE
THUGGEES
THUGGERIES
THUGGERY
THUGGISM
THUGGISMS
THUGGO
THUGGOS
THUGS
THUJA
THUJAS
THULIA
THULIAS
THULITE
THULITES
THULIUM
THULIUMS
THUMB
THUMBED
THUMBIER
THUMBIEST
THUMBING
THUMBKINS
THUMBLESS
THUMBLIKE
THUMBLING
THUMBLINGS
THUMBNAIL
THUMBNAILS
THUMBNUT
THUMBNUTS
THUMBPOT
THUMBPOTS
THUMBS
THUMBTACK
THUMBTACKS
THUMBY
THUMP
THUMPED
THUMPER
THUMPERS
THUMPING
THUMPS
THUNDER
THUNDERED
THUNDERER
THUNDERERS
THUNDERIER
THUNDERIEST
THUNDERING
THUNDERINGS
THUNDERS
THUNDERY
THUNDROUS
THURIBLE
THURIBLES
THURIFER
THURIFERS
THURIFIED
THURIFIES
THURIFY
THURIFYING
THUS
THUSES
THUSNESS
THUSNESSES
THUSWISE
THUYA
THUYAS
THWACK
THWACKED
THWACKER
THWACKERS
THWACKING
THWACKINGS
THWACKS
THWAITE
THWAITES
THWART
THWARTED
THWARTER
THWARTERS
THWARTING
THWARTINGS
THWARTLY

THWARTS
THY
THYINE
THYLACINE
THYLACINES
THYLOSE
THYLOSES
THYLOSIS
THYME
THYMES
THYMI
THYMIC
THYMIDINE
THYMIDINES
THYMIER
THYMIEST
THYMINE
THYMINES
THYMOCYTE
THYMOCYTES
THYMOL
THYMOLS
THYMUS
THYMY
THYRATRON
THYRATRONS
THYREOID
THYREOIDS
THYRISTOR
THYRISTORS
THYROID
THYROIDS
THYROXIN
THYROXINE
THYROXINES
THYROXINS
THYRSE
THYRSES
THYRSI
THYRSOID
THYRSUS
THYSELF
TI
TIAR
TIARA
TIARAED
TIARAS
TIARS
TIBIA
TIBIAE
TIBIAL
TIBIAS
TIC
TICAL
TICALS
TICCA
TICE
TICED
TICES
TICH
TICHES
TICHIER
TICHIEST
TICHY
TICING
TICK
TICKED
TICKEN
TICKENS
TICKER
TICKERS
TICKET
TICKETED
TICKETING
TICKETS
TICKEY
TICKEYS
TICKIES
TICKING
TICKINGS
TICKLE
TICKLED
TICKLER
TICKLERS
TICKLES
TICKLIER
TICKLIEST
TICKLING
TICKLINGS
TICKLISH
TICKLY
TICKS
TICKY
TICS
TID
TIDAL
TIDBIT
TIDBITS
TIDDIER
TIDDIES
TIDDIEST
TIDDLE
TIDDLED
TIDDLER
TIDDLERS
TIDDLES
TIDDLEY
TIDDLEYS
TIDDLIER
TIDDLIES
TIDDLIEST
TIDDLING
TIDDLY
TIDDY
TIDE
TIDED
TIDELAND
TIDELANDS
TIDELESS
TIDEMARK
TIDEMARKS
TIDEMILL
TIDEMILLS
TIDES
TIDESMAN
TIDESMEN
TIDEWATER
TIDEWATERS
TIDEWAVE
TIDEWAVES
TIDEWAY
TIDEWAYS
TIDIED
TIDIER
TIDIES
TIDIEST
TIDILY
TIDINESS
TIDINESSES
TIDING
TIDINGS
TIDIVATE
TIDIVATED
TIDIVATES
TIDIVATING
TIDS
TIDY
TIDYING
TIE
TIEBACK
TIEBACKS
TIED
TIELESS
TIEPIN
TIEPINS
TIER
TIERCE
TIERCED
TIERCEL
TIERCELET
TIERCELETS
TIERCELS
TIERCERON
TIERCERONS
TIERCES
TIERCET
TIERCETS
TIERED
TIERING
TIEROD
TIERODS
TIERS
TIES
TIETAC
TIETACK
TIETACKS
TIETACS
TIFF
TIFFANIES
TIFFANY
TIFFED
TIFFIN
TIFFING
TIFFINGS
TIFFINS
TIFFS
TIFOSI
TIFOSO
TIFT
TIFTED
TIFTING
TIFTS
TIG
TIGE
TIGER
TIGERISH
TIGERISM
TIGERISMS
TIGERLY
TIGERS
TIGERY
TIGES
TIGGED
TIGGING
TIGHT
TIGHTEN
TIGHTENED
TIGHTENER
TIGHTENERS
TIGHTENING
TIGHTENS
TIGHTER
TIGHTEST
TIGHTISH
TIGHTLY
TIGHTNESS
TIGHTNESSES
TIGHTROPE
TIGHTROPES
TIGHTS
TIGHTWAD
TIGHTWADS
TIGLON
TIGLONS
TIGON
TIGONS
TIGRESS
TIGRESSES
TIGRINE
TIGRISH
TIGRISHLY
TIGROID
TIGS
TIKA
TIKAS
TIKE
TIKES
TIKI
TIKIS
TIKKA
TIL
TILAPIA
TILAPIAS
TILBURIES
TILBURY
TILDE
TILDES
TILE
TILED
TILEFISH
TILEFISHES
TILER
TILERIES
TILERS
TILERY
TILES
TILING
TILINGS
TILL
TILLABLE
TILLAGE
TILLAGES
TILLED
TILLER
TILLERED
TILLERING
TILLERS
TILLIER
TILLIEST
TILLING
TILLINGS
TILLITE
TILLITES
TILLS
TILLY
TILS
TILT
TILTABLE
TILTED
TILTER
TILTERS
TILTH
TILTHS
TILTING
TILTINGS
TILTS
TIMARAU
TIMARAUS
TIMARIOT
TIMARIOTS
TIMBAL
TIMBALE
TIMBALES
TIMBALS
TIMBER
TIMBERED
TIMBERING
TIMBERINGS
TIMBERS
TIMBO
TIMBOS
TIMBRE
TIMBREL
TIMBRELS
TIMBRES
TIME
TIMECARD
TIMECARDS
TIMED
TIMEFRAME
TIMEFRAMES
TIMELESS
TIMELIER
TIMELIEST
TIMELINE
TIMELINES
TIMELY
TIMENOGUY
TIMENOGUYS
TIMEOUS

TIMEOUSLY
TIMEPIECE
TIMEPIECES
TIMER
TIMERS
TIMES
TIMESCALE
TIMESCALES
TIMETABLE
TIMETABLED
TIMETABLES
TIMETABLING
TIMID
TIMIDER
TIMIDEST
TIMIDITIES
TIMIDITY
TIMIDLY
TIMIDNESS
TIMIDNESSES
TIMING
TIMINGS
TIMIST
TIMISTS
TIMOCRACIES
TIMOCRACY
TIMON
TIMONEER
TIMONEERS
TIMONS
TIMOROUS
TIMORSOME
TIMOTHIES
TIMOTHY
TIMOUS
TIMOUSLY
TIMPANI
TIMPANIST
TIMPANISTS
TIMPANO
TIMPS
TIN
TINAJA
TINAJAS
TINAMOU
TINAMOUS
TINCAL
TINCALS
TINCHEL
TINCHELS
TINCT
TINCTED
TINCTING
TINCTS
TINCTURE
TINCTURED
TINCTURES
TINCTURING
TIND
TINDAL
TINDALS
TINDED
TINDER
TINDERBOX
TINDERBOXES
TINDERS
TINDERY
TINDING
TINDS
TINE
TINEA
TINEAL
TINEAS
TINED
TINEID
TINEIDS
TINES
TINFOIL
TINFOILS
TINFUL
TINFULS
TING
TINGE
TINGED
TINGEING
TINGES
TINGING
TINGLE
TINGLED
TINGLER
TINGLERS
TINGLES
TINGLIER
TINGLIEST
TINGLING
TINGLINGS
TINGLISH
TINGLY
TINGS
TINGUAITE
TINGUAITES
TINHORN
TINHORNS
TINIER
TINIES
TINIEST
TINILY
TININESS
TININESSES
TINING
TINK
TINKED
TINKER
TINKERED
TINKERER
TINKERERS
TINKERING
TINKERINGS
TINKERS
TINKING
TINKLE
TINKLED
TINKLER
TINKLERS
TINKLES
TINKLIER
TINKLIEST
TINKLING
TINKLINGS
TINKLY
TINKS
TINMAN
TINMEN
TINNED
TINNER
TINNERS
TINNIE
TINNIER
TINNIES
TINNIEST
TINNING
TINNINGS
TINNITUS
TINNITUSES
TINNY
TINPLATE
TINPLATED
TINPLATES
TINPLATING
TINPOT
TINPOTS
TINS
TINSEL
TINSELED
TINSELING
TINSELLED
TINSELLING
TINSELLY
TINSELRIES
TINSELRY
TINSELS
TINSEY
TINSEYS
TINSMITH
TINSMITHS
TINSNIPS
TINSTONE
TINSTONES
TINT
TINTACK
TINTACKS
TINTED
TINTER
TINTERS
TINTIER
TINTIEST
TINTINESS
TINTINESSES
TINTING
TINTINGS
TINTLESS
TINTS
TINTY
TINTYPE
TINTYPES
TINWARE
TINWARES
TINY
TIP
TIPCAT
TIPCATS
TIPI
TIPIS
TIPPABLE
TIPPED
TIPPER
TIPPERS
TIPPET
TIPPETS
TIPPIER
TIPPIEST
TIPPING
TIPPINGS
TIPPLE
TIPPLED
TIPPLER
TIPPLERS
TIPPLES
TIPPLING
TIPPY
TIPS
TIPSIER
TIPSIEST
TIPSIFIED
TIPSIFIES
TIPSIFY
TIPSIFYING
TIPSILY
TIPSINESS
TIPSINESSES
TIPSTAFF
TIPSTAFFS
TIPSTAVES
TIPSTER
TIPSTERS
TIPSY
TIPT
TIPTOE
TIPTOED
TIPTOEING
TIPTOES
TIPTOP
TIPTOPS
TIPULA
TIPULAS
TIRADE
TIRADES
TIRAMISU
TIRAMISUS
TIRASSE
TIRASSES
TIRE
TIRED
TIREDER
TIREDEST
TIREDLY
TIREDNESS
TIREDNESSES
TIRELESS
TIRELING
TIRELINGS
TIRES
TIRESOME
TIRING
TIRINGS
TIRL
TIRLED
TIRLING
TIRLS
TIRO
TIROES
TIROS
TIRR
TIRRED
TIRRING
TIRRIT
TIRRITS
TIRRIVEE
TIRRIVEES
TIRRIVIE
TIRRIVIES
TIRRS
TIS
TISANE
TISANES
TISICK
TISICKS
TISSUE
TISSUED
TISSUES
TISSUING
TISWAS
TISWASES
TIT
TITAN
TITANATE
TITANATES
TITANESS
TITANESSES
TITANIC
TITANIS
TITANISES
TITANISM
TITANISMS
TITANITE
TITANITES
TITANIUM
TITANIUMS
TITANOUS
TITANS
TITBIT
TITBITS
TITCH
TITCHES
TITCHIER
TITCHIEST
TITCHY
TITE
TITELY
TITER
TITERS
TITFER
TITFERS
TITHABLE
TITHE
TITHED
TITHER
TITHERS
TITHES
TITHING

TITHINGS
TITI
TITIAN
TITIANS
TITILLATE
TITILLATED
TITILLATES
TITILLATING
TITIS
TITIVATE
TITIVATED
TITIVATES
TITIVATING
TITLARK
TITLARKS
TITLE
TITLED
TITLELESS
TITLER
TITLERS
TITLES
TITLING
TITLINGS
TITMICE
TITMOSE
TITMOUSE
TITOKI
TITOKIS
TITRATE
TITRATED
TITRATES
TITRATING
TITRATION
TITRATIONS
TITRE
TITRES
TITS
TITTED
TITTER
TITTERED
TITTERER
TITTERERS
TITTERING
TITTERINGS
TITTERS
TITTIES
TITTING
TITTISH
TITTIVATE
TITTIVATED
TITTIVATES
TITTIVATING
TITTLE
TITTLEBAT
TITTLEBATS
TITTLED
TITTLES
TITTLING
TITTUP
TITTUPED
TITTUPING
TITTUPPED
TITTUPPING
TITTUPS
TITTUPY
TITTY
TITUBANCIES
TITUBANCY
TITUBANT
TITUBATE
TITUBATED
TITUBATES
TITUBATING
TITULAR
TITULARIES
TITULARLY
TITULARS
TITULARY
TITULE
TITULED
TITULES
TITULING
TITUP
TITUPED
TITUPING
TITUPPED
TITUPPING
TITUPS
TITUPY
TIZWAS
TIZWASES
TIZZ
TIZZES
TIZZIES
TIZZY
TJANTING
TJANTINGS
TMESES
TMESIS
TO
TOAD
TOADFISH
TOADFISHES
TOADFLAX
TOADFLAXES
TOADGRASS
TOADGRASSES
TOADIED
TOADIES
TOADRUSH
TOADRUSHES
TOADS
TOADSTONE
TOADSTONES
TOADSTOOL
TOADSTOOLS
TOADY
TOADYING
TOADYISH
TOADYISM
TOADYISMS
TOAST
TOASTED
TOASTER
TOASTERS
TOASTIE
TOASTIES
TOASTING
TOASTINGS
TOASTS
TOASTY
TOAZE
TOAZED
TOAZES
TOAZING
TOBACCO
TOBACCOES
TOBACCOS
TOBIES
TOBOGGAN
TOBOGGANED
TOBOGGANING
TOBOGGANINGS
TOBOGGANS
TOBOGGIN
TOBOGGINED
TOBOGGINING
TOBOGGINS
TOBY
TOC
TOCCATA
TOCCATAS
TOCCATINA
TOCCATINAS
TOCHER
TOCHERED
TOCHERING
TOCHERS
TOCK
TOCKED
TOCKING
TOCKS
TOCO
TOCOLOGIES
TOCOLOGY
TOCOS
TOCS
TOCSIN
TOCSINS
TOD
TODAY
TODAYS
TODDE
TODDED
TODDES
TODDIES
TODDING
TODDLE
TODDLED
TODDLER
TODDLERS
TODDLES
TODDLING
TODDY
TODIES
TODS
TODY
TOE
TOEA
TOEAS
TOECAP
TOECAPS
TOECLIP
TOECLIPS
TOED
TOEHOLD
TOEHOLDS
TOEIER
TOEIEST
TOEING
TOELESS
TOENAIL
TOENAILED
TOENAILING
TOENAILS
TOERAG
TOERAGGER
TOERAGGERS
TOERAGS
TOES
TOETOE
TOETOES
TOEY
TOFF
TOFFEE
TOFFEES
TOFFIER
TOFFIES
TOFFIEST
TOFFISH
TOFFS
TOFFY
TOFORE
TOFT
TOFTS
TOFU
TOFUS
TOG
TOGA
TOGAED
TOGAS
TOGATE
TOGATED
TOGE
TOGED
TOGES
TOGETHER
TOGGED
TOGGERIES
TOGGERY
TOGGING
TOGGLE
TOGGLED
TOGGLES
TOGGLING
TOGS
TOGUE
TOGUES
TOHEROA
TOHEROAS
TOHO
TOHOS
TOHUNGA
TOHUNGAS
TOIL
TOILE
TOILED
TOILER
TOILERS
TOILES
TOILET
TOILETED
TOILETING
TOILETRIES
TOILETRY
TOILETS
TOILETTE
TOILETTES
TOILFUL
TOILINET
TOILINETS
TOILING
TOILINGS
TOILLESS
TOILS
TOILSOME
TOISE
TOISEACH
TOISEACHS
TOISECH
TOISECHS
TOISES
TOISON
TOISONS
TOITOI
TOITOIS
TOKAMAK
TOKAMAKS
TOKAY
TOKAYS
TOKE
TOKED
TOKEN
TOKENED
TOKENING
TOKENISM
TOKENISMS
TOKENS
TOKES
TOKING
TOKO
TOKOLOGIES
TOKOLOGY
TOKOLOSHE
TOKOLOSHES
TOKOS
TOLA
TOLAS
TOLBOOTH
TOLBOOTHS
TOLD
TOLE
TOLED
TOLERABLE
TOLERABLY
TOLERANCE
TOLERANCES
TOLERANT
TOLERATE
TOLERATED

TOLERATES
TOLERATING
TOLERATOR
TOLERATORS
TOLES
TOLEWARE
TOLEWARES
TOLING
TOLINGS
TOLL
TOLLABLE
TOLLAGE
TOLLAGES
TOLLBOOTH
TOLLBOOTHS
TOLLDISH
TOLLDISHES
TOLLED
TOLLER
TOLLERS
TOLLHOUSE
TOLLHOUSES
TOLLING
TOLLINGS
TOLLMAN
TOLLMEN
TOLLS
TOLSEL
TOLSELS
TOLSEY
TOLSEYS
TOLT
TOLTER
TOLTERED
TOLTERING
TOLTERS
TOLTS
TOLU
TOLUATE
TOLUATES
TOLUENE
TOLUENES
TOLUIC
TOLUIDINE
TOLUIDINES
TOLUOL
TOLUOLS
TOLUS
TOLZEY
TOLZEYS
TOM
TOMAHAWK
TOMAHAWKED
TOMAHAWKING
TOMAHAWKS
TOMALLEY
TOMALLEYS
TOMAN
TOMANS
TOMATILLO
TOMATILLOES
TOMATILLOS
TOMATO
TOMATOES
TOMATOEY
TOMB
TOMBAC
TOMBACS
TOMBAK
TOMBAKS
TOMBED
TOMBIC
TOMBING
TOMBLESS
TOMBOC
TOMBOCS
TOMBOLA
TOMBOLAS
TOMBOLO
TOMBOLOS
TOMBOY
TOMBOYISH
TOMBOYS
TOMBS
TOMBSTONE
TOMBSTONES
TOMCAT
TOMCATS
TOME
TOMENTA
TOMENTOSE
TOMENTOUS
TOMENTUM
TOMES
TOMFOOL
TOMFOOLED
TOMFOOLING
TOMFOOLS
TOMIA
TOMIAL
TOMIUM
TOMMIED
TOMMIES
TOMMY
TOMMYING
TOMOGRAM
TOMOGRAMS
TOMOGRAPH
TOMOGRAPHS
TOMORROW
TOMORROWS
TOMPION
TOMPIONS
TOMPON
TOMPONED
TOMPONING
TOMPONS
TOMS
TOMTIT
TOMTITS
TON
TONAL
TONALITE
TONALITES
TONALITIES
TONALITY
TONALLY
TONANT
TONDI
TONDINI
TONDINO
TONDINOS
TONDO
TONDOS
TONE
TONED
TONELESS
TONEME
TONEMES
TONEMIC
TONEPAD
TONEPADS
TONER
TONERS
TONES
TONETIC
TONEY
TONG
TONGA
TONGAS
TONGED
TONGING
TONGS
TONGSTER
TONGSTERS
TONGUE
TONGUED
TONGUELET
TONGUELETS
TONGUES
TONGUING
TONGUINGS
TONIC
TONICITIES
TONICITY
TONICS
TONIER
TONIES
TONIEST
TONIGHT
TONIGHTS
TONING
TONINGS
TONISH
TONISHLY
TONITE
TONITES
TONK
TONKED
TONKER
TONKERS
TONKING
TONKS
TONLET
TONLETS
TONNAG
TONNAGE
TONNAGES
TONNAGS
TONNE
TONNEAU
TONNEAUS
TONNEAUX
TONNELL
TONNELLS
TONNES
TONNISH
TONNISHLY
TONOMETER
TONOMETERS
TONOMETRIES
TONOMETRY
TONS
TONSIL
TONSILLAR
TONSILS
TONSOR
TONSORIAL
TONSORS
TONSURE
TONSURED
TONSURES
TONSURING
TONTINE
TONTINER
TONTINERS
TONTINES
TONUS
TONUSES
TONY
TOO
TOOART
TOOARTS
TOOK
TOOL
TOOLBAG
TOOLBAGS
TOOLBAR
TOOLBARS
TOOLBOX
TOOLBOXES
TOOLED
TOOLER
TOOLERS
TOOLHOUSE
TOOLHOUSES
TOOLING
TOOLINGS
TOOLKIT
TOOLKITS
TOOLMAKER
TOOLMAKERS
TOOLMAN
TOOLMEN
TOOLROOM
TOOLROOMS
TOOLS
TOOM
TOOMED
TOOMER
TOOMEST
TOOMING
TOOMS
TOON
TOONS
TOORIE
TOORIES
TOOT
TOOTED
TOOTER
TOOTERS
TOOTH
TOOTHACHE
TOOTHACHES
TOOTHCOMB
TOOTHCOMBS
TOOTHED
TOOTHFUL
TOOTHFULS
TOOTHIER
TOOTHIEST
TOOTHILY
TOOTHING
TOOTHLESS
TOOTHLIKE
TOOTHPICK
TOOTHPICKS
TOOTHS
TOOTHSOME
TOOTHWASH
TOOTHWASHES
TOOTHWORT
TOOTHWORTS
TOOTHY
TOOTING
TOOTLE
TOOTLED
TOOTLES
TOOTLING
TOOTS
TOOTSED
TOOTSES
TOOTSIE
TOOTSIES
TOOTSING
TOOTSY
TOP
TOPARCH
TOPARCHIES
TOPARCHS
TOPARCHY
TOPAZ
TOPAZES
TOPAZINE
TOPCOAT
TOPCOATS
TOPE
TOPECTOMIES
TOPECTOMY
TOPED
TOPEE
TOPEES
TOPEK
TOPEKS
TOPER
TOPERS
TOPES
TOPFULL
TOPHI
TOPHUS

TOPI
TOPIARIAN
TOPIARIES
TOPIARIST
TOPIARISTS
TOPIARY
TOPIC
TOPICAL
TOPICALLY
TOPICS
TOPING
TOPIS
TOPKNOT
TOPKNOTS
TOPLESS
TOPLINE
TOPLINED
TOPLINER
TOPLINERS
TOPLINES
TOPLINING
TOPLOFTY
TOPMAKER
TOPMAKERS
TOPMAKING
TOPMAKINGS
TOPMAN
TOPMAST
TOPMASTS
TOPMEN
TOPMINNOW
TOPMINNOWS
TOPMOST
TOPOI
TOPOLOGIC
TOPOLOGIES
TOPOLOGY
TOPONYM
TOPONYMAL
TOPONYMIC
TOPONYMICS
TOPONYMIES
TOPONYMS
TOPONYMY
TOPOS
TOPOTYPE
TOPOTYPES
TOPPED
TOPPER
TOPPERS
TOPPING
TOPPINGLY
TOPPINGS
TOPPLE
TOPPLED
TOPPLES
TOPPLING
TOPS
TOPSAIL
TOPSAILS
TOPSIDE
TOPSIDES
TOPSMAN
TOPSMEN
TOPSOIL
TOPSOILS
TOPSPIN
TOPSPINS
TOQUE
TOQUES
TOQUILLA
TOQUILLAS
TOR
TORAN
TORANA
TORANAS
TORANS
TORBANITE
TORBANITES
TORC
TORCH
TORCHED
TORCHER
TORCHERE
TORCHERES
TORCHERS
TORCHES
TORCHIER
TORCHIERE
TORCHIERES
TORCHIERS
TORCHING
TORCHINGS
TORCHON
TORCHONS
TORCHWOOD
TORCHWOODS
TORCS
TORCULAR
TORCULARS
TORDION
TORDIONS
TORE
TOREADOR
TOREADORS
TORERO
TOREROS
TORES
TOREUTIC
TOREUTICS
TORGOCH
TORGOCHS
TORI
TORIC
TORII
TORMENT
TORMENTA
TORMENTED
TORMENTER
TORMENTERS
TORMENTIL
TORMENTILS
TORMENTING
TORMENTINGS
TORMENTOR
TORMENTORS
TORMENTS
TORMENTUM
TORMENTUMS
TORMINA
TORMINAL
TORMINOUS
TORN
TORNADE
TORNADES
TORNADIC
TORNADO
TORNADOES
TORNADOS
TOROID
TOROIDAL
TOROIDS
TOROSE
TOROUS
TORPEDO
TORPEDOED
TORPEDOER
TORPEDOERS
TORPEDOES
TORPEDOING
TORPEDOS
TORPEFIED
TORPEFIES
TORPEFY
TORPEFYING
TORPID
TORPIDITIES
TORPIDITY
TORPIDLY
TORPIDS
TORPITUDE
TORPITUDES
TORPOR
TORPORS
TORQUATE
TORQUATED
TORQUE
TORQUED
TORQUES
TORR
TORREFIED
TORREFIES
TORREFY
TORREFYING
TORRENT
TORRENTS
TORRET
TORRETS
TORRID
TORRIDER
TORRIDEST
TORRIDITIES
TORRIDITY
TORRIDLY
TORRS
TORS
TORSADE
TORSADES
TORSE
TORSEL
TORSELS
TORSES
TORSI
TORSION
TORSIONAL
TORSIONS
TORSIVE
TORSK
TORSKS
TORSO
TORSOS
TORT
TORTE
TORTEN
TORTES
TORTILE
TORTILITIES
TORTILITY
TORTILLA
TORTILLAS
TORTIOUS
TORTIVE
TORTOISE
TORTOISES
TORTONI
TORTONIS
TORTRICES
TORTRICID
TORTRICIDS
TORTRIX
TORTS
TORTUOUS
TORTURE
TORTURED
TORTURER
TORTURERS
TORTURES
TORTURING
TORTURINGS
TORTUROUS
TORUFFLED
TORULA
TORULAE
TORULI
TORULIN
TORULINS
TORULOSE
TORULOSES
TORULOSIS
TORULUS
TORUS
TOSA
TOSAS
TOSE
TOSED
TOSES
TOSH
TOSHACH
TOSHACHS
TOSHED
TOSHER
TOSHERS
TOSHES
TOSHIER
TOSHIEST
TOSHING
TOSHY
TOSING
TOSS
TOSSED
TOSSEN
TOSSER
TOSSERS
TOSSES
TOSSIER
TOSSIEST
TOSSILY
TOSSING
TOSSINGS
TOSSPOT
TOSSPOTS
TOSSY
TOST
TOSTADA
TOSTADAS
TOT
TOTAL
TOTALISE
TOTALISED
TOTALISER
TOTALISERS
TOTALISES
TOTALISING
TOTALITIES
TOTALITY
TOTALIZE
TOTALIZED
TOTALIZER
TOTALIZERS
TOTALIZES
TOTALIZING
TOTALLED
TOTALLING
TOTALLY
TOTALS
TOTANUS
TOTANUSES
TOTAQUINE
TOTAQUINES
TOTARA
TOTARAS
TOTE
TOTED
TOTEM
TOTEMIC
TOTEMISM
TOTEMISMS
TOTEMIST
TOTEMISTS
TOTEMS
TOTES
TOTHER
TOTIENT
TOTIENTS
TOTING
TOTITIVE
TOTITIVES
TOTS
TOTTED
TOTTER

TOTTERED
TOTTERER
TOTTERERS
TOTTERING
TOTTERINGS
TOTTERS
TOTTERY
TOTTIE
TOTTIER
TOTTIES
TOTTIEST
TOTTING
TOTTINGS
TOTTY
TOUCAN
TOUCANET
TOUCANETS
TOUCANS
TOUCH
TOUCHABLE
TOUCHBACK
TOUCHBACKS
TOUCHDOWN
TOUCHDOWNS
TOUCHE
TOUCHED
TOUCHER
TOUCHERS
TOUCHES
TOUCHIER
TOUCHIEST
TOUCHILY
TOUCHING
TOUCHINGS
TOUCHLESS
TOUCHLINE
TOUCHLINES
TOUCHMARK
TOUCHMARKS
TOUCHTONE
TOUCHWOOD
TOUCHWOODS
TOUCHY
TOUGH
TOUGHEN
TOUGHENED
TOUGHENER
TOUGHENERS
TOUGHENING
TOUGHENINGS
TOUGHENS
TOUGHER
TOUGHEST
TOUGHIE
TOUGHIES
TOUGHISH
TOUGHLY
TOUGHNESS
TOUGHNESSES
TOUGHS
TOUK
TOUKED
TOUKING
TOUKS
TOUN
TOUNS
TOUPEE
TOUPEES
TOUPET
TOUPETS
TOUR
TOURACO
TOURACOS
TOURED
TOURER
TOURERS
TOURIE
TOURIES
TOURING
TOURINGS
TOURISM
TOURISMS
TOURIST
TOURISTIC
TOURISTS
TOURISTY
TOURNEDOS
TOURNEY
TOURNEYED
TOURNEYER
TOURNEYERS
TOURNEYING
TOURNEYS
TOURNURE
TOURNURES
TOURS
TOUSE
TOUSED
TOUSER
TOUSERS
TOUSES
TOUSIER
TOUSIEST
TOUSING
TOUSINGS
TOUSLE
TOUSLED
TOUSLES
TOUSLING
TOUSTIE
TOUSTIER
TOUSTIEST
TOUSY
TOUT
TOUTED
TOUTER
TOUTERS
TOUTIE
TOUTIER
TOUTIEST
TOUTING
TOUTS
TOUZE
TOUZED
TOUZES
TOUZIER
TOUZIEST
TOUZING
TOUZLE
TOUZLED
TOUZLES
TOUZLING
TOUZY
TOVARICH
TOVARICHES
TOVARISCH
TOVARISCHES
TOVARISH
TOVARISHES
TOW
TOWABLE
TOWAGE
TOWAGES
TOWARD
TOWARDLY
TOWARDS
TOWBAR
TOWBARS
TOWBOAT
TOWBOATS
TOWED
TOWEL
TOWELED
TOWELHEAD
TOWELHEADS
TOWELING
TOWELLED
TOWELLING
TOWELLINGS
TOWELS
TOWER
TOWERED
TOWERIER
TOWERIEST
TOWERING
TOWERLESS
TOWERS
TOWERY
TOWHEE
TOWHEES
TOWIER
TOWIEST
TOWING
TOWINGS
TOWLINE
TOWLINES
TOWMON
TOWMOND
TOWMONDS
TOWMONS
TOWMONT
TOWMONTS
TOWN
TOWNEE
TOWNEES
TOWNHOUSE
TOWNHOUSES
TOWNIE
TOWNIER
TOWNIES
TOWNIEST
TOWNISH
TOWNLAND
TOWNLANDS
TOWNLESS
TOWNLIER
TOWNLIEST
TOWNLING
TOWNLINGS
TOWNLY
TOWNS
TOWNSCAPE
TOWNSCAPED
TOWNSCAPES
TOWNSCAPING
TOWNSCAPINGS
TOWNSFOLK
TOWNSFOLKS
TOWNSHIP
TOWNSHIPS
TOWNSKIP
TOWNSKIPS
TOWNSMAN
TOWNSMEN
TOWNY
TOWPATH
TOWPATHS
TOWROPE
TOWROPES
TOWS
TOWSE
TOWSED
TOWSER
TOWSERS
TOWSES
TOWSIER
TOWSIEST
TOWSING
TOWSY
TOWT
TOWTED
TOWTING
TOWTS
TOWY
TOWZE
TOWZED
TOWZES
TOWZIER
TOWZIEST
TOWZING
TOWZY
TOXAEMIA
TOXAEMIAS
TOXAEMIC
TOXAPHENE
TOXAPHENES
TOXEMIA
TOXEMIAS
TOXEMIC
TOXIC
TOXICAL
TOXICALLY
TOXICANT
TOXICANTS
TOXICITIES
TOXICITY
TOXIN
TOXINS
TOXOCARA
TOXOCARAS
TOXOID
TOXOIDS
TOXOPHILIES
TOXOPHILY
TOY
TOYED
TOYER
TOYERS
TOYING
TOYINGS
TOYISH
TOYISHLY
TOYLESOME
TOYLESS
TOYLIKE
TOYLSOM
TOYMAN
TOYMEN
TOYS
TOYSHOP
TOYSHOPS
TOYSOME
TOYWOMAN
TOYWOMEN
TOZE
TOZED
TOZES
TOZIE
TOZIES
TOZING
TRABEATE
TRABEATED
TRABECULA
TRABECULAE
TRACE
TRACEABLE
TRACEABLY
TRACED
TRACELESS
TRACER
TRACERIED
TRACERIES
TRACERS
TRACERY
TRACES
TRACHEA
TRACHEAE
TRACHEAL
TRACHEARIES
TRACHEARY
TRACHEATE
TRACHEID
TRACHEIDE
TRACHEIDES
TRACHEIDS
TRACHINUS
TRACHINUSES
TRACHITIS
TRACHITISES
TRACHOMA

TRACHOMAS
TRACHYTE
TRACHYTES
TRACHYTIC
TRACING
TRACINGS
TRACK
TRACKABLE
TRACKAGE
TRACKAGES
TRACKBALL
TRACKBALLS
TRACKED
TRACKER
TRACKERS
TRACKING
TRACKINGS
TRACKLESS
TRACKMAN
TRACKMEN
TRACKROAD
TRACKROADS
TRACKS
TRACKWAY
TRACKWAYS
TRACT
TRACTABLE
TRACTABLY
TRACTATE
TRACTATES
TRACTATOR
TRACTATORS
TRACTED
TRACTILE
TRACTING
TRACTION
TRACTIONS
TRACTIVE
TRACTOR
TRACTORS
TRACTRICES
TRACTRIX
TRACTS
TRACTUS
TRACTUSES
TRAD
TRADABLE
TRADE
TRADEABLE
TRADED
TRADEFUL
TRADELESS
TRADEMARK
TRADEMARKS
TRADENAME
TRADENAMES
TRADER
TRADERS
TRADES
TRADESMAN
TRADESMEN
TRADING
TRADINGS
TRADITION
TRADITIONS
TRADITIVE
TRADITOR
TRADITORES
TRADITORS
TRADS
TRADUCE
TRADUCED
TRADUCER
TRADUCERS
TRADUCES
TRADUCING
TRADUCINGS
TRAFFIC
TRAFFICKED
TRAFFICKING
TRAFFICKINGS
TRAFFICS
TRAGEDIAN
TRAGEDIANS
TRAGEDIES
TRAGEDY
TRAGELAPH
TRAGELAPHS
TRAGI
TRAGIC
TRAGICAL
TRAGOPAN
TRAGOPANS
TRAGULE
TRAGULES
TRAGULINE
TRAGUS
TRAHISON
TRAHISONS
TRAIK
TRAIKED
TRAIKING
TRAIKIT
TRAIKS
TRAIL
TRAILABLE
TRAILED
TRAILER
TRAILERED
TRAILERING
TRAILERS
TRAILING
TRAILS
TRAIN
TRAINABLE
TRAINBAND
TRAINBANDS
TRAINED
TRAINEE
TRAINEES
TRAINER
TRAINERS
TRAINING
TRAININGS
TRAINLESS
TRAINS
TRAIPSE
TRAIPSED
TRAIPSES
TRAIPSING
TRAIPSINGS
TRAIT
TRAITOR
TRAITORLY
TRAITORS
TRAITRESS
TRAITRESSES
TRAITS
TRAJECT
TRAJECTED
TRAJECTING
TRAJECTS
TRAM
TRAMCAR
TRAMCARS
TRAMLINE
TRAMLINED
TRAMLINES
TRAMMED
TRAMMEL
TRAMMELLED
TRAMMELLING
TRAMMELS
TRAMMING
TRAMP
TRAMPED
TRAMPER
TRAMPERS
TRAMPET
TRAMPETS
TRAMPETTE
TRAMPETTES
TRAMPING
TRAMPINGS
TRAMPISH
TRAMPLE
TRAMPLED
TRAMPLER
TRAMPLERS
TRAMPLES
TRAMPLING
TRAMPLINGS
TRAMPOLIN
TRAMPOLINED
TRAMPOLINING
TRAMPOLINS
TRAMPS
TRAMROAD
TRAMROADS
TRAMS
TRAMWAY
TRAMWAYS
TRANCE
TRANCED
TRANCEDLY
TRANCES
TRANCHE
TRANCHES
TRANCHET
TRANCHETS
TRANCING
TRANECT
TRANECTS
TRANGAM
TRANGAMS
TRANGLE
TRANGLES
TRANKUM
TRANKUMS
TRANNIE
TRANNIES
TRANNY
TRANQUIL
TRANQUILLER
TRANQUILLEST
TRANSACT
TRANSACTED
TRANSACTING
TRANSACTS
TRANSAXLE
TRANSAXLES
TRANSCEND
TRANSCENDED
TRANSCENDING
TRANSCENDS
TRANSE
TRANSECT
TRANSECTED
TRANSECTING
TRANSECTS
TRANSENNA
TRANSENNAS
TRANSEPT
TRANSEPTS
TRANSES
TRANSEUNT
TRANSFARD
TRANSFECT
TRANSFECTED
TRANSFECTING
TRANSFECTS
TRANSFER
TRANSFERRED
TRANSFERRING
TRANSFERS
TRANSFIX
TRANSFIXED
TRANSFIXES
TRANSFIXING
TRANSFORM
TRANSFORMED
TRANSFORMING
TRANSFORMINGS
TRANSFORMS
TRANSFUSE
TRANSFUSED
TRANSFUSES
TRANSFUSING
TRANSHIP
TRANSHIPPED
TRANSHIPPING
TRANSHIPPINGS
TRANSHIPS
TRANSHUME
TRANSHUMED
TRANSHUMES
TRANSHUMING
TRANSIENT
TRANSIENTS
TRANSIRE
TRANSIRES
TRANSIT
TRANSITED
TRANSITING
TRANSITS
TRANSLATE
TRANSLATED
TRANSLATES
TRANSLATING
TRANSMEW
TRANSMEWED
TRANSMEWING
TRANSMEWS
TRANSMIT
TRANSMITS
TRANSMITTED
TRANSMITTING
TRANSMOVE
TRANSMOVED
TRANSMOVES
TRANSMOVING
TRANSMUTE
TRANSMUTED
TRANSMUTES
TRANSMUTING
TRANSOM
TRANSOMS
TRANSONIC
TRANSONICS
TRANSPIRE
TRANSPIRED
TRANSPIRES
TRANSPIRING
TRANSPORT
TRANSPORTED
TRANSPORTING
TRANSPORTINGS
TRANSPORTS
TRANSPOSE
TRANSPOSED
TRANSPOSES
TRANSPOSING
TRANSPOSINGS
TRANSSHIP
TRANSSHIPPED
TRANSSHIPPING
TRANSSHIPPINGS
TRANSSHIPS
TRANSUDE
TRANSUDED
TRANSUDES
TRANSUDING
TRANSUME
TRANSUMED
TRANSUMES
TRANSUMING
TRANSUMPT
TRANSUMPTS
TRANSVEST
TRANSVESTED

TRANSVESTING
TRANSVESTS
TRANT
TRANTED
TRANTER
TRANTERS
TRANTING
TRANTS
TRAP
TRAPAN
TRAPANNED
TRAPANNING
TRAPANS
TRAPDOOR
TRAPDOORS
TRAPE
TRAPED
TRAPES
TRAPESED
TRAPESES
TRAPESING
TRAPESINGS
TRAPEZE
TRAPEZED
TRAPEZES
TRAPEZIA
TRAPEZIAL
TRAPEZII
TRAPEZING
TRAPEZIUM
TRAPEZIUMS
TRAPEZIUS
TRAPEZIUSES
TRAPEZOID
TRAPEZOIDS
TRAPING
TRAPLIKE
TRAPPEAN
TRAPPED
TRAPPER
TRAPPERS
TRAPPIER
TRAPPIEST
TRAPPING
TRAPPINGS
TRAPPY
TRAPROCK
TRAPROCKS
TRAPS
TRAPUNTO
TRAPUNTOS
TRASH
TRASHCAN
TRASHCANS
TRASHED
TRASHERIES
TRASHERY
TRASHES
TRASHIER
TRASHIEST
TRASHILY
TRASHING
TRASHMAN
TRASHMEN
TRASHTRIE
TRASHTRIES
TRASHY
TRASS
TRASSES
TRAT
TRATS
TRATT
TRATTORIA
TRATTORIAS
TRATTORIE
TRATTS
TRAUCHLE
TRAUCHLED
TRAUCHLES
TRAUCHLING
TRAUMA
TRAUMAS
TRAUMATA
TRAUMATIC
TRAVAIL
TRAVAILED
TRAVAILING
TRAVAILS
TRAVE
TRAVEL
TRAVELED
TRAVELER
TRAVELERS
TRAVELING
TRAVELINGS
TRAVELLED
TRAVELLER
TRAVELLERS
TRAVELLING
TRAVELLINGS
TRAVELOG
TRAVELOGS
TRAVELS
TRAVERSAL
TRAVERSALS
TRAVERSE
TRAVERSED
TRAVERSER
TRAVERSERS
TRAVERSES
TRAVERSING
TRAVERSINGS
TRAVERTIN
TRAVERTINS
TRAVES
TRAVESTIED
TRAVESTIES
TRAVESTY
TRAVESTYING
TRAVIS
TRAVISES
TRAVOIS
TRAWL
TRAWLED
TRAWLER
TRAWLERS
TRAWLING
TRAWLINGS
TRAWLS
TRAY
TRAYBIT
TRAYBITS
TRAYFUL
TRAYFULS
TRAYNE
TRAYNED
TRAYNES
TRAYNING
TRAYS
TREACHER
TREACHERIES
TREACHERS
TREACHERY
TREACHOUR
TREACHOURS
TREACLE
TREACLED
TREACLES
TREACLIER
TREACLIEST
TREACLING
TREACLY
TREAD
TREADER
TREADERS
TREADING
TREADINGS
TREADLE
TREADLED
TREADLER
TREADLERS
TREADLES
TREADLING
TREADLINGS
TREADMILL
TREADMILLS
TREADS
TREAGUE
TREAGUES
TREASON
TREASONS
TREASURE
TREASURED
TREASURER
TREASURERS
TREASURES
TREASURIES
TREASURING
TREASURY
TREAT
TREATABLE
TREATED
TREATER
TREATERS
TREATIES
TREATING
TREATINGS
TREATISE
TREATISES
TREATMENT
TREATMENTS
TREATS
TREATY
TREBLE
TREBLED
TREBLES
TREBLING
TREBLY
TREBUCHET
TREBUCHETS
TRECENTO
TRECENTOS
TRECK
TRECKED
TRECKING
TRECKS
TREDDLE
TREDDLED
TREDDLES
TREDDLING
TREDILLE
TREDILLES
TREDRILLE
TREDRILLES
TREE
TREED
TREEING
TREELESS
TREEN
TREENAIL
TREENAILS
TREENS
TREENWARE
TREENWARES
TREES
TREESHIP
TREESHIPS
TREETOP
TREETOPS
TREF
TREFA
TREFOIL
TREFOILED
TREFOILS
TREGETOUR
TREGETOURS
TREHALA
TREHALAS
TREIF
TREILLAGE
TREILLAGES
TREILLE
TREILLES
TREK
TREKKED
TREKKER
TREKKERS
TREKKING
TREKS
TRELLIS
TRELLISED
TRELLISES
TRELLISING
TREMA
TREMAS
TREMATIC
TREMATODE
TREMATODES
TREMATOID
TREMATOIDS
TREMBLANT
TREMBLE
TREMBLED
TREMBLER
TREMBLERS
TREMBLES
TREMBLIER
TREMBLIEST
TREMBLING
TREMBLINGS
TREMBLY
TREMIE
TREMIES
TREMOLANT
TREMOLANTS
TREMOLITE
TREMOLITES
TREMOLO
TREMOLOS
TREMOR
TREMORED
TREMORING
TREMORS
TREMULANT
TREMULANTS
TREMULATE
TREMULATED
TREMULATES
TREMULATING
TREMULOUS
TRENAIL
TRENAILS
TRENCH
TRENCHAND
TRENCHANT
TRENCHARD
TRENCHARDS
TRENCHED
TRENCHER
TRENCHERS
TRENCHES
TRENCHING
TREND
TRENDED
TRENDIER
TRENDIES
TRENDIEST
TRENDILY
TRENDING
TRENDS
TRENDY
TRENDYISM
TRENDYISMS
TRENISE
TRENISES
TRENTAL
TRENTALS
TREPAN
TREPANG
TREPANGS

TREPANNED
TREPANNER
TREPANNERS
TREPANNING
TREPANNINGS
TREPANS
TREPHINE
TREPHINED
TREPHINER
TREPHINERS
TREPHINES
TREPHINING
TREPHININGS
TREPID
TREPIDANT
TREPONEMA
TREPONEMAS
TREPONEMATA
TREPONEME
TREPONEMES
TRES
TRESPASS
TRESPASSED
TRESPASSES
TRESPASSING
TRESS
TRESSED
TRESSEL
TRESSELS
TRESSES
TRESSIER
TRESSIEST
TRESSING
TRESSURE
TRESSURED
TRESSURES
TRESSY
TREST
TRESTLE
TRESTLES
TRESTS
TRET
TRETS
TREVALLIES
TREVALLY
TREVIS
TREVISES
TREVISS
TREVISSES
TREW
TREWS
TREWSMAN
TREWSMEN
TREY
TREYBIT
TREYBITS
TREYS
TREZ
TREZES
TRIABLE
TRIACID
TRIACT
TRIACTINE
TRIAD
TRIADIC
TRIADIST
TRIADISTS
TRIADS
TRIAGE
TRIAGES
TRIAL
TRIALISM
TRIALISMS
TRIALIST
TRIALISTS
TRIALITIES
TRIALITY
TRIALLED
TRIALLING
TRIALLIST
TRIALLISTS
TRIALOGUE
TRIALOGUES
TRIALS
TRIANGLE
TRIANGLED
TRIANGLES
TRIAPSAL
TRIARCH
TRIARCHIES
TRIARCHS
TRIARCHY
TRIATHLON
TRIATHLONS
TRIATIC
TRIATICS
TRIATOMIC
TRIAXIAL
TRIAXIALS
TRIAXON
TRIAXONS
TRIBADE
TRIBADES
TRIBADIC
TRIBADIES
TRIBADISM
TRIBADISMS
TRIBADY
TRIBAL
TRIBALISM
TRIBALISMS
TRIBALIST
TRIBALISTS
TRIBALLY
TRIBASIC
TRIBBLE
TRIBBLES
TRIBE
TRIBELESS
TRIBES
TRIBESMAN
TRIBESMEN
TRIBLET
TRIBLETS
TRIBOLOGIES
TRIBOLOGY
TRIBRACH
TRIBRACHS
TRIBUNAL
TRIBUNALS
TRIBUNATE
TRIBUNATES
TRIBUNE
TRIBUNES
TRIBUTARIES
TRIBUTARY
TRIBUTE
TRIBUTER
TRIBUTERS
TRIBUTES
TRICAR
TRICARS
TRICE
TRICED
TRICEPS
TRICEPSES
TRICERION
TRICERIONS
TRICES
TRICHINA
TRICHINAE
TRICHINAS
TRICHITE
TRICHITES
TRICHITIC
TRICHOID
TRICHOME
TRICHOMES
TRICHORD
TRICHORDS
TRICHOSES
TRICHOSIS
TRICHROIC
TRICHROME
TRICING
TRICK
TRICKED
TRICKER
TRICKERIES
TRICKERS
TRICKERY
TRICKIER
TRICKIEST
TRICKILY
TRICKING
TRICKINGS
TRICKISH
TRICKLE
TRICKLED
TRICKLES
TRICKLESS
TRICKLET
TRICKLETS
TRICKLIER
TRICKLIEST
TRICKLING
TRICKLINGS
TRICKLY
TRICKS
TRICKSIER
TRICKSIEST
TRICKSOME
TRICKSTER
TRICKSTERS
TRICKSY
TRICKY
TRICLINIA
TRICLINIC
TRICOLOR
TRICOLORS
TRICOLOUR
TRICOLOURS
TRICORN
TRICORNE
TRICORNES
TRICORNS
TRICOT
TRICOTS
TRICROTIC
TRICUSPID
TRICYCLE
TRICYCLED
TRICYCLER
TRICYCLERS
TRICYCLES
TRICYCLIC
TRICYCLING
TRICYCLINGS
TRIDACNA
TRIDACNAS
TRIDACTYL
TRIDARN
TRIDARNS
TRIDE
TRIDENT
TRIDENTAL
TRIDENTED
TRIDENTS
TRIDUAN
TRIDUUM
TRIDUUMS
TRIDYMITE
TRIDYMITES
TRIE
TRIECIOUS
TRIED
TRIENNIAL
TRIER
TRIERARCH
TRIERARCHS
TRIERS
TRIES
TRIETERIC
TRIETHYL
TRIFACIAL
TRIFECTA
TRIFECTAS
TRIFF
TRIFFER
TRIFFEST
TRIFFIC
TRIFFID
TRIFFIDS
TRIFFIDY
TRIFID
TRIFLE
TRIFLED
TRIFLER
TRIFLERS
TRIFLES
TRIFLING
TRIFOCAL
TRIFOCALS
TRIFOLIES
TRIFOLIUM
TRIFOLIUMS
TRIFOLY
TRIFORIA
TRIFORIUM
TRIFORM
TRIFORMED
TRIG
TRIGAMIES
TRIGAMIST
TRIGAMISTS
TRIGAMOUS
TRIGAMY
TRIGGED
TRIGGER
TRIGGERED
TRIGGERING
TRIGGERS
TRIGGEST
TRIGGING
TRIGLOT
TRIGLOTS
TRIGLY
TRIGLYPH
TRIGLYPHS
TRIGNESS
TRIGNESSES
TRIGON
TRIGONAL
TRIGONIC
TRIGONOUS
TRIGONS
TRIGRAM
TRIGRAMS
TRIGRAPH
TRIGRAPHS
TRIGS
TRIGYNIAN
TRIGYNOUS
TRIHEDRAL
TRIHEDRALS
TRIHEDRON
TRIHEDRONS
TRIHYBRID
TRIHYBRIDS
TRIHYDRIC
TRIKE
TRIKES
TRILBIES
TRILBY
TRILBYS
TRILD
TRILEMMA
TRILEMMAS
TRILINEAR
TRILITH

TRILITHIC
TRILITHON
TRILITHONS
TRILITHS
TRILL
TRILLED
TRILLING
TRILLINGS
TRILLION
TRILLIONS
TRILLIUM
TRILLIUMS
TRILLO
TRILLOES
TRILLS
TRILOBATE
TRILOBE
TRILOBED
TRILOBES
TRILOBITE
TRILOBITES
TRILOGIES
TRILOGY
TRIM
TRIMARAN
TRIMARANS
TRIMER
TRIMERIC
TRIMEROUS
TRIMERS
TRIMESTER
TRIMESTERS
TRIMETER
TRIMETERS
TRIMETHYL
TRIMETRIC
TRIMLY
TRIMMED
TRIMMER
TRIMMERS
TRIMMEST
TRIMMING
TRIMMINGS
TRIMNESS
TRIMNESSES
TRIMS
TRIMTAB
TRIMTABS
TRIN
TRINAL
TRINARY
TRINDLE
TRINDLED
TRINDLES
TRINDLING
TRINE
TRINED
TRINES
TRINGLE
TRINGLES
TRINING
TRINITIES
TRINITRIN
TRINITRINS
TRINITY
TRINKET
TRINKETED
TRINKETER
TRINKETERS
TRINKETING
TRINKETINGS
TRINKETRIES
TRINKETRY
TRINKETS
TRINKUM
TRINKUMS
TRINOMIAL
TRINOMIALS
TRINS
TRIO
TRIODE
TRIODES
TRIOLET
TRIOLETS
TRIONES
TRIONYM
TRIONYMAL
TRIONYMS
TRIOR
TRIORS
TRIOS
TRIOXIDE
TRIOXIDES
TRIP
TRIPE
TRIPEDAL
TRIPERIES
TRIPERY
TRIPES
TRIPEY
TRIPHONE
TRIPHONES
TRIPIER
TRIPIEST
TRIPITAKA
TRIPITAKAS
TRIPLANE
TRIPLANES
TRIPLE
TRIPLED
TRIPLES
TRIPLET
TRIPLETS
TRIPLEX
TRIPLEXES
TRIPLIED
TRIPLIES
TRIPLING
TRIPLINGS
TRIPLOID
TRIPLOIDIES
TRIPLOIDY
TRIPLY
TRIPLYING
TRIPOD
TRIPODAL
TRIPODIES
TRIPODS
TRIPODY
TRIPOLI
TRIPOLIS
TRIPOS
TRIPOSES
TRIPPANT
TRIPPED
TRIPPER
TRIPPERS
TRIPPERY
TRIPPET
TRIPPETS
TRIPPIER
TRIPPIEST
TRIPPING
TRIPPINGS
TRIPPLE
TRIPPLED
TRIPPLER
TRIPPLERS
TRIPPLES
TRIPPLING
TRIPPY
TRIPS
TRIPSES
TRIPSIS
TRIPTANE
TRIPTANES
TRIPTOTE
TRIPTOTES
TRIPTYCH
TRIPTYCHS
TRIPTYQUE
TRIPTYQUES
TRIPUDIA
TRIPUDIUM
TRIPUDIUMS
TRIPWIRE
TRIPWIRES
TRIPY
TRIQUETRA
TRIQUETRAS
TRIRADIAL
TRIREME
TRIREMES
TRISAGION
TRISAGIONS
TRISECT
TRISECTED
TRISECTING
TRISECTOR
TRISECTORS
TRISECTS
TRISEME
TRISEMES
TRISEMIC
TRISHAW
TRISHAWS
TRISKELE
TRISKELES
TRISKELIA
TRISMUS
TRISMUSES
TRISOME
TRISOMES
TRISOMIC
TRISOMIES
TRISOMY
TRIST
TRISTE
TRISTESSE
TRISTESSES
TRISTFUL
TRISTICH
TRISTICHS
TRISUL
TRISULA
TRISULAS
TRISULS
TRITE
TRITELY
TRITENESS
TRITENESSES
TRITER
TRITES
TRITEST
TRITHEISM
TRITHEISMS
TRITHEIST
TRITHEISTS
TRITIATE
TRITIATED
TRITIATES
TRITIATING
TRITICAL
TRITICALE
TRITICALES
TRITICISM
TRITICISMS
TRITIDE
TRITIDES
TRITIUM
TRITIUMS
TRITON
TRITONE
TRITONES
TRITONIA
TRITONIAS
TRITONS
TRITURATE
TRITURATED
TRITURATES
TRITURATING
TRIUMPH
TRIUMPHAL
TRIUMPHALS
TRIUMPHED
TRIUMPHER
TRIUMPHERS
TRIUMPHING
TRIUMPHINGS
TRIUMPHS
TRIUMVIR
TRIUMVIRI
TRIUMVIRIES
TRIUMVIRS
TRIUMVIRY
TRIUNE
TRIUNES
TRIUNITIES
TRIUNITY
TRIVALENT
TRIVALVE
TRIVALVED
TRIVALVES
TRIVET
TRIVETS
TRIVIA
TRIVIAL
TRIVIALLY
TRIVIUM
TRIVIUMS
TRIZONAL
TRIZONE
TRIZONES
TROAD
TROADE
TROADES
TROADS
TROAT
TROATED
TROATING
TROATS
TROCAR
TROCARS
TROCHAIC
TROCHAICS
TROCHAL
TROCHE
TROCHEE
TROCHEES
TROCHES
TROCHI
TROCHILIC
TROCHILUS
TROCHILUSES
TROCHISK
TROCHISKS
TROCHITE
TROCHITES
TROCHLEA
TROCHLEAR
TROCHLEAS
TROCHOID
TROCHOIDS
TROCHUS
TROCHUSES
TROCK
TROCKED
TROCKEN
TROCKING
TROCKS
TROD
TRODDEN
TRODE
TRODES
TRODS
TROELIE
TROELIES
TROELY
TROG
TROGGED

ROGGING
ROGGS
ROGON
ROGONS
ROGS
ROIKA
ROIKAS
ROILISM
ROILISMS
ROILIST
ROILISTS
ROILITE
ROILITES
ROKE
ROKED
ROKES
ROKING
ROLL
ROLLED
ROLLER
ROLLERS
ROLLEY
ROLLEYED
ROLLEYING
ROLLEYS
ROLLIES
ROLLING
ROLLINGS
ROLLIUS
ROLLIUSES
ROLLOP
ROLLOPED
ROLLOPEE
ROLLOPEES
ROLLOPING
ROLLOPS
ROLLOPY
ROLLS
ROLLY
ROMBONE
ROMBONES
ROMINO
ROMINOES
ROMINOS
ROMMEL
ROMMELS
ROMP
ROMPE
ROMPED
ROMPES
ROMPING
ROMPS
RON
RONA
RONAS
RONC
RONCS
RONE
RONES
RONS
ROOLIE
ROOLIES
ROOP
ROOPED
TROOPER
TROOPERS
TROOPIAL
TROOPIALS
TROOPING
TROOPS
TROPARIA
TROPARION
TROPE
TROPED
TROPES
TROPHESIES
TROPHESY
TROPHI
TROPHIC
TROPHIED
TROPHIES
TROPHY
TROPHYING
TROPIC
TROPICAL
TROPICS
TROPING
TROPISM
TROPISMS
TROPIST
TROPISTIC
TROPISTS
TROPOLOGIES
TROPOLOGY
TROPPO
TROSSERS
TROT
TROTH
TROTHED
TROTHFUL
TROTHING
TROTHLESS
TROTHS
TROTLINE
TROTLINES
TROTS
TROTTED
TROTTER
TROTTERS
TROTTING
TROTTINGS
TROTTOIR
TROTTOIRS
TROTYL
TROTYLS
TROUBLE
TROUBLED
TROUBLER
TROUBLERS
TROUBLES
TROUBLING
TROUBLINGS
TROUBLOUS
TROUGH
TROUGHS
TROULE
TROULED
TROULES
TROULING
TROUNCE
TROUNCED
TROUNCER
TROUNCERS
TROUNCES
TROUNCING
TROUNCINGS
TROUPE
TROUPED
TROUPER
TROUPERS
TROUPES
TROUPIAL
TROUPIALS
TROUPING
TROUSE
TROUSER
TROUSERED
TROUSERING
TROUSERINGS
TROUSERS
TROUSES
TROUSSEAU
TROUSSEAUS
TROUSSEAUX
TROUT
TROUTER
TROUTERS
TROUTFUL
TROUTIER
TROUTIEST
TROUTING
TROUTINGS
TROUTLESS
TROUTLET
TROUTLETS
TROUTLING
TROUTLINGS
TROUTS
TROUTY
TROUVERE
TROUVERES
TROUVEUR
TROUVEURS
TROVER
TROVERS
TROW
TROWED
TROWEL
TROWELLED
TROWELLER
TROWELLERS
TROWELLING
TROWELS
TROWING
TROWS
TROWSERS
TROY
TROYS
TRUANCIES
TRUANCY
TRUANT
TRUANTED
TRUANTING
TRUANTRIES
TRUANTRY
TRUANTS
TRUCAGE
TRUCAGES
TRUCE
TRUCELESS
TRUCES
TRUCHMAN
TRUCHMANS
TRUCHMEN
TRUCIAL
TRUCK
TRUCKAGE
TRUCKAGES
TRUCKED
TRUCKER
TRUCKERS
TRUCKIE
TRUCKIES
TRUCKING
TRUCKINGS
TRUCKLE
TRUCKLED
TRUCKLER
TRUCKLERS
TRUCKLES
TRUCKLING
TRUCKLINGS
TRUCKMAN
TRUCKMEN
TRUCKS
TRUCULENT
TRUDGE
TRUDGED
TRUDGEN
TRUDGENS
TRUDGEON
TRUDGEONS
TRUDGER
TRUDGERS
TRUDGES
TRUDGING
TRUDGINGS
TRUE
TRUED
TRUEING
TRUEMAN
TRUEMEN
TRUENESS
TRUENESSES
TRUEPENNIES
TRUEPENNY
TRUER
TRUES
TRUEST
TRUFFLE
TRUFFLED
TRUFFLES
TRUFFLING
TRUFFLINGS
TRUG
TRUGS
TRUING
TRUISM
TRUISMS
TRUISTIC
TRULL
TRULLS
TRULY
TRUMEAU
TRUMEAUX
TRUMP
TRUMPED
TRUMPERIES
TRUMPERY
TRUMPET
TRUMPETED
TRUMPETER
TRUMPETERS
TRUMPETING
TRUMPETINGS
TRUMPETS
TRUMPING
TRUMPINGS
TRUMPS
TRUNCAL
TRUNCATE
TRUNCATED
TRUNCATES
TRUNCATING
TRUNCHEON
TRUNCHEONED
TRUNCHEONING
TRUNCHEONS
TRUNDLE
TRUNDLED
TRUNDLER
TRUNDLERS
TRUNDLES
TRUNDLING
TRUNK
TRUNKED
TRUNKFISH
TRUNKFISHES
TRUNKFUL
TRUNKFULS
TRUNKING
TRUNKINGS
TRUNKS
TRUNNION
TRUNNIONS
TRUQUAGE
TRUQUAGES
TRUQUEUR
TRUQUEURS
TRUSS
TRUSSED
TRUSSER
TRUSSERS
TRUSSES
TRUSSING
TRUSSINGS
TRUST
TRUSTED
TRUSTEE
TRUSTEES

TRUSTER
TRUSTERS
TRUSTFUL
TRUSTIER
TRUSTIES
TRUSTIEST
TRUSTILY
TRUSTING
TRUSTLESS
TRUSTS
TRUSTY
TRUTH
TRUTHFUL
TRUTHIER
TRUTHIEST
TRUTHLESS
TRUTHLIKE
TRUTHS
TRUTHY
TRY
TRYE
TRYER
TRYERS
TRYING
TRYINGLY
TRYINGS
TRYP
TRYPS
TRYPSIN
TRYPSINS
TRYPTIC
TRYSAIL
TRYSAILS
TRYST
TRYSTED
TRYSTER
TRYSTERS
TRYSTING
TRYSTS
TSADDIK
TSADDIKIM
TSADDIKS
TSADDIQ
TSADDIQIM
TSADDIQS
TSAMBA
TSAMBAS
TSAR
TSARDOM
TSARDOMS
TSAREVICH
TSAREVICHES
TSAREVNA
TSAREVNAS
TSARINA
TSARINAS
TSARISM
TSARISMS
TSARIST
TSARISTS
TSARITSA
TSARITSAS
TSARS
TSESSEBE
TSESSEBES
TSETSE
TSETSES
TSIGANE
TSIGANES
TSOTSI
TSOTSIS
TSOURIS
TSOURISES
TSUBA
TSUBAS
TSUNAMI
TSUNAMIS
TSURIS
TSURISES
TSUTSUMU
TSUTSUMUS
TUAN
TUANS
TUART
TUARTS
TUATARA
TUATARAS
TUATH
TUATHS
TUB
TUBA
TUBAE
TUBAGE
TUBAGES
TUBAL
TUBAR
TUBAS
TUBATE
TUBBED
TUBBER
TUBBERS
TUBBIER
TUBBIEST
TUBBINESS
TUBBINESSES
TUBBING
TUBBINGS
TUBBISH
TUBBY
TUBE
TUBECTOMIES
TUBECTOMY
TUBED
TUBEFUL
TUBEFULS
TUBELESS
TUBELIKE
TUBENOSE
TUBENOSES
TUBER
TUBERCLE
TUBERCLED
TUBERCLES
TUBERCULA
TUBERCULE
TUBERCULES
TUBEROSE
TUBEROSES
TUBEROUS
TUBERS
TUBES
TUBFAST
TUBFASTS
TUBFISH
TUBFISHES
TUBFUL
TUBFULS
TUBICOLAR
TUBICOLE
TUBICOLES
TUBIFEX
TUBIFEXES
TUBIFORM
TUBING
TUBINGS
TUBS
TUBULAR
TUBULATE
TUBULATED
TUBULATES
TUBULATING
TUBULE
TUBULES
TUBULIN
TUBULINS
TUBULOUS
TUCHUN
TUCHUNS
TUCK
TUCKAHOE
TUCKAHOES
TUCKED
TUCKER
TUCKERBAG
TUCKERBAGS
TUCKERBOX
TUCKERBOXES
TUCKERED
TUCKERING
TUCKERS
TUCKET
TUCKETS
TUCKING
TUCKS
TUCOTUCO
TUCOTUCOS
TUCUTUCO
TUCUTUCOS
TUFA
TUFACEOUS
TUFAS
TUFF
TUFFE
TUFFES
TUFFET
TUFFETS
TUFFS
TUFT
TUFTED
TUFTER
TUFTERS
TUFTIER
TUFTIEST
TUFTING
TUFTINGS
TUFTS
TUFTY
TUG
TUGBOAT
TUGBOATS
TUGGED
TUGGER
TUGGERS
TUGGING
TUGGINGLY
TUGGINGS
TUGHRA
TUGHRAS
TUGHRIK
TUGHRIKS
TUGRA
TUGRAS
TUGRIK
TUGRIKS
TUGS
TUI
TUILLE
TUILLES
TUILLETTE
TUILLETTES
TUILYIE
TUILYIED
TUILYIEING
TUILYIES
TUILZIE
TUILZIED
TUILZIEING
TUILZIES
TUINA
TUINAS
TUIS
TUISM
TUISMS
TUITION
TUITIONAL
TUITIONS
TULAREMIA
TULAREMIAS
TULAREMIC
TULBAN
TULBANS
TULCHAN
TULCHANS
TULE
TULES
TULIP
TULIPANT
TULIPANTS
TULIPS
TULIPWOOD
TULIPWOODS
TULLE
TULLES
TULWAR
TULWARS
TUM
TUMBLE
TUMBLED
TUMBLER
TUMBLERS
TUMBLES
TUMBLING
TUMBLINGS
TUMBREL
TUMBRELS
TUMBRIL
TUMBRILS
TUMEFIED
TUMEFIES
TUMEFY
TUMEFYING
TUMESCE
TUMESCED
TUMESCENT
TUMESCES
TUMESCING
TUMID
TUMIDITIES
TUMIDITY
TUMIDLY
TUMIDNESS
TUMIDNESSES
TUMMIES
TUMMY
TUMOR
TUMOROUS
TUMORS
TUMOUR
TUMOURS
TUMP
TUMPED
TUMPHIES
TUMPHY
TUMPIER
TUMPIEST
TUMPING
TUMPS
TUMPY
TUMS
TUMSHIE
TUMSHIES
TUMULAR
TUMULARY
TUMULI
TUMULT
TUMULTED
TUMULTING
TUMULTS
TUMULUS
TUN
TUNA
TUNABLE
TUNABLY
TUNAS
TUNBELLIES
TUNBELLY
TUND
TUNDED
TUNDING
TUNDRA

TUNDRAS
TUNDS
TUNDUN
TUNDUNS
TUNE
TUNEABLE
TUNED
TUNEFUL
TUNEFULLY
TUNELESS
TUNER
TUNERS
TUNES
TUNESMITH
TUNESMITHS
TUNGSTATE
TUNGSTATES
TUNGSTEN
TUNGSTENS
TUNIC
TUNICATE
TUNICATED
TUNICATES
TUNICIN
TUNICINS
TUNICKED
TUNICLE
TUNICLES
TUNICS
TUNIER
TUNIEST
TUNING
TUNINGS
TUNNAGE
TUNNAGES
TUNNED
TUNNEL
TUNNELED
TUNNELER
TUNNELERS
TUNNELING
TUNNELLED
TUNNELLER
TUNNELLERS
TUNNELLING
TUNNELLINGS
TUNNELS
TUNNIES
TUNNING
TUNNINGS
TUNNY
TUNS
TUNY
TUP
TUPEK
TUPEKS
TUPELO
TUPELOS
TUPIK
TUPIKS
TUPPED
TUPPENCE
TUPPENCES
TUPPENNIES
TUPPENNY
TUPPING
TUPS
TUPTOWING
TUQUE
TUQUES
TURACIN
TURACINS
TURACO
TURACOS
TURBAN
TURBAND
TURBANDS
TURBANED
TURBANS
TURBANT
TURBANTS
TURBARIES
TURBARY
TURBID
TURBIDITE
TURBIDITES
TURBIDITIES
TURBIDITY
TURBIDLY
TURBINAL
TURBINALS
TURBINATE
TURBINATES
TURBINE
TURBINED
TURBINES
TURBIT
TURBITH
TURBITHS
TURBITS
TURBO
TURBOCAR
TURBOCARS
TURBOFAN
TURBOFANS
TURBOJET
TURBOJETS
TURBOND
TURBONDS
TURBOPROP
TURBOPROPS
TURBOS
TURBOT
TURBOTS
TURBULENT
TURCOPOLE
TURCOPOLES
TURD
TURDINE
TURDION
TURDIONS
TURDOID
TURDS
TUREEN
TUREENS
TURF
TURFED
TURFEN
TURFIER
TURFIEST
TURFINESS
TURFINESSES
TURFING
TURFINGS
TURFITE
TURFITES
TURFMAN
TURFMEN
TURFS
TURFY
TURGENT
TURGENTLY
TURGID
TURGIDER
TURGIDEST
TURGIDITIES
TURGIDITY
TURGIDLY
TURGOR
TURGORS
TURION
TURIONS
TURKEY
TURKEYS
TURKIES
TURKIESES
TURKIS
TURKISES
TURLOUGH
TURLOUGHS
TURM
TURME
TURMERIC
TURMERICS
TURMES
TURMOIL
TURMOILED
TURMOILING
TURMOILS
TURMS
TURN
TURNABOUT
TURNABOUTS
TURNAGAIN
TURNAGAINS
TURNBACK
TURNBACKS
TURNCOAT
TURNCOATS
TURNCOCK
TURNCOCKS
TURNDUN
TURNDUNS
TURNED
TURNER
TURNERIES
TURNERS
TURNERY
TURNING
TURNINGS
TURNIP
TURNIPED
TURNIPING
TURNIPS
TURNKEY
TURNKEYS
TURNOFF
TURNOFFS
TURNOUT
TURNOUTS
TURNOVER
TURNOVERS
TURNPIKE
TURNPIKES
TURNROUND
TURNROUNDS
TURNS
TURNSKIN
TURNSKINS
TURNSOLE
TURNSOLES
TURNSPIT
TURNSPITS
TURNSTILE
TURNSTILES
TURNSTONE
TURNSTONES
TURNTABLE
TURNTABLES
TURPETH
TURPETHS
TURPITUDE
TURPITUDES
TURPS
TURQUOISE
TURQUOISES
TURRET
TURRETED
TURRETS
TURRIBANT
TURRIBANTS
TURTLE
TURTLED
TURTLER
TURTLERS
TURTLES
TURTLING
TURTLINGS
TURVES
TUSCHE
TUSCHES
TUSH
TUSHED
TUSHERIES
TUSHERY
TUSHES
TUSHIE
TUSHIES
TUSHING
TUSHKAR
TUSHKARS
TUSHKER
TUSHKERS
TUSHY
TUSK
TUSKAR
TUSKARS
TUSKED
TUSKER
TUSKERS
TUSKIER
TUSKIEST
TUSKING
TUSKINGS
TUSKLESS
TUSKS
TUSKY
TUSSAH
TUSSAHS
TUSSAL
TUSSEH
TUSSEHS
TUSSER
TUSSERS
TUSSIS
TUSSISES
TUSSIVE
TUSSLE
TUSSLED
TUSSLES
TUSSLING
TUSSOCK
TUSSOCKS
TUSSOCKY
TUSSORE
TUSSORES
TUT
TUTANIA
TUTANIAS
TUTEE
TUTEES
TUTELAGE
TUTELAGES
TUTELAR
TUTELARIES
TUTELARS
TUTELARY
TUTENAG
TUTENAGS
TUTIORISM
TUTIORISMS
TUTIORIST
TUTIORISTS
TUTMAN
TUTMEN
TUTOR
TUTORAGE
TUTORAGES
TUTORED
TUTORESS
TUTORESSES
TUTORIAL
TUTORIALS
TUTORING
TUTORINGS
TUTORISE
TUTORISED
TUTORISES
TUTORISING
TUTORISM

TUTORISMS
TUTORIZE
TUTORIZED
TUTORIZES
TUTORIZING
TUTORS
TUTORSHIP
TUTORSHIPS
TUTRESS
TUTRESSES
TUTRICES
TUTRIX
TUTRIXES
TUTS
TUTSAN
TUTSANS
TUTSED
TUTSES
TUTSING
TUTTED
TUTTI
TUTTIES
TUTTING
TUTTINGS
TUTTIS
TUTTY
TUTU
TUTUS
TUTWORK
TUTWORKER
TUTWORKERS
TUTWORKS
TUX
TUXEDO
TUXEDOES
TUXEDOS
TUXES
TUYERE
TUYERES
TUZZ
TUZZES
TWA
TWADDLE
TWADDLED
TWADDLER
TWADDLERS
TWADDLES
TWADDLIER
TWADDLIEST
TWADDLING
TWADDLINGS
TWADDLY
TWAE
TWAES
TWAFALD
TWAIN
TWAINS
TWAITE
TWAITES
TWAL
TWALHOURS
TWALPENNIES
TWALPENNY
TWALS
TWANG
TWANGED
TWANGIER
TWANGIEST
TWANGING
TWANGINGS
TWANGLE
TWANGLED
TWANGLES
TWANGLING
TWANGLINGS
TWANGS
TWANGY
TWANK
TWANKAY
TWANKAYS
TWANKS
TWAS
TWASOME
TWASOMES
TWAT
TWATS
TWATTLE
TWATTLED
TWATTLER
TWATTLERS
TWATTLES
TWATTLING
TWATTLINGS
TWAY
TWAYS
TWEAK
TWEAKED
TWEAKING
TWEAKINGS
TWEAKS
TWEE
TWEED
TWEEDIER
TWEEDIEST
TWEEDLE
TWEEDLED
TWEEDLER
TWEEDLERS
TWEEDLES
TWEEDLING
TWEEDS
TWEEDY
TWEEL
TWEELED
TWEELING
TWEELS
TWEELY
TWEENESS
TWEENESSES
TWEENIES
TWEENY
TWEER
TWEERED
TWEERING
TWEERS
TWEEST
TWEET
TWEETED
TWEETER
TWEETERS
TWEETING
TWEETS
TWEEZE
TWEEZED
TWEEZERS
TWEEZES
TWEEZING
TWELFTH
TWELFTHLY
TWELFTHS
TWELVE
TWELVEMO
TWELVEMOS
TWELVES
TWENTIES
TWENTIETH
TWENTIETHS
TWENTY
TWENTYISH
TWERP
TWERPS
TWIBILL
TWIBILLS
TWICE
TWICER
TWICERS
TWICHILD
TWICHILDREN
TWIDDLE
TWIDDLED
TWIDDLER
TWIDDLERS
TWIDDLES
TWIDDLIER
TWIDDLIEST
TWIDDLING
TWIDDLINGS
TWIDDLY
TWIER
TWIERS
TWIFOLD
TWIFORKED
TWIFORMED
TWIG
TWIGGED
TWIGGEN
TWIGGER
TWIGGERS
TWIGGIER
TWIGGIEST
TWIGGING
TWIGGY
TWIGHT
TWIGHTED
TWIGHTING
TWIGHTS
TWIGLOO
TWIGLOOS
TWIGS
TWIGSOME
TWILIGHT
TWILIGHTED
TWILIGHTING
TWILIGHTS
TWILIT
TWILL
TWILLED
TWILLIES
TWILLING
TWILLS
TWILLY
TWILT
TWILTED
TWILTING
TWILTS
TWIN
TWINE
TWINED
TWINER
TWINERS
TWINES
TWINGE
TWINGED
TWINGES
TWINGING
TWINIER
TWINIEST
TWINING
TWININGLY
TWININGS
TWINK
TWINKED
TWINKING
TWINKLE
TWINKLED
TWINKLER
TWINKLERS
TWINKLES
TWINKLING
TWINKLINGS
TWINKS
TWINLING
TWINLINGS
TWINNED
TWINNING
TWINNINGS
TWINS
TWINSET
TWINSETS
TWINSHIP
TWINSHIPS
TWINTER
TWINTERS
TWINY
TWIRE
TWIRED
TWIRES
TWIRING
TWIRL
TWIRLED
TWIRLER
TWIRLERS
TWIRLIER
TWIRLIEST
TWIRLING
TWIRLS
TWIRLY
TWIRP
TWIRPS
TWISCAR
TWISCARS
TWIST
TWISTABLE
TWISTED
TWISTER
TWISTERS
TWISTIER
TWISTIEST
TWISTING
TWISTINGS
TWISTOR
TWISTORS
TWISTS
TWISTY
TWIT
TWITCH
TWITCHED
TWITCHER
TWITCHERS
TWITCHES
TWITCHIER
TWITCHIEST
TWITCHING
TWITCHINGS
TWITCHY
TWITE
TWITES
TWITS
TWITTED
TWITTEN
TWITTENS
TWITTER
TWITTERED
TWITTERER
TWITTERERS
TWITTERING
TWITTERINGS
TWITTERS
TWITTERY
TWITTING
TWITTINGS
TWIZZLE
TWIZZLED
TWIZZLES
TWIZZLING
TWO
TWOCCER
TWOCCERS
TWOCCING
TWOCCINGS
TWOER
TWOERS
TWOFOLD
TWONESS
TWONESSES
TWOPENCE
TWOPENCES
TWOPENNIES
TWOPENNY
TWOS

TWOSEATER
TWOSEATERS
TWOSOME
TWOSOMES
TWOSTROKE
TWP
TWYER
TWYERE
TWYERES
TWYERS
TWYFOLD
TWYFORKED
TWYFORMED
TYCHISM
TYCHISMS
TYCOON
TYCOONATE
TYCOONATES
TYCOONERIES
TYCOONERY
TYCOONS
TYDE
TYE
TYED
TYEING
TYES
TYG
TYGS
TYING
TYKE
TYKES
TYKISH
TYLECTOMIES
TYLECTOMY
TYLER
TYLERS
TYLOPOD
TYLOPODS
TYLOSES
TYLOSIS
TYLOTE
TYLOTES
TYMBAL
TYMBALS
TYMP
TYMPAN
TYMPANA
TYMPANAL
TYMPANI
TYMPANIC
TYMPANICS
TYMPANIES
TYMPANIST
TYMPANISTS
TYMPANO
TYMPANS
TYMPANUM
TYMPANY
TYMPS
TYND
TYNDE
TYNE
TYNED
TYNES
TYNING
TYPAL
TYPE
TYPECAST
TYPECASTING
TYPECASTS
TYPED
TYPES
TYPESET
TYPEWRITE
TYPEWRITES
TYPEWRITING
TYPEWRITINGS
TYPEWRITTEN
TYPEWROTE
TYPHLITIC
TYPHLITIS
TYPHLITISES
TYPHOID
TYPHOIDAL
TYPHOIDS
TYPHON
TYPHONIAN
TYPHONIC
TYPHONS
TYPHOON
TYPHOONS
TYPHOUS
TYPHUS
TYPHUSES
TYPIC
TYPICAL
TYPICALLY
TYPIFIED
TYPIFIER
TYPIFIERS
TYPIFIES
TYPIFY
TYPIFYING
TYPING
TYPINGS
TYPIST
TYPISTS
TYPO
TYPOLOGIES
TYPOLOGY
TYPOMANIA
TYPOMANIAS
TYPOS
TYPTO
TYPTOED
TYPTOING
TYPTOS
TYRAMINE
TYRAMINES
TYRAN
TYRANED
TYRANING
TYRANNE
TYRANNED
TYRANNES
TYRANNESS
TYRANNESSES
TYRANNIC
TYRANNIES
TYRANNING
TYRANNIS
TYRANNISE
TYRANNISED
TYRANNISES
TYRANNISING
TYRANNIZE
TYRANNIZED
TYRANNIZES
TYRANNIZING
TYRANNOUS
TYRANNY
TYRANS
TYRANT
TYRANTED
TYRANTING
TYRANTS
TYRE
TYRED
TYRELESS
TYRES
TYRO
TYROES
TYRONES
TYROS
TYROSINE
TYROSINES
TYSTIE
TYSTIES
TYTE
TYTHE
TYTHED
TYTHES
TYTHING
TZADDIK
TZADDIKIM
TZADDIKS
TZADDIQ
TZADDIQIM
TZADDIQS
TZAR
TZARS
TZATZIKI
TZATZIKIS
TZETSE
TZETSES
TZIGANIES
TZIGANY
TZIMMES

U

UAKARI
UAKARIS
UBEROUS
UBERTIES
UBERTY
UBIETIES
UBIETY
UBIQUE
UBIQUITIES
UBIQUITY
UCKERS
UDAL
UDALLER
UDALLERS
UDALS
UDDER
UDDERED
UDDERFUL
UDDERLESS
UDDERS
UDO
UDOMETER
UDOMETERS
UDOMETRIC
UDOS
UDS
UEY
UEYS
UFO
UFOLOGIES
UFOLOGIST
UFOLOGISTS
UFOLOGY
UFOS
UG
UGGED
UGGING
UGH
UGHS
UGLIED
UGLIER
UGLIES
UGLIEST
UGLIFIED
UGLIFIES
UGLIFY
UGLIFYING
UGLILY
UGLINESS
UGLINESSES
UGLY
UGLYING
UGS
UGSOME
UHLAN
UHLANS
UHURU
UHURUS
UINTAHITE
UINTAHITES
UINTAITE
UINTAITES
UITLANDER
UITLANDERS
UJAMAA
UJAMAAS
UKASE
UKASES
UKE
UKELELE
UKELELES
UKES
UKULELE
UKULELES
ULCER
ULCERATE
ULCERATED
ULCERATES
ULCERATING
ULCERED
ULCERING
ULCEROUS
ULCERS
ULE
ULEMA
ULEMAS
ULES
ULEX
ULEXES
ULICHON
ULICHONS
ULICON
ULICONS
ULIGINOSE
ULIGINOUS
ULIKON
ULIKONS
ULITIS
ULITISES
ULLAGE
ULLAGED
ULLAGES
ULLAGING
ULLING
ULLINGS
ULMACEOUS
ULMIN
ULMINS
ULNA
ULNAE
ULNAR
ULNARE
ULNARIA
ULOSES
ULOSIS
ULOTRICHIES
ULOTRICHY
ULSTER
ULSTERED
ULSTERS
ULTERIOR
ULTIMA
ULTIMACIES
ULTIMACY
ULTIMAS
ULTIMATA
ULTIMATE
ULTIMATES
ULTIMATUM
ULTIMO
ULTION
ULTIONS
ULTRA
ULTRAISM
ULTRAISMS
ULTRAIST
ULTRAISTS
ULTRARED
ULTRAS
ULULANT
ULULATE
ULULATED
ULULATES
ULULATING
ULULATION
ULULATIONS
ULVA
ULVAS
ULYIE
ULYIES
ULZIE
ULZIES
UM
UMBEL
UMBELLAR
UMBELLATE
UMBELLULE
UMBELLULES
UMBELS
UMBER
UMBERED
UMBERING
UMBERS
UMBERY
UMBILICAL
UMBILICI
UMBILICUS
UMBILICUSES
UMBLES
UMBO
UMBONAL
UMBONATE
UMBONES
UMBOS
UMBRA
UMBRACULA
UMBRAE
UMBRAGE
UMBRAGED
UMBRAGES
UMBRAGING
UMBRAL
UMBRAS
UMBRATED
UMBRATIC
UMBRATILE
UMBRE
UMBREL
UMBRELLA
UMBRELLAS
UMBRELLO
UMBRELLOES
UMBRELLOS
UMBRELS
UMBRERE
UMBRERES
UMBRES
UMBRETTE
UMBRETTES
UMBRIERE
UMBRIERES
UMBRIL
UMBRILS
UMBROSE
UMBROUS
UMIAK
UMIAKS
UMLAUT
UMLAUTED
UMLAUTING
UMLAUTS
UMPH
UMPIRAGE
UMPIRAGES
UMPIRE
UMPIRED
UMPIRES
UMPIRING
UMPTEEN
UMPTEENTH
UMPTIETH
UMPTY
UMQUHILE
UMWHILE
UN
UNABASHED
UNABATED
UNABLE
UNACCUSED
UNACHING
UNACTABLE
UNACTED
UNACTIVE
UNADAPTED
UNADMIRED
UNADOPTED
UNADORED
UNADORNED
UNADVISED
UNAFRAID
UNAIDABLE
UNAIDED
UNAIMED
UNAIRED
UNAKING
UNALIGNED
UNALIKE
UNALIST
UNALISTS
UNALIVE
UNALLAYED
UNALLIED
UNALLOYED
UNALTERED
UNAMAZED
UNAMENDED
UNAMERCED
UNAMIABLE
UNAMUSED
UNAMUSING
UNANCHOR
UNANCHORED
UNANCHORING
UNANCHORS
UNANELED
UNANIMITIES
UNANIMITY
UNANIMOUS
UNANXIOUS
UNAPPAREL

UNAPPARELLED
UNAPPARELLING
UNAPPARELS
UNAPPLIED
UNAPT
UNAPTLY
UNAPTNESS
UNAPTNESSES
UNARGUED
UNARISEN
UNARM
UNARMED
UNARMING
UNARMS
UNARTFUL
UNASHAMED
UNASKED
UNASSAYED
UNASSUMED
UNASSURED
UNATONED
UNATTIRED
UNAU
UNAUS
UNAVENGED
UNAVOIDED
UNAVOWED
UNAWARE
UNAWARES
UNAWED
UNBACKED
UNBAFFLED
UNBAG
UNBAGGED
UNBAGGING
UNBAGS
UNBAITED
UNBAKED
UNBALANCE
UNBALANCED
UNBALANCES
UNBALANCING
UNBANDED
UNBANKED
UNBAPTISE
UNBAPTISED
UNBAPTISES
UNBAPTISING
UNBAPTIZE
UNBAPTIZED
UNBAPTIZES
UNBAPTIZING
UNBAR
UNBARBED
UNBARE
UNBARED
UNBARES
UNBARING
UNBARK
UNBARKED
UNBARKING
UNBARKS
UNBARRED
UNBARRING
UNBARS
UNBASHFUL
UNBATED
UNBATHED
UNBE
UNBEAR
UNBEARDED
UNBEARING
UNBEARS
UNBEATEN
UNBED
UNBEDDED
UNBEDDING
UNBEDS
UNBEEN
UNBEGET
UNBEGETS
UNBEGETTING
UNBEGGED
UNBEGOT
UNBEGOTTEN
UNBEGUILE
UNBEGUILED
UNBEGUILES
UNBEGUILING
UNBEGUN
UNBEING
UNBEINGS
UNBEKNOWN
UNBELIEF
UNBELIEFS
UNBELIEVE
UNBELIEVED
UNBELIEVES
UNBELIEVING
UNBELOVED
UNBELT
UNBELTED
UNBELTING
UNBELTS
UNBEND
UNBENDED
UNBENDING
UNBENDINGS
UNBENDS
UNBENIGN
UNBENT
UNBEREFT
UNBERUFEN
UNBESEEM
UNBESEEMED
UNBESEEMING
UNBESEEMS
UNBESPEAK
UNBESPEAKING
UNBESPEAKS
UNBESPOKE
UNBESPOKEN
UNBIAS
UNBIASED
UNBIASES
UNBIASING
UNBIASSED
UNBIASSES
UNBIASSING
UNBID
UNBIDDEN
UNBIND
UNBINDING
UNBINDINGS
UNBINDS
UNBISHOP
UNBISHOPED
UNBISHOPING
UNBISHOPS
UNBITT
UNBITTED
UNBITTING
UNBITTS
UNBLAMED
UNBLENDED
UNBLENT
UNBLESS
UNBLESSED
UNBLESSES
UNBLESSING
UNBLEST
UNBLIND
UNBLINDED
UNBLINDING
UNBLINDS
UNBLOCK
UNBLOCKED
UNBLOCKING
UNBLOCKS
UNBLOODED
UNBLOODY
UNBLOTTED
UNBLOWED
UNBLOWN
UNBLUNTED
UNBODIED
UNBODING
UNBOLT
UNBOLTED
UNBOLTING
UNBOLTS
UNBONE
UNBONED
UNBONES
UNBONING
UNBONNET
UNBONNETED
UNBONNETING
UNBONNETS
UNBOOKED
UNBOOKISH
UNBOOT
UNBOOTED
UNBOOTING
UNBOOTS
UNBORE
UNBORN
UNBORNE
UNBOSOM
UNBOSOMED
UNBOSOMER
UNBOSOMERS
UNBOSOMING
UNBOSOMS
UNBOUGHT
UNBOUND
UNBOUNDED
UNBOWED
UNBOX
UNBOXED
UNBOXES
UNBOXING
UNBRACE
UNBRACED
UNBRACES
UNBRACING
UNBRAIDED
UNBRASTE
UNBRED
UNBREECH
UNBREECHED
UNBREECHES
UNBREECHING
UNBRIDGED
UNBRIDLE
UNBRIDLED
UNBRIDLES
UNBRIDLING
UNBRIZZED
UNBROKE
UNBROKEN
UNBRUISED
UNBRUSED
UNBRUSHED
UNBUCKLE
UNBUCKLED
UNBUCKLES
UNBUCKLING
UNBUDDED
UNBUILD
UNBUILDING
UNBUILDS
UNBUILT
UNBUNDLE
UNBUNDLED
UNBUNDLER
UNBUNDLERS
UNBUNDLES
UNBUNDLING
UNBUNDLINGS
UNBURDEN
UNBURDENED
UNBURDENING
UNBURDENS
UNBURIED
UNBURIES
UNBURNED
UNBURNT
UNBURROW
UNBURROWED
UNBURROWING
UNBURROWS
UNBURTHEN
UNBURTHENED
UNBURTHENING
UNBURTHENS
UNBURY
UNBURYING
UNBUSY
UNBUTTON
UNBUTTONED
UNBUTTONING
UNBUTTONS
UNCAGE
UNCAGED
UNCAGES
UNCAGING
UNCALLED
UNCANDID
UNCANDOUR
UNCANDOURS
UNCANNIER
UNCANNIEST
UNCANNILY
UNCANNY
UNCANONIC
UNCAP
UNCAPABLE
UNCAPE
UNCAPED
UNCAPES
UNCAPING
UNCAPPED
UNCAPPING
UNCAPS
UNCAREFUL
UNCARING
UNCART
UNCARTED
UNCARTING
UNCARTS
UNCASE
UNCASED
UNCASES
UNCASHED
UNCASING
UNCATE
UNCAUGHT
UNCAUSED
UNCE
UNCEASING
UNCERTAIN
UNCES
UNCESSANT
UNCHAIN
UNCHAINED
UNCHAINING
UNCHAINS
UNCHANCIER
UNCHANCIEST
UNCHANCY
UNCHANGED
UNCHARGE
UNCHARGED
UNCHARGES
UNCHARGING
UNCHARITIES
UNCHARITY
UNCHARM
UNCHARMED

UNCHARMING
UNCHARMS
UNCHARNEL
UNCHARNELLED
UNCHARNELLING
UNCHARNELS
UNCHARTED
UNCHARY
UNCHASTE
UNCHECK
UNCHECKED
UNCHECKING
UNCHECKS
UNCHEERED
UNCHEWED
UNCHILD
UNCHILDED
UNCHILDING
UNCHILDS
UNCHOSEN
UNCHRISOM
UNCHURCH
UNCHURCHED
UNCHURCHES
UNCHURCHING
UNCI
UNCIAL
UNCIALS
UNCIFORM
UNCINATE
UNCINATED
UNCINI
UNCINUS
UNCIPHER
UNCIPHERED
UNCIPHERING
UNCIPHERS
UNCITED
UNCIVIL
UNCIVILLY
UNCLAD
UNCLAIMED
UNCLASP
UNCLASPED
UNCLASPING
UNCLASPS
UNCLASSED
UNCLASSY
UNCLE
UNCLEAN
UNCLEANED
UNCLEANER
UNCLEANEST
UNCLEANLY
UNCLEAR
UNCLEARED
UNCLEARER
UNCLEAREST
UNCLEARLY
UNCLED
UNCLENCH
UNCLENCHED
UNCLENCHES
UNCLENCHING
UNCLES
UNCLESHIP
UNCLESHIPS
UNCLEW
UNCLEWED
UNCLEWING
UNCLEWS
UNCLING
UNCLIPPED
UNCLIPT
UNCLOAK
UNCLOAKED
UNCLOAKING
UNCLOAKS
UNCLOG
UNCLOGGED
UNCLOGGING
UNCLOGS
UNCLOSE
UNCLOSED
UNCLOSES
UNCLOSING
UNCLOTHE
UNCLOTHED
UNCLOTHES
UNCLOTHING
UNCLOUD
UNCLOUDED
UNCLOUDING
UNCLOUDS
UNCLOUDY
UNCLOVEN
UNCLUTCH
UNCLUTCHED
UNCLUTCHES
UNCLUTCHING
UNCO
UNCOATED
UNCOCK
UNCOCKED
UNCOCKING
UNCOCKS
UNCOIL
UNCOILED
UNCOILING
UNCOILS
UNCOINED
UNCOLT
UNCOLTED
UNCOLTING
UNCOLTS
UNCOMBED
UNCOMBINE
UNCOMBINED
UNCOMBINES
UNCOMBINING
UNCOMELY
UNCOMMON
UNCOMMONER
UNCOMMONEST
UNCONCERN
UNCONCERNS
UNCONFINE
UNCONFINED
UNCONFINES
UNCONFINING
UNCONFORM
UNCONGEAL
UNCONGEALED
UNCONGEALING
UNCONGEALS
UNCOOKED
UNCOOL
UNCOPE
UNCOPED
UNCOPES
UNCOPING
UNCORD
UNCORDED
UNCORDIAL
UNCORDING
UNCORDS
UNCORK
UNCORKED
UNCORKING
UNCORKS
UNCORRUPT
UNCOS
UNCOSTLY
UNCOUNTED
UNCOUPLE
UNCOUPLED
UNCOUPLES
UNCOUPLING
UNCOURTLY
UNCOUTH
UNCOUTHER
UNCOUTHEST
UNCOUTHLY
UNCOVER
UNCOVERED
UNCOVERING
UNCOVERS
UNCOWL
UNCOWLED
UNCOWLING
UNCOWLS
UNCOYNED
UNCRATE
UNCRATED
UNCRATES
UNCRATING
UNCREATE
UNCREATED
UNCREATES
UNCREATING
UNCROPPED
UNCROSS
UNCROSSED
UNCROSSES
UNCROSSING
UNCROWDED
UNCROWN
UNCROWNED
UNCROWNING
UNCROWNS
UNCRUDDED
UNCRUMPLE
UNCRUMPLED
UNCRUMPLES
UNCRUMPLING
UNCTION
UNCTIONS
UNCTUOUS
UNCULLED
UNCURABLE
UNCURBED
UNCURDLED
UNCURED
UNCURIOUS
UNCURL
UNCURLED
UNCURLING
UNCURLS
UNCURRENT
UNCURSE
UNCURSED
UNCURSES
UNCURSING
UNCURTAIN
UNCURTAINED
UNCURTAINING
UNCURTAINS
UNCURVED
UNCUS
UNCUT
UNDAM
UNDAMAGED
UNDAMMED
UNDAMMING
UNDAMNED
UNDAMPED
UNDAMS
UNDASHED
UNDATE
UNDATED
UNDAUNTED
UNDAWNING
UNDAZZLE
UNDAZZLED
UNDAZZLES
UNDAZZLING
UNDE
UNDEAD
UNDEAF
UNDEAFED
UNDEAFING
UNDEAFS
UNDEALT
UNDEAR
UNDEBASED
UNDECAYED
UNDECEIVE
UNDECEIVED
UNDECEIVES
UNDECEIVING
UNDECENT
UNDECIDED
UNDECIMAL
UNDECK
UNDECKED
UNDECKING
UNDECKS
UNDEE
UNDEEDED
UNDEFACED
UNDEFIDE
UNDEFIED
UNDEFILED
UNDEFINED
UNDEIFIED
UNDEIFIES
UNDEIFY
UNDEIFYING
UNDELAYED
UNDELIGHT
UNDELIGHTS
UNDELUDED
UNDER
UNDERACT
UNDERACTED
UNDERACTING
UNDERACTS
UNDERARM
UNDERBEAR
UNDERBEARING
UNDERBEARINGS
UNDERBEARS
UNDERBID
UNDERBIDDING
UNDERBIDS
UNDERBIT
UNDERBITE
UNDERBITES
UNDERBITING
UNDERBITTEN
UNDERBORE
UNDERBORNE
UNDERBOUGHT
UNDERBRED
UNDERBUSH
UNDERBUSHED
UNDERBUSHES
UNDERBUSHING
UNDERBUY
UNDERBUYING
UNDERBUYS
UNDERCARD
UNDERCARDS
UNDERCART
UNDERCARTS
UNDERCAST
UNDERCASTS
UNDERCLAD
UNDERCLAY
UNDERCLAYS
UNDERCLUB
UNDERCLUBBED
UNDERCLUBBING
UNDERCLUBS
UNDERCOAT
UNDERCOATS
UNDERCOOK
UNDERCOOKED
UNDERCOOKING
UNDERCOOKS

UNDERCOOL
UNDERCOOLED
UNDERCOOLING
UNDERCOOLS
UNDERCUT
UNDERCUTS
UNDERCUTTING
UNDERDECK
UNDERDECKS
UNDERDID
UNDERDO
UNDERDOER
UNDERDOERS
UNDERDOES
UNDERDOG
UNDERDOGS
UNDERDOING
UNDERDONE
UNDERDRAW
UNDERDRAWING
UNDERDRAWINGS
UNDERDRAWN
UNDERDRAWS
UNDERDREW
UNDERFED
UNDERFEED
UNDERFEEDING
UNDERFEEDS
UNDERFELT
UNDERFELTS
UNDERFIRE
UNDERFIRED
UNDERFIRES
UNDERFIRING
UNDERFISH
UNDERFISHED
UNDERFISHES
UNDERFISHING
UNDERFLOW
UNDERFLOWS
UNDERFONG
UNDERFONGED
UNDERFONGING
UNDERFONGS
UNDERFOOT
UNDERFOOTED
UNDERFOOTING
UNDERFOOTS
UNDERFUND
UNDERFUNDED
UNDERFUNDING
UNDERFUNDINGS
UNDERFUNDS
UNDERFUR
UNDERFURS
UNDERGIRD
UNDERGIRDED
UNDERGIRDING
UNDERGIRDS
UNDERGIRT
UNDERGO
UNDERGOES
UNDERGOING
UNDERGONE
UNDERGOWN
UNDERGOWNS
UNDERGRAD
UNDERGRADS
UNDERHAND
UNDERHANDS
UNDERHUNG
UNDERKEEP
UNDERKEEPING
UNDERKEEPS
UNDERKEPT
UNDERKING
UNDERKINGS
UNDERLAID
UNDERLAIN
UNDERLAP
UNDERLAPPED
UNDERLAPPING
UNDERLAPS
UNDERLAY
UNDERLAYING
UNDERLAYS
UNDERLET
UNDERLETS
UNDERLETTING
UNDERLETTINGS
UNDERLIE
UNDERLIES
UNDERLINE
UNDERLINED
UNDERLINES
UNDERLING
UNDERLINGS
UNDERLINING
UNDERLIP
UNDERLIPS
UNDERLYING
UNDERMAN
UNDERMANNED
UNDERMANNING
UNDERMANS
UNDERMEN
UNDERMINE
UNDERMINED
UNDERMINES
UNDERMINING
UNDERMININGS
UNDERMOST
UNDERN
UNDERNOTE
UNDERNOTED
UNDERNOTES
UNDERNOTING
UNDERNS
UNDERPAID
UNDERPART
UNDERPARTS
UNDERPASS
UNDERPASSES
UNDERPAY
UNDERPAYING
UNDERPAYS
UNDERPEEP
UNDERPEEPED
UNDERPEEPING
UNDERPEEPS
UNDERPIN
UNDERPINNED
UNDERPINNING
UNDERPINNINGS
UNDERPINS
UNDERPLAY
UNDERPLAYED
UNDERPLAYING
UNDERPLAYS
UNDERPLOT
UNDERPLOTS
UNDERPROP
UNDERPROPPED
UNDERPROPPING
UNDERPROPS
UNDERRAN
UNDERRATE
UNDERRATED
UNDERRATES
UNDERRATING
UNDERRUN
UNDERRUNNING
UNDERRUNNINGS
UNDERRUNS
UNDERSAID
UNDERSAY
UNDERSAYE
UNDERSAYES
UNDERSAYING
UNDERSAYS
UNDERSEA
UNDERSEAL
UNDERSEALED
UNDERSEALING
UNDERSEALINGS
UNDERSEALS
UNDERSELF
UNDERSELL
UNDERSELLING
UNDERSELLS
UNDERSELVES
UNDERSET
UNDERSETS
UNDERSETTING
UNDERSHOT
UNDERSIDE
UNDERSIDES
UNDERSIGN
UNDERSIGNED
UNDERSIGNING
UNDERSIGNS
UNDERSKIES
UNDERSKY
UNDERSOIL
UNDERSOILS
UNDERSOLD
UNDERSONG
UNDERSONGS
UNDERTAKE
UNDERTAKEN
UNDERTAKES
UNDERTAKING
UNDERTAKINGS
UNDERTANE
UNDERTIME
UNDERTIMES
UNDERTINT
UNDERTINTS
UNDERTONE
UNDERTONES
UNDERTOOK
UNDERTOW
UNDERTOWS
UNDERUSE
UNDERUSED
UNDERUSES
UNDERUSING
UNDERVEST
UNDERVESTS
UNDERWAY
UNDERWEAR
UNDERWEARS
UNDERWENT
UNDERWING
UNDERWINGS
UNDERWIT
UNDERWITS
UNDERWOOD
UNDERWOODS
UNDERWORK
UNDERWORKED
UNDERWORKING
UNDERWORKS
UNDERWROUGHT
UNDESERT
UNDESERTS
UNDESERVE
UNDESERVED
UNDESERVES
UNDESERVING
UNDESIRED
UNDEVOUT
UNDID
UNDIES
UNDIGHT
UNDIGHTING
UNDIGHTS
UNDIGNIFIED
UNDIGNIFIES
UNDIGNIFY
UNDIGNIFYING
UNDILUTED
UNDIMMED
UNDINE
UNDINES
UNDINISM
UNDINISMS
UNDINTED
UNDIPPED
UNDIVIDED
UNDIVINE
UNDO
UNDOCK
UNDOCKED
UNDOCKING
UNDOCKS
UNDOER
UNDOERS
UNDOES
UNDOING
UNDOINGS
UNDONE
UNDOOMED
UNDOUBLE
UNDOUBLED
UNDOUBLES
UNDOUBLING
UNDOUBTED
UNDRAINED
UNDRAPED
UNDRAW
UNDRAWING
UNDRAWN
UNDRAWS
UNDREADED
UNDREAMED
UNDREAMT
UNDRESS
UNDRESSED
UNDRESSES
UNDRESSING
UNDRESSINGS
UNDREW
UNDRIED
UNDRILLED
UNDRIVEN
UNDROSSY
UNDROWNED
UNDRUNK
UNDUBBED
UNDUE
UNDUG
UNDULANCIES
UNDULANCY
UNDULANT
UNDULATE
UNDULATED
UNDULATES
UNDULATING
UNDULLED
UNDULOSE
UNDULOUS
UNDULY
UNDUTEOUS
UNDUTIFUL
UNDYED
UNDYING
UNDYINGLY
UNEARED
UNEARNED
UNEARTH
UNEARTHED
UNEARTHING
UNEARTHLIER
UNEARTHLIEST
UNEARTHLY
UNEARTHS
UNEASE
UNEASES
UNEASIER

UNEASIEST
UNEASILY
UNEASY
UNEATABLE
UNEATEN
UNEATH
UNEATHES
UNEDGE
UNEDGED
UNEDGES
UNEDGING
UNEDITED
UNEFFACED
UNELATED
UNELECTED
UNEMPTIED
UNENDING
UNENDOWED
UNENGAGED
UNENTERED
UNENVIED
UNENVIOUS
UNENVYING
UNEQUABLE
UNEQUAL
UNEQUALLY
UNEQUALS
UNERRING
UNESPIED
UNESSAYED
UNESSENCE
UNESSENCED
UNESSENCES
UNESSENCING
UNETH
UNETHICAL
UNEVEN
UNEVENER
UNEVENEST
UNEVENLY
UNEXALTED
UNEXCITED
UNEXPIRED
UNEXPOSED
UNEXTINCT
UNEXTREME
UNEYED
UNFABLED
UNFACT
UNFACTS
UNFADABLE
UNFADED
UNFADING
UNFAILING
UNFAIR
UNFAIRED
UNFAIRER
UNFAIREST
UNFAIRING
UNFAIRLY
UNFAIRS
UNFAITH
UNFAITHS
UNFALLEN
UNFAMED
UNFANNED
UNFASTEN
UNFASTENED
UNFASTENING
UNFASTENS
UNFAULTY
UNFAZED
UNFEARED
UNFEARFUL
UNFEARING
UNFED
UNFEED
UNFEELING
UNFEIGNED
UNFELLED
UNFELT
UNFENCED
UNFETTER
UNFETTERED
UNFETTERING
UNFETTERS
UNFEUDAL
UNFEUED
UNFIGURED
UNFILDE
UNFILED
UNFILIAL
UNFILLED
UNFILMED
UNFINE
UNFIRED
UNFIRM
UNFISHED
UNFIT
UNFITLY
UNFITNESS
UNFITNESSES
UNFITS
UNFITTED
UNFITTER
UNFITTEST
UNFITTING
UNFIX
UNFIXED
UNFIXES
UNFIXING
UNFIXITIES
UNFIXITY
UNFLAWED
UNFLEDGED
UNFLESH
UNFLESHED
UNFLESHES
UNFLESHING
UNFLESHLY
UNFLOORED
UNFLUSH
UNFLUSHED
UNFLUSHES
UNFLUSHING
UNFOCUSED
UNFOLD
UNFOLDED
UNFOLDER
UNFOLDERS
UNFOLDING
UNFOLDINGS
UNFOLDS
UNFOOL
UNFOOLED
UNFOOLING
UNFOOLS
UNFOOTED
UNFORBID
UNFORCED
UNFORGED
UNFORGOT
UNFORM
UNFORMAL
UNFORMED
UNFORMING
UNFORMS
UNFORTUNE
UNFORTUNES
UNFOUGHT
UNFOUND
UNFOUNDED
UNFRAMED
UNFRANKED
UNFRAUGHT
UNFRAUGHTED
UNFRAUGHTING
UNFRAUGHTS
UNFREE
UNFREED
UNFREEMAN
UNFREEMEN
UNFREEZE
UNFREEZES
UNFREEZING
UNFRETTED
UNFRIEND
UNFRIENDS
UNFROCK
UNFROCKED
UNFROCKING
UNFROCKS
UNFROZE
UNFROZEN
UNFUELLED
UNFUMED
UNFUNDED
UNFUNNY
UNFURL
UNFURLED
UNFURLING
UNFURLS
UNFURNISH
UNFURNISHED
UNFURNISHES
UNFURNISHING
UNFURRED
UNGAG
UNGAGGED
UNGAGGING
UNGAGS
UNGAIN
UNGAINFUL
UNGAINLIER
UNGAINLIEST
UNGAINLY
UNGALLANT
UNGALLED
UNGARBLED
UNGAUGED
UNGEAR
UNGEARED
UNGEARING
UNGEARS
UNGENIAL
UNGENTEEL
UNGENTLE
UNGENTLY
UNGENUINE
UNGERMANE
UNGET
UNGETS
UNGETTING
UNGHOSTLY
UNGIFTED
UNGILD
UNGILDED
UNGILDING
UNGILDS
UNGILT
UNGIRD
UNGIRDED
UNGIRDING
UNGIRDS
UNGIRT
UNGIRTH
UNGIRTHED
UNGIRTHING
UNGIRTHS
UNGIVING
UNGLAD
UNGLAZED
UNGLOSSED
UNGLOVE
UNGLOVED
UNGLOVES
UNGLOVING
UNGLUE
UNGLUED
UNGLUES
UNGLUING
UNGOD
UNGODDED
UNGODDING
UNGODLIER
UNGODLIEST
UNGODLIKE
UNGODLILY
UNGODLY
UNGODS
UNGORD
UNGORED
UNGORGED
UNGOT
UNGOTTEN
UNGOWN
UNGOWNED
UNGOWNING
UNGOWNS
UNGRACED
UNGRADED
UNGRASSED
UNGRAVELY
UNGRAZED
UNGROOMED
UNGROUND
UNGROWN
UNGRUDGED
UNGUAL
UNGUARD
UNGUARDED
UNGUARDING
UNGUARDS
UNGUENT
UNGUENTS
UNGUES
UNGUESSED
UNGUIDED
UNGUIFORM
UNGUILTY
UNGUIS
UNGULA
UNGULAE
UNGULATE
UNGULATES
UNGULED
UNGUM
UNGUMMED
UNGUMMING
UNGUMS
UNGYVE
UNGYVED
UNGYVES
UNGYVING
UNHABLE
UNHACKED
UNHAILED
UNHAIR
UNHAIRED
UNHAIRING
UNHAIRS
UNHALLOW
UNHALLOWED
UNHALLOWING
UNHALLOWS
UNHALSED
UNHAND
UNHANDED
UNHANDILY
UNHANDING
UNHANDLED
UNHANDS
UNHANDY
UNHANG
UNHANGED
UNHANGING
UNHANGS
UNHAPPIED
UNHAPPIER
UNHAPPIES

UNHAPPIEST
UNHAPPILY
UNHAPPY
UNHAPPYING
UNHARBOUR
UNHARBOURED
UNHARBOURING
UNHARBOURS
UNHARDY
UNHARMED
UNHARMFUL
UNHARMING
UNHARNESS
UNHARNESSED
UNHARNESSES
UNHARNESSING
UNHASP
UNHASPED
UNHASPING
UNHASPS
UNHASTING
UNHASTY
UNHAT
UNHATCHED
UNHATS
UNHATTED
UNHATTING
UNHATTINGS
UNHAUNTED
UNHEAD
UNHEADED
UNHEADING
UNHEADS
UNHEAL
UNHEALED
UNHEALING
UNHEALS
UNHEALTH
UNHEALTHIER
UNHEALTHIEST
UNHEALTHS
UNHEALTHY
UNHEARD
UNHEARSE
UNHEARSED
UNHEARSES
UNHEARSING
UNHEART
UNHEARTED
UNHEARTING
UNHEARTS
UNHEATED
UNHEDGED
UNHEEDED
UNHEEDFUL
UNHEEDILY
UNHEEDING
UNHEEDY
UNHELE
UNHELED
UNHELES
UNHELING
UNHELM
UNHELMED
UNHELMING
UNHELMS
UNHELPED
UNHELPFUL
UNHEPPEN
UNHEROIC
UNHERST
UNHEWN
UNHIDDEN
UNHINGE
UNHINGED
UNHINGES
UNHINGING
UNHIP
UNHIRED
UNHITCH
UNHITCHED
UNHITCHES
UNHITCHING
UNHIVE
UNHIVED
UNHIVES
UNHIVING
UNHOARD
UNHOARDED
UNHOARDING
UNHOARDS
UNHOLIER
UNHOLIEST
UNHOLILY
UNHOLPEN
UNHOLY
UNHOMELY
UNHONEST
UNHOOD
UNHOODED
UNHOODING
UNHOODS
UNHOOK
UNHOOKED
UNHOOKING
UNHOOKS
UNHOOP
UNHOOPED
UNHOOPING
UNHOOPS
UNHOPED
UNHOPEFUL
UNHORSE
UNHORSED
UNHORSES
UNHORSING
UNHOUSE
UNHOUSED
UNHOUSES
UNHOUSING
UNHUMAN
UNHUMBLED
UNHUNG
UNHUNTED
UNHURRIED
UNHURT
UNHURTFUL
UNHUSK
UNHUSKED
UNHUSKING
UNHUSKS
UNI
UNIAXIAL
UNICITIES
UNICITY
UNICOLOR
UNICOLOUR
UNICORN
UNICORNS
UNICYCLE
UNICYCLES
UNIDEAL
UNIFIABLE
UNIFIC
UNIFIED
UNIFIER
UNIFIERS
UNIFIES
UNIFILAR
UNIFORM
UNIFORMED
UNIFORMING
UNIFORMLY
UNIFORMS
UNIFY
UNIFYING
UNIFYINGS
UNILLUMED
UNILOBAR
UNILOBED
UNIMBUED
UNIMPEDED
UNIMPOSED
UNINCITED
UNINDEXED
UNINJURED
UNINSTALL
UNINSTALLED
UNINSTALLING
UNINSTALLS
UNINSURED
UNINURED
UNINVITED
UNION
UNIONISE
UNIONISED
UNIONISES
UNIONISING
UNIONISM
UNIONISMS
UNIONIST
UNIONISTS
UNIONIZE
UNIONIZED
UNIONIZES
UNIONIZING
UNIONS
UNIPAROUS
UNIPED
UNIPEDS
UNIPLANAR
UNIPOD
UNIPODS
UNIPOLAR
UNIQUE
UNIQUELY
UNIQUER
UNIQUES
UNIQUEST
UNIRAMOUS
UNIRONED
UNIS
UNISERIAL
UNISEX
UNISEXUAL
UNISON
UNISONAL
UNISONANT
UNISONOUS
UNISONS
UNIT
UNITAL
UNITARD
UNITARDS
UNITARIAN
UNITARIANS
UNITARY
UNITE
UNITED
UNITEDLY
UNITER
UNITERS
UNITES
UNITIES
UNITING
UNITINGS
UNITION
UNITIONS
UNITISE
UNITISED
UNITISES
UNITISING
UNITIVE
UNITIVELY
UNITIZE
UNITIZED
UNITIZES
UNITIZING
UNITS
UNITY
UNIVALENT
UNIVALENTS
UNIVALVE
UNIVALVES
UNIVERSAL
UNIVERSALS
UNIVERSE
UNIVERSES
UNIVOCAL
UNIVOCALS
UNJADED
UNJEALOUS
UNJOINT
UNJOINTED
UNJOINTING
UNJOINTS
UNJOYFUL
UNJOYOUS
UNJUST
UNJUSTER
UNJUSTEST
UNJUSTLY
UNKED
UNKEMPT
UNKENNED
UNKENNEL
UNKENNELLED
UNKENNELLING
UNKENNELS
UNKENT
UNKEPT
UNKET
UNKID
UNKIND
UNKINDER
UNKINDEST
UNKINDLED
UNKINDLIER
UNKINDLIEST
UNKINDLY
UNKING
UNKINGED
UNKINGING
UNKINGLIER
UNKINGLIEST
UNKINGLY
UNKINGS
UNKISS
UNKISSED
UNKISSES
UNKISSING
UNKNELLED
UNKNIGHT
UNKNIGHTED
UNKNIGHTING
UNKNIGHTS
UNKNIT
UNKNITS
UNKNITTED
UNKNITTING
UNKNOT
UNKNOTS
UNKNOTTED
UNKNOTTING
UNKNOWING
UNKNOWN
UNKNOWNS
UNLACE
UNLACED
UNLACES
UNLACING
UNLADE
UNLADED
UNLADEN
UNLADES
UNLADING
UNLADINGS
UNLAID
UNLASH
UNLASHED

UNLASHES
UNLASHING
UNLAST
UNLASTE
UNLATCH
UNLATCHED
UNLATCHES
UNLATCHING
UNLAW
UNLAWED
UNLAWFUL
UNLAWING
UNLAWS
UNLAY
UNLAYING
UNLAYS
UNLEAD
UNLEADED
UNLEADING
UNLEADS
UNLEAL
UNLEARN
UNLEARNED
UNLEARNING
UNLEARNS
UNLEARNT
UNLEASED
UNLEASH
UNLEASHED
UNLEASHES
UNLEASHING
UNLED
UNLESS
UNLET
UNLICH
UNLICKED
UNLID
UNLIDDED
UNLIDDING
UNLIDS
UNLIGHTED
UNLIKABLE
UNLIKE
UNLIKELIER
UNLIKELIEST
UNLIKELY
UNLIKES
UNLIMBER
UNLIMBERED
UNLIMBERING
UNLIMBERS
UNLIME
UNLIMED
UNLIMES
UNLIMING
UNLIMITED
UNLINE
UNLINEAL
UNLINED
UNLINES
UNLINING
UNLINK
UNLINKED
UNLINKING
UNLINKS
UNLISTED
UNLIT
UNLIVABLE
UNLIVE
UNLIVED
UNLIVELY
UNLIVES
UNLIVING
UNLOAD
UNLOADED
UNLOADER
UNLOADERS
UNLOADING
UNLOADINGS
UNLOADS
UNLOCATED
UNLOCK
UNLOCKED
UNLOCKING
UNLOCKS
UNLOGICAL
UNLOOKED
UNLOOSE
UNLOOSED
UNLOOSEN
UNLOOSENED
UNLOOSENING
UNLOOSENS
UNLOOSES
UNLOOSING
UNLOPPED
UNLORD
UNLORDED
UNLORDING
UNLORDLY
UNLORDS
UNLOSABLE
UNLOST
UNLOVABLE
UNLOVE
UNLOVED
UNLOVELIER
UNLOVELIEST
UNLOVELY
UNLOVES
UNLOVING
UNLUCKIER
UNLUCKIEST
UNLUCKILY
UNLUCKY
UNMADE
UNMAILED
UNMAIMED
UNMAKABLE
UNMAKE
UNMAKES
UNMAKING
UNMAKINGS
UNMAN
UNMANACLE
UNMANACLED
UNMANACLES
UNMANACLING
UNMANAGED
UNMANLIER
UNMANLIEST
UNMANLIKE
UNMANLY
UNMANNED
UNMANNING
UNMANS
UNMANTLE
UNMANTLED
UNMANTLES
UNMANTLING
UNMANURED
UNMARD
UNMARKED
UNMARRED
UNMARRIED
UNMARRIES
UNMARRY
UNMARRYING
UNMASK
UNMASKED
UNMASKER
UNMASKERS
UNMASKING
UNMASKINGS
UNMASKS
UNMATCHED
UNMATED
UNMATURED
UNMEANING
UNMEANT
UNMEEK
UNMEET
UNMEETLY
UNMELTED
UNMERITED
UNMET
UNMETED
UNMEW
UNMEWED
UNMEWING
UNMEWS
UNMILKED
UNMILLED
UNMINDED
UNMINDFUL
UNMINGLED
UNMIRY
UNMISSED
UNMIXED
UNMIXEDLY
UNMOANED
UNMODISH
UNMONEYED
UNMONIED
UNMOOR
UNMOORED
UNMOORING
UNMOORS
UNMORAL
UNMOTIVED
UNMOULD
UNMOULDED
UNMOULDING
UNMOULDS
UNMOUNT
UNMOUNTED
UNMOUNTING
UNMOUNTS
UNMOURNED
UNMOVABLE
UNMOVABLY
UNMOVED
UNMOVEDLY
UNMOVING
UNMOWN
UNMUFFLE
UNMUFFLED
UNMUFFLES
UNMUFFLING
UNMUSICAL
UNMUZZLE
UNMUZZLED
UNMUZZLES
UNMUZZLING
UNMUZZLINGS
UNNAIL
UNNAILED
UNNAILING
UNNAILS
UNNAMABLE
UNNAMED
UNNANELD
UNNATIVE
UNNATURAL
UNNEATH
UNNEEDED
UNNEEDFUL
UNNERVE
UNNERVED
UNNERVES
UNNERVING
UNNEST
UNNESTED
UNNESTING
UNNESTS
UNNETHES
UNNETTED
UNNOBLE
UNNOBLED
UNNOBLES
UNNOBLING
UNNOTED
UNNOTICED
UNOBEYED
UNOBVIOUS
UNOFFERED
UNOFTEN
UNOILED
UNOPENED
UNOPPOSED
UNORDER
UNORDERED
UNORDERING
UNORDERLY
UNORDERS
UNOWED
UNOWNED
UNPACED
UNPACK
UNPACKED
UNPACKER
UNPACKERS
UNPACKING
UNPACKINGS
UNPACKS
UNPAGED
UNPAID
UNPAINED
UNPAINFUL
UNPAINT
UNPAINTED
UNPAINTING
UNPAINTS
UNPAIRED
UNPALSIED
UNPANEL
UNPANELLED
UNPANELLING
UNPANELS
UNPANGED
UNPANNEL
UNPANNELLED
UNPANNELLING
UNPANNELS
UNPAPER
UNPAPERED
UNPAPERING
UNPAPERS
UNPARED
UNPARTIAL
UNPATHED
UNPAVED
UNPAY
UNPAYABLE
UNPAYING
UNPAYS
UNPEELED
UNPEERED
UNPEG
UNPEGGED
UNPEGGING
UNPEGS
UNPEN
UNPENNED
UNPENNIED
UNPENNING
UNPENS
UNPENT
UNPEOPLE
UNPEOPLED
UNPEOPLES
UNPEOPLING
UNPERCH
UNPERCHED
UNPERCHES
UNPERCHING
UNPERFECT
UNPERPLEX
UNPERPLEXED
UNPERPLEXES

UNPERPLEXING
UNPERSON
UNPERSONED
UNPERSONING
UNPERSONS
UNPERVERT
UNPERVERTED
UNPERVERTING
UNPERVERTS
UNPICK
UNPICKED
UNPICKING
UNPICKS
UNPIERCED
UNPILOTED
UNPIN
UNPINKED
UNPINKT
UNPINNED
UNPINNING
UNPINS
UNPITIED
UNPITIFUL
UNPITYING
UNPLACE
UNPLACED
UNPLACES
UNPLACING
UNPLAGUED
UNPLAINED
UNPLAIT
UNPLAITED
UNPLAITING
UNPLAITS
UNPLANKED
UNPLANNED
UNPLANTED
UNPLAYED
UNPLEASED
UNPLEATED
UNPLEDGED
UNPLIABLE
UNPLIABLY
UNPLIANT
UNPLUCKED
UNPLUG
UNPLUGGED
UNPLUGGING
UNPLUGS
UNPLUMB
UNPLUMBED
UNPLUMBING
UNPLUMBS
UNPLUME
UNPLUMED
UNPLUMES
UNPLUMING
UNPOETIC
UNPOINTED
UNPOISED
UNPOISON
UNPOISONED
UNPOISONING
UNPOISONS
UNPOLICED
UNPOLISH
UNPOLISHED
UNPOLISHES
UNPOLISHING
UNPOLITE
UNPOLITIC
UNPOLLED
UNPOPE
UNPOPED
UNPOPES
UNPOPING
UNPOPULAR
UNPOSED
UNPOSTED
UNPOTABLE
UNPRAISE
UNPRAISED
UNPRAISES
UNPRAISING
UNPRAY
UNPRAYED
UNPRAYING
UNPRAYS
UNPREACH
UNPREACHED
UNPREACHES
UNPREACHING
UNPRECISE
UNPREDICT
UNPREDICTED
UNPREDICTING
UNPREDICTS
UNPREPARE
UNPREPARED
UNPREPARES
UNPREPARING
UNPRESSED
UNPRETTY
UNPRICED
UNPRIEST
UNPRIESTED
UNPRIESTING
UNPRIESTS
UNPRIMED
UNPRINTED
UNPRISON
UNPRISONED
UNPRISONING
UNPRISONS
UNPRIZED
UNPROP
UNPROPER
UNPROPPED
UNPROPPING
UNPROPS
UNPROVED
UNPROVEN
UNPROVIDE
UNPROVIDED
UNPROVIDES
UNPROVIDING
UNPROVOKE
UNPROVOKED
UNPROVOKES
UNPROVOKING
UNPRUNED
UNPULLED
UNPURGED
UNPURSE
UNPURSED
UNPURSES
UNPURSING
UNPURSUED
UNQUALIFIED
UNQUALIFIES
UNQUALIFY
UNQUALIFYING
UNQUEEN
UNQUEENED
UNQUEENING
UNQUEENLIER
UNQUEENLIEST
UNQUEENLY
UNQUEENS
UNQUELLED
UNQUIET
UNQUIETED
UNQUIETING
UNQUIETLY
UNQUIETS
UNQUOTE
UNQUOTED
UNQUOTES
UNQUOTING
UNRACED
UNRACKED
UNRAISED
UNRAKE
UNRAKED
UNRAKES
UNRAKING
UNRATED
UNRAVEL
UNRAVELLED
UNRAVELLING
UNRAVELLINGS
UNRAVELS
UNRAZORED
UNREACHED
UNREAD
UNREADIER
UNREADIEST
UNREADILY
UNREADY
UNREAL
UNREALISE
UNREALISED
UNREALISES
UNREALISING
UNREALISM
UNREALISMS
UNREALITIES
UNREALITY
UNREALIZE
UNREALIZED
UNREALIZES
UNREALIZING
UNREALLY
UNREAPED
UNREASON
UNREASONS
UNREAVE
UNREAVED
UNREAVES
UNREAVING
UNREBATED
UNREBUKED
UNRECKED
UNRED
UNREDREST
UNREDUCED
UNREDY
UNREEL
UNREELED
UNREELING
UNREELS
UNREEVE
UNREEVED
UNREEVES
UNREEVING
UNREFINED
UNREFUTED
UNREIN
UNREINED
UNREINING
UNREINS
UNRELATED
UNRELAXED
UNREMOVED
UNRENEWED
UNRENT
UNREPAID
UNREPAIR
UNREPAIRS
UNRESERVE
UNRESERVES
UNREST
UNRESTFUL
UNRESTING
UNRESTS
UNREVISED
UNREVOKED
UNRHYMED
UNRIBBED
UNRID
UNRIDABLE
UNRIDDEN
UNRIDDLE
UNRIDDLED
UNRIDDLER
UNRIDDLERS
UNRIDDLES
UNRIDDLING
UNRIFLED
UNRIG
UNRIGGED
UNRIGGING
UNRIGHT
UNRIGHTS
UNRIGS
UNRIMED
UNRINGED
UNRIP
UNRIPE
UNRIPENED
UNRIPER
UNRIPEST
UNRIPPED
UNRIPPING
UNRIPPINGS
UNRIPS
UNRISEN
UNRIVEN
UNRIVET
UNRIVETED
UNRIVETING
UNRIVETS
UNROBE
UNROBED
UNROBES
UNROBING
UNROLL
UNROLLED
UNROLLING
UNROLLS
UNROOF
UNROOFED
UNROOFING
UNROOFS
UNROOST
UNROOSTED
UNROOSTING
UNROOSTS
UNROOT
UNROOTED
UNROOTING
UNROOTS
UNROPE
UNROPED
UNROPES
UNROPING
UNROSINED
UNROTTED
UNROTTEN
UNROUGED
UNROUGH
UNROUND
UNROUNDED
UNROUNDING
UNROUNDS
UNROUSED
UNROVE
UNROYAL
UNROYALLY
UNRUBBED
UNRUDE
UNRUFFE
UNRUFFLE
UNRUFFLED
UNRUFFLES
UNRUFFLING
UNRULE
UNRULED
UNRULES
UNRULIER

UNRULIEST
UNRULY
UNRUMPLED
UNS
UNSADDLE
UNSADDLED
UNSADDLES
UNSADDLING
UNSAFE
UNSAFELY
UNSAFER
UNSAFEST
UNSAFETIES
UNSAFETY
UNSAID
UNSAILED
UNSAINED
UNSAINT
UNSAINTED
UNSAINTING
UNSAINTLIER
UNSAINTLIEST
UNSAINTLY
UNSAINTS
UNSALABLE
UNSALTED
UNSALUTED
UNSAPPED
UNSASHED
UNSATABLE
UNSATED
UNSATIATE
UNSATING
UNSAVED
UNSAVOURY
UNSAY
UNSAYABLE
UNSAYING
UNSAYS
UNSCALE
UNSCALED
UNSCALES
UNSCALING
UNSCANNED
UNSCARRED
UNSCARY
UNSCATHED
UNSCENTED
UNSCOURED
UNSCREW
UNSCREWED
UNSCREWING
UNSCREWS
UNSCYTHED
UNSEAL
UNSEALED
UNSEALING
UNSEALS
UNSEAM
UNSEAMED
UNSEAMING
UNSEAMS
UNSEASON
UNSEASONED
UNSEASONING
UNSEASONS
UNSEAT
UNSEATED
UNSEATING
UNSEATS
UNSECRET
UNSECULAR
UNSECURED
UNSEDUCED
UNSEEABLE
UNSEEDED
UNSEEING
UNSEEL
UNSEELED
UNSEELING
UNSEELS
UNSEEMING
UNSEEMINGS
UNSEEMLIER
UNSEEMLIEST
UNSEEMLY
UNSEEN
UNSEENS
UNSEIZED
UNSELDOM
UNSELF
UNSELFED
UNSELFING
UNSELFISH
UNSELFS
UNSELVES
UNSENSE
UNSENSED
UNSENSES
UNSENSING
UNSENT
UNSERIOUS
UNSET
UNSETS
UNSETTING
UNSETTLE
UNSETTLED
UNSETTLES
UNSETTLING
UNSETTLINGS
UNSEVERED
UNSEW
UNSEWED
UNSEWING
UNSEWN
UNSEWS
UNSEX
UNSEXED
UNSEXES
UNSEXING
UNSEXIST
UNSEXUAL
UNSHACKLE
UNSHACKLED
UNSHACKLES
UNSHACKLING
UNSHADED
UNSHADOW
UNSHADOWED
UNSHADOWING
UNSHADOWS
UNSHAKED
UNSHAKEN
UNSHALE
UNSHALED
UNSHALES
UNSHALING
UNSHAMED
UNSHAPE
UNSHAPED
UNSHAPELIER
UNSHAPELIEST
UNSHAPELY
UNSHAPEN
UNSHAPES
UNSHAPING
UNSHARED
UNSHAVED
UNSHAVEN
UNSHEATHE
UNSHEATHED
UNSHEATHES
UNSHEATHING
UNSHED
UNSHELL
UNSHELLED
UNSHELLING
UNSHELLS
UNSHENT
UNSHEWN
UNSHIP
UNSHIPPED
UNSHIPPING
UNSHIPS
UNSHOCKED
UNSHOD
UNSHOE
UNSHOED
UNSHOEING
UNSHOES
UNSHOOT
UNSHOOTED
UNSHOOTING
UNSHOOTS
UNSHORN
UNSHOT
UNSHOUT
UNSHOUTED
UNSHOUTING
UNSHOUTS
UNSHOWN
UNSHRIVED
UNSHRIVEN
UNSHROUD
UNSHROUDED
UNSHROUDING
UNSHROUDS
UNSHRUBD
UNSHUNNED
UNSHUT
UNSHUTS
UNSHUTTER
UNSHUTTERED
UNSHUTTERING
UNSHUTTERS
UNSHUTTING
UNSICKER
UNSICKLED
UNSIFTED
UNSIGHING
UNSIGHT
UNSIGHTED
UNSIGHTLIER
UNSIGHTLIEST
UNSIGHTLY
UNSIGNED
UNSINEW
UNSINEWED
UNSINEWING
UNSINEWS
UNSISTING
UNSIZABLE
UNSIZED
UNSKILFUL
UNSKILLED
UNSKIMMED
UNSKINNED
UNSLAIN
UNSLAKED
UNSLICED
UNSLING
UNSLINGING
UNSLINGS
UNSLUICE
UNSLUICED
UNSLUICES
UNSLUICING
UNSLUNG
UNSMART
UNSMILING
UNSMITTEN
UNSMOOTH
UNSMOOTHED
UNSMOOTHING
UNSMOOTHS
UNSMOTE
UNSNAP
UNSNAPPED
UNSNAPPING
UNSNAPS
UNSNARL
UNSNARLED
UNSNARLING
UNSNARLS
UNSNECK
UNSNECKED
UNSNECKING
UNSNECKS
UNSNUFFED
UNSOAPED
UNSOCIAL
UNSOCKET
UNSOCKETED
UNSOCKETING
UNSOCKETS
UNSOD
UNSODDEN
UNSOFT
UNSOILED
UNSOLACED
UNSOLD
UNSOLDER
UNSOLDERED
UNSOLDERING
UNSOLDERS
UNSOLEMN
UNSOLID
UNSOLIDLY
UNSOLVED
UNSONSY
UNSOOTE
UNSORTED
UNSOUGHT
UNSOUL
UNSOULED
UNSOULING
UNSOULS
UNSOUND
UNSOUNDED
UNSOUNDER
UNSOUNDEST
UNSOUNDLY
UNSOURCED
UNSOURED
UNSOWN
UNSPAR
UNSPARED
UNSPARING
UNSPARRED
UNSPARRING
UNSPARS
UNSPEAK
UNSPEAKING
UNSPEAKS
UNSPED
UNSPELL
UNSPELLED
UNSPELLING
UNSPELLS
UNSPENT
UNSPHERE
UNSPHERED
UNSPHERES
UNSPHERING
UNSPIDE
UNSPIED
UNSPILLED
UNSPILT
UNSPOILED
UNSPOILT
UNSPOKE
UNSPOKEN
UNSPOTTED
UNSPRUNG
UNSPUN
UNSQUARED
UNSTABLE
UNSTABLER
UNSTABLEST
UNSTACK

UNSTACKED
UNSTACKING
UNSTACKS
UNSTAID
UNSTAINED
UNSTAMPED
UNSTARCH
UNSTARCHED
UNSTARCHES
UNSTARCHING
UNSTATE
UNSTATED
UNSTATES
UNSTATING
UNSTAYED
UNSTAYING
UNSTEADIED
UNSTEADIER
UNSTEADIES
UNSTEADIEST
UNSTEADY
UNSTEADYING
UNSTEEL
UNSTEELED
UNSTEELING
UNSTEELS
UNSTEP
UNSTEPPED
UNSTEPPING
UNSTEPS
UNSTERILE
UNSTICK
UNSTICKING
UNSTICKS
UNSTIFLED
UNSTILLED
UNSTINTED
UNSTIRRED
UNSTITCH
UNSTITCHED
UNSTITCHES
UNSTITCHING
UNSTOCK
UNSTOCKED
UNSTOCKING
UNSTOCKS
UNSTOP
UNSTOPPED
UNSTOPPER
UNSTOPPERED
UNSTOPPERING
UNSTOPPERS
UNSTOPPING
UNSTOPS
UNSTOW
UNSTOWED
UNSTOWING
UNSTOWS
UNSTRAP
UNSTRAPPED
UNSTRAPPING
UNSTRAPS
UNSTRING
UNSTRINGED
UNSTRINGING
UNSTRINGS
UNSTRIP
UNSTRIPED
UNSTRIPPED
UNSTRIPPING
UNSTRIPS
UNSTRUCK
UNSTRUNG
UNSTUCK
UNSTUDIED
UNSTUFFED
UNSTUFFY
UNSTUFT
UNSUBDUED
UNSUBJECT
UNSUBTLE
UNSUCCESS
UNSUCCESSES
UNSUCKED
UNSUIT
UNSUITED
UNSUITING
UNSUITS
UNSULLIED
UNSUMMED
UNSUNG
UNSUNNED
UNSUNNY
UNSUPPLE
UNSURE
UNSURED
UNSURER
UNSUREST
UNSUSPECT
UNSWADDLE
UNSWADDLED
UNSWADDLES
UNSWADDLING
UNSWATHE
UNSWATHED
UNSWATHES
UNSWATHING
UNSWAYED
UNSWEAR
UNSWEARING
UNSWEARINGS
UNSWEARS
UNSWEET
UNSWEPT
UNSWORE
UNSWORN
UNTACK
UNTACKED
UNTACKING
UNTACKLE
UNTACKLED
UNTACKLES
UNTACKLING
UNTACKS
UNTAILED
UNTAINTED
UNTAKEN
UNTAMABLE
UNTAMABLY
UNTAME
UNTAMED
UNTAMES
UNTAMING
UNTANGLE
UNTANGLED
UNTANGLES
UNTANGLING
UNTANNED
UNTAPPED
UNTARRED
UNTASTED
UNTAUGHT
UNTAX
UNTAXED
UNTAXES
UNTAXING
UNTEACH
UNTEACHES
UNTEACHING
UNTEAM
UNTEAMED
UNTEAMING
UNTEAMS
UNTEMPER
UNTEMPERED
UNTEMPERING
UNTEMPERS
UNTEMPTED
UNTENABLE
UNTENANT
UNTENANTED
UNTENANTING
UNTENANTS
UNTENDED
UNTENDER
UNTENT
UNTENTED
UNTENTING
UNTENTS
UNTENTY
UNTESTED
UNTETHER
UNTETHERED
UNTETHERING
UNTETHERS
UNTHANKED
UNTHATCH
UNTHATCHED
UNTHATCHES
UNTHATCHING
UNTHAW
UNTHAWED
UNTHAWING
UNTHAWS
UNTHINK
UNTHINKING
UNTHINKS
UNTHOUGHT
UNTHREAD
UNTHREADED
UNTHREADING
UNTHREADS
UNTHRIFT
UNTHRIFTS
UNTHRIFTY
UNTHRONE
UNTHRONED
UNTHRONES
UNTHRONING
UNTIDIED
UNTIDIER
UNTIDIES
UNTIDIEST
UNTIDILY
UNTIDY
UNTIDYING
UNTIE
UNTIED
UNTIES
UNTIL
UNTILE
UNTILED
UNTILES
UNTILING
UNTILLED
UNTIMELIER
UNTIMELIEST
UNTIMELY
UNTIMEOUS
UNTIN
UNTINGED
UNTINNED
UNTINNING
UNTINS
UNTIRABLE
UNTIRED
UNTIRING
UNTITLED
UNTO
UNTOILING
UNTOLD
UNTOMB
UNTOMBED
UNTOMBING
UNTOMBS
UNTONED
UNTORN
UNTOUCHED
UNTOWARD
UNTRACE
UNTRACED
UNTRACES
UNTRACING
UNTRACKED
UNTRADED
UNTRAINED
UNTREAD
UNTREADING
UNTREADS
UNTREATED
UNTRESSED
UNTRIDE
UNTRIED
UNTRIM
UNTRIMMED
UNTRIMMING
UNTRIMS
UNTROD
UNTRODDEN
UNTRUE
UNTRUER
UNTRUEST
UNTRUISM
UNTRUISMS
UNTRULY
UNTRUSS
UNTRUSSED
UNTRUSSER
UNTRUSSERS
UNTRUSSES
UNTRUSSING
UNTRUSSINGS
UNTRUST
UNTRUSTS
UNTRUSTY
UNTRUTH
UNTRUTHS
UNTUCK
UNTUCKED
UNTUCKING
UNTUCKS
UNTUMBLED
UNTUNABLE
UNTUNABLY
UNTUNE
UNTUNED
UNTUNEFUL
UNTUNES
UNTUNING
UNTURBID
UNTURF
UNTURFED
UNTURFING
UNTURFS
UNTURN
UNTURNED
UNTURNING
UNTURNS
UNTUTORED
UNTWINE
UNTWINED
UNTWINES
UNTWINING
UNTWIST
UNTWISTED
UNTWISTING
UNTWISTINGS
UNTWISTS
UNTYING
UNTYINGS
UNTYPABLE
UNTYPICAL
UNURGED
UNUSABLE
UNUSABLY
UNUSED
UNUSEFUL
UNUSHERED
UNUSUAL
UNUSUALLY

UNUTTERED
UNVAIL
UNVAILE
UNVAILED
UNVAILES
UNVAILING
UNVAILS
UNVALUED
UNVARIED
UNVARYING
UNVEIL
UNVEILED
UNVEILER
UNVEILERS
UNVEILING
UNVEILINGS
UNVEILS
UNVENTED
UNVERSED
UNVETTED
UNVEXED
UNVIABLE
UNVIEWED
UNVIRTUE
UNVIRTUES
UNVISITED
UNVISOR
UNVISORED
UNVISORING
UNVISORS
UNVITAL
UNVIZARD
UNVIZARDED
UNVIZARDING
UNVIZARDS
UNVOCAL
UNVOICE
UNVOICED
UNVOICES
UNVOICING
UNVOICINGS
UNVULGAR
UNWAGED
UNWAKED
UNWAKENED
UNWALLED
UNWANTED
UNWARDED
UNWARE
UNWARELY
UNWARES
UNWARIE
UNWARIER
UNWARIEST
UNWARILY
UNWARLIKE
UNWARMED
UNWARNED
UNWARPED
UNWARY
UNWASHED
UNWASHEN
UNWASTED
UNWASTING
UNWATCHED
UNWATER
UNWATERED
UNWATERING
UNWATERS
UNWATERY
UNWAYED
UNWEAL
UNWEALS
UNWEANED
UNWEAPON
UNWEAPONED
UNWEAPONING
UNWEAPONS
UNWEARIED
UNWEARY
UNWEAVE
UNWEAVES
UNWEAVING
UNWEBBED
UNWED
UNWEDDED
UNWEEDED
UNWEENED
UNWEETING
UNWEIGHED
UNWELCOME
UNWELDY
UNWELL
UNWEPT
UNWET
UNWETTED
UNWHIPPED
UNWHIPT
UNWIELDIER
UNWIELDIEST
UNWIELDY
UNWIFELIER
UNWIFELIEST
UNWIFELY
UNWIGGED
UNWILFUL
UNWILL
UNWILLED
UNWILLING
UNWILLS
UNWIND
UNWINDING
UNWINDINGS
UNWINDS
UNWINGED
UNWINKING
UNWIPED
UNWIRE
UNWIRED
UNWIRES
UNWIRING
UNWISDOM
UNWISDOMS
UNWISE
UNWISELY
UNWISER
UNWISEST
UNWISH
UNWISHED
UNWISHES
UNWISHFUL
UNWISHING
UNWIST
UNWIT
UNWITCH
UNWITCHED
UNWITCHES
UNWITCHING
UNWITS
UNWITTED
UNWITTILY
UNWITTING
UNWITTY
UNWIVE
UNWIVED
UNWIVES
UNWIVING
UNWOMAN
UNWOMANED
UNWOMANING
UNWOMANLIER
UNWOMANLIEST
UNWOMANLY
UNWOMANS
UNWON
UNWONT
UNWONTED
UNWOODED
UNWOOED
UNWORDED
UNWORK
UNWORKED
UNWORKING
UNWORKS
UNWORLDLIER
UNWORLDLIEST
UNWORLDLY
UNWORMED
UNWORN
UNWORRIED
UNWORTH
UNWORTHIER
UNWORTHIEST
UNWORTHS
UNWORTHY
UNWOUND
UNWOUNDED
UNWOVE
UNWOVEN
UNWRAP
UNWRAPPED
UNWRAPPING
UNWRAPS
UNWREAKED
UNWREATHE
UNWREATHED
UNWREATHES
UNWREATHING
UNWRINKLE
UNWRINKLED
UNWRINKLES
UNWRINKLING
UNWRITE
UNWRITES
UNWRITING
UNWRITTEN
UNWROTE
UNWROUGHT
UNWRUNG
UNYEANED
UNYOKE
UNYOKED
UNYOKES
UNYOKING
UNZEALOUS
UNZIP
UNZIPPED
UNZIPPING
UNZIPS
UNZONED
UP
UPADAISY
UPAITHRIC
UPAS
UPASES
UPBEAR
UPBEARING
UPBEARS
UPBEAT
UPBIND
UPBINDING
UPBINDS
UPBLEW
UPBLOW
UPBLOWING
UPBLOWN
UPBLOWS
UPBOIL
UPBOILED
UPBOILING
UPBOILS
UPBORE
UPBORNE
UPBOUND
UPBOUNDEN
UPBRAID
UPBRAIDED
UPBRAIDER
UPBRAIDERS
UPBRAIDING
UPBRAIDINGS
UPBRAIDS
UPBRAST
UPBRAY
UPBRAYED
UPBRAYING
UPBRAYS
UPBREAK
UPBREAKING
UPBREAKS
UPBRING
UPBRINGING
UPBRINGINGS
UPBRINGS
UPBROKE
UPBROKEN
UPBROUGHT
UPBUILD
UPBUILDING
UPBUILDINGS
UPBUILDS
UPBUILT
UPBURNING
UPBURST
UPBURSTING
UPBURSTS
UPBY
UPBYE
UPCAST
UPCASTING
UPCASTS
UPCATCH
UPCATCHES
UPCATCHING
UPCAUGHT
UPCHEARD
UPCHEER
UPCHEERED
UPCHEERING
UPCHEERS
UPCHUCK
UPCHUCKED
UPCHUCKING
UPCHUCKS
UPCLIMB
UPCLIMBED
UPCLIMBING
UPCLIMBS
UPCLOSE
UPCLOSED
UPCLOSES
UPCLOSING
UPCOAST
UPCOIL
UPCOILED
UPCOILING
UPCOILS
UPCOME
UPCOMES
UPCOMING
UPCURL
UPCURLED
UPCURLING
UPCURLS
UPCURVED
UPDATE
UPDATED
UPDATES
UPDATING
UPDRAG
UPDRAGGED
UPDRAGGING
UPDRAGS
UPDRAW
UPDRAWING
UPDRAWN
UPDRAWS
UPDREW
UPEND
UPENDED

UPENDING
UPENDS
UPFILL
UPFILLED
UPFILLING
UPFILLINGS
UPFILLS
UPFLOW
UPFLOWED
UPFLOWING
UPFLOWS
UPFLUNG
UPFOLLOW
UPFOLLOWED
UPFOLLOWING
UPFOLLOWS
UPFRONT
UPFURL
UPFURLED
UPFURLING
UPFURLS
UPGANG
UPGANGS
UPGATHER
UPGATHERED
UPGATHERING
UPGATHERS
UPGAZE
UPGAZED
UPGAZES
UPGAZING
UPGO
UPGOES
UPGOING
UPGOINGS
UPGONE
UPGRADE
UPGRADED
UPGRADER
UPGRADERS
UPGRADES
UPGRADING
UPGREW
UPGROW
UPGROWING
UPGROWINGS
UPGROWN
UPGROWS
UPGROWTH
UPGROWTHS
UPGUSH
UPGUSHED
UPGUSHES
UPGUSHING
UPHAND
UPHANG
UPHANGING
UPHANGS
UPHAUD
UPHAUDING
UPHAUDS
UPHEAP
UPHEAPED
UPHEAPING
UPHEAPINGS
UPHEAPS
UPHEAVAL
UPHEAVALS
UPHEAVE
UPHEAVED
UPHEAVES
UPHEAVING
UPHELD
UPHILD
UPHILL
UPHILLS
UPHOARD
UPHOARDED
UPHOARDING
UPHOARDS
UPHOIST
UPHOISTED
UPHOISTING
UPHOISTS
UPHOLD
UPHOLDER
UPHOLDERS
UPHOLDING
UPHOLDINGS
UPHOLDS
UPHOLSTER
UPHOLSTERED
UPHOLSTERING
UPHOLSTERS
UPHOORD
UPHOORDED
UPHOORDING
UPHOORDS
UPHROE
UPHROES
UPHUDDEN
UPHUNG
UPHURL
UPHURLED
UPHURLING
UPHURLS
UPJET
UPJETS
UPJETTED
UPJETTING
UPKEEP
UPKEEPS
UPKNIT
UPKNITS
UPKNITTED
UPKNITTING
UPLAID
UPLAND
UPLANDER
UPLANDERS
UPLANDISH
UPLANDS
UPLAY
UPLAYING
UPLAYS
UPLEAD
UPLEADING
UPLEADS
UPLEAN
UPLEANED
UPLEANING
UPLEANS
UPLEANT
UPLEAP
UPLEAPED
UPLEAPING
UPLEAPS
UPLEAPT
UPLED
UPLIFT
UPLIFTED
UPLIFTER
UPLIFTERS
UPLIFTING
UPLIFTINGS
UPLIFTS
UPLIGHTED
UPLIGHTER
UPLIGHTERS
UPLINK
UPLINKING
UPLINKINGS
UPLINKS
UPLOAD
UPLOADED
UPLOADING
UPLOADS
UPLOCK
UPLOCKED
UPLOCKING
UPLOCKS
UPLOOK
UPLOOKED
UPLOOKING
UPLOOKS
UPLYING
UPMAKE
UPMAKER
UPMAKERS
UPMAKES
UPMAKING
UPMAKINGS
UPMANSHIP
UPMANSHIPS
UPMOST
UPON
UPPED
UPPER
UPPERCUT
UPPERCUTS
UPPERMOST
UPPERS
UPPILED
UPPING
UPPINGS
UPPISH
UPPISHLY
UPPITY
UPRAISE
UPRAISED
UPRAISES
UPRAISING
UPRAN
UPRATE
UPRATED
UPRATES
UPRATING
UPREAR
UPREARED
UPREARING
UPREARS
UPREST
UPRESTS
UPRIGHT
UPRIGHTED
UPRIGHTING
UPRIGHTLY
UPRIGHTS
UPRISAL
UPRISALS
UPRISE
UPRISEN
UPRISES
UPRISING
UPRISINGS
UPRIST
UPRISTS
UPRIVER
UPROAR
UPROARED
UPROARING
UPROARS
UPROLL
UPROLLED
UPROLLING
UPROLLS
UPROOT
UPROOTAL
UPROOTALS
UPROOTED
UPROOTER
UPROOTERS
UPROOTING
UPROOTINGS
UPROOTS
UPROSE
UPROUSE
UPROUSED
UPROUSES
UPROUSING
UPRUN
UPRUNNING
UPRUNS
UPRUSH
UPRUSHED
UPRUSHES
UPRUSHING
UPRYST
UPS
UPSCALE
UPSEE
UPSEES
UPSEND
UPSENDING
UPSENDS
UPSENT
UPSET
UPSETS
UPSETTER
UPSETTERS
UPSETTING
UPSETTINGS
UPSEY
UPSEYS
UPSHOOT
UPSHOOTING
UPSHOOTS
UPSHOT
UPSHOTS
UPSIDE
UPSIDES
UPSIES
UPSILON
UPSILONS
UPSITTING
UPSITTINGS
UPSPAKE
UPSPEAK
UPSPEAKING
UPSPEAKS
UPSPEAR
UPSPEARED
UPSPEARING
UPSPEARS
UPSPOKE
UPSPOKEN
UPSPRANG
UPSPRING
UPSPRINGING
UPSPRINGS
UPSPRUNG
UPSTAGE
UPSTAGED
UPSTAGES
UPSTAGING
UPSTAIR
UPSTAIRS
UPSTAND
UPSTANDING
UPSTANDS
UPSTARE
UPSTARED
UPSTARES
UPSTARING
UPSTART
UPSTARTED
UPSTARTING
UPSTARTS
UPSTATE
UPSTAY
UPSTAYED
UPSTAYING
UPSTAYS
UPSTOOD
UPSTREAM
UPSTREAMED
UPSTREAMING
UPSTREAMS
UPSTROKE
UPSTROKES

UPSURGE
UPSURGED
UPSURGES
UPSURGING
UPSWARM
UPSWARMED
UPSWARMING
UPSWARMS
UPSWAY
UPSWAYED
UPSWAYING
UPSWAYS
UPSWEEP
UPSWEEPS
UPSWELL
UPSWELLED
UPSWELLING
UPSWELLS
UPSWEPT
UPSWING
UPSWINGS
UPSWOLLEN
UPSY
UPTAK
UPTAKE
UPTAKEN
UPTAKES
UPTAKING
UPTAKS
UPTEAR
UPTEARING
UPTEARS
UPTHREW
UPTHROW
UPTHROWING
UPTHROWN
UPTHROWS
UPTHRUST
UPTHRUSTING
UPTHRUSTS
UPTHUNDER
UPTHUNDERED
UPTHUNDERING
UPTHUNDERS
UPTIE
UPTIED
UPTIES
UPTIGHT
UPTIGHTER
UPTIGHTEST
UPTILT
UPTILTED
UPTILTING
UPTILTS
UPTOOK
UPTORE
UPTORN
UPTOWN
UPTOWNER
UPTOWNERS
UPTOWNS
UPTRAIN
UPTRAINED
UPTRAINING
UPTRAINS
UPTREND
UPTRENDS
UPTRILLED
UPTURN
UPTURNED
UPTURNING
UPTURNINGS
UPTURNS
UPTYING
UPVALUE
UPVALUED
UPVALUES
UPVALUING
UPWAFT
UPWAFTED
UPWAFTING
UPWAFTS
UPWARD
UPWARDLY
UPWARDS
UPWELL
UPWELLED
UPWELLING
UPWELLINGS
UPWELLS
UPWENT
UPWHIRL
UPWHIRLED
UPWHIRLING
UPWHIRLS
UPWIND
UPWINDING
UPWINDS
UPWOUND
UPWRAP
UPWRAPS
UPWROUGHT
UR
URACHI
URACHUS
URACHUSES
URACIL
URACILS
URAEI
URAEMIA
URAEMIAS
URAEMIC
URAEUS
URAEUSES
URALI
URALIS
URALITE
URALITES
URALITIC
URALITISE
URALITISED
URALITISES
URALITISING
URALITIZE
URALITIZED
URALITIZES
URALITIZING
URANIAN
URANIC
URANIDE
URANIDES
URANIN
URANINITE
URANINITES
URANINS
URANISCI
URANISCUS
URANISM
URANISMS
URANITE
URANITES
URANITIC
URANIUM
URANIUMS
URANOLOGIES
URANOLOGY
URANOUS
URANYL
URANYLIC
URANYLS
URAO
URAOS
URARI
URARIS
URATE
URATES
URBAN
URBANE
URBANELY
URBANER
URBANEST
URBANISE
URBANISED
URBANISES
URBANISING
URBANITE
URBANITES
URBANITIES
URBANITY
URBANIZE
URBANIZED
URBANIZES
URBANIZING
URCEOLATE
URCEOLI
URCEOLUS
URCEOLUSES
URCHIN
URCHINS
URD
URDE
URDEE
URDS
URDY
URE
UREA
UREAL
UREAS
UREDIA
UREDINE
UREDINES
UREDINIA
UREDINIAL
UREDINIUM
UREDINOUS
UREDIUM
UREDO
UREDOSORI
UREIC
UREIDE
UREIDES
UREMIA
UREMIAS
UREMIC
URENA
URENAS
URENT
URES
URESES
URESIS
URETER
URETERAL
URETERIC
URETERS
URETHAN
URETHANE
URETHANES
URETHANS
URETHRA
URETHRAE
URETHRAL
URETHRAS
URETIC
URGE
URGED
URGENCE
URGENCES
URGENCIES
URGENCY
URGENT
URGENTLY
URGER
URGERS
URGES
URGING
URGINGS
URIAL
URIALS
URIC
URICASE
URICASES
URIDINE
URIDINES
URINAL
URINALS
URINANT
URINARIES
URINARY
URINATE
URINATED
URINATES
URINATING
URINATION
URINATIONS
URINATIVE
URINATOR
URINATORS
URINE
URINED
URINES
URINING
URINOLOGIES
URINOLOGY
URINOSE
URINOUS
URITE
URITES
URMAN
URMANS
URN
URNAL
URNED
URNFIELD
URNFIELDS
URNFUL
URNFULS
URNING
URNINGS
URNS
UROCHORD
UROCHORDS
UROCHROME
UROCHROMES
URODELAN
URODELANS
URODELE
URODELES
URODELOUS
UROGENOUS
UROGRAPHIES
UROGRAPHY
UROKINASE
UROKINASES
UROLAGNIA
UROLAGNIAS
UROLITH
UROLITHIC
UROLITHS
UROLOGIC
UROLOGIES
UROLOGIST
UROLOGISTS
UROLOGY
UROMERE
UROMERES
UROPOD
UROPODS
UROPYGIA
UROPYGIAL
UROPYGIUM
UROPYGIUMS
UROSCOPIC
UROSCOPIES
UROSCOPY
UROSES
UROSIS
UROSOME
UROSOMES
UROSTEGE
UROSTEGES

UROSTOMIES
UROSTOMY
UROSTYLE
UROSTYLES
URSINE
URSON
URSONS
URTEXT
URTEXTS
URTICA
URTICANT
URTICARIA
URTICARIAS
URTICAS
URTICATE
URTICATED
URTICATES
URTICATING
URUBU
URUBUS
URUS
URUSES
URVA
URVAS
US
USABILITIES
USABILITY
USABLE
USABLY
USAGE
USAGER
USAGERS
USAGES
USANCE
USANCES
USE
USED
USEFUL
USEFULLY
USELESS
USELESSLY
USER
USERS
USES
USHER
USHERED
USHERESS
USHERESSES
USHERETTE
USHERETTES
USHERING
USHERINGS
USHERS
USHERSHIP
USHERSHIPS
USING
USNEA
USNEAS
USTION
USTIONS
USUAL
USUALLY
USUALNESS
USUALNESSES
USUALS
USUCAPION
USUCAPIONS
USUCAPT
USUCAPTED
USUCAPTING
USUCAPTS
USUFRUCT
USUFRUCTED
USUFRUCTING
USUFRUCTS
USURE
USURED
USURER
USURERS
USURES
USURESS
USURESSES
USURIES
USURING
USURIOUS
USUROUS
USURP
USURPED
USURPEDLY
USURPER
USURPERS
USURPING
USURPINGS
USURPS
USURY
USWARD
USWARDS
UT
UTAS
UTASES
UTE
UTENSIL
UTENSILS
UTERI
UTERINE
UTERITIS
UTERITISES
UTEROTOMIES
UTEROTOMY
UTERUS
UTES
UTILE
UTILISE
UTILISED
UTILISER
UTILISERS
UTILISES
UTILISING
UTILITIES
UTILITY
UTILIZE
UTILIZED
UTILIZER
UTILIZERS
UTILIZES
UTILIZING
UTIS
UTISES
UTMOST
UTMOSTS
UTOPIA
UTOPIAN
UTOPIANS
UTOPIAS
UTOPIAST
UTOPIASTS
UTOPISM
UTOPISMS
UTOPIST
UTOPISTS
UTRICLE
UTRICLES
UTRICULAR
UTRICULI
UTRICULUS
UTS
UTTER
UTTERABLE
UTTERANCE
UTTERANCES
UTTERED
UTTERER
UTTERERS
UTTEREST
UTTERING
UTTERINGS
UTTERLESS
UTTERLY
UTTERMOST
UTTERMOSTS
UTTERNESS
UTTERNESSES
UTTERS
UTU
UTUS
UVA
UVAE
UVAROVITE
UVAROVITES
UVAS
UVEA
UVEAL
UVEAS
UVEITIC
UVEITIS
UVEITISES
UVEOUS
UVULA
UVULAE
UVULAR
UVULARLY
UVULAS
UVULITIS
UVULITISES
UXORIAL
UXORIALLY
UXORICIDE
UXORICIDES
UXORIOUS

V

VAC
VACANCE
VACANCES
VACANCIES
VACANCY
VACANT
VACANTLY
VACATE
VACATED
VACATES
VACATING
VACATION
VACATIONED
VACATIONING
VACATIONS
VACATUR
VACATURS
VACCINAL
VACCINATE
VACCINATED
VACCINATES
VACCINATING
VACCINE
VACCINES
VACCINIA
VACCINIAL
VACCINIAS
VACCINIUM
VACCINIUMS
VACHERIN
VACHERINS
VACILLANT
VACILLATE
VACILLATED
VACILLATES
VACILLATING
VACKED
VACKING
VACS
VACUA
VACUATE
VACUATED
VACUATES
VACUATING
VACUATION
VACUATIONS
VACUIST
VACUISTS
VACUITIES
VACUITY
VACUOLAR
VACUOLATE
VACUOLE
VACUOLES
VACUOUS
VACUOUSLY
VACUUM
VACUUMED
VACUUMING
VACUUMS
VADE
VADED
VADES
VADING
VADOSE
VAE
VAES
VAGABOND
VAGABONDED
VAGABONDING
VAGABONDS
VAGAL
VAGARIES
VAGARIOUS
VAGARISH
VAGARY
VAGI
VAGILE
VAGILITIES
VAGILITY
VAGINA
VAGINAE
VAGINAL
VAGINALLY
VAGINANT
VAGINAS
VAGINATE
VAGINATED
VAGINITIS
VAGINITISES
VAGINULA
VAGINULAE
VAGINULE
VAGINULES
VAGITUS
VAGITUSES
VAGRANCIES
VAGRANCY
VAGRANT
VAGRANTS
VAGROM
VAGUE
VAGUED
VAGUELY
VAGUENESS
VAGUENESSES
VAGUER
VAGUES
VAGUEST
VAGUING
VAGUS
VAHINE
VAHINES
VAIL
VAILED
VAILING
VAILS
VAIN
VAINER
VAINESSE
VAINESSES
VAINEST
VAINGLORIED
VAINGLORIES
VAINGLORY
VAINGLORYING
VAINLY
VAINNESS
VAINNESSES
VAIR
VAIRE
VAIRIER
VAIRIEST
VAIRS
VAIRY
VAIVODE
VAIVODES
VAKASS
VAKASSES
VAKEEL
VAKEELS
VAKIL
VAKILS
VALANCE
VALANCED
VALANCES
VALE
VALENCE
VALENCES
VALENCIES
VALENCY
VALENTINE
VALENTINES
VALERIAN
VALERIANS
VALES
VALET
VALETA
VALETAS
VALETE
VALETED
VALETES
VALETING
VALETINGS
VALETS
VALGOUS
VALGUS
VALGUSES
VALI
VALIANCE
VALIANCES
VALIANCIES
VALIANCY
VALIANT
VALIANTLY
VALIANTS
VALID
VALIDATE
VALIDATED
VALIDATES
VALIDATING
VALIDER
VALIDEST
VALIDITIES
VALIDITY
VALIDLY
VALIDNESS
VALIDNESSES
VALINE
VALINES
VALIS
VALISE
VALISES
VALLAR
VALLARY
VALLECULA
VALLECULAE
VALLEY
VALLEYS
VALLONIA
VALLONIAS
VALLUM
VALLUMS
VALONEA
VALONEAS
VALONIA
VALONIAS
VALOR
VALORISE
VALORISED
VALORISES
VALORISING
VALORIZE
VALORIZED
VALORIZES
VALORIZING
VALOROUS
VALORS
VALOUR
VALOURS
VALSE
VALSED
VALSES
VALSING
VALUABLE
VALUABLES
VALUABLY
VALUATE
VALUATED
VALUATES
VALUATING
VALUATION
VALUATIONS
VALUATOR
VALUATORS
VALUE
VALUED
VALUELESS
VALUER
VALUERS
VALUES
VALUING
VALUTA
VALUTAS
VALVAL
VALVAR
VALVASSOR
VALVASSORS
VALVATE
VALVE
VALVED
VALVELESS
VALVELET
VALVELETS
VALVES
VALVING
VALVULA
VALVULAE
VALVULAR
VALVULE
VALVULES
VAMBRACE
VAMBRACED
VAMBRACES
VAMOOSE
VAMOOSED
VAMOOSES
VAMOOSING
VAMOSE
VAMOSED

VAMOSES
VAMOSING
VAMP
VAMPED
VAMPER
VAMPERS
VAMPING
VAMPINGS
VAMPIRE
VAMPIRED
VAMPIRES
VAMPIRIC
VAMPIRING
VAMPIRISE
VAMPIRISED
VAMPIRISES
VAMPIRISING
VAMPIRISM
VAMPIRISMS
VAMPIRIZE
VAMPIRIZED
VAMPIRIZES
VAMPIRIZING
VAMPISH
VAMPLATE
VAMPLATES
VAMPS
VAN
VANADATE
VANADATES
VANADIC
VANADIUM
VANADIUMS
VANADOUS
VANDAL
VANDALISE
VANDALISED
VANDALISES
VANDALISING
VANDALISM
VANDALISMS
VANDALIZE
VANDALIZED
VANDALIZES
VANDALIZING
VANDALS
VANDYKE
VANDYKED
VANDYKES
VANDYKING
VANE
VANED
VANELESS
VANES
VANESSA
VANESSAS
VANG
VANGS
VANGUARD
VANGUARDS
VANILLA
VANILLAS
VANILLIN
VANILLINS
VANISH
VANISHED
VANISHER
VANISHERS
VANISHES
VANISHING
VANISHINGS
VANITAS
VANITASES
VANITIES
VANITORIES
VANITORY
VANITY
VANNED
VANNER
VANNERS
VANNING
VANNINGS
VANQUISH
VANQUISHED
VANQUISHES
VANQUISHING
VANS
VANT
VANTAGE
VANTAGED
VANTAGES
VANTAGING
VANTBRACE
VANTBRACES
VANTS
VANWARD
VAPID
VAPIDER
VAPIDEST
VAPIDITIES
VAPIDITY
VAPIDLY
VAPIDNESS
VAPIDNESSES
VAPOR
VAPORABLE
VAPORED
VAPORETTI
VAPORETTO
VAPORETTOS
VAPORIFIC
VAPORING
VAPORISE
VAPORISED
VAPORISER
VAPORISERS
VAPORISES
VAPORISING
VAPORIZE
VAPORIZED
VAPORIZER
VAPORIZERS
VAPORIZES
VAPORIZING
VAPOROUS
VAPORS
VAPORWARE
VAPORWARES
VAPOUR
VAPOURED
VAPOURER
VAPOURERS
VAPOURING
VAPOURINGS
VAPOURISH
VAPOURS
VAPOURY
VAPULATE
VAPULATED
VAPULATES
VAPULATING
VAQUERO
VAQUEROS
VARA
VARACTOR
VARACTORS
VARAN
VARANS
VARAS
VARDIES
VARDY
VARE
VAREC
VARECH
VARECHS
VARECS
VARES
VAREUSE
VAREUSES
VARGUENO
VARGUENOS
VARIABLE
VARIABLES
VARIABLY
VARIANCE
VARIANCES
VARIANT
VARIANTS
VARIATE
VARIATED
VARIATES
VARIATING
VARIATION
VARIATIONS
VARIATIVE
VARICELLA
VARICELLAS
VARICES
VARICOSE
VARIED
VARIEDLY
VARIEGATE
VARIEGATED
VARIEGATES
VARIEGATING
VARIER
VARIERS
VARIES
VARIETAL
VARIETALS
VARIETIES
VARIETY
VARIFOCAL
VARIFOCALS
VARIFORM
VARIOLA
VARIOLAR
VARIOLAS
VARIOLATE
VARIOLATED
VARIOLATES
VARIOLATING
VARIOLE
VARIOLES
VARIOLITE
VARIOLITES
VARIOLOID
VARIOLOIDS
VARIOLOUS
VARIORUM
VARIORUMS
VARIOUS
VARIOUSLY
VARISCITE
VARISCITES
VARISTOR
VARISTORS
VARIX
VARLET
VARLETESS
VARLETESSES
VARLETRIES
VARLETRY
VARLETS
VARLETTO
VARLETTOS
VARMENT
VARMENTS
VARMINT
VARMINTS
VARNA
VARNAS
VARNISH
VARNISHED
VARNISHER
VARNISHERS
VARNISHES
VARNISHING
VARNISHINGS
VARROA
VARROAS
VARSAL
VARSITIES
VARSITY
VARTABED
VARTABEDS
VARUS
VARUSES
VARVE
VARVED
VARVEL
VARVELLED
VARVELS
VARVES
VARY
VARYING
VARYINGS
VAS
VASA
VASAL
VASCULA
VASCULAR
VASCULUM
VASCULUMS
VASE
VASECTOMIES
VASECTOMY
VASES
VASIFORM
VASOMOTOR
VASSAIL
VASSAILS
VASSAL
VASSALAGE
VASSALAGES
VASSALESS
VASSALESSES
VASSALLED
VASSALLING
VASSALRIES
VASSALRY
VASSALS
VAST
VASTER
VASTEST
VASTIDITIES
VASTIDITY
VASTIER
VASTIEST
VASTITIES
VASTITUDE
VASTITUDES
VASTITY
VASTLY
VASTNESS
VASTNESSES
VASTS
VASTY
VAT
VATABLE
VATFUL
VATFULS
VATIC
VATICIDE
VATICIDES
VATICINAL
VATMAN
VATMEN
VATS
VATTED
VATTER
VATTERS
VATTING
VATU
VATUS
VAU
VAUDOO
VAUDOOS
VAUDOUX
VAULT

VAULTAGE
VAULTAGES
VAULTED
VAULTER
VAULTERS
VAULTING
VAULTINGS
VAULTS
VAULTY
VAUNCE
VAUNCED
VAUNCES
VAUNCING
VAUNT
VAUNTAGE
VAUNTAGES
VAUNTED
VAUNTER
VAUNTERIES
VAUNTERS
VAUNTERY
VAUNTFUL
VAUNTIER
VAUNTIEST
VAUNTING
VAUNTINGS
VAUNTS
VAUNTY
VAURIEN
VAURIENS
VAUS
VAUT
VAUTE
VAUTED
VAUTES
VAUTING
VAUTS
VAVASORIES
VAVASORY
VAVASOUR
VAVASOURS
VAWARD
VAWARDS
VAWTE
VAWTED
VAWTES
VAWTING
VEAL
VEALE
VEALER
VEALERS
VEALES
VEALIER
VEALIEST
VEALS
VEALY
VECTOR
VECTORED
VECTORIAL
VECTORING
VECTORINGS
VECTORISE
VECTORISED
VECTORISES
VECTORISING
VECTORIZE
VECTORIZED
VECTORIZES
VECTORIZING
VECTORS
VEDALIA
VEDALIAS
VEDETTE
VEDETTES
VEDUTA
VEDUTE
VEDUTISTA
VEDUTISTI
VEE
VEENA
VEENAS
VEEP
VEEPS
VEER
VEERED
VEERIES
VEERING
VEERINGLY
VEERINGS
VEERS
VEERY
VEES
VEG
VEGA
VEGAN
VEGANIC
VEGANISM
VEGANISMS
VEGANS
VEGAS
VEGELATE
VEGELATES
VEGES
VEGETABLE
VEGETABLES
VEGETABLY
VEGETAL
VEGETALS
VEGETANT
VEGETATE
VEGETATED
VEGETATES
VEGETATING
VEGETATINGS
VEGETE
VEGETIVE
VEGETIVES
VEGGED
VEGGES
VEGGIE
VEGGIES
VEGGING
VEGIE
VEGIES
VEHEMENCE
VEHEMENCES
VEHEMENCIES
VEHEMENCY
VEHEMENT
VEHICLE
VEHICLES
VEHICULAR
VEHM
VEHME
VEHMIC
VEHMIQUE
VEIL
VEILED
VEILIER
VEILIEST
VEILING
VEILINGS
VEILLESS
VEILLEUSE
VEILLEUSES
VEILS
VEILY
VEIN
VEINED
VEINIER
VEINIEST
VEINING
VEININGS
VEINLET
VEINLETS
VEINOUS
VEINS
VEINSTONE
VEINSTONES
VEINSTUFF
VEINSTUFFS
VEINY
VELA
VELAMEN
VELAMINA
VELAR
VELARIA
VELARIC
VELARISE
VELARISED
VELARISES
VELARISING
VELARIUM
VELARIZE
VELARIZED
VELARIZES
VELARIZING
VELARS
VELATE
VELATED
VELATURA
VELATURAS
VELD
VELDS
VELDSKOEN
VELDSKOENS
VELDT
VELDTS
VELE
VELES
VELETA
VELETAS
VELIGER
VELIGERS
VELL
VELLEITIES
VELLEITY
VELLENAGE
VELLENAGES
VELLET
VELLETS
VELLICATE
VELLICATED
VELLICATES
VELLICATING
VELLON
VELLONS
VELLS
VELLUM
VELLUMS
VELOCE
VELOCITIES
VELOCITY
VELODROME
VELODROMES
VELOUR
VELOURS
VELOUTE
VELOUTES
VELOUTINE
VELOUTINES
VELSKOEN
VELSKOENS
VELUM
VELURE
VELURED
VELURES
VELURING
VELVERET
VELVERETS
VELVET
VELVETED
VELVETEEN
VELVETEENS
VELVETIER
VELVETIEST
VELVETING
VELVETINGS
VELVETS
VELVETY
VENA
VENAE
VENAL
VENALITIES
VENALITY
VENALLY
VENATIC
VENATICAL
VENATION
VENATIONS
VENATOR
VENATORS
VEND
VENDACE
VENDACES
VENDAGE
VENDAGES
VENDANGE
VENDANGES
VENDED
VENDEE
VENDEES
VENDER
VENDERS
VENDETTA
VENDETTAS
VENDEUSE
VENDEUSES
VENDIBLE
VENDIBLES
VENDIBLY
VENDING
VENDIS
VENDISES
VENDISS
VENDISSES
VENDITION
VENDITIONS
VENDOR
VENDORS
VENDS
VENDUE
VENDUES
VENEER
VENEERED
VENEERER
VENEERERS
VENEERING
VENEERINGS
VENEERS
VENEFIC
VENEFICAL
VENERABLE
VENERABLY
VENERATE
VENERATED
VENERATES
VENERATING
VENERATOR
VENERATORS
VENEREAL
VENEREAN
VENEREANS
VENEREOUS
VENERER
VENERERS
VENERIES
VENERY
VENEWE
VENEWES
VENEY
VENEYS
VENGE
VENGEABLE
VENGEABLY
VENGEANCE
VENGEANCES
VENGED
VENGEFUL
VENGEMENT

VENGEMENTS
VENGER
VENGERS
VENGES
VENGING
VENIAL
VENIALITIES
VENIALITY
VENIALLY
VENIDIUM
VENIDIUMS
VENIN
VENINS
VENIRE
VENIREMAN
VENIREMEN
VENIRES
VENISON
VENISONS
VENITE
VENITES
VENNEL
VENNELS
VENOM
VENOMED
VENOMING
VENOMOUS
VENOMS
VENOSE
VENOSITIES
VENOSITY
VENOUS
VENT
VENTAGE
VENTAGES
VENTAIL
VENTAILE
VENTAILES
VENTAILS
VENTANA
VENTANAS
VENTAYLE
VENTAYLES
VENTED
VENTER
VENTERS
VENTIDUCT
VENTIDUCTS
VENTIFACT
VENTIFACTS
VENTIGE
VENTIGES
VENTIL
VENTILATE
VENTILATED
VENTILATES
VENTILATING
VENTILS
VENTING
VENTINGS
VENTOSE
VENTOSITIES
VENTOSITY
VENTRAL
VENTRALLY
VENTRALS
VENTRE
VENTRED
VENTRES
VENTRICLE
VENTRICLES
VENTRING
VENTRINGS
VENTROUS
VENTS
VENTURE
VENTURED
VENTURER
VENTURERS
VENTURES
VENTURI
VENTURING
VENTURINGS
VENTURIS
VENTUROUS
VENUE
VENUES
VENULE
VENULES
VENUS
VENUSES
VENVILLE
VENVILLES
VERACIOUS
VERACITIES
VERACITY
VERANDA
VERANDAH
VERANDAHS
VERANDAS
VERATRIN
VERATRINE
VERATRINES
VERATRINS
VERATRUM
VERATRUMS
VERB
VERBAL
VERBALISE
VERBALISED
VERBALISES
VERBALISING
VERBALISM
VERBALISMS
VERBALIST
VERBALISTS
VERBALITIES
VERBALITY
VERBALIZE
VERBALIZED
VERBALIZES
VERBALIZING
VERBALLED
VERBALLING
VERBALLY
VERBALS
VERBARIAN
VERBARIANS
VERBATIM
VERBENA
VERBENAS
VERBERATE
VERBERATED
VERBERATES
VERBERATING
VERBIAGE
VERBIAGES
VERBICIDE
VERBICIDES
VERBID
VERBIDS
VERBIFIED
VERBIFIES
VERBIFY
VERBIFYING
VERBLESS
VERBOSE
VERBOSELY
VERBOSER
VERBOSEST
VERBOSITIES
VERBOSITY
VERBOTEN
VERBS
VERDANCIES
VERDANCY
VERDANT
VERDANTLY
VERDELHO
VERDELHOS
VERDERER
VERDERERS
VERDEROR
VERDERORS
VERDET
VERDETS
VERDICT
VERDICTS
VERDIGRIS
VERDIGRISED
VERDIGRISES
VERDIGRISING
VERDIN
VERDINS
VERDIT
VERDITE
VERDITER
VERDITERS
VERDITES
VERDITS
VERDOY
VERDURE
VERDURED
VERDURES
VERDUROUS
VERECUND
VERGE
VERGED
VERGENCE
VERGENCES
VERGENCIES
VERGENCY
VERGER
VERGERS
VERGES
VERGING
VERGLAS
VERGLASES
VERIDICAL
VERIER
VERIEST
VERIFIED
VERIFIER
VERIFIERS
VERIFIES
VERIFY
VERIFYING
VERILY
VERISM
VERISMO
VERISMOS
VERISMS
VERIST
VERISTIC
VERISTS
VERITABLE
VERITABLY
VERITIES
VERITY
VERJUICE
VERJUICED
VERJUICES
VERKRAMP
VERLIG
VERLIGTE
VERLIGTES
VERMAL
VERMEIL
VERMEILED
VERMEILING
VERMEILLE
VERMEILLED
VERMEILLES
VERMEILLING
VERMEILS
VERMELL
VERMELLS
VERMES
VERMIAN
VERMICIDE
VERMICIDES
VERMICULE
VERMICULES
VERMIFORM
VERMIFUGE
VERMIFUGES
VERMIL
VERMILIES
VERMILION
VERMILIONED
VERMILIONING
VERMILIONS
VERMILLED
VERMILLING
VERMILS
VERMILY
VERMIN
VERMINATE
VERMINATED
VERMINATES
VERMINATING
VERMINED
VERMINOUS
VERMINS
VERMINY
VERMIS
VERMOUTH
VERMOUTHS
VERNAL
VERNALISE
VERNALISED
VERNALISES
VERNALISING
VERNALITIES
VERNALITY
VERNALIZE
VERNALIZED
VERNALIZES
VERNALIZING
VERNALLY
VERNANT
VERNATION
VERNATIONS
VERNICLE
VERNICLES
VERNIER
VERNIERS
VERONAL
VERONALS
VERONICA
VERONICAS
VERONIQUE
VERQUERE
VERQUERES
VERQUIRE
VERQUIRES
VERREL
VERRELS
VERREY
VERRUCA
VERRUCAE
VERRUCAS
VERRUCOSE
VERRUCOUS
VERRUGA
VERRUGAS
VERRY
VERS
VERSAL
VERSALS
VERSANT
VERSANTS
VERSATILE
VERSE
VERSED
VERSELET
VERSELETS
VERSER
VERSERS
VERSES

VERSET
VERSETS
VERSICLE
VERSICLES
VERSIFIED
VERSIFIER
VERSIFIERS
VERSIFIES
VERSIFORM
VERSIFY
VERSIFYING
VERSIN
VERSINE
VERSINES
VERSING
VERSINGS
VERSINS
VERSION
VERSIONAL
VERSIONER
VERSIONERS
VERSIONS
VERSO
VERSOS
VERST
VERSTS
VERSUS
VERSUTE
VERT
VERTEBRA
VERTEBRAE
VERTEBRAL
VERTED
VERTEX
VERTEXES
VERTICAL
VERTICALS
VERTICES
VERTICIL
VERTICILS
VERTICITIES
VERTICITY
VERTIGINES
VERTIGO
VERTIGOES
VERTIGOS
VERTING
VERTIPORT
VERTIPORTS
VERTS
VERTU
VERTUE
VERTUES
VERTUOUS
VERTUS
VERVAIN
VERVAINS
VERVE
VERVEL
VERVELLED
VERVELS
VERVEN
VERVENS
VERVES
VERVET
VERVETS
VERY
VESICA
VESICAE
VESICAL
VESICANT
VESICANTS
VESICATE
VESICATED
VESICATES
VESICATING
VESICLE
VESICLES
VESICULA
VESICULAE
VESICULAR
VESPA
VESPAS
VESPER
VESPERAL
VESPERS
VESPIARIES
VESPIARY
VESPINE
VESPOID
VESSAIL
VESSAILS
VESSEL
VESSELS
VEST
VESTA
VESTAL
VESTALS
VESTAS
VESTED
VESTIARIES
VESTIARY
VESTIBULA
VESTIBULE
VESTIBULED
VESTIBULES
VESTIBULING
VESTIGE
VESTIGES
VESTIGIA
VESTIGIAL
VESTIGIUM
VESTIMENT
VESTIMENTS
VESTING
VESTINGS
VESTITURE
VESTITURES
VESTMENT
VESTMENTS
VESTRAL
VESTRIES
VESTRY
VESTRYMAN
VESTRYMEN
VESTS
VESTURAL
VESTURE
VESTURED
VESTURER
VESTURERS
VESTURES
VESTURING
VESUVIAN
VESUVIANS
VET
VETCH
VETCHES
VETCHIER
VETCHIEST
VETCHLING
VETCHLINGS
VETCHY
VETERAN
VETERANS
VETIVER
VETIVERS
VETKOEK
VETKOEKS
VETO
VETOED
VETOES
VETOING
VETS
VETTED
VETTING
VETTURA
VETTURAS
VETTURINI
VETTURINO
VEX
VEXATION
VEXATIONS
VEXATIOUS
VEXATORY
VEXED
VEXEDLY
VEXEDNESS
VEXEDNESSES
VEXER
VEXERS
VEXES
VEXILLA
VEXILLARIES
VEXILLARY
VEXILLUM
VEXING
VEXINGLY
VEXINGS
VEXT
VEZIR
VEZIRS
VIA
VIABILITIES
VIABILITY
VIABLE
VIADUCT
VIADUCTS
VIAE
VIAL
VIALFUL
VIALFULS
VIALLED
VIALS
VIAMETER
VIAMETERS
VIAND
VIANDS
VIAS
VIATICA
VIATICALS
VIATICUM
VIATICUMS
VIATOR
VIATORES
VIATORIAL
VIATORS
VIBE
VIBES
VIBEX
VIBICES
VIBIST
VIBISTS
VIBRACULA
VIBRAHARP
VIBRAHARPS
VIBRANCIES
VIBRANCY
VIBRANT
VIBRANTLY
VIBRATE
VIBRATED
VIBRATES
VIBRATILE
VIBRATING
VIBRATION
VIBRATIONS
VIBRATIVE
VIBRATO
VIBRATOR
VIBRATORS
VIBRATORY
VIBRATOS
VIBRIO
VIBRIOS
VIBRIOSES
VIBRIOSIS
VIBRISSA
VIBRISSAE
VIBRONIC
VIBS
VIBURNUM
VIBURNUMS
VICAR
VICARAGE
VICARAGES
VICARATE
VICARATES
VICARESS
VICARESSES
VICARIAL
VICARIATE
VICARIATES
VICARIES
VICARIOUS
VICARS
VICARSHIP
VICARSHIPS
VICARY
VICE
VICED
VICELESS
VICENARY
VICENNIAL
VICEREINE
VICEREINES
VICEROY
VICEROYS
VICES
VICESIMAL
VICHIES
VICHY
VICIATE
VICIATED
VICIATES
VICIATING
VICINAGE
VICINAGES
VICINAL
VICING
VICINITIES
VICINITY
VICIOSITIES
VICIOSITY
VICIOUS
VICIOUSLY
VICOMTE
VICOMTES
VICTIM
VICTIMISE
VICTIMISED
VICTIMISES
VICTIMISING
VICTIMIZE
VICTIMIZED
VICTIMIZES
VICTIMIZING
VICTIMS
VICTOR
VICTORESS
VICTORESSES
VICTORIA
VICTORIAS
VICTORIES
VICTORINE
VICTORINES
VICTORS
VICTORY
VICTRESS
VICTRESSES
VICTRIX
VICTRIXES
VICTROLLA
VICTROLLAS
VICTUAL
VICTUALLED
VICTUALLING
VICTUALS
VICUNA
VICUNAS

VID
VIDAME
VIDAMES
VIDE
VIDELICET
VIDENDA
VIDENDUM
VIDEO
VIDEODISC
VIDEODISCS
VIDEOED
VIDEOFIT
VIDEOFITS
VIDEOGRAM
VIDEOGRAMS
VIDEOING
VIDEOS
VIDEOTAPE
VIDEOTAPED
VIDEOTAPES
VIDEOTAPING
VIDEOTEX
VIDEOTEXES
VIDEOTEXT
VIDEOTEXTS
VIDETTE
VIDETTES
VIDIMUS
VIDIMUSES
VIDS
VIDUAGE
VIDUAGES
VIDUAL
VIDUITIES
VIDUITY
VIDUOUS
VIE
VIED
VIELLE
VIELLES
VIER
VIERS
VIES
VIEW
VIEWABLE
VIEWDATA
VIEWDATAS
VIEWED
VIEWER
VIEWERS
VIEWIER
VIEWIEST
VIEWINESS
VIEWINESSES
VIEWING
VIEWINGS
VIEWLESS
VIEWLY
VIEWPHONE
VIEWPHONES
VIEWPOINT
VIEWPOINTS
VIEWS
VIEWY
VIFDA
VIFDAS
VIGESIMAL
VIGIA
VIGIAS
VIGIL
VIGILANCE
VIGILANCES
VIGILANT
VIGILANTE
VIGILANTES
VIGILS
VIGNERON
VIGNERONS
VIGNETTE
VIGNETTED
VIGNETTER
VIGNETTERS
VIGNETTES
VIGNETTING
VIGOR
VIGORISH
VIGORISHES
VIGORO
VIGOROS
VIGOROUS
VIGORS
VIGOUR
VIGOURS
VIHARA
VIHARAS
VIHUELA
VIHUELAS
VIKING
VIKINGISM
VIKINGISMS
VIKINGS
VILAYET
VILAYETS
VILD
VILDE
VILDLY
VILDNESS
VILDNESSES
VILE
VILELY
VILENESS
VILENESSES
VILER
VILEST
VILIACO
VILIACOES
VILIACOS
VILIAGO
VILIAGOES
VILIAGOS
VILIFIED
VILIFIER
VILIFIERS
VILIFIES
VILIFY
VILIFYING
VILIPEND
VILIPENDED
VILIPENDING
VILIPENDS
VILL
VILLA
VILLADOM
VILLADOMS
VILLAGE
VILLAGER
VILLAGERIES
VILLAGERS
VILLAGERY
VILLAGES
VILLAGIO
VILLAGIOES
VILLAGIOS
VILLAGREE
VILLAGREES
VILLAIN
VILLAINIES
VILLAINS
VILLAINY
VILLAN
VILLANAGE
VILLANAGES
VILLANIES
VILLANOUS
VILLANS
VILLANY
VILLAR
VILLAS
VILLATIC
VILLEIN
VILLEINS
VILLENAGE
VILLENAGES
VILLI
VILLIAGO
VILLIAGOES
VILLIAGOS
VILLIFORM
VILLOSE
VILLOSITIES
VILLOSITY
VILLOUS
VILLS
VILLUS
VIM
VIMANA
VIMANAS
VIMINEOUS
VIMS
VIN
VINA
VINACEOUS
VINAL
VINAS
VINASSE
VINASSES
VINCA
VINCAS
VINCIBLE
VINCULA
VINCULUM
VINDALOO
VINDALOOS
VINDEMIAL
VINDICATE
VINDICATED
VINDICATES
VINDICATING
VINE
VINED
VINEGAR
VINEGARED
VINEGARING
VINEGARS
VINEGARY
VINER
VINERIES
VINERS
VINERY
VINES
VINEW
VINEWED
VINEWING
VINEWS
VINEYARD
VINEYARDS
VINIER
VINIEST
VINING
VINO
VINOLENT
VINOLOGIES
VINOLOGY
VINOS
VINOSITIES
VINOSITY
VINOUS
VINS
VINT
VINTAGE
VINTAGED
VINTAGER
VINTAGERS
VINTAGES
VINTAGING
VINTAGINGS
VINTED
VINTING
VINTNER
VINTNERS
VINTRIES
VINTRY
VINTS
VINY
VINYL
VINYLS
VIOL
VIOLA
VIOLABLE
VIOLABLY
VIOLAS
VIOLATE
VIOLATED
VIOLATER
VIOLATERS
VIOLATES
VIOLATING
VIOLATION
VIOLATIONS
VIOLATIVE
VIOLATOR
VIOLATORS
VIOLD
VIOLENCE
VIOLENCES
VIOLENT
VIOLENTED
VIOLENTING
VIOLENTLY
VIOLENTS
VIOLER
VIOLERS
VIOLET
VIOLETS
VIOLIN
VIOLINIST
VIOLINISTS
VIOLINS
VIOLIST
VIOLISTS
VIOLONE
VIOLONES
VIOLS
VIPER
VIPERINE
VIPERISH
VIPEROUS
VIPERS
VIRAEMIA
VIRAEMIAS
VIRAEMIC
VIRAGO
VIRAGOES
VIRAGOISH
VIRAGOS
VIRAL
VIRANDA
VIRANDAS
VIRANDO
VIRANDOS
VIRE
VIRED
VIRELAY
VIRELAYS
VIREMENT
VIREMENTS
VIRENT
VIREO
VIREOS
VIRES
VIRESCENT
VIRETOT
VIRETOTS
VIRGA
VIRGAS
VIRGATE
VIRGATES
VIRGE
VIRGER
VIRGERS

VIRGES
VIRGIN
VIRGINAL
VIRGINALLED
VIRGINALLING
VIRGINALS
VIRGINED
VIRGINING
VIRGINITIES
VIRGINITY
VIRGINIUM
VIRGINIUMS
VIRGINLY
VIRGINS
VIRGULATE
VIRGULE
VIRGULES
VIRICIDAL
VIRICIDE
VIRICIDES
VIRID
VIRIDIAN
VIRIDIANS
VIRIDITE
VIRIDITES
VIRIDITIES
VIRIDITY
VIRILE
VIRILISED
VIRILISM
VIRILISMS
VIRILITIES
VIRILITY
VIRILIZED
VIRING
VIRINO
VIRINOS
VIRION
VIRIONS
VIRL
VIRLS
VIROGENE
VIROGENES
VIROID
VIROIDS
VIROLOGIES
VIROLOGY
VIROSE
VIROSES
VIROSIS
VIROUS
VIRTU
VIRTUAL
VIRTUALLY
VIRTUE
VIRTUES
VIRTUOSA
VIRTUOSE
VIRTUOSI
VIRTUOSIC
VIRTUOSO
VIRTUOSOS
VIRTUOUS
VIRTUS
VIRUCIDAL
VIRUCIDE
VIRUCIDES
VIRULENCE
VIRULENCES
VIRULENCIES
VIRULENCY
VIRULENT
VIRUS
VIRUSES
VIS
VISA
VISAED
VISAGE
VISAGED
VISAGES
VISAGIST
VISAGISTE
VISAGISTES
VISAGISTS
VISAING
VISAS
VISCACHA
VISCACHAS
VISCERA
VISCERAL
VISCERATE
VISCERATED
VISCERATES
VISCERATING
VISCID
VISCIDITIES
VISCIDITY
VISCIN
VISCINS
VISCOSE
VISCOSES
VISCOSITIES
VISCOSITY
VISCOUNT
VISCOUNTIES
VISCOUNTS
VISCOUNTY
VISCOUS
VISCUM
VISCUMS
VISCUS
VISE
VISED
VISEED
VISEING
VISES
VISIBLE
VISIBLES
VISIBLY
VISIE
VISIED
VISIEING
VISIER
VISIERS
VISIES
VISILE
VISILES
VISING
VISION
VISIONAL
VISIONARIES
VISIONARY
VISIONED
VISIONER
VISIONERS
VISIONING
VISIONINGS
VISIONIST
VISIONISTS
VISIONS
VISIT
VISITABLE
VISITANT
VISITANTS
VISITATOR
VISITATORS
VISITE
VISITED
VISITEE
VISITEES
VISITER
VISITERS
VISITES
VISITING
VISITINGS
VISITOR
VISITORS
VISITRESS
VISITRESSES
VISITS
VISIVE
VISNE
VISNES
VISNOMIE
VISNOMIES
VISNOMY
VISON
VISONS
VISOR
VISORED
VISORING
VISORS
VISTA
VISTAED
VISTAING
VISTAL
VISTALESS
VISTAS
VISTO
VISTOS
VISUAL
VISUALISE
VISUALISED
VISUALISES
VISUALISING
VISUALIST
VISUALISTS
VISUALITIES
VISUALITY
VISUALIZE
VISUALIZED
VISUALIZES
VISUALIZING
VISUALLY
VISUALS
VITA
VITAE
VITAL
VITALISE
VITALISED
VITALISER
VITALISERS
VITALISES
VITALISING
VITALISM
VITALISMS
VITALIST
VITALISTS
VITALITIES
VITALITY
VITALIZE
VITALIZED
VITALIZER
VITALIZERS
VITALIZES
VITALIZING
VITALLY
VITALS
VITAMIN
VITAMINE
VITAMINES
VITAMINS
VITAS
VITASCOPE
VITASCOPES
VITATIVE
VITE
VITELLARY
VITELLI
VITELLIN
VITELLINE
VITELLINES
VITELLINS
VITELLUS
VITEX
VITEXES
VITIABLE
VITIATE
VITIATED
VITIATES
VITIATING
VITIATION
VITIATIONS
VITIATOR
VITIATORS
VITICETA
VITICETUM
VITICETUMS
VITICIDE
VITICIDES
VITILIGO
VITILIGOS
VITIOSITIES
VITIOSITY
VITRAGE
VITRAGES
VITRAIL
VITRAIN
VITRAINS
VITRAUX
VITREOUS
VITREUM
VITREUMS
VITRIC
VITRICS
VITRIFIED
VITRIFIES
VITRIFORM
VITRIFY
VITRIFYING
VITRINE
VITRINES
VITRIOL
VITRIOLIC
VITRIOLS
VITTA
VITTAE
VITTATE
VITTLE
VITTLES
VITULAR
VITULINE
VIVA
VIVACE
VIVACIOUS
VIVACITIES
VIVACITY
VIVAED
VIVAING
VIVAMENTE
VIVANDIER
VIVANDIERS
VIVARIA
VIVARIES
VIVARIUM
VIVARIUMS
VIVARY
VIVAS
VIVAT
VIVATS
VIVDA
VIVDAS
VIVE
VIVELY
VIVENCIES
VIVENCY
VIVER
VIVERRA
VIVERRAS
VIVERRINE
VIVERS
VIVES
VIVIANITE
VIVIANITES
VIVID
VIVIDER
VIVIDEST
VIVIDITIES
VIVIDITY
VIVIDLY

VIVIDNESS
VIVIDNESSES
VIVIFIC
VIVIFIED
VIVIFIER
VIVIFIERS
VIVIFIES
VIVIFY
VIVIFYING
VIVIPARIES
VIVIPARY
VIVISECT
VIVISECTED
VIVISECTING
VIVISECTS
VIVO
VIVRES
VIXEN
VIXENISH
VIXENLY
VIXENS
VIZAMENT
VIZAMENTS
VIZARD
VIZARDED
VIZARDING
VIZARDS
VIZCACHA
VIZCACHAS
VIZIED
VIZIER
VIZIERATE
VIZIERATES
VIZIERIAL
VIZIERS
VIZIES
VIZIR
VIZIRATE
VIZIRATES
VIZIRIAL
VIZIRS
VIZIRSHIP
VIZIRSHIPS
VIZOR
VIZORED
VIZORING
VIZORS
VIZSLA
VIZSLAS
VIZY
VIZYING
VIZZIE
VIZZIED
VIZZIEING
VIZZIES
VLEI
VLEIS
VLIES
VLY
VOAR
VOARS
VOCAB
VOCABLE
VOCABLES
VOCABS
VOCABULAR
VOCAL
VOCALESE
VOCALESES
VOCALIC
VOCALION
VOCALIONS
VOCALISE
VOCALISED
VOCALISER
VOCALISERS
VOCALISES
VOCALISING
VOCALISM
VOCALISMS
VOCALIST
VOCALISTS
VOCALITIES
VOCALITY
VOCALIZE
VOCALIZED
VOCALIZER
VOCALIZERS
VOCALIZES
VOCALIZING
VOCALLY
VOCALNESS
VOCALNESSES
VOCALS
VOCATION
VOCATIONS
VOCATIVE
VOCATIVES
VOCES
VOCODER
VOCODERS
VOCULAR
VOCULE
VOCULES
VODKA
VODKAS
VOE
VOES
VOGIE
VOGIER
VOGIEST
VOGUE
VOGUED
VOGUEING
VOGUEINGS
VOGUER
VOGUERS
VOGUES
VOGUEY
VOGUIER
VOGUIEST
VOGUING
VOGUINGS
VOGUISH
VOICE
VOICED
VOICEFUL
VOICELESS
VOICER
VOICERS
VOICES
VOICING
VOICINGS
VOID
VOIDABLE
VOIDANCE
VOIDANCES
VOIDED
VOIDEE
VOIDEES
VOIDER
VOIDERS
VOIDING
VOIDINGS
VOIDNESS
VOIDNESSES
VOIDS
VOILA
VOILE
VOILES
VOISINAGE
VOISINAGES
VOITURE
VOITURES
VOITURIER
VOITURIERS
VOIVODE
VOIVODES
VOL
VOLA
VOLABLE
VOLAE
VOLAGE
VOLAGEOUS
VOLANT
VOLANTE
VOLANTES
VOLAR
VOLARIES
VOLARY
VOLATIC
VOLATILE
VOLATILES
VOLCANIAN
VOLCANIC
VOLCANISE
VOLCANISED
VOLCANISES
VOLCANISING
VOLCANISM
VOLCANISMS
VOLCANIST
VOLCANISTS
VOLCANIZE
VOLCANIZED
VOLCANIZES
VOLCANIZING
VOLCANO
VOLCANOES
VOLE
VOLED
VOLENS
VOLERIES
VOLERY
VOLES
VOLET
VOLETS
VOLING
VOLITANT
VOLITATE
VOLITATED
VOLITATES
VOLITATING
VOLITIENT
VOLITION
VOLITIONS
VOLITIVE
VOLITIVES
VOLK
VOLKS
VOLKSRAAD
VOLKSRAADS
VOLLEY
VOLLEYED
VOLLEYER
VOLLEYERS
VOLLEYING
VOLLEYS
VOLOST
VOLOSTS
VOLPINO
VOLPINOS
VOLPLANE
VOLPLANED
VOLPLANES
VOLPLANING
VOLS
VOLT
VOLTA
VOLTAGE
VOLTAGES
VOLTAIC
VOLTAISM
VOLTAISMS
VOLTE
VOLTES
VOLTIGEUR
VOLTIGEURS
VOLTINISM
VOLTINISMS
VOLTMETER
VOLTMETERS
VOLTS
VOLUBIL
VOLUBLE
VOLUBLY
VOLUCRINE
VOLUME
VOLUMED
VOLUMES
VOLUMETER
VOLUMETERS
VOLUMINAL
VOLUMING
VOLUMISE
VOLUMISED
VOLUMISES
VOLUMISING
VOLUMIST
VOLUMISTS
VOLUMIZE
VOLUMIZED
VOLUMIZES
VOLUMIZING
VOLUNTARIES
VOLUNTARY
VOLUNTEER
VOLUNTEERED
VOLUNTEERING
VOLUNTEERS
VOLUSPA
VOLUSPAS
VOLUTE
VOLUTED
VOLUTES
VOLUTIN
VOLUTINS
VOLUTION
VOLUTIONS
VOLUTOID
VOLVA
VOLVAS
VOLVATE
VOLVE
VOLVED
VOLVES
VOLVING
VOLVOX
VOLVOXES
VOLVULI
VOLVULUS
VOLVULUSES
VOMER
VOMERINE
VOMERS
VOMICA
VOMICAE
VOMICAS
VOMIT
VOMITED
VOMITING
VOMITINGS
VOMITIVE
VOMITIVES
VOMITO
VOMITORIA
VOMITORIES
VOMITORY
VOMITOS
VOMITS
VOMITUS
VOMITUSES
VOODOO
VOODOOED
VOODOOING
VOODOOISM
VOODOOISMS
VOODOOIST
VOODOOISTS
VOODOOS

VOR
VORACIOUS
VORACITIES
VORACITY
VORAGO
VORAGOES
VORANT
VORPAL
VORRED
VORRING
VORS
VORTEX
VORTEXES
VORTICAL
VORTICES
VORTICISM
VORTICISMS
VORTICIST
VORTICISTS
VORTICITIES
VORTICITY
VORTICOSE
VOTARESS
VOTARESSES
VOTARIES
VOTARIST
VOTARISTS
VOTARY
VOTE
VOTED
VOTEEN
VOTEENS
VOTELESS
VOTER
VOTERS
VOTES
VOTING
VOTIVE
VOTRESS
VOTRESSES
VOUCH
VOUCHED
VOUCHEE
VOUCHEES
VOUCHER
VOUCHERS
VOUCHES
VOUCHING
VOUCHSAFE
VOUCHSAFED
VOUCHSAFES
VOUCHSAFING
VOUCHSAFINGS
VOUDOU
VOUDOUED
VOUDOUING
VOUDOUS
VOUGE
VOUGES
VOULGE
VOULGES
VOULU
VOUSSOIR
VOUSSOIRED
VOUSSOIRING
VOUSSOIRS
VOUTSAFE
VOUTSAFED
VOUTSAFES
VOUTSAFING
VOW
VOWED
VOWEL
VOWELISE
VOWELISED
VOWELISES
VOWELISING
VOWELIZE
VOWELIZED
VOWELIZES
VOWELIZING
VOWELLED
VOWELLESS
VOWELLING
VOWELLY
VOWELS
VOWER
VOWERS
VOWESS
VOWESSES
VOWING
VOWS
VOX
VOXEL
VOXELS
VOYAGE
VOYAGED
VOYAGER
VOYAGERS
VOYAGES
VOYAGEUR
VOYAGEURS
VOYAGING
VOYEUR
VOYEURISM
VOYEURISMS
VOYEURS
VOZHD
VOZHDS
VRAIC
VRAICKER
VRAICKERS
VRAICKING
VRAICKINGS
VRAICS
VRIL
VRILS
VROOM
VROOMED
VROOMING
VROOMS
VROUW
VROUWS
VROW
VROWS
VUG
VUGGIER
VUGGIEST
VUGGY
VUGS
VULCAN
VULCANIAN
VULCANIC
VULCANISE
VULCANISED
VULCANISES
VULCANISING
VULCANISM
VULCANISMS
VULCANIST
VULCANISTS
VULCANITE
VULCANITES
VULCANIZE
VULCANIZED
VULCANIZES
VULCANIZING
VULCANS
VULGAR
VULGARER
VULGAREST
VULGARIAN
VULGARIANS
VULGARISE
VULGARISED
VULGARISES
VULGARISING
VULGARISM
VULGARISMS
VULGARITIES
VULGARITY
VULGARIZE
VULGARIZED
VULGARIZES
VULGARIZING
VULGARLY
VULGARS
VULGATE
VULGATES
VULGO
VULGUS
VULGUSES
VULN
VULNED
VULNERARIES
VULNERARY
VULNERATE
VULNERATED
VULNERATES
VULNERATING
VULNING
VULNS
VULPICIDE
VULPICIDES
VULPINE
VULPINISM
VULPINISMS
VULPINITE
VULPINITES
VULSELLA
VULSELLAE
VULSELLUM
VULTURE
VULTURES
VULTURINE
VULTURISH
VULTURISM
VULTURISMS
VULTURN
VULTURNS
VULTUROUS
VULVA
VULVAE
VULVAL
VULVAR
VULVAS
VULVATE
VULVIFORM
VULVITIS
VULVITISES
VUM
VUMMED
VUMMING
VUMS
VYING
VYINGLY

W

WABAIN
WABAINS
WABBIT
WABBLE
WABBLED
WABBLER
WABBLERS
WABBLES
WABBLING
WABOOM
WABOOMS
WABSTER
WABSTERS
WACK
WACKE
WACKER
WACKERS
WACKES
WACKIER
WACKIEST
WACKINESS
WACKINESSES
WACKO
WACKS
WACKY
WAD
WADD
WADDED
WADDIE
WADDIED
WADDIES
WADDING
WADDINGS
WADDLE
WADDLED
WADDLER
WADDLERS
WADDLES
WADDLING
WADDS
WADDY
WADDYING
WADE
WADED
WADER
WADERS
WADES
WADI
WADIES
WADING
WADINGS
WADIS
WADMAAL
WADMAALS
WADMAL
WADMALS
WADMOL
WADMOLL
WADMOLLS
WADMOLS
WADS
WADSET
WADSETS
WADSETT
WADSETTED
WADSETTER
WADSETTERS
WADSETTING
WADSETTS
WADT
WADTS
WADY
WAE
WAEFUL
WAENESS
WAENESSES
WAES
WAESOME
WAESUCKS
WAFER
WAFERED
WAFERING
WAFERS
WAFERY
WAFF
WAFFED
WAFFING
WAFFLE
WAFFLED
WAFFLER
WAFFLERS
WAFFLES
WAFFLIER
WAFFLIEST
WAFFLING
WAFFLINGS
WAFFLY
WAFFS
WAFT
WAFTAGE
WAFTAGES
WAFTED
WAFTER
WAFTERS
WAFTING
WAFTINGS
WAFTS
WAFTURE
WAFTURES
WAG
WAGE
WAGED
WAGELESS
WAGENBOOM
WAGENBOOMS
WAGER
WAGERED
WAGERER
WAGERERS
WAGERING
WAGERS
WAGES
WAGGED
WAGGERIES
WAGGERY
WAGGING
WAGGISH
WAGGISHLY
WAGGLE
WAGGLED
WAGGLES
WAGGLIER
WAGGLIEST
WAGGLING
WAGGLY
WAGGON
WAGGONED
WAGGONER
WAGGONERS
WAGGONING
WAGGONS
WAGHALTER
WAGHALTERS
WAGING
WAGMOIRE
WAGMOIRES
WAGON
WAGONAGE
WAGONAGES
WAGONED
WAGONER
WAGONERS
WAGONETTE
WAGONETTES
WAGONFUL
WAGONFULS
WAGONING
WAGONLOAD
WAGONLOADS
WAGONS
WAGS
WAGTAIL
WAGTAILS
WAHINE
WAHINES
WAHOO
WAHOOS
WAID
WAIDE
WAIF
WAIFED
WAIFING
WAIFS
WAIFT
WAIFTS
WAIL
WAILED
WAILER
WAILERS
WAILFUL
WAILING
WAILINGLY
WAILINGS
WAILS
WAIN
WAINAGE
WAINAGES
WAINED
WAINING
WAINS
WAINSCOT
WAINSCOTED
WAINSCOTING
WAINSCOTINGS
WAINSCOTS
WAINSCOTTED
WAINSCOTTING
WAINSCOTTINGS
WAIST
WAISTBAND
WAISTBANDS
WAISTBELT
WAISTBELTS
WAISTBOAT
WAISTBOATS
WAISTCOAT
WAISTCOATS
WAISTED
WAISTER
WAISTERS
WAISTLINE
WAISTLINES
WAISTS
WAIT
WAITE
WAITED
WAITER
WAITERAGE
WAITERAGES
WAITERING
WAITERINGS
WAITERS
WAITES
WAITING
WAITINGLY
WAITINGS
WAITRESS
WAITRESSES
WAITS
WAIVE
WAIVED
WAIVER
WAIVERS
WAIVES
WAIVING
WAIVODE
WAIVODES
WAIWODE
WAIWODES
WAKA
WAKANE
WAKANES
WAKAS
WAKE
WAKED
WAKEFUL
WAKEFULLY
WAKELESS
WAKEMAN
WAKEMEN
WAKEN
WAKENED
WAKENER
WAKENERS
WAKENING
WAKENINGS
WAKENS
WAKER
WAKERIFE
WAKERS
WAKES
WAKF
WAKFS
WAKIKI
WAKIKIS
WAKING
WAKINGS
WALD
WALDFLUTE
WALDFLUTES

WALDGRAVE
WALDGRAVES
WALDHORN
WALDHORNS
WALDRAPP
WALDRAPPS
WALDS
WALE
WALED
WALER
WALERS
WALES
WALI
WALIER
WALIES
WALIEST
WALING
WALIS
WALISE
WALISES
WALK
WALKABLE
WALKABOUT
WALKABOUTS
WALKATHON
WALKATHONS
WALKED
WALKER
WALKERS
WALKING
WALKINGS
WALKMILL
WALKMILLS
WALKS
WALKWAY
WALKWAYS
WALL
WALLA
WALLABA
WALLABAS
WALLABIES
WALLABY
WALLAH
WALLAHS
WALLAROO
WALLAROOS
WALLAS
WALLBOARD
WALLBOARDS
WALLCHART
WALLCHARTS
WALLED
WALLER
WALLERS
WALLET
WALLETS
WALLFISH
WALLFISHES
WALLIE
WALLIER
WALLIES
WALLIEST
WALLING
WALLINGS
WALLOP
WALLOPED
WALLOPER
WALLOPERS
WALLOPING
WALLOPINGS
WALLOPS
WALLOW
WALLOWED
WALLOWER
WALLOWERS
WALLOWING
WALLOWINGS
WALLOWS
WALLPAPER
WALLPAPERS
WALLS
WALLSEND
WALLSENDS
WALLWORT
WALLWORTS
WALLY
WALLYDRAG
WALLYDRAGS
WALNUT
WALNUTS
WALRUS
WALRUSES
WALTIER
WALTIEST
WALTY
WALTZ
WALTZED
WALTZER
WALTZERS
WALTZES
WALTZING
WALTZINGS
WALY
WAMBENGER
WAMBENGERS
WAMBLE
WAMBLED
WAMBLES
WAMBLIER
WAMBLIEST
WAMBLING
WAMBLINGS
WAMBLY
WAME
WAMED
WAMEFUL
WAMEFULS
WAMES
WAMMUS
WAMMUSES
WAMPEE
WAMPEES
WAMPISH
WAMPISHED
WAMPISHES
WAMPISHING
WAMPUM
WAMPUMS
WAMPUS
WAMPUSES
WAMUS
WAMUSES
WAN
WANCHANCY
WAND
WANDER
WANDERED
WANDERER
WANDERERS
WANDERING
WANDERINGS
WANDEROO
WANDEROOS
WANDERS
WANDLE
WANDOO
WANDOOS
WANDS
WANE
WANED
WANES
WANEY
WANG
WANGAN
WANGANS
WANGLE
WANGLED
WANGLER
WANGLERS
WANGLES
WANGLING
WANGLINGS
WANGS
WANGUN
WANGUNS
WANHOPE
WANHOPES
WANIER
WANIEST
WANIGAN
WANIGANS
WANING
WANINGS
WANK
WANKED
WANKER
WANKERS
WANKIER
WANKIEST
WANKING
WANKLE
WANKS
WANKY
WANLE
WANLY
WANNA
WANNABE
WANNABEE
WANNABEES
WANNABES
WANNED
WANNEL
WANNER
WANNESS
WANNESSES
WANNEST
WANNING
WANNISH
WANS
WANT
WANTAGE
WANTAGES
WANTED
WANTER
WANTERS
WANTHILL
WANTHILLS
WANTIES
WANTING
WANTINGS
WANTON
WANTONED
WANTONER
WANTONEST
WANTONING
WANTONISE
WANTONISED
WANTONISES
WANTONISING
WANTONIZE
WANTONIZED
WANTONIZES
WANTONIZING
WANTONLY
WANTONS
WANTS
WANTY
WANWORDY
WANWORTH
WANWORTHS
WANY
WANZE
WANZED
WANZES
WANZING
WAP
WAPENSHAW
WAPENSHAWS
WAPENTAKE
WAPENTAKES
WAPINSHAW
WAPINSHAWS
WAPITI
WAPITIS
WAPPED
WAPPEND
WAPPER
WAPPERED
WAPPERING
WAPPERS
WAPPING
WAPS
WAQF
WAQFS
WAR
WARATAH
WARATAHS
WARBIER
WARBIEST
WARBLE
WARBLED
WARBLER
WARBLERS
WARBLES
WARBLING
WARBLINGS
WARBY
WARD
WARDCORN
WARDCORNS
WARDED
WARDEN
WARDENED
WARDENING
WARDENRIES
WARDENRY
WARDENS
WARDER
WARDERED
WARDERING
WARDERS
WARDING
WARDINGS
WARDMOTE
WARDMOTES
WARDOG
WARDOGS
WARDRESS
WARDRESSES
WARDROBE
WARDROBER
WARDROBERS
WARDROBES
WARDROOM
WARDROOMS
WARDROP
WARDROPS
WARDS
WARDSHIP
WARDSHIPS
WARE
WARED
WAREHOUSE
WAREHOUSED
WAREHOUSES
WAREHOUSING
WAREHOUSINGS
WARELESS
WARES
WARFARE
WARFARED
WARFARER
WARFARERS
WARFARES
WARFARIN
WARFARING
WARFARINGS
WARFARINS
WARHABLE
WARHEAD

WARHEADS
WARHORSE
WARHORSES
WARIBASHI
WARIBASHIS
WARIER
WARIEST
WARILY
WARIMENT
WARIMENTS
WARINESS
WARINESSES
WARING
WARISON
WARISONS
WARK
WARKS
WARLIKE
WARLING
WARLINGS
WARLOCK
WARLOCKRIES
WARLOCKRY
WARLOCKS
WARLORD
WARLORDS
WARM
WARMAN
WARMBLOOD
WARMBLOODS
WARMED
WARMEN
WARMER
WARMERS
WARMEST
WARMING
WARMINGS
WARMISH
WARMLY
WARMNESS
WARMNESSES
WARMONGER
WARMONGERS
WARMS
WARMTH
WARMTHS
WARN
WARNED
WARNER
WARNERS
WARNING
WARNINGLY
WARNINGS
WARNS
WARP
WARPATH
WARPATHS
WARPED
WARPER
WARPERS
WARPING
WARPINGS
WARPLANE
WARPLANES
WARPS
WARRAGAL
WARRAGALS
WARRAGLE
WARRAGLES
WARRAGUL
WARRAGULS
WARRAN
WARRAND
WARRANDED
WARRANDING
WARRANDS
WARRANED
WARRANING
WARRANS
WARRANT
WARRANTED
WARRANTEE
WARRANTEES
WARRANTER
WARRANTERS
WARRANTIES
WARRANTING
WARRANTINGS
WARRANTOR
WARRANTORS
WARRANTS
WARRANTY
WARRAY
WARRAYED
WARRAYING
WARRAYS
WARRE
WARRED
WARREN
WARRENER
WARRENERS
WARRENS
WARREY
WARREYED
WARREYING
WARREYS
WARRIGAL
WARRIGALS
WARRING
WARRIOR
WARRIORS
WARRISON
WARRISONS
WARS
WARSHIP
WARSHIPS
WARSLE
WARSLED
WARSLES
WARSLING
WARST
WART
WARTED
WARTHOG
WARTHOGS
WARTIER
WARTIEST
WARTIME
WARTIMES
WARTLESS
WARTLIKE
WARTS
WARTWEED
WARTWEEDS
WARTWORT
WARTWORTS
WARTY
WARWOLF
WARWOLVES
WARY
WAS
WASE
WASEGOOSE
WASEGOOSES
WASES
WASH
WASHABLE
WASHBALL
WASHBALLS
WASHBASIN
WASHBASINS
WASHBOARD
WASHBOARDS
WASHBOWL
WASHBOWLS
WASHCLOTH
WASHCLOTHS
WASHDAY
WASHDAYS
WASHED
WASHEN
WASHER
WASHERED
WASHERIES
WASHERING
WASHERMAN
WASHERMEN
WASHERS
WASHERY
WASHES
WASHHOUSE
WASHHOUSES
WASHIER
WASHIEST
WASHINESS
WASHINESSES
WASHING
WASHINGS
WASHLAND
WASHLANDS
WASHOUT
WASHOUTS
WASHPOT
WASHPOTS
WASHRAG
WASHRAGS
WASHROOM
WASHROOMS
WASHSTAND
WASHSTANDS
WASHTUB
WASHTUBS
WASHWIPE
WASHWIPES
WASHY
WASM
WASMS
WASP
WASPIE
WASPIER
WASPIES
WASPIEST
WASPISH
WASPISHLY
WASPNEST
WASPNESTS
WASPS
WASPY
WASSAIL
WASSAILED
WASSAILER
WASSAILERS
WASSAILING
WASSAILINGS
WASSAILRIES
WASSAILRY
WASSAILS
WASSERMAN
WASSERMEN
WAST
WASTABLE
WASTAGE
WASTAGES
WASTE
WASTED
WASTEFUL
WASTEL
WASTELAND
WASTELANDS
WASTELOT
WASTELOTS
WASTELS
WASTENESS
WASTENESSES
WASTER
WASTERED
WASTERFUL
WASTERIES
WASTERIFE
WASTERIFES
WASTERING
WASTERS
WASTERY
WASTES
WASTFULL
WASTING
WASTINGS
WASTNESS
WASTNESSES
WASTREL
WASTRELS
WASTRIES
WASTRIFE
WASTRIFES
WASTRY
WASTS
WAT
WATAP
WATAPS
WATCH
WATCHABLE
WATCHBOX
WATCHBOXES
WATCHCASE
WATCHCASES
WATCHDOG
WATCHDOGS
WATCHED
WATCHER
WATCHERS
WATCHES
WATCHET
WATCHETS
WATCHFUL
WATCHING
WATCHMAN
WATCHMEN
WATCHWORD
WATCHWORDS
WATE
WATER
WATERAGE
WATERAGES
WATERED
WATERER
WATERERS
WATERFALL
WATERFALLS
WATERFOWL
WATERFOWLS
WATERHEN
WATERHENS
WATERIER
WATERIEST
WATERING
WATERINGS
WATERISH
WATERLESS
WATERLILIES
WATERLILY
WATERLINE
WATERLINES
WATERLOG
WATERLOGGED
WATERLOGGING
WATERLOGS
WATERMAN
WATERMARK
WATERMARKED
WATERMARKING
WATERMARKS
WATERMEN
WATERPOX
WATERPOXES
WATERS
WATERSHED
WATERSHEDS
WATERSIDE
WATERSIDES
WATERWAY

WATERWAYS
WATERWEED
WATERWEEDS
WATERWORK
WATERWORKS
WATERY
WATS
WATT
WATTAGE
WATTAGES
WATTER
WATTEST
WATTLE
WATTLED
WATTLES
WATTLING
WATTLINGS
WATTMETER
WATTMETERS
WATTS
WAUCHT
WAUCHTED
WAUCHTING
WAUCHTS
WAUFF
WAUFFED
WAUFFING
WAUFFS
WAUGH
WAUGHED
WAUGHING
WAUGHS
WAUGHT
WAUGHTED
WAUGHTING
WAUGHTS
WAUK
WAUKED
WAUKER
WAUKERS
WAUKING
WAUKMILL
WAUKMILLS
WAUKRIFE
WAUKS
WAUL
WAULED
WAULING
WAULINGS
WAULK
WAULKED
WAULKER
WAULKERS
WAULKING
WAULKMILL
WAULKMILLS
WAULKS
WAULS
WAUR
WAURED
WAURING
WAURS
WAURST
WAVE
WAVEBAND
WAVEBANDS
WAVED
WAVEFORM
WAVEFORMS
WAVEFRONT
WAVEFRONTS
WAVEGUIDE
WAVEGUIDES
WAVELESS
WAVELET
WAVELETS
WAVELIKE
WAVELLITE
WAVELLITES
WAVEMETER
WAVEMETERS
WAVER
WAVERED
WAVERER
WAVERERS
WAVERIER
WAVERIEST
WAVERING
WAVERINGS
WAVEROUS
WAVERS
WAVERY
WAVES
WAVESHAPE
WAVESHAPES
WAVESON
WAVESONS
WAVEY
WAVEYS
WAVIER
WAVIES
WAVIEST
WAVILY
WAVINESS
WAVINESSES
WAVING
WAVINGS
WAVY
WAW
WAWE
WAWES
WAWL
WAWLED
WAWLING
WAWLINGS
WAWLS
WAWS
WAX
WAXBERRIES
WAXBERRY
WAXBILL
WAXBILLS
WAXCLOTH
WAXCLOTHS
WAXED
WAXEN
WAXER
WAXERS
WAXES
WAXIER
WAXIEST
WAXILY
WAXINESS
WAXINESSES
WAXING
WAXINGS
WAXWING
WAXWINGS
WAXWORK
WAXWORKER
WAXWORKERS
WAXWORKS
WAXY
WAY
WAYBILL
WAYBILLS
WAYBOARD
WAYBOARDS
WAYBREAD
WAYBREADS
WAYED
WAYFARE
WAYFARED
WAYFARER
WAYFARERS
WAYFARES
WAYFARING
WAYFARINGS
WAYGONE
WAYGOOSE
WAYGOOSES
WAYING
WAYLAID
WAYLAY
WAYLAYER
WAYLAYERS
WAYLAYING
WAYLAYS
WAYLEAVE
WAYLEAVES
WAYLESS
WAYMARK
WAYMARKED
WAYMARKING
WAYMARKS
WAYMENT
WAYMENTED
WAYMENTING
WAYMENTS
WAYPOST
WAYPOSTS
WAYS
WAYSIDE
WAYSIDES
WAYWARD
WAYWARDLY
WAYWISER
WAYWISERS
WAYWODE
WAYWODES
WAYWORN
WAYZGOOSE
WAYZGOOSES
WAZIR
WAZIRS
WE
WEAK
WEAKEN
WEAKENED
WEAKENER
WEAKENERS
WEAKENING
WEAKENS
WEAKER
WEAKEST
WEAKFISH
WEAKFISHES
WEAKLIER
WEAKLIEST
WEAKLING
WEAKLINGS
WEAKLY
WEAKNESS
WEAKNESSES
WEAL
WEALD
WEALDS
WEALS
WEALSMAN
WEALSMEN
WEALTH
WEALTHIER
WEALTHIEST
WEALTHILY
WEALTHS
WEALTHY
WEAMB
WEAMBS
WEAN
WEANED
WEANEL
WEANELS
WEANER
WEANERS
WEANING
WEANLING
WEANLINGS
WEANS
WEAPON
WEAPONED
WEAPONRIES
WEAPONRY
WEAPONS
WEAR
WEARABLE
WEARED
WEARER
WEARERS
WEARIED
WEARIER
WEARIES
WEARIEST
WEARIFUL
WEARILESS
WEARILY
WEARINESS
WEARINESSES
WEARING
WEARINGLY
WEARINGS
WEARISH
WEARISOME
WEARS
WEARY
WEARYING
WEASAND
WEASANDS
WEASEL
WEASELED
WEASELER
WEASELERS
WEASELING
WEASELLED
WEASELLER
WEASELLERS
WEASELLING
WEASELLY
WEASELS
WEATHER
WEATHERED
WEATHERING
WEATHERINGS
WEATHERLY
WEATHERS
WEAVE
WEAVED
WEAVER
WEAVERS
WEAVES
WEAVING
WEAVINGS
WEAZAND
WEAZANDS
WEAZEN
WEAZENED
WEAZENING
WEAZENS
WEB
WEBBED
WEBBIER
WEBBIEST
WEBBING
WEBBINGS
WEBBY
WEBER
WEBERS
WEBFEET
WEBFOOT
WEBFOOTED
WEBS
WEBSITE
WEBSITES
WEBSTER
WEBSTERS
WEBWHEEL
WEBWHEELS
WEBWORM
WEBWORMS
WECHT
WECHTS

WED
WEDDED
WEDDER
WEDDERED
WEDDERING
WEDDERS
WEDDING
WEDDINGS
WEDELN
WEDELNED
WEDELNING
WEDELNS
WEDGE
WEDGED
WEDGES
WEDGEWISE
WEDGIE
WEDGIER
WEDGIES
WEDGIEST
WEDGING
WEDGINGS
WEDGY
WEDLOCK
WEDLOCKS
WEDS
WEE
WEED
WEEDED
WEEDER
WEEDERIES
WEEDERS
WEEDERY
WEEDICIDE
WEEDICIDES
WEEDIER
WEEDIEST
WEEDINESS
WEEDINESSES
WEEDING
WEEDINGS
WEEDLESS
WEEDS
WEEDY
WEEING
WEEK
WEEKDAY
WEEKDAYS
WEEKE
WEEKEND
WEEKENDED
WEEKENDER
WEEKENDERS
WEEKENDING
WEEKENDINGS
WEEKENDS
WEEKES
WEEKLIES
WEEKLY
WEEKNIGHT
WEEKNIGHTS
WEEKS
WEEL
WEELS
WEEM
WEEMS
WEEN
WEENED
WEENIER
WEENIES
WEENIEST
WEENING
WEENS
WEENY
WEEP
WEEPER
WEEPERS
WEEPHOLE
WEEPHOLES
WEEPIE
WEEPIER
WEEPIES
WEEPIEST
WEEPING
WEEPINGLY
WEEPINGS
WEEPS
WEEPY
WEER
WEES
WEEST
WEET
WEETE
WEETED
WEETEN
WEETER
WEETEST
WEETING
WEETINGLY
WEETLESS
WEETS
WEEVER
WEEVERS
WEEVIL
WEEVILED
WEEVILLED
WEEVILLY
WEEVILS
WEEVILY
WEFT
WEFTAGE
WEFTAGES
WEFTE
WEFTED
WEFTES
WEFTING
WEFTS
WEID
WEIDS
WEIGELA
WEIGELAS
WEIGH
WEIGHABLE
WEIGHAGE
WEIGHAGES
WEIGHED
WEIGHER
WEIGHERS
WEIGHING
WEIGHINGS
WEIGHS
WEIGHT
WEIGHTED
WEIGHTIER
WEIGHTIEST
WEIGHTILY
WEIGHTING
WEIGHTINGS
WEIGHTS
WEIGHTY
WEIL
WEILS
WEIR
WEIRD
WEIRDED
WEIRDER
WEIRDEST
WEIRDIE
WEIRDIES
WEIRDING
WEIRDLY
WEIRDNESS
WEIRDNESSES
WEIRDO
WEIRDOS
WEIRDS
WEIRED
WEIRING
WEIRS
WEISE
WEISED
WEISES
WEISING
WEIZE
WEIZED
WEIZES
WEIZING
WEKA
WEKAS
WELAWAY
WELCH
WELCHED
WELCHER
WELCHERS
WELCHES
WELCHING
WELCOME
WELCOMED
WELCOMER
WELCOMERS
WELCOMES
WELCOMING
WELD
WELDABLE
WELDED
WELDER
WELDERS
WELDING
WELDINGS
WELDLESS
WELDMENT
WELDMENTS
WELDMESH®
WELDMESHES
WELDOR
WELDORS
WELDS
WELFARE
WELFARES
WELFARISM
WELFARISMS
WELFARIST
WELFARISTS
WELK
WELKE
WELKED
WELKES
WELKIN
WELKING
WELKINS
WELKS
WELKT
WELL
WELLADAY
WELLANEAR
WELLAWAY
WELLBEING
WELLBEINGS
WELLED
WELLHEAD
WELLHEADS
WELLHOUSE
WELLHOUSES
WELLIE
WELLIES
WELLING
WELLINGS
WELLNESS
WELLNESSES
WELLS
WELLY
WELSH
WELSHED
WELSHER
WELSHERS
WELSHES
WELSHING
WELT
WELTED
WELTER
WELTERED
WELTERING
WELTERS
WELTING
WELTS
WEM
WEMB
WEMBS
WEMS
WEN
WENCH
WENCHED
WENCHER
WENCHERS
WENCHES
WENCHING
WEND
WENDED
WENDIGO
WENDIGOS
WENDING
WENDS
WENNIER
WENNIEST
WENNISH
WENNY
WENS
WENT
WENTS
WEPT
WERE
WEREGILD
WEREGILDS
WEREWOLF
WEREWOLVES
WERGILD
WERGILDS
WERNERITE
WERNERITES
WERSH
WERSHER
WERSHEST
WERT
WERWOLF
WERWOLVES
WESAND
WESANDS
WEST
WESTBOUND
WESTED
WESTER
WESTERED
WESTERING
WESTERINGS
WESTERLIES
WESTERLY
WESTERN
WESTERNER
WESTERNERS
WESTERNS
WESTERS
WESTING
WESTINGS
WESTLIN
WESTLINS
WESTMOST
WESTS
WESTWARD
WESTWARDS
WET
WETA
WETAS
WETBACK
WETBACKS
WETHER
WETHERS
WETLAND
WETLANDS
WETLY
WETNESS

WETNESSES
WETS
WETTED
WETTER
WETTEST
WETTING
WETTISH
WETWARE
WETWARES
WEX
WEXE
WEXED
WEXES
WEXING
WEY
WEYARD
WEYS
WEYWARD
WEZAND
WEZANDS
WHA
WHACK
WHACKED
WHACKER
WHACKERS
WHACKIER
WHACKIEST
WHACKING
WHACKINGS
WHACKO
WHACKOES
WHACKOS
WHACKS
WHACKY
WHAISLE
WHAISLED
WHAISLES
WHAISLING
WHAIZLE
WHAIZLED
WHAIZLES
WHAIZLING
WHALE
WHALEBACK
WHALEBACKS
WHALEBOAT
WHALEBOATS
WHALEBONE
WHALEBONES
WHALED
WHALEMAN
WHALEMEN
WHALER
WHALERIES
WHALERS
WHALERY
WHALES
WHALING
WHALINGS
WHALLY
WHAM
WHAMMED
WHAMMIES
WHAMMING
WHAMMO
WHAMMOS
WHAMMY
WHAMPLE
WHAMPLES
WHAMS
WHANG
WHANGAM
WHANGAMS
WHANGED
WHANGEE
WHANGEES
WHANGING
WHANGS
WHAP
WHAPPED
WHAPPING
WHAPS
WHARE
WHARES
WHARF
WHARFAGE
WHARFAGES
WHARFED
WHARFING
WHARFINGS
WHARFS
WHARVE
WHARVES
WHAT
WHATEN
WHATEVER
WHATNA
WHATNESS
WHATNESSES
WHATNOT
WHATNOTS
WHATS
WHATSIS
WHATSISES
WHATSIT
WHATSITS
WHATSO
WHATTEN
WHAUP
WHAUPS
WHAUR
WHAURS
WHEAL
WHEALS
WHEAR
WHEARE
WHEAT
WHEATEAR
WHEATEARS
WHEATEN
WHEATIER
WHEATIEST
WHEATMEAL
WHEATMEALS
WHEATS
WHEATWORM
WHEATWORMS
WHEATY
WHEE
WHEECH
WHEECHED
WHEECHING
WHEECHS
WHEEDLE
WHEEDLED
WHEEDLER
WHEEDLERS
WHEEDLES
WHEEDLING
WHEEDLINGS
WHEEL
WHEELBASE
WHEELBASES
WHEELED
WHEELER
WHEELERS
WHEELIE
WHEELIER
WHEELIES
WHEELIEST
WHEELING
WHEELINGS
WHEELMAN
WHEELMEN
WHEELS
WHEELWORK
WHEELWORKS
WHEELY
WHEEN
WHEENGE
WHEENGED
WHEENGES
WHEENGING
WHEENS
WHEEPLE
WHEEPLED
WHEEPLES
WHEEPLING
WHEESH
WHEESHED
WHEESHES
WHEESHING
WHEESHT
WHEESHTED
WHEESHTING
WHEESHTS
WHEEZE
WHEEZED
WHEEZES
WHEEZIER
WHEEZIEST
WHEEZILY
WHEEZING
WHEEZINGS
WHEEZLE
WHEEZLED
WHEEZLES
WHEEZLING
WHEEZY
WHEFT
WHEFTS
WHELK
WHELKED
WHELKIER
WHELKIEST
WHELKS
WHELKY
WHELM
WHELMED
WHELMING
WHELMS
WHELP
WHELPED
WHELPING
WHELPS
WHEMMLE
WHEMMLED
WHEMMLES
WHEMMLING
WHEN
WHENAS
WHENCE
WHENCES
WHENCEVER
WHENEVER
WHENS
WHERE
WHEREAS
WHEREAT
WHEREBY
WHEREFOR
WHEREFORE
WHEREFORES
WHEREFROM
WHEREIN
WHEREINTO
WHERENESS
WHERENESSES
WHEREOF
WHEREON
WHEREOUT
WHERES
WHERESO
WHERETO
WHEREUNTO
WHEREUPON
WHEREVER
WHEREWITH
WHEREWITHS
WHERRET
WHERRETED
WHERRETING
WHERRETS
WHERRIES
WHERRY
WHERRYMAN
WHERRYMEN
WHET
WHETHER
WHETS
WHETSTONE
WHETSTONES
WHETTED
WHETTER
WHETTERS
WHETTING
WHEUGH
WHEUGHED
WHEUGHING
WHEUGHS
WHEW
WHEWED
WHEWING
WHEWS
WHEY
WHEYEY
WHEYIER
WHEYIEST
WHEYISH
WHEYS
WHICH
WHICHEVER
WHICKER
WHICKERED
WHICKERING
WHICKERS
WHID
WHIDAH
WHIDAHS
WHIDDED
WHIDDER
WHIDDERED
WHIDDERING
WHIDDERS
WHIDDING
WHIDS
WHIFF
WHIFFED
WHIFFER
WHIFFERS
WHIFFET
WHIFFETS
WHIFFIER
WHIFFIEST
WHIFFING
WHIFFINGS
WHIFFLE
WHIFFLED
WHIFFLER
WHIFFLERIES
WHIFFLERS
WHIFFLERY
WHIFFLES
WHIFFLING
WHIFFLINGS
WHIFFS
WHIFFY
WHIFT
WHIFTS
WHIG
WHIGGED
WHIGGING
WHIGS
WHILE
WHILED
WHILERE
WHILES
WHILING
WHILK
WHILLIED

WHILLIES
WHILLY
WHILLYING
WHILLYWHA
WHILLYWHAED
WHILLYWHAING
WHILLYWHAS
WHILOM
WHILST
WHIM
WHIMBERRIES
WHIMBERRY
WHIMBREL
WHIMBRELS
WHIMMED
WHIMMIER
WHIMMIEST
WHIMMING
WHIMMY
WHIMPER
WHIMPERED
WHIMPERER
WHIMPERERS
WHIMPERING
WHIMPERINGS
WHIMPERS
WHIMPLE
WHIMPLED
WHIMPLES
WHIMPLING
WHIMS
WHIMSEY
WHIMSEYS
WHIMSICAL
WHIMSIER
WHIMSIES
WHIMSIEST
WHIMSILY
WHIMSY
WHIN
WHINBERRIES
WHINBERRY
WHINCHAT
WHINCHATS
WHINE
WHINED
WHINER
WHINERS
WHINES
WHINGE
WHINGED
WHINGEING
WHINGEINGS
WHINGER
WHINGERS
WHINGES
WHINIARD
WHINIARDS
WHINIER
WHINIEST
WHININESS
WHININESSES
WHINING
WHININGLY
WHININGS
WHINNIED
WHINNIER
WHINNIES
WHINNIEST
WHINNY
WHINNYING
WHINS
WHINSTONE
WHINSTONES
WHINY
WHINYARD
WHINYARDS
WHIP
WHIPBIRD
WHIPBIRDS
WHIPCAT
WHIPCATS
WHIPCORD
WHIPCORDS
WHIPCORDY
WHIPJACK
WHIPJACKS
WHIPLASH
WHIPLASHED
WHIPLASHES
WHIPLASHING
WHIPLIKE
WHIPPED
WHIPPER
WHIPPERS
WHIPPET
WHIPPETS
WHIPPIER
WHIPPIEST
WHIPPING
WHIPPINGS
WHIPPY
WHIPS
WHIPSAW
WHIPSAWED
WHIPSAWING
WHIPSAWS
WHIPSTAFF
WHIPSTAFFS
WHIPSTALL
WHIPSTALLED
WHIPSTALLING
WHIPSTALLS
WHIPSTER
WHIPSTERS
WHIPSTOCK
WHIPSTOCKS
WHIPT
WHIPTAIL
WHIPWORM
WHIPWORMS
WHIR
WHIRL
WHIRLBAT
WHIRLBATS
WHIRLED
WHIRLER
WHIRLERS
WHIRLIER
WHIRLIEST
WHIRLIGIG
WHIRLIGIGS
WHIRLING
WHIRLINGS
WHIRLPOOL
WHIRLPOOLS
WHIRLS
WHIRLWIND
WHIRLWINDS
WHIRLY
WHIRR
WHIRRED
WHIRRET
WHIRRETED
WHIRRETING
WHIRRETS
WHIRRIED
WHIRRIES
WHIRRING
WHIRRINGS
WHIRRS
WHIRRY
WHIRRYING
WHIRS
WHIRTLE
WHIRTLES
WHISH
WHISHED
WHISHES
WHISHING
WHISHT
WHISHTED
WHISHTING
WHISHTS
WHISK
WHISKED
WHISKER
WHISKERED
WHISKERS
WHISKERY
WHISKET
WHISKETS
WHISKEY
WHISKEYS
WHISKIES
WHISKING
WHISKS
WHISKY
WHISPER
WHISPERED
WHISPERER
WHISPERERS
WHISPERING
WHISPERINGS
WHISPERS
WHISPERY
WHISS
WHISSED
WHISSES
WHISSING
WHIST
WHISTED
WHISTING
WHISTLE
WHISTLED
WHISTLER
WHISTLERS
WHISTLES
WHISTLING
WHISTLINGS
WHISTS
WHIT
WHITE
WHITEBAIT
WHITEBAITS
WHITEBASS
WHITEBASSES
WHITEBEAM
WHITEBEAMS
WHITECAP
WHITECAPS
WHITECOAT
WHITECOATS
WHITED
WHITEFLIES
WHITEFLY
WHITEHEAD
WHITEHEADS
WHITELY
WHITEN
WHITENED
WHITENER
WHITENERS
WHITENESS
WHITENESSES
WHITENING
WHITENINGS
WHITENS
WHITEPOT
WHITEPOTS
WHITER
WHITES
WHITEST
WHITEWALL
WHITEWALLS
WHITEWARE
WHITEWARES
WHITEWASH
WHITEWASHED
WHITEWASHES
WHITEWASHING
WHITEWING
WHITEWINGS
WHITEWOOD
WHITEWOODS
WHITEY
WHITEYS
WHITHER
WHITHERED
WHITHERING
WHITHERS
WHITIER
WHITIES
WHITIEST
WHITING
WHITINGS
WHITISH
WHITLING
WHITLINGS
WHITLOW
WHITLOWS
WHITRET
WHITRETS
WHITS
WHITSTER
WHITSTERS
WHITTAW
WHITTAWER
WHITTAWERS
WHITTAWS
WHITTER
WHITTERED
WHITTERING
WHITTERS
WHITTLE
WHITTLED
WHITTLER
WHITTLERS
WHITTLES
WHITTLING
WHITTLINGS
WHITTRET
WHITTRETS
WHITY
WHIZ
WHIZBANG
WHIZBANGS
WHIZZ
WHIZZED
WHIZZER
WHIZZERS
WHIZZES
WHIZZING
WHIZZINGS
WHO
WHOA
WHODUNNIT
WHODUNNITS
WHOEVER
WHOLE
WHOLEFOOD
WHOLEFOODS
WHOLEMEAL
WHOLEMEALS
WHOLENESS
WHOLENESSES
WHOLES
WHOLESALE
WHOLESALES
WHOLESOME
WHOLESOMER
WHOLESOMEST
WHOLISM
WHOLISMS
WHOLIST
WHOLISTIC
WHOLISTS
WHOLLY
WHOM
WHOMBLE

WHOMBLED
WHOMBLES
WHOMBLING
WHOMEVER
WHOMMLE
WHOMMLED
WHOMMLES
WHOMMLING
WHOOBUB
WHOOBUBS
WHOOP
WHOOPED
WHOOPEE
WHOOPEES
WHOOPER
WHOOPERS
WHOOPING
WHOOPINGS
WHOOPS
WHOOPSIE
WHOOPSIES
WHOOSH
WHOOSHED
WHOOSHES
WHOOSHING
WHOOT
WHOOTED
WHOOTING
WHOOTS
WHOP
WHOPPED
WHOPPER
WHOPPERS
WHOPPING
WHOPPINGS
WHOPS
WHORE
WHORED
WHOREDOM
WHOREDOMS
WHORES
WHORESON
WHORESONS
WHORING
WHORISH
WHORISHLY
WHORL
WHORLBAT
WHORLBATS
WHORLED
WHORLS
WHORT
WHORTS
WHOSE
WHOSEVER
WHOSO
WHOSOEVER
WHOT
WHOW
WHUMMLE
WHUMMLED
WHUMMLES
WHUMMLING
WHUNSTANE
WHUNSTANES
WHY
WHYDAH
WHYDAHS
WHYEVER
WICCA
WICCAN
WICCANS
WICCAS
WICE
WICH
WICHES
WICK
WICKED
WICKEDER
WICKEDEST
WICKEDLY
WICKEDS
WICKEN
WICKENS
WICKER
WICKERED
WICKERS
WICKET
WICKETS
WICKIES
WICKING
WICKIUP
WICKIUPS
WICKS
WICKY
WIDDIES
WIDDLE
WIDDLED
WIDDLES
WIDDLING
WIDDY
WIDE
WIDEAWAKE
WIDEAWAKES
WIDEBODY
WIDELY
WIDEN
WIDENED
WIDENER
WIDENERS
WIDENESS
WIDENESSES
WIDENING
WIDENS
WIDER
WIDES
WIDEST
WIDGEON
WIDGEONS
WIDGET
WIDGETS
WIDGIE
WIDGIES
WIDISH
WIDOW
WIDOWED
WIDOWER
WIDOWERS
WIDOWHOOD
WIDOWHOODS
WIDOWING
WIDOWMAN
WIDOWMEN
WIDOWS
WIDTH
WIDTHS
WIDTHWAYS
WIDTHWISE
WIEL
WIELD
WIELDABLE
WIELDED
WIELDER
WIELDERS
WIELDIER
WIELDIEST
WIELDING
WIELDLESS
WIELDS
WIELDY
WIELS
WIENIE
WIENIES
WIFE
WIFEHOOD
WIFEHOODS
WIFELESS
WIFELIER
WIFELIEST
WIFELIKE
WIFELY
WIFIE
WIFIES
WIG
WIGAN
WIGANS
WIGEON
WIGEONS
WIGGED
WIGGERIES
WIGGERY
WIGGING
WIGGINGS
WIGGLE
WIGGLED
WIGGLER
WIGGLERS
WIGGLES
WIGGLIER
WIGGLIEST
WIGGLING
WIGGLY
WIGHT
WIGHTED
WIGHTING
WIGHTLY
WIGHTS
WIGLESS
WIGLIKE
WIGS
WIGWAG
WIGWAGGED
WIGWAGGING
WIGWAGS
WIGWAM
WIGWAMS
WILD
WILDCAT
WILDCATS
WILDCATTED
WILDCATTING
WILDED
WILDER
WILDERED
WILDERING
WILDERS
WILDEST
WILDFIRE
WILDFIRES
WILDFOWL
WILDFOWLS
WILDGRAVE
WILDGRAVES
WILDING
WILDINGS
WILDISH
WILDLAND
WILDLANDS
WILDLIFE
WILDLIFES
WILDLY
WILDNESS
WILDNESSES
WILDS
WILDWOOD
WILDWOODS
WILE
WILED
WILEFUL
WILES
WILFUL
WILFULLY
WILGA
WILGAS
WILI
WILIER
WILIEST
WILILY
WILINESS
WILINESSES
WILING
WILIS
WILJA
WILJAS
WILL
WILLABLE
WILLED
WILLEMITE
WILLEMITES
WILLER
WILLERS
WILLEST
WILLET
WILLETS
WILLEY
WILLEYED
WILLEYING
WILLEYS
WILLFUL
WILLIE
WILLIED
WILLIES
WILLING
WILLINGLY
WILLIWAW
WILLIWAWS
WILLOW
WILLOWED
WILLOWIER
WILLOWIEST
WILLOWING
WILLOWISH
WILLOWS
WILLOWY
WILLPOWER
WILLPOWERS
WILLS
WILLY
WILLYARD
WILLYART
WILLYING
WILT
WILTED
WILTING
WILTJA
WILTJAS
WILTS
WILY
WIMBLE
WIMBLED
WIMBLES
WIMBLING
WIMBREL
WIMBRELS
WIMP
WIMPIER
WIMPIEST
WIMPISH
WIMPISHLY
WIMPLE
WIMPLED
WIMPLES
WIMPLING
WIMPS
WIMPY
WIN
WINCE
WINCED
WINCER
WINCERS
WINCES
WINCEY
WINCEYS
WINCH
WINCHED
WINCHES
WINCHING
WINCHMAN
WINCHMEN
WINCING

WINCINGS
WINCOPIPE
WINCOPIPES
WIND
WINDAC
WINDACS
WINDAGE
WINDAGES
WINDAS
WINDASES
WINDBAG
WINDBAGS
WINDBLOW
WINDBLOWN
WINDBLOWS
WINDBORNE
WINDBOUND
WINDBREAK
WINDBREAKS
WINDBURN
WINDBURNS
WINDED
WINDER
WINDERS
WINDFALL
WINDFALLS
WINDGALL
WINDGALLS
WINDGUN
WINDGUNS
WINDHOVER
WINDHOVERS
WINDIER
WINDIEST
WINDIGO
WINDIGOS
WINDILY
WINDINESS
WINDINESSES
WINDING
WINDINGLY
WINDINGS
WINDLASS
WINDLASSED
WINDLASSES
WINDLASSING
WINDLE
WINDLES
WINDLESS
WINDMILL
WINDMILLED
WINDMILLING
WINDMILLS
WINDOCK
WINDOCKS
WINDORE
WINDORES
WINDOW
WINDOWED
WINDOWING
WINDOWINGS
WINDOWS
WINDPIPE
WINDPIPES
WINDPROOF
WINDRING
WINDROSE
WINDROSES
WINDROW
WINDROWED
WINDROWING
WINDROWS
WINDS
WINDSAIL
WINDSAILS
WINDSES
WINDSHAKE
WINDSHAKES
WINDSHIP
WINDSHIPS
WINDSOCK
WINDSOCKS
WINDSTORM
WINDSTORMS
WINDSURF
WINDSURFED
WINDSURFING
WINDSURFINGS
WINDSURFS
WINDSWEPT
WINDTHROW
WINDTHROWS
WINDTIGHT
WINDWARD
WINDWARDS
WINDY
WINE
WINEBERRIES
WINEBERRY
WINED
WINEGLASS
WINEGLASSES
WINEPRESS
WINEPRESSES
WINERIES
WINERY
WINES
WINESKIN
WINESKINS
WINEY
WING
WINGBEAT
WINGBEATS
WINGDING
WINGDINGS
WINGE
WINGED
WINGEDLY
WINGEING
WINGER
WINGERS
WINGES
WINGIER
WINGIEST
WINGING
WINGLESS
WINGLET
WINGLETS
WINGS
WINGSPAN
WINGSPANS
WINGY
WINIER
WINIEST
WINING
WINK
WINKED
WINKER
WINKERS
WINKING
WINKINGLY
WINKINGS
WINKLE
WINKLED
WINKLER
WINKLERS
WINKLES
WINKLING
WINKS
WINN
WINNA
WINNABLE
WINNER
WINNERS
WINNING
WINNINGLY
WINNINGS
WINNLE
WINNLES
WINNOCK
WINNOCKS
WINNOW
WINNOWED
WINNOWER
WINNOWERS
WINNOWING
WINNOWINGS
WINNOWS
WINNS
WINO
WINOS
WINS
WINSEY
WINSEYS
WINSOME
WINSOMELY
WINSOMER
WINSOMEST
WINTER
WINTERED
WINTERIER
WINTERIEST
WINTERING
WINTERISE
WINTERISED
WINTERISES
WINTERISING
WINTERIZE
WINTERIZED
WINTERIZES
WINTERIZING
WINTERLY
WINTERS
WINTERY
WINTLE
WINTLED
WINTLES
WINTLING
WINTRIER
WINTRIEST
WINTRY
WINY
WINZE
WINZES
WIPE
WIPED
WIPEOUT
WIPEOUTS
WIPER
WIPERS
WIPES
WIPING
WIPINGS
WIPPEN
WIPPENS
WIRE
WIRED
WIREDRAW
WIREDRAWING
WIREDRAWINGS
WIREDRAWN
WIREDRAWS
WIREDREW
WIRELESS
WIRELESSED
WIRELESSES
WIRELESSING
WIREMAN
WIREMEN
WIREPHOTO
WIREPHOTOS
WIRER
WIRERS
WIRES
WIRETAP
WIRETAPPED
WIRETAPPING
WIRETAPS
WIREWAY
WIREWAYS
WIREWORK
WIREWORKS
WIREWORM
WIREWORMS
WIREWOVE
WIRIER
WIRIEST
WIRILY
WIRINESS
WIRINESSES
WIRING
WIRINGS
WIRRICOW
WIRRICOWS
WIRY
WIS
WISARD
WISARDS
WISDOM
WISDOMS
WISE
WISEACRE
WISEACRES
WISECRACK
WISECRACKED
WISECRACKING
WISECRACKS
WISED
WISELING
WISELINGS
WISELY
WISENESS
WISENESSES
WISENT
WISENTS
WISER
WISES
WISEST
WISH
WISHBONE
WISHBONES
WISHED
WISHER
WISHERS
WISHES
WISHFUL
WISHFULLY
WISHING
WISHINGS
WISING
WISKET
WISKETS
WISP
WISPED
WISPIER
WISPIEST
WISPING
WISPS
WISPY
WISSED
WISSES
WISSING
WIST
WISTARIA
WISTARIAS
WISTED
WISTERIA
WISTERIAS
WISTFUL
WISTFULLY
WISTING
WISTITI
WISTITIS
WISTLY
WISTS
WIT
WITAN
WITBLITS
WITBLITSES
WITCH

WITCHED
WITCHEN
WITCHENS
WITCHERIES
WITCHERY
WITCHES
WITCHETTIES
WITCHETTY
WITCHIER
WITCHIEST
WITCHING
WITCHINGS
WITCHKNOT
WITCHKNOTS
WITCHLIKE
WITCHMEAL
WITCHMEALS
WITCHY
WITE
WITED
WITELESS
WITES
WITGAT
WITGATS
WITH
WITHAL
WITHDRAW
WITHDRAWING
WITHDRAWN
WITHDRAWS
WITHDREW
WITHE
WITHED
WITHER
WITHERED
WITHERING
WITHERINGS
WITHERITE
WITHERITES
WITHERS
WITHES
WITHHAULT
WITHHELD
WITHHOLD
WITHHOLDEN
WITHHOLDING
WITHHOLDS
WITHIER
WITHIES
WITHIEST
WITHIN
WITHING
WITHOUT
WITHOUTEN
WITHS
WITHSTAND
WITHSTANDING
WITHSTANDS
WITHSTOOD
WITHWIND
WITHWINDS
WITHY
WITHYWIND
WITHYWINDS
WITING
WITLESS
WITLESSLY
WITLING
WITLINGS
WITLOOF
WITLOOFS
WITNESS
WITNESSED
WITNESSER
WITNESSERS
WITNESSES
WITNESSING
WITS
WITTED
WITTER
WITTERED
WITTERING
WITTERS
WITTICISM
WITTICISMS
WITTIER
WITTIEST
WITTILY
WITTINESS
WITTINESSES
WITTING
WITTINGLY
WITTINGS
WITTOL
WITTOLLY
WITTOLS
WITTY
WITWALL
WITWALLS
WITWANTON
WITWANTONED
WITWANTONING
WITWANTONS
WIVE
WIVED
WIVEHOOD
WIVEHOODS
WIVERN
WIVERNS
WIVES
WIVING
WIZARD
WIZARDLY
WIZARDRIES
WIZARDRY
WIZARDS
WIZEN
WIZENED
WIZENING
WIZENS
WIZIER
WIZIERS
WO
WOAD
WOADED
WOADS
WOBBEGONG
WOBBEGONGS
WOBBLE
WOBBLED
WOBBLER
WOBBLERS
WOBBLES
WOBBLIER
WOBBLIES
WOBBLIEST
WOBBLING
WOBBLINGS
WOBBLY
WOBEGONE
WOCK
WOCKS
WODGE
WODGES
WOE
WOEBEGONE
WOEFUL
WOEFULLER
WOEFULLEST
WOEFULLY
WOES
WOESOME
WOFUL
WOFULLY
WOFULNESS
WOFULNESSES
WOG
WOGGLE
WOGGLES
WOGS
WOIWODE
WOIWODES
WOK
WOKE
WOKEN
WOKS
WOLD
WOLDS
WOLF
WOLFBERRIES
WOLFBERRY
WOLFED
WOLFER
WOLFERS
WOLFHOUND
WOLFHOUNDS
WOLFING
WOLFINGS
WOLFISH
WOLFISHLY
WOLFKIN
WOLFKINS
WOLFLING
WOLFLINGS
WOLFRAM
WOLFRAMS
WOLFS
WOLFSBANE
WOLFSBANES
WOLFSKIN
WOLFSKINS
WOLLIES
WOLLY
WOLVE
WOLVED
WOLVER
WOLVERENE
WOLVERENES
WOLVERINE
WOLVERINES
WOLVERS
WOLVES
WOLVING
WOLVINGS
WOLVISH
WOLVISHLY
WOMAN
WOMANED
WOMANHOOD
WOMANHOODS
WOMANING
WOMANISE
WOMANISED
WOMANISER
WOMANISERS
WOMANISES
WOMANISH
WOMANISING
WOMANIZE
WOMANIZED
WOMANIZER
WOMANIZERS
WOMANIZES
WOMANIZING
WOMANKIND
WOMANKINDS
WOMANLESS
WOMANLIER
WOMANLIEST
WOMANLIKE
WOMANLY
WOMANS
WOMB
WOMBAT
WOMBATS
WOMBED
WOMBING
WOMBLIKE
WOMBS
WOMBY
WOMEN
WOMENFOLK
WOMENFOLKS
WOMENKIND
WOMENKINDS
WOMERA
WOMERAS
WON
WONDER
WONDERED
WONDERER
WONDERERS
WONDERFUL
WONDERING
WONDERINGS
WONDEROUS
WONDERS
WONDRED
WONDROUS
WONGA
WONGAS
WONGI
WONGIED
WONGIING
WONGIS
WONING
WONINGS
WONK
WONKIER
WONKIEST
WONKS
WONKY
WONNED
WONNING
WONNINGS
WONS
WONT
WONTED
WONTING
WONTLESS
WONTS
WOO
WOOBUT
WOOBUTS
WOOD
WOODBIND
WOODBINDS
WOODBINE
WOODBINES
WOODBLOCK
WOODBLOCKS
WOODCHAT
WOODCHATS
WOODCHIP
WOODCHIPS
WOODCHUCK
WOODCHUCKS
WOODCOCK
WOODCOCKS
WOODCRAFT
WOODCRAFTS
WOODCUT
WOODCUTS
WOODED
WOODEN
WOODENER
WOODENEST
WOODENLY
WOODENTOP
WOODENTOPS
WOODHOLE
WOODHOLES
WOODHORSE
WOODHORSES
WOODHOUSE
WOODHOUSES
WOODIE
WOODIER
WOODIES
WOODIEST

WOODINESS
WOODINESSES
WOODING
WOODLAND
WOODLANDS
WOODLARK
WOODLARKS
WOODLESS
WOODLICE
WOODLOUSE
WOODMAN
WOODMEAL
WOODMEALS
WOODMEN
WOODMICE
WOODMOUSE
WOODNESS
WOODNESSES
WOODNOTE
WOODNOTES
WOODPILE
WOODPILES
WOODREEVE
WOODREEVES
WOODROOF
WOODROOFS
WOODRUFF
WOODRUFFS
WOODRUSH
WOODRUSHES
WOODS
WOODSCREW
WOODSCREWS
WOODSHED
WOODSHEDDED
WOODSHEDDING
WOODSHEDDINGS
WOODSHEDS
WOODSHOCK
WOODSHOCKS
WOODSIA
WOODSIAS
WOODSIER
WOODSIEST
WOODSKIN
WOODSKINS
WOODSMAN
WOODSMEN
WOODSPITE
WOODSPITES
WOODSTONE
WOODSTONES
WOODSY
WOODWALE
WOODWALES
WOODWARD
WOODWARDS
WOODWAX
WOODWAXEN
WOODWAXENS
WOODWAXES
WOODWIND
WOODWINDS
WOODWORK
WOODWORKS
WOODWORM
WOODWORMS
WOODWOSE
WOODWOSES
WOODY
WOODYARD
WOODYARDS
WOOED
WOOER
WOOERS
WOOF
WOOFED
WOOFER
WOOFERS
WOOFIER
WOOFIEST
WOOFING
WOOFS
WOOFTER
WOOFTERS
WOOFY
WOOING
WOOINGLY
WOOINGS
WOOL
WOOLD
WOOLDED
WOOLDER
WOOLDERS
WOOLDING
WOOLDINGS
WOOLDS
WOOLEN
WOOLENS
WOOLFAT
WOOLFATS
WOOLFELL
WOOLFELLS
WOOLLED
WOOLLEN
WOOLLENS
WOOLLIER
WOOLLIES
WOOLLIEST
WOOLLY
WOOLMAN
WOOLMEN
WOOLPACK
WOOLPACKS
WOOLS
WOOLSACK
WOOLSACKS
WOOLSEY
WOOLSEYS
WOOLSHED
WOOLSHEDS
WOOLWARD
WOOLWORK
WOOLWORKS
WOOMERA
WOOMERANG
WOOMERANGS
WOOMERAS
WOON
WOONED
WOONING
WOONS
WOOPIE
WOOPIES
WOORALI
WOORALIS
WOORARA
WOORARAS
WOOS
WOOSEL
WOOSELL
WOOSELLS
WOOSELS
WOOSH
WOOSHED
WOOSHES
WOOSHING
WOOT
WOOTZ
WOOTZES
WOOZIER
WOOZIEST
WOOZILY
WOOZINESS
WOOZINESSES
WOOZY
WOP
WOPPED
WOPPING
WOPS
WORCESTER
WORCESTERS
WORD
WORDAGE
WORDAGES
WORDBOOK
WORDBOOKS
WORDBOUND
WORDBREAK
WORDBREAKS
WORDED
WORDGAME
WORDGAMES
WORDIER
WORDIEST
WORDILY
WORDINESS
WORDINESSES
WORDING
WORDINGS
WORDISH
WORDLESS
WORDLORE
WORDLORES
WORDPLAY
WORDPLAYS
WORDS
WORDSMITH
WORDSMITHS
WORDY
WORE
WORK
WORKABLE
WORKADAY
WORKADAYS
WORKBAG
WORKBAGS
WORKBENCH
WORKBENCHES
WORKBOAT
WORKBOATS
WORKBOOK
WORKBOOKS
WORKBOX
WORKBOXES
WORKDAY
WORKDAYS
WORKED
WORKER
WORKERIST
WORKERISTS
WORKERS
WORKFARE
WORKFARES
WORKFOLK
WORKFOLKS
WORKFORCE
WORKFORCES
WORKFUL
WORKGIRL
WORKGIRLS
WORKGROUP
WORKGROUPS
WORKHORSE
WORKHORSES
WORKHOUSE
WORKHOUSES
WORKING
WORKINGS
WORKLESS
WORKLOAD
WORKLOADS
WORKMAN
WORKMANLY
WORKMATE
WORKMATES
WORKMEN
WORKPIECE
WORKPIECES
WORKPLACE
WORKPLACES
WORKROOM
WORKROOMS
WORKS
WORKSHEET
WORKSHEETS
WORKSHOP
WORKSHOPPED
WORKSHOPPING
WORKSHOPS
WORKSHY
WORKSOME
WORKTABLE
WORKTABLES
WORKTOP
WORKTOPS
WORKWEAR
WORKWEARS
WORKWEEK
WORKWEEKS
WORKWOMAN
WORKWOMEN
WORLD
WORLDED
WORLDLIER
WORLDLIEST
WORLDLING
WORLDLINGS
WORLDLY
WORLDS
WORLDWIDE
WORM
WORMCAST
WORMCASTS
WORMED
WORMER
WORMERIES
WORMERS
WORMERY
WORMHOLE
WORMHOLED
WORMHOLES
WORMIER
WORMIEST
WORMING
WORMS
WORMSEED
WORMSEEDS
WORMWOOD
WORMWOODS
WORMY
WORN
WORRAL
WORRALS
WORREL
WORRELS
WORRICOW
WORRICOWS
WORRIED
WORRIEDLY
WORRIER
WORRIERS
WORRIES
WORRIMENT
WORRIMENTS
WORRISOME
WORRIT
WORRITED
WORRITING
WORRITS
WORRY
WORRYCOW
WORRYCOWS
WORRYGUTS
WORRYING
WORRYINGS
WORRYWART
WORRYWARTS
WORSE
WORSED

WORSEN
WORSENED
WORSENESS
WORSENESSES
WORSENING
WORSENS
WORSER
WORSES
WORSHIP
WORSHIPPED
WORSHIPPING
WORSHIPS
WORSING
WORST
WORSTED
WORSTEDS
WORSTING
WORSTS
WORT
WORTH
WORTHED
WORTHFUL
WORTHIED
WORTHIER
WORTHIES
WORTHIEST
WORTHILY
WORTHING
WORTHLESS
WORTHS
WORTHY
WORTHYING
WORTLE
WORTLES
WORTS
WOS
WOSBIRD
WOSBIRDS
WOST
WOT
WOTCHER
WOTS
WOTTED
WOTTEST
WOTTETH
WOTTING
WOUBIT
WOUBITS
WOULD
WOULDS
WOULDST
WOUND
WOUNDABLE
WOUNDED
WOUNDER
WOUNDERS
WOUNDILY
WOUNDING
WOUNDINGS
WOUNDLESS
WOUNDS
WOUNDWORT
WOUNDWORTS
WOUNDY
WOURALI
WOURALIS
WOVE
WOVEN
WOW
WOWED
WOWEE
WOWF
WOWFER
WOWFEST
WOWING
WOWS
WOWSER
WOWSERS
WOX
WOXEN
WRACK
WRACKED
WRACKFUL
WRACKING
WRACKS
WRAITH
WRAITHS
WRANGLE
WRANGLED
WRANGLER
WRANGLERS
WRANGLES
WRANGLING
WRANGLINGS
WRAP
WRAPOVER
WRAPOVERS
WRAPPAGE
WRAPPAGES
WRAPPED
WRAPPER
WRAPPERED
WRAPPERING
WRAPPERS
WRAPPING
WRAPPINGS
WRAPROUND
WRAPROUNDS
WRAPS
WRAPT
WRASSE
WRASSES
WRAST
WRASTED
WRASTING
WRASTS
WRATE
WRATH
WRATHED
WRATHFUL
WRATHIER
WRATHIEST
WRATHILY
WRATHING
WRATHLESS
WRATHS
WRATHY
WRAWL
WRAWLED
WRAWLING
WRAWLS
WRAXLE
WRAXLED
WRAXLES
WRAXLING
WRAXLINGS
WREAK
WREAKED
WREAKER
WREAKERS
WREAKFUL
WREAKING
WREAKLESS
WREAKS
WREATH
WREATHE
WREATHED
WREATHEN
WREATHER
WREATHERS
WREATHES
WREATHIER
WREATHIEST
WREATHING
WREATHS
WREATHY
WRECK
WRECKAGE
WRECKAGES
WRECKED
WRECKER
WRECKERS
WRECKFISH
WRECKFISHES
WRECKFUL
WRECKING
WRECKINGS
WRECKS
WREN
WRENCH
WRENCHED
WRENCHES
WRENCHING
WRENCHINGS
WRENS
WREST
WRESTED
WRESTER
WRESTERS
WRESTING
WRESTLE
WRESTLED
WRESTLER
WRESTLERS
WRESTLES
WRESTLING
WRESTLINGS
WRESTS
WRETCH
WRETCHED
WRETCHEDER
WRETCHEDEST
WRETCHES
WRETHE
WRETHED
WRETHES
WRETHING
WRICK
WRICKED
WRICKING
WRICKS
WRIED
WRIER
WRIES
WRIEST
WRIGGLE
WRIGGLED
WRIGGLER
WRIGGLERS
WRIGGLES
WRIGGLIER
WRIGGLIEST
WRIGGLING
WRIGGLINGS
WRIGGLY
WRIGHT
WRIGHTS
WRING
WRINGED
WRINGER
WRINGERS
WRINGING
WRINGINGS
WRINGS
WRINKLE
WRINKLED
WRINKLES
WRINKLIER
WRINKLIES
WRINKLIEST
WRINKLING
WRINKLY
WRIST
WRISTBAND
WRISTBANDS
WRISTIER
WRISTIEST
WRISTLET
WRISTLETS
WRISTS
WRISTY
WRIT
WRITABLE
WRITATIVE
WRITE
WRITER
WRITERESS
WRITERESSES
WRITERLY
WRITERS
WRITES
WRITHE
WRITHED
WRITHEN
WRITHES
WRITHING
WRITHINGS
WRITHLED
WRITING
WRITINGS
WRITS
WRITTEN
WRIZLED
WROATH
WROATHS
WROKE
WROKEN
WRONG
WRONGDOER
WRONGDOERS
WRONGED
WRONGER
WRONGERS
WRONGEST
WRONGFUL
WRONGING
WRONGLY
WRONGNESS
WRONGNESSES
WRONGOUS
WRONGS
WROOT
WROOTED
WROOTING
WROOTS
WROTE
WROTH
WROUGHT
WRUNG
WRY
WRYBILL
WRYBILLS
WRYER
WRYEST
WRYING
WRYLY
WRYNECK
WRYNECKS
WRYNESS
WRYNESSES
WRYTHEN
WUD
WUDDED
WUDDING
WUDS
WULFENITE
WULFENITES
WULL
WULLED
WULLING
WULLS
WUNNER
WUNNERS
WURLEY
WURLEYS
WURLIES
WURST
WURSTS
WURTZITE
WURTZITES

WUS
WUSES
WUSHU
WUSHUS
WUSS
WUSSES
WUTHER
WUTHERED
WUTHERING
WUTHERS
WUZZLE
WUZZLED
WUZZLES
WUZZLING
WYANDOTTE
WYANDOTTES
WYCH
WYCHES
WYE
WYES
WYLIECOAT
WYLIECOATS
WYN
WYND
WYNDS
WYNN
WYNNS
WYNS
WYSIWYG
WYTE
WYTED
WYTES
WYTING
WYVERN
WYVERNS

XANTHAM
XANTHAMS
XANTHAN
XANTHANS
XANTHATE
XANTHATES
XANTHEIN
XANTHEINS
XANTHENE
XANTHENES
XANTHIC
XANTHIN
XANTHINE
XANTHINES
XANTHINS
XANTHOMA
XANTHOMAS
XANTHOMATA
XANTHOUS
XANTHOXYL
XANTHOXYLS
XEBEC
XEBECS
XENIA
XENIAL
XENIAS
XENIUM
XENOCRYST
XENOCRYSTS
XENOGAMIES
XENOGAMY
XENOGRAFT
XENOGRAFTS
XENOLITH
XENOLITHS
XENOMANIA
XENOMANIAS
XENOMENIA
XENOMENIAS
XENON
XENONS
XENOPHILE
XENOPHILES
XENOPHOBE
XENOPHOBES
XENOPHOBIES
XENOPHOBY
XENOPHYA
XENOTIME
XENOTIMES
XENURINE
XERAFIN
XERAFINS
XERANSES
XERANSIS
XERANTIC
XERAPHIM
XERAPHIMS
XERARCH
XERASIA
XERASIAS
XERIC
XEROCHASIES
XEROCHASY
XERODERMA
XERODERMAS
XEROMA
XEROMAS
XEROMATA
XEROMORPH
XEROMORPHS
XEROPHAGIES
XEROPHAGY
XEROPHILIES
XEROPHILY
XEROPHYTE
XEROPHYTES
XEROSES
XEROSIS
XEROSTOMA
XEROSTOMAS
XEROSTOMATA
XEROTES
XEROTIC
XI
XIPHOID
XIPHOIDAL
XIPHOPAGI
XIS
XOANA
XOANON
XU
XYLEM
XYLEMS
XYLENE
XYLENES
XYLENOL
XYLENOLS
XYLIC
XYLITOL
XYLITOLS
XYLOCARP
XYLOCARPS
XYLOGEN
XYLOGENS
XYLOGRAPH
XYLOGRAPHS
XYLOID
XYLOIDIN
XYLOIDINE
XYLOIDINES
XYLOIDINS
XYLOL
XYLOLOGIES
XYLOLOGY
XYLOLS
XYLOMA
XYLOMAS
XYLOMATA
XYLOMETER
XYLOMETERS
XYLONIC
XYLONITE
XYLONITES
XYLOPHAGE
XYLOPHAGES
XYLOPHONE
XYLOPHONES
XYLORIMBA
XYLORIMBAS
XYLOSE
XYLOSES
XYLYL
XYLYLS
XYST
XYSTER
XYSTERS
XYSTI
XYSTOI
XYSTOS
XYSTS
XYSTUS

Y

YABBER
YABBERED
YABBERING
YABBERS
YABBIE
YABBIES
YABBY
YACCA
YACCAS
YACHT
YACHTED
YACHTER
YACHTERS
YACHTIE
YACHTIES
YACHTING
YACHTINGS
YACHTS
YACHTSMAN
YACHTSMEN
YACK
YACKED
YACKER
YACKERS
YACKING
YACKS
YAFF
YAFFED
YAFFING
YAFFLE
YAFFLES
YAFFS
YAGER
YAGERS
YAGGER
YAGGERS
YAH
YAHOO
YAHOOS
YAHS
YAK
YAKHDAN
YAKHDANS
YAKIMONO
YAKIMONOS
YAKITORI
YAKITORIS
YAKKA
YAKKAS
YAKKED
YAKKER
YAKKERS
YAKKING
YAKOW
YAKOWS
YAKS
YAKUZA
YALD
YALE
YALES
YAM
YAMEN
YAMENS
YAMMER
YAMMERED
YAMMERING
YAMMERINGS
YAMMERS
YAMS
YAMULKA
YAMULKAS
YANG
YANGS
YANK
YANKED
YANKER
YANKERS
YANKIE
YANKIES
YANKING
YANKS
YANQUI
YANQUIS
YAOURT
YAOURTS
YAP
YAPOCK
YAPOCKS
YAPOK
YAPOKS
YAPON
YAPONS
YAPP
YAPPED
YAPPER
YAPPERS
YAPPIE
YAPPIER
YAPPIES
YAPPIEST
YAPPING
YAPPS
YAPPY
YAPS
YAPSTER
YAPSTERS
YAQONA
YAQONAS
YARD
YARDAGE
YARDAGES
YARDANG
YARDANGS
YARDBIRD
YARDBIRDS
YARDED
YARDING
YARDLAND
YARDLANDS
YARDMAN
YARDMEN
YARDS
YARDSTICK
YARDSTICKS
YARDWAND
YARDWANDS
YARE
YARELY
YARER
YAREST
YARFA
YARFAS
YARMULKA
YARMULKAS
YARMULKE
YARMULKES
YARN
YARNED
YARNING
YARNS
YARPHA
YARPHAS
YARR
YARRAMAN
YARRAMANS
YARROW
YARROWS
YARRS
YARTA
YARTAS
YARTO
YARTOS
YASHMAK
YASHMAKS
YATAGAN
YATAGANS
YATAGHAN
YATAGHANS
YATE
YATES
YATTER
YATTERED
YATTERING
YATTERINGS
YATTERS
YAUD
YAUDS
YAULD
YAUP
YAUPON
YAUPONS
YAW
YAWED
YAWEY
YAWING
YAWL
YAWLED
YAWLING
YAWLS
YAWN
YAWNED
YAWNIER
YAWNIEST
YAWNING
YAWNINGLY
YAWNINGS
YAWNS
YAWNY
YAWP
YAWPED
YAWPER
YAWPERS
YAWPING
YAWPS
YAWS
YAWY
YBET
YBLENT
YBORE
YBOUND
YBOUNDEN
YBRENT
YCLAD
YCLED
YCLEEPE
YCLEEPED
YCLEEPES
YCLEEPING
YCLEPED
YCLEPT
YCOND
YDRAD
YDRED
YE
YEA
YEAD
YEADING
YEADS
YEAH
YEALDON
YEALDONS
YEALM
YEALMED
YEALMING
YEALMS
YEAN
YEANED
YEANING
YEANLING
YEANLINGS
YEANS
YEAR
YEARBOOK
YEARBOOKS
YEARD
YEARDED
YEARDING
YEARDS
YEARLIES
YEARLING
YEARLINGS
YEARLONG
YEARLY
YEARN
YEARNED
YEARNER
YEARNERS
YEARNING
YEARNINGS
YEARNS
YEARS
YEAS
YEAST
YEASTED
YEASTIER
YEASTIEST
YEASTING
YEASTLIKE
YEASTS
YEASTY
YECH
YEDE
YEDES
YEDING
YEED
YEEDING
YEEDS
YEGG
YEGGMAN
YEGGMEN

YEGGS
YELD
YELDRING
YELDRINGS
YELDROCK
YELDROCKS
YELK
YELKS
YELL
YELLED
YELLING
YELLINGS
YELLOCH
YELLOCHED
YELLOCHING
YELLOCHS
YELLOW
YELLOWED
YELLOWER
YELLOWEST
YELLOWIER
YELLOWIEST
YELLOWING
YELLOWISH
YELLOWS
YELLOWY
YELLS
YELM
YELMED
YELMING
YELMS
YELP
YELPED
YELPER
YELPERS
YELPING
YELPINGS
YELPS
YELT
YELTS
YEN
YENNED
YENNING
YENS
YENTA
YENTAS
YEOMAN
YEOMANLY
YEOMANRIES
YEOMANRY
YEOMEN
YEP
YEPS
YERBA
YERBAS
YERD
YERDED
YERDING
YERDS
YERK
YERKED
YERKING
YERKS
YERSINIA
YERSINIAE
YERSINIAS
YES
YESES
YESHIVA
YESHIVAH
YESHIVAHS
YESHIVAS
YESHIVOT
YESHIVOTH
YESK
YESKED
YESKING
YESKS
YESSES
YEST
YESTER
YESTERDAY
YESTERDAYS
YESTEREVE
YESTEREVES
YESTERN
YESTREEN
YESTS
YESTY
YET
YETI
YETIS
YETT
YETTS
YEUK
YEUKED
YEUKING
YEUKS
YEVE
YEVEN
YEVES
YEVING
YEW
YEWEN
YEWS
YEX
YEXED
YEXES
YEXING
YFERE
YGLAUNST
YGO
YGOE
YIBBLES
YICKER
YICKERED
YICKERING
YICKERS
YIELD
YIELDABLE
YIELDED
YIELDER
YIELDERS
YIELDING
YIELDINGS
YIELDS
YIKE
YIKES
YIKKER
YIKKERED
YIKKERING
YIKKERS
YILL
YILLS
YIN
YINCE
YINS
YIP
YIPPED
YIPPEE
YIPPER
YIPPERS
YIPPIES
YIPPING
YIPPY
YIPS
YIRD
YIRDED
YIRDING
YIRDS
YIRK
YIRKED
YIRKING
YIRKS
YITE
YITES
YLEM
YLEMS
YLIKE
YLKE
YLKES
YMOLT
YMOLTEN
YMPE
YMPES
YMPING
YMPT
YNAMBU
YNAMBUS
YO
YOB
YOBBERIES
YOBBERY
YOBBISH
YOBBISHLY
YOBBISM
YOBBISMS
YOBBO
YOBBOES
YOBBOS
YOBS
YOCK
YOCKED
YOCKING
YOCKS
YOD
YODE
YODEL
YODELLED
YODELLER
YODELLERS
YODELLING
YODELS
YODLE
YODLED
YODLER
YODLERS
YODLES
YODLING
YOGA
YOGAS
YOGH
YOGHOURT
YOGHOURTS
YOGHS
YOGHURT
YOGHURTS
YOGI
YOGIC
YOGIN
YOGINI
YOGINIS
YOGINS
YOGIS
YOGISM
YOGISMS
YOGURT
YOGURTS
YOHIMBINE
YOHIMBINES
YOICK
YOICKED
YOICKING
YOICKS
YOICKSED
YOICKSES
YOICKSING
YOJAN
YOJANA
YOJANAS
YOJANS
YOK
YOKE
YOKED
YOKEL
YOKELISH
YOKELS
YOKES
YOKING
YOKINGS
YOKKED
YOKKING
YOKOZUNA
YOKOZUNAS
YOKS
YOKUL
YOLD
YOLDRING
YOLDRINGS
YOLK
YOLKED
YOLKIER
YOLKIEST
YOLKS
YOLKY
YOMP
YOMPED
YOMPING
YOMPS
YON
YOND
YONDER
YONDERLY
YONDERS
YONGTHLY
YONI
YONIS
YONKER
YONKERS
YONKS
YONT
YOOF
YOOFS
YOOP
YOOPS
YOPPER
YOPPERS
YORE
YORES
YORK
YORKED
YORKER
YORKERS
YORKIE
YORKIES
YORKING
YORKS
YOS
YOU
YOUK
YOUKED
YOUKING
YOUKS
YOUNG
YOUNGER
YOUNGEST
YOUNGISH
YOUNGLING
YOUNGLINGS
YOUNGLY
YOUNGNESS
YOUNGNESSES
YOUNGS
YOUNGSTER
YOUNGSTERS
YOUNGTH
YOUNGTHLY
YOUNGTHS
YOUNKER
YOUNKERS
YOUR
YOURN
YOURS
YOURSELF
YOURSELVES
YOURT
YOURTS
YOUTH
YOUTHFUL
YOUTHHEAD

YOUTHHEADS
YOUTHHOOD
YOUTHHOODS
YOUTHIER
YOUTHIEST
YOUTHLY
YOUTHS
YOUTHSOME
YOUTHY
YOW
YOWE
YOWES
YOWIE
YOWIES
YOWL
YOWLED
YOWLEY
YOWLEYS
YOWLING
YOWLINGS
YOWLS
YOWS
YPIGHT
YPLAST
YPLIGHT
YPSILOID
YPSILON
YPSILONS
YRAPT
YRAVISHED
YRENT
YRIVD
YRNEH
YRNEHS
YSAME
YSHEND
YSHENDING
YSHENDS
YSHENT
YSLAKED
YTOST
YTTERBIA
YTTERBIAS
YTTERBIUM
YTTERBIUMS
YTTRIA
YTTRIAS
YTTRIC
YTTRIOUS
YTTRIUM
YTTRIUMS
YU
YUAN
YUCA
YUCAS
YUCCA
YUCCAS
YUCK
YUCKED
YUCKER
YUCKERS
YUCKIER
YUCKIEST
YUCKING
YUCKS
YUCKY
YUFT
YUFTS
YUG
YUGA
YUGAS
YUGS
YUK
YUKATA
YUKATAS
YUKE
YUKED
YUKES
YUKIER
YUKIEST
YUKING
YUKKIER
YUKKIEST
YUKKY
YUKO
YUKOS
YUKS
YUKY
YULAN
YULANS
YULE
YULES
YULETIDE
YULETIDES
YUMMIER
YUMMIEST
YUMMY
YUMP
YUMPED
YUMPIE
YUMPIES
YUMPING
YUMPS
YUNX
YUNXES
YUP
YUPON
YUPONS
YUPPIE
YUPPIEDOM
YUPPIEDOMS
YUPPIES
YUPPIFIED
YUPPIFIES
YUPPIFY
YUPPIFYING
YUPPY
YUPS
YURT
YURTS
YUS
YWIS
YWROKE

Z

ZABAIONE
ZABAIONES
ZABETA
ZABETAS
ZABRA
ZABRAS
ZABTIEH
ZABTIEHS
ZACK
ZACKS
ZADDIK
ZADDIKIM
ZADDIKS
ZAFFER
ZAFFERS
ZAFFRE
ZAFFRES
ZAG
ZAGGED
ZAGGING
ZAGS
ZAIRE
ZAITECH
ZAITECHS
ZAKAT
ZAKATS
ZAKUSKA
ZAKUSKI
ZAMAN
ZAMANG
ZAMANGS
ZAMANS
ZAMARRA
ZAMARRAS
ZAMARRO
ZAMARROS
ZAMBO
ZAMBOMBA
ZAMBOMBAS
ZAMBOORAK
ZAMBOORAKS
ZAMBOS
ZAMBUCK
ZAMBUCKS
ZAMBUK
ZAMBUKS
ZAMIA
ZAMIAS
ZAMINDAR
ZAMINDARI
ZAMINDARIES
ZAMINDARIS
ZAMINDARS
ZAMINDARY
ZAMOUSE
ZAMOUSES
ZAMPOGNA
ZAMPOGNAS
ZAMPONE
ZAMPONI
ZANDER
ZANDERS
ZANELLA
ZANELLAS
ZANIED
ZANIER
ZANIES
ZANIEST
ZANINESS
ZANINESSES
ZANJA
ZANJAS
ZANJERO
ZANJEROS
ZANTE
ZANTES
ZANTHOXYL
ZANTHOXYLS
ZANY
ZANYING
ZANYISM
ZANYISMS
ZANZE
ZANZES
ZAP
ZAPATA
ZAPATEADO
ZAPATEADOS
ZAPOTILLA
ZAPOTILLAS
ZAPPED
ZAPPER
ZAPPERS
ZAPPIER
ZAPPIEST
ZAPPING
ZAPPY
ZAPS
ZAPTIAH
ZAPTIAHS
ZAPTIEH
ZAPTIEHS
ZARAPE
ZARAPES
ZARATITE
ZARATITES
ZAREBA
ZAREBAS
ZAREEBA
ZAREEBAS
ZARF
ZARFS
ZARIBA
ZARIBAS
ZARNEC
ZARNECS
ZARNICH
ZARNICHS
ZARZUELA
ZARZUELAS
ZASTRUGA
ZASTRUGI
ZATI
ZATIS
ZAX
ZAXES
ZEA
ZEAL
ZEALANT
ZEALANTS
ZEALFUL
ZEALLESS
ZEALOT
ZEALOTISM
ZEALOTISMS
ZEALOTRIES
ZEALOTRY
ZEALOTS
ZEALOUS
ZEALOUSLY
ZEALS
ZEAS
ZEBEC
ZEBECK
ZEBECKS
ZEBECS
ZEBRA
ZEBRAS
ZEBRASS
ZEBRASSES
ZEBRINA
ZEBRINAS
ZEBRINE
ZEBRINNIES
ZEBRINNY
ZEBROID
ZEBRULA
ZEBRULAS
ZEBRULE
ZEBRULES
ZEBU
ZEBUB
ZEBUBS
ZEBUS
ZECCHINE
ZECCHINES
ZECCHINI
ZECCHINO
ZECCHINOS
ZED
ZEDOARIES
ZEDOARY
ZEDS
ZEE
ZEES
ZEIN
ZEINS
ZEITGEIST
ZEITGEISTS
ZEK
ZEKS
ZEL
ZELANT
ZELANTS
ZELATOR
ZELATORS
ZELATRICE
ZELATRICES
ZELATRIX
ZELATRIXES
ZELOSO
ZELOTYPIA
ZELOTYPIAS
ZELS
ZEMINDAR
ZEMINDARI
ZEMINDARIES
ZEMINDARIS
ZEMINDARS
ZEMINDARY
ZEMSTVA
ZEMSTVO
ZEMSTVOS
ZENANA
ZENANAS
ZENDIK
ZENDIKS
ZENITH
ZENITHAL
ZENITHS
ZEOLITE
ZEOLITES
ZEOLITIC
ZEPHYR
ZEPHYRS
ZEPPELIN
ZEPPELINS
ZERDA
ZERDAS
ZEREBA
ZEREBAS
ZERIBA
ZERIBAS
ZERO
ZEROED
ZEROING
ZEROS
ZEROTH
ZERUMBET
ZERUMBETS
ZEST
ZESTED
ZESTER
ZESTERS
ZESTFUL
ZESTFULLY
ZESTIER
ZESTIEST
ZESTING
ZESTS
ZESTY
ZETA
ZETAS
ZETETIC
ZETETICS
ZEUGMA
ZEUGMAS
ZEUGMATIC
ZEUXITE
ZEUXITES
ZEX
ZEXES
ZEZE
ZEZES
ZHO
ZHOMO
ZHOMOS
ZHOS
ZIBELINE
ZIBELINES
ZIBELLINE
ZIBELLINES
ZIBET
ZIBETS
ZIFF
ZIFFIUS
ZIFFIUSES
ZIFFS
ZIG
ZIGAN

ZIGANKA
ZIGANKAS
ZIGANS
ZIGGED
ZIGGING
ZIGGURAT
ZIGGURATS
ZIGS
ZIGZAG
ZIGZAGGED
ZIGZAGGING
ZIGZAGGY
ZIGZAGS
ZIKKURAT
ZIKKURATS
ZILA
ZILAS
ZILCH
ZILCHES
ZILLAH
ZILLAHS
ZILLION
ZILLIONS
ZILLIONTH
ZILLIONTHS
ZIMB
ZIMBI
ZIMBIS
ZIMBS
ZIMMER
ZIMMERS
ZIMOCCA
ZIMOCCAS
ZINC
ZINCED
ZINCIER
ZINCIEST
ZINCIFIED
ZINCIFIES
ZINCIFY
ZINCIFYING
ZINCING
ZINCITE
ZINCITES
ZINCKED
ZINCKIER
ZINCKIEST
ZINCKIFIED
ZINCKIFIES
ZINCKIFY
ZINCKIFYING
ZINCKING
ZINCKY
ZINCO
ZINCODE
ZINCODES
ZINCOID
ZINCOS
ZINCOUS
ZINCS
ZINCY
ZINE
ZINEB
ZINEBS
ZINES
ZINFANDEL
ZINFANDELS
ZING
ZINGED
ZINGEL
ZINGELS
ZINGER
ZINGERS
ZINGIBER
ZINGIBERS
ZINGIER
ZINGIEST
ZINGING
ZINGS
ZINGY
ZINKE
ZINKED
ZINKENITE
ZINKENITES
ZINKES
ZINKIER
ZINKIEST
ZINKIFIED
ZINKIFIES
ZINKIFY
ZINKIFYING
ZINKING
ZINKY
ZINNIA
ZINNIAS
ZIP
ZIPLOCK
ZIPPED
ZIPPER
ZIPPERED
ZIPPERS
ZIPPIER
ZIPPIEST
ZIPPING
ZIPPO
ZIPPOS
ZIPPY
ZIPS
ZIPTOP
ZIRCALOY
ZIRCALOYS
ZIRCON
ZIRCONIA
ZIRCONIAS
ZIRCONIC
ZIRCONIUM
ZIRCONIUMS
ZIRCONS
ZIT
ZITE
ZITHER
ZITHERN
ZITHERNS
ZITHERS
ZITI
ZITS
ZIZ
ZIZANIA
ZIZANIAS
ZIZEL
ZIZELS
ZIZYPHUS
ZIZYPHUSES
ZIZZ
ZIZZED
ZIZZES
ZIZZING
ZLOTY
ZLOTYS
ZO
ZOA
ZOARIA
ZOARIUM
ZOBO
ZOBOS
ZOBU
ZOBUS
ZOCCO
ZOCCOLO
ZOCCOLOS
ZOCCOS
ZODIAC
ZODIACAL
ZODIACS
ZOEA
ZOEAE
ZOEAL
ZOEAS
ZOECHROME
ZOECHROMES
ZOEFORM
ZOETIC
ZOETROPE
ZOETROPES
ZOETROPIC
ZOIATRIA
ZOIATRIAS
ZOIATRICS
ZOIC
ZOISITE
ZOISITES
ZOISM
ZOISMS
ZOIST
ZOISTS
ZOMBI
ZOMBIE
ZOMBIES
ZOMBIFIED
ZOMBIFIES
ZOMBIFY
ZOMBIFYING
ZOMBIISM
ZOMBIISMS
ZOMBIS
ZOMBORUK
ZOMBORUKS
ZONA
ZONAE
ZONAL
ZONARY
ZONATE
ZONATED
ZONATION
ZONATIONS
ZONDA
ZONDAS
ZONE
ZONED
ZONELESS
ZONES
ZONING
ZONINGS
ZONK
ZONKED
ZONKING
ZONKS
ZONOID
ZONULA
ZONULAE
ZONULAR
ZONULAS
ZONULE
ZONULES
ZONULET
ZONULETS
ZONURE
ZONURES
ZOO
ZOOBIOTIC
ZOOBLAST
ZOOBLASTS
ZOOCHORE
ZOOCHORES
ZOOCHORIES
ZOOCHORY
ZOOCYTIA
ZOOCYTIUM
ZOOEA
ZOOEAE
ZOOEAL
ZOOEAS
ZOOECIA
ZOOECIUM
ZOOGAMETE
ZOOGAMETES
ZOOGAMIES
ZOOGAMOUS
ZOOGAMY
ZOOGENIC
ZOOGENIES
ZOOGENOUS
ZOOGENY
ZOOGLOEA
ZOOGLOEAE
ZOOGLOEAS
ZOOGLOEIC
ZOOGONIES
ZOOGONOUS
ZOOGONY
ZOOGRAFT
ZOOGRAFTS
ZOOGRAPHIES
ZOOGRAPHY
ZOOID
ZOOIDAL
ZOOIDS
ZOOKS
ZOOLATER
ZOOLATERS
ZOOLATRIA
ZOOLATRIAS
ZOOLATRIES
ZOOLATRY
ZOOLITE
ZOOLITES
ZOOLITH
ZOOLITHIC
ZOOLITHS
ZOOLITIC
ZOOLOGIES
ZOOLOGIST
ZOOLOGISTS
ZOOLOGY
ZOOM
ZOOMANCIES
ZOOMANCY
ZOOMANTIC
ZOOMED
ZOOMETRIC
ZOOMETRIES
ZOOMETRY
ZOOMING
ZOOMORPH
ZOOMORPHIES
ZOOMORPHS
ZOOMORPHY
ZOOMS
ZOON
ZOONAL
ZOONIC
ZOONITE
ZOONITES
ZOONITIC
ZOONOMIA
ZOONOMIAS
ZOONOMIC
ZOONOMIES
ZOONOMIST
ZOONOMISTS
ZOONOMY
ZOONOSES
ZOONOSIS
ZOONOTIC
ZOONS
ZOOPATHIES
ZOOPATHY
ZOOPERAL
ZOOPERIES
ZOOPERIST
ZOOPERISTS
ZOOPERY
ZOOPHAGAN
ZOOPHAGANS
ZOOPHAGIES
ZOOPHAGY
ZOOPHILE
ZOOPHILES
ZOOPHILIA
ZOOPHILIAS

ZOOPHILIES
ZOOPHILY
ZOOPHOBIA
ZOOPHOBIAS
ZOOPHORI
ZOOPHORIC
ZOOPHORUS
ZOOPHYTE
ZOOPHYTES
ZOOPHYTIC
ZOOPLASTIES
ZOOPLASTY
ZOOS
ZOOSCOPIC
ZOOSCOPIES
ZOOSCOPY
ZOOSPERM
ZOOSPERMS
ZOOSPORE
ZOOSPORES
ZOOSPORIC
ZOOTAXIES
ZOOTAXY
ZOOTECHNIES
ZOOTECHNY
ZOOTHECIA
ZOOTHEISM
ZOOTHEISMS
ZOOTHOME
ZOOTHOMES
ZOOTOMIC
ZOOTOMIES
ZOOTOMIST
ZOOTOMISTS
ZOOTOMY
ZOOTOXIN
ZOOTOXINS
ZOOTROPE
ZOOTROPES
ZOOTROPHIES
ZOOTROPHY
ZOOTYPE
ZOOTYPES
ZOOTYPIC
ZOOZOO
ZOOZOOS
ZOPILOTE
ZOPILOTES
ZOPPA
ZOPPO
ZORGITE
ZORGITES
ZORI
ZORIL
ZORILLE
ZORILLES
ZORILLO
ZORILLOS
ZORILS
ZORINO
ZORINOS
ZORIS
ZORRO
ZORROS
ZOS
ZOSTER
ZOSTERS
ZOUK
ZOUKS
ZOUNDS
ZOWIE
ZUCCHETTO
ZUCCHETTOS
ZUCCHINI
ZUCCHINIS
ZUCHETTA
ZUCHETTAS
ZUCHETTO
ZUCHETTOS
ZUFFOLI
ZUFFOLO
ZUFOLI
ZUFOLO
ZUGZWANG
ZUGZWANGS
ZULU
ZULUS
ZUMBOORUK
ZUMBOORUKS
ZUPA
ZUPAN
ZUPANS
ZUPAS
ZURF
ZURFS
ZUZ
ZUZIM
ZYDECO
ZYDECOS
ZYGA
ZYGAENID
ZYGAENINE
ZYGAENOID
ZYGAL
ZYGANTRA
ZYGANTRUM
ZYGANTRUMS
ZYGOCACTI
ZYGODONT
ZYGOMA
ZYGOMAS
ZYGOMATA
ZYGOMATIC
ZYGON
ZYGOPHYTE
ZYGOPHYTES
ZYGOSE
ZYGOSES
ZYGOSIS
ZYGOSPERM
ZYGOSPERMS
ZYGOSPORE
ZYGOSPORES
ZYGOTE
ZYGOTES
ZYGOTIC
ZYLONITE
ZYLONITES
ZYMASE
ZYMASES
ZYME
ZYMES
ZYMIC
ZYMITE
ZYMITES
ZYMOGEN
ZYMOGENIC
ZYMOGENS
ZYMOID
ZYMOLOGIC
ZYMOLOGIES
ZYMOLOGY
ZYMOLYSES
ZYMOLYSIS
ZYMOLYTIC
ZYMOME
ZYMOMES
ZYMOMETER
ZYMOMETERS
ZYMOSES
ZYMOSIS
ZYMOTIC
ZYMOTICS
ZYMURGIES
ZYMURGY
ZYTHUM
ZYTHUMS

Dictionary of 2- and 3-letter words allowable for Scrabble®

Note that, although these are complete lists of all the 2- and 3-letter words allowable for Scrabble, the meanings are not necessarily comprehensive; the full range can be found in *The Chambers Dictionary.*

The definitions have been selected to help players to remember the words, and at the same time to act as guides to possible derivatives. For example, CUE is defined both as 'a signal to begin a speech, etc' (the plural CUES being implied) and as 'to give such a signal' (implying the forms CUES (again), CUEING, and CUED). Remember however that this dictionary is intended only as an aide-mémoire. *Official Scrabble® Words*, in conjunction with *The Chambers Dictionary,* is the final authority.

Different parts of speech are separated by '❑', and different meanings of the same word by ';'.

Bold type is used when reference is being made to other words. Often these words are defined in the lists; when, however, the reference is to longer words, definitions have been given for those that are felt to be less familiar.

2-LETTER WORDS

AA a type of lava
AD colloquial for **advertisement**
AE Scots word for **one** (adjective)
AH interjection expressing surprise, joy, etc ❑ to make such an interjection
AI the three-toed sloth; same as **ayu**
AM present tense of **be**
AN the indefinite article used before a vowel
AR the letter 'R'
AS in whatever way ❑ so ❑ a mythological Norse god; a Roman unit of weight; a Roman coin
ÅS a **kame**, a gravel ridge
AT preposition denoting position in space or time
AW interjection expressing disappointment, sympathy, etc
AX US form of **axe**
AY always ❑ yes ❑ an affirmative vote or voter

BA in ancient Egyptian religion, the soul
BE to exist or live
BI colloquial short form of **bisexual**, (a person who is) attracted sexually to both sexes
BO interjection intended to startle ❑ in US slang, a term of address to a man
BY beside; near; through ❑ same as **bye**

CH obsolete dialect pronoun meaning **I**

DA a Burmese knife; a dialect form of **dad**, a father
DI a plural of **deus**, Latin word for **god**
DO to perform ❑ a celebration; same as **doh**

EA dialect word meaning **river**
EE Scots word for **eye** (noun)
EF the letter 'F'
EH interjection expressing inquiry ❑ to say 'eh'
EL the letter 'L', or anything of that shape; an elevated railway
EM the letter 'M'; a unit of measurement in printing
EN the letter 'N'; in printing, half of an **em**
ER interjection expressing hesitation
ES the letter 'S', or anything of that shape
EX the letter 'X'; someone no longer in a previous relationship

FA a musical note (in sol-fa)
FY same as **fie**

GI same as **gie**, a judo or karate costume
GO to pass from one place to another ❑ energy or activity; a Japanese board game
GU same as **gue**

HA interjection expressing a wide range of emotions or responses
HE pronoun used in referring to a male person or thing ❑ a male
HI interjection calling attention
HO interjection calling attention, expressing surprise, etc ❑ stopping, cessation ❑ obsolete word meaning to stop

ID a fish of the carp family; part of the human personality
IF on condition that; whether ❑ a condition
IN not out ❑ someone or something that is in ❑ to take in
IO interjection expressing joy, triumph or grief ❑ a cry of 'io'
IS present tense of **be**
IT pronoun referring to an inanimate thing ❑ an indefinable quality; Italian vermouth

JO Scots word for a loved one

KA the spirit or soul; a god; same as **kae**, a jackdaw
KO a Maori digging-stick
KY same as **kye**

LA a musical note (in sol-fa) ❑ interjection with various meanings
LI a Chinese unit of distance
LO interjection meaning see, look or behold

MA childish or familiar word for **mother** (noun)
ME pronoun representing oneself
MI a musical note (in sol-fa)
MO old word for **more**

MU a letter in the Greek alphabet
MY of or belonging to me

NA Scots word for **no**, not at all
NE obsolete word meaning not
NÉ (of a man) born
NO a word of negation; not at all ❑ a negative vote or voter
NU a letter in the Greek alphabet
NY obsolete spelling of **nigh** (adjective and verb)

OB an objection
OD a hypothetical force; old word for **god**, often used as a mild oath
OE same as **oy**
OF belonging to
OH interjection expressing surprise, interest, pain, etc
OI interjection used to attract attention
OM an intoned Hindu sacred symbol
ON not off; available ❑ in cricket, the on-side ❑ to go on
OO Scots form of **wool** ❑ Scots form of **we**
OP short form of **operation**
OR in heraldry, the tincture gold or yellow ❑ a word expressing alternatives
OS a bone
OU Scots interjection expressing concession
OW interjection expressing pain; same as **ou**
OX a general name for a bovine animal
OY Scots word for **grandchild**

PA childish or familiar word for **father**; a Maori fort
PH a number used to express degree of acidity or alkalinity
PI a letter in the Greek alphabet ❑ pious or sanctimonious
PO short form of **chamberpot**

QI an individual's life force

RE a musical note (in sol-fa) ❑ about

SH interjection requesting silence
SI an earlier form of **ti**, a musical note
SO in such a way ❑ same as **sol**, a musical note
ST interjection requesting silence

TA interjection expressing thanks
TE same as **ti**, a musical note
TI a musical note (in sol-fa); a small Pacific tree
TO in the direction of, towards

UG to loathe
UM interjection expressing doubt or hesitation
UN dialect word for **one** (noun)
UP in a higher place ❑ a rise; a spell of prosperity ❑ to move up
UR interjection expressing hesitation
US pronoun used in referring to oneself and others
UT a syllable representing **doh**

WE pronoun used in referring to oneself and others
WO variant of **woe**

XI a letter in the Greek alphabet
XU a Vietnamese coin

YE old word for **you**; old spelling of **the**
YO interjection calling for effort or attention
YU precious jade

ZO same as **zho**

3-LETTER WORDS

AAS plural of **aa**
ABA an outer garment worn by some Arab women
ABB a textile yarn
ABY to pay (as) a penalty
ACE a winning serve in tennis ❑ outstanding ❑ to play an ace
ACH same as **och**
ACT to do in a specified way ❑ something done
ADD to make an addition
ADO bustle or fuss
ADS plural of **ad**
ADZ US form of **adze**, a cutting tool
AFT behind; near the stern of a vessel, etc
AGA a Turkish commander or chief officer
AGE the time during which a person has existed ❑ to grow old
AGO past; since
AHA interjection expressing exultation, pleasure, surprise, etc
AHS present tense of **ah**
AIA an Indian or South African nursemaid
AID to help or assist ❑ help; something that helps
AIL to be indisposed ❑ a trouble
AIM to point or direct ❑ a purpose
AIN Scots word for **own** (adjective)
AIR the mixture of gases breathed by people and animals; an appearance or manner ❑ to make known publicly
AIS plural of **ai**
AIT a small island
AKE old spelling of **ache** (verb)
ALA an outgrowth on a fruit
ALB a priest's long white vestment
ALE a kind of beer
ALL comprising the whole amount, extent, etc of ❑ the whole; everybody or everything
ALP a high mountain; a mountain pasture
ALS obsolete form of **also**, or **as** (adverb)
ALT a high tone; a halt or rest
AMI French word for **friend**
AMP short form of **ampere** and **amplifier**
ANA in equal quantities (in recipes and prescriptions)
AND also; indicating addition ❑ something added
ANE Scots word for **one**
ANI a tropical American bird
ANN old Scots word for a payment to a parish minister's widow
ANT a small industrious insect
ANY some; whichever, no matter which
APE a monkey ❑ to imitate
APT suitable ❑ obsolete word meaning to adapt
ARB short form of **arbitrageur**, a person who profits by judicious dealing in stocks and shares
ARC a part of the circumference of a circle ❑ to form an arc
ARD a primitive type of plough
ARE present tense of **be** ❑ a unit of metric land measure
ARK a floating vessel ❑ obsolete word meaning to put in an ark
ARM a limb; a weapon ❑ to provide with weapons
ARS plural of **ar**
ART the creation of works of beauty; a human skill
ARY dialect word for **any**
ASH a kind of tree; the remains of anything burnt
ASK to request, inquire, or invite ❑ dialect word for **newt**
ASP a venomous snake
ASS a long-eared animal like a small horse; a stupid person
ATE past tense of **eat**
AUF obsolete word for an elf's child
AUK a heavy black-and-white seabird
AVA Scots word meaning **at all**
AVE a recitation of the address or prayer to the Virgin Mary
AWA Scots word for **away**
AWE fear or dread ❑ to strike with or influence by awe
AWL a pointed instrument for boring
AWN the beard of barley, etc ❑ to shelter with an awning
AXE a tool for chopping ❑ to chop or cut down
AYE ever; yes ❑ an affirmative vote or voter
AYS plural of **ay**
AYU a small edible Japanese fruit

BAA the cry of a sheep ❑ to bleat
BAC colloquial short form of **baccalaureate**, a degree or diploma

BAD evil; wicked; faulty ❑ something evil, wicked, etc
BAG a receptacle for containing something ❑ to put into a bag
BAH interjection expressing disgust or contempt
BAM a hoax ❑ to hoax or cheat
BAN a prohibition ❑ to forbid or prohibit
BAP a large, flat breakfast roll
BAR a block of a solid substance; an obstruction ❑ to obstruct or prevent
BAS plural of **ba**
BAT a flying mammal; an implement for striking a ball ❑ to strike with a bat
BAY an inlet of the sea; the barking (of hounds) ❑ to bark or howl
BED a place to sleep on ❑ to put to bed
BEE an insect that makes honey; the letter 'B'
BEG to ask for ❑ another word for **bey**
BEL a measure of noise
BEN Scots or Irish word for **mountain**
BET a sum of money, etc, gambled ❑ to gamble (money, etc)
BEY a Turkish governor
BEZ the second tine of a deer's horn
BIB a protective piece of material fastened under a child's chin ❑ to tipple
BID an offer ❑ to make an offer
BIG large; very important ❑ Scots word for **build** (verb)
BIN a container for rubbish; a case for wine ❑ to put into a bin
BIO short form of **biography**
BIS twice
BIT a small piece; a curb or restraint ❑ to curb or restrain
BIZ slang word for **business**
BOA a large constricting snake
BOB to move quickly up and down ❑ a curtsy
BOD a person
BOG a marsh ❑ to sink
BOH same as **bo** (interjection)
BOK South African word for a goat or an antelope
BON French word for **good**
BOO a sound expressing disapproval or contempt ❑ to make such a sound
BOP short for **bebop**, a variety of jazz music ❑ to dance to pop music
BOR East Anglian form of address meaning **neighbour**
BOS plural of **bo**
BOT the maggot of a botfly ❑ Australian word meaning to cadge
BOW a bending of the neck or body in greeting ❑ to bend or incline downwards
BOX a case or receptacle for holding anything; a blow with the hand or fists ❑ to put into a box; to strike with the hand or fists
BOY a male child ❑ Shakespearean word meaning to play (a female part) as a boy
BRA short for **brassière**, an undergarment worn to support a woman's breasts
BRO a place for which one feels a strong affinity
BUB old word for a strong drink
BUD a flower not yet opened ❑ to produce buds
BUG a kind of insect ❑ to pester or irritate
BUM a tramp or sponger ❑ to sponge or live dissolutely
BUN a kind of sweet roll or cake
BUR a prickly seed-case; a throaty sound of 'r' ❑ to whisper hoarsely
BUS a road vehicle for passengers ❑ to transport by bus
BUT except; nevertheless ❑ an objection ❑ to put forward as an objection
BUY to purchase ❑ something purchased
BYE a pass to the next round (of a competition, etc)
BYS plural of **by**

CAB a taxi-cab
CAD a dishonourable man
CAM a projection on a revolving shaft; a whitening stone ❑ to whiten with a cam
CAN a container of tin-plate ❑ to store in such a container
CAP a covering for the head, a chimney, etc ❑ to put a cap on or cover the top of
CAR a self-propelled wheeled vehicle
CAT a small, furry domestic animal ❑ to vomit
CAW to cry as a crow ❑ the cry of a crow
CAY a low islet
CEE the letter 'C', or anything of that shape
CEL short form of **celluloid**, a strong, often transparent, plastic material
CEP a kind of edible mushroom
CHA tea

CHE dialect form of **I**, used by Shakespeare
CHI feminine of **chal**, a fellow or person
CID a chief, captain or hero
CIG colloquial short form of **cigarette**
CIT contemptuous term for someone who is not a gentleman
CLY old word meaning to seize or steal
COB a male swan; a wicker basket ❑ to strike
COD a kind of fish; a hoax ❑ to hoax or make fun of
COG a projection on a toothed wheel ❑ to furnish with cogs
COL a pass in a mountain range
CON a trick or swindle ❑ to trick; to persuade by dishonest means
COO to make a sound like a dove ❑ the sound made by a dove
COP to capture ❑ a policeman; a capture or arrest
COR interjection expressing surprise ❑ a Hebrew measure
COS a crisp, long-leaved lettuce
COT a small bed for a young child
COW the female of bovine and some other animals ❑ to subdue
COX short for **coxswain**, (to act as) a person who steers a boat
COY bashful or modest ❑ Shakespearean word meaning to caress or to disdain
COZ short for **cousin**
CRU French word meaning **vineyard** or **vintage**
CRY to utter a sound of pain or grief, or loudly ❑ such a sound
CUB the young of some animals, eg a fox ❑ to produce cubs
CUD food chewed again by a ruminating animal
CUE a signal to begin a speech, etc ❑ to give such a signal
CUM combined with; with the addition of
CUP a small round drinking-vessel ❑ to form into a cup shape
CUR a worthless mongrel dog
CUT to make an incision in; to reduce ❑ an incision or reduction
CUZ obsolete form of **coz**
CWM Welsh word for **valley**

DAB to touch or press gently ❑ a gentle touch or wipe; an expert ❑ expert
DAD a father; a thump ❑ to thump
DAE Scots form of **do** (verb)
DAG a dirty tuft of wool on a sheep ❑ to cut off dags
DAH same as **da**, a Burmese knife
DAK in India, the mail or post; a letter
DAL a kind of Indian edible pea
DAM an embankment to restrain water ❑ to restrain (water) with an embankment or bank
DAN a level of efficiency (in Japanese combative sports)
DAP to dip bait gently into the water (in fishing) ❑ bait so dipped
DAS plural of **da**
DAW a jackdaw ❑ to dawn
DAY the time when it is light; 24 hours
DEB colloquial form of **débutante**, a young woman making her first formal appearance in society
DEE the letter 'D', or anything of that shape ❑ euphemism for **damn**
DEF excellent, brilliant
DEI a plural of **deus**, Latin word for **god**
DEL another word for **nabla**, a mathematical symbol
DEN the lair of a wild animal; a private place ❑ to retire to a den
DEW moisture deposited from the air on cooling ❑ to moisten (as) with dew
DEY formerly, the pasha of Algiers
DIB to fish by dapping ❑ a small bone in a sheep's leg
DID past tense of **do**
DIE to lose life ❑ a small cube, a dice
DIG to use a spade; to excavate ❑ an act of digging
DIM not bright ❑ to make dim
DIN a loud jarring noise ❑ to annoy with such a noise
DIP to immerse briefly; to lower ❑ an act or period of dipping
DIT named or reputed (French) ❑ Scots word meaning to block
DIV an evil spirit of Persian mythology
DOB to inform on or betray
DOC contraction of **doctor** (noun)
DOD dialect word meaning to cut the hair of ❑ Scots word for a rounded hill
DOE the female of a deer, rabbit, and some other animals
DOG one of a family of four-legged animals, often the domestic variety ❑ to follow like a dog
DOH a musical note (in sol-fa)
DON a university lecturer, etc ❑ to put on (clothes, etc)
DOO Scots word for **dove**, a pigeon

DOP a kind of brandy ❑ obsolete word meaning to dip
DOR a dung-beetle ❑ obsolete word meaning to mock
DOS plural of **do**, a musical note
DOT a very small spot ❑ to make such a spot
DOW same as **dhow**, an Arab sailing vessel ❑ obsolete and Scots word meaning to be able
DRY without liquid ❑ to make or become dry
DSO same as **zho**
DUB to add sound effects, etc, to ❑ Scots word for **puddle**
DUD something or someone ineffectual ❑ ineffective; useless
DUE something owed ❑ Shakespearean word meaning to endue
DUG past tense of **dig** ❑ a nipple of an animal
DUN greyish brown ❑ a greyish-brown horse ❑ to press for payment
DUO two people considered a pair for a specific reason
DUP Shakespearean word meaning to undo
DUX a leader
DYE to stain ❑ a colour produced by dyeing
DZO same as **zho**

EAN Shakespearean word meaning to give birth to
EAR the organ of hearing; the part of corn, etc, containing the seeds ❑ to produce (corn) ears; obsolete word meaning to plough
EAS plural of **ea**
EAT to take in food ❑ an archaic word for **food**
EAU French word for **water**; same as **ea**
EBB to move back from the land (of the tide) ❑ such a movement of the tide
ECH Shakespearean word meaning to eke out
ECU a European unit of currency
EDH same as **eth**
EEK interjection expressing fright
EEL a long, smooth cylindrical fish
EEN plural of **ee**
EFF euphemism for **fuck**
EFS plural of **ef**
EFT a newt
EGG an oval or round body from which young are hatched ❑ to add eggs to (in cooking, etc)
EGO the 'I' or self
EHS present tense of **eh**
EIK Scots form of **eke**
EKE to add ❑ an addition
ELD old word for age or old age
ELF a diminutive, mischievous supernatural being ❑ Shakespearean word meaning to entangle (hair)
ELK a kind of large deer
ELL a measure of length
ELM a tree with serrated leaves
ELS plural of **el**
ELT dialect word for a young sow
EME obsolete word for **uncle**
EMS plural of **em**
EMU a flightless, fast-running bird
END the last point; termination or close ❑ to finish or close
ENE obsolete, dialect or poetic word for **even**
ENG a phonetic symbol
ENS plural of **en**; being or existence
EON same as **aeon**, an eternity
ERA a series of years; an age
ERE before ❑ same as **ear**, to plough
ERF South African word for a garden plot
ERG a unit of work
ERK slang word for **aircraftsman**
ERN old spelling of **earn**
ERR to make a mistake
ERS the bitter vetch
ESS same as **es**
EST a programme designed to develop human potential
ETA a letter in the Greek alphabet
ETH a letter used in Old English
EUK dialect word meaning to itch ❑ an itching
EVE poetic word for **evening**
EWE a female sheep
EWK same as **euk**
EWT old form of **newt**, a tailed amphibious animal
EYE the organ of sight ❑ to look at carefully

FAB marvellous
FAD an interest intensely but briefly pursued; a craze
FAG a cigarette; drudgery ❑ to work, or be worked, hard
FAH same as **fa**

FAN an instrument used for cooling ❑ to cool, (as) with a fan
FAP Shakespearean word meaning fuddled or drunk
FAR remote or distant ❑ dialect word meaning to remove to a distance
FAS plural of **fa**
FAT plump; obese ❑ solid vegetable or animal oil ❑ to make or grow fat
FAW a gypsy
FAX a machine that scans electronically ❑ to send messages by such a machine
FAY poetic word for a fairy ❑ dialect word meaning to clean out (eg a ditch) ❑ same as **fey** (adjective)
FED past tense of **feed** ❑ US slang for a Federal agent
FEE the price paid for services ❑ to pay a fee to
FEN low marshy land
FET obsolete form of **fetch** (verb)
FEU a Scottish form of land tenure ❑ to grant or hold land in feu
FEW not many
FEY whimsical; fairylike; foreseeing the future ❑ same as **fay** (verb)
FEZ a red brimless cap of wool or felt
FIB a little lie ❑ to tell such a lie
FID a conical pin of hard wood
FIE old interjection expressing disapproval ❑ same as **fey** (adjective)
FIG a kind of tropical fruit packed with seeds ❑ Shakespearean word meaning to make an insulting gesture at
FIL Shakespearean word for the shaft of a vehicle
FIN a steering, swimming, or balancing organ on an aquatic animal
FIR a kind of conifer
FIT healthy; suitable ❑ something that fits ❑ to make suitable
FIX to make firm; to arrange ❑ a difficulty; something fraudulently arranged
FIZ to make a hissing or sputtering sound ❑ such a sound; a fizzy drink
FLU short form of **influenza**
FLY to move through the air ❑ a kind of flying insect ❑ surreptitious or sly
FOB a small watch pocket ❑ obsolete word meaning to pocket
FOE an enemy
FOG a thick mist ❑ to be affected by fog
FOH an expression of disgust or contempt
FON obsolete word for a fool ❑ to play the fool
FOP an affected dandy
FOR in the place of; in favour of; towards
FOU Scots word for **drunk** (adjective)
FOX a wild animal related to the dog ❑ to act cunningly, to cheat
FOY Spenserian word meaning **allegiance**, loyalty
FRA Italian word meaning **brother** or **friar**
FRO obsolete word for **from**
FRY to cook in oil or fat ❑ a dish so cooked; a number of young fish
FUB old word meaning to put off
FUD Scots word for a rabbit's or hare's tail
FUG a very hot, close atmosphere ❑ to cause a fug in
FUM same word as **fung**, a fabulous Chinese bird
FUN pleasure, enjoyment, merriment ❑ to play
FUR the thick, soft, fine hair of some animals; a crust formed by hard water ❑ to cover or coat with fur

GAB to chatter ❑ idle talk
GAD to wander about idly ❑ a miner's chisel
GAE Scots word for **go** (verb)
GAG to silence ❑ something that gags the mouth
GAL dialect word for **girl**
GAM a school of whales ❑ to join up in a gam
GAN past tense of the old verb **gin**, to begin
GAP an opening ❑ to make a gap in
GAR Scots word meaning to compel ❑ a garfish
GAS a substance which is neither solid nor liquid ❑ to poison with gas
GAT slang word for a gun
GAU under the Nazi regime, a German political district
GAY lively ❑ a homosexual
GED dialect word for **pike** (fish)
GEE the letter 'G' ❑ of horses, to move on
GEL a jelly-like solution ❑ to form a gel
GEM a precious stone ❑ old word meaning to adorn with gems
GEN general information
GEO a gully or creek
GET to obtain ❑ a stupid person
GEY Scots word meaning **fairly** ❑ Scots word meaning **considerable**

GHI clarified butter
GIB a wedge-shaped piece of metal ❑ to fasten with a gib
GID a sheep disease
GIE Scots word for **give** (verb) ❑ a judo costume
GIF old word meaning **if**
GIG a band or pop group's engagement ❑ to play a gig
GIN an alcoholic spirit ❑ to snare in a gin trap
GIO same as **geo**
GIP same as **gyp** (noun)
GIS plural of **gis**
GIT a stupid person
GJU same as **gue**
GNU an African antelope
GOA a Tibetan gazelle
GOB slang word for the mouth ❑ to spit
GOD an object of worship ❑ to deify
GOE older form of **geo** ❑ old form of **go** (verb)
GON a geometrical grade
GOO a sticky substance
GOS plural of **go**
GOT past tense of **get**
GOV short form of **governor**
GOY a Gentile
GUB Australian word for a white man
GUE a kind of violin formerly used in Shetland
GUM a sticky substance ❑ to smear, coat, etc with gum
GUN a weapon for discharging explosive projectiles, etc ❑ to discharge such projectiles, etc
GUP slang word for gossip or prattle
GUR an unrefined cane sugar
GUS plural of **gu**
GUT the intestine ❑ to take the guts out of (fish, etc)
GUV same as **gov**
GUY colloquial term for a person generally ❑ to make fun of
GYM short form of **gymnasium**, **gymnastics**, etc
GYP slang word for a cheat ❑ to swindle

HAD past tense of **have**
HAE Scots form of **have**
HAG an ugly old woman ❑ Scots word meaning to hack or hew
HAH an interjection expressing various emotions, such as surprise, exultation, dismay
HAJ a Muslim pilgrimage to Mecca
HAM salted and smoked flesh from the leg of a pig; a bad actor ❑ to overact, exaggerate
HAN Spenserian plural form of **have** (verb)
HAP chance, fortune ❑ to happen by chance
HAS present tense of **have**
HAT a covering for the head ❑ to provide or cover with a hat
HAW the fruit of the hawthorn ❑ to make indecisive noises
HAY cut grass, used for fodder ❑ to make hay
HEM an edge or border ❑ to form a hem on
HEN a female domestic fowl ❑ to challenge to a daring act
HEP slang word meaning knowing, abreast of knowledge and taste ❑ a rosehip
HER pronoun representing a female person or thing ❑ of or belonging to such a person or thing
HES plural of **he**
HET slang word for **heterosexual**
HEW to cut with blows ❑ Spenserian form of **hue**
HEX something that brings misfortune ❑ to bring misfortune
HEY interjection calling attention, etc ❑ a winding country-dance ❑ to dance this dance
HIC interjection representing a hiccup
HID past tense of **hide**
HIE to turn (a horse) to the left ❑ a cry requesting such a turn
HIM pronoun representing a male person or thing
HIN a Hebrew liquid measure
HIP part of the thigh ❑ to carry on the hip
HIS of or belonging to a male person or thing
HIT to strike ❑ an act of striking
HOA interjection expressing exultation, surprise, etc ❑ cessation ❑ obsolete word meaning to stop
HOB a flat surface on a cooker
HOC Latin word for **this**
HOD a trough for carrying bricks ❑ Scots word meaning to bob or jog
HOE a tool for loosening the earth ❑ to use a hoe
HOG a kind of pig ❑ to use selfishly
HOH same as **ho**
HOI interjection used to attract attention

HON short for **honey**, as a term of endearment
HOO Shakespearean interjection expressing boisterous emotion
HOP to leap on one leg ❑ a leap on one leg
HOS plural of **ho**
HOT very warm ❑ to heat
HOW in what way ❑ a manner or means
HOX Shakespearean word meaning to hock or hamstring
HOY a large one-decked boat ❑ interjection requesting someone or something to stop ❑ to incite
HUB the centre of a wheel
HUE a colour or tint
HUG to embrace ❑ an embrace
HUH interjection expressing disgust
HUI a Maori gathering; a social gathering
HUM to make a sound like bees ❑ the noise of bees
HUP to turn (a horse) to the right ❑ a cry requesting such a turn
HUT a small house or shelter ❑ to settle in a hut
HYE obsolete form of **hie** or **high**
HYP old word for **hypochondria**, excessive worry about one's health ❑ to offend

ICE frozen water ❑ to cool with ice
ICH Shakespearean word meaning to eke or augment ❑ dialect word for **I**
ICY covered with ice; frosty
IDE same as **id**, a fish
IDS plural of **id**
IFF conjunction used in logic to express 'if and only if'
IFS plural of **if**
ILK a type or kind
ILL unwell ❑ harm; misfortune
IMP a mischievous child; a wicked spirit ❑ to engraft (a hawk) with new feathers
INK a coloured liquid used in writing ❑ to colour with ink
INN a small hotel ❑ old word meaning to lodge
INS plural of **in**
ION an electrically-charged particle
IOS plural of **io**
IRE anger
IRK to annoy or weary
ISH Scottish legal word meaning issue or expiry
ISM any distinctive theory or fad
ISO short for **isolated replay**, a TV and film facility
ITA the miriti palm
ITS of or belonging to something
IVY a climbing evergreen plant

JAB to poke or stab ❑ a poke or stab, an injection
JAG a sharp projection ❑ to pierce
JAK same as **jack**, an East Indian tree
JAM a conserve made with fruit and sugar; a blockage ❑ to block up (eg a street) by crowding
JAP same as **jaup**, a Scots word meaning to splash or a splash
JAR a wide-mouthed container ❑ to put in jars
JAW part of the skull holding the teeth ❑ to chatter at length
JAY a bird of the crow family
JEE same as **gee**
JET a stream of liquid; a jetplane ❑ to spout; to travel by jet
JEU French word for **game**
JEW offensive word meaning to cheat or get the better of
JIB a triangular sail ❑ to show objection
JIG a lively dance ❑ to dance a jig; to jump up and down
JIZ same as **gizz**, Scots word for a wig
JOB a piece of work ❑ to work at jobs
JOE same as **jo**
JOG to run at a slow, steady pace ❑ a spell of jogging
JOR the second movement of a raga
JOT a little bit, an iota ❑ to note down
JOW Scots word meaning to toll ❑ a stroke of a bell
JOY gladness, delight ❑ an obsolete word meaning to rejoice
JUD a mass of coal
JUG a container for liquids ❑ to stew (eg hare) in a closed pottery jar
JUS Latin word for a law or a legal right
JUT to project ❑ a projection

KAE Scots word for **jackdaw** ❑ to serve
KAI in New Zealand, etc, food, a meal
KAM Shakespearean word meaning **awry**, twisted or distorted
KAS plural of **ka**
KAT same as **khat**, an E African shrub; an ancient Egyptian unit of weight
KAW same as **caw**
KAY the letter 'K'
KEA a large New Zealand parrot

KEB Scots word meaning to give birth to a premature or stillborn lamb ❑ a ewe giving birth to such a lamb
KED a wingless fly that infests sheep
KEF a drug that produces a dreamy repose; such repose
KEG a small cask
KEN to know ❑ a range of knowledge
KEP dialect word meaning to catch ❑ a catch
KET Scots word for **carrion**, rotting flesh of an animal
KEX a dry stalk
KEY an instrument for locking, tuning, etc ❑ to enter (data) into a computer
KID a young goat; a child ❑ to hoax or deceive
KIF same as **kef**
KIN one's relations
KIP a nap ❑ to have a nap or sleep
KIR a wine and blackcurrant drink
KIT equipment ❑ to provide with equipment
KOA a Hawaiian acacia
KOB an African waterbuck
KOI a Japanese carp, an edible fish (plural also **koi**)
KON Spenserian word meaning to know
KOP South African word for **hill**
KOS same as **coss**, an Indian measure of distance
KOW same as **cow**, Scots word for a bunch of twigs
KYE Scots word for **cows**, cattle
KYU in judo, one of the novice grades

LAB contraction of **laboratory**
LAC a dark-red resin
LAD a boy or youth
LAG a delay; insulating material ❑ to fall behind; to cover (eg pipes) with insulating material
LAH same as **la**, a musical note
LAM to beat ❑ a hurried flight from the police (US slang)
LAP a circuit of a race-track ❑ to scoop up with the tongue
LAR the god relating to a house
LAS plural of **la**
LAT short form of **latrine**, a lavatory
LAV short form of **lavatory**
LAW a rule or statute ❑ obsolete word meaning to take to court
LAX slack, careless, or negligent ❑ a kind of salmon
LAY to place or set down; to produce eggs ❑ a lyric or song
LEA meadow or pasture ❑ fallow
LED past tense of **lead**
LEE shelter; the sheltered side ❑ Scots word meaning to tell a lie
LEG a limb for walking and standing ❑ to walk briskly
LEI a garland or wreath; plural of **leu**
LEK the unit of Albanian currency ❑ of blackcocks, etc, to gather and display
LEP dialect word meaning to leap
LES same as **lez**
LET to allow; to grant use of in return for payment ❑ a hindrance; an instance of letting for payment
LEU the unit of Romanian currency
LEV the unit of Bulgarian currency
LEW same as **lev** ❑ tepid
LEX Latin word for **law**
LEY a straight line between landscape features; same as **lea**
LEZ short form of **lesbian**, a female homosexual
LIB short form of **liberation**, setting free, from discrimination, prejudice, etc ❑ dialect word meaning to geld
LID a cover or covering
LIE a false statement ❑ to tell a lie; to be in a horizontal position
LIG a dialect form of **lie**
LIN Spenserian word meaning to cease ❑ same as **linn**, a waterfall
LIP one of the folds of flesh round the mouth ❑ to use or touch with the lips
LIS a fleur-de-lis
LIT past tense of **light**
LOB a ball hit (in tennis) or thrown (in cricket) in a specific way ❑ to hit or throw a ball in this way
LOD in statistics, the logarithm of the odds
LOG a fallen or cut tree-trunk ❑ to enter in a record
LOO colloquial form of **lavatory**; a card game ❑ to subject to a forfeit at loo
LOP to cut off unnecessary parts ❑ an act of lopping
LOR colloquial form of **lord**, interjection expressing surprise
LOS praise, reputation
LOT a great deal; a set of things offered together for sale ❑ to allot
LOW not tall or high ❑ an area where things (eg spirits, health, finances, etc) are low ❑ to make the noise of cattle

LOX liquid oxygen; a kind of smoked salmon
LOY in Ireland, a long, narrow spade
LUD a form of **lord**, a judge
LUG to pull or drag with difficulty ❑dialect word for **ear**
LUM Scots word for **chimney**
LUR same as **lure**, a Bronze Age trumpet
LUV love, a term of endearment
LUX a unit of illumination
LUZ a supposedly indestructible bone, possibly the sacrum
LYE a short branch of a railway; an alkaline solution
LYM Shakespearean for **lyam**, a leash

MAA of a goat, to bleat
MAC contraction of **mackintosh**
MAD insane; angry ❑Shakespearean word meaning to drive mad
MAE Scots word for **mo**
MAG short form of **magazine**; an old word for a halfpenny ❑dialect word for to tease or to chatter
MAK Scots word meaning to make
MAL French word for **pain**, **sickness**
MAM dialect word for **mother**
MAN an adult human male ❑to provide with a (human) operator
MAP a diagram of the surface of the earth, etc ❑to make a map of
MAR to spoil or damage
MAS a house or farm in the south of France; plural of **ma**
MAT a floor covering ❑to tangle
MAW the stomach of an animal
MAX obsolete word for **gin**, the drink
MAY may blossom ❑to gather may blossom
MEG variant form of **mag**, a halfpenny
MEL honey
MEN plural of **man**
MES plural of **me**
MET past tense of **meet** ❑short form of **meteorology**, the study of weather
MEU the plant spignel
MEW (of a cat) to make a thin, high-pitched cry ❑this cry; a gull
MHO a former unit of electrical inductance
MID middle ❑the middle; short for **midshipman**
MIL a unit of wire measurement; a Cyprian coin
MIM Scots and dialect word meaning **prim**
MIR a Russian peasant farming commune; a Muslim ruler
MIS Spenserian word meaning to fail ❑plural of **mi**
MIX to mingle ❑a mixture
MIZ short form of **misery** or **miserable**
MNA same as **mina**, a Greek unit of weight or money
MOA a gigantic extinct bird like an ostrich
MOB a disorderly crowd ❑to form into a mob
MOD a Highland Gaelic festival
MOE obsolete form of **mo**, more ❑obsolete form of **mow**, a wry face
MOG same as **moggy**, a cat
MOI French word meaning **me**, facetiously used in English
MOM US colloquial word for **mother**
MON a Japanese family badge or crest
MOO (of cattle) to low ❑a cow's low
MOP a sponge, etc, on a stick ❑to clean with a mop
MOR a layer of humus
MOT French word meaning **word**
MOU Scots word for a mouth
MOW to cut the grass on ❑a pile of hay; obsolete word for a wry face
MOY Shakespearean word for a coin or a measure
MOZ Australian word meaning a type of curse
MUD wet soft earth ❑to bury or hide in mud
MUG a cup with vertical sides ❑to attack from behind
MUM child's word for **mother** (noun) ❑silent ❑to act in a mime
MUN dialect word for **must** (verb) ❑dialect word for **man** (noun)
MUS plural of **mu**
MUX US and dialect word meaning to spoil, botch ❑a mess

NAB to seize ❑a hilltop
NAE Scots form of **no**, not any, certainly not
NAG a small horse ❑to worry or annoy constantly
NAM same as **naam**, distraint ❑past tense of **nim**
NAN same as **naan**, slightly leavened bread
NAP to take a short sleep ❑a short sleep
NAS form of obsolete **ne has**, has not, and **ne was**, was not

NAT colloquial form of **nationalist**, a person who strives for the unity or independence of a nation
NAY old form of **no** ❑ a denial
NEB a beak or bill ❑ to put a bill on
NED a young hooligan
NÉE (of a woman) born
NEF obsolete word for a church nave
NEK South African word for **col**
NEP dialect word for **catmint**, a plant attractive to cats
NET an open material, formed into meshes ❑ to catch (fish) in a net
NEW recently made, bought, produced, etc ❑ something new ❑ old word meaning to renew
NIB the writing point of a pen ❑ to provide with a nib
NID a pheasant's nest or brood
NIE obsolete spelling of **nigh** (adjective and verb)
NIL nothing; zero
NIM obsolete word meaning to take or steal ❑ an old game involving taking objects (usually matches) alternately from heaps
NIP a small quantity of spirits ❑ to pinch
NIS in Scandinavian folklore, a brownie or goblin
NIT a young louse; a fool; a unit of information
NIX nothing; ❑ to veto or cancel
NOB a person of high social rank
NOD to move the head forward in assent or greeting ❑ such a movement of the head
NOG an egg and alcohol drink; a wooden peg or cog ❑ to fix with a nog
NOH same as **no**, a traditional style of Japanese drama
NOM French word for **name**
NON Latin word for **not**
NOR and not; neither
NOS plural of **no**
NOT word expressing denial, negation, or refusal
NOW at the present time; immediately ❑ the present time
NOX nitrogen oxide
NOY Spenserian word meaning to hurt or annoy ❑ vexation, hurt or trouble
NTH adjective implying a large number
NUB the point or gist; same as **knub**, a knob ❑ to hang
NUN a female member of a religious order
NUR same as **knur**, a knot on a tree
NUS plural of **nu**
NUT an edible seed in a hard shell ❑ to look for and gather nuts
NYE obsolete spelling of **nigh** (adjective and verb) ❑ another word for **nid**
NYS Spenserian word meaning **is not**

OAF a lout; an idiot
OAK a kind of tree; its wood
OAR a pole with a blade for rowing a boat ❑ to row a boat
OAT a kind of grass, the seeds of which are used as food
OBA in West Africa, a chief or ruler
OBI West Indian, etc witchcraft; a fetish or charm ❑ to bewitch
OBO a vessel for carrying oil and bulk ore
OBS plural of **ob**
OCA a South American wood-sorrel
OCH Scots or Irish interjection expressing impatience or regret
ODA a room in a harem
ODD strange; unpaired, left over ❑ in golf, an additional or allowed stroke
ODE an elaborate lyric addressed to someone or something
ODS plural of **od**
OES plural of **oe**
OFF not on; away; not available ❑ in cricket, the off-side ❑ to go off
OFT often
OHM a unit of electrical resistance
OHO an expression of triumph and surprise or gratification
OIK an inferior person; a lout
OIL a greasy, flammable liquid ❑ to smear or lubricate with oil
OKE a Turkish weight
OLD advanced in years; worn out ❑ times past, olden times
OLE Spanish interjection expressing approval or support
OLM a blind salamander
OMS plural of **om**
ONE single; undivided; only ❑ an individual thing or person; the number or figure 1; a symbol representing it
ONS plural of **on**
OOF slang word for money
OOH an expression of pleasure, surprise, etc ❑ to make such an expression
OOM South African word for **uncle**
OON Scots word for **oven**
OOP same as **oup**
OOR Scots word for **our**

OOS plural of **oo**, Scots word for **wool**
OPE poetic word meaning to open
OPS plural of **op**
OPT to decide or choose
ORB a circle or sphere ❑ to form into an orb
ORC an orca, a killer whale
ORD obsolete word meaning a point, eg of a weapon
ORE a solid mineral aggregate
ORF a viral infection of sheep
ORS plural of **or**
ORT dialect word for a leftover from a meal
OUD an Arab stringed instrument
OUK Scots word for **week**
OUP Scots word meaning to bind with thread or to join
OUR of or belonging to us
OUT not in; excluded ❑ someone or something that is out ❑ to put or throw out; to make public
OVA plural of **ovum**, an egg
OWE to be in debt for
OWL a nocturnal predacious bird; a wiseacre ❑ to behave like an owl
OWN to possess ❑ belonging to oneself
OWT dialect word for **anything**
OYE same as **oy**
OYS plural of **oy**

PAD a wad of soft material used to cushion, protect, fill out, etc ❑ to cover or fill with soft material
PAH same as **pa**, a Maori fort or settlement
PAL colloquial word for **friend** ❑ to associate as a pal
PAM the knave of clubs
PAN a broad, shallow container ❑ to wash earth for gold
PAP soft food for infants ❑ to feed with such food
PAR a state of equality; same as **parr**, a young fish, especially a young salmon
PAS French word for **step**; plural of **pa**
PAT a gentle stroke with the palm of the hand ❑ to stroke gently
PAW a clawed foot ❑ to scrape with a paw
PAX the kiss of peace; Latin word for **peace**
PAY to hand over money; to be profitable ❑ salary or wages
PEA a vegetable, the rounded seed of a climbing plant
PEC colloquial short form for a pectoral muscle
PED short for **pedestrian**, a person who travels on foot
PEE the letter 'P' ❑ to urinate
PEG a pin or fixture ❑ to fasten with a peg
PEN an implement for writing ❑ to write down on paper
PEP vigour or spirit ❑ to put pep into
PER for each; by
PET a tame animal; a favourite ❑ to treat as a pet
PEW a bench in a church
PHI a letter in the Greek alphabet
PHO same as **foh**
PHS plural of **ph**
PIA a tropical plant
PIC colloquial word for **picture** (noun)
PIE meat, fruit, etc baked in a pastry; confusion ❑ to reduce to confusion
PIG a farm animal bred for food ❑ slang word meaning to eat greedily
PIN a piece of wood or metal used for fastening ❑ to fasten with a pin
PIP a small hard seed in a fruit; offence or disgust ❑ to offend or disgust
PIR a Muslim title of honour, given to a holy man
PIS plural of **pi**
PIT a hole in the earth ❑ to put in a pit
PIU Italian word for **more**
PIX same as **pyx**
PLY a fold ❑ to bend or fold
POA a meadow-grass plant
POD the shell of leguminous plants ❑ to shell (eg peas)
POH interjection expressing impatient contempt
POI a Hawaiian dish, fermented taro
POM colloquial word for a Pomeranian dog
POO slang word for **faeces**, excrement ❑ to defecate
POP a mild explosive sound ❑ to make a pop
POS plural of **po**
POT a utensil for cooking or storing ❑ to cook or put in a pot
POW Scots word for **head** (noun)
POX any of several viral diseases with pustules ❑ obsolete word meaning to infect with pox
POZ old short form of **positive** (adjective)
PRE colloquial word meaning **before**
PRO in favour ❑ someone who is in favour; colloquial short form

of **professional** and **prostitute** (nouns)
PRY to examine things with curiosity ❑ an act of prying
PSI a letter in the Greek alphabet
PST interjection used to attract attention
PUB a public house
PUD colloquial word for **pudding**
PUG a small dog with a wrinkled face; clay, ground with water ❑ to grind with water
PUH Shakespearean spelling of **pooh**, interjection expressing disgust, etc
PUN to play on words ❑ a play on words
PUP a young dog ❑ to give birth to pups
PUR obsolete spelling of **purr**, (of a cat) to make a contented sound ❑ the sound made
PUS thick yellowish fluid formed by suppuration
PUT to place; to throw ❑ a push; a throw
PUY a small volcanic cone
PYE same as **pie**, confusion ❑ to reduce to confusion
PYX a box in which coins are kept for testing ❑ to test

QAT same as **kat**, an E African shrub
QIS plural of **qi**
QUA in the capacity of

RAD a unit of radiation dosage
RAG a worn scrap of cloth ❑ to tease or ridicule
RAH an expression of approbation or joy ❑ to make such an expression
RAI a modern, North African form of popular music
RAJ rule, government, or sovereignty
RAM a male sheep ❑ to push or cram down hard
RAN past tense of **run**
RAP a sharp blow ❑ to strike sharply
RAS a headland; an Ethiopian prince
RAT a rodent like a large mouse ❑ to hunt rats
RAW uncooked
RAX dialect word meaning to stretch ❑ a stretch
RAY a beam of light ❑ to radiate
REC a recreation ground
RED of a colour like blood ❑ the colour of blood; something that is red ❑ Scots word meaning to tidy
REE Scots word for an enclosure (for sheep, etc)
REF short form of **referee**, (to act as) an umpire or judge
REH an efflorescence of salts on soil in India, etc
REM a unit of radiation dosage
REN old spelling of **run**
REP a commercial representative ❑ to work or act as a rep
RES short form of (North American Indian) **reservation**
RET to expose to moisture; to soak
REV a revolution in an internal-combustion engine ❑ to increase the speed of revolution
REW Spenserian spelling of **row** (noun)
REX obsolete plural word meaning tricks or pranks
REZ same as **res**
RHO a letter in the Greek alphabet
RHY Spenserian spelling of **rye**, the grass
RIA a drowned valley
RIB a bone curving forward from the backbone ❑ to tease
RID to free or clear
RIG to fit with sails; to equip or clothe ❑ an arrangement of sails and masts; an outfit
RIM an edge or border ❑ to provide with a rim
RIN Scots form of **run**
RIP to tear open or apart ❑ a rent or tear
RIT Scots word meaning to slit ❑ a slit
RIZ US past tense of **rise**
ROB to steal ❑ a fruit syrup
ROC an enormous bird in Arabian legend
ROD a slender stick or bar ❑ to push a rod through
ROE a mass of fish eggs; a small species of deer
ROK same as **roc**
ROM a gypsy man
ROO short form of **kangaroo**
ROT to decay ❑ decay or corruption
ROW a line or rank; a noisy squabble ❑ to quarrel ❑ to propel through water with oars
RUB to apply friction ❑ an impediment or difficulty
RUC same as **roc**
RUD archaic or dialect word meaning redness or complexion ❑ Spenserian word meaning to redden
RUE a strong smelling plant; regret ❑ to regret
RUG a heavy floor-mat ❑ Scots word meaning to pull roughly

RUM a spirit distilled from sugar cane ❑ odd, droll
RUN to move quickly ❑ an act or instance of running
RUT a furrow made by wheels ❑ to make such a furrow
RYA a type of Scandinavian rug
RYE a cereal grass; its grain

SAB a saboteur
SAC in biology, a baglike structure
SAD unhappy, sorrowful
SAE Scots form of **so**, in this way, accordingly, etc
SAG to bend or hang down ❑ an act or instance of sagging
SAI the capuchin monkey
SAL a large North Indian tree; a salt
SAM Spenserian word meaning **together**
SAN old short form of **sanatorium**, a kind of hospital; a Japanese form of address
SAP a liquid circulating through plants ❑ to drain
SAR Scots form of **savour**, (to) taste; a sea bream
SAT past tense of **sit**
SAW a cutting tool with a toothed blade ❑ to use a saw; past tense of **see**
SAX short form of **saxophone**, a musical instrument; a chopper for trimming slates
SAY to utter in words, speak ❑ something said or stated
SAZ a stringed instrument of Turkey, North Africa, etc
SEA a great expanse of water
SEC a secant ❑ of wines, dry
SED Miltonic spelling of **said** (verb)
SEE to perceive by the eye ❑ an area under the authority of a bishop
SEG a stud in the sole of a shoe
SEI a whale, a kind of rorqual
SEL Scots form of **self**
SEN a monetary unit (in Japan, etc) of various values ; a coin of these values
SET to put or place in position ❑ a group; a complete series
SEW to work on with a needle and thread
SEX the quality of being male or female ❑ to identify the sex of
SEY Scots word for a part of a carcase of beef
SEZ slang spelling of **says** (verb)
SHE pronoun used in referring to a female person or thing ❑ a female
SHY embarrassed; bashful ❑ to jump aside; to recoil
SIB a blood relation, a kinsman
SIC thus ❑ Scots word for **such** ❑ to incite (a dog to attack)
SIM short for **Simeonite**, an evangelical
SIN moral offence ❑ to commit sin
SIP to drink in small mouthfuls ❑ a quantity sipped
SIR a word used in addressing a man ❑ to address as 'sir'
SIS contracted form of **sister**
SIT to rest on the buttocks ❑ a spell of sitting
SIX the number after five
SKA Jamaican music similar to reggae
SKI a narrow strip attached to a boot for gliding over snow ❑ to move on skis
SKY the space visible above the earth ❑ to hit high into the air
SLY cunning, wily; surreptitious
SMA Scots word for **small**
SNY same as **snye**, a side channel of a river
SOB to cry uncontrollably, taking intermittent breaths ❑ the sound of a breath so taken
SOC historically, the right of holding a local court
SOD an obnoxious person; a piece of cut turf ❑ to cover with sods
SOG dialect word for a soft, wet place ❑ to soak
SOH same as **sol**, a musical note
SOL a musical note (in sol-fa); a colloidal suspension in a liquid
SON a male offspring
SOP bread, etc soaked in liquid ❑ to soak
SOS plural of **so**, a musical note
SOT a habitual drunkard ❑ to act as a sot
SOU an old small French coin
SOV short form of **sovereign**, a gold coin
SOW a female pig ❑ to scatter seed on the ground
SOX slang spelling of **socks** (plural noun)
SOY dark, salty sauce made from fermented beans
SPA a resort with a mineral spring ❑ to stay at a spa
SPY a secret agent employed to watch ❑ to watch secretly
STY a pen for pigs ❑ to keep in a sty
SUB colloquial shortening of **subscription**, **subeditor**, and many other words ❑ to subscribe, subedit, etc

SUD rare singular form of **suds**, froth of soapy water
SUE to prosecute at law
SUI Latin word meaning of himself, herself, itself
SUK same as **souk**, a market-place
SUM the total, whole amount ❑ to add, make up the total of
SUN the star that is the source of light ❑ to expose to the sun's rays
SUP to take (liquid) into the mouth ❑ a small mouthful
SUQ same as **souk**, a market-place
SUR French word for **on, above**
SUS a suspect ❑ to arrest for suspicious behaviour
SWY an Australian game, two-up
SYE dialect word meaning to strain ❑ a sieve

TAB a small tag, flap, or other attachment ❑ to fix a tab to
TAD a small amount
TAE Scots form of **toe**, **too**, and **to**
TAG a tab or label ❑ to put a tag on
TAI a Japanese sea bream
TAJ a crown; a dervish's conical cap
TAK Scots form of **take**
TAM a cap with a broad circular flat top
TAN brown colour of the skin after exposure to the sun's rays ❑ to become brown in the sun
TAP a gentle knock or its sound ❑ to knock gently
TAR a black bituminous substance ❑ to coat with tar
TAT shabby articles ❑ to touch up
TAU a letter in the Greek alphabet
TAW to prepare skins for white leather ❑ a thong
TAX a contribution levied towards a country's revenue ❑ to impose a tax on
TAY dialect, especially Irish, word for **tea**
TEA a drink made from the dried leaves of a shrub ❑ to take tea
TED a Teddy boy or girl ❑ to spread out (cut grass) for drying
TEE a support for a golf ball ❑ to place on a tee
TEF an Ethiopian cereal grass
TEG a sheep in its second year
TEL in Arab countries, a hill or mound
TEN the number after nine
TES plural of **te**
TEW to hustle ❑ excitement
THE the definite article
THO Spenserian word for **those** or **then**
THY of thee
TIC an involuntary twitching of muscles
TID Scots word meaning mood, a temporary state of mind
TIE to bind, fasten or knot ❑ something for tying
TIG a touch; a game involving touching ❑ to touch
TIL sesame
TIN a silvery-white metal ❑ to coat with tin
TIP a gratuity; a helpful piece of advice ❑ to give a tip
TIS plural of **ti**
TIT a nipple; a small bird; a tug ❑ to tug
TOC telecommunications code for signalling the letter 'T'
TOD an old wool weight ❑ to yield a tod
TOE a digit at the end of a foot ❑ to kick or touch with the toes
TOG a unit of measurement of thermal insulation ❑ to dress
TOM a male cat
TON a unit of weight
TOO also
TOP the highest point, part or level ❑ to cover the top; to surpass
TOR a hill
TOT a small child or drink ❑ to add or total
TOW to pull along (behind) ❑ an act of towing; prepared fibres of flax or hemp
TOY an object for playing with ❑ to play idly with
TRY to attempt; to make an effort ❑ an effort
TUB a small carton; a bath ❑ to bath in a tub
TUG to pull forcibly ❑ a forcible pull, a jerk
TUI a New Zealand bird, a honey-guide
TUM colloquial word for **stomach**
TUN a large cask ❑ to put in a tun
TUP a ram ❑ of a ram, to copulate
TUT interjection expressing rebuke or disapproval ❑ to say 'tut'
TUX short for **tuxedo**, a dinner-jacket
TWA Scots form of **two**
TWO the number after one
TWP dim-witted, stupid (Welsh)
TYE a trough for washing ore ❑ to wash in a tye
TYG an old drinking-cup with two or more handles

UDO a Japanese ivy
UDS old interjection meaning **God's** or **God save**
UEY a U-turn
UFO an unidentified flying object
UGH interjection expressing repugnance ❑ an old representation of a cough or grunt
UGS present tense of ug
UKE a ukulele
ULE a Central American rubber tree
UNI colloquial for **university**
UNS plural of **un**
UPS plural and present tense of **up**
URD an Indian bean
URE an extinct wild ox
URN a type of vase ❑ to put in an urn
USE to put to some purpose ❑ the purpose for which something is used
UTE Australian short form of **utility**, a small truck
UTS plural of **ut**
UTU settlement of a debt (Maori)
UVA a grape or grape-like berry

VAC vacation; a vacuum-cleaner ❑ to clean with a vac
VAE same as **voe**
VAN a light transport vehicle ❑ to go or send in a van
VAS a duct carrying liquid
VAT a large vessel or tank ❑ to put or treat in a vat
VAU an obsolete letter in the Greek alphabet
VEE the letter 'V', or anything of that shape or angle
VEG short for **vegetable(s)** ❑ to laze about
VET a veterinary surgeon ❑ to treat an animal medically; to examine
VEX to distress or annoy ❑ Scots word meaning **grief**
VIA Latin word for **way** or **road** ❑ by way of, through
VID short form of **video**
VIE to contend in rivalry ❑ obsolete word meaning a bid
VIM energy, vigour
VIN French word for **wine**
VIS Latin word for **force**
VLY low-lying wet ground, a swamp
VOE in Orkney and Shetland, a bay or creek
VOL in heraldry, two wings displayed and conjoined
VOR Shakespearean word meaning to warn
VOW a solemn promise ❑ to make a vow or vows
VOX voice
VUG Cornish word for a cavity in a rock
VUM US word meaning to vow

WAD a pad or mass of loose material ❑ to form into a wad
WAE Scots word for **woe**
WAG to move from side to side ❑ an act of wagging; a habitual joker
WAN lacking colour, pale ❑ to make or become wan
WAP to throw or pull quickly ❑ a sharp blow
WAR a state of conflict ❑ to make war
WAS past tense of **be**
WAT a Thai Buddhist temple or monastery
WAW Spenserian or Scott word meaning a wave
WAX a fatty substance ❑ to treat with wax; to grow larger
WAY a route or passage ❑ Spenserian word meaning to journey
WEB a fine structure spun by a spider ❑ to envelop with a web
WED to marry ❑ a pledge, security
WEE small ❑ a short distance ❑ to urinate
WEM old word for **wame**, the womb or belly
WEN a sebaceous cyst; former name for **wyn**
WET containing, or soaked or covered with, liquid ❑ to make wet
WEX obsolete form of **wax**
WEY a measure for dry goods
WHA Scots form of **who**
WHO pronoun used in referring to a person or people
WHY for what reason; because of which
WIG an artificial covering of hair ❑ to scold
WIN to gain; to be successful ❑ a gain or victory
WIS sham archaic word meaning to know
WIT humour; intelligence ❑ archaic word meaning to know
WOE misery
WOG offensive word for a non-white foreigner
WOK a pan used in Chinese cookery
WON past tense of **win** ❑ the monetary unit of Korea

WOO to court; to seek the support of
WOP offensive word for someone of a Mediterranean or Latin race; ❑ variant of **whop**, to whip or thrash
WOS plural of **wo**, woe
WOT facetious spelling of **what** ❑ variant of **wit**, to know
WOW interjection expressing wonder ❑ to impress ❑ anything thrillingly impressive
WOX obsolete past tense of **wax**
WRY twisted to one side; sardonic ❑ to give a twist to
WUD Scots form of **wood**
WUS a term used in addressing a companion (Welsh)
WYE the letter 'Y', or anything shaped like it
WYN a rune, having the value of modern English 'w'

XIS plural of **xi**

YAH variant of **yea** ❑ interjection expressing derision, etc
YAK a species of ox; persistent talk ❑ to talk persistently
YAM a sweet potato
YAP to bark sharply or constantly ❑ a yelp
YAW to deviate from course ❑ such a deviation
YEA yes ❑ an affirmative vote or voter
YEN a Japanese coin; an intense desire ❑ to desire or yearn
YEP variant of **yes**
YES a word of affirmation ❑ an affirmative vote or voter
YET in addition, besides; nevertheless
YEW a type of evergreen tree
YEX Scots word for **hiccup**
YGO Spenserian past participle of **go**
YIN one of the two opposing principles of Chinese philosophy
YIP to give a short, sudden cry ❑ such a cry
YOB a lout
YOD past tense of Spenserian **yead**, to go
YOK a laugh ❑ to laugh
YON that, the thing known ❑ yonder
YOS plural of **yo**
YOU pronoun referring to the person being spoken or written to
YOW variant of **ewe**
YUG same as **yuga**, one of the four Hindu ages of the world
YUK something unpleasantly messy, disgusting or sickly
YUP same as **yep**
YUS plural of **yu**

ZAG a change of direction on a zigzag course ❑ to change direction on such a course
ZAP to destroy ❑ vitality or force
ZAX variant of **sax**, a chopper for trimming slates
ZEA part of a cereal plant, once used as a diuretic
ZED the letter 'Z'; a bar of metal of this shape
ZEE US form of **zed**
ZEK in the former USSR, an inmate of a prison or labour camp
ZEL an Oriental cymbal
ZEX variant of **zax**
ZHO in the Himalayas, an animal that is a cross between a yak and a cow
ZIG same as **zag**
ZIP energy, vitality ❑ to be full of or act with energy
ZIT a pimple
ZIZ a nap or sleep ❑ to take a nap
ZOA plural of **zoon**, a unified individual creature
ZOO a garden or park where animals are kept
ZOS plural of **zo**
ZUZ an ancient Palestinian coin